The Professional Edition of

J.K. LASSER'S
YOUR INCOME TAX

1988

PREPARED BY THE
J. K. LASSER TAX INSTITUTE

EDITOR
BERNARD GREISMAN
Member of the New York Bar

J.K. LASSER TAX INSTITUTE
New York

THIS PROFESSIONAL EDITION is prepared as a service to subscribers who have asked for the technical sources of YOUR INCOME TAX. It is divided into five parts:

PART ONE: The complete 1988 edition of YOUR INCOME TAX, which, for 51 years, has helped subscribers to solve their tax problems. During this time, it has proven a solid work of reference for professionals who prepare tax returns for others.

PART TWO: An explanation of tax authorities, legislative, administrative, and judicial—and their relative importance in the practice of tax law.

PART THREE: The citations of authority for the text of YOUR INCOME TAX. A complete collection of income tax references is beyond the scope of one volume. Here, in the Professional Edition, the practitioner will find: (1) A quick reference guide which can save him time and effort in finding authority for common income tax problems, (2) a selection of authorities, with particular stress on the Internal Revenue Code, the Treasury regulations, and the leading cases which provide a beginning for further research. Law review and professional tax journal articles also are cited as an additional aid.

PART FOUR: Practice before the IRS. Primarily, this section is devoted to the means by which taxpayers and their representatives can negotiate with the tax authorities up to the time when a tax dispute may have to be litigated.

PART FIVE: Preparing and Filing a Federal Estate Tax Return: This section provides a sample filled-in estate tax form and explanation of how to prepare and file an estate tax return.

BERNARD GREISMAN

 J.K. LASSER TAX INSTITUTE

Simon & Schuster, Inc.
Gulf + Western Plaza
One Gulf + Western Plaza
New York, N.Y. 10023

Distributed by Prentice Hall Trade, New York

PUBLISHER'S NOTE: YOUR INCOME TAX is published in recognition of
the great need for a clarification of the income tax laws for
the millions of men and women who must make out tax returns. We
believe the research and interpretation by the J.K. LASSER TAX
INSTITUTE to be authoritative and of service to taxpayers.

We acknowledge the editorial contribution of co-editor Elliott
Eiss, member of the New York Bar, and the assistance of
Katherine Torak.

ISBN: 0-13-510430-0

Library of Congress Card Number: 62-51991

CONTENTS

PART ONE

YOUR INCOME TAX

CONTENTS

v

INCOME TAX BASICS

In this part, you will learn these income tax basics:

Whether you must file a return.

When and where to file your return.

Which type of return to file.

How to claim dependency exemptions and the dependent care credit.

How to handle alimony arrangements.

How to report your income—pay, interest, dividend capital gain, pensions, annuity, rents, royalties, self-employment income, prizes, awards, scholarships and insurance.

How to set up IRAs and Keogh Plans.

WHO MUST FILE A RETURN

Your personal tax status and age determines the income limits that require you to file a tax return. In the charts below, find your personal status in the first column, and in the second column, you will find the income limit.

IF YOU ARE—	YOU MUST FILE IF GROSS INCOME IS AT LEAST—
Single	
Under 65 and not blind	$4,440
Under 65 and blind	4,900
65 or older	5,650
Married Filing Joint Return*	
Both spouses under 65 and neither blind	7,560
Both spouses under 65 and one or both spouses blind	8,800
One spouse 65 or over	9,400
Both spouses 65 or older	10,000
Married Filing Separate return	1,900

IF YOU ARE—	YOU MUST FILE IF GROSS INCOME IS AT LEAST—
Head of Household	
Under 65 but not blind	$4,440
Under 65 and blind	6,300
65 and older	7,050
Qualifying Widow(er)	
Under 65 but not blind	5,660
Under 65 and blind	6,900
65 or older	7,500
Married living apart at end of 1987	1,900
Nonresident alien	1,900
Individual with tax year of less than 12 months	1,900

* These filing floors for joint returns apply only if the spouses live together at the end of 1987 and neither spouse is claimed as a dependent on another return.

Dependents. If you may be claimed as a dependent on another individual's tax return for 1987, you generally must file a return if your gross income exceeds $500. However, if you have only earned income, such as salary, and no investment income, you do not have to file unless your earned income exceeds your allowable standard deduction under chapter 13. For example, an unmarried dependent under age 65 with only earned income does not have file a 1987 return unless such income exceeds $2,540, the allowable standard deduction. A single dependent with only earned income who is either age 65 or older or blind must file a 1987 return if such earned income exceeds $3,750; $4,500 if both 65 or older and also blind. Tax legislation would increase the filing limits for dependents who are 65 or over or blind; see the Supplement to this book.

You must also file a return in these cases:

Your net self-employment earnings are $400 or more, or

You are entitled to a refund of taxes withheld from your wages or a refund based on the earned income credit for low income householders (see chapter 24), or

You received any earned income credit payments in advance from your employers (see chapter 24), or

You owe any tax, such as alternative minimum tax (chapter 23); IRA penalty (chapter 8); FICA on tips (chapter 25).

THIS IS GROSS INCOME

Salary, wages, bonuses, commissions
Professional fees
Interest
Dividends
Rents
Royalties
Gains from property sales
Pension Income
Annuity income
Alimony (meeting the rules of chapter 1)
Business gross income
Gambling winnings
Lottery winnings
Jury fees
Director fees
Sick vacation or severance pay
Employer contributions to SEP
Foreign earned income even though tax free
Gain from home sale qualifying for $125,000 exclusion
Social Security benefits taxable under the rules of chapter 34

THIS IS NOT TAXABLE INCOME

Gifts from relatives and friends
Inheritances
Scholarship and fellowships (meeting rules of chapter 12)
Employee educational assistance payments
Certain medical benefits paid by employers; *see* chapter 2
Rental value of parsonage
Fringe benefits (meeting the rules of chapter 2)
Meals and lodging furnished for the employer's convenience
Benefits under qualified group legal services plans. cafeteria plans, qualified transportation, dependent care assistance programs, group term life insurance up to $50,000.
Child support payments
Social Security benefits tax free under the rules of chapter 34
Life insurance proceeds (meeting rules of chapter 12)

WHEN TO FILE

April 15 is the general filing due date. However, you may qualify for a later date by filing for an extension or if you are abroad.

IF YOU ARE—	YOU FILE BY—
Citizen or resident of the U.S.	April 15
If abroad on April 15	June 15
Filing the last return of a person who died during the year	April 15
Resident of Canada or Mexico and U.S. taxes were withheld from your wages	April 15
Nonresident alien if no taxes were withheld from wages	June 15

IF YOU ARE—	YOU FILE BY—
Executor, administrator, or trustee of estate or trust	April 15
Resident alien about to leave U.S.	Within 10 days before departure
Committee for a person unable to manage his own affairs	April 15
Reporting for a fiscal year	15th day of the 4th month after close of fiscal year.

For a timely filing, be sure your return is postmarked by midnight of the due date. The return is considered to have been filed on the postmark date, even though received by the IRS afterwards. Where a filing date falls on a Saturday, Sunday, or legal holiday, the filing date is extended to the next business day.

Apply for an extension if you cannot file on time. You may get an automatic four-month extension without waiting for the IRS to act on your request by filing Form 4868 and paying the full amount of tax you estimate that you owe; for further details on this subject *see* chapter 27.

Outside the U.S. on April 15. You are entitled to an automatic extension to June 15 without filing Form 4868. Attach a statement to your return saying that you were outside the U.S. or Puerto Rico on April 15 and include interest on any unpaid tax from due date.

A general extension of time to file outside of the automatic extension rules above may be granted by showing undue hardship.

WHERE TO FILE

IF YOU ARE FILING—	DO THIS—
Personal return	File with Service Center listed for your place of legal residence. Use the envelope included in the IRS packet of forms if the envelope address is the same as the Center listed for your residence. *See* chapter 27 for Service Center addresses.
Business return	File with Service Center where your principal place of business is located.

IF YOU ARE FILING—	DO THIS—
As a U.S. citizen abroad who claims exclusion benefits of chapter 36.	File with the Service Center at Philadelphia, Pa. 19255. If you do not claim tax free benefits abroad, file with the Service Center listed for your legal residence. If you have no legal residence or business in the U.S. file with the Service Center, Philadelphia, Pa. 19255.
As a nonresident alien	File with the Service Center, Philadelphia, Pa. 19255.
As a Serviceman	File with the Service Center listed for your civilian legal residence.

Do not allow your inability to pay the tax stop you from filing a return. Inability to pay the tax is not a reason for which an extension is granted. If you cannot pay your tax, file your return and apply for an extension of time to pay your tax on Form 1127; *see* chapter 27.

Filing an amended return. If, after filing your return, you find that an error has been made, you should file an amended return, Form 1040X, which may be used to correct a return filed in 1986 or an earlier year; *see* chapter 27.

FILING POINTERS FOR MARRIED PERSONS

FILING JOINTLY

Married couples pay less tax by filing jointly. Filing jointly allows the use of joint return rates.

You may file a joint return if you are legally married on the last day of 1987.

You need not live together provided you are legally married. A couple legally separated under a final decree of divorce or separate maintenance may *not* file a joint return.

You may file jointly if your spouse died during 1987. *See* ¶1.1.

If one spouse is a nonresident alien, you must file jointly *only* if you make a special election to be taxed on your world-wide income. *See* ¶1.8.

You *must* file jointly to make an IRA deduction on behalf of an non-working spouse (¶8.7), to claim the credit for the elderly (chapter 34), dependent care credit (¶1.30), or earned income credit (chapter 24).

On a joint return, each spouse is liable for the entire tax. If one spouse does not pay, the other spouse may be liable even though all of the income was earned by the spouse who failed to pay the tax. A spouse who files a joint return may be relieved of fraud penalties and tax liability in certain circumstances. *See* ¶1.3.

For community property rules, *see* ¶1.9.

FILING SEPARATELY

You may not file joint return and must use tax rates for married persons filing separately in these cases:

1. You and your spouse have different tax reporting years. If you report on the calendar year but your spouse reports on a fiscal year, you must file separately unless you get permission from the IRS to change your reporting year (Form 1128). This bar to joint filing does not apply when your tax year begins on the same day, but ends because of the death of either or both spouses. A spouse who has never filed a tax return may elect to use the other spouse's tax year as his first tax year. Then they can file a joint return. That a husband and wife had different tax years before their marriage is no bar to a joint return.
2. You or your spouse is a nonresident alien and you do not make an election to be taxed on your world-wide income. *See* ¶1.8.
3. Your spouse files a separate return. If you are experiencing marital discord, you may be forced to file separately unless your spouse consents to a joint return.
4. You or your spouse is claimed by someone else as a dependent. *See* ¶1.27.

LIVING APART FROM SPOUSE: FILING AS UNMARRIED HEAD OF HOUSEHOLD

If you live apart from your spouse, you may qualify for tax purposes as "unmarried" and use head of household rates which are less than single person rates.

You qualify if:

1. You file a separate return.
2. Your spouse was not a member of your household during the last six months of 1987.
3. You maintain your home as a household which was the principal place of abode for your child, or adopted child, foster child, or stepchild, for more than half of 1987. However, a foster child must be a member of your household for the entire year.
4. You are entitled to claim the child as a dependent. Ignore this test if the non-custodial spouse claims the exemption for the child under the rules of ¶1.34.
5. You provide over half of the cost of supporting the household.

FILING POINTERS FOR SINGLE PERSONS

SINGLE PERSON

If you are not married at the end of 1987, use the rate for "unmarried" single individuals, unless you qualify as a surviving spouse or a head of household.

If you are widowed, you are "unmarried" and use rates for single individuals regardless of the number of years you were married. There is an exception for recent widows or widowers supporting children, as explained in the column "surviving spouse."

HEAD OF HOUSEHOLD

You may use special head of household rates if you meet these tests:

1. You are not married at the end of the year.
2. You maintain a household for more than half of 1987 for your child or a dependent relative. The household must be your home and the main residence of your dependent relative except that a dependent parent need not live with you. However, you must maintain a dependent parent's separate household for the entire year to claim head of household status based on that support.
3. You pay more than one-half the cost of the household.
4. You are a U.S. citizen or resident alien during the entire tax year.

These rules are explained in detail in ¶1.10.

SURVIVING SPOUSE

If you are a widow or widower and your spouse died in 1985 or 1986, you may use 1987 joint return tax rates if you meet these four test:

1. You maintain your home as the main home of your child for the entire year and you furnish over half the cost of maintaining the household.
2. You are entitled to claim the child as a dependent; *see* ¶1.14.
3. In the year your spouse died, you could have filed a joint return.
4. You did not remarry before January 1, 1988.

The 1987 tax rate schedules are in chapter 22.

1

HOW YOUR PERSONAL AND FAMILY STATUS AFFECTS YOUR TAXES

¶ **1.1** Your family and personal status directly affects the tax you pay.

For each qualified dependent, you claim a deduction of $1,900. The tax-saving rules for claiming exemptions for yourself, your spouse and dependents are discussed at ¶1.14.

For paying care costs of dependent children while you work you may claim a tax credit as explained in ¶1.29–¶1.34.

For paying qualifying alimony, you may claim a deduction. If you receive such alimony, you report it as income. Pay special attention to the rules at ¶1.35–¶1.50 in planning alimony agreements so that you achieve favorable tax consequences.

Your tax rates depend on your personal status. There are four tax rate classes: Rates for married persons filing jointly, unmarried person rates, head of household rates, and rates for married persons filing separate returns. The lowest tax rates are provided to married persons filing jointly; the next lowest to unmarried persons filing as head of household; the highest rates apply to married persons filing separate returns. Joint return rates favor married couples where only one spouse earns income. When both spouses have income, the joint return rates usually result in a higher tax than if the two were reporting as single persons and applying single person rates. The difference in tax is called the "marriage penalty." Under prior law, this "penalty" was eased by a special deduction of up to $3,000. In 1987 and later years, this deduction is no longer allowed.

If you are married your best tax-saving choice is probably to file jointly; filing separately often results in a higher combined tax because of the tax rates applied to separate returns of married couples, as explained in ¶1.4. In special cases, a recently widowed individual may use joint return rates, which is an advantage to a single person; and certain separated married persons may use head of household rates under ¶1.10 rather than the higher rates applied to married persons filing separately. Tax rate schedules are in chapter 22.

	See ¶
Signing the joint return	1.2
Innocent spouse rules	1.3
Married persons may choose to file separately	1.4
Death of spouse during the year	1.5
Death of spouse in prior two years	1.6
Effect of divorce or separation decree	1.7

	See ¶
Joint return if spouse is a nonresident alien	1.8
Community property rules	1.9
Unmarried head of household	1.10
Tax returns for your children	1.11
Filing income tax returns for a decedent	1.12
Return for an incompetent person	1.13

SIGNING THE JOINT RETURN

¶ **1.2** Both you and your spouse must sign the return. Under the following rules, if your spouse is unable to sign, you may sign for him or her.

You may sign your spouse's name as agent by adding these words: "By _____ Husband (or Wife)," and attaching to the return your authorization.

If, because of illness, your spouse is physically unable to sign the joint return, you may, with the oral consent of your spouse, sign his or her name on the return followed by the words "By _____, Husband (or Wife)." You then sign the return again in your own right and attach a signed and dated statement with the following information: (1) The return or declaration being filed, (2) the tax year, (3) the reason for the inability of the sick spouse to sign, and (4) that the sick spouse has consented to your signing.

You might be able to prove you filed a joint return even if your spouse did not sign and you did not sign as your spouse's agent where:

You intended it to be a joint return—your spouse's income was included (or the spouse had no income).

Your spouse agreed to have you handle tax matters and you filed a joint return.

Your answers to the questions on the tax return indicate you intend to file a joint return.

Your spouse's failure to sign can be explained.

EXAMPLE

The Hills generally filed joint returns. In one year, Hill claimed joint return filing status and reported his wife's income as well as his own; in place of her signature on the return, he indicated that she was out of town caring for her sick mother. She did not file a separate return. The IRS refused to treat the return as joint. The Tax Court disagreed. Since Mrs. Hill testified that she would have signed had she been available, her failure to do so does not bar joint return status. The couple intended to make a joint return at the time of filing.

If a third party signs as agent for your spouse, power of attorney, Form 2848, must accompany the return.

Joint liability. When you sign a joint return, you and your spouse may be held individually liable for the entire tax due, plus interest and any penalties. You may be held liable if your spouse does not pay the tax, even if he or she earned all the income.

If you divorce, you remain jointly liable for joint returns filed before the divorce.

In limited cases, an innocent spouse may avoid liability, as discussed below.

INNOCENT SPOUSE RULES

¶ **1.3** To a limited extent, a spouse who files a joint return may be relieved of tax liability based on omitted income or invalid tax deductions or credits. These conditions must be met: (1) There is a tax underpayment exceeding $500 due to the omission of gross income attributable to the other spouse or inflated deductions or credits claimed by the other spouse, provided the "innocent" spouse's tax liability exceeds certain limits discussed below. In determining gross income, community property rules are disregarded, except for income from property. (2) In signing the joint return, the innocent spouse did not know of and had no reason to know of the omission of income or inflated deductions or credits. (3) Taking into account all the circumstances, it would be inequitable to hold the innocent spouse liable for the tax. The IRS will consider the extent to which the "innocent" spouse benefited from the tax underpayment in deciding the "equity" issue.

Innocent spouse's tax liability must exceed percentage of income. Where relief is based on the other spouse's claiming of invalid deductions or credits, the innocent spouse's tax liability must exceed $500 and a specific percentage of adjusted gross income for the taxable year preceding the year in which the IRS mails a deficiency notice. If the innocent spouse's adjusted gross income in the year preceding the mailing of a deficiency notice was $20,000 or less, the tax liability attributable to the other spouse's improper deductions must exceed 10% of the preceding year's adjusted gross income. If adjusted gross income was more than $20,000, the tax liability for which relief is sought must exceed 25% of the preceding year's adjusted gross income. If the innocent spouse has remarried as of the end of the preceding year, the new spouse's income must be included to determine the innocent spouse's adjusted gross income for purposes of the 10% and 25% tests.

Important. The above innocent spouse rules apply to all preceding taxable years which are not closed by the statute of limitations.

MARRIED PERSONS MAY CHOOSE TO FILE SEPARATELY

¶ 1.4 It is generally advisable to file jointly even though your spouse may have earned a small sum and could get a refund by filing separately. If your spouse files separately, you must file separately and your tax may be substantially higher than if you had filed jointly.

> Filing separately may reduce the overall taxes for a husband and a wife when both have separate incomes and one spouse may deduct a larger amount of medical expenses, casualty losses, and/or miscellaneous expenses because a lower adjusted gross income floor applies. Do not file separately if you want to take advantage of the $25,000 rental allowance deduction discussed in ¶11.4. For the effect of separate returns on IRA deductions, see chapter 8. To determine if there is a savings by filing separate returns, figure the tax on both types of returns taking these items into consideration, plus the effect of filing separately on computing taxable Social Security benefits and claiming credits such as the elderly and disabled credit (see chapter 34 and the box below).

Effect of filing separate returns. If you and your spouse file separate returns, you have three years from the due date to change to a joint return. If a joint return is filed and the due date has passed, you may not elect to file separate returns. The choice of filing a joint return is irrevocable once the due date is passed.

The filing of separate or joint estimated tax does not commit you to a similar tax return.

> You must file jointly to claim the following tax benefits: The IRA deduction for a nonworking spouse, and the credit for the elderly, dependent care credit, and the earned income credit. Further, if you receive Social Security benefits, one-half of your benefits are generally subject to tax on a separate return, because on a separate return you are not allowed a base amount exemption, *see* ¶34.8.

DEATH OF A SPOUSE DURING THE YEAR

¶ 1.5 You do not lose the right to file a joint return when your spouse dies during the year. Generally, a joint return is filed by you and the executor or administrator. But you alone may file a joint return if you are otherwise entitled to file jointly and:

1. The deceased has not filed a separate return, and
2. No executor or administrator has been appointed when the joint return is made, or no executor or administrator was appointed before the last day required to file the return of the surviving spouse.

As a surviving spouse, you may not file a joint return if:
1. You remarry before the end of the year of your spouse's death (but you may file a joint return with your new spouse).
2. You or your deceased spouse has a short year because of a change in the accounting period.
3. Either spouse was a nonresident alien at any time during the tax year. But *see* ¶1.8.
4. The executor or administrator disaffirms. When the executor or administrator is later appointed, he may disaffirm the joint return by filing a separate return for the decedent. The executor or administrator is the person who is actually appointed to that office. It is not the person who may be in charge of the property of the decedent. Even if a surviving spouse has properly filed a joint return for himself and the deceased spouse (*see* above)—the executor or administrator is given the right to disaffirm the joint return. But in one case, a state court held that a co-executrix could not refuse to sign a joint return where it would save the estate money.

The executor may disaffirm, within one year after the time required to file, the return of the surviving spouse by filing a separate return. The executor's separate return is treated as a late return. He has to pay interest and a penalty for a late filing. The return of the surviving spouse is deemed to be his or her separate return. Tax on that return is computed by excluding all items belonging to the deceased spouse.

Signing the return. A joint return reporting a decedent's income should list the names of the surviving spouse and the deceased. Where there is an executor or administrator, the return is signed by the surviving spouse and the executor or administrator in his official capacity. If the surviving spouse is the executor or administrator, he signs once as surviving spouse and again as the executor or administrator. Where there is no executor or administrator, the surviving spouse signs, followed by the words, "Taxpayer and surviving spouse."

If a joint return is filed and the estate cannot pay its share of the joint income tax liability, the surviving spouse may be liable for the full amount. Once the return is filed and the time for filing passes, the survivor can no longer change the joint return election and file a separate return unless an administrator or executor is appointed after the due date of the return. In that case, as explained above, the executor may disaffirm the joint return.

If a surviving spouse who will be appointed executor or administrator is concerned about insolvency, it may be advisable to hedge as follows: (1) File separate returns and if it is later seen that a joint return is preferable, the surviving spouse has three years to change to a joint return. (2) File jointly but postpone being appointed executor or administrator until after the due date of the joint return. In this way, the joint return may be disaffirmed if the estate cannot cover its share of the taxes.

DEATH OF SPOUSE IN PRIOR TWO YEARS

¶ 1.6 If your spouse died in either 1985 or 1986, you may use joint return rates on your 1987 return provided all the following requirements are met:

1. You did not remarry before 1988 (if you did remarry you may file a joint return with your new spouse).
2. A dependent child, stepchild, adopted child or foster child lived with you during 1987 and you paid over half the cost of maintaining your home,
3. You were able to file jointly in the year of your spouse's death, even if you did not actually do so.

If you meet all these tests, your 1987 filing status is "qualified widow or widower," which entitles you to compute your tax using favorable joint return rates. *See* chapter 22 for rate schedules.

If your spouse died before 1985 and you did not remarry before 1988, you may be able to use head of household rates if you qualify under the rules of ¶1.10.

EFFECT OF DIVORCE OR SEPARATION DECREE ON JOINT RETURN

¶ 1.7 *A decree of divorce or separate maintenance before the end of the year.* A decree entered before the end of 1987 prevents you from filing a joint return. Unless you qualify as head of household (¶1.10), you must use the rates for single individuals. You may not claim an exemption for a divorced or legally separated spouse, even if you contribute all support.

If you are married but live apart from your spouse and care for a child, you may be able to qualify as a head of household, *see* ¶1.10.

You may file a joint return after an interlocutory decree of divorce. Once the decree is made final, the privilege to file jointly ends. Alimony paid during the period covered by the interlocutory decree is deducted by the husband and reported by the wife as income if separate returns are filed.

If a divorce decree is interlocutory but another state waives the waiting period and permits a spouse to remarry, the IRS will recognize the new marriage and allow the filing of joint returns by the newly married couple. But a court has refused to allow a joint return where a new marriage took place in Mexico during the interlocutory period in violation of California law.

> The IRS and an appeals court conflict over whether a joint return with a new spouse is permissible if a prior divorce decree has been declared invalid by a state court. The appeals court allows the joint return; the IRS does not.

Year-end foreign divorce may not be recognized. A married couple with two incomes may pay more tax on a joint return than unmarried couples who file separately using single person rates. To avoid it, some married couples made quick year-end divorces to file as unmarried persons and then remarried the next year. The Tax Court has ruled two Caribbean divorces obtained by a Maryland couple during a two-year period were ineffective for tax purposes; the couple remained married and could not use unmarried person rates.

JOINT RETURN IF SPOUSE IS A NONRESIDENT ALIEN

¶ 1.8 You may not be able to file a joint return if either you or your spouse was a nonresident alien during any part of the year. Thus, a joint return may be barred if the alien spouse enters the United States in the middle of the taxable year or departs before it ends. Nevertheless, you may be able to claim your nonresident alien spouse as an exemption on a return filed as married filing separately if the spouse had no income and could not be claimed as a dependent by another taxpayer (*see* ¶1.15). If the alien spouse becomes a resident before the beginning of the next tax year, you may file jointly thereafter.

Election to file a joint return. Where a U.S. citizen or resident is married to a nonresident alien, the couple may file a joint return if both elect to be taxed on their worldwide income. The requirement that one spouse be a U.S. citizen or resident need be met only at the close of the year. Joint returns may be filed in the year of the election and all later years until the election is terminated.

A couple that makes the election must keep books and records of their worldwide income and give the IRS access to such books and records. If either spouse does not provide the necessary information to the IRS, the election is terminated. Further, the election is terminated if either spouse revokes or dies. Revocation before the due date of return is effective for that return. The election automatically terminates for the year of death of either spouse. However, if the survivor is a U.S. citizen or resident, he or she may claim the benefits of being a surviving spouse (*see* ¶1.1). The election to file jointly also terminates if the couple is legally separated under a decree of divorce or separate maintenance. Termination is effective as of the beginning of the taxable year of the legal separation. If neither spouse is a citizen or resident for any part of the taxable year, an election may not be made and an existing election is revoked. Once the election is terminated, neither spouse may ever again make the election.

Electing to file a joint return does not terminate the special withholding on the nonresident alien's income.

> *Special election where one spouse is a U.S. citizen or resident and the other is a nonresident alien who becomes a resident during the tax year.* The couple may file a joint return for that year if both elect to be taxed on their worldwide income. This is a one-time election; neither spouse may make the election again even if married to a new spouse.

If a couple does not make the election to file jointly, certain community property rules do not apply. *See* ¶1.9.

COMMUNITY PROPERTY RULES

¶ 1.9 If you live in Arizona, California, Idaho, Louisiana, Nevada, New Mexico, Texas, Washington, or Wisconsin, the income and property you and your spouse acquire during the marriage is generally regarded as "community property." But note that there are some instances in which community property rules are disregarded for tax purposes; these instances are clearly highlighted in the pertinent sections of this book.

Community property means that each of you owns half of the community income and community property, even if legal title is held by only one spouse.

Separate property may be owned. Property owned before marriage generally remains "separate property"; it does not become community property when you marry. Property received during the marriage by one spouse as a gift or inheritance from a third party is generally separate property. In some states, if the nature of ownership cannot be fixed, the property is presumed to be community property.

In some states, income from "separate property" may be treated as community property income. In other states, income from "separate property" remains the separate property of the individual owner.

Divorce or separation. If you and your spouse divorce, your community property automatically becomes separate property. A wife, while separated from her husband, does not generally report temporary alimony payments. She reports her share of community income until the date of the interlocutory divorce decree.

When community income rules do not apply to separated couples. If a husband and wife in a community property state file separate returns, each spouse must generally report one-half of the community income. However, a spouse may be able to avoid reporting income earned by his or her spouse if they live apart during the entire calendar year and do not file a joint return. To qualify, one or both spouses must have earned income for the year and none of that earned income may be transferred, directly or indirectly, between the spouses during the year. One spouse's payment to the other spouse solely to support the couple's dependent children is not a disqualifying transfer. If the separated couple qualifies under these tests, community income is allocated as follows: Earned income (excluding business or partnership income) is taxed to the spouse who performed the personal services. Business income (other than partnership income) is treated as the husband's income, unless the wife exercises substantially all of the management and control of the business. However, a similar rule for self-employment income was held unconstitutional on the basis of sex, and the IRS agreed to follow the court rule that the spouse actually carrying on the business is the spouse subject to self-employment tax. Partnership income is taxed to the spouse entitled to a distributive share of partnership profits.

Innocent spouse rules applied to community property. As discussed above, community property rules may not apply to earned income where spouses live apart for the entire year and file separate returns. In addition, a spouse who files a separate return may be relieved of tax liability on community income which is attributable to the other spouse if he or she does not know (or have reason to know) about the income and if it would be inequitable under the circumstances for him or her to be taxed on such income. This rule applies to all tax years not closed by the statute of limitations.

The IRS may disregard community property rules and tax income to a spouse who treats such income as if it were solely his or hers and who fails to notify the other spouse of the income before the due date of the return (including extensions).

Death of spouse. The death of a spouse dissolves the community property relationship, but income earned and accrued from community property before death is community income.

Moving from a community property to a common law (separate property) state. Most common law states (those which do not have community property laws) recognize that both spouses have an interest in property accumulated while residents of a community property state. If the property is not sold or reinvested, it may continue to be treated as community property. If you and your spouse sell community property after moving to a common law state and reinvest the proceeds, the reinvested proceeds are generally separate property, which may be held as joint tenants, or in another form of ownership recognized by common law states.

Moving from a common law state to a community property state. Separate property brought into a community property state generally retains its character as separately owned property. Property acquired by a couple after moving to a community property state is generally owned as community property. In at least one state (California), personal property which

qualifies as community property is treated as such, even though it was acquired when the couple lived in a common law state.

> *Claiming dependents on separate returns.* Married parents in community property states who plan to file separate returns should be aware that neither parent may be able to claim an exemption for a dependent child. Where all of the couple's income is considered community income, each parent on a separate return is treated as having provided exactly one-half of the child's support, regardless of who actually paid the support. Since neither parent has provided more than one-half of the support, neither can claim the child as a dependent.
>
> To avoid this result, parents whose sole income is community income and who want to file separately should consider signing a multiple support agreement, Form 2120, designating which parent may claim the exemption. Filing Form 2120 is not necessary where either parent can prove that he or she has income which is considered separate income rather than community income; that parent may be able to satisfy the more than 50% support test. In certain community property states, the law may provide that income of a husband and wife living apart is considered separate income rather than community income.

FILING AS HEAD OF HOUSEHOLD

UNMARRIED "HEAD OF HOUSEHOLD"

¶ **1.10** If you are an unmarried head of a household, you may compute your tax at a rate lower than that imposed on unmarried persons who do not qualify as heads of households. Tax rates are at chapter 22. If you live apart from your spouse, you may also qualify for head of household rates that are lower than rates for married persons filing separately; *see* rule 1 below.

You have to meet the following five tests to qualify as head of household.

1. You are not married at the end of the year.
You are any one of the following:
Single.
A widow or widower and your spouse died before the beginning of 1987. (Also see ¶ 1.6 if you may use joint return rates.)
Separated or divorced under a final court decree. A custody and support order does not qualify as a legal separation. An interlocutory decree, such as a support order pendente lite, has no effect for tax purposes until the decree is made final.
Married but living apart from your spouse. You are considered unmarried for 1987 if your spouse was not a member of your household during the last six months of 1987, you file separate returns, and you maintain a household for more than half the year for a dependent child, stepchild or adopted child. A foster child qualifies if a member of your household for the whole year. You must be able to claim the child as a dependent unless your spouse (the noncustodial parent) has the right to the exemption under rules of ¶ 1.23.
Your spouse was a nonresident alien during any part of 1987, and you do not qualify to file a joint return.

2. You maintain a household for your child or a dependent relative.

> *Your parent* must qualify as an exemption on your return and live in a home maintained by you, although not necessarily the home in which you live. Supporting a parent in a separate household or a home for the aged qualifies. Support in an outside household must be for the whole year.

EXAMPLE
Your mother lived with your sister in your sister's apartment, which cost $4,000 to maintain. Of this amount, you contributed $2,500, your sister $1,500. Your mother has no income and did not contribute any funds to the household. You qualify as head of household: For 1987, you paid over half the cost of maintaining the home for your mother who also qualifies as an exemption on your return.

Your child, stepchild, adopted child, foster child, or grandchild must live with you in your principal residence for more than half of 1987 (see 3 below). An unmarried child, stepchild, adopted child or grandchild does not have to be your dependent; a foster child does have to be your dependent. If the child is married, he must qualify as a dependent for you to claim head of household status unless you are divorced or separated and you have waived the exemption for your married child or the child's other parent may claim the exemption under a pre-1985 agreement. See ¶ 1.23. A person married on the last day of the year is considered married for the whole year.

If you are married and living apart from your spouse, you must be able to claim your child, married or unmarried, as an exemption unless you waive the exemption or your spouse (the noncustodial parent) may claim the exemption under a pre-1985 instrument, as explained at ¶ 1.23.

Any other relative must live with you (*see* 3 below) in your principal residence for more than half of 1987 and qualify as an exemption. Dependent relatives, other than children or parents, who may qualify you for head of household status are: Sons- or daughters-in-law, father- or mother-in-law, brothers- or sisters-in-law, brothers, sisters, grandparents, stepparents, stepbrothers or sisters, half-brothers or sisters, and uncles, aunts, nieces or nephews by blood.

If a child or other relative qualifies as an exemption on the basis of a multiple support agreement (*see* ¶ 1.22), you do not qualify as head of household.

A spouse who is a nonresident alien during any part of the year is not a dependent who can qualify you for head of household status, even though you maintain a home for him or her.

The support of an unrelated family, such as a mother and her children, does not qualify you as head of household, even if you are entitled to dependency exemptions for the children. See ¶ 1.17.

3. The household must be your home and the main residence of a dependent relative (described in 2 above). The home maintained for your dependent relative must be his or her principal residence for more than half of 1987, or for all of 1987 in the case of a dependent parent's separate household. That same home must also be *your* principal residence unless the dependent is your parent. For example, an IRS ruling held that a serviceman who supports his illegitimate child may not be a head of a household unless the child lives in the same house with him. However, an appeals court disagreed in one case; it allowed a mother to claim head of household status where she maintained a home for a child in one state and had her principal residence in another state.

The household relationship is not disqualified by your or your dependent's temporary absences, such as for illness, education, business, vacation, military service or child custody agreement. You must continue to maintain the household during the temporary absence.

You may claim head of household status when your dependent is confined to a hospital or sanitarium and his absence is temporary and you continue to maintain a household in expectation of his return.

A dependent who was born or died during the year is considered as having lived with you the entire year.

Custody decree does not determine child's residence for head of household purposes. A divorce decree will generally specify the parent who has custody of the children. In one case, a decree gave custody to the mother, but the child attended boarding school and lived with his father during vacations. The IRS held that the father could not claim head of household status. The child's principal place of abode could not be with his father because the mother had legal custody. The child's principal place of abode was the boarding school because the child lived there. The Tax Court disagreed, allowing the father to use head of household rates. Legal custody of a child does not determine the child's principal place of abode. The school was not the child's home; he lived there only temporarily. The father maintained a home with a room for him where his clothes and other belongings were kept. He furnished all his support, including tuition. The son could not live with his mother because of extreme hostility between them.

4. You pay more than one-half the cost of the household you maintain. The costs of maintaining a household include: property taxes, mortgage interest, rent, utility charges, upkeep and repairs, domestic help, property insurance, and food eaten in the household. You do not, as in the case of figuring support for a dependency exemption, consider the rental value of the lodgings provided the dependent. Also not included in the cost of maintaining a household are: clothing, education costs, medical expenses, vacation costs, life insurance premiums, transportation costs, and the value of your work around the house.

You may be head of household although not head of the family.

EXAMPLE

A son who earns more than his father and contributes more than half of the cost of maintaining the family may be a head of a household. That his father, not he, "exercises family control" does not matter. The important factor is a dollar test, whether he contributed more than half the cost of maintaining the household which is his home and the principal home of his qualifying dependents.

Two-family house. A mother was allowed head of household status by the Tax Court in the following case. She and her unmarried daughter rented one floor of a multilevel home. A married daughter lived on a different floor with her family. Parts of the home were shared. According to the court, the mother was a head of household, based on support of her unmarried daughter. Although she did not pay more than half of the total household expenses, she paid more than half the expenses attributable to her and her unmarried daughter.

5. You are a U.S. citizen or resident alien during the entire tax year.

FILING RETURNS FOR CHILDREN, DECEDENTS, AND INCOMPETENT PERSONS

TAX RETURNS FOR YOUR CHILDREN

¶ **1.11** The income of your minor child is not included in your return. A minor is considered a taxpayer in his own right. If the child is required to file a return (*see* chapter 22) but is unable to do so because of age or for any other reason, his parent or guardian is responsible for filing the return. If the child is unable to sign the return, the parent or guardian should sign the child's name in the proper place, followed by the words "By (signature), Parent (or guardian) for minor child." A parent is liable for tax due on pay earned by the child for services, but not on investment income.

A child who is not required to file a return should still do so for a refund of taxes withheld, if any.

Filing tests for dependent children and rules for computing tax of a child with investment income are at chapter 22.

A parent or guardian must obtain a Social Security number for a child before filing the child's first income tax return. The child's Social Security number must also be provided to banks, brokers and other payers of interest and dividends to avoid penalties and backup withholding (¶25.12). To obtain a Social Security number, file Form SS-5 with your local Social Security office. If you have applied for a Social Security number but not yet received it by the filing due date, write "Applied for" on the tax return.

Children with wages are generally subject to withholding and should file Form W-4 with their employer. An exemption from withholding may be claimed only in limited cases where the child can be claimed as a dependent by a parent or other taxpayer. If a dependent child has any investment income, the exemption from withholding is allowed only if the expected amount of investment income plus wages is $500 or less. Further, the child must certify on Form W-4 that he or she had no federal tax liability in the prior year and expects to have no liability in the current year.

You may deduct wages paid to your children in your business. Keep records showing that their activities are of a business rather than household nature.

If your child pays you for board and lodging, the payments probably are not income to you. The amount contributed by the child is usually less than the cost of his board. If the child works for you, you may not take a deduction for board and lodging you provide unless the child has been freed from your parental control.

TAX RETURN FOR A DECEASED PERSON

¶ **1.12** When a person dies, another taxpaying entity is created—the decedent's estate. Until the estate is fully distributed, it will generally earn income for which a return must be filed. For example, decedent had a savings account. Decedent dies on June 30. Income earned on the account through June 30 is reported on decedent's final income tax return, Form 1040. Income earned on the account from July 1 is reported in the estate's income tax return, fiduciary Form 1041. See ¶10.16.

What income tax returns must be filed? If decedent died after close of taxable year, but before income tax return was filed, the following must be filed:
1. Income tax return for prior year
2. Final income tax return, covering earnings in period from beginning of taxable year to date of death, and
3. Estate income tax return, covering earnings in period after decedent's death.

If decedent died after filing a return for prior tax year, then only (2) and (3) are filed.

EXAMPLE

Jones died on March 31, 1988, before he could file his 1987 tax return due April 15, 1988. A regular income tax return must be filed by April 15, 1988. A final income tax return to report earnings from January 1, 1988 through March 31, 1988 will have to be filed on April 15, 1989. Similarly, an estate income tax return to report earnings on or after April 1, 1988 will have to be filed. The due date for the estate income tax return depends on the tax year of the estate. If the estate adopts a fiscal year beginning April 1, the first return is due July 15, 1989.

For purposes of determining whether a final income tax return is due, the annual gross income test on page 2 is considered in full. You do not prorate it to the part of the year decedent lived.

An income tax return for the estate must be filed if the estate has gross income of $600 or more.

Who is responsible for filing? The executor, administrator, or other legal representative is responsible for filing all returns. A surviving spouse may assume responsibility for filing a joint return for the year of death if no executor or administrator has been appointed and other tests are met (¶1.5). However, if a legal representative has been appointed, he or she must consent to the filing of a joint return for the year of decedent's death.

How do you report the decedent's income and deductions? You follow the method used by the decedent during his life to account for the income up to his death. The income does *not* have to be put on an annual basis. Each item is taxed in the same manner as it would have been taxed had he lived for the entire year.

If the deceased owned U.S. savings bonds *see* ¶4.15.

Do not report on the decedent's final return income that is received after his death or accrues after or because of his death. It is taxed to the estate or beneficiary receiving the income in the year of the receipt. On the decedent's final return, only deductible expenses paid up to and including the date of death may be claimed. If the decedent reported on the accrual basis, those deductions accruable up to and including the date of death are deductible. If a check for payment of a deductible item was delivered or mailed before the date of the decedent's death, a deduction is allowable on the decedent's last return, even though the check was not cashed or deposited until after the decedent's death. If the check was not honored by the bank, the item is not deductible. Also *see* ¶11.03.

The payment of medical expenses of the decedent by his estate within one year after his death is treated as having been paid by the decedent when incurred. Consequently, the expenses are deductible on the decedent's last return. However, the expenses are not deductible for income tax purposes if they are deducted for estate tax purposes. To deduct such medical expenses on the decedent's last return, a statement must be filed affirming that no estate tax deduction has been taken and waiving the rights to the deduction.

Partnership income. The final return includes partnership income or loss only from a partnership year that ends within the decedent's tax year. Thus, if a partner dies in July, 1987 and the partnership's calendar year ends December 31, 1987, no partnership income or loss is included on the partner's final 1987 return. It is reported by the partner's executor or other successor in interest on the estate's income tax return.

What exemptions are allowed on a final return? Generally, the same exemptions the decedent would have had if he had not died. You do not reduce them because of a shorter taxable year. If the deceased had contributed more than one-half of a dependent's annual support, a dependency exemption is claimed on his final return.

Does estimated tax have to be paid? No estimated tax need be paid after the death of an unmarried individual by the executor; the entire tax is paid when filing the final tax return. But where the deceased and a surviving spouse paid estimated tax jointly, the rule is different. The surviving spouse is still liable for the balance of the estimated tax unless an amended estimated tax voucher is filed. Further, if the surviving spouse plans to file a joint return (¶1.5) which includes the decedent's income, estimated tax payments may be required. *See* chapter 26.

What if a refund is due? The decedent's return may also be used as a claim for a refund of an overpayment of withheld or estimated taxes. But to get the refund, Form 1310 must be filed with the final return with an attached certificate of death. Form 1310 is available from your local District Director. A surviving spouse who files a joint return for the year of death does not have to file Form 1310.

When one spouse dies in a community property state (*see* ¶1.9), how should the income from the community property be reported during the administration of the estate? The IRS says that half the income is the estate's and the other half belongs to the surviving spouse.

Signing the return. An executor or administrator of the estate signs the return. If it is a joint return, *see* ¶1.5.

To expedite the closing of the decedent's estate, an executor or other personal representative of the decedent may file a written request for a prompt assessment. Once filed, the IRS has 18 months to assess additional taxes. Without the request, the IRS has three years from the due date of the return to make assessments. In making a request, state that it is being made under Section 6501(d) of the Code. The request must be filed *separately* from the return but should be sent to the District Director for the district in which the return is filed.

RETURN FOR AN INCOMPETENT PERSON

¶ 1.13 A legal guardian of an incompetent person files Form 1040 for him if the incompetent's gross income meets the filing tests at page 2. Where a spouse becomes incompetent, the IRS says the other spouse may file a return for the incompetent without a power of attorney, if no legal guardian has been appointed. For example, during the period an individual was in a mental hospital, and before he was adjudged legally incompetent, his wife continued to operate his business. She filed an income tax return for him and signed it for him although she had no power of attorney. The IRS accepted the return as properly filed. Until a legal guardian was appointed, she was charged with the care of her husband and his property.

The IRS had accepted a joint return filed by a wife and in her capacity as legal guardian for her missing husband. However, the Tax Court has held that where one spouse is mentally incompetent, a joint return may not be filed because the incompetent spouse was unable to consent to a joint return; an appeals court agreed.

CLAIM ALL YOUR EXEMPTIONS

Illustrations listing exemptions may be found in the Supplement to YOUR INCOME TAX.

¶ 1.14 New law increases personal exemptions. Each exemption you claim on your 1987 return is the equivalent of a $1,900 deduction. You may claim an exemption for:

Yourself. Every taxpayer is allowed one exemption unless he or she is the dependent of another taxpayer. If you are claimed as a dependent by another person for 1987, you may not claim a personal exemption for yourself on your own return. This rule prevents a child or other dependent from claiming an exemption on his or her return if you may claim an exemption for the child or other dependent.

No extra exemptions are allowed for being 65 or for being blind but such individuals are allowed an additional standard deduction; *see* chapter 13.

Your spouse. You claim your spouse as an exemption when you file a joint return. If you file a separate return, you claim your spouse as an exemption if he or she has no income and is not a dependent of another person.

Children, parents, and other dependents. There is no limit to the number of dependents you may claim, provided you satisfy five tests for each dependent—a relationship test, a support test, an income test, a citizenship or residency test, and for married dependents, a joint return test. These tests are fully discussed starting at ¶ 1.16.

You must report on your 1987 return the Social Security number of each dependent who is at least five years old.

EXEMPTIONS FOR SPOUSE, CHILDREN AND OTHER DEPENDENTS

CLAIMING YOUR SPOUSE AS AN EXEMPTION

¶ 1.15 Your spouse is not your dependent for tax purposes. An exemption for a wife or husband is based on the marital relationship, not support.

On a joint return, each spouse receives an exemption as a taxpayer.

On a separate return, you may claim your spouse as an exemption if he or she has no gross income and is not the dependent of another taxpayer. You may not claim an exemption for your spouse who has income, *unless you file a joint return which includes that income.* For example, if a wife files a separate return, her husband may not claim her as an exemption, even if she filed the return merely for a refund of taxes withheld on her wages.

You are divorced or legally separated. You may not claim your spouse as an exemption if you are divorced or legally separated under a *final* decree of divorce or separate maintenance, even though you support your spouse and do not deduct alimony. However, an interlocutory decree does not bar you from claiming your spouse as an exemption.

EXAMPLE
An interlocutory decree of divorce is entered in 1987; a final decree in 1988. For 1987, the couple may file a joint return on which exemptions for both are claimed. A marriage is not dissolved until a final decree is entered, which here is in 1988.

Your spouse died during the year. If you did not remarry and your deceased spouse had no gross income, you may claim an exemption for the deceased on a joint return or on a separate return if the deceased was not a dependent of another taxpayer. If the deceased had gross income, to claim the exemption, you must file a joint return that includes the deceased's income.

EXAMPLE
Mrs. Smith dies on June 27. Mr. Smith files a joint return and claims her as an exemption. They were married as of the date of Mrs. Smith's death. The joint return includes all of Mr. Smith's income for the year, but only that part of Mrs. Smith's income earned up to June 27 (*see* ¶ 1.5).

If you remarry before the end of the year in which your spouse died, you may not claim an exemption for your deceased spouse. If a widow remarries, she may be an exemption on her deceased husband's separate return and on her present husband's joint return or separate return, provided she had no income and was not a dependent of another taxpayer.

If your spouse is a nonresident alien, *see* ¶ 1.8.

TESTS FOR CLAIMING DEPENDENTS

¶ 1.16 Here are the five tests that determine whether or not you may claim an exemption for a dependent.

1. Relationship or member of household test
A relative—Child, stepchild, adopted child, grandchild, great grandchild, son- or daughter-in-law, father- or mother-in-law, brother- or sister-in-law, parent, brother, sister, grandparent, stepparent, stepbrother or sister, half-brother or sister, uncle, aunt, niece or nephew by blood. A foster child qualifies if, for the entire year, he made your home his principal home and is a member of your household. *See* ¶ 1.17.

Or—any person, whether or not related, who for the entire year made your home his principal home and is a member of your household (except if the relationship between you and such person is in violation of state law.) *See* ¶ 1.18.

2. Support test

You either contribute more than half the dependent's support or contribute more than 10%, and together with others contribute more than half. *See ¶1.19.*

Total the dollar amount of support spent on a dependent by you, by others, and by the dependent. If your contribution is:

More than 50% of the total spent—you claim the exemption.

More than 10% of the total spent and together with what you and the other contributors gave is more than 50% of the total spent—you or one of the others who also contributed more than 10% may claim the exemption. You and the others must decide who is to claim the exemption. If you take it, you must attach to your return a Form 2120, Multiple Support Declaration, signed by each person who contributed more than 10%.

Less than 50%, either alone or with the contribution to his own support—neither you nor the other contributors may claim the exemption for the dependent.

3. Gross income test

Your dependent had less than $1,900 of gross income for the year. *See ¶1.24.*

Or—your dependent is your child, who is under 19 or a full-time student, in which case the amount of the dependent's gross income is not considered and may be $1,900 or over.

4. Citizenship or resident test

Your dependent is a United States citizen or national, or a resident of the United States, Canada or Mexico. *See ¶1.26.*

5. Joint return test

Your married dependent does not file a joint return with his or her spouse. *See ¶1.27.*

TEST 1. DEPENDENT'S RELATIONSHIP

¶ 1.17 Your dependent must be related to you (*see above* for a list of qualifying relatives). That he is an adult, healthy, and capable of self-support does not bar you from claiming him as an exemption—provided all the other tests are met.

The following rules apply to these relationships.

Infants. A child born during the year is a dependent. For example, you may claim an exemption for the year for a child born on December 31.

A stillborn child may not be claimed as an exemption. The exemption is allowed for a child who was born alive even if the infant lived for only a moment.

Adopted children. A legally adopted child is considered your child. A child is legally adopted when a court decree is entered. In states allowing interlocutory decrees, you may claim the exemption in the year the interlocutory decree is entered. If a court decree has not been entered, a child may be your dependent provided he was placed with you for adoption by an authorized adoption agency and was a member of your household. If he has not been placed with you for adoption by an agency, you may claim him as a dependent *only if* he was a member of your household for the entire tax year (*see* ¶1.18).

Foster child. A foster child is considered to be your child if your home is his principal residence and he is a member of your household for the entire year.

Death during the year. If a dependent died during 1987 but while he was alive you supported him and you meet the other tests listed in this chapter, you may claim an exemption for him.

EXAMPLE

On January 21, 1987, your father died. Until that date, you contributed all of his support. You may claim him as an exemption for 1987. The full deduction is taken. Exemptions are not prorated.

Nephew, niece, uncle, and aunt. They must be your blood relatives to qualify as your dependents. For example, the brother or sister of your father or mother qualifies as your relative; their spouses do not. You may not claim your spouse's nephews, nieces, uncles, or aunts unless you file a joint return.

EXAMPLE

You contribute more than half of the support of the sister of your wife's mother (your wife's aunt). If you and your wife file a joint return, her aunt is allowed as an exemption on your joint return. But even on a joint return, you may not claim an exemption for supporting your wife's aunt's husband. He is not related by blood to you or your wife.

In-laws. Brother-in-law, sister-in-law, father-in-law, mother-in-law, son-in-law, and daughter-in-law are relatives by marriage. You may claim them as exemptions if you meet the other tests in this chapter.

You may claim an exemption for a dependent who was related to you by marriage and whom you continue to support after divorce or death of your spouse.

EXAMPLE

Allen has contributed all the support of his father-in-law since he was married. His wife died in 1986. He continued as sole support of his wife's father in 1987. He may claim him as an exemption.

Stepchild's husband or wife or child. Your stepchild's spouse does not meet the relationship test. Nor may you claim an exemption for a step-grandchild if you file a separate return. They are not on the list of relatives for whose support you may claim an exemption. (*See* ¶1.16.) But you may claim them as exemptions on a joint return. On a joint return, it is not necessary that the close relationship exist between the dependent and the spouse who furnishes the chief support. It is sufficient that the relationship exists with either spouse.

UNRELATED OR DISTANTLY RELATED DEPENDENT MEMBERS OF YOUR HOUSEHOLD

¶ 1.18 A friend, foster child (not legally adopted), and a relative not listed in ¶1.16—such as a cousin who lives with you—can be your dependent. You may claim an unrelated or distantly related person as a dependent if:

1. He is a member of your household, and
2. Your home is his principal home for the entire year, except for absences when attending school, vacationing, or being confined to a hospital.

EXAMPLES

1. You support a friend who lives in your house all year. You can claim him as a dependent member of your household.

2. You provide a home for an orphan for seven months. You cannot claim him as a dependent. He did not live in your home for an entire year. However, if the child had been placed in your home for adoption by an authorized adoption agency, you may claim him as a dependent although he was not a member of your household for the entire year (*see* adopted children rule at ¶1.17).

3. You support a cousin who lives in a house you own. However, you live elsewhere. You may not claim him as a dependent. You do not live in the same house.

You may not claim a friend as an exemption when you live in his house even though you support him. You are living in his household, not your own. Also, you cannot claim an exemption for a friend who lives in your house and renders you services in return for your care.

The following are not considered dependents, even if they technically meet the above two rules:

Your spouse. Under the tax law, one spouse is not considered a dependent of the other (*see* ¶1.15).

A boarder in your house.

Housekeeper, servant, or maid.

An exemption for an unmarried mate depends on local law. Where the relationship violates local law, no exemption may be claimed.

EXAMPLE

Ensminger lived in North Carolina with a woman whom he supported. When he claimed an exemption for her, the IRS disallowed the exemption, claiming that under North Carolina law, it is a misdemeanor for an unmarried man and woman to live together. When the Tax Court supported the IRS position, Ensminger appealed, arguing that the North Carolina law was an unconstitutional invasion of his right to privacy. The appeals court held that constitutionality was not an issue for the IRS and Tax Court to decide. The states are responsible for regulating domestic affairs. Federal tax law merely follows the direction of state law. If Ensminger lived in a state that did not hold his relationship illegal, he could claim the exemption.

In a similar case, a dependency exemption was allowed where the court ruled cohabitation did not violate Missouri law.

TEST 2. SUPPORT PROVIDED THE DEPENDENT

¶ 1.19 If your dependent has no financial means and you are the only person contributing to his support during the year, you can skip the following discussion on support. You meet the support test. You contribute 100% of the dependent's support. If, however, the dependent or other persons or organizations contribute to his support, you have to determine whether your contribution meets the support test.

Divorced or separated parents contributing to support of their children may have to figure support under special rules. *See* ¶ 1.23.

Follow these steps to figure support: (1) Total the value of the support contributed by you, by the dependent himself, and by others. (2) Determine your share of the total. If your share is more than 50% of the dependent's total support, you meet the support test. If the dependent or some other person or organization contributed 50% or more to his support, you may not take the exemption. If the dependent or someone else did not contribute 50% or more to his support, and you contributed more than 10% of the total support, you may be able to claim the exemption under the multiple support agreement rule of ¶ 1.24.

> You do not consider the number of days or months in which you or anyone else paid his support. You claim the exemption in the year you furnish the support, not the year you pay any debts you incurred in providing the support. Furnishing support requires more than a promise or unfulfilled duty or obligation to pay. There must be an unconditional obligation to pay for the items of support.
>
> **EXAMPLE**
>
> Your son's college tuition is due in September, 1987. His school has allowed you to postpone payment until 1988. You include that part of the tuition covering the school months in 1987 as support contributions.

You now have a general outline of how to compare support contributions. To fill in the details, you need to know what are and what are not support items. For this purpose, see the checklists of includable and nonincludable support items. Following the checklists, you will find a discussion of how to value and allocate lodging and food items and further examples of figuring support.

These Are Support Items:

Lodging, food, and clothing
Social Security benefits if used for support
Education—tuition payments and cost of books and supplies
Tax-free income, such as life insurance proceeds and tax-exempt interest, used to pay maintenance expenses, is counted as support.

EXAMPLES

1. Your father uses his Social Security benefits for his support. You must count these amounts to find the total he uses for support.

2. Social Security benefits paid to children of deceased workers *which are used for their support* are treated as the children's contribution to their own support. Follow this rule even though benefits are paid to you as the child's parent or custodian, *and you use them for the child's support*. If the Social Security benefits used for a child's support are more than half of his total support, no one may claim him as a dependent.

Medical and dental care, including premiums paid for medical care insurance policies. Federal basic Medicare benefits under Part A and supplementary benefits under Part B are not treated as a dependent's contribution to his own support. According to the IRS, Medicaid payments are considered support in the nature of welfare payments, furnished by the dependent for his own support. A Tax Court decision rejects the IRS view.

Recreation and entertainment—including summer camp costs
Transportation
Singing and dancing lessons and cost of musical instruments
Wedding clothes and reception for a child
Purchase of auto and certain appliances (*see* discussion below)
Dependent care payments (baby sitter fees, nursery school costs)
Care provided a relative in an institution, orphanage, or old-age home supported by a state, a religious, or a fraternal organization

EXAMPLE

In 1987, your father was a patient in a state hospital. The state required you to pay part of his expenses and you paid the state $1,600. In the state budget report for 1987, the average cost of maintaining an individual in the hospital was listed at $3,000. As you contributed over half of your father's support, you may claim him as a dependent. If he required special care, such as private nursing or a major operation, the actual cost to the state agency for maintaining him during the year, rather than the average cost, would be used to measure his total support.

Educational benefits received by a student from the government as subsidy allowances under the GI Bill, U.S. Naval Educational Assistance scholarships, and Armed Forces Academies such as West Point. (However, note that courts have ruled that payments received under the Naval R.O.T.C. Program are scholarship payments that are not treated as items of support.) War Orphans Educational Assistance Act payments are not counted as support.

Student loans. If your child has obtained a loan to pay educational costs and is the primary obligor, the loan proceeds are treated as his contribution to support. That a parent is a guarantor does not change the rule.

State welfare payments. These are considered to have been furnished by the dependent for his own support, unless evidence is shown that he has used these payments for others or for nonsupport items, such as life insurance premiums.

Foster care payments by a child-placing agency to foster parents are support furnished by the agency and not the parent. A parent's unreimbursed expenses are deductible either as a charitable contribution

> Lump-sum contribution covering a dependent's stay in an old-age home. The lump sum is prorated over the dependent's life expectancy.
>
> **EXAMPLE**
>
> A son secures his father's placement in a religious home for a lump sum payment of $9,600. The payment was determined on the basis of $1,200 a year over the father's life expectancy of eight years. The home makes no refund if the father dies within eight years. The son counts $1,200 as an annual contribution to his father's support. If this is more than half of his father's yearly support costs, the son may claim the exemption. If the father fails to reach his life expectancy, the son may not deduct any unused part of the $9,600 as a charitable deduction.

or as a business expense (if payments in addition to reimbursements are received).

Tax-free payments by a state social service to adoptive parents to help finance the adopted child's care. This is support contributed by the state. To claim an exemption for the child, the parents must prove they contributed more to the child's support than the state.

Armed Forces support of a dependent who joined or left the Armed Forces during 1987. In determining his support, you must include the value of the board, lodging, clothing, etc., he received while in service, and any pay that he used for his support. If he has been in service for the entire year, you may not claim him as an exemption.

Armed Forces dependency allotments. Both the part of a dependency allotment contributed by the government, as well as the part withheld from a serviceman's pay, are considered as support being furnished by the serviceman. If the allotment is used to support dependents other than those for whom the allotment is authorized, an exemption may be claimed for those other dependents if they otherwise qualify as the serviceman's dependents.

EXAMPLE

You are in the Armed Forces and authorize a dependency allotment for your widowed mother. She uses the payment to support herself and your younger brother. You provide no other funds for their support. If more than half of their support is provided by your allotment, you claim exemptions for both your mother and your brother, even though the allotment was authorized only for your mother.

Serviceman's allowance for quarters paid to or on behalf of a specified dependent. If an allowance is actually used by the dependent, the serviceman is considered to have furnished the allowance. He may include it in figuring whether he contributed more than half the dependent's support.

Auto and appliances may be support items. The purchase price of an auto may be treated as a support cost item.

EXAMPLE

A dependent child buys a car for $4,500. In the same year, his parent contributes $4,000 to his support. The automobile bought by the child is treated as the child's own support contribution in the year of purchase. As the $4,000 of support furnished by the parent for the youth is less than half of the total support of $8,500, the parent may not claim him as an exemption. If the parent had purchased the automobile as a gift for the child and registered title in the child's name, the parent would have provided all the child's support.

What if a parent buys a car, registers it in his own name, but allows his dependent child to use it? The automobile itself is not a support item. However, the out-of-pocket expenses of operating the automobile for the benefit of the dependent child are support items.

A power lawn mower purchased by a parent for a child who is made responsible for keeping the lawn trimmed is not a support item even if the mower was supplied to make mowing more palatable to the child.

A TV receiver bought as a gift by a *noncustodial* parent for his child and placed in the child's bedroom was held to be a support item. If the set is bought on credit, it is a support item in the year of the gift, even though no payment for the set may have been made in the year of the gift.

These Items Are Not Counted as Support:

Life insurance premiums

Federal, state, and local income taxes and Social Security taxes paid by the dependent from his own income

Funeral expenses

Value of personal services you perform for a dependent, such as nursing

Scholarships received by your child (or stepchild or legally adopted child) who is a full-time student for at least each of five calendar months during the year. Scholarship aid is counted as support contributed by the child if he is not a full-time student during each of five calendar months of the year. Note also the exceptions above for certain government educational benefits.

EXAMPLE

Your child attends college on a $5,000 scholarship. She has no income of her own. You contribute $4,000 to her support. You may claim her as a dependent. The scholarship is not counted in figuring whether you give more than half her support.

Value of food and lodging furnished student nurses by an accredited nursing school.

Value of education, room, and board provided a handicapped child by a state agency. The state aid is treated as a scholarship.

Medical care benefits paid by an insurance company to a dependent under a policy paid by you or similar payments in compensation of medical expenses paid by a person who caused an accident resulting in injuries to the dependent.

Federal Medicare benefits paid under the supplementary medical care insurance program (Part B) or basic benefits (Part A).

Medical care provided a dependent by the federal government under the Dependents' Medical Care Act of 1956.

HOW TO VALUE LODGING AND ALLOCATE FOOD COSTS AND SOCIAL SECURITY BENEFITS

¶ 1.20 You count as support *the fair rental value* of a room, apartment, or house in which the dependent lives. In your estimate, you include a reasonable allowance for the rental value of furnishing and for heat and other utilities. You do not add payments of rent, taxes, interest, depreciation, paint, insurance, and utilities. These are presumed to be accounted for in the fair rental estimate. The fair rental value of lodging you furnish a dependent is the amount you could reasonably expect to receive from a stranger for the lodging.

If the dependent lives in his own home, he contributes the total fair rental value of his home to his own support. If you help him maintain his home by giving him cash to pay, or you directly pay, such expenses as the mortgage, real estate taxes, fire insurance premiums, and repairs, you reduce the total fair rental value of his home by the amount you contributed.

EXAMPLE

You contribute $1,500 as support to your father who lives in his own home which has a fair rental value of $4,500 a year. He uses $200 of the money you give him to pay real estate taxes on the property. His total support is computed as follows:

Cash contributed by you	$1,500
Fair rental value of house ($4,500 less $200 for taxes)	4,300
Father's total support	$5,800

If you lived with your dependent rent-free in his home, the fair rental value of lodging furnished to you must be offset against the amounts you spent for your dependent in determining the net amount of your contribution to his support.

Food and other similar household expenses. If the dependent lives with you, you divide your total food expenses equally among all the members of your household, unless you have records showing the exact amount spent on the dependent. If he does not live with you, you count the actual amount of food expenses spent by or for the dependent.

Allocating Social Security benefits. Where a couple receives Social Security benefit checks made out in joint names, half of the payment is considered to have been used for the support of each, unless a different use of the money is proved.

EXAMPLE

Your father and mother received $7,500 during the year as joint Social Security benefits. Although under the Social Security Act two-thirds of these benefits belong to your father and one-third to your mother, one-half of the benefits, or $3,750, is considered to have been used by your father and $3,750 by your mother.

EXAMPLES OF HOW SUPPORT IS ALLOCATED

¶ **1.21** The following examples illustrate how you allocate various items of support.

EXAMPLE

1. Your father lives with you, your spouse and three children. He receives Social Security benefits of $2,700, which he spends for his own needs. You spend $4,200 for food during the year. You also paid his dental bill of $200. You estimate the fair rental value of the room furnished him is $2,000. Your father's total support is:

Social Security	$2,700
Share of food costs (1/6 of $4,200)	700
Dental bill paid by you	200
Rental value of room	2,000
	$5,600

You claim him as a dependent. You contributed more than half his total support, or $2,900 ($2,000 lodging, $200 dental, $700 food).

2. Your parents live with you, your spouse and two children in a house you rent. The fair rental value of their room is $2,000. Your father receives a pension of $4,200, all of which he spent equally for your mother and himself for clothing and recreation. Your total expense in providing food for the household is $6,000. You pay heat and utility bills of $1,200. You paid your mother's medical expenses of $600. You figure the total support of your parents as follows:

	Father	Mother
Fair rental value of room	$1,000	$1,000
Pension used for their support	2,100	2,100
Share of food costs (1/6 of $6,000)	1,000	1,000
Medical expense for mother		600
	$4,100	$4,700

The support you furnish your father, $2,000 (lodging, $1,000; food, $1,000), is not over half of his total support of $4,100. The support you furnish your mother, $2,600 (lodging, $1,000; food, $1,000; medical, $600), is over half of her total support of $4,700. You claim an exemption for your mother but not your father. You do not consider the cost of heat and utilities. It is presumed to be in the rental estimate.

3. Your parents live in an apartment which they furnish with their own belongings. You pay rent of $4,800 for the apartment. The fair market value of the apartment with furnishings is $5,800. Your father receives a pension of $5,000 which he uses for his and your mother's personal needs. Their total support is:

	Father	Mother
Fair rental value of furnished apartment	$2,900	$2,900
Pension used for support	2,500	2,500
	$5,400	$5,400

You may not claim either parent as an exemption. Your payment of rent for an unfurnished apartment of $2,400 for each is less than half of their total support. If you had provided the furniture, the amount of their support would be over half for each, or $2,900. You would then have gotten both exemptions.

> *Earmarking support to one dependent in a household.* If you are contributing funds to a household consisting of several persons and the amount you contribute does not exceed 50% of the total support cost of the household, you may be able to claim an exemption for at least one dependent by earmarking your support to his or her use, if your contribution will exceed 50% of their support costs. You may do this by marking your checks for the benefit of the dependent, or by having a statement of your support arrangement at the time you start your payments. The IRS says its agents will generally accept such evidence of your arrangement. If you do not designate for whom you are providing support, your contribution is allocated equally among all members of a household (*see* example 1 above).

EXAMPLES

1. A husband who lives apart from his family without a divorce or legal separation sends his wife $3,240 to meet household expenses. A son and daughter live with her. The wife contributes from her own funds $6,480; an uncle sends her $1,080. The total amount going to meet household expenses from all sources is $10,800. On a separate return, the husband may not claim any exemptions for his children; his contributions are less than 50% of their total support. As he has not earmarked who is to get his contributions, his payments are allocated equally among the three members of the household. Each is considered to have received $1,080 from him. His contribution of $1,080 is less than half of the total support of $3,600 allocated to each child.

Contributed by:	Allocated to:		
	Wife	Son	Daughter	Total
Wife	$2,160	$2,160	$2,160	$6,480
Husband	1,080	1,080	1,080	3,240
Uncle	360	360	360	1,080
Total	$3,600	$3,600	$3,600	$10,800

2. Same facts as above except that the husband notes on his monthly checks of $270 that $180 is for his son; $90 for his daughter. He may claim his son as an exemption on a separate return; he has contributed more than half of the son's support. As total household costs of $10,800 are allocated equally among the three household members, the wife's contribution is reallocated to make up for the difference created by the husband's increased support to the son. Here, the wife is considered to have contributed $3,240 to her own support.

Contributed by:	Allocated to:		
	Wife	Son	Daughter	Total
Wife	$3,240	$1,080	$2,160	$6,480
Husband		2,160	1,080	3,240
Uncle	360	360	360	1,080
Total	$3,600	$3,600	$3,600	$10,800

3. Assume in the above example the mother contributed only $6,240 and her son contributed $240. There would be no change in tax consequences; however, the allocation of support contributions would differ. The son's contribution is added to the total household costs which are allocated equally among the family members to find how much applies to each person's support. However, in determining support contributions, the son is treated as contributing $240 to his own support.

Contributed by:	Allocated to:		
	Wife	Son	Daughter	Total
Wife	$3,240	$840	$2,160	$6,240
Son		240		240
Husband		2,160	1,080	3,240
Uncle	360	360	360	1,080
Total	$3,600	$3,600	$3,600	$10,800

MULTIPLE SUPPORT AGGREEMENTS

¶ **1.22** Are you and others sharing the support of one person, but with no one individual providing more than half his total support? You may claim the dependent as an exemption if:

1. You gave more than 10% of the support;
2. The amount contributed by you and others to the dependent's support equals more than half the support;
3. Each contributor could have claimed the exemption—except that he gave less than half support; *and*
4. Each contributor who gave more than 10% agrees to let you take the exemption. Each signs a Form 2120, Multiple Support Agreement. You then attach the forms to your return.

EXAMPLES

1. You and your two brothers contribute $2,000 each toward the support of your mother. She contributes $1,000 of her own to support herself. Your two sisters contribute $500 each. Thus, the total support comes to $8,000. Of this, each brother gave 25% ($2,000/$8,000) for a total of 75%. Each sister gave less than 10%—6 ¼% ($500 ÷ $8,000). You or one of your brothers may claim the exemption. The total of your contributions is more than half of your mother's support. Each of

you contributed more than 10%. Among yourselves, you must decide who is to claim the exemption. If you claim the exemption, your brothers must sign Forms 2120 which you attach to your return. If one of your brothers claims the exemption, you sign a Form 2120 which is attached to the return of the brother who claims the exemption. Since neither of your sisters furnished more than 10%, neither can claim the exemption. Consequently, they need not sign Forms 2120.

2. You and your sister each furnished $1,000 to your mother's support. Her two cousins who did not live with her each contributed $1,500. No one may claim her as an exemption. Half of her support of $5,000 was not furnished by persons, such as you and your sister, who but for the support test, could claim an exemption for her. A cousin does not meet the relationship or member of household test.

3. Your mother's support totals $6,000; you contribute $1,800, your brother $1,200, your father $600, and your mother from her savings contributes $2,400. Assume your father does not file a tax return claiming your mother as an exemption. You and your brother cannot use your father's contribution to meet the more than 50% test required by rule 2 above. Your father may not join in a multiple support agreement because your mother is not his dependent for tax purposes although an exemption may be claimed for a wife on the basis of the marital relationship; see ¶1.15.

4. Same facts as in (3) above, but another brother contributed $200. Then you and your brothers may join in a multiple support agreement; your contributions exceeded 50% of the support costs.

DIVORCED OR SEPARATED PARENTS FOLLOW SPECIAL RULES FOR FIGURING SUPPORT OF CHILDREN

¶ **1.23** Divorced or separated parents have to apply special custodial rules to determine which parent has met the support test for a dependent child.

If you had custody of the child for more than half the year, the exemption is generally yours if these tests are met:

Marital status: You are divorced or legally separated under a decree of divorce or separate maintenance, or separated under a written agreement, or live apart at all times during the last six months of 1987.

Support: In 1987, over half of the child's total support is from you and your former or separated spouse.

Custody: The child is in the custody of one or both parents for more than half of 1987. If you had custody for a greater portion of 1987, you claim the exemption unless you waive it or the noncustodial parent may claim it under a pre-1985 agreement.

Custodial parent's waiver. You may waive the exemption by signing a written declaration on Form 8332. On the form, you indicate whether you are waiving the exemption for 1987 only or for future years as well. The noncustodial parent attaches the declaration to his or her 1987 return and claims the exemption for the child.

> *Pre-1985 agreement specifying noncustodial parent.* If a pre-1985 agreement gives you, as noncustodial parent, the exemption, you must provide at least $600 for the support of the child in 1987. The exemption must be specifically allocated to you in a decree of divorce or separate maintenance or a written agreement executed before January 1, 1985. Attach a copy of the agreement to your return.

Do relatives or friends have custody of the children? If the children are not in the custody of either or both parents for more than half of 1987 the exemption is claimed by the person who contributed more than 50% of the child's support.

Do persons other than the parents contribute to the children's support? The above rules for custodial and noncustodial parents do not apply, and thus neither parent may claim the exemption, unless the parents together give more than 50% of the child's support. If a parent remarries, support contributions made by the new spouse are treated as contributions of the parent. They are not treated as contributions of a third person.

The above custodial rules also do not apply if the parties contributing support enter into a multiple support agreement under which one of them claims the exemption under the rules at ¶1.22.

TEST 3. GROSS INCOME EARNED BY YOUR DEPENDENT

¶ **1.24** The gross income test does *not* apply to your dependent child who is under 19 or a full-time student. He or she may earn any amount, and be claimed as an exemption, provided you meet the support test of ¶1.19.

The gross income test applies only to—

Dependents who are not your children— such as parents, in laws, sisters, brothers, uncles, aunts, and members of your household; *and*

Children who are 19 or over and not full-time students. *See* ¶1.25.

The gross income test requires your dependent to have a gross income of less than $1,900 in 1987. If a dependent earns $1,900 or more, he or she may not be claimed as an exemption, even if all of their support is provided by you.

Gross income here means income items included in the dependent's tax return. It does not include non-taxed items such as gifts and dividends excluded by the exclusion. *See* chapter 40 for a list of tax-free receipts. Gross income for a service type business is gross receipts without deductions of expenses and for a manufacturing or merchandising business is total sales less cost of goods sold. Partner's share of partnership gross income, not his share of net income, is treated as part of his gross income.

Social Security benefits are treated as gross income only to the extent they are taxable under the rules of ¶34.8.

Gross income does not include income earned by a totally and permanently disabled individual at a school operated by a government agency or tax-exempt organization, if the school provides special instruction for alleviating the disability and the income is incidental to medical care received.

EXAMPLES

1. Jones gives $1,800 a year for his father's support. The father owns a two-family house. He lives in one apartment and rents the other for $200 a month, giving him a gross annual income of $2,400. After deducting interest and taxes, his net income is $1,200. Nevertheless, Jones may not take his father as a dependent as his gross income is not under $1,900.

2. Your son, age 25 and *not* a full-time student, received $2,900 for disabilities incurred while a member of the Armed Forces. You contributed $3,000 for his support. You get the exemption although his income exceeded the $1,900 test. Tax-free income is not considered gross income.

3. Your father received $2,400 in Social Security benefits. The benefits were not subject to tax. He used this amount to support himself. You contributed $2,600 to his support. You may claim him as an exemption. The Social Security benefits are not considered gross income. However, if you contributed $2,400 or less to his support, you could not take the exemption because you did not meet the support test at ¶1.19.

CHILDREN WHO ARE UNDER 19 OR FULL-TIME STUDENTS

¶ **1.25** The tax law provides the following tax break for dependent children. There is no gross income test for—
1. Your children *regardless of age* who are full-time students at an educational institution, *and*
2. Your children under 19.

This rule applies to your child, stepchild, and adopted child. It also applies to a foster child who, for the entire year, has made your home his principal home and is a member of your household. It does not apply to a grandchild, or a son- or daughter-in-law, or brother or sister who is a full-time student.

EXAMPLE

Your son is 19 on December 8, 1987. He does not attend school and has earned $2,000 during the year. You may not claim him as an exemption because he reached 19 during the year and his earnings exceeded the $1,900 limit. You may not prorate the exemption for the time he was under 19.

A full-time student is one who attends school full time during at least five calendar months in the tax year. For example: Attendance from February through some part of June—or from February through May and then from September through December—qualifies. The five months do not have to run consecutively.

EXAMPLES

1. Your child who is 22 was a June graduate. The gross income test does not apply to his earnings in 1987.

2. Your child who is 19 worked during the first half of the year and then starts college in September. You may not claim him as an exemption if he earned $1,900 or more. Although he is a full-time student, he did not attend school for at least five months during the year.

Attending night classes. Your child who attends night school is considered a full-time student only if he is enrolled for the number of hours or classes that is considered full-time attendance at a similar daytime school.

A child taking a full-time course of institutional on-farm training is a full-time student if the training is supervised by an official agent of an educational institution or of a state or other government agency in a state.

A "co-op" job that is part of a child's prescribed course of classroom study at a vocational high school qualifies. But do not confuse a "co-op" job with "on-the-job" training. "On-the-job" training is generally not part of a prescribed study course supervised by a school and does not qualify a child as a full-time student.

An educational institution is one with a regular faculty, established courses, and an organized student body. It does not include correspondence schools, job training schools, night schools, or a hospital which trains interns. An intern is not a student but an employee of the hospital.

Where your child has income of his own that may be used for his support, be prepared to show that he does not use it for support or that your contributions exceed his.

The filing of tax returns for children is discussed at ¶1.11.

TEST 4. THE DEPENDENT IS A CITIZEN OR RESIDENT

¶ **1.26** To claim an exemption for a dependent, the dependent must have at some time during 1987 qualified as:

Citizen or resident of the United States, or

United States national (one who owes permanent allegiance to the U.S.; principally, a person born in American Samoa who has not become a naturalized American citizen), or

Resident of Canada or Mexico.

Dependents in Puerto Rico. A U.S. citizen or resident may take as an exemption a dependent who is living in Puerto Rico and is a citizen of Puerto Rico, provided he is not a citizen of a foreign country. Most citizens of Puerto Rico are also citizens of the United States. All persons born in Puerto Rico on or after April 11, 1899, and prior to January 13, 1941 (and who resided in Puerto Rico or other territory over which the United States exercised rights on January 13, 1941) are citizens of the U.S. So are all persons born in Puerto Rico on or after January 13, 1941, and who are subject to the jurisdiction of the United States.

A child born in a foreign country whose one parent is a nonresident alien and whose other parent is a U.S. citizen qualifies as a dependent. If you are a U.S. citizen living abroad, you may claim as a dependent a legally adopted child who is not a U.S. citizen or resident if for the entire year your home was the child's principal residence and he is a member of your household.

Resident status is discussed at ¶37.1.

TEST 5. THE DEPENDENT DOES NOT FILE A JOINT RETURN

¶ **1.27** You may not claim an exemption for a dependent who files a joint return with another. For example, you meet all of the four tests entitling you to an exemption for your married daughter as your dependent. She files a joint return with her husband. You may not claim her as your dependent on your tax return.

The loss of the exemption may cost a parent more than the joint return saves the couple. In such a case, it may be advisable for the couple to file separate returns so that the parent may benefit from the larger tax saving.

If the couple files a joint return and decides to revoke their election to file jointly and then file separate returns in order to preserve the exemption for a parent, they must do so before the filing date for the return. Once a joint return is filed, the couple may not, after the filing deadline, file separate returns for the same year.

The IRS allows a limited opportunity for avoiding the rule that no exemption may be claimed for a dependent filing a joint return where the income of each spouse is under the income limit required for filing a return and the couple files a return merely to obtain a refund of withheld taxes. Under these circumstances, their return is considered a refund claim, and a dependency exemption may be claimed.

REPORTING SOCIAL SECURITY NUMBER OF DEPENDENTS

¶ **1.28** On your 1987 return, you must list the Social Security number of each dependent who is at least five years old. This requirement applies to parents or other adults who you claim as dependents, as well as to dependent children who reach age five before 1988.

To obtain a Social Security number for a dependent child, contact your local Social Security Administration office.

A $5 penalty may be imposed for each failure to file a Social Security number, or for filing an incorrect number, unless you can show reasonable cause for the omission or error.

Individuals who are exempt from self-employment tax because of their religious beliefs may continue to obtain Social Security numbers directly from the IRS, instead of obtaining the number from the Social Security Administration. The IRS also provides Social Security numbers for nonresident aliens.

TAX CREDIT FOR DEPENDENT CARE EXPENSES

¶ 1.29 Did you hire a sitter or maid to care for your children or other dependents while you work? If so, you may qualify for a tax credit for the expenses. You may claim the credit even if you work part-time. The credit is generally available to the extent you have earnings from employment.

The credit is claimed on Form 2441.

The size of the credit depends on the amount of care expenses and income. Depending on your income, the credit is 20% to 30% of up to $2,400 of care expenses for one dependent and up to $4,800 of expenses for two or more dependents.

To qualify for the credit, you must:

1. Incur the care expenses in order to earn income. In the case of a married couple, this requires both spouses to work either at full- or part-time positions. An exception to the earned income rule is made for a spouse who is a full-time student or incapacitated.
2. Maintain a household for the dependent.
3. File a joint return if you are married, unless you are separated under the rules of ¶1.34.
4. Hire someone other than your child under age 19 or a person you can claim as a dependent (¶1.33).

Withholding tax for housekeeper. Note that where you employ help to care for your dependent, you are liable for FICA taxes if you pay wages of $50 or more in a calendar quarter. As an employer, you pay FICA at the rate of 7.15% of wages (up to $43,800) in 1987. For example, you pay a housekeeper $125 a week ($6,500 for the year). You must pay $464.75 in FICA as well as withhold the same amount from the housekeeper's wages. If you do not withhold, you are liable for the full amount.

You report and pay this tax on a quarterly Form 942. Under an exception, FICA tax does not apply to wages paid to your spouse. Further, FICA tax does not apply to wages paid to your son or daughter under 21, but note the rule that bars you from basing a dependent care credit on payments made to a child under age 19 (¶1.33). Further, FICA generally does not apply to wages paid to your father or mother unless (1) you are divorced, widowed or your spouse is disabled, and (2) you have a child living at home who is under 18 or is disabled. If your housekeeper wants income tax to be withheld and you agree, he or she must fill out a Form W-4 (Withholding Allowances) and you include the withholdings on quarterly Form 942. As an employer, you are also liable for FUTA (unemployment) taxes if you paid wages of $1,000 or more in any calender quarter during 1987 or 1986. The tax is deposited quarterly if the tax due exceeds $100; deposits are made using coupons from Form 8109 (the Federal Tax Deposit Coupon Book). You also report FUTA annually on Form 940. Wages paid to a spouse, your parents, or children under 21 are exempt from FUTA. Obtain Form 940 for details. FICA and FUTA taxes are not separately deductible but are included with your other dependent care expenses. The amount of these taxes may more than offset your dependent care credit.

OVERALL VIEW OF THE CARE CREDIT

¶ 1.30 The credit is a percentage of expenses paid for the care of a dependent to allow you to work and earn income. The credit percentage depends on your income. For families with adjusted gross income of $10,000 or less, a 30% credit may be claimed on care expenses of up to $2,400 for one dependent; $4,800 for two or more dependents. For adjusted gross income over $10,000, the 30% credit is reduced by 1% for each $2,000 of adjusted gross income or fraction of $2,000 over $10,000, but not below 20%. The 20% credit applies to adjusted gross incomes exceeding $28,000.

The applicable credit percentage applies to a credit base of dependent care expenses which may not exceed $2,400 for one qualifying dependent or $4,800 for two or more qualifying dependents. This is true, even if expenses exceed $2,400 or $4,800. Further, a credit base may be less than the maximum if your earned income is less (see ¶1.31).

EXAMPLE

You paid care expenses of $4,000 for two qualifying dependents but had earned income of $3,000 from a job. Your credit base is limited to $3,000. If you had earned income of at least $4,000, you then could have figured the credit on the base of $4,000.

The dependent care credit is added to the credits for the elderly, and disabled, and mortgage credit certificates. The total credit is allowed up to your tax liability, figured without regard to alternative minimum tax, self-employment tax and certain penalty taxes.

If adjusted gross income is	Credit percentage	Your maximum credit for	
		One dependent	Two or more dependents
$10,000 or less	30%	$720	$1,440
10,001–12,000	29	696	1,392
12,001–14,000	28	672	1,344
14,001–16,000	27	648	1,296
16,001–18,000	26	624	1,248
18,001–20,000	25	600	1,200
20,001–22,000	24	576	1,152
22,001–24,000	23	552	1,104
24,001–26,000	22	528	1,056
26,001–28,000	21	504	1,008
28,001 and over	20	480	960

EARNED INCOME TEST

¶ 1.31 You must earn wage, salary or self-employment income figured without regard to community property laws.

Earned income rule for married couples. Generally, both spouses must work at least part-time, unless one is incapable of self-care or is a full-time student. The income limitation for the credit base is figured, not on combined joint income, but on the smaller income earned by either you or your spouse.

EXAMPLE

John and Mary are married. John earns $23,500. Mary earns $1,500. They incur care costs of $3,000 for their two children, ages 5 and 7. Their adjusted gross income is $25,000; their credit percentage is 22%. The child care credit base is limited to Mary's lower income of $1,500. They may claim a credit of $330 ($1,500 × 22%).

Expenses for dependent care incurred while looking for a job may be included. However, you must have earnings during the year to claim the credit.

An incapacitated spouse or a spouse who is a full-time student is considered to have earned income of $200 a month if expenses are incurred for one dependent; $400 a month for two or more such dependents.

A full-time student is one who attends school full time during each of five calendar months during the year. If both husband and wife are full-time students and neither works, they may not claim the credit for dependent care costs. While one spouse may be considered to have earned income of $200 (or $400) each month, the other spouse's earned income is zero. Care costs are limited to the lesser amount of earned income, which in this case is zero.

HOUSEHOLD AND DEPENDENT TESTS

¶ 1.32 You must maintain as your principal home a household for at least one of the following dependents who lives with you:

1. A dependent child under the age of 15 for whom you are entitled to deduct a dependency exemption. If you are divorced or separated, you do not have to be entitled to claim an exemption if you have custody for a greater part of the year than your former spouse (the child's other parent) (see ¶1.34).

2. Your spouse, if physically or mentally incapable of caring for himself or herself.
3. A dependent, regardless of age, who is physically or mentally incapable of caring for himself. A dependent who cannot dress himself or provide for his hygiene or nutritional needs, or who needs constant attention to avoid hurting himself or others is incapable of self-care. Relatives who qualify, if disabled, are listed at ¶1.16. A nonrelative may qualify if he made your home his principal home for the entire year and is a member of your household.

That a disabled dependent has gross income of $1,900 or more, so that you may not claim an exemption, does not bar you from claiming a credit for his care costs.

If your child becomes 15 during the year, you take into account expenses incurred for his or her care prior to the birthday. However, you do not prorate the $2,400 limitation. For example, if your child becomes 15 on May 1 and you incurred $2,400 in care expenses between January 1 and April 30, the entire $2,400 qualifies for the credit.

The costs of caring for a child under the age of 15 outside the home may be counted. The costs of caring for other dependents outside the home are taken into account only if the dependent regularly spends at least eight hours per day in your home. Expenses at dependent care centers qualify only if the centers are in compliance with state and local law.

EXAMPLES

1. You live with your mother who is physically incapable of caring for herself. You hire a practical nurse to care for her in the home while you are at work. Payments to the nurse qualify as care costs. However, if you placed her in a nursing home, the cost of the nursing home would not qualify as dependent care costs; but see ¶17.11 for possible medical expense deduction.

2. You have a dependent child, 10 years old, who has been attending public school. You are offered a job which you can accept only if the child is placed in a boarding school. You take the position, and enroll the child in a boarding school. The expenses paid to the school are allocated between those covering the child's care and those covering tuition. Expenses for care qualify as dependent care costs; the tuition costs do not.

Maintaining a household. You are considered to have maintained a household if you (or you and your spouse) provided more than half the maintenance costs in 1987. You also qualify if you paid more than half the costs during a lesser period in which you had care cost expenses. Rent, mortgage interest, property tax and insurance, utility bills, upkeep, repairs, and groceries are considered maintenance expenses. Costs of clothing, education, medical expenses, vacations, life insurance, mortgage principal and capital improvements are not.

In determining costs of maintaining a household for a care period of less than a year, the annual household costs are prorated over the number of calendar months within the period care costs were incurred. A period of less than a calendar month is treated as a calendar month.

EXAMPLE

The annual cost of maintaining a household is $6,600, and the period during which child care costs qualified for the deduction is from June 20 to December 31. To meet the household test, you must furnish more than $1,925 in maintaining the household from June 1 to December 31. The allocation covers seven months (June 1 to December 31).

7/12 of $6,600	$3,850
50% of $3,850	$1,925

Household of two or more families. If two or more families occupy common living quarters, each family is treated as a separate household.

EXAMPLE

Two unrelated women, each with children, occupy common living quarters; each pays more than one-half of the household costs for her own family. Each is treated as maintaining her separate household.

EXPENSES QUALIFYING FOR THE CREDIT

¶ **1.33** The tax law allows the following expenses to be figured in the base amount of credit.

1. Care expenses of your child, incapacitated spouse, or incapacitated dependent in your home. If you pay FICA or FUTA taxes on your housekeeper's wages, you may include your share of the tax (employer) as part of the wages when figuring the credit.
2. Ordinary domestic services in your home, such as laundry, cleaning, and cooking (but not payments to a gardener or chauffeur). Expenses for the dependent's food, clothing or entertainment do not qualify. Food costs for a housekeeper who eats in your home may be added to qualifying expenses.
3. Outside-the-home care costs for a child under 15, as in a day care center, day camp, nursery school, or in the home of a baby sitter. Outside-the-home care costs also qualify if incurred for a handicapped dependent, regardless of age, provided he or she regularly spends at least eight hours per day in your home.

The IRS has agreed to follow a Tax Court decision allowing a working parent to include the costs of sleep-away camp. It held that summer camp was a reasonable way to provide care for a child of a working parent. The full amount you pay to a day care center or nursery school is also counted, even if it covers such incidental benefits as lunch. Tuition for a child in first grade or higher is not taken into account. The cost of transportation between home and a day care facility is not included in care expenses. Outside-the-home care for other qualified dependents qualifies where the dependent regularly spends at least eight hours per day in your home. Expenses of outside-the-home care are treated the same as expenses for care in the home. Up to $2,400 (or $4,800) a year of outside-the-home care expenses may be taken into account in figuring the credit.

The manner of care need not be the least expensive alternative. For example, where a grandparent resides with you and may provide adequate care for your child to enable you to work, the cost of hiring someone to care for the child is still eligible for the credit.

If a portion of expenses is for other than dependent care or household services, only the portion allocable to dependent care or household services qualifies. No allocation is required if the non-dependent care services are minimal.

EXAMPLES

1. A person accepts a full-time position and sends his 12-year-old child to boarding school. The expenses paid to the school must be allocated; the part representing care of the child qualifies; the part representing tuition does not.

2. A full-time housekeeper is hired to care for two children, ages 9 and 12. In addition, the housekeeper drives the mother to and from work each day. The driving is no more than thirty minutes. No allocation is required because the nondependent care services of chauffeuring are minimal.

Care costs which also qualify as medical expenses. Care costs, such as a nurse's wages, may also qualify as medical expenses, but you may not claim both the dependent care credit and the medical expense deduction. If your care costs exceed the amount allowed as dependent care costs, the excess, to the extent it qualifies as a medical expense, may be added to your other deductible medical costs.

EXAMPLE

You pay $6,000 for care of your child in your home. The expenses also qualify as medical expenses. Assume your adjusted gross income is $17,000. Your dependent care costs are limited to $2,400 and you may claim a credit of $624 ($2,400 × 26%). The balance of $3,600 is deductible as medical expenses. If you had no other medical costs, your medical deduction would be $2,325 after deducting the 7.5% limitation on medical costs ($3,600–$1,275 or 7.5% of $17,000).

Payments to relatives. No credit may be claimed for payments made to relatives for whom a dependency exemption is allowable (see ¶1.16) or to your child who is under 19 years at the close of the tax year. Thus, if you pay your mother to care for your child and you cannot claim your mother as a dependent, such payments qualify for the credit.

Allocating expenses when employed less than entire year. When an expense covers a period part of which you were gainfully employed or in active search of gainful employment and part of which you were not employed or seeking employment, you must allocate expenses on a daily basis.

EXAMPLE
You are employed for only two months and 10 days. Monthly care expenses are $300. Eligible care expenses amount to $700 ($300 × 2 months, plus ⅓ of $300).

RULES FOR SEPARATED COUPLES

¶ 1.34 Where you are living apart from your spouse, you may claim the credit on a separate return if you meet these tests:
1. You maintain as your home a household which is the principal place of abode of your dependent for more than half the year;

2. You furnish over half the cost of maintaining the household for the entire year;
3. Your spouse was not a member of the household during *the last six months* of the year.

If you satisfy the above tests, you are treated as unmarried and may claim the credit on a separate return. You do not have to take your spouse's income into account or show that he or she is employed in order to claim a credit.

If you are legally divorced or separated, separated under a written agreement, or you live apart from your spouse during the last six months of 1987 and you are the custodial parent (have custody longer than the other parent), the following favorable rule applies: You may claim the credit for care of a dependent child who is under 15 or physically or mentally incapable of caring for himself even if you waive the dependency exemption for the child or may not claim the exemption under a pre-1985 divorce or separation agreement. The child must be in your custody or the custody of yourself and the other parent for more than half of 1987.

ALIMONY PAYMENTS

Alimony under the new law. The projected reduction of tax rates will lessen the value of alimony deductions. As a result, a couple may pay less attention to the tax consequences in negotiating a settlement.

The recapture period for a decrease in payments is reduced from six years to three years. Prior agreements may be amended to take advantage of this new rule.

DUAL TAX CONSEQUENCES OF ALIMONY PAYMENTS

¶ 1.35 The same rules determine whether alimony is deductible and taxable. For example, if a husband makes deductible alimony payments to his ex-wife, the payments are taxable to her. He may not deduct payments that are not taxable to her.

The deductible and taxable portion of alimony is determined by two different sets of rules, depending on whether the payments are made under decrees and agreements entered into:
Before 1985. These rules are discussed in ¶1.39–¶1.44.
After 1984. These rules are discussed in ¶1.45–¶1.50
A test common to both sets of rules is that the alimony must be paid under a decree or written separation agreement, *see* ¶1.37.
Child support payments are neither deductible nor taxable; *see* ¶1.38 for pre-1985 rules and ¶1.50 for post-1984 rules.

How to report alimony deduction or income. On Form 1040, you deduct alimony in the year of payment. You claim the deduction whether or not you claim itemized deductions. Payment of arrears is also deductible in the year of payment. A third party who pays alimony for you may not claim a deduction for his payment.

On Form 1040, you must enter the Social Security number and last name (if different from yours) of your ex-spouse. Otherwise, your deduction may be disallowed, and you may have to pay a $50 penalty. Your ex-spouse is required to give his or her Social Security number and is subject to a $50 penalty for failure to do so.

Trust payments. To meet your alimony obligations, you may transfer income producing property to a trust that is to pay the income to your spouse. You may not deduct payments made by the trust. You are not taxable on the income earned by the trust even though it pays your alimony obligations. This tax treatment is the equivalent of receiving a tax deduction for paying alimony. Your spouse reports the payments as trust income on Schedule E. You may deduct out-of-pocket payments that make up a shortage in the trust payments.

Funds for payments of alimony may be provided through the purchase of an annuity or endowment policy. You may not deduct payments made under the policies assigned or purchased for your spouse.

EXAMPLES
1. To meet an alimony obligation of $500 a month, H purchases or assigns for the benefit of W a commercial annuity contract. The full $500 a month received by W is includible in her income. No part of these payments is deductible by H.
2. H transfers property to a trust which pays $1,000 a year to W as alimony. The annual $1,000 received by W, whether or not it is principal, is to be reported by W. H gets no deduction.

Court decisions have held that payment of tax-exempt interest is not taxable. The IRS, however, claims that the payment is taxable regardless of its source.

Alimony to nonresident alien. If you pay alimony payments to a nonresident alien, and you are a U.S. citizen or resident, you must withhold 30% (or at a lower treaty rate) on each payment for income tax purposes. *See* IRS Publication 515 for more information.

Tax refund diversion for delinquent child support. The IRS can give your tax refund to a state which is paying support to your child, if you fail to make support payments. The IRS has the authority to make the diversion where the delinquency is $150 or more and is overdue for at least three months. The IRS will not notify you of the diversion until it is made to the state. However, a federal court has held that a state must provide notice to all those whose refunds may be intercepted, specifying possible defenses and how to challenge the diversion before it is made; judicial review of the state's administrative decision must also be available.

DEDUCTING LEGAL FEES IN MARITAL ACTIONS

¶ **1.36** **Wife's payment of legal fees.** If you are receiving taxed alimony, you may deduct part of your legal fees. Ask your attorney to divide his fees into charges for arranging:
1. The divorce or separation; *and*
2. Details of the alimony payments.

You may deduct the legal fees allocated to (2), but you may not deduct the fee attributed to the divorce or separation negotiation. The deduction is subject to the 2% adjusted gross income floor on miscellaneous deductions. *See* Chapter 19. If the alimony is not taxed to you, you may not deduct any part of the fee. However, part of a fee allocated to a property settlement may be added to the basis of the property obtained in the settlement.

Husband's payment of legal fees. You may not deduct legal fees paid for arranging a divorce or for resisting your wife's demands for alimony. Furthermore, you may not deduct legal fees incurred in resisting your wife's claims to income producing property, the loss of which would affect your earnings. However, these rules do not bar a husband from deducting that part of his legal fee that is identified as being paid for tax advice. The type of proof that may support a deduction is as follows:
1. The fee is charged by a firm that limits its practice to state and federal tax matters and is engaged to advise on the tax consequences of a property settlement involving the transfer of property in exchange for other property and the release of the wife's marital rights in the husband's property.
2. The fee is charged by a firm engaged in general practice which assigns tax problems, such as the tax consequences of creating an alimony trust, to its special tax department. On the bill, an allocation is made for tax advice based on time, complexity of the case, and the amount of tax involved.
3. An attorney handles the divorce for a fixed fee and also gives advice on the right to claim exemptions for the children following the divorce. The bill allocated part of the fee to the tax advice, based on time, results obtained by his negotiations, and fees customarily charged in the locality for similar services.

You may not deduct your payment of your wife's legal fees, even if the fees are only for tax advice.

DECREE OR AGREEMENT REQUIRED

¶ **1.37** Alimony, to be deductible and taxable, must be required by one of the following: (1) a decree of divorce or legal separation, (2)

a written separation agreement, or (3) a decree of support. This rule applies to both pre-1985 and post-1984 decrees and agreements. Voluntary payments are not deductible.

Divorced or legally separated. The obligation to pay alimony must be imposed by the decree of divorce or separate maintenance or a written agreement incident to the divorce or separation.

Alimony paid under a Mexican divorce decree qualifies. Payments under a Mexican or state decree declared invalid by another jurisdiction do not qualify according to present IRS policy. Two appeals courts reject the IRS position.

Support payments ordered by a court in a wife's home state qualify as alimony, even though not provided for by an *ex parte* divorce decree obtained by the husband in another state. Similarly, payments qualified when a state court increased support originally ordered before the husband obtained an uncontested Mexican divorce.

Payments made under a separation approved by a Roman Catholic ecclesiastical board do not qualify.

When the decree fails to mention alimony, payments qualify as long as they are made under a written agreement considered "incident to" the divorce or separated status of the couple.

Payments made under an agreement *amended* after a divorce or legal separation may also qualify, if the amendment is considered "incident" to the divorce or separation. For example, the IRS agrees that a *written* amendment changing the amount of alimony payments is incident to the divorce where the legal obligation to support under the original agreement survived the divorce. However, payments under an amended agreement did not qualify where the original agreement settled all rights between the husband and wife and made no provision for future support. The legal obligation to support the wife did not survive the divorce and could not be revived by the new agreement.

Annulments. Payments made under an annulment decree qualify as deductible (and taxable) alimony.

Where a couple is separated and living apart, alimony is deductible by the husband and taxable to the wife if paid under either a written separation agreement or decree of support. A written separation agreement made before August 17, 1954 does not qualify unless materially modified after August 16, 1954.

Oral changes agreed to by the parties will not be recognized for tax purposes unless they are incorporated into the written separation agreement.

A decree of support. Any court decree or order requiring support payments qualifies, including alimony *pendente lite* (temporary alimony while the action is pending), and an interlocutory (not final) divorce decree.

In certain community property states, payments under a decree of alimony *pendente lite* which do not exceed the wife's interest in community income are not deductible by the husband nor taxable to the wife; payments exceeding the wife's interest are taxable to her and deductible by the husband.

ALIMONY PAID UNDER PRE-1985 DECREES AND AGREEMENTS

¶ **1.38** Under a pre-1985 decree or agreement, a husband may deduct alimony payments and the wife must report the alimony as income, if these four rules are met:
1. Payments must be required by a decree of divorce or legal separation, a written separation agreement, or a decree of support, *see* ¶1.37.
2. There must be an obligation to support, *see* ¶1.39.
3. The payments must be periodic, *see* ¶1.40.
4. The payments must not be specifically designated for child support, *see* ¶1.44.

If the amount or terms of payment under a pre-1985 arrangement are changed after 1984 by a new decree or agreement, the rules for post-1984 instruments will apply.

SUPPORT OBLIGATION—PRE-1985

¶ **1.39** Alimony, to be deductible (and taxable), must be paid because of the marital obligation to support the spouse. Payment of any other obligation does not qualify. These are examples of nondeductible (and nontaxable) payments:

Repayment of a bona fide loan.

EXAMPLE
During their marriage, a husband borrowed $10,000 from his wife. The divorce decree now provides that he return the $10,000 in installments over a period of 12 years. He may not deduct these payments.

Payments to settle property rights, including payment of a spouse's share of community property.

Voluntary payments in excess of required alimony. This is true even if the wife reports them as income or a court order denies temporary alimony on condition that the voluntary payments continue. Payments made in excess of the amount required by a decree or separation agreement are considered to be voluntary. Amending the decree retroactively to cover an increase does not qualify the increase as deductible and taxable alimony. The increase has to be approved by the court before the increased payments are made.

Payments to spouse who remarries. The tax deduction allowed for alimony payments made under a pre-1985 decree or agreement hinges on the obligation to support. Once the spouse receiving alimony remarries, the obligation to support generally ends under state law. In these states, any payment after remarriage is not considered alimony and is not deductible. The payments made after remarriage are considered tax-free gifts, if the former husband knows of the remarriage and that he is no longer obligated to pay. If she does not inform him of her remarriage, his payments are taxable to her but are not deductible by him.

Voluntary alimony payments may also be subject to gift tax.

The decree or agreement may combine payments for support and non-marital obligations. If the decree or agreement does not separately identify the two types of payments, the amounts paid for support may not be deductible by the husband and are not taxable to the wife.

> Where an estranged couple continues to share the same home, courts disagree over the tax status of alimony paid under pre-1985 decrees or agreements. An appeals court holds that a couple does not have to live in separate quarters to be considered separated for tax purposes, as long as the evidence indicates the couple is in fact living separately. On the other hand, the Tax Court does not treat a couple living under the same roof as separated for tax purposes.

PERIODIC PAYMENTS—PRE-1985

¶ **1.40** To be deductible (and taxable), alimony payments must meet a "periodic" test. The term "periodic" as used in the law is misleading. The ordinary meaning of "periodic" implies payments at regular intervals. However, Treasury regulations state that there is no requirement to pay at regular intervals. "Periodic" is then what the law and regulations have labeled as "periodic." Not periodic payments are non-contingent payments of a fixed sum over a period of 10 years or less. These types of payments are considered periodic:

1. *Payments over an indefinite period of time.* For example, a husband agrees to pay $500 a month to his wife for as long as she lives or remains unmarried.
2. *A fixed sum payable in installments over a period of more than 10 years.* However, each year only 10% of the fixed amount is considered a periodic payment. Thus, to the extent that payments in one year exceed 10%, the excess is not deductible by the husband or taxable to the wife. The 10% limit does not apply to payments in arrears.
3. *Fixed payments over a period of 10 years or less, subject to one or more of these contingencies:* Death of either spouse, wife's remarriage, a change of economic status of either spouse, or the court's power to modify, alter or amend. Even if the agreement does not have such a provision, the alimony may still be deductible if state law subjects the alimony to similar contingencies. For example, in your state, a court may modify the alimony agreement for the benefit of children, and by statute, the obligation to pay alimony ends at the death of either spouse. Such contingencies imposed by state law qualify the payments as periodic.
4. *Payments of an indefinite amount, such as payments based on a percentage of annual income which fluctuates.* For example, a husband agreed to pay 20% of his yearly income. Here, even if the alimony period is 10 years or less, the payments qualify.

EXAMPLE

After deductions, you have an income of roughly $40,000 a year. If you agreed to pay your spouse $50,000 in five annual payments of $10,000, you get no deductions. But if you agreed to pay 25% of your

income for five years, the payments are fully deductible by you and taxable to your spouse.

Lump-sum payments. Even if provided for in the decree or written separation agreement, a lump-sum payment is not deductible because it is not a periodic payment.

If a husband has been making periodic payments and agrees to a lump-sum settlement, the lump sum is not deductible by him nor taxable to his wife except to the extent that it includes arrears of periodic alimony. To avoid loss of the deduction for the arrears, the part of your payment representing arrears should be specifically designated as such.

EXAMPLE

H has been paying W $3,600 a year in alimony. H and W agree on a $20,000 lump-sum settlement. If H pays the entire $20,000 with no mention of arrears, he gets no deduction. Had the payment been made in two checks for $16,400 and $3,600 or had $3,600 been specifically designated as being for arrears, H would get a $3,600 alimony deduction.

Alimony in arrears. Alimony in arrears is deductible by the husband and taxable to his wife in the year paid, even if paid in a lump sum. The 10% limitation on a fixed sum paid in installments over a period of more than 10 years does not apply to arrears.

RENT-FREE HOME AS ALIMONY—PRE-1985

¶ **1.41** A portion of an alimony award may be allocated to the payment of expenses on a residence, such as mortgage interest and principal, taxes, and insurance. The tax consequences of the payments depends upon how the residence is owned.

Tenancy with right of survivorship (tenancy by the entirety or joint tenancy). If you and your spouse are jointly liable on the mortgage, you may deduct as alimony one-half of each principal and interest payment. You may deduct as interest the other half of your interest payments. You may not deduct the other half of principal payments as they are nondeductible personal expenses. Your spouse must include as income one-half of each interest and principal payment, but she may deduct her one-half share of interest if she itemizes deductions.

If your spouse is not personally liable on the mortgage, your payments are not deductible alimony. However, you may deduct your payments of interest and taxes as itemized deductions.

Tenants in common. Each of you owns one-half of the home; there is no right of survivorship. You may deduct as alimony amounts you pay for mortgage principal and interest, taxes, and insurance on your spouse's one-half of the home. You may separately deduct the other one-half of interest and taxes. Principal and insurance payments on your half of the property are nondeductible personal expenses.

Your spouse must include in income the payments on her half of the property, but she may deduct interest and taxes as itemized deductions.

Your spouse is sole owner of the house. If you pay real estate taxes, mortgage payments, and insurance premiums on the home your spouse owns, you may deduct your payments as alimony. Your spouse must include the payments, but may deduct taxes and interest as itemized deductions.

You are the sole owner of the house. You may agree to allow your spouse to live rent-free in a house you own. You may not deduct your mortgage payments. Nor may you deduct the fair rental value of the home. You may, however, deduct interest and taxes as itemized deductions.

Rent-free use of cooperative apartment. In one case, a husband's payments of leasing charges on his co-op apartment in which his estranged wife lived were treated as deductible alimony. However, not all co-op payments are alimony. Rent payments to a co-op apartment corporation on behalf of an ex-spouse are alimony, except for the portion allocable to mortgage interest, real estate taxes, and principal amortization. The payment of mortgage principal and interest and real estate taxes directly and primarily benefits the owner of the co-op stock.

Paying utilities. Regardless of the way title is held, your payments for utilities are considered periodic payments, deductible as alimony by you and taxable to your spouse.

A court held that a husband's payment of rent for a house owned by his corporation and occupied by his divorced wife was deductible as alimony and taxable to his wife.

Note: Interest deductions for home mortgages are subject to the rules of ¶15.7.

PAYMENT OF SPOUSE'S MEDICAL OR OTHER EXPENSES—PRE-1985

¶ 1.42 If you pay your spouse's medical expenses as part of your alimony obligation, the payments are deductible as alimony, provided they are considered to be periodic. If she is required to report such payments as income, she may deduct them as medical expenses under the rules of chapter 17.

> Tuition payments and support payments for a wife's relatives may be deductible alimony.

EXAMPLES

1. Christiansen agreed to pay the cost of educating his former wife's nephew and niece. He deducted the expense as alimony. The IRS disallowed the deduction because his wife did not actually receive the payments. The Tax Court allowed the deduction. Mrs. Christiansen felt obligated to educate the children. Her husband's payments discharged that obligation, giving her an economic benefit. Whether her obligation was moral rather than legal does not matter.

2. Under a divorce settlement, a husband had to pay his former wife $20,000 a year and his former mother-in-law $5,000 a year. This arrangement was made because the wife was her mother's sole support. The $5,000 received by the mother is considered part of the taxable alimony paid to the wife.

INSURANCE PREMIUMS AS ALIMONY—PRE-1985

¶ 1.43 As part of your alimony obligation, you may pay premiums on insurance assigned to your spouse. You may deduct the premium payments if the policy is assigned to her absolutely and she is irrevocably named as beneficiary. This is true even though, under the decree or agreement, your obligation to pay the premiums will cease on the death or remarriage of your spouse. Your spouse reports as income the full amount of the premium, not the smaller amount by which the premium increases the cash surrender value of the policy. If she has only a contingent interest in the policy, the deduction is lost and the premium is not taxable. Contingent interests that have barred deductions are:

The policy comes back to the husband if the wife dies first, even if the wife had the right to get the cash surrender value or borrow on the policy during her life.

Wife loses her interest in the policy if she remarries (*but see* case below).

Husband keeps rights to surrender the policy or to make a loan against it, even though the wife has power to veto his action.

If the wife's rights to the policy do not vest under the divorce decree, the premiums are not deductible, even if she later becomes absolute owner of the policy after the later assignment. The decree may require only a limited transfer, for example, to prevent you from borrowing against the policy. If, under these circumstances, you assign the policy

absolutely, you may not deduct your premium payments. Your assignment is voluntary.

Premiums paid on a decreasing term policy which has no loan or cash surrender value are not deductible alimony.

You may not deduct as alimony a lump-sum payment for a policy purchased for your spouse or the cash surrender value of a policy assigned to her.

CHILD SUPPORT PAYMENTS—PRE-1985

¶ 1.44 Payments specifically designated for support of a minor child of the husband are neither deductible by the husband nor taxable to the wife. Where periodic payments are not specifically earmarked for child support, the entire amount paid is taxable alimony to the wife, even where it appears child support was intended. Payments for the support of the wife's child who is not a child of the husband are not child support payments. They are deductible alimony payments if they qualify as periodic and are taxable to the wife.

EXAMPLE

Under a decree of divorce, H is ordered to pay $50 for W's support and $100 for the support of his minor children. Only $50 is taxable to W and deductible by H.

The tax law does not state at what age a child ceases to be a minor. The Tax Court has held that for tax purposes a minor is anyone under the age of 21, regardless of the age fixed by state law.

The Supreme Court holds that an allocation between taxable (deductible) alimony and child support may be made only if the agreement specifically fixes an amount as child support. Without a specific child support provision, all payments made under an agreement are alimony, although the children benefit from them. Merely stating that child support payments are fixed "for tax purposes" is not a specific designation. Amendments to the original decree to specifically fix the amount for child support do not have retroactive effect unless the amendment corrects an error by the court in the original decree.

The Supreme Court rule does not apply to support payments under post-1984 agreements, *see* ¶1.49.

Assume your spouse remarries and you continue alimony payments under an agreement that does not fix child support payments. You may deduct the alimony although you intend it for your children's support. Until a court changes the terms of the alimony agreement and provides for child support, the payments are deductible by you and taxable to your spouse. This is true, even if the court order is retroactive to the date of your spouse's remarriage. Of course, payments of child support after the court order are not deductible.

When you fail to pay the entire amount under a decree or agreement requiring both alimony and child support, the amount actually paid is applied first to child support.

EXAMPLE

Under a divorce decree, H is to pay $200 a month, $100 for support of W and $100 for support of his minor children. During 1984, H pays only $150 a month. $100 for each monthly payment in 1984 is considered support of the children. Only $50 of each month's payment is included in W's return and is deducted by H.

Paid vacation expenses for wife and children were not treated as nondeductible support payments, although payments were contingent on the children accompanying the wife. No specific amount could be allocated to the children.

While the husband may not deduct child support payments, they count in determining if he is entitled to the dependency exemption for the child. *See* ¶1.23.

ALIMONY PAID UNDER POST-1984 DECREES AND AGREEMENTS

PLANNING ALIMONY AGREEMENTS.

¶ **1.45** You can arrange beforehand how the costs of a divorce are to be borne. You may specifically state in the decree or agreement that the alimony is neither taxable to the payee-spouse (under IRC section 71) nor deductible by the payer-spouse (under IRC section 215). Such a statement effectively disqualifies payments that otherwise would be taxable to the payee-spouse and deductible by the payer-spouse. The payee-spouse must attach a copy of the agreement that includes the statement to the tax return for the years in which it applies.

Planning the after-tax consequences of alimony is difficult. The first problem is for a couple to be convinced that they may have a common financial interest; the second, projecting future tax consequences.

For example, assume that the husband is to make payments to the wife. If tax planning is approached from the viewpoint of each spouse separately, the tax deduction is an advantage for the husband; tax-free income is an advantage for the wife. However, both advantages cannot be acheived, and the couple must face the reality of the tax law. They must compromise and approach the setting of amounts and tax consequences by balancing their interests.

One equitable approach is to view both spouses as a single economic tax unit. If this is done and the husband will be in a higher tax bracket during the payout period than the wife, an agreement should generally provide for taxable and deductible alimony. The tax savings provided by the deduction can conserve more of the husband's assets while providing funds required by the wife. The final amount of alimony to be paid depends on the spouses tax brackets. Where there is no favorable difference in tax brackets, there may be no advantage in tailoring an agreement for taxable and deductible alimony when viewing the positions of the two parties as a unit.

If you agree that one spouse is to pay deductible alimony and the other spouse is to report the alimony as income, these rules must be met:

1. The alimony must be paid under the decree of divorce or legal separation agreement or decree of support. See ¶1.37.
2. The agreement must provide for cash payments. See ¶1.46. There is no minimum payout period for annual alimony payments of $15,000 or less. One payment of $15,000 can qualify as deductible and taxable alimony. Technically, there is also no minimum payout period for annual alimony payments exceeding $15,000. However, recapture of alimony deductions claimed in the first or second year may occur where annual payments of over $15,000 are scheduled and paid, but in the second or third year a reduced payment is made. To avoid recapture of deductions for payments exceeding $15,000, carefully plan schedules of declining payments within the rules of ¶1.48.
3. In providing for the support of children, a specific allocation to their support or the setting of certain contingencies disqualifies payments as deductible and taxable alimony. See ¶1.50
4. Divorced and legally separated parties may not live in the same household. If they live in the same household, alimony payments are not deductible or taxable. However, there are these exceptions: A spouse who makes payments while preparing to leave the common residence may deduct payments made within one month before the departure. Also, where you are separated under a written agreement but not legally separated under a decree of divorce or separation maintenance, you may deduct alimony payments even if you both are members of the same household.
5. The payer spouse's liability to pay alimony must end on the death of the payee spouse. The alimony agreement does not have to state expressly that payments end on death if liability ends under state law, see ¶1.49.

CASH PAYMENTS REQUIRED—POST-1984

¶ **1.46** Only payments of cash, checks, and money orders payable on demand qualify as taxable and deductible alimony.

Providing services or transferring or providing property do not qualify. For example, you may not deduct as alimony your note, the assignment of a third party note, or an annuity contract.

Your cash payment to a third party for a spouse qualifies if made under the terms of a divorce decree or separation instrument. For example, you pay the rent, mortgage, tax, or tuition liabilities of your former spouse. The payments qualify if made under the terms of the divorce or separation instrument. However, you may not deduct payments to maintain property owned by you but used by your spouse. For example, you pay the mortgage expenses, real estate taxes, and insurance premiums for a house which you own and in which your former spouse lives. You may not deduct those payments, even if required by a decree or agreement.

> You may deduct payments made to a third party at the written request of the payee spouse. For example, your former spouse asks you to make a cash donation to a charitable organization instead of paying alimony installments to her. Her request must be in writing and state that both she and you intend the payment to be treated as an alimony. You must receive the written request before the date of filing your return of tax for the taxable year in which the payment was made.

Premiums paid for term or whole life insurance on your life made under the terms of the divorce or separation instrument qualify as deductible alimony to the extent your former spouse owns the policy.

MINIMUM PAYMENT PERIOD FOR ALIMONY—POST-1984

¶ **1.47** Payments exceeding $10,000 under agreements and decrees made in 1985 and 1986 were subject to a minimum six-year payment period. Under this rule, if the agreement did not require payments exceeding $10,000 to continue for at least six years, payments over $10,000 were not treated as taxable and deductible alimony.

For agreements executed after 1986, there is no minimum payout period, but a recapture rule applies where payments fall by more than $15,000 within the first three years. See ¶1.48 for recapture rules.

Pre-1987 agreements may be amended to allow deductions for payments subject to the prior law minimum payment period rule. To make the amendment, you merely add a statement to your 1985 or 1986 agreement that the amendments made by the 1986 Tax Reform Act apply. It is not necessary to redraft the agreement. If the agreement is not amended, the six-year payout rule continues to apply.

EXAMPLE

In 1986, an alimony agreement is signed providing for a $20,000 payment in each of 1986, 1987, and 1988. The agreement did not meet the prior law six-year payment rule. Thus in 1986, only $10,000 of the first $20,000 payment was deductible. In 1987, the agreement is modified to incorporate the new law changes. The $20,000 payments in 1987 and 1988 are deductible. If the agreement had not been modified, only $10,000 in each year would be deductible.

RECAPTURE RULES FOR DECLINE OF PAYMENTS—POST-1984

¶ **1.48** The recapture rules are designed to prevent the "so-called"front loading of payments intended as a property settlement rather than alimony. For agreements executed *after 1986*, deductible payments made in the first year or second year may have to be recaptured in the third year where payments within the first three years fall by more than $15,000. The same rule applies to 1985 and 1986 agreements that are amended to conform to the new law. See below for the prior law recapture rule applicable to 1985 and 1986 agreements that are not amended.

Where recapture is required under the following rules, the payer reports the recaptured amount as income in the third year and the payee claims a deduction for the same amount.

Recapture under post-1986 rule. For agreements executed after 1986, and for 1985 and 1986 agreements that are amended to expressly provide that the new law changes apply, follow these steps in computing recapture:

1. Recapture of the second-year payment is determined before recapture of the first-year payment. The second-year payment is recaptured to the extent it exceeds the third-year payment by more than $15,000.

2. The first-year payment is recaptured to the extent it exceeds by more than $15,000 the average payment made in the second and third years. In figuring the average payment, reduce the second-year payment by any recaptured amount for the second year figured under Step 1.

The three-year recapture period begins with the first calendar year in which you pay deductible alimony under a decree of divorce or separate maintenance, or written separation agreement. The three-year period need not begin with the year of divorce or separation if no qualifying payments are made in that year.

EXAMPLES

1. In 1987, Jones obtains a divorce and pays deductible alimony of $50,000. His wife reports $50,000 as income. In 1988, and 1989, he makes no payments. On his 1989 return, $35,000 of the first year 1987 deduction is recaptured ($50,000–$15,000) as income by Jones. His ex-spouse deducts $35,000.

2. In 1987, Smith makes his first alimony payment of $50,000; in 1988, $20,000, and in 1989 nothing. On his 1989 return, $32,500 is recaptured as follows:

Recapture of second-year payment:		
Payment in 2nd year		$20,000
Less 3rd-year payment	$0	
Less allowance	15,000	15,000
Recapture—second year		$ 5,000
Recapture of first-year payment:		
Average calculation:		
Payment over the 2nd and 3rd years	$20,000	
Less recapture in the 2nd year	5,000	
	15,000	
Average ($15,000 ÷ 2)	$ 7,500	
Payment in first year		50,000
Less average	$ 7,500	
Less allowance	15,000	$22,500
Recapture—first year		$27,500
Total ($5,000 + $27,500)		$32,500

1985 and 1986 agreements. If a 1985 or 1986 agreement is not amended to conform to the new law, recapture applies where payments decline by more than $10,000 in the three-year period. Recapture may be required in the second or third year under this rule.

EXAMPLES

1. Under a 1986 decree, Ross pays and deducts alimony payments of $25,000. In 1987, he pays only $12,000. As there has been a decrease of more than $10,000, recapture applies. The recaptured amount of $3,000 is the $13,000 decrease less $10,000. He reports $3,000 as income. His former spouse may also claim a $3,000 deduction.

1986 deduction		$25,000
Less:		
Payment in 1987	$12,000	
Plus $10,000	10,000	22,000
Recaptured in 1987		$ 3,000

2. Same facts as in (1) but in 1988 Ross pays only $1,000; the excess amount recaptured in 1988 is $12,000.

1986 deduction after recapture			$22,000
Less:			
Payment in 1988		$ 1,000	
Plus $10,000		10,000	11,000
Excess (1)			11,000
1987 deduction		12,000	
Less:			
Payment in 1988	1,000		
Plus $10,000	10,000	11,000	
Excess (2)			1,000
Recaptured in 1988 (Total of excess 1 and 2)			$12,000

PAYMENTS MUST STOP AT DEATH—POST-1984

¶ **1.49** Under a post-1984 agreement or decree, payments must stop on the death of the payee-spouse. If not, none of the payments, whether made before or after the payee's death, qualify as taxable or deductible alimony.

Under prior law, an agreement or decree had to specifically state that payments end at death. Under current law, such a statement is not necessary, if under state law, the liability to pay ends on the death of the payee-spouse.

To the extent that one or more payments are to begin, increase in amount, or accelerate after the death of the payee-spouse, such payments may be treated as a substitute for the continuation of payments terminating on the death of the payee-spouse.

EXAMPLES

1. Under the terms of a divorce decree, Smith is obligated to make annual alimony payments of $30,000, terminating on the earlier of the end of six years or the death of Mrs. Smith. She also is to keep custody of their two minor children. The decree also provides that if on her death the children are still minors, Jones is to pay annually $10,000 to a trust each year. The trust income and corpus are to be used for the children until the youngest child reaches the age of majority. Under these facts, Smith's possible liability to make annual $10,000 payments to the trust is treated as a substitute for $10,000 of the $30,000 annual payments. $10,000 of each of the $30,000 annual payments does not qualify as alimony.

2. Same facts as in (1) but the alimony is to end on the earlier of the expiration of 15 years or the death of Mrs. Smith. Further if Mrs. Smith dies before the end of the 15 year period, Smith will pay her estate the difference between the total amount that he would have paid had she survived less the amount actually paid. For example, if she dies at the end of the tenth year, he will pay her estate $150,000 ($450,000–$300,000). Under these facts, his liability to make a lump-sum payment to the estate is a substitute for the full amount of each of the annual $30,000 payments. Accordingly, none of the annual $30,000 payments qualifies as alimony.

CHILD SUPPORT PAYMENTS ARE NOT ALIMONY—POST-1984

¶ **1.50** A payment is fixed as payable for the support of your child if the divorce or separation instrument specifically fixes an amount payable for support.

> Even in the absence of a support allocation, a payment will be treated as payable for support if it is to be reduced on the happening of a contingency relating to the child or at a time clearly associated with such a contingency. Reducing payments for the following events falls within this rule: the child reaches a specified age or income level, dies, marries, leaves school, leaves the parent's household, or begins to work.

EXAMPLE

On July 1, 1985, a couple is divorced when their children John (born July 15, 1970) and Jane (born September 23, 1972) are 14 and 12. Under the divorce decree, the husband is to make monthly alimony payments of $2,000. The monthly payments are to be reduced to $1,500 on January 1, 1991 and to $1,000 on January 1, 1995. On January 1, 1991, the date of the first reduction, John will be almost 20 and a half years old. On January 1, 1995, the date of the second reduction, Jane will be over 22 years old. As each reduction is to occur not more than one year before or after a child reaches the age of 21 years, the IRS will presume that the deductions are associated with the happening of a contingency relating to the children. The two reductions total $1,000 per month and are treated as the amount fixed for the support of the children. $1,000 of the $2,000 monthly payment does not qualify as alimony. The husband must prove that the reductions were not related to the support of the children.

If both alimony and child support are specified and a payment is less than the total of the two amounts, then the payment is first allocated to child support.

2

TAXABLE PAY AND TAX FREE PAY BENEFITS

Illustrations of entering wage and salary income on a tax return may be found in the Supplement to YOUR INCOME TAX.

¶ **2.1** Practically everything you receive for your work or services is taxed, whether it is paid in cash, property, or services. Taxed pay includes: salaries, wages expense allowances, honoraria, commissions, tips, bonuses, jury fees, director fees, employee prizes or awards, severance pay, dismissal pay, back pay, sick pay, and vacation pay.

The amount of your pay is shown on Form W-2. Report the full pay listed on the form. Do not decrease the amount by the amount your employer withholds for income taxes, Social Security taxes, disability insurance payments, hospitalization insurance premiums, U.S. Savings Bonds, pension funds, union dues, or payments to a creditor who has attached your salary.

If you are self-employed, do not report your fees on Form 1040 as salary or wages, even if you consider your drawings as salary. Report your business or professional income on Schedule C.

Tax-free pay benefits. Fringe benefits provided you by your employer may be tax free. The most common tax-free benefit is employer-paid premiums for health and accident plans and certain group-term life insurance plans for coverage up to $50,000. Other tax-free fringes are discussed in the section beginning at ¶2.2.

TAX FREE BENEFITS

EMPLOYER-FURNISHED MEALS OR LODGING

¶ **2.2** The value of employer-financed food or lodging is not taxable if furnished on your employer's business premises for his convenience. The value of lodgings is not taxable if you must accept the lodging as a condition of your employment. The key words here are: "business premises," "convenience of the employer," and "conditions of employment." For meals, you must satisfy the "business premises" and "convenience of employer" tests. For lodging, you must satisfy these two tests plus the "condition of employment" test.

Convenience of employer. This requires proof that an employer provides the free meals or lodging for a business purpose other than providing extra pay. However, that the board and lodging are described in a contract or state statute as extra pay does not bar tax-free treatment provided they are *also* furnished for other substantial, noncompensatory business reasons, for example, you are required to be on call 24 hours a day.

Generally, the value of meals furnished before or after working hours

or on nonworking days is not treated as tax-free income, but see examples (1) and (3) following.

> **Business premises.** The IRS generally defines "business premises" as the place of employment, such as a company cafeteria in a factory or an employer's home for a domestic. The Tax Court has a liberal view, extending the area of "business premises" beyond the actual place of business in these cases:
>
> A house provided a hotel manager, although located across the street from the hotel. The IRS has agreed to the decision.
>
> A house provided a motel manager, two blocks from the motel. However, a court of appeals reversed the decision and held in the IRS's favor.
>
> A rented hotel suite used daily by executives for a luncheon conference.

EXAMPLES

1. A waitress who works from 7 A.M. to 4 P.M. is furnished two meals a day without charge. Her employer encourages her to have her breakfast at the restaurant before working, but she is required to have her lunch there. The value of her breakfast and lunch is not income, because it is furnished during her work period or immediately before or after the period. But say she is also allowed to have free meals on her days off and a free supper on the days she works. The value of these meals is taxable income because they are not furnished during or immediately before or after her work period.

2. A hospital maintains a cafeteria on its premises where all of its employees may eat during their working hours. No charge is made for these meals. The hospital furnishes meals to have the employees available for emergencies. The employees are not required to eat there. Since the hospital furnishes the meals in order to have employees available for emergency call during meal periods, the meals are not income to any of the hospital employees who obtain their meals at the hospital cafeteria.

3. You are required to occupy living quarters on your employer's business premises as a condition of employment. The value of *any* meal furnished you without charge on your employer's premises is not taxable income.

> The IRS does not consider partners or self-employed persons as employees and so does not allow them an exclusion under the rules of this section. The IRS also does not allow a partnership to deduct the cost of meals and lodging provided a partner-manager of a hotel. Courts split on this issue.

Meal charges. Your company may charge for meals on company premises and give you an option to accept or decline the meals. The IRS may not point to this option as evidence that the meals are not furnished for the convenience of your employer.

Where you must incur a fixed charge for your meals (furnished for your employer's convenience) on a periodic basis, you may claim an exclusion for the meal costs, provided you incur the meal charge whether or not you accept the meals.

Condition of employment. This test requires evidence that the lodging is needed for you to perform your job properly. For example, you are required to be available for duty at all times. If you are given the choice of free lodging at your place of employment or a cash allowance, the lodging is not considered as a "condition of employment," and its value is taxable, if elected.

"Lodging" includes heat, electricity, gas, water, sewerage, and other utilities. Where these services are furnished by the employer and their value is deducted from your salary, the amount deducted is also not included as part of your wage income. But if you pay for the utilities yourself, you may not exclude their cost from your income.

EXAMPLE

Jones is employed at a construction project at a remote job site. His pay is $200 a week. Because there are no accessible places near the site for food and lodging, the employer furnishes meals and lodging for which it charges $40 a week, which is taken out of Jones's pay. Jones reports only the net amount he receives, $160. The value of the meals and lodging is a tax-free benefit.

An employer may furnish unprepared food, such as groceries, rather than prepared meals. Courts are divided on whether the value of the gro-

ceries is excludable from income. One court allowed an exclusion for the value of non-food items, such as napkins and soap, as well as for groceries, furnished to a doctor who ate at his home on hospital grounds so he would be available for emergencies.

Cash allowances. A cash allowance for meals and lodging is taxable. Only meals furnished in kind are permitted tax-free treatment.

EXAMPLE

A hotel manager's wife bought groceries, the cost of which was reimbursed by the hotel. Milk was delivered to their apartment and paid for by the hotel. The reimbursement of the grocery bills was taxable because the groceries were not "furnished in kind" by the hotel. However, the cost of the milk was not taxable because the delivery to the apartment and the payment of the bill by the hotel was considered "furnishing in kind."

Peace Corps and VISTA volunteers. Peace Corps volunteers working overseas may exclude subsistence allowances from income under a specific Code provision. The law does not provide a similar exclusion for the small living expense allowances received by VISTA volunteers.

ARE YOUR BOARD AND LODGING TAX FREE?

Yes	No
A state civil service employee works at a state institution. His job requires him to live at the institution and eat there so he may be available for duty at any time. Under state law, the value of his meals and lodgings are considered part of his pay. Hotel executives, managers, housekeepers, and auditors who are required to live at the hotel. The following employees usually meet the above tests: domestics, farm laborers, fishermen, canners, seamen, servicemen, building superintendents, hospital and sanitarium employees. Restaurant and other food service employees for meals furnished during or immediately before or after working hours. Employees who must be available during meal periods for emergencies. Employees who, because of the nature of the business, are given short meal periods. Workers who have no alternative but to use company-supplied facilities in remote areas. Park employees who voluntarily live in rent-free apartments provided by a park department in order to protect the park from vandalism.	Your employer gives you a cash allowance for your meals or lodgings. He supplies neither. You have a choice of accepting cash or getting the meals or lodgings. For example, under a union contract you get meals, but you may refuse to take them and get an automatic pay increase. A state hospital employee is given a choice: He may live at the institution rent free or live elsewhere and get an extra $30 a month. Whether he stays at the institution or lives outside, the $30 a month is included in his income. A waitress, on her days off, is allowed to eat free meals at the restaurant where she works. You may buy lunch in the company's cafeteria or bring your own. There are no other eating facilities near the company's premises.

TAX FREE FRINGE BENEFITS

¶ 2.3 The tax law specifically exempts the following types of fringe benefits from tax:

Group hospitalization premiums paid by an employer or former employer, if you are retired. If you retire and have the option of receiving continued coverage under the medical plan or a lump-sum payment covering unused accumulated sick leave instead of coverage, the lump sum amount is reported as income at the time you have the option to receive it. If you elect continued coverage, the amount reported in income may be deductible as medical insurance. Medical coverage provided to the family of a deceased employee is tax free since it is treated as a continuation of the employee's fringe-benefit package.

Child or dependent care services provided by an employer under a written, nondiscriminatory plan. However, the value of services excluded from an employee's gross income may not exceed $5,000 or $2,500 for married persons filing separately. Expenses are excludable if they would qualify under ¶1.33 for the dependent care credit. The exclusion is not allowed if dependent care is provided by a relative who is your dependent (or your spouse's dependent) or by your child under the age of 19.

Group-term life insurance premiums paid by your employer, provided the policy does not exceed $50,000. *See* ¶2.5.

Medicare premiums paid by your employer for voluntary hospital coverage (Part B).

Qualified group legal services plan contributions paid by your employer for prepaid personal legal services for you and your family. The value of legal services provided are also tax free.

Employer contributions to a qualified pension or profit-sharing plan.

Employer's payment of education costs under a nondiscriminatory plan. The annual tax-free benefit may not exceed $5,250 per employee for tuition, books, fees, supplies and equipment for any courses. Courses do not have to be job related, provided they do not involve sports, games, or hobbies. Benefits above $5,250 are taxable.

Employer-provided services that are sold to the public and offered to employees at no additional cost to the employer.

Not taxable are free or low-cost flights provided by an airline to its employees, free or discount lodging for employees of a hotel, and telephone service provided to employees of telephone companies. These tax-free fringes also may be provided to the employee's spouse and dependent children; retired employees, including employees retired on disability; and widows or widowers of deceased or retired employees. Benefits received by officers, owners and highly compensated employees are subject to nondiscrimination rules. Benefits provided by another company under a reciprocal arrangement, such as standby tickets on another airline, also qualify.

If a company has two lines of business, such as an airline and a hotel, an employee of the airline may not receive tax-free benefits provided by the hotel. There are exceptions. An employee who provides services to both business lines may receive benefits from both business lines. Benefits may also be available under a special election made by the company. Your employer should notify you of this tax benefit.

Qualified employee discounts on company goods and services. The tax-free exclusion for merchandise discounts may not exceed your employer's gross profit percentage. For example, if a company's profit percentage is 40%, the maximum tax-free employee discount for merchandise is 40% of the regular selling price; the employer has a choice of methods for figuring profit percentage. Discounts on services provided by the employer also qualify, with the maximum exclusion limited to 20% of the selling price charged customers. An insurance policy is treated as a service. Thus, insurance company employees are not taxed on a discount of up to 20% of the policy's price.

Some company products do not qualify for exclusion. Discounts on real estate and investment property such as securities, commodities, currency or bullion are taxable. Interest-free or low-interest loans given by banks or other financial institutions to employees are not excludable. The loan is subject to tax under the rules of ¶4.17.

The same line of business limitation discussed above for no-additional cost services also applies to qualified employee discounts. Thus, if a company operates an airline and a hotel, employees who work for the airlines may generally not receive tax-free hotel room discounts. However, by making a special election the company may allow its employees to receive tax-free benefits from any line of business.

Owners and key employees are subject to the nondiscrimination rules discussed below.

Employer paid subscriptions to business periodicals are a tax-free working condition fringe, as are employer reimbursements for membership dues in a professional association.

Working condition fringes. The value of a company car or airplane is tax free to the extent that you use it for business, *see* ¶2.4.

Free or reduced-rate parking provided to employees on or near the business premises is a tax-free working condition fringe benefit.

A limited product testing exclusion applies to company manufactured goods used by employees away from company premises in order to test and evaluate the product.

De minimis fringes. There are small benefits that are administratively impractical to tax, such as typing of a personal letter by a company secretary, personal use of the company copy machine, occasional supper money or company cocktail party or picnic, and occasional theater or sporting event tickets.

The operation of an eating facility for employees is a tax-free *de minimis* fringe if it is located on or near the business premises, and the cost of the meals to employees equals or exceeds the company's operating costs. Do not confuse this type of meal benefit with employer-supplied meals for employees who must be on call on an employer's premises; these are tax free under ¶2.2. Executive dining room meals do not qualify as a *de minimis* fringe although the meals may be tax free under rules of ¶2.2 if meals must be taken on company premises.

Tuition reductions. Employees and retired employees of educational institutions, their spouses and dependent children are not taxed on tuition reductions for courses below the graduate level furnished after June 30, 1985. Widows or widowers of deceased employees or of former employees also qualify. Officers and highly paid employees may claim the exclusion only if the employer plan does not discriminate on their behalf. The exclusion applies to tuition for education at any educational institution, not only the employer's school. Graduate students who teach or do research at educational organizations are not taxable on tuition reductions received during 1987.

Athletic facilities. The fair market value of athletic facilities, such as gyms, swimming pools, golf courses and tennis courts is tax free if the facilities are on the employer's property (not necessarily the main business premises) and substantially all of the use of the facilities is by employees, their spouses, and dependent children. Such facilities must be open to all employees on a nondiscriminatory basis in order for the company to deduct related expenses.

Nondiscrimination rules. Qualified employee discounts, no additional-cost services, and eating facility services received by officers, owners, and highly compensated employees are tax free only if the same benefits are available to other employees on a nondiscriminatory basis. The nondiscrimination rule does not apply to working condition fringes or *de minimis* fringes other than eating facilities. For 1987, a highly compensated employee is any employee who has compensation greater than the compensation of 90 percent of all employees employed by the employer. There are two exceptions to the 90 percent test: (1) any employee who has compensation of $50,000 or more during a calendar year is a highly compensated employee for that year, regardless of the 90% test, and (2) any employee who has compensation of $20,000 or less during a year is not a highly compensated employee for that year, unless no employee of the employer has compensation in excess of $35,000.

Interest-free and low-interest loans. Interest-free loans received from your employer may be taxed. See ¶4.17.

Employee Achievment Awards. Special rules apply to awards given to you in recognition of length of service or safety achievement. As a general rule, if your employer is allowed to deduct the cost of the award, you are not taxed. If your employer's deduction is less than the item's cost, you are taxed on (1) the difference between the cost and your employer's deduction, or if greater, (2) the excess of the item's fair market value over your employer's deduction. Deduction tests for achievement awards are discussed at ¶19.48. Therefore, it is up to your employer to tell you the tax consequences of the award.

An award will not be treated as a tax-free safety achievement award if employee safety achievement awards (other than those of *de minimis* value) were granted during the year to more than 10 percent of employees (not counting managers, administrators, clerical employees and other professional employees) or were granted to a manager, administrator, clerical employee or other professional employee.

The tax-free treatment also does not apply when you receive an award for length of service during the first five years of employment or when you previously received such awards during the last five years, unless the prior award qualified as a *de minimis* fringe benefit; *see above.*

COMPANY CARS AS FRINGE BENEFITS

¶ **2.4** The use of a company car is tax free under the working condition fringe rule, provided you use the car for business. If you use the car for personal driving, you may be taxed on the value of such personal use. Your company has the responsibility of calculating taxable income based on Treasury tables that specify the value of various priced cars. For certain cars, a flat mileage allowance may be used to measure personal use. You are also required to keep for your employer a mileage log or similar record to substantiate your business use. Your employer should tell you what type of records are required. Similarly, employees who use a company airplane for personal trips are taxable on the value of the flights, as determined by the employer using Treasury tables.

Regardless of personal use, you are not subject to tax for a company vehicle that the IRS considers to be of limited personal value. These are ambulances or hearses; flatbed trucks; dump, garbage or refrigerated trucks; one passenger delivery trucks (including truck with folding jump seat); tractors, combines, other farm equipment, or forklifts. Also not taxable is personal use of school buses, passenger buses (seating at least 20), and moving vans where such personal use is restricted; police or fire vehicles, or an unmarked law enforcement vehicle, where personal use is authorized by a government agency.

The value of a demonstration car used by a full-time auto salesperson is tax free as a working condition fringe, if the use of the car facilitates job performance, and there are substantial personal use restrictions, including a prohibition on use by family members and for vacation trips. Further, total mileage outside of normal working hours must be limited and personal driving must generally be restricted to a 75 mile radius around the dealer's sales office.

Reporting taxable automobile benefits. Social Security tax must be withheld. Income tax withholding is not required, but your employer may choose to withhold income tax. You must be notified by your employer that he is not withholding income tax so that you may consider the taxable benefits when determining your estimated tax; *see* chapter 26. Whether or not withholdings are taken, the taxable value of the benefits is entered on your Form W-2 along with other compensation or on a separate Form W-2 for fringe benefits. A special IRS rule allows your employer to include on Form W-2 100% of the value of using the car, even if you used the car primarily for business. In this case, you must report the 100% value as income and then deduct expenses attributable to business driving on Form 2106. On Form 2106, you must claim actual expenses; the flat IRS mileage allowance may not be used since you are not the owner.

Your employer may also decide to treat fringe benefits provided during the last two months of the calendar year as if paid during the following year. For example, if this election is made for a company car in 1987, only the value of personal use from January through October is taxable in 1987; personal use in November and December is taxable in 1988. If your employer has elected this special year-end rule, you should be notified near the end of the year or when you receive Form W-2.

GROUP INSURANCE, DEATH, AND OTHER BENEFITS

GROUP-TERM LIFE INSURANCE PREMIUMS

¶ **2.5** You are not taxed on your employer's payments of premiums on a policy of up to $50,000 on your life. You are taxed only on his cost of premiums for coverage of over $50,000 as determined by the Treasury rates listed below. Your employer will give you a written statement of the amount of income you must report for coverage on policies exceeding $50,000. The taxable amount is not subject to withholding tax. You may not avoid tax by assigning the policy to another person.

> If you pay for a part of the insurance, reduce the amount includable as income by your payments.

If two or more employers provide you with group-term insurance coverage, the amount of taxable income is computed on the basis of only one exclusion of $50,000.

Retirees. If you retired before 1984 at normal retirement age or on disability and are still covered by a company group-term life insurance policy, you are not taxed on premium payments made by your employer even if coverage is over $50,000. If you retired after 1983 because of disability and remain covered by your company's plan, you are not taxed even if coverage exceeds $50,000. Further, if you retired after 1983 and are not disabled, you may still qualify for tax-free coverage over $50,000 if the following tests are met: The insurance is provided under a plan existing on January 1, 1984, or under a comparable successor plan; you were employed during 1983 by the company having the plan, or a predecessor employer; and you were age 55 or over on January 1, 1984.

Key employees. The $50,000 exclusion is not available to "key employees," generally officers and certain employees with ownership interests, unless the group plan meets nondiscrimination tests. If the plan discriminates, a key employee's taxable benefit is based on the larger of (1) the actual cost of coverage, or (2) the amount using the table below for coverage over $50,000. The nondiscrimination rules also apply to retired "key employees."

Age	Rates for coverage over $50,000 *Monthly premium per $1,000 of coverage above $50,000*
Under 30	$ .08
30–34	.09
35–39	.11
40–44	.17
45–49	.29
50–54	.48
55–59	.75
60 and over	1.17

Based on the above table, a 50-year-old executive provided with $200,000 of group-term coverage has income of $864 (150 × .48 premium × 12 months).

Important: After 1987, group-term life insurance plans are subject to new nondiscrimination rules and other restrictions.

Permanent life insurance. If your employer pays premiums on your behalf for permanent nonforfeitable life insurance, you report the cost of the benefit as taxable wages. A permanent benefit is an economic value that extends beyond one year and includes paid-up insurance or cash surrender value, but does not include, for example, the right to convert or continue life insurance coverage after group coverage is terminated. Where permanent benefits are combined with term insurance, the permanent benefits are taxed under formulas found in Treasury regulations.

GIFTS FROM EMPLOYERS

¶ **2.6** A payment may be called a gift but still be taxable income. Any payment made in recognition of past services or in anticipation of future services or benefits is taxable even if the employer is not obligated to make the payment. *See also* ¶12.3. To prove a gift is tax free, you must show that the employer acted with pure and unselfish motives of affection, admiration, or charity. This is difficult to do, given the employer-employee relationship.

A gift of stock by majority stockholders to key employees has been held to be taxable income.

EMPLOYEES' DEATH BENEFITS MAY BE TAX FREE UP TO $5,000

¶ **2.7** An employer's payment to his deceased employee's beneficiary is tax free up to $5,000 if: (1) Paid solely because of the employee's death; *and* (2) the employee did not have a nonforfeitable right to the payment while he was alive. An employee had a nonforfeitable right if he could have received the amount on demand or when he left his job. Where benefits were payable under an annuity contract, ask the company paying the benefits what part of the payments, if any, qualify for the $5,000 exclusion. The nonforfeitable requirement does not apply to payments that qualify as a lump-sum distribution from a qualified pension or profit-sharing plan (¶7.7) or qualified annuity plan for employees of tax-exempt schools and charities (¶7.30).

Beneficiaries of retired employees who retired on disability before reaching mandatory retirement age under Federal Civil Service laws or the Retired Servicemen's family Protection Plan may claim the $5,000 exclusion.

Payments received from a qualified Keogh plan by beneficiaries of self-employed individuals also qualify (see ¶7.7).

EXAMPLES

1. Products Co. pays Brown's widow a $5,000 bonus due Brown. The bonus is fully taxable. Brown had a right to the payment while he was alive. Similarly, payments for unused leave and uncollected salary are not tax free up to $5,000.
2. When an employee dies, Grand Co. pays the deceased's widow or other family beneficiary a death benefit of $1,000. The amount is tax free. It is paid because of the death of an employee who had no right to the amount while alive.

The death benefit exclusion may not exceed $5,000 regardless of the number of employers making payment or beneficiaries receiving pay-

ments. The $5,000 exclusion is divided among all the beneficiaries. Each claims a part of the exclusion in the same ratio as his share bears to the total benefit paid. Interest paid on tax-free death benefits is taxed.

Where benefits are paid over several years, the $5,000 exclusion must be applied to the first payments.

> **Voluntary payments as gifts.** The IRS holds that if a death benefit exceeds $5,000, the excess is taxable even if the payment was voluntarily made by the employer. Some federal district courts have allowed tax-free gift treatment for amounts over $5,000; the Tax Court has supported the IRS position.
>
> As a practical matter, a tax law provision usually forces an employer who wants to deduct amounts over $5,000 as compensation to decide whether the payment is a gift or pay. If he calls the payment a gift, he may not deduct more than $25 of the payment that exceeds $5,000. For the full deduction, he must treat it as compensation.

RENTAL VALUE OF A PARSONAGE IS NOT INCOME

¶ **2.8** A duly ordained minister of the gospel pays no tax on the rental value of a home provided as part of his pay. If he is not provided a home but is paid a rental allowance, he pays no tax on the allowance if he uses the entire amount to pay his rent (including the rent of a furnished or unfurnished apartment or house and garage and utilities). Where a minister buys or owns his own home, he pays no tax on the allowance used as a down payment on the house, mortgage installments, or for utilities, interest, tax and repair expenses of the house. Any part of the allowance not used for these housing purposes is taxed. For example, that part of an allowance used to pay rent on business or farm property or for food or the services of a maid is taxed.

The IRS has generally barred an exclusion to ordained ministers working as executives of non-religious organizations even where services or religious functions are performed as part of the job. The Tax Court has focused on the duties performed; exclusions have been allowed in some cases and not in others.

EXCLUSION FOR PARSONAGE ALLOWANCE

Allowed to:	*Not allowed to:*
A teacher or executive director or administrator who is a minister of the gospel if he teaches in a school, college, or theological seminary which is part of a church organization and his position requires the services of a minister of the gospel. Cantor Ordained ministers in interdenominational organizations, if they serve in the exercise of their ministry. A traveling evangelist who is ordained and receives rental allowances from out-of-town churches, if the allowances are used to maintain his permanent home. More than one minister of the gospel for the same congregation, if the allowances are authorized by the church or congregation. A retired minister, if the allowance is furnished in recognition of past services.	Church officers who are not ordained, such as ministers of music or education. Theological students Civilian chaplains at VA hospitals. Minister-administrator of an old-age home which is not under the authority of a church. Rabbi employed by service organization as director of interreligious affairs. He was not assigned to his job by a religious body or employed as a minister to lead religious worship, but performed public relations services for his employer. Minister directing anticommunist drive. An ordained priest living as a layman while he teaches college and receiving pay directly from the college, rather than from his order.

Allowance must be authorized by church or congregation. To qualify rental allowances for tax-free treatment, official church action by the local congregation designating the allowance must be made in advance of the payments. Official action may be shown by an employment contract, minutes, a resolution, or a budget allowance. The local congregation must officially designate the part of the clergyman's compensation that is a rental allowance.

Allowance subject to self-employment tax. Although parsonage allowances are not taxed income, they are reported as self-employment income for Social Security purposes (*see* ¶5.51). If you do not receive a cash allowance, report the rental value of the parsonage as self-employment income. Rental value is usually equal to what you would pay for similar quarters in your locality. Also include as self-employment income the value of house furnishings, utilities, appurtenances supplied, such as a garage, and the value of meals furnished that meet the rules at ¶2.2.

A minister who rents his home while abroad on church business may exclude his rental allowance only up to amounts used for capital improvements. These amounts are treated as expenses of keeping up his regular home. The balance of his rental allowance is taxable compensation even though he had expenses for maintenance, interest, taxes, repairs, and utilities during the rental period. The expenses may be deducted from rental income.

CAFETERIA PAY PLANS

¶ **2.9** "Cafeteria plans" is a nickname for plans that give an employee a choice of selecting tax-free fringe benefits or taxable benefits. You are generally not taxed when you elect nontaxable benefits.

A qualified cafeteria plan must be written and not discriminate in favor of highly compensated employees and stockholders. If the plan provides for health benefits, a special rule applies to determine whether the plan is discriminatory.

Employees with three years of employment must be eligible to participate in the plan. If a plan is held discriminatory, the highly compensated participants are taxed to the extent they could have elected taxable benefits.

The law restricts the types of benefits that a cafeteria plan may offer and bars cash refunds for unused benefits. Your employer should tell you the tax status of the benefits you select.

Note: New law restrictions and nondiscrimination tests apply to cafeteria plans in plan years starting after 1987.

WHEN IS YOUR PAY TAXED?

REPORTING WAGES

¶ **2.10** The cash basis and the accrual basis are the two usual methods of reporting income. Most individuals use the cash basis to report all income items in the year they are actually received and deduct expenses in the year they are actually paid. Under the accrual basis, income is reported when earned, even though not received. The accrual basis is used primarily to report business income. The right to use the accrual basis is conditioned on accurate bookkeeping accounts which are generally unnecessary and burdensome for personal income (*see* ¶5.2).

As a cash-basis taxpayer, you are subject to the "constructive receipt rule." The rule requires you to report income not actually received but which has been credited to your account, subject to your control, or put aside for you.

Examples of Taxed Wages—

Salaries, wages, expense allowances, honoraria, commissions, tips, bonuses, severance pay, dismissal pay, back pay, sick pay, vacation pay, and cash payment received upon the exercise of stock appreciation rights (SARs).

Withholdings from your wages for taxes (income, Social Security, unemployment insurance, etc.), hospitalization and life insurance premiums, savings bond payments, union dues, your pension fund contributions.

Wages garnished by creditors. If your wages are attached and your employer pays part of them to your creditor, you report your entire pay.

Wages received by your agent for your account.

You must pay tax on a paycheck received before the end of the year even though you do not cash or deposit it to your account. If your employer does not have funds in the bank and asks you to hold the check before depositing it, you do not have taxed income until the check is cashed. Where an employee was not at home to take delivery of a year-end check, the Tax Court held the funds were taxable in the year following the year of receipt.

Sick pay. Sick pay is generally taxable as wages unless it qualifies as worker's compensation under the rules of ¶2.19. Further, payments received under accident or health plans are tax free if you paid the premiums or your employer provides benefits for certain serious physical injuries, as explained at ¶2.21.

Assigning your pay. You may not avoid tax on income earned by you by assigning the right to payment to another person. For example, you report earnings donated by you but paid directly by your employer to a charity. You may claim a contribution deduction for the donation (*see* chapter 14). The IRS allowed an exception for doctors working in a clinic. They were required to assign to a foundation all fees derived from treating patients with limited income (teaching cases). The fees were not taxable.

Withholdings for retirement plans. Amounts withheld as your contribution to your pension or profit-sharing account are generally taxable. Courts have held that amounts withheld from the pay of both U.S. Civil Service employees and city and county civil service employees are taxable to the employees.

Wages withheld for compulsory forfeitable contributions to a nonqualified pension plan are not taxable if these conditions exist: (1) The contribution is forfeited if employment is terminated prior to death or retirement. (2) The plan does not provide for a refund of employee contributions and, in the administration of the plan, no refund will be made. Where only part of the contribution is subject to forfeiture, the amount of withheld contribution not subject to forfeiture is taxable income.

Check with your employer to determine the status of your contributions.

Deferring tax on pay. Under certain conditions, you may contract with your employer to defer the taxable receipt of current compensation to future years. To defer pay to a future period, you must take some risk. You cannot have any control over your deferred pay account. If you are not confident of your employer's ability to pay in the future, you should not enter into a deferred pay plan.

An employee is not taxed on employer contributions to a qualified cash or deferred arrangement (401(k) plan) even though the employee had the option to take the cash. *See* ¶32.4. Qualified salary reductions under a simplified employee pension plan (SEP, *see* ¶8.12) or tax-sheltered annuity plan (¶7.30) are also not taxed even though you could have received cash currently.

An employee of a state or local government or tax-exempt organization which has established a nonqualified deferred pay plan may defer the lesser of $7,500 or 33 1/3% of his or her pay, reduced by amounts deferred under tax-sheltered annuity programs, 401(k) plans or SEP plans. The deferred pay is not taxed until it is paid or made available to you.

Salary advances. Salary paid in advance for services to be rendered in the future is generally taxable in the year received if it is subject to your free and unrestricted use.

Barter transactions. The value of the trades by members of a barter club is subject to income tax. For example, an attorney and a housepainter, both members of a barter club, arrange for the housepainter to paint the attorney's home in exchange for legal services. The fair market value of the services received by the attorney and the housepainter are taxable. Even where no goods or services are received, a club member is taxable on the value of "credit units" credited during the year.

If you exchanged services or goods through a barter exchange during 1987, you should receive Form 1099-B from the exchange by January 31, 1988, showing the value received during the year. The IRS also gets a copy of Form 1099-B.

Child's wages. A parent is not taxed on wages paid for a child's services even if payment is made to the parent. However, a parent is taxed on income from work contracted for by the parent even if the child assists in the labor. For example, a parent whose children helped her with part-time work at home claimed that the children should be taxed on 70% of the income since they did 70% of the work. The IRS claimed that the parent was taxable on all the income because she, not the children, was the true earner, and the Tax Court agreed. Although the company knew that the children were doing part of the work, it had no agreement with them.

PAY RECEIVED IN PROPERTY IS TAXED

¶ 2.11 Your employer may pay you with property instead of cash. You report the fair market value of the property as wages.

EXAMPLE
For services rendered, you receive a check for $1,000 and property having a fair market value of $500. You report $1,500 as wages.

If you receive your company's stock as payment for your services, you include the value of the stock as pay in the year you receive it. However, if the stock is non-transferrable and subject to substantial risk of forfeiture, you do not have to include its value as pay. See ¶32.7.

If you receive your employer's note which has a fair market value, you are taxed on the value of the note, less what it would cost you to discount it. If the note bears interest, report the full face value. But do not report income if the note has no fair market value. Report income on the note only when payments are made on it.

A debt cancelled by an employer is taxable income.

A salesman employed by a dealer has taxable income on receipt of "prize points" redeemable for merchandise from a distributor.

WHEN COMMISSIONS ARE TAXED

¶ 2.12 *Earned commissions.* Earned commissions are taxable in the year they are credited to your account and subject to your drawing, whether or not you actually draw them.

On your 1987 tax return, you do not report commissions which were earned in 1987 but which cannot be computed or collected until a later year.

EXAMPLE
You earn commissions based on a percentage of the profits. In 1987, you draw $10,000 from your account. However, at the end of 1987 the full amount of your commissions is not known because profits for the year have not been figured. In January, 1988, your 1987 commissions are computed to be $15,000, and the $5,000 balance is paid to you. The $5,000 is taxable in 1988 even though earned in 1987.

You may not postpone tax on earned commissions credited to your account in 1987 by not drawing them until 1988 or a later year. However, where a portion of earned commissions is not withdrawn because your employer is holding it to cover future expenses, you are not taxed on the amount withheld.

Advances against unearned commissions. Under standard insurance industry practice, an agent who sells a policy does not earn his commission

until premiums are received by the insurance company. However, the company may issue a cash advance on the commissions before the premiums are received. Agents have claimed that they may defer reporting the income until the year the premiums are earned. The IRS, recognizing that in practice companies rarely demand repayment, requires that advances be included in income in the year received if the agent has full control over the advanced funds. A repayment of unearned commissions in a later year is deducted as an itemized deduction.

> Some courts have recognized that an advance may constitute a loan if there is an unconditional personal obligation to repay the advanced amount. Factors to be considered: A note or other evidence of indebtedness, a repayment schedule, how the advance is carried on the books of the company, and an attempt on the part of the company to collect advances.

Salesmen have been taxed on commissions received on property bought for their personal use. In one case, an insurance agent was taxed on commissions paid to him on his purchase of an insurance policy. In another case, a real estate agent was taxed on commissions he received on his purchase of land. A salesman was also taxed for commissions waived on policies he sold to friends, relatives, and employees.

An insurance agent's kickback of his commission is taxable where agents may not under local law give rebates or kickbacks of premiums to their clients.

UNEMPLOYMENT BENEFITS ARE TAXABLE

¶ 2.13 All unemployment benefits you receive in 1987 from a state agency or the federal government are taxable. You should receive Form 1099-G, showing the amount of the payments.

Supplemental unemployment benefits paid from company financed funds are fully taxable. Such benefits are usually paid under guaranteed annual wage plans made between unions and employers. Unemployment benefits from a private or union fund to which you voluntarily contribute dues are taxable only to the extent the benefits exceed your contributions to the fund. Your contributions to the fund are not deductible.

Worker's compensation payments are not taxable. See ¶2.19.

If you had to repay supplemental unemployment benefits because of receipt of Trade Readjustment Assistance payments, taxable unemployment benefits are reduced by repayments made in the same year. If you repay the benefits in a later year, a deduction may be claimed in the later year under the rules of ¶2.15.

STRIKE PAY BENEFITS AND PENALTIES

¶ 2.14 *Pay penalty charged striking teachers not deductible.* State law may prohibit public school teachers from striking and charge a penalty equal to one day's pay for each day on strike if they do strike. For example, when striking teachers returned to work after a one week strike, a penalty of one week's salary was deducted from their pay. Although they did not actually receive pay for the week they worked after the strike, they earned taxable wages. Further, the penalty is not deductible. No deduction is allowed for a fine or penalty paid to a government for the violation of a law.

> Strike benefits paid by a union are taxable unless you can show they are in the nature of "gifts" or "charity." Evidence tending to show that strike benefits are gifts: Payments are based on individual need; they are paid to both union and nonunion members; and no conditions are imposed on the strikers who receive benefits. If you receive benefits under conditions by which you are to participate in the strike and the payments are tied to your scale of wages, the benefits are taxable.

DID YOU HAVE TO RETURN INCOME RECEIVED IN AN EARLIER YEAR?

¶ 2.15 When you return income, such as salary or commissions, which you reported in a prior taxable year, a deduction in the year of repayment may be allowed under a special statute (Section 1341), if in the year you received the income "it appeared you had an unrestricted right to the income." Further, if the repayment qualifies under Section 1341 and exceeds $3,000, you have an alternative: Instead of claiming the deduction from 1987 income, you may recompute your tax for the prior year by claiming a credit for the amount of tax overpaid in the prior year on your 1987 tax return. Choose the alternative which gives you the larger tax reduction. See IRS Publication 525 and Treasury regulations for how tax computations are made under Section 1341.

Section 1341 does not apply to the refund of income arising from the sale of inventory items.

Note: To claim the repayment as a 1987 deduction, you must itemize deductions on Schedule A. However, the deduction is not subject to the 2% adjusted gross income floor for miscellaneous expenses; *see also* chapter 19.

Repayment of supplemental unemployment benefits. Where repayment is required because of the receipt in an earlier year of trade readjustment allowances, you may deduct the repayment from gross income. If repayment is $3,000 or more, you have the choice of a deduction or claiming a credit against your 1987 tax by recomputing your tax for the year supplemental unemployment benefits were received, as explained above. If a deduction is claimed, the deduction is allowed even if you do not itemize.

> *Repayment of disallowed salary or T & E expenses.* If a "hedge" agreement between you and your company requires you to repay salary or T & E expenses if they are disallowed to the company by the IRS, you may claim a deduction in the year of repayment. According to the IRS, you may not recalculate your tax for the prior year and claim a tax credit under the rules of Section 1341. An appeals court has rejected the IRS position and allowed a tax recomputation under Section 1341 to an executive who returned part of a disallowed salary under the terms of a corporate by-law.

WAIVER OF EXECUTOR'S AND TRUSTEE'S COMMISSIONS

¶ 2.16 Commissions received by an executor are taxable as compensation. An executor may waive commissions without income or gift tax consequences by giving a principal legatee or devisee a formal waiver of his right to commissions within six months after his initial appointment or by not claiming commissions at the time of filing the usual accountings.

The waiver may not be recognized if he takes any action that is inconsistent with the waiver. An example of an inconsistent action would be the claiming of an executor's fee as a deduction on an estate, inheritance, or income tax return.

A bequest to an executor is tax free.

DISABILITY PENSIONS, ACCIDENT AND HEALTH BENEFITS, WORKMEN'S COMPENSATION

DISABILITY PENSION EXCLUSION REPEALED

¶ 2.17 Disability pensions financed by your employer are reported as wage income unless they are tax free under the rules of ¶2.21. Turn to ¶34.2 to see if you may claim a tax credit for the receipt of a disability pension. A credit, subject to income limitations, is allowed for disability payments received while you are under the age of 65 and permanently and totally disabled.

HEALTH AND ACCIDENT INSURANCE BENEFITS

¶ 2.18 You pay no tax on benefits received from a health or accident insurance policy on which you paid all of the premiums. However, if a payment reimburses a medical expense which you deducted in a prior year, you may have to report all or part of the payment. See ¶17.5.

If you and your employer each pay part of the premiums for accident and health insurance, you have, for tax purposes, two plans: One financed by you; the other financed by your employer. For treatment of benefits from a plan financed by your employer, *see* ¶2.21.

WORKER'S COMPENSATION ARE TAX FREE

¶ 2.19 You do not pay tax on worker's compensation payments for job-related injuries or illness. However, your employer might continue paying your regular salary but require you to turn over to him your worker's compensation payments. Then you may be taxed on the difference between what he paid you and what you returned to him.

EXAMPLE
You are injured while at work and are out of work for two months. Your company continues your salary of $175. You also receive workmen's compensation of $35 a week which you give to your employer. The $35 is tax free. The balance of $140 a week is considered taxable wages.

> A teacher, injured while working, received full salary during a two-year sick leave. She argued that the payments were similar to worker's compensation and thus were tax free. The IRS disagreed on the grounds that the payments were not paid under a worker's compensation statute. The Tax Court supported the teacher. The payments were like worker's compensation; they were paid because of injuries sustained in the line of duty. Although not made under a worker's compensation statute, they were authorized by board of education regulations which have the force of law.

Not all payments for job-related illness or injury qualify as tax-free worker's compensation. For example, payments to a government employee under the Civil Service Retirement Act are not in the nature of worker's compensation because the payments are made regardless of whether disability is caused by on-the-job injuries. Payments are taxable even if a particular employee's payments are in fact based on job related injuries.

DISABILITY PENSION RULES FOR MEMBERS OF THE MILITARY, PUBLIC HEALTH SERVICE AND FOREIGN SERVICE

¶ 2.20 Tax-free treatment of disability pensions for members of the military, the Public Health Service, and Foreign Service are not available generally to individuals who joined these government services after September 24, 1975. Under prior law, tax-free treatment covered pensions or similar allowances for personal injuries or sickness resulting from active service in the Armed Forces of any country, as well as similar amounts received by disabled members of the National Oceanic and Atmospheric Administration (NOAA, formerly called the Coast and Geodetic Survey), the Public Health Service, or the Foreign Service.

Also, a portion of a disability pension based on years of active service could be treated as tax-free sick pay by a disabled retiree before he reached retirement age. Finally, benefits paid by the Veterans Administration were fully exempt from tax.

Under current law, the above prior tax-exempt rules (except for the abolished sick pay exclusion) continue to apply to your disability payments if:

1. On or before September 24, 1975, you were entitled to receive disability payments, or
2. On September 24, 1975, you were a member of one of the above services (or reserve component) or under a binding written commitment to become a member.

If you do not meet either rule (1) or (2), the following tax-free benefits are available to members of the military:

Veterans Administration disability payments or an amount equivalent to benefits a member would be entitled to receive from the V.A.

Pension based on combat-related injuries. A combat-related injury or sickness which is incurred as a result of any one of the following activities: (1) as a direct result of armed conflict; (2) while engaged in extra-hazardous service, even if not directly engaged in combat; (3) under conditions simulating war, including maneuvers or training; or (4) which is caused by an instrumentality of war, such as weapons.

Tax-free treatment applies to a disability pension paid to a civilian U.S. employee for injuries incurred as a direct result of a violent attack which the Secretary of State determines to be a terrorist attack and which occurred while the employee was working for the United States in the performance of his official duties outside the United States.

Disability pensions meeting the rules of this section generally are fully tax free.

TAX-FREE BENEFITS FROM ACCIDENT AND HEALTH PLANS FINANCED BY EMPLOYER

¶ **2.21** *Employer contributions.* Employees are generally not taxed on their employer's contributions for health or accident plan coverage. However, in plan years starting after June 30, 1986, highly compensated employees in companies with 20 or more employees are taxed on the employer's contribution unless all of the employer's group health plans meet the continuing coverage requirements discussed below. For purposes of this rule, highly compensated employees generally include employees with compensation over $75,000, employees paid over $50,000 who are in the top-paid 20% of all employees, employees with ownership interests over 5%, and officers with pay exceeding $45,000. Highly compensated employees who are covered by a government plan or a church plan may exclude their employee's contributions; the continuing coverage rules do not apply to such plans.

Plan benefits . You are not taxed on benefits received under your employee's plan if:

1. They are specific reimbursements of medical expenses (not amounts you would have received anyway) you had for yourself, your spouse, or any of your dependents. If the reimbursement is for medical expenses you deducted in a previous year, the reimbursement may be taxed income to you. (See ¶17.5 for the rules on how reimbursements affect the medical deduction.) Payment does not have to come directly to you; it may go directly to those to whom you owe money for medical expenses. A special rule applies to discriminatory self-insured reimbursed plans; *see* below.
2. They are for the permanent loss or loss of use of part of the body or for permanent disfigurement of yourself, your spouse, or a dependent. The payments are based on the kind of injury and have no relation to the length of time you are out of work. These payments are not for medical expenses and are tax free. In addition, you may also deduct any medical expenses you have in connection

with these injuries. An appeals court held that severe hypertension does not involve loss of a bodily part or function.

Benefits not coming within the above two categories are fully taxable if (1) your employer paid all the premiums, and (2) you were not required to report his premium payments as taxable income. If you and your employer each paid part of the premiums and you were not taxable on your employer's payment, the part of the proceeds allocated to the employer's contribution is taxed to you. Assume the annual premium is $240; you pay $80, your employer, $160. Two-thirds of your health and accident insurance proceeds is taxable. Ask your employer for the allocation ratio.

Continuing coverage for group health plans. For plan years starting after June 30, 1986, employers may not deduct their expenses for group-health plans unless they offer continuing group health and accident coverage to employees who leave the company and to spouses and dependent children who would lose coverage in the case of divorce or the death of the employee. The cost of the continuing coverage is paid by the employee or beneficiary. Continuing coverage rules do not apply to small employers who in the previous calendar year had less than 20 employees on a typical day, or government agencies and churchs. For other employers, continuing coverage must be offered in these situations:

1. Employee with coverage voluntarily or involuntarily leaves the company—unless termination is for gross misconduct. Employees who would lose coverage because of a reduction in hours must also be offered continuing coverage. If accepted, the coverage must last for at least 18 months.
2. On the death of a covered employee, continuing coverage must be offered to the surviving spouse and dependent children who are beneficiaries under the plan on the day before the death. Coverage must be for at least 36 months.
3. If a covered employee is divorced or legally separated, continuing coverage must be offered to the spouse and dependent children for at least 36 months.
4. If a covered employee becomes eligible for medicare benefits, continuing coverage under the employer's plan must be offered to the employee's spouse and dependent children for at least 36 months.
5. If a dependent child becomes ineligible under the plan upon reaching a certain age, continuing coverage must be offered for at least 36 months.

Employers must provide written notice of the continuing coverage option. If one of the above qualifying events occurs, eligible employees, spouses and/or dependent children generally have 60 days to elect continuing coverage.

Discriminatory medical reimbursement plans. Reimbursements from an employer plan for medical expenses of an employee, his or her spouse, and dependents are generally tax free. However, the exclusion does not apply to certain highly compensated employees and stockholders if the plan is self-insured and it discriminates on their behalf. These rules apply to employees owning more than 10% of the employer's stock, the highest paid 25% of all employees (other than employees who do not have to be covered under the law) and the five highest paid officers. If the plan discriminates on their behalf, they are taxed on the amount of the discriminatory benefit not received by other employees. A plan is self-insured if reimbursement is not provided by an unrelated insurance company. If coverage is provided by an unrelated insurer, these discriminatory restrictions do not apply.

Taxable reimbursements are considered received in the taxable year of the employee in which the plan year ends. The particular plan year to which reimbursements relate is determined under plan provisions. If there are no provisions, reimbursements are attributed to the year of payment.

Note: Highly compensated employees in insured as well as self-insured plans may be subject to tax under new nondiscrimination rules for plan years starting after 1987.

3

DIVIDEND INCOME

Illustrations of reporting dividend income may be found in the Supplement to YOUR INCOME TAX.

REPORTING DIVIDEND INCOME

¶ **3.1** Dividends paid out of current or accumulated earnings of a corporation are subject to tax. Most dividends fall into this class, except for stock dividends and stock rights on common which are generally not taxed. *See* ¶3.6.

The prior law $100 dividend exclusion ($200 on joint returns) has been repealed.

Dividends paid to you during 1987 are reported to the IRS by the company on Form 1099-DIV. The IRS uses this information as a check on your reporting of dividends. You receive a copy of Form 1099-DIV. Do not attach it to your tax return.

Publicly held corporations generally inform stockholders of the tax consequences of stock dividends and other distributions. Keep such letters with your tax records. You may also want to consult investment publications such as Moody's or Standard and Poor's annual dividend record books for details of dividend distributions and their tax treatment.

DIVIDENDS FROM A PARTNERSHIP, S CORPORATION, ESTATE, OR TRUST

¶ **3.2** You report dividend income you receive as a member of a partnership or as a beneficiary of an estate or trust. The fiduciary of the estate or trust should advise you of the dividend income to be reported on your return. The amount of dividends a partner reports is listed in Schedule K-1 of the partnership tax return, Form 1065.

Distributions from S corporations. Distributions of an S corporation (*see* ¶10.7) are generally not treated as dividends. You report your pro rata share of each item of income, loss, deduction, or credit in a special schedule of your return. Allocated long-term capital gains are reported in Schedule D.

HOW MUTUAL FUND DIVIDENDS ARE TAXED

¶ **3.3** Mutual funds (open-ended regulated investment companies) pay their shareholders five kinds of dividends:

1. Ordinary dividends—income from the mutual fund's investments in corporate stock and other securities, including bonds. Included here are short-term capital gain dividends representing the fund's short-term profits.

2. Capital gain dividends—proceeds from the mutual fund's long-term profits on its sale of securities.
3. Exempt-interest dividends—proceeds from the fund's interest income from tax-exempt bonds is tax exempt to investors.
4. Return of capital—proceeds from the receipt by the mutual fund of corporation distributions which were not out of earnings.
5. Dividends from foreign corporations—income from the fund's investments in foreign corporations.

Whether the dividend is received by you or reinvested by the fund, you must report it on your return. The fund on an information return, Form 1099-DIV (or a similar written form), gives you a breakdown of the type of dividends paid during the taxable year. Each identified part of the dividend is treated as follows:

Ordinary dividends. Ordinary dividends from a mutual fund are fully taxable.

Capital gain dividends. You report the capital gain dividend as a long-term capital gain regardless of how long you have held your mutual fund shares.

A few mutual funds retain their long-term capital gains and pay capital gains tax on those amounts. Even though not actually received by you, you include as a capital gain dividend on your return the amount of the undistributed capital gain dividend allocated to you by the fund. If the mutual fund paid a tax on the undistributed capital gain, you are entitled to a credit (¶24.5).

A loss on the sale of mutual fund shares held for six months or less is treated as a long-term capital loss to the extent of the capital gain dividend received before the sale. This restriction does not apply to dispositions under periodic redemption plans.

Nontaxable distributions. The mutual fund designates amounts representing return of capital as nontaxable distributions. They reduce the cost basis of the mutual fund shares. A return of capital is not taxed unless the distribution (when added to other such distributions received in the past) exceeds your investment in the fund. *See* ¶3.11.

Exempt-interest dividends are also nontaxable. They do not reduce your basis in the mutual fund shares.

Deferred annuity plans. Certain deferred annuity plans invest in high yielding investments, such as money market funds. Earnings may or may not be taxed currently depending on the terms of the plan.

Fund expenses. You may deduct your share of fund expenses as a miscellaneous itemized deduction subject to the 2% AGI floor provided you do not claim the standard deduction.

HOW REAL ESTATE INVESTMENT TRUST DIVIDENDS ARE TAXED

¶ 3.4 Ordinary dividends from a real estate investment trust are fully taxable. Dividends designated by the trust as capital gain dividends are reported as long-term capital gains regardless of how long you have held your trust shares.

The rule for losses incurred within six months discussed above for mutual funds applies also to sales of REIT shares.

DIVIDENDS ARE TAXED WHEN CORPORATION HAS EARNINGS AND PROFITS

¶ 3.5 You pay tax on dividends only when the corporation distributing the dividends has earnings and profits. Publicly held corporations will tell you whether their distributions are taxable. If you hold stock in a close corporation, you may have to determine the tax status of its distribution. You need to know earnings and profits at two different periods:

1. Current earnings and profits as of the *end of the current taxable year.* A dividend is considered to have been made from earnings most recently accumulated.
2. Accumulated earnings and profits as of the *beginning of the current year.* However, when current earnings and profits are large enough to meet the dividend, you do not have to make this computation. It is only when the dividends *exceed* current earnings (or there are no current earnings) that you match accumulated earnings against the dividend. The tax term "accumulated earnings and profits"is similar in meaning to the accounting term "retained earnings." Both stand for the net profits of the company after deducting distributions to stockholders. However, "tax" earnings may differ from "retained earnings" for the following reasons: Surplus accounts, the additions to which are not deductible for income tax purposes, are ordinarily included as tax earnings.

EXAMPLES

1. During 1987, Corporation A paid dividends of $25,000. At the beginning of 1987 it had accumulated earnings of $50,000. It lost $25,000 during 1987. You are fully taxed on your dividend income in 1987, because the corporation's net accumulated surplus exceeds its dividends.

2. At the end of 1986, Corporation B had a deficit of $200,000. Earnings for 1987 were $100,000. In 1987 it paid stockholders $25,000. The dividends are taxed; earnings exceeded the dividends.

STOCK DIVIDENDS ON COMMON STOCK

¶ 3.6 If you own common stock in a company and receive a dividend of stock in the same company, the dividend is generally not taxable. *See* ¶6.50 and ¶6.51 for the method of computing cost basis of stock dividends and rights and sales of such stock.

Exceptions to tax-free rule. A stock dividend on common is taxable when you may elect to take either stock or cash; there are different classes of common, one class receiving cash dividends and another class receiving stock; or the dividend is of convertible preferred. *See* ¶3.8 below for further details of taxable stock dividends.

Fractional shares. When a stock dividend is declared, you may be entitled to a fractional share redeemable for cash. The fractional share is not taxable if a full share would be considered a tax-free stock dividend. Gain or loss on the sale of the fractional share is handled like any other sale of stock and is long- or short-term depending on the holding period of the original stock.

Where you receive cash or redeemable scrip instead of a fractional share without any option to take a fractional share, the cash or scrip is taxed as a cash dividend, unless the company paid the cash in order to save trouble and expense and not to change stockholder interests.

Stock rights. The rules that apply to stock dividends also apply to distributions of stock rights. If you, as a common stockholder, receive rights to subscribe to additional common, the receipt of the rights is not taxable provided the terms of the distribution do not fall within the taxable distribution rules of ¶3.8.

> *Stock splits.* Stock splits resemble the receipt of stock dividends, but they are not dividends. They do not represent a distribution of surplus as in the case of stock dividends. The receipt of stock under a split-up is not taxable. The purpose of a split-up is generally to reduce the value of individual shares in order to increase their marketability. The basis of the old holding is divided among the new shares in order to find the basis for the new shares (*see* ¶6.50).

DIVIDENDS PAID IN PROPERTY

¶ 3.7 A dividend may be paid in property such as securities of another corporation or merchandise. You report as income the fair market value of the property. A dividend paid in property is sometimes called a dividend in kind.

EXAMPLE

You receive one share of X corporation stock as a dividend from the G company of which you are a stockholder. You receive the X stock when it had a market value of $25. You report $25, the value of the property received.

Corporate benefits. On an audit, the IRS may charge that a benefit given to a shareholder-employee is a taxable dividend.

TAXABLE STOCK DIVIDENDS

¶ 3.8 The following stock dividends are taxable:

Stock dividends paid to holders of preferred stock. However, no taxable income is realized where the conversion ratio of convertible preferred stock is increased only to take account of a stock dividend or split involving the stock into which the convertible stock is convertible.

Stock dividend elected by a shareholder of common stock who had the choice of taking stock, property or cash. (A distribution of stock that was immediately redeemable for cash at the stockholder's option was treated as a taxable dividend.)

Stock dividend paid in a distribution where some shareholders receive property or cash and other shareholders' proportionate interests in the assets or earnings and profits of the corporation are increased.

Distributions of preferred stock to some common shareholders and common stock to other common shareholders.

Distributions of convertible preferred stock to holders of common stock, unless it can be shown that the distribution will not result in the creation of disproportionate stock interests.

> *Dividend reinvestment plan in company stock.* Some companies provide plans whereby stockholders may elect to take either cash dividend or automatically reinvest the dividends in company stock at a discount price. If you elect the stock plan, the amount of the taxable dividend is the fair market value of the stock at the time of dividend distribution plus the service fee charged for the acquisition. The basis of the stock is also fair market value at the time of dividend distribution; the service charge may be claimed as an itemized deduction. If at the same time you also have the option to buy additional stock at a discount and you exercise the option, you have additional dividend income for the difference between the fair market value of the optional shares and the amount paid for the shares.

Constructive stock dividends. You may not actually receive a stock dividend, but under Treasury regulations you may be treated as having received a taxable distribution. This may happen when a company increases the ratio of convertible preferred stock.

WHO REPORTS THE DIVIDEND?

¶ 3.9 Stock held by broker in street name. If your broker holds stock for you in a street name, dividends earned on this stock are received by the broker and credited to your account. You report all dividends credited to your account in 1987. The broker is required to file an information return on all such dividends.

If your statement shows only a gross amount of dividends, check with your broker if any of the dividends represented nontaxable returns of capital.

Dividends on stock sold or bought between ex-dividend date and record date. Record date is the date set by a company on which you must be listed as a stockholder on its records to receive the dividend. However, in the case of publicly traded stock, an ex-dividend date, which usually precedes the record date by several days, is fixed by the exchange to determine who is entitled to the dividend.

If you buy stock before the ex-dividend date, the dividend belongs to you and is reported by you. If you buy on or after the ex-dividend date, the dividend belongs to the seller.

If you sell stock before the ex-dividend date, you do not have a right to the dividend. If you sell on or after the ex-dividend date, you receive the dividend and report it as income.

The dividend declaration date and date of payment do not determine who receives the dividend.

Stock sold short. For a discussion of how to treat a payment to a broker for dividends paid on stock sold short, *see* ¶ 6.52.

YEAR DIVIDENDS ARE REPORTED

¶ 3.10 Dividend income is usually reported on the tax return for the year in which the dividend is unqualifiedly credited to your account or when you receive the dividend check.

EXAMPLES
1. A corporation declares a dividend payable on December 31, 1987. It follows a practice of paying dividends by checks which are mailed so that stockholders do not receive them until January, 1988. You report this dividend in your 1988 return.
2. On December 31, 1987, a dividend is credited to a stockholder's account. The dividend is taxable in 1987, as the crediting is considered constructive receipt in 1987, even though the dividend is not paid until 1988 or a later year.

Dividends received in a year after the one in which they were declared, when you held the stock on the record date, are taxed in the year they are received.

EXAMPLE
You own stock in a corporation. In April, 1985 the corporation declared a dividend. But it provided that the dividend will be paid when it gets the cash. It finally pays the dividend in September, 1987. The dividend is taxable in 1987.

Back dividends on preferred stock accumulated before you bought the stock but paid after you acquired it are taxed in the year you receive them.

DISTRIBUTION NOT OUT OF EARNINGS: RETURN OF CAPITAL

¶ 3.11 A return of capital or "nontaxable distribution" reduces the cost basis of the stock. If the cost basis is reduced to zero, further distributions of capital are taxed as capital gains. Whether short- or long-term depends on the length of time you have held the stock. The company paying the dividend will usually inform you of the tax treatment of the payment.

Dividends on insurance policies are not true dividends. They are returns of premiums previously paid. They reduce the cost of the policy and are not subject to tax until they exceed the net premiums paid for the contract. Interest paid or credited on dividends left with the insurance company is taxable. Dividends on VA insurance are tax free. Where insurance premiums are deducted as a business expense in prior years, receipts of insurance dividends are either included in income or taken as a reduction of the insurance expense deduction of the current year. Dividends on capital stock of an insurance company are taxable dividends.

4

INTEREST INCOME

Illustrations of reporting interest income may be found in the Supplement to YOUR INCOME TAX.

GUIDE TO INTEREST INCOME RULES

Item	Pointer
Form 1099	Information returns, Forms 1099-INT, sent by payers of interest income, simplify the reporting of interest income. The forms give you the amount of interest to enter on your tax return. Although they are generally correct, you should check for mistakes and notify payers of any error and request a form marked "corrected." If tax was withheld (¶ 25.12), claim this tax as a payment on your tax return. The IRS will check interest reported on your return against the Forms 1099-INT sent by banks and other payers.
Deposits in savings account	Interest credited to your savings account for 1987 is taxable even though you do not present your passbook to have the interest entered. Dividends on deposits or accounts in the following institutions are reported as interest income: Mutual savings banks, cooperative banks, domestic building and loan associations, domestic and federal savings and loan associations.
Savings certificates, deferred interest or bonus plan	The interest element on certificates of deposit and similar plans of more than one year is treated as original issue discount (OID) and is taxable on an annual basis. The bank notifies you of the taxable OID amount on Form 1099-OID. If you discontinue a savings plan before maturity, you may have a loss deduction for forfeited interest, which is listed on Form 1099-INT or Form 1099-OID. Tax on interest can be deferred on a savings certificate with a term of one year or less. Interest is taxable in the year it is available for withdrawal without substantial penalty. Where you invest in a six-month certificate before July 1, the entire amount of interest is paid six months later and is taxable in the year of payment. However, when you invest in a six-month certificate after June 30, only interest actually paid or made available for withdrawal is taxable in the year of issuance. The balance is taxable in the year of maturity. You can defer interest to a later year by investing in a six-month certificate after June 30, provided the payment of interest is specifically deferred to the year of maturity by the terms of the certificate.
U.S. Savings Bonds, Series E, EE	The increase in redemption value is interest income. You do not have to report the annual increase in value until the year in which you cash the bond or the year in which the bond finally matures, whichever is earlier.
U.S. Savings Bonds, Series H, HH	Semi-annual interest is taxable when received.
U.S. Treasury bills	You report as interest the difference between the cost and amount received on a sale or redemption of the bills at maturity in 1986. It is possible to sustain a capital loss on the sale of Treasury bills before maturity.

Item	Pointer
Bearer or coupon bonds	Interest coupons due and payable in 1987 are taxable on your 1987 return regardless of when they were presented for collection. For example, a coupon due January 1987 and presented for payment in 1986 is taxable in 1987. Similarly, a coupon due December 1987 but presented for payment in 1988 is taxable in 1987.
Corporate obligations in registered form	You report interest when received or made available to you. *See* ¶ 4.4 on how to treat interest when you buy or sell bonds between interest dates.
Interest on state and local government obligations	Although you may receive a Form 1099-INT for interest on state or municipal bonds, you do not pay federal tax on the interest. You are required to list the tax-exempt interest on your tax return, although it is not taxable. The interest may be subject to state income tax.
Borrow to meet minimum deposit requirements for savings certificates	Interest expenses are deductible as itemized deductions. Report the full amount of interest income listed on Form 1099-INT even if you do not take interest deductions.
Insurance proceeds	You report interest paid on insurance proceeds left with an insurance company or included in installment payments (under options modes of payment). Exception: A surviving spouse of a decedent who died before October 23, 1986 is not taxed on up to $1,000 a year of interest included in installment payments.
Interest on prepaid premium	Taxable interest is reported by insurance company on Form 1099-INT.
Interest on tax refunds	Interest on tax refunds is fully taxable.
Bank gifts	The value of gifts is taxable. To attract new deposits, banks and thrifts offer cash, televisions, toasters, and the like, as inducements. The gifts are taxable as interest and reported on Form 1099-INT.
Interest on unwithdrawn life insurance dividends	If you can withdraw the interest annually, you report the interest in the year it is credited to your account. However, if, under the terms of the insurance policy, the interest can be withdrawn only on the anniversary date of the policy (or some other specified date), then you report the interest in the year in which the anniversary date of the policy (or some other specified date) falls. Interest on GI insurance dividends on deposit with the VA is taxable, although the dividends were not taxable.
Interest on funds invested abroad	Interest must be reported in U.S. dollars. If foreign tax has been paid, you may be entitled to a deduction or credit, *see* ¶ 36.16. *See also* ¶ 36.13 for blocked currency reporting rules.

FORFEITURE OF INTEREST ON PREMATURE WITHDRAWAL OF TIME SAVINGS ACCOUNT

¶ 4.1 A bank may pay a fixed interest rate on a savings account, provided principal is not withdrawn during the specified period. If you prematurely withdraw funds in order to switch to higher paying investments or for any other reason, you may forfeit part of the interest earned and even the principal. In some cases, the penalty may exceed the interest earned so that principal is forfeited to make up the difference. You report the full amount of interest credited to your account; the principal as well as interest forfeited is deductible. The deductible amount is shown on the information return sent to you. You may claim the deduction even if you do not claim excess itemized deductions. On Form 1040, the line for deducting forfeited interest is included in the section "Adjustments to Income" as "penalty on early withdrawal of savings."

Loss on redemption before maturity. If you redeem a long-term savings certificate for a price less than the stated redemption price at maturity, you are allowed a loss deduction for the amount of original issue discount reported as income but not received. The amount of the loss is the excess of (1) the original issue discount reported as income for the period you held the certificate over (2) the excess of the amount received upon the redemption over the issue price. Do not include in the computation any amount based on a fixed rate of simple or compound interest which is actually payable or is treated as constructively received at fixed periodic intervals of one year or less. Basis of the obligation is reduced by the amount of the deductible loss.

EXAMPLE

In 1984, you buy a four-year savings certificate from a building and loan corporation for $4,000 redeemable on December 31, 1988 for $5,000. The original issue discount is $1,000 of which $250 is reported each year. In 1987, when you redeem the certificate, you receive $4,660. In 1984, 1985 and 1986, you reported $250 of original issue discount for a total of $750. As the excess of $660 received on redemption is less than the original issue discount of $750 which was reported as income, the difference of $90 is a deductible loss claimed on Form 1040 on the line for entry "Penalty on early withdrawal of savings."

Partial redemption. Under the terms of a plan, you may be allowed to withdraw principal but not interest. In such a case, when you withdraw principal, you may be entitled to deduct a loss based on part of the previously reported interest. Ask your bank for a computation of your tax and investment position or check Treasury regulations for details of the computation.

INTEREST ON FROZEN ACCOUNTS NOT TAXED

¶ 4.2 If you have funds in a bankrupt or insolvent financial institution that "freezes" your account by limiting withdrawals, you do not pay tax on interest allocable to the "frozen" deposits. The interest is taxable when withdrawals are permitted. Officers and owners of at least a 1% interest in the financial institution, or their relatives may not take advantage of this rule and must report interest on frozen deposits.

If you lose funds because of a financial institution's bankruptcy or insolvency, or you can reasonably estimate such a loss, you may deduct the loss either as a nonbusiness bad debt (¶6.55) or as a casualty loss (¶18.19).

Refund opportunity. If you reported interest on a frozen deposit on a prior return, you may file a refund claim for the tax paid on the interest.

INTEREST INCOME ON DEBTS OWED YOU

¶ 4.3 You report interest earned on money which you loan to another person. If you are on the cash basis, you report interest in the year you actually receive it or when it is considered received under the "constructive receipt rule," see ¶5.2. If you are on the accrual basis, you report interest when it is earned, whether or not you have received it.

See ¶4.17 for minimum interest rates required for loans and ¶4.4 when OID rules apply.

Where partial payment is being made on a debt or a debt is being compromised, the parties may agree in advance what part of the payment covers interest and principal. If a payment is not identified as either principal or interest, the payment is first applied against interest due and reported as interest income to the extent of the interest due.

Interest income is not realized when a debtor gives a new note for an old note including the interest due on the old note. The new note is considered a payment of the interest.

If you give away obligations, you report as income collectible interest due at the date of the gift. To avoid tax on the interest, the obligations must be transferred before interest becomes due.

REPORTING INTEREST ON BONDS BOUGHT OR SOLD DURING THE YEAR

¶ 4.4 Where you buy or sell bonds between interest dates, interest is included in the price of the bonds. The purchaser does not report as income interest accrued before he owned the bond. (The purchaser reduces the basis of the bond by the accrued interest reported by the seller.) The seller reports the accrued amount. The following examples illustrate these rules.

EXAMPLES

1. *Purchase.* On April 30, you buy a $5,000 corporate bond bearing interest at 8% per year, payable January 1 and July 1. The purchase price of the bond included accrued interest of $133.

Interest received 7/1	$200
Less: Accrued interest	133
Taxable interest	$ 67

Form 1099 sent to you includes accrued interest. On Schedule B, you report the total amount of interest of $300 and also subtract the accrued interest of $133 paid to the seller with the note "Accrued Interest."

2. *Sale.* On April 30, you sell for $3,125 a $5,000 3% bond with interest payable January 1 and July 1. You receive $3,175.

Sales price of the bond	$3,125
Accrued interest from Jan. 1 to Apr. 30	50
You receive	$3,175

You report interest of $50.

On a redemption, interest received in excess of the amount due at that time is not treated as interest income.

EXAMPLE

You hold a $5,000 9% bond with interest payable January 1 and July 1. The company can call the bonds for redemption on any interest date. In May 1987, the company announces it will redeem the bonds on July 1. But you may present the bond for redemption beginning with June 1 and it will be redeemed with interest to July 1. On June 1 you present the bond and receive $5,225; $5,000 principal, $187.50 interest to June 1, and $37.50 extra interest to July 1. The $37.50 is treated as a capital gain, not interest income. The $187.50 is interest.

Taxable interest may continue on bonds after the issuer becomes bankrupt if a guarantor continues to pay the interest when due. The loss on the bonds will occur only when they mature and are not redeemed or when they are sold below your cost. In the meantime, the interest received from the guarantor is taxed.

Bondholders exchanging their bonds for stock, securities, or other property in a tax-free reorganization, including a reorganization in bankruptcy, have interest income to the extent the property received is attributable to accrued but unpaid interest. See the Bankruptcy Tax Act of 1980 for further details.

Bonds selling at a flat price. When you buy bonds with defaulted interest at a "flat" price, a later payment of the defaulted interest is not taxed. It is a tax-free return of capital that reduces your cost of the bond. This rule applies only to interest in default at the time the bond is purchased. Interest that accrues after the date of your purchase is taxed as ordinary income.

The above rules also apply to contingent interest attributed to a period before you owned the bond. The payment of such interest is considered a return of capital; however, the payment of contingent interest covering a period during which you owned the bond is fully taxable.

Treatment of original issue discount on corporate and government obligations is discussed at ¶4.6 and ¶6.10.

AMORTIZATION OF BOND PREMIUM

¶ 4.5 Bond premium is the extra amount paid for a bond in excess of its principal or face amount. You may elect to amortize bond premium and reduce basis or leave the basis of the bond unchanged. If you do not amortize the premium, you will realize a capital loss when the bond is redeemed at par or you sell it for less than you paid for it.

EXAMPLES

1. On July 11, 1986, you pay $1,200 for a $1,000 bond which was issued before September 28, 1985, and which matures on July 1, 1996. You elected to amortize the premium. Amortization is allowed for the months you held the bond. You include the month of acquisition (July) since you held the bond for more than half of that month. Here, the number of months from acquisition to maturity is 120 months, which gives you a monthly amortization write-off of $1.67 per month. In 1986, you deducted amortization of $10; $167 × 6 months. Basis of the bond at the end of 1986 was $1,190 ($1,200 cost less $10 amortization).

In 1987, you may claim a 1987 amortization deduction of $20: $1.67 × 12 months. The basis of the bond at the end of 1987 is $1,170 ($1,200 cost less $30 amortized in 1986 and 1987).

2. Several years ago, you bought a $1,000 corporate bond for $1,300. You did not amortize the premium of $300. The bond is redeemed at par. You realize a long-term loss of $300. The premium is treated as part of the basis of the bond.

Redemption proceeds	$1,000
Cost basis	1,300
Loss	($300)

For bonds *issued* after September 27, 1985, amortization is based not on the straight line method illustrated in example 1 above but on a constant yield method. For the computation, *see* Treasury regulations and IRS Publication 535.

Electing amortization. If you choose to amortize, the election applies to all bonds owned by you at the beginning of the first year you make the choice, and to all bonds acquired thereafter. You make an election to amortize by taking the deduction on your income tax return in the first year you decide to amortize the bond premium. If you file your return without claiming the deduction, you may not change your mind and make the election by filing an amended return or refund claim.

If you claim the amortization deduction, the deducted bond premium is treated as investment interest when figuring the limit on deductible investment interest expense. See ¶15.14.

Amortizing the premium annually is usually the preferred method because it gives a current deduction against ordinary income, provided you claim itemized deductions. You deduct amortized bond premium as a miscellaneous deduction but the deduction is not subject to the 2% adjusted gross income floor (*see* chapter 19). You also reduce the cost basis of the bond by the amount of the premium taken as a deduction. If you hold the bond to maturity, the entire premium is amortized and you have neither gain nor loss on redemption of the bond. If in 1987 you sell the bond at a gain (selling price exceeds your basis for the bond), you realize long-term capital gain if you hold the bond long term. A sale of the bond for less than its adjusted basis gives a capital loss.

Callable bonds. On fully taxable bonds bought after 1957, amortization is based on either the maturity or earlier call date, depending on which date gives a smaller yearly deduction. This rule applies regardless of the issue date of the bond. If the bond is called before maturity, you may deduct as an ordinary loss the unamortized bond premium in the year the bond is redeemed.

EXAMPLES

1. On January 1, 1982, you pay $1,200 for a $1,000 bond which matures on December 31, 2000. The bond is callable on January 1, 1987 at $1,165. The premium computed with reference to the maturity date is $200 ($1,200–$1,000). The premium computed with reference to the earlier call date is $35 ($1,200–1,165). The premium of $200 gives a yearly $15 deduction ($200 divided by 20 years). The premium of $35 gives a yearly deduction of $7 ($35 divided by 5 years). You amortize to the earlier call date because that gives a lower yearly deduction until 1987. If the bond is not called by then, the deduction for each taxable year from 1987 to the end of 2001 will be $11 ($165 divided by 15 years).

2. Use the same figures as in example 1, but say the earlier call date is January 1, 1986. You amortize the premium based on the maturity date. This gives you a lower deduction than if you used the period of the earlier call date.

If you paid a premium for a convertible bond, the premium allocated to the conversion feature may not be amortized.

Tax-exempt bonds. You may not take a deduction for the amortization of premium paid on a tax-exempt bond. When you dispose of the bond, you amortize the premium for the period you held the bond and reduce the basis of the bond by the amortized amount.

If the bond has call dates, the IRS may require the premium to be amortized to the earliest call date.

EXAMPLE

In 1978, a tax-exempt bond par $1,000 is bought for $1,055. Between January 1, 1979, and December 31, 1980, it is callable at $105; between January 1, 1982, and December 31, 1982, at $104; between January 1, 1983, and December 31, 1988, at $104; it matures on January 1, 1989, at par. Amortization is figured as follows:

1. $5 is amortizable in 1978.
2. $10 is amortizable over 1979 and 1980.
3. $10 is amortizable over 1981 and 1982.
4. $30 is amortizable over 1983 through 1988.

If the bond were sold on December 31, 1987, the basis of the bond would be reduced by $50 to $1,005.

Premium paid on bonds with original issue discount. If you paid more than the original issue price plus accumulated OID from the date of issue, that excess, called acquisition premium, reduces the amount of OID which you have to include in income. The rules for computing the reduction to OID depend on when the bond was purchased. For bonds purchased after July 18, 1984, OID is reduced by a fraction, the numerator of which is the acquisition premium; the denominator is the OID remaining after your purchase date to the maturity date. *See* IRS Publication 1212 for making the computation.

DISCOUNT ON BONDS AND OTHER OBLIGATIONS

¶ **4.6** There are two types of bond discounts:

Original issue discount (OID). OID arises when a bond is issued for a price less than its face or principal amount. OID is the difference between the principal amount and the issue price. For publicly offered obligations, the issue price is the initial offering price to the public at which a substantial amount of such obligations was sold. All obligations that pay no interest before maturity, such as zero coupon bonds, are considered to be issued at a discount. For example, a bond with a face amount of $1,000 is issued at an offering price of $900. The $100 difference is OID. Depending on the issue date of the bond, you may have to report a portion of the OID as interest income each year. OID is explained at ¶4.7 for publicly offered corporate and government bonds.

Market discount. Market discount arises when the price of a bond declines because its interest rate is less than the current interest rate. For example, a bond originally issued at its face amount of $1,000 declines in value to $900 because the interest payable on the bond is less than the current interest rate. The difference of $100 is called market discount. The tax treatment of market discount is explained in ¶4.5.

Form 1099-OID. For bonds with a term of more than one year, the issuer of the bond will send you Form 1099-OID, reporting the amount of OID which is taxable as interest for the year. Discount on obligations with a term of one year or less is reported as interest on Form 1099-INT. In some cases, the amount on Form 1099-OID may have to be reduced to avoid reporting too much income, for example, if you do not own the bond for the entire period covered by the reported OID, *see* ¶4.7. If you are reporting less OID than shown on Form 1099-OID, first include in the interest schedule the full amount of OID listed on the Form 1099-OID; then subtract from the total the OID you are not required to report.

If you do not receive the Form 1099-OID, contact the issuer to obtain the amount or check IRS Publication 1212, which lists OID amounts for publicly offered OID instruments as well as rules for figuring OID.

Original discount bond bought at premium. If you pay more than face amount for a bond originally issued at a discount, you do not report OID as ordinary income. When you dispose of a bond bought at a premium, the difference between the sale or redemption price and your basis is a capital gain or loss, *see* ¶4.5. However, this rule does not apply if you pay more than the original issue price plus accumulated OID. Your excess payment, called acquisition premium, reduces the amount of OID you must report as income. *See* ¶4.5.

Exceptions to OID. OID rules do not apply to: (1) Obligations with a term of one year or less held by cash basis taxpayers (*see* ¶4.9); (2) tax-exempt obligations; (3) U.S. savings bonds; (4) an obligation issued by an individual before March 2, 1984, and (5) loans of $10,000 or less from individuals that come within the rules of ¶4.7.

You may disregard OID that is less than one fourth of one percent of the principal amount multiplied by the number of full years from the rate of original issue to maturity. On most long-term bonds, the OID will exceed this amount and will have to be reported.

EXAMPLES
1. A 10-year bond with face amount of $1,000 is issued at $980. One fourth of one percent of $1,000 times 10 is $25. As the $20 OID

is less than $25, it may be ignored for tax purposes.
2. Same facts as in (1) except that the bond is issued at $950. As OID of $50 is more than the $25, OID must be reported under the rules explained at ¶4.6.

REPORTING ORIGINAL ISSUE DISCOUNT (OID) ON PUBLICLY OFFERED OBLIGATIONS

¶ **4.7** The way you report OID depends on the issue date of the obligation. The following are the general rules and several examples. For further details, see IRS Publication 1212.

Corporate obligations issued after 1954 but before May 28, 1969 and government obligations issued before July 2, 1982. You pay no tax on the OID until the year the obligation is disposed of. If a gain results and the obligation is a capital asset, part of the OID is taxed as ordinary income, part capital gain. If there is a loss on the disposition, the entire loss is capital loss; no OID is taxed.

The amount of gain treated as ordinary income is figured as follows:

$$\frac{\text{Number of full months you held the bond}}{\text{Number of full months from date of original issue to date of maturity}} \times \text{OID} = \text{Ordinary Income}$$

EXAMPLES
1. On the original issue date of February 1, 1967, you purchased a 30-year 5% bond for $910—a $90 discount from the face amount of $1,000. You sell the bond on February 20, 1987 for $950. You have held the bond for 240 full months; the additional days amounting to less than a full month are not counted. The number of complete months from date of issue to date of maturity is 360 (30 years). Multiplying the fraction 240/360 by the discount of $90 gives $60, the OID attributable to your holding period. Therefore, on the sale in 1987 the entire gain of $40 is ordinary income since it is less than the allocable $60 OID.
2. Same facts as in (1) except that you sell the bond for $980. Here $60 of the $70 gain is ordinary income, the balance of $10 is long-term capital gain.
3. Same facts as in (1) except you sold for $800. You have a long-term capital loss of $110.

Corporate obligations issued after May 27, 1969 and before July 2, 1982. If you held the bond as a capital asset, you report OID as income and increase the basis of the bond by the amount of OID reported. For each year you hold the bond, you report the ratable monthly portion of OID.

If you bought the bond at OID and held it for all of 1987 or the part of 1987 they were outstanding, report the total OID from Form 1099-OID. If you bought it at issue and it was outstanding for all of 1987 but you did not hold it for all of 1987, figure taxable OID by dividing the total OID by 12 and multiplying the result by the number of complete and partial months you held it in 1987.

If you bought it after original issue, the OID shown on Form 1099-OID may not be the correct amount for you to report. For example, your purchase exceeded the original issue price (but less than redemption price) and included the amount of accumulated OID from the date of issue. Here, the excess (called acquisition premium) reduces the amount of OID you report. In this case, you must recalculate OID. *Step 1:* Divide the OID by 12 to figure the ratable monthly portion. *Step 2:* Subtract from your cost the issue price and the amount of accumulated OID from the date of issue. If the result is zero or less, do not reduce the ratable monthly portion. *Step 3:* Divide (2) by the number of complete months and any part of a month from the date of your purchase to the stated maturity date. *Step 4:* Subtract (3) from (1). The amount you report as income each month is (1) or (4), whichever is less.

If you buy or sell an obligation on any day other than the day of the month that is the same as the date of original issue, you divide the ratable monthly portion of OID between you and the seller or the buyer, according to the number of days each of you held the obligation. Your holding period begins the day you acquired the obligation and ends the day before you dispose of it.

EXAMPLES

1. On June 1, 1982, 10-year bonds at 95% of principal amount were issued. On February 1, 1987, you bought for $9,737 a $10,000 bond. Form 1099-OID lists OID of $50. Here you bought the bonds for an amount equal to the original issue price plus accumulated OID. In 1987, $45.87 is taxed ($4.17 monthly OID times 11 months). In the interest schedule, you report $50 and then reduce the amount by $4.17.

2. Same facts as in (1) except that you buy the bonds for $9,450. You report $45.87, even though you paid less than the original issue price.

3. Same facts as in (1) except that you pay more than $9,737. Here the premium may reduce the amount of the OID following the steps outlined above.

Corporate and government obligations issued after July 1, 1982, and before January 1, 1985. The amount of the reportable OID is based on the daily portion of the increase in the adjusted price of the bond. If you held the bond as a capital asset for all of 1987, or it was outstanding for only part of 1987 and you held it for the entire period, report the total OID from Form 1099-OID. If the obligation was outstanding for all of 1987 but you did not hold it for the entire year, figure taxable OID by dividing the total OID by 365 and multiplying the result by the number of days you held it in 1987.

If you bought the obligation after its original issue, the amount of OID on Form 1099-OID may not be the correct amount for you. For figuring OID in such a case, see IRS Publication 1212.

Basis in the bond is increased by the OID reported on income.

The daily portion of OID for the initial accrual period is computed by applying the following formula:

$$\frac{(\text{Issue Price} \times \text{Yield to Maturity}) - \text{Stated Interest}}{\text{Number of Days in the Accrual Period}}$$

The daily portion of OID for later accrual periods is computed in the same manner except that the issue price is increased by OID reported in earlier years.

Corporate and government obligations issue after December 31, 1984. OID is reported without regard to whether you hold the obligation as a capital asset. Further, OID is computed for six-month accrual periods that generally correspond to the maturity date of the obligation and to the date which is six months before such maturity date (or the shorter period from date of issue). For example, if a bond issued April 1, 1986, matures January 1, 1988, the first six-month period for which OID must be computed is April 1, 1986 to June 30, 1986; the second is July 1, 1986, to December 31, 1986; the third January 1, 1987, to June 30, 1987; and the fourth July 1, 1987, to December 31, 1987.

REPORTING INCOME ON MARKET DISCOUNT BONDS

¶ 4.8 Market discount arises where the price of a bond declines below its face amount because it carries an interest rate that is below the current rate of interest. The treatment of market discount depends on the issue date of the bond.

Bonds issued before July 19, 1984. Gain attributable to the market discount on the sale of the bond *issued* before July 19, 1984, is generally treated as capital gain. However, you may have ordinary income if you borrow money to purchase or carry a market discount bond acquired after July 18, 1984. Under a restrictive rule discussed below, the interest deduction on the loan is subject to special rules. In the year the bond is sold, you may claim an interest deduction for any interest expense that could not be deducted in prior years under the restrictive rule. Gain on the disposition is ordinary income to the extent of deductible interest; the balance is capital gain.

EXAMPLE

You paid $910 for a bond that had been originally issued at its face amount of $1,000. The difference of $90 is market discount. In 1987, you sell the bond for $980. The $70 profit is long-term capital gain.

Bonds issued after July 18, 1984. Generally, market discount is taken into account when a bond is sold. However, under a new law, market discount on bonds *acquired* after October 22, 1986, may have to be included in income currently where the issuer of the bond pays you part of the bond principal. *See* below.

On a sale of a bond *issued* after July 18, 1984, gain is taxed as ordinary interest income to the extent of the market discount accrued to the date of sale. The daily accrual is figured by dividing market discount by the number of days in the period from the date you bought the bond until the date of maturity. This method of computing the daily accrual is called the ratable accrual method.

EXAMPLE

Market discount on a bond issued after July 18, 1984, is $200, and there are 1,000 days between the date of your purchase and maturity date. The daily accrual rate is twenty cents. You hold the bond for 600 days before selling it for a price exceeding what you paid for the bond. Under the ratable accrual method, up to $120 of your profit is market discount taxable as interest income ($600 × $.20).

Instead of using the ratable accrual method to compute accrual of market discount, you may elect to figure the accrual discount under the constant rate method. If you make the election, you may not change the election. The complex constant rate method is explained in IRS Publication 1212.

Exceptions to ordinary income rules. The following bonds are not subject to the ordinary income rules for market discount bonds: (1) bonds acquired after July 18, 1984 that were issued on or before that date; (2) bonds with a maturity date of up to six months from date of issuance; (3) tax-exempt obligations; (4) installment obligations; and (5) U.S. Savings Bonds. Further, you may treat as zero any market discount that is less than one-fourth of one percent of the redemption price multiplied by the number of full years after you acquire the bond to maturity. Such minimal discount will not affect capital gain on a sale.

Electing to report market discount rate currently. Rather than report market discount in the year you sell the bond, you may elect to report market discount currently as interest income. You may use either the ratable accrual method or the constant interest rate method explained in IRS Publication 550.

EXAMPLE

Using the same figures as in the above example. During a taxable year, you held the bond for 300 days. You elect to report the market discount currently. Under the ratable accrual method, you report $60 as interest income (300 × $.20).

Your election to report currently applies to all market discount bonds issued after July 18, 1984 that you later acquire. You may not revoke the election without the IRS consent.

Partial principal payments are taxable. If the issuer of a market discount bond makes a partial payment of the principal (face amount) you must include the payment as ordinary interest income to the extent it does not exceed the accrued market discount on the bond. A taxable partial principal payment reduces the amount of remaining accrued market discount when figuring your tax on a later sale or receipt of another partial principal payment.

Market discount on a bond originally issued at a discount. A bond issued at original issue discount may later be acquired at a market discount because of an increase in interest rates. If you acquire at market discount an OID bond issued after July 18, 1984, the market discount is the excess of (1) the issue price of the bond plus the total original issue discount includible in the gross income of all prior holders of the bond, over (2) what you paid for the bond.

Exchanging market discount bond in corporate reorganizations. If you hold a market discount bond and exchange it for another bond as part of a merger or other reorganization, the new bond is subject to the market discount rules when you sell it. However, under an exception, market discount rules will not apply to the new bond if the old market discount bond was issued before July 19, 1984, and the terms and interest rates of both bonds are identical.

Interest deduction limited if you borrow to buy market discount bonds after July 18, 1984. If you took such a loan, deductible interest expense is generally limited to the excess of the interest expense over the interest income earned on the bond for the year (including OID income, if any) *less* any market discount allocated to the days you held the bond during the year. The limitation on the interest deduction applies to bonds you acquire after July 18, 1984 regardless of the issue date of the bond. The allocation of market discount follows the rules explained above. *See* IRS Publication 550 for further details.

EXAMPLE

In 1987, you borrowed to buy a market discount bond. During 1987, your interest expense is $1,000. Income from the bond is $900 and ratable market discount allocated to the annual holding period is $75. Then, $25 is deductible interest ($1,000 – 975), subject to the limitations on investment interest; *see* ¶15.14.

> In the year the bond is disposed of, you may deduct any interest expense disallowed in prior years because of the limitation. However, in a year in which you have net interest income from the bond, you may choose to deduct disallowed interest in expense before the year of disposition. Net interest income is interest income for the year less the interest expense incurred during the year. This election lets you deduct any disallowed interest expense to the extent it does not exceed the net interest income of that year. The balance of the disallowed interest expense is deductible in the year of disposition.

Exception. If you elect to report ratably market discount on bonds issued after July 18, 1984, the above limitations on the interest deduction do not apply.

DISCOUNT ON SHORT-TERM OBLIGATIONS

¶ 4.9 Short-term obligations (maturity of a year or less) may be purchased at a discount from face. If you are on the cash basis, interest income is realized when the obligation is paid. The interest is reported on Form 1099-INT.

EXAMPLE

In May 1986, you paid $920 for a short-term note with a face amount of $1,000. In January 1987, you receive payment of $1,000 on the note. On your 1987 tax return, you report $80 as interest.

In 1987, you borrowed to buy a market discount bond. During 1987, your interest expense is $1,000. Income from the bond is $900 and ratable market discount allocated to the annual holding period is $75.

Governmental obligations. Accrual basis taxpayers report as income that part of the acquisition discount allocated to the period the note was held during the taxable year. For short-term obligations other than tax-exempts acquired after July 18, 1984, accrual basis taxpayers accrue the discount following the daily ratable accrual method, unless an election to use the constant interest method is made, as explained in ¶4.8. The accrual rule also applies to short-term discount on an obligation held primarily for sale to customers in the ordinary course of your trade or business, by a bank, regulated investment company, or common trust fund, by certain pass through entities, or identified as part of a hedging transaction. In addition, the accrual rule applies to a person who separates or strips the interest coupon from a bond and then retains the stripped bond or stripped coupon; the daily accrual rule applies to the retained obligation.

Further, for discount bonds acquired after September 27, 1985, accrual basis taxpayers and others subject to the above reporting rule must report as income any interest payable on the obligation that has accrued during the year.

Nongovernmental obligations. Accrual basis taxpayers and others listed above who are subject to current income reporting for governmental obligations are also subject to current reporting for short-term nongovern-

mental obligations. For a short-term nongovernmental obligation, OID is generally taken into account instead of acquisition discount, but an election may be made to accrue the discount. *See* IRS Publication 550 for details.

Interest deduction limitation for cash basis investors. A cash basis investor who takes a loan to buy a short-term discount obligation may not claim a full interest deduction. Under a complicated formula, deductible interest is generally limited to the excess of the interest expense for the year over the taxable interest from the bond during the year *less* (1) the portion of the discount allocated to the days you held the bond during the year, and (2) for bonds acquired after September 27, 1985, the portion of interest not taxable for the year under your method of accounting. Any interest expense disallowed under this limitation is deductible in the year in which the obligation is disposed.

The interest deduction limitation does *not* apply if you elect to report the accruable discount as explained in ¶4.8. *See* IRS Publication 550 for further details.

Gain on disposition. If you have a gain on the sale or exchange of a discounted short-term governmental obligation (other than tax-exempt local obligations) the gain is ordinary income to the extent of the ratable share of the discount received when you bought the obligation. Follow the computation shown in ¶4.14 for Treasury bills to figure this ordinary income portion. Any gain over this ordinary income portion is capital gain (*see* chapter 6).

Gain on short-term nongovernmental obligations is treated as ordinary income up to the ratable share of OID. The formula for figuring this ordinary income portion is similar to that used for short-term governmental obligations. Gain above this amount is capital gain (*see* chapter 6). *See* IRS Publication 550 for further details.

STRIPPED COUPON BONDS

¶ 4.10 To create tax losses, investors holding coupon bonds separated or stripped the coupons from the bonds and sold either the bonds or coupons. A law bars a deduction for such losses on bonds bought or sold after July 1, 1982. However, for certain investment purposes, brokers continue to offer stripped bonds and coupons for sale. Zero-coupon instruments sold by brokerage houses (such as CATS, TIGRS) are examples.

If you buy a stripped bond or coupon, the spread between the lower cost of the bond or coupon and its face amount is treated as original issue discount. This means that you annually report a part of the spread as explained in ¶4.6. For a stripped bond, the amount of the original issue discount is the difference between the stated redemption price of the bond at maturity and the cost of the bond. For a stripped coupon, the amount of the discount is the difference between the amount payable on the due date of the coupon and the cost of the coupon.

If you strip a coupon bond, interest accrual and allocation rules prevent you from creating a tax loss on a sale of the bond or coupons. You are required to report interest accrued up to the date of the sale and also add the amount to the basis of the bond. If you acquired the obligation after October 22, 1986, you must also include in income any market discount that accrued before the date you sold the stripped bond or coupons. The accrued market discount is also added to the basis of the bond. You then allocate this basis between the bond and the coupons. The allocation is based on the relative fair market values of the bond and coupons at the date of sale. Gain or loss on the sale is the difference between the sales price of the stripped item (bond or coupons) and its allocated basis. Furthermore, the original issue discount rules apply to the stripped item which you keep (bond or coupon). Original issue discount for this purpose is the difference between the basis allocated to the retained item and the redemption price of the bond (if retained) or the amount payable on the coupons (if retained). You annually report a ratable portion of the discount under the rules of ¶4.6.

TAX FREE INTEREST ON STATE AND LOCAL GOVERNMENT BONDS AND OBLIGATIONS

STATE AND CITY INTEREST GENERALLY EXEMPT

¶ 4.11 Generally, you pay no tax on interest on bonds or notes of states, cities, counties, the District of Columbia or a possession of the United States. This includes bonds or notes of port authorities, toll road commissions, utility services activities, community redevelopment agencies and similar bodies created for public purposes. Bonds issued after June 30, 1983 must be in registered form for the interest to be tax exempt.

Check with the issuer of the bond to verify the tax status of the interest.

Private activity bonds. Interest on so-called private activity bonds is generally taxable (*see* ¶4.12 for taxable bonds) but there are certain exceptions. For example, interest on the following bonds is tax exempt even if the bond may technically be in the category of private activity bonds: qualified student loan bonds, exempt facility bonds, qualified small issue bonds, qualified mortgage bonds and veterans' mortgage bonds, and qualified 501(c)(3) bonds issued by charitable organizations.

However, while interest on such bonds is not subject to regular tax, interest that you receive after 1986 on such bonds issued after August 7, 1986 is considered a tax preference that may be subject to alternative minimum tax; *see* ¶23.4.

Check with the issuer for the tax status of a private activity bond.

On your 1987 return, you must list the amount of tax-exempt interest received during the year. *See* the Supplement for an example of interest reporting.

TAXABLE STATE AND CITY INTEREST

¶ 4.12 Interest on certain state and city obligations is taxable.

Federally guaranteed obligations. Interest on state and local obligations issued after 1983 is generally taxable if the obligation is federally guaranteed, but there are exceptions allowing tax exemptions for obligations guaranteed by the Federal Housing Administration, Veterans Administration and Student Loan Marketing Associations.

Mortgage subsidy bonds. Interest on bonds issued by a state or local government after April 24, 1979, may not be tax exempt if funds raised by the bonds are used for home mortgages. There are exceptions for certain qualified mortgage bonds and veterans' bonds. Check on the tax-exempt status of mortgage bonds with the issuing authority.

Private activity bonds. Generally, a private activity bond is any bond where more than 10% of the issue's proceeds are used by a private business whose use secures the issue, or if at least 5% of the proceeds are used for loans to parties other than governmental units. Interest on such bonds is generally taxable, but there are exceptions as discussed in ¶4.11. Check on the tax status of the bonds with the issuing authority.

Arbitrage bonds. These are state and local bonds issued after October 9, 1969, used to provide funds for reinvestment in higher yielding instruments. Interest on arbitrage bonds is taxable.

TAX-EXEMPT BONDS BOUGHT AT A DISCOUNT

¶ 4.13 Gain attributed to original issue discount is tax-exempt; gain attributed to market discount is taxable income.

Market discount. This arises when a bond originally issued at not less than par is bought at below par. If you sell a tax-exempt bond purchased at a market discount for a price exceeding your purchase price, the excess is taxable gain. If the bond was held long term, the gain is long term. A redemption of the bond at a price exceeding your purchase price is similarly treated. The market discount rules of ¶4.8 do not apply to tax exempts.

Original issue discount. This arises when a bond is issued for a price less than the face amount of the bond. The discount is considered tax-exempt interest. Thus, if you are the original buyer and hold the bond to maturity, the entire amount of the discount is tax free. If you sell the bond before maturity, the amount of tax-free discount is based on the period of your holding compared to the period from issue date to maturity date. A succeeding holder of the bond may treat as tax-free income the remaining discount allocated up to the time he disposes of the bond. Depending on the issue and acquisition date, the allocation of OID may be on the straight line or economic constant interest method. The economic constant interest method applies to obligations issued after September 3, 1982, and acquired after March 1, 1984. Under this method, less discount accrues in the early years than under the straight line method.

EXAMPLE

In 1981, you bought a 10-year $1,000 state bond issued at $950. In 1987, you sell it for $985. Under the straight line method, you treat 60% (6/10) of the $50 discount or $30 as tax-free income. You also have a long-term gain of $5.

Amount realized on sale	$985
Less: Tax-free original issue discount	30
	$955
Cost basis	950
Taxable gain	$ 5

When bonds are redeemed before maturity, the same rule applies: That portion of the original issue discount earned to the date of redemption is tax-free interest; the balance is capital gain. Bonds issued with an intention to redeem before maturity are not subject to this rule: All interest is tax exempt.

Amortization of premiums is discussed at ¶4.5.

INTEREST ON U.S. OBLIGATIONS

¶ 4.14 Interest on securities issued by the federal government is fully taxable on your federal return. However, interest on federal obligations is not subject to state income taxes. Interest on Treasury bills, notes and bonds is reported on Form 1099-INT.

Treasury bonds and notes. You report the fixed or coupon interest as interest income in the year the coupon becomes due and payable. Treasury bonds and notes are capital assets; gain or loss on their sale, exchange or redemption is reported as capital gain or loss in Schedule D (*see* Chapter 6). If you purchased a federal obligation below par (at a discount) after July 1, 1982, *see* ¶4.6 for the rules on reporting original issue discount. If you purchased a Treasury bond or note above par (at a premium), you may elect to amortize the premium (*see* ¶4.5). If you do not elect to amortize and you hold the bond or note to maturity, you have a capital loss.

Treasury bills. These are short-term U.S. obligations issued at a discount with maturities of three, six, or twelve months. Treasury bills are capital assets and a loss on the disposition is taxed as a capital loss. If there is a gain on a sale or exchange, ordinary income is realized up to the amount of the ratable share of the discount received when you bought the obligation. This amount is treated as interest income and is figured as follows:

$$\frac{\text{Days T-bill was held}}{\text{Days from acquisition to maturity}} \times \frac{\text{T-bill's value at maturity}}{\text{minus your cost}}$$

Any gain over this amount is capital gain. *See* chapter 6.

On a bill held to maturity, you report as interest the difference between the discounted price and the amount you receive on a redemption of the bills at maturity.

> You may postpone the receipt of interest income this year by selecting a Treasury bill maturing next year. Income is not recognized until the date on which the Treasury bill is paid at maturity, unless it has been sold or otherwise disposed of earlier.

Accrual basis taxpayers are required to report ratably the acquisition discount element on Treasury bills acquired after July 18, 1984 using the method explained in ¶4.8. An irrevocable election to accrue under a special accrual formula is also available.

Interest incurred on loans used to buy Treasury bills after July 18, 1984 is deductible by a cash basis investor only to the extent that interest expenses exceed the acquisition discount for each day during the year that the bill is held. The deferred interest expense is deductible in the year the bill is disposed of. If an election is made to report ratably acquisition discount, the interest expense may also be deducted ratably. The election applies to all future acquisitions.

HOW U.S SAVINGS BOND INTEREST IS TAXED

¶ **4.15** **Series E and EE.** These bonds may be cashed for what you paid for them plus an increase in their value over stated periods of time. The increase in redemption value is taxed as interest. You do not have to report the annual increase in value. You may defer the interest income until the year in which you cash the bond or the year in which the bond finally matures, whichever is earlier. But if you want, you may report the annual increase by merely including it on your tax return. If you own bonds which have increased in value in prior years and make an election to report annual increases this year, make sure you report the total of all these increases in value. But next year, report only the increases accruing then, plus increases accruing on bonds newly purchased. That is, once you make the election you must continue reporting annual increases unless you get IRS permission to change your method of reporting. If you use the accrual method of reporting, you must include the interest each year as it accrues.

Suppose you do not include the annual increase on your return and later change your mind. If the due date of the return has passed, it is too late to make the election. You may not file an amended return reporting the increase in value for that year. You have to wait until next year's return to make the election.

E bonds may be held for additional periods of maturity after their initial maturity dates. Bonds held for additional periods increase in value and may be cashed in at any time. If you chose to postpone paying tax on accumulated interest, you may continue to postpone the tax during the extended period. You would then report the entire accumulated interest at the final maturity date or in the year you redeem the bond, whichever occurs earlier. If you have reported the increase in value each year, you must continue to do that during the extended maturity periods. However, E-bondholders may not indefinitely defer the tax on interest. E bonds will cease earning interest once the bonds reach their final maturity date. For example, bonds issued during 1947 cease earning interest in 1987, 40 years from the date of issuance. On your 1987 return, you must pay tax on all the accumulated interest unless the bonds are traded for new HH bonds in multiples of $500. Exchanging E bonds for HH bonds will continue the tax deferral on interest. *See* ¶30.14 for a listing of final maturity dates.

Bonds for child. Interest on savings bonds bought in the name of a child is taxed to the child, even if the parent paid for the bonds and is named as beneficiary. *See* ¶30.14.

If you redeem an E or EE bond you will receive a Form 1099-INT. The amount listed on the form reports the difference between the cost of the bond and the redemption price. This amount may not be correct if you or a prior owner reported interest in prior years. List the gross amount and then subtract the prior interest reported and describe the subtraction as "U.S. Savings Bond interest previously reported."

Series EE bonds will not earn interest beyond maturity. *See* ¶30.14.

Changing the form of registration. Changing the form of registration of an E or EE bond may result in tax. Assume a father uses his own funds to purchase a bond issued in his name, payable on his death to his son. Later, at the father's request, a new bond is issued in the son's name only. The increased value of the original bond up to the date it was redeemed and reissued in the son's name is taxed as interest to the father.

> The following changes in registration do not result in an immediate tax.
> **EXAMPLES**
> 1. Jones buys an E bond and has it registered in his name and in the name of his son as co-owner. Jones has the bonds reissued solely in his own name; he is not required to report the accrual interest at that time.
> 2. You and your spouse each contributed an equal amount toward the purchase of a $1,000 E bond which was issued to you as co-owners. You later have the bond reissued as two $500 bonds, one in your name and one in your spouse's name. Neither of you has to report the interest earned to the date of reissue.
> 3. You add another person's name as co-owner to facilitate a transfer of the bond on death. The change in registration does not result in a tax.

Co-owners of E and EE bonds follow these rules:

1. You paid for the entire bond: Either you or the co-owner may redeem it. You are taxed on all the interest, even though the co-owner cashes the bond and you receive no proceeds.
2. You paid for only part of the bond: Either of you may redeem it. You are taxed on that part of the interest which is in proportion to your share of the purchase price. This is so even though you do not receive the proceeds.
3. You paid for part of the bond, and then had it reissued in another's name. You pay tax only on the interest accrued while you held the bond. The new co-owner picks up his share of the interest accruing afterwards.
4. You and another person were named co-owners on a bond bought as a gift by a third party. You are taxed on 50% of the interest income; your co-owner on the remaining half.

> **Transfer of an E or EE bond because of owner's death.** The death of the original owner does not result in a taxable event for income tax purposes if that owner did not report the interest annually. The income tax liability on the interest accumulated during the deceased's lifetime passes to the survivor unless an election is made to report the accrued interest in the decedent's final income tax return (*see* ¶1.12). If the election is made on the decedent's final return, the new owner is taxable on interest earned after the date of death.

Where an estate tax has been incurred, the new bondholder may claim a deduction for estate tax paid on the accrued interest included in the estate when he reports interest accumulated during the decedent's lifetime (*see* ¶10.18).

Transfer to a trust. If you transfer U.S. Savings Bonds to a trust giving up all rights of ownership, you are taxed on the interest to date of transfer. If, however, you are considered to be the owner of the trust and the interest earned before and after the transfer is taxable to you, you may continue to defer reporting the interest.

Transfer to a charity. Tax on the accumulated E or EE bond interest is not avoided by having the bonds reissued to a philanthropy. Further, tax may not be deferred by first converting E bonds to HH bonds and then reissuing the HH bonds in the philanthropy's name. The IRS held that by having the bonds reissued in the philanthropy's name, the owner realized taxable income on the accumulated bond interest.

Interest on U.S. Savings Bonds transferred by spouses in a divorce or settlement is not subject to tax because of the transfer. *See* ¶6.49.

Treasury regulations on transferring E or EE bonds. Assume you have bought E or EE bonds and had them registered in joint names of yourself and your daughter. The law of your state provides that jointly-owned property may effectively be transferred to a co-owner by delivery or possession. You deliver the bonds to your daughter and tell her they now belong to her alone. According to Treasury regulations, this is not a valid gift of the bonds. The bonds must be surrendered and reissued in your daughter's name.

If you do not have the bonds reissued and you die, the bonds are taxable in your estate. Ownership of the bonds is a matter of contract between the United States and the purchaser of the bonds. The bonds are nontransferrable. A valid gift cannot be accomplished by manual delivery to a donee unless the bonds also are surrendered and reissued in the name of the donee in accordance with Treasury regulations.

Reporting interest on Freedom shares must be the same as the method used for reporting E bonds.

Series H. These bonds were available before 1980. They were bought at face value and pay semi-annual interest that is taxable when received. Do you own Series H bonds purchased through the exchange of Series E or J bonds, interest on which you did not report annually? You do not have to report the interest due on the old bonds until the H bonds are redeemed or mature, whichever occurs first. Interest earned on Series H bonds is taxable in the year received.

If you receive cash when exchanging E bonds for H bonds, you report the cash received as interest income to the extent of the interest earned on the bonds exchanged.

H bonds purchased before July, 1959 will cease earning interest when they mature between February, 1982 and May, 1989. Final maturity dates are listed at ¶30.14. These matured bonds may not be traded but must be cashed in. You report the accumulated interest in the year the bond matures.

Series HH. These bonds are issued at face value and pay semi-annual interest that is taxable when received.

Form 1099-INT for U.S. Savings Bonds interest. When you cash in an E or EE bond, you receive Form 1099-INT that lists as interest the difference between the amount received and the amount paid for the bond. The form may show more taxable interest than you are required to report because you have regularly reported the interest or a prior owner reported the interest. Report the full amount shown on Form 1099-INT on the interest schedule of your return and then, on the same schedule, reduce the amount by the interest previously reported and identify the reduction as "previously reported interest."

Table of Redemption Values for U.S. Savings Bonds—Series E and EE

The following tables list the redemption value of E and EE bonds through October 1987. The year-end tables were not available at the time of publication as the tables were being revised to reflect a change in the interest rate starting in November. You can obtain the year-end redemption values from your bank or by requesting a copy of the tables from the Department of the Treasury, U.S. Savings Bond Division, 1111 20th Street N.W., Washington, D.C., 20226.

U.S. SAVINGS BONDS, SERIES EE
REDEMPTION VALUES BY DENOMINATION—THROUGH OCTOBER 1987

ISSUE YEAR	ISSUE MONTHS	$50	$75	$100	$200	$500	$1,000	$5,000	$10,000
1987	May thru Oct.	NOT ELIGIBLE FOR PAYMENT							
	Apr.	25.52	38.28	51.04	102.08	255.20	510.40	2,552.00	5,104.00
	Mar.	25.60	38.40	51.20	102.40	256.00	512.00	2,560.00	5,120.00
	Feb.	25.70	38.55	51.40	102.80	257.00	514.00	2,570.00	5,140.00
	Jan.	25.78	38.67	51.56	103.12	257.80	515.60	2,578.00	5,156.00
1986	Dec.	25.88	38.82	51.76	103.52	258.80	517.60	2,588.00	5,176.00
	Nov.	25.98	38.97	51.96	103.92	259.80	519.60	2,598.00	5,196.00
	Oct.	26.40	39.60	52.80	105.60	264.00	528.00	2,640.00	5,280.00
	Sep.	26.54	39.81	53.08	106.16	265.40	530.80	2,654.00	5,308.00
	Aug.	26.68	40.02	53.36	106.72	266.80	533.60	2,668.00	5,336.00
	July	26.80	40.20	53.60	107.20	268.00	536.00	2,680.00	5,360.00
	June	26.94	40.41	53.88	107.76	269.40	538.80	2,694.00	5,388.00
	May	27.08	40.62	54.16	108.32	270.80	541.60	2,708.00	5,416.00
	Jan. thru Apr.	27.22	40.83	54.44	108.88	272.20	544.40	2,722.00	5,444.00
1985	Nov. thru Dec.	27.22	40.83	54.44	108.88	272.20	544.40	2,722.00	5,444.00
	May thru Oct.	28.14	42.21	56.28	112.56	281.40	562.80	2,814.00	5,628.00
	Jan. thru Apr.	29.16	43.74	58.32	116.64	291.60	583.20	2,916.00	5,832.00
1984	Nov. thru Dec.	29.16	43.74	58.32	116.64	291.60	583.20	2,916.00	5,832.00
	May thru Oct.	30.30	45.45	60.60	121.20	303.00	606.00	3,030.00	6,060.00
	Jan. thru Apr.	31.54	47.31	63.08	126.16	315.40	630.80	3,154.00	6,308.00
1983	Nov. thru Dec.	31.54	47.31	63.08	126.16	315.40	630.80	3,154.00	6,308.00
	May thru Oct.	32.94	49.41	65.88	131.76	329.40	658.80	3,294.00	6,588.00
	Jan. thru Apr.	34.46	51.69	68.92	137.84	344.60	689.20	3,446.00	6,892.00
1982	Nov. thru Dec.	34.46	51.69	68.92	137.84	344.60	689.20	3,446.00	6,892.00
	May thru Oct.	37.90	56.85	75.80	151.60	379.00	758.00	3,790.00	7,580.00
	Jan. thru Apr.	39.72	59.58	79.44	158.88	397.20	794.40	3,972.00	7,944.00
1981	Nov. thru Dec.	39.72	59.58	79.44	158.88	397.20	794.40	3,972.00	7,944.00
	May thru Oct.	41.66	62.49	83.32	166.64	416.60	833.20	4,166.00	8,332.00
	Jan. thru Apr.	43.34	65.01	86.68	173.36	433.40	866.80	4,334.00	8,668.00
1980	Nov. thru Dec.	43.34	65.01	86.68	173.36	433.40	866.80	4,334.00	8,668.00
	May thru Oct.	45.00	67.50	90.00	180.00	450.00	900.00	4,500.00	9,000.00
	Jan. thru Apr.	46.68	70.02	93.36	186.72	466.80	933.60	4,668.00	9,336.00

U.S. SAVINGS BONDS, SERIES E
REDEMPTION VALUES BY DENOMINATION—THROUGH OCTOBER 1987

ISSUE YEAR	ISSUE MONTHS	$10	$25	$50	$75	$100	$200	$500	$1,000
1980	May thru June		32.47	64.94	97.41	129.88	259.76	649.40	1,298.80
	Jan. thru Apr.		33.35	66.70	100.05	133.40	266.80	667.00	1,334.00
1979	Nov. thru Dec.		33.35	66.70	100.05	133.40	266.80	667.00	1,334.00
	June thru Oct.		34.27	68.54	102.81	137.08	274.16	685.40	1,370.80
	May		34.20	68.40	102.60	136.80	273.60	684.00	1,368.00
	Jan. thru Apr.		35.13	70.26	105.39	140.52	281.04	702.60	1,405.20
1978	Dec.		35.13	70.26	105.39	140.52	281.04	702.60	1,405.20
	Nov.		35.04	70.08	105.12	140.16	280.32	700.80	1,401.60
	June thru Oct.		36.01	72.02	108.03	144.04	288.08	720.20	1,440.40
	May		35.91	71.82	107.73	143.64	287.28	718.20	1,436.40
	Jan. thru Apr.		36.91	73.82	110.73	147.64	295.28	738.20	1,476.40
1977	Dec.		36.91	73.82	110.73	147.64	295.28	738.20	1,476.40
	Nov.		36.81	73.62	110.43	147.24	294.48	736.20	1,472.40
	June thru Oct.		39.71	79.42	119.13	158.84	317.68	794.20	1,588.40
	May		39.60	79.20	118.80	158.40	316.80	792.00	1,584.00
	Jan. thru Apr.		40.89	81.78	122.67	163.56	327.12	817.80	1,635.60
1976	Dec.		40.89	81.78	122.67	163.56	327.12	817.80	1,635.60
	Nov.		40.78	81.56	122.34	163.12	326.24	815.60	1,631.20
	June thru Oct.		42.12	84.24	126.36	168.48	336.96	842.40	1,684.80
	May		42.02	84.04	126.06	168.08	336.16	840.40	1,680.80
	Jan. thru Apr.		43.38	86.76	130.14	173.52	347.04	867.60	1,735.20
1975	Dec.		43.38	86.76	130.14	173.52	347.04	867.60	1,735.20
	Nov.		43.29	86.58	129.87	173.16	346.32	865.80	1,731.60
	June thru Oct.		44.70	89.40	134.10	178.80	357.60	894.00	1,788.00
	May		44.59	89.18	133.77	178.36	356.72	891.80	1,783.60
	Jan. thru Apr.		46.04	92.08	138.12	184.16	368.32	920.80	1,841.60
1974	Dec.		46.04	92.08	138.12	184.16	368.32	920.80	1,841.60
	Nov.		45.92	91.84	137.76	183.68	367.36	918.40	1,836.80
	June thru Oct.		47.42	94.84	142.26	189.68	379.36	948.40	1,896.80
	May		47.31	94.62	141.93	189.24	378.48	946.20	1,892.40
	Jan. thru Apr.		48.86	97.72	146.58	195.44	390.88	977.20	1,954.40
1973	Dec.		48.86	97.72	146.58	195.44	390.88	977.20	1,954.40
	Aug. thru Nov.		49.67	99.34	149.01	198.68	397.36	993.40	1,986.80
	July		49.56	99.12	148.68	198.24	396.48	991.20	1,982.40
	June		51.17	102.34	153.51	204.68	409.36	1,023.40	2,046.80
	Feb. thru May		51.05	102.10	153.15	204.20	408.40	1,021.00	2,042.00
	Jan.		50.92	101.84	152.76	203.68	407.36	1,018.40	2,036.80
1972	Dec.		52.58	105.16	157.74	210.32	420.64	1,051.60	2,103.20
	Aug. thru Nov.		52.46	104.92	157.38	209.84	419.68	1,049.20	2,098.40
	July		52.34	104.68	157.02	209.36	418.72	1,046.80	2,093.60
	June		54.05	108.10	162.15	216.20	432.40	1,081.00	2,162.00
	Feb. thru May		53.90	107.80	161.70	215.60	431.20	1,078.00	2,156.00
	Jan.		53.76	107.52	161.28	215.04	430.08	1,075.20	2,150.40
1971	Dec.		55.51	111.02	166.53	222.04	444.08	1,110.20	2,220.40
	Aug. thru Nov.		55.37	110.74	166.11	221.48	442.96	1,107.40	2,214.80
	July		55.27	110.54	165.81	221.08	442.16	1,105.40	2,210.80
	June		56.37	112.74	169.11	225.48	450.96	1,127.40	2,254.80
	Feb. thru May		56.20	112.40	168.60	224.80	449.60	1,124.00	2,248.00
	Jan.		56.07	112.14	168.21	224.28	448.56	1,121.40	2,242.80
1970	Dec.		58.04	116.08	174.12	232.16	464.32	1,160.80	2,321.60
	Aug. thru Nov.		57.91	115.82	173.73	231.64	463.28	1,158.20	2,316.40
	July		57.77	115.54	173.31	231.08	462.16	1,155.40	2,310.80
	June		59.36	118.72	178.08	237.44	474.88	1,187.20	2,374.40
	Feb. thru May		59.08	118.16	177.24	236.32	472.64	1,181.60	2,363.20
	Jan.		58.93	117.86	176.79	235.72	471.44	1,178.60	2,357.20

ISSUE YEAR	ISSUE MONTHS	$10	$25	$50	$75	$100	$200	$500	$1,000
1969	Dec.		60.56	121.12	181.68	242.24	484.48	1,211.20	2,422.40
	Aug. thru Nov.		60.25	120.50	180.75	241.00	482.00	1,205.00	2,410.00
	July		60.11	120.22	180.33	240.44	480.88	1,202.20	2,404.40
	June		61.76	123.52	185.28	247.04	494.08	1,235.20	2,470.40
	May		60.18	120.36	180.54	240.72	481.44	1,203.60	2,407.20
	Jan. thru Apr.		61.84	123.68	185.52	247.36	494.72	1,236.80	2,473.60
1968	Dec.		61.84	123.68	185.52	247.36	494.72	1,236.80	2,473.60
	Nov.		61.01	122.02	183.03	244.04	488.08	1,220.20	2,440.40
	June thru Oct.		62.69	125.38	188.07	250.76	501.52	1,253.80	2,507.60
	May		61.95	123.90	185.85	247.80	495.60	1,239.00	2,478.00
	Jan. thru Apr.		63.65	127.30	190.95	254.60	509.20	1,273.00	2,546.00
1967	Dec.		63.65	127.30	190.95	254.60	509.20	1,273.00	2,546.00
	Nov.		62.89	125.78	188.67	251.56	503.12	1,257.80	2,515.60
	June thru Oct.		64.62	129.24	193.86	258.48	516.96	1,292.40	2,584.80
	May		63.92	127.84	191.76	255.68	511.36	1,278.40	2,556.80
	Jan. thru Apr.		65.68	131.36	197.04	262.72	525.44	1,313.60	2,627.20
1966	Dec.		65.68	131.36	197.04	262.72	525.44	1,313.60	2,627.20
	Nov.		64.96	129.92	194.88	259.84	519.68	1,299.20	2,598.40
	June thru Oct.		66.75	133.50	200.25	267.00	534.00	1,335.00	2,670.00
	May		66.06	132.12	198.18	264.24	528.48	1,321.20	2,642.40
	Jan. thru Apr.		67.89	135.78	203.67	271.56	543.12	1,357.80	2,715.60
1965	Dec.		67.89	135.78	203.67	271.56	543.12	1,357.80	2,715.60
	Sep. thru Nov.		68.00	136.00	204.00	272.00	544.00	1,360.00	2,720.00
	Aug.		67.66	135.32	202.98	270.64	541.28	1,353.20	2,706.40
	June thru July		69.52	139.04	208.56	278.08	556.16	1,390.40	2,780.80
	Mar. thru May		69.14	138.28	207.42	276.56	553.12	1,382.80	2,765.60
	Feb.		68.80	137.60	206.40	275.20	550.40	1,376.00	2,752.00
	Jan.		74.19	148.38	222.57	296.76	593.52	1,483.80	2,967.60
1964	Dec.		74.19	148.38	222.57	296.76	593.52	1,483.80	2,967.60
	Sep. thru Nov.		73.72	147.44	221.16	294.88	589.76	1,474.40	2,948.80
	Aug.		73.35	146.70	220.05	293.40	586.80	1,467.00	2,934.00
	June thru July		75.74	151.48	227.22	302.96	605.92	1,514.80	3,029.60
	Mar. thru May		75.25	150.50	225.75	301.00	602.00	1,505.00	3,010.00
	Feb.		74.89	149.78	225.75	299.56	599.12	1,497.80	2,995.60
	Jan.		77.34	154.68		309.36	618.72	1,546.80	3,093.60
1963	Dec.		77.34	154.68		309.36	618.72	1,546.80	3,093.60
	Sep. thru Nov.		76.84	153.68		307.36	614.72	1,536.80	3,073.60
	Aug.		76.48	152.96		305.92	611.84	1,529.60	3,059.20
	June thru July		78.97	157.94		315.88	631.76	1,579.40	3,158.80
	Mar. thru May		78.36	156.72		313.44	626.88	1,567.20	3,134.40
	Feb.		78.00	156.00		312.00	624.00	1,560.00	3,120.00
	Jan.		80.55	161.10		322.20	644.40	1,611.00	3,222.00
1962	Dec.		80.55	161.10		322.20	644.40	1,611.00	3,222.00
	Sep. thru Nov.		80.21	160.42		320.84	641.68	1,604.20	3,208.40
	Aug.		79.64	159.28		318.56	637.12	1,592.80	3,185.60
	June thru July		82.24	164.48		328.96	657.92	1,644.80	3,289.60
	Mar. thru May		82.03	164.06		328.12	656.24	1,640.60	3,281.20
	Feb.		81.45	162.90		325.80	651.60	1,629.00	3,258.00
	Jan.		84.09	168.18		336.36	672.72	1,681.80	3,363.60
1961	Dec.		84.09	168.18		336.36	672.72	1,681.80	3,363.60
	Sep. thru Nov.		83.85	167.70		335.40	670.80	1,677.00	3,354.00
	Aug.		82.92	165.84		331.68	663.36	1,658.40	3,316.80
	June thru July		85.62	171.24		342.48	684.96	1,712.40	3,424.80
	Mar. thru May		85.38	170.76		341.52	683.04	1,707.60	3,415.20
	Feb.		84.40	168.80		337.60	675.20	1,688.00	3,376.00
	Jan.		87.15	174.30		348.60	697.20	1,743.00	3,486.00

U.S. SAVINGS BONDS, SERIES E
REDEMPTION VALUES BY DENOMINATION—THROUGH OCTOBER 1987

ISSUE YEAR	ISSUE MONTHS	$10	$25	$50	$75	$100	$200	$500	$1,000
1960	Dec.		87.15	174.30		348.60	697.20	1,743.00	3,486.00
	Sep. thru Nov.		86.98	173.96		347.92	695.84	1,739.60	3,479.20
	Aug.		85.99	171.98		343.96	687.92	1,719.80	3,439.60
	June thru July		88.78	177.56		355.12	710.24	1,775.60	3,551.20
	Mar. thru May		88.63	177.26		354.52	709.04	1,772.60	3,545.20
	Feb.		87.62	175.24		350.48	700.96	1,752.40	3,504.80
	Jan.		90.48	180.96		361.92	723.84	1,809.60	3,619.20
1959	Dec.		90.48	180.96		361.92	723.84	1,809.60	3,619.20
	Sep. thru Nov.		90.27	180.54		361.08	722.16	1,805.40	3,610.80
	Aug.		89.27	178.54		357.08	714.16	1,785.40	3,570.80
	June thru July		91.06	182.12		364.24	728.48	1,821.20	3,642.40
	Jan. thru May		92.43	184.86		369.72	739.44	1,848.60	3,697.20
1958	Dec.		91.36	182.72		365.44	730.88	1,827.20	3,654.40
	July thru Nov.		93.93	187.86		375.72	751.44	1,878.60	3,757.20
	June		92.83	185.66		371.32	742.64	1,856.60	3,713.20
	Jan. thru May		94.31	188.62		377.24	754.48	1,886.20	3,772.40
1957	Dec.		93.19	186.38		372.76	745.52	1,863.80	3,727.60
	July thru Nov.		96.06	192.12		384.24	768.48	1,921.20	3,842.40
	June		94.96	189.92		379.84	759.68	1,899.20	3,798.40
	Feb. thru May		97.15	194.30		388.60	777.20	1,943.00	3,886.00
	Jan.		96.30	192.60		385.20	770.40	1,926.00	3,852.00
1956	Dec.		96.30	192.60		385.20	770.40	1,926.00	3,852.00
	Oct. thru Nov.		95.77	191.54		383.08	766.16	1,915.40	3,830.80
	Sep.		94.67	189.34		378.68	757.36	1,893.40	3,786.80
	June thru Aug.		97.27	194.54		389.08	778.16	1,945.40	3,890.80
	Apr. thru May		97.04	194.08		388.16	776.32	1,940.80	3,881.60
	Mar.		94.41	188.82		377.64	755.28	1,888.20	3,776.40
	Jan. thru Feb.		97.01	194.02		388.04	776.08	1,940.20	3,880.40
1955	Dec.		97.01	194.02		388.04	776.08	1,940.20	3,880.40
	Oct. thru Nov.		96.76	193.52		387.04	774.08	1,935.20	3,870.40
	Sep.		95.47	190.94		381.88	763.76	1,909.40	3,818.80
	June thru Aug.		98.10	196.20		392.40	784.80	1,962.00	3,924.00
	Apr. thru May		97.84	195.68		391.36	782.72	1,956.80	3,913.60
	Mar.		96.60	193.20		386.40	772.80	1,932.00	3,864.00
	Jan. thru Feb.		99.25	198.50		397.00	794.00	1,985.00	3,970.00
1954	Dec.		99.25	198.50		397.00	794.00	1,985.00	3,970.00
	Oct. thru Nov.		99.05	198.10		396.20	792.40	1,981.00	3,962.00
	Sep.		97.73	195.46		390.92	781.84	1,954.60	3,909.20
	June thru Aug.		100.41	200.82		401.64	803.28	2,008.20	4,016.40
	Apr. thru May		100.16	200.32		400.64	801.28	2,003.20	4,006.40
	Mar.		98.90	197.80		395.60	791.20	1,978.00	3,956.00
	Jan. thru Feb.		101.61	203.22		406.44	812.88	2,032.20	4,064.40
1953	Dec.		101.61	203.22		406.44	812.88	2,032.20	4,064.40
	Oct. thru Nov.		101.36	202.72		405.44	810.88	2,027.20	4,054.40
	Sep.		100.09	200.18		400.36	800.72	2,001.80	4,003.60
	June thru Aug.		102.85	205.70		411.40	822.80	2,057.00	4,114.00
	Apr. thru May		102.59	205.18		410.36	820.72	2,051.80	4,103.60
	Mar.		101.34	202.68		405.36	810.72	2,026.80	4,053.60
	Jan. thru Feb.		101.61	203.22		406.44	812.88	2,032.20	4,064.40
1952	Dec.		109.27	218.54		437.08	874.16	2,185.40	4,370.80
	Oct. thru Nov.		108.99	217.98		435.96	871.92	2,179.80	4,359.60
	Sep.		107.64	215.28		430.56	861.12	2,152.80	4,305.60
	June thru Aug.		111.14	222.28		444.56	889.12	2,222.80	4,445.60
	May		110.88	221.76		443.52	887.04	2,217.60	4,435.20
	Jan. thru Apr.		111.31	222.62		445.24	890.48	2,226.20	4,452.40

ISSUE YEAR	Note	ISSUE MONTHS	$10	$25	$50	$75	$100	$200	$500	$1,000
1951		Dec.		111.31	222.62		445.24	890.48	2,226.20	4,452.40
		Nov.		109.71	219.42		438.84	877.68	2,194.20	4,388.40
		June thru Oct.		113.29	226.58		453.16	906.32	2,265.80	4,531.60
		May		111.64	223.28		446.56	893.12	2,232.80	4,465.60
		Jan. thru Apr.		115.26	230.52		461.04	922.08	2,305.20	4,610.40
1950		Dec.		115.26	230.52		461.04	922.08	2,305.20	4,610.40
		Nov.		113.58	227.16		454.32	908.64	2,271.60	4,543.20
		June thru Oct.		117.26	234.52		469.04	938.08	2,345.20	4,690.40
		May		115.67	231.34		462.68	925.36	2,313.40	4,626.80
		Jan. thur Apr.	47.77	119.42	238.84		477.68	955.36	2,388.40	4,776.80
1949		Dec.	47.77	119.42	238.84		477.68	955.36	2,388.40	4,776.80
		Nov.	47.18	117.94	235.88		471.76	943.52	2,358.80	4,717.60
		June thru Oct.	48.71	121.78	243.56		487.12	974.24	2,435.60	4,871.20
		May	46.74	116.84	233.68		467.36	934.72	2,336.80	4,673.60
		Jan. thru Apr.	48.26	120.64	241.28		482.56	965.12	2,412.80	4,825.60
1948		Dec.	48.26	120.64	241.28		482.56	965.12	2,412.80	4,825.60
		Nov.	47.49	118.72	237.44		474.88	949.76	2,374.40	4,748.80
		June thru Oct.	49.03	122.57	245.14		490.28	980.56	2,451.40	4,902.80
		May	48.24	120.61	241.22		482.44	964.88	2,412.20	4,824.40
		Jan. thru Apr.	49.82	124.54	249.08		498.16	996.32	2,490.80	4,981.60
1947		Dec.	49.82	124.54	249.08		498.16	996.32	2,490.80	4,981.60
		Nov.	49.03	122.58	245.16		490.32	980.64	2,451.60	4,903.20
	A	June thru Oct.	50.63	126.57	253.14		506.28	1,012.56	2,531.40	5,062.80
	A	May	49.83	124.57	249.14		498.28	996.56	2,491.40	4,982.80
	A	Jan. thru Apr.	49.35	123.38	246.76		493.52	987.04	2,467.60	4,935.20
1946	A	Dec.	49.35	123.38	246.76		493.52	987.04	2,467.60	4,935.20
	A	Nov.	48.57	121.42	242.84		485.68	971.36	2,428.40	4,856.80
	A	June thru Oct.	48.10	120.25	240.50		481.00	962.00	2,405.00	4,810.00
	A	May	47.36	118.41	236.82		473.64	947.28	2,368.20	4,736.40
	A	Jan. thru Apr.	46.91	117.28	234.56		469.12	938.24	2,345.60	4,691.20
1945	A B	Dec.	46.91	117.28	234.56		469.12	938.24	2,345.60	4,691.20
	A B	Nov.	45.77	114.43	228.86		457.72	915.44	2,288.60	4,577.20
	A B	June thru Oct.	45.33	113.33	226.66		453.32	906.64	2,266.60	4,533.20
	A B	May	44.62	111.54	223.08		446.16	892.32	2,230.80	4,461.60
	A B	Jan. thru Apr.	44.19	110.47	220.94		441.88	883.76	2,209.40	4,418.80
1944	A B	Dec.	44.19	110.47	220.94		441.88	883.76	2,209.40	4,418.80
	A B	Nov.	43.50	108.75	217.50		435.00	870.00	2,175.00	4,350.00
	A B	June thru Oct.	43.08	107.70	215.40		430.80	861.60	2,154.00	4,308.00
	A B	May		106.11	212.22		424.44	848.88	2,122.20	4,244.40
	A B	Jan. thru Apr.		105.09	210.18		420.36	840.72	2,101.80	4,203.60
1943	A B	Dec.		105.09	210.18		420.36	840.72	2,101.80	4,203.60
	A B	Nov.		103.48	206.96		413.92	827.84	2,069.60	4,139.20
	A B	June thru Oct.		102.48	204.96		409.92	819.84	2,049.60	4,099.20
	A B	May		100.91	201.82		403.64	807.28	2,018.20	4,036.40
	A B	Jan. thru Apr.		99.95	199.90		399.80	799.20	1,999.00	3,998.00
1942	A B	Dec.		99.95	199.90		399.80	799.20	1,999.00	3,998.00
	A B	Nov.		98.40	196.80		393.60	787.20	1,968.00	3,936.00
	A B	June thru Oct.		97.45	194.90		389.80	779.60	1,949.00	3,898.00
	A B	May		96.00	192.00		384.00	768.00	1,920.00	3,840.00
	A B	Jan. thru Apr.		94.35	188.70		377.40	754.80	1,887.00	3,774.00
1941	A B	Dec.		94.35	188.70		377.40	754.80	1,887.00	3,774.00
	A B	Nov.		92.86	185.72		371.44	742.88	1,857.20	3,714.40
	A B	June thru Oct.		91.96	183.92		367.84	735.68	1,839.20	3,678.40
	A B	May		90.59	181.18		362.36	724.72	1,811.80	3,623.60

A BONDS WITH THESE ISSUE DATES HAVE REACHED FINAL MATURITY AND WILL EARN NO ADDITIONAL INTEREST.
B BONDS WITH ISSUE DATES OF SEPTEMBER 1946 AND PRIOR ARE NOT ELIGIBLE FOR EXCHANGE TO SERIES HH BONDS.

MINIMUM INTEREST FOR LOANS AND SELLER-FINANCED DEBT

¶ 4.16 The law requires minimum interest on loan transactions unless a specific exception covers the transaction. Where minimum interest is not charged, the law imputes interest as if the parties agreed to the charge.

The rules are complicated and have been subject to several revisions. There are different minimum interest rates and reporting rules depending on the nature of the transaction. The following discussion provides the important details for understanding the rules. For specific cases and computations, we suggest that you consult Treasury regulations for details not covered in this book.

There are two broad classes of transactions:

Loans. These are generally covered by Internal Revenue Code Section 7872. Below-market or low rate interest loans are discussed at ¶ 4.17.

Seller-financed sales of property. These are covered by either Internal Revenue Code Section 1274 or Section 483. Seller-financed sales are discussed at ¶ 4.18. Under prior law, there was a rate differential between the minimum interest rate and the imputed rate that was applied if the minimum rate was not charged. Under current law, the minimum rate is the same as the imputed rate. Thus, if parties fail to charge the minimum rates, the same minimum rate is imputed by law.

INTEREST-FREE OR BELOW MARKET INTEREST LOANS

¶ 4.17 For many years, the IRS tried to tax interest-free or below-market interest loans. However, court decisions supported taxpayers who argued that such loans did not result in taxable income or gifts. To reverse these decisions, the IRS convinced Congress to pass a law imposing tax on interest-free or low-interest loans made by individuals and businesses. You may no longer make interest-free or low-interest loans to a relative who uses the loan for investment purposes without adverse tax consequences unless the exception for $10,000 or $100,000 loans applies (*see* below).

The law generally treats a loan as two transactions:

1. The law assumes that the lender has transferred to the borrower an amount equal to the foregone interest element of the loan. In the case of a loan between individuals, such as a parent and child, the parent is subject to gift tax on this element; in the case of a stockholder borrowing from a company, the element is a taxable dividend; in the case of a loan made to an employee, taxable pay. For gift tax purposes, a term loan is treated as if the lender gave to the borrower the excess of the amount of the loan over the present value of all payments due during the loan term. Demand loans are treated as if the lender gave to the borrower annually the amount of the foregone interest.

2. The law assumes that imputed interest is paid by the borrower to the lender. The lender must report the imputed interest as income; the borrower claims an interest deduction if itemized deductions are claimed.

A husband and wife are treated as one person for purposes of imputing interest.

No tax withholding is required on interest imputed by the rules of the section.

There are two general classes of loans:

1. Gift loans, whether term or demand, and nongift demand loans.
2. Nongift term loans.

The distinction is important for figuring and reporting imputed interest. For example, in the case of nongift term loans, the imputed interest element is treated as original issue discount.

A demand loan is any loan payable in full at any time on the demand of the lender. This includes any nontransferable loan on which the interest arrangement is conditioned on future performance of substantial services by an individual. A term loan is any type of loan that is not a demand loan.

A demand loan is subject to the rules of this section if no interest is payable or the interest rate is less than the applicable federal rate. A term loan is subject to the rules if the amount of loan exceeds the present value

of all payments due under the loan. In case of a demand note, the lender is treated as giving the borrower an amount equal to the foregone interest on an annual basis.

The amount of imputed interest is generally the excess of the amount of interest which would have been payable on the loan for the period at the applicable federal rate and any interest payable on the loan.

Refer to Treasury regulations for calculating taxable amounts.

Applicable federal rate. In the case of a term loan, the applicable federal rate is the one in effect as of the day on which the loan was made, compounded semiannually.

Loan	*Federal Rate*
Not more than three years	Short-term rate
Over three years but not over nine	Mid-term rate
Over nine years	Long-term rate

A demand loan is considered as a series of one-day term loans and interest on such a loan is computed on a daily basis using the federal short-term rate.

To avoid interest imputation, set the interest at the applicable federal rate at the time of the loan or modification of the loan. *See* Treasury regulations for examples of interest terms which may require compound interest values. The applicable federal rates (AFR) are released in IRS Bulletins and may be available at your local IRS office.

$10,000 exception. In the case of a gift loan, no interest is imputed to any day on which the aggregate outstanding amount of all loans between the parties is not over $10,000, provided the loan is not attributed to the purchase or carrying of income-producing assets.

The $10,000 exception also applies for compensation-related and corporate-shareholder loans, provided the principal purpose of the loan is not tax avoidance. Certain low-interest loans given to employees by their employers to purchase a new residence in connection with a move to a new job location are exempt from the imputed interest requirements.

Limitation on imputed interest for gift loans up to $100,000. Interest is not imputed to the lender for any day if (1) the borrower's net investment income for the year in which the day falls does not exceed $1,000, and (2) the aggregate outstanding balance on all loans from the lender to the borrower on such day does not exceed $100,000 (taking into account all loans by the lender to the borrower regardless of the rate of interest). If net investment income is over $1,000, imputed interest is limited to the borrower's net income provided the maximum aggregate amount owned for any day during a year does not exceed $100,000. Net investment income is the excess of investment income over investment expenses.

The net investment income limitations do not apply if a principal purpose of a loan is the avoidance of federal taxes.

Reporting rules. Imputed interest is generally treated as transferred by the lender to the borrower and retransferred by the borrower to the lender on December 31 in the calendar year of imputation and is reported under the regular accounting method of the borrower and lender.

EXAMPLE

On January 1, 1987, Jones Company makes a $200,000 interest-free demand loan to Frank, an employee. The loan remains outstanding for the entire 1987 calendar year. Jones Company has a taxable year ending September 30. Frank is a calendar year taxpayer. For 1987, the imputed compensation payment and the imputed interest payment is treated as made on December 31, 1987.

With gift loans between individuals, interest computed during the borrower's taxable year is treated for both the lender and the borrower as earned on the last day of the borrower's taxable year. Treasury regulations to Section 7872 provide rules for figuring "foregone" interest. Where a demand loan is in effect for the entire calendar year, an "annual blended rate" issued by the IRS to simplify reporting may be used to compute the imputed interest. The blended rate is not available if the loan was not outstanding for the entire year or if the loan balance fluctuated; computations provided by Treasury regulations must be used.

Tax return statement requirements. Both a lender and borrower must attach statements to their income tax returns reporting the interest, how it was calculated, and the name of the parties and their tax identification numbers.

MINIMUM INTEREST AND REPORTING RULES FOR SELLER FINANCING

¶ 4.18 The law requires minimum interest charges for seller-financed sales. If the minimum rate is not charged, the IRS imputes interest at the minimum applicable rate. For example, property is sold on the installment basis for $100,000 and the parties fail to charge adequate interest. Assume the IRS imputes interest of $5,000. For tax purposes, $95,000 is allocated to the sale of the property and the principal amount of the debt; the balance is imputed interest of $5,000, taxable to the seller and deductible by the buyer. However, when the property is *personal use* property, such as a residence to be used by the buyer, imputed interest rules do not apply to the buyer. Thus, the buyer may not deduct the imputed interest. His deduction is limited to his payment of interest stated in the contract.

Two statute classes. The minimum or imputed interest rules are covered by two Internal Revenue Code statutes: Sections 1274 and 483. Under both, the same minimum interest rates apply. Section 483 applies to any payment due more than six months after the date of sale under a contract which calls for some or all payments more than one year after the date of sale. Section 1274 applies where some or all payments are due more than six months after the date of sale. Section 483 does not apply if the sales price is $3,000 or less. Transactions within Section 483 are sales or exchanges of: (1) personal residences, (2) any property if total consideration received by the seller is $250,000 or less, (3) farms if the total price is $1 million or less and (4) sales of land between family members to the extent the sales price does not exceed $500,000. All other transactions involving nonpublicly traded debt instruments for nonpublicly traded property are within Section 1274. Interest is generally figured in the same manner under both statutes.

One important practical difference between the two statutes involves the timing of the reporting and deducting of interest.

Under Section 483, a seller and buyer use their regular reporting method for imputed interest. For a cash-basis seller, interest is taxed when received; a cash-basis buyer deducts interest when paid. However, if too much interest is allocated to a payment period, the excess interest is treated as prepaid interest, and the deduction is postponed to the year or years interest is earned. Section 483 also describes imputed interest as *unstated interest.*

Under Section 1274, the interest element is generally reported by both buyer and seller ratably according to the OID accrual rules, even if they otherwise report on the cash basis. Where the sales price is $2 million or less, the parties can elect the cash method to report the interest regardless of the OID and accrual rules if: (1) the seller-buyer is on a cash basis method and is not a dealer of the property sold, (2) the seller and buyer jointly elect to use the cash method; and (3) the property is not eligible for the investment credit. The cash basis election binds any cash basis successor of the buyer or seller. If the lender transfers his interest to an accrual basis taxpayer, the election no longer applies; interest is thereafter taxed under the accrual method rules. The OID rules also do not apply to a cash-basis buyer of *personal use* property; here, the cash-basis debtor deducts only payments of interest required by the contract.

Rates. The following are rates for seller-financed sales:

General rate. If seller financing is $2.8 million or less, the minimum required interest is the lower of 9% compounded semi-annually or the applicable federal rate (AFR). The amount of seller financing is

the stated principal amount under the contract. If the seller-financed amount exceeds $2.8 million, the minimum interest rate is 100% of the AFR. After 1989, the $2.8 million threshold will be indexed for inflation.

The IRS has authority to write regulations allowing the parties to use an interest rate lower than the AFR if it is shown that the borrower could obtain a loan on an arm's length basis at lower interest.

Seller-financed sale-leaseback transactions. Interest equal to 110% of AFR must be charged.

Sales of land between family members. To the extent that sales price does not exceed $500,000 during a calendar year, the minimum interest rate is 6%, compounded semiannually. To prevent multiple sales from being used to avoid the $500,000 limit, the $500,000 ceiling applies to all land sales between family members during the same year. To the extent that the $500,000 sales price limit is exceeded, the general 9% or 100% of AFR rules apply.

Figuring AFR. Monthly, the IRS determines the AFR rate applying to the following month. The rates are listed in the Internal Revenue Bulletin. There are three AFR rates depending on the length of the contract:

Short-term AFR—a term of three years or less

Mid-term—a term of over three years but not over nine years.

Long-term—a term of over nine years.

The parties may choose the lowest AFR for the three-month period ending with the month in which a binding written sales contract is entered into. Thus, if the AFR for either of the prior two months is lower than the AFR for the month of contract, the lowest of the three AFRs applies.

The total unstated interest is allocated ratably to payments under an OID computation.

Where the contract provides adequate interest and the amount of principal and interest payments do not exceed $250,000, the IRS will recognize the parties' allocation of interest and principal payments, even if it does not match the actual interest accruing during the period.

EXAMPLES

1. On July 1, 1987, Jones sells rental property to Smith for $100,000. Smith is required to make two installment payments of $64,857.18: one on June 30, 1989, the second on June 30, 1991. Each payment includes $50,000 principal and $14,857.18 interest. The loan provides for adequate stated interest. But Jones and Smith have allocated less interest to the first installment than the amount accruing as of that date. The interest accruing as of that date is $19,246.40: $9,200 in the first year ($100,000 × .092), $10,046.40 in the second year ($109,200 × .092). However, as the total amount payable under the contract is less than $250,000, the IRS will accept the allocation.

2. Same facts as in example (1), except that the first installment includes principal of $35,142.82 and $29,714.36 interest; the second installment is entirely principal. The parties have allocated more interest than has accrued. The excess is $10,467.96 ($29,714.36–$19,246.40). In 1989, Jones reports the full amount of interest paid when received. In 1989, Smith may deduct only that part of the paid interest accruing up to the end of 1989. The excess is deductible in later years as it is considered to have been earned.

Assumptions of loans. The imputed interest rules of Sections 1274 and 483 do not generally apply to debt instruments assumed as part of a sale or exchange, or if the property is taken subject to the debt, provided that neither the terms of the debt instrument nor the nature of the transactions are changed.

A change in payment terms may require an adjustment of interest to come within the minimum rate.

If a contract provides for carrying charges, then buyer is not subject to imputed interest.

Imputed interest rules do not apply to sales of patents coming within the rules of ¶6.17.

Safe harbor for points. Under proposed regulations in cases of seller-financed residence sales, generally one-sixth of a point per year of amortization will not be counted as OID.

Important: In planning deferred or installment sales, review Treasury regulations to Sections 483 and 1274 for further examples and details.

5

INCOME OR LOSS FROM YOUR BUSINESS OR PROFESSION

A sample Schedule C may be found in the Supplement to YOUR INCOME TAX.

¶ 5.1 New Law Pointers. The new law makes numerous changes for reporting business income and expenses. The most important are new rules for depreciating property and a drastic cutback of loss deductions from business activities in which you do not materially participate.

Passive activity restrictions. If you are the sole proprietor and do not regularly, continuously and substantially participate in the business, your self-employment income or loss is subject to passive activity restrictions. A loss is deductible only against other passive activity income. The passive activity restrictions are discussed in detail in chapter 11.

New depreciation rules. Business assets other than real estate placed in service after 1986 are depreciable over 3, 5, 7, 10, 15, or 20 years. Automobiles and light trucks, computers and office equipment are in the five-year class. Property in the 3-, 5-, 7-, and 10-year classes are depreciable using the double declining balance method, switching to the straight line method so as to maximize the deduction. The new rates may be elected for assets placed in service after July 31, 1986. See ¶5.22 for details on depreciation.

First-year expensing increased. The first-year expensing deduction for property placed in service after 1986 increases to $10,000 from the $5,000 limit in 1986. However, the annual $10,000 limit is reduced for every $1 of qualifying investment in excess of $200,000. Further, the expensing deduction may not exceed the taxable income from any business which you actively conduct; amounts in excess of taxable income are carried forward and added to the amount eligible for expensing in the later year.

Bad debt reserve method repealed. The reserve method of deducting business bad debts for all taxpayers other than financial institutions is repealed for taxable years beginning after 1986. Bad debts will be deductible only when the debt becomes worthless. The balance of any existing reserve must be taken into account as income ratably over a four-year period. Further, partners or S corporation shareholders who are required to report more than 12 months of income in a single year as a result of the repeal may report the excess income ratably over four years.

Profit presumption period for hobby losses extended. Under pre-1987 law, if you showed a profit in an activity in two or more years during a period of five consecutive years, the law presumed that you are in the activity in order to make a profit. The new law requires you to show a profit in at least three out of five years for the presumption to apply. In the case of horse breeding, training, racing or showing, the profit presumption rule applies if you show profits in two of seven consecutive years. The IRS may rebut the presumption.

Health insurance deduction for self-employed. If you are self-employed you may deduct in 1987, 1988, and 1989 25% of the amounts paid for health insurance on behalf of yourself, your spouse and dependents. The deduction may not exceed your net earnings from self-employment. You may not claim the deduction if you or your spouse is covered by an employer health plan.

Fiscal year restrictions. For taxable years beginning after 1986, partnerships, S corporations, and personal service corporations will generally have to use the same taxable year as their owners, usually calendar years, unless a business purpose is shown. Deferring income to partners or shareholders will not be considered a business purpose. Partners or S corporation shareholders required by the new rules to include more than 12 months of income during a year may be allowed to report the excess over a four-year period.

WHAT ACCOUNTING BASIS CAN YOU USE?

¶ 5.2 Your business income is reported on either the accrual or cash basis. You may figure your business income on the accrual basis even if you report your nonbusiness income on the cash basis. If you have more than one business, you may have a different accounting method for each business. If you have inventories, you *must* use the accrual basis in your business.

Cash basis. You report income items in the taxable year in which they are received; you deduct all expenses in the taxable year in which they are paid. Under the cash basis, income is also reported if it is "constructively" received. You have "constructively" received income when an amount is credited to your account, subject to your control, or set apart for you and may be drawn by you at any time. For example, in 1987 you receive a pay check, but you do not cash it until 1988. You have constructively received the wage income in 1987, and it is taxable in 1987.

In general, you deduct expenses in the year of payment. Expenses paid by credit card are deducted in the year they are charged. Expenses paid through a "pay by phone" account with a bank are deducted in the year the bank sends the check. This date is reported by the bank on its monthly statement.

Advance payments. You may not deduct advance rent payments covering charges of a later tax year. The IRS applies a similar rule to advance payments of insurance premiums; however, an appeals court has allowed an immediate deduction.

Cash method of accounting limited. For taxable years starting after 1986, the following entities may not use the cash method: a regular C corporation, a partnership with a C corporation as a partner, a tax shelter or a tax-exempt trust with unrelated business income. Exceptions: The cash method may be used by professional corporations, entities other than tax shelters with average annual gross receipts of $5 million or less, and farming and timber businesses.

Accrual basis. You report income that has been earned, whether or not received, unless a substantial contingency affects your right to collect the income. The treatment of expenses is subject to more rigid rules. Under prior law, accrual basis taxpayers could deduct accrued expenses that were not payable for several years. You were allowed to deduct an accrued expense if liability was fixed and the amount could be determined with reasonable accuracy. The IRS believed that this so-called "all events" test gave a premature tax savings where performance was delayed beyond the taxable year.

> The cash basis has this advantage over other accounting methods: You may defer reporting income by postponing the receipt of income. For example, if 1987 is a high income year or income tax rates will be lower in 1988, you might extend the date of payment of some of your customers' bills until 1988. But make certain that you avoid the constructive receipt rule. You may also postpone the payment of presently due expenses to a year in which the deduction gives you a greater tax saving.

Under current law a deduction may not be claimed until economic performance has occurred. Economic performance occurs for:

Rent—as the property is used.
Services—when they are performed.
Goods—when they are delivered.
Work of subcontractor hired by the taxpayer—when the subcontractor performs services.

EXAMPLE
You are a calendar-year taxpayer using the accrual method. In December 1987, you buy office supplies. You receive the supplies and are billed for them before the end of the year but make payment in 1988. You may deduct the cost of supplies in 1987. You meet the "all events" test as liability was fixed in 1987; economic performance also occurred in 1987 with the delivery.

Even if delivery were delayed until 1988, the supplies could qualify as a recurring expense as explained below, thereby allowing a 1987 deduction.

Under an exception, a deduction may be allowed for recurring expenses incurred in normal business practice even though economic performance has not yet occurred. All of these tests must be met:

1. The item meets the general "all events" test and economic performance occurs within a reasonable period after the end of the taxable year for which the expense is accrued, but not exceeding 8½ months.
2. The item is recurring in nature and the taxpayer consistently from year to year treats such items as accrued in the year the all events test is satisfied.
3. Either (1) the item is not a material item, or (2) the accrual in the year the "all events" test is met results in a better matching against income than accrual in the year of economic performance. For example, where income from shipping goods is recognized in 1987 but the goods are not shipped until 1988, the shipping costs are more properly matched to income in 1987, the year of sale, than in 1988 when the goods are shipped.

Workmen's Compensation and tort liability do not qualify under the above exceptions. Such liabilities are deductible only when paid.

Contested liability. Under prior law, a deduction for a contested liability was allowed if the amount of the liability was paid into a trust. Under the new law, a deduction may be claimed only if the economic performance test is met, even though payment is made to a trust. Further, if economic performance itself is the actual payment of the liability, payment to a trust is not treated as economic performance.

The above restrictions do not affect the deduction of items that are covered by specific tax law provisions, such as vacation pay, bad debts, and employee-benefits plans.

A 10-year carryback period for losses arising from deferred deductions related to state or federal statutory liability or from tort liability is allowed by statute.

Deductions for lease expenses under deferred rental agreements are subject to the accrual rules of ¶9.10.

> The accrual basis has this advantage over the cash basis: It generally gives a more even and balanced financial report.

Although the accrual method and cash method of accounting are the most common methods of reporting, other methods are allowed if they clearly reflect your income. Special accounting methods include the installment method for dealers in personal property and the percentage of completion or completed contract method for construction contractors. The details of these methods are described in Treasury regulations.

Inventory. Requirements for allocating costs to inventory are detailed in Treasury regulations and IRS Publication 538.

Accrual deferral of service income. Starting in 1987, a new accrual rule applies to income due for services which (based on experience) will not be collected in that year. Part of the income may be deferred until the year of collection. However, if interest or a penalty is charged for a failure to make a timely payment, income is reported when the amount is billed. Further, if discounts for early payments are offered, the full amount of the bill must be accrued; the discount for early payment is treated as an adjustment to income in the year payment is made.

The amount of income to be deferred is based on a percentage that considers billing and uncollectibles over the past five most recent years. The percentage is found by dividing the uncollectible amounts by the total billings during the five-year period. That percentage applied to the total billings during the tax year may be deferred. For example, if $200,000 was billed during the five-year period and $20,000 was uncollectible, the percentage is 10%, and 10% of the current billings may be deferred. If you do not have a five-year experience, you use the period during which you were in business.

> **Changing your accounting method.** Generally, you must obtain the consent of the Internal Revenue Service prior to any change in accounting method. Apply for consent by filing Form 3115 with the Commissioner of Internal Revenue, Washington, D.C. 20224, within 180 days after the beginning of the tax year in which you wish to make the change. Thus, if you are on the calendar-year basis and want to change methods for 1988, file by June 30, 1988.

TAX REPORTING FOR SELF-EMPLOYED

¶ 5.3 Your taxable year must be the same for both your business and nonbusiness income. If you report your business income on a fiscal year basis, you must also report your nonbusiness income on a fiscal year basis.

Generally, you report the tax consequences of transactions that have occurred during a 12-month period. If the period ends on December 31, it is called a calendar year. If it ends on the last day of any month other than December, it is called a fiscal year. A reporting period, technically called a taxable year, can never be longer than 12 months unless you report on a 52-53 week fiscal year basis (details of which can be found in

Treasury regulations). A reporting period may be less than 12 months whenever you start or end your business in the middle of your regular taxable year, or change your taxable year.

A change of reporting periods requires the consent of the IRS. Form 1128 must be filed with the Commissioner of Internal Revenue, Washington, D.C. 20224, prior to any change.

Fiscal year limitations. For tax years starting after 1986, all partnerships, S corporations, and personal service corporations must change their fiscal tax years to the tax year of the partnerships and stockholders. As almost all individuals report on the calendar year, the law is an order to adopt calendar years.

Under the law, a partnership must have the same tax year as that of partners owning a majority interest, unless a good business reason is established for having the fiscal year. A partnership is not required to adopt the tax year of majority interest partners unless the partners having the same tax year have owned a majority interest for the preceding three tax years. If the majority owners do not have the same taxable year, the partnership must adopt the same tax year as its principal partners. If the principal partners do not have the same taxable year, and no majority of partners have the same taxable year, the partnership must adopt a calendar year.

A personal service corporation must use a calendar year for tax years starting after 1986, unless a business purpose for a fiscal year is shown.

All S corporations are required to use a calendar year for tax years beginning after 1986 regardless of the year the S election was made, unless a business purpose is given for a fiscal year.

If a business purpose is shown for a fiscal year, the Treasury will allow the fiscal year. Deferral of income to owners for three months or less no longer justifies the use of a fiscal year. Partnerships or corporations that have already obtained Treasury permission for a fiscal year do not have to get permission again because of the new law unless that year was based on a deferral of income.

Under an election, excess income generated by changes in tax years may be reported ratably over the first four tax years by the partners or stockholders.

REPORTING BUSINESS CASH RECEIPTS TO THE IRS

¶ 5.4 Did you receive in the course of business, cash of more than $10,000 in one transaction or two or more related transactions? If you did, you must file an information return, Form 8300, with the IRS for each transaction. There are penalties for failure to file.

File Form 8300 with the IRS within 15 days of the transaction. Only cash payments are reported; do not report funds received by bank check

or wire transfer where cash was not physically transferred. Foreign currency is considered cash. If multiple payments from a single payer (or a payer's agent) are received within a 24-hour period, the payments are aggregated, and the total must be reported if over $10,000.

The reporting requirement applies to individuals, corporations, partnerships, trusts, and estates, except for certain financial institutions that are already required to report cash transactions to the Treasury. Cash received in transactions occurring entirely outside the U.S. does not have to be reported.

The filing requirement applies to cash received for providing goods or services. Thus, an attorney, doctor, or other professional must report cash payments of over $10,000 from a client. Further, cash received for setting up a trust of more than $10,000 for a client must be reported.

On an installment sale of business property you generally report each payment exceeding $10,000 within 15 days of receipt. If the initial installment is $10,000 or less, you must aggregate all payments received within one year of the initial payment and report the total after it exceeds $10,000.

The IRS warns that the reporting requirement may not be avoided by splitting up a single transaction into separate transactions. Thus, a sale of property for $36,000 may not be broken down into four separate sales of $9,000 to avoid reporting. Similarly, an attorney who represents a client in a case must aggregate all cash payments by the client, although payments may be spread over several months. If the total exceeds $10,000 it must be reported.

There is an exception to the reporting requirement for persons who act as agents if they receive cash of over $10,000 from their principal and use it within 15 days in a cash transaction, provided they identify the principal to the payee in the cash transaction.

On Form 8300, you provide the payer's home address and tax identification number to the IRS. You also must provide the payer with a copy of the form or a similar statement by January 31 of the following year.

A $50 penalty may be imposed for each failure to file Form 8300 or provide the payer with a statement, unless reasonable cause is shown. The maximum penalty is $100,000 per calendar year for each type of statement (IRS or payee). If failure to file is intentional, the penalty for each failure increases to 10% of the reportable amount, with no annual limitation; criminal penalties could also be imposed.

You must keep a copy of each Form 8300 you file with the IRS for five years from the date of filing.

REPORTING INCOME AND EXPENSES ON SCHEDULE C

REPORTING INCOME AND EXPENSES ON SCHEDULE C

¶ 5.5 The following explanations of reporting income and expenses on Schedule C are keyed to a sample schedule on the following page. A 1987 filled-in Schedule C may be found in the Supplement.

Gross receipts or sales. The sample schedule illustrates the reporting of gross receipts by a service business operated by a self-employed person. If you do not produce or sell goods but provide only services, you do not determine cost of goods sold but report only your receipts from services on line 1, as in the case illustrated here. (A sample of Schedule C in the Supplement illustrates the case of a retail business selling merchandise that is required to determine the cost of goods sold using the special section, Part III, of Schedule C.)

Do not report as receipts on Schedule C the following items:

Gains or losses on the sale of property used in your business or profession. These transactions are reported on Schedule D and Form 4797.
Dividends from stock held in the ordinary course of your business. These are reported as dividends from stocks held for investment.

Deductions. Deductible business expenses are claimed in Part II; the descriptive breakdown of items is generally self-explanatory. However, note these points:

Bad debts (line 7): In prior years, accrual basis taxpayers could use the reserve method of charging bad debts. Starting in 1987, you deduct bad debts only when a specific debt becomes partially or wholly worthless.

You also must report any balance in the bad debt reserve ratably as income over a four-year period. Rules for deducting business bad debts are at ¶6.55. Cash basis taxpayers also follow the rules at ¶6.55.

Depreciation (line 12): Enter here the amount of your annual depreciation deduction. A complete discussion of depreciation may be found in ¶5.22 and following. Form 4562, which is used for figuring MACRS and ACRS deductions, may be found in the Supplement.

Employee benefit programs (line 14): Enter your cost for the following programs you provide for your employees: wage continuation, accident or health plans, self-insured medical reimbursement plans; educational assistance programs; supplemental unemployment benefits; and prepaid legal expenses. Retirement plans are reported separately, as discussed below. Employee benefits supported by insurance premiums, such as group hospitalization and medical plans, are deducted as insurance, line 16.

Insurance (line 16): Premiums on insurance policies written for the protection of your business are deductible, such as accident, burglary, embezzlement, marine risks, plate glass, public liability, workmen's compensation, fire, storm, or theft and indemnity bonds upon employees. State unemployment insurance payments are deducted here or as taxes if they are considered taxes under state law.

Premiums paid on an insurance policy on the life of an employee or one financially interested in a business, for the purpose of protecting you from loss in the event of the death of the insured, are not deductible.

Prepaid insurance premiums are deducted ratably over the term covered by the policy, whether you are on a cash or accrual basis. However, an appeals court allowed a cash basis taxpayer to take an immediate deduction for premiums paid on a policy covering more than a year.

Premiums for disability insurance to cover loss of earnings when out ill or injured are nondeductible personal expenses. But you may deduct premiums in policies covering business overhead expenses.

A self-employed doctor may deduct the premium costs of malpractice insurance. However, a doctor who is not self-employed but employed by someone else, say a hospital, may deduct the premium costs only as an itemized deduction. Whether malpractice premiums paid to a physician-owned carrier are deductible depends on how the carrier is organized. If there is a sufficient number of policyholders who are not economically related and none of them owns a controlling interest in the insuring company, a deduction is allowed provided the premiums are reasonable and are based on sound actuarial principles.

In one case, physicians set up a physician-owned carrier which was required by state insurance authorities to set up a surplus fund. The physicians contributed to the fund and received nontransferable certificates that were redeemable only if they retired, moved out of the state or died. The IRS and Tax Court held the contributions to the fund were nondeductible capital expenses.

In another case, a professional corporation of anesthesiologists set up a trust to pay malpractice claims, up to specified limits. The IRS and Tax Court disallowed deductions for the trust contributions on the grounds that the PC remained potentially liable. Malpractice claims within the policy limits might exceed trust funds and the PC would be liable for the difference. Since risk of loss was not shifted to the trust, the trust was not a true insurance arrangement.

Interest (line 17). Include interest on business debts, but prepaid interest that applies to future years is not deductible.

A new law limits your interest deduction if you borrow against a life insurance policy covering yourself as an employee or the life of any other employee, officer or other person financially interested in your business. Interest on a loan used for business is deductible only if the loan is no more than $50,000 per employee or other covered person. If you own

policies covering the same employees (or other persons) in more than one business, the $50,000 limit applies on an aggregate basis to all the policies. The interest deduction limit applies even if a sole proprietor borrows against a policy on his own life and uses the proceeds in his business; interest is not deductible to the extent the loan exceeds $50,000. The loan applies to all policies purchased after June 20, 1986, in taxable years ending after that date.

Pension and profit-sharing plans (line 21): Keogh plan contributions made for your employees are entered here; contributions made for your account are entered directly on Form 1040 as an "Adjustment to Income." In addition, you must file an information return by the last day of the seventh month following the end of the plan year.

Rent on business property (line 22): Rent paid for the use of lofts, buildings, trucks, and other equipment is deductible. However, you may not deduct the entire amount of an advance rental in the year of its payment. This is true even if you are on the cash basis. You deduct only that portion of the payment attributed to the use of the property in the taxable year. For example, you sign a 10-year lease calling for yearly rental payments of $2,000. You pay the first year's rent on July 1. In your tax return for the calendar year, you may deduct only $1,000 ($\frac{6}{12}$ of $2,000). However, an appeals court allowed a calendar year cash basis lessee to deduct advance rentals where the rental payments covered a period of a year or less. For example, on December 1, 1986, the lessee pays the entire rental due for the lease ending November 30, 1987. While the IRS would allow only $\frac{1}{12}$ of the payment to be deductible in 1986, the appeals court would allow a deduction for the entire payment. The court believes this approach is within the spirit of the cash basis rule. In the case of a long-term lease where advance rental payments cover no more than a year beyond the year of payment, the IRS proration rule sacrifices the simplicity of the cash basis method without a meaningful change in the timing of deductions; according to the appeals court. *See also* ¶9.10.

Taxes on leased property that you pay to the lessor are deductible as additional rent.

Repairs (line 23): The cost of repairs is deductible provided they do not materially add to the value of the property or appreciably prolong its life. Expenses of replacements that arrest deterioration and appreciably increase the value of the property are capitalized and their cost recovered through depreciation.

Taxes (line 25): Deduct real estate and personal property taxes on business assets here. Also deduct your share of Social Security taxes paid on behalf of employees and payments of Federal unemployment tax. Federal highway use tax is deductible. Federal import duties, excise and stamp taxes normally not deductible as itemized deductions are deductible as business taxes if incurred by the business. Taxes on business property, such as an *ad valorem* tax, must be deducted here; they are not to be treated as itemized deductions. However, the IRS holds that you may not deduct state income taxes on business income as a business expense. Its reasoning: Income taxes are personal taxes even when paid on business income. As such, you may deduct state income tax only as an itemized deduction.

The Tax Court supports the IRS rule on the grounds that it reflects Congressional intent toward the treatment of state income taxes in figuring taxable income. However, the Tax Court's position is inconsistent. In somewhat similar cases, it has allowed business expense deductions from gross income for interest paid on state and federal income tax deficiencies and legal fees incurred on tax audits of business income.

For purposes of computing a net operating loss, state income tax on business income is treated as a business deduction.

Travel, meals, and entertainment (line 26). Travel expenses and 80% of meals and entertainment for business are deductible. Total meals and entertainment expenses are listed here and then reduced by 20%.

Wages (line 28): You do not deduct your drawings. You may deduct reasonable wages paid to family members who work for you. If you have an employee who works in your office and also in your home, such as a domestic, you deduct that part of the salary allocated to the work in your office. If you take a targeted jobs credit, the credit offsets the wage deduction.

Part I Income

1a Gross receipts or sales	**1a**	
b Less: Returns and allowances	**1b**	
c Subtract line 1b from line 1a and enter the balance here	**1c**	
2 Cost of goods sold and/or operations (from Part III, line 8)	**2**	
3 Subtract line 2 from line 1c and enter the **gross profit** here	**3**	
4 Other income (including windfall profit tax credit or refund received in 1987).	**4**	
5 Add lines 3 and 4. This is the **gross income** . . . . ▶	**5**	

Part II Deductions

6 Advertising		**23** Repairs		
7 Bad debts from sales or services (Cash method taxpayers, see Instructions.) . .		**24** Supplies (not included in Part III) . .		
8 Bank service charges		**25** Taxes		
9 Car and truck expenses		**26** Travel, meals, and entertainment:		
10 Commissions		**a** Travel		
11 Depletion		**b** Total meals and entertainment .		
12 Depreciation and section 179 deduction from Form 4562 (not included in Part III)		**c** Enter 20% of line 26b subject to limitations (see Instructions) .		
13 Dues and publications		**d** Subtract line 26c from 26b . . .		
14 Employee benefit programs . . .		**27** Utilities and telephone		
15 Freight (not included in Part III) . . .		**28a** Wages . . .		
16 Insurance		**b** Jobs credit . .		
17 Interest:		**c** Subtract line 28b from 28a		
a Mortgage (paid to financial institutions)		**29** Other expenses (list type and amount):		
b Other		. . . .		
18 Laundry and cleaning		. . . .		
19 Legal and professional services . .		. . . .		
20 Office expense				
21 Pension and profit-sharing plans . .				
22 Rent on business property				
30 Add amounts in columns for lines 6 through 29. These are the **total deductions** . . . . ▶		**30**		

DEDUCTIONS FOR PROFESSIONALS

¶ 5.6 The following expenses incurred by professionals in the course of their work are generally allowed as deductions from income:

Dues to professional societies
Operating expenses and repairs of car used on professional calls
Supplies
Subscriptions to professional journals
Rent for office space
Cost of fuel, light, water, telephone used in office
Salaries of assistants
Malpractice insurance (see ¶ 5.5)
Cost of books, professional instruments, and equipment with a useful life of a year or less.

Professional libraries are depreciable. Depreciation rules are discussed at ¶ 5.22.

Employees. Professionals who are not in their own practice may not deduct professional expenses on Schedule C. A salaried professional may deduct his professional expenses only as itemized expenses on Schedule A subject to the 2% AGI floor (see ¶ 19.3).

The cost of preparing for a profession. You may *not* deduct the cost of a professional education and the cost of establishing a professional reputation.

The IRS does not allow a deduction for the cost of a license to practice. However, courts have allowed an attorney to amortize the cost of a bar admission over his life expectancy.

The costs of courses taken to keep abreast of professional developments are usually deductible (see chapter 21).

A doctor may depreciate part of the purchase price of a medical practice, if he can show he bought a wasting asset, such as patients' records, the useful life and value of which can be estimated. The IRS on an audit may disallow the deduction. However, there is court authority which has allowed the deduction. Similarly, a doctor may be able to deduct payment for the right to practice in a hospital over his life expectancy.

Payment of clients' expenses. An attorney may follow a practice of paying his clients' expenses in pending cases. He may not deduct the payments as the expenses are those of his clients. Nor are they bad debts if reimbursement is doubtful. For a bad debt deduction, it must be shown that the claim is worthless (see ¶ 6.57).

An attorney might deduct a payment to his client reimbursing the client for a bad investment recommended by the attorney. A court upheld the deduction on the grounds that the reimbursement was required to protect the reputation of an established law practice. However, no deduction is allowed when malpractice insurance reimbursement is available but the attorney fails to make a claim.

Daily business lunches with associates have been held to lack business purpose. Courts agree with the IRS that professionals do not need to have lunch together every day to talk shop. The cost of the meals are therefore not deductible.

EXAMPLES

1. A law partnership deducted the meal costs of the staff attorneys who lunched every day at the same restaurant to discuss cases and court assignments. The deductions were disallowed as personal expenses. A court agreed with the IRS that daily lunches are not necessary. Co-workers generally do not need luncheons to provide social lubrication for business talk as is true with clients.

2. A physician held luncheon meetings three or four times a week with other physicians. He argued that the purpose of the luncheons was to generate referrals. A court held that such frequent luncheons became a routine personal event not tied to specific business. The cost of the meals was not deductible.

NONDEDUCTIBLE EXPENSE ITEMS

¶ **5.7** *Capital expenditures* may not be deducted. Generally, the cost of acquiring an asset or of prolonging its life is a capital expenditure.

EXAMPLE

A new roof is installed on your office building. If the roof increases the life of the building, its cost is a capital expenditure recovered by depreciation deductions. The cost of repairing a leak in the roof is a deductible operating expense. A deduction was allowed for the cost of a major roof renovation on evidence that the work was not designed to increase the value of the building but to correct the defect.

If the useful life of an item is less than a year, its cost is deductible. Otherwise, you may recover your cost only through depreciation except to the extent first-year expensing applies (¶5.34).

Expenses while you are not in business. You are not allowed to deduct business expenses incurred during the time you are not engaged in your business or profession.

EXAMPLE

A lawyer continued to maintain his office while he was employed by the government. During that time he did no private law work. He only kept the office to have it ready at such time as he quit the government job and returned to practice. His costs of keeping up his office while he was working for the government were not deductible.

Payments of fines. You may not deduct the payment of a fine even though your violation was unintentional.

Bribes, kickbacks. Bribes and kickbacks are not deductible if they are illegal under a federal or a generally enforced state law which subjects the payor to a criminal penalty or provides for the loss of license or privilege to engage in business. A kickback, even if not illegal, is not deductible by a physician or other person who has furnished items or services that are payable under the Social Security Act (including state programs). A kickback includes payments for referral of a client, patient, or customer.

In one case, the IRS, with support from the Tax Court and a federal appeals court, disallowed a deduction for legal kickbacks paid by a subcontractor. The courts held that the kickbacks were not a "necessary" business expense because the contractor had obtained nearly all of its other contracts, without paying kickbacks, including contracts from the same general contractor bribed here.

COSTS OF WRITING A BOOK MUST BE CAPITALIZED

¶ **5.8** Under prior law (IRC 280), the IRS and Tax Court held that the costs of writing a book had to be capitalized and deducted over the period during which the author reasonably expected to receive income from the book. However, an appeals court held that these capitalization rules did not apply to authors. According to the appeals court, the prior law was intended to apply to book publishers and tax shelter ventures, but not to authors.

For taxable years after 1986, Section 280 has been repealed and the requirement to capitalize costs incurred after 1986 is covered by a new Section 263A. Committee reports to the new law specifically state that the costs of researching and writing a book are subject to the new law. At the time this book went to press, the method of amortizing the capitalized costs under the new law was not yet clarified by Treasury regulations.

DEDUCTING EXPENSES OF A SIDELINE BUSINESS OR HOBBY

¶ **5.9** There is a one-way tax rule for hobbies: Income from a hobby is taxable; losses are not deductible. The losses are considered nondeductible personal losses.

A profitable sale of a hobby collection held long-term is taxable at capital gain rates; losses are not deductible (*see* ¶6.8).

> The question of whether an activity, such as dog breeding or collecting and selling coins and stamps, is a hobby or sideline business arises when losses are incurred. As long as you show a profit, you may deduct the expenses of the activity. But when expenses exceed income and your return is examined, an agent may allow expenses only up to the amount of your income and disallow the remaining expenses that make up your loss. At this point, to claim the loss deduction, you may be able to take advantage of a "presumption" explained below, or you may have to prove that you are engaged in the activity to make a profit.

Allowance and disallowance of expenses. If an activity is held not to be engaged in for profit, expenses are deductible up to the extent of income from the activity; a deduction for expenses exceeding the income is disallowed. A special sequence is followed in determining which expenses are deductible from income. Deducted first are amounts allowable without regard to whether the activity is a business engaged in for profit, such as interest, state and local taxes and bad debts. If any income remains, "business" expense such as repairs, maintenance, and depreciation may be deducted to the extent of remaining income. The order and allocation of deductible items are detailed in Treasury regulations.

Presumption of profit-seeking. For taxable years beginning before January 1, 1987, if you show a profit in two or more years during a period of five consecutive years, the law presumes that you are in an activity for profit. For taxable years beginning after December 31, 1986, you must show a profit for three or more years in the five-year period to take advantage of the presumption. If the activity is horse breeding, training, racing or showing, the profit presumption applies if you show profits in two of seven consecutive years. The presumption does not necessarily mean that losses will automatically be allowed; the IRS may rebut the presumption (*see* below).

Election postpones determination of profit presumption. If you have losses in the first few years of an activity, and the IRS tries to disallow them as hobby losses, you have this option: You may make an election on Form 5213 to postpone the determination of whether the above profit presumption applies. The postponement is until after the end of the fourth taxable year following the first year of the activity. For example, if you enter a farming activity in 1986, you can elect to postpone the profit motive determination until after 1990. Then, if you have realized profits in at least two of the five years (1986–1990), the profit presumption applies. When you make the election on Form 5213, you agree to waive the statute of limitations for all activity-related items in the taxable years involved. The waiver generally gives the IRS an additional two years after the filing due date for the last year in the presumption period to issue deficiencies related to the activity.

To make the election, you must file Form 5213 within three years of the due date of the return for the year you started the activity. Thus, if you started your activity during 1987, you have until April 15, 1991, to make the election. If before the end of this three-year period you receive a deficiency notice from the IRS disallowing a loss from the activity and you have not yet made the election, you can still do so within 60 days of receiving the notice.

These election rules apply to individuals, partnerships and S corporations. An election by a partnership or S corporation is binding on all partners or S corporation shareholders holding interests during the presumption period.

DEDUCTING EXPENSES OF LOOKING FOR A NEW BUSINESS

¶ **5.10** When you are planning to invest in a business, you may incur preliminary expenses for traveling to look at the property and for legal or accounting advice. Expenses incurred during a general search or preliminary investigation of a business are not deductible, including expenses related to the decision whether or not to enter a transaction. However, when you go beyond a general search and focus on acquiring a particular business, you may deduct the start-up expenses. The timing of the deduction depends on whether or not you actually go into the business.

> **Amortization election when you go into business.** If you go into a business, you may elect to amortize over at least a 60-month period the costs of investigating, such as expenses of surveying potential markets, products, labor supply, transaction facilities; travel and other expenses incurred in lining up prospective distributors, suppliers, or customers; and salaries or fees paid to consultants and similar professional services. The amortization period starts when you begin or acquire a going business. You make the election on the return for the year the business begins.

You may not amortize expenses incurred in acquiring or selling securities or partnership interests, such as securities registration expenses, or underwriters' commissions. You may not amortize costs of acquiring property to be held for sale or property which may be depreciated or amortized, including expenses incident to a lease and leasehold improvements.

Amortizable expenses are restricted to expenses incurred in investigating an active business; expenses of looking for investment property may not be amortized. For rental activities to qualify as an active business, there must be significant furnishings of services incident to the rentals. For example, the operation of an apartment complex, an office building, or a shopping center would generally be considered an active business.

You may not claim any deduction for start-up expenses if you do not elect to amortize. For example, if you incur expenses prior to completion of a building to be used in an active rental business, such as rental pay-

ments for leasing the land on which the building is to be constructed, you must elect to amortize the expenses or you will lose a deduction. If you do not elect to amortize, you treat expenses as follows: Costs connected with the acquisition of capital assets are capitalized and depreciated; costs related to assets with unlimited or indeterminable useful lives are recovered only on the future sale or liquidation of the business.

If the acquisition fails. Where you have gone beyond a general search and have focused on the acquisition of a particular business, but the acquisition falls through, you may deduct the expenses as a loss incurred in a transaction entered into for profit.

EXAMPLES

1. In search of a business, you place newspaper advertisements and travel to investigate various prospective ventures. You pay for audits to evaluate the potential of some of the ventures. You then decide to purchase a specific business and hire a law firm to draft necessary documents. However, you change your mind and later abandon your plan to acquire the business. According to the IRS, you may not deduct the related expenses for advertisements, travel, and audits. These are considered investigatory. You may deduct the expense of hiring the law firm.

2. Domenie left his job to invest in a business. He advertised and was contacted by a party who wished to sell. He agreed to buy, hired an attorney, transferred funds to finance the business, and worked a month with the company manager to familiarize himself with the business. Discovering misrepresentations, he refused to buy the company and deducted over $5,000 for expenses, including travel and legal fees. The IRS disallowed the deduction as incurred in a business search. The Tax Court disagreed. Domenie thought he had found a business and acted as such in transferring funds and drawing legal papers for a takeover.

Investigating and looking for a new business is treated as a business activity if you are a promoter of new businesses.

For deducting the expenses of looking for a new job, *see* ¶ 19.8.

BUSINESS USE OF A HOME

EXCLUSIVE AND REGULAR USE OF HOME OFFICE

¶ **5.11** You may operate your business from your home, using a room or other space as an office or area to assemble or prepare items for sale. To deduct home expenses allocated to this activity, as a self-employed person, you must be able to prove that you use the home area *exclusively* and on a *regular basis* either as:

A place of business to meet or deal with patients, clients, or customers in the normal course of your business. In one case, the Tax Court held that telephoning clients at home met this requirement, but an appeals court reversed, holding that the physical presence in the office of clients or customers is required.

Your principal place of business. Your home office will qualify as your principal place of business if you spend most of your working time there and most of your business income is attributable to your activities there. In one case, the Tax Court disallowed a deduction where a road stand was operated a mile from a home where items were prepared for sale at the stand. Although the home space was used for a business purpose, the deduction was barred because the home was not the principal place of business; the road stand was.

In another case, an appeals court allowed an owner of a laundromat to deduct the costs of a home office where there was no space in the laundromat for an office, and more time was spent in the home office than at the laundromat.

Restrictive income test. Even if you meet the above tests, your deduction for allocable office expenses may be substantially limited or barred by a restrictive rule that limits deductions to the gross income from the office activity *minus* business expenses that are not allocable to the use of the home area itself, such as salary paid to an assistant or office supplies. This rule bars a deduction if business related expenses such as salaries equal or exceed the gross receipts for the business. *See* ¶ 5.14.

Employees. Employees who use a home office must also meet the above tests. Because of the conditions of employment, most employees may be unable to prove that the office is the principal place of business. The IRS and the Tax Court generally hold that an employee's home office is not the principal place of his or her business. For example, the IRS and Tax Court did not allow an employed orchestral musician to deduct his home studio costs even though it was his only place to practice. An appeals court allowed the deduction. Home practice was the focal point of his position as concert musician. Rehearsals and performances at the opera house were made possible by the solo practice at home. Since the opera company did not provide space to its musicians for solo practice, maintaining a practice room at home was a business necessity, not a personal convenience.

> The appeals court also allowed a professor to deduct the costs of a home office where his school office was inadequate. The professor showed that he spent most of his work week in his home office doing research. The appeals court held that where employer-provided space is unsuitable to do substantial work, the home office may be treated as a principal place of business. The IRS does not follow this approach.

Home office expenses of employees are discussed further at ¶19.10.

Exclusive use and regular basis tests. If you use a room, such as a den, both for business and family purposes, you must be prepared to show that a specific section of the den is used exclusively as office space. A partition or other physical separation of the office area is helpful but not required.

Under the regular basis test, expenses attributable to incidental or occasional trade or business use are not deductible even if the room is used for no other purpose but business.

> The above tests will generally not present problems in deducting home expenses where the home area is the principal place of business or professional activity. For example, you are a doctor and see most of your patients at an office set aside in your home. Problems may arise where you have a principal office elsewhere and use a part of your home for occasional work. If your deduction is questioned, you must prove that the area is used regularly and exclusively to receive customers, clients, or patients. For example, evidence that you have actual office facilities is important. Furnish the room as an office with a desk, files, and a phone used only for business calls. Also keep a record of work done and business visitors.

Separate structure. If in your business you use a separate structure not attached to your home, such as a studio adjacent but unattached to your home, the expenses are generally deductible if you satisfy the exclusive use and regular basis tests discussed above. A separate structure does not have to qualify as your principal place of business or a place for meeting patients, clients or customers. However, the gross income limitation discussed at ¶5.14 applies.

In one case, a taxpayer argued that an office located in a separate building in his backyard was not subject to the exclusive and regular business use tests and the gross income limitation. However, the IRS and Tax Court held that it was. The office building was "appurtenant" to the home and thus part of it, based on these facts: The office building was 12 feet away from the house and within the same fenced-in residential area; it did not have a separate address; it was included in the same title and subject to the same mortgage as the house, and all taxes, utilities and insurance were paid as a unit for both buildings.

Day care services. The exclusive use test does not apply to business use of a home to provide day care service for children and handicapped or elderly persons, provided certain state licensing requirements are met. When day care services are provided, the allocation of expenses is made on the basis of space used for such services and then multiplied by a fraction representing the hours such space is used for business purposes. Specifically, the amount of expenses allocated to business space is then multiplied by a fraction, the numerator of which is the *time* the space was used for day care services over the total time available for use.

Storage space and inventory. If your home is the only location of a business selling products, expenses allocated to space regularly used for inventory storage is deductible if the space is separately identifiable and suitable for storage.

DEDUCTIBLE EXPENSES OF A HOME AREA USED FOR BUSINESS

¶ 5.12 Depending on your income (*see* ¶5.14), a deduction for home business use may include real estate taxes, mortgage interest, operating expenses (e.g., home insurance premiums, utility costs), and depreciation allocated to the area used for business. Household expenses and repairs that do not benefit that space are not deductible. However, a pro rata share of the cost of painting the outside of a house or repairing a roof may be deductible. Costs of lawn care and landscaping are not deductible.

Figuring depreciation. For depreciation purposes, the cost basis of the house is the lower of the fair market value of the entire house at the time you started to use a part of it for business, or its adjusted basis (exclusive of the land). Only that part of the cost basis allocated to the office is depreciable.

How to claim the deduction. There is no specific form for deducting home office expenses. If you are self-employed, you deduct your business expenses for real estate taxes, mortgage interest, insurance, utilities, and repairs on the appropriate lines of Schedule C. Depreciation is computed on Form 4562 and then entered in Schedule C. On Schedule C, you must also answer a question regarding home office expenses in the affirmative.

Employees who qualify for a home office deduction claim the deduction on Schedule A as a miscellaneous itemized deduction which is subject to the 2% AGI floor, *see* ¶19.1.

ALLOCATING EXPENSES TO BUSINESS USE

¶ 5.13 You may allocate expenses as follows: Compare the number of square feet of space used for business with the total number of square feet in the home and then apply the resulting fraction or percentage to the total deductible expenses.

If all rooms in your home are approximately the same size, you may base the allocation on a comparison of the number of rooms used as an office to the total number of rooms.

EXAMPLE

A doctor rents a 10-room apartment using three rooms for his office and seven rooms for his residence. Applying a percentage based on the ratio of rooms used as an office to the the total rooms in the apartment, he deducts 30% (3 ÷ 10) of the following expenses.

	Total	Office	Residence
Rent	$ 7,200	$2,160	$5,040
Light	600	180	420
Heat	1,000	300	700
Wages of domestic	2,000	600	1,400
	$10,800	$3,240	$7,560

$3,240 is deductible as professional expenses, subject to the income limitation of ¶5.14.

BUSINESS INCOME MAY LIMIT HOME OFFICE EXPENSE DEDUCTIONS

¶ 5.14 Deductible expenses allocated to the business use of an area in your home may not exceed net income derived from that use, as explained below. If you do not realize income during the year, no deduction is allowed. For example, you are a full-time writer and use an office in your home. You do not sell any of your work this year or receive any advances or royalties. You may not claim a home office deduction for this year.

If you do receive income, follow these steps to determine your deductible office expenses:

1. First reduce gross income from the business activity in your home office by business expenses that are *not* allocable to the use of the office itself, such as salaries paid to employees, telephone and supply costs. The resulting amount is the income base against which allocable office expenses may be claimed. If these non-office expenses exceed your gross receipts, no office related expenses are deductible.
2. From the balance of income under Step 1, you deduct the business

portion of allowable mortgage interest and real estate taxes (and casualty losses if any).

3. From the balance of income, if any, you deduct operating expenses allocable to the office, such as maintenance, utilities and insurance.
4. If a balance still remains, you deduct allocable depreciation up to the amount of remaining business income.

The amount of taxes, interest, or casualty losses not allocable to the home office under Step 2 may be claimed as itemized deductions.

Carryover. Expenses disallowed because of the income limitation may be carried forward and treated as home office expenses in the next year. The carryover, when added to expenses of the next year, is also subject to the gross income limitation. This carryover rule applies only to expenses after 1986 that are disallowed by the income limitation.

EXAMPLES

1. Smith does sideline business consulting from a home office. His gross income from consulting services is $1,900. He paid an office secretary salary of $500, office telephone expenses of $150 and office supply costs of $200.

In addition, he allocated 10% of his home costs to the business space, as follows:

	Total	10% allocation
Mortgage interest	$5,000	$ 500
Real estate taxes,	2,000	200
Insurance	600	60
Utilities	900	90
Depreciation	3,200	320

Because of the restrictive definition of gross income, the allowable deduction for business use is computed as follows:

Gross income from consulting		$1,900
Less: Secretary's salary	500	
Business phone	150	
Office supplies	200	850
Income from office		$1,050
Less: Interest	500	
Taxes	200	700
Balance		$ 350
Less: Insurance	60	
Utilities	90	150
Balance		200
Less: Depreciation		200

Only $200 of the allowable depreciation of $320 is deductible. The disallowed balance of $120 is carried over to the next year. The balance of interest and taxes is deductible if itemized deductions are claimed.

2. A teacher uses a home office as the principal place of a sideline retail business. He also uses the office to correct student papers. The home office deductions are limited to gross income from the retail business. Teaching-related income is not counted towards the home office expenses since the home office is not the principal place of his teaching job.

AN OFFICE IN A HOME FOR SIDELINE BUSINESS

¶ 5.15 You may have an occupation and also manage rental property or run a sideline business from an office in your home. The home office expenses are deductible if it is a principal place of operating the rental or sideline business.

EXAMPLE

A doctor is employed full time by a hospital. He also owns six rental properties which he personally manages. He uses one bedroom in his two-bedroom home exclusively as an office to manage the properties. The room is furnished with a desk, bookcase, filing cabinet, calculators, and answering service; furnishings and other materials for preparing rental units for tenants are stored there. He may deduct expenses allocable to the home office.

> In claiming home office expenses of a sideline business, it is important to be ready to prove that you are actually in business. (See ¶ 5.9). A court has held that activities in seeking new tenants, supplying furnishings, and cleaning and preparing units for tenants are sufficiently systematic and continuous to put a person in the business of real estate rental. In some cases, the rental of even a single piece of real property may be a business.

Investors managing their own securities portfolio may find it difficult to convince a court that investment management is a business activity. According to Congressional committee reports, a home office deduction should be denied to an investor who uses a home office to read financial periodicals and reports, clip bond coupons, and perform similar activities. In one case, the Claims Court allowed a deduction to Moller who spent about 40 hours a week at a home office managing a substantial stock portfolio. The Claims Court held these activities amounted to a business. However, an appeals court reversed the decision. According to the appeals court, the test is whether or not a person is a trader. A trader is in a business; an investor is not. A trader buys and sells frequently to catch daily market swings. An investor buys securities for capital appreciation and income without regard to daily market developments. Therefore, to be a trader, one's activities must be directed to short-term trading, not the long-term holding of investments. Here Moller was an investor; he was primarily interested in the long-term growth potential of stock. He did not earn his income from the short-term turnovers of stocks. He had no significant trading profits. His interest and dividend income was 98% of his income.

DEPRECIATION ON A COOPERATIVE APARTMENT USED AS AN OFFICE

¶ 5.16 If your home office meets the tests of ¶ 5.11, you may deduct depreciation on your stock interest in the cooperative. The basis for depreciation may be the cooperative corporation's basis for the building or an amount computed from the price you paid for the stock. The method you use depends on whether you are the first or a later owner of the stock.

You are the first owner. In figuring your depreciation, you start with the basis of the building to the cooperative in which you own stock. You then take your share of depreciation according to the percentage of stock interest you own.

If space in the building is rented to commercial tenants who do not have stock interests in the corporation, the total allowable depreciation is reduced by the amount allocated to the space used by the commercial tenants.

You are a later owner of the cooperative's stock. When you buy stock from a prior owner, the basis of depreciation is determined from the price of the stock and the outstanding mortage on the property at the time you bought the stock.

FIGURING NET OPERATING LOSSES FOR REFUND OF PRIOR TAXES

NET OPERATING LOSSES FOR REFUND OF PRIOR TAXES

¶ 5.17 A loss incurred in your profession or unincorporated business is deducted from other income reported on Form 1040. If the 1987 loss (plus any casualty loss) exceeds income, the excess may be first carried back to 1984, 1985, 1986 and *then* forward 15 years to 1988 through 2002 until it is used up. A loss carried back to a prior year reduces income of that year and entitles you to a refund. A loss applied to a later year reduces income for that year.

You may elect to carry forward your loss for 15 years, forgoing the three-year carryback (*see* ¶5.21).

The rules below apply not only to self-employed individuals, farmers, and professionals but also to individuals whose casualty losses exceed income, stockholders in S corporations, and partners whose partnerships have suffered losses. Each partner claims his share of the partnership loss.

The following example shows you how a 1987 loss would be carried back and forward:

EXAMPLE
You have a 1987 operating loss of $650.

Year	Income	Loss	*Loss carried back or forward to income*
1984	$ 50		($ 50)
1985	80		(80)
1986	60		(60)
1987		($650)	
1988	20		(20)
1989	40		(40)
1990	50		(50)
1991	100		(100)
1992	100		(100)
1993	125		(125)
1994	150		(25)

Net operating losses from product liability may be carried back ten years for taxable years beginning after September 19, 1979. Product liability losses do not include liabilities under a warranty or resulting from services (e.g., legal or medical malpractice).

Passive activity limitation. Losses subject to passive activity rules of chapter 11 are not deductible as net operating losses. However, losses of rental operations coming within the $25,000 allowance of ¶11.4 may be treated as a net operating loss if the loss exceeds passive and other income.

Carryover of loss from prior year to 1987. If you had a net operating loss in an earlier year which is being carried forward to 1987, the loss carryover is reported as a minus figure in the miscellaneous income section of your 1987 return. You must attach a detailed statement showing how you figured the carryover.

Restrictions on loss after accounting method change. You may realize a net operating loss for a short taxable year created by the accounting change. As a condition of allowing the accounting method change, the IRS may require you to forgo the right to a loss carryback and agree to a six-year carryforward period.

EXAMPLE
You want to change from a calendar year to a fiscal year ending April 30. Assume further that May through October is your peak selling period. Thus, you may have a net operating loss for the short taxable year January 1–April 30 because of slack business. According to the IRS, if the net operating loss is $10,000 or less, you may apply the regular net operating loss rules that allow you to carryback the loss three years and then forward 15 years. But if the net operating loss exceeds $10,000 and the short period is less than nine months, the operating loss must be deducted ratably over a six-year period starting with the first tax year after the short period.

YOUR NET OPERATING LOSS

¶ 5.18 A net operating loss is generally the excess of deductible business expenses over business income. The net operating loss may also include the following losses and deductions:

Casualty and theft losses, even if the property was used for personal purposes (*see* ¶chapter 18).

Deductible expenses of moving to a new job location (*see* ¶19.13).

Deductible job expenses, such as travel expenses, work clothes, costs and union dues

Your share of an operating loss from a partnership or an S corporation

Loss incurred in sale of Small Business Investment Company stock (*see* ¶6.11)

Loss incurred in stock coming within the rules of Section 1244 (*see* ¶6.12)

An operating loss may *not* include:

Net operating loss carryback or carryover from any year

Capital losses that exceed capital gain

Excess of nonbusiness deductions over nonbusiness income plus nonbusiness net capital gain

Deductions for personal exemptions

A self-employed's contribution to a Keogh plan

An IRA deduction

Income from other sources may eliminate or reduce your operating loss.

EXAMPLE
You are self-employed and incur a business loss of $10,000. Your spouse earns a salary of $10,000. When you file a joint return, your business loss will be eliminated by your spouse's salary. Similarly, if you also had salary from another position, the salary would reduce your business loss.

FIGURING A NET OPERATING LOSS

¶ 5.19 Form 1045 has a schedule for computing your net operating loss deduction. On the schedule, you start with adjusted gross income and personal deductions shown on your tax return. As these figures include items not allowed for net operating loss purposes, you follow the line by line steps of Form 1045 to eliminate them. That is, you reduce the loss by the nonallowed items, such as deductions for personal exemptions, net capital loss, and nonbusiness deductions exceeding nonbusiness income. On the schedule, the reductions are described as adjustments. The example below illustrates the steps in the schedule.

Adjustment for nonbusiness deductions. Nonbusiness expenses that exceed nonbusiness income may not be included in a net operating loss deduction. Nonbusiness deductions include deductions for IRA and Keogh plans and itemized deductions such as charitable contributions, interest expense, state taxes, and medical expenses. Do not include in this nonallowed group deductible casualty and theft losses, which for net operating loss purposes are treated as business losses. If you do not claim itemized deductions in the year of the loss, you treat the standard deduction as a nonbusiness deduction.

Nonbusiness income is income that is *not* from a trade or business— such as dividends, interest, and annuity income. The excess of nonbusiness capital gains over nonbusiness capital losses is also treated as part of nonbusiness income.

EXAMPLE

Income from dividends and interest is $6,000 and nonbusiness deductions are $6,500. The excess deduction of $500 is an adjustment that reduces your loss on Form 1045.

Adjustment for capital losses. A net nonbusiness capital loss may not be included in a net operating loss. If nonbusiness capital losses exceed nonbusiness capital gains, the excess is an adjustment that reduces your loss on Form 1045. In figuring your loss, you may take into account business capital losses only up to the total of business capital gains plus any nonbusiness capital gains remaining after the nonbusiness deduction adjustment discussed above.

EXAMPLE

In 1987, you have a salary of $2,000, interest of $1,000, a net business loss of $10,000 (income $50,000 and expenses of $60,000); itemized deductions of $4,000, and a net nonbusiness capital gain of $1,000. Your net operating loss is $8,000. The following computation approximates the steps of the Form 1045 computation schedule starting from the line showing your adjusted gross income of ($6,000).

Salary		$2,000
Interest		1,000
Capital gain income		1,000
Business loss		($10,000)
Adjusted gross income	(6,000)	
Add: Exemption and itemized deductions	(5,900)	
		($11,900)
Adjustments:		
Exemptions	$1,900	
Excess nonbusiness deduction*	2000	3,900
Net operating loss		8,000

The excess nonbusiness expenses deduction was figured as follows:

Itemized deductions		$4,000
Net capital gain income	$1,000	
Interest	1,000	$2,000
Excess		2,000

At risk loss limitations. The loss used to figure your net operating loss deduction is subject to the at risk rules discussed at ¶ 11.11. If part of your investment is in nonrecourse loans or is otherwise not at risk, you must compute your deductible loss on Form 6198 which you attach to Form 1040. The deductible loss from Form 6198 is reflected in the income and deduction figures you enter in the Form 1045 schedule to compute your net operating loss deduction.

HOW TO CLAIM YOUR NET OPERATING LOSS DEDUCTION

¶ **5.20** Tax year 1984 is the first year to which you may carry back your 1987 net operating loss. When you carryback the loss to 1984, you recompute your 1984 tax on Form 1045 by deducting the 1987 net operating loss. The net operating loss is deducted from the amount of your original 1984 adjusted gross income. Because of the reduction to adjusted gross income, you have to increase any 1984 medical expense and casualty loss deduction when recomputing 1984 income. You do not have to change the amount of your 1984 charitable deduction. *See* the instruc-

tions to Form 1045 and also Publication 536 for details of the recomputation calculation.

After recomputing the 1984 tax on Form 1045, your refund is the difference between the tax originally paid for 1984 and the lower tax figured after deducting the net operating loss deduction.

Use Form 1045 as a "quick refund" claim. The IRS will usually allow or reject your claim within 90 days from the time you file Form 1045. Do not attach Form 1045 to your 1987 Form 1040. File Form 1045 separately, together with a copy of your return. You may file Form 1045 within 12 months after the end of your tax year. Thus, if you are a calendar year taxpayer, you have until December 31, 1988, to carryback a 1987 loss to 1984 on Form 1045. If the IRS allows the refund, it may still determine later that the refund was excessive and assess additional tax.

Although using Form 1045 is the quickest way to obtain the refund, you may instead file an amended return on Form 1040X to claim the refund. You have three years after the due date (including extensions) of your 1987 tax return to file Form 1040X. Thus, to claim a refund on Form 1040X for 1984, because of a net operating loss carried back three years from 1987, you have until April 15, 1991, to file. On Form 1040X, you must attach a statement detailing how the loss carryback was figured; the schedule from Form 1045 for computing the loss may be used.

Operating losses from more than one year. If you have more than one year net operating loss to be carried to the same taxable year, you apply the loss from the earliest year first.

EXAMPLE

You had net operating losses in both 1986 and 1987 of $6,000 and $10,000 respectively. Your taxable income in 1984 was $5,000. You carried the $6,000 loss from 1986 to 1983, leaving an unused portion of $1,000 to be carried to 1984. Therefore, you have two losses to be applied against 1984 income, the unused portion of the 1986 loss and the 1987 loss. First apply the unused portion of the 1986 loss and then apply the 1987 loss.

On Form 1045 or Form 1040X you must attach a detailed schedule showing how the net operating loss for each year was computed.

Any part of the loss that may not be deducted in 1984 is carried to 1985. *See* the instructions to Form 1045 and also IRS Publication 536 for details of this computation.

ELECTION TO RELINQUISH THE CARRYBACK

¶ **5.21** The discussion above is based on the general carryback and carryforward rules. You may elect to forgo the carryback. Instead, you just carry forward losses. The carryforward period is still 15 years under the election. The election is irrevocable.

> You will generally make the election to relinquish the carryback if you expect greater tax savings by carrying the loss forward. You might also make the election if you are concerned you might be audited for earlier years if you carry back a loss for a refund. You make the election by attaching a statement to this effect to your return for the year of the loss, which must be filed by the due date plus extensions. The IRS refused to allow a late election and received court approval for its position.

CLAIMING DEPRECIATION DEDUCTIONS

Starting in 1987, the new law cuts back some of the accelerated writeoff advantages of ACRS depreciation system. The new method is called "modified ACRS" or MACRS. The new law—

Restructures several class life groups. Business autos and light trucks are removed from the three-year class life and placed in a five-year class life. Office furniture and fixtures are removed from the five-year class and placed in a new seven-year class. The recovery period for real estate is increased from 19 years to 27.5 years for residential rental property and to 31.5 years for non-residential property.

Replaces ACRS rate percentages with a double-declining method for business equipment in the three, five, seven, and ten year classes, and limits depreciation of realty to straight line.

Sets a half-year convention or mid-quarter convention for the year business equipment is placed in service. Generally, regardless of the placement date, only 50% of the annual deduction is allowed in the first year. Consequently, the effective write-off period for three-year property is four years, for five-year property, six years, for seven-year property, eight years. A mid-quarter convention applies when asset acquisitions in the last three months are at least 40% of total acquisitions during the year. In such a case, a mid-quarter convention replaces the half-year convention and the depreciation rate for each asset is based on the particular quarter in which the equipment was placed in service. A mid-month convention applies to realty.

Increases the first-year expensing deduction from $5,000 to $10,000. However, if the cost of qualifying assets exceeds $200,000, the limit is reduced dollar-for-dollar by the cost of payments exceeding $200,000.

Applies different depreciation rates and useful lives for purposes of the alternative minimum tax (AMT). Thus, if you are subject to AMT, you must account for two types of depreciation, regular and AMT, and two basis computations when the property is disposed of, see ¶ 5.27 and ¶ 23.3.

Using ACRS and MACRS

The objective of ACRS and MACRS is to provide rapid depreciation for most asset purchases and to eliminate disputes over useful life, salvage value, and depreciation methods. Useful life and depreciation methods are fixed by law; salvage value is not considered or is treated as zero. If you do not want to use MACRS rates, you may elect the straight line method.

ACRS and MACRS apply to new and used property. They do not apply to intangible property such as patents or covenants not to compete. Except for certain railroad property not discussed in this book, ACRS and MACRS do not apply to property for which an election is made to claim depreciation under a method not expressed in terms of years, such as the unit-of-production or income forecast methods. If you may not use ACRS or MACRS, use pre-1981 rules. Pre-1981 rules are not discussed in this book; see IRS Publication 534.

Depending on when assets were placed in service, assets may be depreciated under pre-1981 depreciation rules, the original ACRS rules for assets placed in service from 1981-1986, and the MACRS rules for assets placed in service after 1986. Assets placed in service after July 31, 1986, and before January 1, 1987, could be depreciated under MACRS on 1986 returns if an election was made to use MACRS instead of ACRS. There was an advantage to electing MACRS in 1986 for assets that were not transferred to longer class lives where double declining rates gave larger deductions in the first two years than provided by the original ACRS rates. The election to use MACRS for assets placed in service after July 31, 1986, and before January 1, 1987, is made on Form 4562-A.

ACRS applies to transition property. Property with a class life of at least seven years which you place in service during 1987 is depreciable under prior law ACRS rules instead of the new MACRS rules, provided you acquired it or constructed it under a written contract binding on March 1, 1986.

Prior law ACRS also applies to property which you started to construct or reconstruct on or before March 1, 1986, if by that date you incurred or committed the lesser of (1) $1 million or (2) 5% of the cost.

Finally, prior law ACRS applies to equipped buildings or plant facilities where construction began on or before March 1, 1986 pursuant to a specific written plan and more than 50% of the cost was incurred or committed by that date.

Transition property is subject to the ACRS rules discussed at ¶ 5.29 and ¶ 5.32.

WHAT PROPERTY MAY BE DEPRECIATED?

¶ **5.22** Depreciation is an expense deduction that allows you to charge off your capital investments in equipment, machines, fixtures, autos, trucks, and buildings used in your business, profession, or rental or other income-producing activities.

Depreciation may be claimed only on property used in your business or other income-producing activity.

EXAMPLES

1. An anesthesiologist suspended his practice indefinitely because of malpractice premium rate increases. He continued to maintain his professional competence by taking courses and keeping up his equipment. The IRS ruled that he could not take depreciation on his equipment. Since he is no longer practicing, the depreciation does not relate to a current trade or business.

2. An electrician spent $1,325 on a trailer to carry his tools and protective clothing. Based on a useful life of three years less salvage value of $25, annual depreciation deductions came to $433. However, the IRS claimed that he could not claim depreciation during the months he was unemployed and the trailer was not used. The Tax Court disagrees. Depreciation is allowed as long as the asset is held for use in a trade or business, even though the asset is idle or its use is temporarily suspended due to business conditions.

Depreciation may not be claimed on property held for personal purposes, such as a personal residence or pleasure car. If property, such as a car, is used both for business and pleasure, only the business portion may be depreciated (*see* ¶19.60 and ¶29.40).

Property bought for income-producing purposes, although yielding no current income, may still be depreciated.

Not all assets used in your business or for the production of income may be depreciable. Property having no determinable useful life (property that will never be used up or become obsolete), such as treasured art works or good will, may not be depreciated. Although land is not depreciable, the cost of landscaping business property may be depreciated. While good will is not depreciable, a restrictive covenant (a covenant not to compete), if separately bargained and paid for, may be "amortized," that is, deducted in equal amounts over the term of the covenant. If a business is purchased and its former owners agree not to compete for a specified period of time, be sure that the covenant is segregated and severable from good will, which may also have been purchased at the same time, in order to be able to amortize the cost of the covenant. *See* ¶5.46. Similarly, customer lists or records, if segregated from good will, may also be amortized.

Property held primarily for sale to customers or property includible in inventory is not depreciable, regardless of its useful life.

Farm property. Farm land is not depreciable; farm machinery and buildings are depreciable. Livestock acquired for work, breeding or dairy purposes and not included in inventory may also be depreciated. For a detailed explanation of the highly technical rules for depreciating farm property and livestock, *see* IRS Publication No. 225, Farmer's Tax Guide.

For depreciation of rental residences, *see* ¶29.41.

For depreciation of a sublet cooperative apartment or one used in business, *see* ¶5.16.

Depreciation is deducted annually. Even though the deduction may give you no tax benefit in a particular year because your other deductions already exceed your income, you may not choose to forego the depreciation deduction and, instead, accumulate it for high income years. Similarly, incorrect deductions claimed in prior years may not be corrected by an adjustment to your present depreciation deduction. If the year in which the error was made is not yet closed by the statute of limitations, you may file an amended return to adjust the depreciation deduction for that year. *See also* ¶6.32 for other adjustments of incorrect depreciation taken in prior years.

MACRS CLASS LIVES FOR PROPERTY PLACED IN SERVICE AFTER 1986

¶ **5.23** Depreciable assets (other than buildings) fall within a 3-, 5-, 7-, 10-, 15-, or 20-year class life. For property in the 3-, 5-, 7-, and 10-year classes, the depreciation method is 200% declining balance, with a switch to straight line. For 15- and 20-year property, the 150% declining balance method is used with a switch to straight line. The conversion to straight line is made when larger annual deductions may be claimed over the remaining life.

Straight-line recovery for buildings is discussed at ¶5.31.

Three-year property. This class includes property with a four-year-or-less midpoint life under the ADR (Asset Depreciation Range) system, other than cars and light-duty trucks (which are in the five-year class).

Property with a midpoint life of four years or less includes: special handling devices for the manufacture of food and beverages; special tools and devices for the manufacture of rubber products; special tools for the manufacture of finished plastic products, fabricated metal products, or motor vehicles; and breeding hogs. By law, racehorses more than 2 years old when placed in service and other horses more than 12 years old when placed in service, are also in the 3-year class.

Five-year class. This includes property with an ADR midpoint of more than four years and less than ten years, such as computers, typewriters, copiers, duplicating equipment, heavy general purpose trucks, trailers, cargo containers, and trailer-mounted containers. Also included by law in the five-year class are cars, light-duty trucks, computer-based telephone central office switching equipment, computer related peripheral equip-

ment, semiconductor manufacturing equipment, and property used in research and experimentation.

Seven-year property. This is a new class and includes any property with an ADR midpoint of 10 years or more and less than 16 years, and property with no ADR midpoint that is not assigned to another class. In this class are: office furniture and fixtures, railroad track, and single purpose agricultural or horticultural structures.

Ten-year property. This includes property with an ADR midpoint of 16 years or more and less than 20 years, such as vessels and water transportation equipment, assets used in petroleum refining, or in the manufacture of tobacco products and certain food products.

Fifteen-year property. This includes property with an ADR midpoint of 20 years or more and less than 25 years, such as municipal sewage treatment plants, telephone distribution plants, and comparable equipment used by nontelephone companies for the two-way exchange of voice and data communications.

Twenty-year property. This is a new class and includes property with an ADR midpoint of 25 years and more, other than real property with an ADR midpoint of 27.5 years and more.

MACRS BASED ON DECLINING BALANCE METHOD

¶ **5.24** The double declining rate for five-year property is 40%; for seven-year property it is 28.58%. The rate is applied each year to the declining cost basis (basis less prior depreciation). When the declining rate provides a lower annual deduction than the straight line rate, the double declining rate is replaced by the straight line rate. Under MACRS, these general rules are modified because of the half-year and mid-quarter conventions. Under the half-year convention, all property acquired during the year, regardless of when acquired during the year, is treated as acquired in the middle of the year. As a result, only one half of the first-year depreciation is deductible and in the year after the last class life year, the balance of the depreciation is written off. Further, in the year property is sold, only half of the depreciation of that year is deductible.

The half-year convention applies unless the total cost bases of depreciable assets placed in service during the last three months of the taxable year exceed 40% of the total bases of all property placed in service during the entire year. If this 40% test is met, you must use a mid-quarter convention to figure your annual depreciation deduction, as explained at ¶5.26.

You may follow these steps to apply the declining rate in the year the property is placed in service.

Step 1. Apply the declining rate to the adjusted basis of the property.

EXAMPLE
You are depreciating an asset that cost $10,000 and is in a MACRS class life of five years. The double declining balance rate is 40%, or double the straight-line rate of 20%. The depreciation allowance before applying the convention adjustment (Step 2) is $4,000 ($10,000 × 40%). If the property is in the seven-year class, the double declining balance rate is 28.58% (straight line rate of 14.29% × 2). For property in the fifteen or twenty-year class, the declining rate is 150% of the straight-line rate.

Step 2. Adjust the Step 1 depreciation allowance for the convention. The rules for applying the conventions are at ¶5.25 (half-year) and ¶5.26 (mid-quarter). If the half-year convention applies, the depreciation deduction in the first year is reduced by 50%.

If the mid-quarter convention applies, multiply the first year allowance determined under Step 1 by the following percentages for the quarter in which the asset was placed in service:

Quarter placed in service	Percentage
1st	87.5%
2nd	62.5
3rd	37.5
4th	12.5

EXAMPLE
The depreciation allowance under Step 1 for five-year property is $4,000. If the half-year convention applies, the first-year deduction is $2,000 ($4,000 × 50%). If the mid-quarter convention applies to all

assets placed in service for the year (¶ 5.26) and the asset was placed in service in the third quarter, the deduction for the first year would be $1,500 ($4,000 × 37.5%).

Annual limitation for business automobiles. The deduction figured under Steps 1 and 2 for a car purchased in 1987 may not exceed $2,560; *see* ¶ 19.60.

Figuring depreciation in later years. You continue to apply the applicable rate to the remaining basis of the property. A switch to straight line is made in the fifth year.

EXAMPLE

Same facts as in the above example using the half-year convention for five-year property.

2nd year: 40% of $8,000 ($10,000 less $2,000 depreciation of first year) or $3,200

3rd year: 40% of $4,800 ($8,000 less $3,200 depreciation) or $1,920.

4th year: 40% of $2,880 ($4,800 less depreciation of $1,920) or $1,152

5th year: a switch to the straight-line method provides a greater deduction for the remaining balance of $1,728. The straight-line rate for 1.5 years is 66.66%. The deduction is therefore $1,152 ($1,728 × 66.66%) in the fifth year, as this exceeds the $691 deduction allowed under the declining method (40% × $1,728). The remaining basis is deducted in the sixth year.

Summary of Deductions:

Year	Deduction
1st	$2,000
2nd	3,200
3rd	1,920
4th	1,152
5th	1,152
6th	576
Total	$10,000

HALF-YEAR CONVENTION FOR MACRS

¶ 5.25 Generally, you must use a half-year convention to figure your first-year MACRS deduction. However, if more than 40% of your depreciable costs are incurred during the last three months of the year, you must apply the mid-quarter convention rules of ¶ 5.26.

The half-year convention treats all business equipment placed in service during a tax year as placed in service in the mid-point of that tax year. The same rule applies in the year in which the property is disposed of. The effect of this rule is as follows: A half-year of depreciation is claimed in the first year property is placed in service, regardless of when the property is placed in service during the tax year. For each of the remaining years of the recovery period, a full year of depreciation is claimed. If you hold the property for the entire recovery period, a half-year of depreciation is claimed for the year following the end of the recovery period. If you dispose of the property before the end of the recovery period, a half-year of depreciation is allowable for the year of disposition.

As a shortcut to applying the 40% rate to the declining basis of five-year property each year (¶ 5.24), you may apply the following rates against original basis, assuming the half-year convention applies.

Year	Half-year convention rates for five-year property
1	20%
2	32
3	19.20
4	11.52
5	11.52
6	5.76

FINAL QUARTER ASSET PLACEMENTS—MID-QUARTER CONVENTION FOR MACRS

¶ 5.26 A mid-quarter convention applies if the total cost bases of business equipment placed in service during the last three months of the tax year exceed 40% of the total bases of all the property placed in

service during the year. You must use a mid-quarter convention for *all property* (other than nonresidential real property and residential rental property) placed in service during the year. In applying the 40% rule, you do not count residential rental property and nonresidential realty.

Under the mid-quarter convention, the first-year depreciation allowance is based on the number of quarters that the asset was in service. Property placed in service at any time during a quarter is treated as having been placed in service in the middle of the quarter.

The mid-quarter convention also applies to sales and disposals of property. The disposal is treated as occurring in the midpoint of the quarter.

To figure your MACRS deduction for property subject to the mid-quarter convention, you first figure your depreciation for the full tax year and then multiply by a percentage for the quarter of the tax year the property is placed in service. The percentages are listed in ¶ 5.24.

EXAMPLE

During 1987, you place in service in September office furniture costing $1,000, and in October a computer costing $5,000. You are on the calendar year. The total bases of all property placed in service in 1987 is $6,000. As the basis of the computer of $5,000 placed in service in the last quarter exceeds 40% of the total basis of all property placed in service during 1987, you must use the mid-quarter convention for the furniture and the computer. The office furniture which is seven-year property and the computer which is five-year property are depreciated using MACRS and a mid-quarter convention.

You first multiply the basis of $1,000 by 28.58%, the seven-year property rate. This gives depreciation of $286 for a full year. As the furniture was placed in service in the third quarter of the tax year, you multiply the $286 by 37.5% (mid-quarter percentage for the third quarter) for depreciation deduction of $107 for the furniture.

You multiply the basis of $5,000 by 40%, the five-year property rate. The deduction is $2,000 for a full year. But as the computer was placed in service in the fourth quarter, you multiply the $2,000 by 12.5% (mid-quarter percentage for the fourth quarter). This gives a deduction of $250.

As a shortcut to applying the 40% rate for five-year property to the declining basis each year, you may apply the following rates against original basis:

	Mid-quarter convention rates for five-year property			
		Quarter placed in service		
Year	*First*	*Second*	*Third*	*Fourth*
1	35%	25%	15%	5%
2	26	30	34	38
3	15.6	18	20.4	22.8
4	11.01	11.37	12.24	13.68
5	11.01	11.37	11.30	10.94
6	1.38	4.26	7.06	9.58

ALTERNATIVE MACRS DEPRECIATION

¶ 5.27 You may not want to use an accelerated rate and may prefer to write off depreciation at an even pace. You may make an irrevocable election to use the alternative depreciation method which is the straight-line method (without regard to salvage value) over the recovery period for the class life. For example, for purposes of the alternative straight-line rule, class life for cars, light trucks and computers is 5 years; business furniture class life is 7 years; the recovery period for personal property with no class life is 12 years; the recovery period for nonresidential real and residential rental property is 40 years.

Accelerated rates of MACRS do not give any greater depreciation than your investment in an asset. They merely give you an opportunity to advance the time of taking your deduction. This may be a decided advantage where the immediate increased annual deductions will provide you with cash for working capital or for investments in other income-producing sources. That is, by taking increased deductions, you defer the payment of taxes that would be due if you claimed smaller depreciation deductions, using more conservative estimates of depreciation. The tax deferral lasts until the rapid method provides less depreciation deductions than would the more conservative method. Your ability to receive the benefits of MACRS generally is more feasible in an ongoing business.

If you are starting a new business in which you expect losses or low income at the start, MACRS may waste depreciation deductions that could be used in later years when your income increases. Therefore, before deciding to use the faster writeoffs of MACRS, consider your own income prospects and allocate your deduction accordingly.

Except for real estate, the alternative election applies to all property within the same class, placed in service during the taxable year. For real estate, the election to use alternative depreciation method may be made on a property by property basis. An election to use the alternative depreciation method is irrevocable.

The alternative method must also be used to determine alternative minimum tax (AMT). The allowable AMT depreciation deduction for personal property placed in service after 1986 (other than transition property) is figured using the 150% declining balance method. You figure this rate by multiplying the straight line rate for the class by 1.5. For real estate placed in service after 1986, AMT depreciation is figured using the 40-year. alternative straight-line method. *See also* ¶ 000.

You are also required to use the alternative depreciation system for automobiles (*see* ¶ 19.63) and computers used 50% or less for business.

Figuring earnings and profits

Any tangible property which during the taxable year is used predominantly outside the United States

Any tax-exempt use property

Any tax-exempt bond financed property

Any imported property covered by an Executive order.

Half-year and quarter-year conventions apply to alternative method depreciation. *See* ¶ 5.25 and ¶ 5.26. For real estate, the mid-month convention applies; *see* ¶ 5.31.

The alternative rate for five-year property assuming a half-year convention is as follows:

Year	Rate
1	10
2	20
3	20
4	20
5	20
6	10

WRITING OFF THE COST OF A COMPUTER IN 1987

¶ **5.28** If you are an employee, you may claim MACRS (five-year life) and/or first-year expensing only if the computer was required for your job. In addition, the unit must be used more than 50% of the time for business. The more than 50% test also applies to self-employed persons. If the computer is not used more than 50% for business, MACRS and first-year expensing may not be claimed; you claim alternative depreciation over a six-year period. *See* ¶ 5.27. The more than 50% test does not apply to computers used exclusively in a business establishment that you operate. A home office qualifying under the rules of ¶ 5.11 is treated as a business establishment.

Merely getting an employer letter stating that a computer is needed for a position does not meet the terms of the law. Even where the employer encourages use of a computer that is used for basic job requirements, a deduction may not be allowed.

EXAMPLES

1. An electric company offers to help pay for its engineers' personal computers where they will improve productivity. Qualifying engineers receive extra pay and must buy a computer meeting company specifications, take approved computer courses, and agree to restrictions on resale of the computer. An engineer buys a computer, uses it 95% of the time for writing business memos and reports and studying business flow charts. He does not use the computer for entertainment.

2. A professor of nursing, trying to keep her temporary position, buys a personal computer, needing a word processor for independent research papers and to document her qualifications for research grants. The research and external grant support were implied university requirements for faculty appointment. She did not have access to university word-processing equipment during regular work hours and because of her classroom responsibilities, her research and grant development work had to be done on her own time. To help her pursue

outside grants, the university bought her a "modem" that allowed a phone hookup with its computer system at night. The computer was used 100% for her research and grant work.

The IRS disallows depreciation writeoffs in both examples. According to the IRS, the computer use by the engineer and the professor, although work-related and benefiting their employers, was not "inextricably related" to proper job performance. In each case, there was no evidence that employees who did not use computers were professionally disadvantaged. As for the engineer, his participation in the computer program was optional, not mandatory.

The IRS held that an insurance agent could not deduct depreciation for a portable computer he used to help develop insurance plans for clients. The insurance company encouraged its agents to buy the computer because office computers were not generally accessible. According to the IRS, it is not enough that the agent's productivity increased or that he used the computer solely for business. Purchasing the computer was optional, not a mandatory job requirement. Employees who did not purchase computers were not professionally disadvantaged.

Investors who use home computers for managing portfolios must use alternate depreciation (¶ 5.27), unless the computer is *also* used more than 50% of the time for business. Further, unless the 50% business use test is met, they may not claim first-year expensing. Business and investment uses are combined for determining the allowable part of deductible depreciation.

EXAMPLES

1. In 1987 Jane buys a computer; she uses it 50% of the time to manage her investment and 40% in a part-time research business. The business-use test is not met for claiming MACRS. She must use alternate depreciation of which 90% is deductible.

2. Assume that Jane used the computer 60% of the time for business and 30% for investment. As business use exceeds 50%, she may claim MACRS, and the allowable deductible percentage is 90% of the MACRS deduction. First-year expensing may be available under the rules of ¶ 5.34.

When you buy a computer with software and the cost of software is not separately stated, the cost of the software may be added to the cost of the computer for figuring depreciation. Software which may be used for only one year, such as a program for preparing your 1987 return, may be deducted as a miscellaneous itemized deduction subject to the 2% floor; *see* ¶ 19.1.

ACRS RECOVERY PERIODS FOR BUSINESS ASSETS PLACED IN SERVICE BEFORE 1987

¶ **5.29** Assets placed in service before 1987 fall within one of the following classes:

Three-year property. This class includes automobiles, taxis, light duty trucks (actual unloaded weight of less than 13,000 pounds), and equipment used for research and experimentation. The following animals also qualify as three-year property: hogs used for breeding, racehorses more than two years old, and any other horse more than twelve years old when placed in service.

The recovery rate for three-year property placed in service before 1987 is:

First year	25%
Second year	38
Third year	37

However, in the case of automobiles, the full 25%, 38% or 37% deduction may not be allowed because of the so-called luxury car limitations, *see* ¶ 19.62.

Five-year property. All tangible personal property has a five-year recovery period unless specifically included in the three-year or ten-year class. Thus, most equipment and other business assets qualify for a five-year writeoff, including office furniture, typewriters, computers, calculators, copiers, and general purpose cultural structures and facilities used for the storage of petroleum and its primary products fall within the five-year class.

The recovery rate for five-year property placed in service before 1987 is:

First year	15%
Second year	22
Third year	21
Fourth year	21
Fifth year	21

Ten-year property. This is a limited category covering assets used in theme and amusement parks, residential mobile homes, railroad tank cars, public utility equipment with an ADR class life of more than 18 but not more than 25 years (except research and experimentation equipment included in the three-year class) and public utility equipment used in coal conversions.

A special 15-year period applies to public utility property with an ADR class life exceeding 25 years as of January 1, 1981. These rules are not discussed further in this book.

Special tools whose ADR class life as of January 1, 1981, was four years or less are also placed in the three-year class; this group includes special tools (not general purpose tools such as wrenches or drills) used in manufacturing motor vehicles, fabricated metal products, rubber products, glass products, and finished plaster products. Specialized containers and other handling devices used in manufacturing food and beverages also qualify as three-year property.

Real estate is discussed at ¶ 5.32

FIGURING ACRS ON BUSINESS EQUIPMENT PLACED IN SERVICE BEFORE 1987

¶ **5.30** To figure depreciation for assets placed in service before 1987 follow these steps:

Step 1. Start with the depreciable basis of the asset. This is usually the cost of the asset. If you acquired the asset other than by purchase, *see* ¶ 6.29. If you claimed a full investment credit when the credit was allowed, basis was reduced by 50% of the credit. If you elected first-year expensing, basis is reduced by the amount of the first-year deduction.

Step 2. Apply the particular year rate for the asset class to the basis. The result is the depreciation deduction for the year. Depreciation is not prorated in the year of acquisition or year of sale except in the case of real estate. Pay special attention to this rule. This means that in the year you acquired depreciable personal property, the entire depreciation allowed by law for the first year was allowable, regardless of when during the year the asset was purchased. However, in the year of disposal, no depreciation whatsoever is allowed, even if the asset is sold on the last day of the taxable year. This rule requires planning asset dispositions to save depreciation deductions. (In the year real estate is acquired or sold, depreciation may be claimed for the months it was in service.)

EXAMPLE

In October 1985, you bought equipment for $5,000. It is in the five-year class; you claimed the full investment credit of $500 (10% of $5,000). Depreciation for 1987 is $998.

Cost	$5,000
Less 50% of credit	250
Depreciable basis	$4,750
Rate for 3rd year	21%
Depreciation	$ 998

Did you elect straight line depreciation before 1987? If you did, the straight line percentages for ACRS property placed in service before 1987 are as given at the top of the next column:

Recovery Period	Percentage
3 years	33.333%
5 years	20%
10 years	10%
12 years	8.333%
25 years	4%
35 years	2.857%

Because of the half-year convention, only 50% of the above percentages are allowed in the year the property is placed in service. If the property is held for the entire elected recovery period, another half-year of depreciation is allowed for the year following the end of the recovery period. If property is disposed of prior to the end of the recovery period, no cost recovery is allowable in the year of disposition.

EXAMPLE

In 1985, you placed in service business equipment (five-year property) for $5,000 and elected the straight line method over five years. In 1985, you claim a half-year's cost recovery, a full year of cost recovery in the next four years and a half-year in the sixth year.

Year	Rate	Amount of Deduction
1985	10	$ 500
1986	20	1,000
1987	20	1,000
1988	20	1,000
1989	20	1,000
1990	10	500

MACRS FOR REAL ESTATE PLACED IN SERVICE AFTER 1986

¶ **5.31** The recovery period for buildings placed in service after December 31, 1986, is 27.5 years for residential rental property and 31.5 years for nonresidential real property. The method of recovery is the straight-line method using a mid-month convention. To figure the MACRS deduction, you divide the adjusted basis of the property by the number of years of the recovery period. This gives you the annual depreciation deduction. Depreciation in the first and last year varies with the month placed in service; *see* example below.

Residential rental property is a rental building or structure for which 80% or more of the gross rental income for the tax year is rental income from dwelling units. If you occupy any part of the building, the gross rental income includes the fair rental value of the part you occupy.

A dwelling unit is a house or an apartment used to provide living accommodations in a building or structure, but not a unit in a hotel, motel, inn, or other establishment where more than one-half of the units are used on a transient basis.

Mid-month convention. Under a mid-month convention, all property placed in service or disposed of during any month is treated as placed in service or disposed of on the mid-point of that month. You may determine the first-year deduction by applying the percentage from the table below to the original depreciable basis.

EXAMPLE

In December 1987, you buy and place in service an office building for $100,000 and land for $20,000. You use the calendar year. The table below gives a first-year depreciation rate of 0.1323% for nonresidential property placed in service during December. Applying this rate, you get a deduction of $132.

Additions or improvements to property. The depreciation deduction for any additions to, or improvement of, any property is figured in the same way as the deduction for the property would be figured if the property had been placed in service at the same time as the addition or improvement.

FIRST-YEAR REALTY DEPRECIATION RATE												
Buildings placed in service in												
For–	Jan.	Feb.	Mar.	Apr.	May	Jun.	July	Aug.	Sept.	Oct.	Nov.	Dec.
Residential	3.4848%	3.1818%	2.8788%	2.5758%	2.2727%	1.9697%	1.6667%	1.3636%	1.0606%	0.7576%	0.4545%	0.1515%
Non-residential	3.0423%	2.7778%	2.5132%	2.2487%	1.9841%	1.7196%	1.4550%	1.1905%	0.9259%	0.6614%	0.3968%	0.1323%

The MACRS class for the addition or improvement is determined by the MACRS class of the property to which the addition or improvement is made. The period for figuring depreciation begins on the date on which the addition or improvement is placed in service, or if later, the date on which the property to which the addition or improvement was made is placed in service.

DEPRECIATING REAL ESTATE PLACED IN SERVICE BEFORE 1987

¶ 5.32 The ACRS recovery period of a building that is not low-income housing depends on the year the building was placed in service:

For buildings placed in service after May 8, 1985, and before 1987, the recovery period is 19 years.

For buildings placed in service after March 15, 1984, and before May 9, 1985, the recovery period is 18 years.

For buildings placed in service before March 16, 1984, and for all low-income housing, the recovery period is 15 years.

Mobile homes and theme parks are in a 10-year class and agricultural, horticultural and petroleum storage structures are in the 5-year class.

Under transitional rules, some 19-year buildings may be depreciated over 18 years, and some 18-year buildings over 15 years, if placed in service before 1987. Specifically, recovery over 18 years is allowed for a building placed in service after May 8, 1985, provided that *before* May 9, 1985, (1) you began construction or had a binding contract to buy the building and (2) you placed the building in service before the end of 1986. The 18-year period also applies if construction was begun, or a contract entered into by a person who transferred the rights to you and you placed the building in service before 1987. Recovery over 15 years is allowed for a building that you (or a prior owner who transferred the right to you) began constructing or contracted for before March 16, 1984, provided you placed it in service before the end of 1986.

Election to use straight line depreciation. You could elect to use the straight line method over the regular recovery period: 19 years for 19-year property, 18 years for 18-year property, 15 years for 15-year property. Further, for any building, a longer recovery period of either 35 or 45 years was available. An election of the straight line method for real property had to be made on a property-by-property basis, by the return due date, plus extensions, for the year the property was placed in service.

Rate of recovery. The rate of recovery is listed in Treasury tables which are available in IRS Publication 534. Also see Form 4562. The specific rates are adjusted according to the month in the first year in which a building or improvement is placed in service.

Tables found in IRS Publication 534 provide straight line rates over the statutory life and longer optional periods.

Real estate depreciated under straight line method is not subject to depreciation recapture.

Substantial improvements made after 1986 to a building are depreciable under MACRS, not ACRS.

If you dispose of 15-year real property, the ACRS deduction for the year of disposition is based on the number of months in use. However, no deduction is allowed for the month of disposition.

EXAMPLE

On March 2, 1984, you purchase and place in service a building. The building is depreciated over 15 years. The cost of the building is $98,000. On June 1, 1987, you sell the building. The ACRS deduction for 1987 is first figured for the full year; the amount is then prorated for the months of use. The full 1987 ACRS deduction is 8% of $98,000 or $7,840. This amount is then prorated to the five months of full use in 1987. The ACRS deduction is $3,267 (7,840 × ⁵⁄₁₂).

If you dispose of 18-year or 19-year real property, the ACRS deduction for the year of disposition is based on the number of months in use; the number of months in use is determined under a mid-month convention. Under the mid-month convention, real property disposed of any time during a month is treated as disposed of in the middle of that month. You count the month of disposition as one half of a month of use.

EXAMPLE

On July 2, 1984, you buy a building; cost allocated to it is $100,000.

On September 25, 1987, you sell it. The ACRS _____ is figured for the months of use. The full ACRS d_____ 8% of $100,000 or $8,000. This is prorated for th_____ in 1987. The ACRS deduction for 1987 is $5,667 _____.

See ¶ 5.38 for recapture rules on the sale of ACRS property.

WHEN MACRS IS NOT ALLOWED

¶ 5.33 If you place in service personal property which you previously used or which was previously owned by a related taxpayer in 1986, you may not be able to apply MACRS rules. This anti-churning restriction is designed to discourage asset transfers between related persons to take advantage of the MACRS deduction. The anti-churning restriction does not apply to personal property if, for the first full taxable year of service, the deduction allowable under ACRS would be greater than the deduction allowable under MACRS.

The anti-churning rule also does not bar MACRS rules for real estate acquired after 1986, unless you lease back the real estate to a related party who owned it before 1987.

Special rules also apply to the transfer of property in certain tax-free transactions. If you receive property in a tax-free exchange, you may have to use the method used by the transferor in computing the ACRS deduction for that part of basis that does not exceed what was the transferor's basis in the property. To the extent that basis exceeds the transferor's the MACRS rules may apply, for example, when you paid boot in addition to transferring property.

Where property is disposed of and reacquired, the depreciation deduction is computed as if the disposition had not occurred.

FIRST-YEAR EXPENSING

¶ 5.34 You may elect to deduct up to $10,000 of the cost of business equipment subject to the limitations discussed below. Under the election, all or part of your cost for personal property used in a business may be written off in the year of acquisition instead of depreciating the cost under MACRS rules. The election is limited to personal property bought for use in a business. It is not available for realty or property held merely for the production of income. The portion of cost not eligible for first-year expensing is recovered under the regular MACRS rules.

The election must be made on your original return for the year in which the property is acquired. You may not revoke the election without the consent of the IRS.

In 1987, you may deduct up to $10,000 of cost ($5,000 in the case of a married individual filing a separate return).

For property bought by a partnership of an S corporation, the dollar limits apply to the business as well as the owners as individual taxpayers.

EXAMPLE

In 1987, you buy equipment for $13,000. You may deduct up to $10,000 of the cost as an expense and depreciate $3,000 over the five-year recovery period.

> You may claim the full $10,000 in 1987, even if the equipment was placed in service on the last day of the taxable year.

Property does not qualify for the expense election if: (1) it is acquired from a person whose relationship to you would result in a disallowance of loss on a transaction between the taxpayers. *See* ¶ 34.9. For purposes of the expense election, a corporation is controlled by you and thus subject to the loss disallowance rule of ¶ 34.9 if 50% or more of the stock is owned by you, your spouse, your ancestors or descendants; (2) the property is acquired by a member of the same group (using a 50% control test) or (3) the basis of the property is determined in whole or in part (a) by reference to the adjusted basis of the property of the person from whom you acquired it, or (b) under the stepped-up basis rules for property acquired from a decedent.

The cost of property eligible for expensing does not include that part of the basis of such property determined by the basis of property traded in.

Restriction on autos and home computers. To claim the first-year expensing deduction for an auto or a computer placed in service in 1987, you must show business use of more than 50%. Further in the case of an auto placed in service in 1987 the first-year deduction may not exceed $2,560, *see* ¶19.62. The 50% test does not apply to a computer used exclusively at your regular business establishment. A home office qualifying under the rules of ¶5.11 may qualify as a business establishment. The 50% test may also apply to other property such as a plane or boat.

Recapture of expensing deduction. The amount expensed is treated as depreciation taken for purposes of recapture rules. *See* ¶5.39. Gain recognized on disposition of the property is treated as ordinary income to the extent of expense deductions and depreciation taken. Further, if the more than 50% business use test is not met for an automobile or computer in a year after the year it is placed in service, the expensing deduction as well as prior ACRS deductions are subject to recapture. *See* ¶19.65 for recapture details.

Limitations. (1) If the total cost of qualifying property placed in service during a taxable year is over $200,000, the $10,000 limit is reduced dollar-for-dollar by the cost of qualifying property exceeding $200,000. (2) The deduction may not exceed the total taxable income from all businesses which you actively conduct. Taxable income from business is computed without regard to the amount expensed. If qualified costs exceed taxable income, the cost may be carried forward to the next tax year and added to expenses in that year. (3) If a married couple files separate returns, the $10,000 expensing limit and the $200,000 cost limit for qualifying property applies to both taxpayers as a unit. Unless they elect otherwise, 50% of the cost of qualifying property is allocated to each spouse.

SALES OF BUSINESS ASSETS AND PROPERTY

¶ 5.35 The new law leaves intact the following two items concerning the sale of business assets and property:

1. Section 1231 which distinguishes between capital gain and loss and ordinary income and loss. For 1987, the distinction between capital gains and ordinary income still has tax significance because of the maximum tax rate of 28% placed on individual long-term capital gains and the $3,000 limitation placed on capital loss deductions from ordinary income.

2. The depreciation recapture rules of prior taxable years. However, real property acquired after 1986 and subject to MACRS lives of 27.5 years and 31.5 years are not subject to recapture because they are depreciable only under the straight line method.

The following checklist summarizes how sales of assets and property used in business are taxed.

Sales of	Tax treatment
Merchandise, stock in trade, etc.	Profits are taxable as ordinary income; losses are fully deductible. Sales of merchandise are reported in Schedule C if you are self-employed.
Machinery, buildings, office equipment, fixtures, van, truck, and other business property subject to depreciation	Gain is taxable as ordinary income if depreciation recapture rules of ¶5.35 or ¶5.38 apply. Capital gain may apply, if sale comes within rules of ¶5.44. Losses may be deductible as ordinary

Sales of	Tax treatment
	rules of ¶5.44. Sales are reported on Form 4797.
Land	If used in your business, capital gain or ordinary income may be realized under the rules of Section 1231. If held as investment, gain or loss is subject to capital gain treatment. Sales of capital assets are reported on Schedule D.

	See ¶
Sales of depreciable property: Depreciation recapture on property placed in service before 1981	5.35(1)
Recapture on business equipment and other personal property placed in service before 1981	5.36
Recapture on depreciable realty placed in service before 1981	5.37
Recapture of ACRS deductions	5.38
Recapture of first-year expensing	5.39
Additional amortization realized on leasehold improvements	5.40
Gifts and inheritances of depreciable property	5.41

	See ¶
Involuntary conversions and tax-free exchanges of depreciable property	5.42
Installment sale of depreciable property	5.43
Property used in a business (Section 1231 assets)	5.44
Sale of a business	5.45
Covenants not to compete and sale of good will	5.46
Sale of securities purchased to protect business interests	5.47
Sale of property used for business and personal purposes	5.48
Tax-free trades of investment or business property	5.49
Should you trade in business equipment?	5.50

PROFITABLE SALES OF DEPRECIABLE PROPERTY PLACED IN SERVICE BEFORE 1981

¶ 5.35(1) Taxable gain may be realized on the sale of depreciable property when depreciation reduces the basis of the asset to an amount below its current selling price. The gain resulting from depreciation is generally taxable as ordinary income under the rules explained in this section.

EXAMPLE

Assume a truck cost $4,000; depreciation claimed was $3,000. It was sold for $1,200.

Sale proceeds		$1,200
Cost	$4,000	
Less: Depreciation	3,000	1,000
Profit		$ 200

The profit of $200 is attributed to depreciation that reduced the cost basis of $4,000 to $1,000. The profit is taxed as ordinary income.

Recapture rules are not uniform. Different calculations apply to types of property as follows below.

Depreciable business equipment (Section 1245 assets). Profit on sale of depreciable business equipment is taxed as ordinary income to the extent of depreciation taken on the property. (*See* ¶5.36). Intangibles, such as patents and copyrights and elevators and escalators, may be treated as Section 1245 assets. Recapture rules for sports franchise contracts are not discussed in this book.

Livestock (Section 1245 assets). Profit on sale of livestock is ordinary income to the extent of depreciation claimed.

Depreciable real property (Section 1250 assets) Complex rules apply to realty acquired before 1987. Depending on the type of realty held, the method of depreciation and the period held, all, part, or none of the depreciation may be subject to recapture. *See* ¶5.37.

There is no recapture of depreciation for real property held for more than one year and depreciated on the straight line method. After a holding period of a year, recapture applies, under varying formulas, to buildings depreciated under a rapid method of depreciation (such as the 150% or double declining method or the sum of years-digits method). If you sell depreciable realty at a profit within a year after you acquired it, that part of your gain attributed to depreciation is subject to ordinary income tax, regardless of the depreciation method you use.

RECAPTURE ON BUSINESS EQUIPMENT PLACED IN SERVICE BEFORE 1981

¶ 5.36 Profit attributed to depreciation on Form 4797 is taxable as ordinary income. If the actual gain is less than the depreciation subject to recapture, only the gain is taxed as ordinary income. If the gain exceeds the amount of depreciation subject to recapture, the portion of the gain attributable to recapture is ordinary income while the excess may be capital gain under Section 1231 (*see* ¶5.44).

EXAMPLE

You sell equipment for $5,000 when its adjusted basis is $4,000. The gain is $1,000. If the amount of depreciation taken on the equipment is $1,000 or more-all of the gain is taxable as ordinary income. If the depreciation is $600, the $600 is taxable as ordinary income and the balance of the gain of $400 may be capital gain.

Generally, the depreciation deduction taken into account for each year is the amount allowed or allowable, whichever is greater. For purposes of assigning ordinary income (but not for purposes of figuring gain or loss), the depreciation deductions taken into account for any year will be the amount "allowed" rather than the amount "allowable," if the allowed deduction is smaller and you can prove its amount.

Exchanges of property (¶5.48 and ¶6.44), involuntary conversions (¶18.20), and corporate distributions may result in recapture of depreciation. For distributions which are not sales, exchanges, or involuntary conversions, the amount of recapture is all depreciation claimed, but not in excess of the difference between fair market value at disposition or original cost, whichever is less, and adjusted basis.

RECAPTURE ON DEPRECIABLE REALTY PLACED IN SERVICE BEFORE 1981

¶ 5.37 Real property for recapture purposes (Section 1250) includes buildings and structural components, *except* for elevators and escalators or other tangible property used as an integral part of manufacturing, production or extraction, or of furnishing transportation and communications. Property may initially be Section 1250 property and then, on a change of use, become Section 1245 property. Such property may not be reconverted to Section 1250 property.

EXAMPLE

A company builds a parking lot for its employees. Five years later, it converts the lot into a loading area for its trucks. The parking lot, which was originally Section 1250 property, is now Section 1245 property.

General recapture pattern in Form 4797. The amount of recapture depends on the rate of depreciation claimed, the length of time you held the property, and the type of realty. If the realty was held for less than one year, all depreciation taken is subject to recapture. If the realty was held for more than one year, only rapid depreciation claimed after 1969 in *excess* of the amount allowed under the straight line method is subject to recapture. The amount actually recaptured will vary, depending upon whether the property is residential or nonresidential realty, low-income housing, or rehabilitation expenditures. The special rules relating to low-income housing and rehabilitation expenditures are not discussed in this book; *see* Treasury regulations and IRS Publication 544.

Depreciation claimed on realty during the years 1964 through 1969. Depreciation claimed during this period is not recaptured.

Depreciation claimed after 1969. One hundred percent of the excess depreciation claimed after 1969 is subject to recapture, but not in excess of the actual gain. For residential realty, this percentage is reduced, depending on the holding period, for depreciation claimed from 1970 through 1975. For this period, the amount subject to recapture on residential property is reduced 1% per month for each month the property is held beyond 100 months. Only full months are counted (*see* table below).

Real property is considered residential realty for periods after 1975 if 85% or more of gross income is from dwelling units. For periods before 1976, the gross income test was 80% or more.

1970-1975 Percentage Reductions for Residential Realty

Held	%	Held	%
Up to 100 months	100	156 months (13 years)	44
108 months (9 years)	92	168 months (14 years)	32
120 months (10 years)	80	180 months (15 years)	20
132 months (11 years)	68	192 months (16 years)	8
144 months (12 years)	56	200 months (16 years, 8 months) or longer	0

Special recapture rules not discussed here apply to property under certain financial arrangements sponsored by the National Housing Act or similar state of local laws.

Special recapture rules not discussed here also apply to separate elements of improvements.

EXAMPLES

1. Starting in January 1969, you depreciate on the declining balance method a newly constructed office building with a cost of $100,000 (exclusive of land). You take double declining depreciation using a 40-year useful life. After holding the building 18 years, in January 1987, you sell for $90,000. At that time, the adjusted basis of the building is $39,721 ($100,000 less depreciation of $60,279). If straight line depreciation had been taken, the total depreciation would have been $45,000 ($2,500 × 18 years) if salvage value is zero.

   A. Profit on the sale is $50,279 ($90,000–$39,721)

epreciation:

	Claimed	Str. Line	Excess
	$5,000	$2,500	$2,500
	4,750	2,500	2,250
1971	4,513	2,500	2,013
1972	4,287	2,500	1,787
1973	4,072	2,500	1,572
1974	3,869	2,500	1,369
1975	3,675	2,500	1,175
1976	3,492	2,500	992
1977	3,317	2,500	817
1978	3,151	2,500	651
1979	2,994	2,500	494
1980	2,844	2,500	344
1981	2,702	2,500	202
1982	2,567	2,500	67
1983	2,438	2,500	(62)
1984	2,316	2,500	(184)
1985	2,201	2,500	(299)
1986	2,091	2,500	(409)

C. Post-1969 excess at 100% ($55,279–$42,500 $12,779

D. Pre-1970 excess of $2,500 not recaptured   0

    Amount subject to recapture (ordinary income) $12,779

    Amount subject to Section 1231 ($50,279– $12,779)   37,500

2. Same facts as in (1) above except the building was residential realty.

A. Profit on the sale   50,279

B. Additional depreciation—see chart above

C. Post-1975 excess at 100% ($30,113–$27,500) $12,613

    Excess from 1970 through 1975 not subject to recapture (building held for more than 16 years, 8 months)

    Amount subject to recapture (ordinary income) $2,613

    Amount subject to Section 1231 $47,666

The useful life and salvage value for determining depreciation on the straight line method is the same as that used under the rapid depreciation method.

Change in method of depreciation. Where you initially used a rapid method of depreciation but switched to the straight line, *see* Treasury regulations for how to compute depreciation subject to recapture.

RECAPTURE OF ACRS AND MACRS DEDUCTIONS

¶ **5.38** Profitable dispositions of assets depreciable under ACRS are subject to recapture as ordinary income. To figure gain or loss, you subtract ACRS deductions from original cost to determine the adjusted basis of the asset.

Form 4797 is used to figure gain or loss on depreciable property, including the recapture of cost recovery deductions.

Personal property. Adjusted basis of personal property, such as business equipment and machinery, is fixed as of the beginning of the year of disposition because no ACRS deductions are allowed in the year of disposition.

EXAMPLE
In 1985, you bought for $10,000 a truck for your business. In 1985, ACRS deductions were $2,500 and $3,800 in 1986. In November 1987 you sell the truck for $4,000. In 1987, no ACRS deduction is allowed

and basis of the truck is $3,700. Gain on the sale is $300 ($4,000–$3,700) and taxable as ordinary income.

If business use of an automobile drops to 50% or less, recapture of prior ACRS deductions is required; *see* ¶ 19.65.

Real property. For real property subjected to ACRS, adjusted basis for computing gain or loss is the adjusted basis at the beginning of the year reduced by the ACRS deduction allowed for the number of months the realty is in service in the year of disposition (*see* ¶ 5.32).

All gain on the disposition of property held for less than one year is ordinary income. If held more than one year, gain may be taxed as ordinary income due to the recapture of prior cost recovery deductions, according to the following rules:

Personal property and real property not in the ACRS recovery period (Section 1245 assets). Gain on the disposition of personal property is ordinary income to the extent of prior ACRS deductions and the first-year expensing deduction. Further, basis adjustment required on investment credit property placed in service after 1982 will affect recapture in later years. *See* Form 4797.

These recapture rules also apply to gain in the disposition of theme park structures, single purpose agricultural and horticultural structures, and petroleum storage facilities. Gain in excess of prior cost recovery deductions is capital gain subject to the netting rules for Section 1231 assets (*see* ¶ 5.44). These recapture rules follow the pre-1981 recapture rules for personal property (*see* ¶ 5.36).

Nonresidential ACRS recovery period building. If the prescribed accelerated method is used to recover the most of nonresidential property, all gain on the disposition of the realty is recaptured as ordinary income to the extent of recovery allowances previously taken. Thus, nonresidential realty will be treated the same as personal property for purposes of recapture if the accelerated recovery allowance is claimed. If the straight line method is elected, there is no recapture; all gain is capital gain subject to the netting rules of Section 1231 (¶ 5.44).

If accelerated cost recovery is used for a nonresidential building and straight line depreciation is used for a substantial improvement to that building which you are allowed to depreciate separately (*see* ¶ 5.27), all gain on a disposition of the entire building is treated as ordinary income to the extent of the accelerated cost recovery claimed; remaining gain is capital gain taxed under the rules for Section 1231 assets.

Residential ACRS recovery period building. Gain is ordinary income to the extent the recovery allowed under the prescribed accelerated method exceeds the recovery that would have been allowable if the straight line method over the ACRS recovery period had been used. Thus, recapture for residential realty essentially follows the pre-1981 recapture rules discussed at ¶ 5.35. If the straight line method is elected, there is no recapture; all gain is capital gain, subject to Section 1231 netting (¶ 5.44).

15-year low-income rental housing. The same rule as for residential realty applies except that recapture is phased out at the rate of one percentage point per month for property held at least 100 months, so that there is no recapture of cost recovery deductions for property held at least 200 months (16 years, 8 months).

Sale of partnership interest. If a partner sells his interest in a partnership which holds business assets subject to ACRS, gain on the sale is subject to recapture. *See* Treasury regulations.

Mass asset account elections. If mass asset accounts are maintained, computation of gain or loss on account assets may be avoided by making an election to recognize gain to the extent of the proceeds received upon the asset's disposition. The asset's cost basis is fully written off under ACRS and then removed from the account. Check Treasury regulations for details.

Recapture of first-year expensing is discussed at ¶ 5.39.

Recapture of ACRS deductions claimed on an auto because of business use of 50% or less is discussed at ¶ 19.65.

MACRS recapture. Depreciation taken on property acquired after 1986 is claimed under modified ACRS (MACRS). The above recapture rules also apply to depreciation claimed under MACRS.

RECAPTURE OF FIRST-YEAR EXPENSING

¶ 5.39 The first-year expensing deduction under ¶5.34 is treated as depreciation for purposes of recapture. When expensed property is sold or exchanged, gain is ordinary income to the extent of the first year expense deduction plus ACRS deductions, if any. *See* ¶5.38. When expensed property is no longer used more than 50% of the time in a business before the close of the second taxable year following the year it is placed in service, the expensed amount is also subject to recapture to the extent of the tax benefit derived from the expensing deduction.

Automobiles and computers. If the more than 50% business use test for a business automobile or a computer is not met in a year after the auto is placed in service, any first-year expensing deduction is subject to recapture on Form 4797.

Installment sale. If you sell property on the installment basis, the first-year expensing deduction claimed for the property in a prior year is recaptured in the year of sale. An installment sale does not defer recapture of the first-year deduction.

ADDITIONAL AMORTIZATION REALIZED ON LEASEHOLD IMPROVEMENTS

¶ 5.40 If an improvement or cost of acquiring a lease is amortized over the life of the lease including all renewal periods (or the life of the improvement, if that period is shorter), gain on the sale of the lease or leasehold improvement is not subject to ordinary income treatment. However, an amount called excess or additional amortization is subject to ordinary income treatment, Excess or additional amortization is the excess of the actual amortization taken over the lesser period of (1) the original term of the lease plus all renewal periods, or (2) 166⅔% (⅗) of the period of which actual amortization was taken.

If as a lessee, you depreciate an improvement over a useful life that is less than the remaining term of the lease, you follow the rules applying to depreciable property.

GIFTS AND INHERITANCES OF DEPRECIABLE PROPERTY

¶ 5.41 Gifts and charitable donations of depreciable property may be affected by the recapture rules. On the gift of depreciable property, the ordinary income potential of the depreciation carries over into the hands of the donee. When he later sells the property at a profit he will realize ordinary income to the extent described in ¶5.35 or ¶5.38. For purposes of the applicable percentage, the person receiving the gift includes in his holding period the period for which the donor held the property.

On the donation of depreciable property, the amount of the contribution deduction is reduced by the amount which would be taxed as ordinary income if the donor sold the equipment at its fair market value.

On the death of a decedent, the transfer of depreciable property to an heir through inheritance is not a taxable event for recapture purposes. The ordinary income potential does not carry over to the heir because his basis is usually fixed as of the date of the decedent's death.

Important: A gift of depreciable property subject to a mortgage may be taxed to the extent that the liability exceeds the basis of the property. *See* ¶14.6 and ¶31.11.

INVOLUNTARY CONVERSIONS AND TAX-FREE EXCHANGES OF DEPRECIABLE PROPERTY

¶ 5.42 **Involuntary conversions:** Gain may be taxed as ordinary income in either of these two cases: (1) You do not buy a qualified replacement; or (2) you buy a qualified replacement, but the cost of the replacement is less than the amount realized on the conversion. The amount taxable as ordinary income may not exceed the amount of gain that is normally taxed under involuntary conversion rules when the replacement cost is less than the amount realized on the conversion. Also, the amount of ordinary income is increased by the value of any nondepreciable property which is bought as a qualified replacement property, for example, the purchase of 80% or more of stock in a company that owns property similar to the converted property.

Further details may be found in Treasury regulations.

Tax-free exchanges: Ordinary income generally is not realized on a tax-free exchange or trade-in (unless some gain is taxed because the exchange is accompanied by "boot" such as money). The ordinary income potential is assumed in the basis of the new property.

Distributions by a partnership to a partner: A distribution of depreciable property by a partnership to a partner does not result in ordinary income to the distributee at the time of the distribution. But the partner assumes the ordinary income potential of the depreciation deduction taken by the partnership on the property. When he later disposes of the property, he may realize ordinary income.

INSTALLMENT SALE OF DEPRECIABLE PROPERTY

¶ 5.43 If you report on an installment basis a profitable sale of depreciable property made before June 7, 1984, "recaptured" ordinary income is reported before any of the capital gain is reported. You do not allocate the profit element of each installment payment between ordinary income and capital gain. As installments are received, you report all of the ordinary income until that amount is exhausted. For a sale after June 6, 1984, all recaptured ordinary income is fully taxable in the year of sale, without regard to the time of payment. However, this rule does not apply to installment sales made under a contract binding on March 22, 1984, and all times thereafter.

Recapture is figured on Form 4797.

PROPERTY USED IN A BUSINESS (SECTION 1231 ASSETS)

¶ 5.44 The following properties used in a business are considered "Section 1231 assets:"

Depreciable assets such as buildings, machinery, and other equipment held long-term.

Land (including growing crops and water rights underlying farm land) held long-term.

Timber, coal or domestic iron ore subject to special capital gain treatment.

Leaseholds held long-term.

An unharvested crop on farm lands, if the crop and land are sold, exchanged or involuntarily converted at the same time and to the same person and the land has been held long-term. Such property is not included here if you retain an option to reacquire the land.

Dairy, breeding, or draft animals acquired before 1970 and held for at least 12 months.

Cattle and horses acquired after 1969 and held for draft, breeding, dairy or sporting purposes, and held for at least 24 months.

Livestock (other than cattle and horses) acquired after 1969 and held for draft, breeding, dairy or sporting purposes and held for at least 12 months. Poultry is not treated as livestock for purposes of Section 1231.

Long-term holding period. The long-term holding period for property is more than six months. Note however, that unless Congress amends the law, the long-term holding period for property acquired after 1987 is scheduled to increase to more than one year. *See* the supplement.

Capital gain or ordinary loss. Sales and involuntary conversions of Section 1231 property are subject to a rule that allows profit to be taxed as capital gain (except for profits on equipment and real estate allocated to depreciation, see ¶5.35 and ¶5.38) and loss to be deducted as ordinary loss. The exact tax result depends on the net profit and loss realized for all sales of such property made during the tax year. The net result of these sales determines the tax treatment of each individual sale. In making the computation on Form 4797, you must consider also losses and gains from casualty, theft, and other involuntary conversions involving business and investment property held long term.

Recapture of net ordinary losses. Starting in taxable years beginning after December 31, 1984, net Section 1231 gain is not treated as capital gain but as ordinary income to the extent of net Section 1231 losses realized in the five most recent prior taxable years beginning after December 31, 1981. Losses are recaptured in chronological order on Form 4797.

Section 1231 netting. Add all losses and gains (except gains allocated to depreciation recapture) from:

Sale of Section 1231 assets (listed above).

The involuntary conversion of such assets and capital assets held long-term for business or investment purposes. You include casualty and theft losses incurred on business or investment property held long term, whether or not insured. *See exception* below if losses exceed gains from involuntary conversion in one taxable year.

Involuntary conversions of capital assets held for personal purposes are not subject to a Section 1231 computation but are subject to a separate computation, *see* ¶ 18.27.

A net gain is taxed as a long-term capital gain. A net loss is fully deductible and is included as an ordinary asset transaction.

EXAMPLES

1. You realize these gains and losses:

	Gain	Loss
Gain on sale of rental property held six years (no part attributed to rapid depreciation)	$5,000	
Loss on sale of business assets held four years		$3,000
	$5,000	$3,000
Net gain treated as long-term capital gain	$2,000	

As your gain exceeded the loss, each sale is treated as a sale of a capital asset held for more than one year. The net gain is included in Schedule D along with your other long-term gains and losses, if any. The effect of this treatment is to give you a long-term capital gain of $2,000, unless you realized a net Section 1231 loss in 1982, 1983, 1984, 1985, or 1986.

2. Assume the same facts as above but that your gain on the sale of rental property was $2,500. Since the gain does not exceed the loss and a net loss of $500 was realized, all of the transactions are treated as dispositions of noncapital assets. The net result is an ordinary loss of $500.

Involuntary conversion losses exceed involuntary conversion gains from casualties or thefts. You must compute the net financial result from all involuntary conversions arising from fire, storm, shipwreck, or other casualty or theft of assets used in your business and capital assets held for business or income-producing purposes and held long-term. The purpose of the computation is to determine whether these involuntary conversions enter into the above Section 1231 computation. If the net result is a gain, all of the assets enter into the Section 1231 computation. If the net result is a loss, then these assets do not enter into the computation; the losses are deducted separately as casualty losses, the gains reported separately as ordinary income. If you incur only losses, the losses similarly do not enter into the Section 1231 computation.

EXAMPLE

You suffer an uninsured fire loss of $2,000 on equipment used in your business and gain of $1,000 on other insured investment property damaged by a storm. All of the property was held long term. Because loss exceeds gain, neither transaction enters into a Section 1231 computation. The gain is reported as ordinary income and the loss is deducted as an ordinary loss. The effect is a net $1,000 loss deduction. If the figures were reversed, that is, if the gain was $2,000 and the loss $1,000, both assets would enter into the Section 1231 computation. If they are the only two transactions in the year, the net effect may be a net capital gain of $1,000. If only the fire loss had occurred, the loss would be treated as a casualty loss and would not enter into the Section 1231 computation.

Installment sale. Gain realized on the installment sale of business or income-producing property held long-term may be long-term gain one year and ordinary gain another year. Actual treatment in each year depends on the net result of all sales including installment payments received in that year. *See also* ¶ 5.43.

If one spouse has a long-term capital gain and the other has the above type of fully deductible loss, separate returns might be filed to preserve the capital gain treatment and the fully deductible loss.

For an explanation of the ordinary income treatment of gain attributed to depreciation, *see* ¶ 5.35 and ¶ 5.38 .

Reporting Section 1231 transactions. Form 4797 (Supplementary Schedule of Gains and Losses) is used to report Section 1231 transactions and dispositions of property subject to ordinary income recapture. A sample Form 4797 is in the Supplement to this book.

SALE OF A BUSINESS

¶ 5.45 Proprietorship. The sale of a sole proprietorship is not considered as the sale of a business unit but as sales of individual business assets. Each sale is reported separately on your tax return.

Assets Held Over One Year	Capital Asset Yes	No
Customer's accounts		x
Inventory and supplies and stock in trade		x
Stocks and bonds held as investments	x	
Machinery, building, and other equipment used in your business	x*	
Land used in business	x	
Good will and nondepreciable franchises	x	
Depreciable franchises		x
Copyrights by a playwright of dramatic works		x
Literary manuscripts, etc., of a playwright		x
Assignable liquor license	x	
Noncompete contract (officer or employee)		x
Life insurance policy	x	

*See ¶ 5.44 for the rule governing assets used in business. It is possible to get a full deduction for a net loss on a sale or treat net gain as long-term capital gain; but gain allocated to depreciation may be taxed as ordinary income (see ¶ 5.35 and ¶ 5.38).

A purchase of a business involves the purchase of various individual business assets of the business. Under prior law, the seller would generally assign a larger portion of the sales price to capital assets such as goodwill to realize capital gain. The buyer would assign a larger part of the same price to inventory and deductible costs items in order to get larger current deductions. To force buyers and sellers to follow the same allocation rules, a new law requires both the buyer and the seller to allocate the purchase price of a business among the transferred assets using a residual method formula. Generally, under the formula, the sales price is first allocated to the assets other than goodwill and going concern value. Allocations are based on the proportion of sales price to an asset's fair market value and allocations are made in the following order: first allocate selling price to cash, demand deposits and similar accounts; then to certificates of deposit, U.S. government securities, marketable stock or securities and foreign currency, and then to other assets except goodwill and going concern value. Any balance of the selling price is allocated to goodwill. Thus, goodwill is the excess of the purchase price over the aggregate fair market values of the tangible assets and the identifiable intangible assets other than goodwill. Further details of the residual methods of allocation are in Temporary Reg. Sec. 1.338 (b)-2(T).

The new law applies to an "applicable asset acquisition" which is a sale of a group of assets considered a business in which the basis of assets of the business are determined by the price paid for the business. A group of assets is considered a business if their character is such that goodwill or going concern value could under any circumstances attach to the assets.

The new law applies to transactions after May 6, 1986, except for a transaction made under a contract binding on and after that date.

Partnership. A sale of a partnership interest generally gives capital gain. But you have ordinary income to the extent the sales price covers unrealized partnership receivables, appreciated inventory items, and depreciation "recapture" on assets held by the partnership.

Unrealized receivables include any partnership rights to payment for goods delivered or services rendered that have not yet been included in the partnership income under its regular accounting method. Appreciated inventory items are those whose value is more than 120% of the partnership's basis for them: *and* more than 10% of the fair market value of all the partnership's property (except cash).

To compute the amount of ordinary income when you sell out, part of the basis of your partnership interest must be allocated to the interest in the receivables, inventory, and depreciation recapture items. You must attach a statement to your return showing the allocation of basis to receivables and inventory. Further, you must notify the partnership within 30 days of transferring a partnership interest that includes unrealized receivables or appreciated inventory. The partnership in turn notifies the IRS. *See* chapter 10 for these reporting rules.

Poor timing of the sale of your partnership interest may be costly if the partnership reports on a fiscal year basis. In the year of sale, you may bunch more than a year of partnership income. The sale of a partnership interest closes the partnership year or the selling partner. Thus, in the year that you sell out, you must report your share of earnings up to the time of sale, in addition to the earnings from the regular partnership fiscal year.

In the liquidation of a retiring partner's or deceased partner's interest, ordinary income is realized on the amount of the distribution attributed to the partner's distributive share of income or guaranteed salaries or interest. Capital gain treatment is extended only to the value attributed to his partnership interest. And for this purpose, the partnership interest does not include payments for unrealized receivables which, if present, will be reflected as ordinary income. However, good will may be included as part of the partnership interest if the partnership agreement provides for such payment. It may not exceed the reasonable value of the distributee's share of the partnership good will. If the distribution includes appreciated inventory, ordinary income may also be realized.

A sale of only a part interest does not close your partnership tax year.

COVENANTS NOT TO COMPETE AND SALE OF GOOD WILL

¶ **5.46** Payments for the sale of the good will of a business are subject to capital gain treatment. If, along with the sale of good will, a covenant not to compete is also given, the amount allocated to the covenant is subject to capital gain treatment provided the covenant is given to protect the transferred good will. If the covenant is not tied to good will, the payments received for the covenant are taxed as ordinary income. Payments for a noncompete covenant are treated as a form of compensation, that is, compensation not to perform services.

Professionals (lawyers, accountants, engineers, consultants, etc.) have good will in their firm names, which they can sell and have taxed at capital gain rates. The IRS will allow capital gain if the seller remains a member of the firm after the sale, provided good will is shown and the incoming partner has paid for part of it.

For effect of covenants not to compete on self-employment tax, *see* ¶5.51.

SALE OF SECURITIES PURCHASED TO PROTECT BUSINESS INTERESTS

¶ **5.47** To protect a business interest, you may purchase securities of a company, or you may make the purchase of the securities to guarantee the supply of merchandise produced by the company. Under such circumstances, you may argue that your securities are not capital assets. You might take this position when you sell the securities at a loss or when they become worthless. The loss would be fully deductible as an ordinary loss rather than a capital loss. In some cases, courts have allowed such treatment. However, the IRA and Tax Court refuse to allow an ordinary loss deduction where there was an investment motive mixed with a business reason for buying stock. To deduct an ordinary loss, be prepared to show that you had no expectation of making a profit on a rise in value of the shares. In one case, an executive claimed that when he joined a new firm, he was pressured into buying stock by the company's president. The Tax Court and an appeals court allowed only a capital loss. Although he may have felt pressured, his employment contract did not require him to buy the stock as a condition of getting or keeping his job. His invest-

ment motive was evidenced by these facts: (1) He admitted at trial that he thought he would eventually realize a profit on sale of the stock; (2) the contract he signed when buying the stock stated that the stock was being bought as an investment. The court rejected his argument that the contract language was necessary to avoid stock registration problems with the SEC.

If you are selling at a gain, your business motives in buying the stock might be used by IRS as a reason for barring capital gain treatment. However, according to the Tax Court, you may get capital gain treatment even if you had a business motive provided some investment considerations also motivated your decision. The IRS has adopted the Tax Court approach.

Sale of partnership interest bought for business reasons. A purchase of a partnership interest for business reasons does not support ordinary loss deduction on later sale of the interest.

SALE OF PROPERTY USED FOR BUSINESS AND PERSONAL PURPOSES

¶ **5.48** One sale will be reported as two separate sales for tax purposes when you sell a car or any other equipment used for business and personal purposes, or a house used partly as a residence and partly as a place of business or to produce rent income.

You allocate the sales price and the basis of the property between the business portion and the personal portion. The allocation is based on use. For example, with a car, the allocation is based on mileage used in business and personal driving.

EXAMPLE

Two partners bought an airplane for about $54,000. They used approximately 75% of its flying time for personal flights and 25% for business flights. After using the plane for eight years, they sold it for about $35,000. Depreciation taken on the business part of the plane amounted to $13,000. The partners figured they incurred a loss of $6,000 on the sale. The IRS, allocating the proceeds and basis between business and personal use, claimed they realized a profit of $8,250 on the business part of the plane and a nondeductible loss of $14,250 on the personal part. The allocation was as follows:

	Partners' claim	IRS Business (25%)	IRS Personal (75%)
Original cost	$54,000	$13,500	$40,500
Depreciation	13,000	13,000	
Adjusted basis	41,000	500	40,500
Selling price	35,000	8,750	26,250
Gain (Nondeductible loss)	($ 6,000)	$ 8,250	($14,250)

The partners argued that the IRS could not split the sale into two separate sales. They sold only one airplane and therefore there was only one sale. A federal district court and appeals court disagreed and held that the IRS method of allocation is practical and fair.

Other references: Allocation of a partly rented residence, *see* ¶29.15. Trade-in of car, *see* ¶19.64. Recapture of depreciation, *see* ¶5.35 and ¶5.38.

TAX-FREE TRADES OF INVESTMENT OR BUSINESS PROPERTY

¶ **5.49** You may defer tax on gain realized on the "like-kind" exchange of business or investment property. If a loss is incurred on a like-kind exchange, the loss is not deductible (*see* ¶5.50).

EXAMPLES

1. Jones, a real estate investor, purchased a parcel for investment in 1944 for $5,000. In 1982, he exchanged it for another parcel, Parcel B, which had a fair market value of $50,000. The gain of $45,000 is not taxed in 1982.

2. Same facts as above, except that in 1987 Jones sells Parcel B for $50,000. His taxable gain is $45,000. The "tax-free" rules have the effect of deferring tax on appreciation. Tax is finally imposed when the exchanged item is sold.

3. Same facts as in (1) above, but the value of Parcel B was $3,000. Jones may not deduct the loss. The basis of the parcel is $5,000. If Jones sells Parcel B in 1987 for $3,000, he may deduct a loss of $2,000.

For tax-free exchanges, the term "like-kind" refers to the character of the property; that is, whether real estate is traded for real estate, or whether business equipment is traded for business equipment. The term does not refer to the grade, quality or use of the property; that is whether the property is new or used or whether a building is traded for land. Here are examples of approved like-kind trades:

An apartment house for an office building
Farmland for city lots
A building for a lot
Used business truck for a new business truck
Business machine for a business truck
Used business automobile for a new business automobile
Business automobile for a business truck
A leasehold interest of 30 years or more for an outright ownership in realty

However, trading a machine for a building would *not* be a like-kind exchange.

Whether you are holding property as an investment or as a dealer is an issue of fact (see ¶ 31.4).

Receipt of cash or other property. If, in addition to the exchanged property, you receive cash or other property, gain is taxable up to the amount of the cash or other property. The additional cash or other property is called "boot."

EXAMPLE
You received cash of $4,500 in addition to property you exchanged. $4,500 of the gain is subject to immediate tax, provided the gain realized in the exchange was $4,500 or more.

If a loss was incurred on the exchange, the receipt of boot does not permit you to deduct the loss.

Adjustments to basis for unrecognized gain or loss are discussed at ¶ 6.29.

If you give cash or other property in addition to the property exchanged, you add the amount of the boot to the basis of the property received.

If you trade mortgaged property, the amount of the mortgage is part of your boot.

EXAMPLE
A has an office building costing $30,000. It is subject to a $20,000 mortgage. He exchanges this for B's building (having a $35,000 cost) and $5,000 in cash. B takes A's building subject to the mortgage. The $5,000 in cash and B's taking subject to the $20,000 mortgage are both boot. The gain is computed this way:

Received by A:	
Cash received from B	$ 5,000
Building received from B	35,000
Mortgage on building traded to B	20,000
Total	$60,000
Less: Tax cost of building traded to B	30,000
Gain on sale	$30,000
Gain recognized (up to amount of boot)	$25,000

If depreciable property is exchanged, ordinary income may be realized if cash or other boot is taken (see ¶ 5.42).

Property not within the tax-free trade rules:
Property used for personal purposes (except for exchanges of personal residences; see ¶ 29.6)
Property held for sale
Inventory or stock-in-trade

Securities (see ¶ 6.45 for exception)
Notes
Partnership interest, *see* below
See also ¶ 31.5 for tax-free exchange of realty.

Exchange of partnership interests. Exchanges of partnership interests in different partnerships are not within tax-free exchange rules, if made after July 18, 1984, in taxable years ending after July 18, 1984. Prior tax-free exchange rules will apply to: (1) an exchange of partnership interests made under a binding contract effective on March 1, 1984, and at all times afterwards; (2) an exchange of a general partnership interest following a plan of reorganization of ownership interests under a contract taking effect on March 29, 1984, provided that all of the exchanges under the plan are completed on or before December 31, 1984.

Time limits for deferred exchanges. One of the parties to an exchange may not have at the time of contract property which he has promised to exchange. Under prior law, a delay in closing the exchange was not fatal to tax-free treatment. Under current law, the exchange must generally be completed within a 180-day period. The qualifying period may even be shorter than 180 days.

Property will *not* be treated as like-kind property if received after (1) 180 days after the date you relinquished property, or (2) the due date of your return for the year in which you made the transfer, *whichever date is earlier.* Further, the property to be received must be identified within 45 days after the date on which you transferred property. According to committee reports, the 45-day test may be met by describing the property in the contract or by listing a limited number of properties that may be transferred, provided the particular property to be transferred depends on contingencies beyond the control of both parties. For example, you transfer real estate for Smith's promise to transfer property X if zoning changes are approved or property Z if they are not. The exchange will qualify provided the contract covers these points and is made within the time limit. The 45/180–day rules apply to transfers after July 18, 1984, and to transfers on or before that date if the property to be received in exchange is not received before January 1, 1987. For transfers on or before July 18, 1984, the assessment period for a deficiency attributed to the new rule will not expire before January 1, 1988.

The rules do not apply if the property to be received in an exchange is identified in a binding contract in effect on June 13, 1984, and at all times after the transfer, and the property is received before January 1, 1989. The assessment period for these transfers will not expire before January 1, 1990.

SHOULD YOU TRADE IN BUSINESS EQUIPMENT?

¶ **5.50** The purchase of new business equipment is often partially financed by trading in old equipment. For tax purposes, a trade-in may not be a good decision. If the market value of the equipment is below its adjusted basis, it may be preferable to sell the equipment to realize an immediate deductible loss. You may not deduct a loss on a trade-in. However, if you do trade, the potential deduction reflected in the cost basis of the old equipment is not forfeited. The undepreciated basis of the old property becomes part of the basis of the new property and may be depreciated. Therefore, in deciding whether to trade or sell where a loss may be realized, determine whether you will get a greater tax reduction by taking an immediate loss on a sale or by claiming larger depreciation deductions.

If the fair market value of the old equipment exceeds its adjusted basis, you have a potential gain. To defer tax on this gain, you may want to trade the equipment in for new equipment. Your decision to sell or trade will generally be based on a comparison between (1) tax imposed on an immediate sale and larger depreciation deductions taken on the cost basis of the new property; and (2) the tax consequences of a trade-in in which the tax is deferred but reduced depreciation deductions are taken on a lower cost basis of the property. In making this comparison, you will have to estimate your future income and tax rates. Also pay attention to the possibility that gain on the sale may be taxed as ordinary income under the depreciation recapture rules. See ¶ 5.35 and ¶ 5.38.

The tax consequences of a trade-in may not be avoided by first selling the used property to the dealer who sells you the new property. The IRS will disregard the sale made to the same dealer from whom you purchase the new equipment. The two transactions will be treated as one trade-in.

When you trade in a car used partly for business and partly for plea-sure, treat the deal as if you had exchanged and received two different types of assets: A personal asset and a business asset. Allocate part of the costs of the old and new car to your business use and part to your personal use. Figure the results on each part. Trade-in rules for a business auto are discussed at ¶19.64.

SELF-EMPLOYMENT TAX

SELF-EMPLOYMENT TAX RULES

¶ **5.51** You are liable for self-employment tax if you make a profit of $400 or more from operating a business or profession as sole proprietor, in partnership with others, or as an independent contractor. Self-employment tax is figured on Schedule SE, which must be attached to your Form 1040.

For 1987, you pay 12.3% tax on net self-employment income of up to $43,800 ($5,387.40 maximum) when you pay your income tax. The self-employment tax provides funds for Social Security and Medicare benefits.

If you have more than one self-employed operation, your net earnings from all the operations are combined. A loss in one self-employed business will reduce the income from another business.

You continue to pay self-employment tax on self-employment income regardless of age and even if you receive Social Security benefits.

If you also received wages, see ¶5.53.

You must include the self-employment tax on your estimated tax declaration. Self-employment tax is added to your income tax liability. The two taxes are paid as one amount. Tax changes for 1988 self-employment tax are in the Supplement.

Self-employment tax rules for various positions or activities

Clergy. An ordained minister, priest or rabbi (other than a member of a religious order who has taken a vow of poverty) is subject to self-employment tax, unless he elects not to be covered on the grounds of conscientious or religious objection to Social Security benefits. Before 1968, a minister had to elect Social Security coverage.

An application for exemption from Social Security coverage must be filed on or before the due date of a minister's income tax return for the second taxable year for which he has net earnings from his services as a clergyman of $400 or more (Form 4361).

An exemption, once granted, is generally irrevocable. However, a law did allow revocation of the exemption for 1977 or 1978. An exemption will not be granted to a minister who elected coverage under prior law.

Consultant. The IRS generally takes the position that income earned by a consultant is subject to self-employment tax. The IRS has also held that a retired executive hired as a consultant by his former firm received self-employment income, even though he was subject to an agreement prohibiting him from giving advice to competing companies. According to the IRS, consulting for one firm is a business; it makes no difference that he acts as a consultant only with his former company. The IRS has also imposed self-employment tax on fees although no services were performed for them.

The courts have generally approved the IRS position.

Director of a company. You are taxed as a self-employed person if you are not an employee of the company. Fees for attendance at meetings are self-employment income.

Employees of foreign governments or international organizations. If you are a U.S. citizen and you work in the United States, you pay tax as a self-employed worker although you are an employee of a foreign government or its wholly-owned instrumentality, or of an international organization given privileges, exemptions, and immunities by the International Organizations Immunities Act.

Executor. As a professional fiduciary, you will always be treated as having self-employment income, regardless of the assets held by the estate. But if you serve as a nonprofessional executor or administrator for the estate of a deceased friend or relative, you will not be treated as having self-employment income unless all of the following tests are met: (1) The estate includes a business. (2) You actively participate in the operation of the business. (3) All or part of your fee is related to your operation of the business.

Public officials and employees of a state or political subdivision. You may be subject to self-employment tax if you are compensated solely by fees. However, you do not have to pay self-employment tax on your fees if your services are covered by a state Social Security coverage agreement, or you elected exemption. (The election must have been made in 1968 and is irrevocable.)

Farmers. Cash or a payment-in-kind under the Payment-in-Kind program is considered earned income subject to self-employment tax.

Lecturer. You are not taxed as a self-employed person if you give only occasional lectures. If, however, you seek lecture engagements and get them with reasonable regularity, your lecture fees are treated as self-employment income.

Writer. Royalties from writing books are self-employment income to a writer. Royalties on books by a professor employed by a university may also be self-employment income despite employment as a professor.

Nurse. A registered nurse or a licensed practical nurse, when hired for private nursing services, is considered self-employed. He or she is an employee when hired by a hospital or a private physician in his practice and works for a salary following a strict routine during fixed hours.

> Nurses' aides, domestics, and other unlicensed individuals who classify themselves as practical nurses are employees. They do not pay self-employment tax. This is true regardless of whether they work for a medical institution, a private physician, or a private household.

Technical service contractors. Consulting engineers and computer technicians who receive assignments from technical service agencies are generally treated as employees and do not pay self-employment tax. The IRS distinguishes between (1) technicians who in three-party arrangements are assigned clients by a technical services agency and (2) those who directly enter into contracts with clients. Employee status covers only technicians in group (1).

Technical specialists who contract directly with clients may be classified as independent contractors by showing that they have been consistently treated as independent contractors by the client, and that other workers in similar positions have also been treated as independent contractors. Thus, they may treat their income as self-employment income.

Firms that are now considered employers of technical specialists are responsible for withholding and payroll taxes.

Babysitters. Where you perform services in your own home and determine the nature and manner of the services to be performed, you are considered to have self-employment income. However, where services are performed in the parent's home according to instructions by the parents, you are an employee of the parents and do not have earnings.

Nonresident alien. You do not pay Social Security tax on your self-employment income derived from a trade, business, or profession. This is so even though you pay income tax. Your exemption from self-employment tax is not influenced by the fact that your business in the United States is carried on by an agent, employee, or partnership of which you are a member. However, if you live in Puerto Rico, the Virgin Islands, American Samoa, or Guam, you are not considered a nonresident alien and are subject to self-employment tax.

Dealers in commodities and options. Registered options dealers and commodities dealers are subject to self-employment tax on net gains from trading in Section 1256 contracts, which include regulated futures contracts, foreign currency contracts, dealer equity options and nonequity options. Self-employment tax also applies to net gains from trading property related to such contracts, such as stock used to hedge options. Long-term gains are considered in full without regard to the capital gains deduction.

Real estate agents and door-to-door salespersons. Licensed real estate agents are considered self-employed if they have a contract specifying that they are not to be treated as employees and if substantially all of their pay is related to sales rather than number of hours worked.

The same rule also applies to door-to-door salesmen with similar contracts who work on a commission basis selling products in homes or other non-retail establishments.

PARTNERS PAY SELF-EMPLOYMENT TAX

¶ 5.52 A partner includes his share of partnership income or loss in his net earnings from self-employment, including guaranteed payments. If your personal tax year is different from the partnership's tax year, you include your share of partnership income or loss for the partnership tax year which ends within 1987.

A limited partner is not subject to self-employment tax on his share of partnership income except for guaranteed payments which are subject to the tax.

If a partner dies within the partnership's tax year, his self-employment income includes his distributive share of the income earned by the partnership through the end of the month in which his death occurs. This is true even though his estate succeeds to his partnership rights. For this purpose, partnership income for the year is considered to be earned ratably each month.

Retirement payments you receive from your partnership are not subject to self-employment tax if the following conditions are met:
   1. The payments are made under a qualified written plan providing for periodic payments on retirement of partners with payments to continue at least until death.
   2. You rendered no service in any business conducted by the partnership during the tax year of the partnership ending within or with your tax year.
   3. By the end of the partnership's tax year, your share in the partnership's capital has been paid to you in full, and there is no obligation from the other partners to you other than with respect to the retirement payments under the plan.

WHAT IS SELF-EMPLOYMENT INCOME?

¶ 5.53 Your self-employment income is generally your net profit from your business or profession whether you participate in its activities full or part time. However, according to the Tax Court, business interruption insurance proceeds are not subject to self-employment tax. Even though the proceeds are a substitute for lost profits, they do not arise from some actual income-producing activity, but rather, from the lack of such activity.

The following types of income or items are *not* included as self-employment income on Schedule SE:

1. Rent from real estate is not self-employment income— *unless* it is the business income of a real estate dealer or income in a business where some services are rendered the occupant as in the leasing of—

Rooms in a hotel or in a boardinghouse.
Apartments (extra services).
Cabins or cabanas in tourist camps where you provide maid services, linens, utensils, and swimming, boating, fishing and other facilities, for which you do not charge separately.
Rents from the leasing of farm land in which the landlord materially participates in the actual production of the farm or in the management of production is considered self-employment income. For purposes of "material participation," the activities of a landlord's agent are not counted; only the landlord's actual participation.

The owner of one office building, who holds it for investment (rather than sale in the ordinary course of business), is not a real estate dealer. His rent income is not self-employment income. Furnishing heat, light, water, and trash and garbage collection to tenants is not services producing self-employment income.

2. Dividends and interest are not self-employment income. However, dividends earned by a dealer in securities and interest on accounts receivable are treated as self-employment income. A dealer is one who buys stock as inventory to sell to customers.

Income reported under an S election is not subject to self-employment tax.

3. Capital gains are not self-employment income. Similarly not treated as self-employment income are gains from the sale of property which is not inventory or held for sale to customers in the ordinary course of business. See exception for dealers in commodities and options in ¶5.51.

Net operating loss deduction. A loss carryover from past years does not reduce business income for self-employment tax purposes. Similarly, the personal exemption may not be used to reduce self-employment income.

Where you and your spouse *each* have self-employment income, each spouse must figure separate self-employment income on separate schedules. Each pays the tax on the separate self-employment income. Both schedules are attached to the joint return.

If you live in a community property state, business income is not treated as community property for self-employment tax purposes. The spouse who is actually carrying on the business is subject to self-employment tax on the earnings.

In 1987, you do not pay self-employment tax on more than $43,800. If your net earnings from self-employment are over $43,800, you pay $5,387.40 (12.3% of $43,800).

In 1987, if you also had wages of $43,800 or more as an employee in covered employment, you do not pay self-employment tax on your net earnings from self-employment. If you had wages of less than $43,800, you pay on the difference between your wages and $43,800. If that difference exceeds your net earnings from self-employment, you pay on your net earnings.

EXAMPLE
In 1987, you have $44,000 net earnings from self-employment and $2,000 of wages subject to Social Security (FICA) tax. Only $41,800 earned from your business ($43,800–$2,000) is subject to the self-employment tax. If your net earnings from self-employment had been $5,000, then $5,000 would be subject to the self-employment tax.

When net self-employment earnings are less than $400, you pay no self-employment tax.

Optional self-employment income base. If your net self-employment income is less than $1,600, you may be allowed to pay self-employment tax on an increased base of up to $1,600. This option may allow you to increase your Social Security benefit base. If you are regularly self-employed, an optional method may be elected if your net earnings from non-farm self-employment are (1) less than $1,600 and (2) less than two-thirds of gross non-farm income and (3) you had net earnings of $400 or more from self-employment (both farm and non-farm) for two out of these three years: 1984, 1985, 1986.

6

CAPITAL GAINS AND LOSSES ON SALES OF PROPERTY

Sample illustrations of reporting gains and losses on the sale of property may be found at ¶6.60.

¶ 6.1 Long-term capital gain may still provide tax savings in 1987 despite repeal of the capital gains deduction.

How sales are taxed. Your gains and losses from sales and exchanges of property are not treated equally under the tax law. The varying tax effects on your sale depend generally on your purpose in holding the property.

WHAT KIND OF GAIN OR LOSS DO YOU HAVE?

Sale of Property Held for	Your Gain Is—	Your Loss Is—
Investment (stock, bonds, land, etc.) See ¶6.6.	Capital	Capital
Personal use (home, car, jewelry, etc.) See ¶6.7.	Capital	Nondeductible
Sale to customers (merchandise, etc.) See ¶5.5.	Ordinary income	Ordinary
Use in your business (Section 1231 property, such as depreciable buildings, trucks, machines, and equipment) See ¶5.44.	Capital or ordinary income	Capital or ordinary

Your 1987 gain is treated as capital gain if:
1. *You have a capital asset or the kind of asset the gain on which qualifies as capital gain.* For example, securities which you hold for investment are capital assets. Other capital assets are described at ¶6.6.
2. *You sold or exchanged the property or your transaction was the kind that is treated as a sale or exchange.* This test is automatically met when you sell property; for example, securities, real estate, etc. Nonsale dispositions that may qualify for capital gains treatment are discussed at ¶6.9.
3. *How long have you held the property?* Capital gains and losses are either short term or long term, according to the length of time the asset has been held. This is an important distinction. Net short-term capital gains are fully taxable at ordinary income rates. Net long-term capital gains are also fully taxable, but the maximum 1987 rate on long-term gains is 28%, if your top rate on other income is higher. *See* ¶6.2. A short-term gain results from the sale or exchange of property held for six months or less; long-term gain after a holding period of more than six months.

You may be able to spread the tax on gain. If the sale qualifies as an installment sale, you do not pay all the tax in one year, but over several years. *See* ¶6.34.

You may be able to defer tax. Tax may be deferred on certain sales or exchanges. The gain on the sale of your personal residence is not taxed when you use the proceeds to buy or build another (chapter 29). You also defer tax when you exchange investment real estate (¶6.44 and ¶31.5). If your property is destroyed or appropriated by government action and with the indemnity proceeds you buy other property, you may also defer tax (*see* ¶18.21).

Before 1987, the 60% capital gain deduction allowed long-term capital gain to be taxed at low income tax rates by leaving only 40% of net long-term capital gains to be taxed along with your other income. Thus, if you were in the 50% bracket, the effective tax rate on long-term capital gains was 20% (40% × 50%). In 1987, the 60% capital gain deduction is not available but the top tax on net long-term gains cannot exceed 28%. This is a tax break if your taxable income is subject to rates exceeding 28%. To allow this benefit to long-term gains, the law retains all of the distinctions between short- and long-term capital gain. Further, by leaving the structure for capital gains and losses intact, Congress has left the door open to a possible reinstatement of a capital gains deduction should tax rates be increased in future years.

As for 1987 capital losses, they first offset capital gains, and any remainder is deductible up to $3,000 from other income ($1,500 for married persons filing separately). Net long-term losses do not have to be reduced by 50% before being deducted against other income as was required before 1987.

HOW CAPITAL GAINS AND LOSSES ARE REPORTED

¶ 6.2 You use Schedule D to report capital gains and losses.

If your regular 1987 tax bracket does not exceed 28% (*see* rate schedules at chapter 22), net long-term capital gains are fully taxable at your regular rate, the same as your short-term gains. However, if your regular 1987 tax bracket exceeds 28%, the tax on your 1987 net long-term gains will be limited to 28%. Specifically, the 28% top rate applies to *net capital gains*, which are net long-term gains less net short-term capital losses.

Computing the 28% tax ceiling on net capital gains. You will not be concerned with computing the 28% ceiling if your 1987 taxable income including net capital gain income (excess of long-term capital gains over short-term capital losses) is—

$45,000 or less using joint return rates (including qualifying widow(er))
$38,000 or less using head-of-household rates
$27,000 or less using single return rates
$22,500 or less using married filing separately rates

These amounts are the levels at which the 28% tax bracket ends and the 35% bracket begins. If your taxable income exceeds these amounts and you have any net capital gain, you will save taxes by applying the 28% ceiling. There is an alternative method of computing your tax so that net capital gain is not taxed at rates exceeding 28%. Compute your tax using the 28% ceiling by following these steps:

1. Enter your taxable income $____
2. Subtract your net capital gain (net long-term capital gain less net short-term capital loss)   ____
3. Taxable income without net capital gain   ____
4. Enter $16,800 if you are single*
      $28,000 if you use joint return rates*
      $23,000 if you use head of household rates*
      $14,000 if you are married filing separately*   ____
5. Enter the greater of line 3 or line 4   ____
6. Subtract line 5 from line 1   ____
7. Figure the amount of tax on line 5   ____
8. Multiply line 6 by 28% and enter the result   ____
9. Add lines 7 and 8. This is your tax for 1987. $____

*These amounts are the taxable income levels at which the 28% rate starts in the 1987 schedules, which are in chapter 22.

EXAMPLE

In 1987, you file a joint return showing a taxable income of $50,000, including a net capital gain of $5,000. Your 1987 tax is $10,240.

1. Taxable income	$50,000
2. Net capital gain	5,000
3. Taxable income without net capital gain	$45,000
4. Starting point for 28% tax rate on joint return	28,000
5. Greater of line 3 or 4	45,000
6. Net capital gain subject to ceiling	5,000
7. Tax before adding capital gain tax	8,840
8. 28% of $5,000 on line 6	1,400
9. Add lines 7 and 8. This is the alternative tax for 1987	$10,240

Without the alternative tax, the tax on $50,000 would be $10,590. The alternative tax provides a tax savings of $350 for the $5,000 of net capital gain that would otherwise be taxed at 35%. The amount of the saving is the 7% difference between the 28% ceiling and the 35% regular rate or $350 (7% of $5,000).

Capital gains deduction retained for dairy cattle. The repeal of the 60% capital gain deduction does not apply to certain gains from the sale of cattle under the U.S. Department of Agriculture milk production termination program. The capital gains deduction applies only to gains realized (under your method of accounting) after January 1, 1987, and before September 1, 1987.

Form 1099-B. You should receive a statement from your broker, Form 1099-B (or equivalent), reporting your total sales of stocks and bonds during 1987. Income from a bartering exchange is also reported on Form 1099-B. Amounts shown on Form 1099-B (or equivalent) must be listed on a specific line of Schedule D. The IRS may compare the amounts reported on Form 1099-B with the amounts reported on your return. There may be a difference between the gains and losses you enter on Schedule D and the amounts reported on the Forms 1099-B. If so, you must attach a statement reconciling the differences. For example, you may receive a Form 1099-B for a transaction that is not reportable as a sale, such as a distribution that is a tax-free return of capital. You would enter the amount shown on the Form 1099-B on the designated line but not report the details of the transaction; on a separate statement you would explain that no gain or loss was realized. You may not receive a Form 1099-B for a 1987 sale which you are reporting on Schedule D, such as a year-end sale which your broker incorrectly reported on 1988 Form 1099-B instead of a 1987 form. You would include the details of the sale in the appropriate short-term or long-term section of Schedule D and on an attached statement note that a Form 1099-B for 1987 was not received.

FIGURING CAPITAL GAINS AND LOSSES

¶ 6.3 You segregate 1987 transactions into two groups: (1) Sales of property held long-term; (2) sales of property held short-term. A short-term gain or loss results from the sale or exchange of property held for six months or less; long-term gain or loss after a holding period of more than six months. In each group, offset gains and losses. In the long-term group, offset long-term gains and losses from each other. In the short-term group, offset short-term gains and losses from each other. Depending upon all your transactions in 1987, you will have one of these results:

1. Net long-term gain. Your net long-term gain is added to your other income reported on Form 1040. Long-term gains are fully includable in 1987 income. However, the maximum 1987 tax rate on net long-term gains is 28%.

2. Net long-term loss. You may deduct 100% of your long-term loss from other income, up to a maximum deduction of $3,000 ($1,500 if married filing separately). The prior law rule that limited the deduction to only 50% of net long-term loss does not apply to 1987 losses. If your net long-term loss exceeds the $3,000 (or $1,500) maximum deduction, you may carryover the excess. The computation of the carryover is discussed at ¶6.4.

EXAMPLE

Your only capital asset transaction is a sale of securities held long-term. You realize a loss of $7,000. Your other income from salary, dividends, and interest is $28,000. You deduct $3,000 from your other income of $28,000. You have a carryover loss of $4,000 to 1988 and later years.

3. Net short-term gain. Add the full amount of it to your other income on Form 1040. Short-term gain is fully taxed as ordinary income.

EXAMPLE

Your only capital asset transaction is a sale of stock held for five months. You realize a profit of $8,000, which is shown on Schedule D, and then added to your ordinary income on Form 1040.

4. Net short-term loss. You deduct this loss from your other income up to $3,000 ($1,500 if married filing separately). If the loss exceeds your ordinary income or is over $3,000 (or $1,500), the unused loss is carried over as a short-term loss to 1988 and later years.

EXAMPLE

Your only capital asset transaction is a sale of stock held for four months. You realize a loss of $800. You have ordinary income of $20,000 from salary. You deduct the $800 from your ordinary income on Form 1040. If the loss were $3,200, only $3,000 of the loss would be deducted from your ordinary income. The remaining $200 is carried over as a short-term loss to 1988.

5. Net long-term gain and net short-term gain. 100% of the net long-term gain and 100% of the net short-term gain are added to your other income on Form 1040. However, the tax rate on the net long-term gain may not exceed 28% in 1987.

EXAMPLE
You sell one lot of securities held for two years at a profit of $6,000. You sell another lot held for two months at a profit of $4,000. The total profit of $10,000 is added to your other income on Form 1040 but the tax rate on long-term profit may not exceed 28%.

6. Net long-term gain and net short-term loss. Deduct the net short-term loss from the net long-term gain. If the net short-term loss exceeds the net long-term gain, the remaining loss is deductible from other income up to $3,000 ($1,500 for married individuals filing separately). After this deduction from ordinary income, any remaining loss is carried over to later years as a short-term loss. If the long-term gain exceeds the short-term loss, 100% of the remaining long-term gain is added to other income but subject to a top tax rate of 28%.

EXAMPLE
You sell two lots of securities held for two years at a profit of $9,000. You also sell a lot of securities held for three months at a loss of $10,000. Combining both the loss and the gain leaves a short-term capital loss of $1,000, which may be deducted from ordinary income. If the short-term loss were $4,000, a net long-term capital gain of $5,000 ($9,000–$4,000) would have resulted and would be added to income and subject to a tax rate not exceeding 28%.

7. Net short-term gain and net long-term loss. Deduct the long-term loss from the short-term gain. If the gain exceeds the loss, add the full amount of the remaining gain to your other income. If the loss exceeds the gain, the remaining long-term loss is deductible from other income up to $3,000 ($1,500 for married filing separately).

EXAMPLE
You realize a net short-term gain of $3,000 and net long-term loss of $4,000. By combining both figures, you get a net loss of $1,000, which is deductible from ordinary income on Form 1040. If the long-term loss were $2,500, net gain of $500 would be added to your ordinary income.

8. Net long-term loss and net short-term loss. The losses are combined and reduce up to $3,000 of ordinary income on your 1987 return. Losses in excess of $3,000 are carried over to 1988. On your 1987 Schedule D, the short-term loss carryover is figured separately from your long-term loss carryover. The distinction between short-term loss carryovers and long-term carryovers has been retained even though long-term losses no longer have to be reduced by 50%.

CAPITAL LOSS CARRYOVERS

¶ 6.4 You have a capital loss carryover when the ordinary income ceiling of up to $3,000 prevents you from deducting the full amount of your net capital loss. You have an unlimited period of time to deduct the loss from future gains, but you do not have the option to defer claiming the deduction in a year in which the deduction provides no tax benefit.

EXAMPLE
In 1973, Smith had a long-term capital loss and no income. In 1974, he had a small adjusted gross income which was almost offset by itemized deductions and exemptions. He decided not to deduct any part of

his carryover loss in 1974 so that he could deduct it in later years when his income would be larger. The IRS ruled he had no choice but to reduce the loss carried over to 1975 by the amount deductible from his 1974 gross income.

On Schedule D, you compute the carryover for both long- and short-term losses, which keep their character over the carryover period. If the original loss is short-term, the carryover is short-term; if long-term, the carryover is long-term.

EXAMPLES
1. From 1986, you have a long-term capital loss carryover of $2,000. In 1987, you have ordinary income of $15,000, a long-term gain of $2,000, and short-term gain of $3,000. The long-term capital loss carryover is applied to and offsets the long-term capital gain.

2. From 1986, you have a short-term capital loss carryover of $5,000. In 1987, you have ordinary income of $15,000, a short-term gain of $1,000, and a long-term gain of $1,000. The carryover is first applied to the short-term gain which is eliminated. The remaining loss of $4,000 is then applied to the long-term gain which is eliminated. The remaining $3,000 of loss is deducted from ordinary income. The carryover has been eliminated.

Nonresident aliens who are not in business in the United States are not allowed a carryover.

Unused carryovers of a deceased person may not be used by his estate.

Pre-1970 losses. Special carryover rules for pre-1970 long-term losses no longer apply in 1987. Under prior law, a long-term capital loss carryover from pre-1970 years was not reduced by 50% before it was deducted from ordinary income.

CAPITAL LOSSES OF MARRIED COUPLES

¶ 6.5 On a joint return, the capital asset transactions of both spouses are combined in one Schedule D. A carryover loss of one spouse may be applied to capital gains of the other spouse. Where both spouses incur net capital losses, only one capital loss deduction of up to $3,000 is allowed. This rule may not be avoided by filing separate returns. If you file separately, the deduction limit for each return is $1,500.

EXAMPLE
You and your spouse individually incurred capital losses of $5,000 and $4,000. If you file separate returns, the maximum amount deductible from ordinary income on each return is $1,500.

Death of spouse. The IRS holds that if a capital loss is incurred by a spouse on his or her own property and that spouse dies, the surviving spouse may not claim any unused loss carryover on a separate return.

EXAMPLE
In 1983, Smith realized a substantial long-term capital loss on separately owned property, which was reported on his 1983 joint return. Part of the excess loss was carried over to the couple's 1984 joint return, and in 1985, before the carryover loss was used up, Smith died. His widow could claim the unused carryover, up to the $3,000 limit, on a joint return filed for 1985, the year of death. However, any remaining loss carryover to 1986 or later years is lost. Although the loss was originally reported on a joint return, the widow may only claim her allocable share of the loss on her separate returns. Since the loss property was owned solely by the deceased husband, no loss is allocable to the widow's separate returns.

CAPITAL ASSET TRANSACTIONS

WHAT ARE CAPITAL ASSETS?

¶ 6.6 Generally, all properties that you own are capital assets if you are not in a business or other income-producing activity. This means that gains and losses on sales of these assets are subject to capital gain or loss treatment as explained at ¶6.1. There is, however, one important limitation applied to losses on sales of property used for personal purposes: The losses are not deductible. See ¶6.7.

If you are in a business or other income-producing activity, your property may be capital assets, Section 1231 assets, or inventory or stock-in-trade assets. Tax treatment of Section 1231 assets is discussed at ¶5.44. Profit from the sale of inventory or stock-in-trade assets is taxable at ordinary income tax rates; loss is generally fully deductible.

The following are not capital assets:
1. Inventory items
2. Stock in trade
3. Property held primarily for sale to customers in the ordinary course of business; for example, subdivided lots held by a real estate dealer.
4. Depreciable property or real estate used in a trade or business (but see ¶5.44).
5. Copyrights, literary, musical, or artistic compositions, a letter or memorandum or similar property held by the creator of the property or other persons who obtained the property from the creator in a tax-free exchange or as a gift. A letter or memorandum that was prepared or produced for you is also not a capital asset.
6. Accounts or notes receivable acquired in the ordinary course of business from the sale of inventory or property held primarily for sale to customers, or for services rendered as an employee.

EXAMPLES OF CAPITAL ASSETS

¶ 6.6(1) All assets that fit into any of the following categories are considered capital assets (provided you are not a dealer in those assets and they are not your regular stock in trade)—
Stocks, bonds, and other securities.
Land, buildings, and other property not used in your business.
Warehouse receipts in which you trade or speculate.
Notes you purchased and did not hold for sale to customers in the ordinary course of your business.
Commodity and other futures bought or sold when you are speculating. You realize ordinary income or loss when you hedge with futures. For example, a cotton merchant before or at the time of contract, to sell and deliver cotton at a future date, also contracts to buy cotton for future delivery. He is insuring himself against price fluctuations. His activity is considered a true hedge. See also ¶6.16.
Expiration records sold by an insurance agent. An insurance agent generally owns the expiration records of fire and casualty insurance sold by him. These records show the beginning and expiration dates and types of policies sold. With this information, the agent can obtain renewals from clients when their policies are about to expire.
Patents, royalty interests, etc., not used in your business.

Literary properties bought for investment; for example, stories bought by a radio commentator and a motion picture director for a hoped-for resale to the movies. These are isolated dealings, not part of their business.
Trademarks.
Obligations of state or federal governmental bodies. See ¶4.14 for special ordinary income rules for Treasury Bills.

Dealers: Property you own may be treated as a capital asset even though you sell similar property in your business. For example, not all securities held by a dealer in securities are stock-in-trade assets. Securities held for investment or speculation, not as stock in trade, are capital assets. Real estate dealers, see ¶31.4.

PROPERTY USED FOR PERSONAL PURPOSES

¶ 6.7 Your residence, personal automobile, jewelry, home equipment, furniture, antiques, clothing, and similar property used for personal purposes are capital assets.

Profits from the sale of personal assets are subject to capital gains treatment. Losses are not deductible unless the properties are acquired in a transaction entered into for profit (see ¶6.8).

Some assets may be held both for personal and business purposes, such as an automobile used by a salesman in his work and used on weekends for pleasure. As explained in ¶5.48, the asset is treated as two separate assets for purposes of figuring gain or loss from its sale.

CAN YOU DEDUCT LOSSES ON SALE OF PERSONAL ASSETS?

¶ 6.8 Here are deduction rules for the following types of property:

Pleasure auto, yacht, or other vehicle

Yes...
If acquired for the purpose of making a profit on resale and used for pleasure purposes to a slight degree.
If acquired and used for business purposes except for an occasional pleasure trip.
If used solely to demonstrate to prospective purchasers.
If sold by an executor for an estate. All transactions of an executor for an estate are assumed to be profit-seeking. The estate may claim a loss on the sale of a personal asset for less than its fair market value, even though the decedent could not if he had sold it.

No...
If acquired for pleasure use—only incidentally with the hope of making a profit on resale.

Jewelry, furs, and other personal effects

Yes...

If acquired for the purpose of making a profit on resale even if worn incidentally for ornamentation.

No...

If acquired for personal adornment—even though believed to be a safer investment than stocks, bonds, or real estate.

Paintings and works of art

Yes...

If acquired for the purpose of making a profit on resale. You indicate a profit motive when, for example, you employ an artist to clean and prepare a painting for sale, or place it with an art gallery for sale.

No...

If acquired for personal use and enjoyment and held for many years without attempting to make a profit from it.

Coins, postage stamps, or autograph collections

Yes...

If acquired primarily for financial gain even though you derive some incidental pleasure from the collection.

If you bought a collection, you do not have to wait until you sell all of it before you may take your loss. You may allocate a portion of your cost to each part. Then find your gain or loss when each unit is sold. If an apportionment is impracticable, you may wait until you sell the entire collection before taking the loss.

No...

If acquired mainly for personal pleasure.

Residences— *See* ¶ 29.11.

Sublease of apartment. Instead of breaking a lease, a tenant who finds that he must move decides to sublet his apartment but finds he can rent it only at a rental lower than he pays. According to the IRS, he may not deduct his loss, the difference between his rent and the rent he collects.

SALE OR EXCHANGE USUALLY REQUIRED FOR CAPITAL ASSET TREATMENT

¶ **6.9** Capital asset treatment generally requires a sale or exchange of a capital asset.

Exchanges treated as tax-free transactions are discussed at ¶ 6.44, ¶ 12.20, ¶ 29.3, ¶ 31.5.

> A forced or involuntary sale, such as a foreclosure sale of mortgaged property, a condemnation of property, or the sale of property pledged as collateral, is treated as a sale. The IRS and some courts also consider a voluntary conveyance of mortgaged property to the mortgagee as a sale, whether or not the mortgagor is personally liable on the debt. The IRS, Tax Court and some appeals courts also treat an abandonment of mortgaged property as a sale. If your mortgaged property is foreclosed or repossessed, and the bank or other lender reacquires it, you will receive from the lender Form 1099-A. Form 1099-A will also be sent if a lender knows that you have abandoned the property. The Form 1099-A indicates the fair market value of the property when abandoned or reacquired by the lender, the amount of your debt and whether you were personally liable. The IRS may compare its copy of Form 1099-A with your return to check if you have reported income from the foreclosure or abandonment. *See* IRS Publication 544 for further details.

A debtor who gives property to his creditor in satisfaction of a debt transacts a sale or exchange. Gain or loss is the difference between adjusted basis of the property and the amount of debt. Similarly, an execu-

tor who transfers property to an heir in satisfaction of a cash bequest transacts a taxable sale for the estate.

A property settlement accompanying a divorce is treated as a tax-free transfer, *see* ¶ 6.49.

The IRS and most courts treat a gift of mortgaged property as a sale if the amount of the mortgage exceeds the donor's basis; the excess is taxable gain to the donor.

Capital asset treatment applies to the following transactions even though a sale or exchange has not occurred:

A nonbusiness bad debt becomes worthless. The loss is a short-term capital loss (see ¶ 6.55).

> **Cancellation of lease.** Payments received by the tenant on the cancellation of a business lease held long-term are treated as proceeds received in a Section 1231 transaction, *see* ¶ 5.44. Payments received by the tenant on cancellation of a lease on a personal residence or apartment are treated as proceeds of a capital asset transaction. Gain is long-term capital gain if the lease was held long-term; losses are not deductible.

Cancellation of a distributor's agreement if you made a substantial capital investment in the distributorship. For example, you own facilities for storage, transporting, processing, or dealing with the physical product covered by the franchise. You do not get capital gain if you have an office mainly for clerical work, or where you handle just a small part of the goods covered by the franchise.

Pension and profit-sharing trust distributions to employees may be long-term capital gain (see ¶ 7.3).

Timber. Under prior law, the owner of timber (or a contract right to cut timber) could elect to treat the cutting of the timber as a sale or exchange qualifying for long-term capital gains treatment, even though the timber was sold or used in the taxpayer's trade or business. Such an election applied to all later years, unless the IRS consented to a revocation of the election.

Since, under the new law, capital gains after 1986 will no longer be taxed at preferential rates, income from the sale of timber is generally taxable as ordinary income in 1987. However, under the new law, any prior election to treat the cutting of timber as a sale may be revoked without Treasury permission. If the election is revoked without permission and later a new election is made, any future revocations will require Treasury permission. See IRS Publication 544, Sales and Other Dispositions of Assets, for details.

SALE OR RETIREMENT OF BONDS AND NOTES

¶ **6.10** *Retirement of an obligation issued by an individual debtor.* Capital gain treatment does not apply to retirement of a debt by an individual. Capital gain treatment, however, may apply if you sell the obligation to a third party and the obligation is a capital asset (see ¶ 6.6). A note acquired by you in your business for services rendered or for the sale of merchandise is not a capital asset. The treatment of periodic payments made on obligations purchased at a discount is discussed at ¶ 31.10.

EXAMPLE

You bought for $6,000 a second trust note of $10,000 from an individual. You receive payments totaling $4,000. Then 60% ($6,000 ÷ $10,000) of the $4,000 is treated as a return on your investment; the balance as discount or interest income. You sell the note for $3,800. To determine your profit or loss, you reduce your cost by $2,400 ($4,000 × 60%). Your capital gain is $200.

Selling price of note		$3,800
Less: Cost of note	$6,000	
Return on investment	2,400	
Adjusted basis of note		3,600
Capital		$ 200

Retirement of bonds. Gain or loss on the retirement of debt obligations issued by a government or corporation is generally capital gain or loss. If the bond was issued before 1955, there is capital gain or loss only if the obligation was issued with interest coupons or in registered form on or before March 1, 1954.

Corporate bonds with OID issued before May 28, 1969, and government bonds with OID issued before July 2, 1982. If the bonds were originally issued at a discount (OID), you report the OID element as ordinary income when the bonds are sold or redeemed; any gain exceeding OID is reported as capital gain. A loss is a capital loss. The method of figuring the taxable OID element is explained at ¶4.6.

Corporate bonds with OID issued after May 27, 1969 and government bonds with OID issued after July 1, 1982. The ratable amount of OID is reported annually as ordinary income and added to basis; *see* ¶4.6. If the bonds are sold or redeemed before maturity, you realize capital gain for the amount over the adjusted basis of the bond, provided there was no intention to call the bond before maturity. If there was an intention to call the obligation before maturity, the unearned discount is taxable as ordinary income; the balance is capital gain.

Market discount on bonds issued after July 18, 1984, is taxable under the rules explained at ¶4.8.

Discount on tax-exempt bonds is discussed at ¶4.13.

WORTHLESS SECURITIES

¶ **6.11** You may deduct as a capital loss on Schedule D the cost basis of securities that have become worthless in 1987. A loss of worthless securities is deductible only in the year the securities become completely worthless. The loss cannot be deducted in any other year.

To support a deduction for 1987 you must show:

1. The stock had some value in 1986. That is, you must be ready to show that the stock did not become worthless in a year prior to 1987.
2. The stock became worthless in 1987. You must be able to present facts fixing the time of loss during this year. For example, the company went bankrupt, stopped doing business, and is insolvent. Despite evidence of worthlessness, such as insolvency, the stock may be considered to have some value if the company continues to do business, or there are plans to reorganize the company.

If a company is in financial trouble but you are not sure whether its condition is hopeless, it is advisable to claim the deduction in 1987 to protect your claim. This advice was given by a court: "The taxpayer is at times in a very difficult position in determining in what year to claim a loss. The only safe practice, we think, is to claim a loss for the earliest year when it may possibly be allowed and to renew the claim in subsequent years if there is a reasonable chance of its being applicable for those years."

Sometimes you can avoid the problem of proving worthlessness. If there is still a market for the security, you can sell. For example, the company is on the verge of bankruptcy, but in 1987 there is some doubt about the complete worthlessness of its securities. You might sell the securities for whatever you can get for them and claim the loss on the sale. However, if the security became worthless in a prior year, say in 1985, a sale in 1987 will not give you a deduction in 1987.

If you are making payments on a negotiable note you used to buy the stock that became worthless and you are on the cash basis method, your payments are deductible losses in the years the payments are made, rather than in the year the stock became worthless.

If the security is a bond, note, certificate or other evidence of a debt incurred by a corporation, the loss is deducted as a capital loss, provided the obligation is in registered form or has attached interest coupons. A loss on a worthless corporate obligation is always deemed to have been sustained on the last day of the year, regardless of when the company failed during the year. No deduction may be claimed for a partially worthless corporate bond.

If the obligation is not issued with interest coupons or in registered form or if it is issued by an individual, the loss is treated as a bad debt. If you received the obligation in a business transaction, the loss is fully deductible. You may also make a claim for a partially worthless business bad debt. If it is a nonbusiness debt, the loss is a capital loss and no claim may be made for partial worthlessness. See ¶6.55.

Stock that becomes worthless is deducted as a capital loss unless it fits within the rules of ¶6.12. A sale is presumed to have occurred at the end of the year, regardless of when worthlessness actually occurred during the year. You may not claim a loss for partially worthless stock.

EXAMPLE

You buy 100 shares of Z Co. stock on June 1, 1960. On March 17, 1987, the stock is considered wholly worthless. The loss is deemed to have been incurred on December 31, 1987. The loss is deducted as a long-term capital loss; the holding period is from June 1, 1960, to December 31, 1987.

Claim for refund. You have seven years from the due date of your return to claim a refund based on a deduction of a bad debt or worthless security. *See* ¶27.2.

EXAMPLE

You have held securities that you learn became worthless in 1980. You still have until April 15, 1988 to file for a refund of 1980 taxes by claiming a deduction for the worthless securities.

Small Business Investment Company stock losses. Investors in such stock may take ordinary loss deductions for losses on the worthlessness or sale of such stock. The loss may also be treated as a business loss for net operating loss purposes. However, a loss realized on a short sale of SBIC stock is deductible as a capital loss. A Small Business Investment Company is a company authorized to provide small businesses with equity capital. Do not confuse investments in these companies with investments in small business stock (Section 1244 stock) discussed at ¶6.12.

Bad debts of political parties are generally not deductible.

S corporation stock. If an S corporation's stock becomes worthless during the taxable year, the basis in the stock is adjusted for the stockholder's share of corporate items of income, loss, and deductions before a deduction for worthlessness is claimed.

Bank deposit loss, *see* ¶18.19.

SECTION 1244 STOCK (SMALL BUSINESS STOCK)

¶ **6.12** A law (Internal Revenue Code Section 1244) allows an ordinary loss deduction on Section 1244 stock losses, subject to the limits stated below. You may have your company plan a special issue of stock (voting or nonvoting) that will be treated as Section 1244 stock if certain tests are met.

An ordinary loss of up to $50,000 ($100,000 on a joint return) may be claimed on Section 1244 stock. Losses in excess of these limits are deductible as capital losses.

An ordinary loss may be claimed only by the original owner of the stock. If a partnership sells Section 1244 stock at a loss, an ordinary loss deduction may be claimed by individuals who were partners when the stock was issued. If a partnership distributes the Section 1244 stock to the partners, the partners may not claim an ordinary loss on their disposition of the stock.

To qualify as Section 1244 stock:

1. The corporation's equity may not exceed $1,000,000 at the time the stock is issued, but including amounts received for the stock to be issued. Thus, if the corporation already has $600,000 equity from stock previously issued, it may not issue more than $400,000 worth of Section 1244 stock.

    Preferred stock issued after July 18, 1984 may also qualify for Section 1244 loss treatment

2. The stock must be issued for money or property (other than stock and securities).
3. The corporation for the five years preceding your loss must generally have derived more than half of its gross receipts from business operations and not from passive income such as rents, royalties, dividends, interest, annuities or gains from the sales or exchanges

of stock or securities. This requirement is waived if the corporation's deductions (other than for dividends received or net operating losses) exceed gross income. If the corporation has not been in existence for the five years before your loss, then generally the period for which the corporation has been in existence is examined for the gross receipts test.

CORPORATE LIQUIDATION

¶ **6.13** Liquidation of a corporation and distribution of its assets for your stock is generally subject to capital gain or loss treatment. For example, on a corporate liquidation, you receive property worth $10,000 from the corporation. Assume the basis of your shares, which you have held long term, is $6,000. You have realized a long-term gain of $4,000.

The corporation may distribute contracts or other assets whose value cannot be figured at the time you receive them. Later, when you receive money for these assets, treat the money as if received from a liquidation. You thus get a capital gain instead of ordinary income. It makes no difference that the corporation would have had ordinary income realized on the assets if it had not liquidated.

If you incur legal expenses in pressing payment of a claim, you treat the fee as a capital expense according to the IRS. The Tax Court and an appeals court hold that the fee is deductible from ordinary income as an expense incurred to earn income.

If you recover a judgment against the liquidator of a corporation for misuse of corporate funds, the judgment is considered part of the amount you received on liquidation and gives you capital gain, not ordinary income.

If you paid a corporate debt after liquidation, the payment reduces the gain realized on the corporate liquidation in the earlier year; thus, in effect, it is a capital loss.

If the corporation distributes liquidating payments over a period of years, gain is not reported until the distributions exceed the adjusted basis of your stock.

SALE OF AN OPTION

¶ **6.14** The tax treatment of the sale of an option depends on the tax classification of the property to which the option relates.

If the option is for the purchase of property that will be a capital asset in your hands, you realize capital gain or loss on the sale of the option. Whether the gain or loss is long term or short term depends on your holding period.

EXAMPLES
1. You pay $500 for an option to purchase a house. After holding the option for five months, you sell the option for $750. Your profit of $250 is short-term capital gain.
2. The same facts as in (1) above, except that you sell the option for $300. The loss is not deductible because the option is related to a sale of a personal residence (see ¶ 6.8).

If the option is for a "Section 1231 asset" (see ¶ 5.44), gain or loss on the sale of the option is combined with other Section 1231 asset transactions to determine if there is capital gain or ordinary loss.

If the option relates to an ordinary asset in your hands, then gain or loss would be ordinary income or loss.

If you fail to exercise an option and allow it to lapse, the option is considered to have been sold on the expiration date. Gain or loss is computed according to the rules explained above.

The party granting the option realizes ordinary income on its expiration, regardless of the nature of the underlying property. If the option is exercised, the option payment is added to the selling price of the property.

CALLS OR OPTION TRANSACTIONS ON OPTION EXCHANGES

¶ **6.15** Option exchanges, such as the Chicago Board of Option Exchange (CBOE) and Amex market, provide a market for standardized options on a specific number of listed stocks, eliminating any relationship between option seller and buyer. The details and risk of these options are more fully discussed in ¶ 30.4. The following paragraphs give the tax consequences of call options transacted by investors on option exchanges, such as CBOE and Amex.

Buyers of options. If you buy an option, the treatment of your investment in the option depends on what you do with it.
1. If you sell it, you realize short-term or long-term capital gain or loss, depending upon how long you held the option.
2. If you allow the option to expire without exercise, you incur a short-term or long-term capital loss, depending on the holding period of the option. The expiration date is treated as the date the option is disposed of.
3. If you exercise the option and buy the stock, you add the cost of the option to the basis of the stock.

Grantors of options. If you write an option through the exchange, you do not treat the premium received for writing the option as income at the time of receipt. You do not realize profit or loss until the option transaction is closed. This may occur when the option expires or is exercised or when you "buy in" on the exchange an option similar to the one you gave to end your obligation to deliver the stock. Here are the rules for these events:
1. If the option is not exercised, you report the premium as short-term capital gain in the year the option expires.
2. If the option is exercised, you add the premium to the sales proceeds of the stock to determine gain or loss on the sale of the stock. Gain or loss is short-term or long-term depending upon the holding period of the stock.
3. If you "buy in" an equivalent option in a closing transaction, you realize profit or loss for the difference between the premium of the option you sold and the cost of the closing option. The profit or loss is treated as short-term capital gain or loss. However, a loss on a covered call that has a stated price below the stock price may be long-term capital loss if, at the time of the loss, long-term gain would be realized on the sale of the stock. Further, the holding period of such stock is suspended during the period in which the option is open. Finally, year-end losses from covered call options are not deductible, unless the stock is held uncovered for more than thirty days following the date on which the option is closed.

Index options. Nonequity options and dealer equity options, which include options based on regulated stock indexes and interest rate futures, are taxed like regulated futures contracts. This means that they are reported annually under the mark-to-market accounting system. You treat all such options held at the end of the year as if they were disposed of at year-end for a price equal to fair market value. Any gain or loss is arbitrarily taxed as if it were 60% long-term and 40% short-term, which gives a maximum tax rate of 32%. It is advisable to ask your broker whether the specific options which you hold come within this special rule.

STRADDLE LOSSES AND DEDUCTIONS RESTRICTIONS

¶ **6.16** Straddles are tax shelter devices to spot losses in one year and gains in another year and to convert ordinary income into capital gain. These maneuvers are now effectively barred by tax accounting rules. Straddle rules apply to commodities and actively traded stock and to stock options used in straddle positions. Straddle positions include any stock that is part of a straddle in which at least one of the offsetting positions is (1) an option tied to the stock or to substantially identical stock or securities or (2) a position in substantially similar or related property other than stock. For example, there is a straddle of stock and substantially similar or related property if offsetting positions of stock and convertible debentures of the same corporation are held and price movements of the two positions are related. Straddle rules apply also to stock of a corporation formed or used to take positions in personal property that offset positions taken by any shareholder. True hedging transactions are not subject to the straddle tax rules. Also, a call option is not treated as part of a straddle position if it is considered a qualified covered call option. A qualified covered call option is an option that a stockholder, who is not a dealer, grants on stock traded on a national securities exchange. Further, the option must be granted more than 30 days before its expiration date and must not be "deep-in-the-money." A covered call option will not qualify if gain on the sale of the stock to be purchased by the option is reported in a year after the year in which the option is closed or if the stock is not held for more than 30 days after the date on which the option is closed. In such a case, the option is subject to the straddle loss deferral rules. The same loss deferment rule applies where the stock is sold at a loss and gain on the related option held less than 30 days is reported in the next year.

Loss on a qualified covered call option with a strike price less than its applicable stock price is treated as long-term capital loss if loss realized on the sale of the stock would be long term. The holding period for stock subject to the option does not include any period during which the tax-payer is the grantor of the option.

A "deep-in-the-money option" is an option with a strike or exercise price that is below the lowest qualified benchmark. The technical rules for determining these values are not discussed in this book.

Tax rules for straddles. The following is an overview of the subject and if you have transacted straddles, we suggest that you consult with an experienced practitioner.

Realized straddle losses are deductible at the close of a taxable year only if they exceed unrealized gains in an offsetting position. Thus, an investor may not deduct losses incurred in 1987 to the extent that he has an unrealized gain position in the open end of the straddle. Form 6781 is used for straddle reporting.

Straddle positions of related persons (such as spouse or child) or controlled flow-through entities (such as a partnership or an S corporation) are considered in determining whether offsetting positions are held.

Realized losses that are not deductible at the end of the year are carried forward and become deductible when there is no unrealized appreciation in an offsetting position bought before the disposition of the loss position. This loss deferral rule may be avoided by identifying straddles before the close of the day of acquisition or at an earlier time that the IRS may set. Gain or loss in identified positions is generally netted; that is, a loss is recognized when the offsetting gain position has been closed.

If you are in a straddle arrangement you must disclose all positions of unrealized gains at the close of a tax year or you may be subject to a negligence penalty unless failure to disclose is due to a reasonable cause.

The loss deferral rule does not apply to positions in a regulated futures contract or other Section 1256 contract subject to the "mark-to-market" system explained below.

The loss deferral rule also does not apply to businesses that must hedge in order to protect their supplies of inventory or financial capital. Hedging transactions are subject to ordinary income or loss treatment. Hedging transactions entered into by syndicates do not qualify for the exception and are subject to the loss deferral rule if more than 35% of losses for a taxable year are allocable to limited partners or entrepreneurs. Further, hedging losses of limited partners or limited entrepreneurs are generally limited to their taxable income from the business in which the hedging transaction was entered into.

Regulated futures contracts and other Section 1256 contracts. Gain or loss on regulated futures contracts is reported annually under the mark-to-market accounting system of regulated commodity exchanges. To settle margin requirements, regulated exchanges determine a party's account for futures contracts on a daily basis. Each regulated futures contract is treated as if sold at fair market value on the last day of the taxable year. Any capital gain or loss is arbitrarily allocated: 40% is short term and 60% is long term.

Under the law, a regulated futures contract is considered a Section 1256 contract. Other Section 1256 contracts subject to the mark-to-market rules are foreign currency contracts and also non-equity listed options and dealer equity options for positions established after July 18, 1984.

The mark-to-market rules do not apply to true hedging transactions executed in the normal course of business to reduce risks and which result in ordinary income or loss. Syndicates may generally not take advantage of this hedging exception if more than 35% of their losses during a taxable year are allocable to limited partners or entrepreneurs. Furthermore, the ability of limited partners or entrepreneurs to deduct losses from hedging transactions is generally limited to taxable income from the business to which the hedging transaction relates.

Capital losses realized on regulated futures contracts or other Section 1256 contracts may be carried back three years. The carryback applies to positions established after June 23, 1981, and to taxable years ending after

that date. Thus, losses may not be carried back to 1980 and earlier years. Estates and trusts are not allowed the carryback. To claim the carryback, file an amended Form 6781 for the prior year together with an amended return (Form 1040X).

> You may elect to avoid the mark-to-market rules for contracts that are part of a mixed straddle. The election is irrevocable unless the Treasury allows a revocation. Further, in temporary regulations, the Treasury allows an election to offset gains and losses from positions that are part of mixed straddles if you separately identify each mixed straddle or establish mixed straddle accounts for a class of activities for which gain and loss will be recognized and offset on a periodic basis.

Contract cancellations. Investors buying forward contracts for currency or securities may not realize ordinary loss by canceling the unprofitable contract of the hedge transaction. Loss realized on a cancellation of the contract is treated as a capital loss.

Cash and carry transactions. Carrying costs for any period during which the commodity or stock or option is part of a balanced position are not deductible. The costs must be capitalized and added to basis. The rule does not apply to hedging. For positions established after July 18, 1984, capitalized items are reduced by dividends on stock included in a straddle, market discounts and acquisition discounts. These reductions, however, are limited to so much of the dividends and discounts as is included in income.

SALES OF PATENTS AND COPYRIGHTS

¶ 6.17 A special law allows long-term capital gain to sales of patents by inventors and their backers. There are advantages to qualifying under this law: Long-term gain is not dependent on any "holding period." The invention can be transferred even before an application for the patent is made. The imputed interest rules do not apply (*see* ¶ 6.39). The sale can be in the form of an outright sale, exclusive license, assignment, or royalty agreement.

> *Capital gain rules for an inventor.* You must transfer all *substantial rights* to the patent to a party who is not your employer and not any of the following related persons:
> 1. Member of your immediate family, such as your husband or wife, ancestors, and lineal descendants, but not brothers and sisters.
> 2. A corporation of which 25% or more in value of the outstanding stock is owned, directly or indirectly, by or for you. Stock owned by your brother or sister is not considered indirectly owned by you.
> 3. Certain beneficiaries, trusts, and grantors (*see* chapter 11).
> The following are *not* considered substantial rights and may be retained:
> right to prohibit sublicensing or subassignment of rights;
> the retention of a security interest such as a lien; and
> the reservation of rights providing for forfeiture for non-performance.

The retention of rights that limit the period of duration of the patent to a period less than the remaining life of the patent will bar capital gain treatment. Capital gain is also not allowed where the patent license limits use to a particular industry. For example, an inventor restricted production of his patented clutch to marine use only. The clutch could have been used in other industries. An appeals court agreed with the IRS that the inventor retained a substantial right. Treasury regulations also bar capital gain treatment where the license is restricted to a geographic area and the inventor keeps the right to exploit the patent elsewhere. The Tax Court holds that it is a question of fact whether geographic restrictions affect the transfer of substantial rights. Previously, it held that capital gain treatment automatically applied to a transfer limited to an exclusive geographic area.

If you are a financial backer, you must buy all of the substantial rights to the patent before the invention is reduced to practice. You will not get capital gain under the special rules if, at the time you bought your interest, you were the employer of the inventor or one of the related parties listed above.

If you cannot meet the special rules, for example, you bought the patent after it was put into operation, you may be able to get capital gain if your interest meets the general capital gain tests: You hold the patent as a capital asset or as a "Section 1231" asset, and you dispose of it in a transaction that is considered a sale or exchange after a long-term holding period. However, one court has said you may not get capital gain unless you do meet the special rules, regardless of whether you meet the general capital gain tests.

Copyrights. If you are the creator of the property covered by the copyright, you may not get capital gain on its sale. This rule applies to literary, musical, artistic compositions, letters, and memoranda, as well as to theatrical productions, radio programs, and newspaper cartoon strips. Ordinary income treatment also applies if you obtained the copyright from its creator by gift or in a tax-free exchange. If a copyright is purchased, however, it may later be sold for capital gain treatment. In such a case, capital gain treatment applies to amounts received for granting the exclusive use or right to exploit the copyrighted work throughout the life of the copyright. This is true whether the payment is measured by a fixed amount or a percentage of the receipts from the sale, performance, exhibition, or publication of the copyrighted work, or by the number of copies sold, performances given, or exhibitions.

GRANTING OF AN EASEMENT

¶ 6.18 Granting an easement presents a practical problem of determining whether all or part of the basis of the property is allocable to the easement proceeds. This requires an opinion of whether the easement affects the entire property or just a part of the property. There is no hard and fast rule to determine whether an easement affects all or part of the property. The issue is factual. For example, an easement for electric lines will generally affect only the area over which the lines are suspended and for which the right of way is granted. In such a case, an allocation may be required (see example (1) below). If the entire property is affected, no allocation is required and the proceeds reduce the basis of the property. If only part of the property is affected, then the proceeds are applied to the cost allocated to the area affected by the easement. If the proceeds exceed the amount allocated to basis, a gain is realized. Capital gain treatment generally applies to grants of easements. The granting of a perpetual easement which requires you to give up all or substantially all of a beneficial use of the area affected by the easement is treated as a sale. The contribution to a government body of a scenic easement in perpetuity is a charitable contribution, not a sale.

In reviewing an easement, the IRS will generally try to find grounds for making an allocation, especially where the allocation will result in a taxable gain. In opposition, a property owner will generally argue that the easement affects the entire property or that it is impossible to make an allocation because of the nature of the easement or the particular nature of the property. If he can sustain his argument, the proceeds for granting the easement reduce the basis of the entire property.

EXAMPLES

1. The owner of a 600 acre farm was paid $5,000 by a power company for the right to put up poles and power lines. The right of way covered 20 acres along one boundary which the owner continued to farm. The cost basis of the farm was $60,000 or $100 an acre. The IRS ruled that he had to allocate basis. At $100 an acre, the allocated basis for the 20 acres was $2,000. Thus, a gain of $3,000 was realized ($5,000–$2,000).

2. The owner of a tract of unimproved land gave a state highway department a perpetual easement affecting only part of the land. He wanted to treat the payment as reduction of the basis of the entire tract and so report no gain. The IRS ruled that he had to allocate basis to the portion affected by the road.

3. The owner of farmland gave a transmission company a 50-foot right of way for an underground pipeline that did not interfere with farming. During construction, the right of way was 150 feet. The owner received payments for damages covering loss of rental income during construction and for the 50-foot permanent right of way. The IRS ruled that the damage payment was taxable as ordinary income; the payment for the right of way was a taxable gain to the extent that it exceeded the basis allocated to the acreage within the 50-foot strip.

If you realize a gain on a grant of an easement under a condemnation or threat, you may defer tax by investing in replacement property.

EXAMPLE

Under threat of condemnation, a farmer in a flood control area gave the government the right to flood his farm. This was expected to occur every six years and did not interfere with farming in the intervening periods. The award exceeded basis. The IRS ruled that the farmer could defer tax by reinvesting in other farmland to keep up crop production. That he retained use of the farm was no bar to the election to defer tax.

RELEASE OF RESTRICTIVE COVENANT

¶ 6.19 A payment received for a release of a restrictive covenant is treated as a capital gain.

EXAMPLE

You sell several acres of land to a construction company subject to a covenant that restricts construction to residential dwellings. Later, the company wants to erect structures other than individual homes and pays you for the release of the restrictive covenant in the deed. You realize capital gain on receipt of the payment. The restrictive covenant is a property interest and a capital asset in your hands.

TRANSACTIONS NOT SUBJECT TO CAPITAL GAIN OR LOSS

¶ 6.20 **Accounts or notes receivable** sold by you and you originally received them for merchandise or services. Receivables are usually discounted or sold at a loss which is fully deductible. If you make a profit (you reported a note at less than face and later sold it for a higher amount), you realize ordinary income.

Abandonment of property. Taxpayers have argued that abandonment of property is not subject to capital asset treatment. The IRS disagrees and has succeeded in getting court support for its position in treating an abandonment of mortgaged property as a sale. *See* ¶6.9.

The holder of property under a land sale contract may not abandon the property for tax purposes if the seller has the right to sue for specific performance of the contract.

Annuity contract surrendered for its cash value.

Damages received in suit for breach of contract even if contract was for sale of a capital asset.

Employment contract canceled. Lump-sum payment received on cancellation is taxed compensation.

Endowment policy paid off on maturity. *See* ¶7.17 on your choices before maturity.

Estate's collection on a claim in excess of estate's basis.

Forfeited deposit on agreement to sell property. Seller has ordinary income and buyer has ordinary loss if the breached contract was for property to be used in a business. A deposit forfeited for the purchase of property used for personal purposes, such as residence, is not deductible by the buyer but is income to seller. However, where the seller breaches the contract and fails to repay because of bankruptcy, the lost deposit may be deductible as a bad debt (*see* ¶6.55). Where a contractor absconds with a deposit, the loss may be deducted as a theft loss (*see* ¶18.5).

Franchises. A transfer of a franchise, trademark, or trade name is not a sale or exchange of a capital asset if the grantor retains a significant power, right, or interest in it such as the right to: Disapprove further assignment of all or part of the franchise; set quality standards for products, services, equipment, or facilities; require that only his products or services be sold or advertised; require that substantially all supplies or equipment be purchased from him and to receive payments contingent on use of the franchise, if such payments are a substantial element of the agreement. In addition, if the grantor has an operational control over the franchise, payment may be treated as ordinary income. Operational control includes the right to: receive periodic reports, approve business methods, prevent removal of equipment from the territory, and withdraw the franchise if the territory is not developed.

To receive capital gain treatment on the sale of a franchise, the grantor must avoid the retention of any of the specified powers of operational control and, in addition, he must meet the general tests for capital gains, such as not dealing in franchises.

Insurance policy sold to a third party.

Insurance renewal commission assigned by insurance agent to insurance company in return for annuity income.

Investment in notes written off as worthless. Later disposal at a bankruptcy sale gives ordinary income.

Liquidated damages on the breach of a contract to sell.

EXAMPLE

You agree to sell property for $60,000, payable $12,000 on the signing of the contract, the balance on the delivery of the deed. The contract calls for liquidated damages of $12,000. After paying $12,000 on the contract, the buyer defaults and you keep the down payment as liquidated damages. Several months later, you sell the property for $55,000 to another party. You cannot bunch the liquidated damages of $12,000 with the sales proceeds of $55,000 and get capital gain for the total. The liquidated damages are treated separately from the later sale and taxed as ordinary income.

Mortgaging property.

Note payment received after getting judgment on the note.

Property received in settlement of suit for its recovery. But if cash is received, you have a sale.

Payments under a contract right to share profits which you bought for a definite sum. The receipts are ordinary income.

Realization of full face value of land contracts purchased at a discount and held to maturity. In Michigan, land contracts require a down payment and the balance in installments over a period of years. They are somewhat similar to mortgages. Contracts bought at less than their unpaid balances and held to maturity give ordinary income for the difference between the purchase price and the amount realized.

Release of debt to the other party of a contract giving you rights to future income. Your receipt is ordinary income. You have merely released a debt.

Release of employment contract.

Release of rights to a pension.

Release of a right to receive profits from sale of gas.

Return of property to you by borrower.

Sale of right to receive income —salary, dividends, or interest. Proceeds are ordinary income.

Satisfaction of a judgment for more than you paid for it gives ordinary income. Suppose you buy a $75,000 court judgment for $11,000. Later you collect $21,000 in satisfaction of the entire judgment. You have $10,000 ordinary income. Satisfaction of a judgment is not a sale or exchange.

Termination of insurance agency contract to solicit business and receive commissions. Termination does not involve the transfer of a capital asset but the relinquishment of a right to render personal services for commissions.

Topsoil. Sale of topsoil gives ordinary income. You may be entitled to depletion (*see* ¶9.13).

COUNTING THE HOLDING PERIOD

¶ 6.21 The period of time you own a capital asset before its sale or exchange determines whether gain or loss is short term or long term.

The short-term holding period is six months or less; a long-term period is more than six months.

Warning: The long-term holding period is scheduled to increase to more than one year for assets acquired after December 31, 1987. *See* the Supplement for any late developments.

Rules for counting the holding period:
1. A holding period is figured in months and fractions of months.
2. The beginning date of a holding month is generally the day after the asset was acquired. The same numerical date of each following month starts a new holding month regardless of the number of days in the preceding month.
3. The last day of the holding period is the day on which the asset is sold.

As a rule of thumb, use the numerical date on which you acquired the asset as the numerical date ending a holding month in each following month. However, if you acquire an asset on the last day of a month, a holding month ends on the last day of a following calendar month, regardless of the number of days in each month.

EXAMPLES
1. On March 12, you buy stock. Holding months begin on March 13, April 13, May 13, June 13, and end on April 12, May 12, June 12, etc.
2. You buy stock on February 28. A holding month ends on March 31, April 30, etc. To realize long-term gain on the sale of these securities, you must hold them at least one day longer than the short-term holding period.
3. You buy stock on November 30. A holding month as in example (2) ends on December 31, January 31, February 28 (or 29 in a leap year), etc.

SECURITIES TRANSACTIONS

¶ 6.22 *Stock sold on a public exchange.* The holding period starts on the day after your purchase order is executed (trading date). The day your sale order is executed (trade date) is the last day of the holding period even if delivery and payment are not made until several days after the actual sale (settlement date). This rule applies even where a gain on a year-end sale is not reported until the next year in which the proceeds are received.

EXAMPLES
1. On June 2, you sell a stock at a profit. Your holding period ends on June 2 although proceeds are not received until June 7.
2. You sell land at a gain on December 31, 1987. The holding period ends on December 31, although the sale is reported in 1988 when the proceeds are received. A sale at a loss is reported in 1987. (*See* chapter 30 for strategy in planning year-end sales.) Note that the December 31st gain transaction can be reported in 1987 by making an election to "elect out" of installment reporting (*see* ¶ 6.35).
3. Same as in example (2) except that stock is sold at a gain on a public exchange on December 31, 1987. Under a new law, the gain must be reported in 1987 even though the proceeds are received in 1988. The installment sale election does not apply. (*See* ¶ 6.33).

Stock subscriptions. If you are bound by your subscription but the corporation is not, the holding period begins the day after the date on which the stock is issued. If both you and the company are bound, the acceptance of the subscription by the corporation is the date of acquisition, and your holding period begins the day after.

Tax-free stock rights. When you exercise rights to acquire corporate stock from the issuing corporation, your holding period for the stock begins on the day of exercise, *not* on the day after. You are deemed to exercise stock rights when you assent to the terms of the rights in the manner requested or authorized by the corporation. An option to acquire stock is not a stock right.

Stock sold from different lots. If you purchased shares of the same stock on different dates and cannot determine which shares you are selling, the shares purchased at the earliest time are considered the stock sold first (*see also* ¶ 30.3).

EXAMPLE
You purchased 10 shares of ABC stock on May 3, 1975, 10 shares of ABC stock on May 1, 1977, and 10 shares of ABC stock on September 2, 1978. In 1987, you sell 25 shares of ABC stock, and are unable to determine when those particular shares were bought. Using the "first-in, first-out" method, 10 shares are from May 3, 1975, 10 shares from May 1, 1977, and five shares from September 2, 1978.

Commodities. If you acquired a commodity futures contract, the holding period of a commodity accepted in satisfaction of the contract includes your holding period of the contract, unless you are a dealer in commodities.

Employee stock options. When an employee exercises a stock option, the holding period of the acquired stock begins on the day after the option is exercised. If an employee option plan allows the exercise of an option by giving notes, the terms of the plan should be reviewed to determine when ownership rights to the stock are transferred. The terms may affect the start of the holding period for the stock.

EXAMPLE
In April 1964, Arnold exercised a stock option by giving a note. He had to pay up by June 1965, at which time he received his stock certificate. In October 1965, he sold the shares, realizing a profit of $20,000, which he reported as a long-term gain. The IRS taxed the profit as short-term gain, claiming that he owned the stock for only four months, that is, from the time he paid the note. Arnold argued that he acquired the stock when he gave the note.

The Tax Court agreed with the IRS. The plan called for cash payment by a deadline date as a condition of issuing the stock. The note was not intended as a substitute for cash and did not entitle Arnold·to delivery of shares. He did not own the optioned stock until he paid the notes.

Other references: Stock dividends, *see* ¶ 6.5; short sales, *see* ¶ 6.52; wash sales, *see* ¶ 6.63; convertible securities, *see* ¶ 6.54.

REAL ESTATE TRANSACTIONS

¶ 6.23 The date of acquisition is the earlier of these two dates: (1) The date title passes to you, or (2) the date you take possession and you assume the burdens and privileges of ownership.

If your purchase of a new residence qualifies under the rules discussed at ¶ 29.3, the holding period for the new home includes the holding period of the former residence. If you convert a residence to rental property and later sell the house, the holding period includes the time you held the house for personal purposes.

Holding period of a newly constructed house. When you sell a newly constructed house after its completion, you may have long-term capital gain on the underlying land and both long-term and short-term capital gain on the house. The holding periods of the land and building are figured separately. The holding period of the land begins from the date of the purchase of the land (which you may have held long term before the sale). The holding period of the building follows this peculiar rule: You get long-term capital gain for that portion of the gain allocable to the cost of the building erected in the applicable long-term period before the sale. You realize short-term capital gain on the balance.

To avoid the allocation and short-term capital gain, hold the house long-term after its completion. But if you have to sell before then, make sure you have records on which to base an allocation so at least part of your gain is long-term.

In disputes involving the starting and closing dates of a holding period, you may refer to the state law that applies to your sale or purchase agreement. State law determines when title to property passes.

GIFT, INHERITED, OR PARTNERSHIP PROPERTY OR INVOLUNTARY CONVERSIONS

¶ 6.24 *Gift property.* If, in figuring a gain or loss, your basis for the property is the same as the donor's basis, you add the donor's holding period to the period you held the property. If you sell the property at a loss for which you use as your basis the fair market value at the date of the gift, your holding period begins the day after the date of the gift (*see* ¶ 6.29).

Inherited property. The holding period for inherited property begins on the day after the date of decedent's death, rather than the date you receive the property from the estate. You do not use the alternate valuation date elected by an executor to fix values for estate tax purposes. Further, the law gives an automatic long-term holding period for inherited property, regardless of the actual length of time you held the property.

Where property is purchased by the executor or trustee and distributed to you, your holding period begins the day after the date on which the property was purchased.

Partnership property. When you receive property as a distribution in kind from your partnership, the period your partnership held the property is added to your holding period. But there is no adding on of holding periods if the partnership property distributed was inventory and was sold by you within five years of distribution.

Involuntary conversions. When you have an involuntary conversion and elect to defer tax on gain, the holding period for the qualified replacement property generally includes the period you held the converted property. A new holding period begins for new property if you do not make an election.

COMPUTING FRACTIONS OF MONTHS

¶ 6.25 Figuring fractions of months is required in computing the holding period of stock purchased after a wash sale (*see* ¶ 6.53).

To figure a fraction of a holding month, follow two rules:

1. When a fraction falls in one calendar month, take the number of days from the end of your last holding month to the date of sale and put it over the number of days in the calendar month of sale.

EXAMPLE
You bought stock January 15 and sold it March 28. On March 15 you have two holding months. From March 15 to March 28 (the date of sale), you have 13 days. Your fraction is $13 \div 31$—March has 31 days. Your holding period is $2\frac{13}{31}$ months.

2. When a fraction falls in two calendar months, figure the number of days from the end of your last holding month. You place this figure over the number of days in the first of the two calendar months over which the fraction extends.

EXAMPLE
You bought stock on January 21 and sold it March 7. On February 21 you have one holding month. From February 21 to March 7 (date of sale), you have 14 days. Since the fraction extends over two calendar months—February and March—you put that figure over the number of days in the first of those two months (February). Your holding period is $1\frac{14}{28}$ or $1\frac{1}{2}$ months.

After a wash sale, the holding period of a new stock includes the holding period of the old lots. If you had more than one old lot in wash sales, you add the holding periods of all the old lots to the holding period of the new lot. You do this even if your holding periods overlapped because you bought another lot before you sold the first. You do not count the periods between sale and purchase when you have no stock.

EXAMPLE
You buy and sell 100 shares of the same stock as follows:

	Date bought	Date sold at loss	"Months" held
Lot 1	Feb. 12	April 2	$1 + \frac{21}{31}$
Lot 2	Mar. 12	May 12	2
Lot 3	June 10	Aug. 4	$1 + \frac{25}{31}$
Holding period of Lot 3	(Total)		$5 + \frac{15}{31}$

IMPORTANT: *For property acquired after 1987, a one-year long-term holding period will apply unless Congress acts to change the law. Thus, gain or loss on the sale of assets acquired in 1988 will be short-term capital gain if the assets are held one year or less; long-term capital gain if held more than one year. See the Supplement for changes, if any, to the scheduled one-year holding period rule.*

FIGURING YOUR PROFIT OR LOSS

¶ **6.26** In most cases, you know if you have realized an economic profit or loss on the sale or exchange of property. You know your cost and selling price. The difference between the two is your profit or loss. The tax computation of gain or loss is similarly figured, except that the rules explained below may require you to increase or decrease your cost or selling price. As a result, your gain or loss for tax purposes may differ from your initial calculation.

GUIDE TO FIGURING GAIN OR LOSS

1. Selling price (*see* ¶6.27) $_____
2.   Less: Selling expenses (*see* ¶6.27)   _____
3. Amount realized (*see* ¶6.27) $_____
4.   Cost or unadjusted basis of
       property (*see* ¶6.28, ¶6.29) $_____
5.   Add: Improvements, commissions
       (*see* ¶6.32) $_____
6.   Less: Depreciation, losses
       (*see* ¶6.32) $_____
7. Less: Adjusted basis (4 plus 5 less 6) $_____
8. Net gain or loss (3 less 7) $_____

EXAMPLE
You sell property to a buyer who pays you cash of $50,000. You bought the property for $30,000. Selling expenses were $2,000. Your gain on the sale is figured as follows:

1. Selling Price	$50,000
2. Less: Selling Expenses	$ 2,000
3. Amount Realized	$48,000
4. Less: Cost	$30,000
5. Net Gain	$18,000

Note: The columns in Schedule D may not follow the above order and may include step 2 *selling expenses* with step 4 cost in order to save space. See ¶6.6. If so, on Schedule D, you report the gross selling price of $50,000 in column (d) "gross sales price"; in column (e) the cost of $30,000 plus selling expenses of $2,000. The final result is the same, a net gain of $18,000 ($50,000–$32,000). In some years, the IRS has required selling expenses to be deducted from gross sales in column (d). A preliminary 1987 Schedule D is included in the back of this book and a final filled-in 1987 Schedule D in the mail-in Supplement.

SELLING PRICE AND AMOUNT REALIZED

¶ **6.27** Selling price is cash plus the fair market value of any additional property received. The buyer's note is included in the selling price at fair market value. This is generally the discounted amount that a bank or other party will pay for the note.

Sale of mortgaged property. The selling price includes the amount of the unpaid mortgage, whether or not you are personally liable on the debt or the buyer assumes the mortgage. The full amount of the unpaid mortgage is included, even where the value of the property is less than the unpaid mortgage.

EXAMPLES
1. You sell property subject to a mortgage of $60,000. The seller pays you cash of $30,000 and takes the property subject to the mortgage. The sales price is $90,000.
2. A partnership receives a nonrecourse mortgage of $1,851,500 from a bank to build an apartment project. Several years later, the partnership sells the project for the buyer's agreement to assume the unpaid mortgage. At the time, the value of the project is $1,400,000 and the partnership basis in the project is $1,455,740. The partnership figures a loss of $55,740, the difference between basis and the value of the project. The IRS figures a gain of $395,760, the difference between the unpaid mortgage and basis. The partnership claims the selling price is limited to the lower fair market value and is supported by an appeals court. The Supreme Court reverses, supporting the IRS position. That the value of property is less than the amount of the mortgage has no effect on the rule requiring the unpaid mortgage to be part of the selling price. A mortgagor realizes value to the extent that his obligation to repay is relieved by a third party's assumption of the mortgage debt.

If at the time of the sale the buyer pays off the existing mortgage or your other liabilities, you include his payment as part of the sales proceeds.

Amount realized. This is the tax term for net selling price. To figure amount realized, you reduce the selling price by commissions, legal fees, transfer taxes, advertising costs and other selling expenses.

EXAMPLE
Same facts as in example (1) above except that on the sale of the property you paid broker fees of $1,000, attorney fees of $350, and advertising cost of $50. The amount realized is $88,600 ($90,000 less $1,400).

FINDING YOUR COST

¶ **6.28** In figuring gain or loss, you need the "unadjusted basis" of the property sold. This term refers to the original cost of your property, if you purchased it. If you received it by gift, inheritance, or other means, you can determine unadjusted basis in the checklist below at ¶6.29. Keep in mind that you have to adjust this figure for improvements to the property, depreciation, or losses. These adjustments are explained at ¶6.32.

UNADJUSTED BASIS OF YOUR PROPERTY

¶ **6.29** In the following order, you will find the unadjusted basis of any property acquired by—
Your cash or obligations
Rendering services
Taxable exchange of property
"Tax-free" exchange of property
Gift after December 31, 1920
Sale of old residence and you acquired new residence
Sale of residence converted to rental
Gift or transfer in trust before January 1, 1921
Life estate or remainder interest in property created by will or gift
Inheritance from a deceased person

Survivor of joint tenancy or tenancy by the entirety
Distribution from a trust to a beneficiary
Compulsory or involuntary conversion
Prenuptial agreement
Nondeductible "wash sale"
Any method—property purchased prior to March 1, 1913
Distribution on orders of the Securities and Exchange Commission
Dividends in property
Bonus on stock owned
Complete liquidation of a corporation
Settlement of debt owed to you
When, as, and if issued contract to buy securities

Your cash or obligations. Basis is your cash cost, where purchased after February 28, 1913. If you assumed a mortgage or bought property subject to a mortgage, the amount of the mortgage is part of your unadjusted basis.

EXAMPLE
You bought a building for $20,000 in cash and a purchase money mortgage of $60,000. The unadjusted basis of the building is $80,000.

Rendering services. The value of the property, when you receive it as taxable income, is your unadjusted basis.

Taxable exchange of property. Technically, your unadjusted basis is the fair market value at the time of exchange of the property surrendered. In practice, however, the basis usually is equal to the fair market value of the property received. (But note the exception below under "tax-free" exchanges.)

EXAMPLE
You acquire real estate in 1950 for $5,000. When the property has a fair market value of $10,000, you exchange it for machinery also worth $10,000. You have a gain of $5,000, and the basis of the machinery is $10,000.

"Tax-free" exchange of property—within the rules explained at ¶5.49 and ¶6.44. Your basis is that of the property which you exchange, decreased by any cash received and increased by any taxed gain or decreased by recognized loss. Gain is taxed to the extent cash is also received, see ¶5.49 for discussion on boot.

EXAMPLE
1. You exchange real estate, which cost you $20,000, for other real estate. You pay no tax on the exchange. The unadjusted basis of the new property received in the exchange is $20,000.
2. Same facts as in (1) but you receive real estate worth $30,000 and cash of $5,000. On this transaction, you realize gain of $15,000 (of which $5,000 is taxed to the extent of the cash). Your basis for the new property is $20,000 figured this way:

Basis of old property	$20,000
Less: Cash received	5,000
	15,000
Plus: Gain recognized	5,000
Basis of new property	$20,000

Sale of property received by gift after December 31, 1920. If you have a gain from the sale of property received as a gift, your basis is the original cost to the person who made the gift. If a loss results to you, you use the donor's cost or market value (whichever is lower) at the date of the gift. This rule applies also to gifts transferred in trust after 1920.

EXAMPLE
Assume that in 1955 you received a gift from your father which you sold in 1987. His cost was $1,000. Then—

If value of the gift at receipt was—	And you sold it for—	Your basis is—	Your taxed gain is—	Your loss is—
$3,000	$2,000	$1,000	$1,000	
700	500	700		$200
300	500	*	none	none
1,500	500	1,000		500

*In the third example, there is neither gain nor loss. To compute gain, cost is used ($1,000). Thus, there is no gain. But there is no loss because the property was sold for more than its value at the time of gift. To compute loss, you must use market value, which in this case is lower than donor's cost.

If a gift tax is paid on the gift of property, the basis of the property is increased under these rules: (1) For property received after December 31, 1976, the basis is increased for the gift tax paid by an amount which bears the same ratio to the amount of tax paid as the net appreciation in the value of the gift bears to the amount of the gift. The increase may not exceed the tax paid. Net appreciation in the value of any gift is the amount by which the fair market value of the gift exceeds the donor's adjusted basis immediately before the gift. (2) For property received after September 1, 1958 but before 1977, basis is increased by the gift tax paid on the property but not above the market value of the property at the time of

the gift. (3) For property received before September 2, 1958, basis is increased by the gift tax paid. But this increase may not be more than the excess of the market value of the property at the time of the gift over the basis of the property in the donor's hands. Ask the donor or his advisor for these amounts.

EXAMPLES
1. In 1975, your father gave you rental property with a market value of $78,000. The basis of the property in his hands was $60,000. He paid a gift tax of $15,000 on the gift. The basis of the property in your hands is $75,000 ($60,000 + $15,000).
2. In 1977, your father gave you rental property with a market value of $78,000. His basis in the property was $60,000. He paid a gift tax of $15,000 on the gift. The basis of the property in your hands is your father's basis increased by the gift tax attributable to the appreciation. Gift tax attributable to the appreciation is:

$$\frac{\text{Appreciation}}{\text{Market value}} \times \text{Gift tax paid}$$

$$\frac{\$18,000}{\$78,000} \times \$15,000 = \$3,462$$

Your basis for figuring gain or loss or depreciation is $63,462.

If you received a gift of property which was used by the donor or by someone before him as depreciable business property, see ¶5.41. You may have to adjust the basis for depreciation taken on the property, and if you sell the property at a gain, you may realize ordinary income.

Sale of old residence, and you acquired the new residence— under the tax deferral rules of ¶29.3. Your basis is what you paid for the new residence, less any gain that was not taxed on the sale of the old residence. See also example of basis computation at the end of ¶29.3.

Sale of residence converted to rental. See ¶29.18.

Gift of transfer in trust before January 1, 1921. Your basis is the fair market value at the time the gift or transfer was made.

EXAMPLE
No matter what the gift cost the donor, if its fair market value at the time he made the gift prior to 1921 was $1,000, your cost basis in a sale is $1,000.

Life estate or remainder interest in property created by will or gift. Your basis is constantly changing. The life tenant's basis is found by applying a formula based on an "annuity" factor taken from a table in the Treasury's regulations. It varies with age of the life tenant at the time of sale. The person who owns the remainder interest makes a similar computation using a "reversion" factor from the same table. If both sell their interests together, the adjusted basis of the property must be apportioned ratably between the life tenant and the remainderman (see Treasury regulations).

If only the life tenant sells his interest, he is considered to have a zero basis so that the entire amount received on the sale is taxable. This zero-basis rule applies also to sales of interests in property for a term of years and income interests in trusts. The zero-basis rule does not apply where both the life tenant and remainderman sell their interests. It also does not apply to sales made on or before October 9, 1969.

Inheritance of property. Basis is generally the value of the property at date of the death of the decedent, regardless of when you acquire the property. If decedent died after October 21, 1942, and the executor elected to use an *alternate valuation date* after the death, your basis is the alternate value at that date. The same rule applies to property:
1. Placed in trust by the deceased to pay the income to him, or at his direction, if he had the right at all times before his death to get back the property.
2. Placed in trust by the deceased to pay the income to him, or at his direction, if he had the right at all times before his death to alter, amend or end the trust, and he died after December 31, 1951.
3. Passing under a general power of appointment.
4. Acquired from deceased before he died if it was subjected to estate tax at his death and he died after December 31, 1953. (You have to reduce the basis for depreciation which you claimed for the property before the deceased's death.)

If the property is subject to a mortgage, though you did not assume the mortgage, your cost is still the value of the property, and not its equity at the date of death. If the property is subject to a lease under which no income is to be received for years, the basis is the value of the property—not the equity.

You might be given the right to buy the deceased person's property under his will. This is not the same as inheriting that property. Your basis is what you pay—not what the property is worth on the date of the deceased's death.

If property was inherited from a decedent dying after 1976 and before November 7, 1978, and the executor elected to apply carryover basis to all estate property, your basis is figured with reference to the decedent's basis. The executor must inform you of the basis of such property.

Survivor of joint tenancy, see ¶ 6.30.

Distribution from a trust to a beneficiary. Generally, you take the same basis the trust had for the property. But if the distribution is made to settle a claim you had against the trust, your basis for the property is the amount of the settled claim.

If you receive a distribution in kind for your share of trust income, the basis of the distribution before June 2, 1984, is generally the value of the property to the extent allocated to distributable net income. For distributions in kind after June 1, 1984, in taxable years ending after June 1, 1984, your basis is the basis of the property in the hands of the trust. If the trust elects to treat the distribution as a taxable sale, your basis is generally fair market value.

See above rules covering inheritance when decedent retained powers over trust he created.

Involuntary conversion. If the property was acquired as a result of an involuntary conversion before 1951, basis is the cost of the property converted. You adjust basis this way: Decrease it by money received not expended for replacement of the converted property and increase it for gain or decrease it for the loss recognized upon the conversion.

If the conversion occurred after 1950, basis is the cost of the new property decreased by gain not reported. If the replacement property consists of more than one piece of property, basis is allocated to each piece in proportion to its respective cost.

EXAMPLE

A building with an adjusted basis of $100,000 is destroyed by fire. The owner receives an insurance award of $200,000, realizing a gain of $100,000. He buys a building as a replacement for $150,000. Thus, $50,000 of his gain is taxable, and the remaining $50,000 is not taxable. The basis of the new building is $100,000.

Cost of the new building	$150,000
Less: Unrecognized gain	50,000
Basis	$100,000

Prenuptial agreement in release of dower and marital rights. The basis of property received under the agreement is its value when acquired if the transfer took place before July 19, 1984.

EXAMPLE

Jones bought stock for $50,000. Under a prenuptial agreement, he later gave this stock to his prospective wife in release of her dower and marital rights. The fair market value at the time she acquired the stock was $150,000. Her basis is $150,000. She is considered to have acquired the stock by purchase not by gift.

Where transfers between spouses take place after July 18, 1984, the transfer is treated as a tax-free exchange and the transferee takes a carryover basis, see ¶ 6.49. In the above example, the carryover basis to the wife would be $50,000.

Nondeductible "wash sale." If you transact a "wash sale," your basis is the cost of the new stock plus the loss not allowed. See ¶ 6.53.

Any method—property purchased prior to March 1, 1913. Your basis is the cost or the fair market value at March 1, 1913, whichever is greater, if a gain results. However, if you sustain a loss, your basis is the cost.

Distribution on orders of the Securities and Exchange Commission. Your basis is the same as that of the property exchanged.

EXAMPLE

Securities of a utility company cost you $1,000. The company is dissolved by order of the Securities and Exchange Commission, and you receive four classes of stock of subsidiaries owned by the utility at the time of its dissolution. You must prorate your $1,000 cost over the four new stocks on the basis of their market values at the time you received them.

Dividends in property (except stock of the issuing corporation). Fair market value of date of distribution is basis.

Bonus on stock owned. If you received common stock as a bonus upon the acquisition of preferred stock or bonds, cost of the preferred stock or bonds should be apportioned between such securities and the common stock. If this is not practicable, you do not realize any taxed profit from the sale of any of the stock or bonds until you first recover your entire cost.

EXAMPLE

You bought 100 shares of preferred stock and received 100 shares of common stock as a bonus. If there was a market for both, you could easily allocate your cost. If the common did not have a market, you are first permitted to recover your cost before a profit is determined on the sale.

Accumulated value of variable annuities on death of contract owner. Decedent's cost.

Complete liquidation of a corporation to an individual. Your basis is generally the fair market value of the property at the time of the liquidation.

EXAMPLE

If you receive securities having a market value of $1,000 in a liquidation, that is your cost when you sell them. Report gain or loss due to the liquidation at the time it occurs.

Settlement of debt owed to you. Your cost of the obligation or any value you and your debtor agree upon is your basis.

When, as, and if issued contract to buy securities. If the contract has cost you nothing, your basis is zero in computing gain or loss on the sale of the contract before its performance.

JOINT TENANCY BASIS RULES FOR SURVIVING TENANTS

¶ **6.30** For deaths occurring after 1981, the law provides different basis rules for joint tenancies between husbands and wives than for tenancies between persons who are not married to each other.

For a joint tenancy by the entirety between a husband and wife, the rule for deaths occurring after 1981 is as follows: The surviving spouse's basis includes one-half of the decedent's interest fixed at fair market value used for estate tax purposes. This is generally fair market value at date of death or six months later if an estate tax return is filed and the optional valuation date is elected. The 50% decedent share applies regardless of the actual amount contributed by the decedent to the property.

EXAMPLE

Jones and his wife jointly own a house that cost them $50,000 in 1970. In 1987, Jones dies when the house is worth $200,000; $100,000 is included in his estate. For income tax purposes, Mrs. Jones's basis for the house is $125,000.

Her original basis	$ 25,000
Basis for inherited portion	100,000
New basis	$125,000

On a sale of the home for $200,000, Mrs. Jones would realize a $75,000 long-term capital gain ($200,000–$125,000).

The following rules apply to joint tenancies between—
Persons who are not married to each other, and
A husband and wife where one spouse died before 1982.
Basis to the survivor for the entire property is your basis for your share before the joint owner died plus the fair market value of the decedent's interest at death (or on the alternate valuation date if the estate uses the alternate date). The decedent's interest does not have to be included on

an estate tax return (as where the estate is too small to be taxable) for you to use the date-of-death value. If no estate tax return is required, you may not use the alternative valuation date basis.

EXAMPLES

1. You and your sister bought a home for $10,000. She paid $6,000, and you, $4,000. Title to the house was held by both of you as joint tenants. In 1987, when she died, the house was worth $30,000. Since she paid 60% of the cost of the house, 60% of the value at her death, $18,000, is included in an estate tax return (or would be included if an estate tax return was due). Basis for the house now becomes $22,000—the $4,000 you originally paid plus the $18,000 fair market value of your sister's share at her death.

2. Husband and wife owned rental property as tenants by the entirety that they purchased for $30,000. The husband furnished two-thirds of the purchase price ($20,000) and the wife furnished one-third ($10,000). Depreciation deductions taken before the husband's death were $12,000. On the date of his death in 1979, the property had a fair market value of $60,000. Under the law of the state in which the property is located, as tenants by the entirety, each had a half interest in the property. The wife's basis in the property at the date of her husband's death is computed as follows:

Interest acquired with her own funds	$10,000	
Interest acquired from husband (⅔ of $60,000)	40,000	$50,000
Less: Depreciation of ½ interest not acquired by reason of death (½ of $12,000)		6,000
Basis at date of husband's death		$44,000

If she had not contributed any part of the purchase price, her basis at the date of her husband's death would be $54,000 ($60,000 fair market value less $6,000 depreciation).

Where property was held in joint tenancy and one of the tenants died before January 1, 1954, no part of the interest of the surviving tenant is treated, for purposes of determining the basis of the property, as property transmitted at death.

Qualified joint interest. Where, after 1976, a deceased dying before 1982 elected to treat realty as a "qualified joint interest" subject to gift tax, such joint property included in his estate is treated as owned fifty-fifty by each spouse. Thus, for income tax purposes, the basis of one half of the property is the estate tax value; the other half is determined under the gift rules detailed above. Personal property is treated as a "qualified joint interest" only if it was created or deemed to have been created after 1976 by a husband and wife and was subject to gift tax.

Eligible joint interest. Where death occurred before 1982 and a surviving spouse materially participated in the operation of a farm or other business, an estate may elect to treat the farm or business property as an "eligible joint interest," which means that that part of the investment in the property may be attributed to the surviving spouse's services and is not included in the deceased spouse's estate. Where such an election is made, the survivor's basis for income tax purposes includes the estate tax value of property included in decedent's estate.

WHEN TO ALLOCATE COST

¶ **6.31** Allocation of basis is generally required in these cases:

Purchase of land and building. To figure depreciation on the building, part of the purchase price must be allocated to the building. The allocation is made according to the fair market values of the building and land. The amount allocated to land is not depreciated.

Purchase of land to be divided into lots. The purchase price of the tract is allocated to each lot, so that the gain or loss from the sale of each lot may be reported in the year of its sale. Allocation is not made ratably, that is, with an equal share to each lot or parcel. It is based on the relative value of each piece of property. Comparable sales, competent appraisals, or assessed values may be used as guides.

See ¶30.3 for methods of identifying securities bought at different dates.

See ¶6.50 for allocating basis of stock dividends and stock splits; ¶6.51 for allocating the basis of stock rights.

See ¶5.45 for allocation rule applied to purchase price of a business.

HOW TO FIND ADJUSTED BASIS

¶ **6.32** After determining the unadjusted cost basis from the checklist starting at ¶6.29, you find your "adjusted basis" in two steps—

1. Additions to basis. You add to basis the cost of all improvements and additions to the property and other capital costs, purchase commissions, legal fees such as the cost of defending or perfecting title, title insurance, legal fees for obtaining a reduction of an assessment levied against property to pay for local benefits, and similar items that were not deductible as current expenses. Note that the instruction to Schedule D may also require you to add to basis selling expenses such as commissions (*see* ¶16.4).

When you buy real estate, you usually pay a portion of the taxes paid by the seller before you took title. If you bought the property before 1954, you add such payments to basis. If you bought the property after 1953, taxes paid are not added to basis because they are immediately deductible in the year paid (*see* ¶16.4). However, if you also paid taxes attributable to the time the seller held the property, you add such taxes to basis.

If you sell land with unharvested crops, add the cost of producing the crops to the basis of the property sold.

2. Deductions from basis. You reduce cost for items such as—

Return of capital, such as dividends on stock paid out of capital or out of a depletion reserve when the company has no available earnings or surplus (*see* ¶3.11).

Losses from casualties, including insurance awards and payments in settlement of damages to your property.

EXAMPLE

Your residence, which cost $15,000, is damaged by fire. You deducted the uninsured loss of $1,000. Several years later, you sell the house for $16,000. To figure your profit, you reduce the original cost of the house by the loss to get an adjusted basis of $14,000. Your gain on the sale is then $2,000 ($16,000–$14,000).

Depletion allowances.

Depreciation, ACRS deductions, amortization, and obsolescence on property used in business or for the production of income. In some years, you may have taken more or less depreciation than was allowable. If you took more depreciation than was allowable, you may have to make the following adjustments: If you have deducted more than what was allowable, and if you received a tax benefit from the deduction, you deduct the full amount of the depreciation. But if the excess depreciation did not give you a tax benefit, because income was eliminated by other deductions, the excess is not deducted from basis.

If you claim less than what was allowable, you must deduct the allowable amount. These rules affect all tax years after 1951. However, the rule covering the treatment of excessive depreciation does not affect pre-1952 years unless you made a special election before January 1, 1955, to come within that rule. Under pre-1952 law, basis is reduced by excessive depreciation even though no tax benefit is received by the deduction. (Property held before March 1, 1913 is reduced by depreciation actually sustained prior to that date.)

No adjustment is made for any first-year expensing claimed.

If you hold bonds bought at a premium, *see* ¶4.5. If you did not pay tax on certain cancellations of debt on your business property (*see* ¶12.15), you reduce basis for the amount forgiven.

Investment credit. Where the full investment credit was claimed in 1983 or later years, basis was reduced by one-half the credit.

REPORTING AN INSTALLMENT SALE

¶ 6.33 Installment selling offers you the opportunity to defer tax on a profitable sale of property. The new law, however, has reduced this advantage for sales of rental and business real estate that exceeds $150,000, *see* ¶6.43. Further such installment sales may not be recognized for alternative minimum tax (AMT) purposes, *see* ¶23.3. The new law has also repealed a favorable rule for profitable sales of publicly-traded securities. If you sell securities on an established exchange at the end of 1987 and do not receive the proceeds until early 1988, your profit is taxable in 1987, the year of the sale, and not in 1988 when the proceeds are received. The installment sale reporting rules no longer apply to sales of securities on a public exchange.

Finally under the new law, sellers of property under a revolving credit plan may no longer use the installment method after 1986, even if the sales were made before 1987. Sellers using revolving credit plans who are denied installment reporting may report adjusted income over a four-year period.

When installment sale rules apply. In 1987, if you sell property and receive one or more payments in a later year or years, you must report the sale as an installment sale, unless you elect otherwise or the sale is outside installment rules, such as a sale of publicly held stock. Form 6252 is used to compute installment sale income.

EXAMPLES

1. In 1987, you sell real estate for $50,000, receiving $10,000 in 1987, 1988 and 1989, and $20,000 in 1990. You realized a profit of $25,000 giving you a profit percentage of 50%. When the buyer pays the notes, you report the following:

In	You report payment of:	income of:
1987	$10,000	$ 5,000
1988	10,000	5,000
1989	10,000	5,000
1990	20,000	10,000
Total	$50,000	$25,000

In 1987, you file Form 6252 to figure your profit. You report only $5,000 as profit on Schedule D (or Form 4797 if applicable). If you do not want to use the installment method, you make an election by reporting the entire gain of $25,000 on Schedule D or Form 4797. Schedule D provides a special box to check your election *out* of the installment method.

2. On December 20, 1987, you sell a building for $50,000, realizing a profit of $25,000. You take a note payable in January 1988. You report the gain in 1988. Receiving a lump-sum payment in a taxable year after the year of sale is considered an installment sale.

The installment method may not be used for reporting a loss.

A farmer may use the installment method to report gain from the sale of property that does not have to be inventoried under his method of accounting. This is true, even though such property is held for regular sale.

Dealers selling personal property on the installment plan are subject to special rules not discussed in this book.

Depreciation recapture. If you make an installment sale of depreciable property after June 6, 1984, any depreciation recapture is reported as income in the year of disposition. Recaptured income increases the basis of the property for purposes of figuring the gross profit ratio for the balance of gain to be reported, if any, over the installment period, *see also* ¶5.43.

FIGURING THE TAXABLE PART OF INSTALLMENT PAYMENTS

¶ 6.34 On the installment method, a portion of each payment represents part of your gain. The profit percentage or ratio applied to each payment is figured by dividing gross profit by contract price. What you include in the selling price, contract price, and gross profit is explained in the following paragraphs.

Selling price. Include cash, fair market value of property received from the buyer, his notes (at face value), and any existing mortgage on the property whether or not assumed by the buyer. If, under the contract of sale, the buyer pays off an existing mortgage or assumes liability for any other liens on the property or pays the sales commissions, such payments are also included in the selling price.

Interest is not included in the selling price.

Notes of a third party given to you by the buyer are valued at fair market value.

Contract price. If there is no mortgage on the property, the contract price is usually the same as the gross selling price. If there is a mortgage, the selling price is reduced by the amount of the mortgage, unless it exceeds the adjusted basis of the property. If the mortgage exceeds the adjusted basis of the property, reduce the contract price only by the amount of the mortgage equal to the amount of the adjusted basis. Do this whether or not the buyer assumes the mortgage. Wrap-around mortgages are discussed below. An obligation of the seller which the buyer assumes, whether related to the sale, such as legal fees, or unrelated, such as medical bills, is not treated as part of the contract price.

EXAMPLE

You sell a building for $160,000. The property is subject to a mortgage of $60,000. The buyer will assume the mortgage and pay the $100,000 in five equal annual installments. The contract price is $100,000; the $160,000 selling price less the mortgage of $60,000.

Payments received. Payments include cash, the fair market value of property, and payments on the buyer's notes. Payments do not include receipt of the buyer's notes or other evidence of indebtedness, unless payable on demand or readily tradable. "Readily tradable" means registered bonds, bonds with coupons attached, debentures, and other evidences of indebtedness of the buyer that are readily tradable in an established securities market. This rule is directed mainly at corporate acquisitions.

Payments in the year of sale include mortgages that the buyer assumes or takes subject to only to the extent the mortgage exceeds the basis of property.

EXAMPLE

You sell a building for $160,000, subject to a mortgage of $60,000. Installments are to be paid over five years. Your basis in the property is $40,000. The buyer assumes the mortgage. In the year of the sale, you are treated as having received payment of $20,000, the amount by which the $60,000 mortgage exceeds basis of $40,000. The basis of the property is treated as being fully recovered in the year of sale. Thus, all of the installment payments received on the sale are fully taxable. The gross profit ratio is 100% (gross profit of $120,000 divided by contract price of $120,000). The contract price is selling price less that part of the mortgage that did not exceed basis.

A third party guarantee (including a standby letter of credit) is not treated as a payment received on an installment obligation.

Gross profit. Gross profit is the selling price less the adjusted basis of the property sold. Selling expenses, such as brokers' commissions and legal fees, are added to basis for purposes of computing gross profit. If you change the selling price during the period payments are outstanding, the gross profit percentage is refigured on the basis of the new selling price. The adjusted profit ratio is then applied to payments received after the adjustment.

EXAMPLE

Jones sells real estate for $100,000 and realizes a gain of $60,000. The purchase price is to be paid in five annual installments of $20,000. Jones reported profit of $12,000 (60% of $20,000) on each installment received in 1985 and 1986. In 1987, the sales price is reduced to $85,000 and payments for 1987, 1988, and 1989 are reduced to $15,000. Jones's original profit of $60,000 is reduced to $45,000. Of this amount, $24,000 was reported in 1985 and 1986. Thus, the profit to be received is $21,000, or $7,000 each year over the three remaining installments of $15,000.

Figuring the profit percentage or ratio. The profit percentage or ratio is found by dividing gross profit by contract price. The computation may be made by following the line-by-line instructions to Form 6252.

EXAMPLE

On December 19, 1987, you sell real estate for $100,000. The property had an adjusted basis of $56,000. Selling expenses are $4,000. You are to receive installment payments of $25,000 in 1987, 1988, 1989, and 1990. The gross profit ratio is determined as follows:

Selling price (contract price)	$100,000
Less: Adjusted basis and selling expenses	60,000
Gross profit	$ 40,000

$$\frac{\text{Gross profit}}{\text{Contract price}} = \frac{\$40,000}{\$100,000} = 40\%$$

In 1987, you report a profit of $10,000 (40% of $25,000). Similarly, in each of the following three years, a profit of $10,000 is reported so that by the end of four years, the entire $40,000 profit will have been reported.

Wrap-around mortgage. For purposes of figuring contract price in the year of sale, the IRS regulations treat a wrap-around mortgage as if the buyer had assumed or taken the property subject to it, even though title does not pass to the buyer in the year of sale and the seller continues to make direct payments on the mortgage. The IRS rule requires a reduction of the contract price by the amount of the mortgage as explained in the above discussion of contract price. As a result, all of the initial payments may be subject to tax as the gross profit ratio may be 100%. Further, under the regulations, a second gross profit ratio must be computed for reporting gain on the installment obligations. Examples of the computation may be found in Temporary Regulation Sec. 15A.453-1(b)(3)(ii). Recently, however, the Tax Court ruled that these regulations are invalid and incomprehensible. Under the Tax Court approach, the contract price is *not* reduced by the amount of the mortgage on which the seller makes direct payments, and only one gross profit ratio would apply to the payments under the general rules discussed above.

EXAMPLE

The seller sells real property worth $2 million, encumbered by a mortgage of $900,000. His basis is $700,000. The buyer pays $200,000 cash and gives an interest-bearing wrap-around mortgage note for $1.8 million. The seller remains obligated to pay off the $900,000 mortgage. The $900,000 mortgage is treated as if the buyer assumed it or the property was taken subject to it. Thus, in the year of sale, the seller is

treated by the IRS as receiving $400,000—$200,000 cash plus $200,000 excess of the mortgages ($900,000) over the basis ($700,000). Since the seller's gross profit ratio is 1 ($1,300,000 gross profit ÷ $1,300,000 contract price), the seller is taxed on the entire $400,000 in the year of sale.

Sale of depreciable property. For the effect of recapture, see ¶5.43.

Recapture of first-year expensing deduction. The entire recaptured amount under ¶5.39 is reported in the year of sale, even though you report the sale on the installment basis. An installment sale does not defer the reporting of the recaptured deduction. You also add the recaptured amount to the basis of the sold asset to compute the amount of the remaining gain to be reported on each installment.

ELECTING NOT TO REPORT ON THE INSTALLMENT METHOD

¶ 6.35 Unless you make a timely election, an installment sale is automatically reported on the installment basis. If you want to report the entire gain in the year of sale, you must elect to do so within the time for filing your return (plus extensions) for the year of sale by reporting the entire gain on Schedule D, or Form 4797.

If you report on the cash basis and receive an obligation whose fair market value is less than face value, you report fair market value of the note. You also must show how you found your value. Fair market value of an obligation may not be set for an amount less than the fair market value of the property, less other payments received on the sale. If you report on the accrual basis, you report the full face amount of the obligation.

An election not to report on the installment method may be revoked only with the consent of the IRS. A revocation will not be permitted for tax avoidance purposes. The IRS in a private ruling refused to allow a seller to use the installment method after inadvertently including the entire gain from the sale on his return. Although reporting of the entire gain was a mistake, this was treated as an election not to use the installment method. The IRS refused permission to revoke the election on the grounds that a second chance to apply the installment method would be tax avoidance.

An election after the due date must be made with IRS consent.

> *When to "elect out" of installment reporting.* Where you have losses to offset your gain in the year of sale, installment sale reporting may be disadvantageous. In such a case, you may want to elect not to report on the installment basis. There is a risk to electing out if the deduction for the losses may be disallowed. If the losses are later disallowed by an IRS audit, you may not have a second chance to use the installment method to spread the gain over the payment period. For example, a seller elected out in a year in which he planned to deduct a net operating loss carryforward from an installment sale gain. In a later year, the IRS substantially reduced the loss. The seller then asked the IRS to allow him to revoke the election to elect out of the installment method. The IRS refused, claiming that the seller had a tax avoidance purpose in asking for the revocation. The installment sale would defer gain to a later year.

Year-end sales of publicly traded securities. You have no choice about when to report the gain from a sale of publicly traded stock or securities made at the end of 1987. Any gain must be reported in 1987, even if the proceeds are not received until early 1988. The sale is not considered an installment sale.

RESTRICTION OF INSTALLMENT SALES TO RELATIVES AND OTHER RELATED PARTIES

¶ 6.36 The installment sale method may not be allowed where you (1) sell to a relative who then sells the property or (2) sell depreciable property to a spouse or to a controlled business (50% control by seller and/or spouse).

The restrictions are primarily aimed at the following types of transactions:

1. A buyer insists on paying cash, but the seller who wants the tax

deferment advantage of installment reporting arranges an installment sale with a family member who then resells the property for cash to the buyer.

2. Securities traded on the exchange cannot be sold on the exchange on the installment basis. To get installment basis reporting an investor would sell to a related party on the installment basis, and the related party would then sell the securities on the exchange.

The tax deferral advantages of installment reporting are generally lost in the above cases when the related party sells the property to the third party; at the time of the second sale, the original seller must report income.

EXAMPLE

In 1987, Jones sells stock to his son for $25,000, realizing a profit of $10,000. The son agrees to pay in five annual installments of $5,000 starting in 1988. Later in 1987, the son sells the stock to a third party for $26,000. Jones Sr. reports his profit of $10,000 in 1987 even though he received no payment that year. Payments received by Jones Sr. from his son after 1987 are tax free because he reported the entire profit in 1987.

The amount to be reported as a result of a second sale by a related party is figured on Form 6252.

Two-year rule. If nondepreciable property other than marketable securities is sold, you are taxed on a second sale by a related party only if it occurs within two years of the initial installment sale. The two-year period is extended during any period in which the buyer's risk is lessened by a put on the property, an option by another person to acquire the property, or a short-sale or other transactions lessening the risk of loss. The two-year rule does not apply to the sale of marketable securities. Marketable securities are: (1) Securities listed on the New York Stock Exchange, the American Stock Exchange, or any city or regional exchange in which quotations appear on a daily basis, including foreign securities listed on a recognized foreign, national or regional exchange; (2) securities regularly traded in the national or regional over-the-counter market, for which published quotations are available; (3) securities locally traded for which quotations can readily be obtained from established brokerage firms; (4) units in a common trust fund; and (5) mutual fund shares for which redemption prices are published.

Related parties include a spouse, child, grandchild, parent, brother or sister, controlled corporation (50% or more direct or indirect ownership) and related partnerships or family trusts. There are exceptions to this related party rule. Second dispositions resulting from an involuntary conversion of the property will not be subject to the related party rule so long as the first disposition occurred before the threat or imminence of conversion. Similarly, transfers after the death of the person making the first disposition or the death of the person acquiring the property in first disposition are not treated as second dispositions. Also, a sale or exchange of stock to the issuing corporation is not treated as a first disposition. Finally, you may avoid tax on a related party's second sale by satisfying the IRS that neither the initial nor the second sale were made for tax avoidance purposes.

Where you transfer property to a related party, the IRS has two years from the date you notify it that there has been a second disposition to assess a deficiency with respect to your transfer.

Sales of depreciable property to related party. Installment reporting is not allowed for sales of depreciable property made to a controlled corporation or partnership (50% control by seller and/or spouse) and between such controlled corporations and partnerships. Installment reporting is also disallowed on a sale to a trust in which you or a spouse is a beneficiary unless your interest is considered a remote contingent interest whose actuarial value is 5% or less of the trust property's value. On these related party sales, the entire gain is reported in the year of sale, unless the seller convinces the IRS that the transfer was not motivated by tax avoidance purposes. Installment reporting may be allowed if at the time of the sale the couple was legally separated under a decree of divorce or separate maintenance, or if the sale was pursuant to a settlement in a proceeding which culminates in such a decree.

On a sale of depreciable property to a related party, if the amount of payments are contingent, for example payments are tied to profits, the seller must make a special calculation. He must treat as received in the year of sale all noncontingent payments plus the fair market value of the contingent payments if such value may be reasonably ascertained. If the fair market value of the contingent payments may not be reasonably calculated, the seller recovers basis ratably. The purchaser's basis for the acquired property includes only amounts that the seller has included in income under the basis recovery rule. Thus, the purchaser's basis is increased annually as the seller recovers basis.

CONTINGENT PAYMENT SALES

¶ **6.37** Where the final selling price or payment period of an installment sale is not fixed at the end of the taxable year of sale, you are considered to have transacted a "contingent payment sale." Special rules apply where a maximum selling price may be figured under the terms of the agreement or there is no fixed price but there is a fixed payment period, or there is neither a fixed price nor fixed payment period.

Stated maximum selling price. Under Treasury regulations, a stated maximum selling price may be determined by assuming that all of the contingencies contemplated by the agreement are met. When the maximum amount is later reduced, the gross profit ratio is recomputed.

EXAMPLE

Smith sells stock in Acme Co. for a down payment of $100,000 plus an amount equal to 5% of the net profits of Acme for the next nine years. The contract provides that the maximum amount payable, including the $100,000 down payment but exclusive of interest, is $2,000,000. Smith's basis for the stock is $200,000; $2,000,000 is the selling price and contract price. Gross profit is $1,800,000. The gross profit ratio is 90% ($1,800,000 ÷ $2,000,000). Thus, $90,000 of the first payment is reportable as gain, $10,000 as a recovery of basis.

Fixed period. When a stated maximum selling price is not determinable but the maximum payment period is fixed, basis, including selling expenses, is allocated equally to the taxable years in which payment may be received under the agreement. If in any year, no payment is received or the amount of payment received is less than the basis allocated to that taxable year, no loss is allowed unless the taxable year is the final payment year or the agreement has become worthless. When no loss is allowed in a year, the basis allocated to the taxable year is carried forward to the next succeeding taxable year.

EXAMPLE

Brown sells property for 10% of the property's gross rents over a five-year period. Brown's basis is $5,000,000. The sales price is indefinite and the maximum selling price is not fixed under the terms of the contract; basis is recovered ratably over the five-year period.

Year	Payment	Basis recovered	Gain
1987	$1,300,000	$1,000,000	$ 300,000
1988	1,500,000	1,000,000	500,000
1989	1,400,000	1,000,000	400,000
1990	1,800,000	1,000,000	800,000
1991	2,100,000	1,000,000	1,100,000

No stated maximum selling price or fixed period. If the agreement fails to specify a maximum selling price and payment period, the IRS may view the agreement as a rent or royalty income agreement. However, if the arrangement qualifies as a sale, basis (including selling expenses) is recovered in equal annual increments over a 15-year period commencing with the date of sale. If in any taxable year, no payment is received or the amount of payment received (exclusive of interest) is less than basis allocated to the year, no loss is allowed unless the agreement has become worthless. Excess basis not recovered in one year is reallocated in level amounts over the balance of the 15-year term. Any basis not recovered at the end of the 15th year is carried forward to the next succeeding year, and to the extent unrecovered, carried forward from year to year until basis has been recovered or the agreement is determined to be worthless. The rule requiring initial level allocation of basis over 15 years may not apply if you prove to the Service that a 15-year general rule will substantially and inappropriately defer recovery of basis. *See* Treasury regulations for further details.

In some cases, basis recovery under an income forecast type of method may also be allowed under Treasury regulations.

An installment sale with payments to be made in foreign currency or fungible payment units (such as bushels of wheat) is a contingent payment sale, but basis is allocated as if payment was fixed in U.S. dollars.

EXAMPLE

In 1987, Jones sells property for 10,000 English pounds. In 1988, 2,500 pounds are payable. In 1989, the balance of 7,500 pounds is payable. Basis in the property is $2,000. In 1988, 25% of the basis or $500 (25% of $2,000) is allocated to the first payment. In 1989, $1,500 (75% of $2,000) is allocated to the second payment.

USING ESCROW AND OTHER SECURITY ARRANGEMENTS

¶ **6.38** You sell property and the sales proceeds are placed in escrow pending the possible occurrence of an event such as the approval of title or your performance of certain contractual conditions. The sale proceeds are not taxed until the year in which the escrow agent releases the funds to you.

The escrow agreement may authorize you to receive the income it produces or it may even authorize you to control the manner in which the fund is to be invested. According to a court decision, these facts do not make the fund taxable to you before the year you actually have it. You are, of course, taxable on the income earned by the fund when it is received by you.

EXAMPLE

Anderson sold stock and mining property for almost $5 million. He agreed to place $500,000 in escrow to protect the buyer against his possible breaches of warranty and to provide security for certain liabilities. The escrow agreement called for Anderson to direct the investments of the escrow fund and receive income from the fund in excess of $500,000.

The IRS claimed that in the year of sale Anderson was taxable on the $500,000 held in escrow on the grounds that Anderson's control of the fund rendered the fund taxable immediately. Anderson argued that he was only taxable as the funds were released to him and the Tax Court agreed. The fund was not under his unqualified control. He might never get the fund if the liabilities materialize. Although Anderson had a free hand with investment of the money, he still lacked ultimate ownership.

If the terms of the escrow involve no genuine conditions that prevent you from demanding immediate payment, there will be immediate tax.

EXAMPLE

Rhodes sold a tract to a buyer who was willing to pay at once the entire purchase price of $157,000. But Rhodes wanted to report the sale on the installment basis over a period of years. The buyer refused to execute a purchase money mortgage on the property to allow the installment sale election (required under prior law), because he wanted clear and unencumbered title to the tract. As a solution, Rhodes asked the buyer to turn over the purchase price to a bank, as escrow agent, which would pay the sum over a five-year period.

The escrow arrangement failed to support an installment sale. Rhodes was fully taxable on the entire price in the year of the sale. The buyer's payment was unconditional and irrevocable. The escrow arrangement involved no genuine conditions that could defeat Rhodes's right to payment, as the buyer could not revoke, alter, or end the arrangement.

Substitution of an escrow account for unpaid notes or deed of trust disqualifies installment reporting.

EXAMPLE

In January, an investor sold real estate for $100,000. He received $10,000 as a down payment and six notes, each for $15,000, secured by a deed of trust on the property. The notes, together with interest, were due annually over the next six years. In July, the buyer deposited the remainder of the purchase price with an escrow agent and got the seller to cancel the deed of trust.

The agreement provides that the escrow agent will pay off the buyer's notes as they fall due. The buyer remains liable for the installment payments. The escrow deposit is irrevocable, and the payment schedule may not be accelerated by any party under any circumstances. Accord-

ing to the IRS the sale, which initially qualified as an installment sale, is disqualified by the escrow account.

If an escrow arrangement imposes a substantial restriction, the IRS may allow installment reporting. An example of a substantial restriction: Payment of the escrow is tied to the condition that the seller refrain from entering a competing business for a period of five years. If, at any time during the escrow period, he engaged in a competing business, he forfeits all rights to the amount then held in escrow.

MINIMUM INTEREST MAY BE REQUIRED ON DEFERRED PAYMENT SALES

¶ **6.39** The tax law requires a minimum amount of interest to be charged on deferred payment sales.

The rules for imputing interest are discussed at ¶4.18.

Imputed interest is included in the taxable income of the seller. Imputed interest is deductible by the buyer if the property is business or investment property but not if it is used substantially all the time for personal purposes.

SALE OR OTHER TRANSFER OR CANCELLATION OF INSTALLMENT NOTES

¶ **6.40** A sale, a gift, or other transfer or cancellation of mortgage notes or other obligation received in an installment sale has tax consequences. If you sell or exchange the notes at other than face value, gain or loss results to the extent of the difference between the basis of the notes and the amount realized. Gain or loss is long term if the original sale was entitled to long-term capital gain treatment. This is true even if the notes were held short term. If the original sale resulted in short-term gain or ordinary income, the sale of the notes gives short-term gain or ordinary income, regardless of the holding period of the notes.

The basis of an installment note or obligation is the face value of the note less the income that would be reported if the obligation were paid in full.

EXAMPLE

You sell a lot for $2,000 which cost you $1,000. In the year of the sale, you received $500 in cash and the purchaser's notes for the remainder of the selling price, or $1,500. A year later, before the buyer makes a payment on the notes, you sell them for $1,300 cash:

Selling price of property	$2,000
Cost of property	1,000
Total profit	$1,000
(Percentage of profit, or proportion of each payment returnable as income, is 50%)	
Unpaid balance of notes	$1,500
Amount of income reportable if notes were paid in full (50% of $1,500)	750
Adjusted basis of the notes	$ 750

Your profit on the sale is $550 ($1,300–$750). It is capital gain if the sale of the lot was taxable as capital gain.

Suppose you make an installment sale of your real estate. taking back a land contract. Later a mortgage is substituted for the unpaid balance of the land contract. The IRS has ruled that the substitution is not the same as a disposition of the unpaid installment obligations. There is no tax on the substitution.

If the installment obligations are disposed of other than by sale or exchange, gain or loss is the difference between the basis of the obligations and their fair market value at the time of the disposition. If an installment obligation is canceled or otherwise becomes unenforceable, it is subject to the same rule for determining gain or loss.

A gift of installment obligations to a person or charitable organization is treated as a taxable disposition. Gain or loss is the difference between the basis of the obligations and their fair market value at the time of the gift. If the notes are donated to a qualified charity, you may claim a contribution deduction for the fair market value of the obligations at the time of the gift.

Not all dispositions of installment obligations result in recognition of gain or loss. A transfer of installment obligations to your spouse or a transfer to a former spouse that is incident to a divorce is treated as a tax-free exchange under the rules of ¶6.49 unless the transfer is in trust. A transfer of installment obligations at death is not taxed. As the notes are paid, the estate or beneficiaries report income in the same proportion as the decedent would have, had he lived. A transfer of installment obligations to a revocable trust is also not taxed.

REPOSSESSION OF PERSONAL PROPERTY SOLD ON INSTALLMENT

¶ **6.41** When the buyer defaults and you repossess property, either through a voluntary surrender or a foreclosure, you may realize gain or loss. The method of calculating gain or loss is similar to the method used for disposition of installment notes (see ¶6.40 above). Gain or loss is the difference between the fair market value of the repossessed property and your basis for the installment obligations satisfied by the repossession. This rule is followed whether or not title has been kept by you or transferred to the buyer. The amount realized is reduced by costs incurred during the repossession. The basis of the obligation is face value less unreported profit.

If the property repossessed is bid in at a lawful public auction or judicial sale, the fair market value of the property is presumed to be the purchase or bid price, in the absence of proof to the contrary.

Gain or loss in the repossession is reported in the year of the repossession.

EXAMPLE

In December 1986, you sell personal property for $1,500—$300 down and $100 a month beginning January 1987. You reported the installment sale on your 1986 tax return. The buyer defaulted after making three monthly payments. You foreclosed and repossessed the property; the fair market value was $1,400. The legal costs of foreclosure were $100. The gain on the repossession in 1987 is computed as follows:

Fair market value of property repossessed		$1,400
Basis of the buyer's notes at time of repossession:		
Selling price	$1,500	
Less: Payments made	600	
Face value of notes at repossession	$ 900	
Less: Unrealized profit (assume gross profit percentage of 33⅓ × $900)	300	600
Gain on repossession		$ 800
Less: Repossession costs		100
Taxable gain on repossession		$ 700

Repossession gain or loss keeps the same character as the gain or loss realized on the original sale. If the sale originally resulted in a capital gain, the repossession gain is also a capital gain.

Repossessions of real property are discussed at ¶31.7. Your basis in the repossessed property is its fair market value at the time of repossession.

BOOT IN A LIKE-KIND EXCHANGE PAYABLE IN INSTALLMENTS

¶ **6.42** An exchange of like-kind property is generally tax free unless boot, such as cash or notes, is received. The boot is taxable, and if payable in installments, the following rules apply. Contract price is reduced by like-kind property received. Gross profit is reduced by gain not recognized. "Payment" does not include like-kind property.

EXAMPLE

Property with a basis of $400,000 is exchanged for like-kind prop-

erty worth $200,000 plus installment obligations of $800,000, of which $100,000 is payable in the year of sale. The contract price is $800,000 ($1 million less $200,000 like-kind property received); the gross profit is $600,000 ($200,000 basis attributed to notes). The gross profit ratio is 75% (gross profit of $600,000 ÷ contract price of $800,000); like-kind property is not treated as a payment received in the year of sale.

The same treatment applies to certain tax-free reorganizations which are not treated as dividends, and to exchanges of certain insurance policies, exchanges of the stock of the same corporation, and exchanges of United States obligations.

INCOME ACCELERATION ON CERTAIN INSTALLMENT SALES

¶ **6.43** The Treasury has convinced Congress that the installment sale method defers too much tax for dealers of property and certain real estate investors and business owners. To cripple or defeat the tax deferment benefits of installment sales, a new law effective for 1987 returns applies a complicated calculation that accelerates taxable income currently even though installment payments are not made. That is, part of the outstanding installment obligation is treated as if it were paid to you at the end of 1987, even though it was not actually paid. The income rule is determined under IRC Section 453C and treats "allocable installment indebtedness" (AII) as a deemed payment.

The rules apply to dealers of personal and real property. They also apply to sales of real estate used in a business, or rental real estate held for income-producing purposes if the sales price exceeds $150,000. The rules do not apply to sales of property you use for personal purposes or sales of property used in a farming business. Certain sales by manufacturers of tangible personal property to a dealer are also exempted as well as certain sales by individual dealers of timeshares and lots.

Specifically, the income rule applies to installment obligations from the following sales:

1. Sales by dealers after February 28, 1986, of real estate or personal property
2. Sales after August 16, 1986, of business real estate or rental real estate held for the production of income where the sales price exceeds $150,000.

Thus, if you sell a rented vacation home for more than $150,000 on the installment basis, you will have to report as income a portion of the outstanding installment debt. A sale of rental real estate for $150,000 or less is not subject to this income reporting rule.

Exceptions. A sale of your personal residence or other personal property is not subject to these rules regardless of the sales price. Property used or produced on a farm is also exempted.

Method of computing income. In general, the amount of reportable income is based on a percentage applied to an average of your installment obligations and other outstanding debts. All forms of debt must be taken into account, including accounts payable and accrued expenses. It does not matter that the debt is unrelated to the installment sale. However, debt secured by property for personal use or farming is not counted.

The debt is computed on a quarterly basis, unless you have no installment obligations outstanding during the year from dealer property sales. In such a case, the computation is done at the end of the taxable year. If AII income is reported because of outstanding debt, payments in a later year of the installment obligations are treated as a tax-free recovery of the previously reported AII income.

Several calculations are necessary to determine income to be reported. At the time this book went to press, specific guidelines for making the calculations were not available. *See* the Supplement for further information and follow tax return instructions if you are subject to the income reporting rule.

AMT consequences. Sales subject to the above rules are not recognized as installment sales for computing income for alternative minimum tax purposes. Gain is treated as received in the year of sale, regardless of when payments are received.

TAX FREE EXCHANGES

¶ 6.44 The term "gain is not recognized" means that the gain is not taxed in the year it is realized. Gain may be taxed at a later disposition of the property because the basis of the property received in the exchange is usually the same as the basis of the property surrendered in the exchange. Thus, if you make a tax-free exchange of property with a tax basis of $10,000 for property worth $50,000, the basis of the property received in exchange is fixed at $10,000, even though its fair market value is $50,000. The gain of $40,000 ($50,000–$10,000) is not recognized. If you later sell the property for $50,000, you realize taxable gain of $40,000 ($50,000–$10,000).

Where property received in a tax-free exchange is held until death, the nonrecognized gain escapes tax forever because basis of the property in the hands of an heir is generally the value of the property at the death of the descendent. *See* ¶6.29.

A tax-free exchange may also involve the transfer of boot such as cash or other property. Gain on the exchange is taxable to the extent of the value of boot.

EXAMPLE

You make a tax-free exchange of property. The tax basis of the property you exchanged was $30,000; the value of the new property is $60,000. You also received cash of $20,000. Gain on the exchange is $50,000 ($80,000–$30,000). Of this amount, $20,000 is taxed in the year of exchange.

Tax-free exchange rules for certain corporate reorganizations are not discussed in this book.

See ¶5.49 for restrictions on deferred exchanges and exchanges of partnership interests.

TAX FREE EXCHANGES OF STOCK

¶ 6.45 Gain on the exchange of common stock for other common stock (or preferred for other preferred) of the same company is not taxable. Similarly, loss realized on such an exchange is not deductible. The exchange may take place between the stockholder and the company or between two stockholders.

An exchange of preferred stock for common, or common for preferred in the same company, is generally not tax free, unless the exchange is part of a tax-free recapitalization. In such exchanges, the company should inform you of the tax consequences.

Convertible securities. Conversion of securities under a conversion privilege is tax free under the rules discussed at ¶6.54

EXCHANGES OF JOINT OWNERSHIP INTERESTS

¶ 6.46 The change to a tenancy in common from a joint tenancy is tax free. You may convert a joint tenancy in corporate stock to a tenancy in common without income tax consequences. The transfer is tax free even though survivorship rights are eliminated. Similarly, a partition and issuance of separate certificates in the names of each joint tenant is also tax free.

A joint tenancy and a tenancy in common differ in this respect. On the death of a joint tenant, this ownership passes to the surviving joint tenant or tenants. But on the death of a tenant holding property in common, his ownership passes to his heirs, not to the other tenant or tenant who held the property with him.

A tenancy by the entirety is a form of joint ownership recognized in some states and can be only between a husband and wife.

A division of properties held as tenants in common may qualify as tax-free exchanges.

EXAMPLE

Three men owned three pieces of real estate as tenants in common. Each man wanted to be the sole owner of one of the pieces of property. They disentangled themselves by exchanging interests in a three-way exchange. No money or property other than the three pieces of real estate changed hands, and none of the men assumed any liability of the others. The transactions qualified as tax-free exchanges and no gain or loss was recognized.

Receipt of boot. Exchanges of jointly owned property are tax free as long as no "boot" such as cash or other property passes between the parties. Boot may not be offset by an assumption of the other party's liabilities.

EXAMPLE

Two farmers, A and B, each owned a one-half interest in two parcels of land used in their farming businesses. Each parcel cost $10,000 and had a fair market value of $200,000. One parcel was subject to a $100,000 mortgage on which they were jointly liable. They decided to exchange interests in the properties so that each owned 100% of one of the parcels: B received the nonmortgaged property; A, the mortgaged property, plus B's note of $50,000 to compensate him for taking the property subject to the mortgage.

The IRS holds that there was a tax free exchange, but at the same time, A received taxable boot of $50,000 in the form of B's note. Further, he may not offset this amount from his assumption of the additional mortgage liability. B did not realize any taxable boot. A's assumption of B's liability on the mortgage may be offset by the $50,000 note he gave to A.

TAX FREE TRANSFERS ALLOWED IN SETTING UP A CLOSELY HELD CORPORATION

¶ 6.47 Tax-free exchange rules facilitate the organization of a corporation. When you transfer property to a corporation that you control solely in exchange for corporate stock or securities, no gain or loss is recognized on the transfer. For control, you alone or together with other transferors (such as partners, where a partnership is being incorporated) must own at least 80% of the combined voting power of the corporation and 80% of all other classes of stock immediately after the transfer to the corporation.

The corporation takes your basis in the property, and your basis in the stock received in the exchange is the same as your basis in the property. Thus, gain not recognized on the organization of the corporation may be taxed when you sell your stock, or the corporation disposes of the property.

EXAMPLE

You transfer a building worth $100,000, which cost you $20,000, to your newly organized corporation in exchange for all of its outstanding stock. You realize an $80,000 gain ($100,000 – $20,000) which is not recognized. Your basis in the stock is $20,000; the corporation's basis in the building is $20,000. The following year, you sell all your stock to a third party for $100,000. The $80,000 gain is now recognized.

Transfer of liabilities. When assets subject to liabilities are transferred to the corporation, the liability assumed by the corporation is not treated as a taxable "boot," but your stock basis is reduced by the amount of liability. The transfer of liabilities may be taxable when the transfer is part of a tax avoidance scheme, or the liabilities exceed the basis of the property transferred to the corporation.

Consult an accountant or an attorney before undertaking a tax-free transfer to a closely held corporation to determine the tax consequences of intended transfers. Also, it may not be to your advantage to fall within the tax-free exchange rules. This is so when you have property with potential losses or you wish the corporation to take a stepped-up basis for property.

EXCHANGES OF COINS AND BULLION

¶ **6.48** An exchange of "gold for gold" coins or "silver for silver" coins may qualify as a tax-free exchange of like-kind investment property. An exchange is tax free if both coins represent the same type of underlying investment. An exchange of bullion-type coins for bullion-type coins is a tax-free like-kind exchange. For example, the exchange of Mexican pesos for Austrian coronas has been held to be a tax-free exchange as both are bullion-type coins.

However, an exchange of silver bullion for gold bullion is not tax free. Silver and gold bullion represent different types of property. Silver is an industrial commodity, whereas gold is primarily an investment in itself. Similarly, an exchange of U.S. gold collector's coins for South African Krugerrands is taxable. Krugerrands are bullion-type coins whose value is determined solely by metal content, whereas the U.S. gold coins are numismatic coins whose value depends on age, condition, number minted, and artistic merit, as well as metal content. Although both coins appear to be similar because of gold content, each represents a different type of investment.

PROPERTY TRANSFERS BETWEEN SPOUSES

¶ **6.49** Tax-free exchange rules apply to all transfers between spouses other than certain trust transfers of mortgaged property (*see* below). The tax-free exchange rules apply to transfers during marriage as well as to those incident to divorce. A transfer "incident to a divorce," must either occur within one year after the date the marriage ceases or, if later, be related to the cessation of the marriage, such as a transfer authorized by a divorce decree. Under temporary regulations, any transfer pursuant to a divorce or separation agreement occurring within six years of the end of the marriage is considered "incident to a divorce." Later transfers qualify only if a transfer within the six-year period was hampered by legal or business disputes, such as a fight over the property value.

Nonresident alien. The tax-free exchange rule does not apply to transfers to a nonresident alien spouse. But it does apply to a transfer to a former spouse who is a nonresident alien, provided that the "incident to a divorce" test is met.

Basis. The basis of the property to the transferee-spouse is the same as the basis of the property to the transferor-spouse. Thus, the transferee bears the tax consequences of a later sale. In a marital settlement, he or she can lessen the tax burden by negotiating for assets that have little or no unrealized appreciation.

EXAMPLE

In a property settlement accompanying a divorce, a husband plans to transfer to his wife stock worth $250,000 that cost him $50,000. In deciding whether to agree to the transfer, the wife should be aware that her basis for the stock will be $50,000; if she sells the stock, she will have to pay tax on the $200,000 gain. She should consider this tax cost in arriving at the settlement.

Transfers in trust. The above tax-free exchange rules generally apply to transfers in trust for the benefit of a spouse or a former spouse if incident to a divorce. However, if the trust property is mortgaged, the transferor spouse must report a taxable gain to the extent that the liabilities assumed by the transferee spouse plus the liabilities to which the property is subject (even if not assumed) exceed the transferor's adjusted basis for the property. If the transferor realizes a taxable gain under this rule, the transferee's basis for the property is increased by the gain.

Under temporary IRS regulations, the tax-free exchange rules even apply to a sale of business property by a sole proprietor to a spouse. The buyer spouse assumed a carryover basis even if fair market value is paid. The transferor is not required to recapture previously claimed deductions or investment credits. However, the transferee is subject to the recapture rules on a premature disposition of the property or if the property is not used for business purposes.

Effective date. The tax-free rules generally apply to transfers made after July 18, 1984. Transfers made under agreements in effect before July 19, 1984, are subject to the tax-free rule only if both spouses make an election to have the tax-free rule apply. The election must be made on a signed statement attached to the first tax return filed by the transferor-spouse for the year in which the first transfer occurs. The transferor must also attach the statement to returns for later years in which a transfer is made under the election.

The rule taxing certain trust transfers of mortgaged property was enacted by the 1986 Tax Act but made retroactive so that transfers in trust after July 18, 1984, could be taxed under the new provision.

SALES OF STOCK DIVIDENDS AND RIGHTS, SHORT SALES, AND WASH SALES

SALE OF STOCK RECEIVED AS DIVIDEND AND IN A STOCK SPLIT

¶ **6.50** A sale of stock originally received as a dividend is treated as any other sale of stock. The holding period of a taxable stock dividend begins on the day after the date of distribution. The holding period of a tax-free stock dividend or stock received in a split starts from the time you acquired the original stock.

EXAMPLE
You bought 100 shares of X Co. stock on December 3, 1986. On August 13, 1987, you receive 10 shares of X Co. stock as a tax-free stock dividend. On December 10, 1987, you sell the 10 shares at a profit. You report the sale as long-term capital gain because the holding period of the 10 shares goes back to your original purchase date of December 3, 1986, not August 13, 1987.

Basis of tax-free dividend in the same class of stock. Assume you receive common on common. You divide the original cost by the total number of old shares and new shares to find the new basis per share.

EXAMPLE
You bought 100 shares of common stock for $1,000, so that each share has a basis of $10. You receive 100 shares of common as a tax-free stock dividend. The basis of your 200 shares remains $1,000. The new cost basis of each share is now $5 ($1,000 ÷ 200 shares). You sell 50 shares for $560. Your profit is $310 ($560–$250).

Basis of tax-free dividend in a different class of stock. Assume you receive preferred on common. You divide the basis of the old shares over the two classes in the ratio of their values at the time the stock dividend was distributed.

EXAMPLE
You bought 100 shares of common for $1,000. You receive a tax-free dividend of 10 shares of preferred. On the date of distribution, the market value of the common is $9 a share; the preferred, $30. That makes the market value of your common stock $900 and your preferred $300. So you allocate 9/12 of your $1,000 original cost (or $750) to your common and 3/12 (or $250) to the preferred.

Basis of taxable stock dividend. The basis of a taxable stock dividend is its fair market value at the time of the distribution. Its holding period begins on the date of distribution. The basis of the old stock remains unchanged.

EXAMPLE
You bought 1,000 shares of stock for $10,000. The company gives you a choice of a dividend in cash or in stock (one share for every hundred held). You elect the stock. On the date of the distribution, its market value was $15 a share. The basis of the new stock is $150 (10×$15). The basis of the old stock remains $10,000.

The tax treatment of the receipt of stock as a dividend and in a split is discussed at ¶3.6.

Basis of public utility stock received under dividend reinvestment plan. For several years before 1987, an exclusion was allowed for stock dividends received from public utility companies if the dividends were reinvested in stock. If you claimed the exclusion, the stock takes a zero basis. If you sell the stock in 1987, the entire sales proceeds of the stock is reported as long-term capital gain.

SALE, EXERCISE, OR EXPIRATION OF STOCK RIGHTS

¶ **6.51** The tax consequences of the receipt of stock rights is discussed at ¶3.6. The following is an explanation of how to treat the sale, exercise, or expiration of nontaxable stock rights.

Expiration of nontaxable distributed stock rights. When you allow nontaxable rights to expire, you do not realize a deductible loss.

Sale of nontaxable distributed stock rights. If you sell stock rights distributed on your stock, you treat the sale as the sale of a capital asset.

The holding period begins from the date you acquired the original stock on which the rights were distributed.

Purchased rights. If you buy stock rights, your holding period starts the day after the date on the purchase. Your basis for the rights is the price paid; this basis is used in computing your capital gain or loss on their sale.

If you allow purchased rights to expire without sale or exercise, you realize a capital loss. The rights are treated as having been sold on the day of expiration. When purchased rights become worthless during the year prior to the year they lapse, you have a capital loss which is treated as having occurred on the last day of the year in which they became worthless.

Exercise of stock rights. You realize no taxable income on the exercise of stock rights. Capital gain or loss on the new stock is recognized when you later sell the stock. The holding period of the new stock begins on the date you exercised the rights. Your basis for the new stock is the subscription price you paid plus your basis for the rights exercised.

Figuring the basis of nontaxable stock rights. The basis of purchase stock rights is cost.

Whether rights received by you as a stockholder have a basis depends on their fair market value when distributed. If the market value of rights is less than 15% of the market value of your old stock, the basis of your rights is zero, unless you elect to allocate the basis over the rights and your original stock. You make the election on your tax return for the year in which the rights are received. The statement of election is made on a separate sheet of paper which you attach to your tax return. Keep a copy of the election and return.

If the market value of the rights is 15% or more of the market value of your old stock, you spread the tax cost of the stock between the old stock and the rights according to their respective values on the date of distribution.

EXAMPLE
You own 100 shares of M Co. that cost $10 a share. On September 15, there is a distribution of stock rights allowing for the purchase of one additional share of common for each 10 rights held at a price of $13 a share. The common is now worth $15 (ex-rights). The rights have a market value of 20¢ each. This is less than 15% of the market value of the stock. You can either (a) choose not to spread the tax cost of the stock between the old stock and the rights; or (b) elect to spread the tax cost as follows:

Cost of your old stock, 100 shares at $10, or $1,000.
Fair market value of old stock, 100 shares at $15, or $1,500.
Market value of 100 rights at 20¢, or $20.
Market value of both old stock and rights, $1,520.

Apportionment of old stock:

$$\frac{\$1,500}{\$1,520} \times \$1,000 = \$986.84$$

Your new basis of old stock is $986.84 for 100 shares, or $9.87 a share. The tax cost of the rights is then calculated:

$$\frac{\$20}{\$1,520} \times \$1,000 = \$13.16$$

Basis of the rights is $13.16 for 100 rights.
When you exercise your rights and 10 shares are bought, your basis for the new stock is $130 plus the cost of the rights of $13.16 or $143.16.
If the option of allocation is not exercised, the rights have a basis of zero and the basis of the new stock is $130. The basis of the old stock remains $1,000.

No basis adjustment is required for stock rights which become worthless during the year of issue.

EXAMPLE
A corporation issued nontaxable stock rights to its common shareholders. The rights were worth more than 15% of the fair market value

of the common stock. Shortly after issue, the stock market values fell and the price of common stock fell below the subscription offer. As the rights were valueless, the company decided to refund subscriptions to shareholders who exercised the option and paid the subscription price. Although the stock rights were originally 15% or more of value of stock, the IRS held that the stockholders receiving the refunds did not have to allocate basis. The allocation is not necessary as the subscription price was returned in the same taxable year in which the rights were issued.

The basis of taxable rights is their fair market value at the time of distribution.

HOW TO TREAT SHORT SALES

¶ **6.52** You sell short when you sell borrowed securities. You usually borrow the securities from your broker. When you sell short, you may (1) own the identical securities but do not want to sell them just now, or (2) not own the securities. You *close* the short sale when you deliver to the broker the identical securities you have been holding or identical securities you have bought after the short sale.

Some objectives of selling short: You may want to profit from a declining market in the hope you can buy the replacement stock at lower prices, or freeze paper profits in an uncertain market, or postpone gain to another year.

EXAMPLES
1. In December 1987, you want to freeze your profit in Z stock, but you want to report the sale in 1988. You sell Z short on December 10, 1987. On January 3, 1988, you close the short sale by delivering your Z stock. The short sale is reported as gain on your 1988 return. You report a short sale in the year in which you close the short sale.
2. You sell short 100 shares of Steel Co. for $5,000. You borrowed the stock from your broker. The market declines. Five months later, you buy 100 shares of Steel Co. stock for $3,000, which you deliver to your broker to close the short sale. Your profit of $2,000 is taxed as short-term capital gain. Your profit would be short term regardless of how long you kept the sale open (*see* below).

One objective of the short sale tax rules is to prevent you from converting short-term gains into long-term gains on transactions of substantially identical securities. Another objective is to prevent you from realizing short-term losses on securities that are substantially identical to securities you are holding long-term.

When analyzing short sale transactions, ask yourself these two questions:
1. When you sold short, did you or your spouse hold short-term securities substantially identical to the securities sold short? (Substantially identical securities are described at ¶6.53.)
2. After the short sale, did you or your spouse acquire substantially identical securities on or before the date of the closing of the short sale?

If you answered "yes" to either or both of these questions, apply the following two rules:

Rule 1. Gains realized on the closing of the short sale. The gain is short term regardless of the period of time you have held the securities by the time you close the short sale.

Rule 2. The beginning date of the holding period of substantially identical stock is suspended. The holding period of substantially identical securities owned or bought under the facts of questions (1) or (2) above does not begin until the date of the closing of the short sale (or the date of the sale, gift, or other disposition of the securities, whichever date occurs first). But note this rule applies only to the number of securities that do not exceed the quantity sold short.

EXAMPLES
1. *Short-term gain on closing short sale (Rule 1 above)*

Feb.1: You buy 100 shares of Steel Co. at $10 a share.
July 1: You sell short 100 shares of Steel Co. at $16 a share.

Aug.1: You close the short sale by delivering the stock bought on Feb.1.
Result:
  You have a short-term gain of $600. On the date of the short sale (July 1), you held 100 shares of Steel Co. stock short term, as they were not held for more than six months. That more than six months elapsed between the purchase and closing date is immaterial.

2. *Holding period suspended (Rule 2 above)*

Feb.1: You buy 100 shares of Steel Co. at $10 a share.
July 1: You sell short 100 shares of Steel Co. at $16 a share.
Aug. 1: You close the short sale with 100 shares you buy today at $18.
Aug. 2: You sell at $18 a share the lot bought on Feb. 1.
Result:
  (a) You have a short-term loss of $200 on the closing of the short sale:

Sales Price	$1,600
Cost	1,800
Loss	($ 200)

  (b) You have a short-term gain of $800 on the sale of the Feb. 1 lot ($1,800—$1,000). Gain is short term although you held the lot for more than six months. The Aug. 1 lot was substantially identical stock held short term at the time of the short sale on July 1. Under the special holding period rule, the holding period of the Feb. 1 lot did not begin until the closing of the short sale on Aug. 1.
  The effect of the holding period rule is to give the same tax result that would have been realized if you had sold the Feb. 1 lot on July 1, instead of making a short sale on that date. On July 1 a sale would have given you a short-term gain of $600.

A put as a short sale. The acquisition of a *put* (an option to sell) is treated as a short sale if you hold substantially identical securities short-term at the time you buy the put. The exercise or failure to exercise the put is treated as the closing of the short sale. However, the short sale rules do not apply if on the same day you buy a put and stock which is identified as covered by the put. If you do not exercise the put which is identified with the stock, add its cost to the basis of the stock.

Losses on short sales. You may not realize a short-term loss on the closing of a short sale if you held substantially identical securities long-term on the date of the short sale. The loss is long-term. This rule prevents you from creating short-term losses when you held the covering stock long term. Loss deductions on short sales may be disallowed under the wash sale rules of ¶6.53.

A loss on a short sale is not deductible until shares closing the short sale are delivered to the broker.

EXAMPLE
Feb. 1: You buy 100 shares of Oil stock at $10 a share.
Sept. 1.: You sell short 100 shares of Oil stock at $16 a share.
Oct. 1: You sell 100 shares bought Feb. 1 for $18 a share. You also close the short sale by buying 100 shares at $18 and delivering them to the broker.

Result:
  You have a long-term gain of $800 on the sale of the Feb. 1 lot. This sale is not affected by the short sale rules because at the time of the short sale the stock was held for more than six months. However, the special loss rule applies: The loss of $200 incurred on the closing of the short sale is long-term, not short-term. You held substantially identical securities for more than six months when you made the short sale. The effect of the rule is to give the same tax result you would have realized if you closed the short sale with the Feb. 1 lot instead of buying stock. That is, your net long-term gain is $600 ($800–$200).

Expenses of short sales. Before you buy stock to close out a short sale, you pay the broker for dividends paid on stock you have sold short. For an investor, the payment of an ordinary cash dividend is deductible as investment interest, if the short sale is held open at least 46 days, or more than a year in the case of extraordinary dividends. The deduction is subject to the 2% floor on miscellaneous itemized deductions; *see* chapter 19. If the 46-day test (or one year) is not met, the payment is generally not deductible and is added to basis; in counting the short sale period, do not count any period during which you have an option to buy or are obligated to buy substantially identical securities, or are protected from the risk of loss from the short sale by a substantially similar position.

Under an exception to the 46-day test, if you receive compensation from the lender of the stock for the use of collateral and you report the compensation as ordinary income, your payment for dividends is deductible to the extent of the compensation; only the excess of your payment over the compensation is disallowed. This exception does not apply to payments with respect to extraordinary dividends. An extraordinary dividend is generally a dividend that exceeds in value 10% of the adjusted basis of the stock or 5% in the case of a preferred stock. For purposes of this test, dividends on stock received within an 85-day period are aggregated; a one-year aggregation period applies if dividends exceed 20% of the adjusted basis in the stock.

Arbitrage transactions. Special holding period rules apply to short sales involved in identified arbitrage transactions in convertible securities and stock into which the securities are convertible. These rules can be found in Treasury regulations.

SECURITY LOSSES FROM WASH SALES

¶ 6.53   The objective of the wash-sale rule is to disallow a loss deduction where you recover your market position in a security within a short period of time after the sale. Under the wash-sale rule, your loss deduction is barred if you purchase, or buy an option to purchase, *substantially identical* stock or securities within 30 days of the sale. The wash-sale period is 61 days— running from 30 days before to 30 days after the date of sale. The end of a taxable year during this 61-day period does not affect the wash-sale rule. The loss is still denied. If you sell at a loss and your spouse buys substantially identical stock, the loss is also barred.

The wash-sale rule does not apply to gains or to acquisitions by gift, inheritance, or tax-free exchange.

The wash-sale rule applies to investors and traders. It does not apply to dealers.

What is substantially identical stock or securities? Buying and selling General Motors stock is dealing in an identical security. Selling General Motors and buying Chrysler stock is not dealing in an identical security.

Bonds of the same obligor are substantially identical if they carry the same rate of interest; that they have different issue dates and interest payment dates will not remove them from the wash-sale provisions. Different maturity dates will have no effect, unless the difference is economically significant. Where there is a long time span between the purchase date and the maturity date, a difference of several years between maturity dates may be considered insignificant. A difference of three years between maturity dates was held to be insignificant where the maturity dates of the bonds, measured from the time of purchase, were 45 and 48 years away. There was no significant difference where the maturity dates differed by less than one year, and the remaining life, measured from the time of purchase, was more than 15 years. The wash-sale rules do not apply if you buy bonds of the same company with substantially different interest rates; buy bonds of a different company; or buy substantially identical bonds outside of the wash-sale period.

A warrant falls within the wash-sale rule if it is an option to buy substantially identical stock. Consequently, a loss on the sale of common stocks of a corporation is disallowed when warrants for the common of the same corporation are bought within the period 30 days before or after the sale. But if the timing is reversed, that is, you sell warrants at a loss and simultaneously buy common of the same corporation, the wash-sale rules may or may not apply depending on whether the warrants are substantially identical to the purchased stock. This is determined by comparing the relative values of the stock and warrants. The wash-sale rule will apply only if the relative values and price changes are so similar that the warrants become fully convertible securities.

The wash-sale rule applies to an oral sale-repurchase agreement between business associates.

EXAMPLE
An investor wanted to offset a substantial capital gain with a loss on stock he wanted to retain. An investment counselor suggested that he and his wife sell stock on which they had a substantial paper loss to a business associate with the understanding that they would rebuy the stock after a 30-day period. The agreement was oral. The investor also loaned his associate funds to buy the stock. The stock, which was traded over the market, was sold at market price, and the couple claimed a loss of almost $190,000, which was used to offset their capital gain. Within 34 days, they bought back the stock. The IRS disallowed the loss claiming that the sale was a sham and also came within the wash-sale rules. The Tax Court agrees that the sale was a sham, and even if not a sham, fell within the wash-sale rules although the repurchase occurred more than 30 days after the sale. The wash-sale provision was triggered by the oral agreement to repurchase which was made *within* the 30-day period. The law does not require a written contract. It requires only that there be an agreement to buy substantially identical securities.

Although the loss deduction is barred if the wash-sale rule applies, the economic loss is not forfeited for tax purposes. Because of the following basis rules, the loss may be realized at a later date when the repurchased stock is sold. After the disallowance of the loss, the cost basis of the new lot is fixed as the basis of the old lot and adjusted (up or down) for the difference between the selling price of the old stock and purchase price of the new stock.

EXAMPLES
1. You bought common stock of Appliance Co. for $10,000 in 1980. On June 30, 1984 you sold the stock for $8,000, incurring a $2,000 loss. A week later, you repurchased the same number of shares of Appliance stock for $9,000. Your loss of $2,000 on the sale is disallowed because of the wash-sale rule. The basis of the new lot becomes $11,000. The basis of the old shares ($10,000) is increased by $1,000, which is the excess of the purchase price of the new shares ($9,000) over the selling price of the old shares ($8,000).

2. Assume the same facts as in example (1) except that you repurchase the stock for $7,000. The basis of the new lot is $9,000. The basis of the old shares ($10,000) is decreased by $1,000, which is the excess of the selling price of the old shares ($8,000) over the purchase price of the new shares ($7,000).

3. Assume that in February 1987, you sell the stock acquired in example (1) above for $9,000 and do not run afoul of the wash-sale rule. On the sale, you realize a loss of $2,000 ($11,000–$9,000).

The number of shares of stock reacquired in a wash sale may be less than the amount sold. Then only a proportionate part of the loss is disallowed.

EXAMPLE
You bought 100 shares of A stock for $10,000. On December 19, 1987, you sell the lot for $8,000, incurring a loss of $2,000. On January 6, 1988, you repurchase 75 shares of A stock for $6,000. Three quarters ($^{75}/_{100}$) of your loss is disallowed or $1,500 (¾ of $2,000). You deduct the remaining loss of $500 on your return for 1988. The basis of the new shares is $7,500.

After a wash sale, the holding period of the new stock includes the holding period of the old lots. If you sold more than one old lot in wash sales, you add the holding periods of all the old lots to the holding period of the new lot. You do this even if your holding periods overlapped as you purchased another lot before you sold the first. You do not count the periods between the sale and purchase when you have no stock.

Losses incurred on short sales are subject to the wash-sale rules. A loss on the closing of a short sale is denied if you sell the stock or enter into a second short sale within the period beginning 30 days before and ending 30 days after the closing of the short sale. Under prior law applying to sales before July 19, 1984, a loss on a short sale was treated as incurred on the day the short sale was transacted, not on the day it was closed. Consequently, the loss was disallowed as incurred on the same day as the purchase of identical stock.

Loss on sale of part of a stock lot bought less than 30 days before the sale is deductible.

EXAMPLE

You buy 200 shares of stock. Within 30 days, you sell 100 shares at a loss. The loss is not disallowed by the wash-sale rule. The wash-sale rule does not apply to a loss sustained in a bona fide sale made to reduce your market position. It does apply when you sustain a loss for tax purposes with the intent of recovering your position in the security within a few days. Thus, if after selling the 100 shares, you repurchase 100 shares of the same stock within 30 days after the sale, the loss is disallowed.

Sometimes the wash-sale rule can work to your advantage. Assume that during December, you are negotiating a sale that will bring you a large capital gain. You want to offset a part of that gain by selling certain securities at a loss. You are unsure just when the gain transaction will go through. It may be on the last day of the year. Then it may be too late to sell the loss securities before the end of the year.

You can do this: Sell the loss securities during the last week of December. If the profitable deal goes through before the end of the year, you need not do anything further. If it does not, buy back the loss securities early in January. The December sale will be a wash sale and the loss disallowed. When the profitable sale occurs next year, you can sell the loss securities again. This time the loss will be allowed and will offset the gain.

CONVERTIBLE STOCKS AND BONDS

¶ **6.54** You realize no gain or loss when you convert a bond into stock, or preferred stock into a common, of the same corporation if the conversion privilege was allowed by the bond or preferred stock certificate.

Holding period. Stock acquired through the conversion of bonds or preferred stock takes the same holding period as the securities exchanged. However, where the new stock is acquired partly for cash and partly by tax-free exchange, each new share of stock has a split holding period. The portion of each new share allocable to the ownership of the converted bonds (or preferred stock) includes the holding period of the bonds (or preferred stock). The portion of the new stock allocable to the cash purchase takes a holding period beginning with the day after acquisition of the stock.

Basis. Securities acquired through the conversion of bonds or preferred stock into common take the same basis as the securities exchanged. Where there is a partial cash payment, the basis of the portion of the stock attributable to the cash is the amount of cash paid.

EXAMPLES

1. On January 4, you paid $100 for the debenture of A Co. Your holding period for the debenture begins on January 5 (*see* ¶6.21). The debenture provides that the holder may receive one share of A Co. common stock upon surrender of one debenture and the payment of $50. On October 19, you convert the debenture to stock on payment of $50. For tax purposes, you realize no gain or loss upon the conversion regardless of whether the fair market value of the stock is more or less than $150 on the date of the conversion. The basis and holding period for the stock is as follows: $100 for the portion attributed to the ownership of the debenture with the holding period beginning January 5; and $50 attributed to the cash payment with the holding period for this portion beginning October 20.

2. Same as above, but you acquired the debenture on January 4 through the exercise of rights on that date. Since the holding period for the debenture includes the date of exercise of the rights (*see* ¶6.51), the portion of the stock allocable to the debenture takes a holding period beginning on January 4.

If you paid a premium for a convertible bond, you may not amortize the amount of the premium attributable to the conversion feature.

BAD DEBT DEDUCTIONS

¶ **6.55** When you lend money or sell on credit and your debtor does not repay, you may deduct your loss. The type of deduction depends on whether the debt was incurred in a business or personal transaction. This distinction is important because business bad debts receive favored tax treatment.

Business bad debt is fully deductible from gross income. In addition, you may deduct partially worthless business debts.

Examples of business debt transactions:

1. You sell merchandise on credit and later the buyer becomes insolvent and does not pay.
2. You are in the business of making loans and a loan goes bad.
3. You sell your business, but retain some accounts receivable. Later, some of these become worthless.
4. You liquidate your business and are unable to collect its outstanding accounts.
5. You operate as a promoter of corporations.
6. You finance your lessees, customers, or suppliers to help your business.
7. You lend money to protect your professional and business reputation.
8. You lend money to insure delivery of merchandise from a supplier.
9. You make a loan to your employer to keep your job.

Reserve method repealed. For taxable years beginning after 1986, you must use the specific charge-off method for deducting business bad debts. The reserve method is no longer allowed to taxpayers other than financial institutions. If before 1987 you used the reserve method, you must change to the specific charge-off method. You do not need specific IRS permission. Any balance from your pre-1987 bad debt reserve is generally taxable to you in equal amounts over the four year period starting with your first tax year beginning after 1986.

Nonbusiness bad debt is deducted as a short-term capital loss on Schedule D. This is a limited deduction. In 1987, you deduct it from capital gains, if any, and $3,000 of other income. Any excess is deductible as a carryover in 1988 and later years (*see* ¶6.4). You may not deduct partially worthless nonbusiness bad debts.

Examples of nonbusiness bad debts:

1. You enter into a deal for profit which is not connected with your business—for example, debts arising from investments are nonbusiness bad debts.
2. You make casual personal advances with a reasonable hope of recovery and are not in the business of making loans.
3. You are assigned a debt that arose in the assignor's business. That he could have deducted it as a business bad debt does not make it your business debt. A business debt must arise in your business.

4. You pay liens filed against your property by mechanics or suppliers who have not been paid by your builder or contractor. Your payment is considered a deductible bad debt when there is no possibility of recovering reimbursement from the contractor, and a judgment obtained against him is uncollectible.
5. You lose a deposit on a house when the contractor becomes insolvent.
6. You had an uninsured savings account in a savings association which went into default.

PROVING A BAD DEBT DEDUCTION

¶ 6.56 To determine whether you have a bad debt deduction in 1987, read the four rules explained below. Pay close attention to the fourth rule which requires proof that the debt became worthless in the year the deduction is claimed. Your belief that your debt is bad, or the mere refusal of the debtor to pay, is not sufficient evidence. There must be an event, such as the debtor's bankruptcy, to fix the debt as worthless.

FOUR RULES FOR BAD DEBT DEDUCTION

¶ 6.57 The following four rules must be met in order to be able to claim a bad debt deduction for 1987.

Rule 1. You must have a valid debt.

You have no loss if your right to repayment is not fixed or depends upon some event which may not happen. Thus, advances to a corporation already insolvent are not valid debts. Nor are advances that are to be repaid only if the corporation has a profit. Voluntary payment of another's debt is also nondeductible. If usurious interest was charged on a worthless debt, and under state law the debt was void or voidable, the debt is not deductible as a bad debt. However, where the lender was in the business of lending money, a court allowed him to deduct the unpaid amounts as business losses.

Rule 2. A debtor-creditor relationship must exist at the time the debt arose.

You have a loss if there was a promise to repay at the time the debt was created and you had the right to enforce it. If the advance was a gift and you did not expect to be repaid, you may not take a deduction. Loans to members of your family, to a controlled corporation or trust may be treated as gifts or contributions to capital.

Rule 3. The funds providing the loan or credit were previously reported as income or part of your capital.

If you are on the cash basis, you may not deduct unpaid salary, rent, or fees. On the cash basis, you do not include these items in income until you are paid.

Rule 4. You must show that the debt became worthless during 1987.
To prove the debt became worthless in 1987, you must show
First, that the debt had some value at the end of the previous year (1986), and that there was a reasonable hope and expectation of recovering something on the debt. Your personal belief unsupported by other facts is not enough: For example, would a businessman have placed some value on the debt on December 31, 1986?
Second, that an identifiable event occurred in 1987—such as a bankruptcy proceeding—that caused you to conclude the debt was worthless. You do not have to go to court to try to collect the debt, if you can show that a court judgment would be uncollectible. Additionally, reasonable collection steps must have been undertaken. That you cancel a debt does not make it worthless. You must still show that the debt was worthless when you canceled it.

> You do not have to wait until the debt is due in order to prove worthlessness.

Third, that there is no hope the debt may have some value in a later year. You are not required to prove that there is no possibility of ever receiving some payment on your debt. You are not expected to be an extreme optimist.

Effect of statute of limitations. A debt is not deductible merely because a statute of limitations has run against the debt. Although the debtor has a legal defense against your demand for payment, he may still recognize his obligation to pay. A debt is deductible only in the year it become worthless. This event, for example, the debtor's insolvency, may have occurred even before the statute became effective.

What if your debtor recognized his moral obligation to pay in spite of the expiration of the statute of limitations, but dies before paying? His executor defeats your claim by raising the statute of limitations. You have a bad debt deduction in the year you made the claim against the estate.

Guarantor or endorsement losses as business bad debts. Loss on a guarantee made after December 31, 1975 is deductible as a business bad debt deduction (ordinary loss deduction) only if the guarantee arose out of the guarantor's business of guarantying, endorsing, or indemnifying debts. If a loss arose out of a guarantee made before December 31, 1975, the loss is a business bad debt under these conditions: The borrower was not a corporation, the proceeds of the guaranteed loan were used in the borrower's trade or business, and at the time the guarantor made the payment the borrower's obligation was worthless.

A loss on a guarantee may be a nonbusiness bad debt if the guarantee was made under circumstances that would have given rise to a nonbusiness bad debt deduction if a direct loan had been made by the guarantor.

Bank deposit losses. See ¶ 18.12.

LOANS BY STOCKHOLDERS

¶ 6.58 It is a common practice for stockholders to make loans to their corporations or to guarantee loans made by banks or other lenders. If the corporation fails and the stockholder is not repaid or has to make good on the guarantee, he is generally left with a nonbusiness bad debt unless he can prove he made a business loan. To prove a business loan, the stockholder usually has to show one of these facts: (1) He is in the business of making loans and the loan was made in that capacity, or he is in the business of promoting corporations for a fee or for profits on their sale. (2) He made the loan to safeguard his business. Or (3) he wanted to protect his job with the company. The Supreme Court has ruled that a stockholder who claims he made the loan to protect his job must show that protection of his job was the *primary and dominant* motive of the loan.

EXAMPLE
To determine an executive's motive for making a loan, the Supreme Court reviewed his salary, outside income, investment in the company, and the size of his loan. His pay was $12,000 ($7,000 after tax), his outside income, $30,000. He had a $38,900 investment in the company and loaned it $165,000. On the basis of these figures, the Court concluded he could not have advanced $165,000 to protect an after-tax salary of $7,000.

The Tax Court followed this approach to determine the motive for a stockholder-employee's guarantee of company loans which went bad. His salary was $12,000 ($11,000 after tax); he had little outside income. His stock investment in the company was $22,100, and he guaranteed $13,000 of corporate debt. He claimed he hoped that his salary would increase to $20,000 if the company was successful. If it was not, he would lose his job. The Court accepted his explanation. An advance of $13,000 to protect an after-tax salary of $11,000 was not unreasonable, particularly since he expected pay increases. Also, his stock investment in the corporation was modest in relation to his salary.

A loan by a stockholder to key employees was held to be a business bad debt in the following case.

EXAMPLE
Carter, the president and majority owner of two corporations, loaned money to two key employees to buy stock in the corporations. He wanted to guarantee their future participation in the company. Both corporations went bankrupt, and the employees defaulted on the loans. Carter deducted both loans as business bad debts, contending he was protecting his job. The IRS argued he had a nonbusiness bad debt; he was merely protecting his investment as a stockholder. The Tax Court disagreed. He made the loans to encourage the future of a business which would provide him salary income rather than dividends or appreciation on his stock.

When liquidation proceeds are insufficient to repay a stockholder for his loan and redeem his stock, the proceeds are first applied to the loan and then to the stock.

FAMILY BAD DEBTS

¶ 6.59 The IRS views loans to relatives, especially to children and parents, as gifts, so that it is rather difficult to deduct family bad debts.

Husband's default on child support—a basis for wife's deductible bad debt? A wife who supports her children when her husband defaults on court-ordered support payments may consider claiming her expenses as a nonbusiness bad debt deduction, arguing that her position is similar to a guarantor who pays a creditor when the principal debtor defaults. The IRS does not agree to the grounds of such a claim and will disallow the deduction; its position is supported by the Tax Court. However, an appeals court left open the possibility that such a claim may have merit if a wife can show: (1)What she spent on the children and (2)her husband's obligation to support was worthless in the year the deduction is claimed. The appeals court barred a bad debt deduction to the wife who could not prove these points, but refused to back the Tax Court position that defaulted support payments may never be treated as a bad debt. The Tax Court has subsequently reiterated its position that defaulted child support payments are no basis for a bad debt deduction.

> To overcome the presumption of a gift when you advance money to a relative, take the same steps you would in making a business loan. Take a note, set a definite payment date, and require interest and collateral. If the relative fails to pay, make an attempt to collect. Failure to enforce collection of a family debt is viewed by the courts as evidence of a gift, despite the taking of notes and interest.

HOW TO SHOW TRANSACTIONS ON SCHEDULE D

¶ 6.60 You report many different types of transactions in a separate Schedule D: sales of securities, worthless personal loans, sales of stock rights and warrants, and sale of a personal residence. This section illustrates the treatment of transactions on Schedule D. The form has been altered to show more transactions than can be entered on an actual Schedule D. A blank proof copy of Schedule D for 1987 may be found at the back of this book; a filled-in final version in the Supplement.

The number of each transaction is keyed to the table below.

1. Sale of stock (long-term gain)— You bought 100 shares of Acme Steel stock on October 1, 1960, for $5,000. On March 3, 1987, you sell the 100 shares for $6,000.

In this and other applicable examples, broker's commissions are added to the cost of the stock. It is assumed that state transfer taxes, if any, are deducted as itemized deductions.

2. Sale of stock (short-term gain)— You bought 200 shares of Buma Rubber stock on July 20, 1987 for $400. On October 9, 1987, you sell the 200 shares for $600.

3. Sale of stock received as a gift (long-term gain)— Your father gave you a gift of 100 shares of Crown Auto stock on March 15, 1987, which he had bought in 1960 for $4,000. The fair market value of the stock at the time of the gift was $5,900. On March 20, 1987, you sell the stock for $6,000. (No gift tax was due on the gift, see ¶6.29 and ¶6.24.)

4. Sale of stock received as a gift (short-term loss)— Same facts as above but the value of the stock at the time of the gift is $3,000. You sell the stock on March 27, 1987, for $2,500. This sale is short-term because, when stock received as a gift is sold at a loss and its value at time of gift is less than cost, the holding period begins at the date of gift (see ¶6.29 and ¶6.24).

5. Sale of stock received as inheritance (long-term gain)— You inherited 300 shares of Davis Textile preferred stock from your father who died on January 2, 1975. He had bought them in 1941 for $1,500. When he died, they were selling on the exchange for $15,000, at which value they were reported for estate tax purposes. You received the stock on February 23, 1980, when they were selling at $16,500. You sold the stock for $18,000 on June 4, 1987 (see ¶6.29).

6. Sale of stock including stock dividends— You bought 100 shares of Box Co. stock for $1,000 on June 20, 1968. Last year, you received a stock dividend of 10 shares; this year, a stock dividend of 40 shares. On March 20, 1987, you sell the 150 shares for $3,000 (see ¶6.50)

7. Sale of stock dividend— You bought 100 shares of Bale Co. stock for $1,200 on January 5, 1978. You receive a stock dividend for 20 shares on April 19, 1982. You sell the 20 shares received as a stock dividend on June 5, 1987 for $300 (see ¶6.50).

8. Sale of stock rights— You bought 100 shares of Tel. Co. stock for $5,000 on January 30, 1962. On January 5, 1987, you receive stock rights to subscribe to 10 shares at $53 a share. The stock is worth $55 a share (ex-rights). You sell the rights for $20 on February 6, 1987 (see ¶6.51).

9. Worthless bond— On August 10, 1950, you bought two $1,000 bonds of Rail Co. at par. These bonds became completely worthless during 1987 (see ¶6.11).

10. Worthless personal loan— You loaned $500 to a person on May 1, 1981. He was adjudged bankrupt on March 5, 1987 (see ¶6.55).

The IRS requires that you explain the deduction in a statement attached to your return. The statement should show: (1)The nature of the debt, (2) the name of the debtor and his business or family relationship, if any, to you, (3) when debt was due, (4) how you tried to collect it, (5) how you determined it was worthless.

11. Short sale— You sold "short" 100 shares of Fast Co. on September 4, 1987, for $9,000. You covered this sale on October 22, 1987, by buying 100 shares for $8,500 and delivering them to your broker (see ¶6.52).

12. Call— On June 4, 1987, you bought a 60-day call on 100 shares of Sand Corp. for $500. You did not exercise it (see ¶6.15).

13. Capital distribution— On June 25, 1987, you receive a return of capital distribution of $500 from Filmco, Inc. You purchased 25 shares on May 3, 1966, for $700 and had received a return of capital dividend for $400 in a previous year, which reduced your cost basis to $300. You report that part of the return of capital distribution that exceeds your cost basis (see ¶3.11).

A return of capital distribution that results in neither gain nor loss is not reported in Schedule D.

14. Liquidating dividends—On August 6, 1987, you receive, in redemption of your stock, a final distribution of $150 in complete liquidation from Derby Corp. You purchased this stock on January 6, 1961, for $250 and had received a liquidating distribution of $50 in a prior year, which reduced your cost to $200 (see ¶3.11).

15. Lump-sum or pension payment (pre-1974 participation) —On Form 1099 R, your employer will generally give you a breakdown of the amounts reported as capital gain and as ordinary income. The method of computing these figures is also explained at ¶7.5. On Schedule D, you report only the amount subject to capital gain treatment. Assume in 1987, on retirement, you receive a lump-sum payment of $100,000 of which $15,000 is allocated as capital gain because of your participation in the plan before 1974. You report $15,000 on Schedule D. The tax on the ordinary income element is figured on Form 4972 (see ¶7.3).

Caution: If the effective tax rate of 10-year averaging is less than the effective capital gain rate and you qualify for 10-year averaging (see ¶7.4), do not report the item as capital gain. Compute the tax under both methods, reporting the capital gain separately or treating the entire distribution as ordinary income. Choose the method giving the lower tax. The election to treat the entire sum as ordinary income is made on Form 4972 by simply entering the entire distribution as ordinary income.

16. Bargain sale of appreciated property to charity. On June 4, 1987, you sell to a charity 100 shares of Long Co. stock for your cost of $12,000. You acquired the stock in 1961. The present value is $20,000. You allocate 60% ($12,000 ÷ $20,000) of your cost to the "sold" portion; 60% of your cost of $12,000 is $7,200. You report long-term gain $4,800 ($12,000–$7,200). You may claim a charitable deduction for $8,000 in the itemized deduction schedule.

Short-term Capital Gains and Losses*

a. Description of property (Example, 100 shares of Z Co.)	b. Date acquired (mo., day, yr)	c. Date sold (mo., day, yr)	d. Sales price	e. Cost or other basis plus expense of sale	f. Loss	g. Gain
(2) 200 sh Buma Rubber	7/20/87	10/9/87	600	400		200
(4) 100 sh Crown Auto	3/15/87	3/27/87	2,500	3,000	(500)	
(10) Worthless loan**	5/1/81		Worthless	500	(500)	
(11) 100 sh Fast Co.	10/22/87	9/4/87	9,000	8,500		500
(12) Call Sand Co.	6/4/87	Expired		500		(500)

Long-term Capital Gains and Losses*

a. Description of property	b. Date acquired	c. Date sold	d. Sales price	e. Cost or other basis	f. Loss	g. Gain
(1) 100 sh Acme Steel	10/1/60	3/3/87	6,000	5,000		1,000
(3) 100 sh Crown Auto	1960	3/20/87	6,000	4,000		2,000
(5) 300 sh Davis Textile	1/2/75	6/4/87	18,000	15,000		3,000
(6) 150 sh Box Co.	6/20/68	3/20/87	3,000	1,000		2,000
(7) 20 sh Bale Co.	1/5/78	6/5/87	300	200		100
(8) 100 rights Tel.Co.	1/30/62	2/6/87	20			20
(9) 2 bonds Rail Co.	8/10/50	12/31/87	Worthless	2,000	(2,000)	
(13) 25 sh Filmco, Inc.	5/3/66	6/25/87	500	300		200
(14) 5 sh Derby Corp.	1/6/61	8/6/87	150	200	(50)	
(15) Lump-sum distribution from Form 4972						15,000
(16) 100 sh Long Co.	1961	6/4/87	12,000	7,200		4,800

*The parenthetical numbers leading off the first column on the left refer to the numbered paragraphs in this section.

**See item (10) above for details about required explanation you must attach.

7

RETIREMENT AND ANNUITY INCOME

Illustrations of reporting annuity and pension income on Form 1040 may be found in the Supplement to YOUR INCOME TAX.

ROUNDUP OF TAX-FAVORED RETIREMENT PLANS

¶ 7.1 There are several tax-favored retirement plans. If you are an employee, you are bound to the plan provided by your employer. If you are self-employed, you may set up a Keogh plan, but at the same time, your plan must generally also cover your employees. Finally if you have earned income, whether employed or self-employed, you may invest in an IRA and make either deductible or nondeductible contributions, depending on your plan coverage and income.

Type	General Tax Considerations	Tax Treatment on 1987 Distributions
Company qualified plan	A company qualified pension or profit-sharing plan offers these benefits: (1) You do not realize current income on your employer's contributions to the plan on your behalf. (2) Income earned on funds contributed to your account compound tax free. (3) Your employer may allow you to make voluntary contributions. Although these contributions may not be deducted, income earned on the voluntary contributions is not taxed until withdrawn.	If you receive a lump sum, tax on employer contributions may be reduced by a special averaging rule, *see* ¶ 7.3. If you receive a lump-sum distribution in company securities, unrealized appreciation on those securities is not taxed until you finally sell the stock, *see* ¶ 7.10. Distributions before age 59½ are generally subject to penalties, but there are exceptions. *See* ¶ 7.13. Further, a penalty may also apply for distributions exceeding specified ceilings. *See* ¶ 7.14). Rather than pay an immediate tax, you may elect to rollover a lump-sum payment to an IRA account, *see* ¶ 7.8. If you decide to collect your retirement benefits over a period of years, *see* ¶ 7.24.
Keogh or self-employed plans	You may set up a self-employed retirement plan called a Keogh plan if you earn self-employment income through your performance of personal services. You may deduct contributions up to limits discussed in chapter 8; income earned on assets held by the plan are not taxed. You must include employees under rules explained in chapter 8.	As a self-employed person, you may generally not withdraw funds until age 59½ unless you are disabled. Premature withdrawals are subject to a 10% penalty. Qualified distributions to a self-employed person or to their beneficiaries at death may qualify for favored lump-sum treatment under the rules of ¶ 7.3. Employees of Keogh plans follow rules of ¶ 7.3 applied to qualified plans.
IRA	Anyone who has earned income may contribute to an IRA, but the contribution is deductible only if new law requirements are met. Your status as a participant in an employer retirement plan and your income determines whether you may claim a full $2,000 IRA deduction, a partial deduction, or no deduction at all. *See* chapter 8 for these deduction limitations. Where deductible contributions are allowed, IRAs offer the following benefits: (1) Deductions of up to $2,000 for single persons; $4,000 for working couples; and $2,250 on a joint return where only one spouse works. (2) Income earned on IRA accounts is not taxed until the funds are withdrawn. This tax-free build-up of earnings also applies where you make nondeductible IRA contributions under the rules of Chapter 8.	You may not withdraw funds without penalty unless you are 59½ or disabled or receive IRA distributions in the form of a life-annuity. Premature withdrawals are subject to a 10% penalty. If you delay withdrawals, you must begin to take money out of the account at 70½. *See* ¶ 8.20. Distributions are fully taxable as ordinary income. *See* ¶ 8.19. Special averaging is not allowed. Distributions exceeding $150,000 are subject to a penalty for "excess" distributions. *See* ¶ 7.14.
SEP	A simplified employee pension plan set up by your employer allows the employer to contribute to an IRA more than you can under regular IRA rules. You do not have to include in 1987 income any employer contributions for your account. If your employer qualifies, you may be allowed to make elective deferrals of salary to the plan, but not more than $7,000. See also ¶ 7.22.	Withdrawals are taxable under rules explained above for IRAs.
Deferred salary or 401(k) plans	If your company has a profit-sharing or stock bonus plan, the tax law allows the company to add a cash or deferred pay plan which can operate in one of two ways: (1) Your employer contributes an amount for your benefit to your trust account. You are not taxed on your employer's contribution. (2) You agree to take a salary reduction or to forgo a salary increase. The reduction is placed in a trust account for your benefit. The reduction is treated as your employer's contribution. Starting in 1987, the maximum salary reduction is $7,000. Income earned on the trust account accumulates tax free until it is withdrawn.	Withdrawals are penalized unless you have reached age 59½, become disabled, or meet other exceptions listed at ¶ 7.13. At the time of withdrawal, the tax on proceeds may be computed under rules of ¶ 7.3.

¶ 7.2 New law changes substantially affect the tax treatment of retirement benefits:

IRA's. Starting in 1987, you may not deduct IRA contributions if you are covered by an employer plan and your adjusted gross income exceeds $35,000 if you are single, or $40,000 if you file jointly with your spouse. On a joint return, the $40,000 limit applies to your combined income if either of you has employer coverage. *See* chapter 8 for full IRA details.

Lump-sum retirement distributions. Favorable averaging rules are still allowed to persons who were *age 50 or over before January 1, 1986.* You have a choice of averaging methods: ten-year averaging using 1986 tax rates or five-year averaging using 1987 tax rates. Averaging may be elected only once after 1986.

Averaging is no longer allowed for younger persons. If you were under 50 as of January 1, 1986, you may not qualify for averaging until you are age 59½. Under pre-1987 law, averaging was allowed to those under age 59½ upon separation from serv-

ice. Thus, under the new law, if you left your job and received a plan distribution in 1987 and were not age 50 or over on January 1, 1986, averaging is barred.

The new lump sum distribution rules are further discussed at ¶7.3 and ¶7.4. An election to treat the pre-1974 portion of a lump-sum distribution as capital gain is discussed at ¶7.5.

Starting date for distributions. Unless you reached age 70½ before 1988, you will have to begin receiving distributions from your employer's qualified plan by April 1 of the year following the year you reach age 70½. A penalty may apply if you fail to take a minimum distribution. *See* ¶7.12.

Penalties for premature distributions and excess distributions. The new law generally imposes a 10% penalty on distributions from a qualified plan before age 59½, but there are exceptions. *See* ¶7.13.

You may also be penalized if you receive a distribution exceeding the limits discussed at ¶7.14.

DISTRIBUTIONS FROM QUALIFIED RETIREMENT PLANS

LUMP-SUM DISTRIBUTIONS

¶ 7.3 The following favorable tax elections may apply to qualified lump-sum distributions from a company retirement plan or Keogh plan.

Special averaging if you were at least age 50 before January 1, 1986; see ¶7.4.

Capital gain treatment for gains realized before 1974 and special averaging (for those age 50 on January 1, 1986), on the taxable balance of the distribution; see ¶7.5.

Tax-free rollover to an IRA or another qualified company plan; see ¶7.8.

Choose the election that gives you the greatest after-tax return. If you do not meet the age-50 test and are therefore barred from averaging (see ¶7.4), a lump-sum distribution will be subject to tax at regular rates unless it is rolled over to an IRA or other qualified plan within 60 days.

Distributions from an IRA or redemptions of retirement bonds do not qualify for special averaging or capital gain treatment.

You may be subject to a 10% penalty for a lump-sum distribution received before age 59½; see ¶7.13 for details and exceptions. Further, lump-sum distributions exceeding $750,000 may be subject to a separate 15% penalty for excess distributions, as explained at ¶7.14.

Lump-sum requirements. To qualify as a lump-sum distribution, these tests must be met:

1. Payment must be from a qualified pension or profit-sharing plan. A qualified plan is one approved by the IRS. A civil service retirement system that has a trust fund may be treated as a qualified plan. Ask your retirement plan administrator whether the plan qualifies.
2. You must receive all that is due you under the plan. A distribution of only part of your account is not a lump-sum distribution. If your employer's plan uses more than one trust, you must receive a distribution of all that is due you from each trust. However, lump-sum

treatment is not lost by receipt of a payment in a later year for your last year of work. The later payment is reported as ordinary income; it is not part of the lump sum.

3. The payment or payments must be made within one of your taxable years (usually a calendar year). For example, you retired on October 31, 1987, and start receiving monthly annuity payments under your company's plan on November 1, 1987. On February 4, 1988, you take the balance to your credit in lieu of any future annuity payments. The payments do not qualify as a lump sum; you did not receive them within one taxable year. However, if you had taken the balance of your account on or before December 31, 1987, all the payments would have qualified.
4. If you are an employee, the distribution must be made because you are separated from service, reach the age of 59½, or die. If you are self-employed, the lump-sum distribution from your Keogh plan must be made after you reach age 59½, become disabled, or die. See ¶7.6 for "separation-from-service" if you are an employee.
5. For special averaging, you must also have been a plan participant for five years or more before the year of distribution. This rule does not apply to payments made because of death. See ¶7.7.

> **Important:** If you are married, you must generally obtain your spouse's consent to elect a lump-sum distribution. See ¶7.11.

Should you make a rollover? If you cannot take advantage of special averaging because you do not meet the age test or five-year participation test, you will avoid current tax by making a rollover within 60 days of receiving the lump-sum distribution. If you do qualify for averaging, you should determine whether paying tax currently using the averaging method will be more favorable to you than making a tax free rollover. You have only 60 days to make up your mind. After 60 days, a rollover may not be made. Also if you elect a rollover you cannot change your mind and cancel the IRA account and apply special averaging. The rollover election is irrevocable, according to the IRS. If you need the funds immediately, take the distribution and pay the tax. Similarly, if you think you may have to withdraw the entire account in a few years, a rollover may be unwise because a distribution of the rolled-over account will be taxed as ordinary income; special averaging is not allowed for an IRA distribution.

If you qualify for special averaging but do not plan to use the funds until retirement, estimate whether you will build a larger retirement fund by rolling over the distribution and letting earnings accumulate tax free, or by using special averaging and investing the funds to give you the greatest after-tax return. This is not an easy projection. You must consider the number of years to retirement, your expected tax bracket at retirement, and the estimated yield you can earn on your funds. Generally speaking, a younger person who is not planning to retire for many years may get a greater after-tax return by making a rollover and investing at peak rates, and then taking withdrawals over his life expectancy at retirement.

However, if you make the rollover to an IRA and later decide to withdraw funds before age 59½, you will be subject to a penalty unless you are disabled or you receive payments over your life expectancy; see ¶8.10. Finally, keep in mind the tax rule that allows you to elect averaging *only once after 1986*. If you receive a lump-sum distribution that qualifies for averaging but you plan to continue working, a later lump-sum distribution will not qualify for averaging if you elect averaging for the current distribution. If you make a rollover to an IRA and later join a company with a retirement plan that accepts rollovers, you may transfer the funds to the company plan and averaging could apply when you receive a qualifying lump sum from that plan.

Disqualification of retirement plan. If you receive a lump-sum distribution from a plan which loses its exempt status, the IRS may argue that the distribution does not qualify for lump-sum treatment. Under the IRS position, you may not roll over the distribution to an IRA or elect special averaging. The Tax Court holds that if the plan qualified when contributions were made, an allocable portion of the distribution is a qualified lump sum. However, the majority of appeals courts that have reviewed Tax Court decisions on this issue have supported the IRS position.

TEN-YEAR OR FIVE-YEAR AVERAGING ON FORM 4972

¶ **7.4** Your age determines whether you can use averaging on your 1987 return for a lump-sum distribution meeting the test of ¶7.3. You must have reached age 50 or over *before* January 1, 1986. If you meet this age test, and if you were a participant in the plan for five or more years before the 1987 taxable year, you may elect averaging on Form 4972 using either: (1) a ten-year averaging method based on 1986 tax rates, or (2) a five-year averaging method based on current 1987 tax rates.

If you were not at least age 50 before 1986, the new law does not allow you to claim averaging until you receive a lump-sum distribution after age 59½. For example, assume that in 1988, at age 52, you change jobs and receive a lump-sum distribution from the plan of your old employer. You may not claim either ten-year averaging or five-year averaging for the 1988 distribution. The distribution will be taxed at regular 1988 rates unless a tax-free rollover is made under the rules of ¶7.8. If you continue to work and receive a distribution after reaching age 59½, you will be able to make a one-time election of five-year averaging; ten-year averaging will not be permitted.

Limited 1986 averaging opportunity for retirees under age 50. If you separated from service during *1986* and received a lump-sum distribution after 1986 but before March 16, 1987, a special rule allows a tax break. You may elect to treat the distribution as if it were received in 1986 for averaging purposes. Thus, if you would be barred from electing averaging under the new law because you were under age 50 on January 1, 1986, the special rule allows you to claim averaging on your 1986 return under prior law rules. The election must be made on an original or an amended return for 1986 filed by April 15, 1988, the due date for 1987 returns. A statement should be attached to the return, noting that the distribution is being treated as a "Section 1124 lump-sum distribution." If the election

increases your 1986 tax liability, no estimated tax penalty will be imposed, but you could be billed for interest due after April 15, 1987, the due date for the 1986 return. If you make the election, you will be barred from electing averaging for a later distribution under the new law rule allowing only one lifetime averaging election.

Averaging on 1987 returns. If you meet the age 50 test and were a participant in the plan for five years before 1987, follow IRS instructions to Form 4972 for applying either the ten-year averaging or the five-year averaging methods. Ten-year averaging will provide a lower tax in most cases, except for extremely large distributions. Figure the tax under both methods and choose the one providing the lower tax. On Form 4972, the ordinary income part of the distribution is taxed as if it had been received evenly over ten years under the ten-year averaging method, or over five years under five-year averaging. The tax is taken from the unmarried individuals' tax rate schedule (single) even if you use joint return or head of household rates for your other income. The separate tax figured under averaging is added to your regular tax which is computed on your other income reported on Form 1040.

You are allowed to elect averaging only once after 1986. If you reached age 50 before 1986 and elect averaging for a 1987 distribution after separating from service (¶7.6), you will not be able to claim averaging again if you join another company and receive a lump-sum distribution from the new employer.

The taxable portion of a lump-sum distribution does not include your contributions to the plan and net unrealized appreciation on a distribution of securities of the employer. *See* also ¶7.10.

EXAMPLE
In 1987, you receive a lump-sum distribution of $65,000, including stock of your employer. The stock had a basis of $10,000 when put in the plan; it is valued at $25,000 when distributed. You did not contribute to the plan. The taxable portion of the distribution is $50,000 ($65,000– $15,000, the unrealized appreciation). If you participated in the plan before 1974, you may elect to allocate the $50,000 between the capital gain and ordinary income portions; see ¶7.5.

Community property. Only the spouse who has earned the lump sum may use averaging. Community property laws are disregarded for this purpose. If a couple files separate returns and one spouse elects averaging, the other spouse is not taxable on the amount subject to the computation.

EXAMPLE
A husband in a community property state receives a lump-sum distribution of which the ordinary income portion is $10,000. He and his wife file separate returns. If averaging is not elected, $5,000, or one-half, is taxable in the husband's return and the other $5,000 in his wife's return. However, if he elects the averaging method, only he reports the $10,000 on Form 4972.

"Look-back" rule for annuity contracts or receipt of more than one lump sum during a six-year period. A "look-back" provision requires that the lump-sum distributions for the taxable year be aggregated with all lump-sum distributions made during the five previous tax years. This increases the bracket at which the ordinary income portion of the current year's lump-sum distribution is taxed. You do not aggregate lump sums which were not subject to the ten-year averaging rule before 1987. *See* the instructions to Form 4972.

A "look-back" rule is also applied to the distribution of an annuity contract, although its total value is not taxable when distributed. The current actuarial value is included in the six-year aggregation computation to determine the tax bracket of the ordinary income portion of a current lump-sum distribution. An example of computing tax when a distribution includes an annuity contract is in the instructions accompanying Form 4972.

Pre-1974 portion of distribution. If a portion of your lump-sum distribution is attributable to plan participation before 1974 (*see* ¶7.5), you may elect to treat it as capital gain. If you make the capital gain election and you were at least age 50 before 1986, the capital gain portion is taxed at a flat 20% rate, with the ordinary income portion of the distribution subject to the averaging computation. *See* also ¶7.5.

If you were *not* at least age 50 before 1986, you may not elect averaging, but you may elect to treat the pre-1974 portion as capital gain, subject to the phaseout rules discussed at ¶7.5.

CAPITAL GAIN TREATMENT FOR PRE-1974 PARTICIPATION

¶ **7.5** Under pre-1987 law, if you received a qualifying lump-sum distribution, long-term capital gain treatment was available for the portion of the distribution attributable to participation in the plan before 1974. Employees (but not the self-employed) qualified for capital gain treatment even if averaging was not allowed under prior law rules.

Under the new law, capital gain opportunities are still available for distributions after 1986, but the tax benefit may be limited. If you were at least age 50 before January 1, 1986, you may elect a special 20% capital gain rate as discussed below. If you were under age 50 before 1986, you may elect capital gain treatment subject to a phase-out rule to offset capital losses; *see* below.

On Form 1099-R, the company paying the lump-sum distribution lists the capital gain and ordinary income parts of the distribution. If you are an employee, capital gain treatment is available to the extent allowed by the following new law rules, even if you do not qualify for averaging.

Age 50 or over before 1986. The law allows one lifetime election for a lump-sum distribution received after 1986. You may elect to treat the pre-1974 portion as capital gain subject to a flat rate of 20%. If you meet the five-year plan participation test (¶7.4), the tax on the balance of the distribution may be figured under the averaging method. The 20% rate for the capital gain portion is fixed by law, and applies regardless of the tax rate imposed on your other capital gains. The phase-out rules discussed below do not apply if you were age 50 or over before 1986.

You do not have to elect 20% capital gain treatment for the pre-1974 portion. You may elect to treat the entire taxable portion of the lump-sum distribution as ordinary income eligible for averaging. Thus, you should elect 20% capital gain treatment if the effective tax rate under averaging is more than the flat 20% capital gain rate for the pre-1974 portion. Verify effective tax rates by computing the tax under both methods. Follow the instructions to Form 4972 for treating the entire sum as ordinary income, or for making the special capital gain election.

Under the one-election rule, if you elect to apply the above averaging and/or capital gain rules for a 1987 distribution, you may not elect averaging or capital gain treatment for any later distribution.

Phase-out of capital gain treatment for individuals below age 50 on January 1, 1986. If you were not age 50 before January 1, 1986, capital gain phase-out rules apply. Between 1987 and 1991, a decreasing percentage of the pre-1974 portion will qualify as long-term capital gain. An election must be made to obtain capital gain treatment. In 1987, 100% of the pre-1974 portion qualifies as capital gain. However, if the election is made, the capital gain portion is taxable in 1987 at regular rates, subject to the 28% ceiling (See ¶6.2). There is no special tax rate for the capital gain portion, such as the 20% flat rate for those who were over age 50 on January 1, 1986. As the capital gain portion of the distribution will be taxed at regular rates, the only advantage of electing capital gain treatment is that the capital gain may be used to offset capital losses. Making the election has this disadvantage: Electing capital gain treatment under the phase-out rule will bar you from electing five-year averaging for a lump sum received after age 59½.

Under the five-year phase-out, 95% of the pre-1974 portion will qualify as capital gain in 1988, 75% in 1989, 50% in 1990, and 25% in 1991. In each of these years, the qualifying percentage is subject to tax at regular rates but may be used to offset capital loss. Thus, as the qualifying percentage decreases, the advantage of electing capital gain treatment will become even less, particularly since the election bars five-year averaging for a distribution after age 59½. After 1991, no part of a lump-sum distribution will qualify as capital gain if you were not age 50 before 1986.

SEPARATION-FROM-SERVICE TEST FOR EMPLOYEES UNDER 59½

¶ **7.6** Employees who have not reached the age of 59½ must be "separated-from-service" or disabled for a distribution to qualify as a lump-sum distribution. However, even though you are separated from service, you may elect averaging (¶7.4) only if you reached age 50 before

January 1, 1986. If you were not age 50 or over before 1986, a lump-sum distribution received upon separation from service before age 59½ may be rolled over tax free under the rules of ¶7.8, but averaging may not be claimed.

The separation-from-service test requires that you have retired, resigned, or have been discharged. If a plan is terminated but you continue on the job, distributions are not entitled to special lump-sum treatment if you have not reached age 59½. Under the law, you do not have to be separated from service after you reach age 59½. However, in rulings, the IRS has held that if you receive a lump-sum distribution from a pension plan (not a profit-sharing plan) after age 59½ but continue to work for the company, you also must reach the normal retirement age as fixed in the company plan to get lump-sum treatment unless the plan was terminated.

The separation-from-service test generally prevents lump-sum treatment when a qualified plan is terminated following a reorganization or merger of a company. According to the IRS, an employee under age 59½ who remains with a successor corporation and who receives a lump-sum distribution following reorganization, liquidation, or merger may not claim lump-sum treatment.

> Court decisions follow the IRS position. However, the Tax Court has held that an executive working for a successor firm was "separated-from-service" on evidence of substantial changes in staff, duties, and company business. Finally, the IRS, in a private letter ruling, eased its position and allowed 20 employees of a merged company lump-sum tax benefits. They were given new jobs or took on additional responsibilities. The manager of engineering and maintenance of the old company became responsible for energy conservation and security; the former personnel manager was rehired as the purchasing and planning manager. Further, the new company reduced salaries and employee benefits and eliminated the former profit-sharing plan. Given these changes in job positions and pay benefits, employees were considered "separated from service."

A lump sum paid on account of termination of a plan may be rolled over tax free to an IRA (*see* ¶7.8).

Partnership plans. Lump-sum payments paid on the termination of a plan when a partnership dissolves do not qualify for special lump-sum treatment when the employees continue to work for the successor partnership. Similarly, an employee of a partnership, who becomes a partner and has to quit the firm's employee profit-sharing plan, may not treat his payment as a lump sum. He is still serving the firm.

LUMP-SUM PAYMENTS RECEIVED BY DECEASED EMPLOYEE'S BENEFICIARY

¶ **7.7** A beneficiary of a deceased employee may apply the lump-sum rules of ¶7.3 to a 1987 payment received because of the employee's death. In addition, the $5,000 death benefit exclusion may also be claimed (*see* ¶7.28). If the payment qualifies, Form 4972 is used to compute tax under the ten-year or five-year averaging method. Any federal estate tax attributable to the distribution is deductible.

A lump sum paid because of an employee's death may qualify for capital gain and averaging treatment, although the employee received annuity payments before he died.

The $5,000 death benefit exclusion also applies to payments received by Keogh plan beneficiaries following the death of a self-employed person after December 31, 1983.

An estate or trust receiving a lump-sum payment may also apply the lump-sum rules.

A beneficiary may elect averaging, even though the deceased employee was in the plan for less than five years. However, because of an ambiguity in the wording of the new law, it is not clear whether the beneficiary must have been at least age 50 before 1986 in order to claim special averaging or the special 20% capital gain rate (*see* ¶7.5) for pre-1974 participation. Taken literally, the law requires the age 50 test to be met by the beneficiary. Under pre-1987 law, the age of the beneficiary was not relevant.

This change may not have been intended. *See* the instructions for Form 4972 and the Supplement for further developments, if any.

A qualifying beneficiary may elect averaging or capital gain treatment only once for distributions received as the beneficiary of the deceased.

Payment received by a second beneficiary (after the death of the first beneficiary) is not entitled to lump-sum treatment or the death benefit exclusion.

EXAMPLES

1. Gunnison's father was covered by a company benefit plan. The father died as did Gunnison's mother before benefits were fully paid out. Gunnison received a substantial lump sum. He argued that he collected on account of his father's death. The IRS disagreed. The Tax Court and an appeals court sided with the IRS. Gunnison was entitled to the payment following his mother's death, not his father's death. For special lump-sum treatment, the payout must arise solely on account of the death of the covered employee.

2. Robert's employer announced the termination of its pension plan. Before benefits were distributed, Robert died. His widow received a lump-sum distribution as his beneficiary. After subtracting the amount attributable to Robert's contributions, she excluded $5,000 as a death benefit and treated the balance as a lump-sum distribution. The IRS claimed she received the distribution on the termination of the plan, not because of Robert's death. The Tax Court agreed. Distribution was made to her under the termination provision, not the provisions for withdrawal due to separation-from-service or death. She could not take a death benefit exclusion, and the entire distribution (less Robert's contributions) could not be treated as a lump-sum distribution.

> *Lump-sum distribution to more than one beneficiary.* A lump-sum distribution to two or more individuals may qualify for capital gain treatment and the averaging method. The distribution is first treated as made to one recipient to determine whether it is a lump sum and what portion is taxable as capital gain (*see* ¶ 7.4). Each beneficiary may separately elect the averaging method for the ordinary income portion, even though other beneficiaries do not so elect.

Distribution to trust or estate. If a qualifying 1987 lump sum is paid to a trust or an estate, the employee, or his personal representative if he is deceased, may elect averaging. This is true, even though the ordinary income portion is distributed to the beneficiaries in the year the lump sum was received. If the fiduciary makes the election, the ordinary income is taxable to the trust or estate, even if a distribution is made to the beneficiary. However, the capital gain portion, if distributed to the beneficiaries in the year received by the trust or estate, is taxable to the beneficiaries as long-term capital gain, not to the trust. *See* Form 4972 and Publication 575 for further details.

TAX-FREE ROLLOVER OF LUMP SUM

¶ **7.8** You can defer tax on a lump-sum distribution from a qualified company plan by transferring it within 60 days to a qualified plan of your new employer or to an individual IRA account(*see* ¶ 8.11). Your employer is required by law to inform you of these options if your distribution qualifies for tax-free rollover treatment.

The amount you roll over may not include your contributions (after tax contributions) to the qualified plan.

You may not claim a deduction for your rollover contribution to an IRA.

You may not make a tax-free rollover of a distribution which you are required to take under the rules of ¶ 7.12 because you have reached age 70½ or retired.

Note: Under pre-1987 law, an employee or self-employed person who had more than a 5% ownership interest (at any time in the five plan years before the plan year in which the distribution was made) could make a rollover only to an IRA but not to another qualified plan. Under the new law, a rollover after 1986 may be made by a more than 5% owner to a qualified plan as well as to an IRA.

For a tax-free rollover, the lump-sum distribution must meet these tests:

1. The distribution must be all that is due you under the plan. If the employer plan uses more than one trust, you must receive a distribution of all that is due you from each trust.
2. The payment or payments must be made within one of your taxable years.
3. The distribution must be made because you are separated from service, reached age 59½, or the plan has been terminated.

You do not have to roll over the entire distribution; you may make a partial rollover. While the amount rolled over is not taxed, the part *not* rolled over is taxable and you may not apply capital gain treatment or special averaging to the distribution.

A surviving spouse may roll over to an IRA a lump-sum distribution paid on the death of a spouse or upon termination of a qualified retirement plan. The distribution may not be rolled over to a qualified plan of the surviving spouse's current employer.

> A rollover to an IRA after March 20, 1986 is irrevocable. At the time of the rollover, you must elect in writing to irrevocably treat the contribution as a rollover. You may not later change your mind in order to claim averaging. Before making a rollover, figure what the current tax would be on the lump-sum distribution under the special averaging method. Compare it with an estimate of tax payable on a later distribution of the rolled-over account. Consider further that if you make a rollover to an IRA and not to a new employer's qualified plan, you lose the right to apply the special averaging method to the sum. Special averaging applies only to a lump-sum distribution from a qualified plan. It does not apply to a withdrawal from an IRA account. If you are under the age of 59½, also consider that a rollover to an IRA locks in your funds. If you withdraw from the IRA, you may be subject to a penalty, *see* ¶ 7.20. Other points to consider in deciding whether to make a rollover are discussed at ¶ 7.3.

Rollover of partial distributions. If a distribution equals at least 50% of your plan account balance, you may elect to roll it over to an IRA provided it is paid upon your separation from service or upon disability. A self-employed person who separates from service may make a rollover as well as an employee. This separation from service requirement did not apply under prior law to pre-1987 distributions. The rollover must be made within 60 days.

Under the 50% test, you may disregard amounts credited to you under other kinds of qualified plans maintained by the same employer. A surviving spouse of a deceased employee may elect to rollover a qualifying partial distribution. If you elect rollover treatment, a later distribution of your entire account balance will not qualify for special averaging or capital gain treatment (¶ 7.4 and ¶ 7.5).

> *Rollover to new employer's plan.* An IRA may be used as a conduit between two company plans. The funds in the IRA may be transferred to another qualified plan of a company which employs you, provided the plan of your new employer accepts rollovers. The IRA must consist of only the assets (or proceeds from the sale of such assets) distributed from the first qualified plan and income earned on the account. You may not contribute to the account set up as a conduit. You may set up another IRA to which you make annual contributions. In such a case, you will have two accounts; one consisting of the assets (or proceeds from the sale of such assets) of the plan of your prior employer and the other of your own contributions.
>
> ### EXAMPLE
>
> You leave your employer and receive a lump-sum distribution of $5,000 from his qualified plan to which you did not contribute. You place the amount in an IRA. Four years later, you start work for another company that has a qualified plan. The new plan permits you to transfer the assets of the IRA to the plan. You must make the transfer within 60 days after closing the account (*see* ¶ 7.21).

Figuring the 60-day period for more than one payment. The IRS held in a private letter ruling that if you receive several payments, the 60-day period starts from the date of the last payment, provided all of the payments are made within one taxable year. For example, you retired in July 1986 and received a partial distribution from your company plan. You were told that you would receive the balance by December 1986. Provided all payments are received before the end of 1986, the payments received in July and December are considered a lump-sum distribution eligible for rollover. You have 60 days from the date of the final December payment to complete the rollover.

Extension of 60-day rollover period for frozen deposits. If you receive a qualifying distribution from a retirement plan and deposit the funds in a financial institution which becomes bankrupt or insolvent, you may be prevented from withdrawing the funds in time to complete a rollover within 60 days. If this happens, the 60-day period is extended while your account is "frozen." The 60-day rollover period does not include days on which your account is frozen. Further, you have a minimum of 10 days after the release of the funds to complete the rollover.

Distribution includes life insurance policy. Your employer's retirement plan may invest in a limited amount of life insurance which is then distributed to you as part of a lump-sum retirement distribution. You may be able to roll over the life insurance contract to the qualified plan of your new employer but not to an IRA. The law specifically bars investment of IRA funds in life insurance contracts.

Diversification. You may wish to diversify a distribution in different investments. There is no limit on the number of rollover accounts you may have. A lump-sum distribution may be rolled over to several IRAs or retirement annuities.

Rollover of annuities for employees of tax-exempt groups and schools. If you participate in a tax-sheltered annuity program described in ¶7.30, you may roll over a qualifying distribution to an IRA.

On your return, you report a rollover only for information purposes. *See* the Supplement for the line for reporting 1987 rollovers.

ROLLOVER OF PROCEEDS FROM SALE OF PROPERTY RECEIVED IN LUMP-SUM DISTRIBUTION

¶ **7.9** A lump-sum distribution from a qualified plan may include property, such as stock. If you plan to roll over the distribution, you may find a bank may not want to take the property. If you sell the property, you may roll over the sale proceeds to an IRA as long as the sale and rollover occur within 60 days of receipt of the distribution. If you roll over all of the proceeds, neither gain nor loss is recognized. The proceeds are treated as part of the distribution. If you make a partial rollover, you incur tax on the retained proceeds, and in reporting the taxable amount, you allocate between ordinary income and capital gain elements. *See* Treasury regulations for how to make the allocation.

If you receive cash and property, and you sell the property but make a partial rollover, you must designate how much of the cash is to be treated as part of the rollover. The designation must be made by the time for filing your return (plus any extensions) and is irrevocable. If you do not make a timely designation, the allocation between cash and proceeds is made on a ratable basis.

If you contributed to the plan, you may not rollover to an IRA the portion of the distribution equal to your contributions. *See* Treasury regulations for the effect of employee contributions on an allocation.

SECURITIES OF EMPLOYER COMPANY RECEIVED AS PART OF A DISTRIBUTION

¶ **7.10** When a plan distributes securities of your company, the value of the securities may or may not be subject to tax at the time of the distribution. The amount reported as income depends on the value of the securities, the amount contributed by the company toward their purchase, and whether or not the distribution qualifies as a total lump-sum payment.

Lump-sum payments. If the distribution is of appreciated securities and is part of a lump-sum payment meeting the tests of ¶7.3, the unrealized appreciation is not subject to tax at the time of distribution unless

you elect to treat it as taxable; *see* below. Assuming the election is not made, only the amount of the employer's contribution is subject to tax. Tax on the appreciation is delayed until the shares are later sold by you at a price exceeding cost basis. If, when distributed, the shares are valued at below the cost contribution of the employer, the fair market value of the shares is subject to tax. If you contributed to the purchase of the shares and their value is less than your contribution, you do not realize a loss deduction on the distribution. You realize a loss only when the stock is sold or becomes worthless at a later date. If a plan distributes worthless stock, you may deduct your contributions to the stock as an ordinary loss if you itemize deductions.

EXAMPLES

1. *Shares valued below your cost contribution.* You contributed $500 and your employer contributed $300 to buy ten shares of company stock having at the time a fair market value of $80 per share. When you retire, the fair market value of the stock is $40 per share, or a total of $400. You do not realize income on the distribution, and you do not have a deductible loss for the difference between your cost contribution and the lower fair market value. Your contribution to the stock is its basis. This is $50 per share. If you sell the stock for $40 per share, you have a capital loss of $10 per share. However, if you sell the stock for $60 per share, you have gain of $10 per share.

2. *Appreciated shares.* You receive ten shares of company stock to which only the employer contributed toward their purchase. Your employer's cost was $50 a share. At the time of distribution, the shares are valued at $80 a share. Your employer's contribution of $50 a share or $500 is included as part of your taxable distribution. The appreciation of $300 is not included. The cost basis of the shares in your hands is $500 (the amount currently taxable to you). The holding period of the stock starts from the date of distribution. However, if you sell the shares for any amount exceeding $500 and up to $800, your profit is long-term gain even if the sale is within six months from the date of the distribution. If you sell for more than $800, the gain exceeding the original unrealized appreciation of $300 is subject to long-term capital gain treatment only if the sale is long-term from the date of distribution. Thus, if within a month of the distribution, you sold the shares for $900, $300 would be long-term gain; $100 would be short-term gain.

Election to waive tax-free treatment. You may elect to include the unrealized appreciation in employer securities as income. You might consider making this election when you want to accelerate income to the current year by taking into account the entire lump-sum distribution. The IRS has not yet released rules for making the election; *see* the Supplement.

Other than lump-sum payments. If you receive appreciated securities in a distribution that does not meet the lump-sum tests of ¶7.3, you report as ordinary income the amount of the employer's contribution to the purchase of the shares and the appreciation allocated to his cost contribution. You do not report the amount of appreciation allocated to your contribution to the purchase.

EXAMPLE

A qualified plan distributes ten shares of company stock with an average cost of $100, of which the employee contributed $60 and the employer, $40. At the date of distribution, the stock had fair market value of $180. The portion of the unrealized appreciation attributable to the employee's contribution is $48 (60% of $80); the employer's is $32 (40% of $80). The employee reports $72 as income; the employer's cost of $40 and share of appreciation of $32. The basis of each share is $132 which includes employee contribution of $60 and the $72 reported as taxable income. Net unrealized appreciation and cost contributions must be supplied by the company distributing the stock.

SURVIVOR ANNUITY BENEFITS GENERALLY REQUIRED FOR SURVIVING SPOUSE

¶ **7.11** If you have been married for at least a year, the law generally requires that payments be in a specific annuity form to protect your surviving spouse. All defined benefit and money purchase plans must provide benefits in the form of a qualified joint and survivor annuity unless you, with the written consent of your spouse, elect a different form of benefit. A qualified joint and survivor annuity must also be provided by profit-sharing or stock bonus plans, unless you do not elect a life annuity payment and the plan provides that your nonforfeitable benefit is payable in full upon your death to your surviving spouse, or to another beneficiary if the spouse consents or there is no surviving spouse.

Under a qualified joint and survivor annuity, you receive an annuity for your life and your surviving spouse receives an annuity for his or her life that is no less than 50% of the amount payable during your joint lives. Unless you obtain spousal consent, you must take this type of annuity; you may not take a lump-sum distribution or a single life annuity ending when you die. A single life annuity pays higher monthly benefits during your lifetime than the qualified joint and survivor annuity.

The law also requires that a pre-retirement survivor's annuity be paid to your surviving spouse if you die before the date benefits become payable. For example, under a defined contribution plan such as a profit sharing plan, the pre-retirement annuity payments must be equal to those under a single life annuity valued at 50% or more of your account balance. The pre-retirement annuity is automatic unless you, with your spouse's consent, agree to a different benefit.

> Your spouse must consent in writing to any waiver and the selection of a different type of distribution. A spouse's consent must be witnessed by a plan representative or notary public. An election to waive the qualified joint and survivor annuity may be made during the 90-day period ending on the annuity starting date. An election to waive the qualified pre-retirement survivor annuity may be made from the first day of the plan year in which you reach age 35 up until your date of death. A waiver is revocable during the time permitted to make the election.

These survivor annuity requirements generally do not apply to couples who have been married for less than one year as of the participant's annuity starting date or, if earlier, the date of the participant's death.

Your plan should provide you with a written explanation of these annuity rules within a reasonable period before the annuity starting date as well as the rules for electing to waive the joint and survivor annuity benefit and the pre-retirement survivor annuity.

Cash out of annuity. If the present value of the qualified joint and survivor annuity is $3,500 or less, your employer may "cash out" your interest without your consent by making a lump-sum distribution of the present value of the annuity before the annuity starting date. After the annuity starting date, you and your spouse must consent to a cash out. Written consent is required for a cash out if the present value of the annuity exceeds $3,500. Similar cash out rules apply to pre-retirement surviving annuities.

WHEN RETIREMENT BENEFITS MUST BEGIN

¶ **7.12** The longer you can defer taking retirement distributions from your company plan or Keogh plan, the greater will be the tax free buildup of your retirement fund. To cut off this tax deferral, the law requires distributions to begin by a specified date. Unless you have reached age 70½ before 1988, you will have to begin receiving distributions in the year after you reach age 70½. This is true even if you do not retire and continue to work. If you did reach age 70½ before 1988 and you continue to work, you may be able to delay the start of distribution until after you retire, as discussed below.

If you reached age 70½ before 1988. If you are an employee or self-employed person who reached age 70½ before January 1, 1988, and do not own more than a 5% ownership interest, you do not have to start to receive distributions until April 1 of the calendar year following the calendar year in which you retire. For example, if you reached age 70½ in 1987 or in an earlier year and you retired in 1987, you must start to receive distributions by April 1, 1988. If you do not retire until 1989, your first distribution does not have to be made until April 1, 1990, the year after the year of retirement.

You qualify to delay distributions until after retirement only if you did not own more than a 5% ownership interest in the employer during the plan year ending with or within the calendar year in which you reached 66½ or in any later year.

If you reach age 70½ after 1987. You will have to start to receive distributions no later than April 1 of the calendar year following the calendar year in which you reach age 70½. For example, if you reach age 70½ during 1988, your first distribution must be no later than April 1, 1989, even if you continue to work.

This required beginning date applies to distributions from all qualified corporate and Keogh plans, as well as eligible deferred compensation plans (Section 457 plans) of state and local governments and tax-exempt employers. Further, the rules also apply to distributions from tax-sheltered annuities (¶7.30) but only for benefits accrued after 1986. The law does not specify a mandatory beginning date for tax-sheltered annuity benefits accrued before 1987.

Pre-1984 designations. Individuals who made a special election before 1984 to receive distributions under pre-1984 rules are not subject to the age 70½ rule or the beneficiary distribution methods discussed below.

Distribution methods for employees and self-employed. All qualified retirement plans, including Keogh plans for the self-employed, are subject to the same distribution rules.

When you retire or begin distributions under the age 70½ rule, you may spread payments over your life, over the joint lives of yourself and any designated beneficiary, or over a specific period that does not exceed your life expectancy or the joint life expectancies of yourself and any designated beneficiary. In figuring the payout schedule, your life expectancy may be recalculated annually. If payments are made over the joint life expectancies of you and your spouse, your spouse's life expectancy may also be recalculated annually. To determine your life expectancy, use Table V shown at ¶7.20; use IRS Table VI for joint life expectancies.

Basing payments on the joint life expectations of yourself and a younger beneficiary will extend the withdrawal period, but the law imposes a limit. Generally, the present value of the projected payments to you must exceed 50% of the present value of the total projected payments to you and your beneficiaries. This requirement does not affect payments required for spouses under the qualified joint and survivor annuity rule of ¶7.11. As discussed at ¶7.11, your plan must automatically provide annuity benefits in the form of a qualified joint and survivor annuity if you are married, unless you and your spouse elect otherwise.

Minimum distributions that you are required to take under these rules may not be rolled over tax free.

These distribution rules do not apply to collectively bargained plans ratified on or before July 18, 1984, until the earlier of January 1, 1988, or the date on which the bargaining agreement terminates (without regard to extensions after July 18, 1984).

> If an employee or self-employed person dies before receiving benefits, distribution rules depend on who is the beneficiary. A surviving spouse who is not receiving annuity payments under the rules of ¶7.11 may delay distributions until the date on which the deceased spouse would have reached age 70½, or if later, one year after the decedent's death. Starting on that date, the surviving spouse must receive distributions over his or her life expectancy. If someone other than a surviving spouse is beneficiary, payments generally have to be completed within five years of the decedent's death, but there is an important exception. If the beneficiary was designated by the employee, distributions may be spread over the beneficiary's life or life expectancy provided that distributions began no later than one year after the employee's death. The IRS may extend the one-year limit if circumstances warrant delay. Life expectancy is determined under Table 5 shown at ¶7.20.

Penalty warning. Starting in 1989, you may be subject to a 50% penalty if you fail to take a distribution from a qualified plan by the required beginning date or you receive a distribution that is insufficient under the above distribution methods. Unless waived by the IRS, the 50% penalty will apply to the difference between the amount you should have received and the amount you did receive. This penalty does not apply to 1987 or 1988 returns. Individuals who made a special election before 1984 to receive distributions under pre-1984 rules will not be subject to the penalty. For employees covered by collective bargaining agreements ratified before March 1, 1986, the penalty will not apply to distributions in plan years beginning before the earlier of (1) the date on which the agreement terminates (disregarding extensions after February 28, 1986) but no later than January 1, 1989, or (2) January 1, 1991.

Payout period for beneficiaries. Where an employee or self-employed individual dies after benefits have begun, beneficiaries must continue to take distributions at least as rapidly as the participant did during his or her lifetime. For example, if an employee had elected to receive benefits in equal annual installments over his 20-year life expectancy, but died after 10 years, the beneficiary would have to receive equal annual installments over the remaining 10 years but could elect to accelerate payments over a shorter period.

A surviving spouse receiving an annuity under the survivor benefit rules of ¶7.11 receives payments over his or her lifetime, starting at the participant's death.

PENALTY FOR PREMATURE DISTRIBUTIONS

¶ **7.13** Under prior law, distributions before age 59½ from a qualified plan were not subject to a penalty unless the recipient owned more than a 5% interest in the employer making the distribution. Starting in 1987, the new law imposes a 10% penalty on distributions before age 59½, regardless of ownership interest, unless you are disabled or one of the other exceptions discussed below applies. Distributions payable to a beneficiary after the death of a plan participant are exempt from the penalty. A similar 10% penalty applies to IRA distributions before age 59½; see ¶8.10 for IRA penalty rules.

Distributions before 59½ from a qualified corporate or Keogh plan, qualified annuity plan, and tax-sheltered annuity are subject to the penalty. The penalty does not apply to Section 457 plans of tax-exempt employees or State or local governments.

The penalty is 10% of the taxable distribution.

Exceptions to the penalty. The penalty does not apply to distributions made on or after the date you reach 59½, on account of your disability or to a beneficiary after your death. Further, the following distributions are also exempt from the 10% penalty, even if received before age 59½:

- Distributions under the plan for early retirement after age 55—you must be age 55 or over when you retire;
- Distributions used to pay deductible medical expenses exceeding 7.5% of adjusted gross income (whether or not an itemized deduction for medical expenses is claimed);
- Distributions received after separation from service which are part of a series of substantially equal payments (at least annually) over your life expectancy, or over the joint lives of yourself and your beneficiary. If before age 59½ you receive a lump sum or change the distribution method so that it does not qualify for the exception, and you are not disabled, a recapture penalty tax will apply to all amounts received before age 59½, as if the exception had never been allowed. The recapture tax also applies to payments received before age 59½ if substantially equal payments are not received for at least five years.
- Distributions paid to an alternate payee pursuant to a qualified domestic relations court order;
- Lump-sum distribution received before March 16, 1987, if you separated from service in 1986 and you pay 1986 tax on the distribution;
- Distributions made pursuant to a designation under the 1982 Tax Act (TEFRA);
- Distributions to an employee who separated from service by March 1, 1986, provided that accrued benefits were in pay status as of that date under a written election specifying the payout schedule;
- Certain distributions before 1990 from an employee stock ownership plan (ESOP) if a majority of plan assets have been invested in employer securities for five plan years; or
- Dividend distributions from an ESOP.

Further, if you are considered a highly compensated employee and excess elective deferrals or excess contributions are made on your behalf, a distribution of the excess to you is not subject to the penalty.

PENALTY FOR EXCESS DISTRIBUTIONS

¶ **7.14** You may be penalized if you withdraw amounts from an employer retirement plan or IRA *over* the following limits—
$750,000 for lump sums qualifying for averaging
$150,000 for all other types of distributions including IRA distributions
A 15% penalty is imposed on the excess amount. For example, in 1987, if you receive a $200,000 IRA distribution, and the following exceptions do not apply, the penalty is $7,500 (15% × $50,000 excess).

Exceptions. The following amounts are not counted as distributions for purposes of the $150,000 or $750,000 limit and may help you avoid the penalty: (1) distributions equal to your after-tax contributions to a plan or your investment in the contract: (2) distributions from a qualified plan which you rollover to an IRA; (3) distributions to a former spouse ordered by a domestic relations court; the former spouse takes the distributions into account in determining whether the penalty applies; (4) distributions received by a beneficiary of a deceased individual.

Special 1987 and 1988 election. If your accrued benefit as of August 1, 1986, exceeded $562,500, an election may be made to exempt such accrued benefits from the penalty. *See* the IRS instructions to Form 1040 for making this election.

RESTRICTIONS ON LOANS FROM COMPANY PLANS

¶ **7.15** You may borrow from an employer retirement plan without incurring tax, if the loan is within certain limits and you repay it within a specified period. The restrictions apply to loans from a qualified company plan, tax-sheltered annuity plan, or government plan.

After 1986, loans repayable within five years are not taxed if they fall within the following limits:

If your vested accrued benefit is $20,000 or less, you are not taxed if the loan, when added to other outstanding loans from all plans of the employer, is $10,000 or less. If total loans exceed $10,000, the excess is treated as a taxable distribution.

If your vested accrued benefit exceeds $20,000, then the maximum tax-free loan depends on whether you borrowed from any employer plan within the one-year period ending on the day before the date of the new loan. If you did not borrow within the year, you are not taxed on a loan that does not exceed the *lesser* of $50,000 or 50% of the vested benefit.

If there were loans in the one-year period, the $50,000 limit must be further reduced. The loan, when added to the outstanding loan balance, may not exceed $50,000 *less* the excess of (1) the highest outstanding loan balance during the one-year period (ending the day before the new loan), over (2) the outstanding balance on the date of the new loan. This reduced $50,000 limit applies where it is less than 50% of the vested benefit; if 50% of the vested benefit was the smaller amount, that would be the maximum tax-free loan.

EXAMPLE

Your vested plan benefit is $200,000. Assume that in January 1987, you borrow $30,000 from the plan. On November 1, 1987, when the outstanding balance on the first loan is $20,000, you want to take another loan without incurring tax. You may borrow an additional $20,000 without incurring tax: The $50,000 limit is first reduced by the outstanding loan balance of $20,000—leaving $30,000. The reduced $30,000 limit is in turn reduced by $10,000, the excess of $30,000 (the highest loan balance within one year of the new loan) over $20,000 (the balance on November 1).

The $20,000 loan limit applies because it is less than 50% of the vested benefit of $200,000.

Repayment period. Generally, loans within the above limits must be repayable within five years to be tax free. However, if you use the loan to purchase a principal residence for yourself, the repayment period may be longer than five years. This exception does not apply if the plan loan is used to improve your existing principal residence, to buy a second home, or to finance the purchase of a home or home improvements for other family members; such loans are subject to the five-year repayment rule.

Level loan amortization required. A new law allows tax free treatment for a loan only if you are required to repay using a level amortization schedule, with payments at least quarterly. According to Congressional Committee Reports, you may accelerate repayment, and the employer may use a variable interest rate and require full repayment if you leave the company.

Spousal consent generally required. If you are married and want to borrow from your plan, you may be required to obtain your spouse's consent. The new law requires that all plans subject to the joint and survivor rules of ¶7.11 must require spousal consent in order to be able to use your account balance as security for the loan in case you default. Check with your plan administrator for consent requirements.

Interest deduction limitations. Interest deductions on plan loans are limited under the new law restrictions for personal consumer loans and investment loans; *see* chapter 15. In addition, new law rules bar *any* interest deduction in these cases: (1) you are a key employee (generally owners or officers), or (2) you borrow your own elective deferrals of salary (or income earned on the deferrals) from a 401(k) plan or tax-sheltered annuity plan.

Loan limits for self-employed. Loans to a self-employed person from a Keogh plan are subject to the same restrictions discussed above for employees and in addition, borrowing usually results in penalties; *see* ¶8.21.

COMMERCIAL ANNUITIES

¶ 7.16 New law pointers:

New actuarial tables. If you made any investment in an annuity contract after June 30, 1986, you must use new unisex life expectancy tables to figure the taxable portion of your annuity payments. If your entire investment was before July 1, 1986, the old actuarial tables generally apply. *See* the discussion at 7.17.

Exclusion limited to investment. It was possible under prior law for individuals living longer than the life expectancy predicted by Treasury tables to exclude from income more than their total annuity investment. This rule has been changed if you have an annuity starting date after 1986. You may not exclude more than your total investment in the policy.

Penalty for premature withdrawals. The penalty for withdrawals from deferred annuity contracts before age 59½ is now 10%, up from 5%. The penalty and several exceptions are discussed at ¶7.17.

REPORTING COMMERCIAL ANNUITIES

¶ 7.17 That part of the annuity payment allocated to your cost investment is treated as a nontaxable return of the cost; the balance is taxable income earned on the investment. You may find the taxable part of your annuity payment by following the six steps below:

1. *Figure your investment in the annuity contract.*

If your annuity is	Your cost is
Single premium annuity contract	The single premium paid
Deferred annuity contract	The total premiums paid
A gift	Your donor's cost
An employee annuity	The total of your contributions to the plan plus your employer's contributions which you were required to report as income. See ¶7.24–¶7.28.
With a refund feature	What was paid for the annuity, less the value of the refund feature

If you have no investment in the contract, annuity income is fully taxable; ignore steps 2 through 6 below.
From cost, you subtract the following items:
Any premiums refunded, rebates, or dividends received on or before the annuity starting date.
Additional premiums for double indemnity or disability benefits.
Amounts received under the contract before the annuity starting date to the extent these amounts were not taxed.
Value of refund feature (*see* ¶7.18).
Amounts received before the annuity starting date which are allocable to investments made before August 14, 1982, reduce the cost of the annuity contract. If they exceed your cost, the excess is subject to tax. The same rule applies if payment is made to a beneficiary where the annuitant dies before annuity payments begin. Generally, these payments will not be more than the cost—unless they are lump-sum payments to cancel the contract. The reduced cost, where the contract continues, is the investment in the contract. For investments after August 13, 1982; *see* withdrawal rules in the next column.

Dividends received on or after the date annuity payments begin (and the annuity payments continue) are fully taxed.

2. *Find your expected return.* This is the total of all the payments you are to receive. If the payments are to be made to you for life, your expected return is figured by multiplying the amount of the annual payment by a multiple based on your life expectancy as of the annuity starting date. These multiples are listed in tables published by the Treasury. The tables are in IRS Publication 575. Further, you can get the tables from your local District Director, or you can write to your insurance company, requesting the amount of your expected return.

If the payments are for a fixed number of years (as in an endowment contract), find your expected return by multiplying your annual payments by the number of years you are to receive them. (Variable annuities are discussed at ¶7.21).

3. *Divide the investment in contract (step 1) by the expected return (step 2).* This will give you a percentage. This percentage of your yearly annuity payments is tax free. The percentage remains the same for the remaining years of the annuity.

4. *Find your total annuity receipts for the year.* (For example, you received ten monthly payments as your annuity began in March. Your total is the monthly payment multiplied by ten.)

5. *Multiply the percentage in step 3 by the total in step 4.* The result is the nontaxable portion (or excludable amount) of your annuity payments.

6. *Subtract the amount in step 5 from the amount in step 4.* This is the part of your annuity for the year which is subject to tax.

Examples of reporting annuities may be found at ¶7.20.

New IRS actuarial tables. The IRS has new unisex actuarial tables that you must use if you made any investment in the annuity contract *after* June 30, 1986. Generally, life expectancies are longer under the new tables than under the old tables. The old tables are still used if your entire investment was *before* July 1, 1986. The new tables are Tables V through VIII. The old tables are Tables I through IV. All of the tables are included in

IRS Publication 575; they may also be available from the issuer of the annuity contract.

You may make an irrevocable election to use the new tables for all payments received under the contract, even if you did not make an investment after June 30, 1986.

If you invested in the contract both before July 1, 1986, and after June 30, 1986, and you are the first person to receive annuity payments under the contract, you may make a special election to use Tables I through IV for the pre-July 1986 investment and Tables V through VIII for the post-June 1986 investment. *See* IRS Publication 575 for further information. Treasury Regulation 1.72-6(d) has examples showing how to figure the post-June 1986 and pre-July 1986 investments.

Types of Annuity Contracts

Annuity	Description
One annuitant annuity	You receive payments for the rest of your life. For an example of how to find the expected return of this type of annuity, see ¶ 7.19 and ¶ 7.20.
Temporary annuity	You receive payment until death or until the end of a specified limited period, whichever occurs earlier. To get your expected return, you find your multiple in Treasury Table IV if your entire investment was before July 1, 1986; Table VIII if any investment was after June 30, 1986.*
Uniform joint and survivor annuity	You receive payments for the rest of your life, and after your death the same amount is paid to the other annuitant. The expected return is based on the combined life expectancies of both of you. You use Treasury Table II to get a multiple based on joint lives if the entire investment was before July 1, 1986; Table VI if any investment was after June 30, 1986.* The exclusion ratio remains the same for both you and the survivor.
One annuitant stepped-up annuity	You receive smaller payments at first and when you reach a certain age, usually on retiring, you receive larger payments. This contract is treated as a combination of a one annuitant contract for the larger amount minus a temporary annuity for the difference between the larger and smaller amounts. To get your expected return, you find your multiple in Treasury Tables I and IV, or in Tables V and VIII, depending on when you invested.
One annuitant stepped-down annuity	You receive larger payments at first and then, when you reach a certain age, smaller payments, usually on reaching age 65. This contract is treated as a combination of a one annuitant contract for the smaller amount plus a temporary annuity for the difference between the larger and smaller amounts. To get your expected return, you find your multiple in Treasury Tables I and IV if all investments were before July 1, 1986; Tables V and VIII if any investments after June 30, 1986.*
Variable payment joint and survivor annuity with lesser annuity to survivor	You receive payments while both are alive and on the death of one of you, a lesser amount is paid to the survivor—regardless of which annuitant dies first. To get your expected return, you use Treasury Tables II and IIA if all investments were before July 1, 1986; otherwise use Tables VI and VI-A if any investment was after June 30, 1986.*
Variable payment joint and survivor annuity with first and second annuitants specified	You receive payments of a certain amount, and on your death the other annuitant gets a lesser amount. To get your expected return, you use Treasury Tables I and II if all investments were before July 1, 1986; otherwise use Tables V and VI.* The exclusion ratio remains the same for both you and the survivor.

*See the paragraph above this chart, "New IRS actuarial tables," for applying the new actuarial tables.

Exclusion limited to investment for annuities starting after 1986. If your annuity starting date is after 1986, your lifetime exclusion may not exceed your cost contribution. Under prior law, it was possible for individuals who lived longer than their projected life expectancies (according to Treasury tables) to exclude more than their contributions. Under the new law, this is still possible only for individuals with an annuity starting date before 1987.

If you have an annuity starting date after July 1, 1986, and die before recovering your investment, a deduction is allowed on your final tax return for the unrecovered cost. If a refund of the investment is made under the contract to a beneficiary, the beneficiary is allowed the deduction. The deduction is claimed as an itemized deduction and is not subject to the 2% floor; *see* chapter 19.

Withdrawals from deferred annuities. Cash withdrawals before the annuity starting date may be taxable to the extent that the cash value of the contract exceeds your investment in the contract. Withdrawals are taxable if attributed to investments made after August 13, 1982, even if the contract was purchased before August 14, 1982. Loans under the contract or pledges are treated as cash withdrawals. Withdrawals from contracts bought by a qualified retirement plan are discussed at ¶ 7.19.

Premature withdrawals are also subject to a penalty of 10% of the amount includible in income. A withdrawal in 1987 from an annuity contract is penalized *unless:*

1. You have reached age 59½ or have become disabled.
2. The distribution is part of a series of substantially equal payments, made at least annually over your life expectancy or life expectancies of you and a beneficiary.
3. The payment is received by a beneficiary or estate after the policyholder's death.
4. Payment is from a qualified retirement plan, tax-sheltered annuity or IRA; in this case the penalty rules of ¶ 7.13 (qualified plans) or chapter 8 (IRAs) apply.
5. Payment is allocable to investments made before August 14, 1982;
6. Payment is from an annuity contract under a qualified personal injury settlement.
7. Payment is from a single premium annuity where the starting date is no more than one year from the date of purchase.
8. Payment is from an annuity purchased by an employer upon the termination of a qualified retirement plan and held until you separated from service.

If you can avoid the penalty under exception (3) for substantial equal payments and you change to a nonqualifying distribution method within five years or before age 59½, such as where you receive a lump sum, a recapture tax will apply to the payments received before age 59½.

COST OF ANNUITY WITH A REFUND FEATURE

¶ 7.18 If your annuity has a refund feature, your investment in the contract is the cost of your annuity less the value of the refund feature.

Your annuity has a refund feature when these three requirements are present:

1. The refund under the contract depends, even in part, on the life expectancy of at least one person.
2. The contract provides for payments to a beneficiary or the annuitant's estate after the annuitant's death.
3. The payments to estate or beneficiary are in the nature of a refund of the amount paid for the annuity.

Where an employer paid part of the cost, the refund is figured on only the part paid by the employee.

The amount of the reduction for the refund feature is figured by using a multiple which your local District Director will give you at your request, or the company which has issued your contract will give you this net investment figure. The multiple is included in Treasury Table III or Table VII, depending on the date of your investment.

The surviving beneficiary receiving the balance of guaranteed payment does not include any amount as taxed income until the payments, when added to that portion of the payments excluded by the first annuitant, equal the investment in the contract. All later payments are taxed in full.

FINDING YOUR EXPECTED RETURN

¶ 7.19

Payments for fixed number of years. If you receive payments for a fixed number of years, multiply the amount of the annual payment by the number of years you are to receive payments. The result is your expected return. For example, if you are to receive $1,000 a year for ten years, your expected return is $10,000. Assuming you paid $7,500 for the policy, the nontaxable portion of your annuity each year is $750 (7,500 ÷ 10,000) or 75% of $1,000; the taxable portion is $250 ($1,000–$750).

Payments for life. The expected return is reached by multiplying the annual annuity income by the life expectancy multiple found in the Treasury table for your particular kind of annuity.

Before using the table, you must know two things:

1. Your annuity starting date. The annuity starting date is the first day of the first period for which an annuity payment is received. For example, on January 1 you complete payment under an annuity contract providing for monthly payments starting on July 1 for the period beginning June 1. The annuity starting date is June 1. Use that date in computing your investment in the contract and your expected return. (Those who were collecting annuities before 1954 use January 1, 1954, as the annuity starting date.)
2. Adjustments to the life expectancy multiple. Adjustments are required when your annuity income is received quarterly, semiannually, or annually.

EXAMPLE

You receive quarterly annuity payments. Your first payment comes on January 15, covering the first quarter of the year. Since the period between the starting date of January 1 and the payment date of January 15 is less than one month, you adjust the multiple according to the table below by adding 0.1.

When your annuity payments come to you more frequently than quarterly (for example, monthly), the multiple is not adjusted.

Increases in annuity payments are taxable in full. The excluded amount attributed to your cost remains the same as before the increase.

MULTIPLE ADJUSTMENT TABLE

If the number of whole months from the annuity starting date to the first payment date is—	0–1	2	3	4	5	6	7	8	9	10	11	12
And payments under the contract are to be made:												
Annually	+ .5	+ .4	+ .3	+ .2	+ .1	0.0	0.0	− .1	− .2	− .3	− .4	− .5
Semiannually	+ .2	+ .1	0.0	0.0	− .1	− .2						
Quarterly	+ .1	0.0	− .1									

COMPUTING THE EXPECTED RETURN OF A ONE-ANNUITANT ANNUITY

¶ 7.20 The payments go to one individual for life; on death, the payments stop. To find the multiple here, use Table 1 or Table V below.

Find your age at the nearest birthday to your annuity starting date in the proper column—"Male" or "Female." Then look opposite your age to find the proper multiple. (This multiple may have to be adjusted. See ¶7.19.) You then multiply this number by the total annuity payments you are to receive in one full year. If you have a monthly annuity, you multiply it by 12 times the monthly payments. The product is your expected return.

TABLE 1: Investments Before July 1, 1986. (See ¶ 7.17.)

Male	Female	Multiples	Male	Female	Multiples	Male	Female	Multiples
6	11	65.0	41	46	33.0	76	81	9.1
7	12	64.1	42	47	32.1	77	82	8.7
8	13	63.2	43	48	31.2	78	83	8.3
9	14	62.3	44	49	30.4	79	84	7.8
10	15	61.4	45	50	29.6	80	85	7.5
11	16	60.4	46	51	28.7	81	86	7.1
12	17	59.5	47	52	27.9	82	87	6.7
13	18	58.6	48	53	27.1	83	88	6.3
14	19	57.7	49	54	26.3	84	89	6.0
15	20	56.7	50	55	25.5	85	90	5.7
16	21	55.8	51	56	24.7	86	91	5.4
17	22	54.9	52	57	24.0	87	92	5.1
18	23	53.9	53	58	23.2	88	93	4.8
19	24	53.0	54	59	22.4	89	94	4.5
20	25	52.1	55	60	21.7	90	95	4.2
21	26	51.1	56	61	21.0	91	96	4.0
22	27	50.2	57	62	20.3	92	97	3.7
23	28	49.3	58	63	19.6	93	98	3.5
24	29	48.3	59	64	18.9	94	99	3.3
25	30	47.4	60	65	18.2	95	100	3.1
26	31	46.5	61	66	17.5	96	101	2.9
27	32	45.6	62	67	16.9	97	102	2.7
28	33	44.6	63	68	16.2	98	103	2.5
29	34	43.7	64	69	15.6	99	104	2.3
30	35	42.8	65	70	15.0	100	105	2.1
31	36	41.9	66	71	14.4	101	106	1.9
32	37	41.0	67	72	13.8	102	107	1.7
33	38	40.0	68	73	13.2	103	108	1.5
34	39	39.1	69	74	12.6	104	109	1.3
35	40	38.2	70	75	12.1	105	110	1.2
36	41	37.3	71	76	11.6	106	111	1.0
37	42	36.5	72	77	11.0	107	112	.8
38	43	35.6	73	78	10.5	108	113	.7
39	44	34.7	74	79	10.1	109	114	.6
40	45	33.8	75	80	9.6	110	115	.5
						111	116	0

TABLE V: Investments After June 30, 1986. (See ¶ 7.17.)

AGE	MULTIPLE	AGE	MULTIPLE	AGE	MULTIPLE
5	76.6	42	40.6	79	10.0
6	75.6	43	39.6	80	9.5
7	74.7	44	38.7	81	8.9
8	73.7	45	37.7	82	8.4
9	72.7	46	36.8	83	7.9
10	71.7	47	35.9	84	7.4
11	70.7	48	34.9	85	6.9
12	69.7	49	34.0	86	6.5
13	68.8	50	33.1	87	6.1
14	67.8	51	32.2	88	5.7
15	66.8	52	31.3	89	5.3
16	65.8	53	30.4	90	5.0
17	64.8	54	29.5	91	4.7
18	63.9	55	28.6	92	4.4
19	62.9	56	27.7	93	4.1
20	61.9	57	26.8	94	3.9
21	60.9	58	25.9	95	3.7
22	59.9	59	25.0	96	3.4
23	59.0	60	24.2	97	3.2
24	58.0	61	23.3	98	3.0
25	57.0	62	22.5	99	2.8
26	56.0	63	21.6	100	2.7
27	55.1	64	20.8	101	2.5
28	54.1	65	20.0	102	2.3
29	53.1	66	19.2	103	2.1
30	52.2	67	18.4	104	1.9
31	51.2	68	17.6	105	1.8
32	50.2	69	16.8	106	1.6
33	49.3	70	16.0	107	1.4
34	48.3	71	15.3	108	1.3
35	47.3	72	14.6	109	1.1
36	46.4	73	13.9	110	1.0
37	45.4	74	13.2	111	.9
38	44.4	75	12.5	112	.8
39	43.5	76	11.9	113	.7
40	42.5	77	11.2	114	.6
41	41.5	78	10.6	115	.5

EXAMPLES

1. Jones was 66 years old on March 14, 1987. On April 1, he received his first monthly annuity check of $100. This covered his annuity payment for March. His annuity starting date is March 1, 1987, and his entire investment was before July 1, 1986. Looking at Table 1 under "Male" at age 66, Jones finds the multiple 14.4. (Jones does not have to adjust that multiple according to the rules explained in ¶7.19 because the payments are monthly.) Jones multiplies the 14.4 by $1,200 ($100 a month for a year) to find his expected return of $17,280. Say the annuity cost Jones $12,960. He divides his expected return into the investment in the contract (the cost) and gets his exclusion percentage of 75%. Thereafter, in every year for the rest of his life, Jones receives tax free 75% of his annuity payments and is taxable on 25%. For 1987 Jones reports his annuity income as follows:

Amount received	$900
Amount excludable	675
Taxable portion	$225

For 1988 and later years, Jones will receive annuity payments for the full year. The amount received will be $1,200; amount excludable, $900, and taxable portion, $300.

2. Same facts as in example (1) except there was an investment after June 30, 1986 and Table V is used. Looking at Table V under age 66, Jones finds the multiple 19.2. The same multiple applies to males and females. Multiplying the 19.2 by $1,200 gives an expected return of $23,040. Using a cost of $12,960, the exclusion percentage is 56.25% ($12,960 ÷ $23,040). For 1987 Jones reports annuity income as follows:

Amount received	$900
Amount excludable	506.25
Taxable portion	$393.75

For 1988 and later years in which annual payments of $1,200 are received, the amount excludable will be $675, and the taxable portion, $525.

VARIABLE ANNUITIES

¶ **7.21** Variable annuity policies pay different benefits depending on cost-of-living indices, profits earned by the annuity fund, or similar fluctuating standards.

You figure the tax due by considering your investment in the contract (adjusted for the refund feature, if any), and the number of periodic payments you expect to receive under the contract. If the annuity is for a definite period, the number of payments is determined by multiplying the number of payments to be made each year by the number of years you will receive payments.

If the annuity is for life, you divide the amount you invested in the contract by a multiple obtained from an appropriate actuarial table (see ¶7.17). The figure you obtain is the amount of annual annuity income which is not taxed.

EXAMPLE

Your total investment in the contract was $12,000. Your annuity is to start at age 65 and will be paid starting January 1, 1987 in varying annual installments for your life. The amount of each payment excluded from tax is:

Investment in the contract	$12,000
Multiple (from Table 1)	15.0
Amount of each payment excluded from tax ($12,000 ÷ 15)	$ 800

If your first payment is $920, then $120 ($920–$800) is included in your 1987 income.

If you receive a payment which is less than the nontaxable amount, you may elect when you receive the next payment to recalculate the nontaxable portion. The amount by which the periodic nontaxable portion exceeded the payment you received is divided by the number of payments you expect as of the time of the next payment. The result is added to the previously calculated periodic nontaxable portion. The sum is the amount of each future payment to be excluded from tax.

EXAMPLE

Using the facts of the example above, assume that after your 1987 payment you receive $700 in 1988 and $1,200 in 1989. None of the 1988 payment is taxed; you exclude $800 for each annual annuity payment. Also you may elect to recompute your annual exclusion when you receive your payment in 1989. You elect to recompute your exclusion as follows:

Amount excludable in 1988	$800
Amount received in 1988	700
Difference	$100
Multiple as of 1/1/89 (see actuarial table)	13.8
Amount added to previously determined annual exclusion ($100 ÷ 13.8)	$ 7.25
Revised annual exclusion for 1988 and later years ($800 + $7.25)	$807.25
Amount taxable in 1989 ($1,200–$807.25)	$392.75

WHEN YOU CONVERT YOUR MATURED ENDOWMENT POLICY

¶ **7.22** When an endowment policy matures, you may elect to receive a lump sum, an annuity, an interest option, or a paid-up life insurance policy. If you elect—

A lump sum. You report the difference between your cost (premium payments less dividends) and what you receive.

An annuity before the policy matures or within 60 days after maturity. You report income in the years you receive your annuity. (See ¶7.17 for how to report annuity income.) Use as your investment in the annuity contract the cost of the endowment policy less premiums paid for other benefits, such as double indemnity or disability income. If you elect the annuity option more than 60 days after maturity, you report income on the matured policy as if you received the lump sum (see above rule). The lump sum is treated as the cost investment in the annuity contract.

An interest option before the policy matures. You report no income on the matured policy as long as you do not have the right to withdraw the proceeds of the policy. If you make the election after maturity or have the right to withdraw proceeds, you report income as if you received a lump sum. The interest is taxed in the years received.

Paid-up insurance. You report the difference between the present value of the paid-up life insurance policy and the premium paid for the endowment policy. In figuring the value of the insurance policy, you do not use its cash surrender value, but the amount you would have to pay for a similar policy with the company at the date of exchange. Your insurance company can give you this figure. The difference is taxed at ordinary income tax rates.

Tax-free exchange rules apply to the policy exchanges listed at ¶12.20.

Sales of endowment, annuity, or life insurance policies are taxable as ordinary income, not as capital gains.

The proceeds of a veteran's endowment policy paid before the death of the veteran are not taxable.

EMPLOYEE ANNUITIES

¶ **7.23** **New law pointers.** New tax law has affected how you are taxed on payments from employee annuities.

The three-year rule for recovering cost is available only to employees whose annuity started on or before July 1, 1986. If your annuity starting date was after July 1, 1986, the three-year rule is not available and you must use the regular annuity rules of ¶7.17. *See* ¶7.26.

If you invested in an annuity contract on or after June 30, 1986, you must use new unisex annuity tables to compute the taxable portion of annuity payments. *See* ¶7.17.

Under prior law, you did not have to pay tax on distributions from a qualified plan before the annuity starting date unless your withdrawals exceeded your investment. Now, only a proportionate part of each withdrawal is tax free. *See* ¶7.29.

Starting in 1987, the maximum tax free salary reduction allowed under tax-sheltered annuity plans is generally $9,500. However, employees with more than 15 years of service may defer up to $12,500 annually. *See* ¶7.30.

REPORTING EMPLOYEE ANNUITIES

¶ **7.24** Retirement benefits paid as annuities are generally taxed in the same manner as commercial annuities. That part of the annuity payment allocated to your cost investment is treated as a nontaxable return of cost; the balance is treated as taxable income.

If your pension was completely financed by your employer and you did not report your employer's premium contributions, you report all payments as ordinary income. You have no cost investment in the annuity contract. To determine if you have a cost investment, see the next paragraph, ¶7.25.

COST OF EMPLOYEE ANNUITY

¶ **7.25** Cost of an employee annuity includes the following items:

Premiums paid by you or by withholdings from your pay.

Payments made by your employer and reported as additional pay. Premiums paid by an employer in a nonapproved plan for your benefit give you immediate income if you have nonforfeitable rights to the policy.

Premiums paid by your employer, which, if the amounts had been paid to you directly, would have been tax free to you because you were working abroad (*see* chapter 36).

Pre-1939 contributions by a city or state to its employees' pension fund. (Before 1939, salary payments to state and city employees were tax free for federal income tax purposes.)

If you are a beneficiary collecting because of the death of an employee, cost may include all or part of the death benefit exclusion up to $5,000 (*see* ¶7.28).

THREE-YEAR RECOVERY OF COST

¶ **7.26** If your annuity starting date was *before* July 2, 1986, and within three years of the first payment you will receive payments under the contract which equal or exceed your cost investment, payments are not taxable as income until after they equal your cost investment.

Under the new law, this favorable three-year cost recovery method is not available if your annuity starting date was *after* July 1, 1986. If your annuity starting date was July 2, 1986 or later, you must use the general rules of ¶7.17 to allocate part of each payment between the excludable and taxable portions. According to Congressional Committee Reports, if under the terms of your employer plan, your annuity starting date was July 1, 1986, you may use the three-year rule even if you do not actually receive an annuity payment on July 1; you qualify as long as the first annuity payment was for the period commencing no later than July 1, 1986.

EXAMPLES

1. Starting July 1, 1985, you receive a pension annuity of $300 a month for the rest of your life. You contributed $9,000 to the policy; your company paid the balance. Because payments will equal or exceed your cost within three years, payments received before January 1, 1988, are not taxable income.

Payments in	Total
1985 (six months)	$1,800
1986	3,600
1987	3,600
	$9,000

2. Same facts as above except you contributed only $6,000 to the policy.

Payments in	Total
1985 (six months)	$1,800
1986	3,600
1987 (two months)	600
	$6,000

Taxable payments (ten months) reported in 1987 total $3,000.

After you have received payments equaling your investment, all future payments are ordinary income.

If you will not recover your cost within three years after your pension starts, or if the annuity starting date was after July 1, 1986, follow the regular annuity rules at ¶7.17.

An increase in the amount of payments during the three-year period does not permit use of the three-year rule if you could not have used it initially.

An employee is taxed on the full value of a nonforfeitable annuity contract which his employer buys him if the employer does not have a qualified pension plan. Tax is imposed in the year the policy is purchased. A qualified plan is one approved by the IRS for special tax benefits.

You may receive benefits from more than one program under a single trust or plan of an employer or from several trusts or plans. Check with your former employer if you are covered by more than one pension or annuity contract. If so, you have to account for each contract separately even though benefits are included in one check.

Variable annuity. The three-year cost rules apply to periodic payments under a variable annuity contract financed by you and your employer. To determine whether you will recover your cost within three years, multiply the amount of the first periodic payment by the number of periodic payments to be made within the three years beginning on the date of its receipt.

CIVIL SERVICE RETIREMENT

¶ 7.27 Almost all U.S. Civil Service retirees receive annuity benefits sufficient to recover their cost within three years after they retire. Thus, provided the annuity date was before July 2, 1986, the three-year cost recovery rule of ¶7.26 may be used. If the annuity starting date was after July 1, 1986, the general rules of ¶7.17 must be used to compute the tax free and taxable portions of each withdrawal. If you elected a reduced annuity in order to receive a lump-sum credit for your total contributions to the plan, *see* IRS Publication 721 for figuring the taxable portion of the lump-sum.

While you worked for the federal government, contributions to the Civil Service retirement fund were withheld from your pay. These contributions represent your cost. Also, if you repaid to the retirement fund amounts that you previously had withdrawn, or paid into the fund to receive full credit for certain uncovered service, the entire amount you paid, including that designated as interest, is part of your cost. You may not claim an interest deduction for any amount designated as interest.

The annuity statement you received when your annuity was approved shows your "total contributions" to the retirement fund (your cost) and the "monthly rate" of your annuity benefit. The monthly rate is the rate before adjustment for health benefits coverage and life insurance, if any. To determine whether you will recover your cost within three years, multiply your initial monthly rate by 36. If the result equals or exceeds your cost, you must use the three-year rule provided the annuity starting date was before July 2, 1986. If you will not recover your cost within the three-year period or if the annuity starting date was after July 1, 1986, you report your annuity by following the rules at ¶7.17.

An increase in the monthly rate of your annuity resulting from a cost-of-living increase does not affect the method of reporting your annuity on your tax return. If you determine that you must use the three-year rule, your entire annuity, including the increase, is fully taxable after you have received payments equaling your cost. If, at the time you received your first annuity payment, you determined that you may not use the three-year rule, a later increase in your monthly rate thereafter will not enable you to use it; you must use the general rules at ¶7.17. A future increase in a civil service pension to the retiree or his survivor is not treated as annuity income but is reported in full as miscellaneous income and is not reduced by the exclusion ratio. However, an increase effective on or before a survivor's civil service annuity commences must be taken into account in computing the expected return or in determining the aggregate amount receivable under the annuity.

If you retired during the past year and filed your application for retirement late or are entitled to accrued payments because your application was processed late, you may receive a lump-sum payment representing the unpaid accrued monthly installments for the period before your regular monthly payments begin. If the lump sum is less than your cost of the annuity, you determine whether the three-year rule applies as explained above. Disregarding the lump sum, multiply the monthly rate of your annuity by 36; and if that amount plus the lump sum equals or exceeds your cost, you must use the three-year rule. In determining your tax for the year under the three-year rule, the lump sum is treated as a tax free recovery of part of your cost. If the lump sum exceeds your cost of the annuity, the excess is fully taxable. Also, all the regular monthly annuity payments you receive thereafter are fully taxable.

A lump-sum payment for accrued annual leave received upon retirement is not part of your annuity. It is treated as a salary payment and is taxable as ordinary income.

If you made voluntary contributions to the retirement fund, you report the portion of your annuity attributable to the voluntary contributions as a separate annuity, taxable under the rules at ¶7.17. If you made voluntary contributions, an information return which you receive each year will state the portion of your monthly payments attributable to your voluntary contributions.

$5,000 DEATH BENEFIT EXCLUSION ADDED TO THE COST OF AN ANNUITY

¶ 7.28 A pension annuity paid to you as the beneficiary of a deceased employee may qualify for a death benefit exclusion, up to $5,000. The amount of the exclusion is added to the cost of the annuity in calculating the investment in the contract as of the annuity starting date.

The $5,000 exclusion may not be added to the investment if the deceased had received any payment under a joint and survivor contract after reaching his retirement age.

If, after taking the $5,000 exclusion into account in computing the investment in the contract, the three-year rule is not applicable, the beneficiary follows the regular annuity rules to compute taxable income (*see* ¶7.17). If the annuity is payable over the lifetime of the beneficiary, actuarial tables are used to determine the expected return on the contract. Ask the company paying the annuity to give you these amounts. The maximum amount of the death benefit exclusion is fixed at $5,000 without regard to the number of beneficiaries or the number of employers funding pension payments.

The death benefit exclusion may also be available to beneficiaries of a self-employed person who died after December 31, 1983.

WITHDRAWALS FROM EMPLOYER PLAN BEFORE ANNUITY STARTING DATE

¶ 7.29 Under prior law, an employee could withdraw funds from an employer plan before the annuity starting date without incurring tax until his or her investment was recovered. Only withdrawals exceeding the employee's investment were taxed. Under the new law, you must generally pay tax on a portion of each withdrawal before the annuity date. The portion of the withdrawal allocable to your investment is recovered tax free; the portion allocable to employer contributions and income earned on the contract is taxed. To compute the tax free recovery, multiply the withdrawal by this fraction:

$$\frac{\text{Your total investment}}{\text{Your vested account balance or accrued benefit}}$$

Your investment and vested benefit are generally determined as of the date of distribution.

Exceptions. More favorable investment recovery rules are allowed in the following cases:

1. *Plans in effect May 5, 1986.* If on May 5, 1986, your employer's plan allowed distributions of employee contributions before separation from service, the above pro-rata recovery rule applies only to the extent that the withdrawal exceeds the total investment in the contract on December 31, 1986. For example, assume that as of December 31, 1986, you had an account balance of $9,750, which included $4,000 of your own contributions. If the plan on May 5, 1986, allowed pre-retirement distributions of employee contributions, you may receive withdrawals up to your $4,000 investment without incurring tax. Thus, if you receive a $3,000 distribution in 1987, it is not subject to tax.

2. *Separate accounts for employee contributions.* A defined contribution plan (such as a profit-sharing plan) is allowed to account for employee contributions (and earnings on the contributions) separately from employer contributions. If separate accounting is maintained, withdrawals of employee contributions from the separate account may be made tax free. A defined benefit pension plan may also maintain employee contributions (and earnings) in a separate account to which earnings and losses are allocated.

Note: Both of the above exceptions are complicated and you should consult your plan administrator to determine if the exceptions apply and how to make the required calculations.

ANNUITIES FOR EMPLOYEES OF TAX-EXEMPT GROUPS AND SCHOOLS

¶ 7.30 If you are employed by a tax-exempt religious, charitable, or educational organization, or are on the civilian staff or faculty of the Uniformed Services University of the Health Services (Department of Defense), you may be able to arrange for the purchase of nonforfeitable tax-deferred retirement annuities.

The purchase is generally made through a reduction of salary which is used to pay for the contract. The amount of the salary reduction used to buy the contract is not taxable if it comes within specified limits. The tax rules for computing the excludable amount are complicated, as there are several limitations and exceptions.

The tax-sheltered contribution is generally 20% of your pay multiplied by the number of years of service with your employer *less* tax-free contributions made in prior years by your employer to any qualified plan: Salary reductions count as tax free employer contributions. Under this formula, you may not be allowed to exclude any part of the current year's salary reduction because of employer contributions in prior years. Further, even though allowed by the 20% of pay/years of service formula, the maximum tax-free salary reduction may not exceed the *lower* of 25% of your pay or $9,500. The new $9,500 limit takes effect in 1987. However, employees with at least 15 years of service may be able to defer up to $12,500. *See* below for details of the $9,500 limit and the exceptions.

A tax-deferred plan may be funded in mutual fund shares.

You may make a rollover of a distribution to an IRA account (*see* ¶7.8), but may not use the special averaging method to report the distribution.

EXAMPLE

A public school teacher earning $10,000 agrees to a $1,000 salary reduction to be used to purchase an annuity contract. The employer also contributes $1,800 per year to a pension trust for the teacher's account. In the first year, the entire salary reduction contribution is tax free as it is within the 20% exclusion of $1,800 (20% of the reduced salary of $9,000 × one year service). In the second and third year, there is a taxable amount.

Second year		
20% of pay	$1,800	
Years of service	× 2	$3,600
Less prior tax-free contributions		2,800
Tax-free exclusion		$ 800

Third year		
20% of pay	$1,800	
Years of service	× 3	5,400
Less prior tax-free contributions		5,400
No exclusion		–0–

The entire $1,000 salary reduction in the third year is taxable to the teacher.

Subject to the maximum $9,500 limit, employees of schools, hospitals, churches, health and welfare service agencies, and home health services may be able to elect tax free contributions exceeding 25% of pay. Such employees may elect a limitation equal to the lower of (1) the general 20% of pay exclusion, (2) 25% of pay plus $4,000, or (3) $15,000. Once an election is made, it is irrevocable. Such employees may also make an irrevocable election to disregard the general 20% of pay test. If the election is made, the annual tax free contribution equals the contribution limit for defined-contribution plans which is the lesser of 25% of pay or $30,000.

A special alternative test applies to a church employee whose adjusted gross income is $17,000 or less. A church employee is allowed a minimum exclusion allowance equal to the lesser of $3,000 or his or her includable compensation, even if this exceeds the amount otherwise allowable under the general 20% of pay/year of service test. Further, such church employees who elect the minimum exclusion allowance may make an election which allows contributions to be made on their behalf that exceed 25% of pay. Church employees include duly ordained, commissioned or licensed ministers and lay employees of the church.

$9,500 limit. Even if allowed by the general 20% of pay/years of service exclusion rule, the maximum tax free salary reduction from a tax-sheltered annuity plan cannot exceed the lower of $9,500 or 25% of pay. If you work for more than one employer, the $9,500 limit applies to all tax-sheltered annuity arrangements in which you participate. The $12,500 limit for certain employees with 15 years of service is discussed below.

If you defer more than $9,500, the excess is taxable. Further, if a salary reduction deferral in excess of the $9,500 limit is made and the excess is not distributed to you by April 15 of the following year, the excess will be

taxed twice; not only in the year of deferral but again in the year it is actually distributed. To avoid the double tax, a distribution of any excess deferral *plus* the income attributable to such excess should be distributed no later than April 15 of the year following the year in which the excess deferral is made. A distribution by the following April 15 is not subject to the premature withdrawal penalty if you are under age 59½ (¶7.13) or the penalty for excess distributions (¶7.14).

The $9,500 limit applies only to elective contributions from your pay under a salary-reduction arrangement. If your employer makes separate contributions, the total of elective salary reductions (not to exceed $9,500) plus the employer contributions may be up to the contribution limit for defined contribution plans, which is generally the lower of 25% of pay or $30,000. As discussed above, certain employees may elect to exceed the 25% of pay ceiling.

The $9,500 limit will remain in effect until the $7,000 limit on elective 401(k) plan deferrals (*See* chapter 32) is increased by inflation adjustments to more than $9,500. At that time, the $9,500 limit for tax-sheltered annuity plans will also be increased.

Special catch-up election may allow $12,500 deferral. If allowed under the general 20% of pay/years of service exclusion formula, and by the 25% of pay limit, the $9,500 salary reduction ceiling is increased to $12,500 for employees of educational organizations, hospitals, churches, home health service agencies, and health and welfare service agencies who have completed 15 years of service. However, the extra $3,000 annual deferral may not be claimed indefinitely. There is a lifetime limit of $15,000 on the amount of extra deferrals (over $9,500) allowed. Further, the extra deferrals may not be claimed after lifetime elective deferrals to the plan exceed $5,000 multiplied by your years of service.

Note: As the annuity contribution rules have been stated in general terms and are also subject to temporary Treasury regulations, we suggest that you rely on the amount computed by your employer or the issuer of the contract. Also *see* IRS Publication 571 for detailed examples.

RETIRED MILITARY PERSONNEL ALLOWED TAX EXCLUSION ON ANNUITY ELECTION

¶ **7.31** If, when you retire from the military, you elect to receive reduced retirement pay to provide an annuity for your spouse or certain child beneficiaries, you do not report that part of your retirement pay used to fund the annuity.

EXAMPLE

You are eligible to receive retirement pay of $500 a month. You elect to receive $400 a month to obtain an annuity of $200 a month for your spouse on your death. You report $400 a month for tax purposes during your lifetime, rather than the $500. On your death, your spouse generally will report the full $200 a month received as income.

If you received retirement pay before 1966 and elected reduced benefits, you reported more retirement pay than you actually received. In this case, amounts attributed to the reduction in retirement pay reported in prior years offset retirement pay received in 1966 and later years.

> If you elected to receive veteran's benefits instead of some or all of your retirement pay, you may have been required to deposit with the U.S. Treasury an amount equal to the reduction for the annuity. If so, you do not report retirement pay until it equals the amount deposited.

If all of the retired person's consideration for the contract (previously taxed reductions) has not been offset against retirement income at the time of death, the beneficiary excludes all payments under the contract until the exclusions equal the remaining consideration for the contract not previously excluded by the deceased. As soon as this amount is excluded, the beneficiary reports all later payments as income.

The $5,000 death benefit exclusion is treated as a cost investment to be added to the spouse's annuity contract if the deceased serviceman retired because of disability and dies before reaching retirement age.

8

IRAs AND KEOGHS

Illustrations of reporting IRA and Keogh plan contributions, deductions, and income on Form 1040 may be found in the Supplement to YOUR INCOME TAX.

New Law Guide to IRA Rules

Points to Consider	Tax Rule
Active participation in retirement plans	If your employer has a pension plan and you are eligible to participate, you are considered an active participant, even if you decline participation. If your employer has a profit sharing plan or 401(k) plan and any contributions are made to your account, you are considered a participant. Whether you have vested rights to benefits does not matter under these tests. If you have a Keogh plan, you may be considered an active participant. *See* ¶8.4 for details on active participation.
Deduction limits for an active participant who is single or a head of household	You may deduct IRA contributions if your adjusted gross income (AGI)* is $25,000 or less. Partial deductions are allowed if your AGI is over $25,000 but less than $35,000. No deduction is allowed if your AGI is $35,000 or more. *See* ¶8.3.
Deduction limits for an active participant who is married and files jointly	You may deduct IRA contributions only if your adjusted gross income (AGI)* is $40,000 or less. Partial deductions are allowed if AGI is between $40,000–$50,000. No deduction is allowed if AGI is $50,000 or over. These limits apply even if only one spouse is covered by an employer plan. *See* ¶8.3.
Deduction limits for an active participant who is married and files separately.	You are allowed only a partial deduction if your AGI* is less than $10,000. No deduction is allowed if your AGI is $10,000 or more.
Nonparticipant who is single or a head of household.	You may deduct contributions to an IRA of $2,000 of earned income regardless of the amount of your adjusted gross income.
Nonparticipant who is married and files jointly.	If your spouse is an active participant in a retirement plan, the AGI* limit of $40,000–$50,000 applies even if you are not a plan participant. If you and your spouse do not have plan coverage, you may each deduct contributions up to $2,000 of earned income or, if only one of you works, up to $2,250 if you contribute to a spousal IRA. *See* ¶8.7.
Nonparticipant who is married and files separately	You may claim your full IRA deduction on a separate return, even if your spouse has coverage.

New Law Guide to IRA Rules

Points to Consider	Tax Rule
Anyone over age 70½	*You may not* contribute to an IRA in the year you reach 70½. Thus, if you were born in June 1917 or earlier, you may not contribute to an IRA for 1987 or later years. The ban on IRAs applies both to nondeductible as well as deductible contributions.
Anyone withdrawing an IRA before age 59½	A 10% premature withdrawal applies to distributions before age 59½ unless you are disabled or the distributions are paid under a life annuity exception explained at ¶8.10.
Borrowing from IRAs	Prohibited transaction rules prevent you from borrowing from an IRA or using it as security for a loan or selling property to an IRA. If you do, your IRA is considered terminated and the entire IRA is considered to have been distributed to you as of the first day of that year.
Nondeductible IRA contributions by active participants	Make nondeductible contributions only if you believe that the tax free accumulation of nondeductible contributions within the IRA will build a larger retirement fund than if you invested outside the IRA. Nondeductible contributions may not be withdrawn tax free if you also have made deductible contributions; an allocable part of each IRA distribution will be tax free, the rest taxable. *See* ¶8.9 for IRA distribution rules.
When to make IRA contributions	You have until the April 15 filing due date to make either deductible or nondeductible contributions. Waiting until after the end of the year has an advantage if during the year you are unsure whether contributions will be deductible. After the end of the year, you are then in a position to determine your AGI and to verify your participation status if your employer has a retirement plan. If your employer has no retirement plan, making contributions earlier in the year allows greater tax free IRA accumulations. This is also true if you are a plan participant but can project that a full deduction will be allowed because your AGI will be less than the $25,000 threshold for unmarried persons, or the $40,000 threshold for married couples filing jointly.

*Adjusted gross income. In figuring adjusted gross income, follow the rules of ¶13.8, but do not take into account IRA contributions. Foreign earned income eligible for the exclusion (chapter 36) is counted in AGI; the exclusion is disregarded. Include in adjusted gross income taxable Social Security benefits. If you are allowed a passive loss under new law restrictions (chapter 11), the loss reduces AGI.

INDIVIDUAL RETIREMENT ACCOUNTS (IRAS)

RETIREMENT SAVINGS THROUGH IRAs

¶ 8.1 If you are allowed an IRA deduction for 1987 contributions, you can obtain a substantial tax savings. For example, if you are in the 35% bracket and qualify for a full deduction, a $2,000 contribution reduces your taxes by $700 in 1987. If you are in the maximum 38.5% bracket, a $2,000 deductible contribution reduces your tax by $770.

All IRA contributions, whether deductible or nondeductible, accumulate tax free. That is, income earned on funds in the account is not taxed until the funds are withdrawn. Tax-free interest compounding can produce the following funds for retirement:

$2,000 invested annually	*With interest compounded daily*		
	8%	*10%*	*12%*
	gives you—		
5 years	$12,794	$13,633	$14,540
10 years	31,879	36,109	41,030
15 years	60,349	73,164	89,294
20 years	102,820	134,252	177,227
25 years	166,176	234,962	337,437
30 years	260,688	400,993	629,329

Weigh the above benefits against these restrictions: You may not freely withdraw IRA funds until the year you reach 59½ or become disabled. If you take money out or even borrow using the account as collateral before that time, you are subject to a penalty. In the year you reach 70½, you may no longer make IRA contributions, and you must start to withdraw from the account. All IRA withdrawals are fully taxable; special averaging for lump-sum distribution does not apply. Finally, unauthorized contributions and distributions are penalized.

Whether you should make nondeductible IRA contributions is discussed at ¶8.5.

CONTRIBUTIONS MUST BE BASED ON EARNINGS

¶ 8.2 IRA contributions must be based on payments received for rendering personal services such as salary, wages, commissions, tips, fees, bonuses, or net earnings from self-employment (less Keogh plan contributions on behalf of the self-employed). Compensation does *not* include:

1. Income earned abroad for which the foreign earned income exclusion is claimed;
2. Deferred compensation, pensions, or annuities; or
3. Investment income such as interest, dividends, or profits from sales of property.

EXAMPLE

A trader, whose sole income was derived from stock dividends and gains in buying and selling stocks, contributed to an IRA. The IRS disallowed the deduction on the grounds that his income was not earned income. The trader argued that compensation is a broad term which should include his profits from investments. His trading activities were more than those of a mere investor. He had his own desk at a national brokerage house, spent full time at his investment activities, and traded over $3 million during the year. Despite his substantial investment activities, the Tax Court sides with the IRS. His profits came from property holdings and are not considered earned income.

If you work for your spouse, you may make an IRA contribution provided you actually perform services and receive an actual payment of wages. A wife who worked as a receptionist and assistant to her husband, a veterinarian, failed to meet the second test. Her husband did not pay her a salary. Instead, he deposited all income from his business into a joint bank account held with the wife. In addition, no federal income tax was withheld from her wages. In a ruling, the IRS held that the wife could not set up her own IRA, even though she performed services. She failed to receive actual payment. Depositing business income in a joint account is neither actual nor constructive payment of the wife's salary. Further, any deduction claimed for the wife's wages was disallowed.

If you live in a community property state, the fact that one-half of your spouse's income is considered your income does not entitle you to make contributions to an IRA. The contribution must be based on pay earned through your services.

Only cash contributions are deductible; contributions paid by check are considered cash for this purpose.

If you have more than one self-employed activity, you must aggregate profits and losses from all of your self-employed businesses to determine if you have net income on which to base an IRA contribution. For example, if one self-employed business produces a net profit of $15,000 but another a net loss of $20,000, you may not make an IRA contribution based on the net profit of $15,000. This netting rule does not apply to salary or wage income. If you are an employee who also has an unprofitable business, you may make an IRA contribution based on your salary.

FIGURING YOUR IRA CONTRIBUTION AND DEDUCTION

¶ 8.3 You may make IRA contributions of up to $2,000, provided you have wage, salary, or self-employment earnings. If your earned income is less than $2,000, the contribution limit is 100% of your pay or net earned income if self-employed. The contribution limit is $2,250, if you file a joint return with your spouse and only one of you has compensation; *see* ¶8.7.

Contributions are deductible, if you meet either one of these tests:
1. Your adjusted gross income (AGI) does not exceed $25,000 if unmarried or $40,000 if married on a joint return; or,
2. You are not an active participant in an employer-maintained retirement plan for any part of the plan year ending within your taxable year. If you are married and file a joint return, neither you nor your spouse must be an active participant in such a plan. Active participation is explained at ¶8.4.

If your AGI exceeds $25,000 (unmarried) or $40,000 (married filing jointly) and you are an active participant, your deduction is phased out over the next $10,000 of AGI. If you are unmarried and your AGI is $35,000 or over, you may not claim a deduction. If you are married and filing jointly, you and your spouse may not claim a deduction when your combined AGI is $50,000 or over. The $40,000–$50,000 phase-out range also applies to qualified widows and widowers.

If you are a married person filing separately and you are an active participant in a company retirement plan, you may not make a deductible IRA contribution if your AGI is $10,000 or more; if your AGI is less than $10,000, you are allowed a partial deduction.

Filing status	AGI range for phase-out of IRA deduction
Unmarried	$25,000–35,000
Married filing jointly or qualified widow(er)	40,000–50,000
Married filing separately	0–10,000

If you are an active participant and your AGI is *within* the phaseout range, you may figure your reduced deduction as follows:

Step 1. Figure how much your adjusted gross income (AGI) exceeds the $25,000 threshold for unmarried individuals, the $40,000 threshold for married filing jointly (and qualified widows), or the zero threshold for married filing separately, whichever applies to you.

Step 2. Subtract Step 1 from $10,000.

Step 3. Multiply Step 2 by .20 if your contribution limit is $2,000; .225 if $2,250 for spousal account. This is your deductible contribution. If the result is not a multiple of $10, the allowable deduction is *increased* to the next highest $10; *see* example (3) below.

EXAMPLES (All examples assume company coverage)

1. You are single and your AGI is $26,000. Your maximum deductible IRA contribution is $1,800.
   Step 1. $1,000 ($26,000–$25,000).
   Step 2. $9,000 ($10,000–$1,000).
   Step 3. $1,800 ($9,000 × .20).
   If you contributed $2,000 to the IRA, $200 will be treated as a nondeductible contribution.

2. You and your spouse have a joint adjusted gross income of $43,000. You file a joint return. You each work and one of you is an active participant in an employer plan. The maximum IRA deduction for each of you is $1,400.
   Step 1. $3,000 ($43,000–$40,000).
   Step 2. $7,000 ($10,000–$3,000).
   Step 3. $1,400 ($7,000 × .20).
   Note: If one spouse had compensation of less than $1,400, that spouse's contribution could not exceed such compensation.

3. Same as example (2), but only you work and are an active participant in an employer plan. You set up a spousal IRA for your nonworking spouse. The maximum deductible contribution for both accounts is $1,580.
   Step 1. $3,000 ($43,000–$40,000).
   Step 2. $7,000 ($10,000–$3,000).
   Step 3. $1,575 ($7,000 × .225).
   Since $1,575 is not a multiple of $10, the allowable deduction is *increased* to the next highest $10, or $1,580. You may divide the $1,580 contribution between you and your spouse however you choose, but according to the IRS, neither of you may deduct more than $1,400, the deductible limit per spouse for a couple with a $43,000 AGI, as figured under example (2).

4. You are married, file a separate return, and are an active participant in an employer plan. Your adjusted gross income is $7,500. Your maximum deductible IRA contribution is $500.
   Step 1. $7,500 ($7,500–$0).
   Step 2. $2,500 ($10,000–$7,500).
   Step 3. $500 ($2,500 × .20).
   If you file a separate return and are *not* an active participant in an employer plan, you may claim a $2,000 IRA deduction regardless of your separate AGI.

$200 IRA deduction floor. A special rule gives a $200 deduction if your AGI falls within the last $1,000 of the phaseout range. Using the above three-step formula, your reduced deduction would be less than $200 when your AGI is over $34,000 (unmarried) or over $49,000 (married filing jointly). However, a $200 deduction may be claimed by a single person with an AGI of over $34,000 but under $35,000; by a married person filing jointly with an AGI of over $49,000 but under $50,000; and by a married person filing separately with an AGI of over $9,000 but under $10,000.

EXAMPLE

Your AGI is $34,400 and you file as a head of household.
Step 1. $9,400 ($34,400–$25,000).
Step 2. $600 ($10,000–$9,400).
Step 3. $120 ($600 × .20).
Although $120 is the deductible limit under the above computation, you may deduct $200.

Nondeductible contributions. Any contributions above the amount allowed under the above rules is treated as a nondeductible IRA contribution. *See* ¶8.5 for further details on nondeductible contributions.

ACTIVE PARTICIPATION TESTS

¶ 8.4 Active participants in an employer retirement plan are subject to the adjusted gross income tests for deducting contributions as discussed at ¶8.3. An employer retirement plan means:
1. A qualified pension, profit sharing, or stock bonus plan;
2. A qualified annuity plan;
3. A simplified employee pension;
4. A plan established for its employees by the United States, by a state or political subdivision, or by any agency or instrumentality of the United States or a state or political subdivision; or
5. A tax sheltered annuity.

If you are self-employed and set up a Keogh plan, you are considered to be a member of an employer retirement plan.

Your Form W-2 from your employer indicates whether you are an active participant. If you want to make a contribution before you receive your Form W-2, check the following guidelines and consult your plan administrator for your status. The rules for determining active participation status generally depend on the type of plan your employer has. As discussed below, the tests for defined benefit pension plans are different from the tests for defined contribution plans such as profit sharing plans and 401(k) plans. Under any type of plan, if you are considered an active participant for any part of the plan year ending with or within your taxable year, you are treated as an active participant. Because of this plan year rule, you may be an active participant even if you were with the employer for only part of the year.

In general, you are treated as an active participant in a defined benefit pension plan if for the plan year ending with or within your taxable year, you are eligible to participate in the plan. Under this rule, as long as you are eligible, you are treated as an active participant, even if you decline participation in the plan or you fail to make a mandatory contribution specified in the plan. Further, you are treated as an active participant even if your rights to benefits are not vested.

For a defined contribution plan, you are generally considered an active participant if "with respect to" the plan year ending with or within the taxable year (1) you make elective deferrals to the plan; (2) your employer contributes to your account; or (3) forfeitures are allocated to your account. You can be an active participant even if you do not have a vested right to receive benefits from your account.

Under IRS guidelines, it is possible to be treated as an active participant in the year of retirement and even in the year after retirement if your employer maintains a fiscal year plan.

EXAMPLE

Your employer has a defined benefit pension plan with a plan year starting July 1 and ending the following June 30. You are not excluded from participating. If you retired during September 1987, you are considered an active participant for 1987, because you were eligible to participate during the plan year ending during 1987. You will also be considered an active participant for 1988. Although you will retire before the end of the 1987–1988 plan year, you will still be eligible to participate during part of that plan year, and since that plan year ends within your 1988 tax year, you will be considered an active participant for 1988.

NONDEDUCTIBLE IRA CONTRIBUTIONS

¶ 8.5 If you are barred from making any deductible contributions for 1987 or a later year (*see* ¶8.3), you may still make *nondeductible* IRA contributions of up to $2,000 (or $2,250, in the case of a spousal IRA). If you are allowed a partial IRA deduction, you may make a nondeductible contribution to the extent the maximum contribution limit of $2,000, $2,250, or $4,000 exceeds the deductible limit figured under ¶8.3. Thus, if you are limited to an $1,800 deduction because of your adjusted gross income, you may make a $200 nondeductible contribution. As with deductible contributions, nondeductible contributions may be made up to the April 15 filing due date (without extensions). The advantage of making nondeductible contributions is that earnings on the account accumulate tax free until withdrawn.

You must file Form 8606 to report nondeductible IRA contributions. You may file an amended return for a taxable year and change the designa-

contributions from deductible to nondeductible or nondeductible to deductible.

If you make contributions during the year, you may not know whether you will be allowed to claim a deduction. For example, you may have employer plan coverage but might not know whether your AGI will exceed the $35,000 limit (single) or $50,000 limit (married filing jointly). You can make your contribution without knowing whether it is deductible or not, and figure your deduction when you file your return. However, if you do not want to make nondeductible contributions, you may wait until after the end of the year when you can determine your AGI and active participant status; you have until the April 15 filing due date to make your contribution.

Further, you may withdraw IRA contributions before the April 15 filing due date. If you do, you must also withdraw the earnings allocable to the withdrawn contribution and include the earnings as income for the year the contribution was made. You might want to make the withdrawal if you incorrectly determined that a contribution would be deductible and you do not want to leave nondeductible contributions in your account. However, making the withdrawal could subject you to bank penalties for premature withdrawals, or other withdrawal penalties imposed by the IRA trustee. Further, if you are under 59½ and not disabled, the 10% premature withdrawal penalty applies to the withdrawn earnings.

Recordkeeping for IRA distributions. Keep separate records showing nondeductible and deductible contributions. When you make IRA withdrawals, the portion of each withdrawal allocable to nondeductible contributions is not taxed. You may not completely avoid tax even if you withdraw an amount equal to your nondeductible contributions. The rules for figuring tax on withdrawals are at ¶8.9.

Should you make nondeductible IRA contributions? Yes, if in your case, the accumulation of tax free income in the account will, when you withdraw the account, give you a greater return than other types of investments. However, if you have other IRA accounts based on deductible contributions, withdrawals from a nondeductible account may be taxable as explained in ¶8.9. This is a disadvantage as you may not treat the account as a regular savings account from which you can make tax free withdrawals at any time. Generally a nondeductible account should be considered when you intend to leave it intact until you retire.

SETTING UP AN IRA

¶ **8.6** Banks, brokerage firms, insurance companies, and credit unions offering IRA investment plans provide all of the necessary forms for setting up your IRA. You do not have to file any forms with your tax return when you set up or make contributions to your IRA. Form 5498 listing your contribution will be filed with the IRS by the company with which you set up your IRA.

You may set up an IRA as:

1. *An individual retirement account* with a bank, savings and loan association, federally insured credit union, or other qualified person as trustee or custodian. An individual retirement account is technically a trust or custodial account. Your contribution may be invested in vehicles such as certificates of deposit, mutual funds, and certain limited partnerships.

If you wish to take a more active role in managing your IRA investments, you may set up a "self-directed" IRA using a Treasury model form. The model trust (Form 5305) and the model custodial account agreement (Form 5305A) meet the requirements of an exempt individual retirement account and so do not require a ruling or determination letter approving the exemption of the account and the deductibility of contributions made to the account. If you use this method, you still have to find a bank or other institution or trustee to handle your account or investment. If you have a self-directed IRA, you may not invest in collectibles, such as stamps, antiques, rugs, metals, guns, or coins, except for U.S. minted gold and silver coins. Assets used to acquire a collectible are treated as distributions and are taxed.

2. *An individual retirement annuity,* by purchasing an annuity contract (including a joint and survivor contract for the benefit of you and your spouse) or an endowment contract issued by an insurance company. No trustee or custodian is required. The contract, endorsed to meet the terms of an IRA, is all that is required. In the case of an endowment contract, however, no deduction is permitted for the portion of the premium allocated to life insurance. This nondeductible amount is generally called a P.S. 85 cost. As borrowing or pledging of the contract is not allowed under an IRA, the contracts will not contain loan provisions.

Annuity and endowment contracts may not have fixed premiums nor annual premiums exceeding $2,000. Further, a refund of premiums must be applied toward the payment of future premiums or to purchase additional benefits. If you contracted for a fixed premium contract before November 7, 1978, you may continue with the contract or exchange it. Tax free exchanges were allowed prior to January 1981. However, this change in the tax law does not govern the terms of the contract between you and the insurance company. Thus, you may suffer substantial nondeductible losses in the exchange of contracts because of fees and other charges by the insurance company.

Broker's restriction on transferring IRA accounts. Before you invest in an IRA carefully review the terms of the agreement for restrictions. One investor, who put his IRA in a brokerage account, was not allowed by the trustee to transfer from one account to another. Further, the trustee reserved some of the IRA funds to cover broker fees and other transfer costs. The investor asked the IRS if these restrictions violated the tax law. The IRS, in a private letter ruling, said there was no violation. An IRA is a contractual agreement between the IRA trustee and the participant. Although the tax laws do not place limitations on direct IRA-to-IRA transfers, the trustees of a particular account may restrict such transfers.

In the past, there was a third IRA alternative: Special U.S. Retirement bonds, which the Treasury stopped issuing in 1982.

Trustees' or custodians' fees. Payments to set up or manage an IRA are not considered IRA contributions if separately paid. They are investment expenses which may be deducted as a miscellaneous itemized deduction subject to the 2% floor; see ¶19.1.

Contributions after the end of the taxable year. You have until the due date for filing your 1987 return, April 15, 1988, to make deductible or nondeductible IRA contributions for 1987. If you are short of cash, you may borrow the funds without jeopardizing the deduction. If an IRA deduction entitles you to a refund, you can file your return early, claim the IRA deduction, and if you receive the refund in time, apply it towards an IRA contribution before the due date.

A contribution must be made by the April 15, 1988, due date even if you get an extension to file your return.

Diversifying your investments. You may set up one type of IRA one year and choose another form the next year. You may also split your contribution between two or more investment vehicles. For example, you are eligible to contribute $2,000. You may choose to put $1,000 into an investment retirement annuity and $1,000 into an individual retirement account with your local bank.

IRAS FOR MARRIED COUPLES

¶ **8.7** *Both spouses have compensation.* If both spouses have compensation and each is eligible to set up an IRA account, each may contribute to his or her separate IRA account up to $2,000. If a joint return is filed and either spouse is an active participant in an employer plan, contributions are fully deductible if joint adjusted gross income (AGI) is $40,000 or less; partial deductions are allowed if joint AGI is between $40,000 and $50,000. For a married person filing separately who is an active participant in an employer plan, an IRA deduction is allowed only if AGI is less than $10,000. See ¶8.3 for figuring partial deductions.

EXAMPLES

1. You earn a salary of $20,000; your spouse earns $10,000 and neither of you is covered by an employer retirement plan. On a joint return, the maximum deduction is up to $4,000. If only one of you works and qualifies to set up an IRA, the maximum deduction is $2,000, unless an account for a nonworking spouse is set up.

If you both work and either of you were an active participant in an employer plan, you would still be allowed the maximum $4,000 deduction provided your joint AGI on a joint return was $40,000 or less.

2. You live in a community property state. You earn a salary of $20,000. Your spouse does not work. The maximum deduction for an IRA is $2,000, even though, under the community property laws, your spouse is considered to have earned half of your salary. You may set up an IRA for your nonworking spouse. In that case, your maximum deduction may not exceed $2,250, assuming the deduction is not limited under the rules of ¶8.3.

Account for nonworking spouse. If you are working, you may make a 1987 contribution on behalf of your nonworking spouse provided you file a joint return. You may have two separate IRAs, one for you and one for your spouse, or a single IRA which has a subaccount for you and another subaccount for your spouse. A joint account is not allowed. However, each spouse may have a right of survivorship in the subaccount of the other.

Generally, the maximum contribution is $2,250 and may be allocated between spouses in any way as long as no spouse receives a contribution exceeding $2,000. However, where deductions are limited under the rules of ¶8.3, the amount of deductible contributions which may be made for either spouse may be reduced; *see* example (3) in ¶8.3.

Generally, you may set up an account (or subaccount) for your spouse only if your spouse received no compensation for the year, including tax-exempt foreign earned income. However, there is this limited exception: You may contribute to a spousal IRA if your spouse had compensation of $250 or less; your spouse is treated as if he or she had no compensation. You may set up a spousal account regardless of the amount of your spouse's unearned income, such as interest, dividends or Social Security benefits.

A working spouse who is over age 70½ may contribute to an IRA for a nonworking spouse who is under age 70½, but the entire contribution must be allocated to the nonworking spouse, no contribution may be made for the spouse over age 70½.

A spouse may start withdrawing from his or her spousal account (or subaccount) on reaching age 59½ and must start withdrawing on reaching age 70½.

If you are divorced, you may not maintain a spousal account for your former spouse. If you contributed to an account on behalf of your nonworking spouse and then divorce later in the year, the contribution is an excess contribution. IRAs based on alimony are discussed at ¶8.8.

An amount distributed to one spouse may not be rolled over to an IRA account of the other spouse, except in the case of divorce (*see* ¶8.11).

If you already have an IRA for yourself and you want to make contributions on behalf of your nonworking spouse, you may do so by merely opening a new IRA for your spouse and continue your present IRA for yourself. However, if you have an annuity or endowment contract, check with your insurance agent about any contract restrictions on reducing your premium payments. Before setting up a single IRA with subaccounts for you and your spouse, check Treasury regulations covering their use.

Should a married person file separately to claim an IRA deduction? If a married couple has combined AGI of between $40,000 and $50,000, and either spouse is an active participant in an employer plan, only a partial IRA deduction is allowed if they file jointly; no deduction is allowed if AGI is $50,000 or more on a joint return. To avoid the deduction pase-out, a married couple might consider filing separate returns if only one spouse is covered by an employer plan. The spouse who is not covered may deduct IRA contributions of up to $2,000 of earned income, regardless of his or her separate AGI. The spouse who has employer plan coverage may claim a partial IRA deduction only if AGI is less than $10,000, and no deduction if AGI is $10,000 or more.

Is filing separately advisable? The answer depends on your respective incomes and separate deductions. Filing separate returns where one spouse can claim an IRA deduction will sometimes result in an overall tax saving despite the loss of joint return rates. However, in other cases, the loss of joint return rates makes it inadvisable to file separately. Further, other tax benefits can be lost if you file separately, which might tip the balance in favor of a joint return:

1. If you file separately and receive Social Security benefits, 50% of your benefits are subject to tax. If you filed jointly, a $32,000 base could reduce or eliminate any tax on benefits; *see* ¶34.8.
2. The $25,000 rental loss allowance under the new passive loss rules (*see* ¶11.4) may not be claimed on a separate return.

To determine which method is better in your particular case, figure the tax both ways. Compare the total tax on two separate returns against the tax on a joint return and choose the method providing the lower tax.

Important: Tax legislation being considered by Congress would allow less favorable IRA deduction rules for married persons who live together at any time during the year and file separate returns. *See* the Supplement.

IRAS FOR DIVORCEES

¶ 8.8 A divorced spouse with little or no earnings in 1987 may treat taxable alimony as compensation, giving a basis for deductible IRA contributions. A divorced spouse may make an IRA contribution equal to 100% of taxable alimony up to $2,000. If you are divorced, you make an IRA contribution equal to 100% of taxable alimony up to $2,000. However, the deduction may be reduced or eliminated if you are an active participant in an employer plan and your adjusted gross income exceeds the $25,000 threshold for unmarried individuals. *See* ¶8.3. Taxable alimony is alimony paid under a decree. of divorce or legal separation or a written agreement incident to such a decree, *see* ¶1.35. It does not include alimony payments made under a written agreement that is not incident to such a decree.

IRA DISTRIBUTIONS

¶ 8.9 Withdrawals from an IRA account are reported as ordinary income in the year received. However, if you have made nondeductible IRA contributions as well as deductible contributions, the portion of a distribution allocable to nondeductible contributions is tax free. The allocation rules are discussed below.

If you have an individual retirement annuity, your investment in the contract is treated as zero so all payments are fully taxable. Distributions from an endowment policy because of death are taxed as ordinary income to the extent allocable to retirement savings; to the extent allocable to life insurance, they are considered insurance proceeds.

Proceeds from U.S. retirement bonds are taxable in the year the bonds are redeemed. However, you must report the full proceeds in the year you reach age 70½ even if you do not redeem the bonds.

Your entire interest in an IRA must be, or begin to be, distributed not later than the April 1 following the end of the taxable year during which you reach age 70½. For example, if you reach age 70½ during 1987, you must start taking IRA distributions no later than April 1, 1988. *See* ¶8.10 for figuring minimum distributions to avoid a penalty.

Withdrawals from an IRA may be subject to bank interest penalties for premature withdrawals, even if no tax penalty is imposed under the rules of ¶8.10.

Distributions from an IRA are subject to withholding unless you file for exemption. *See* ¶25.11.

After the death of an IRA owner, distributions to beneficiaries may be spread over the same periods discussed above for pension and profit-sharing plans at ¶7.12.

Tax on withdrawals if nondeductible contributions were made. All of your IRAs are treated as one contract. All distributions during a taxable year are treated as one distribution. If you withdraw an amount from an IRA during a taxable year and you previously made both deductible and nondeductible IRA contributions, part of your withdrawal will be tax free and part will be taxable. The nontaxable amount is based on the ratio of the nondeductible IRA contributions over the year-end balance of all of your IRA accounts plus the amount of the distribution (see example below). This withdrawal rule will penalize you if you make nondeductible contributions and later decide to make withdrawals from the "nondeduct-ible account." You may not claim that you are withdrawing only your tax free contributions, even if your withdrawal is less than your nondeductible contributions. If you withdraw amounts from your nondeductible account, you will incur tax.

The payer of an IRA account, such as a bank, will report withdrawals from an IRA account to the IRS as if they are taxable. It is up to you to keep records that show otherwise and to indicate the nondeductible contributions on your tax return as required by IRS instructions.

Follow these steps in determining the tax free and taxable portion of IRA withdrawals:

Step 1. Total IRA withdrawals during the year.
Step 2. Total nondeductible contributions to all IRAs for all years. Prior tax free withdrawals of nondeductible contributions reduce the total.
Step 3. Add Step 1 to the balance of all your IRAs at the end of the year. If you received a distribution near the end of the year and rolled it over tax free to another IRA at the beginning of the following year (within 60 days), add the rollover to the year-end balance.
Step 4. Divide Step 2 by Step 3. This is the tax free percentage of your IRA withdrawal.
Step 5. Multiply the Step 4 percentage by Step 1. This amount is tax free. The balance of your IRA withdrawal is fully taxable.

EXAMPLE

In 1990, you withdraw $5,000 from your IRA having made deductible IRA contributions of $8,000 and nondeductible contributions of $6,000 as follows:

Year	Deductible	Nondeductible
1984	$2,000	–0–
1985	2,000	–0–
1986	2,000	–0–
1987	1,000	$1,000
1988	1,000	1,000
1989	-0-	2,000
1990	-0-	2,000
	$8,000	$6,000

Assume that at the end of 1990, your total IRA account balance, including earnings, is $17,500, and that this is your first IRA withdrawal. On your 1990 return, $1,350 of the $5,000 IRA withdrawal will be tax free and $3,650 will be taxable.

Step 1.	IRA withdrawal	$5,000
Step 2.	Nondeductible contributions	6,000
Step 3.	IRA balance at end of the year ($17,500) plus Step 1.	22,500
Step 4.	Tax free percentage ($6,000 ÷ $22,500)	27%
Step 5.	Tax free withdrawal (27% × $5,000)	1,350
	Taxable withdrawal: $5,000–$1,350	$3,650

Deductible IRA loss based on unrecovered nondeductible contributions. According to the IRS, a loss may be allowed if all IRA funds have been distributed and you have not recovered your basis in nondeductible contributions.

EXAMPLE

You make nondeductible IRA contributions of $10,000 from 1987–1991. At the end of 1991, when the total IRA balance is $14,000, you withdraw $6,000. The tax free portion of the withdrawal is $4,286:

$$\frac{\$10,000 \text{ (nondeductible contributions)}}{\$14,000 \text{ (IRA balance)}} \times \$6,000 = \$4,286$$

After the withdrawal, your account balance is $8,000 and your basis in the account is $5,714 ($10,000–$4,286). If because of poor investments the value of the IRA fell to $3,000 by the end of the next year and you withdrew the entire $3,000 balance, you could claim a $2,714 loss ($5,714 basis–$3,000 distributed balance).

PENALTIES FOR PREMATURE DISTRIBUTIONS, EXCESS DISTRIBUTIONS, EXCESS CONTRIBUTIONS, INSUFFICIENT WITHDRAWALS

¶ 8.10 You must file Form 5329 with your 1987 return if you are liable for any of the penalties discussed below. Failure to file Form 5329 may result in an additional penalty.

Premature distributions. If you receive a distribution in 1987 before age 59½ and you are not disabled, you will incur a penalty tax of 10% on the premature distribution, unless the distribution is part of a scheduled series of substantially equal payments over your life expectancy or over the joint life expectancies of you and a beneficiary. The 10% penalty does *not apply* to IRA distributions payable to a beneficiary (or estate) upon the death of an IRA owner.

The 10% penalty is in addition to the tax that will be incurred when you include the distribution as ordinary income with your other income. If part of a premature distribution is tax free because it is allocable to nondeductible contributions (¶8.9), the 10% penalty applies only to the taxable portion of the distribution.

EXAMPLE

An unmarried person, age 40, withdraws $3,000 from his IRA plan. All contributions were deductible. Assume his regular tax on his income (after including in income the $3,000 distribution) is $5,100. To this amount, he must add 10% of $3,000 or $300. His total tax becomes $5,400.

Redemption of U.S. retirement bonds before age 59½ is considered a premature distribution.

If you borrow from your IRA plan, you are considered to have received your entire interest. Borrowing will subject the account or the fair market value of the contract to tax at ordinary income rates as of the first day of the taxable year of the borrowing. Your IRA account loses its tax-exempt status. If you use the account or part of it as security for a loan, the pledged portion is treated as a distribution.

Exception for substantially equal payments. The 10% penalty will not apply if before age 59½ you start to receive distributions over your life expectancy or joint life expectancy of yourself and a beneficiary. However, a penalty may be incurred in a later year if (1) you change the distribution method before reaching age 59½ or becoming disabled, or (2) you change the distribution method after reaching age 59½, are not disabled, and have not received substantially equal payments for at least five years. In such case, a 10% penalty will be applied to payments received before age 59½.

Excess distributions. As discussed at ¶7.14, an IRA distribution exceeding $150,000 may be subject to a 15% penalty. The penalty is imposed on the excess over $150,000 unless an exception to the penalty is available. For example, the penalty on a $200,000 IRA distribution would be $7,500 (15% × $50,000 excess over $150,000). If you receive an IRA distribution and make a tax free rollover to another IRA within 60 days, the penalty does not apply. Other exceptions are listed at ¶7.14.

Insufficient distributions. If you do not start receiving distributions by the April 1 following the year you reach age 70½ or you receive an insufficient distribution after this date, a penalty tax of 50% applies to the difference between the amount you should have received and the amount you did receive.

EXAMPLE

You receive $500 from your IRA plan. The minimum amount required to be paid to you was $700. You pay a penalty tax of $100 (50% of $200).

The first required installment amount is generally fixed by the amount of the account at age 70½ and your life expectancy as determined under the unisex IRA actuarial tables at ¶7.20. If you are married, you may figure the minimum distribution using joint lives which will result in a smaller minimum distribution requirement than the one life table. Use IRS Table VI for determining joint life expectancies, which may be found in IRS Publication 575.

If you have an individual retirement annuity, your insurance company should gear your payments to meet minimum distribution requirements.

Payouts at 70½. If you were born any time between July 1, 1916, and June 30, 1917, you must begin distributions by April 1, 1988; if between July 1917 and through June 1918, distributions must start by April 1, 1989.

Minimum payouts. The minimum distributable amount each year is found by dividing the amount of all of your IRA accounts as of the beginning of the taxable year by your life expectancy.

If you are married, you may elect to use the joint and last survivor expectancy of you and your spouse. Each year, you may redetermine your life expectancy and refigure the minimum distribution for that year. You may find that such a recomputation may allow you to take a smaller minimum distribution.

The IRS extended the deadline for making minimum 1985 and 1986 distributions until December 31, 1987. For individuals required to take minimum distributions for 1985 and 1986, December 31, 1987, was also the deadline for receiving the minimum distribution for 1987. *See* the guidelines for calculating minimum required distributions in IRS Proposed Regulation 1.408-8. Also *see* the Supplement and the instructions to Form 5329 for further details.

> The IRS may waive the penalty for insufficient withdrawals if due to reasonable error and steps are being taken to remedy the situation. You must submit evidence to account for shortfalls in withdrawals and how you are rectifying the situation. The IRS has indicated that examples of acceptable reasons for insufficient withdrawals include erroneous advice from the sponsoring organization or other pension advisors or that your own good faith efforts to apply the required withdrawal formula produced a miscalculation or misunderstanding of the formula. You should attach your letter of explanation to Form 5329. You must pay the penalty; if the IRS grants a waiver, it will refund the penalty.

Excess contributions. If you contribute more than the allowable amount, whether deductible or nondeductible, the excess contribution may be subject to a penalty tax of 6%. The penalty tax is cumulative. That is, unless you correct the excess, you will be subject to another penalty on the excess contribution in the following year. The penalty tax is not deductible.

The 6% penalty may be avoided by withdrawing the excess contribution by the due date for your return, including extensions. Further, if you did not contribute more than $2,250 to your IRA and you withdraw by the filing due date for your return (including extensions) the excess plus any income earned on the excess contribution, the withdrawn excess is not taxable provided no deduction was allowed for it. The withdrawn income must be reported on your return for the year of the excess contribution. If you are under age 59½ (and not disabled) when you receive the income, the 10% premature withdrawal penalty applies to the income.

If an excess contribution for 1987 is not withdrawn by the due date for your 1987 return, the 6% penalty may be avoided for 1988 by withdrawing the excess by the end of 1988. *See* Form 5329 for details.

If you deducted an excess contribution in an earlier year for which total contributions were $2,250 or less, you may make a tax free withdrawal of the excess by filing an amended return to correct the excess deduction. However, the 6% penalty tax applies for each year that the excess was still in the account at the end of the year.

See IRS Publication 590 for further information on correcting excess contributions made in a prior year.

ROLLOVERS OF IRAs; TRANSFERS INCIDENT TO DIVORCE

¶ 8.11 You may transfer assets tax free from one IRA to another or from a qualified corporate plan to an IRA. Such transfers are treated as a distribution of the assets from your old plan to you. To avoid tax on the transfer, these tests must be met: (1) The amount you receive from your old plan must be transferred to the new plan within 60 days of

your receiving it. (2) A tax free rollover may occur only once in a one-year period. If a second rollover occurs within the same one-year period, you are taxed on the plan assets.

The 60-day limit for completing a rollover is extended if the funds are "frozen" and may not be withdrawn from a bankrupt or insolvent financial institution. The 60-day period is extended while the account is frozen and you have a minimum of 10 days after the release of the funds to complete the rollover.

A direct transfer of funds from one bank to another is not considered a rollover subject to the one-year restriction.

EXAMPLE
Smith sets up an IRA at Bank A. In January 1987, he instructs Bank A to transfer the funds to Bank B. The transfer from Bank A to Bank B is not subject to the one-year restriction on rollovers because there was no payment or distribution of the funds to Smith.

> A person over age 70½ may roll over a lump-sum distribution from a company plan to an IRA, although contributions to an IRA are specifically barred to him. The rollover must be made within 60 days of the distribution and, in the year of the rollover, the individual must receive a minimum distribution from the IRA (*see* ¶ 8.10).

Rollover contributions are not deductible.

For transfers of a lump-sum distribution of a tax-qualified plan to an IRA (*see* ¶ 7.8).

Tax free transfer of IRAs because of divorce. A spouse may transfer tax free his IRA account to his former spouse as long as the transfer is made under a valid divorce decree or written agreement incident to the divorce. The transferred account, policy, or bond must be maintained in the name of the spouse who receives it.

Surviving spouse may make tax-free rollover of inherited account. A surviving spouse who receives an IRA account upon the death of his or her spouse may make a tax-free rollover to an IRA. Beneficiaries other than surviving spouses may not make a rollover; the payout rules are similar to those for pension and profit sharing plan beneficiaries. *See* ¶ 7.12.

SIMPLIFIED EMPLOYEE PENSION PLANS

¶ 8.12 A simplified employee pension plan set up by an employer allows the employer to contribute and deduct to an employee's IRA account more money than allowable under regular IRA rules. For 1987, your employer may contribute up to 15% of your compensation or $30,000, whichever is less.

> An employee over age 70½ may still participate in an employer SEP plan but may not make his own personal IRA contribution.

Starting in 1987, your employer's SEP contributions are excluded from your pay. In years before 1987, you were required to report the contribution as income and then claim an offsetting deduction.

SEP salary reduction arrangements. Qualifying small employers may set up salary reduction SEPs which allow employees to contribute a portion of their pay to the plan instead of receiving it in cash.

Only qualifying small companies may offer such plans. Salary reductions are allowed for a year only if the employer had no more than 25 employees at any time during the prior taxable year. Further, at least 50% of the employees must elect the salary reduction option, and the deferral percentage for highly compensated employees may not exceed 125% of the average contribution of regular employees. State or local government agencies and tax-exempt organizations may not set up salary reduction SEPs.

If salary reductions are allowed, the maximum salary reduction contribution is $7,000. The $7,000 limit may be increased starting in 1988 by an inflation factor. Deferrals over $7,000 are taxable, and if not timely distributed to the employee, can be taxed again when distributed from the plan.

If an employee contributes to both a SEP and a 401(k) plan, the $7,000 limit applies to the total salary reductions from both plans. If an employee makes salary reduction contributions to an SEP and also to a tax-sheltered annuity plan (¶7.23), the maximum salary reduction to the SEP is $7,000,

and an additional $2,500 salary reduction may be made to the tax-sheltered annuity plan. If salary reductions were made only to the tax-sheltered annuity plan, a $9,500 limit generally applies. See ¶7.30.

If an employer makes separate contributions to an SEP apart from an employee's salary reduction contributions, the total tax free contribution is the lesser of 15% of pay or $30,000,

TAX RETIREMENT PLANS FOR SELF-EMPLOYED

TAX BENEFITS OF KEOGH PLANS

¶ **8.13** The advantages of setting up a self-employed retirement plan (Keogh plan) flow from: (1) tax deductions allowed for contributions made to the plan (a form of forced savings); (2) accumulations of tax-free income earned on assets held by the plan; and (3) special averaging provisions for benefits paid on retirement.

The following discussion assumes that you are a self-employed person in your own business or profession or are a partner in a business. Most self-employed persons are considered key employees and may be subject to the restrictions on top-heavy plans discussed at ¶8.16.

Keogh plan distributions. Distributions from a Keogh plan are subject to the rules explained at ¶7.1 to ¶7.15.

Further details on Keogh plans are discussed in the following sections:

	See ¶
Who may set up a Keogh plan	8.14
Choosing a plan	8.15
Top-heavy plan restrictions	8.16
How much you may contribute and deduct	8.17
How to claim the deduction	8.18
How to qualify a plan	8.19
Annual information returns	8.20
Restrictions on loans	8.21

WHO MAY SET UP A KEOGH PLAN

¶ **8.14** You may set up a self-employed retirement plan called a Keogh plan if you earn self-employment income from personal services. For purposes of a Keogh plan, this income is called earned income and is your net profit (gross business or professional income less allowable business deductions). Income earned abroad and excluded from federal income tax is not considered earned income for purposes of the plan. If you are an inactive owner, such as a limited partner, you may not qualify for a Keogh plan.

If you control more than one business (own more than 50% of the capital or profits interest in a partnership or the entire share of an unincorporated business): (1) You must set up pension or profit-sharing plans for all businesses under your control. These may be incorporated in one plan or remain separate. (2) Any additional plans must also conform to all regulations governing the original plan. (3) The additional plans must make contributions in an equal ratio and provide equal benefits.

The above rules prevent you from increasing your deductible contribution for your own benefit by contributing to more than one retirement plan. However, if you are an employee-member of a company retirement plan, you may set up a Keogh plan if you carry on a self-employed enterprise or profession on the side. For example, you are an attorney employed by a company that has a qualified pension plan in which you are a member. At the same time, you have an outside practice. You may set up a Keogh plan based on your self-employed earnings. Each plan is independent of the other.

A plan may not discriminate in favor of officers or other highly compensated personnel. Benefits must be for the employees and their beneficiaries, and their plan rights may not be subject to forfeiture. A plan may not allow any of its funds to be diverted for purposes other than pension benefits. Contributions made on your behalf may not exceed the ratio of contributions made on behalf of employees.

An individual partner or partners, although self-employed, may not set up a Keogh plan. The plan must be established by the partnership.

You must formally set up your plan in writing on or before the end of the taxable year in which you want the plan to be effective. For example, if you want to make a contribution for 1987, your plan must be set up on or before December 31, 1987, if you report on a calendar-year basis; see ¶8.19.

Including employees in your plan. You must include in your plan all employees who have reached age 21 with at least one year of service. If your plan provides for full and immediate vesting of benefits, an employee may be required to complete three years of service before participating. You are not required to cover seasonal or part-time employees who work less than 1000 hours during a 12-month period. If you set up a defined benefit plan, you may exclude an employee who is within five years of normal retirement age (which may not be later than age 65) when his or her period of service begins.

CHOOSING A KEOGH PLAN

¶ **8.15** There are two general types of Keogh plans: defined-benefit plans and defined-contribution plans. A defined-benefit plan provides in advance for a specific retirement benefit funded by contributions based on an IRS formula and actuarial assumptions. A defined-contribution plan does not fix a specific retirement benefit, but rather sets the amount of annual contributions so that the amount of retirement benefits depends on contributions and income earned on those contributions. If contributions are geared to profits, the plan is a profit sharing plan. A plan that requires fixed contributions regardless of profits is a money-purchase plan.

A defined-benefit plan may prove costly if you have older employees who also must be provided with proportionate defined benefits. Further, a defined-benefit plan requires you to contribute to their accounts even if you do not have profits. The maximum annual retirement benefit for basing annual contributions may not exceed $90,000 and the $90,000 limit may have to be reduced if benefits begin before the Social Security age, currently 65. You may not adopt a defined-benefit plan unless it provides benefits for all your employees without taking into account benefits under Social Security. All plans of a controlled group of businesses are aggregated for purposes of the limitations applied to defined benefits.

If you are interested in following an aggressive investment policy for funds in your Keogh plan, you will set up a trust to receive Keogh contributions. You may name yourself or an independent trustee to oversee the plan.

As an owner-employee (owning more than 10% of the business), your dealings with the trust are subject to restrictions. You are subject to penalties if you borrow funds from the trust; buy property from or sell property to the trust; or charge any fees for services you render to the trust. These restrictions also apply to any member of your immediate family and any corporation in which you own more than half the voting stock, directly or indirectly.

If you are considering an investment in savings certificates, you need not set up a trust; you may use a custodial account with the bank.

If you use funds to buy nontransferable annuity contracts from an insurance company, no trust may be necessary. Premium payments are made directly to the insurance company. The annuity contract may pay a fixed monthly income for life, or for a fixed period of years, or may be a variable annuity contract.

TOP-HEAVY PLAN RESTRICTIONS

¶ 8.16 "Top-heavy" plan rules, which apply to corporate plans favoring "key employees," may also apply to a Keogh plan of a self-employed person. The top-heavy rules apply if more than 60% of the account balances or accrued benefits are for key employees; *see* below for definition of key employees. Even if your Keogh plan is not currently considered top heavy, your plan may be disqualified unless it includes provisions that would automatically take effect if the plan becomes top heavy.

Vesting. A top-heavy plan must provide for faster vesting of your employees' benefits. The plan must provide either 100% vesting after three years of service, or graded vesting at the rate of at least 20% after two years of service, 40% after three years of service, 60% after four years of service, 80% after five years of service, and 100% after six years of service.

> There may be an advantage in electing three-year vesting if you have a high turnover of employees. Further, under three-year vesting, a plan may ignore some years of service if the employee has a break in service.

The $200,000 pay limit. Under the top-heavy plan rules, only the first $200,000 of a self-employed person's earned income may be considered in determining contributions.

Distributions before age 59½. For 1987, the 10% penalty for distributions before age 59½ (¶7.13) applies whether or not the plan is top heavy. The penalty does not apply to distributions made because you are disabled. Other exceptions to the penalty are listed at ¶7.13.

The IRS has ruled that a tax free rollover may be made where the Keogh plan is terminated. A timely rollover will avoid the 10% penalty on premature distributions if the recipient is under 59½.

Retirement plan bonds. If you invested Keogh plan funds in Treasury Department Retirement Plan Bonds before May 1, 1982, you may redeem them at any time, even if you are under age 59½. To avoid immediate tax, a rollover may be made within 60 days to an IRA or qualified pension or profit sharing plan.

Who are key employees? The above top-heavy restrictions apply if more than 60% of a defined-contributions plan account balances or more than 60% of the accrued benefits of a defined-benefit plan are for key employees. Key employees are employees who at any time during the plan year or in any of the four preceding plan years own (1) one of the ten largest ownership interests and have compensation exceeding $30,000; (2) more than a 5% interest; or (3) more than a 1% interest and also earn compensation of more than $150,000. Officers of corporations are also considered key employees if they have compensation exceeding $45,000.

HOW MUCH YOU MAY CONTRIBUTE AND DEDUCT

¶ 8.17 You may contribute up to the lower of 25% of earned income or $30,000 to a defined contribution plan, such as a money-purchase pension plan or a profit sharing plan. However, for purposes of fig-

uring contributions, earned income is net earnings from self-employment *less* the deductible Keogh contribution. Because net earnings must be reduced by the deductible contribution, your maximum contribution to a money-purchase plan is reduced from 25% to 20% of net earnings (before Keogh deduction is considered). The entire 20% contribution is deductible.

However, if you have a profit sharing plan, you may not claim a 20% deduction. The maximum deductible profit sharing contribution is technically 15% of earned income, but because net earnings must be reduced, your maximum deductible contribution is reduced from 15% to 13.0435% of your net earnings (before Keogh deduction is considered). *See* the reduction formula and example below. To maximize your deductible contributions, you may establish a separate money-purchase plan to supplement a profit sharing plan. A bank or other Keogh plan trustee can help you set up separate plans and stay within the overall contribution limit of 25% of earned income.

Only the first $200,000 of a self-employed person's earned income may be considered for purposes of computing contributions if the plan is top heavy.

No minimum contribution is permitted. Prior to 1984, if your adjusted gross income did not exceed $15,000 and your self-employment income was $750 to $5,000, you could make a minimum contribution of up to $750.

The IRS gives the following method of reducing your earnings by the deductible Keogh contribution for purposes of figuring the maximum deductible contribution to a defined-contribution plan:

Step 1. Rate of contribution in your plan.
Step 2. Add 1 to the rate in Step 1. For example, if your profit sharing plan provides for a 15% contribution, the result would then be 1.15 (1 plus 0.15).
Step 3. Divide Step 1 by Step 2. This is the deductible percentage of your net earnings after taking into account the deductible contribution.
Step 4. Multiply the Step 3 percentage by your net earnings (before considering Keogh deductions). The result is your allowable maximum deduction.

EXAMPLE

You are a sole proprietor with no employees and have a profit sharing plan which provides for a 15% contribution rate. Your net earnings (without considering your Keogh plan contribution deductions) are $200,000. Your maximum deductible contribution is $26,087:

Step 1.	Contribution rate	15%
Step 2.	Add 1 to Step 1 rate	1.15
Step 3.	Divide Step 1 by Step 2	13.0435%
Step 4.	Net earnings of $200,000 multiplied by 13.0435% from Step 3. This is your maximum deduction.	$26,087

Contributions for your employees. The above earned income reduction rule does not affect contributions for employees. You continue to make contributions for your employees at the rate specified in your plan, based upon their compensation. Thus, in the above example, you would contribute 15% of your employees' pay to the plan. You deduct contributions for employees when figuring your net earnings from self-employment on Schedule C before figuring your own deductible contribution using the above formula.

Contributions after age 70½. You may continue to make contributions as long as you have self-employment income. At the same time, if you reached age 70½, you may have to begin to receive minimum distributions from the plan no later than the April 1 in the year following the year you reach age 70½. *See* ¶7.12. A penalty may be imposed if the minimum distribution is not received. The minimum distribution must be based on your life expectancy. If you are married, withdrawals may be spread over the joint lives of you and your spouse. Use the new IRS actuarial tables to figure life expectancy, as explained at ¶7.17.

Carryover of excess and unused contributions. Contributions to a profit sharing plan exceeding the 15% deduction ceiling (13.0435% after reduction) may be carried over and deducted in later years subject to the 15% ceiling for those years. However, if contributions exceed the lesser of $30,000 or 15% of net earnings (after reduction by deductible contribution), a 10% penalty could be imposed on the nondeductible contribution for taxable years starting after 1986.

If you contribute less than the allowable deduction limit for a profit sharing plan in taxable years starting after 1986, you may not carryforward the unused limit to a later year. However, the deduction limit for years after 1986 is increased by any unused pre-1987 carryforwards, but the increased limit may not exceed 25% of net earnings (after reduction for deductible contributions).

Contributions to defined-benefit plan. Generally, you may deduct contributions needed to produce the accrued benefits provided for by the plan. This is a complicated calculation requiring actuarial computations requiring the services of a pension expert.

HOW TO CLAIM THE DEDUCTION

¶ **8.18** Contributions made for your account as a self-employed person are deducted from gross income to find your adjusted gross income. However, a deduction for a contribution made for your benefit may not be part of a net operating loss.

> Contributions for your employees are entered as deductions on Schedule C for purposes of computing profit or loss from your business. Trustees' fees not provided for by contributions are deductible in addition to the maximum contribution deduction.

Deductible contributions may generally be made at any time up to the due date of your return, including any extension of time. However, the plan itself must be set up before the close of the taxable year for which the deduction is sought. If you miss the December 31 deadline for setting up a Keogh plan, you still have up to April 15, 1988, to set up an SEP for 1987 (*see* ¶ 8.12).

HOW TO QUALIFY A PLAN

¶ **8.19** You may set up your plan and contribute to it without advance approval. But, since advance approval is advisable, you may, in a determination letter, ask your local District Director to review your plan. Approval requirements depend on whether you set up your own administered plan or join a master plan administered by a bank, insurance company, mutual fund, or a prototype plan sponsored by a trade or professional association. If you start your own individually designed plan, you apply for a determination letter on Form 5300 for a defined-benefit plan, or Form 5301 for a defined-contribution plan. Schedule T must be filed with the appropriate form to comply with new law requirements.

If you join a master or prototype plan, the sponsoring organization applies to the IRS for approval of its plan. You should be given a copy of the approved plan and copies of any subsequent amendments.

ANNUAL INFORMATION RETURNS

¶ **8.20** You must file an annual information return with the IRS. The return must be filed by the last day of the seventh month after the end of the plan year. Thus, if you have a calendar year Keogh plan, you must file your 1987 plan year return by July 31, 1988. The filing requirement applies even if you have no employees.

You may file a short form, Form 5500EZ, if the plan covers only you and your spouse and you are the only owners of the business. A partnership may also use Form 5500EZ if the plan covers only the partners or the partners and their spouses. If your business has employees other than yourself and your spouse, or your partnership has employees other than the partners' spouses, the plan must meet minimum coverage requirements for Form 5500EZ to be used.

If you cannot use Form 5500EZ, you must file either Form 5500-C or Form 5500-R. Form 5500-R is a simpler form that may be used for the 1987 plan year if there are fewer than 100 plan participants and 1987 was not your first plan year or final plan year and if you filed a Form 5500-C for your 1985 or 1986 plan year. Otherwise, you must file the more extensive Form 5500-C.

The form instructions warn that a penalty of $25 per day will be imposed for late or incomplete filing unless you attach an explanation showing reasonable cause for the improper filing.

RESTRICTIONS ON LOANS

¶ **8.21** Keogh plan loans to an owner-employee (more than 10% ownership) are subject to prohibited transaction penalties. There are two penalties: (1) A 5% penalty and (2) a 100% penalty.

The 5% penalty applies in the year of the loan and in later years until the loan is repaid with interest. The penalty is figured on a fair market interest factor which is explained in the instructions to Form 5330. You are required to report loans to the IRS on Form 5330 and pay the 5% penalty when you file the form. Form 5330 must be filed within seven months after the end of the taxable year; extensions may be granted by the IRS if you apply in writing before the due date.

The 100% penalty is imposed if the loan is not repaid. The penalty may be avoided by repaying the loan within 90 days after the IRS sends a deficiency notice for the 100% tax. The 90-day period may be extended by the IRS to allow a reasonable time for repayment.

New law exception. A provision of the 1986 Tax Act permits an owner-employee to apply to the Department of Labor for a special exemption from the prohibited transaction penalties. Details of the exemption procedure were not available at the date of publication of this book.

Loans treated as taxable distributions. Self-employed individuals are taxable on loans from their plan under the same rules applied to regular employees, as discussed at ¶ 7.15.

9

INCOME FROM RENTS AND ROYALTIES

Illustrations of reporting rental income and expenses may be found in the Supplement to YOUR INCOME TAX.

¶ **9.1** New law changes substantially affect the tax treatment of rental income and loss:

1. Depreciation write-off periods have been lengthened and accelerated depreciation benefits have been eliminated for rental property acquired after 1986. Depreciation is discussed at ¶5.22.

2. Rental losses must generally be deducted only from rental income and other passive activity income. Your rental activity is now treated as a passive activity, even if you actively participate in operating the property. This means that you may not generally deduct rental losses from other income (such as salary, interest, and dividends).

Rental losses may offset only other rental and passive activity income. However, if you perform some management role you may be able to deduct from other income real estate rental losses of up to $25,000, provided your adjusted gross income does not exceed $100,000. The passive activity restrictions have one positive effect in making rental income attractive. Property providing rental income may be sought by persons who have tax losses which may be used to offset rental income.

The full details of these restrictions, which also affect tax credits, are discussed in chapter 11.

RENTAL INCOME AND DEDUCTIONS

REPORTING RENT INCOME

¶ **9.2** On the cash basis, you report rent income on your tax return for the year in which you receive payment.

On the accrual basis, you report income on your tax return for the year in which you are entitled to receive payment. You do not report accrued income if the financial condition of the tenant makes collection doubtful. If you sue for payment, you do not report income until you win a collectible judgement.

Advance rentals. Advance rentals or bonuses are reported in the year received, whether you are on the cash or accrual basis.

Payment of landlord's expenses. The tenant's payment of your taxes, interest, insurance, mortgage amortization (even if you are not personally liable on the mortgage), repairs, or other charges is considered additional rental income to you.

Insurance proceeds for loss of rental income because of fire or other casualty are rental income.

A tenant's payment for canceling a lease or modifying its terms is ordinary income when received. You may deduct expenses incurred because of the cancellation and any unamortized balance of expenses paid in negotiating the lease.

Security deposits. Distinguish advance rentals, which are income, from security deposits, which are not. Security deposits are amounts deposited with you solely as security for the tenant's performance of the terms of his lease, and as such are usually not taxed, particularly where local law treats security deposits as trust funds. If the tenant breaches the lease, you are entitled to apply the sum as rent, at which time you report it as income.

Improvements by tenants. You do not realize taxable income when your tenant improves the leased premises, provided the improvements are not substitute rent payments. Furthermore, when you take possession of the improvements at the time the lease ends, you do not realize income. However, you may not depreciate the value of the improvements as the basis to you is considered zero.

Where to report rent income. Rental income and expenses are reported on Schedule E (see *the Supplement to Your Income Tax*). You also file Forms 4562 and 4562-A to claim depreciation deductions. If you are in the real estate business, rental income and expenses are reported on

Schedule C. You are in the real estate business when you provide additional services for the convenience of the tenants, such as maid service. Payments received for the use and occupancy of rooms or other areas in a boarding house, apartment, tourist home, motel, or trailer court where services are provided primarily for the occupant are also reported on Schedule C.

See ¶9.10 for the treatment of deferred rental agreements.

CHECKLIST OF DEDUCTIONS FROM RENT INCOME

¶ 9.3 The following items are deductible from rental income in determining your profit from this activity.

Real estate taxes. But special assessments for paving, sewer or other local improvements are not deductible; they are added to the cost of the land. See ¶16.6 through ¶16.9 for real estate tax deductions.

Depreciation.

Management expenses.

Maintenance expenses: heating, repairs, lighting, water, electricity, gas, telephone, coal, and other service costs. See ¶9.4.

Salaries and wages paid to superintendents, janitors, elevator operators, service and maintenance personnel.

Traveling expenses to look after the properties.

Legal expenses for dispossessing tenants. But expenses of long-term leases are capital expenditures deductible over the term of the lease.

Interest on mortgages and other indebtedness. But expenses and fees for securing loans are capital expenditures.

Commissions paid to collect rentals. But commissions paid to secure long-term rentals must be deducted over the life of the lease. Commissions paid to acquire the property are capitalized.

Premiums for fire, liability, plate glass insurance. If payment is made in one year for insurance covering a period longer than one year, you amortize and deduct the premium over the life of the policy, even though you are on a cash basis.

Premium paid to secure a release from a mortgage in order to get a new loan.

Construction period interest and taxes may have to be amortized. See ¶16.5.

If you rent your property to a friend or relative for less than the fair rental value, you may deduct expenses and depreciation only to the extent of the rent income. See ¶29.17.

Limitations on renting a residence. The law limits deductions you may claim if you rent out part of your home or a vacation home. See ¶29.15 and ¶29.17.

Co-tenants. One of two tenants in common may deduct only half of the maintenance expenses although he pays the entire bill. A tenant in common who pays all of the expenses of the common property is entitled to reimbursement from the other co-tenant. So one-half of the bill is not his ordinary and necessary expense. Each co-tenant owns a separate property interest in the common property which produces separate income for each. Each tenant's deductible expense is that portion of the entire expense which each separate interest bears to the whole, and no more.

> The Tax Court rejected the above rule for co-tenants in a case involving the deduction of real estate taxes. According to the court, the deductibility test for real estate taxes is whether the payment satisfied a personal liability or protects a beneficial interest in the property. In the case of co-tenants, nonpayment of taxes by the other co-tenants could result in the property being lost or foreclosed. To prevent this, a co-tenant who pays the tax is protecting his beneficial interest and so is entitled to deduct the payment of the full tax.

Costs of canceling lease. A landlord may pay the tenant to cancel an unfavorable lease. The way the payment is treated by the landlord depends on the reason for the cancellation. If the purpose of the cancellation is to enable the landlord to construct a new building in place of the old, the cancellation payment is added to the basis of the new building.

If the purpose is to sell the property, the payment is added to the cost of the property. If the landlord wants the premises for his own use, the payment is deducted over the remaining term of the old lease. If the landlord gets a new tenant to replace the old one, the cancellation payment is also generally deductible over the remaining term of the old lease.

EXAMPLE

Handlery Hotels, Inc., had to pay its lessee $85,000 to terminate a lease on a building three years before the lease term expired. Handlery entered into a new 20-year lease at more favorable terms with another lessee. Handlery amortized the $85,000 cancellation payment over the three-year unexpired term of the old lease. The IRS claimed that the payment had to be amortized over the 20-year term of the new lease, because it was part of the cost of obtaining the new lease. A federal district court agreed with the IRS, but an appeals court sided with Handlery. Since the unexpired lease term is the major factor in determining the amount of the cancellation payment, the cost of cancellation should be amortized over that unexpired term.

DISTINGUISH BETWEEN A REPAIR AND AN IMPROVEMENT

¶ 9.4 Maintenance and repair expenses are not treated the same as expenses for improvements and replacements. Only maintenance and incidental repair costs are deductible against rental income. Repairs that add to the value or prolong the life of the property are capital improvements. They may not be deducted but may be added to the basis of the property.

EXAMPLE

The costs of painting the outside of a building used for business purposes and the costs of papering and painting the inside are repair costs and may be deducted. The replacement of a roof or a change in the plumbing system is a nondeductible capital expenditure which may be added to the basis of the property.

Repairs may not be separated from capital expenditures when part of an improvement program.

EXAMPLE

Jones buys a dilapidated business building and has the building renovated and repaired. The total cost comes to about $13,000, of which $7,800 is deducted as repairs. But the repair deduction is disallowed because it is a capital expenditure. When a general improvement program is undertaken, you may not separate repairs from improvements. They become an integral part of the overall betterment and a capital investment, although they could be characterized as repairs when viewed independently.

What if the repairs and improvements are unconnected and not part of an overall improvement program? Assume you repair the floors of one story and improve another story by cutting new windows. You may probably deduct the cost of repairing the floors provided you have separate bills for the jobs. To safeguard the deduction, schedule the work at separate times so that the two jobs are not lumped together as an overall improvement program.

SALE OF A LEASE

¶ 9.5 Payments to a lessee-tenant on the assignment or cancellation of a lease used in the tenants' business is subject to Section 1231 treatment; see ¶5.44. Payments to a tenant for cancelling the lease on a personal residence are treated as proceeds from a sale of a capital asset; gain is capital gain if the lease was held long term but losses are not deductible.

Payments received by a landlord for cancellation of a lease are ordinary income, not capital gain.

DEDUCTING COST OF DEMOLISHING A BUILDING

¶ 9.6 When you buy improved property, the purchase price is allocated between the land and the building; only the building may be depreciated; the land may not; see ¶5.22. If you later demolish the building you may not deduct the cost of the demolition or the undepreciated basis of the building as a loss in the year of demolition. In taxable years beginning after 1983, expenses or losses in connection with the demolition of any structure, including certified historic structures, are not deductible. They must be capitalized and added to the basis of the land on which the structure is located.

In taxable years beginning before 1984, whether a demolition loss was allowed generally depended on whether you bought the property with the intention of demolishing the building. If you purchased with the intent to demolish the building, the entire purchase price was attributed to the land and no part to the building. Since the building was given no basis, there was no loss when it was demolished. The costs of the demolition were added to the basis of the new property.

DEDUCTING THE COST OF A BUSINESS LEASE

¶ **9.7** The cost of buying a business lease is amortized over the term of the lease. However, the lease terms may have to include optional renewal periods. Where less than 75% of the cost of acquiring the lease is attributed to the remaining lease term on the date of acquisition, the lease term includes all renewal options and any other period for which there is a reasonable expectation of a renewal of the lease. In determining the period of the remaining lease term on the date of acquisition, options renewable by the lessee are not considered. Your annual deduction will be smaller if the renewal periods are added to the amortization term.

HOW LESSEES DEDUCT LEASEHOLD IMPROVEMENTS

¶ **9.8** Leasehold improvements placed in service after 1986 by a lessee are depreciated under MACRS; 27 ½ years for residential property or 31 ½ years for commercial property. You ignore the term of the lease. If the lease term is shorter than the MACRS life and you do not retain the improvements at the end of the term, the remaining undepreciated basis is considered in computing gain or loss at that time.

For leasehold improvements placed in service before 1987, the cost of improvements is deductible over the *shorter* of the following periods:

The useful life of the improvement (in this case, you recover cost by depreciation); *or*

The remaining term of the lease (in this case, you recover cost by amortization).

If there is an option to renew the lease, the renewal period is added to the remaining term of the lease to make the above comparison with the useful life of the improvement if the useful life of the improvement excess the original term of the lease. If the useful life is less than the original term, it is not necessary to determine if the renewal period is to be added. The improvement is depreciable over its useful life because, in any event, the useful life will be less than the original term or the original term plus the renewal period. If the useful life of the improvement exceeds the original term of the lease but is less than the original term plus the renewal period, the improvement is depreciated over useful life. If the useful life exceeds the original term plus the renewal period, the improvement is amortized over the period of the original and renewal term of the lease. A percentage test is used to determine whether a renewal is intended. You include a renewal period if the remaining term of the original lease at the completion of an improvement is less than 60% of the useful life of the improvement.

SPECIAL TAX CREDITS FOR CERTAIN REAL ESTATE INVESTMENTS

¶ **9.9** To encourage certain real estate investments, the tax law offers the following tax credits—

Low-income housing credit for buildings placed in service after 1986. The credit applies to newly constructed low-income housing and also to certain existing structures that are substantially rehabilitated. In 1987 the credit is 9% for new buildings that are not federally subsidized. It is 4% for new federally subsidized buildings and existing buildings. To claim the credit, you as the building owner must receive a certification from an authorized housing credit agency. The agency allocates a credit to you on Form 8609, which you use to claim the credit on Form 8586. You must attach both Form 8609 and Form 8586 to your tax return.

Rehabilitating a certified historical structure. The amount of the credit is 20%. Use Form 3468 to claim the credit.

Rehabilitating a building first placed in service before 1936. The amount of the credit is 10%. Claim the credit on Form 3468.

For further details and conditions for claiming these credits, check Treasury regulations and releases, and IRS publications 535 and 572.

DEFERRED OR STEPPED-UP RENTAL AGREEMENTS

¶ **9.10** Cash basis lessors and accrual basis lessees through the use of deferred rental or stepped-up rental leases were able to coordinate tax savings benefits. Stepped-up rentals are rent payments that substantially increase during the later period of a lease. In effect, rent for the early years is deferred and repaid with interest in the later years. Through such an arrangement, a cash basis lessor did not report rent income until the year of payment while the accrual basis tenant deducted the rent by accruals to the rental period.

To prevent this type of planning, a law imposes uniform reporting for both the lessor and lessee regardless of their accounting basis if the rental agreement is within the terms of Code Section 467. A Section 467 rental agreement is any agreement which provides for stepped-up rents or defers rent for use of the property until after the close of the year following the year of rental use. Section 467 does not apply if the total rental payments are $250,000 or less. It also does not apply to agreements entered into before June 9, 1984, or to later agreements pursuant to a binding written contract made on or before June 8, 1984.

The lessor and lessee of a "Section 467 rental agreement" must report rental income or expense under the accrual basis and report imputed interest based on the deferred rent. The calculation of imputed interest is similar to the 110% rule of ¶ 4.18.

> If the rental agreement allocates rent, rent accruals may be based on the agreement. However, rents payable after the end of the rental period are accounted for according to their present value.

Stricter accrual rules apply: (1) if the agreement does not allocate rents; (2) the lease term exceeds 75% of the ACRS recovery period for such property; or (3) the agreement is considered a disqualified leaseback. In these cases, rents are "leveled" under a constant accrual method.

ROYALTY INCOME AND DEDUCTIONS

REPORTING ROYALTY INCOME

¶ **9.11** Royalties are payment for use of patents or copyrights or for the use and exhaustion of mineral properties. Royalties are taxable as ordinary income and are reported in Schedule E (Form 1040). Depletion deductions relating to the royalties are also reported in Schedule E. If you own an operating oil, gas, or mineral interest, or are a self-employed writer, investor, or artist, you report royalty income, expenses, and depletion in Schedule C.

Examples of royalty income—

License fees received for use, manufacture, or sale of patented article. *See* ¶ 6.17 for capital gain opportunities.

Renting fees received from patents, copyrights and depletable assets (such as oil wells).

Authors' royalties including advance royalties if not a loan.

Royalties for musical compositions, works of art, etc.

Proceeds of sale of part of your rights in an artistic composition or book—for example, sale of motion picture or television rights.

Royalties from oil, gas, or other similar interests (*see* ¶ 9.12).
Lessee's payment of taxes on mineral property.

To have a royalty, you must retain an economic interest in the minerals deposited in the land which you have leased to the producer. You usually have a royalty when payments are based on the amount of minerals produced. However, if you are paid regardless of the minerals produced, you have a sale which is taxed as capital gain if the proceeds exceed the basis of the transferred property interest. Bonuses and advance royalties which are paid to you before the production of minerals are taxable as royalty income and are entitled to an allowance for depreciation. Under a new law, bonuses and advanced royalties for gas and oil wells and geothermal deposits are not treated as gross income for purposes of calculating percentage depletion. If the lease is terminated without production and you received a bonus or advanced royalty, you report as income previously claimed depletion deductions. You increase the basis of your property by the restored depletion deductions.

INTANGIBLE DRILLING COSTS

¶ 9.12 *Deducting intangible drilling costs.* Intangible drilling and development costs may be deducted as current expenses or treated as capital expenditures. They include wages, fuel, repairs, hauling and supplies incident to and necessary for the drilling of wells and the preparation of wells for the production of oil or gas and geothermal wells.

The election applies only to costs of drilling and developing items, exclusive of depreciable items that do not have a salvage value. You must make this election in your income tax return for the first tax year in which you pay or incur the costs.

Tax shelter investors may deduct prepayments of drilling expenses made after March 31, 1984, only if the well is "spudded" within 90 days after the close of the taxable year in which the prepayment is made. The prepayment must also have a business purpose, not be a deposit and not materially distort income. The investor's deduction is limited to his cash investment in the tax shelter. For purposes of this limitation, an investor's cash investment includes loans that are not secured by his shelter interest or the shelter's assets and loans that are not arranged by the organizer or promoter. If the above tests are not met, a deduction may be claimed only as actual drilling services are provided.

Recapture of intangible drilling costs for oil, gas, or geothermal property. Deductions previously claimed for intangible drilling expenses and development costs on productive wells are subject to ordinary income treatment upon disposition of a working or operating interest in oil and gas property. The amounts are treated as ordinary income to the extent that the deduction exceeded what would have been allowed if the intangible costs had been capitalized and deducted through cost depletion. In no event may the amount recaptured exceed the gain upon the disposition of the property. The recapture rule for geothermal property applies only to wells commenced after September 30, 1978.

Special allocation rules apply when you dispose of less than your entire interest.

Treasury regulations explain how the recapture provisions apply to sales of partnership interests and stock in S corporations. The regulations exempt certain dispositions from the recapture provisions, such as gifts, transfers at death, and transfers in certain tax-free incorporations and reorganization.

Certain intangible drilling costs are also treated as tax preference items subject to alternative minimum tax. *See* ¶ 23.4.

DEPLETION DEDUCTION

¶ 9.13 Properties subject to depletion deductions are mines, oil and gas wells, timber, and exhaustible natural deposits.

Two methods of computing depletion are: (1) cost depletion, and (2) percentage depletion. If you are allowed to compute under either method, you must use the one that produces the larger deduction. In most cases, this will be percentage depletion.

Cost depletion. The cost depletion of minerals is computed as follows: (1) Divide the total number of units (tons, barrels) remaining in the deposit to be mined into the adjusted basis of the property. (2) Multiply

the unit rate found in step 1 by the number of units for which payment is received during the taxable year if you are on the cash basis.

Adjusted basis is the original cost of the property, less depletion allowed, whether computed on the percentage or cost depletion method. It does not include nonmineral property such as mining equipment. Adjusted basis may not be less than zero.

Timber depletion is based on the cost of timber (or other basis in the owner's hands) and does not include any part of the cost of land. Depletion takes place when standing timber is cut. Depletion must be computed by the cost method, not by the percentage method. For further details, *see* Treasury regulations.

> You claim depletion deductions if you are an operating owner or an owner of an economic interest in mineral deposits in place or standing timber. You have an economic interest when your return of capital depends on income received from the extraction of minerals or the cutting of timber. (*See* ¶ 9.12 above.)

Percentage depletion. Percentage depletion is based on a certain percentage rate applied to annual gross income derived from the resource. A deduction for percentage depletion is allowed even if the basis of the property is already fully recovered by prior depletion deductions. However, the excess of depletion deductions over the basis at the end of the year (without regard to the current year's deduction) is an item of tax preference (*see* ¶ 23.4). The percentage to be applied depends upon the mineral involved; the range is from 5% up to 22%. In determining gross income for percentage depletion, do not include any lease bonuses, advance royalties, or any other amount payable without regard to production.

Restrictions on the application of percentage depletion for gas and oil property are discussed below.

The percentage depletion deduction may not exceed 50% of taxable income from the property computed without the depletion deduction. In computing the 50% limitation, a net operating loss deduction is not deducted from gross income.

Percentage depletion for oil and gas wells was repealed as of January 1, 1975, except for exemptions allowed (1) small independent producers and royalty owners, and (2) for gas well production. The independent owner exemption is not generally available to transfers of proven oil and gas interests made after 1974. The following discussion covers only the general pattern of the restrictions on percentage depletion.

> *Small independent producers and royalty owner exemption.* A 15% rate applies to the extent that average daily production does not exceed certain daily rate exemptions fixed by the law. The daily rate production (called depletable oil quantity exemption) is fixed at 1,000 barrels of oil a day and 6,000,000 cubic feet of gas a day. Total production is averaged over the entire year to reach the daily rate regardless of when production actually occurred. Where you have both oil and natural gas production, the exemption is allocated between the oil and natural gas production.

Average daily production of oil is found by dividing your aggregate production during the taxable year by the number of days in the taxable year. If you hold a partial interest in the production (including a partnership interest), production rate is found by multiplying total production of such property by your income percentage participation in such property.

The depletable natural gas quantity depends on an election made annually by independent producers or royalty owners to have crude oil treated as natural gas. The depletable quantity of natural gas is 6,000 cubic feet times the barrels of depletable oil for which an election has been made. The election is made on an original or amended return or on a claim for credit or refund. The election applies to secondary or tertiary production, subject to a limitation found in Treasury regulations.

The 65% taxable income test limit. Percentage depletion may not exceed 50% of the taxable income from the property. Further, the depletion deduction for a small producer or royalty owner is subject to this additional limitation. The deduction attributable to the application of the exemption may not exceed 65% of your taxable income computed without regard to depletion deduction allowed under the small producer's exemption and net operating loss carry-back. Trusts may compute the 65% of taxable income limitation without regard to any deduction for distributions to the beneficiaries.

If your average daily production exceeds the above exemption limit, the exemption must be allocated among all the properties in which you have an interest.

Secondary or tertiary production. There is no longer a distinction between primary and secondary or tertiary production. The 15% depletion rate applies to up to 1,000 barrels of all production. However, percentage depletion may not be claimed for secondary or tertiary production from proven properties transferred after 1974 unless one of the exceptions discussed below applies.

Limitations where family members or related businesses own interests. The daily depletable oil quantity rate is allocated among members of the same family in proportion to their respective production of oil. Similar allocation is required where business entities are under common control. This affects interests owned by you, your spouse and minor children; by corporations, estates and trusts in which 50% of the beneficial interest is owned by the same or related persons; and by a corporation which is a member of the same controlled group.

Transfers of oil or gas property after 1974. No depletion exemption is allowed for a transfer (including the subleasing of a lease) after December 31, 1974, of an interest (including an interest in a partnership or trust) in any proven oil or gas property. A property is treated as a proven oil or gas property if, at the time of the transfer, the principal value of the property has been demonstrated by prospecting or exploration or discovery work. This limitation does not apply to a transfer of property at death, or certain tax-free transfers between an individual and his corporation under Section 351 of the Internal Revenue Code. For taxable years beginning after December 31, 1974, oil or natural gas property is not treated as "transferred" property because of changes in beneficiaries of a trust provided the changes occur because of birth, adoption, or death involving a single family.

The small producer exemption is not allowed to any producer who owns or controls a retail outlet for the sale of oil or natural gas or petroleum products. It is also not allowed to a refiner who refines more than 50,000 barrels of oil on any one day of the taxable year. A taxpayer is not treated as a retailer where gross sales of oil and gas products are less than $5 million in any one year or if all sales of oil or natural gas products occur outside the United States, and none of the taxpayer's domestic production is exported. Bulk sales of oil or natural gas to industrial or utility customers are not to be treated as retail sales.

Gas well exemptions. The 22% depletion allowance is allowed for the following two classes: (1) domestic natural gas sold under a fixed contract in effect on February 1, 1975, and (2) domestic "regulated natural gas" produced and sold before July 1, 1976.

Windfall profit tax. Holders of oil and gas interests may be subject to a windfall profit tax. Any windfall profit tax paid is deductible on Schedule E.

For 1987, up to three barrels of oil a day are exempt from the windfall profit tax. To claim the three-barrel-a-day exclusion, Form 6783 is filed with the party that withholds the tax from royalty payments. This excise tax and an exemption for oil from stripper wells are not discussed further here.

For a partnership, property cost or percentage depletion is figured separately by each partner and not by the partnership. However, the partnership first allocates to each partner his share of the adjusted basis of each partnership property. The allocation is made as of the date the partnership acquires the oil or gas property or January 1, 1975, whichever is later. The partner's share of the adjusted basis depends on his interest in partnership capital or income or by the partnership agreement. A partner reduces his share of the adjusted basis of each property by the amount of depletion claimed each year.

The partner reports his share of royalty income and deducts depletion on Schedule E. Each interest in a partnership is reported separately.

Each stockholder of an S corporation figures the depletion allowance separately in the same way as a partner in a partnership. The S corporation allocates to each shareholder his basis of each oil or gas property held by the corporation. The allocation is made as of the date the corporation acquired the property or, if later, generally the first day of the taxable year beginning in 1983.

COAL AND TIMBER ROYALTIES

¶ **9.14** Royalties are usually taxed at ordinary income tax rates. However, royalties from coal and timber operations may get capital gain treatment if—

Coal royalties are received by a lessor or sublessor on coal owned long term before it was mined. Gain is the difference between the payments received and the basis of the coal sold. However, percentage depletion may not be deducted; only cost depletion may be deducted. Capital gains are not applied to royalties received through a joint venture or partnership.

Timber royalties are received by a lessor or sublessor on timber owned long term before it was disposed of. This date of disposal is usually the date the timber was cut. However, if payment under a contract is made before this time, the date of payment may be treated as the date of disposal. Gain is the difference between the payments received and the basis of the timber sold.

DEDUCTING THE COST OF PATENTS OR COPYRIGHTS

¶ **9.15** You may deduct costs incurred to license the property or to improve it.

> Deduct depreciation over the life of the patent or copyright. Basis for depreciation includes all expenses which you are required to capitalize in connection with creating the work, such as the cost of drawings and experimental models, stationery and supplies; travel expenses to obtain material for a book, fees to counsel; government charges for patent or copyright; litigation costs in protecting or perfecting title.

If you purchased the patent or artistic creation, depreciate your cost over the remaining life of the patent or copyright.

If you inherited the patent or rights to an artistic creation, your cost is the fair market value either at the time of death of the person from whom you inherited it or the alternate valuation date if elected by the executor. You get this cost basis even if the decedent paid nothing for it. Figure your depreciation by dividing the fair market value by the number of years of remaining life.

If your patent or copyright becomes valueless, you may deduct your unrecovered cost or other basis in the year it became worthless. Abnormal obsolescence does not give rise to a loss deduction. You may, however, adjust the useful life depreciation rate to reflect such obsolescence.

AMORTIZATION OF PRODUCTION COSTS

¶ **9.16** Under prior law (IRC Section 280), the cost of producing a book, motion picture, record or other similar property had to be amortized and deducted over the period you reasonably expect to receive substantially all of the income from the particular film, book, or record. The rate of deduction was based on the ratio of income received in the year over total income expected to be received. For costs incurred after 1986, Section 280 has been repealed and under a new law Code Section 263A, such costs must be similarly capitalized. However, at the time this book went to press, the Treasury had not clarified the method of amortizing the capitalized expenses.

10

REPORTING INCOME FROM PARTNERSHIPS, S CORPORATIONS, TRUSTS, ESTATES, AND FARMING

¶ **10.1** **New law changes substantially affect the tax treatment of income from partnerships, S corporations, and farms.** Effective for tax years beginning after 1986, if you do not materially participate in the business activity, income or loss is treated as incurred in a passive activity. This means that you may not deduct from other income (salary, interest, dividends, annuity, self-employment income, etc.) losses from any business in which you do not materially participate. Such losses may offset only income from passive activities. Similarly, tax credits from passive activities are likewise limited to the tax allocable to income from passive activities. These restrictions are being phased in for interests held before October 23, 1986, so that in 1987, 65% of a passive activity loss will be allowed from other non-passive income.

Disallowed losses and credits are suspended and carried forward to the next taxable year, where they may be used only against passive income. Any remaining suspended loss may be deducted when you sell your interest. However, a suspended credit may not be claimed in the year you sell your interest.

The passive loss restrictions apply to all passive investments (unless excepted by law)—even to a business in which you invest money but do not manage, for example, you invest in a business operated by your children.

Income received for the performance of personal services in a passive activity, however, is not treated as income from a passive activity. For example, as a limited partner, if you are paid for performing services for the partnership, the payments may not be offset by passive losses from the partnership or from any other passive activity. For further details, see chapter 11 which discusses passive activity rules.

PARTNERSHIP INCOME

HOW PARTNERS REPORT PARTNERSHIP PROFIT AND LOSS

¶ **10.2** A partnership files Form 1065 which informs the IRS of partnership profit or loss and each partner's share. The partnership pays no tax on partnership income; each partner reports his or her share of partnership net profit or loss and special deductions and credits, whether or not distributions are received from the partnership. Income that is not distributed or withdrawn increases the basis of a partner's partnership interest.

Your share is generally based on your proportionate capital interest in the partnership, unless the partnership agreement provides for another allocation. The following types of items are reported by partners on their personal tax return:

Net profit or loss from the partnership activity. This is listed on Schedule E.

Dividends and interest earned on partnership investments. These are reported on Schedule E.

A partner's share of tax-exempt interest keeps its tax free status.

Capital gains and losses from the sale and exchange of partnership assets. These are listed in Schedule D.

Charitable contributions made by the partnership. These are claimed on Schedule A, if itemized deductions are taken.

Tax preference items (see ¶ 23.4).

Depletion allowances.

Credit or deduction for taxes paid to foreign countries or U.S. possessions.

Partnership elections. The partnership, not the individual partners, makes elections affecting the computation of partnership income, such as the election to defer involuntary conversion gains, to amortize organization and rehabilitation costs, and to modify ACRS depreciation. An election to claim a foreign tax credit is made by the partners.

Guaranteed salary and interest. A guaranteed salary which is fixed without regard to partnership income is reported as salary income. If you receive a percentage of the partnership income with a stipulated minimum payment, the guaranteed payment is the amount by which the minimum guarantee exceeds your share of the partnership income before taking into account the minimum guarantee.

Interest on capital is reported as interest income.

Self-employment tax. You pay self-employment tax on up to $43,800 of your partnership profits, including a guaranteed salary and other guaranteed payments. Limited partners do not pay self-employment tax.

Special allocations. Partners may agree to special allocations of gain, income, loss, deductions or credits disproportionate to their capital contributions. The allocation should have a substantial economic effect to avoid an IRS disallowance. The IRS will not issue an advance ruling on whether an allocation has a substantial economic effect. If the allocation is rejected, a partner's share is determined by his or her partnership interest.

To have substantial economic effect, a special allocation must be reflected by adjustments to the partner's capital account; liquidation proceeds must be distributed in accordance with the partners' capital accounts, and following a liquidating distribution, the partners must be liable to the partnership to restore any deficit in their capital.

If there is a change of partnership interests during the year, items are allocated to a partner for that part of the year he or she is a member of the partnership. Thus, a partner who acquires an interest late in the year is barred from deducting partnership expenses incurred prior to his entry into the partnership. If the partners agree to give an incoming partner a disproportionate share of partnership losses for the period after he becomes a member, the allocation must meet the substantial economic effect test to avoid IRS disallowance. *See* Treasury regulations and IRS Publication 541 for further details.

Organization expenses. The costs of organizing a partnership may be deducted ratably over a period of not less than 60 months. Organizational expenses include legal fees for the negotiation and preparation of the partnership agreement, accounting fees for establishing the partnership accounting system, and necessary filing fees. If the partnership is liquidated before the end of the 60-month period, the balance can be deducted as a loss. A partnership must make an election to amortize organization expenses on a statement attached to the partnership return for the first year of business, filed by the due date, plus extensions.

Syndication expenses are not deductible. These are the costs of issuing and marketing interests in a partnership, such as brokerage commissions, legal and accounting fees relating to tax and securities law disclosures in the offering materials, and printing costs of the prospectus and other promotional materials. Such syndication costs are nondeductible capital expenses.

Reporting transfers of interest to IRS. If you transfer a partnership interest that includes an interest in partnership receivables and appreciated inventory, you must report the disposition to the partnership within 30 days. The partnership in turn files a report with the IRS on Form 8308. You must also attach a statement to your income tax return describing the transaction and allocating basis to the receivables and inventory items. The IRS wants to keep track of such dispositions because partners have to pay ordinary income tax on the portion of profit attributable to the receivables and inventory.

Under a new law, gains on the sale or exchange of property between a partner and partnership, or between two partnerships, are treated as ordinary income if more than 50% of the capital or profits interest is owned, directly or indirectly, by the same person or persons.

Within 30 days of your transfer, provide the partnership with a statement that includes the date of the exchange and that identifies the transferee (include Social Security number if known). You can be penalized $50 for failure to notify the partnership. You and your transferee should receive a copy of the Form 8308 which the partnership will send to the IRS along with its Form 1065.

Generally, the partnership must file a separate Form 8308 for each transfer but the IRS may allow a composite Form 8308 for the calendar year if there were at least 25 reportable transfers.

WHEN A PARTNER REPORTS INCOME OR LOSS

¶ **10.3** You report your share of the partnership gain or loss for the partnership year which ends in your tax reporting year. If you and the partnership are on a calendar year basis, you report your share of the 1987 partnership income on your 1987 income tax return. If the partnership is on a fiscal year ending March 31, for example, a partner (reporting on a calendar year) reports on his 1987 return his share of the partnership income for the whole fiscal year ending March 31, 1987—that is, partnership income for the fiscal year April 1, 1986, through March 31, 1987.

In 1987, most partnerships must change from a fiscal tax year to the tax year of the partners. As almost all individuals report on the calendar year, the law is essentially an order to adopt a calendar year unless a business purpose for a fiscal year is shown.

Unless a good business reason is established for having a fiscal year, a partnership must have the same tax year as that of partners owning a majority interest (more than 50%). However, if the majority interest partners have not owned a majority interest for the preceding three tax years, the partnership must adopt the same tax year as its principal partners. If the principal partners do not have the same taxable year, and no majority of partners have the same taxable year, the partnership must adopt a calendar year.

If a business purpose is shown for using a fiscal year, the Treasury will allow the fiscal year. Deferral of income for three months or less no longer justifies a fiscal year. Partnerships that have already obtained Treasury permission for a fiscal year do not have to get permission again because of the law, unless that fiscal year was based on a deferral of income.

Under an election, excess income generated by changes in tax years may be reported ratably over the first four tax years by the partners.

PARTNERSHIP LOSS LIMITATIONS

¶ **10.4** Your share of partnership losses may not exceed the adjusted basis of your partnership interest. If the loss exceeds basis, the excess loss may not be deducted until you have partnership earnings to cover the loss or contribute capital to cover the loss. The basis of your partnership interest is generally the amount paid for the interest (either through contribution or purchase), less withdrawals plus accumulated taxed earnings that have not been withdrawn.

Partners, except those whose partnership's principal activity is real estate, are subject to the "at risk" loss limitation rules. These rules limit the amount of loss that may be deducted to the amount each partner personally has at stake in the partnership, such as contributions of property and loans for which the partner is personally liable. *See* ¶ 11.11 for a discussion of the "at risk" rules.

Further, if the IRS determines that a tax shelter partnership is not operated to make a profit, deductions may be disallowed even where there is an "at risk" investment.

Finally, any loss not barred by the above limitations may be disallowed under the passive activity rules discussed at chapter 11. For partnership fiscal years starting in 1986 and ending in 1987, the passive activity rules may limit the entire year's loss deductions and tax credits, even if the losses or credits were incurred during the 1986 portion of the 1986-1987 fiscal year. Follow the instructions accompanying Form 1065 for applying the passive activity rules.

UNIFIED TAX AUDITS OF PARTNERSHIPS WITH MORE THAN TEN PARTNERS

¶ **10.5** For partnership taxable years beginning after September 3, 1982, tax audits of both a partnership of more than ten partners and its partners must be at the partnership level. To challenge the partnership treatment of an item, the IRS must generally audit the partnership, not the individual partners. To avoid a personal audit of a partnership item, a partner should report partnership items as shown on the partnership return or identify any inconsistent treatment on his or her return. Otherwise the IRS may assess a deficiency without auditing the partnership.

For a partnership level audit, the partnership names a "tax matters partner" (TMP) to receive notice of the audit. If one is not named, the

IRS will treat as a TMP the general partner having the largest interest in partnership profits at the end of the taxable year involved in the audit. Notice of the audit must also be given to the other partners at least 120 days before the IRS mails the TMP notice of its final determination. All partners may participate in the partnership audit. If the IRS settles with some partners, similar settlement terms must be offered to the other partners.

Within 90 days after the IRS mails its final determination, the TMP may appeal to the Tax Court; individual partners have an additional 60 days to file a court petition if the TMP does not do so. An appeal may also be filed in a federal district court or the Claims Court if the petitioning partner first deposits with the IRS an amount equal to the tax that would be owed if the IRS determination were sustained. A Tax Court petition takes precedence over petitions filed in other courts. The first Tax Court petition filed is heard; if other partners have also filed petitions, their cases will be dismissed. If no Tax Court petitions are filed, the first

petition filed in federal district court or the Claims Court takes precedence. Regardless of which petition takes precedence, all partners who hold an interest during the taxable year involved will be bound by the decision (unless the statute of limitations with respect to that partner has run out).

Partnerships with ten or fewer partners may elect to come within the unified audit procedures, provided all of the partners are individuals or estates.

Important: The above discussion covers only the general features of partnership tax reporting. It also does not cover new law changes in other partnership areas, such as contributions of property. Specific partnership rules are complex and their implementation requires the services of an experienced tax practitioner. IRS Publication 541 has further information on partnership reporting.

S CORPORATION ELECTION

¶ 10.6 An S corporation election allows an incorporated business to avoid paying a corporate income tax, thus eliminating the double tax feature of corporate operations while retaining limited liability and other advantages of doing business as a corporation.

The S corporation files a return on Form 1120S, informing the IRS of corporate net earnings and losses and the stockholders' shares of income or loss items which they report on their personal tax returns. This tax reporting procedure is similar to that of partnerships.

An election is not advisable for an existing company which has an operating loss carryover. The loss may not be used by the corporation after the election and it may not be passed through to the stockholders. The loss may be revived if the election is terminated. Each year the election is in force counts as a year in figuring the carryover period even though the loss has not been used.

> You will generally make an S election when your personal tax rates do not exceed the corporate tax rates, when you cannot take sufficient money out of a corporation without subjecting some or all of it to the double tax, or when a special advantage is offered by an S election. For example, in the early years of the corporation's existence, substantial losses are expected. The S election allows the pass-through of operating losses to stockholders who may have substantial income from other sources to offset these losses.

Important: The following sections discuss general features of the election, the implementation and review of which require the services of an experienced tax accountant or attorney. A detailed discussion of these issues along with the particular objectives of an election may be found in tax services dealing with corporate tax problems and in IRS Publication 589.

STOCKHOLDER REPORTING OF S CORPORATION INCOME AND LOSS

¶ 10.7 S corporations are subject to tax reporting rules similar to those applied to partnerships. However, shareholders who work for the corporation are treated as employees for FICA purposes. They do not pay self-employment tax on their salary income or other receipts from the corporation.

Each stockholder reports his or her share of corporate items of income and loss, deductions, and credits, as shown on Schedule K-1 of Form 1120S.

The allocation of items is based on the proportion of stock held in the

corporation. If your interest changed during the year, the pro rata share must also consider on a daily basis the time you held the stock.

The following items are allocated to and pass through to the stockholders:

Gains and losses from the sale and exchange of capital assets and Section 1231 property. Each stockholder reports his or her share of capital gains and aggregates Section 1231 transactions with his or her other Section 1231 transactions, if any.

Interest and dividends on corporate investments and losses. Investment interest expenses subject to the rules of ¶15.14 also pass through.

Tax-exempt interest. Tax-exempt interest remains tax free in the hands of the stockholders but increases the basis of their stock. Dividends from other companies may qualify for the exclusion.

First-year expense deduction.

Charitable contributions made by the corporation.

Foreign income or loss.

Foreign taxes paid by the corporation. Each stockholder elects whether to claim these as a credit or deduction.

Tax preference items.

Recovery of bad debts and prior taxes.

Fiscal year corporations. If the corporation reports on a fiscal year, the stockholders report their shares of corporate items on their tax returns for the year in which the corporate tax year ends.

For fiscal years starting in 1986 and ending in 1987, the passive activity rules apply and loss deductions may be disallowed. *See* chapter 11. Follow the instructions to Form 1120S for applying the passive activity rules to your 1987 return.

Basis limits loss deductions. Deductible losses may not exceed your basis in corporate stock and loans to the corporation. If losses exceed basis, the excess loss is carried over and becomes deductible when you invest or lend an equivalent amount of money to the corporation. This rule may allow for timing a loss deduction. In a year in which you want to deduct the loss, you may contribute capital to the corporation. If a carryover loss exists when an S election terminates, a limited loss deduction may be allowed.

Passive activity rules limit loss deductions. Losses allocated to you may be disallowed under the passive activity rules discussed at chapter 11.

Basis adjustments. Because of the nature of S corporation reporting, the basis of each stockholder's stock is subject to change. Basis is *increased* by the passthrough of income items and *reduced* by the passthrough of loss items and the receipt of distribution. Because income and loss items pass through to stockholders, an S corporation has no current earnings and profits. An income item will not increase basis unless you actually report the amount on your tax return. The specific details and order of basis adjustments are listed in Treasury Publication 589.

Family corporations. The IRS has the authority to change the amounts of items passed through to stockholders to properly reflect the value of services rendered or capital contributed by family members of one or more S corporation shareholders. If you are the member of a family of an S corporation shareholder and perform services or furnish capital to the corporation without receiving reasonable compensation, the IRS may reallocate salary or interest income to you from the other shareholders to reflect the value of your services or capital. The term "family" includes only a spouse, parents, ancestors, children, and any trusts for the benefit of such relatives.

Allocating income and loss for changes in stock ownership during the year. In a year stock ownership changes, income and loss items are either allocated on a daily basis or all persons who were stockholders during the entire taxable year may elect to allocate income and loss items as if there were two short taxable years, the first year ending on the date the shareholder's interest ended. The allocation of items for each short taxable year is determined according to corporate records and workpapers. The following examples illustrate how the allocation on a daily basis is made.

EXAMPLES

1. A calendar year corporation incurs a loss of $10,000. Smith and Jones each own 50% of the stock. On May 1, Smith sells all of his stock to Harris. For the year, Smith was a shareholder for 120 days, Jones for 365 days, and Harris for 245 days. The loss is allocated on a daily basis; the daily basis of the loss is $27.2973 ($10,000 divided by 365 days). The allocation is as follows:

   Smith: $1,644 ($27.3973 × 120 days × 50% interest)
   Jones: $5,000 ($27.3973 × 365 days × 50% interest)
   Harris: $3,356 ($27.3973 × 245 days × 50% interest)

2. Same facts as in example (1) except that on May 1, Smith sells only 50% of his stock to Harris. The allocation for Smith accounts for his 50% interest for 120 days and his 25% interest for the remainder of the year.

   Smith: $3,322 ($27.3973 × 120 days × 50% plus $27.3973 × 245 days × 25%)
   Jones: $5,000 (as above)
   Harris: $1,678 ($27.3973 × 245 days × 25%)

In a year in which stock ownership changes, determine tax consequences both ways: using the daily allocation method and the method using two short periods. Choose the method providing the best overall tax consequences for the shareholders. Different tax results will occur, especially if substantial loss items were incurred in one short year and income items in the other short year. The daily allocation method will average the items between the two years. The short-period method basis will place the items in the period they were incurred.

Expenses owed to shareholders. An S corporation is deemed to be on the cash method of accounting for purposes of deducting business expenses and interest owed to cash basis shareholders who own at least 2% of the corporate stock. Therefore expenses accruing to such stockholders are deductible only when paid to the stockholders.

EXAMPLE

In 1987, a calendar-year S corporation accrues $5,000 of salary to an employee-stockholder. It does not pay the salary until February 1987. In 1987, the $5,000 is deductible by the corporation and reported by the employee-stockholder as income.

An S corporation recognizes taxable gain if it distributes to a stockholder corporate property which has appreciated in value, except in the case of a complete liquidation of the corporation. Gain is also not recog-

nized on distribution of stock in a reorganization to the extent that the receipt of stock is tax free under Section 354, 355, or 356.

QUALIFYING TESTS FOR AN S ELECTION

¶ **10.8** The election may be made for a domestic corporation which is not a member of an affiliated group and which has—

1. No more than 35 stockholders, all of whom must agree to the election. For purposes of the stockholder test, a husband and wife (and their estates) are counted as one shareholder, regardless of how they hold the stock. However, when consenting to S corporation status, each spouse must separately consent. When spouses divorce, each spouse is treated as a separate stockholder, even though they own stock jointly.

For purposes of the stockholder test, each beneficiary of a voting trust is counted as a stockholder.

Each minor owning stock held by a custodian is counted. The minor, his legal or natural guardian, or custodian who is also his guardian must consent to the election. The same rule applies to incompetents.

2. Stockholders who are either U.S. citizens or residents, estates, or certain trusts. You may not make the election if a nonapproved trust, partnership, or another corporation owns stock in your company. The following trusts may be electing shareholders: (1) A trust all of which is treated for tax purposes as owned by an individual who is a U.S. citizen or resident. The trust may continue as a shareholder for a 60-day period following the death of the owner; if the entire corpus is includible in the deemed owner's gross estate, the trust may continue as a shareholder for a two-year period following the date of death. (2) A voting trust. (3) A testamentary trust which receives the stock under the terms of a will, but only for a 60-day period beginning on the day on which such stock is transferred to it. The creation of a bankruptcy estate by filing a petition for bankruptcy does not result in a non-qualified stockholding. (4) A qualified Subchapter S trust. A qualified trust is one in which all of the income is distributed currently to a beneficiary who is a U.S. citizen or resident and who has elected to have the trust qualify. There may be only one income beneficiary at any one time and a new election must be made for each successive income interest. Where the trust terminates during the life of the income beneficiary, all the assets must be distributed to that beneficiary. Trust shares that are treated as separate trusts by the tax law also qualify.

3. One class of stock. You may not make the election if your company has common and preferred stock. Differences in voting rights will not cause one class of stock to be treated as two classes. Only outstanding stock is counted in determining whether there is one class of stock. Treasury stock or unissued preferred stock of a different class does not disqualify the election.

The issuance of options and warrants to acquire its stock and convertible debentures does not disqualify the election.

Straight debt instruments are not treated as a second class of stock. Shareholder loans are treated as straight debt provided: (1) the loan is a written unconditional promise by the corporation to pay a specified sum on demand or on a set date; (2) the interest rate and payment date are not contingent on corporate profits or on the discretion of the corporation; and (3) the debt is not convertible into stock.

A corporation with an inactive subsidiary may make the election as long as the subsidiary has no gross income.

FILING AN S ELECTION

¶ **10.9** The corporation makes an election by filing Form 2553 with the Internal Revenue officer designated in the instructions to the form. All shareholders must sign written consents to the election in the space provided on Form 2553 or in an attached statement. If the election is made after the start of the first year for which the election is to be effective, consents must be filed by all shareholders who held interests *before* the date of election, even if they have sold their interests.

An election may be filed during the entire taxable year before the year in which the election is to be effective and before the 16th day of the third month of the current taxable year. An election which is ineffective because of late filing is automatically effective in the following year. Even if the election is filed on time within the first two months and 15 days of the current year, the election will not take effect until the following year unless all those with shareholders interests before the filing date consent to the election.

EXAMPLES

1. A calendar year corporation wants to elect S corporation status for 1988. It may file an election of Form 2553 any time during 1987 upon or before March 15, 1988.

If Form 2553 were filed after March 15, 1988, the election would take effect in 1989.

2. A Form 2553 filed on March 10, 1988 does not contain the written consent of a shareholder who sold his interest in February 1988. The election will not take effect until 1989.

Once a valid election is made, it is effective for all following tax years unless revoked or terminated under the rules of ¶ 10.10.

A valid election may not be filed before a corporation is formally incorporated. The first day of a tax year of a new corporation does not begin until one of these events occurs: It has shareholders, acquires assets, or begins doing business. However, if, under state law, corporate existence begins with filing articles of incorporation, even though the corporation has no assets and does not begin doing business until a later date, the first day of the tax year begins on the date of such filing.

> *Newly organized corporation.* Usually, the first tax year of a newly organized corporation will be for a period less than 12 months. An election may be made for this short tax year as long as it is made before the 16th day of the third months of the corporation's first taxable year. If the first taxable year of a new corporation is for a period of less than two and a half months, the election may be made for that year within two and a half months from the beginning of the taxable year. The first taxable year begins when the corporation has shareholders, acquires assets, or begins doing business, whichever occurs first.

New stockholders. A new shareholder does not have to file any consent nor can he terminate the election. However, a majority stockholder may revoke the election; see ¶ 10.10.

Built-in-gains tax. If an S election is made by a C corporation, that is, one already in existence and subject to regular corporation tax, the S corporation may have to pay tax on the sale of appreciated property held by the company before the election. The gain must be reported by the S corporation if the property is sold or distributed within 10 years of the date of the S election. The new rule applies to elections made after December 31, 1986, but not to S elections made before or on that date. Small qualifying S corporations may be able to avoid this built-in gains tax if more than 50% of the stock is owned by 10 or less individuals, estates or certain trusts, and the value of the corporation does not exceed $10 million. For further details, *see* Form 1120S and Publication 589.

Corporations making S elections before 1987 are subject to the capital gains tax discussed at ¶ 10.14.

REVOCATION OR TERMINATION OF AN S ELECTION

¶ 10.10 An election may be revoked or may automatically terminate because the corporation no longer qualifies as an S corporation.

Revocation. Shareholders owning a majority of stock may agree to revoke the election by filing a statement of revocation. They may specify the future effective date of the revocation. If they do not fix a date, the revocation is effective on the first day of the taxable year in which the revocation is filed if filed on or before the 15th day of the third month of that year; if filed later in the year, the effective date is the first day of the following taxable year.

Termination. An election terminates when a company no longer qualifies under the rules of ¶ 10.8. A termination is effective as of the date the corporation no longer qualifies as an S corporation. The last day of the S

corporation's short taxable year is the day before termination is effective; the day that termination is effective starts a short taxable year as a C corporation. The corporation's items of income and loss are allocated to the two short taxable years on a daily basis unless a unanimous election to have items assigned to the two short years under normal accounting rules is made by all of the persons who are shareholders in the corporation at any time during the S short taxable year and all persons who are shareholders on the first day of the C short year. For purposes of computing the corporate tax, the taxable income for the C short year must be annualized. This is true regardless of the method of allocation used for allocating income and loss items.

The pro rata allocation requirement does not apply if there is a sale or exchange of 50% or more of stock during the year of termination.

> It is important to determine tax consequences under the daily allocation method and the normal accounting method. Choose the method providing the best overall tax consequences for the shareholders reporting their shares for the first short year and for the corporation reporting as a C corporation for the second short year. Different tax results will occur especially if substantial loss items were incurred in one short year and income items in the other short year. The daily allocation basis will average these between the two years. The actual allocation basis will place the items in the period they were incurred.

Election following termination. When the election is revoked or terminated, you may not make another election until the fifth year following the year in which the election was revoked or terminated, unless the IRS gives its consent. The five-year rule does not apply to terminations and revocations under prior law. An exception to the five-year rule also applies to inadvertent termination (see below). Based on prior law (pre-1983 Subchapter S rules), the IRS will not consent to an election before the end of the five-year period if the termination is considered reasonably within the control of the corporation or controlling shareholders.

Inadvertent termination. If the IRS decides that the termination was inadvertent and steps are taken by the corporation to reestablish its qualified status within a reasonable time after discovering the disqualifying event, then the corporation is treated as an S corporation. The corporation and each shareholder must agree to adjustments required by the IRS.

TAX ON FRINGE BENEFITS RECEIVED BY STOCKHOLDERS

¶ 10.11 For S elections made after September 28, 1982, owners of more than 2% of the stock will realize taxable income for receiving fringe benefit coverage such as in employee group insurance and accident and health plans. This tax rule does not apply until 1988 to shareholders of an S corporation existing as of September 28, 1982, provided the corporation does not have passive income of more than 20% of gross receipts or does not have a change of majority stockholders after 1982.

PASSIVE INVESTMENT INCOME

¶ 10.12 The receipt of passive investment income does not disqualify an S election as long as the corporation does not have accumulated earnings from taxable years prior to the election. Passive investment income includes dividends, interest, rents, royalties, and securities sale gains.

If a corporation does have accumulated earnings and passive investment income exceeding 25% of gross receipts, a portion of the excess passive income is subject to tax. A worksheet included in the instructions to Form 1120S is used to compute the tax. The tax does not apply if the corporation has been an S corporation since the date of incorporation.

The IRS has authority to waive this tax where the corporation proves that it had determined in good faith that it did not have accumulated earnings and profits at the close of the taxable year, and the earnings and profits were distributed within a reasonable period of time after the corporation determined that it did have accumulated earnings and profits.

Further, the election may be lost if for three consecutive years the company has prior accumulated earnings and passive investment income exceeding 25% of gross receipts.

FISCAL YEAR RESTRICTIONS

¶ **10.13** For tax years beginning after 1986, all S corporations must change their fiscal tax years to the tax year of the stockholders. As almost all individuals report on the calendar year, the law is an order to adopt calendar years. All S corporations are required to follow the new rules regardless of the year the S election was made.

If a business purpose is shown for a fiscal year, the Treasury will allow the fiscal year. Deferral of income for three months or less no longer justifies a fiscal year. Companies that have already obtained the Treasury permission for a fiscal year do not have to get permission again because of the law, unless that year was based on a deferral of income. Under an election, excess income generated by changes in years may be reported ratably over the first four tax years by the stockholders.

TAX ON CAPITAL GAINS

¶ **10.14** For corporations that made an S election before 1987, a special tax is imposed to prevent the use of the election for the pass-through of substantial capital gains. The tax applies if taxable income for the year exceeds $25,000 and the net capital gains exceed $25,000 and 50% of taxable income.

The tax does not apply to a corporation that has been an S corporation for the three preceding taxable years or to a new corporation that has been in existence for less than four years and has been an S corporation for that entire period. *See* Form 1120S instructions for details.

The tax does not apply if the S election was made after 1986. However, such corporations are subject to the built-in-gains tax discussed at ¶ 10.9.

AUDITS OF S CORPORATIONS AND SHAREHOLDERS

¶ **10.15** S corporations and shareholders are subject to audit rules similar to those for partnerships discussed in ¶ 10.5. These rules require the tax treatment of disputed items to be determined in a unified administrative proceeding at the corporate level rather than in separate proceedings with the individual shareholders. The IRS must give all shareholders notice of their right to participate in any corporate-level administrative proceeding.

Under an exception, corporate level proceedings do not apply to S corporations with five shareholders or less, all of whom are individuals or estates. Husbands and wives are considered one person under this rule. S corporations with five or fewer shareholders may elect to come within the unified audit procedure by attaching a statement to the first S corporation return; the election is binding for all later years.

TRUST AND ESTATE INCOME

HOW BENEFICIARIES REPORT ESTATE OR TRUST INCOME

¶ **10.16** Tax accounting for trust or estate income is complicated. As a beneficiary, you are not required to understand the rules governing the taxing of trusts and estates. That is the trustee's or executor's responsibility. After he or she has computed trust or estate income, the fiduciary should inform you of your share of taxable income and its source on Schedule K-1 of Form 1041. The fiduciary should also tell you whether the distribution is out of current income or accumulated income. If it is out of accumulated income, *see* ¶ 10.17.

Trust or estate income is treated as if you had received the income directly from the original source instead of from the estate or trust. This means capital gain remains capital gain, ordinary income is fully taxed, and tax-exempt income remains tax free. Dividends received from the trust are no longer allowed an exclusion. Tax preference items of a trust or estate are apportioned between the estate or trust and beneficiaries according to allocation of income (*see* ¶ 23.4).

Following these rules and the allocation of income provided by the fiduciary, you report trust or estate income as follows:

Dividend income. The dividends are added to your other dividend income.

EXAMPLE
According to the trustee, $400 of the trust income paid to you is from dividends received by the trust. You are single and have dividend income of $25 from your own investments. Total dividend income is $425.

Capital gains. Report these in Schedule D. Report short-term capital gain in the regular short-term section. Report long-term capital gains with your other long-term capital gains.

Tax-exempt income. This income is not taxable.

EXAMPLE
The trustee paid you $1,500 during the year; $700 was interest received from municipal bonds, $800 interest from bank deposits. Since municipal bond interest is tax free, the $700 is tax free in your hands.

Foreign income. Check with the trustee for how to report items from a foreign trust. New law changes not discussed in this book may affect the trust income reporting.

Depreciation and depletion. Income beneficiaries and the trustee share depreciation and depletion deductions in proportions provided by the trust agreement. If directions are omitted, the deduction is apportioned on the basis of trust income allocated to each.

Losses. A trust or estate takes a deduction for losses; not the beneficiaries. Unused capital loss carryovers, net operating loss carryovers, or deductions in excess of gross income in the final year of the trust or estate are passed on to the beneficiaries who receive the trust property.

Tax preference items. You report your share of tax preference items.

Employee benefit payments, see ¶ 7.7.

Reporting rule for revocable grantor trusts. A grantor who sets up a revocable trust or keeps certain powers over trust income or corpus must report all of the trust income, deductions, and credits. If a grantor is also a trustee, filing Form 1041 is not necessary. The grantor simply reports the trust income, deductions, and credits on Form 1040.

This reporting rule is optional for revocable trusts created before 1981. Grantors of such trusts who want to report trust income on their own returns without having to file Form 1041 must first file a final Form 1041 for the current tax year with a notation on the form alerting the IRS that in later years they will report trust income on their own returns.

Distributions of property. The trustee should give you the basis of distributed property. See ¶ 6.29 for basis rules.

Multiple trusts. If two or more trusts have the same grantor and substantially the same beneficiaries, the IRS may treat the trusts as one trust if tax avoidance is the principal purpose for setting them up.

DISTRIBUTIONS OF ACCUMULATED TRUST INCOME

¶ **10.17** Where you are the beneficiary of an accumulation trust, the trust accumulates income on which it pays tax. When the trust distributes income to you, the trustee tells you what part of the distribution is attributable to accumulations of prior income. Distributions of current income are reported according to the rules of ¶ 10.16.

Distributions of accumulated income are subject to tax, provided the accumulation exceeds the accounting income of the trust for the year. However, only that portion of the accumulation distribution that would have been included in the beneficiary's income had it been distributed when earned is currently taxed. Thus, tax-exempt interest is never taxed. Taxes imposed on the trust on an accumulation distribution are considered an additional distribution. Taxes imposed on the trust are the gross federal income taxes before credits.

Although a beneficiary pays a tax in the year of receiving the accumulation distribution, tax is computed as if the accumulated income were actually distributed in the years in which it was earned. The tax is the sum of: (1) A tax on taxable income exclusive of the accumulation distribution; (2) a tax, computed by a shortcut method, on the accumulation distribution; and (3) an interest charge in the case of a foreign trust.

In preparing your return, the tax on your regular taxable income is computed on Form 1040; the tax on the distribution is computed on Form 4970 and added to the tax on Form 1040.

Where a trust has already been subject to estate tax or the generation-skipping transfer tax, the partial tax on a distribution is reduced by the estate or generation-skipping tax attributable to the accumulated income. The reduction is limited by a special statutory formula for determining the pre-death portions. Consult Treasury regulations for more details. The reduction is only for estate tax from a decedent dying after 1979 or for generation-skipping transfer taxes after June 11, 1976.

Where the beneficiary receives an accumulation distribution from more than two trusts for the same year, tax for the distributions from the third trust is computed under the method described above, except that no credit is given for any taxes previously paid by the trust with respect to the accumulation distribution. A *de minimis* rule provides that accumulation distributions are not subject to the multiple trust rule unless the distribution equals or exceeds $1,000.

Income accumulated prior to the beneficiary's attaining the age of 21 and the years before a beneficiary was born are not subject to the throwback rule unless distributions are made under the multiple trust rule.

No refunds or credits are made to any beneficiary or trust, even though the taxes paid by the trust exceed the accumulation distributions.

If you receive a distribution of accumulated income from a trust, contact the trustee or an experienced tax practitioner for advice in computing your tax on the accumulation.

Sale of capital gain property by trust within two years of transfer. Capital gain is not subject to the throwback rules. However, if the trust sells property within two years of receiving it by gift or bargain sale, gain is taxed at the same rate that the grantor would have paid if the grantor sold the property. This rule for taxing gain does not apply if the grantor dies within the two-year period.

Trust for the benefit of a spouse. Where a spouse creates a trust for the benefit of the other spouse after October 9, 1969, income of the trust is taxed to the spouse who created the trust as income is earned.

There are special rules for foreign trusts. *See* Treasury regulations.

DEDUCTIONS FOR INCOME SUBJECT TO ESTATE TAX

¶ **10.18** If you receive income which was earned by, but not paid to, a decedent before death, you are said to have "income in respect of a decedent." You report the income, and if an estate has paid a federal estate tax on the income, you may deduct part of the estate tax allocated to the income. No deduction is allowed for state death taxes. Ask the executor of the estate for data in computing the deduction.

EXAMPLE
When your uncle died, he was owed a fee of $1,000. He also had not collected accrued bond interest of $500. You, as the sole heir, will collect both items and pay income tax on them. These items are called income in respect of a decedent. Assume that an estate tax of $390 was paid on the $1,500. You collect the $1,000, which you report on your income tax return. You may deduct $260, computed as follows:

$$\frac{\$1,000}{\$1,500} \times \$390, \text{ or } \$260$$

When you collect the $500, you will deduct the balance, or $130 ($390–$260).

The deduction is generally claimed as an itemized deduction and is *not* subject to the 2% AGI floor of chapter 19. However, if you receive long-term capital gain income, such as an installment payment on a sale transacted before decedent's death, the estate tax attributed to the capital gain item is not claimed as a miscellaneous deduction. The deduction is treated as if it were an expense of sale and thus reduces the amount of gain before the computation of the capital gain deduction. This rule applies to capital gain received because of a decedent dying after November 6, 1978.

Lump-sum distributions from qualified retirement plans. When a beneficiary receiving a lump-sum distribution because of an employee's death reports the distribution using the special averaging method, the distribution is subject to estate tax. However, beneficiaries of decedents dying after April 1, 1980, may reduce the taxable amount of the distribution by the deduction for estate taxes attributable to the distribution.

REPORTING FARM INCOME OR LOSS

WHO IS A FARMER?

¶ **10.19** The term "farmer" includes all individuals, partnerships, syndicates and corporations that cultivate, operate or manage a farm for profit or gain, either as owners or tenants. Thus, partners in a partnership which operates a farm are considered farmers.

The term "farm" includes stock, dairy, poultry, fruit and truck farms, plantations, ranches and all land used for farming operations. A fish farm where fish are specially fed and raised, and not just caught, is a farm. Animal breeding farms, such as mink, fox, and chinchilla farms, are also considered farms.

> *Gentleman farming.* To be treated as farmers, individuals must be engaged in farming for gain or profit. Farm losses of part-time or "gentlemen" farmers may be disallowed on the grounds that the farm is not operated to make a profit but is a hobby. The hobby rules explained at ¶5.9 apply in determining the existence of a profit motive in farming operations. Favorable evidence of an intention to make a profit are: You do not use your farm just for recreation. You have tried to cut losses by switching from unsuccessful products to other types of farming. Losses are decreasing. Losses were caused by unexpected events. You have a bookkeeping system. You consult experts. You devote personal attention to the farm.

Farm loss deductions may also be restricted by at risk rules and passive activity rules of chapter 11.

If your farm losses exceed your other income, *see* ¶5.17.

Important: A guide to reporting farm income and loss may be obtained at your local Internal Revenue office or from your County Farm Agent. It is called Farmer's Tax Guide (Publication No. 225).

FORMS FARMERS FILE

¶ **10.20** Use Schedule F to report income from a farm you operate as an individual. The profit or loss computed on Schedule F is then included in Form 1040. Schedule F is also used as a basis for figuring self-employment tax on Schedule SE, which must also be filed with Form 1040. Sales of farm equipment and dairy or breeding livestock are reported on Form 4797.

If you operate through a partnership, the details of your farm operation are shown on Schedule F and Form 1065. Your share of the partnership net income or loss is included in Form 1040.

Individual farmers on a calendar year basis (ending December 31) may file a 1987 declaration of estimated tax by January 15, 1988, if at least two-thirds of 1987 estimated gross income is from farming, or if at least two-thirds of 1986 total gross income was from farming. A final return is required by April 15, 1988. However, you may file your final return by March 1, 1988, instead of filing a 1987 declaration of estimated tax in January.

If you are on a fiscal year (any year not ending on December 31), ask your District Director for filing rules.

FARMERS' SOCIAL SECURITY

¶ **10.21** Farmers follow special rules for figuring their self-employment income and tax. If your gross income from farming is not more than $2,400, you may figure your self-employment income in either of two ways:

   You may reduce your self-employment income by your allowable deductions (as any other self-employed person would do), and pay the self-employment tax on the difference; or

   You may consider your next self-employment income from farming to be two-thirds of your gross farming income.

If your gross income from farming is more than $2,400 but your net self-employment income (figuring it in the usual manner by reducing gross income by the farm's expenses) is less than $1,600, you may take the net amount or $1,600 as self-employment income.

Self-employment tax on farm income is figured on Schedule SE. *See* ¶5.53.

Treasury regulations and IRS Publication 225 should also be consulted for the computation of self-employment income of share-farmers and landlords.

11

LOSS RESTRICTIONS: PASSIVE ACTIVITIES AND AT RISK LIMITS

¶ **11.1** The motivating force behind tax shelter investments was the chance to use substantial deductions generated by the investments to offset salary and other investment income such as dividends and interest. This tax-saving technique is no longer effective. Starting in 1987, you may not generally deduct from other income (such as salary, interest, dividends, annuity, and self-employment income) losses from tax shelters and from any business in which you do *not* materially participate. Such losses may offset only income from passive activities. Similarly, tax credits from passive activities are limited to the tax allocable to income from passive activities. Under a phase-in rule, losses and credits will be only partially disallowed in 1987 for those investors who acquired interests on or before October 22, 1986— the date the 1986 Tax Act was enacted.

Disallowed losses and credits are suspended and carried forward to the next taxable year, when they may offset passive income. Any remaining suspended loss may be deducted when you sell your interest. However, a suspended credit may not be claimed in the year you sell your interest. It remains in suspense until it may be used against tax liability allocable to future passive income. Thus the passive activity rules reverse in the government's favor the order of claiming deductions for tax shelter plans. They defer the deduction of losses until the passive activity produces income or is disposed of.

The passive loss restrictions apply to all passive investments (unless excepted by law), even to your rental of an apartment in a two-family house that you own and to a business in which you invest money but do not manage; for example, you invest in a business operated by your children.

If you are considered a real estate dealer, your income or loss from dealer holdings is not subject to passive activity rules. If you personally invest in real estate, you must distinguish between your holdings as a dealer which are outside passive activity limits, and your personal holdings which may be subject to passive loss restrictions.

Another tax provision, the at risk limits, prevents the deduction of losses that exceed actual cash investments in a venture.

Form 8582. You must file the new Form 8582 to compute deductible passive activity losses.

PASSIVE ACTIVITY

TWO CLASSES OF PASSIVE ACTIVITY

¶ **11.2** There are two classes or types of passive activity:

1. **Rental operations.** Your status is fixed by law. The ownership of rental property is treated as a passive activity, regardless of whether or not you participate in operating the property. Thus, rental losses are generally deductible only against passive income. However, by showing that you *do* manage rental real estate, you may be able to deduct up to $25,000 of your rental loss as explained at ¶11.4.

Rental activities, where payments are principally for the use of property, are presumed by law to be a passive activity. This passive loss restriction applies to rentals of apartments and commercial office space (whether long- or short-term), long-term rentals of office equipment, automobiles, and/or a vessel under a bare-boat charter or a plane under a dry lease (no pilot or captain and no fuel), and net-leased property. A property is under a net-lease if the deductions (other than rents and reimbursed amounts) are less than 15% of rental income or where the lessor is guaranteed a specific return or is guaranteed against loss of income. Rental activities, however, do not include short-term car rentals and rentals of hotel rooms or similar space to transients. Providing incidental services, such as a laundry room in an apartment building, is considered part of the rental activity.

Real estate *dealers* are generally not treated as engaging in a passive activity.

2. **Passive investor status in all other businesses.** Your status is fixed by fact, that is, your actual relationship to the business. If you do not "materially participate" in the business your share of losses from the business is tainted as a passive loss. As such, you may not deduct the loss from your other (non-passive) income.

Material participation generally requires involvement in daily business operations. Your services must be regular, continuous, and substantial. You must personally meet the material participation test whether you do business as a sole proprietor, in an S corporation, or partnership. Losses and credits passed through S corporations and partnerships are subject to the passive activity rules. Whether you materially participate in a business is determined each year. If you are a limited partner, you do not by law meet the material participation test unless Treasury regulations permit an exception.

Details of the test are at ¶ 11.5.

Closely held corporations and personal service corporations. The passive activity rules apply to personal service corporations. Thus, a personal service corporation may not offset passive losses and credits against either income from non-passive sources or portfolio income; *see* ¶ 11.7

Closely held corporations are subject to a less restrictive limitation: Passive losses and credits may offset active business income but not portfolio income. *See* ¶ 11.7.

Working oil and gas interests outside of passive activity restrictions. The passive activity rules do not apply to an investor who holds a working interest in an oil and gas property. This is true even for an investor who does not materially participate in the activity. A working interest is one burdened with the cost of developing and operating the property, such as a share in tort liability (for example, uninsured losses from a fire); some responsibility to share in additional costs; responsibility for authorizing expenses; receiving periodic reports about drilling, completion, and expected production; the possession of voting rights and rights to continue operations if the present operator steps out. If your liability is limited, you are not treated as owning a working interest. For example, you are a limited partner or a stockholder in an S corporation. Rights to overriding royalties or production payments, and contract rights to extract or share in oil and gas profits without liability for a share of production costs are not working interests.

Exception for certain low income housing investments. The rules barring passive activity losses do not apply to qualifying investments in low income housing, as discussed at ¶ 11.10.

See the Supplement and IRS Publication 925 for further details.

PARTIAL DEDUCTIONS FOR PRE-OCTOBER 23, 1986, INVESTMENTS

¶ **11.3** The full effect of the passive loss rule will not apply until 1991 for investments you held on October 22, 1986, the date the 1986 Tax Act was enacted.

During a five-year period, passive losses and credits from pre-October 23, 1986, interests are deductible at this rate:

In—	Rate is—
1987	65%
1988	40
1989	20
1990	10

EXAMPLES

1. In 1985, you invested as a limited partner in a syndicate holding rental property. In 1987, your loss from the syndicate is $6,000. Under the phase-out rule, you may deduct 65% of the loss or $3,900 from your 1987 salary and other (non-passive) income. The nondeductible 35% or $2,100, is carried forward and deductible in a later year in which there is net passive income or in the year you dispose of your interest in a taxable transaction (¶ 11.9).

2. Assume you invested in the syndicate in November 1986. In 1987, you may not deduct any part of the loss from your salary and other non-passive income because you made the investment after October 22, 1986. The loss may only be used to offset income from other passive activities. Further, you do not qualify for the $25,000 rental allowance (¶ 11.4), because as a limited partner you cannot meet the active participant test. The disallowed loss may be carried forward to 1988 (¶ 11.9).

After 1991, deductions or credits are allowable only if they meet the new passive loss rules.

To take advantage of the phase-in, your investment interests in passive activities must have been acquired on or before October 22, 1986. Interests acquired after that date are not eligible for the phase-in and are fully subject to the passive loss rule.

A contractual obligation to purchase an interest in a passive activity binding on October 22, 1986, may be treated as an acquisition of the interest in the activity. A binding contract qualifies even if your obligation to acquire an interest is subject to contingencies, provided the contingencies are beyond your control. Thus, if you signed on or before October 22, 1986, a subscription agreement to buy a limited partnership interest contingent upon the agreement of other purchasers to acquire interests in the limited partnership amounting to a particular total, then if the contingency is satisfied, you are eligible for the phase-in rule. On the other hand, a conditional obligation to purchase or one subject to contingencies within your control does not qualify.

Where, after October 22, 1986, you contribute additional capital to the activity, you still qualify in full for the phase-in to the extent that your percentage ownership interest does not change as a result of the contribution. However, if your ownership interest is increased after October 22, 1986, then that part of your interest attributable to the increase does not qualify for the phase-in.

EXAMPLES

1. After October 22, 1986, you increase your ownership interest in a partnership from 25% to 50%. Only the losses attributable to the 25% interest qualify for the phase-in relief. Phase-in relief applies only with respect to the percentage interest held by the taxpayer at all times after the date of enactment.

2. After October 22, 1986, you reduce your interest from 50% to 25%, and later purchase additional interests restoring your share to 50%. Only the 25% share held throughout qualifies for phase-in relief.

To qualify for the phase-in relief, the interest must be in an activity that has commenced by October 22, 1986. For example, a rental activity has commenced when the rental property has been placed in service in the activity. When the venture in which you own an interest liquidates or disposes of one activity and begins another after October 22, 1986, the new activity does not qualify. In the case of a house purchased for personal use but converted to rental use, the residence must be held out for rental by October 22, 1986.

Where the activity did not commence by October 22, 1986, phase-in treatment may apply if the venture has entered into a binding contract effective on or before August 16, 1986, to acquire the assets used to conduct the activity. Similarly, phase-in treatment applies to self-constructed business property of an entity (or direct owner), where construction of the property to be used in the activity commenced on or before August 16, 1986.

When you own both pre-October 23, 1986, and post-October 22, 1986, interests in passive activities, this order is followed in calculating the phase-in. Determine the amount that would be disallowed in the absence of the phase-in. Phase-in relief then applies to the lower of the total passive loss, or the passive loss taking into account only pre-October 23, 1986, interests.

EXAMPLE

You have $100 of passive loss relating to pre-October 23, 1986, interests and $60 of net passive income from post-October 22, 1986, interests, resulting in a total passive loss of $40. The phase-in treatment applies to the lesser of $100 and $40.

Carryover. Any passive loss that is disallowed for a taxable year during the phase-in period and carried forward is allowable in a later year only to the extent that there is net passive income in the later year (or there is a fully taxable disposition of the activity).

EXAMPLE

You have a passive loss of $100 in 1987, $65 of which is allowed under the phase-in, $35 is carried forward. The $35 is not allowed in a later year under the phase-in percentage applying for that year. If you have a passive loss of $35 in 1988, including the amount carried over from 1987, then no relief under the phase-in is provided. If you have a passive loss of $50 in 1988 ($35 from 1987 and $15 from 1988, all attributable to pre-October 23, 1986, interests) then $6 of losses (40% of the $15 loss arising in 1988) is allowed against active income under the phase-in rule. The $35 loss carryover from 1987 is disallowed in 1988 and is carried forward (along with the disallowed $9 from 1988) and allowed in any later year in which you have net passive income.

The phase-in percentage applies to the passive loss net of any part of the loss that may be allowed under the $25,000 allowance rule for rental activity, *see* ¶11.4.

REAL ESTATE RENTALS GET LIMITED LOSS ALLOWANCE

¶ 11.4 You may take advantage of a limited break if you perform some management role in a real estate rental. You may deduct up to $25,000 of your loss to offset income from any source if your adjusted gross income is $100,000 or less. The allowance is phased out for adjusted gross incomes between $100,000 and $150,000 as discussed below. The allowance applies only to real estate rentals, not rentals of equipment or other personal property.

EXAMPLE
You rent out an apartment in a two-family house which you own and live in. If your expenses exceed your rental income, and your 1987 adjusted gross income is under $100,000, you may deduct up to $25,000 of the loss.

> A trust may not qualify for the $25,000 allowance. Thus you cannot circumvent the $25,000 ceiling or multiply the number of $25,000 allowances, simply by transferring various rental real properties to one or more trusts. However, an estate may qualify for the allowance if the decedent actively participated in the operation. The estate is treated as an active participant for two years following the death of the decedent.

The limited allowance is phased out when your adjusted gross income is over $100,000. For every dollar of income over $100,000, the loss allowance is reduced by 50¢. When your income reaches $150,000, there is no allowance.

If AGI is—	Loss Allowance is—
Up to $100,000	$25,000
110,000	20,000
120,000	15,000
130,000	10,000
140,000	5,000
150,000 or more	–0–

Married filing separately. If you file separately but at any time during the taxable year live with your spouse, no allowance at all may be claimed. If you are married but live apart from your spouse for the entire year and file a separate return, the $25,000 allowance, and the adjusted gross income phase-out range is reduced by 50%. Thus, the maximum allowance on your separate return is $12,500 and this amount is phased out by 50% of AGI over $50,000. Therefore, if your AGI exceeds $75,000, no allowance is allowed.

Qualifying for the allowance. You must meet an *active-participation test.* Having an agent manage your property does not prevent you from meeting the test. You may meet the test by showing that you or your spouse participate in decisions, such as selecting tenants, setting rental terms, and reviewing expenses. You must also have at least a 10% interest in the property. By law, limited partners are not considered active participants and thus do not qualify for the allowance.

In the case of an estate of a deceased taxpayer who owned an interest in a rental real estate activity in which he actively participated, the estate is deemed to actively participate for the two years following the death of the taxpayer. Trusts do not qualify for the allowance.

Figuring the $25,000 allowance. First match income and loss from all of your rental real estate activities in which you actively participate. A net loss from these activities is then applied to net passive income (if any) from other activities to determine the $25,000 allowance. Mortgage interest on a principal residence or second residence is not subject to the passive loss rule when you rent out the residence.

EXAMPLE
You have $25,000 of losses from a rental activity in which you actively participate. You also actively participate in another real estate

rental activity, from which you had a $25,000 gain. There is no net loss from rental estate activities in which you actively participate and no $25,000 allowance is permitted.

The allowance may not be used against carryover losses from prior taxable years when you were not an active participant.

Adjusted gross income, for purposes of the phase-out is figured without considering IRA contributions and taxable social security benefits.

Real estate allowance for tax credits. A *deduction equivalent* of up to $25,000 may allow a credit that otherwise would be disallowed. You must meet the active participation test in the year the credit arose. The $25,000 allowance is generally subject to the regular AGI phase-out rule. In the case of the low-income housing and rehabilitation credits (¶9.9), however, you need not meet the active participant test. Further, the phase-out for the $25,000 allowance starts at AGI of $200,000; thus, while the deduction equivalent is completely disallowed when AGI reaches $250,000. In the case of the low-income housing credit, the increase in the phase-out range and waiver of the active participation rule apply only to property placed in service before 1990, and during the original credit compliance period for the property, except if the property is placed in service before 1991 and 10% or more of the total project costs are incurred before 1989.

The *deduction equivalent* of a credit is the amount which, if allowed as a deduction, would reduce your tax by an amount equal to the credit. For example, a tax credit of $1,000 for a taxpayer in the 35% bracket equals a deduction of $2,857 and would come within the $25,000 allowance provided you actively participated. In the 35% bracket, the equivalent of a $25,000 deduction is a tax credit of $8,750 ($25,000 × 35%). In the 28% bracket, it is $7,000. Thus, if you have a rehabilitation credit of $8,000 and you are in the 28% bracket, the $25,000 allowance may allow you to claim $7,000 of the credit, while $1,000 of the credit would be held in suspense.

If in one year you have both losses and a credit, the $25,000 allowance applies to both the losses and credit.

The allowance and net operating losses. If losses are allowed by the $25,000 allowance but your non-passive income and other income are less than the loss, the balance of the loss may be treated as a net operating loss and may be carried back and forward, *see* ¶5.17.

A firm that has both rental and nonrental operations must treat each activity separately for purposes of the passive activity rule.

EXAMPLE
A partnership operates a travel agency that has offices on two floors on an eight-story building. The partnership owns the building and rents out the other six floors. The partnership is treated as engaged in two separate activities. Income, deductions, and credits allocated to the partners from the travel agency activity are subject to the material participation test (¶11.5). Income, deductions, and credits allocated to the rental activity are subject to the passive activity rules. Limited partners may not claim the $25,000 allowance.

MATERIAL PARTICIPATION TEST FOR BUSINESSES OTHER THAN RENTAL REAL ESTATE

¶ 11.5 By meeting the material participation test, you avoid the passive activity loss limitations. You must be regularly involved in daily business operations. By law, limited partners do not qualify as material participants.

In determining material participation, congressional committee reports suggest these tests:

1. **Is the activity your principal business?** For example, if your main business is farming, you are more likely to materially participate in a farm than an executive who invests in a farm venture. By law, a farmer who materially participates in a farm and retires retains that status after retirement, as does the spouse.
2. **Do you live near the activity?** You are likely to be actively involved in a business close to your home.
3. **What is your knowledge and experience in the business?** A full-time manager of a business including several business activities may be considered to be materially participating in those activities although he is involved in management rather than operations. You are likely to be materially participating in an activity, if you do everything

...e to conduct the activity, even though the actual ...be done to conduct the activity is low in compari-...ies.

...d continuous decision making may be considered ...

Crop rotation, selection, and pricing;

The incursion of embryo transplant or breeding expenses;

The purchase, sale, and leasing of capital items, such as cropland, animals, machinery, and equipment;

Breeding and mating decisions; and

The selection of herd or crop managers who then act for you, rather than as paid advisors directing your decisions.

Providing professional services, such as accounting or legal services is not generally considered material participation.

Research and experimentation deductions. If you have an interest in a venture involving research and experimentation, and you do not materially participate in the activity, losses (including the research and experimentation expenditures) are subject to the passive loss rules.

TAX CREDITS OF PASSIVE ACTIVITIES LIMITED

¶ 11.6 You may not claim a tax credit from a passive activity unless you report and pay taxes on income from a passive activity. Further, the tax allocated to that income must be at least as much as the credit. If the tax credit exceeds your tax liability on income allocable to passive activities, the excess credit is not allowed.

EXAMPLE

You have a $1,000 credit from a passive activity. You do not report income from any passive activity. You may not deduct the credit because no part of your tax is attributed to passive activity income. The credit is suspended until you have income from a passive activity and you incur tax on that income. All or part of the credit may then be claimed to offset the tax. If you dispose of your interest before using a suspended credit, the credit may no longer be claimed.

The real estate allowance for a credit is discussed at ¶11.4.

Suspended credits are not allowed when property is disposed of. The credits may be used only when passive income is earned.

Basis adjustment for suspended credits. If the basis of property was reduced when tax credits were claimed, you may elect to add back a suspended credit to the basis when the property is disposed of.

EXAMPLE

Jones places in service rehabilitation credit property and claims an allowable credit of $50, which also reduces basis by $50. However, under the passive loss rule, he is prevented from claiming the credit. In a later year, he disposes of his entire interest in the activity, including the property whose basis was reduced. He may elect to increase basis of the property by the amount of the original basis adjustment.

If the property is disposed of in a transaction that, under the passive loss rule, is not treated as a fully taxable disposition, then no basis adjustment is allowed.

PORTFOLIO INCOME OF A PASSIVE ACTIVITY IS NOT PASSIVE INCOME

¶ 11.7 Portfolio income such as interest, dividends, royalty, or annuity income earned on funds set aside for future use in the activity is not treated as passive income from the activity and must be accounted for separately. Gain or loss from sales or exchanges of portfolio assets (including property held for investment) is treated as portfolio gain or loss. Portfolio income is reduced by the deductible expenses (other than interest) that are directly allocable to such income. Properly allocable interest expense also reduces portfolio income. Thus, such deductions are not treated as attributable to a passive activity. Allocation of interest to portfolio income may be made on the basis of assets or traced to a particular transaction.

Closely held or personal service corporations. To prevent avoidance of the passive activity rules through use of corporations, the law imposes restrictions on income and loss offsets in closely held C corporations and personal service corporations. A personal service corporation may not offset passive losses against either active income or portfolio income. A closely held C corporation that is not a personal service corporation may offset passive losses against net active income, but not against portfolio income. These limits do not apply if stockholders holding more than a 50% interest materially participate in the activity; the losses are not considered passive. Alternatively, a closely held C corporation may avoid the loss limits, if during the prior year (1) at least one full-time employee actually managed the activity, (2) at least three non-owner employees worked full-time in the activity, and (3) business deductions exceeded 15% of gross income from the activity.

EXAMPLE

A closely held corporation has $300,000 of passive losses from a rental operation, $250,000 of active business income, and $50,000 of portfolio income. Passive losses of $300,000 eliminate the active business income of $250,000. The remaining $50,000 of passive losses may not be used to eliminate portfolio income.

If a corporation stops being closely held, its passive losses and credits from prior years are not allowable against portfolio income, but continue to be allowable only against passive income and net active income.

A closely held C corporation is a corporation in which more than 50% in value of whose stock is owned by five or fewer persons during the last half of the tax year.

A personal service corporation is a corporation the principal activity of which is the performance of personal services by employee-owners. An employee-owner is any employee who on any day in the tax year owns any stock in the corporation. If an individual owns any stock in a corporation which in turn owns stock in another corporation, the individual is deemed to own a proportionate part of the stock in the other corporation. Further, more than 10% of its stock by value must be owned by owner-employees.

INTEREST EXPENSES AND OTHER DEDUCTIONS OF PASSIVE ACTIVITIES

¶ 11.8 Interest deductions attributable to passive activities are subject to the passive loss rule but not to the investment interest limitations. For example, in 1987, if you have net passive loss of $100, $40 of which is of interest expense, the entire $100 is subject to limitation under the passive loss rule. No portion of the loss is subject to limitation under the investment interest limitation. Similarly, income and loss from passive activities generally are not treated as investment income or loss in calculating the amount of the investment interest limitation.

However, interest on a vacation home elected as a qualified second residence is not treated as passive activity interest and is deductible as residential interest, see ¶15.11 and ¶29.17. The passive loss rule applies to all other deductions that are from passive activities, including deductions for state and local property taxes incurred with respect to passive activities whether or not such deductions are claimed above-the-line or as itemized deductions.

SUSPENDED LOSSES ALLOWED ON DISPOSITION OF YOUR INTEREST

¶ 11.9 Losses and credits that may not be claimed in 1987 because of the passive active limitations are suspended and carried forward to 1988 and later years. The carryover lasts indefinitely, until you have passive income against which to claim the losses and credits. No carryback is allowed.

Worthlessness of a security in a passive activity is treated as a disposition.

A disposition of your entire interest will allow you to claim suspended deductions from the activity. However, the fact that the nature of an activity changes in the course of its development is not a disposition.

On a disposition, the deduction of the loss is taken in this order:

1. Income of the passive activity disposed of
2. Income of other passive activities
3. Other income.

Gifts. When a passive activity interest is given away, the donee's basis in the property is increased by the suspended loss if the property is sold at a gain. If a loss is realized by the donee on a sale of the interest, the donee's basis may not exceed fair market value of the gift at time of the gift.

Death. On the death of an investor in a passive interest, suspended losses are deductible on the decedent's final return to the extent gains would have been realized on a sale of the interest.

> Suspended losses are allowed in full when you sell your entire interest in property or transfer it in a taxable exchange. The suspended losses are not allowed in tax-free exchanges and in sham transactions involving a repurchase option. A sale to a related party may not be treated as a disposition. This rule applies only to suspended losses and not to credits. If you have credits that were barred under the passive activity rules, they may be claimed only in future years when you have tax liability attributable to passive income. However, in the year you dispose of your interest, a special election may be available to decrease your gain by the amount of your suspended credit.

EXAMPLE
Brown dies owning a limited partnership interest in a building. The basis of the interest is $30,000; its fair market value is $60,000. Suspended losses amount to $45,000. On Brown's final return, $15,000 of the loss may be deducted—that is, the suspended loss of $45,000 less gain of $30,000. If the suspended loss was $30,000 or less, there would be no deduction.

Installment sales. If the passive activity interest is sold at a profit on the installment basis, the release of suspended losses in a year is based on a percentage of the gain reported in the year over the total gain realized on the sale.

Abandonment of property will allow a deduction of suspended passive loss.

Basis election for suspended credits. If you qualify for an investment credit (under transition rules) or a rehabilitation credit, you are required to reduce the basis of the property even if you are unable to claim the credit because of the passive activity rules. If this occurs and you later dispose of your entire interest in the passive activity, including the property whose basis was reduced, your gain will be increased by virtue of the basis reduction although you never benefited from the credit. To prevent this, you may reduce the taxable gain by electing to increase the pre-transfer basis of the property by the amount of the unused credit. This election is allowed only if you make a fully taxable disposition of your interest.

EXAMPLE
Brown places in service rehabilitated credit property qualifying for a $50 credit, but the credit is not allowed under the passive loss rules. However, basis is still reduced by $50. In a later year, Brown makes a taxable disposition of his entire interest in the activity and in the rehabilitation property. Assuming that no part of the suspended $50 credit has been used, Brown may elect to increase his basis in the property by the unused $50 credit.

LOW INCOME HOUSING EXEMPTION

¶ **11.10** A transitional rule applies to qualified investors in certain qualified low-income housing projects. Losses during a fixed period are not treated as passive activity losses. The period begins with the tax year in which you made an initial investment in the qualified low-income housing project and ending with whichever of the following is the earliest: (1) the sixth tax year after the tax year in which you made your initial investment, (2)the first tax year after the tax year in which you are obligated to make your last investment, or (3) the tax year preceding the first tax year for which such project ceases to be a qualified low-income housing project.

A qualified low income housing project is generally a project constructed or acquired under a binding written contract entered into on or before August 16, 1986, and placed in service before January 1, 1989.

A qualified investment had to be made after 1983, and if the project was placed in service on or before August 16, 1986, the investor must have held an interest in the project or had a binding contract to acquire an interest on August 16, 1986. If the project was placed in service after August 16, 1986, the investor must have made the initial investment after 1983 and held an interest in the project (or had a binding contract) on December 31, 1986.

AT RISK RULES

AT RISK LIMITS

¶ **11.11** Even before you apply the passive loss rules explained beginning in ¶11.1, your loss deductions are subject to at risk limits. The at risk rules prevent investors from claiming losses in excess of their actual tax investment, by barring them from including nonrecourse liabilities as part of the tax basis for their interest. Before 1987, all ventures except real estate were subject to the at risk limits. Under the new law, real estate placed in service after 1986 is technically subject to at risk rules as well, but most real estate nonrecourse financing can qualify for an exception. See ¶11.12.

EXAMPLE
You invest cash of $1,000 in a venture and sign a nonrecourse note for $8,000. In 1987, your share of the venture's loss is $1,200. The at risk rules limit your deduction to $1,000, the amount of your cash investment; as you are not personally liable on the note, the amount of the liability is not included as part of your basis for loss purposes.

If you have amounts that are not at risk, you must file Form 6198. A separate form must be filed for each activity. Further, if you have an interest in a partnership or S corporation that has more than one investment in any of the following activities, check the instructions to Form 6198 to see whether you must file a separate Form 6198 for each investment:
1. Holding, producing, or distributing motion picture films or video tapes;
2. Leasing business equipment subject to depreciation recapture;
3. Exploring for, or exploiting, geothermal deposits (for wells commenced on or after October 1, 1978) and;
4. Farming. For this purpose, farming is defined as the cultivation of land, raising or harvesting of any agricultural or horticultural commodity including raising, shearing, breeding, caring for or management of animals. Forestry and timber activities are not included, but orchards bearing fruits and nuts are within the definition of farming. Certain activities carried on within the physical boundaries of the farm may not necessarily be treated as farming.

The IRS also has authority to apply the at risk rules to business or income-producing activities which have tax shelter characteristics.

Exempted from the at risk rules are C corporations which meet active business tests and are not in the equipment leasing business or any business involving master sound recording, films, video tapes, or other artistic, literary, or musical property. The active business tests are not discussed in this book.

The at risk limitation applies only to tax losses produced by expense deductions which are not disallowed by reason of another provision of the law. For example, if a prepaid interest expense is deferred under the prepaid interest limitation (¶15.4), the interest will not be included in the loss subject to the risk limitation. When the interest accrues and becomes deductible, the expense may be considered within the at risk provision. Similarly, if a deduction is deferred because of farming syndicate rules, that deduction will enter into the computation of the tax loss subject to the risk limitation only when it becomes deductible under the farming syndicate rules.

WHAT IS AT RISK

¶ **11.12** The following amounts are considered at risk in determining your tax position in a business or investment:

Cash

Adjusted basis of property that you contribute

Borrowed funds for which you are personally liable to pay

Pledges of other property as security. If you pledge personally owned real estate to secure a nonrecourse debt and invest the proceeds in an at risk activity, the proceeds may be considered part of your risk investment. The proceeds included in basis are limited by the fair market value of the property used as collateral (determined as of the date the property is pledged as security) less any prior (or superior) claims to which the collateral is subject.

Personal liability alone does not assure that the borrowed funds are considered at risk. The lender must have no interest in the venture other than as creditor.

EXAMPLE

An investor pays a promoter of a book purchase plan $45,000 for a limited partnership interest. The promoter is the general partner. The investor pays $30,000 cash and gives a note for $15,000 on which he is personally liable. His amount at risk is $30,000; the $15,000 personal liability note is not counted because it is owed to the general partner.

Basis, limiting losses, is figured at the end of a taxable year.

EXAMPLES

1. On January 1, 1984, an investor contributes $5,000 cash to a farming venture. He also borrows $3,000 from a bank for which he is personally liable. By the end of 1984, he pays off $750 of the loan. The venture has no income or losses in 1984. The investor's at risk basis as of December 31, 1984, is $7,250, determined as follows:

Contributions	$5,000	
Recourse financing	3,000	$8,000
Less: Partial loan repayment		750
Amount at risk as of 12/31/84		$7,250

2. Same as example (1) but on February 1, 1985, he borrows $10,000 on a nonrecourse basis. He pays off $1,000 on the personal liability loan and $500 on the nonrecourse loan. The venture earns $3,000 and distributes $2,000 to him. The at risk basis as of December 31, 1985 is $7,250, determined as follows:

Amount at risk as of 1/1/85		$7,250
Plus: Income		3,000
		$10,250
Less: Repayment of personal liability loan	$1,000	
Distribution	2,000	3,000
Amount at risk as of 12/31/85		$7,250

Payment on the nonrecourse loan with funds or other nonrecourse loans from only the activity does not affect the amount at risk.

3. Same as example (2) but on March 1, 1986, the investor contributes $2,500 and pays off the personal liability loan. The venture has losses of $10,500 for 1986. As of December 31, 1986, the investor's amount at risk is $8,500, determined as follows:

Amount at risk as of 1/1/86		$7,250
Plus: Contribution		2,500
		9,750
Less: Payment of personal liability loan		1,250
Amount at risk as of 12/31/86		$8,500

The investor's loss deduction is limited to the amount at risk of $8,500. The $2,000 disallowed loss is carried over to 1987.

The above adjustments of basis are only for at risk purposes. Basis for depreciation and computing gain or loss on a sale is controlled by the adjusted basis rules at ¶6.32.

Activities begun before 1976. A special rule determines the amount at risk as of the first day of the first tax year after 1975. Again, you start with the amounts considered at risk. Losses incurred and deducted in taxable years before 1976 first reduce the basis allocated to amounts considered

not at risk, such as nonrecourse loans. If the losses exceed the amount not at risk, the excess reduces the at risk investment. Distributions reduce at risk amounts. If records are insufficient to establish the amount at risk, the amount at risk is your basis in the activity reduced (but not below zero) by your share of nonrecourse or other similar financing or loans from interested persons.

If a loss is partly disallowed, deductible items are claimed in the following order:

1. All capital losses
2. Section 1231 losses
3. Losses from deductions other than tax preference items (such as taxes and interest)
4. All tax preference items

Special at risk rule for real estate financing. For real property placed in service after 1986, you may treat nonrecourse financing from unrelated commercial lenders as amounts at risk if the financing is secured by the real estate. Third party nonrecourse debt from a related lender, other than the seller or a promoter, may also escape at-risk rules providing the terms of the loan are commercially reasonable and on substantially the same terms as loans involving unrelated persons.

If you acquired an interest after 1986 in a partnership or S corporation, the above at risk rules apply to your share of real estate losses regardless of when the partnership or S corporation placed the property in service.

AMOUNTS NOT AT RISK

¶ **11.13** The following may not be treated as part of basis for at risk purposes in determining your tax position in a business or investment:

Liabilities for which you have no personal liability, except in the case of certain real estate financing, *see* ¶11.12.

Liabilities for which you have personal liability, but the lender also has a capital or profit-sharing interest in the venture.

EXAMPLE

An investor purchases cattle from a rancher for $10,000 cash and a $30,000 note payable to the rancher. The investor is personally liable on the note. In a separate agreement, the rancher agrees to care for the cattle for 6% of the investor's net profits from the cattle activity. The investor is considered at risk to $10,000; he may not increase the amount at risk by the $30,000 borrowed from the rancher.

Recourse liabilities convertible to a nonrecourse basis.

EXAMPLE

A tax shelter promoter offered an equipment leasing deal which required $25,000 cash and an investor's recourse note of $250,000 subject to 10% annual interest. The equipment had a seven-year useful life (under pre-1981 law). In the first seven years, the note was payable in annual installments of $25,000. Payments were first applied to unpaid interest. Principal would be reduced if certain excess rentals were made. At the end of seven years, the investor could extend the note for another term or convert the balance of the note to nonrecourse liability by paying $10,000. The promoter claimed the investor was at risk for the full purchase price so that he could deduct depreciation based on a $275,000 investment. The IRS disagreed, ruling that the investor's basis is only $35,000 ($25,000 cash plus $10,000 to be paid after seven years). The liability of $250,000 may not be considered part of basis, although the note on its face entailed personal liability.

The way the plan was structured, annual payments covered only interest, and at the end of seven years, the investor could avoid personal liability on the balance by paying $10,000. The seven-year term over which the investor was personally liable was arranged solely for the depreciation deduction and served no business purpose.

Money borrowed from a relative listed at ¶33.11, who has an interest in the venture, other than as a creditor, or from a partnership in which you own more than a 10% interest.

Funds borrowed from a person whose recourse is either your interest in the activity or property used in the activity.

Amounts for which your economic loss is limited by nonrecourse financing guarantee, stop-loss agreement, or other similar arrangement.

Investments protected by insurance or loss reimbursement agreement between you and another person. If you are personally liable on a mortgage but you separately obtain insurance to compensate you for any mortgage payments, you are at risk only to the extent of the uninsured portion of the personal liability. You may, however, include as at risk any amount of premium paid from your personal assets. Taking out casualty insurance or insurance protecting you against tort liability is not considered within the at risk provisions, and such insurance does not affect your investment basis.

Potential cash call. The IRS and Tax Court held that a limited partner was not at risk with respect to a partnership note where under the terms of the partnership agreement, he could be required to make additional capital contributions if the general partners did not pay off the note at maturity. The possibility of such a potential cash call was too uncertain; the partnership might earn profits to pay off the note and even if there were losses, the general partners might not demand additional contributions from the limited partners.

EXAMPLES

1. Some commercial feedlots in livestock feeding operations may reimburse investors against any loss sustained on sales of the livestock above a stated dollar amount per head. Under such "stop loss" orders, an investor is at risk only to the extent of the portion of his capital against which he is not entitled to reimbursement. Where a limited partnership agrees with a limited partner that, at the partner's election, his partnership interest will be bought at a stated minimum dollar amount (usually less than the investor's original capital contribution), the partner is considered at risk only to the extent of his investment exceeding the guaranteed repurchase price.

2. A promoter of TV films sold half-hour programs in a TV series to individual investors. Each investor gave a cash down payment and a note for which he was personally liable for the balance. Each investor's note, which was identical in face amount, terms and maturity date, was payable out of the distribution proceeds from the film. Each investor also bought from the promoter the right to the unpaid balance on another investor's note. The promoter arranged the distribution of the films as a unit and was to apportion the sales proceeds equally among the investors. The IRS held that each investor is not at risk on the investment evidenced by the note. Upon maturity, each may receive a payment from another investor equal to the one that he owes.

3. A gold mine investment offered tax write-offs of four times the cash invested. For $10,000 cash, an investor buys from a foreign mining company a seven-year mineral claim lease to a gold reserve. Under the lease, he can develop and extract all of the gold in the reserve. At the same time, he agrees to spend $40,000 to develop the lease before the end of the year. To fund this commitment, the investor authorizes the promoter to sell an option for $30,000 to a third party who is to buy all the gold to be extracted. The $30,000 along with the $10,000 down payment is to be used to develop the reserve. The promoter advises the investor that he may claim a $40,000 deduction for certain development costs.

The IRS ruled that $30,000 is not deductible because the amount is not "risk capital." The investor gets $30,000 by selling an option that can be exercised only if gold is found. If no gold is found, he is under no obligation to the option holder. His risk position for the $30,000 is substantially the same as if he had borrowed from the option holder on a nonrecourse basis repayable only from his interest in the activity. The Tax Court struck down a similar plan on different grounds. Without

deciding the question of what was at risk, the court held that the option was only a right of first refusal. Thus, $30,000 was taxable income to the investor in the year of the arranged sale.

According to regulatons, a partner is treated as at risk to the extent that his basis in the partnership is increased by his share of partnership income. That partnership income is then used to reduce the partnership's nonrecourse indebtedness will have no effect on a partner's amount at risk. If the partnership makes actual distributions of the income in the taxable year, the amount distributed reduces the partner's amount at risk. A buy-sell agreement, effective at a partner's death or retirement, is not considered for at risk purposes.

AT RISK INVESTMENT IN SEVERAL ACTIVITIES

¶ 11.14 If you invest in several activities, each is generally treated separately when applying the at risk limitation on Form 6198. You may not aggregate basis, gains and losses from the activities for purposes of at risk limitations. Thus, income from one activity may not be offset by losses from another; the income from one must be reported while the losses from the other may be nondeductible because of at risk limitations.

The law allows partnerships and S corporations to treat as a single activity all Section 1245 properties (*see ¶5.35*) *which are leased or held for lease.*

The IRS also has authority to set guidelines for aggregating or separating the other activities listed at ¶11.11. See Form 6198 instructions.

The at risk rules are not applied at the corporate level to S corporations.

For pre-1987 tax years, losses are allocated between real estate and nonreal estate portions of a business and the losses attributable to real estate were not subject to at risk rules before 1987.

CARRYOVER OF DISALLOWED LOSSES

¶ 11.15 A loss disallowed in a current year by the at risk limitation may be carried over and deducted in the next taxable year, provided it does not fall within the at risk limits in that year. The loss is subject to an unlimited carryover period until there is an at risk basis to support the deduction. This may occur when additional contributions are made to the business or when the activity has income which has not been distributed.

Gain from the disposition of property used in an at risk activity is treated as income from the activity. In general, the reporting of gain will allow a deduction for losses disallowed in previous years to be claimed in the year of disposition.

RECAPTURE OF LOSSES WHERE AT RISK LESS THAN ZERO

¶ 11.16 To prevent manipulation of at risk basis after a loss is claimed, there is a special recapture rule. If the amount at risk is reduced to below zero because of a distribution or a change in the status of an indebtedness from recourse to nonrecourse, income may be realized to the extent the at risk basis is below zero. The taxable amount may not exceed the amount of losses previously deducted.

The recaptured amount is not treated as income from the activity for purposes of determining whether current or suspended losses are allowable.

12

PRIZES, SCHOLARSHIPS, DAMAGES, LIFE INSURANCE, AND OTHER INCOME

Illustrations of reporting other income on Form 1040 are in the Supplement to YOUR INCOME TAX.

¶ **12.1** **New tax law pointers.** The new tax law has significantly affected the tax treatment of the following types of income.
Prizes and awards. All prizes and awards are taxable except for *certain* awards which are not taxable provided you give them away as a charitable donation, see ¶12.4.
Scholarships. Grants after August 16, 1986, are subject to restrictive tax rules. Tax-free treatment is restricted to degree candidates to the extent the funds are used for tuition, books, supplies,

and equipment related to the course of study; *see* ¶12.8.
Debt cancellations. Solvent taxpayers outside of bankruptcy may no longer defer tax on a debt discharge. However, a solvent farmer may still defer tax under conditions explained in ¶12.18.
Interest exclusion for surviving spouse. The $1,000 interest exclusion is no longer allowed for the payment of interest on an insurance installment where the insured dies after October 22, 1986, *see* ¶12.17.

GIFTS AND INHERITANCES, BARGAIN PURCHASES, PRIZES AND AWARDS, AND GAMBLING WINNINGS

GIFTS AND INHERITANCES

¶ **12.2** Gifts and inheritances are not taxable. Income earned from gift or inherited property after you receive it is taxable.

Describing a payment as a gift or inheritance will not necessarily shield it from tax, if it is, in fact, a payment for services.

EXAMPLES

1. An employee is promised by his employer that he will be remembered in his will if he continues to work for him. The employer dies but fails to mention the employee in his will. The employee sues the estate which settles his claim. The settlement is taxable.

2. A nephew left his uncle a bequest of $200,000. In another clause of the will, the uncle was appointed executor, and the bequest of the $200,000 was described as being made in lieu of all commissions to which he would otherwise be entitled as executor. The bequest is con-

sidered tax-free income. It was not conditioned upon the uncle performing as executor. If the will had made the bequest contingent upon the uncle acting as executor, the $200,000 would have been taxed.

3. An attorney performed services for a friend without expectation of pay. The friend died and in his will left the attorney a bequest in appreciation for his services. The payment was considered a tax-free bequest. The amount was not bargained for.

4. A lawyer agreed to handle a client's legal affairs without charge; she promised to leave him securities. Twenty years later, under her will, he inherited the securities. The IRS taxed the bequest as pay. Both he and the client expected that he would be paid for legal services. If she meant to make a bequest from their agreement, she could have said so in her will.

A sale of an expected inheritance from a living person is taxable as ordinary income.

Campaign contributions. Campaign contributions are not taxable income to a political candidate if the funds are used for political campaign expenses or some similar purposes. Detailed records of receipts and disbursements are advisable to avoid tax on the political funds. Also nontaxable are contributions which are intended for the candidate's unrestricted personal use and qualify as gifts.

Treatment of gifts to employees is covered at ¶2.6.

BARGAIN PURCHASES

¶ 12.3 Whether a bargain purchase is taxable depends on the relationship of the parties. When you make a bargain purchase from your employer, the difference between what you pay and the value of the property may be taxable as compensation. If you are a stockholder purchasing from your corporation, the difference may be taxable as a dividend.

EXAMPLE

A corporation takes out an insurance policy on the life of a key executive, pays the premiums, and names itself as beneficiary. Several years later, the executive buys the policy from the company for its cash surrender value so he can name his own beneficiary. He has taxable income on the bargain purchase from his company. The true value of the policy to him is not its cash surrender value but what it would cost him to buy such a policy at his present age.

Courtesy discounts are discussed at ¶2.3.

PRIZES AND AWARDS

¶ 12.4 Prizes and awards are taxable income except for an award or prize that meets all these tests:
1. It is for outstanding educational activities, literary or civic achievement.
2. You were selected without any action on your part.
3. You do not have to perform services.
4. You assign the prize or award to a government unit or tax-exempt charitable organization. You must make the assignment before you benefit from the award. You may *not* claim a charitable deduction for the assignment.

A prize of merchandise is taxed at fair market value. For example, where a prize of first-class steamship tickets was exchanged for tourist class tickets for a winner's family, the taxable value of the prize was the price of the tourist tickets. The taxable value of an automobile won as a prize is its immediate trade-in value, not its list price.

SWEEPSTAKE AND LOTTERY WINNINGS

¶ 12.5 Sweepstake, lottery, and raffle winnings are taxable. You deduct the price of the ticket from the winnings. If you do not win, you may not deduct the cost of the ticket. If you frequently buy state lottery chances and win a drawing, you may also deduct the cost of your prior losing tickets bought in 1987 up to the amount of your winnings.

> To split income, potential sweepstakes winnings may be divided among family members or others before the prize is won. You might buy the sweepstakes or lottery ticket in your name and the names of others. The prize is shared and each portion separately taxed. Income-splitting is generally not possible after the prize is won if you bought the ticket.

Where a minor wins a state lottery and the prize is held by his parents as custodians under the Uniform Gifts to Minors Act, the prize is taxed to the minor in the year the prize is won.

GAMBLING WINNINGS AND LOSSES

¶ 12.6 Gambling winnings are taxable. Losses from gambling are deductible only up to the gains from gambling. You may not deduct a net gambling loss even though a particular state says gambling is legal. Nor does it matter that your business is gambling. You may not deduct the loss.

If you are not a professional gambler, gambling income is included on your tax return with your other income. Gambling losses (but not exceeding the amount of the gains) are deductible as "miscellaneous deductions" on Schedule A. The losses are not subject to the 2% AGI floor (covered in chapter 19). According to the IRS, professional gamblers who bet only for their own account are not in a business and must deduct losses (up to gains) as itemized deductions. However, the Supreme Court has held that full-time gamblers may deduct losses as business expenses even if they place wagers only for themselves. According to the Supreme Court, a gambler must prove that he bets full-time to earn a livelihood and not merely as a hobby to be considered in a business.

To prove your losses in the event your return is questioned, you must retain evidence of losses.

SCHOLARSHIPS, FELLOWSHIPS, AND GRANTS

¶ 12.7 The law distinguishes between grants made before August 17, 1986, and those made after August 16, 1986. Starting in 1987, scholarships and fellowships granted after August 16, 1986, are tax free only for degree candidates, and only to the extent the grant pays for tuition and course-related fees, books, supplies, and equipment. Amounts for room, board, and incidental expenses are taxable. Further, no tax-free exclusion is allowed for grants or tuition reductions that pay for teaching or other services or for federal grants where the recipient agrees to future work with the federal government.

Degree test. Scholarships given to students attending a primary or secondary school, or pursuing a degree at a college or university meet the degree test. Also qualifying are full-time or part-time scholarships for study at an educational institution that (1) provides an educational program acceptable for full credit towards a higher degree, or offers a program of training to prepare students for gainful employment in a recognized occupation, and (2) is authorized under federal or state law to provide such a program and is accredited by a nationally recognized accreditation agency.

Rules for pre-August 17, 1986, grants. After 1986, favorable prior tax rules still apply to pre-August 17, 1986, grants, unless the grantor did not make a firm committment for payments covering later semesters, see example 2.

EXAMPLES
1. In May 1986, you were notified of a scholarship that will pay your tuition, room and board for four years. The total amount of the scholarship is determinable and thus prior law rules will apply to tax shelter all payments, including payments for room and board.
2. In May 1986, you are granted a four-year scholarship. The amount for the first year is specified at $5,000. You need not reapply for the scholarship after the first year, but no specific amount is provided for years two through four. According to the IRS, up to $5,000 per year will be subject to the prior law rules. If you receive $4,000 in the second year, the entire amount is subject to prior law exclusion rules. If you receive $6,000, then $5,000 is subject to the prior law and $1,000 subject to the new law and may be taxable to the extent that it is used to pay room and board costs.

AWARDS TO DEGREE CANDIDATES BEFORE AUGUST 17, 1986

¶ 12.8 If you are a degree candidate, the following amounts paid under a grant are tax free: tuition, matriculation fees, room, board, laundry and other services, and family allowances.

Studies leading to your certification to practice a profession, such as psychiatric nurse, are not equivalent to being a candidate for a degree.

Work-study programs. Tuition and work payments are tax free if your college requires all its students to take part in the work-study program. Payments for services not required by the program are taxable.

Travel and other expenses. You are not taxed on allowances specifically designated for expenses incident to the grant, such as for travel (including meals and lodging while traveling and a family travel allowance), research, clerical help, and equipment. You are taxable to the extent the allowance is not spent for these purposes.

Payments for teaching or research. Where the primary purpose of teaching or research is to further your own training and education, payment for such services is tax free if the services are required of all degree candidates. Where the primary purpose is to pay you for services, the payments are taxable, even if teaching or research is required for the degree. Where you are paid for services not required of all degree candidates, a portion of the grant attributable to the services is taxed according to the going rate paid for similar services.

EXAMPLES

1. You are studying for a bachelor's degree in education. Teaching certain classes is a degree requirement. You do not report any part of your grant as income.

2. You are a candidate for a masters degree in education for which internship teaching is required. You are taxable on payments paid to you by a municipal school system where you assume full classroom responsibilities and receive a salary in accordance with the pay scale for all teachers. The payments are considered compensation for services.

3. You are earning a degree in mathematics. You do not need teaching experience for your degree. You receive a university grant requiring you to instruct certain classes. You report as income that part of the grant attributed to your teaching services. The taxed portion is found by multiplying the number of hours worked by the going hourly rate of pay for similar work. If you taught for 100 hours and the going hourly rate is $20, then $2,000 of your grant is taxable income and the remaining portion is tax free.

4. For a bachelor of science degree, a university required students of medical technology to complete a year of study at a hospital laboratory. Apart from regular lecture and study hours in the training year, they spent 35 hours a week at the hospital, three quarters of the time in supervised on-the-job training, and one quarter on independent work projects. The hospital paid them $250 a month, the same amount paid to employees doing similar work. The IRS treats these stipends as taxable pay. Even though they had to work at the hospital to get the university degree, the students were paid for services.

AWARDS TO NONDEGREE CANDIDATES BEFORE AUGUST 17, 1986

¶ 12.9 If you are not working for a degree, your scholarship or fellowship grant is tax free up to $300 a month for each month during the year in which you receive payments under the grant. You may claim the $300-a-month exclusion for only 36 months during your lifetime. The months do not have to run consecutively. A grant does not qualify for this tax-free exclusion if it represents payment for services or for research or studies primarily for the grantor's benefit.

After you exclude income for 36 months, all further grants are taxable.

EXAMPLES

1. In March 1986, Smith is awarded a post-doctoral fellowship to start in September and to end on June 1, 1987. The fellowship grant is for $4,500. He receives this in monthly installments of $500. During 1987, he received $2,000 for the five months. He excludes $1,500 ($300 per month × 5) from gross income. He reports the remaining $1,000 on his 1987 return.

2. Under a fellowship grant granted in 1985, Brown receives $200 a month for 40 months. Only $7,200 ($200 per month × 36 months) is

tax free. The remaining $800 ($200 per month × 4 months) is taxable—even though he could not, in any of the 36 months, make use of the full $300 exclusion.

If you receive two or more grants during the year, total all payments to figure the tax-free exclusion. If the payments are received during the same month or months, each month counts only once for the purpose of determining the number of months for which you are paid.

> Keep records to show whether your grants are taxable or tax free. Months in which you could have excluded payments under a grant may be counted in the 36 months, even if you did not claim the exclusion. It is up to you to show that you could not have excluded the payment.

The $300-a-month exclusion is the maximum set by law. There is no authority to increase it because of particular circumstances. For example, the IRS refused a request to allow a larger exclusion for a researcher who had a family to support.

Travel and other expense allowances. In addition to the $300 monthly exclusion, allowances specifically designated for expenses incident to the grant, such as for travel (including meals and lodgings while traveling and a family travel allowance), research, clerical help, and equipment are not taxable to the extent spent for such expenses.

EXAMPLE

An executive of a state agency, who received a grant to travel and study foreign rehabilitation programs, was allowed to exclude $300 a month, but not amounts exceeding $300 a month, for travel expenses. His entire grant was intended to cover travel expenses, but he was not required to use it for travel; in fact, there were no restrictions on how he used the money. Therefore, tax-free treatment was limited to payments to $300 a month; no part of the excess was allowed for travel expenses. To come within the expense exclusion, the allowance had to be specifically restricted to travel costs.

Who makes the grant. To qualify for the 36-month exclusion, the grant must be received from one of the following sources:

The United States, or any agency or instrumentality of the United States.

A state, territory, or possession of the United States, or any of the subdivisions, or the District of Columbia.

A tax-exempt nonprofit organization operated exclusively for religious, charitable, scientific, literary, testing for public safety, prevention of cruelty to children or animals, or educational purposes.

A foreign government.

An organization under the Mutual Educational and Cultural Exchange Act of 1961.

FELLOWSHIPS FOR INTERNS AND RESIDENT PHYSICIANS MADE BEFORE AUGUST 17, 1986

¶ 12.10 According to the IRS, payments interns and resident physicians receive from hospitals are generally taxable as compensation for services performed even though training and experience are gained while working. Most court decisions follow this IRS position. In the following cases, however, residents' grants were treated as tax-free fellowships.

EXAMPLES

1. A doctor, who had been a public health officer for two years, entered a medical school research program designed to prepare physicians for careers in academic medicine. The school was under contract to provide medical services to a hospital, and the doctor spent approximately 25% of his time on hospital clinical work. The school withheld taxes from his stipend and paid his malpractice insurance. The doctor joined the staff when he finished the research program.

The IRS taxed the doctor claiming that he was paid for his work at the hospital and that he was expected to join the staff. The Tax Court rejected both arguments. The doctor did not take care of patients and was not a resident. He did not take calls or keep regular hospital hours and spent most of his clinical time in conferences. His research was of interest to the academic community, but of no special advantage to the medical school. He did not have to work on projects the school was committed to. While the school may have hoped he would join the staff, its purpose was to educate him in a specialty, not to train him as an employee.

2. Two residents, an orthopedist and a pathologist, received stipends from a university medical center; the pathologist also had a VA grant. They convinced a district court jury and an appeals court that they were paid to further their medical training, not as compensation for services to the medical center. The medical center was a teaching institution with a full-time faculty to supervise the residents. Patients were not billed for services from the residents. Residents were not required to work for the center after training. These facts offset evidence that they were treated as employees for purposes of fringe benefits and pay-roll deductions. The pathologist's VA grant was also a fellowship. He spent only three months at the VA hospital as part of his residency at the medical center.

3. A doctor was accepted in a cardio-renal training program at a hospital. Although he went on rounds, the doctor argued that he performed no useful service to the hospital. He was there to learn from the leading experts in his field of study. The IRS, in taxing his stipend, noted that not only did he see patients on rounds but he also accepted a staff position when he finished training. The Tax Court held that the doctor received a tax-free fellowship. He was developing diagnostic skills on hospital rounds, not helping senior staff. The hospital did not pay the grant in the expectation that he would later join their staff, and he was not obliged to do so. Finally, the amount of his grant was geared to his personal financial needs, not to the length or quality of his service to the hospital.

4. Grants to 15 residents at a state university medical center qualified for the $300-per-month exclusion. The grants were designed to defray living expenses during training and were not conditioned on job performance or treatment of patients; the residents were not required to work for the state upon completion of the residency program. Further, fees were not charged for work performed by residents and the residents were always supervised by medical school faculty when seeing hospital patients. An appeals court held that given these facts, a jury verdict in favor of the residents should not be overruled, despite evidence the residents were treated as employees for purposes of fringe benefits and annual increases.

For a list of nontaxed grants, *see* ¶ 12.12.

TUITION PLANS FOR FAMILIES OF FACULTY MEMBERS

¶ **12.11** The law allows an exclusion for free or partially free tuition for undergraduate studies provided to a faculty member by his or her own school or at another similar school. However, such tuition benefits may be taxable to highly compensated employees if the tuition plan discriminates in their favor. Tax-free tuition benefits may be provided to the employee's spouse, dependent child, or to a former employee who retired

or left on disability, widow or widower of an individual who died while employed by the school, or a widow or widower of a retired or disabled employee. If both parents have died and one of the parents qualified as an employee, the fact that the child is a dependent of another person does not affect tax-free treatment of tuition benefits if the child is under age 25; if over 25, tuition reductions are taxed even if both parents are deceased.

CHECKLIST OF NONTAXABLE GRANTS MADE BEFORE AUGUST 17, 1986

¶ **12.12** The following are considered nontaxable grants:

National Science Foundation stipends, and National Institute of Public Affairs grants to government employees for an academic year of study.

National Institute of Health grants. These are generally tax free but may be considered taxable where you are selected on the basis of your experience and the NIH reserves patent and copyright rights arising from your research. NIH grants under Visiting Fellows Programs to residents of the following countries are exempt under tax conventions: Belgium, Finland, France, Iceland, Japan, the Netherlands, Norway, Poland, Romania and Trinidad and Tobago.

National Defense Education Act of 1958 Title IV grants to graduate students to help them prepare for careers as college teachers.

Research fellowships by the American Heart Association. However, "established investigatorship" awards to conduct independent research in the cardiovascular field are taxable.

Grants provided by a private person, if motivated by philanthropic reasons, and if the grant is turned over to a university which then pays the grant to you. Generally, however, grants provided by a private person are not eligible for the tax-free exclusion.

National Research Service Award.

FULBRIGHT AWARDS

¶ **12.13** How your Fulbright award is taxed depends on the purpose of the award. If you receive the award to—

Teach or lecture— the entire amount of the award is taxed as compensation for services, including any supplemental grant you receive under the Smith-Mundt Act. However, provided you are not a U.S. government employee, you may claim the foreign earned income exclusion to avoid tax on the grant (*see* chapter 36). If you do not qualify for the exclusion and if your overseas stay is temporary and you intend to return to your regular teaching position in the United States, you may deduct the cost of your travel, meals, and lodgings overseas.

Further your education as a student or research grantee— all or part of your award is tax free under the rules applied in ¶ 12.7.

TAX REFUNDS, DEBT CANCELLATIONS, AND COURT AWARDS

TAX REFUNDS AND OTHER RECOVERIES OF PREVIOUSLY DEDUCTED ITEMS

¶ **12.14** You may realize taxable income when you receive any of the following items previously deducted:

Refund of state or local taxes which you deducted in a prior year. (A refund of federal income tax is not taxable.)

Payment from a debtor of a debt you deducted as a bad debt in a prior year.

A return of donated property for which you claimed a charitable contribution deduction in a prior year, or

Reimbursement for a loss which you claimed as a casualty loss in a prior year.

Receipt of a state tax refund or other recovery will not be subject to tax in these cases:

You did not itemize deductions for the year in which the expenses, such as state income tax, were paid;

You paid alternative minimum tax (AMT) in that year and the item, such as state taxes, is not deductible for AMT purposes;

Tax credits reduced your tax to zero in that year.

In figuring whether you have a tax-free recovery of an item deducted in a prior year now closed by the statute of limitations, count only deductions taken on the return. Deductions you could have claimed but did not are ignored. *See* chapter 27 for statute of limitations.

If a casualty loss deduction is claimed in one year and in a later year the loss is reimbursed, the reimbursement is taxable income. However, in the case of a personal casualty loss, the reimbursement is not taxable to the extent that the $100 floor reduced the deduction.

For treatment of reimbursed medical costs, see ¶17.5.

EXAMPLE

The Browns file a joint return. In 1986, their adjusted gross income was $30,000, state income tax deduction was $2,000 and other itemized deductions were $5,000. They claimed three exemptions. In 1987, they received a refund of $1,000 of their 1986 state income tax.

	1986 Income	1986 Income Without State Tax Deduction
Adjusted gross income	$30,000	$30,000
Itemized deductions	7,000	$5,000
Zero bracket amount	(3,670)	(3,670)
Excess itemized deductions	(3,330)	(1,330)
Exemptions	(3,240)	(3,240)
Taxable income	$23,430	$25,430
Income without state tax deduction	25,430	
Income actually reported	23,430	
Tax benefit from deduction	$2,000	

Since the entire $2,000 state income tax deduction reduced the 1986 tax, the entire $1,000 refund is taxable in 1987.

Recovery of previously deducted items used to figure carryover. A deductible expense may not reduce your tax because you have an overall loss. If in a later year the expense is repaid or the obligation giving rise to the expense is cancelled, the deduction of that expense will be treated as having produced a tax reduction if it increased a carryover that has not expired by the beginning of the taxable year in which the forgiveness occurs. For example, you are on the accrual basis and deducted, but did not pay, rent in 1986. The rent obligation is forgiven in 1987. The 1986 rent deduction is treated as having produced a reduction in tax even if it resulted in no tax saving in 1986, if it figured in the calculation of a net operating loss that has not expired or been used by the beginning of 1987, the year of forgiveness. The same rule applies to other carryovers, such as the investment credit carryover.

Price rebate on energy credit equipment. If you claimed a home energy credit before 1986 and in a later year receive a manufacturer's rebate for the product on which the credit was based, the tax benefit rule applies and taxable income may be realized. The amount of income equals the portion of the credit attributable to the rebate. For example, in 1985, you buy solar-energy equipment costing $5,000 and claim a $2,000 credit (40% of $5,000). In 1987, you receive a price rebate of $500 on the item. You must recapture $200 of the credit (40% of $500). You add the recaptured $200 to your 1987 tax.

This recapture rule for price rebates does not apply to the investment tax credit, the business energy credit, the rehabilitation credit, the employer-plan credit, or the foreign tax credit.

CANCELLATION OF DEBTS YOU OWE

¶ 12.15 If your creditor cancels a debt you owe, you may realize taxable income. For example, a prepayment of a home mortgage at a discount is taxable.

EXAMPLE

A bank allows a homeowner to prepay a low-interest mortgage of $20,000 for $18,000. The discount of $2,000 is taxable as ordinary income.

You are not taxed if you can prove that your creditor intended a gift or you meet the following exceptions.

Cancellation of student loans. A student loan canceled after 1982 is taxable income with this exception: If a loan by a government agency or a qualified hospital organization is canceled because you worked for a period of time in certain geographical areas (such as practice medicine in rural areas) or because you worked for certain employers (such as an inner city school), then the canceled amount is not taxable.

Debts discharged in bankruptcy or insolvency. A discharge of a debt in a Title 11 bankruptcy case is not taxable, but is used to reduce specified "tax attributes" in this order:

1. Net operating losses and carryovers—dollar for dollar of debt discharge;
2. Carryovers of investment tax credit, WIN credit, jobs credit, research credit, low-income housing credit, and credit for alcohol used as a fuel—33⅓ cents for each dollar or debt cancellation;
3. Capital losses and carryovers—dollar for dollar;
4. Basis of depreciable and nondepreciable assets—dollar for dollar (but not below the amount of your total undischarged liabilities);
5. Foreign tax credit carryovers—33⅓ cents for each dollar of debt cancellation.

After these reductions, any remaining balance of the debt discharge is disregarded. On Form 982, you may make a special election to first reduce the basis of any depreciable assets and realty held as inventory or for sale to customers before reducing other tax attributes in the order shown above. The election allows a bankrupt or insolvent debtor to maximize the advantages of a net operating loss or other carryovers by first reducing basis of depreciable assets or realty held as inventory.

In a Title 11 case, the tax attribute reductions are made to the attributes in the bankruptcy estate. Reductions are not made to attributes of an individual debtor that come into existence after the bankruptcy case begins or that are treated as exempt property under bankruptcy rules. Basis reduction does apply to property transferred by the bankruptcy estate to the individual.

Similar rules apply to a debt discharged outside of bankruptcy while you are insolvent. Insolvency means that liabilities exceed the value of your assets immediately before the discharge. The discharged debt is not taxed to the extent of your insolvency (liabilities in excess of assets) and is applied to the reduction of tax attributes in the same manner as a bankrupt individual. Any remaining balance of the canceled debt is treated as if it were a debt cancellation of a solvent person and thus it is taxable unless it is a qualifying farming debt as discussed below.

The above rules for bankrupt and insolvent individuals apply for debt discharges occurring, or court proceedings beginning, on or after January 1, 1982. For debt discharges occurring after December 30, 1980, and before January 1, 1982, or in a court proceeding commencing before 1982, a bankrupt or insolvent taxpayer applies the discharged amount to reduce the basis of all depreciable and nondepreciable assets, but not below the property's fair market value on the date of the discharge.

Partnership debts. When a partnership's debt is discharged, the discharged amount is allocated among the partners. A bankrupt or insolvent partner applies the allocated amount to reduce tax attributes, as discussed above; a solvent partner cannot avoid tax on the discharged amount.

Solvent taxpayers outside bankruptcy. Under prior law, solvent taxpayers could defer tax on a debt discharge related to property used in a trade or business. This break was repealed for discharges occurring after 1986 for all taxpayers other than farmers who may qualify for the following exception.

Farmers. A solvent farmer may avoid tax from a discharge of indebtedness by an unrelated lender if the debt was incurred in farming or is farm business debt secured by farmland or farm equipment used in the farming business. You are eligible for this relief only if 50% or more of your average annual gross receipts for the preceding three taxable years was derived from farming. The excluded amount first reduces tax attributes such as net operating loss carryovers and business tax credits, then reduces the farmer's basis in all property other than farmland, and then the basis in land used in the farming business. The new rules for farmers are effective for discharges of indebtedness after April 9, 1986.

Effect of basis reduction on later disposition of property. Where basis is reduced under the above rules, the reduction is treated as a depreciation deduction. The effect of this rule is that when the asset is later sold at a gain, the gain may be taxed as ordinary income under the recapture rules of Section 1245, regardless of the nature of the asset. See ¶5.35(1).

Effect of basis reduction on investment credit. Where you reduce the basis of your property under the above rules, the basis reduction is not treated as a disposition of the property triggering recapture of a previously claimed investment credit. *See* ¶ 24.8.

RECEIPTS IN COURT ACTIONS FOR DAMAGES

¶ **12.16** *Tax-free damages.* You do not report damages received from suits for personal injuries, slander or libel of personal reputation, breach of promise to marry, alienation of affection, annulment of marriage, or amounts received for child support. Alimony may be taxed. *See* ¶1.35.

Taxable damages. According to the IRS and Tax Court, you report as taxable income damages collected for loss of profits. *See* below for defamation. Damages received for patent or copyright infringement or breach of contract are considered to be for loss of profits and thus are taxable. Courts reason that payments for loss of profits are taxable because the profits themselves would have been taxable if realized.

> When a payment compensates for loss of profits and good will or capital, make sure to have evidence for allocating the award between profits and good will or capital assets. Otherwise, the entire amount may be taxed as a recovery of profits. Be certain that your complaint is drawn so that it clearly demands a recovery both for loss of profits *and* injury to property. Seek to have any lump-sum award divided between the two in any judgment. If your action is settled, make sure the settlement agreement specifically earmarks the nature of the payments. To support a claim that good will was damaged, have evidence of the specific customers lost.

When damages compensate for the loss of property, you have taxable gain if the damages exceed adjusted basis of the property. A deductible loss will generally be allowed when the recovery is less than adjusted basis. The nature of the gain or loss takes on the same character (that is, gain or loss or ordinary income gain or loss) as the property lost.

Payments compensating for an anticipated invasion of the right of privacy are taxable in the absence of proof that actual damage has been suffered.

Punitive damages are taxable. The IRS will impose tax on punitive damages received for personal injuries or wrongful death. Under an exception, damages will not be taxed if received in consideration of a release from liability signed before July 16, 1984, under a wrongful death statute that provides exclusively for punitive damages.

An award from the National Labor Relations Board as a result of a discharge in violation of the National Labor Relations Act is taxable income.

Awards received in arbitration and amounts received in settlement of a dispute are treated according to the above rules.

Employment contracts. A settlement of an employment contract is generally taxable, unless a part of the settlement is allocated to a personal injury claim.

EXAMPLE

A corporate executive refused to leave when he was fired. The company sued, and the incident was widely reported in newspapers. The executive threatened a countersuit. He settled for a year's salary of $60,000 plus $45,000 for personal embarrassment. He argued that $45,000 was a tax-free payment for personal injuries. The Tax Court agreed. His "embarrassment" was part of a personal injury claim.

Defamation. The IRS holds that where a libelous statement damages both personal and business reputation, damages compensating for personal injury are tax free; damages for business reputation are taxable. If the award does not specify the character of the damages the IRS may tax all of the payments as a replacement of lost earnings due to injury to business reputation. The Tax Court and an appeals court disagree with the IRS approach. According to these courts, if state law treats defamation as a personal injury, the award is tax free, even if business reputation has been damaged.

Legal fees. The rules for deducting legal fees closely follow the above

rules. If the damages are tax free, you may not deduct your litigation costs. If your damages are fully taxed, you deduct all of your litigation costs. If your damages are only partially taxed, then you deduct only that portion of your litigation costs attributed to the taxed damages.

When your attorney receives payment of taxable damages and then turns over the money after deducting his fee, you are taxed in the year you receive your share.

Legal fees that are deductible as miscellaneous expenses are subject to the 2% adjusted gross income floor, *see* chapter 19.

HOW LIFE INSURANCE PROCEEDS ARE TAXED TO A BENEFICIARY

¶ **12.17** Life insurance proceeds received because of the death of the insured are generally tax free. However, insurance proceeds may be subject to estate tax so that the beneficiary actually receives a reduced amount (*see* ¶38.12). Interest paid on proceeds left with the insurer is taxable except in this case: A surviving spouse who elects to receive installments rather than a lump sum does not pay tax on the first $1,000 of interest received each year if the decedent died before October 23, 1986. Read the following checklist to find how your insurance receipts are taxed—

A lump-sum payment of the full face value of a life insurance policy: The proceeds are generally tax free.

The tax-free exclusion also covers death benefits payments under endowment contracts, workmen's compensation insurance contracts, employers' group insurance plans, or accident and health insurance contracts. The exclusion does not apply to a policy combined with a nonrefund life annuity contract where a single premium equal to the face value of the insurance is paid.

Insurance proceeds may be taxable where the policy was transferred for valuable consideration. Exceptions to this rule are made for transfers among partners and corporations and their stockholders and officers.

Installment payments spread over your life under a policy that could have been paid in a lump sum: Part of each installment attributed to interest may be taxed. Divide the face amount of the policy by the number of years the installments are to be paid. The result is the amount which is received tax free each year.

If you are the surviving spouse of an insured who died before October 23, 1986, up to $1,000 of interest paid with the annual installment is also tax free. You are still treated as a spouse if separated from the insured at the date of his death, but not if divorced. (If you receive payments under a policy with a "family income rider," *see* ¶12.18). The $1,000 interest exclusion is not allowed where the insured died after October 22, 1986.

EXAMPLE

Alice is the wife and beneficiary under her husband John's life insurance policy of $100,000. He died September 30, 1986. She elected to take installment payments for the rest of her life. Alice's life expectancy is 20 years. Then $5,000 ($100,000 ÷ 20) is the principal amount spread to each year. The first $6,000 received each year ($5,000 principal plus $1,000 of the spouse's special interest exclusion) is exempt from tax. If Alice lives more than 20 years, she may continue to treat up to $6,000 of annual payments as tax-free receipts.

If the policy guarantees payments to a secondary beneficiary if you should die before receiving a specified number of payments, the tax-free amount is reduced by the present value of the secondary beneficiary's interest in the policy. The insurance company can give you this figure.

Installment payments for a fixed number of years under a policy which could have been paid in a lump sum: Divide the full face amount of the policy by the number of years you are to receive the installments. The result is the amount which is received tax free each year.

EXAMPLE

Same facts as in example above, but Alice elects to take installment payments for 10 years. Then $10,000 ($100,000 ÷ by 10) is the principal amount received tax free. So, up to $11,000 per year may be received tax free by Alice, $10,000 of principal sum plus up to $1,000 of interest, under the surviving spouse's interest exclusion.

Installment payments when there is no lump-sum option in the policy: You must find the discounted value of the policy at the date of the insured's death and use that as the principal amount. The insurance company can give you that figure. After you find the discounted value, you divide it (as above) by the number of years you are to receive installments. The result is the amount that is tax free. The remainder is taxed.

EXAMPLE

Insured died in 1987. Under an insurance policy, the surviving wife is entitled to $5,000 a year for life. Her life expectancy is 20 years. There is no lump sum stated in the policy. Say the discounted value of the wife's rights is $60,000. The principal amount spread to each year for the wife is $3,000 ($60,000 ÷ 20). Subtracting $3,000 from each annual $5,000 payment gives her taxed income of $2,000.

Payments to you along with other beneficiaries under the same policy, by lump-sum or varying installments.

EXAMPLE

Under one life insurance policy of an insured who died in 1987, a surviving wife, daughter, and nephew of the insured are all beneficiaries. The wife is entitled to a lump sum of $60,000. The daughter and nephew are each entitled to a lump sum of $35,000. Under the installment options, the wife chooses to receive $5,000 a year for the rest of her life. (She has a 20-year life expectancy). The daughter and the nephew each chooses a yearly payment of $5,000 for 10 years. This is how each yearly installment is taxed:

WIFE: The principal amount spread to each year is $3,000. Subtracting $3,000 from the yearly $5,000 payment gives the wife taxed income of $2,000.

DAUGHTER AND NEPHEW: Both are taxed the same way. The principal amount spread to each of the 10 years is $3,500. Subtracting this $3,500 from the yearly $5,000 installment gives the daughter and the nephew each taxable income of $1,500 each.

Interest, when proceeds are left on deposit under the "interest only" option, is fully taxed; the lump sum is not taxed. A surviving spouse of an insured who died before October 23, 1986, may not exclude $1,000 interest under the "interest only" option. However, if the surviving spouse later elects to receive proceeds from the policy in installments, the interest exclusion applies from the time of the election.

Universal life policy. A universal life policy allows a policy-holder to apply premium payments to cash value instead of to death benefits. Death benefits may be tax free if the policies meet certain technical tests. These tests must be determined by the insurance company. Therefore you must check with the company paying the proceeds whether the payments qualify as tax-free life insurance payments.

Other names applied to universal life may be "flexible premium" or "adjustable life premium" policies.

A POLICY WITH A FAMILY INCOME RIDER

¶ **12.18** Payments received under a family income rider are taxed under a special rule. A family income rider provides additional term insurance coverage for a fixed number of years from the date of the basic policy. Under the terms of a rider, if the insured dies at any time during the term period, his beneficiary receives monthly payments during the balance of the term period, and then at the end of the term period, he receives the lump-sum proceeds of the basic policy. If the insured dies after the end of the term period, the beneficiary receives only the lump sum from the basic policy.

When the insured dies during the term period, part of each monthly payment received during the term period includes interest on the lump-sum proceeds of the basic policy (which is held by the company until the end of the term period). That interest is fully taxed. The balance of the monthly payment consists of an installment (principal plus interest) of the proceeds from the term insurance purchased under the family income rider. You may exclude from this balance: (1) A prorated portion of the present value of the lump sum under the basic policy, and (2) an additional amount of up to $1,000 attributable to interest if you are a surviving spouse of an insured who died before October 23, 1986. The lump sum under the basic policy is tax free when you eventually receive it.

The rules here also apply to an integrated family income policy and to family maintenance policies, whether integrated or with an attached rider.

In figuring your taxable portions, ask the insurance company for its interest rate and the present value of term payments.

HOW OTHER INSURANCE PROCEEDS ARE TAXED

¶ **12.19** Dividends paid by the insurance company as reduction of premiums (taken in cash, left as interest with the company, or used to accelerate the maturity of the policy) are not taxable. They serve to reduce the cost basis of your policy, thus increasing gain sometimes computed upon maturity of some policies. (But interest on these "dividends" is taxed even if the policy is issued by the Veterans Administration, *see* chapter 4.)

Matured endowment policies. Gain is taxable, *see* ¶ 7.22. The payment on an endowment contract because of the insured's death is treated as the payment of tax-free life insurance proceeds provided the policy meets certain technical definitions not discussed in this book.

Sale of an endowment contract before maturity. Taxed as ordinary income. *See* ¶ 7.22.

Surrender of policy for cash. Taxed as ordinary income (not capital gain), if the cash received exceeds the premiums paid, less dividends received. If you take, instead, a paid-up policy, you may avoid tax. *See* ¶ 12.20. You get no deduction if there is a loss on the surrender of a policy.

Collection of proceeds on policy purchased by or assigned to you on the life of someone else. Where a policy is transferred for valuable consideration, only the amount paid and the premiums paid after the transfer are tax free when collected; the balance is taxed. There is no tax on life insurance proceeds paid under contracts which have been transferred to a partner or to a corporation in which the insured was a shareholder or officer.

TAX FREE EXCHANGES OF INSURANCE POLICIES

¶ **12.20** These exchanges of insurance policies are considered tax free—

Life insurance policy for another life insurance policy, endowment policy, or an annuity contract.

Endowment policy for another endowment policy that provides for regular payments beginning no later than the date payments would have started under the old policy, or for an annuity contract.

Annuity contract for another annuity contract with identical annuitants.

These exchanges are not tax free—

Endowment policy for a life insurance policy, or for an endowment policy that provides for payments beginning at a date later than payments would have started under the old policy.

Annuity contract for a life insurance or an endowment policy.

DEDUCTIONS, CREDITS, AND FIGURING YOUR TAX

In this part, you will learn how to reduce your tax liability by claiming expenses and tax credits. Pay special attention to—

The new standard deduction. Although the standard deduction may provide a tax reduction, read the chapters on the itemized deductions to see that you have not overlooked itemized deductions for charitable donations, interests, state and local taxes, medical expenses, casualty and theft losses, and miscellaneous expenses for job costs and investment expenses.

Figuring tax liability for minor children. New complicated rules must be followed if your children under 14 have investment income.

Alternative Minimum Tax (AMT). The AMT tax has been broadened and you may be subject to it if your regular tax liability has been reduced by tax deductions and tax benefit provisions.

Filing for refunds.

Estimated tax. Since the penalty threshold has been tightened, learn how to avoid penalties.

13

CLAIMING THE STANDARD DEDUCTION OR ITEMIZED DEDUCTIONS

What You Should Know About Itemized Deductions and Standard Deductions

Item	Explanation	Limitation
Standard deduction	The law gives a standard deduction which is fixed by law according to your filing status and age. The standard deduction in 1987 is: $3,760 if you are married, filing jointly, or a surviving spouse. $2,540 if you are unmarried (including head of household). $1,880 if you are married, filing separately. If you are 65 or over or blind, your standard deduction is substantially larger. See ¶13.4	The standard deduction may not be claimed by a nonresident person, estate or trust—or on a return filed for a short taxable year caused by a change in accounting period. Married persons filing separately may not use the standard deduction if their spouse itemizes deductions. A lower standard deduction of $500 is allowed dependents with unearned income.
Itemized deductions	You get greater tax savings by claiming itemized deductions which exceed the standard deduction for your filing status. Itemized deductions include charitable contributions, interest expenses, local and state taxes, medical and dental costs, casualty and theft losses, job and investment expenses, and educational costs.	There is no dollar limit on the amount of itemized deductions. But individual itemized deductions are subject to limitations explained below. **EXAMPLE** You are single and may claim the standard deduction of $2,540. However, your itemized deductions are $5,000. You claim $5,000.
Charitable contributions	You may deduct donations to religious, charitable, educational, and other philanthropic organizations that have been approved to receive deductible contributions. See ¶14.15.	The contribution deduction is generally limited to 50% of adjusted gross income. Lower ceilings apply to property donations and contributions to foundations.
Interest expenses	You may deduct interest on loans and other debts. A list of common interest payments is at ¶15.2. You deduct the interest on the tax return of the year in which you paid the interest, unless you are on the accrual basis. Prepaid interest is deductible over the period of the loan; see ¶15.4.	No dollar limit on interest on business loans. But there is a limit on interest on loans to carry investments, consumer loans, and mortgage interest.
Taxes	You may deduct payments of state, local, and foreign real property and income taxes, as well as state and local personal property taxes. You claim your deduction on the tax return of the year in which you paid the taxes unless you report on the accrual basis; see ¶16.6.	No dollar limitation.
Medical expenses	You may deduct payments of medical expenses for yourself and dependents. A checklist of over one hundred deductible medical items is at ¶17.2. Deductible drug costs are limited to drugs prescribed by a physician.	Only expenses in excess of 7.5% of adjusted gross income are deductible.
Casualty and theft losses	You may deduct property losses caused by storms, fires, and other natural events and as the result of theft.	Each individual casualty loss must exceed $100 and the total of all losses during the year must exceed 10% of adjusted gross income.
Job expenses	You may deduct unreimbursed costs of union dues, job educational courses, work clothes, entertainment, travel and looking for a new job.	Included as miscellaneous expenses of which only the excess over 2% of adjusted gross income is deductible.
Investment expenses	You may deduct investment expenses and other expenses of producing and collecting income, expenses of maintaining income-producing property, expenses of tax return preparation, refunds and audits.	Included as miscellaneous expenses of which only the excess over 2% of adjusted gross income is deductible.

STANDARD DEDUCTION

¶ **13.1** **Standard Deduction.** The standard deduction provides larger tax benefits than the zero bracket amount which it replaces.

	The 1987 standard deduction if you are—	
	Under 65 and not blind	65 or older or blind
Married filing jointly	$3,760	from $5,600 to $7,400
Single	2,540	from $3,750 to $4,500
Head of household	2,540	from $5,150 to $5,900
Married filing separately	1,880	from $3,100 to $3,700
Qualifying widow or widower with dependent child	3,760	from $5,600 to $6,200

The standard deduction is not integrated into the tax schedules (as was the zero bracket amount), but is deducted from adjusted gross income if you do not claim itemized deductions.

EXAMPLE

You are age 25 and single. In 1987 you have wage income of $15,000 and interest income of $2,000. You are not covered by a company plan and have contributed $2,000 to an IRA. You have decided to claim the standard deduction because your itemized deductions are less.

Gross Income		
Salary	$15,000	
Interest Income	2,000	$17,000
Deduction from gross income:		
IRA		2,000
Adjusted Gross Income		15,000
Less: Standard Deduction		2,540
		12,460
Less: Exemption		1,900
Taxable income		$10,560

A special standard deduction rule applies to a person claimed as a dependent. A dependent may use up to $500 of the standard deduction to offset unearned income such as interest or dividends, see ¶ 13.5.

ELECT TO ITEMIZE OR TAKE THE STANDARD DEDUCTION

¶ **13.2** Claim the standard deduction only if it exceeds your allowable itemized deductions for charitable donations, certain local taxes, interest, allowable casualty loss, miscellaneous expenses, and medical expenses. If your deductions exceed your standard deduction, you elect to itemize by claiming the deductions on Schedule A of Form 1040.

EXAMPLE

You are single and your adjusted gross income is $35,000. Your itemized deductions total $5,200. As the standard deduction is less than your itemized deductions, you claim itemized deductions of $5,200. You figure your tax after deducting the itemized deductions and personal exemption from your adjusted gross income.

Changing an election. If you filed your return using the standard deduction and want to change to itemized deductions, or you itemized and want to change to the standard deduction, you may do so within the three-year period allowed for amending your return. If you are married and filing separately, each of you must consent to and make the change.

HUSBANDS AND WIVES FILING SEPARATE RETURNS

¶ **13.3** If you file separate returns, you and your spouse must first decide whether you will claim itemized deductions or limit yourselves to a standard deduction of $1,880 each. You must make the same election. That is, if one spouse has itemized deductions exceeding $1,880 and elects to itemize, the other spouse must also itemize, even if his or her itemized deductions are less than $1,880.

On a separate return, each spouse may deduct only those itemized expenses for which he or she is liable. This is true even if one spouse pays expenses for the other. For example, if property is owned by the wife, then the interest and taxes imposed on the property are her deductions, not her husband's. If he pays them, neither one may deduct them on separate returns. The husband may not because they were not his liability. The

wife may not because she did not pay them. This is true also of interest on a personal loan and casualty or theft losses.

Claiming itemized deductions when you are living apart from your spouse. When a husband and wife are legally separated under a decree of divorce or separate maintenance, they are free to compute their tax as they see fit, without reference to the return of the other spouse. They are treated as single. If one spouse has itemized deductions, that spouse may elect to claim them, and the other spouse is not required to itemize. The standard deduction is not limited to $1,880. Head of household tax rates may be available under the rules of ¶ 1.10.

If a husband and wife are separated but do not have a decree of divorce or separate maintenance, both must either itemize or claim the standard deduction of $1,880. There is an exception if you are married and live apart from your spouse and meet the following conditions:

Your spouse was not a member of your household during the last six months of 1987;

You maintained as your home a household which was, for more than half of 1987, the principal place of abode for your child, adopted child, foster child, or stepchild.

You are entitled to claim the child as a dependent (¶ 1.17) or the child's other parent has the right to the exemption under the rules of ¶ 1.23.

You provide over half the cost of supporting the household.

If you satisfy these conditions and file a separate return, you may compute your tax as though you were single. However, if you are under age 65 and not blind, your standard deduction is $2,540 and you may elect to itemize without regard to whether your spouse itemizes or not. You may use head of household rates if you meet the rules at ¶ 1.10.

INCREASED STANDARD DEDUCTION FOR ELDERLY AND BLIND

¶ **13.4** A larger standard deduction is provided for persons who are 65 or over or who are blind. The larger deduction for blindness is allowed regardless of age.

If You Are—	Standard Deduction is
Single 65 or over	$3,750
Single and blind	3,750
Single 65 or over and also blind	4,500
Married filing jointly with:	
One spouse 65 or over	5,600
Both spouses 65 or over	6,200
One spouse blind under 65	5,600
Both spouses blind under 65	6,200
One spouse 65 or over and also blind	6,200
One spouse 65 or over and other spouse blind under 65	6,200
One spouse 65 or over and also blind. Other spouse blind under 65	6,800
Both spouses 65 or over and also blind	7,400
Qualifying widow or widower (¶ 1.6) 65 or over	5,600
Qualifying widow or widower and blind	5,600
Qualifying widow or widower 65 or over and also blind	6,200
Head of household 65 or over	5,150
Head of household and blind	5,150
Head of household 65 or over and also blind	5,900
Married filing separately 65 or over	3,100
Married filing separately and blind	3,100
Married filing separately 65 or over and also blind	3,700

The above standard deduction amounts reflect a basic standard deduction plus an extra amount for blindness and being 65 or over at the end of 1987.

Married. The basic standard deduction is $5,000 for married couples filing jointly where either spouse is age 65 or over or blind. It is also $5,000 for elderly or blind qualified widows or widowers with dependent children who may use joint return rates (¶1.6). For a married person who files separately, the basic standard deduction is $2,500.

The extra amount is $600 for each married person who is 65 or over or blind; a married person who is both age 65 and also blind gets an extra $1,200 deduction, $600 for each status. A married person filing separately and a qualifying widow(er) also get the extra $600 deduction for each status (age or blindness).

Unmarried. The basic standard deduction for a single person who is either age 65 or over or blind is $3,000; $4,400 for a head of household. The extra standard deduction for single persons and heads of households is $750 for each status. Thus, a single person age 65 or over has a standard deduction of $3,750 ($3,000 basic deduction + $750 extra). If also blind, the deduction increases an additional $750 to $4,500.

STANDARD DEDUCTION FOR DEPENDENTS

¶ 13.5 The standard deduction for a person who is claimed as a dependent by another is limited to the greater of $500 or earned income, but no more than the standard deduction allowed for the dependent's filing status.

Therefore, if you claim your child as a dependent and your child has only investment income, the child's standard deduction equals the investment income up to $500; if investment income exceeds $500, the standard deduction is limited to $500. If your dependent has earned income such as wages, the standard deduction is the greater of $500 or earned income but only earnings up to the amount of the regular standard deduction are considered. A dependent may claim itemized deductions if these exceed his or her standard deduction.

EXAMPLES

1. You claim your son, age 15, as a dependent on your return. He has interest income of $600 and wages of $150. His standard deduction is $500; the greater of $500 or earned income of $150.

2. You claim your mother as a dependent. She is 68 years old and has interest income of $700 and wages of $2,000. Her standard deduction is $2,000—because the greater of $500, or her earned income of $2,000 is $2,000. Her earned income is also less than the maximum standard deduction of $3,750 for a single person age 65 or over (*see* ¶13.4).

3. You claim as a dependent your 22-year-old son who is a full-time college student. He is also married and files a separate return. He has $1,500 in interest and $2,400 in wages. His standard deduction is $1,880. Although his earned income is $2,400, his standard deduction

may not exceed the $1,880 maximum allowable standard deduction for a married person filing a separate return (*see* the table at the beginning of the chapter).

New legislation: When this book went to press, Congress was considering a bill that would allow dependents who are elderly (65 or over) or blind to claim a larger standard deduction. Under the bill, the standard deduction would equal the greater of $500 or earned income (up to regular limits in ¶13.4) *plus* $600 if married or $750 if unmarried. *See* the Supplement for further developments and check your tax forms instruction booklet.

STANDARD DEDUCTION INCREASES IN 1988

¶ 13.6 In 1988, the standard deduction for those who are under age 65 and not blind increases to the following amounts:

If you are—	The standard deduction will be—
Married filing jointly	$5,000
Single	3,000
Head of household	4,400
Married filing separately	2,500
Qualifying widow or widower	5,000

For those 65 or over or blind, the standard deduction allowed in 1987 reflects the above increased amounts and so remains the same in 1988. *See* ¶13.4.

ALTERNATE USE OF STANDARD AND ITEMIZED DEDUCTIONS

¶ 13.7 If you find your itemized deductions are equal to or slightly less than the amount of the standard deduction, you may reduce taxes by alternating use of the standard deduction and itemized deductions. Depending on the amount of your expenses, you may:

Prepay deductible expenses so that your itemized deductions exceed the standard deduction. In the next year, you will have less itemized deductions and will claim the standard deduction, or

Postpone payment of expenses to next year and claim the standard deduction this year. Next year, you will claim itemized deductions.

In both instances, the total amount of deductions over the two years will be greater than the amount of standard deductions claimed in both years.

EXAMPLE

In 1988, you are single and you estimate that your itemized deductions will be $2,900. You could choose to take the larger standard deduction of $3,000. But towards the end of 1988, you can prepay a state income tax of $500 to raise your itemized deductions to $3,400. Without increasing your expenditures over a two-year period by making the prepayment, you have increased your deductions by $400. In 1988 you deduct itemized deductions of $3,400, and in 1989 you claim a standard deduction of $3,000. You might follow this practice every other year. Take as many itemized deductions as possible in one year; in the next year, claim the standard deduction.

Deductible items that you may prepay: charitable donations, dues, subscription fees for one year, state and local taxes. You may get a deduction only in the year payment is due for interest, rent, and insurance premiums.

ADJUSTED GROSS INCOME

¶ 13.8 Adjusted gross income is a technical term used in the tax law. It is the amount used in figuring the 7.5% floor for the medical expense deductions, the 10% floor for personal casualty and theft losses, the 2% floor for miscellaneous deductions, and the charitable contribution limitation. If you follow the instructions and order of the tax return, you will arrive at adjusted gross income without having to know or understand the following steps. But if you are planning the tax consequences of a transaction in advance of preparing your return, this is how to figure adjusted gross income.

Adjusted gross income is the difference between gross income (Step 1) and deductions listed in Step 2 below. If you do not have any of these deductions, adjusted gross income is the same as gross income.

Step 1. Figure gross income. This is all income received by you from any source, such as wages, salary, gross business income, income from sales and exchanges, interest and dividends, rents, royalties, annuities, pensions, etc. But gross income does not include such items as tax free interest from state or local bonds, tax free parsonage allowance, tax free insurance proceeds, gifts and inheritances, Social Security benefits which are not subject to tax under the rules of ¶34.8, tax free scholarship grants, tax free board and lodging allowance, and the first $5,000 of death benefits.

Step 2. Deduct from gross income only the following items:
Trade or business expenses. These items are listed on Schedule C.
Reimbursed job expenses of employees. Expenses in this category include local transportation expenses, travel expenses away from home, outside salesperson expenses and meal and entertainment expenses which are reimbursed.
Capital loss deduction. Where capital losses exceed capital gains, capital loss deduction up to $3,000 may be deducted from gross income. Schedule D is used to figure this loss deduction.

Net operating losses.
Certain deductions of life tenants and income beneficiaries of property.
Contributions to a Keogh plan. The deduction for the contribution on your behalf is taken on Form 1040; contributions for your employees on Schedule C.
Deductible contributions to IRAs.
Alimony payments.
Forfeit penalties because of a premature withdrawal of funds from time savings accounts or deposits.
Expenses to produce rent and royalty income.
Repayment of supplemental unemployment benefits required because of receipt of trade readjustment allowances.
Reforestation expenses.
Certain expenses of performing artists.
Required repayments of supplemental unemployment compensation benefits.
Health insurance deduction for self-employed

Step 3. The difference between Steps 1 and 2 is adjusted gross income.

14
CHARITABLE CONTRIBUTION DEDUCTION

Illustrations of deducting charitable contributions may be found in the Supplement to YOUR INCOME TAX.

¶ **14.1** **New law pointers.** Several new provisions take effect for 1987 and later tax years that might dampen charitable writeoffs:
1. In 1987, you may not take advantage of a prior law benefit which allowed charitable contribution deductions to those who did not itemize their deductions. The nonitemized charitable deduction is no longer allowed. Further, a new law bars deductions for charitable travel expenses, where there is a significant element of personal pleasure or recreation in the trip. This provision is primarily directed against trips organized by educational groups as research studies in vacation and exotic areas; *see* ¶14.4.
2. You will not be able to claim a charitable contribution for the appreciation on certain property donations, such as art objects, where the donee organization does not use the property but sells it.
3. Gifts of appreciated property must be considered in figuring any alternative minimum tax (AMT) liability; *see* ¶23.4.

DEDUCTIBLE CONTRIBUTIONS

¶ **14.2** You may deduct donations to religious, charitable, educational, and other philanthropic organizations which have been approved by the IRS to receive deductible contributions (*see* ¶14.15). If you are unsure of the tax status of a philanthropy, ask the organization about its status, or check the IRS list of tax-exempt organizations (IRS Publication No. 78). Donations to federal, state, and local governmental bodies are also deductible.

Charitable contributions are deductible only as itemized deductions.

> *Timing your contributions.* You deduct donations on the tax return filed for the year in which you paid them in cash or property. A contribution by check is deductible in the year you give the check, even if it is cashed in the following year. A check mailed and dated on the last day of 1987 is deductible in 1987. A postdated check with a 1988 date is not deductible until 1988. A pledge or a note is not deductible until paid. Donations made through a credit card are deductible in the year the charge is made. Donations made through a pay-by-phone bank account are not deductible until the payment date shown on the bank statement. Keep a record of canceled checks or receipts from charities.

If you are planning to donate appreciated securities near the end of the year, make sure that you consider these delivery rules in timing the donation. If you unconditionally deliver or mail a properly endorsed stock certificate to the donee or its agent, the gift is considered completed on the date of delivery or mailing, provided it is received in the ordinary course of the mails. If you deliver the certificate to your bank or broker as your agent, or to the issuing corporation or its agent, your gift is not complete until the stock is transferred to the donee's name on the corporation's books. This transfer may take several weeks, so if possible, make the delivery at least three weeks before the end of the year to assure a current deduction.

Limits on deduction. In general, the amount of your charitable deduction is limited to 50% of adjusted gross income. A 30% ceiling applies to deductions for donations of certain types of appreciated property (*see* ¶14.17). Where donations in one year exceed the statutory limit, a five-year carryover of the excess may be allowed (*see* ¶14.18).

Debts. You may assign to a charity a debt payable to you. A contribution deduction may be claimed in the year your debtor pays the charity.

Dues. Dues paid to a tax-exempt organization may be deductible if you receive no benefits or privileges from the organization for the dues, such as monthly bulletins or journals, use of a library, or the right to attend luncheons and lectures.

If dues are paid to a social club with the understanding that a specified part goes to a named charity, you may claim a charitable deduction for dues earmarked for the charity. If the treasurer of your club is actually the agent of the charity, you take the deduction in the year you give him the money. If the treasurer is merely your agent, you may take the deduction only in the year the money is turned over to the charity.

BENEFIT TICKETS, BAZAARS, AND BINGO

¶ **14.3** Tickets to theater events, tours, concerts, and other entertainments are often sold by charitable organizations at prices higher than the regular admission charge. The difference between the regular admission and the higher amount you pay is deductible as a charitable contribution. If you decline to accept the ticket or return it to the charity for resale, your deduction is the price you paid.

If the benefit ticket price is the same or less than the regular admission price, you have no deduction unless you refuse to accept the ticket or you return the ticket to the charity for resale.

If you purchase season tickets to a charity-sponsored series of programs and your average cost per program equals or is less than the cost for individual performances, your deduction for a returned ticket depends upon how long you held the tickets. Generally, you may deduct only your

cost. However, if you have held the ticket for more than a year, you may deduct the fair market value, the price the charity will charge on resale of the ticket.

You may not deduct the cost of raffle tickets, bingo games, or other types of lotteries organized by charities.

Donations tied to football season tickets. To encourage donations to athletic scholarship programs, universities allow donors who contribute a specific amount to buy a season ticket for football games in preferred seating locations. A deduction is allowed to the extent that the donation exceeds the value of the right to buy the season ticket.

EXAMPLES

1. An alumnus pays $300 for the right to buy a season ticket in a designated location before season tickets are offered to noncontributors. There are comparable seats that he could have purchased even if he had not made the contribution. The $300 is deductible. The right to get tickets early and to sit with other contributors is not a substantial benefit.

2. An alumnus must pay $300 for the right to buy a season ticket in a specific section. The university brochure states that the fair market value of the right to buy the ticket is $120 and that $180 is the contribution. Then $180 is deductible unless the IRS claims that the seating privilege is worth more than $120.

UNREIMBURSED EXPENSES OF VOLUNTEER WORKERS

¶ **14.4** If you work without pay for an organization listed at ¶14.15, you may deduct as charitable contributions your unreimbursed travel expenses, including commutation expenses to and from its place of operations, and meals and lodging on a trip away from home for the organization. To qualify for the deduction, the expenses must be incurred for a domestic organization which authorizes your travel.

You may not deduct the value of your donated services.

You may deduct either the actual operating costs of your car in volunteer work, or a flat mileage rate of 12¢ a mile allowed by the IRS. Parking fees and tolls are deductible under both methods.

EXAMPLE

You are a volunteer worker for a philanthropy. In the course of your volunteer work, you drove the car approximately 1,000 miles. You may claim a contribution deduction of $120 plus tolls and parking.

The 12¢ a mile deduction rate is not mandatory. If your out-of-pocket expenses are greater, you may deduct your actual costs of operating the automobile exclusively for charitable work, such as the cost of gas and oil, in addition to tolls and parking fees.

Also deductible as charitable contributions are:

Uniform costs required in serving the organization.

Cost of telephone calls, and cost of materials and supplies you furnished (stamps, stationery).

Convention expenses of official delegates to conventions of church, charitable, veteran, or other similar organizations. Members who are not delegates get no such deduction. However, they may deduct expenses paid for the benefit of their organization at the convention.

Expenses incurred by volunteers in operating their equipment. No deduction, however, is allowed for the rental value of such equipment, depreciation, and premiums paid on liability or property damage insurance.

Expenses of unsalaried city and town officials.

The IRS does not allow a deduction for "babysitting" expenses of charity volunteer workers. Although incurred to make the volunteer work possible, babysitting costs are a nondeductible personal expense. Further, the expense is not a dependent care cost; it is not related to a paying job.

Travel expenses of charity research trips. To claim a charitable deduction for travel expenses of a research project for a charitable organization, you must show the trip had no significant element of personal pleasure, recreation, or vacation.

EXAMPLES

1. Jones sails from one Caribbean Island to another and spends eight hours a day counting whales and other forms of marine life as

part of a project sponsored by a charitable organization. According to the IRS, he may not claim a charitable deduction for the costs of the trip.

2. Smith works on an archaeological excavation sponsored by a charitable organization for several hours each morning, with the rest of the day free for recreation and sightseeing. According to the IRS, he may not deduct the cost of the trip.

The above restrictive rule does not apply to volunteers who travel to transact business for an organization.

EXAMPLE

A member of a chapter of a local charitable organization travels to New York City and spends the entire day at the organizational required meeting. According to the IRS, he may deduct as a charitable donation, his expenses even if he attends a theater in the evening.

SUPPORT OF A STUDENT IN YOUR HOME

¶ **14.5** A limited charitable deduction is allowed for support of an elementary or high school student in your home under an educational program arranged by a charitable organization. If the student is not a relative, you may deduct as a charitable contribution your support payments up to $50 for each month the student stays in your home. For this purpose, 15 days or more of a calendar month is considered a full month. You may not deduct any payments received from the charitable organization in reimbursement for the student's maintenance.

To support the deduction, be prepared to show a written agreement between you and the organization relating to the support arrangement. Keep records of amounts spent for such items as food, clothing, medical and dental care, tuition, books, and recreation in order to substantiate your deduction. No deduction is allowed for depreciation on your house.

PROPERTY DONATIONS

APPRECIATED PROPERTY DONATIONS

¶ **14.6** Donations of property (securities, houses, collectibles, automobiles, paintings, manufactured goods) are deductible. Whether the full amount of the fair market value of the property is deductible depends on the type of property donated, the holding period, the nature of the philanthropy, and the use to which the property is put. You may have to attach an appraisal summary to your return; see ¶ 14.12.

Intangible personal property (such as securities) and real estate held long-term. Fair market value is deductible where such property is given to a publicly supported charity or to a private foundation which distributes donations to publicly supported charities within 2½ months after the end of the tax year in which it receives the donations. Deductions for such appreciated property are limited to 30% of adjusted gross income, with a five-year carryover for the excess. Carryovers are discussed at ¶ 14.18. If the donation exceeds the 30% ceiling you may consider a special election which allows you to apply the 50% ceiling. See ¶ 14.19.

> *Tax advantage of donating securities or realty held long-term.* You may claim a deduction for the fair market value of the property and also avoid tax on the appreciation in value of the property. The amount of tax you avoid further reduces the cost of your donation. However, these advantages may be lost if you are subject to the alternative minimum tax (AMT). If you plan to donate appreciated property, first check whether you may be subject to alternative minimum tax (AMT). If you are, the appreciation element on the donation will be subject to AMT tax. If so, postpone the donation until you incur regular tax. AMT is discussed in chapter 23.

You may figure the reduced cost of such a donation of appreciated property by following these two steps:
1. Figure the tax reduction resulting from the deduction of the fair market value of the property. For example, you donate appreciated stock which is selling at $1,000. Your top tax bracket is 38.5%. The deduction for the donation reduces your taxes by $385.
2. Estimate how much tax you would have paid on a sale of the stock. Assume you would have to pay tax of $140 on a sale of the stock at $1,000. The total tax savings from your donation is $525 ($385 + $140). The cost of your contribution is $475 ($1,000–525).

The IRS ruled that you may not claim a deduction on donated stock if you retain the voting rights, even though the charity has the right to receive dividends and sell the stock. The right to vote is considered a substantial interest and is crucial in protecting a stockholder's financial interest.

Ordinary income property. This is property which, if sold by you at its fair market value, would *not* result in long-term capital gain. The deduction for donations of this kind of property is restricted to your cost for the property. Examples of ordinary income property include: stock held short-term, inventory items donated by business, farm crops, Section 306 stock (preferred stock received as a tax free stock dividend, usually in a closely held corporation), and works of art, books, letters, and memoranda donated by the person who prepared or created them.

EXAMPLES

1. You hold short-term stock which cost you $1,000. It is now worth $1,500. If you donate it to a philanthropy, your deduction would be limited to $1,000. You would get no tax benefit for the appreciation of $500. On the other hand, if the stock were held long-term, you could claim a deduction for the full market value of the stock on its donation.
2. A former Congressman claimed a charitable deduction for the donation of his papers. His deduction was disallowed. His papers were ordinary income property and, since his cost basis in the papers was zero, he could claim no deduction.

Tangible personal property held long-term. Items such as furniture, books, equipment, fixtures (severed from realty), jewelry and art objects are tangible personal property. When held long-term, deductions for donations of this type of asset may be subject to restrictions which will limit your deduction to cost basis. If the philanthropy to which you donate the property does not put it to a use that is related to its charitable function, you have to reduce the deduction by the amount of long-term capital gain that would have been realized if the property had been sold at fair market value. If the charity must sell your gift to obtain cash for its exempt purposes, your deduction is also reduced by the long-term gain element. Where a donation of property is subject to a reduction as a nonrelated gift, the reduced gift is then subject to the 50% annual ceiling. If the gift is related to the organization's charitable purposes, you may deduct the property's fair market value subject to the 30% ceiling, or you may elect to deduct up to 50% of adjusted gross income by reducing the deduction by the long-term gain element. See ¶ 14.19.

Donating capital gain property to private nonoperating foundations. Generally, you may *not* deduct the full fair market value of gifts of capital gain property to private nonoperating foundations that are subject to the 20% deduction ceiling discussed at ¶ 14.17. (Capital gain property is property which, if sold by you at fair market value would result in long-term capital gain.) The deduction must be reduced by the long-term gain that would have been realized if the property had been sold at fair market value. However, you may deduct the full value without reduction of contributed stock for which there is a readily available market quotation on an established securities market on the date of contribution. If you or family members contribute more than 10% of any corporation's stock, the full deduction may be claimed only for the first 10%.

Donation of mortgaged property may be taxable. Before you give mortgaged property to a charity, have an attorney review the transaction. You may deduct the excess of fair market value over the amount of the outstanding mortgage. However, you may realize a taxable gain. The IRS and Tax Court treat the transferred mortgage debt as cash received in a part-gift, part-sale subject to the bargain-sale rules discussed at ¶14.8. This is true even if the charity does not assume the mortgage. You will realize a taxable gain if the transferred mortgage exceeds the portion of basis allocated to the sale part of the transaction.

EXAMPLE

You donate to a college land held long-term which is worth $250,000 and subject to a $100,000 mortgage. Your basis for the land is $150,000. As a charitable contribution, you may deduct $150,000 ($250,000–$100,000). You also are considered to have made a bargain sale for $100,000 on which you realized $40,000 long-term capital gain.

40% of the transaction is treated as a bargain sale.

$$\frac{\$100,000 \ (\text{amount of mortgage})}{\$250,000 \ (\text{fair market value})} = 40\%$$

Basis allocated to sale: 40% of $150,000 or $60,000

Amount realized	$100,000
Allocated basis	60,000
Gain	$ 40,000

Figuring value. When donating securities listed on a public exchange, fair market value is readily ascertainable from newspaper listings of stock prices. It is the average of the high and low sales price on the date of the donation.

To value other property, such as real estate or works of art, you will need the services of an experienced appraiser. Fees paid to an appraiser are not deductible as a contribution, but rather as a miscellaneous itemized deduction.

U.S. Saving Bonds. You may not donate U.S. Saving Bonds, such as EE bonds, because you may not transfer them. They are nonnegotiable. You must first cash the bonds and then give the proceeds to the charity, or surrender the bonds and have new ones registered in the donee's name. When you do this, you have to report the accrued interest on your tax return. Of course, you will get a charitable deduction for the cash gift.

Gift of installment obligations. You may deduct your donation of installment notes to a qualified philanthropy. However, if you received them on your sale of property which you reported on the installment basis, you may realize gain or loss on the gift of the notes (*see* ¶6.40). The amount of the contribution is the fair market value of the obligation, not the face amount of the notes.

Tax return requirements. Save records to support the market value and cost of donated property. Get a receipt or letter from the charitable organization acknowledging and describing the gift. Lack of substantiation may disqualify an otherwise valid deduction. If the total claimed value of your property donations exceeds $500, you must report the donation on Form 8283, which you attach to Schedule A, Form 1040. *See also* ¶14.12 for when you need an appraisal of the value of the property.

PROPERTY THAT HAS DECLINED BELOW COST

¶ 14.7 Unless the charity needs the property for its own use, you should not donate business or investment property whose value has declined below your cost. You may not claim a deductible loss when you make a gift. When the property is held for investment or business purposes, you may get the loss deduction by first selling the property and then a charitable deduction by donating the cash proceeds of the sale.

EXAMPLE

You own securities which cost $20,000 several years ago but which have declined in value to $5,000. A donation of these securities gives a charitable contribution of $5,000. But selling the securities for $5,000 to make a cash donation provides a long-term capital loss of $15,000.

If property is a personal asset (clothing, automobile) you may not deduct a loss on the sale (*see* ¶6.8). It makes no difference whether you sell and donate the sales proceeds or give the property directly to the charity.

BARGAIN SALES OF APPRECIATED PROPERTY

¶ 14.8 A sale of appreciated property to a philanthropy for less than fair market value allows you to claim a charitable deduction for the donated appreciation while receiving proceeds from the sale. However, you must pay a tax on part of the gain attributed to the sale. That is, the transaction is broken down into two parts: (1) The sale and (2) the gift.

To compute gain on the sale, you allocate the adjusted basis of the property between the sale and the gift.
1. Find the percentage of the sales proceeds over fair market value of the property.
2. Apply the percentage to the adjusted basis of the property.
3. Deduct the resulting basis of step (2) from the sales proceeds to find the gain.

EXAMPLE

You sell to a university for $12,000 stock held long-term. The adjusted basis of the stock is $12,000, and the fair market value $20,000. On the sale, you have recouped your investment and donated the appreciation of $8,000, but at the same time, you have realized taxable gain of $4,800 computed as follows:
1. Percentage of basis applied to the sale:

$$\frac{\text{sales proceeds}}{\text{fair market value}} = \frac{\$12,000}{\$20,000} = 60\%.$$

2. Basis allocated to sale: 60% of the adjusted basis of $12,000, or $7,200.
3. Gain on sale:

Sales proceeds	$12,000
Allocated basis	7,200
Gain	$ 4,800

In the case of stock where individual shares may be sold, it will make no practical difference whether you bargain-sell all of your shares to a charity, or you sell some of the shares on the open market for a price that equals your cost and make a donation of the balance of the shares. However, the bargain sale may provide an overall tax benefit if you want to recover part or all of the cost on donating a piece of property that may not be divided for sale.

The above discussion applies to bargain sales of (1) intangible personal property such as securities (including exchanges for an unassigned gift annuity); (2) real estate; and (3) tangible personal property that can be used by the charity. See ¶14.6. The bargain sale allocation rules apply whether or not the taxable gain realized is long- or short-term gain or ordinary income. But the allocation rules apply only where a deduction is allowable.

EXAMPLES

1. You sell to your church ordinary income property worth $10,000 for your adjusted basis of $4,000. The gift of $6,000 must be reduced by the ordinary gain element of $6,000. The contribution deduction is reduced to zero. Consequently, no allocation of basis is required. You have no taxable gain. ($4,000 sale proceeds–$4,000 adjusted basis).
2. You sell securities held short-term to your college for $6,000. Your adjusted basis is $4,000. Fair market value is $10,000. Your charitable contribution of $4,000 is reduced to zero because the gift is

reduced by the $6,000 ordinary income element ($4,000–$6,000). Since no charitable deduction is allowable under the sale, the allocation rules do not apply. Your taxable gain is $2,000 ($6,000–$4,000).

3. You sell to a church for $2,000 stock held short-term which has an adjusted basis of $4,000 and a fair market value of $10,000. Without allocation of basis, a charitable deduction of $2,000 would be allowed (the gift of $8,000 less the ordinary gain element of $6,000). Since a deduction would be allowed, the bargain sale allocation formula is applied. Thus 20% of basis

$$\frac{\$2,000 \text{ proceeds}}{\$10,000 \text{ market value}} \times \$4,000 \text{ adjusted basis}$$

or $800 is the allocated basis of the "sold" property. You have realized a taxable short-term gain of $1,200 ($2,000 less $800). However, your charitable contribution deduction is $3,200 (80% of basis of $4,000).

Where the property is subject to a debt, the amount of the debt is included as part of the amount realized for tax purposes.

The bargain sale computations are more complicated if you sell tangible personal property subject to the percentage reduction explained at ¶14.6, or if you bargain-sell property to a private foundation subject to the 20% ceiling. Basis must be allocated to both the gift portion and the sale portion of the transaction. To determine the allowable deduction, the gift is reduced by the appreciation in the allocated gift portion. *See* Publication 544 and Treasury regulations for details.

ART OBJECTS

¶ **14.9** You may claim a charitable deduction for a painting or other art object donated to a charity. The amount of the deduction depends on (1) whether you are the artist; (2) if you are not the artist, how long you owned it; (3) the type of organization receiving the gift.

If you are the artist, your deduction is limited to cost regardless of how long you held the art work or to what use the charity puts it. In the case of a painting, the deduction would be the lower of cost for canvas and paints or the fair market value.

If you owned the art work short-term, your deduction is limited to cost, under the rules applying to donations of ordinary income property at ¶14.6.

If you held the art object long-term, your deduction depends upon how the charity uses it. If the charity uses it for its exempt purposes, you may deduct the fair market value. However, if the charity uses it for unrelated purposes, your deduction is reduced by 100% of the appreciation. A donation of art work to a general fund raising agency would be reduced because the agency would have no direct use for it. It would have to sell the art work and use the cash for its exempt purposes.

EXAMPLES

1. You give your college a painting which you have owned for many years. Its cost was $100 but is now worth $1,000. The school displays the painting in its library for study by students. This use is related to the school's educational purposes. Your donation is deductible at fair market value. If, however, the school proposed to sell the painting and use the proceeds for general education purposes, its use would not be considered related. Your deduction would be reduced by the $900 appreciation to $100. That the school sells the painting does not necessarily reduce the donation if you show that, when you made the gift, it was reasonable to anticipate that your gift would not be put to such unrelated use.

2. You donate to the Community Fund a collection of first edition books held for many years and worth $5,000. Your cost is $1,000. Since the charity is a general fund raising organization, its use of your gift is not related. Your deduction would be $1,000 ($5,000 less $4,000).

3. You contribute to a charity antique furnishings you owned for years. The antiques cost you $500 and are now worth $5,000. The charity uses the furnishings in its office in the course of carrying on its functions. This is a related use. Your contribution deduction is $5,000.

A sale by the charity of an insubstantial part of a collection does not result in reduction of the contribution deduction.

Be prepared to support your deduction with detailed proof of cost, the date of acquisition, and how value was appraised. The appraisal fee is deductible as an itemized "miscellaneous" expense.

The IRS has its own art advisory panel to assess whether the fair market value of art works is reasonable.

INTERESTS IN REAL ESTATE

¶ **14.10** No deduction is allowable for the fair rental value of property you allow a charity to use without charge even in direct furtherance of its charitable functions as, for example, for a thrift shop.

If you donate an undivided fractional part of your entire interest, a deduction will be allowed for the fair market value of the proportionate interest donated.

A donation of an option is not deductible until the year the option to buy the property is exercised.

Remainder interest in a home or farm. You may claim a charitable deduction for a gift of the remainder value of a residence or farm donated to a charity, even though you reserve the use of the property for yourself and your spouse for a term of years or life. Remainder gifts generally must be made in trust. However, where a residence or farm is donated the remainder interest must be conveyed outright, not in trust. A remainder interest in a vacation home or in a "hobby" farm is also deductible. There is no requirement that the home be your principal residence or that the farm be profit making.

Contribution of real property for conservation purposes. A deduction may be claimed for the contribution of certain partial interests in real property to government agencies or publicly supported charities for exclusively conservation purposes. Deductible contributions include: (1) your entire interest in real property other than retained rights to subsurface oil, gas, or other minerals; (2) a remainder interest; or (3) an easement, restrictive covenant, or similar property restriction granted in perpetuity. The contribution must be in perpetuity and further at least one of these "conservation purposes": preservation of land areas for outdoor recreation, education, or scenic enjoyment; preservation of historically important land areas or structures; the protection of plant, fish, and wildlife habitats or similar natural ecosystems.

To obtain the deduction, there must be legally enforceable restrictions that prevent you from using your retained interest in the property in a way contrary to the intended conservation purpose. The donee organization must be prohibited from transferring the contributed interest except to other organizations that will hold the property for exclusively conservation purposes. If you retain an interest in subsurface oil, gas, or minerals, surface mining must generally be specifically prohibited. However, there is a limited exception where the mineral rights and surface interests have been separately owned since June 12, 1976. A deduction will be allowed if the probability of surface mining is so remote as to be considered negligible. The exception does not apply if you are related to the owner of the surface interest or if you received the mineral interest (directly or indirectly) from the surface owner.

LIFE INSURANCE

¶ **14.11** You may deduct the value of a life insurance policy if the charity is irrevocably named as beneficiary and you make both a legal assignment and a complete delivery of the policy. You should reserve no right to change the beneficiary.

The amount of your deduction generally depends on the type of policy donated. Your insurance company can furnish you with the information necessary to calculate your deduction. In addition, you may deduct premiums you pay after you assign the policy.

APPRAISALS NEEDED FOR PROPERTY DONATIONS

¶ **14.12** If the total value of your property donations exceeds $500, you must provide details for each donation on Form 8283. Further, if you donate property other than publicly traded securities valued at more than $5,000, you must get a written appraisal to support your deduction.

An appraisal is also required if several similar items such as coins or paintings with an aggregate value exceeding $5,000 are donated, even if the donees are different. For nonpublicly traded securities valued at more than $5,000 but not more than $10,000, an appraisal is not required, but gifts over $500 must be reported on Form 8283.

An appraisal must be made by an unrelated professional appraiser no earlier than 60 days before your gift, and you must receive it by the due date, including extensions, of your return.

Keep the appraisal for your records. You do not have to attach the appraisal to your return, but you must complete an appraisal summary on Form 8283. The appraisal summary must be signed by an authorized representative of the donee organization, acknowledging receipt of the property. Further, your appraiser must certify the appraised value and his or her qualifications on the form.

If you do not complete a required appraisal summary on Form 8283, the IRS may disallow the deduction, or it may give you 90 days to provide the information. If you comply, the deduction will be allowed, unless the IRS concludes that the original failure was not a good faith omission.

A professional appraiser is subject to a $1,000 penalty if he knowingly overvalues charitable contribution property; $10,000 for corporate returns. If you rely on the appraisal of a disqualified appraiser, you may avoid penalties for claiming an overvalued deduction by showing that you were not aware of the appraiser's overvaluation. Penalties for overvaluation of property values are discussed at ¶38.9.

A fee paid an appraiser is deductible as a "miscellaneous" expense subject to the 2% adjusted gross income floor, *see* chapter 19.

Charity reports transfers within two years. If the charity sells or otherwise disposes of the appraised property within two years after your gift, it must notify the IRS on Form 8282 and send you a copy. The IRS could compare the selling price received by the charity with the value you claimed on Form 8283.

BUSINESS OR FARM INVENTORY

¶ **14.13** Business owners and accrual basis farmers generally may not deduct more than cost for donations of inventory. Costs incurred in a year prior to the donation must be removed from inventory if a charitable deduction is claimed. No contribution deduction is allowed for a gift of merchandise which was produced or acquired in the year donated. Instead, the cost is deducted as a business expense or added to the cost of goods sold. A business expense deduction is not subject to the percentage limitation applied to donations.

A cash basis farmer may not claim a charitable deduction for a donation of inventory products. This is because the fair market value of his donated property must be reduced under the ordinary income rule to zero.

DONATING INCOME AND REMAINDER INTERESTS THROUGH TRUSTS

¶ **14.14** Outright gifts are not the only way to make deductible gifts to charities. You may transfer property to a charitable income trust or a charitable remainder trust to provide funds for charity.

A charitable income trust involves your transfer of property to a trust directed to pay income to a charity you name, for the term of the trust, and then to return the property to you or to someone else.

A charitable remainder trust is one which provides income for you or another beneficiary for life, after which the property passes to a charity.

Trust arrangements require the services of an experienced attorney who will draft the trust in appropriate form and advise you of the tax consequences.

Deductions for gifts of income interests in trust. Current law is designed to prevent a donor from claiming an immediate deduction for the present value of trust income payable to a charity for a term of years. In limited situations, a donor may claim a deduction if either: (1) He gives away all his interests in the property. For example, he puts his property in trust, giving an income interest for 20 years to a church and the remainder to a college. A deduction is allowed for the value of the property. (2) He creates a unitrust or annuity trust, and he is taxable on the income. A unitrust for this purpose provides that a fixed percentage of trust assets is payable to the charitable income beneficiary each year. An annuity trust provides for payment of a guaranteed dollar amount to the charitable income beneficiary each year. A deduction is allowed for the present value of the unitrust or annuity trust interest.

Alternative (2) will probably not be chosen, unless the income of the trust is from tax-exempt securities. A tax may be due if the donor dies before the trust ends or is no longer the taxable owner of trust income. The law provides for a recapture of a proportion of the tax deduction, even where the income was tax exempt (*see* Treasury regulations).

Charitable remainder trusts. A charitable deduction is allowable for transfers of property to charitable remainder trusts only if the trust meets these requirements: The income payable for a noncharitable income beneficiary's life or a term of up to 20 years must be guaranteed under a unitrust or annuity trust. If a donor gives all of his interests in the property to the charities, the annuity or unitrust requirements need not be satisfied. The value of the charitable deduction allowable for a gift in trust is determined by Treasury tables.

Life income plans. A philanthropy may offer a life income plan (pooled income fund) to which you transfer property or money in return for a guaranteed income for life. After your death, the philanthropy has full control over the property. If you enter such a plan, ask the philanthropy for the amount of the deduction that you may claim for the value of your gift.

LIMITATIONS PLACED ON DONATIONS

ORGANIZATIONS QUALIFIED TO RECEIVE DEDUCTIBLE DONATIONS

¶ **14.15** The following types of organizations may qualify to receive deductible contributions:

1. The United States, a possession or political subdivision, a state, city, or town. The gift must be for public purposes. The gift may be directed to a government unit, or it may be to a government agency, such as a state university, a fire department, a civil defense group, or a committee to raise funds to develop land into a public park. Donations may be made to the Social Security system (Federal Old Age and Survivors Insurance trust fund). Donations may be made to the federal government to help reduce the national debt; checks should be made payable to "Bureau of the Public Debt."

2. A domestic nonprofit organization, trust, community chest, fund or foundation operated exclusively for one of the following purposes—

Religious. Payments for pew rents, assessments, and dues to churches and synagogues are deductible.

Charitable. In this class are organizations such as Boy Scouts, Girl Scouts, American Red Cross, Community Funds, Cancer Societies, CARE, Salvation Army, Y.M.C.A., and Y.W.C.A.

Scientific, literary, and educational. Included in this group are hospitals, research organizations, colleges, universities, and other schools that do not maintain racially discriminatory policies; and leagues or associations set up for education or to combat crime, improve public morals, and aid public welfare.

Prevention of cruelty to children or animals.

Fostering amateur sports competition. However, the organization's activities may not provide athletic facilities or equipment.

3. Domestic nonprofit veteran organizations or auxiliary units.

4. A domestic fraternal group operating under the lodge system, only if contributions are to be used exclusively for religious, charitable,

scientific, literary, or educational purposes, or for the prevention of cruelty to children or animals.

5. Nonprofit cemetery and burial companies, where the voluntary contribution benefits the whole cemetery, not your plot.

6. Legal services corporation established under the Legal Services Corporation Act which provides legal assistance to financially needy people in noncriminal proceedings.

Foreign charities. You may deduct donations to domestic organizations that distribute funds to charities in foreign countries, as long as the American organization controls the distribution of the funds overseas. An outright contribution to a foreign charitable organization may *not* be deducted. Some exceptions to this ban are provided by international treaties. A limited exception applies to contributions to certain Canadian organizations if you have income from Canadian sources. For further details, write IRS, Foreign Operations District, Washington, D.C. 20225.

NONDEDUCTIBLE CONTRIBUTIONS

¶ **14.16** The following types of contributions to philanthropic or other types of organizations are not deductible:

1. Payments to an organization that devotes a substantial part of its activities to lobbying, trying to influence legislation, or carrying on propaganda or whose lobbying activities exceed certain limits set by the law causing the organization to lose its tax-exempt status. The IRS has disallowed contributions to a civic group opposing saloons, nightclubs, and gambling places, although the group also aided libraries, churches, and other public programs.

2. Gifts to needy or worthy individuals, scholarships for specific students, or gifts to organizations to benefit only certain groups. However, the IRS in private rulings has allowed deductions for scholarship funds which are limited to members of a particular religion, so long as that religion is open to all on a racially nondiscriminatory basis, and to scholarship funds open only to male students.

3. Gifts to organizations such as—
   Fraternal groups—except when they set up special organizations exclusively devoted to charitable, educational, or other approved purposes.
   Professional groups—such as those organized by accountants, lawyers, and physicians—except when they are specially created for exclusive charitable, educational, or other philanthropic purposes. The IRS will disallow unrestricted gifts made to state bar associations, although such organizations may have some public purposes. Courts have allowed donations to bar associations on the ground that their activities benefit the general public.
   Clubs for social purposes—fraternities and sororities are generally in this class.

4. Donations to civic leagues, communist or communist-front organizations, chambers of commerce, business leagues, or labor unions.

5. Contributions to a hospital or school operated for profit.

6. Purchase price of church building bond. To claim a deduction, you must donate the bond to the church. The amount of the deduction is the fair market value of the bond when you make the donation. Interest on the bond is income each year, under the original issue discount rules of ¶4.7, where no interest will be paid until the bond matures.

7. Donations of blood to the Red Cross or other blood banks.

8. Contributions to foreign charitable organizations or directly to foreign governments. Thus, a contribution to the State of Israel was disallowed. Similarly, contributions to international charitable organizations are nondeductible.

9. Donations which provide you with goods or services. You may not deduct tuition payments to a parochial or other church-sponsored school for the education of your children. Payments exceeding the usual tuition charge are deductible.

10. Fees paid to a tax-exempt rest home in which you live, or to a hospital for the care of a particular patient. A gift to a retirement home, over and above monthly fees, is not deductible if the size or type of your quarters depends on the gift.

Unless you contribute to an organization exclusively operated for a charitable, religious, or other approved purpose, you may not deduct your contribution, even though your funds are used for a charitable or religious purpose.

Donation of services. You may not deduct the value of volunteer work you perform for charities. But *see* ¶14.4 for the deductions allowed for unreimbursed expenses incurred during such work.

Free use of property. You may not deduct the rental value of property you allow a charity to use without charge. That is, if you allow a charity rent-free use of an office in your building, you may not deduct the fair rental value. You also have no deduction when you lend money to a charity without charging interest.

CEILING ON CHARITABLE DEDUCTIONS

¶ **14.17** Depending on the type of contribution and the organization to which the donation is made, an annual ceiling of 20%, 30%, or 50% may be placed on the amount of contributions allowed as a deduction. The ceiling is based on a technical term called "contribution base." For most purposes, "contribution base" is adjusted gross income (*see* ¶13.8). "Contribution base" is adjusted gross income computed without regard to a net operating loss carryback.

For most individuals, the 50% limit will apply, except where they contribute appreciated securities or other intangible personal property and real estate held long-term. Such contributions are subject to the 30% ceiling if made to organizations qualifying for the 50% ceiling. A 20% limit generally applies to contributions of capital gain property to organizations that do not qualify for the 50% ceiling, such as nonoperating private foundations and charities that do not receive substantial support from the general public. However, for contributions of cash and ordinary income property to such organizations, a 30% ceiling applies. A 30% ceiling also applies to gifts, such as gifts in trust, which are considered to be "for the use of," rather than directly "to" a qualified charity.

A husband and wife filing a joint return figure the ceiling on their total joint adjusted gross income.

The 50% ceiling. Contributions of cash and noncapital gain property generally are subject to the 50% ceiling if *made to* the following types of charitable organizations:

Churches, synagogues and other religious organizations.
Schools, colleges and other educational organizations that normally have regular faculties and student bodies in attendance.
Hospitals and medical research organizations.
Foundations for state colleges.
Publicly supported organizations that receive a substantial part of their financial support from the general public or a government unit. Libraries, museums, drama, opera, ballet and orchestral societies, community funds, the American Red Cross, Heart Fund and other groups providing research and aid in treatment of disease are generally in this category.
Private operating foundations.
Private foundations that distribute their income annually to qualified charities within the time prescribed by law.
Private foundations that pool donations, allow donors to designate the charities to receive their gifts, and pay out all funds received within times stated by IRS rules.
Donations made merely *for the use of* an organization do not qualify for the 50% ceiling. This restriction affects certain trust dispositions (*see* Treasury regulations).

The 30% limit for certain capital gain property. The 30% limit generally applies to donations of appreciated intangible personal property (like securities) and real estate held long-term where the gift is to a publicly supported charity or a foundation that qualifies for the 50% ceiling; *see* list above.

This 30% limit also applies to donations of appreciated tangible personal property held long-term (like a boat, furnishings, and art work) where the charitable organization's use of your gift is directly related to its charitable purposes. However, the 50% ceiling applies to gifts of tangible personal property held long-term where the organization's use of the gift is not directly related to its charitable purposes and the deduction is reduced for appreciation (see ¶14.6). The 50% ceiling may also apply to appreciated intangible personal property under an election providing for a percentage reduction explained in ¶14.19.

The 30% limit for gifts to nonoperating private foundations and certain other organizations. Gifts of cash or ordinary income property are subject to a 30% limit if made to nonoperating private foundations and other charities that are not in the above list of corporations qualifying for the 50% ceiling. For example, a gift of cash or ordinary income property to a veteran's organization, fraternal society or nonprofit cemetery is subject to the 30% ceiling.

Such gifts are deductible only to the extent of the lower of: (1) 30% of your adjusted gross income, or (2) 50% of your adjusted gross income less donations to publicly supported charities or foundations qualifying for the 50% ceiling (including donations of capital gain property which are subject to the 30% ceiling).

Contributions that cannot be deducted due to the 30% ceiling may be carried forward for five years; see ¶14.18.

The 20% limit for capital gain property. Gifts of capital gain property to private nonoperating foundations and other organizations not eligible for the 50% ceiling (see list above) are deductible only to the extent of the lower of: (1) 20% of your adjusted gross income or (2) 30% of adjusted gross income less donations of capital gain property which qualify for the 30% ceiling (contributed to organizations qualifying for the 50% ceiling).

Contributions not deductible due to the 20% limitation may be carried over for five years; see ¶14.18.

Applying the ceiling. To figure your deduction follow this order in applying the various income limitations:

1. Gifts qualifying for the 50% ceiling
2. Gifts of cash and ordinary income property to nonoperating private foundations and other organizations that qualify for the 30% ceiling
3. Gifts of capital gain property to organizations qualifying for the 50% ceiling that are subject to the 30% of income deduction limit
4. Gifts of capital gain property to nonoperating private foundations and other organizations not qualifying under the 50% ceiling.

EXAMPLE

Smith has an adjusted gross income of $100,000. He makes charitable contributions of $40,000 in 30% capital gain property to a college and $30,000 in cash to a nonoperating private foundation subject to the 30% ceiling. The 30% limitation for cash gifts to nonoperating private foundations is applied before the 30% limitation applicable to gifts of capital gain property to public charities. The deduction for the cash gift is reduced to $10,000 (50% of $100,000–$40,000). The amount of the contribution of 30% capital gain property is limited to $30,000 (30% of $100,000). Accordingly, Smith's charitable contributions deduction

is $40,000 ($10,000 + $30,000). Smith is allowed to carry over $10,000 ($40,000–$30,000) from his contributions of 30% capital gain property. He is also allowed to carry over the nondeductible $20,000 cash donation ($30,000– $10,000).

FIVE-YEAR CARRYOVER FOR EXCESS DONATIONS EXCEEDING STATUTORY CEILING

¶ 14.18 If your donations to charities that qualify for the 50% ceiling total more than 50% of your adjusted gross income, you may carry over the excess over the next five years.

Where contributions of appreciated long-term intangible personal property and real estate (or tangible personal property put to a related use by the charity) exceed the 30% ceiling, the excess over 30% also may be carried over for five years. The excess is subject to the 30% ceiling in the carryover years. A five-year carryover applies also to excess contributions to nonoperating private foundations and other organizations qualifying for the 30% or 20% ceiling.

When planning substantial donations that may exceed the annual ceiling, make a projection of your income for at least five years. Although the carryover period of five years will probably absorb most excess donations, it is possible that the excess may be so large that it will not be completely absorbed during the year of the contribution and the five-year carryover period. It is also possible that your income may drop in the future so that you cannot adequately take advantage of the excess.

If a donor dies during the carryover period, the excess carryover for the years after his death is not deductible.

If in any taxable year a deduction is claimed for part or all of a carryover, you attach a statement showing the contribution year or years, and the excess carried over for each year. *See* Treasury regulations for further details and for the effect of a net operating loss carryback.

ELECTION TO REDUCE APPRECIATION OF CERTAIN PROPERTY GIFTS

¶ 14.19 Although the 30% ceiling generally applies to long-term intangible property (such as securities) and real estate, you may elect the 50% ceiling, provided you reduce the deduction by 100% of the appreciation on all donations during the year of long-term intangible property and real estate and tangible personal property related in use to the organization's charitable function. In most cases, this election will be made only where the amount of appreciation is negligible. Where there is substantial appreciation, the increase in the deduction may not make up or exceed the required 100% reduction. If the election is made in a year in which there are carryovers of capital gain property subject to the 30% ceiling, the carryovers are subject to reduction (see Treasury regulations for the adjustment).

The election is made by attaching a statement to your original return or amended return filed by the original due date.

15

DEDUCTIONS FOR INTEREST YOU PAY

¶ **15.1** Starting in 1987, the following new tax law rules regarding deductions for interest you pay take effect:

Personal interest. In 1987, you may deduct 65% of personal interest payments; in 1988 40%; in 1989, 20%; in 1990, 10%. After 1990, no personal interest will be deductible. The term personal interest covers a broad range of interest expense such as credit card finance charges, interest on tax deficiencies, car loans, and educational loans. The phase-out applies to consumer interest paid after 1986 even if the debt was incurred before 1987.

Investment interest. In 1987, only 65% of the first $10,000 of investment interest exceeding net investment income is deductible; 40% in 1988; 20% in 1989; 10% in 1990. After 1990, no deduction will be allowed for interest exceeding net investment income. Disallowed interest may be carried forward if there is net invest-

ment income in excess of investment interest in the later year.

Mortgage interest. Interest on debt secured by a first and/or second home is generally fully deductible. However, where a loan made after August 16, 1986, exceeds the purchase price of the home plus improvement costs, the loan proceeds must be used for educational or medical purposes in order to claim an interest deduction in 1987 and later years.

You must file the new **Form 8598** to figure deductible mortgage interest if *after* August 16, 1986, you took out any home mortgage (or other debt secured by the home, such as a home equity loan) for purposes other than to buy the home. You also file Form 8598 if *after* August 16, 1986, you refinanced a mortgage debt originally incurred before August 17, 1986, or you borrowed additional amounts on the original mortgage.

SEGREGATE YOUR INTEREST PAYMENTS

¶ **15.2** The limitations placed on interest requires you to segregate your interest within the following classes:

Residential mortgage interest. This is generally fully deductible if paid on no more than two residences. If the loan was made after August 16, 1986, part of the interest may not be deductible if the loan proceeds exceed the purchase price of the house; *see* ¶15.11.

Investment interest. This is interest paid on debt to buy or carry investment property, other than property subject to the passive activity limitations of chapter 11. Interest expenses that exceed your net investment income are deductible up to $6,500 in 1987.

Business interest. This is fully deductible. Distinguish between interest paid for personal purposes and interest paid for rental or business purposes. Interest on debts incurred for nonbusiness purposes is deductible only if you have itemized deductions. Interest paid on a debt connected with rental property or a business is deducted from rent or business income, even if you do not claim itemized deductions. Whether interest is a business or a personal expense depends upon the use made of the money borrowed, not on the kind of property used to secure the loan. Interest on a business loan is deductible from business income, even though the loan is secured by a mortgage on nonbusiness assets. Interest on personal loans, even though secured by a business asset, is deductible only if you itemize deductions. If you rent part of your personal residence and you borrow money for the purchase or repair of the house, part of the interest payment allocable to the rented portion is deducted from the rental income. The balance is an itemized deduction. Interest on an income tax deficiency is personal interest, even though the deficiency is related to your business.

Personal interest. All other interest that does not fall into the above categories is considered personal interest. In 1987, 65% of personal interest is deductible. Interest on a tax deficiency is considered personal interest, even if the deficiency is based on business income.

Retirement plan loans. No interest deduction is allowed if you borrow from a qualified employer plan and (1) you are a key employee or (2) the loan is secured by elective deferrals from your salary to a 401(k) plan or a tax-sheltered annuity plan.

Subject to the above limits, you may deduct interest on debts for which you are legally liable. You may not deduct interest due on another person's debt. Other restrictions are discussed at ¶15.8.

Check your payment of personal judgments, loans, and other debts for full interest charges. If you make a late payment of taxes or mortgage payment, or you pay a deficiency at a later date, part of the amount will include deductible interest. A penalty charge may or may not be deductible as additional interest. A penalty for late payment which is merely a service charge is not deductible. A fixed charge having no relationship to the amount borrowed or the time given to pay suggests that the charge is a service charge and not interest.

Some utility companies charge an additional percentage if a bill is not paid within 20 days of the due date. The IRS says that the late-payment charge is deductible interest, if it is not connected to any service provided by the utility but is assessed solely on the basis of late payment.

Imputed interest deductions. Interest imputed under the rules for interest-free loans (¶4.17) and unstated interest within the OID and deferred payment rules (¶4.18) are deductible.

Interest on loans to buy market discount bonds and Treasury bills. Limits apply to the deduction for interest on loans used to buy or carry market discount bonds (*see* ¶4.8) and Treasury bills (*see* ¶4.14) acquired after July 18, 1984.

A creditor may hold a debtor's stock as collateral. If the creditor receives and applies the dividends to the interest, the debtor may claim an interest deduction for such amounts.

Loan fees. Whether a loan fee is deductible as interest in a lump sum in the year of payment or must be amortized over the life of the loan depends on how you structure the initial transfer of funds. To avoid amortization, first obtain the full amount of the loan and then pay the fee to the lender. An immediate deduction is not jeopardized even if the prepayment is an integral part of the loan agreement, and the lender would not have made the loan without charging the fee. Where the lender gives you only the net proceeds of the loan, you must amortize the fee over the life of the loan.

Interest on loan obtained by dummy corporation. You may be forced to set up a dummy corporation to obtain loans that would otherwise violate state usury laws. According to the IRS, you may not deduct interest paid on the loan; the interest is deductible only by the corporation although it is a shell. Courts are split on this issue.

Important: For guidelines on earmarking loan proceeds and allocating interest, *see* ¶ 15.15.

YEAR TO CLAIM AN INTEREST DEDUCTION

¶ **15.3** Subject to the limits of ¶ 15.2, as a cash basis taxpayer, you deduct interest in the year of payment except for prepayments of interest; see ¶15.4.

An accrual basis taxpayer generally deducts interest in the year in which the interest expense accrues.

Giving a promissory note is not considered payment. Increasing the amount of a loan by interest owed, as with insurance loans, is also not considered payment and will not support a deduction (*see* below). If a person pays your interest obligation with the understanding you will repay him, you take the deduction in the year he pays the interest, not when you repay him.

The following paragraphs illustrate how a cash basis taxpayer treats interest in the following situations:

On a life insurance loan, you claim a deduction in the year in which the interest is paid. You may not claim a deduction when the insurance company adds the interest to your debt. You may not deduct your payment of interest on an insurance loan after you assign the policy.

EXAMPLE
You borrow $500 at 5% interest from your insurance company against your life insurance policy. This year, instead of paying the interest ($25), you execute a new note to the company for $525 to replace the old note plus the interest due. This is not payment of interest, and no deduction is permitted. If you allow the interest to accumulate on the loan by executing new notes each year until the cash surrender value of the policy is about equal to the loan plus all the accumulated interest, you might then surrender your policy. This is the same as repayment of the loan and interest, and you claim your interest deduction at that time subject to the percentage limitations for personal interest.

See ¶15.8 below discussing when interest is not deductible on certain insurance purchase plans.

On a margin account with a broker, interest is deductible in the year in which it is paid or your account is credited after the interest has been charged. But an interest charge to your account is not payment if you do not pay it in cash or the broker has not collected dividends, interest, or security sales proceeds which he may apply against the interest due him. Interest on margin accounts is subject to investment interest limitations.

For partial payment of a loan, interest is deductible in the year the payment is credited against interest due. When a loan has no provision for allocating payments between principal and income, the law presumes that a partial payment is applied first to interest and then to principal, unless you agree otherwise. Where the payment is in full settlement of the debt, the payment is applied first to principal, unless you agree otherwise. Where there is an involuntary payment, such as that following a foreclosure sale of collateral, sales proceeds are applied first to principal, unless you agree to the contrary. See also ¶15.15 for the effect of payments on the allocation of debt proceeds.

EXAMPLES
1. Assume you owe $1,000 on a note, plus interest of $120. If you should pay $800 on account, the law presumes that $120 of the $800 represents a payment of interest.
2. Same as above but the payment is accepted in full settlement of the debt. The law presumes that the $800 represents a payment of principal for which no deduction is allowed.

> *Using borrowed funds to pay interest.* To get an interest deduction you must pay the interest; you may not claim a deduction by having the creditor add the interest to the debt. If you do not have funds to pay the interest, you may borrow money to pay the interest. Borrow the funds from a different creditor. The IRS disallows deductions where a debtor borrows from the same creditor to make interest payments on an earlier loan; the second loan is considered merely a device for getting an interest expense deduction without actually making payments. Courts tend to side with the IRS.

Note renewed. You may not deduct interest by merely giving a new note. You claim a deduction in the year the renewed note is paid. The giving of a new note or increasing the amount due is not payment. The same is true when past due interest is deducted from the proceeds of a new loan. This is not deemed payment of the interest.

PREPAID INTEREST ALLOCATED OVER TERM OF LOAN

¶ **15.4** Prepaid interest is deductible over the period of the loan, whether you are a cash basis or accrual taxpayer. In the year of prepayment, you may not deduct a prepayment of interest allocable to any period falling in a later taxable year.

Treatment of interest included in a level payment schedule. Where payments of principal and interest are equal, a large amount of interest allocated to the payments made in early years of a loan will generally not be considered prepaid interest. However, if the loan calls for a variable interest rate, the IRS may treat interest payments as consisting partly of interest, computed under an average level effective rate, and partly of prepaid interest allocable to later years of the loan. An interest rate which varies with the "prime rate" does not necessarily involve a prepaid interest element.

INTEREST ON DISCOUNT LOANS

¶ **15.5** When you borrow money and give a note to the lender, the amount of your loan proceeds may be less than the face value of the note. The difference between the proceeds and the face amount is interest discount. For loans that do not fall within the OID rules of ¶4.6, such as loans of a year or less, interest is deductible in the year of payment if you are on the cash basis. If you use the accrual basis, the interest is deductible as it accrues.

EXAMPLE
In February 1986, you borrow $1,000 and receive $900 in return for your $1,000 note. You repay the full loan in January 1987. You are on the cash basis. You do not deduct the interest of $100 when the note is given. The $100 interest is deductible when the loan is paid in 1987.

For loans that fall within OID rules, your lender should provide a statement showing the interest element and the tax treatment of the interest.

RULE OF 78's

¶ **15.6** When payments of a loan are made in installments, the lender may charge interest under the "rule of 78's." Under the "rule of 78's," more interest is charged to the earlier installments of the loan. If you are on the accrual basis, you must deduct interest under the regular accrual basis; you may not claim a deduction based on the "rule of 78's."

If you are on the cash basis, the IRS will allow interest deductions based on the "rule of 78's" only for interest paid on a short-term consumer loan covering a period of five years or less. If you have borrowed under terms requiring a computation of interest under the "rule of 78's," ask the lender for the amount of deductible interest. For loans other than qualifying short-term consumer loans, the deductible amount must be based on the accrual method even if you are on the cash basis.

According to the IRS, a short-term consumer loan qualifying for the "rule of 78's" is a self-amortizing loan that requires level payments at regular intervals at least annually, over a period of five years or less (with no balloon payment at the end of the loan term). The loan agreement must also provide for the calculation of interest under the "rule of 78's" method.

The "rule of 78's" method. Under this method, interest due for the loan period is allocated by a fraction to determine the amount of interest due for each installment. The denominator of the fraction always remains the same—and is the sum of the digits for the number of installment payments of the loan. The denominator of a 12-installment loan is 78 $(12 + 11 + 10 + \ldots + 1 = 78)$. The denominator of a 10-installment loan is 55 $(10 + 9 + \ldots + 1 = 55)$. The denominator of a 60-installment loan is 1,830 $(60 + 59 + 58 + \ldots + 1 = 1,830)$. The numerator of the fraction changes from installment to installment and is the number of installments remaining on the note. Thus the fraction for figuring the interest due for the second installment of a 12-installment loan is $^{11}/_{78}$.

FINANCE CHARGES

¶ 15.7 In 1987, you may deduct 65% of interest finance charges paid on credit purchases of personal items through:

Credit cards. The finance charge of a bank, gasoline company or department store credit card plan is generally deductible as interest.

Revolving credit accounts. Finance charges on a revolving credit account in a retail store are deductible as interest.

Installment contract where the charge is separately stated as a percentage of the unpaid balance. A prepayment penalty, sometimes called an acquisition charge or minimum fee, may also be incurred and is deductible as interest.

Educational service contract for tuition and lodgings. The separately stated finance charge on the unpaid balance is deductible as interest.

> In addition to monthly finance charges, also deductible is a one-time charge for each new cash advance and each new check and overdraft advance added to your balance, provided it is not a service charge, loan fee, credit investigation fee, or other similar fee.

Fixed fee on installment purchase contract may require averaging. If a fixed or flat fee is charged on an installment contract to buy personal property or educational services provided by educational institutions, the deduction may be limited as follows: If the interest rate is given, then that part of the fee allocated to the interest is deductible. If the interest rate is not given, the deduction is based on 6% of the average balance figured according to Treasury regulations.

Interest paid on deferred tuition plan. Students of some universities are allowed to defer tuition payments until they graduate and earn income. Each student joins a group that is obligated to pay the tuition over a period up to 35 years. The IRS says a participant may not deduct any part of a payment as interest until he has paid up his total tuition and the insurance premiums. Further payments are then deductible as interest.

NONDEDUCTIBLE INTEREST

¶ 15.8 A checklist at chapter 42 lists nondeductible interest charges, some of which are detailed below.

Interest on certain retirement plans. If you are a key employee (generally an owner or officer) you cannot deduct interest on a loan from your

employer's retirement plan. Further, no interest deduction is allowed if you borrow your own elective deferrals from salary (or income on the deferrals) to a 401(k) plan or tax sheltered annuity plan.

Interest paid on another person's debts if you are not legally obligated to make the payment. However, a father was allowed to deduct interest on a mortgage on property owned by a family trust; under state law, he was still liable on the mortgage.

Interest on minimum deposit life insurance plans. If, after August 6, 1963, you bought life insurance policies under a plan whereby loans on the cash value of the policy pay for part of the premiums, you may not deduct the interest paid on the loans, unless you meet *one* of these conditions: (1) The interest paid during the year is not over $100. (2) During the first seven years of the policy, you paid at least four of the annual premiums without having to borrow under the plan. (3) You borrowed because of an unforeseen substantial loss of income or increase in financial obligations. (4) You incurred the debt in your business. For further details, *see* Treasury regulations.

Interest on debts incurred or continued to purchase or carry a single premium life insurance, endowment, or annuity contract if substantially all the premiums are paid within four years (or deposited with the company within that time).

Interest on debts to carry tax-exempt obligations. See ¶ 15.9.

Interest on debts to purchase or carry straddles unless the straddle is a hedging transaction. See ¶ 6.16.

Construction period interest with respect to real property held for business or investment purposes. See ¶ 16.4.

Interest where no real debt exists. If there is no recourse against you personally, you have not incurred a real liability. Loans between family members are particularly vulnerable to attack as being mere gifts.

Interest incurred on loans to finance the purchase of securities in tax avoidance schemes. However, one court allowed the deduction where an actual bank loan was made to finance the purchase of short-term U.S. Treasury notes. In another case, the deduction was disallowed where the loans and interest were merely reflected in "bookkeeping entries."

Interest charged for reinstating GI insurance is not deductible. Lapsed GI insurance may be reinstated on the payment of the back premiums plus interest charged on these premiums. The interest charge is not deductible. It is not real interest because no debt is outstanding between the parties. It is merely a charge for reinstating the policy.

Handling charges, loan commitment fees, insurance, financing charges, and other costs computed without reference to the period of the loan are not deductible as interest. Such charges are added to the basis of the asset financed by the loan. If you want an interest deduction, insist that these charges be called interest if they are the price you have to pay to postpone full payment. Under the "Truth in Lending Act," finance charges on consumer loans must be stated separately. The IRS has ruled that the extra charge by an insurance company against policyholders who choose to pay premiums on other than an annual basis is not interest. The Tax Court held that bank service charges on a checking account are not deductible as interest.

A voluntary payment of additional interest, or a retroactive increase in interest without additional consideration, is not deductible. For example, a loan calls for 7% interest and you voluntarily pay 8%. Only interest at the rate of 7% is deductible.

Interest beyond the limitations of the "at risk" rules. See ¶ 11.11.

INTEREST ON DEBTS TO CARRY TAX-EXEMPT OBLIGATIONS AND SHORT SALES

¶ 15.9 When you borrow money in order to buy or carry tax-exempt bonds, you may not deduct any interest paid on your loan. Application of this disallowance rule is clear where there is actual evidence that loan proceeds were used to buy tax exempts or that tax exempts were used as collateral. But sometimes the relationship between a loan and the purchase of tax exempts is less obvious, as where you hold tax exempts and borrow to carry other securities or investments. IRS guidelines explain when a direct relationship between the debt and an investment in tax exempts will be inferred so that no interest deduction is allowed. The IRS will *not* infer a direct relationship between a debt and an investment in tax exempts in these cases:

1. The investment in tax exempts is not substantial. That is, it is not more than 2% of the adjusted basis of the investment portfolio and any assets held in an actively conducted business.
2. The debt is incurred for a personal purpose. For example, an investor may take out a home mortgage instead of selling his tax exempts and using the proceeds to finance the home purchase. Interest on the mortgage is deductible.
3. The debt is incurred in connection with the active conduct of a business and does not exceed business needs. But, if a person reasonably could have foreseen when he purchased the tax exempts that he would have to borrow to meet ordinary and recurrent business needs, his interest expenses are not deductible.

The guidelines infer a direct relationship between the debt and an investment in tax exempts in this type of case: an investor in tax exempts has outstanding debts not directly related to personal expenses or to his business. The interest will be disallowed even if the debt appears to have been incurred to purchase other portfolio investments. Portfolio investments include transactions entered into for profit, including investments in real estate, which are not connected with the active conduct of a business.

EXAMPLE

An investor owning $360,000 in tax-exempt bonds purchased real estate in a joint venture, giving a purchase money mortgage and cash for the price. He deducted interest on the mortgage. The IRS disallowed the deduction, claiming the debt was incurred to carry tax exempts. A court allowed the deduction. A mortgage is the customary manner of financing such a purchase. Furthermore, since the purchase was part of a joint venture, the other parties' desires in the manner of financing had to be considered.

Note: If you receive exempt interest dividends from a mutual fund during the year, you may not deduct interest on a loan used to buy or carry the mutual fund shares.

Short sale expenses. Expenses incurred to carry personal property used in a short sale occurring after July 18, 1984, are generally treated as interest incurred to carry tax exempts and thus not deductible. This disallowance rule applies to payments to a broker in lieu of dividends which do not have to be capitalized under the rules discussed at ¶6.52. However, a deduction is not barred for short sale expenses if you provide cash as collateral for a short sale and do not receive a material return on the deposited cash.

Investment interest expenses are subject to the limitations of ¶15.14.

DEDUCTIONS FOR OWNERS OF COOPERATIVE AND CONDOMINIUM APARTMENTS

¶ 15.10 **Cooperative apartments.** If you are a tenant-stockholder of a cooperative apartment, you may deduct your portion of:

Interest paid by the cooperative on its debts, provided you do not pay interest on more than two residences; *see* ¶15.11. This includes your pro rata share of the permanent financing expenses (points) of the cooperative on its mortgage covering the housing project.

Taxes paid by the cooperative. (However, if the cooperative does not own the land and building but merely leases them and is required to pay real estate taxes under the terms of the lease, you may not deduct your share of the tax payment.)

In some localities, such as New York City, rent control rules allow tenants of a building converted to cooperatives to remain in their apartments even if they do not buy into the co-op. A holdover tenant may prevent some co-op purchasers from occupying an apartment. The IRS rules that the fact that a holdover tenant stays in the apartment will not bar the owner from deducting his share of the co-op's interest and taxes.

Condominiums. If you own an apartment or unit in a condominium, you have a direct ownership interest in the property and are treated, for tax purposes, just as any other property owner. You may deduct your payments of real estate taxes and mortgage interest. You may also deduct taxes and interest paid on the mortgage debt of the project allocable to your share of the property. The deduction of interest from condominium ownership is also subject to the two residences limit of ¶15.11. If you use your condominium apartment for business, a profession, or for the production of income, or if you rent it to others, you may deduct expenses of maintenance and repairs and claim depreciation deductions subject to rules of ¶29.17.

TWO RESIDENCE RULE FOR HOME MORTGAGE INTEREST

¶ 15.11 Qualifying residential mortgage interest on up to two residences is exempt from the phase-out limitations for personal interest. The tax rules for deducting qualifying residential mortgage interest distinguish between mortgages made before, on, or after August 16, 1986.

Interest on mortgage debt incurred before August 17, 1986. If debt secured by your principal residence or a second residence was incurred on or before August 16, 1986, the interest is fully deductible. It does not matter how you used the loan proceeds. Such pre-August 17, 1986, loans are not subject to the following limitations applied to mortgage debts incurred after August 16, 1986. However, if you increase the debt which was secured as of August 16, 1986, such as by taking a line of credit or refinancing the mortgage, the *increased debt* may be subject to the new tax limits for debts incurred after August 16, 1986. When this book went to press, Congress was considering a bill allowing a full interest deduction for a refinanced mortgage originally incurred on or before August 16, 1986, provided the new mortgage does not exceed the outstanding principal debt immediately before the refinancing. *See* the Supplement.

Interest on mortgage debt incurred after August 16, 1986. Whether interest is deductible on a new mortgage or refinancing after August 16, 1986, depends on:

1. The cost basis of the residence including improvement costs;
2. Existing mortgage debt, if any; and
3. In some cases, how you use the loan proceeds.

If debt secured by the residence does not exceed cost basis plus improvements, the interest is deductible even if you use the loan proceeds to pay personal consumer debts. If you want to borrow above cost basis plus improvements (but not over fair market value of the house), the interest is deductible if you use the loan proceeds to pay medical and educational expenses. If you use the proceeds for other purposes, the interest on the excess debt (debt above cost plus improvements) is treated as personal interest and is subject to the phase-out limitation discussed at ¶15.1.

EXAMPLES

1. The cost basis in your principal residence is $100,000. Fair market value is $125,000. Your residence is subject to a purchase money mortgage of $60,000. You may refinance up to $100,000 (including the original $60,000 plus an additional $40,000). The interest paid on the new mortgage is deductible regardless of the type of personal needs you apply the loan to.
2. You refinance for $110,000. To deduct interest on the $10,000 of the debt above $100,000 cost, you must show that the $10,000 proceeds are used to pay medical or educational expenses, or make improvements to the home. If the $10,000 proceeds were used for other purposes, interest on that $10,000 debt would be treated as personal interest and thus subject to the phase-out limitations discussed at ¶15.1.

Treat as cost basis the purchase price of the home. If you have deferred tax on the sale of a residence and bought a new home, cost basis for purposes of the interest rule is the cost of the new home, not the basis for tax deferral purposes. Cost basis includes improvement costs that under the law are treated as additions to basis. Basis is not reduced by depreciations as, for example, where you rent a second residence to tenants for a part of the year. The basis of an inherited residence is generally the value at the date of death of the decedent.

Qualified medical expenses are unreimbursed amounts paid for medical care of the taxpayer, his or her spouse, and dependents. Qualified educational expenses are amounts paid for reasonable living expenses while away from home, and for any tuition and related expenses incurred that would qualify as scholarships for the taxpayer, his or her spouse or dependent, while a student at an educational organization. Thus, tuition expenses for primary, secondary, college, and graduate level education are generally qualified expenses. The qualified educational expenses or qualified medical expenses must be incurred within a reasonable period of time before or after the debt is incurred. To be treated as qualified residential mortgage interest, the debt used to pay qualified medical or education expenses must be secured by your principal residence or designated personal second residence (see below).

Two residence limit. The above rules for deducting residential mortgage interest apply to loans secured by your principal residence and one other residence. A principal residence may be a condominium or cooperative unit, a houseboat or house trailer. If you own more than two houses, you decide which residence shall be considered your second residence; interest debt secured by the designated second residence is deductible under the above rules. Interest on any other home will be subject to the limits for personal interest. A residence that is rented out for any part of the year may be designated as a second residence only if it is used for personal non-rental purposes for the greater of 14 days or 10% of the rental days. By making the designation, you insure that interest is fully deductible as residential interest. If you do not make the designation, part of the interest allocated to your personal use is deductible only as personal interest subject to the phase-out percentages of ¶15.1 and interest allocated to the rental activity is treated as passive activity interest subject to limitations of Chapter 11.

A married couple filing jointly may designate as a second residence a home owned or used by either spouse.

If a married couple files separately, each spouse may generally deduct interest on debt secured by one residence. However, both spouses may agree in writing to allow one of them to deduct the interest on a principal residence plus a designated second residence.

Cooperatives. In the case of housing cooperatives, debt secured by stock as a tenant-stockholder is treated as secured by a residence.

See the Supplement and IRS Publication 545 for further details.

MORTGAGE PAYMENT RULES

¶ 15.12 Payments to the bank or lending institution holding your mortgage may include interest, principal payments, taxes, and fire insurance premiums. Deduct only the payments of interest and taxes. You may not deduct the payments of mortgage principal and insurance premiums.

> Banks and other lending institutions report mortgage interest payments of $600 or more to the IRS on Form 1098. You should receive a copy of form 1098 or similar statement by February 1, 1988, showing your mortgage payments in 1987. The form does not include payment of points.

In the year you sell your home, check your settlement papers for interest charged up to the date of sale; this amount is deductible.

Mortgage credit. If you qualify for the special tax credit for interest on qualified home mortgage certificates, you only deduct interest in excess of the allowable credit. *See* ¶24.6.

Jointly owned property. When mortgaged property is jointly owned, a joint owner who pays the entire interest charge may deduct the amount of the entire payment.

Prepayment penalty. A penalty for prepayment of a mortgage is deductible as interest.

Mortgage assistance payments. You may not deduct interest paid on your behalf under Section 235 of the National Housing Act.

Interest reduction payments under Section 237 of the National Housing Act. Payments made to sponsors of low income rental apartments must be reported as income; the full amount of HUD interest payments are deductible.

Graduated payment mortgages. Monthly payments are initially smaller than under the standard mortgage on the same amount of principal, but payments increase each year over the first five- or ten-year period and continue at the increased monthly amount for the balance of the mortgage term. As a cash basis taxpayer, you deduct the amount of interest actually paid even though, during the early years of the mortgage, payments are less than the interest owed on the loan. The unpaid interest is added to the loan principal, and future interest is figured on the increased unpaid mortgage loan balance. The bank, in a year-end statement, will identify the amount of interest actually paid. (An accrual basis taxpayer may deduct the accrued interest each year.)

Reverse mortgage loan. Home owners who own their homes outright may in certain states cash in on their equity by taking a "reverse mortgage loan." Typically, 80% of the value of the house is paid by a bank to a homeowner in a lump sum or in installments. Principal is due when the home is sold or the homeowner dies; interest is added to the loan and is payable when the principal is paid. The IRS rules that no interest deduction may be claimed by a cash basis homeowner when the interest is added to the outstanding loan balance.

Zero interest mortgage. Under this type of loan, a buyer makes a cash down payment and then pays off the balance of the purchase price in equal monthly installments over a mortgage term which is generally five years. Although no interest is charged, a portion of each monthly payment may be treated as deductible interest under the imputed interest rule of ¶6.39. The exact amount is determined by Treasury tables. However, no interest deduction may be claimed for payments in the first six months. Cost basis in the house is reduced by the total interest amount allocated during the term of the note.

Shared appreciation mortgage. Under a shared appreciation mortgage (SAM) for a personal residence, the lender agrees to charge a lower rate of interest than the prevailing market rate. In return, the homeowner promises to pay a percentage of the appreciation on the property at a later date to make up the difference. For example, a homeowner agrees to pay interest of 12% plus 40% of the appreciation in the value of the property within 10 years or earlier if he sells the house or pays off the mortgage. If, at the end of ten years, the residence is not sold or the loan repaid, the owner may refinance at the prevailing rate the outstanding balance plus the interest based on the appreciation. If he refinances with the same lender, he may not claim an immediate deduction for the extra interest. The execution of a note is not considered payment. The amount covering the extra interest is deducted ratably over the period of the new loan. If he refinances with another lender and uses the funds to pay off the old loan plus the extra interest, the extra interest is deductible in the year of payment, subject to the limits of ¶15.11.

"POINTS"

¶ 15.13 Lenders charge "points" above the regular interest rate to get around state limits on interest when the cost of money climbs and pushes interest rates above state maximums. Whether points are deductible as interest depends on what the charge covers. As a borrower, you may deduct points if your payment is solely for your use of the money and is not for specific services performed by the lender which are separately charged. Whether a payment is called "points" or "a loan processing fee" does not affect its deductibility if it is actually a charge for the use of money. The purpose of the charge, that is, for the use of the money or the services rendered, will be controlling.

Points treated as prepaid interest. Points are treated as prepaid interest and must be deducted over the period of the loan unless they are charged on a loan to buy or improve your principal residence. In this case, points are deductible in the year paid, provided: (1) The loan is secured by your

the charging of points is an established business
...hic area in which the loan is made; and (3) the
...ceed the points generally charged in the area. For
...est, *see* ¶ 15.4.

Points paid on refinancing. The IRS does not allow a current deduction for points on a refinanced mortgage. The points must be deducted ratably over the loan period. Thus, if you pay points of $2,400 when refinancing a 20-year loan, you may deduct only $10 a month, $120 each full year. The points are not currently deductible because they are incurred for repaying the existing mortgage debt, not buying a home or financing home improvements.

The ratable deduction rule is allowed only to cash basis individuals with home mortgages for 30 years or less where the principal amount of the refinanced loan is $250,000 or less. If the loan exceeds $250,000, the ratable method is allowed, provided the number of points is no more than four on loans for 15 years or less, or no more than six points on loans between 15 and 30 years. If these limits are exceeded, homeowners may not use the ratable deduction formula. Further, partners and S corporation shareholders who have pass-through interest deductions from their partnership or corporation are not entitled to use the ratable deduction rule. At the time of publication of this book, the IRS did not explain what deduction method should be used by such taxpayers.

> Points withheld from the loan principal are not immediately deductible. To deduct loan fees, you should obtain the full amount of the loan and then pay the fee to the lender. If fees are withheld and you receive only the net proceeds, the fees are amortized over the life of the loan.

If a homeowner refinances a home mortgage and uses part of the new loan for home improvements, an allocable portion of the points is deductible.

EXAMPLE

When interest rates are 10%, Smith refinances his 16% home mortgage which has principal of $80,000 outstanding. The new loan is for $100,000, of which $80,000 is used to pay off the old $80,000 balance and the $20,000 balance for home improvements. Assume that at the closing of the new loan, Smith pays from his separate funds 3.6 points or $3,600. In the year of payment he may deduct $720 allocable to the 20% of the loan used for home improvements. The balance of the points, or $2,880, is deducted over the period of the new loan.

If the points had been withheld from the loan proceeds instead of being paid from Smith's separate funds, no current deduction for points would be allowed regardless of how the loan was used. If the points were withheld, he would not be treated as having made a "payment" of points.

A seller who assumes the buyer's payment of points may not claim the points paid as an interest deduction. The payment is subtracted from the amount realized on the sale.

Claiming deductible points. Points are deducted on a separate line in Schedule A and are not subject to the 65% limit for personal interest in 1987.

INVESTMENT INTEREST LIMITATIONS

¶ **15.14** Interest paid on debts to buy or carry investments is deductible up to the amount of net investment income. However, interest exceeding net investment income may be partially deductible until 1990. In 1987, only 65% of the first $10,000 of investment interest exceeding net investment income is deductible; 40% in 1988; 20% in 1989; 10% in 1990. The $10,000 limit is reduced to $5,000 for married persons filing separately. Interest not allowed by the limitation may be carried forward. Interest disallowed under prior law investment interest limits may be carried forward but are subject to the rules of this section.

What is investment interest? It is all interest paid or accrued on debts incurred or continued to buy or carry investment property, such as interest on securities in a margin account. However, investment interest does not include any interest related to a passive activity; *see* chapter 11. It includes any amounts allowable as a deduction on a short sale. It does not include interest related to a residential mortgage.

Investment property includes property producing portfolio income under the passive activity rules of chapter 11, and property in an activity in which one does not materially participate provided the activity is *not* treated as a passive activity.

Net investment income is the excess of investment income over investment expenses. Investment income is gross income from property held for investment, including any net gain attributable to disposition of property held for investment.

Income or expenses considered in figuring profit or loss of a passive activity is not considered investment income or expenses. Property subject to a net lease is not treated as investment property as it is within the passive activity rules.

Investment income is reduced by passive activity losses that can be currently deducted under phase-in rules for interests held before October 23, 1986; *see* ¶ 11.3. No reduction is allowed for a rental real estate activity under the $25,000 allowance; *see* ¶ 11.4.

Investment expenses are deductible expenses, other than interest, directly connected with the production of investment income. Where the 2% adjusted gross income floor applies to an investment expense, only the amount allowed over the floor is considered a deductible investment expense.

Interest that is capitalized under the construction tests at ¶ 16.5 is not treated as investment interest.

Amount of investment interest disallowed. In 1987, the disallowed amount of excess interest expense that is carried forward to future years is the total of:

1. 35% of the first $10,000 of excess interest ($5,000 for a married person filing a separate return).
2. The excess interest over $10,000 ($5,000 if married filing separately).

EXAMPLES

1. In 1987, you paid interest of $8,000 on debt financing your investment property. Your net investment income is $10,000. The full amount of the interest is deductible as it is less than the net investment income. There is no excess interest expense.

2. Same facts as in (1) but your net investment income is $2,000. The interest exceeding investment income is $6,000 ($8,000–2,000). Of this amount, 35% or $2,100 is disallowed; 65% or $3,900 is allowed as a deduction for 1987. The disallowed $2,100 is carried forward to 1988.

EARMARKING USE OF LOAN PROCEEDS FOR INTEREST DEDUCTIONS

¶ **15.15** To safeguard your interest deductions, you must earmark and keep a record of your loans. You should avoid using loan proceeds to fund different types of expenditures. Keep separate accounts for business, personal, and investment borrowing. For example, if you borrow for investment purposes, keep the proceeds of the loan in a separate account and use the proceeds only for investment purposes. Do not use the fund to pay personal expenses. Further, do not deposit loan proceeds in an account funded with unborrowed money, unless you intend to use the proceeds within 15 days of the deposit.

By following these directions, you can pinpoint your use of the proceeds to a specific expenditure, such as for investment, personal, or business purposes, and the interest on the loan may be treated as incurred for that purpose.

The IRS treats undisbursed loan proceeds deposited in an account as investment property, even though the account does not bear interest. When proceeds are disbursed from the account, the use of the proceeds determines how interest is treated.

EXAMPLES

1. On January 1, 1988, you borrow $10,000 and deposit the proceeds in a non-interest-bearing checking account. No other amounts are deposited in the account during the year and no part of the loan is repaid during the year. On April 1, you invest $2,000 of the proceeds in a real estate venture. On September 1, you use $4,000 to buy furniture.

From January 1 through March 31, interest on the entire undisbursed $10,000 is treated as investment interest. From April 1 through August 31, interest on $2,000 of the debt is treated as passive activity interest, and interest on $8,000 of the debt is treated as investment interest. From September 1 through December 31, interest on $4,000 of the debt is treated as personal interest; interest on $2,000 is treated as passive activity interest; and interest on $4,000 is treated as investment interest.

2. On September 1, you borrow money for business purposes and deposit it in a checking account. On October 15, you disburse the proceeds for business purposes. Interest incurred on the loan before the disbursement of the funds is treated as investment interest expense. Interest starting on October 15 is treated as business interest. However, you may elect to treat the starting date for business interest as of the first of the month in which the disbursement was made, that is, October 1, provided all other disbursements from the account during the same month are similarly treated.

The IRS has set down complex record keeping and allocation rules for claiming interest deductions for personal, passive activity, business, or investment purposes. The rules deal primarily with the use of loan proceeds for more than one purpose and the commingling of loan proceeds in an account with unborrowed funds. Where you make more than one disbursement from such an account, you may treat any disbursements within 15 days of the loan as made from the loan proceeds. Thus, you may allocate interest on the loan to that disbursement. If you make the disbursement after 15 days, the IRS requires you to allocate interest on the loan to the first disbursement. Further, if an account includes only loan proceeds and interest earned on the proceeds, disbursements may first be allocated to the interest income.

EXAMPLES

1. On September 1, 1987, you borrow $5,000 to invest in stock and deposit the proceeds in your regular checking account. On September 10, you buy a TV and stereo for $2,500 and on September 11 invest $5,000 in stock. As the stock investment was made within 15 days of the loan, interest on the entire loan is treated as incurred for investment purposes.

2. Same facts as in (1) above but the TV and stereo were bought on October 1 and the stock on October 3. As the stock investment was not made within 15 days, the IRS requires you to treat the purchase of the TV and the stereo for $2,500 as the first purchase made with the loan proceeds of $5,000. Thus, only 65% of the loan interest allocated to the stereo purchase is deductible as personal interest.

3. Same facts as in (2) above but assume the interest cost per month is $40—or $160 for the period September 1 to December 31. For September, when there were no disbursements, $40 is treated as investment interest expense. The $60 of interest allocated to the stereo purchase for the period October 1 to December 31 is personal interest, but only 65% or $39 is deductible. For the remaining interest, interest for two days in October is treated as investment interest; the balance allocated to the stock purchase is also treated as investment interest expense.

The deductibility of interest depends on the use of the loan proceeds, not the nature of pledged property.

Interest is allocated to an expenditure for the period *beginning* on the date the loan proceeds are used or treated as used, and ending on the earlier of the date the debt is repaid or reallocated.

Accrued interest is treated as a debt until it is paid, and any interest accruing on unpaid interest is allocated in the same manner as the unpaid interest is allocated. Compound interest accruing on such debt, other than compound interest accruing on interest that accrued before the beginning of the year, may be allocated between the original expenditure and the new expenditure on a straight-line basis. That is done by allocating an equal amount of such interest expense to each day during the taxable year. In addition, you may treat a year as *twelve 30-day months* for purposes of allocating interest on a straight-line basis.

EXAMPLE

On January 1, Jones borrows $1,000 at an interest rate of 11% compounded semiannually. He immediately uses the loan proceeds to buy stock. On July 1, he sells the stock for $1,000 and uses the sales proceeds to invest in a passive activity. On December 31, he pays accrued

interest of $113 on the $1,000 debt for the entire year. The $1,000 debt is allocated to the stock investment from January 1 through June 30, and to the passive activity from July 1 through December 31. Accrued interest expense of $113 is allocated over the year, even though the debt was allocated to the passive activity on the date the interest was paid. Interest of $55 for the period from January through June 30 is treated as investment interest. Further, an additional $3 of interest expense for the period from July 1 through December 31 is also treated as an investment interest expenditure. This is the additional interest charge made on accrued investment interest of $55 ($55 × .055). The remaining $55 of interest for the period from July 1 through December 31 is treated as passive activity interest. Jones may also elect to allocate the interest on a straight-line basis treating the year as twelve 30-day months. Thus, $56.50 of interest expense (180 ÷ 360 × $113) would be allocated to the investment interest and the remaining $56.50 of interest expense to the passive activity interest.

A disbursement from a checking account is treated as made at the time the check is written on the account, provided the check is delivered or mailed to the payee within a reasonable period after the writing of the check. You may treat checks written on the same day as written in any order. A check is presumed to be written on the date appearing on the check and to be delivered or mailed to the payee within a reasonable period thereafter. However, the fact that a check does not clear within a reasonable period after the date appearing on the check is evidence that the check was not mailed within a reasonable time.

Debt-financed property. You must reallocate interest if you convert debt-financed property to a different use; for example, when you convert a business auto to personal use.

EXAMPLE

You buy a business auto on time. Interest paid on the auto is business interest. Assume during the year you convert the auto to personal use. Interest paid after the conversion is personal interest.

Order of repayment. If you used loan proceeds for several different types of disbursements, a repayment of the debt is treated as repaid in the following order:
1. Repayment of personal debt.
2. Repayment of investment debt and passive activity debt other than (3) below.
3. Repayment of debt in real estate activity in which you actively participate.
4. Repayment of former passive activity debt.
5. Repayment of business debt.
Payments made on the same day may be treated as made in any order.

EXAMPLE

On July 12, Smith borrows $100,000 and immediately deposits the proceeds in an account. He uses the proceeds as follows:

August 31	$40,000 for passive activity
October 5	$20,000 for rental activity
December 24	$40,000 for personal use

On January 19 of the following year, Smith repays $90,000. Of the repayment, $40,000 is allocated as a repayment of the personal expenditure, $40,000 of the passive activity, and $10,000 of the rental activity. The outstanding $10,000 is treated as debt incurred in a rental activity.

Transitional rules. The above rules apply to interest accrued or paid in 1987, including debts incurred before 1986. However, a 90-day period may be substituted for the 15-day disbursement period for disbursements made on or before August 3, 1987. Further, under the second transitional rule, debt outstanding on December 31, 1986, attributable to a business or rental activity may be allocated to the assets held for business or rental activity. You must explain your allocation of business or rental debt on a statement attached to your return for the first taxable year beginning after December 31, 1986. If you do not file a statement or fail to allocate the debt in a reasonable and consistent manner, the IRS will allocate the debt.

This second transitional allocation rule is not allowed if you allocate outstanding debt on December 31, 1986, by applying the 90-day transitional rule. Further, you may elect not to apply this transitional rule if you attach a statement to that effect to your return for the first taxable year beginning after December 31, 1986.

16

DEDUCTIONS FOR TAXES

Illustrations of deducting taxes may be found in the Supplement to YOUR INCOME TAX.

¶ **16.1** **New tax law pointers.** The following rules take effect for 1987 regarding deductions of the taxes you pay.
1. State and local sales taxes are no longer deductible as itemized deductions. Itemized deductions for state and local income taxes, real property taxes, and personal property taxes remain deductible.

2. Sales tax on business property. If you pay sales tax on the purchase of business or investment property, add the tax to the cost of the property. If the tax is incurred on a sale of such property, deduct the tax from the sales proceeds.
3. Construction period costs including taxes must be capitalized under new rules discussed at ¶16.5.

GENERAL RULES FOR DEDUCTING TAXES

¶ **16.2** You may deduct as itemized deductions your payments of state, local, and foreign real property and income taxes as well as state and local personal property taxes. Sales taxes on personal property are no longer deductible as itemized deductions. Stock transfer taxes paid on the sale of securities may be claimed as an itemized deduction if you are an investor.

Claim the deduction on the tax return for the year in which you paid the taxes, unless you report on the accrual basis, see ¶16.6.

The following table lists whether a particular type of tax may be claimed as an itemized deduction in 1987.

Type of tax	Deductible as itemized deduction
Admission	No
Alcoholic beverage	No
Assessments for local benefits	No
Automobile license fees not qualifying as personal property tax	No
Cigarette	No
Customs duties	No
Driver's license	No
Estate—federal or state (except see ¶ 10.12)	No
Excise—federal or state, for example, on telephone service	No
Gasoline—federal	No
Gasoline and other motor fuel—state and local	No
Gift taxes—federal and state	No
Income—federal (including minimum tax)	No
Income—state or local or foreign	Yes
Inheritance tax	No
Mortgage tax	No
Personal property—state or local	Yes
Poll	No
Real estate (state, local or foreign)	Yes
Regulatory license fees—(dog licenses, parking meter fees, hunting and fishing licenses)	No
Sales and use	No
Social Security	No
Tolls	No
Transfer tax on securities and income-producing realty—state and local	Yes
Utility taxes imposed under state or local law if rate is the same as general sales tax	No

Other state, local, and foreign taxes are deductible if paid in a business, for the production or collection of income, or the maintenance, management, or conservation of property held for the production of income. See ¶16.11.

State and local taxes on gasoline used for personal purposes are not deductible, but are deductible as part of the cost of gasoline used for business travel. See ¶19.57.

Windfall profit tax. The tax is deductible in the year withheld from payments received by crude oil purchasers. The tax is deductible from royalty income reported on Schedule E.

DEDUCTING STATE INCOME TAXES

¶ **16.3** You may deduct on your 1987 return state and local income taxes withheld and estimated state and local taxes paid in 1987. If you pay in 1988 additional state income tax on your 1987 income, you deduct the payment on your 1988 tax return.

To increase your itemized deductions on your 1987 return, consider prepaying state income taxes before the end of 1987. The prepayment is deductible provided the state tax authority accepts prepayments and state law recognizes them as tax payments. The IRS has ruled, however, that prepayments are not deductible if you do not reasonably believe that you owe additional state tax. Do not make prepayments if you may be subject to alternative minimum tax; *see* chapter 23.

If you report on the accrual basis and you contest a tax liability, *see* Treasury regulations for how to treat the item.

State and local income taxes allocable to interest income that is exempt from federal but not state and local income tax are deductible. However, state and local taxes allocated to other federal exempt income are not deductible. For example, state income tax allocated to a cost-of-living allowance exempt from federal income tax is not deductible.

State income taxes may be claimed only as itemized deductions, even if attributed solely to business income. That is, state income taxes may not be deducted as business expenses from gross income (*see* ¶5.7).

Mandatory employee contributions to the following state disability insurance funds are deductible as state income taxes: California Nonoccupational Disability Benefit Fund; New Jersey Nonoccupational Disability Benefit Fund; New York Nonoccupational Disability Benefit Fund; and Rhode Island Temporary Disability Benefit Fund. However, employee contributions to a private or voluntary disability plan in California, New Jersey or New York are not deductible.

Mandatory employee contributions to a state unemployment fund are deductible.

Note: A refund of state income taxes claimed as an itemized deduction may have to be reported as income; *see* ¶ 12.14.

TAXES AND OTHER CARRYING CHARGES YOU CAPITALIZE OR DEDUCT

¶ **16.4** For certain property, you may elect to capitalize certain deductible taxes and other carrying charges, such as interest, by adding these amounts to the basis of the property. This may be to your advantage if you do not need the immediate deduction because you have little or no income to offset, or because you do not have itemized deductions or expect a greater tax benefit by adding the taxes to the basis.

An election to capitalize applies not only to taxes but also to interest and other deductible carrying charges incurred during your ownership of the property. The election is limited to—

Unimproved and nonproductive real property.

Real property being improved or developed. You may elect to capitalize costs up to the time the development or construction work has been completed. These costs include interest on loans to furnish funds for this work, taxes on pay to your employees, and taxes on the materials used and other expenses incurred in the development. *See* ¶ 16.5 for mandatory amortization of certain construction period interest and taxes.

Personal property up to the time of its installation or actual use (whichever is later).

EXAMPLES

1. Jones, in 1986 and 1987, pays taxes and interest on a mortgage on vacant and nonproductive property. In 1987, he operates the property as a parking lot. Jones may capitalize the taxes and mortgage interest paid in 1986, but not the tax and interest paid in 1987.

2. Smith began in April 1987 to erect a building for himself. In 1987, he paid $6,000 in employer Social Security taxes in erecting the building. On his 1987 return, he elected to capitalize these taxes. He must continue to capitalize them until the building is finished.

To make the election, indicate your choice on your tax return. IRS permission is not required. The election, once made, may not be revoked when made for personal property or real property being improved or developed. With unimproved and nonproductive realty, the election may be made in any year, regardless of how the items were treated in a prior year.

AMORTIZATION OF CONSTRUCTION PERIOD INTEREST AND TAXES

¶ **16.5** For realty held for business or investment purposes, construction period interest and real estate taxes *must* be capitalized in the year paid or incurred. For costs incurred before 1987, amortization was generally over a 10-year period. The pre-1987 rules are not discussed in this book.

Costs incurred after 1986 on business or investment real estate are subject to uniform capitalization rules. Real property used for your own personal use is not within these capitalization rules. However, where substantial construction occurred before March 1, 1986, costs are capitalized and amortized under prior law rules. At the time this book went to press, the Treasury had not released regulations explaining the application of the cost capitalization rules.

DEDUCTING REAL ESTATE TAXES

¶ **16.6** You may deduct payments of real estate tax on your property if you claim itemized deductions. Real estate taxes included in a mortgage payment to a bank are not deductible until paid to the taxing authority. The monthly mortgage payment to a bank generally includes amounts allocated to real estate taxes, which the bank pays to the taxing authority on their due date. You may not deduct the amounts allocated

to the taxes in the year paid to the bank, unless the [...] to the tax authority. Typically, banks will furnish you w[...] ment of disbursements to taxing authorities, indicatin[...]

Cooperative apartments. Tenant-stockholders of a cooperative housing corporation may deduct their share of the real estate taxes paid by the corporation. However, no deduction is allowed if the corporation does not own the land and building but merely leases them and pays taxes under the lease agreement.

Assessments by homeowner's association not deductible as taxes. Assessments paid to a local homeowner's association for the purpose of maintaining the common areas of the residential project and for promoting the recreation, health, and safety of the residents are not deductible as real property taxes.

Nondeductible governmental charges. Such charges include municipal water bills (even if described as a "tax"); sewer assessments; assessments for sanitation service; title registration fees; permit to build or improve a personal residence (you add the permit fee to the cost basis of the house).

TENANTS' PAYMENT OF TAXES GENERALLY NONDEDUCTIBLE

¶ **16.7** You may not generally deduct a portion of your rent as property taxes. This is so even where state or local law identifies a portion of the rent as being tied to tax increases.

EXAMPLE

A municipal rent control ordinance allowed landlords to charge real property tax increases to the tenants as a monthly "tax surcharge." The ordinance stated that the surcharge was not to be considered rent for purposes of computing cost-of-living rental increases. The IRS ruled that the tenant may not deduct the "tax surcharge" as a property tax.

> Tenants have been allowed a deduction for property taxes in the following areas: In Hawaii, tenants with leases of 15 years or more may deduct the portion of the rent representing taxes. In California, tenants who have their names placed on the tax rolls and who pay the taxes directly to the taxing authority may claim a deduction.

In New York liability for tax is placed directly on the tenant and the landlord is a collecting agent for paying over the tax to the taxing authorities; the landlord also remains liable for the tax. The IRS ruled that it will not permit tenants to deduct a portion of rent as a payment of taxes.

ALLOCATING TAXES WHEN YOU SELL OR BUY REALTY

¶ **16.8** When property is sold, the buyer and seller apportion the real estate taxes imposed on the property during the "real property year." A "real property year" is the period which a real estate tax covers. This allocation is provided for you in a settlement statement at the time of closing. If you want to figure your own allocations, your local tax authority can give you the "real property year" of the taxes you plan to apportion. With this information, you then make the following allocation. If *you* are the:

Seller, you deduct that portion of the tax covering the beginning of the real property year through the day before the sale.

Buyer, you deduct the part of the tax covering the date of the sale through the end of the real property year.

EXAMPLE

The real property year in East County starts April 1 and ends March 31. On July 2, 1987, you sell realty located in East County to Jones. Assume the real estate tax for the real property year ending March 31, 1988 is $366. You deduct $92 (92/366 of $366, since there are 92 days in the period beginning April 1 and ending July 1, 1987). Jones deducts $274 (274/366 of $366, since there are 274 days in the period beginning July 2, 1987 and ending March 31, 1988).

179

The above allocation is mandatory whether or not your contract provides for an allocation. However, you do not allocate taxes of a real property year when:

Property is sold before the real property year. This rule prevents the seller from deducting any part of the tax for that year, even though it became a personal liability or lien while he owned the property. The buyer gets the deduction because the tax covers the property year he owns the property.

Property is sold after the real property year. This rule prevents the buyer from deducting the tax even though it becomes a personal liability or lien after he takes possession of the property. The seller gets the deduction because the tax covers the property year he owns the property.

The allocation is limited to a tax covering a property year during which both the seller and the buyer own the property.

EXAMPLE

The real property tax for the calendar year in 1987 in North County becomes a lien on November 1, 1986. On November 15, 1986, you sell real property in the county to Brown. You apportion the 1986 tax between yourself and Brown. However, you may not deduct any part of the real property tax for the 1987 real property year, even though it became a lien while you owned the property on November 1, 1986. The entire real property tax for the 1987 real property tax year may be deducted by Brown when paid or accrued, depending on his method of accounting.

When to deduct allocated taxes. After you have made the allocation based on the "real property year," you then must fix the year in which you deduct your share of the allocated tax. Here you consider your method of reporting your income—cash or accrual basis—and the date on which either you or the other party became liable for the tax or paid the tax. If neither you nor the other party is liable for the tax under local law, then the party who holds the property at the time the tax became a lien on the property is considered liable. Check the following rules to determine when you deduct the apportioned tax:

Seller on the cash basis—If the buyer is liable for the tax, the seller may deduct the tax either in the year of the sale or, at a later time, in the year the tax is actually paid.

If a buyer is obligated to pay taxes under a land contract but fails to pay, the owner who pays the tax may deduct the payment if the tax is assessed to him.

If the seller is liable for the tax and the tax is not payable until after the date of sale, the seller may deduct the tax either in the year of sale or in the year he pays the tax.

Buyer on the cash basis—If the seller is liable for the tax, the buyer may deduct the tax either in the year of sale or when the tax is actually paid.

If the buyer is liable for the tax, he deducts the tax in the year he pays the tax.

Seller on the accrual basis—The seller accrues his share of the tax on the date of the sale, unless he has been accruing taxes ratably over the years. If this is so, his last accrual is the date of the sale.

Buyer on the accrual basis—If the seller is liable for the tax, the buyer accrues his share of the tax on the date of the sale, unless he accrues taxes ratably. If he accrues taxes ratably, the accrual begins with the date of sale. If he is liable for the tax, he deducts the tax in the return for the year the tax accrues unless he elects to accrue ratably from the date of sale.

Seller's deduction in excess of the allocated amount is taxed as income. If, in the year before the sale, the seller deducts an amount for taxes in excess of the amount allocated above, he reports the excess as income in the year of the sale. This may happen when seller is on the cash basis and pays the tax in the year before the sale.

EXAMPLE

A real property tax is due and payable on November 30 for the following calendar year. On November 30, 1986, Jones, who uses the cash basis and reports on a calendar year, pays the 1987 tax. On June 30, 1987, he sells the real property. Under the apportionment rule, he is allowed to deduct only 181/365 (January 1–June 30, 1987) of the tax for the 1987 real property tax year. But he has already deducted the full amount in the 1986 return. Therefore, he reports as income that part of the tax deduction he was not entitled to under the apportionment.

Buyer's payment of seller's back taxes. A buyer may not deduct his payment of the seller's back taxes. The back taxes paid are added to the cost of the newly purchased property. The amount realized by the seller is increased by the buyer's payment of back taxes.

On the sale of a personal residence, transfer or stamp taxes imposed on and paid by the seller are not deducted as itemized deductions but reduce the sales proceeds. If imposed on and paid by the buyer, they are added to the cost basis of the house.

Seller's payment upon buyer's failure to pay. If a buyer is obligated to pay taxes under a land contract but fails to pay, the owner who pays the tax may deduct the payment if the tax is assessed to him.

Buyer of foreclosed property. If you buy realty at a tax sale, you may not be able to deduct payment of realty taxes for several years if you do not receive immediate title to the property under state law until after a redemption period.

WHO MAY DEDUCT REAL PROPERTY TAXES

¶ **16.9** The following table summarizes who may deduct real property taxes:

If the tax is paid by	Then it is deductible by
You, for your spouse	Neither, if your spouse has title to the property and you each file a separate return. This is true even if the mortgage requires you to pay the taxes. The tax is deductible on a joint return.
You, as owner of a condominium	You deduct real estate tax paid on your separate unit. You also deduct your share of the tax paid on the common property.
A life tenant	A court allowed the deduction to a widow required to pay the taxes under a will for the privilege of occupying the house during her life.
A tenant	The tenant of a business lease may deduct the payment of tax as additional rent, not tax. The tenant of a personal residence may not deduct the payment as either a tax or rent expense, unless he places himself on the real estate assessment rolls, so the tax is assessed directly against him.
You, as a local benefit tax to maintain, repair, or meet interest costs arising from local benefits	You deduct only that part of the tax which you can show is for maintenance, repair, or interest. If you cannot make the allocation, no deduction is allowed. If the benefit increases the value of the property, you add the nondeductible assessment to the basis of the property.
Your cooperative apartment or corporation	You deduct your share of real estate tax paid on the property; see ¶ 15.10. But if the organization leases the land and building and pays the tax under the terms of the lease, you may not deduct your share.
One whose property was foreclosed for failure to pay taxes	You may not deduct the taxes paid out of the proceeds of the foreclosure sale if your interest in the property ended with the foreclosure.
Tenant by the entirety or joint tenant	The tenant who is jointly and severally liable and who pays the tax. If real property is owned by husband and wife as tenants by the entirety or joint tenants, either spouse may deduct the taxes he has paid on a separate return or a joint return. When property is owned as a tenancy in common, under an IRS rule, a tenant may deduct only his share of the tax even if he has paid the entire tax. However, a court has allowed a deduction for the full amount. See ¶ 9.3.
A mortgagee	No deduction. If paid before the foreclosure, it is added to the loan. If paid after the foreclosure, it is added to the cost of property.

AUTOMOBILE LICENSE FEES

¶ **16.10** You may not deduct an auto license fee based on weight, model, year, or horsepower. But you may deduct a fee based on the value of the car if these three tests are met: (1) The fee is an *ad valorem* tax, based on a percentage of value of the property. (2) It is imposed on an annual basis, even though it is collected more or less frequently. (3) It is imposed on personal property. This third test is met even though the tax is imposed on the exercise of a privilege of registering a car or for using a car on the road.

If the tax is based partly on value and partly on weight or other test, the tax attributed to the value is deductible. For example, assume a registration fee based on 1% of value, plus 40¢ per hundred-weight. The part of the tax equal to 1% of value qualifies as an *ad valorem* tax and is deductible.

The majority of state motor vehicle registration fees are not *ad valorem* taxes and so do not qualify for the deduction. Various states and localities impose *ad valorem* or personal property taxes on motor vehicles that may qualify for the deduction. If you pay fees or taxes on your auto in these states, we suggest you contact a state or local authority to verify the amount of tax qualifying: Arizona, California, Colorado, Georgia, Indiana, Iowa, Maine, Massachusetts, Mississippi, Montana, Nebraska, Nevada, Oklahoma, Washington, and Wyoming.

TAXES DEDUCTIBLE AS BUSINESS OR INCOME-PRODUCING EXPENSES

¶ **16.11** That a tax is not deductible as an itemized deduction does not mean you may not deduct it elsewhere on your return. You may deduct taxes incurred as a cost of doing business or producing income. Here are some examples.

If you pay excise taxes on merchandise you sell in your business, you deduct the tax as a business expense.

If you pay Social Security taxes (FICA) on your employees' wages, you deduct the tax as a business expense on Schedule C. You may not generally deduct Social Security taxes paid on the wages of household help. But *see* ¶ 1.29 for dependent and child care expenses. You may not deduct self-employment tax.

If you pay state transfer taxes on the sale of securities, you deduct the tax as an "other" tax on Schedule A.

If you pay sales tax on business property, you add the tax to the cost of the property.

FOREIGN TAXES

¶ **16.12** You may deduct your payment of foreign real property taxes and income and excess profits taxes as itemized deductions. Where you pay foreign income or excess profits tax, you have an election of either claiming the tax as a deduction or a credit. Claiming the credit may provide a larger tax savings; *see* ¶ 36.15.

17

MEDICAL AND DENTAL EXPENSE DEDUCTIONS

Illustrations of deducting your medical and dental expenses may be found in the Supplement to YOUR INCOME TAX.

¶ **17.1** The new tax law has introduced these two significant changes in the handling of medical and dental expense deductions:
1. The medical expense floor is increased from 5% to 7.5% of adjusted gross income. Thus in 1987, only those medical expenses exceeding 7.5% of adjusted gross income are deductible.

2. Handicapped individuals may treat as deductible medical expenses the cost of making structural changes to their residence, such as adding exit ramps, modifying doorways, and installing railings and support bars. Such improvements are treated for deduction purposes as not increasing the value of the house; *see* ¶ 17.13.

ALLOWABLE MEDICAL CARE COSTS

¶ **17.2** A deductible medical expense is any cost of diagnosis, cure, mitigation, treatment, or prevention of disease, or any treatment that affects a part or function of the body. The following is a list of deductible expenses.

PROFESSIONAL SERVICES

Chiropodist
Chiropractor (lic.)
Christian Science Practitioner
Dermatologist
Dentist
Gynecologist
Neurologist
Obstetrician
Oculist
Optician
Optometrist
Orthopedist
Osteopath (lic.)
Pediatrician
Physician
Physiotherapist
Plastic Surgeon
Podiatrist
Practical or other nonprofessional nurse for medical services only; not for care of a healthy person or a small child who is not ill. Costs for medical care of elderly person, unable to get about, or person subject to spells, are deductible. See ¶ 17.12.
Psychiatrist
Psychoanalyst
Psychologist
Registered Nurse
Surgeon
Payments to an unlicensed practitioner are deductible if the type and quality of his services are not illegal.

DENTAL SERVICES

Cleaning teeth
Dental X-rays
Extracting teeth
Filling teeth
Gum treatment
Oral surgery
Straightening teeth

EQUIPMENT AND SUPPLIES

Abdominal supports
Air conditioner where necessary for relief from an allergy or for relieving difficulty in breathing; see ¶17.13.
Ambulance hire
Arches
Artificial teeth, eyes
Autoette (auto device for handicapped person), but not if used to travel to job or business.
Back supports
Braces
Contact lenses
Cost of installing stair-seat elevator for person with heart condition; see ¶ 17.13.
Crutches
Elastic hosiery
Eyeglasses
Fluoridation unit in home
Hearing aids
Heating devices
Invalid chair
Iron Lung
Orthopedic shoes
Reclining chair if prescribed by doctor.
Repair of special telephone equipment for the deaf
Sacroiliac belt
Special mattress and plywood bed boards for relief of arthritis or spine.
Splints
Truss
Wig advised by doctor as essential to mental health of person who lost all her hair from disease.

MEDICAL TREATMENTS

Abortion
Acupuncture
Blood transfusion
Cosmetic surgery
Diathermy
Electric shock treatments
Hearing services

Hydrotherapy (water treatments)
Injections
Insulin treatments
Navajo healing ceremonies ("sings")
Nursing
Organ transplant
Pre-natal and post-natal treatments
Psychotherapy
Sterilization
Radium therapy
Ultra-violet ray treatments
Vasectomy
Whirlpool baths
X-ray treatments

MEDICINES AND DRUGS

Cost of prescriptions only

LABORATORY EXAMINATIONS AND TESTS

Blood tests
Cardiographs
Metabolism tests
Spinal fluid tests
Sputum tests
Stool examination
Urine analyses
X-ray examinations

HOSPITAL SERVICES

Anesthetist
Hospital bills
Oxygen mask, tent
Use of operating room
Vaccines
X-ray technician

PREMIUMS FOR MEDICAL CARE POLICIES

See ¶ 17.6 for how to deduct for:

Blue Cross and Blue Shield
Contact lens replacements
Federal voluntary Medicare (Part B)
Federal Medicare (Part A) by persons not covered by Social Security

Health insurance covering hospital, surgical, and other medical expenses
Membership in medical service cooperative

MISCELLANEOUS

Alcoholic inpatient care costs
Asylum; see ¶ 17.11.
Birth control pills or other birth control items prescribed by your doctor.
Braille books—excess cost of braille works over cost of regular editions
Clarinet lessons advised by dentist for treatment of tooth defects.
Convalescent home—for medical treatment only (see ¶ 17.11).
Drug treatment center—inpatient care costs
Face lifting operation, even if not recommended by doctor
Fees paid to health institute where the exercises, rubdowns, etc., taken there are prescribed by a physician as treatments necessary to alleviate a physical or mental defect or illness.
Hair transplant operation
Kidney donor's or possible kidney donor's expenses
Legal fees for guardianship of mentally ill spouse where commitment was necessary for medical treatment.
Nurse's board and wages, including Social Security taxes you pay on wages.
Remedial reading for child suffering from dyslexia
Sanitarium and similar institutions; see ¶ 17.11.
"Seeing-eye" dog and its maintenance.
Special school costs for physically and mentally handicapped children (see ¶ 17.10).
Wages of guide for a blind person.
Telephone-teletype costs and television adapter for closed caption service for deaf person.

Medicine and drugs. To be deductible, medicines and drugs must *require* a prescription by a doctor. You may not deduct the cost of over-the-counter medicines and drugs, such as aspirin and other cold remedies. The cost of insulin is deductible.

Special foods. According to the IRS, the cost of special food or beverages is not a deductible medical expense if the food or beverages are taken as substitutes for those normally consumed.

EXAMPLE

To alleviate an ulcer, the doctor puts you on a special diet. The cost of your food and beverages is not deductible. The special diet replaces the food you normally eat.

The Tax Court has set its own standard for deducting the extra cost of special foods as medical costs. The test is to show a medical need for taking the special food and the extra cost of the health food over ordinary food. Only the extra cost is deductible.

EXAMPLE

Von Kalb suffered from hypoglycemia and her physician prescribed a special high protein diet, which required her to consume twice as much protein as an average person and exclude all processed foods and carbohydrates. She spent $3,483 for food, and deducted 30%, or $1,045, as the extra costs of her high protein diet. The IRS disallowed the deduction, claiming that the protein supplements were a substitute for foods normally consumed. The Tax Court disagreed. The high protein food did not substitute for her usual diet but helped alleviate her hypoglycemia. Thus, she may deduct its additional expense.

NONDEDUCTIBLE EXPENSES

¶ 17.3 The following expenses, although many are related to health care, are *not* deductible for tax purposes.

Over-the-counter medicines and drugs.
Toothpaste.
Maternity clothes.
Antiseptic diaper service.
Funeral, cremation or burial, cemetery plot, monument, mausoleum.
Illegal operations and drugs.
Your divorced spouse's medical bills—but *see* ¶ 1.42 and ¶ 17.7. You may be able to deduct them as alimony.
Special food or beverage substitutes—but excess cost of chemically uncontaminated foods over what would have ordinarily been spent on normal food was deductible for allergy patients.
Bottled water bought to avoid drinking fluoridated city water.
Health programs offered by resort hotels, health clubs, and gyms.
Domestic help—even if recommended by doctor because of spouse's illness. But part of cost attributed to any nursing duties performed by the domestic is deductible. See ¶ 17.12.
Deductions from your wages for sickness insurance under state law.
Premiums, in connection with life insurance policies, paid for disability, double indemnity, or for waiver of premiums in event of total and permanent disability or policies providing for reimbursement of loss of earnings or a guarantee of a specified amount in the event of hospitalization.
Athletic club expenses to keep physically fit.
Tattooing; ear piercing.

Boarding school fees paid for healthy child while parent is recuperating from illness. It makes no difference that this was done on a doctor's advice.
Tuition and travel expenses to send a problem child to a particular school for a beneficial change in environment. See ¶ 17.10.
Transportation costs of a disabled person to and from work.
Traveling costs to look for a new place to live—on doctor's advice.
Cost of trips for a "change of environment" to boost morale of ailing person. That doctor prescribed the trip is immaterial.
Travel costs to favorable climate when you can live there permanently.
Dance lessons advised by doctors as physical and mental therapy or for the alleviation of varicose veins or arthritis; however, the cost of a clarinet and lessons for the instrument were allowed as deductions when advised as therapy for a tooth defect.
Scientology fees.
Cost of divorce recommended by psychiatrist.
Cost of hotel room suggested for sex therapy.
Marriage counseling fees.
Veterinary fees for pet; pet is not a dependent.
Babysitting fees to enable you to make doctor's visits.
Weight reduction or stop smoking programs undertaken for general health, not for specific ailments.
Cost of moving away from airport noise by person suffering a nervous breakdown.

INCOME FLOOR APPLIED TO MEDICAL EXPENSE DEDUCTION

¶ 17.4 A wide range of expenses, such as those listed at ¶ 17.2, qualify as deductible medical expenses. However, you may not be able to claim the deduction because of a percentage floor. In 1987, you may deduct only expenses exceeding 7.5% of your adjusted gross income. Adjusted gross income is explained at ¶ 13.8.

Married persons filing joint returns figure the 7.5% limit on combined adjusted gross income.

On your 1987 return, you may deduct only expenses paid in 1987 for yourself, your spouse, or dependents. If you borrow to pay medical or dental expenses, you claim the deduction in the year you use the loan proceeds to pay the bill, not in the later year when you repay the loan. If you pay for medical or dental expenses by credit card, the deduction is allowed in the year of the charge.

You may not deduct the payment of expenses you are not legally obliged to pay until 1988 or some later year. You may not deduct medical expenses for which you have been reimbursed by insurance or other awards (see ¶ 17.5). Furthermore, reimbursement of medical expenses deducted in prior tax years may be taxable income (see ¶ 12.14).

EXAMPLE
Your adjusted gross income in 1987 is $16,000. Your unreimbursed medical expenses were $900 for medical care, $187 for prescribed drugs and medicines, and $600 for medical insurance premiums. You deduct medical expenses of $487 figured this way:

Unreimbursed medical care	$900
Premiums	600
Drugs	187
Total	$1,687
Less: 7.5% of adjusted gross income (7.5% of $16,000)	1,200
Medical expense deduction	$ 487

HOW YOUR 1987 MEDICAL EXPENSE DEDUCTION IS REDUCED BY THE 7.5% LIMIT

If your adjusted gross income is	$200	$300	$400	$500	$600	$700	$800	$900	$1,000	$1,500	$2,000
					Your medical expenses are						
						You may deduct					
$ 2,000	50	150	250	350	450	550	650	750	850	1,350	1,850
3,000	0	75	175	275	375	475	575	675	775	1,275	1,775
4,000	0	0	100	200	300	400	500	600	700	1,200	1,700
5,000	0	0	25	125	225	325	425	525	625	1,125	1,625
6,000	0	0	0	50	150	250	350	450	550	1,050	1,550
7,000	0	0	0	0	75	175	275	375	475	975	1,475
8,000	0	0	0	0	0	100	200	300	400	900	1,400
9,000	0	0	0	0	0	25	125	225	325	825	1,325
10,000	0	0	0	0	0	0	50	150	250	750	1,250
11,000	0	0	0	0	0	0	0	75	175	675	1,175
12,000	0	0	0	0	0	0	0	0	100	600	1,100
13,000	0	0	0	0	0	0	0	0	25	525	1,025
14,000	0	0	0	0	0	0	0	0	0	450	950
15,000	0	0	0	0	0	0	0	0	0	375	875
18,000	0	0	0	0	0	0	0	0	0	150	650
20,000	0	0	0	0	0	0	0	0	0	0	500
25,000	0	0	0	0	0	0	0	0	0	0	125
30,000	0	0	0	0	0	0	0	0	0	0	0
40,000	0	0	0	0	0	0	0	0	0	0	0
50,000	0	0	0	0	0	0	0	0	0	0	0

REIMBURSEMENTS OF MEDICAL COSTS

¶ 17.5 Insurance or other reimbursements of your medical costs reduce your medical deductions. Reimbursements for loss of earnings or damages for personal injuries and mental suffering do not.

A reimbursement first reduces the medical expense for which it is paid. The excess is then applied to your other deductible medical costs.

EXAMPLE

Premiums paid for medical insurance totaled $800. You paid doctor and hospital bills totaling $700 and purchased prescribed drugs costing $150. Group hospitalization insurance reimbursed $300 for doctors and hospital bills and $25 for medicines and drugs. Your adjusted gross income is $8,000. Your 1987 deduction is computed as follows:

Prescribed drugs	$150
Medical care expenses	700
Premiums	800
Total	$1,650
Less Reimbursement	325
	1,325
Less 7.5% of $8000	600
Medical expense deduction	$ 725

Personal injury settlements or awards. Generally, a cash settlement recovered in a personal injury suit does not reduce your medical expense deduction. The settlement is not treated as reimbursement of your medical bills. But when part of the settlement is specifically earmarked by a court or by law for payment of hospital bills, the medical expense deduction is reduced.

Reimbursements in excess of your medical expenses. If you paid the entire premium of the policy, the excess payment is not taxed. If you and your employer each contributed to the policy, you may have to include in income that part of the excess reimbursement which is attributable to your employer's premium contributions and which was not included in your gross income and not paid for permanent injury, disfigurement, or as tax free disability pension. *See* ¶2.21.

If your employer paid the total cost of the policy and his contributions were not taxed to you, you report as income all of your excess reimbursement, unless it covers payment for permanent injury, disfigurement or tax free disability pension.

EXAMPLES

1. Smith pays premiums of $240 and $120 for two personal health insurance policies. His total medical expenses are $900. He receives $700 from one insurance company and $500 from the other. The excess of $300 ($1,200–$900) is not taxable.

2. Jones' employer paid premiums of $240 and $120 for two employee health insurance policies covering medical expenses. Jones's medical expenses in one year are $900. He receives $1,200 from the two companies. The entire $300 excess is taxable.

3. Brown's employer paid a premium of $240 for a group health policy covering Brown, and Brown himself paid $120 for a personal health policy. His medical expenses are $900; he recovers $700 under his employer's policy and $500 under his own policy. The taxable portion attributed to his employer's premium contribution is $175, computed this way:

Reimbursement allocated to Brown's policy, 5/12 × $900	$375
Reimbursement allocated to employer's policy, 7/12 × $900	525
Total	$900
Taxable excess allocated to employer's policy ($700– $525)	$175

4. Green's employer paid $240 for a health insurance policy but contributed only $90 and deducted $150 from Green's wages. Green also paid $120 for a personal health insurance policy. His medical expenses are $900. He recovered $700 from the employer's policy and $500 from his personal policy. The excess attributable to the employer's policy is $175 (computed as in example 3 above). However, the taxable portion is only $65.63. Both Green and his employer contributed to the cost of the employer's policy and a further allocation is necessary:

Green's contribution	$150
Employer's contribution	90
Total cost of policy	$240
Ratio of employer's contribution to annual cost of policy (90/240)	
Taxable portion—9/24 of excess reimbursement of $175	$65.63

Reimbursement in a later year. If you took a medical expense deduction in one year and are reimbursed for all or part of the expense in a later year, the reimbursement may be taxed in the year received. The reimbursement is taxable income to the extent the deduction reduced your tax in the prior year.

EXAMPLES

1. In 1986, you had adjusted gross income of $12,000. During that year, you paid medical expenses of $1,300. You deducted $700 computed as follows:

Medical expenses	$1,300
Less: 5% of $12,000	600
Allowable deduction	$ 700

In 1987 you collect $500 insurance reimbursing part of your 1986 medical expenses. If you had collected that amount in 1986, your medical expense deduction would have been $200. The entire reimbursement of $500 is taxable in 1987. It is the amount by which the 1986 deduction of $700 exceeds the deduction of $200 that would have been allowed if the reimbursement had been received in 1986.

2. Same facts as in (1) above but you did not deduct the medical expense because you did not itemize deductions. The reimbursement is not taxable.

PREMIUMS OF MEDICAL CARE POLICIES

¶ 17.6 You may deduct as medical expenses premiums paid for medical care policies covering yourself, your spouse, or dependents. Such policies include Blue Cross, Blue Shield, and Federal Voluntary Medicare insurance (Medicare Part B). Payment for coverage under Medicare (Part A) is deductible by those over age 65 who are not covered by Social Security. Deductions may be claimed for membership payments in associations furnishing cooperative or free-choice medical services, group hospitalization or clinical care policies, and medical care premiums paid to colleges as part of a tuition bill, if the amount is separately stated in the bill.

> Deductible premiums include amounts paid for health insurance providing reimbursements for hospital, surgical, drug costs, and other medical expenses. Also deductible are premiums paid for contact lens replacement and premiums on policies providing solely for indemnity for hospital and surgical expenses, even though benefits are paid regardless of the amount of expenses incurred.

Premiums paid before you reach age 65 for medical care insurance for protection after you reach 65 are deductible in the year paid if they are payable on a level payment basis under the contract (1) for a period of 10 years or more, or (2) until the year you reach age 65 (but in no case for a period of less than five years).

You may *not* deduct premiums for a policy guaranteeing you a specified amount each week (not to exceed a specified number of weeks) in the event you are hospitalized. Also, no deduction may be claimed for premiums paid for a policy which compensates you for loss of earnings while ill or injured, or for loss of life, limb, or sight. If your policy covers both medical care and loss of income or loss of life, limb, or sight, no part of the premium is deductible unless (1) the contract or separate statement from the insurance company states what part of the premium is allocated to medical care, and (2) the premium allocated to medical care is deductible. You may not deduct a portion of car insurance premiums that provides medical insurance coverage for persons injured by or in your car.

There is no separate deduction for health insurance premiums. All qualifying premiums are treated as medical expenses subject to the overall 7.5% limit.

DEPENDENTS' MEDICAL EXPENSES

¶ 17.7 Spouse. You may deduct as medical expenses your payments of medical bills for your spouse. You must have been married either at the time the expenses were incurred or at the time the bills were paid. That is, you may deduct your payment of your spouse's medical bills even though you are divorced or widowed, if, at the time the expenses were incurred, you were married. Further, if your spouse incurred medical expenses before you married and you pay the bills after you marry, you may deduct the expense.

EXAMPLES

1. Your spouse has doctor bills covering an operation performed in 1986, before you were married. You married in 1987. You pay those bills in 1987. You may claim a medical expense deduction for your payment.

2. In October 1986, your spouse had dental work done. In February 1987 you are divorced; in April 1987, you pay your former spouse's dental bills. You may deduct the payment on your 1987 tax return.

3. In 1987, you pay medical expenses for your spouse who died in 1987. You remarry in 1987. In a joint return which you file with your new spouse in 1987, you may deduct your payment of your deceased spouse's medical expenses.

Children and other dependents. You may deduct your payment of medical bills for your children or other dependents. The person must be someone you could claim as a dependent except for the fact that he earned more than $1,900 or filed a joint return. You must be able to prove you: (1) paid the medical expenses and (2) contributed more than half the support. (*See* ¶1.50 for a list of persons you may claim as dependents.) The close family relationship must exist either at the time the expense was incurred or at the time you paid it.

EXAMPLES

1. You contribute more than half of your married son's support, including a payment of a medical expense of $800. Because he filed a joint return with his wife, you may not claim him as a dependent. But you may still deduct your payment of the $800 medical expense. You contributed more than half of his support.

2. Your mother underwent an operation in November 1986. You paid for the operation in February 1987. You may deduct the cost of the operation in 1987 if you furnished more than one-half your mother's support in either 1986 or 1987.

Divorced and separated parents. You may be able to deduct your payment of your child's medical costs, even though your ex-spouse is entitled to claim the child as a dependent. For purposes of the medical deduction, the child is considered to be the dependent of *both* parents if (1) they are divorced or legally separated under a written agreement, separated under a written agreement, or married but living apart during the last six months of 1987; (2) the child was in the custody of one or both parents for more than half of 1987, and (3) more than half of the child's 1987 support was provided by both parents.

A child may not deduct medical expenses paid with his parent's welfare payments.

EXAMPLE

A son is the legal guardian of his mother who is mentally incompetent. As guardian, he received his mother's state welfare and Social Security benefits which he deposited in his personal bank account and used to pay part of his mother's medical expenses. On his tax return, he claimed a deduction for the total medical expenses paid on behalf of his mother. The court held that he could deduct only medical expenses in excess of the amounts received as welfare and Social Security payments. The benefits, to the extent used for medical expenses, represented the mother's payments on her own behalf.

Adopted children. You may deduct medical expenses of an adopted child if you may claim the child as a dependent either when the medical services are rendered or when you pay the expenses. An adopted child may be claimed as a dependent when a court has approved the adoption. In the absence of a court decree, the child is an exemption if he is a member of your household for the entire year. However, you do not have to show that he lived in your home for the entire year if he has been placed in your custody by an authorized agency.

If you reimburse an adoption agency for medical expenses it paid under an agreement with you, you are considered to have paid the

expenses. But reimbursement of expenses incurred and paid before adoption negotiations do not qualify as your medical expenses and you may not deduct them.

You may not deduct medical expenses for services rendered to the natural mother of the child you adopt.

EXAMPLE

A couple adopted a son on the day of his birth. They paid all medical expenses of the birth. They were denied a deduction because they could not show the expenses were for the child, their dependent, and not for the natural mother, a nondependent.

Multiple support agreements. You may be able to deduct your payment of a relative's medical expenses although you do not contribute more than one-half his support. You must meet the tests for a multiple support agreement. *See* ¶1.22. If your relative has gross income over $1,900, you may still deduct your payment of medical expenses provided the other tests for multiple support are met.

You may deduct only the amount you actually pay for the relative's medical expenses. If you are reimbursed by others who signed the multiple support agreement, you must reduce your deduction by the amount of reimbursement.

EXAMPLE

You and your brother and sister share equally in the support of your mother. Part of your mother's support includes medical expenses. Should the three of you share in the payment of the bills or should only one of you pay them? The answer: Payment should be made by the person who may claim her as a dependent under a multiple support agreement. Only he may deduct the payment. If you are going to claim her as an exemption, you should pay the bill. You may deduct the payment although you did not contribute more than half of her support. If your brother and sister reimburse you for part of the bill, you must reduce your medical deduction by the amount of the reimbursement. And neither your brother nor your sister may deduct this share. Thus, a deduction is lost for these amounts.

DECEDENT'S MEDICAL EXPENSES

¶ **17.8** The executor or administrator of a decedent's estate may pay the decedent's medical expenses out of the estate. Where the expenses are paid within one year of death, they may be treated as paid when incurred and claimed as income tax deductions. Thus, a claim for refund or an amended return may be filed for an earlier year when the expenses were incurred but not paid until after death by the executor.

EXAMPLE

Jones incurred medical expenses of $500 in 1986 and $300 in 1987. He died June 1, 1987, without having paid these expenses. He had already filed his 1986 return before the due date. In August 1987, his executor pays the $800 in medical expenses. He may file an amended return for 1986 and claim a medical expense deduction for the $500 and get a refund for the increased deductions. He may claim the remaining $300 as a medical expense deduction on Jones's final return.

A decedent's medical expenses claimed as an income tax deduction may not again be claimed as an estate tax deduction. If the expenses may be claimed as an estate tax deduction but are claimed as an income tax deduction, the executor must file a statement with the decedent's income tax return that the expenses have not been deducted on the estate tax return and the estate waives its right to deduct them for estate tax purposes.

If medical expenses are claimed as an income tax deduction, the portion of the expenses that are below the 7.5% floor and, therefore, not deductible, may not be deducted on the estate tax return. Although the expenses were not actually deducted, the IRS considers them to be part of the overall income tax deduction.

TRAVEL COSTS MAY BE MEDICAL DEDUCTIONS

¶ **17.9** You may deduct the cost of travel to a place where you receive medical treatment or which is prescribed as a place that will help relieve a specific chronic ailment. Trips to and from a doctor's office are the most common type of deductible travel expense.

The amount of the deduction is limited to the cost of transportation, such as the cost of operating a car or fares for public transportation. If you use your automobile, you may deduct a flat rate of 9¢ a mile and, in addition, you may deduct parking fees and tolls. If, however, auto expenses exceed this standard mileage rate, you may deduct your actual out-of-pocket costs for gas, oil, repairs, tolls, and parking fees. Do not include depreciation, general maintenance, or car insurance.

EXAMPLE

You drive your car to a doctor's office for treatment. You made 40 such round trips of 25 miles each. As the total mileage is 1,000 miles, you claim $90 (1,000 × 9¢) as medical expenses. If you incurred tolls or parking fees during the trips, you add these expenses to the deduction.

Important: The 9¢ rate was effective when this edition went to press. Any change in the rate is listed in the Supplement.

Per diem lodging allowance. A daily lodging allowance of up to $50 is allowed on trips to obtain medical care by a physician at a licensed hospital, hospital-related facility, or equivalent facility such as an outpatient clinic. The deduction is allowed only if the lodging is not considered extravagant and there is no significant vacation or recreation element to the trip. Food expenses are not deductible. A separate $50 per diem lodging deduction is also allowed to a parent who accompanies a dependent child on a qualifying trip to obtain medical care. For example, the IRS ruled that the $50 allowance could be claimed by a parent for a six-week hotel stay while her eight-year-old daughter was treated in a nearby hospital for serious injuries received in an automobile accident. The mother's presence was necessary so that she could sign release forms for surgery.

Examples of travel costs which have been allowed as medical deductions by rulings or court decisions are:

Nurse's fare if nurse is required on trip.

Parent's fare if parent is needed to accompany child who requires medical care.

Parent's fare to visit his child at an institution where the visits are prescribed by a doctor.

Trip to visit specialist in another city.

Airplane fare to a distant city in which a patient used to live to have a check up by a family doctor living there. That he could have received the same examination in the city in which he presently lived did not bar his deduction.

Trip to escape a climate that is bad for your health. For example, the cost of a trip from a northern state to Florida made by a person recovering from a throat operation was ruled deductible.

Travel to an Alcoholics Anonymous Club meeting if membership in the group has been advised by a doctor.

Disabled veteran's commuting expenses where a doctor prescribed work and driving as therapy.

Wife's trip to provide nursing care for an ailing husband in a distant city. The trip was ordered by her husband's doctor as a necessity.

Driving prescribed as therapy.

Travel costs of kidney transplant donor or prospective donor.

Nondeductible travel costs—

Trip for the general improvement of your health.

Traveling to areas of favorable climates during the year rather than living permanently in a locality suitable for your health.

Meals while on trip for medical treatment—even if cost of transportation is a valid medical cost, but a court has allowed the deduction of the extra cost of specially prepared food.

Trip for medical treatment at a distant city when you could have been treated in your home city. For example, a trip to Florida for an appendectomy is not deductible.

Trip to get "spiritual" rather than medical aid. For example, cost of trip to the Shrine of Our Lady of Lourdes is not deductible.

Moving a family to a climate more suitable to an ill mother's condition.

Only the mother's travel costs would be deductible.

Moving household furnishings to area advised by physician.

Operating an auto or special vehicle to go to work because of disabled condition. But the cost of wheel chair or autoette or special auto devices for handicapped persons is deductible.

Convalescence cruise advised by a doctor for a patient recovering from pneumonia.

Loss on sale of car bought for medical travel.

Medical seminar cruise taken by patient whose condition was reviewed by physicians taking the cruise.

SCHOOLING COSTS FOR THE HANDICAPPED

¶ 17.10 You may deduct as medical expenses the costs of sending a mentally or physically handicapped person to a special school or institution to overcome or alleviate his handicap. Such costs may cover—

Teaching of braille or lip reading.

Training, caring for, supervising, and treating a mentally retarded person.

Cost of meals and lodgings, if boarding is required at the school.

Costs of regular education courses also taught at the school, provided they are incidental to the special courses and services furnished by the school.

The parent of a problem child may deduct only that part of a private school fee directly related to psychological aid given to the child.

EXAMPLES

1. An emotionally disturbed child is sent to a private school which has a staff of three psychologists. His father deducted the school fee of $6,270 as a medical expense. IRS disallowed the amount claiming that the child, who was neither mentally retarded nor handicapped, was sent to school primarily for an education. The Tax Court allowed the father to deduct $3,000 covering the psychological treatment.

2. A boy could not understand subjects taught in public schools. He was withdrawn and enrolled at a private military academy. The deduction of tuition costs was disallowed by a court. The academy furnished no psychiatric treatment and, furthermore, enrollment in the academy was not recommended by a doctor.

3. A retarded boy with a speech defect attends a state school for therapy. On the advice of school authorities, the boy is sent to a "halfway home" in another community so that he may have major orthodontic work to reduce his speech disability. The state school has neither an orthodontist nor facilities to take the child to one. The halfway home is operated by a private couple who care for several other people, all with disabilities and placed there through a local welfare service. The cost of maintaining the boy at the private home and transportation costs incurred in taking the child from the home to his residence and back on visits are deductible.

4. A retarded boy had been excluded from several schools for the mentally handicapped because he needed close attention. The director of a military academy had extensive experience in training young boys. Although it was not the usual practice of the academy to enroll mentally handicapped children, the director accepted the boy on a day-to-day basis as a personal challenge. The Tax Court holds that the cost of both tuition and transportation to bring the boy to and from the school are deductible medical expenses. The primary purpose of the training given the boy was not ordinary education but remedial training designed to overcome his handicap. But note that in other cases, a deduction for tuition of a military school to which a child was sent in order to remove him from a tense family environment, and the cost of a blind boy's attendance at a regular private school which made a special effort to accommodate his braille equipment, were disallowed.

The fact that a particular school or camp is recommended for an emotionally disturbed child by a psychiatrist will not qualify the tuition as a deduction if the school or camp has no special program geared to the child's problem. However, you may deduct the costs of maintaining a mentally retarded person in a home specially selected to meet the standards set by his psychiatrist to aid him in his adjustment from life in a mental hospital to community living.

Payment for future medical care expenses is deductible if immediate payment is required by contract.

CONVALESCENT HOME COSTS

¶ **17.11** A payment for meals and lodging to a nursing home, convalescent home, home for the aged, or sanitarium is a deductible medical expense if the patient is confined for medical treatment.

> Helpful in establishing the full deductibility of payments to a nursing home, convalescent home, home for the aged, or sanitarium are facts such as these:
>
> The patient entered the institution on the direction or suggestion of a doctor.
>
> Attendance or treatment at the institution had a direct therapeutic effect on the condition suffered by the patient.
>
> The attendance at the institution was for a specific ailment rather than for a "general" health condition. That the patient suffers from an ailment is not sufficient proof that he is in the home for treatment.

If you cannot prove that the patient entered the home for medical care (which would permit a deduction for meals and lodging in addition to medical costs), you may nevertheless deduct that part of the cost covering actual medical and nursing care.

EXAMPLE

A husband and wife pay $500 per month to a rest home for lifetime care. They prove, on the basis of the home's experience, that it costs the home $100 to provide them with medical care, medicines, and hospitalization. Under such circumstances, $100 of each monthly fee is a deductible medical expense.

In an unusual case, a court allowed a medical expense deduction for apartment rent of an aged parent.

EXAMPLE

A doctor recommended to Ungar that his 90-year-old mother, convalescing from a brain hemorrhage, could receive better care at less expense in accommodations away from a hospital. A two-room apartment was rented, hospital equipment installed, and nurses engaged for seven months. The rent totaled $1,400. Ungar's sister, who worked in her husband's shoe store, nursed her mother for six weeks. Ungar paid the wages of a clerk who was hired to substitute for his sister in the store. Ungar deducted both the rent and wages as medical expenses. The IRS disallowed them; a Tax Court reversed the IRS. The apartment rent was no less a medical expense than the cost of a hospital room. As for the clerk's wages, they too were deductible medical costs. The clerk was hired specifically to allow the daughter to nurse her mother, thereby avoiding the larger, though more direct, medical expense of hiring a nurse.

Payment for future lifetime care. Generally, no deduction is allowed for prepayment of medical expenses for services to be performed in a later taxable year. However, this disallowance rule does not apply where there is a current obligation to pay.

EXAMPLES

1. A 78-year-old man entered into an agreement with a retirement home. For a lump-sum payment, the home agreed to provide lifetime care, including medical care, medicine, and hospitalization. The lifetime care fee was calculated without regard to fees received from other patients, and was not insurance. The home allocated 30% of the lump-sum payment to medical expenses based on its prior experience. The IRS holds that this part of the payment is deductible in the year paid. It holds that the legal obligation to pay the medical expenses was incurred at the time the lump-sum payment was made, even though medical services would not be performed until a future time, if at all. Should any portion of the lump-sum payment be refunded, that part attributable to the deducted amount must be reported as income (*see* ¶ 12.14).

2. Parents contracted with an institution to care for their handicapped child after their death. The contract provided for payments as follows: 20% on signing, 10% within 12 months, 10% within 24 months, and the balance when the child enters. Payment of specified amounts at specified intervals was a condition imposed by the institution for its

agreement to accept the child for lifetime care. Since the obligation to pay was incurred at the time payments were made, they are deductible as medical expenses, although the medical services were not to be performed until a future time, if at all.

3. A couple entered a retirement home which would provide them with accommodations, meals, and medical care for life. They agreed to pay a founder's fee of $40,000 and a monthly fee of $800. If they quit the home, they may get a refund of a portion of the founder's fee. Fifteen percent of the monthly fee and 10% of the founder's fee will be used for medical care and 5% of the founder's fee will be used for construction of a health facility. On the basis of these figures, the couple may deduct as medical costs 10% of the founder's fee and 15% of the monthly fee. However, the portion of the founder's fee for the possible health facility does not qualify as a medical expense. Finally, any refund of the founder's fee received in a later year may be income to the extent medical deductions were previously claimed for the fees.

4. An entrance fee to a retirement community gave new residents not only the right to live in the development but also the right to 30 days of free care at a nearby convalescent home in the first year, with additional free days in later years of residency. The community allocated 7% of the $20,000 entrance fee, or $1,400, to the convalescent care. Smith deducted the $1,400 as a medical expense which the IRS disallowed. It claimed that the amount could not be deducted in the year of payment because most of the promised free services would not be received until future years. The Tax Court disagreed and allowed the deduction because the obligation to pay was incurred when the residency agreement was signed.

NURSES' WAGES

¶ **17.12** The costs of a nurse attending an ill person are deductible. Costs include any Social Security (FICA) tax paid by you. That the nurse is not registered or licensed will not bar the deduction, provided the services are performed for the medical aid or treatment of the patient. When you use a nonprofessionally trained person, such as a practical nurse, be prepared to show that the nurse performed medical services. If the nurse also performs domestic services, deduct only that part of the pay attributed to medical aid to the patient.

EXAMPLES

1. Dodge's wife was arthritic. His doctor advised that he have someone take care of her to prevent her from falling. He moved her to his daughter's home and paid the daughter to care for her mother. He deducted the payments to his daughter. The IRS disallowed the deduction, claiming that the daughter was not a trained nurse. The Tax Court allows that part of the deduction attributed to the nursing aid. Whether a medical service has been rendered depends on the nature of the services rendered, not on the qualifications or title of the person who renders them. Here, the daughter's services, following the doctor's advice, qualify as medical care.

2. A husband hires a domestic to care for his home so that his wife can get a complete rest as prescribed by her doctor. He may deduct only that part of the domestic's salary directly attributed to nursing aid given to the wife. No deduction is allowed for the cost of the domestic services in the home. (But see ¶ 1.29, tax credit for dependent care expenses.)

3. An attendant hired by a quadriplegic performs household duties, in addition to caring for his medical and personal needs. The quadriplegic pays him wages and also provides food and lodging. According to the IRS, a medical expense deduction is allowable only for that portion of the wages attributable to medical and personal care. The wages are apportioned on the basis of time spent performing nursing-type services and time spent performing household duties. The same allocation is used to determine the portion of the cost of the attendant's meals which are deductible as a medical expense. However, the attendant's lodging is not deductible as a medical expense unless the quadriplegic shows additional expenditures directly attributable to lodging the attendant, such as paying increased rent for an apartment with another bedroom for the attendant.

The salary of a clerk hired specifically to relieve a wife from her husband's store in order to care for her ill mother was allowed as a medical expense (*see* the example in ¶ 17.11).

If, in order to work, you pay a nurse to look after a physically or mentally disabled dependent, you may be able to claim a credit for all or part of the nurse's wage as a dependent care expense. You may not, however, claim both a credit and a medical expense deduction. First, you claim the nurse's wage as a dependent care cost. If not all of the wages are utilized as a care cost because of the expense limits (see ¶1.29), the remaining balance is deductible as a medical expense.

HOME IMPROVEMENTS AS MEDICAL EXPENSES

¶ **17.13** A disease or ailment may require the construction of special equipment or facilities in a home: A heart patient may need an elevator to carry him upstairs; a polio patient, a pool; an asthmatic patient, an air cleaning system.

You may deduct the full cost of equipment installed for a medical reason if it does not increase the value of your property, as for example, the cost of a detachable window air conditioner. Where equipment increases the value of your property, you may take a medical deduction to the extent that the cost of the equipment exceeds the increase in the value of the property. Of course, if the equipment does not increase the value of the property, its entire cost is deductible, even though it is permanently fixed to the property.

EXAMPLES

1. Gerard's daughter suffered from cystic fibrosis. While there is no known cure for the disease, doctors attempt to prolong life by preventing pulmonary infection. One approach is to maintain a constant temperature and high humidity. A doctor recommended that Gerard install a central air-conditioning unit in his home for his daughter. It cost $1,300 and increased the value of his home by $800. The balance of $500 was deductible as a medical expense.

2. After a three-year-old child had been diagnosed as having lead poisoning, health officials required removal of the lead-based paint and a refinishing of surfaces reachable by the child, or those that were in poor repair. The cost of removing the lead-based paint from surfaces reachable by the child or in poor repair qualifies as a medical expense because of the child's history of lead poisoning and the hazardous condition of his home as certified by local authorities. Also deductible was the cost of installation of wallboard or wall paneling over such surfaces to the extent that the cost of the work exceeds the increase in the value of the house. No deduction was allowed for the cost of painting or repairing any of the surfaces which were not reachable by the child or were not in poor repair.

If swimming is prescribed as physical therapy, the cost of constructing a home swimming pool may be partly deductible as a medical expense. However, the IRS is likely to question the deductions because of the possibility that the pool may be used for recreation. If you can show that the pool is specially equipped to alleviate your condition and is not generally suited for recreation, the IRS will allow the deduction. For example, the IRS allowed a deduction for a pool constructed by an osteoarthritis patient. His physician prescribed swimming several times a day as treatment. He built an indoor lap pool with specially designed stairs and a hydrotherapy device. Given these features, and the fact that the pool did not have a diving board, the IRS concluded that the pool was specially designed to provide medical treatment and was not intended for personal recreation.

In one case the IRS tried to limit the cost of a luxury indoor pool built for therapeutic reasons to the least expensive construction. The Tax Court rejected the IRS position, holding that a medical expense is not to be limited to the cheapest form of treatment, but on appeal, the IRS position was adopted.

If, instead of building a pool, you buy a home with a pool, can you deduct the part of the purchase price allocated to the pool? The Tax Court said no. The purchase price of the house includes the fair market value of the pool. Therefore, there is no extra cost above the increase in the home's value which would support a medical expense deduction.

The operating costs of an indoor pool were allowed as a deduction to an emphysema sufferer.

EXAMPLE

Cherry was advised by his doctor to swim to relieve his severe emphysema and bronchitis. He could not swim at local health spas; they did not open early enough or stay open late enough to allow him to swim before or after work. His home was too small for a pool. He bought a lot and built a new house with an indoor pool. He used the pool several times a day, and swimming improved his condition; if he did not swim, his symptoms returned. Cherry deducted pool operating costs of $4,000 for fuel, electricity, insurance and repairs. The IRS disallowed the deductions claiming that the pool was used for personal recreation. Besides, it did not have special medical equipment. The Tax Court allowed the deduction. Cherry built the pool to swim in in order to exercise his lungs. That there was no special equipment is irrelevant; Cherry did not need special ramps, railings, a shallow floor or whirlpool. Finally, his family rarely used the pool.

No deduction is allowed where the primary purpose of the improvement is for personal convenience rather than medical necessity.

EXAMPLE

Haines broke his leg in a skiing accident and underwent various forms of physical therapy, including swimming. To aid his recovery, his physician recommended that he install a swimming pool at his home. The Tax Court agreed with the IRS that the cost of the pool was not deductible. Although swimming was beneficial to his condition, he needed special therapy for only a limited period of time, and he could have gotten it at less cost at a nearby public pool. Finally, because of weather conditions, the pool could not be used for about half of the year.

Cost of maintaining and operating improvement. The expense of maintaining and operating equipment installed for medical reasons may be claimed as a medical expense, although the cost of the equipment and its installation is not deductible under the above rules.

Handicap exception. The increased-value test does not apply to a handicapped person who makes structural changes to a residence such as adding ramps, modifying doorways, and installing railings and support bars. Such improvements are treated for medical deduction purposes as not increasing the value of the house. The cost of such improvements when added to other deductible expenses are deductible to the extent that they exceed the 7.5% floor.

COSTS DEDUCTIBLE AS BUSINESS EXPENSES

¶ **17.14** The following examples illustrate cases in which expenses are deductible as business expenses rather than as medical expenses. Claiming a business deduction is preferable because the deduction is not subject to the 7.5% adjusted gross income floor.

Costs of a checkup required by your employer are business expenses and are not subject to the 7.5% floor.

EXAMPLE

An airline pilot is required by his company to take a semi-annual physical exam at his own expense. If he fails to produce a resultant certificate of good health, he is subject to discharge. The cost of such checkups certifying physical fitness for a job is an ordinary and necessary business expense. If the doctor prescribes a treatment or further examinations to maintain the pilot's physical condition, the cost of these subsequent treatments or examinations may be deducted only as medical expenses, even though needed to maintain the physical standards required by the job. Thus, a professional singer who consults a throat specialist may not deduct the fee as a business expense. The fee is a medical expense subject to the 7.5% floor.

The Tax Court allowed the costs of psychoanalysis by a licensed social worker working as a therapist to be deducted as an education cost.

Some expenses incurred by a physically handicapped person because of his handicap may be deductible as a business expense rather than as a medical expense. A business expense deduction may be allowed if the expense is necessary for the person to satisfactorily perform his job and is not required or used, except incidentally, for personal purposes.

EXAMPLES

1. A blind person requires a reader to help him perform his job. The costs of the reader's services are deductible as an itemized business deduction.

2. A professor is paralyzed from the waist down and confined to a wheelchair. When he attends out-of-town professional meetings, he has his wife, a friend, or a colleague accompany him to help him with baggage, stairs, narrow doors, and to sit with him on airplanes when air-

lines will not allow wheelchair passengers without an attendant. While he does not pay them a salary, he does pay their travel costs. He may deduct these costs as business expenses. They are incurred solely because of his occupation.

3. An attorney uses prostheses due to bilateral amputation of his legs and takes medication several times a day for other ailments. When he must take out-of-town business trips, his wife or a neighbor accompanies him to help with his wheelchair, luggage, driving, daily removal and replacement of his prostheses, and administration of medication and to help him should he have an allergic reaction to the drugs. The attorney requires many of these services in conducting his personal and business affairs in his home town. He may deduct the out-of-town expenses incurred for his neighbor's services only as a medical expense. The services are not considered business expenses as he regularly uses them for personal purposes. When his wife accompanies him, he may deduct her transportation costs as a medical expense; her food and lodging are nondeductible ordinary living expenses.

18

CASUALTY AND THEFT LOSSES AND INVOLUNTARY CONVERSION GAINS

¶ 18.1 Deductible losses must exceed 10% income floor. A 10% income floor limits the amount of personal casualty and theft losses deductible as itemized deductions. The 10% limit based on adjusted gross income applies to total losses incurred during 1987, after each loss is reduced by $100 (see ¶ 18.10).

EXAMPLE

In January 1987, you have an uninsured theft loss of $1,000, and in July 1987 uninsured car damage of $3,000. Your adjusted gross income is $25,000. Your deduction is $1,300 figured as follows:

Theft loss	$1,000	
Less	100	$900
Car damage	$3,000	
Less	100	2,900
Total loss		$3,800
Less 10% of $25,000		2,500
Deductible loss		$1,300

The 10% limit does not apply to losses of business or income-producing property and certain netting computations explained at ¶ 18.27.

DEDUCTIBLE PERSONAL CASUALTY AND THEFT LOSSES

¶ 18.2 A loss of nonbusiness property must result from a sudden and destructive force. Chance or a natural phenomenon must be present. Examples include earthquakes, hurricanes, tornadoes, floods, severe storms, landslides and fires. Damage to your car from an accident is generally deductible; *see* ¶18.13. Courts have allowed deductions for other types of accidents; *see* example 2 below. The requirement of suddenness is designed to bar deductions for damage caused by a natural action such as erosion, corrosion, and termite infestation occurring over a period of time. The requirement of suddenness does not apply to losses of business or income-producing property.

EXAMPLES
1. A home owner claimed a loss for water damage to wallpaper and plaster. The water entered through the frames of a window. The loss was disallowed. He gave no evidence that the damage came from a sudden or destructive force, such as a storm. The damage might have been caused by progressive deterioration.
2. Unaware that his wife had reached back into their automobile, Mr. White slammed the door on her hand. The impact loosened a large diamond in the ring she wore. In pain, she shook her hand vigorously and the diamond flew out of its loosened setting to the leaf-covered gravel driveway. It was never found. In disallowing White's deduction, the IRS contended that a casualty loss requires a cataclysmic event. The Tax Court disagreed and allowed the deduction. Whenever an accidental force is exerted against property, and its owner is powerless to prevent the damage because of the suddenness, the resulting damage is a deductible casualty loss. The IRS has agreed to accept the decision.

Personal casualty and theft losses after the floor reductions must be taken as itemized deductions. Casualty and theft losses of business and rental or royalty-producing property are deductible, even if you do not itemize deductions.

> *Drought damage.* The IRS does not generally allow deductions for drought damage. An agent may argue that the loss resulted from progressive deterioration which does not fit the legal definition of a personal casualty loss. Courts have allowed deductions for severe drought.

Destruction of a lawn by the careless use of weed killer has been held to be a casualty.

Loss due to vandalism during riots or civil disorders is treated as a casualty loss.

Loss due to buyer resistance because of damage to surrounding property is generally not deductible. However in the following case a deduction was allowed by a federal district court and appeals court.

EXAMPLE
Floods damaged 12 homes which were razed by local authorities for safety reasons. Although Finkbohner's home suffered only minor damage, he claimed that the removal of the neighboring homes decreased the attractiveness of the neighborhood and made it more susceptible to crime. He estimated that the value of his home fell from $120,000 to $95,000 and claimed a casualty loss for the $25,000 difference.

The IRS disallowed the loss on the grounds that it was not based on actual physical damage. It allowed a deduction only for the cost of repairs, about $1,200. A federal district court jury allowed a $12,500 casualty loss after being instructed by the trial judge that permanent buyer resistance after the flood damage to the neighborhood is basis for a loss deduction. An appeals court upheld the loss because permanent buyer resistance affected the value of the home. The court distinguished Finkbohner's case from that of a homeowner who, after a flood and mud slide, was barred from deducting a loss based on fears of future floods. In that situation, the owner was trying to claim a loss that could only be deducted, if and when a future disaster occurred, by the future owner. Here, the buyer resistance confronting Finkbohner was not based on expected future casualties, but on changes to their neighborhood that already occurred.

Termites. Termite damage is generally nondeductible since it often results from long periods of termite infestation. Proving a *sudden* action in the sense of fixing the approximate moment of the termite invasion is difficult. Some courts have allowed a deduction, but the IRS will disallow deductions for termite damage under any conditions based on a study that found that serious termite damage results only after an infestation of three to eight years. Examples of other nondeductible casualty losses are at ¶18.15.

Destruction of trees by southern pine beetles over a period of 5–10 days was held by the IRS to be a casualty. One court held similarly where destruction occurred over a 30-day period. For figuring the deduction for tree and shrub damage, *see* ¶18.14.

Failure to protect against a foreseeable casualty does not bar a deduction for the loss if it does occur.

EXAMPLES
1. Heyn owned a hillside lot on which he contracted for the building of a home. A soil test showed a high proportion of fine-grain dense sandstone, which is unstable. His construction contract called for appropriate shoring up and support. But, because of the contractor's negligence, a landslide occurred. The IRS disallowed the loss on the grounds that it was not due to a "casualty" because the danger was known before Heyn undertook the project and because of the negligence involved. The court disagreed. The contractor's negligence is not a factor in determining whether there was a casualty. For example, an automobile collision is considered a casualty, even if caused by negligent driving. Foreseeability is not a factor. A weather report may warn property owners to take protective steps against an approaching hurricane, but losses caused by the hurricane are deductible. The IRS has agreed to accept the decision.
2. Mrs. Carpenter placed her dirty ring in a glass of ammonia beside the sink. Not knowing the contents of the glass, her husband emptied it into the sink and started the automatic garbage disposal, crushing the ring. The court allowed a full deduction for the loss which it said resulted from a destructive force. That Mr. Carpenter was negligent has no bearing on whether the event was a casualty.

The cost of preventative measures, such as burglar alarms or smoke detectors, is not deductible.

EXAMPLE
A utility company cut down trees interfering with power lines and removed branches of the remaining trees. Later, the property owner feared that the lack of branches on the remaining trees might cause them to uproot during an ice storm and damage his home. So he had all of the trees removed and claimed a $3,900 deduction for the removal. He argued that preventive measures taken to avoid casualty loss damage qualify for a casualty loss deduction. The IRS with Tax Court support disagrees. A casualty loss is allowed only if it is caused by a sudden and unexpected event, such as a storm.

> *Faulty construction no bar to casualty loss.* A plumber stepped on a pipe which was improperly installed two years before. Resulting underground flooding caused damage of over $20,000. The IRS argued that this was caused by a construction fault and did not qualify as a casualty loss. The Tax Court disagreed. The plumber caused the damage. Improper construction was only an element in the causative chain.

WHO MAY CLAIM THE LOSS DEDUCTION

¶ 18.3 The casualty and theft loss deduction may be claimed only by the owner of the property. For example, a husband filing a separate return may not deduct the loss of jewelry belonging to his wife; only she may deduct it on her separate return.

On jointly owned property, the loss is divided among the owners. If you and your spouse own the property jointly, you deduct the entire loss on a joint return. If you file separately, each owner deducts his share of the loss on each separate return.

If you have a legal life estate in the property, the loss is apportioned between yourself and those who will get the property after your death.

The apportionment may be based on actuarial tables that consider your life expectancy.

You may claim a casualty loss deduction for the loss or destruction of property used by your dependent if you own the property. You may not claim a loss deduction for the destruction of property belonging to your child who has reached majority, even though your child is still your dependent.

Lessee. A person leasing property may be allowed to deduct payments to a lessor compensating him for a casualty loss. A tenant was allowed to deduct as a casualty loss payment of a judgment obtained by the landlord for fire damage to the rented premises which had to be returned in the same condition as at the start of the lease. However, the Tax Court does not allow a deduction for the cost of repairing a rented car, as the lessee has no basis in the car.

PROVING A CASUALTY LOSS

¶ **18.4** If your return is audited, you will have to prove that the casualty occurred and the amount of the loss. The time to collect your evidence is as soon after the casualty as possible.

To prove	You need this information
That a casualty actually occurred	With a well-known casualty, like regional floods, you will have no difficulty proving the casualty occurred, but you must prove it affected your property. Photographs of the area, before and after, and newspaper stories placing the damage in your neighborhood are helpful. If only your property is damaged, there may be a newspaper item on it. Some papers list all the fire alarms answered the previous day. Police, fire and other municipal departments may have reports on the casualty.
The cost of repairing the property	Cost of repairs is allowed as a measure of loss if it is not excessive and the repair merely restored your property to its condition immediately before the casualty. Save canceled checks, bills, receipts, vouchers for expenses of clearing debris and restoring the property to its condition before the casualty.
The value immediately before and after the casualty	Appraisals by a competent expert are important. Get them in writing—in the form of an affidavit, deposition, estimate, appraisal, etc. The expert—an appraiser, engineer, architect—should be qualified to judge local values. Any records of offers to buy your property either before or after the casualty, are helpful. Automobile "blue books" may be used as guides in fixing the value of a car. But an amount offered for your car as a trade-in on a new car is not usually an acceptable measure of value.
Cost of your property— the deductible loss cannot be more than that	A deed, contract, bill of sale, or other document probably shows your original cost. Bills, receipts, and canceled checks show the cost of improvements. One court refused to allow a deduction because an owner failed to prove the original cost of a destroyed house and its value before the fire. In another case, estimates were allowed where a fire destroyed records of cost. A court held that the homeowner could not be expected to prove cost by documents lost in the fire that destroyed her property. She made inventories after the fire and again at a later date. Her reliance on memory to establish cost, even though inflated, was no bar to the deduction. The court estimated the market value based on her inventories. If you acquired the property by gift or inheritance, you must establish an adjusted basis in the property from records of the donor or the executor of the estate. See ¶ 6.29 and ¶ 6.31.

THEFT LOSSES

¶ **18.5** The taking of property must be illegal under state law to support a theft loss deduction. That property is missing is not sufficient evidence to sustain a theft deduction. It may have been lost or misplaced. So, if all you can prove is that an article is missing or lost, your deduction

may be disallowed. Sometimes, of course, the facts surrounding the disappearance of an article indicate that it is reasonable to assume that a theft took place.

You deduct a theft loss in the year you discover the property was stolen. If you have a reasonable chance of being reimbursed for your loss, you may not take a deduction until the year in which you learn there is no reasonable prospect of recovery.

A legal fee paid to recover stolen property has been held to be deductible as part of the theft loss.

> **Proving a theft.** Get statements from witnesses who saw the theft or police records of a breaking into your house or car. A newspaper account of the crime might also help.
>
> When you suspect a theft, make a report to the police. Even though your reporting does not prove that a theft was committed, it may be inferred from your failure to report that you were not sure that your property was stolen. But a theft loss was allowed where the loss of a ring was not reported to the police or an attempt made to demand its return from the suspect, a domestic. The owner feared being charged with false arrest.

Fraud by building contractors. A deduction was allowed when a building contractor ran away with a payment he received to build a residence. The would-be home owner was allowed a theft loss deduction for the difference between the money he advanced to the contractor and the value of the partially completed house. In another case, a theft deduction was allowed for payments to subcontractors. The main contractor had fraudulently claimed that he had paid them before he went bankrupt. A deduction has also been allowed for the theft of trees.

Embezzlement losses are deductible as theft losses in the year the theft is discovered. However, if you report on a cash basis, you may not take a deduction for the embezzlement of income you have not reported. For example, an agent embezzled royalties of $46,000 due an author. The author's theft deduction was disallowed. The author had not previously reported the royalties as income; therefore, she could not get the deduction.

The embezzlement must be the direct cause of the loss, not merely a contributing factor.

EXAMPLE

A depositor kept $102,000 in a bank which went bankrupt as a result of a large employee embezzlement. The Federal Deposit Insurance Corporation paid him $100,000, the maximum amount insured by law. He claimed a $1,900 theft loss ($2,000–$100 floor) in a year prior to the 10% floor. The IRS disallowed the deduction on the grounds that the embezzlement was only an indirect factor in his loss. He was allowed to claim a nonbusiness bad debt deductible as a short-term capital loss in the year in which his account became worthless, that is, when the receiver in bankruptcy notified the depositor that payment after liquidation is doubtful. *See* also new law election at ¶ 18.19.

Worthless stock purchased on the representation of false and fraudulent sales offers are deductible as theft losses in the year there is no reasonable prospect of recovery. However, the illegal sale of unregistered stock does not support a theft loss deduction.

Confiscated personal property is not deductible as a theft or casualty loss.

Seizure of a car by creditors under an invalid writ is not a deductible theft loss.

Payment of a ransom to a kidnapper is generally a deductible theft loss. However, the expenses of trying to find an abducted child is not a theft loss.

To figure the amount of a theft loss deduction, *see* ¶ 18.7.

RIOT LOSSES ARE DEDUCTIBLE

¶ **18.6** Losses caused by fire, theft, and vandalism occurring during riots and civil disorders are deductible.

To support your claim of a riot loss, keep evidence of the damage suffered and the cost of repairs. Photographs taken prior to repairs or replacement, lists of damaged or missing property, and police reports would help to establish and support your loss deduction.

When a reception is canceled because of a curfew, no loss deduction is allowed for perishable food that is discarded.

FIGURING YOUR LOSS

¶ **18.7** The deductible loss is usually the difference between the market value of the property before and after the casualty less (1) reimbursements received for the loss, and (2) $100, if the property was used for personal purposes. The deductible loss may not exceed the basis of the property. The total of all deductible personal casualty and theft losses incurred during 1987 is limited by the 10% adjusted gross income ceiling, see ¶ 18.1.

To figure a loss, follow these four steps:

1. Compute the loss in market value of the property. This is the difference between the market value immediately before and immediately after the casualty. You will need written appraisals to support your claim for loss of value.
2. Compute the adjusted basis of the property. This is usually the cost of the property plus the cost of improvements, less previous casualty loss deductions and depreciation if the property is used in business or for income-producing purposes. Basis of property acquired by other than purchase is explained at ¶ 6.29. Adjusted basis is explained at ¶ 6.31.
3. Take the lower amount of step (1) or (2). The lower amount, reduced by the adjustments in step (4), is your casualty loss, with one exception: Where property used for business or income-producing purposes is totally destroyed, and before the casualty its market value is less than its adjusted basis, the measure of the loss is the adjusted basis.
4. Reduce the loss in step (3) by the insurance proceeds or other compensation for the loss (see ¶ 18.9) and $100, if the property was used for personal purposes (see ¶ 18.10).

You reduce the basis of the damaged property by (1) the casualty loss deduction claimed and (2) compensation received for the loss.

EXAMPLES

1. Your home which cost $16,000 was damaged by a fire. The value of the house before the disaster was $67,500, afterwards $62,500. Your household furnishings were destroyed. You separately compute the loss on each item of furnishings and figure a combined loss of $2,000 on the furnishings. The insurance company reimbursed you $2,000 for your house damage and $500 for your furnishings. You figure your loss as follows:

1. Decrease in market value		
Value of house before fire		$67,500
Value of house after fire		62,500
Decrease in value		$ 5,000
2. Adjusted basis		$16,000
3. Loss sustained (lower of 1 or 2)		$ 5,000
Less: Insurance		2,000
Loss on house		$ 3,000
4. Loss on furnishings		$ 2,000
Less: Insurance		500
Loss on furnishings		$ 1,500
5. Total loss ($3,000 and $1,500)		$ 4,500
Less: $100 floor		100
Casualty loss (subject to 10% ceiling)		$ 4,400

2. Depreciable business property with a fair market value of $1,500 and an adjusted basis of $2,000 is totally destroyed. The loss is measured by the larger adjusted basis of $2,000 because the property was used in your business. Disregard the $100 floor applied to casualty

losses on personal property. If the property were used for personal purposes, the loss would have been limited to the lower market value of $1,500 less $100, leaving a casualty loss of $1,400.

For examples of auto losses, see ¶ 18.13.

You may not claim sentimental or aesthetic values or a fluctuation in property values caused by a casualty; you must deal with cost or market values of what has been lost.

Inventory losses are reflected in an adjustment to the cost of goods sold. If the loss is separately deducted, an offsetting credit must be applied either to opening or closing inventory. See IRS Publication No. 549 for further details.

The casualty must have caused damage to your property. Damage to a nearby area which lowered the value of your property does not give you a loss deduction.

EXAMPLE

You buy or lease a lot on which to build a cottage. Along with your purchase or lease, you have the privilege of using a nearby lake. The lake is later destroyed by a storm and the value of your property drops. You may not deduct the loss. The lake is not your property. You had only a privilege to use it, and this is not an ownership right which supports a casualty loss deduction.

For property held partly for personal use and partly for business or income, the loss deduction is computed as if two separate pieces of property were damaged, destroyed, or stolen.

EXAMPLE

A building with two apartments, one used by the owner as his home and the other rented to a tenant, is damaged by a fire. The fair market value of the building before the fire was $69,000 and after the fire, $56,000. Its cost basis was $20,000. Depreciation taken before the fire was $4,000. The insurance company paid $2,000. The owner has adjusted gross income of $20,000. This is his only loss this year. He has a business casualty loss of $5,000 and a deductible personal casualty loss of $3,400.

	Business	Personal
1. Decrease in value of building:		
Value before fire ($69,000)	$34,500	$34,500
Value after fire ($56,000)	28,000	28,000
Decrease in value	$ 6,500	$ 6,500
2. Adjusted basis of building:	$10,000	$10,000
Less: Depreciation	4,000	
Adjusted basis	$ 6,000	$10,000
3. Loss sustained (lower of 1 or 2)	$ 6,000	$ 6,500
Less: Insurance (total $2,000)	$ 1,000	$ 1,000
4. Loss	$ 5,000	$ 5,500
Less: $100 floor and 10% of adjusted gross income		2,100
Deductible casualty loss	$ 5,000	$ 3,400

No deduction may be claimed for estimated decline in value based on buyer resistance in an area subject to landslides. The Tax Court has allowed casualty loss deductions that were not based on market value comparisons, but on cost less depreciation.

EXAMPLE

The fair market rule applied to household items generally limits your deduction to the going price for second-hand furnishings. But one householder claimed that the fair market value should be original cost less depreciation. He based his figures on an inventory prepared by certified public adjusters describing each item, its cost and age. The deduction figured this way came to approximately $27,500 ($55,000 cost, less $13,000 depreciation, a $14,400 insurance recovery, and the $100 floor).

The IRS estimated that the furniture was worth $15,304 before the fire and limited the deduction to $804 after setting off the insurance and the $100 floor. The Tax Court disagreed. The householder's method of valuing his furniture is consistent with methods used by insurance adjusters who have an interest in keeping values low. He is not limited to the amount his property would bring if "hawked off by a second-hand dealer or at a forced sale." However, in another case, the court refused to allow the cost less depreciation formula where the homeowner's inventory list was based on memory.

Indirect expenses. Expenses such as personal injury, temporary lights, fuel, moving or rentals for temporary living quarters, are not deductible as casualty losses.

Appraisal costs of damaged property, see ¶ 18.17.

REPAIRS MAY BE "MEASURE OF LOSS"

¶ **18.8** The cost of repairs may be treated as evidence of the loss of value if the amount is not excessive and the repairs do nothing more than restore the property to its condition before the casualty (*see* ¶18.4). An estimate for repairs will not suffice: only actual repairs may be used as a measure of loss. However, where you are not relying on repairs as a measure of loss but rather are using appraisals of value of the property before and after the casualty, repairs may be considered in arriving at a post-casualty value even though no actual repairs are made.

> A casualty loss deduction is not limited to repair expense where the decline in market value is greater.

EXAMPLES
1. Connor claimed that the market value of his house dropped $93,000 after it was extensively damaged by fire. His cash outlay ($52,000) in repairing the house was reimbursed by insurance. Connor claimed a casualty loss deduction of approximately $40,000, the uncompensated drop in market value. The IRS disallowed the deduction. The house was restored to pre-casualty condition. The cost of the repairs is a realistic measure of the loss, and, as the expense was fully compensated by insurance, Connor suffered no loss. A court disagreed. It found that the house dropped $70,000 in market value, of which $20,000 was uncompensated by insurance. The deduction is measured by the uncompensated difference in value before and after the casualty. It is not limited to the cost of repairs, even where the repair expense is less than the difference in market values. Had the repairs cost more than this difference, the IRS would not have allowed Connor a larger deduction.
2. Seven months after Hagerty bought his house for $78,000, it was severely damaged by fire. The insurance company hired a general contractor to repair the house at a cost of $33,000. Hagerty claimed a casualty loss of $20,000 on the basis of these figures:

Value before fire	$78,000
Value after fire	25,000
	$53,000
Less: Insurance	33,000
Loss	$20,000

The IRS disallowed the deduction, arguing that the loss was completely compensated by the insurance company. It paid for the repairs, which is a measure of the loss here. The Tax Court disagreed. Repairs are not a measure of the loss where they do not completely restore the residence to its pre-fire condition. Hagerty proved that the contractor of the insurance company did not do as thorough a job as contractors hired by him would have done. However, the court set the fair market value of the home after the fire at $35,000, reducing Hagerty's loss to $10,000.

INSURANCE REIMBURSEMENTS

¶ **18.9** You reduce the amount of your loss by insurance proceeds, voluntary payments received from your employer for damage to your property and cash or property received from the Red Cross. However, cash gifts from friends and relatives to help defray the cost of repairs do not reduce the loss where there are no conditions on the use of the

gift. Also, gifts of food, clothing, medical supplies and other forms of subsistence do not reduce the loss deduction nor are they taxable income.

Cancellation of part of a disaster loan under the Disaster Relief Act is treated as a partial reimbursement of the loss and reduces the amount of the loss. Urban renewal agency's payments to acquire property under the Federal Relocation Act of 1970 are considered reimbursements reducing a casualty loss deduction.

Insurance payments for the cost of added living expenses because of damage to a home do not reduce a casualty loss. The payments are treated separate and apart from payments for property damage. Payments for extra living costs are generally not taxable (*see* ¶18.18).

> *Failure to make an insurance claim.* If you are insured for the extent of your loss and do not file a claim because you do not want to risk cancellation of liability coverage, you may not claim a deduction.

HOW THE $100 FLOOR IS APPLIED

¶ **18.10** The $100 floor reduces casualty and theft losses of property used for personal purposes. It does not apply to losses of business property or property held for the production of income, such as securities. If property used both in business and personal activities is damaged, the $100 offset applies only to the loss allocated to personal use.

The $100 reduction applies to a loss arising in each casualty or theft occurring during the year. For example, you are involved in five different casualties during the year. There will be a $100 offset applied to each of the five losses. But when two or more items of property are destroyed in one event, only one $100 offset is applied to the total loss. For example, a storm damages your residence and your car parked in the driveway. Only one $100 offset limits the amount of the loss stemming from storm damage to your house and car.

The $100 floor applies to the entire loss sustained from each casualty. For example, in 1987, you incur a casualty loss of $290, on which you expect a reimbursement of $250. Thus, your unreimbursed loss in 1987 is $40, but you may not deduct the amount as it does not exceed $100. Now assume that in 1988, you learn that you cannot recover the expected reimbursement of $250. In claiming a casualty loss deduction in 1988, you reduce the $250 by $60. $40 of the $100 limitation had applied to part of the same casualty loss in 1987.

The $100 limit applies separately to the loss of each individual whose property has been damaged by a single casualty, even where the damaged property is owned by two or more individuals.

EXAMPLES
1. Two sisters own and occupy a house which sustains a casualty loss of $500. Each sister applies the $100 limit.
2. Your house is partially damaged by a fire which also damages the personal property of a house guest. You are subject to one $100 limitation and the house guest is subject to a separate $100 limitation.

Where a husband and wife own property either jointly or separately and they file a joint return, only one $100 floor applies to their joint return. If they file separate returns, each applies a $100 floor to the respective loss.

Where a single casualty results in losses to a husband and wife in two or more tax years, the rules for deductions are as follows: If a joint return was filed for the first year for which the loss was sustained, only one $100 limitation applies. If they file separate returns in the first year of the loss, each applies a separate $100 limitation to the loss deducted on the separate return. If the couple files a joint return for the first loss year and separate returns for the later years, each allocates any unused portion of the $100 limitation equally between them in the later years.

WHEN TO DEDUCT YOUR CASUALTY LOSS

¶ **18.11** Generally, you deduct a casualty loss in the year the casualty occurs, regardless of when you repair or replace damaged or destroyed property. But say a casualty strikes in one year and you do not discover the damage until a later year. Or you know damage has been inflicted but you do not know the full extent of the loss because you expect reimbursement in a later year. Here is what to do:

If you reasonably expect reimbursement in a later year, deduct in the year the casualty occurred only that part of your loss for which you do not expect reimbursement. For example, if you expect a full insurance recovery next year for a 1987 loss, you would take no deduction in 1987.

If you do not expect reimbursement and deduct a loss in 1987 but you receive insurance or other reimbursement in 1988, you would then report as income in 1988 the amount of the deduction you claimed in 1987 if it gave you a tax benefit by reducing your taxable income (see ¶ 12.14). You may not amend your 1987 tax return.

EXAMPLE

In 1969, Hurricane Camille destroyed oceanfront real estate owned jointly by two brothers. The buildings were insured under two policies which included wind damage but not losses resulting from floods, tidal waves or water. The insurers, claiming the tidal wave had caused the destruction, denied their claim. The brothers consulted an attorney about the possibility of suit against the insurance companies, but there seemed little likelihood of recovery, so they deducted their shares of the casualty loss in 1969. However, in January 1970, the adjusters of both companies changed their decisions, reimbursing the brothers for more than two-thirds of their loss. One of the brothers filed an amended 1969 tax return, reducing the previously reported casualty loss.

The IRS claimed that the insurance recovery is taxable in the year of receipt, 1970, to the extent that the prior deduction reduced 1969 income. The brother claimed that he made an error in claiming the deduction in 1969 because he had a reasonable prospect of reimbursement. Therefore, he was not entitled to the deduction; his amended return reducing the deduction by the reimbursement was proper.

The Tax Court disagreed. Tax liability is based on facts as they exist at the end of each year. A recovery in a later tax year does not prove that a reasonable prospect of recovery existed in the earlier year. Amendments to previously filed tax returns may be made only to correct mathematical errors or miscalculations, not to rearrange facts and readjust income for two years.

Assume you took no loss deduction in 1987 because you expected to recover your entire loss in 1988—but the insurance company refuses to pay your claim. When do you deduct your loss? You deduct your loss in the year you find that you have no reasonable prospect of recovery. For example, you sue the company in 1988, with a reasonable prospect of winning your claim. However, in 1989, a court rules against you. You deduct your loss in 1989.

If you do not discover the loss until a later year, Treasury regulations do not specifically allow the deduction of the loss in the year it is discovered, but court decisions have. In one case, an unseasonable blizzard damaged a windbreak planted to protect a house, buildings, and livestock. The damage to the evergreens did not become apparent until the next year, when about half of the trees died and the others were of little value. The court held that the loss occurred in the later year. In another case, hurricane damage did not become apparent for two years. The Tax Court allowed the deduction in the later year.

If you, as lessee, are liable to the lessor for damage to property, you may deduct the loss in the year you pay the lessor.

DISASTER LOSSES

¶ 18.12 If you suffer a loss to property from a disaster in an area declared by the President as warranting federal assistance, you may deduct the loss either on the return for the year of the loss or on the return of the prior tax year.

You may elect to claim the deduction on a prior return any time on or before the later of (1) the due date (without extensions) of the return for the year of the disaster or (2) the due date considering any extension for filing the return for the prior tax year.

1. *1987 disaster losses.* You have generally until April 15, 1988, to amend a 1986 tax return to claim a disaster loss occurring during 1987.
2. *1988 disaster losses.* You have generally until April 15, 1989, to amend a 1987 tax return to claim a disaster loss occurring during 1988.

After making your election, you have 90 days in which to revoke it. After the 90-day period, the election becomes irrevocable. However where an early election is made, you have until the due date for filing your return for the year of the disaster to change your election.

Your revocation of an election is not effective unless you repay any credit or refund resulting from the election within the revocation period. A revocation made before you receive a refund will not be effective unless you repay the refund within 30 days after you receive it.

You make an election in a signed statement attached to your return (original or amended) or refund claim. List the date of the disaster and where the property was located (city, town, county, and state).

To amend a filed return for a prior year, use Form 1040X.

Homeowners forced to relocate. If you were forced to relocate or demolish your home in a disaster area, you may be able to claim the loss even though the damage, such as from erosion, does not meet the sudden test of ¶ 18.2. For example, after a severe storm, there is a danger to a group of homes from nearby mudslides. State officials order homeowners to evacuate and relocate their homes. Under prior law, a deduction could be barred if there was no actual physical damage to the home. A new law allows disaster loss treatment if these tests are met: (1) The president has determined that the area warrants federal disaster relief; (2) within 120 days of the President's order, you are ordered by the state or local government to demolish or relocate your residence, and (3) the home was rendered unsafe by the erosion or other disaster. The law applies to vacation homes and rental properties as well as to principal residences.

The loss is treated as a disaster loss so that you may elect to deduct the loss either in the year the demolition or relocation order is made or in the prior taxable year.

Fiscal year. If you are on a fiscal year, an election may be made for disaster losses occurring after the close of a fiscal year.

EXAMPLE

You are on a fiscal year ending on April 30, and suffer a disaster loss on or before April 30, 1987. You may elect to deduct the loss on your return for the year ended April 30, 1986.

Should you make an election? Consider making the election if the deduction on the return of the prior year gives a greater tax reduction than if claimed on the return for the year in which the loss occurred or you want a refund of all or part of the tax paid for the prior year.

Cancellation of part of a disaster loan under the Disaster Relief Act is treated as a reimbursement that reduces your loss.

DEDUCTING DAMAGE TO YOUR CAR

¶ 18.13 Damage to your car in an accident may be a deductible loss unless the damage is caused by your willful negligence, such as drunken driving.

You may not deduct legal fees and costs of a court action for damages or money paid for damages to another's property because of your negligence while driving for commuting or other personal purposes. But if at the time of the accident you were using your car on business, you may deduct as a business loss a payment of damages to the other party's car. For purposes of a business loss deduction, driving between two locations of the same business is considered business driving but driving between locations of two separate businesses is considered personal driving. Therefore, the payment of damages arising from an accident while driving between two separate businesses is not deductible.

A court has allowed deductions for damage resulting from a child pressing the starter button of a car and from flying stones while driving over a temporary road. In a private letter ruling, the IRS disallowed a loss for damage to a race car by an amateur racer on the grounds that in races, crashes are not an unusual event and so do not constitute a casualty.

If the deduction is questioned, be prepared to show the amount, if any, of your insurance recovery. A deduction is allowed only for uninsured losses. Not only must the loss be proved, but also that it was not compensated by insurance.

When you use an automobile partly for personal use and partly for business, your loss is computed as though two separate pieces of property were damaged—one business and the other personal. The $100 and 10% floors reduce only the loss on the part used for personal purposes.

Towing costs are not included as part of the casualty loss.

A parent may not claim a casualty loss deduction for damage to a car registered in his son's name, although the parent provided funds for the purchase of the car.

Expenses of personal injuries arising from a car accident are not a deductible casualty loss.

DAMAGE TO TREES AND SHRUBS

¶ **18.14** Not all damage to trees and shrubs qualifies as a casualty loss. The damage must be occasioned by a sudden event (see ¶ 18.2). Destruction of trees over a period of 5–10 days by southern pine beetles is deductible. One court allowed a deduction for similar destruction over a 30-day period. However, damage by Dutch Elm disease or lethal yellowing disease has been held to be gradual destruction not qualifying as a casualty loss. The Tax Court has allowed a deduction for the cost of removing infested trees.

> If shrubbery and trees on nonbusiness property are damaged by a sudden casualty, you figure the loss on the value of the entire property before and after the casualty. You treat the buildings, land, and shrubs as one complete unit; in fixing the loss on business or income producing property, however, shrubs and trees are valued separately from the building.

EXAMPLES

1. Smith bought an office building for $90,000. The purchase price was allocated between the land ($18,000) and the building ($72,000). Smith planted trees and ornamental shrubs on the grounds surrounding the building at a cost of $1,200. When the building had been depreciated to $66,000, a hurricane caused extensive property damage. The fair market value of the land and building immediately before the hurricane was $18,000 and $70,000; immediately afterwards, $18,000 and $52,000. The fair market value of the trees and shrubs immediately before the casualty was $2,000 and immediately afterwards, $400. Insurance of $5,000 is received to cover damage to the building. The deduction for the building is $13,000, computed as follows:

Value of property immediately before casualty	$70,000
Less: Value immediately after casualty	52,000
Value of property actually destroyed	18,000
Less: Insurance received	5,000
Deduction allowed	$13,000

The deduction for the trees and shrubs is $1,200:

Value immediately before casualty	$2,000
Less: Value of trees immediately after casualty	400
Value of property actually destroyed	$1,600*

*However, the loss cannot exceed the adjusted basis of property, $1,200.

2. Same facts as in example (1) except that Smith purchases a personal residence instead of an office building. Smith's adjusted gross income is $25,000, and this is his only 1987 loss. No allocation of the purchase price is necessary for the land and house because the property is not depreciable. Likewise, no individual evaluation of the fair market values of the land, house, trees, and shrubs is necessary. The amount of the deduction for the land, house, trees, and shrubs is $12,000, computed as follows:

Value of property immediately before casualty		$90,000
Less: Value of property immediately after casualty		70,400
Value of property actually destroyed		19,600
Less: Insurance received	$5,000	
10% and $100 floors	2,600	7,600
Deduction allowed		$12,000

NONDEDUCTIBLE LOSSES

¶ **18.15** Certain losses, though casualties for you, may not be deducted if they are not due to theft, fire, or from some other sudden natural phenomenon. The following losses have been held not to be deductible—

Termite damage; see ¶ 18.2.
Carpet beetle damage.
Dry rot damage.
Damages for personal injuries or property damage to others caused by your negligence.
Legal expenses in defending a suit for your negligent operation of your personal automobile.
Legal expenses to recover personal property wrongfully seized by the police.
Expenses of moving to and rental of temporary quarters.
Loss of personal property while in storage or in transit.
Loss of passenger's luggage put aboard a ship. The passenger missed the boat and the luggage could not be traced.
Accidental loss of a ring from your finger.
Injuries resulting from tripping over a wire.
Loss by husband of joint property taken by his wife when she left him.
Loss of a valuable dog which strayed and was not found.
Damages to a crop caused by plant diseases, insects, or fungi.
Damage to property from drought in an area where a dry spell is normal and usual.
Damage to property caused by excavations on adjoining property.
Damages from rust or corroding of understructure of house.
Moth damage.
Dry well.
Losses occasioned by water pockets, erosion, inundation at still water levels. and other natural phenomena. (There was no sudden destruction.)
Amount paid to a public library for damages to a book you borrowed.
Death of a saddle horse after eating a silk hat.
A watch or spectacles dropped on the ground.
Sudden drop in the value of securities.
Loss in earnings of a lawyer resulting from his illness.
Loss of contingent interest in property due to the unexpected death of a child.
Improper police seizure of private liquor stock.
Chinaware broken by a family pet.
Temporary fluctuation in value.
Loss of tree from Dutch Elm disease and lethal yellowing disease.
Loss of trees after horse ate bark.
Damage to property from local government construction project.

Note. But some of the items listed in the above column may be allowed to persons in business.

DO YOUR CASUALTY LOSSES EXCEED YOUR INCOME?

¶ **18.16** If your casualty losses exceed your income, you pay no tax in 1987. You may also carry the excess loss back to 1984 and file a refund claim for that year. Any remaining loss may be carried back to 1985 and 1986 and carried forward to 1988 through 2001 or you may just carry your loss forward 15 years until it is used up. *See* ¶5.17 on figuring your net operating loss for a refund of prior taxes.

Note that the $100/10% of adjusted gross income floors for personal casualty losses apply only in the year of loss; you do not again reduce your loss in the carryback or carryover years.

HOW TO DEDUCT YOUR CASUALTY AND THEFT LOSSES

¶ **18.17** Generally, you deduct nonbusiness casualty or theft losses as itemized deductions on Schedule A. You figure the loss on Form 4684. The amount of the loss is then entered on Schedule A. If you have suffered more than one casualty or theft event, use separate forms 4684 to figure the losses for each event. Where you have realized both gains and losses from personal casualty and theft events, *see* ¶18.27.

Appraisal fees and other incidental costs (photos, etc.) incurred in establishing the amount of your casualty loss do not offset your loss; they are claimed as a miscellaneous itemized deduction on Schedule A.

EXCESS LIVING COSTS PAID BY INSURANCE ARE NOT TAXABLE

¶ **18.18** Your insurance contract may reimburse you for excess living costs when a casualty or a threat of casualty forces you to vacate your house. The payment is not taxable income if these tests are met:

1. Your principal residence is damaged or destroyed by fire, storm, or other casualty or you are denied use of it by a governmental order because of the occurrence or threat of the casualty.
2. You are paid under an insurance contract for living expenses resulting from the loss of occupancy or use of the residence. The living expenses must be paid by the insurance company for yourself and members of your household.

The tax free exclusion covers only excess living costs paid by the insurance company. The excess is the difference between: (1) the actual living expenses incurred during the time you could not use or occupy your house, and (2) the normal living expenses which you would have incurred for yourself and members of your household during the period. Living expenses during the period may include the cost of renting suitable housing and extraordinary expenses for transportation, food, utilities, and miscellaneous services. The expenses must be incurred for items and services (such as laundry) needed to maintain you in the same standard of living that you enjoyed before the loss and must be covered by the policy.

Where a lump-sum settlement does not identify the amount covering living expenses, an allocation is required to determine the tax free portion. In the case of uncontested claims, the tax free portion is that part of the settlement which bears the same ratio to total recovery as increased living expense bears to total loss and expense. If your claim is contested, you must show the amount reasonably allocable to increased living expenses consistent with the terms of the contract, but not in excess of coverage limitations specified in the contract.

The exclusion does not cover insurance reimbursements for loss of rental income or for loss of or damage to real or personal property.

If your home is used for both residential and business purposes, the exclusion does not apply to insurance proceeds and expenses attributable to the nonresidential portion of the house. There is no exclusion for insurance recovered for expenses resulting from governmental condemnation or order unrelated to a casualty or threat of casualty.

The insurance reimbursement may cover part of your normal living expenses as well as the excess expenses due to the casualty. The part covering normal expenses is income; it does not reduce your casualty loss.

EXAMPLES

1. On March 1, your home was damaged by fire. While it was being repaired, you and your spouse lived at a motel and took meals at restaurants. Costs are $200 at the motel, $180 for meals, and $25 for laundry services. You make the required March payment of $190 on your home mortgage. The mortgage payment has no relationship to the casualty and is not considered an actual living expense resulting from the loss of use of your residence. Your customary $40 commuting expense is $20 less for the month because the motel is closer to your work. Your usual commuting expense is therefore treated as not being incurred to the extent of the $20 decrease. Further, you do not incur your customary $150 food expense for meals at home, $75 for utilities, and $10 for laundry at home. The tax free exclusion is limited to $150 computed in the last column.

2. Same facts as example (1) except that you rented the residence for $100 per month and the risk of loss was on the landlord. You did not pay the March rent. The excludable amount is $50 ($150 less $100 normal rent not incurred).

	Actual expenses resulting from casualty	Normal expenses not incurred	Increase (Decrease)
Housing	$200.00		$200.00
Utilities	$ 75.00	(75.00)	
Meals	180.00	150.00	30.00
Transportation		20.00	(20.00)
Laundry	25.00	10.00	15.00
Total	$405.00	$255.00	$150.00

BANK DEPOSIT LOSSES

¶ **18.19** If a bank in which you deposit funds fails and your loss is not covered by insurance you may claim your loss either as a bad debt deduction or casualty loss.

You may claim a bad debt deduction for a loss of a bank deposit in the year there is no reasonable prospect of recovery from the insolvent or bankrupt bank. You claim the loss as a short-term capital loss unless the deposit was made in your business. A lost deposit of business funds is claimed as a business bad debt, *see* ¶6.55.

You may elect to take a casualty loss deduction for the year in which the loss can be reasonably estimated. The loss is subject to the 10% AGI floor for casualty losses. Once the casualty loss election is made, it is irrevocable and will apply to all other losses on deposits in the same financial institution.

The casualty loss election may allow you to claim the loss in an earlier year because you do not have to wait until the year there is no prospect of recovery as required in the case of bad debts. The casualty loss election may also be advisable if other casualty losses may absorb all or part of the 10% AGI floor.

In 1987, nonbusiness bad debt deduction is deductible only from capital gains. If you do not have capital gain or the bad debt loss exceeds capital gain, only $3,000 of the loss may offset other income. The remaining loss is carried over.

The casualty loss election is generally not allowed to stockholders or officers of the bank, or their relatives.

Under the new law, a casualty loss may be elected for pre-1987 years if the time limit for amended returns has not expired.

GAINS FROM INVOLUNTARY CONVERSIONS

¶ 18.20 You may realize a gain when your property is destroyed by a casualty or taken by a government authority if insurance or other compensation exceeds the adjusted basis of the property. Tax on the gain may be postponed if you elect to defer gain and invest the proceeds in replacement property, the cost of which is equal to or exceeds the net proceeds from the conversion. If you do not plan to replace the property or you plan to replace but do not want to defer tax, see ¶5.44 for the tax treatment of gains from involuntary conversions; also see ¶18.27. The following sections discuss the election to defer tax on gains realized from involuntary conversions.

INVOLUNTARY CONVERSIONS QUALIFYING FOR TAX DEFERRAL ELECTION

¶ 18.21 For purposes of an election to defer tax, "involuntary conversion" is more broadly defined than casualty loss. You have an involuntary conversion when your property is—

Damaged or destroyed

Stolen

Seized, requisitioned, or condemned by a governmental authority. If you voluntarily sell land made useless to you by the condemnation of your adjacent land, the sale may also qualify as a conversion. Condemnation of property as unfit for human habitation does not qualify. Condemnation, as used by the tax law, refers to the taking of private property for public use, not to the condemnation of property for non-compliance with housing and health regulations. Similarly a tax sale to pay delinquent taxes is not an involuntary conversion.

Sold under a threat of seizure, condemnation, or requisition. The threat must be made by an authority qualified to take property for public use. A sale following a threat of condemnation made by a government employee is a conversion if you reasonably believe he speaks with authority and could and would carry out the threat to have your property condemned. If you learn of the plan of an imminent condemnation from a newspaper or the radio, the IRS requires you to confirm the report from a government official before you act on the news.

Farmers also have involuntary conversions when—

Land is sold within an irrigation project to meet the acreage limitations of the federal reclamation laws;

Cattle are destroyed by disease or sold because of disease, *or*

Draft, breeding, or dairy livestock is sold because of drought. the election to treat the sale as a conversion is limited to livestock sold over the number which would have been sold but for the drought. In some cases, livestock may be replaced with other farm property where there has been soil or other environmental contamination.

If property subject to depreciation recapture is involuntarily converted, see ¶5.42; if an investment credit was claimed in the purchase of the property and the conversion occurred before the end of the recovery period, part of the credit may be recaptured, see instructions to Form 4255.

If your residence is condemned or destroyed, see ¶29.3.

An election gives an immediate advantage: Tax on gain is postponed and the funds that would have been spent for the payment of tax may be used for other investments.

As a condition of deferring tax, the basis of the replacement property is usually fixed at the same cost basis as the converted property. As long as the value of the replacement property does not decline, tax on the gain is finally incurred when the property is sold.

> To decide whether postponement of gain at the expense of a reduced basis for property is advisable, compare the tax consequences of an election with those resulting if no election is made.

EXAMPLE

Assume a rental building is destroyed by fire and a proper replacement is made. Assume that gain on the receipt of the fire proceeds is taxable as capital gain. An election is generally not advisable if you have capital losses to offset the gain. However, even if you have no net capital losses, you may still decide not to make the election and pay tax in order to fix, for purposes of depreciation, the basis of the new property at its purchase price, if the future depreciation deductions will offset income taxable at a higher rate than the current tax. If there is little or no difference between the two rates so that a net after tax benefit from the depreciation would not arise, an election might be made solely to postpone the payment of tax.

HOW TO ELECT TO DEFER TAX

¶ 18.22 You make an election by omitting the taxable gain as income on the tax return for the year in which gain is realized. However, attach to your return a statement giving details of the transaction, including computation of the gain and your plan to buy a replacement.

If the conversion is directly into similar property, no election is necessary. Postponement of tax on the gain is required. For example, the city condemns a store building and compensates the owner by giving him another store building the value of which exceeds the cost basis of the old one. Gain is not taxed.

Election to defer tax on involuntary conversion gain may be irrevocable. If you change your mind and prefer to pay tax, you may not revoke the election if you have made a qualified replacement within the time limits. Both the IRS and the Tax Court hold that the election is irrevocable once a qualified replacement has been made.

> To nullify the effect of the election to defer tax on involuntary conversion gain and to subject the conversion to tax, these options may be available: You do not make a replacement; you purchase property that does not qualify as a replacement; you invest in the replacement property less than the amount realized from the conversion; or you replace after the time limits have expired.

Partnerships. The election to defer gain must be made at the partnership level. Individual partners may not make separate elections unless the partnership has terminated, with all partnership affairs wound up. Dissolution under state law is not a termination for tax purposes.

TIME PERIOD FOR BUYING REPLACEMENT PROPERTY

¶ 18.23 To defer tax, you must generally buy property similar or related in use to the converted property within two years after the end of the taxable year in which you realize any gain from the conversion. However, if investment or business (noninventory) realty has been condemned, the replacement period is three years after the end of the taxable year in which any gain was realized.

EXAMPLE

On January 10, 1987, a parcel of land is condemned; the parcel cost $1,500. On February 26, 1987, you receive a check for $10,000 from the state. You may defer the tax on the gain of $8,500 if you invest at least $10,000 in other real estate not later than December 31, 1990.

Gain is realized in the year compensation for the converted property exceeds the basis of the converted property. An advance payment of an award which exceeds the adjusted basis of the property starts the running of the replacement period.

EXAMPLE

When Stewart's property was condemned, he received an advance of $70,000 on which he realized gain. Three years later, a final payment was made after a court determined the value of the condemned property. He paid no tax on the advance, claiming that he made a qualified replacement within the allowable period after receiving the full amount of the award.

The IRS argued that the advance payment began the replacement period, which ended before he bought the replacement. The Tax Court agreed. Stewart had unrestricted use of the advance. The advance payment began the period for purchase of replacement property. This is true even though he might have had to return part of the award if the court found it exceeded the value of the condemned property.

Stewart could have deferred tax by applying for an extension of time to replace the condemned property when he realized there would be a delay in getting the final award.

An award is treated as received in the year that it is made available to you without restrictions, even if you contest the amount.

Replacement before actual condemnation. You may make a replacement after a threat of condemnation. If you buy property before the threat of condemnation, it will not qualify as a replacement even though you still own it at the time of the actual condemnation.

EXAMPLE

While condemnation proceedings are under way, you find property to replace the property being condemned. The purchase of the new parcel before the condemnation qualifies as a replacement provided you hold the new property at the time the old property is condemned.

The replacement test may be satisfied by purchasing a controlling interest (80%) in a corporation owning property that is similar or related in service to the converted property (*see* Treasury regulations for further details).

Extension of time to replace. A contract to buy replacement property within the time limits is not considered a qualified replacement. If you cannot replace property within the time required, ask your local District Director for additional time. Apply for an extension before the end of the period. If you apply for an extension within a reasonable time after the statutory period has run out, you must have a reasonable cause for the delay in asking for the extension.

Replacement by an estate. A person whose property was converted may die before he makes a replacement. According to the IRS, his estate may not reinvest the proceeds within the allowed time and postpone tax on the gain. The Tax Court rejects the IRS position and has allowed tax deferral where the replacement was made by the deceased owner's estate. However, the Tax Court agreed with the IRS that a surviving spouse's investment in land did not defer tax on gain realized by her deceased husband on an involuntary conversion of his land. She had received his property as survivor of joint tenancy and could not, in making the investment, be considered as acting for his estate.

Notice of replacement. If you have not bought replacement property by the time you file your return for the year of the involuntary conversions but you intend to do so, attach a statement to your return describing the conversion and the computation of gain and state that you intend to make a timely replacement. Then, on the return for the year of replacement, attach a statement giving the details of your replacement property. This notice starts the running of the period of limitations for any tax on the gain. Failure to give notice keeps the period open. Similarly, a failure to give notice of an intention not to replace also keeps the period open. When you do not buy replacement property after making an election to postpone tax on the gain, file an amended return for the year in which gain was realized and pay the tax (if any) on the gain.

Assume you have the involuntary conversion resulting in a gain and do not expect to reinvest the proceeds. You report the gain and pay the tax. In a later year, but within the prescribed time limits, you buy similar property. You may make an election to defer tax on the gain and file a claim for tax refund.

CHARACTER OF REPLACEMENT PROPERTY

¶ 18.24 Although exact duplication is not required, the replacement must be generally similar or related in use to the converted property. Where real property held for productive use in a business or for investment is converted through a condemnation or threat of condemnation, the replacement test is more liberal. A replacement merely has to be of *like kind* to the converted property. Under the *like kind* test, the replacement of improved property by unimproved qualifies (*see* ¶5.49). Under the *related use* test, the replacement of unimproved land for improved does not. A replacement generally must be closely related in function to the destroyed property. For example, a condemned personal residence must be replaced with another personal residence. The replacement of a house rented to a tenant with a house used as a personal residence does not qualify for tax deferral; the new house is not being used for the same purpose as the condemned one. This functional test, however, is not strictly applied to conversions of rental property. Here, the role of the owner toward the properties, rather than the functional use of the buildings, is reviewed. If an owner held both properties as investments and offered similar services and took similar business risks in both, the replacement may qualify.

You may own several parcels of property, one of which is condemned. You may want to use the condemnation award to make improvements on the other land such as drainage and grading. The IRS generally will not accept the improvements as a qualified replacement. However, an appeals court has rejected the IRS approach in one case.

If it is not feasible to reinvest the proceeds from the conversion of livestock because of soil contamination or other environmental contamination, then other property (including real property) used for farming purposes is treated as similar or related and qualifies as replacement property.

INVESTMENT IN REPLACEMENT PROPERTY

¶ 18.25 To defer tax, the cost of the replacement property must be equal to or exceed the net proceeds from the conversion. If replacement cost is less than the adjusted basis of the converted property, you report the entire gain. If replacement cost is less than the amount realized on the conversion but more than the basis of the converted property, the difference between the amount realized and the cost of the replacement is reported as gain. You may elect to postpone tax on the balance of the gain reinvested (*see* example 2 following).

EXAMPLES

1. The cost basis of a four-family apartment house is $75,000. It is condemned to make way for a thruway. The net award from the state is $100,000. Your gain is $25,000. If you buy a similar apartment house for $75,000 or less, you report the entire $25,000 gain.

2. Using the same figures as in example (1), except that you buy an apartment house for $85,000. Of the gain of $25,000, you report $15,000 as taxed gain ($100,000–$85,000). You may elect to postpone the tax on the balance of the gain, or $10,000.

3. Using the same figures as in example (1), but you buy an apartment house for $100,000. You may elect to postpone tax on the entire gain because you have invested all of the award in replacement property.

Condemnation award. The award received from a state authority may be reduced by expenses of getting the award, such as legal, engineering, and appraisal fees. The treatment of special assessments and severance damages received when part of your property is condemned is explained at ¶18.26. Payments made directly by the authority to your mortgagee may not be deducted from the gross award.

Do not include as part of the award interest paid on the award for delay in its payment; you report the interest as interest income. The IRS may treat as interest part of an award paid late, even though the award does not make any allocation for interest.

Relocation payments are not treated as taxable income to the extent that they are spent for purposes of relocation.

Distinguish between insurance proceeds compensating you for loss of profits because of business interruption and those compensating you for the loss of property. Business interruption proceeds are fully taxed as ordinary income and may not be treated as proceeds of an involuntary conversion.

A single standard fire insurance policy may cover several assets. Assume a fire occurs, and in a settlement the proceeds are allocated to each destroyed item according to its fair market value before the fire. In comparing the allocated proceeds to the tax basis of each item, you find that on some items, you have realized a gain; that is, the proceeds exceed basis. On the other items, you have a loss; the proceeds are less than basis. According to the IRS, you may elect to defer tax on the gain items by buying replacement property. You do not treat the proceeds paid under the single policy as a unit, but as separate payments made for each covered item.

HOW TO TREAT SPECIAL ASSESSMENTS AND SEVERANCE DAMAGES

¶ **18.26** When only part of a property parcel is condemned for a public improvement, the condemning authority may:

1. Levy a special assessment against the remaining property, claiming that it is benefited by the improvement. The authority usually deducts the assessment from the condemnation award.
2. Award severance damages for damages suffered by the remaining property because of the condemnation.

Special assessments reduce the amount of the gross condemnation award. If they exceed the award, the excess is added to the basis of the property. An assessment levied after the award is made may not be deducted from the award.

EXAMPLE

Two acres of a 10-acre tract are condemned for a new highway. The adjusted basis of the land is $30,000 or $3,000 per acre. The condemnation award is $10,000; the special assessment against the remaining eight acres is $2,500. The net gain on the condemnation is $1,500:

Condemnation award		$10,000
Less:		
Basis of two condemned acres	$6,000	
Special assessment	2,500	8,500
Net gain		$ 1,500

When both the condemnation award and severance damages are received, the condemnation is treated as two separate involuntary conversions: (1) A conversion of the condemned land. Here, the condemnation award is applied against the basis of the condemned land to determine gain or loss on its conversion. (2) A conversion of part of the remaining land in the sense that its utility has been reduced by condemnation, for which severance damages are paid.

Severance damages reduce the basis of the retained property. If the damages exceed basis, gain is realized. Tax may be deferred on the gain through the purchase of replacement property under the "similar or related in use test" at ¶ 18.24, such as adjacent land or restoration of the property to its original condition.

Allocating the proceeds between the condemnation award and severance damages will either reduce the gain or increase the loss realized on the condemned land. The IRS will allow such a division only when the condemnation authority specifically identifies part of the award as severance damage in the contract or in an itemized statement or closing sheet. The Tax Court, however, has allowed an allocation in the absence of earmarking where the state considered severance damages, and the value of the condemned land was small in comparison to the damages suffered by the remaining property. To avoid a dispute with the IRS, make sure the authority makes this breakdown. Without such identification, the IRS will treat the entire proceeds as consideration for the condemned property.

IF YOU HAVE GAINS AND LOSSES FROM CASUALTIES AND THEFTS

¶ **18.27** Gains and losses from involuntary conversion of property used for personal purposes are netted against each other. If as a result of the netting, recognized gains exceed recognized losses, all such gains and losses are treated as capital gain transactions. The $100 floor applies to each loss before the netting. The 10% adjusted gross income floor does not apply to the losses if capital gain treatment applies. *See* Form 4684.

If recognized losses exceed recognized gains, all gains and losses are treated as ordinary asset transactions. The net loss is reduced by the 10% adjusted gross income floor. Further, if losses exceed gains, for computing adjusted gross income, the loss is treated as a deduction from gross income to the extent of the gain.

EXAMPLE

Jones has an adjusted gross income of $40,000, a personal involuntary conversion gain of $20,000, and a personal casualty loss of $5,000 after applying the $100 floor. As gains exceed losses, all of the casualty gains and losses are treated as capital gain and losses. The 10% floor does not apply to the losses.

For purposes of netting gains and losses, the 10% adjusted gross income ceiling applies to estates and trusts. Administration expenses are first deducted to compute adjusted gross income.

19

DEDUCTING MISCELLANEOUS EXPENSES

Deductible miscellaneous expenses cover a wide and varied range of items such as employee travel and entertainment expenses, work clothes expenses, union and employee professional dues, investment expenses, legal expenses, tax preparation expenses and educational expenses. They also share this common limitation introduced by the Tax Act: a floor of 2% of adjusted gross income. If your expenses do not exceed this floor, you may not deduct your expenses. If the expenses exceed the floor, you may deduct only the excess as explained in ¶19.1.

NEW TWO PERCENT FLOOR REDUCES MISCELLANEOUS DEDUCTIONS

¶ 19.1 Starting in 1987, a floor of 2% of your adjusted gross income (AGI) applies to the total of most miscellaneous deductions. (Adjusted gross income is explained at ¶13.8).

The purpose of the floor is to curtail or eliminate such deductions. Only expenses above the floor are deductible. The floor applies to the following expense deductions:

Unreimbursed employee travel, meals, and entertainment expenses, ¶19.3
Union dues, ¶19.5
Professional and business association dues, ¶19.5
Work clothes expenses, ¶19.6
Cost of looking for a new job ¶19.8
Job agency fees, ¶19.8
Tax advice and preparation fees, ¶20.2
Appraisal fees related to casualty losses and charitable property contributions, ¶20.3
Investment expenses, such as IRA custodian fees, safe deposit rentals and fees to investment counselors, ¶20.2
Employee home office expenses, ¶19.10
Legal fees, ¶20.4
Education costs, chapter 21

The 2% AGI floor does not apply to these miscellaneous expenses:
Moving expenses to a new job location, *see* ¶19.13
Gambling losses up to gambling income, ¶12.6
Estate tax attributable to income in respect of a decedent, ¶10.18
The deduction for repayment of amounts held under a claim of right, ¶2.15
Impairment-related work expenses for handicapped employees, ¶19.12
Amortizable bond premium, ¶4.5

Certain costs of cooperative housing corporations,
Interest expenses of short sales, ¶6.52
Certain terminated annuity payments.

EXAMPLE

1. In 1987, you pay union dues of $180, work clothes costs of $200, and $50 for the preparation of your return. Your adjusted gross income (AGI) is $15,000. Your miscellaneous deduction after applying the 2% floor is $230:

Union dues	$180
Work clothes	200
Tax preparation	150
	530
Less 2% of $15,000	300
Deductible amount	$230

2. In 1987, your adjusted gross income (AGI) is $90,000. You pay the following deductible miscellaneous expenses:

Professional dues	$100
Investment counsel fee	300
Safe deposit box	50
Tax preparation fee	500
Unreimbursed travel expenses	800
	$1,750

The 2% floor of $1,800 (2% × $90,000) applied to your expenses prevents you from claiming any of the above expenses.

1986 prepayments of 1987 miscellaneous expenses may not be fully deductible. Did you prepay 1987 expenses in 1986 to avoid the effect of the 2% floor on 1987 miscellaneous expenses? Under an IRS ruling, the prepayment was not fully deductible in 1986, if the prepayment covered a period of more than a year. A deduction in 1986 was allowed only for that part of the prepayment covering expenses of one year. The excess is deductible over the period the expense covers.

EXAMPLES

1. The cost of a three-year subscription to a financial service beginning in January 1987 is $720. In December 1986, you paid the $720 expecting to deduct that amount on your 1986 return. According to the IRS, only $240, the one-third portion allocated to the first year of the subscription was deductible in 1986; the balance, subject to the 2% floor, is deductible as follows: in 1987, $240, and in 1988, $240.

2. Assume the $720 prepayment in (1) was for a three-year renewal of an existing subscription expiring in March 1987. In 1986 you may deduct $180, the portion of the payment covering April to December 1987. The remaining $540, subject to the 2% floor, is deductible as follows: In 1987, $240; in 1988, $240; and in 1989, $60.

EFFECT OF TWO PERCENT FLOOR

¶ **19.2** The following tables show the effect of the new 2% floor on miscellaneous deductible expenses. For example, a middle income taxpayer with an AGI of $40,000 can deduct only $2,200 of his or her miscellaneous deductions of $3,000. Higher bracket taxpayers will see even greater reductions in their miscellaneous deductions.

How the New Two Percent Floor Reduces Deductions

If your adjusted gross income is	Miscellaneous expenses must exceed this amount for a deduction—
$ 2,000	$ 40
5,000	100
10,000	200
15,000	300
20,000	400
25,000	500
30,000	600
35,000	700
40,000	800
50,000	1,000
60,000	1,200
70,000	1,400
90,000	1,800
100,000	2,000
200,000	4,000

DEDUCTING JOB EXPENSES

¶ **19.3** You may deduct expenses that are necessary to earn your salary. Typical expenses are those incurred for traveling to see customers or clients, food lodging on business trips away from home, entertaining business customers, work clothes, and union and business association dues.

Job expenses are deducted on different parts of your return. One class of expenses is deductible from income before you itemize; the other class is deductible only if you claim itemized deductions. This difference in treatment is fixed by law. Under *prior* law, you could deduct the following job expenses from gross income on Form 1040 whether or not you itemized deductions: travel expenses away from home, transportation expenses, reimbursed job expenses, and moving expenses. Starting in 1987, *unreimbursed* travel, transportation, and moving expenses to a new job location are no longer deductible by employees from gross income. Unreimbursed travel and transportation expenses are deductible only if you itemize. Moreover, they are claimed as miscellaneous deductions and when added to other miscellaneous deductions are subject to the 2% AGI floor. Similarly, unreimbursed moving expenses are deductible only if you itemize deductions, but as explained in ¶ 19.13, they are not subject to the 2% floor. The only job expenses that may be deducted from gross income rather than as itemized deductions are reimbursed expenses that were included in your pay under a reimbursement arrangement and the special deduction (below) for performing artists.

Outside salesperson. Job expenses of an outside salesperson are no longer deductible from gross income. Thus, if you are an outside salesman, you must claim unreimbursed travel, transportation and entertainment expenses as miscellaneous itemized deductions subject to the 2% floor.

Performing artists. A performing artist may deduct job expenses from gross income whether or not itemized deductions are claimed, if he or she has:

1. Two or more employers in the performing professions during 1987 with at least $200 of earnings from each;
2. Expenses from acting or other services in the performing arts that exceed 10 percent of gross income from such work; and
3. Adjusted gross income (before deducting these expenses) that does not exceed $16,000.

If a performing artist is married, a joint return must be filed to claim the deduction, unless the couple live apart the whole year. If each spouse is a performing artist, the $16,000 adjusted income test applies to the couple's combined income, but each spouse must separately meet the two-employer test and 10 percent expense test to claim the deduction from gross income.

CHECKLIST OF DEDUCTIBLE JOB EXPENSES SUBJECT TO TWO PERCENT FLOOR

¶ **19.4** The following items that are job related—ranging from professional dues and subscriptions to employment agency fees—are subject to the new 2% floor. List the expenses and any employer reimbursements on Form 2106.

	See ¶
Agency fees for job	19.8
Air fares	19.25
Auto club membership	
Auto expenses	19.57
Books used on the job	
Business machines	5.22(1)
Car insurance premiums	
Christmas gifts	19.48
Cleaning costs	19.6
Commerce association dues	19.5
Commuting costs	19.22
Convention trips	19.20
Correspondence course	chapter 21
Depreciation	5.22
Display, samples, room costs	19.25
Dues	19.5
Educational expenses	chapter 21
Employment agency fees	19.8
Entertainment expenses	19.20
Equipment	19.7
Fidelity bond costs	
Foreign travel cost	19.35
Furniture	19.10, 19.18
Garage rent	
Gasoline	19.59
Gasoline taxes	19.59
Gifts	19.48
Helmets, safety	19.6
Home office expenses	19.10

BUSINESS ASSOCIATION AND UNION DUES

¶ **19.5** You may deduct as miscellaneous itemized deductions, subject to the 2% floor, dues paid to a—

Professional society if you are a salaried lawyer, accountant, teacher, physician, or other professional.

Trade association if it is conducted for the purpose of furthering the business interests of its members.

Stock exchange if you are a securities dealer.

Community "booster" club conducted to attract tourists and settlers to the locality where the members do business.

Chamber of Commerce if it is conducted to advance the business interests of its members.

Union costs. Union members may deduct as "miscellaneous" itemized deductions union dues and initiation fees. Similarly, nonunion employees may deduct monthly service charges to a union. An assessment paid for unemployment benefits is deductible if payment is required as a condition of remaining in the union and holding a union job. However, no deduction is allowed for mandatory contributions to a union pension fund applied toward the purchase of a retirement annuity; the contributions are treated as the cost of the annuity. Further, to the extent that an assessment covers sick, accident, or death benefits payable to you or your family, it is not deductible. Similarly, an assessment for a construction fund to build union recreation centers was disallowed by the Tax Court even though the payment was required for keeping the job.

Campaign costs for running for union office are not deductible.

EXPENSES FOR UNIFORMS AND WORK CLOTHES

¶ **19.6** The cost of uniforms and other apparel, including their cleaning, laundering, and repair, is deductible *only* if they are:
1. Especially required to keep your job; *and*
2. Not adaptable to general or continued wear to the extent they replace your regular clothing.

The deduction is subject to the 2% AGI floor.

Courts have held that the cost of special work clothes that protect you from injury is deductible even if you are not required to wear them to keep your job. You may not deduct the cost of special clothing, such as aprons and overalls, which protect your regular street clothing. Nor may you deduct the cost of ordinary clothes used as work clothes on the grounds that:

They get harder use than customary garments receive.

They are soiled after a day's work and cannot be worn socially.

They were purchased for your convenience to save wear and tear on your better clothes. For example, a sanitation inspector, a machinist's helper, a carpenter, and a telephone repairman were not allowed to deduct the cost of their work clothes.

EXAMPLES

1. A painter may not deduct the cost of work clothing consisting of a white cap, a white shirt, white bib overalls, and standard work shoes. The clothing is not distinctive in character as a uniform would be. That his union requires him to wear such clothing does not make it a deductible expense.

2. A tennis pro who taught at private clubs was not allowed to deduct the cost of tennis outfits or shoes required for his job. He did not wear them outside of work and argued that he replaced the shoes every few weeks to reduce the chances of injury. However, the Tax Court upheld the IRS' disallowance of his deductions because the clothes and shoes are suitable for every day wear; warm-up suits and tennis clothes have become fashionable and are frequently worn as casual wear. Further, there was no evidence that his tennis shoes reduced chances of injury.

An allowance paid by an employer for work clothes or a uniform must be reported as income. You may deduct the amount paid for the uniform or work clothes up to the amount of reimbursement, even if you do not claim excess itemized deductions. Any expenses over the allowance are deductible only if you itemize deductions.

An employer may be able to help your claim of a work clothes deduction if he requires you to wear a uniform.

High fashion work clothes. That your job requires you to wear expensive clothing is not, according to the IRS, a basis for deducting the cost of the clothes, if the clothing is suitable for wear off the job. In one case involving the manager of a boutique selling clothes designed by Yves St. Laurent (YSL), the Tax Court allowed a deduction upon proof that the clothes were not worn off the job and were unsuitable to the worker's lifestyle. An appeals court reversed the decision. According to the appeals court, as long as the clothing is suitable off the job, the cost is not deductible.

Deductions for costs of uniforms and work clothes have been allowed to—

Airline pilot

Bakery salesperson—for a uniform with a company label

Baseball player

Bus driver

Civilian faculty members of a military school

Commercial fisherman's protective clothing, such as oil clothes, work gloves, and rubber boots

Dairy worker's rubber boots, white shirts, trousers, and cap worn only while inside the dairy

Entertainer's theatrical clothing used solely for performances

Factory worker's safety shoes

Firefighter

Hospital attendant's work clothes; he came in contact with patients having contagious diseases

Jockey

Letter carrier

Meat cutter's special white shoes

Musician's formal wear

Paint machine operator's high top shoes and long leather gloves

Plumber's special shoes and gloves

Police officer

Railroad conductor

Cleaning and laundering. If you may deduct the cost of work clothes and uniforms under the rules explained above, you may also deduct the cost of cleaning and laundering them. Also, courts have allowed the cost of cleaning and laundering where—

The clothes could only be worn one day at a time because they became so dirty.

Dirty clothes were a hazard—they became baggy and might get caught in the machinery.

Clothes were only worn at work and a place for changing clothes was provided by the employer.

A meat cutter had to wear clean work clothes at all times.

Uniform costs of reservists and servicemen are discussed at ¶35.02.

SMALL TOOLS

¶ 19.7 If you furnished your own small tools used on your job, you may deduct their cost if they are expected to last for a year or less. The deduction is subject to the 2% AGI floor. The cost of tools with a useful life of more than a year must be recovered through depreciation or first-year expensing; see ¶5.22(1). Be prepared to substantiate your deduction with receipts showing the cost and type of tools purchased, and business necessity for the tool.

A deduction for the cost of tools is taken as a miscellaneous itemized deduction.

EXPENSES OF LOOKING FOR A JOB

¶ 19.8 The IRS allows a deduction for the expenses of looking for a new job in the same line of work, whether or not a new job is found. The deduction is subject to the new 2% AGI floor. If you are unemployed when seeking a job, the IRS may disallow the deduction if it finds a substantial lack of continuity of time between the past job and the current job search. It provides no specific guidelines for what it considers a continuity of time.

Expenses of seeking your first job are not deductible, even if a job is obtained.

The IRS may also dispute the deduction of search expenses of a previously employed professional who forms a partnership with others rather than take another position.

EXAMPLE

A CPA working for a firm decided to go out on his own. After a period of investigation, he formed a partnership with another CPA. The IRS disallowed his deduction of search expenses claiming his expenses were incurred in a new business. As an employee he was in a different business than that of a self-employed practitioner. Thus, the expenses should be capitalized as a cost of setting up or organizing the partnership. The Tax Court disagreed, allowing the deduction. The travel expenses were incurred to seek work as a CPA , whether as a self-employed or employed CPA. Further, the expenses were not partnership organization expenses. Although a partnership was formed, the expenses were incurred to determine if he could get sufficient clients to leave his firm, regardless of the business form his new practice might take.

Travel expenses. If you travel to find a new job in the same line of work, such as an interview in a distant city, you may deduct travel expenses, including living costs. If, during the trip, you also do personal visiting, you may deduct the transportation expenses if the trip was primarily related to your job search. Time spent on personal activity is compared with time spent looking for a job to determine the primary purpose of the trip. If the transportation expenses to and from the destination are not deductible under this test, you may still deduct expenses allocated to seeking the new job.

While trying to make a new contact after leaving your job, you continue to see and entertain your former customers. According to the IRS, you may not deduct the costs of entertainment and other business expenses during this period on the grounds that you are not in business

and earning income. However, the Tax Court in the following case allowed the deduction.

EXAMPLE

Haft was a successful jewelry salesman earning as much as $60,000 a year. In the fall of one year, he left his employer and started to look for a new connection. During the following year, he continued to maintain contacts with his former customers by entertaining buyers and their representatives. He deducted the expenses of entertaining and other business costs. The IRS disallowed the deduction, claiming he was not in business. The court disagreed. His lack of business income was temporary and during a period of transition which lasted a reasonable time.

Employment agency fee. If your employer pays the fee under an agreement with an agency, you may disregard the payment for tax purposes. However, if you pay the fee and after a certain period of employment are reimbursed by your employer, you must report the reimbursement as taxable income. This additional income may be offset by deducting the fee as an itemized deduction.

A company interested in your services may invite you to a job interview and agree to pay all of the expenses of the trip to its office, even if you are not hired. The company payment is tax free to the extent it does not exceed your actual expenses.

UNUSUAL JOB EXPENSES

¶ 19.9 The following are not typical deductible expenses. However, courts have allowed deductions in the following cases.

Shoe shine expenses of a pilot.

EXAMPLE

Company rules required a commercial airline pilot to look neat, keep his hair cut, and wear conservative black shoes, properly shined. The pilot deducted as a business expense $100 for his haircuts and $25 for his shoe shines. The IRS disallowed the deductions, but the Tax Court allowed the cost of the shoe shines. The shoes were of a military type which he wore only with his pilot's uniform. The cost of keeping up a uniform is deductible. The haircuts were merely nondeductible personal expenses.

Cost of lobbying for better working conditions.

Depreciation on furnishings bought by executive for his company office.

EXAMPLE

Following a quarrel with an interior decorator, a sales manager bought his own office furniture when his firm moved to new quarters. Rather than complain or ask for reimbursement, he footed the bill and deducted depreciation. The IRS disallowed the deduction, claiming the expense was that of his company. The Tax Court allowed the deduction. The manager's action was unusual, but prudent. He did not want to cause difficulties, and at the same time had to maintain his image as a successful manager. His expenses for furniture were appropriate and helpful.

Salesman's cost of operating a private plane.

EXAMPLE

Sherman flew his own plane to visit clients in six southern states and deducted $18,000 as operating costs of the plane. The IRS disallowed the deduction, claiming there was no business reason for the plane. He could have taken commercial flights or used a company car to reach his clients. Further, his company did not reimburse him for the private airplane costs, although it would cover costs of his car and commercial air travel. Finally, the amount of airplane expenses was unreasonable compared to his salary of $25,000. Sherman convinced the Tax Court that use of a private airplane was the only reasonable way he could cover his six-state sales area. He showed that most of his clients were not near commercial airports. Although the airplane costs were large in relation to his salary, they were still reasonable and, therefore, deductible.

Executive's purchase of blazers for sales force.

EXAMPLE

Jetty, the president of an oil equipment manufacturing firm, thought that he could generate good will for the company if employees who attended industrial trade shows wore a blazer and vest set in the company colors. He personally paid and deducted $6,725 for 27 blazers and vests. The IRS disallowed the deduction on the grounds that it was a company expense and that Jetty should have sought reimbursement from the company.

The Tax Court allowed the deduction. Paying for the clothes was a legitimate business expense for Jetty since he depended on bonuses for a large portion of his pay, and as company president, he had responsibility for seeing to it that there were profits to share in. Further, the outlay was not the type of expense covered by the company's manual on expense reimbursements.

Repayment of lay-off benefits to restore pension credit.

EXAMPLE

When he was laid off, an employee received a lump-sum payment from his company based on his salary and years of service. When he was rehired a year later, he repaid the lump-sum in order to restore his pension credits and other benefit rights. The IRS ruled that he may deduct the repayment as a condition of being rehired; the repayment was required to restore employee benefits.

Extracurricular teaching costs. The IRS does not allow teachers a deduction for school supplies. Some courts have been lenient and have allowed teachers to deduct out-of-pocket outlays. In one case, however, a teacher could not convince a court that his deduction for the cost of paper, pens, glue, and other supplies was a business expense. He could not support his claim that the school did not supply enough equipment.

Release from employment contract. An employee may have to pay his employer for release from an employment contract. Such a situation is rare, and there are no cases or rulings on the issue. However, tax commentators claim the employee's payment, such as for liquidated damages, is deductible as an itemized deduction if the employee takes a new job with another employer. The IRS states in one of its publications that an amount paid as liquidated damages to a former employer for breach of an employment contract is a deductible employee expense. Its statement does not limit the deduction to those who take a new job.

Job dismissal insurance. Some insurance companies offer corporate executives policies to pay lost income if they are fired for reasons other than misconduct or physical disability. For example, one policy covers salary for up to two years after a job dismissal, or if a lower paying job is obtained, the difference between the old and new salaries. In addition, the policy pays for re-employment counseling, secretarial help, and office space. The IRS has ruled that the premium covering career counseling and other reemployment services is deductible provided the executive seeks another position as a corporate executive.

Benefits paid under the policy are taxable income.

Politician's expenses. Elected officials may incur out-of-pocket expenses in excess of the allowances received from the government. They may deduct as miscellaneous deductions their payment of office expenses such as salaries, office rent and supplies. Part-time officials may claim the deduction. The expenses are deductible even if they exceed the official's income.

HOME OFFICE EXPENSES OF EMPLOYEES

¶ 19.10 The law severely limits employees from claiming deductions for home office expenses by setting conditions most employees cannot meet. To deduct office expenses, the office must be exclusively used on a regular basis as your principal place of business or as a place in which patients, clients, or customers meet or deal with you in the normal course of your profession or business. As an employee, it is only in rare situations that your home office is your principal place of business or a place for meeting patients, clients or customers. Both the Tax Court and

an appeals court agree with the IRS that making and receiving telephone calls at a home office is not the equivalent of client's visits.

Even if you qualify for a deduction under the restrictive tests, the deduction is limited by the 2% floor discussed at ¶ 19.1.

An appeals court has developed a pro-taxpayer exception where an employer does not provide adequate working space. It has allowed home office expense deductions to a violinist working for the Metropolitan opera upon proof that the Met did not provide practice space and to a professor who did substantial work at home because his school did not provide adequate office space.

EXAMPLE

An associate professor at the City University of New York taught classes three days a week, three hours per day. He had to do research and writing in his two-room home office. An office provided by the college had to be shared with three other professors and was unsafe for keeping research materials. The IRS, with Tax Court approval, disallowed his home office deduction on the grounds that the college was his principal place of business. An appeals court allows the deduction. Where employer-provided space is unsuitable to do substantial work, the home office may be considered a principal place of business. Here, the professor needed a private place to read, think and write. The college did not provide such a facility.

An anesthesiologist who used a home office for billing and recordkeeping was not allowed to claim a deduction because the focal point of his practice was the hospital where he rendered the bulk of his services.

Exclusive use means that the space used as an office must *not* be used for personal purposes, such as a family den. Further, you must show the office is used for the convenience of your employer. Finally, even if you meet these rules the amount of your deduction may be limited; deductible expenses may not exceed gross income derived from the office.

EXAMPLE

A married couple both teach in an elementary school. Neither can use the school facilities after 5 P.M. and so are required to work at home, preparing lessons, constructing charts and learning materials, and reading education literature. They do this in a room exclusively used for this purpose. The IRS ruled that no home office deduction is available because the room is not their principal place of business.

Office in separate structure. The restrictive tests discussed in the prior paragraphs do not apply to an office located in a separate structure that is not considered part of your home.

EXAMPLES

1. Heineman built an office about 100 yards from his Wisconsin summer home. It had a desk, file cabinets, a telephone, a separate switchboard extension to his office, and a computer terminal connected to the company main computer.

Every August, he used the office to avoid the hot Chicago weather and the distractions of company headquarters. Over a three-year period, he deducted depreciation of $33,700 and office maintenance expenses of $16,800. The IRS stipulated that the office was not part of the home; however, it claimed that the office expenses were not necessary business expenses; Heineman could have worked in an isolated office in Chicago by ordering his staff not to interrupt him. The Tax Court allowed the deduction. The office was helpful and appropriate in his business and thus constituted a necessary business expense. The office allowed him to review long-range plans more effectively than at company headquarters.

2. The Tax Court held that an office in a separate structure was part of a home and subject to the restrictions where (1) the office structure was 12 feet from the residence and within the same fenced-in lot; (2) the structure was under the same title and mortgage; and (3) taxes and upkeep costs were paid as a unit for both the house and structure.

Home office deductions may not be claimed by investors who use a home office to review investments and make investment decisions unless the activity constitutes a business. *See* ¶ 20.2

Home office deductions may not be claimed by employees who rent home office space to their employer. A new law specifically bars deductions for employee-employer rental arrangements starting in 1987. The law overturns a Tax Court decision that held that the home office limits did not apply.

Deductible expenses. Deductible office expenses include real estate taxes, mortgage interest, operating expenses of the office (such as utilities and home insurance premiums) and depreciation. Not deductible are family household expenses and repairs that do not benefit the space used as an office. For example, the costs of painting and repairs to rooms other than the one used as an office are not deductible. However, a pro rata share of the cost of painting the outside of a house, or repairing the roof, may be deductible. The costs of painting and repairing the office space are fully deductible, as well as the cost of an office phone. Costs of lawn care and landscaping are not deductible.

Allocating expenses. Only the expenses attributable to the home office are deductible. You may allocate expenses as follows: Compare the number of rooms or square feet of space used as an office to the total number of rooms or square feet in the home, and then apply the resulting fraction or percentage to the total deductible expenses.

EXAMPLE
One room out of a five-room apartment is used for an office; 1/5 or 20% of deductible home expenses are allocated to the use of the office.

How to claim the deduction. Home office expenses may be claimed only if you claim itemized deductions.

To support your deduction, keep records to show how you allocated the expenses, in addition to canceled checks, receipts and other evidence of the expenses paid.

You need physical evidence of an office. A bare minimum is a desk, chair, and filing cabinet.

Retain business mail directed to your home.

Keep a record of business phone calls you make, particularly charges for long distance telephone calls, and a diary of business visitors, including those who come to your home for entertainment.

The home office provisions as they apply to a self-employed person are explained at ¶5.11.

PHONE AND TELEGRAPH COSTS

¶ **19.11** For business calls made outside the office or at home, keep a record or diary of business calls to support your deduction. To avoid the problem of allocating the costs of a single home phone between business and personal use, consider installing a separate home phone for business use only. For long distance business calls, you might ask the phone company to transfer the charges to your office phone.

IMPAIRMENT-RELATED WORK EXPENSES

¶ **19.12** Starting in 1987, any impairment-related work expenses are deductible as miscellaneous deductions but are not subject to the 2% AGI floor.

To get the deduction, you have to show—

You are handicapped. A handicapped person must have a physical or mental disability which results in a functional limitation to employment or which substantially limits one or more major life activities. Generally, showing blindness or deafness will meet this test, but other disabilities may qualify if they limit the ability to work.

You incur the expenses in order to work. The expenses must be ordinary and necessary to allow you to work. Attendant care services at a place of employment which are necessary for you to work are also deductible.

DEDUCTING MOVING EXPENSES TO A NEW JOB LOCATION

¶ 19.13 Qualifying moving expenses are deductible. Under prior law, moving expenses were deductible from gross income whether or not you claimed itemized deductions. Starting in 1987, you may deduct moving expenses *only* if you claim itemized deductions. If you do not itemize, you may *not* deduct any moving expenses. You may decide not to itemize when the standard deduction exceeds the total of your itemized deductions.

Moving expenses are *not* reduced by the 2% AGI floor.

Use Form 3903 to figure your deduction and attach it to Form 1040. Enter the deductible amount on Schedule A.

	See ¶
The 35-mile distance test	19.14
39-week test for employees	19.15
78-week test for the self-employed and partners	19.16
Claiming the deduction before satisfying the time test	19.17

	See ¶
Moving expenses you may deduct	19.18
You must report reimbursements	19.19
Moving expenses and foreign earned income deduction	chapter 36

THE 35-MILE DISTANCE TEST

¶ 19.14 The distance between your new job location and your former home must be at least 35 miles more than the distance between your old job location and your former home. For this purpose, your home may be a house, apartment, trailer, or even a houseboat, but not a seasonal residence such as a summer cottage. If you had no previous job or you return to full-time work after a long period of unemployment or part-time work, the new job location must be at least 35 miles from your former home. The 35 mile test applies to the self-employed and employees.

> Find the shortest of most commonly traveled routes in measuring the distances under the 35 mile test. The following worksheet may be used as an aid.
>
> | Distance between | In miles |
> |---|---|
> | 1. Old residence and new job location | _____ |
> | 2. Old residence and old job location | _____ |
> | 3. Difference (must be at least 35 miles) | _____ |

The location of your new residence is not considered in applying the 35 mile test. However, if the distance between your new residence and the new job location is more than the distance between your old residence and new job location, your moving expenses may be disallowed unless you can show (1) you are required to live there as a condition of employment, or (2) an actual decrease in commuting time or expense results.

EXAMPLES
1. Your company's office is in the center of a metropolitan area. You live 18 miles from your office. You are transferred to a new office. To deduct moving costs, you must show that the location of the new office is at least 53 miles from your previous residence.

2. Your old job was four miles from your former residence and your new job is 40 miles from your former residence. You move to a house that is less than 35 miles from your old house. Nevertheless, you have met the 35 mile test since your new job is 36 miles further from your former home than your old job was.

If you worked for more than one employer, you find the shortest of the most commonly traveled routes from your old residence to your former principal place of employment.

Your job location is where you spend most of your working time. If you work at various locations, the job location is where you report to work. If you work for several employers on a short-term basis and get jobs through a union hall system, the union hall is considered your job location.

Moving overseas. A member of the Armed Services may deduct the cost of moving his family to an overseas post.

For deducting expenses of moving overseas where you have foreign earned income, *see* chapter 36.

Alien moving to the U.S. The deduction is not limited to U.S. citizens and residents. An alien may deduct the cost of travel here to work at a full-time position.

39-WEEK TEST FOR EMPLOYEES

¶ 19.15 In addition to meeting the 35-mile distance test, you must remain in the new locality as a full-time employee for at least 39 weeks during the 12-month period immediately following your arrival at the new job location. You do not need to have a job prior to your arrival at the new location. Your family does not have to arrive with you nor must you set up a new household. The 39 weeks of work need not be consecutive or with the same employer. You may change jobs provided you remain in the same locality for 39 weeks.

EXAMPLE
You accept a position with a company 600 miles from your former position. You move to the new location. After you have worked in the new position 14 weeks, you resign and take another job with a nearby company. You may add the 14 weeks of work with the first company to 25 weeks with the second company to meet the 39-week requirement.

If you lose your job for reasons other than your willful misconduct, the 39-week requirement is waived. Should you resign or lose your job for willful misconduct, a part-time job will not satisfy the 39-week test. The 39-week period is also waived if you are transferred from your new job for your employer's benefit or are disabled or die. However, it must be shown that you could have satisfied the 39-week test except for the termination, transfer, disablement, or death. The time test is not waived because you reach mandatory retirement age first, where this retirement was anticipated.

If you are temporarily absent from work through no fault of your own, due to illness, strikes, shutouts, layoffs, or natural disasters, your temporary absence is counted in the 39 weeks.

Full-time status. This is determined by the customary practices of your occupation in the area. If work is seasonal, off-season weeks count as work weeks if the off-season period is less than six months and you have an employment agreement covering the off-season.

Joint returns. On a joint return, either spouse may meet the time test. But the work time of one spouse may not be added to the time of the other spouse.

EXAMPLE
Smith moves from New York to a new job at Denver. After working full-time for 30 weeks, he resigns from his job and cannot find another position during the rest of the 12 month period. He may not deduct his moving expenses. But assume that Mrs. Smith also finds a job in Denver at the same time as her husband and continues to work for at least 39 weeks. Since she has met the 39 week test, the moving expenses from New York to Denver paid by her husband are deductible, provided they file a joint return. However, if Mrs. Smith had worked for only nine

weeks, her work period could not be added to her husband's to meet the 39 week test.

78-WEEK TEST FOR THE SELF-EMPLOYED AND PARTNERS

¶ **19.16** In addition to meeting the 35-mile distance test, you must work full time for at least 78 weeks during the 24 months immediately following your arrival, of which at least 39 weeks occur in the first 12 months. The test is waived if death or disability prevents compliance. The full-time work requirement may prevent the semi-retired hobbyists, students, or others who work only a few hours a week in self-employed trades or occupations from claiming the deduction.

You are considered to have obtained employment at a new principal place of work when you have made substantial arrangements to begin such work. You may not deduct expenses for house-hunting or temporary quarters unless you have already made substantial arrangements to begin work at the new location.

Change of employee or self-employed status. If you start work at a new location as an employee and then become self-employed before meeting the 39-week employee time test, you must meet the 78-week test. Time spent as an employee is counted along with the time spent self-employed in meeting the test.

If, during the first 12 months, you change from working as a self-employed person to working as an employee, you may qualify under the 39-week employee time test provided you have 39 weeks of work as an *employee.* If you do not have 39 weeks as an employee in the first 12 months, you must meet the 78-week test.

Joint returns. Where you file a joint return, you deduct moving expenses if either you or your spouse can satisfy the time test based on individual work records.

CLAIMING THE DEDUCTION BEFORE SATISFYING THE TIME TEST

¶ **19.17** Where the time for filing your tax return occurs before you can satisfy the applicable time test, you may nevertheless, deduct moving expenses. If you file your return without taking the deduction, you may file an amended return or a refund claim after meeting the time test. No matter which option you choose, any reimbursement must be reported in the year received. See ¶ 19.19

EXAMPLE

You move to a new location on November 1, 1987. At the end of the year, you have worked in your new position only nine weeks. You deduct your moving expenses on your 1987 tax return even though you did not complete the 39- or 78-week period of work. But if, after you file the return on which you deducted moving expenses, you move from the location before completing the applicable work period, you must, on your 1988 return, report as income the amount of moving expenses deducted in 1987. As an alternative, you may file an amended 1987 return on which you eliminate the deduction and recompute your tax.

MOVING EXPENSES YOU MAY DEDUCT

¶ **19.18** The law distinguishes between two types of deductible moving expense:
1. Direct expenses of moving, which are fully deductible.
2. Indirect expenses involving the disposition of your old residence and the acquisition of a new residence. These expenses are limited by ceilings discussed below.

Direct expenses: You may deduct in full these directly related moving expenses:

1. Traveling costs of yourself and members of your household en route from your old to the new locality. Here, you include the costs of transportation, meals and lodging along the direct route by conventional transportation for yourself and family; food and lodging before departure for one day after the old residence is unusable; food and lodging for the day of arrival at the new locality. If you use your own car, you may either deduct your actual costs of gas, oil, and repairs (but not depreciation) during the

trip or take a deduction based on the rate of 9 ¢ a mile. Also add parking fees and tolls. See the Supplement for late-breaking rate changes, if any.

Meal cost (food and beverage) must be reduced by 20% before they may be deducted as part of your moving expense deduction.

2. The actual cost of moving your personal effects and household goods. This includes the cost of packing, crating, and transporting furniture and household belongings, in-transit storage up to 30 consecutive days, insurance costs for the goods, and the cost of moving a pet or shipping an automobile to your new residence. You may also deduct expenses of moving your effects from a place other than your former home, but only up to the estimated cost of such a move from your former home. Also deduct the cost of connecting or disconnecting utilities when moving household appliances. The cost of connecting a telephone in your new home is not deductible.

It is not necessary for you and members of your household to travel together or at the same time to claim the deduction for the expenses incurred by each member.

Indirect expenses: You may deduct, within certain limits, these indirectly related expenses of moving:

1. The cost of pre-move house-hunting trips. This includes the expenses of transportation, meals and lodging incurred by you and members of your household in traveling from your former home to the general area of your new job location and returning.

You must obtain employment before the trip begins and the trip must be for the principal purpose of finding a place to live.

You may deduct the expenses of more than one house-hunting trip taken by you or a member of your household. Moreover, the trip need not result in your finding a residence.

2. Temporary living quarters at your new job location. This includes meals and lodging for yourself and members of your household while waiting to move into permanent quarters, or while looking for a new residence. You may deduct expenses incurred within any 30 consecutive days after obtaining employment. You do not have to incur these expenses during the first 30 days after starting to work in order to claim the deduction.

3. Expenses of selling, purchasing, or leasing a residence. Selling expenses include real estate agents' commissions, attorneys' fees, escrow fees, and similar costs necessary to effect the sale or exchange of your residence. But do not deduct fix-up expenses (*see* ¶ 29.23).

Purchasing expenses include attorney's fees, escrow fees, appraisal fees, title costs, loan placement charges (which do not represent interest), and similar expenses. Do not include real estate taxes, interest, or any part of the purchase price of your house in your moving expense deduction. A residence includes a house, apartment, cooperative, or condominium unit, or similar dwelling.

Leasing expenses include reasonable expenses in settling an unexpired lease on an old residence or acquiring a lease on a new residence, such as attorney's fees, real estate commissions, consideration paid to lessor to obtain a release, or other similar expenses. You may not deduct security deposits or payments of rent. However, you may deduct a security deposit for your old lease which you forfeit because certain terms of the lease are broken as a result of the move.

You may not use selling expenses which you have deducted as moving expenses to reduce the amount realized on the sale of your house for purposes of determining gain. Similarly, purchase expenses which you deduct as a moving expense are not added to the cost basis of your new residence for purposes of determining gain. However, selling or purchasing expenses which exceed the $3,000 deduction limitation discussed below may be used to reduce your gain on sale of your old house or increase your basis on your new house. See ¶ 29.23.

$3,000 ceiling on indirect expenses. An overall limit of $3,000 is applied to deductions for indirectly related moving expenses (house-hunting expenses, temporary living quarters, and costs related to sale and purchase or lease of your residence). Of this amount, only $1,500 incurred for temporary living expenses during a 30 day period and for house-hunting trips is deductible.

Married couples filing separate returns. Where a married couple files separate returns and each spouse paid and deducts moving expenses, the above ceiling on each return for indirect expenses is $ 1,500 ($750 for house hunting and temporary quarters).

If one spouse did not incur deductible expenses, the other spouse may deduct up to $3,000 of indirect moving expenses on a separate return.

Separated spouses may each deduct up to $3,000 for indirect expenses on separate returns under these conditions: (1) The couple did not reside together in the same residence at the new location and does not plan to within a determinable time. (2) Both incurred expenses in moving to new places of work. (3) Both spouses satisfy the time and distance tests.

Under the same conditions, a separated couple filing a joint return may deduct up to $6,000 for the indirect expenses of moving to new places of work (including $3,000 for house hunting and temporary quarters). Both spouses must satisfy the time and distance tests.

Delay in moving to new job location. You may delay moving to the area of a new job location. A delay of less than one year does not jeopardize a deduction for moving expenses. Further, if you move to the new job area within one year, your family may stay in the old residence for a longer period. Their later moving expenses will generally be deductible, even though incurred after one year. For example, the IRS allowed a moving expense deduction to a husband who immediately moved to a new job location, although his wife and children did not join him until 30 months after he began the new job. They delayed so the children could complete their education. The IRS held that since part of the moving expenses was incurred within one year, the moving expenses incurred later were also deductible.

Nondeductible expenses. You may not deduct the cost of travel incurred for a maid, nurse, chauffeur or similar domestic help (unless the person is also your dependent), the cost of moving a boat, expenses of refitting rugs and drapes, forfeited tuition, car tags or driver's license for the state you move to, losses on disposing of memberships in clubs, mortgage penalties, expenses for trips to sell your old house or loss on the sale of the house. Furthermore, when your employer reimburses you for such costs, you realize taxable income for the amount of the reimbursement.

You may not deduct the cost of transporting furniture which you purchased en route from your old home.

YOU MUST REPORT REIMBURSEMENTS

¶ **19.19** Include all moving expense reimbursements received in 1987 on your return as part of your salary or wage income whether or not it is reflected on your W-2.

You must report as income such items as payments made by your employer directly to a moving company. Your employer will show these payments on Form 4782. Use your copy of the form to figure reimbursements and expenses. You then deduct your actual costs to the extent they qualify as deductible moving expenses, but only if you itemize deductions. If you do not itemize, you report the reimbursements as income, even though you do not get an offsetting deduction; *see* the Supplement for further details.

Reimbursements and the payment of the expenses generally occur in the same year. If, however, you are reimbursed in a year other than the year you pay the expenses, you may elect to deduct the expenses in the year of reimbursement, provided (1) you paid the expenses in a prior year or (2) you pay the expenses in the year following the year of reimbursement but before the due date for filing the return (including extensions).

EXAMPLES

1. You moved and paid expenses in December 1987. Your employer reimburses you in January 1988. You may deduct your expenses on your 1988 return rather than your 1987 return.

2. In 1987, your employer gave you the cash for your move, but you moved in 1988 and paid the expenses in 1988. You may elect to deduct the expense on your 1987 return if you paid the expense before the due date of the 1987 return (including extensions). If you filed the 1987 return before deducting expenses, you may file a refund claim or an amended return.

Reimbursements by employers of deductible moving expenses are not subject to withholding tax.

Reimbursements on sale of home. To encourage or facilitate an employee's move, an employer may reimburse the employee for a loss he incurred on the sale of his house. The IRS taxes such reimbursements as pay.

Servicemen on active duty. A member of the Armed Forces on active duty moving pursuant to a military order and incident to a permanent change of station does not account for or report any in-kind moving and storage expense services he received from the military or any cash reimbursement or allowances to the extent expenses were actually paid. Further, if the Service moves the member and his family to separate locations, in-kind expenses, reimbursements and allowances are generally not taxable. The "distance" test and the "time" test do not apply to either the serviceman or his spouse.

Moving expenses. Payments received under the Uniform Relocation Assistance and Real Property Acquisition Policies Act of 1970 by persons displaced from their homes, farms, or businesses by federal projects are not included income.

TRAVEL AND ENTERTAINMENT EXPENSES

Illustrations of reporting travel and entertainment expenses may be found in the Supplement of YOUR INCOME TAX.

¶ **19.20** If you are an employee, starting in 1987 you must claim itemized deductions to deduct unreimbursed expenses for travel away from home, transportation, meals and entertainment. Under prior law, unreimbursed transportation and travel expenses away from home (including meals and lodging) were deductible whether or not you claimed itemized deductions. Further, your 1987 itemized deduction is limited by the 2% AGI floor of ¶19.1, and deductible meal and entertainment expenses are limited to 80% of cost before the 2% floor is applied.

If you are self-employed, you deduct travel, meals and entertainment expenses from gross income on Schedule C. Your deduction for meals and entertainment is limited to 80% of cost.

EXAMPLE
In 1987, you incur meal costs of $2,000. Only 80% of the costs or $1,600 is deductible. The 80% limit is discussed at ¶19.47. Further, if you are an employee and the costs are not reimbursed, the $1,600 is added to your other miscellaneous deductions and reduced by 2% of your adjusted gross income, *see* ¶19.1.

DEDUCTING TRANSPORTATION EXPENSES

¶ **19.21** You may deduct your business or job related transportation expenses, but not meals or lodging, on one-day business trips within the general area of your income tax home (¶19.26). If you are traveling *away* from home, see the discussion starting at ¶19.25.

You may deduct the cost of transportation:
Required by your job. For example, you travel to see customers or clients or to deliver merchandise.
Between two work locations for the same employer. You deduct the expenses of traveling from one location to the other. If, for personal reasons such as the choice of a place to eat lunch, you do not go directly to the second location, you deduct only the expenses of what a direct trip would have cost. If your employer has several locations in the same city but you do not move from one location to another

in the same day and you spend the entire day in one place, you may not deduct transportation expenses between your home and the various locations even if you report to a different location each day.
To a second job. You may deduct the transportation expenses of getting from one job to another within the same working day. If, for personal reasons you do not go directly to the second location, you deduct only the cost of the direct trip between the two job locations.
To school after work. If you are taking courses the costs of which are deductible under the rules at ¶21.2, you may deduct travel costs under the rules at ¶21.8.
To reserve meetings. See ¶35.6.
Automobile expenses. If you use your automobile for business travel, you may want to figure your travel expense deduction by using the

IRS mileage allowance. The allowance may be used instead of your actual operating costs and depreciation on your car. Details of the IRS mileage allowance may be found at ¶19.58.

COMMUTING EXPENSES: GENERALLY NOT DEDUCTIBLE BUT THERE ARE EXCEPTIONS

¶ **19.22** The cost of travel between your home and place of work is generally not deductible, even if the work location is in a remote area not serviced by public transportation. Nor can you justify the deduction by showing you need a car for faster trips to work or for emergency trips. Travel from union hall to assigned job is also considered commuting. If you join a car pool, you may not deduct expenses of gasoline, repairs or other costs of driving you and your passengers to work.

According to the IRS, if you install a telephone in your car and make calls to clients or business associates while driving to your office, you are still commuting and your expenses are not deductible. Similarly, the deduction is not allowed if you drive passengers to work and discuss business.

Exceptions. The IRS allows these exceptions to its blanket ban on commuting expense deductions.

If you are on a business trip out-of-town, you may deduct taxi fares or other transportation costs from your hotel to the first business call of the day and all other transportation costs between business calls.

If you use your car to carry tools to work, a deduction is allowed where you can prove that transportation costs were incurred in addition to the ordinary, nondeductible commuting expenses. The deduction will be allowed even if you would use a car in any event to commute.

EXAMPLES

1. Jones commuted to and from work by public transportation before he had to carry tools. Public transportation cost $2 per day to commute to and from work. When he had to use the car to carry the tools, the cost of driving was $3 a day and $5 a day to rent a trailer to carry the tools. Jones may deduct only the cost of renting the trailer. The IRS does not allow a deduction for the additional $1 a day cost of operating the car. It is not considered related to the carrying of the tools. It is treated as part of the cost of commuting which is not deductible.

2. Same facts as above but Jones does not rent a trailer. He uses the car trunk to store his tools. He may not claim a deduction because he incurs no additional cost for carrying the tools.

3. Smith uses his car regardless of the need to transport tools. He rents a trailer for $5 a day to carry tools. He may deduct $5 a day under the "additional-cost" rule.

> *If you have your regular office in your home,* you may deduct travel costs beginning with your first business call of the day. However, you may not deduct the cost of commuting from your regular place of employment to your home because you work at home at a second job.

EXAMPLES

1. Dr. St. John practiced industrial medicine; his patients were employees of his industrial clients. He was on call 24 hours a day and maintained a home office with complete records. His working day began at home where he planned his rounds by telephoning his clients and his outside office. Therefore, when he started on his rounds he was traveling on business, not commuting. The cost of these trips is deductible.

2. An IRS agent argued that he could deduct his evening commuting expenses from an IRS office to his home. He claimed that he had a second place of employment at home where he kept an office to transact business as treasurer of a credit union. Therefore, he was traveling between two places of employment. The deduction was disallowed. He would have gone home evenings even if he did not transact credit union business there.

3. A self-employed home repairman deducted the cost of travel from his home, which served as his business headquarters, to the homes of customers where he actually did the repairs. The IRS disallowed the deduction, claiming that his principal place of business was the various

job sites. The Tax Court disagreed. He contacted clients at home, listed his home phone as his place of business in newspaper advertisements, and kept tools and supplies there. Since his home was the sole fixed location of his business, the cost of travel from home to the job sites is deductible.

4. Wicker, a self-employed nurse and anesthetist worked at a hospital as the head of the department of anesthesiology. She deducted her driving costs from home to the hospital. She claimed the expenses were deductible because she maintained a home office as her principal place of business. Although she was the only full-time anesthetist at the hospital, she was not given hospital office space. Her only office was at home where she kept medical reference materials, patient files, billing and tax records, and where she prepared lectures that she was required to give at the hospital one day a month. She also used her home office to write the hospital manual for anesthesia procedure as well as quarterly reports to state authorities covering treatments of patients.

The IRS argued that although Wicker was self-employed, the hospital was her principal place of business; then she assisted in operations and earned all her fees. In her home office, she saw no patients, charged no fees, and performed only incidental duties.

The Tax Court allows the travel cost deductions. Wicker had to use a home office for keeping records and preparing reports and hospital procedures, particularly since the hospital refused to provide her with an office. That no specific income can be traced to her work in the office does not mean that the office is not her principal place of business. Her position is similar to that of a self-employed physician who operates at a hospital or a trial attorney who spends most of his time in court. In these cases, the principal place of business is not the operating room or courtroom but the professional's regular office. They may deduct their transportation costs from that office to the place where they perform their services. The same rule applies here.

When you commute to a temporary job location outside the general area of your principal place of work, the IRS has followed a policy of allowing a deduction for such commutation costs. It can reverse this policy at will *(see* the Supplement for further developments, if any).

OVERNIGHT SLEEP TEST LIMITS DEDUCTION OF MEAL COSTS ON ONE-DAY BUSINESS TRIPS

¶ **19.23** The over-nightsleep rule prevents the deduction of meal costs on one-day business trips. To be deductible, meal costs must be incurred on a business trip that lasts longer than a regular working day (but not necessarily 24 hours) and requires time off to sleep (not just to eat or rest) before returning home. Taking a nap in a parked car off the road does not meet the overnight sleep test.

EXAMPLES

1. A New Yorker flies to Washington, D.C., which is about 250 miles away, to see a client. He arrives at noon, eats lunch, and then visits the client. He flies back to New York. He may deduct the cost of the plane fare, but not the cost of the lunch. He was not away over night nor was he required to take time out to sleep before returning home.

2. Same facts as above except he sleeps overnight in a Washington hotel. He eats breakfast there, and then sees another client and returns home to New York in the afternoon. He may deduct not only the cost of the plane fare but also the cost of the meals while on the trip and the cost of the hotel. He was away overnight.

3. A trucker's run is from Seattle to Portland and return. He leaves at about 2:00 A.M. and returns to Seattle the same day, getting in at about 6:00 P.M. While in Portland, he is released from duty for about four hours layover time to get necessary sleep before returning to Seattle. He may deduct the cost of meals because he is released at the turnaround point to obtain necessary sleep. Official release from duty is not a prerequisite to satisfying the sleep or rest test.

4. A conductor living in Atlanta works for a railroad. His run begins around 7:00 A.M. and the round trip takes about 15 hours. He spends two hours at the turnaround point and eats lunch there. He may not deduct the cost of lunch. The two-hour interval between runs may have been sufficient time to eat, but not to obtain substantial sleep or rest so as to satisfy the sleep or rest rule necessary to deduct the cost of meals on a one-day trip.

Several courts held that the IRS rule was unreasonable and outdated in the world of supersonic travel, and they would have allowed the New Yorker on the one-day trip to Washington, D.C. to deduct the cost of his lunch. The Supreme Court disagreed and upheld the IRS rule as a fair administrative approach.

Meal costs during overtime. Such costs are not deductible if you are not away from your place of business. Thus, for example, a resident physician could not deduct the cost of meals and sleeping quarters at the hospital during overnight or weekend duty.

IRS MEAL ALLOWANCE

¶ **19.24** Starting in 1987, only 80% of meal costs are deductible. The IRS allows an optional meal allowance for overnight business travel. The allowance is designed for salesmen, long-haul truckers, and others who do not charge their meals through credit cards or keep records of cash outlays while on the road. It is $14 per day for business travel of less than 30 days in one general locality and $9 per day for travel of 30 days or more in one locality. In determining whether you are away at one general locality for at least 30 days, weekend trips home do not reduce the number of days you are considered away. If the allowance is elected, it applies to all meal expenses for the year. Self-employed individuals as well as employees may claim the allowance.

The allowance is allocated for the first and last day of a trip. The day is divided into four six-hour periods, starting at midnight. For each six-hour period that you are away, you are entitled to one quarter of the allowance. If you start your business trip between midnight and 6 A.M., you are considered to be away for the entire day and may claim the full $14 or $9 a day allowance for the first day. If you start between 6 A.M. and noon, you claim 75% of the allowance for the first day; if you start between noon and 6 P.M., you claim 50% of the allowance for the first day; 25% if you leave between 6 P.M. and midnight.

> If you claim the meal allowance, you must be ready to support your deduction with a record of the time, place and business purpose of the trip.

A deduction based on the meal allowance is subject to the 80% cost limitation applied to meal costs.

DEDUCTING TRAVEL EXPENSES AWAY FROM HOME

¶ **19.25** The following expenses of a business trip away from home are deductible:

Plane, railroad, taxi, and other transportation fares.

Hotel and lodging expenses.

Meal costs. Only 80% of the cost of the meal is deductible. The business discussion test of ¶ 19.36 does not apply to meal costs on business trips provided you eat alone or with your family or personal acquaintances.

Tips, telephone, and telegraph costs.

Laundry and cleaning expenses.

Baggage charges (including insurance).

Cab fares or other costs of transportation to and from the airport or station and your hotel. Also deductible are cab fares or other transportation costs, beginning with your first business call of the day, of getting from one customer to another or from one place of business to another.

Keep records to support your deduction of the above expenses, *see* ¶ 19.49.

Travel costs to find a new job are deductible, *see* ¶ 19.8.

Entertainment expenses incurred while traveling away from home are deductible under the rules at ¶ 19.36.

Cruise ship. If you travel by cruise ship on a business trip, your deductible cruise costs are limited to twice the highest federal per diem for travel in the United States times the number of days in transit.

EXAMPLE

You sail to Europe on business. Assume that the highest per diem federal rate is $126 and the trip lasts five days. The maximum deduction for the cost of the trip is $1,260 (2 × $126 × 5).

The double per diem rule applies without regard to the 80% limit on meal costs if meals are not separately stated in your bill. If a separate amount for meals or entertainment is included, such amount must be reduced by 20%.

The per diem limitation does not apply to cruise ship convention costs that are deductible up to $2,000 a year, if all the ports of call are in the U.S. or U.S. possessions and if the ship is registered in the United States, *see* ¶ 19.35. The per diem rate also does not apply if the expense comes within an exception to the 80% cost limit rule explained at ¶ 19.47.

How to report. If you are an employee, use Schedule A to deduct unreimbursed travel and entertainment expenses. *See* a sample Schedule A at the back of this book and in the Supplement.

If you are self-employed, deductible travel and entertainment expenses are claimed in Part II of Schedule C; *see* sample schedule at ¶ 5.5.

WHEN ARE YOU AWAY FROM HOME?

¶ **19.26** You have to meet the "away from home" test to deduct the cost of meals and lodgings while traveling.

> *Tax meaning of home.* For travel expense purposes, your *home* is your place of business, employment, or post of duty, regardless of where you maintain your family residence. This *tax home* includes the entire city or general area of your business premises or place of employment. The area of your *residence* may be your tax home if your job requires you to work at widely scattered locations, you have no fixed place of work, and your residence is in a location economically suited to your work.

EXAMPLES

1. Your residence is in a suburb within commuting distance of New York City where you work full time. Your personal home and tax home are the same, that is, within the metropolitan area of New York City. You are away from home when you leave this area, say for Philadelphia. Meals and lodging are deductible only if you meet the overnight-sleep test (¶ 19.23).

2. Your residence is in New York City but you work in Baltimore. Your tax home is Baltimore; you may not deduct living expenses there. But you may deduct travel expenses on a temporary assignment to New York City even while living at your home there.

3. A construction worker works for a utility company on construction sites in a 12 state area. Assignments are sent from his employer's regional office; he is not required to report to the office. The IRS ruled that his residence, which is in a city in the 12 state area, is his tax home.

The above definition of tax home, which is generally applied by the IRS and courts, has been rejected by an appeals court. The IRS disallowed Ethel Merman's deduction of living expenses in New York while appearing in a Broadway show. A court agreed with her claim that her home was in Colorado where she maintained a residence. Since her home was in Colorado, the deduction of her New York living expenses turns on whether her role in the play was temporary. If so, she could deduct "away from home" business expenses. If "indefinite," the deduction was correctly disallowed, not because she acquired a "tax home" in New York, but because her decision to maintain a residence in Colorado was dictated by personal convenience.

No tax home. A worker who is constantly on the road may be considered by an IRS agent to have no tax home. Similarly an unmarried person who does not keep a permanent residence in one area may also face this charge. According to an IRS ruling, in reviewing a single person's away from home expense deduction, agents will look for the following type of data: (1) He does some of his work in the vicinity of his residence, house, apartment, or room and lives there while performing services in the area. (2) He pays rent for the residence even while he is away on the road. (3) The residence is in an area where he was raised or lived for a long time, or a member of his immediate family such as a parent or child lives there or he frequently lives there.

Permanent duty station of serviceman. The Supreme Court held that a member of the Armed forces is not away from home when he is at a permanent duty station. This is true whether or not it is feasible or even permissible for his family to live with him.

FIXING A TAX HOME IF YOU WORK
IN DIFFERENT LOCATIONS

¶ 19.27 If you regularly work in two or more separate areas, your tax home is the area of your principal place of business or employment. You are away from home when you are away from the area of your principal place of business or employment. Therefore, you may deduct your transportation costs to and from your minor place of business and your living costs there.

A principal place of business or employment is determined by comparing: (1) the time ordinarily spent working in each area, (2) the degree of your business activity in each area, and (3) the amount of your income from each area.

The relative importance of each fact will vary, depending on the facts of a particular case. for example, where there are no substantial differences between incomes earned in two places of employment, your tax home is probably the area in which you spend more of your time. Where there are substantial income differences, your tax home is probably the area in which you earn more of your income.

EXAMPLES

1. Sherman lived in Worcester, Mass., where he managed a factory. He opened his own sales agency in New York. He continued to manage the factory and spent considerable time in Worcester. The larger part of his income came from the New York business. However, he was allowed to treat New York as his minor place of business and to deduct his travel expenses to New York and his living expenses there. The reason: He spent most of his time in Worcester and his income there was substantial.

2. Benson, a consulting engineer, maintained a combination residence business office in a home he owned in New York. He also taught four days a week at a Technological Institute in West Virginia under a temporary nine-month appointment. He spent three-day weekends, holidays, and part of the summer at his New York address. At the Institute, he rented a room in the student union building. The IRS disallowed transportation expenses between New York and West Virginia and meals and lodging there as not incurred while away from home. The Tax Court disagreed. A taxpayer may have more than one occupation in more than one city. When his occupations require him to spend a substantial amount of time in each place, he may deduct his travel expenses, including meals and lodging, at the place away from his permanent residence. That Benson's teaching salary happened to exceed his income from his private practice does not change the result.

3. For many years, Markey, a G.M. engineer, worked near and lived in Lewisburg, Ohio. He also owned rental property, farms, and a machine shop in Lewisburg andwas an officer of a bank. When he retired from G.M., it rehired him as a consultant and reassigned him to Warren, Michigan, 250 miles away. He spent five days a week in Warren, returning to Lewisburg every weekend. He claimed Lewisburg as his tax home. The IRS disallowed his away from home deduction and allowed a deduction only for the cost of a dozen trips from Warren to Lewisburg as an expense of managing his investments. It treated Warren as Markey's tax home on the grounds that he earned $12,000 a

year there while his Lewisburg investments returned less than $1,500. The Tax Court sided with Markey. It reasoned that he considered his business and investment activities at Lewisburg more important than his job even though they generated little income. An appeals court reversed, supporting the IRS position. That Markey attached importance to his interests in Lewisburg was not relevant. Warren was his tax home because he spent more time and earned far more money there.

Professional sports players, coaches, and managers. When the only business of such persons is the professional sport, their home is the "club town." But if they are in another business in addition to their professional playing, the above rules determine whether their club's home town or the place of their off-season business is their tax home. If it is the club's home town, they deduct travel and living expenses while away from that town— including the time they are where the second business is. (If the second place is where their families also live, they may not deduct the families' expenses there.) If the town where the other business is located is the tax home, then expenses in the club's home town may be deducted.

TAX HOME OF MARRIED COUPLE
WORKING IN DIFFERENT CITIES

¶ 19.28 When a husband and wife work and live in different cities during the week, one of them may seek to deduct travel expenses away from home. Such deductions have generally been disallowed, although courts have allowed some exceptions. Although for common law purposes the domicile of the husband may be the domicile of the wife, for tax purposes when each spouse works in a different city, each may have a separate tax home.

EXAMPLES

1. Robert worked in Wilmington, Delaware; his wife, Margaret, in New York City. During the weekend, she traveled to Wilmington and deducted, as travel expenses away from home, her living costs in New York and weekend travel expenses to Wilmington. She argued that because she and her husband filed a joint return, they were a single taxable unit, and the tax home of this unit was Wilmington where her husband lived. The deduction was disallowed. That a couple can file a joint return does not give them deductions that are not otherwise available to them as individuals. Margaret's tax home was New York where she worked. Therefore, her expenses there are not deductible. And, as the weekend trips to Wilmington had no relationship to her job, they, too, are not deductible.

2. Hundt and his wife worked in Washington, D.C., and lived in nearby Arlington, Va., for many years. In 1952, he became a free-lance writer and director of industrial motion pictures. He directed and did research for films in various parts of the country from New York to California. He wrote the film scripts at his Arlington home or on location. However, most of his business came from New York City, where he lived in hotels. In 1956, he spent 175 days in New York City on business and rented an apartment for $1,200 because it was cheaper than a hotel. He deducted half the annual rent for the New York apartment, the costs of traveling between Arlington and New York, and the cost of meals in New York. The IRS disallowed the expenses, finding New York to be his tax home. The court disagreed, holding Arlington was his tax home because (1) part of his income came from his creative writing in Arlington and (2) his travel to other parts of the country was temporary. In this case the fact that most of his income came from New York did not make New York his tax home.

3. Leyland worked for the census bureau and his wife as a consultant to IBM in New Haven, Connecticut. At the request of the bureau, he enrolled for a year's in-service training at the Harvard Business School in Boston. When he moved there, the couple decided to give up their apartment in New Haven, and Mrs. Leyland took a room at a club. When Leyland visited New Haven on business, he lived at the club with her. During the period, she also traveled to Boston on behalf of IBM. On their tax return, the couple claimed New Haven as their tax home and deducted living expenses in Boston. The IRS claimed that New Haven was not Leyland's home as he gave up his apartment there to live in Boston. His expenses were disallowed. However, it agreed that his wife remained a resident of New Haven; she did not change her job and was in Boston only on assignment with IBM. Therefore, she could deduct expenses in Boston. The Tax Court agreed. Although Leyland's assignment in Boston was temporary, he chose to

make Boston his home for the period. He moved his furniture there. As for Mrs. Leyland, her Boston expenses were deductible; she went there on business. Each spouse had a separate tax home: Mrs. Leyland in New Haven, Mr. Leyland in Boston.

DEDUCTING LIVING COSTS ON TEMPORARY JOB ASSIGNMENT AWAY FROM HOME

¶ **19.29** A business trip or job assignment away from home may last a few days, weeks, or months. If your assignment is considered temporary, you deduct living costs away from home. If it is viewed as indefinite, you may not deduct your living costs there. An indefinite assignment shifts your tax home to the area of your work. So, if your assignment is indefinite, you may not claim for tax purposes that you are away from home, even though you keep a permanent residence elsewhere.

What costs are deductible? While you are on a temporary job assignment, you may deduct the cost of meals and lodging at the place of your assignment, even for your days off. If you return home, say for weekends, your living expenses at home are not deductible. You may deduct travel expenses, meals, and lodging en route between your home and your job assignment provided they do not exceed your living expenses had you stayed at the temporary job location. If you keep a hotel room at the temporary location while you return home, you may deduct your round-trip expenses for the trip home only up to the amount you would have spent for meals had you stayed at the temporary workplace.

What is a temporary assignment? The law does not define what is meant by a temporary assignment. Before 1983, the IRS adopted an administrative rule which generally treated an anticipated or actual stay of less than one year as temporary; a stay of a year or more as indefinite. In response to judicial rejection of the one-year test, the IRS now recognizes stays of up to two years as temporary if certain tests are met. It will treat an anticipated or actual employment of two years or more as indefinite regardless of circumstances. The IRS two-year test as applied to construction workers is illustrated at ¶ 19.30.

When you take your family with you to a temporary job location, an IRS agent may argue that this is evidence that you considered the assignment to be indefinite. In the following case, however, such a move was not considered detrimental to a deduction of living expenses at the job location.

EXAMPLE
Michaels, a cost analyst for Boeing, lived in Seattle. He traveled for Boeing, but was generally not away from home for more than five weeks. Michaels agreed to go to Los Angeles for a year to service Boeing's suppliers in that area. He rented his Seattle house and brought his family with him to Los Angeles. Ten months later, Boeing opened a permanent office in Los Angeles and asked Michaels to remain there permanently. Michaels argued that his expenses for food and lodging during the ten-month period were deductible as "away from home" expenses. The IRS contended that the Los Angeles assignment was for an indefinite period.
The Tax Court disagreed with the IRS. Michaels was told that the stay was for a year only. He leased his Seattle house to a tenant for one year, planning to return to it. He regarded his work in Los Angeles as temporary until Boeing changed its plans. The one-year period justified his taking the family but did not alter the temporary nature of the assignment.

In another case, a recurrent summer job was not considered "temporary work."

EXAMPLE
A race track manager lived and worked in Arizona. During the summer, he also managed his employer's Florida track. When he lost his job, he was offered similar work by a Florida trackowner, but only for the summer season. He worked at the job for four consecutive seasons, returning to Arizona each fall. He deducted his transportation to Florida and food and lodging there as an "away from home" business

expense. He argued the job was temporary. The IRS disallowed the deduction; the Tax Court agreed. His summer job was not temporary but was recurrent seasonal employment. He knew at the end of each season that he would be rehired for the next. He had no permanent job in Arizona during this time. His decision to live in Arizona and work in Florida was a personal decision and not dictated by business reasons. Accordingly, his transportation and living expenses in Florida were not deductible.

If the manager in the above example had a seasonal position in Arizona during the balance of the year, the travel expenses to Florida would have been deductible under the rules explained at ¶ 19.27.

That you do not have regular employment where you live may prevent a deduction of living costs at a temporary job in another city. The IRS will disallow the deduction on the grounds that the expenses are not incurred while away from home; the temporary job site is the tax home. The Tax Court has allowed the deduction. An appeals court has agreed with the IRS.

EXAMPLES
1. An elderly stenographer who retired to Florida needed temporary work to supplement her Social Security. She traveled to New York and placed newspaper advertisements which brought her jobs substituting for vacationing secretaries. She earned over $3,000 in seven months and returned to Florida. The IRS disallowed her deduction of advertising costs, train fare, and hotel rent while in New York, apparently taking the position that her tax home was in New York while she worked there. The Tax Court allowed the deduction as travel expenses while away from home. Florida was her tax home even though she had no employment there. She lived, voted, and maintained all her permanent ties in Florida. When she could not find work locally, she went to New York for temporary jobs. She intended to return to Florida in a short time and did so. She could not be expected to move her permanent home for jobs lasting one to 11 weeks.
2. A Harvard law student, who took a summer job with a New York law firm, deducted the cost of food and lodging while in New York and the cost of transportation to and from Boston where she lived with her husband. The Tax Court allowed the deduction and held that her tax home was Boston; it would have been unreasonable for her to have moved to New York for a 10 week job. An appeals court reversed. The Boston home was her home for personal reasons, not for business. As she was not required by business to keep two homes, her tax home was New York, even though the job was temporary.

CONSTRUCTION WORKER AT DIFFERENT PROJECTS

¶ **19.30** As explained at ¶ 19.29, you deduct travel expenses away from home if your assignment at the project is considered temporary. If your employment is expected to and does last for one year or more but less than two years, you must be prepared to prove:
1. You expect your employment to last less than two years and to return to the location which you claim as your tax home, *and*
2. Your residence at this location is your regular place of abode. To prove this point, you should meet the following three IRS tests: (a) You used the residence while working in the vicinity immediately prior to the current position and you continue to look for a position there, (b) you incur living expenses for the residence, and (c) your family, spouse and children, continue to live there or you use it frequently as a lodging such as on weekends.
   If you meet all three tests for your residence, the IRS says it will recognize that you are temporarily away from home. If you meet only two, you may still be able to convince the IRS of the temporary nature of the job, but if you meet only one, the IRS will rule that stay is indefinite. The IRS approach favors married workers who provide homes for their families in one place. Bachelors will find it difficult to get the deduction because they often do not keep permanent residences. The same applies if you live in a trailer which you move from project to project and you have no other established home. Each location becomes your principal place of business and, therefore, you are not "away from home."

EXAMPLES

1. Adams, a construction worker and union member regularly employed in Newark, N.J., takes a job in Baltimore, Md., about 200 miles away. The project is scheduled to be completed in 16 months at which time Adams plans to return to Newark. His wife and children continue to stay in the family-owned home in Newark. While in Baltimore, Adams lives in a trailer and returns most weekends to Newark to be with his family and to check on employment opportunities there.

Adams satisfies the three tests that Newark is his regular place of abode. His stay is considered temporary and his living expenses in Baltimore are deductible.

2. Same facts as in (1) except that Adams sells his house and moves to Baltimore. His stay is not considered temporary. He did not incur duplicate living costs and his family did not remain in Newark. His living costs in Baltimore are not deductible.

DEDUCTING EXPENSES OF A BUSINESS-VACATION TRIP

BUSINESS-VACATION TRIPS WITHIN THE UNITED STATES

¶ **19.31** On a business trip to a resort area, you may also spend time vacationing. If the *primary purpose* of the trip is to transact business and is within the United States (50 states and District of Columbia) you may deduct all of the costs of your transportation to and from the area (including meals and lodging costs en route) even if you do spend time vacationing. If the main purpose of the trip was personal, you may not deduct any part of your travel costs to and from the area. The amount of time spent on business as opposed to sightseeing or personal visits is the most important issue in determining your primary purpose. Regardless of the primary purpose of your trip, you are allowed to deduct expenses related to the business you transacted while in the area.

> If your return is examined, proving business purpose depends on presenting evidence to convince an examining agent that the trip, despite your vacationing, was planned primarily to transact business.

If your trip is primarily for business and while at the business destination you extend your stay for a few days to visit relatives or take a nonbusiness sidetrip, you deduct travel expenses to and from the business destination.

EXAMPLE

You work in Atlanta and make a business trip to New Orleans. You stay in New Orleans for six days and your total costs, including round-trip transportation to and from New Orleans, meals and lodging, is $400, which you may deduct. If on your way home, you spend three days in Mobile visiting relatives and incur an additional $100 in travel costs, your deduction is limited to the $400 you would have spent had you gone home directly from New Orleans.

No deductions will be allowed if you attend a convention or seminar where you are given video tapes to view at your own convenience and no other business-related activities or lectures occur during the convention. The trip is considered a vacation.

BUSINESS-VACATION TRIPS OUTSIDE THE UNITED STATES

¶ **19.32** On a business trip abroad, you may deduct all your travel expenses, even though you take time out to vacation, provided you can prove: (1) The primary business purpose of the trip; (2) You did not have control over the assignment of the trip.

If the IRS determines that you were primarily on vacation, it will disallow all travel costs except for costs directly related to your business in the area, such as registration fees at a foreign business convention.

Fixing the date of the trip does not mean that you had control over the assignment. Treasury regulations assume that when you travel for your company under a reimbursement or allowance arrangement, you do not control the trip arrangements, provided also that you are not: (1) A managing executive of the company; or (2) related to your employer or have 10% or more interest in the company. You are considered a managing executive if you are authorized without effective veto procedures to decide on the necessity of the trip.

Rule for managing executives and self-employed persons. If you are a managing executive, self-employed, or related to your employer or have a 10% or more interest, you may deduct all transportation costs if:

1. In planning the trip you did not place a major emphasis on taking a vacation; *or*
2. The trip outside the United States took a week or less, not counting the day you leave the U.S. but counting the day you return, *or*
3. If the trip abroad lasted more than a week, you spent less than 25% of your time, counting the days your trip began and ended, on vacation or other personal activities.

If the vacationing and other personal activities took up 25% or more of your time on a trip lasting more than one week, and you cannot prove that the vacation was a minor consideration in planning the trip, you must allocate travel expenses between the time spent on business and on personal affairs. The part allocated to business is deductible; the balance is not. To allocate, count the number of days spent on the trip outside of the United States. Count days spent on business and on vacationing or other personal activities. Divide the travel costs between the days spent on vacationing and business. You deduct the costs allocated to the days spent on business.

If you vacation near or beyond the city in which you do business, the expense subject to allocation is the cost of travel from the place of departure to the business destination and back. For example, you travel from New York to London on business and then vacation in Paris before returning to New York. The expense subject to allocation is the cost of traveling from New York to London and back.

EXAMPLES

1. You fly from New York to Paris to attend a business meeting for one day. You spend the next two days sightseeing and then fly back to New York. The entire trip, including two days for travel en route, took five days. The plane fare is deductible. The trip did not exceed one week.

2. You fly from Chicago to New York where you spend six days on business. You then fly to London where you conduct business for two days. You then fly to Paris for a five-day vacation after which you fly back to Chicago. You would not have made the trip except for the business that you had to transact in London. The nine days of travel outside the United States away from home, including two days for travel en route, exceeded a week, and the five days devoted to vacationing were not less than 25% of the total travel time outside of the U.S. The two days spent traveling between Chicago and New York, and the six days spent in New York are not counted in determining whether the travel outside the United States exceeded a week and whether the time devoted to personal activities was less than 25%.

Assume you are unable to prove either that you did not have substantial control over the arrangements of the trip or that an opportunity for taking a personal vacation was not a major consideration in your decision to take the trip. Thus, 5/9ths of the plane fare from New York to London and from London to New York is not deductible.

Weekends, holidays, and business standby days. If you have business meetings scheduled before and after a weekend or holiday, the days in between the meetings are treated as days spent on business for purposes of the 25% business test discussed above. This is true although you spend the days for sightseeing or other personal travel. A similar rule applies if you have business meetings on Friday and the next scheduled meeting is the following Tuesday; Saturday through Monday are treated as business days.

DEDUCTING EXPENSES OF BUSINESS CONVENTION AND SEMINARS

¶ **19.33** Conventions and seminars at resort areas usually combine business with pleasure. Therefore, the IRS scrutinizes deductions claimed for attending a business convention where opportunities exist for vacationing. Especially questioned are trips where you are accompanied by your spouse and other members of your family.

You may not deduct expenses of attending investment conventions and seminars. You also may not deduct the costs of business conventions or seminars where you merely receive a video tape of business lectures to be viewed at your convenience and no other business-related activities occur during the event.

In claiming a deduction for convention expenses, be prepared to show that the convention was connected with your business. Cases and IRS rulings have upheld deductions for doctors, lawyers, and dentists attending professional conventions. One case allowed a deduction to a legal secretary for her costs at a secretaries' convention. If you are a delegate to a business convention, make sure you prove you attended to serve primarily your own business interests, not those of the association. However, it is not necessary for you to show that the convention dealt specifically with your job. It is sufficient that attendance at the convention may advance or benefit your position. If you fail to prove business purpose, the IRS will allocate your expenses between the time spent on your business and the time spent as a delegate. You then deduct only the expenses attributed to your business activities.

> Keep a copy of the convention program and a record of the business sessions you attend. If the convention provides a sign-in book, sign it. In addition, keep a record of all of your expenses as explained in ¶ 19.49.

EXAMPLES
1. An attorney practicing general law was interested in international law and relations. He was appointed a delegate to represent the American branch of the International Law Association at a convention in Yugoslavia. The attorney deducted the cost of the trip and convention costs as business expenses which the IRS and a court disallowed. He failed to prove that attending the conference on international law helped his general practice. He did not get any business referrals as a result of his attendance at the convention. Nor did he prove the chance of getting potential business from the conference.
2. An insurance agent doing business in Texas attended his company's convention in New York. One morning of the six-day convention was devoted to a business meeting and luncheon; the rest of the time was spent in sightseeing and entertainment. The company paid for the cost of the trip. The IRS added the reimbursement to the agent's pay and would not let him deduct the amount. The convention in New York served no business purpose. It was merely a method of entertaining company personnel. If there was any valid business to be transacted, the company could have called a meeting in Texas, the area of his home office.

You may not deduct expenses at conventions held by fraternal organizations such as the American Legion, Shriners, etc. even though some incidental business was carried on. However, delegates to fraternal conventions may in some instances deduct their expenses as charitable contributions (see ¶ 14.16).

What expenses are deductible? If the convention trip is primarily for business, you may deduct travel costs both to and from the convention, food costs, tips, display expenses (such as sample room costs), and hotel bills. If you entertain business clients or customers, you may deduct these amounts too.

Food and beverage costs are subject to the 80% cost limitation rule as explained in ¶ 19.47.

Keep records of your payments identifying expenses directly connected with your business dealings at the convention and those which are part of your personal activity, such as sightseeing, social visiting, and entertaining. Recreation costs are not deductible even though a part of your overall convention costs.

EXAMPLE
You attend a business convention held in a coastal resort city primarily for business reasons. During the convention period, you do some local sightseeing, social entertaining, and visiting—all unrelated to your business. You may deduct your traveling expenses to and from the resort, your living expenses at the resort, and other expenses such as business entertaining, sample displays, etc. But you may not deduct the cost of sightseeing, personal entertaining, and social visiting.

Foreign convention limitations are discussed at ¶ 19.35.

DEDUCTING YOUR SPOUSE'S TRAVEL EXPENSES ON A BUSINESS OR CONVENTION TRIP

¶ **19.34** IRS agents generally disallow deductions claimed for a spouse's travel expenses. They assume, for example, that a wife's presence on her husband's business trip is for personal reasons. A spouse's secretarial services such as typing notes of the convention may not be accepted as evidence of business purpose. In one case, a taxpayer could not claim his wife's expenses even though she was the proprietor of the business, signed business checks, and spent some time in the business. In another case, a husband could not deduct his wife's expenses at a convention even though her presence at the convention was required by his company.

However, you may deduct the cost of your spouse's participation in the entertainment of business clients at convention or business trips if the trip or entertainment meets the tests at ¶ 19.42. Generally, you may deduct the cost of goodwill entertaining of associates immediately before or after convention business meetings. A convention meeting qualifies as a bona fide business meeting.

> Where your spouse accompanies you, your bills will probably show costs for both of you. These usually are less than twice the cost for a single person. To find what you may deduct, do not divide the bill in half. Figure what it would have cost you alone for similar accommodations and transportation. Only the excess over the single person's costs is not deductible.
>
> **EXAMPLE**
> You and your spouse travel by car to a convention. You pay $110 a day for a double room. A single room would have cost $100 a day. Your spouse's presence at the convention was for social reasons. You may deduct the total cost of operating your car to and from the convention city. You may deduct $100 a day for your room. If you traveled by plane or railroad, you would deduct only your own fare.

Courts have allowed the travel expenses of spouses in the following cases:

EXAMPLES
1. A court allowed the travel expenses of a wife who nursed her diabetic husband on a business trip. Facts favorable to her case were: (1) The cities visited were not cities usually associated with tourist travel; (2) her expenses were reasonable when compared to the business developed on the trip and her nursing aid; (3) a doctor advised her care; (4) she was trained to nurse her husband's condition. But a court in another case disallowed the travel costs of a wife who attended her husband who was suffering from a heart condition.
2. A manufacturer's sales representative ran his business through a corporation. His wife occasionally helped in the office and was personally acquainted with many of his business clients whom she entertained at home and at conventions. At one meeting, she also set up large selling displays. On the basis of this evidence, the Tax Court allowed the corporation to deduct part of her salary and her expenses at the conventions. It said that her contacts and the entertainment contributed to the successful operation of the company which required the solicitation of supplies and selling to customers.

3. Roy Disney, president of Walt Disney Productions, traveled regularly to supervise and expand foreign operations. On one round-the-world trip, the company authorized his wife to accompany him. The IRS argued that her travels were primarily for vacation and not business. The court disagreed. It was company policy to enhance the Disney image as purveyor of family entertainment, so that wives were encouraged to accompany its executives on business trips. Mrs. Disney's presence helped her husband to more effectively entertain foreign businessmen. She toured production facilities, attended dinners, film screenings, and press gatherings, and incidentally performed clerical functions, such as receiving phone calls.

For restrictions on deducting foreign convention expenses, *see* ¶ 19.35 below.

RESTRICTIONS ON DEDUCTING FOREIGN CONVENTION AND CRUISE EXPENSES

¶ 19.35 You may not deduct expenses at a foreign convention outside the North American area, unless you can show the convention is directly related to your business and it was as reasonable for the meeting to be held outside the North American area as within it.

Apart from the United States, the North American area includes Puerto Rico, the Trust Territory of the Pacific Islands including American Samoa, U.S. Virgin Islands, Guam, Jamaica, Mexico, and Canada.

Conventions may also be held in eligible Caribbean countries that agree to exchange certain data with the U.S. and do not discriminate against conventions held in the U.S. Barbados has qualified and is considered to be within the North American area.

Check with the convention operator about whether the country in which your convention is being held has qualified.

Limited cruise ship deduction. Up to $2,000 a year is allowed for attending cruise ship conventions if all the ports of call are in the U.S. or U.S. possessions and if the ship is registered in the United States. Special reporting requirements must be met by the individual attending the convention as well as by the sponsoring organization. Do not confuse this limitation with the per diem limitation for cruise ship costs discussed at ¶ 19.25. The per diem limitation does not apply to cruises that meet the above tests.

ENTERTAINMENT EXPENSES

¶ 19.36 Under pre-1987 law, the cost of dining was generally deductible if the meal took place in an atmosphere conducive to business discussions. That business was not actually discussed before, during, or after the meal did not jeopardize the deduction. Further, you did not have to show that the meal expenses were either directly related to or associated with the active conduct of a trade or business. Starting in 1987, this "quiet business meal rule" no longer applies. Further, only 80 percent of allowable meal costs and other entertainment expenses are deductible; *see* ¶ 19.47.

With the repeal of the "quiet business meal rule," meal costs must meet the tests that have been applied to other types of entertainment expenses. That is, in addition to having to prove that a meal expense is ordinary and necessary to your business, you must also have evidence that—

    1. A business discussion occurred directly before, during, or following the meal.

    2. You or your employee were present during the meal. You may not deduct costs of dining customers or clients if neither you nor an employee attended the meal. This is true even if the parties discuss business related to your interest. However, where you or an employee are not present, you may treat the cost of the meal as a deductible business gift subject to a $25 annual limit per person; *see* ¶ 19.48. An independent contractor such as an attorney representing you may be treated as an employee.

You do not have to meet the discussion rule when you travel away from home on business and eat alone or with your family or other personal acquaintances, and you claim a deduction only for your meal costs.

The IRS may disallow meal costs on the grounds that they are extravagant or lavish. No guidelines for determining extravagant and lavish dining have been released.

THE RESTRICTIVE TESTS FOR MEALS AND ENTERTAINMENT

¶ 19.37 You have to be prepared to show that meal and entertainment expenses are ordinary and necessary to your business, and
1. Directly related to the active conduct of your business, *or*
2. Directly preceding or following a substantial and bona fide business discussion on a subject associated with the active conduct of your business. This test applies to dining and entertainment in which you seek new business or to goodwill entertainment to encourage the continuation of an existing business relationship. Under this test, you may entertain business associates in nonbusiness settings such as restaurants, theaters, sports arenas and nightclubs, provided the entertainment directly precedes or follows the business discussion. See ¶ 19.39.

Business associates are: established or prospective customers, clients, suppliers, employees, agents, partners, or professional advisers, whether established or prospective.

Not considered as entertainment expenses are a hotel room maintained by an employer for lodging his employees while on a business trip, and an automobile used in business even though used for routine personal purposes, such as commuting to and from work. However, a hotel room or car provided an employee on vacation is an entertainment expense.

The 80% deduction limit for meals and entertainment is discussed ¶ 19.47.

DIRECTLY RELATED DINING AND ENTERTAINMENT

¶ 19.38 The directly related test limits the deduction of dining and entertainment costs at restaurants, night clubs, on yachts, at sporting events, on hunting trips and during social events. If such dining or entertainment fails to meet the directly related tests, it may qualify under the rules discussed in ¶ 19.39, which require the holding of a business discussion before or after the entertainment.

The directly related test may be met in one of the three ways: (1) Under the generally related test; (2) as expenses incurred in a clear business setting; or (3) as expenses incurred for services performed.

Generally related test. Under this test, you must show a business motive for the dining or entertainment and business activity during the entertainment. You must show that you had a general expectation of getting future income or other specific business benefit (other than goodwill). Although you do not have to prove that income or other business benefit actually resulted from the expense, such evidence will help support your claim. What type of business activity will an IRS agent look for? The agent will seek proof that a business meeting, negotiation, or discussion took place during the period of dining or entertainment. It is not necessary that more time be devoted to business than to entertainment. What if you did not talk business? You must prove that you would have done so except for reasons beyond your control.

> The IRS presumes entertainment during a hunting or fishing trip or on a yacht is not conducive to business discussion or activity. You must prove otherwise.

Clear business setting test. Expenses incurred in a clear business setting meet the directly related test provided also that you had no significant motive for incurring the expenses other than to further your business. Entertainment of people with whom you have no personal or social relationship is usually considered to have occurred in a clear business setting. For example, entertainment of business representatives and civic leaders at the opening of a new hotel or theatrical production to obtain business publicity rather than goodwill is considered to be entertainment in a clear business setting. Also, entertainment which involves a price rebate is considered to have occurred in a clear business setting, as, for example, when a hotel owner provides occasional free dinners at the hotel for a customer who patronizes the hotel.

Costs of a hospitality room displaying company products at a convention are also a directly related expense.

Entertainment occurring under the following circumstances or in the following places is generally not considered as directly related:

You are not present during the entertainment.

The distractions are substantial, as at night clubs, sporting events, or during a social gathering such as a cocktail party.

You meet with a group which includes persons other than business associates at cocktail lounges, country clubs, golf and athletic clubs, or at vacation resorts.

Services performed test. An expense is directly related if it was directly or indirectly made for the benefit of an individual (other than an employee) either as taxable compensation for services he rendered or as a taxable prize or award. The amount of the expense must be reported on an information Form 1099 (unless the amount is less than $600).

EXAMPLE
A manufacturer of products provides a vacation trip for retailers of his products who exceed sales quotas. The value of the vacation is a taxable prize. The vacation cost is a directly related entertainment expense.

GOODWILL DINING AND ENTERTAINMENT

¶ **19.39** Goodwill entertaining may qualify as deductible entertainment. Dining and entertainment costs may be deductible if a substantial and bona fide business discussion directly preceded or followed the dining or entertainment.

A meeting at a convention is considered a bona fide business discussion if it is officially scheduled as part of a convention program and if (1) the expenses necessary for your attendance at the convention are ordinary and necessary business expenses, and (2) a scheduled program of business activity is the principal activity of the convention.

EXAMPLES
1. During the day, you negotiate with a group of business associates. In the evening, you entertain the group and their spouses at a theater and night club. The cost of the entertainment is deductible, even though arranged to promote goodwill.
2. In the evening after a business meeting at a convention, you entertain associates or prospective customers and their spouses. You may deduct the entertainment costs.

> The business discussion generally must take place the same day as the dining or entertainment. If not, and your deduction is questioned, you must give an acceptable reason for the interval between the discussion and the dining or entertainment. Treasury regulations recognize that a day may separate a business meeting and the entertainment of an out-of-town customer. He may come to your office to have a business discussion one day and you may entertain him the next day; or you may entertain him during his first day in town and discuss business the day after.
>
> The IRS does not estimate how long a business discussion should last. But it does warn that a meeting must involve a discussion or negotiation to obtain income or business benefits. It does not require that more time be devoted to the meeting than to the entertainment.

HOME ENTERTAINING

¶ **19.40** The cost of entertaining business customers or clients at home is deductible provided a business discussion occurs before, during, or after the meal. When you claim such a deduction, be ready to prove that your motive for dining with them was commercial rather than social. Have a record of the entertainment costs, names of the guests and their business affiliations.

YOUR PERSONAL SHARE OF ENTERTAINMENT COSTS

¶ **19.41** If the entertaining occurred while on a business trip away from home, you deduct the meal cost as travel expenses away from home. If the entertaining occurred within the locality of your regular place of business, whether you will be allowed a deduction for this cost will depend on the agent examining your return. The IRS said in a ruling that an agent will not disallow your deduction of your own part of the meal cost unless he finds that you are claiming a substantial amount that includes personal living expenses. In such a case, the agent will follow the stricter Tax Court rule (sometimes referred to as the "Sutter" rule) and allow only that part of the meal cost that exceeds what you would usually spend on yourself when alone.

DEDUCTING THE ENTERTAINMENT COSTS OF SPOUSES

¶ **19.42** A deduction is allowed for the spouses' share of the entertainment costs if they were present during entertainment that qualified as directly related entertainment under the general rule discussed in ¶19.38. For goodwill entertainment, the cost of entertainment of the spouses is deductible if your share and the business associate's share of the entertainment is deductible. The IRS recognizes that when an out-of-town customer is accompanied by his or her spouse, it may be impracticable to entertain the customer without your spouse. Under such circumstances, the cost of the spouse's entertainment is deductible if the customer's entertainment costs are also deductible. Furthermore, if your spouse joined the party because the customer's spouse was present, the expenses of your spouse are also deductible.

COSTS OF MAINTAINING AND OPERATING ENTERTAINMENT FACILITIES ARE NOT DEDUCTIBLE

¶ **19.43** You may not deduct the expenses of maintaining and operating facilities used to entertain. By law, entertainment facilities are not considered business assets. Examples of entertainment facilities are yachts, hunting lodges, fishing camps, automobiles, airplanes, apartments, hotel suites or homes in a vacation area. A season box seat or pass at a sporting event or theater is not considered an entertainment facility.

The above disallowance rule applies also to depreciation and the investment credit, but not to such expenses as interest, taxes, and casualty losses which are deductible without having to show business purpose. Country club and other club dues are deductible under the rules of ¶19.44.

Entertainment expenses (such as the cost of food and drinks) incurred at an entertainment facility are deductible if they meet the rules of ¶19.37 to ¶19.40.

Dues paid to a business luncheon club are not within the limitation of entertainment facility rules, as a luncheon club is not considered an entertainment facility under Treasury regulations.

CLUB DUES

¶ 19.44 To deduct dues for a country club or any other social, athletic, or sporting club, you first have to show that you used the club more than 50% of the time during the year to further your business. (Business or personal use is figured on a day-by-day basis, see ¶19.41.) But this percentage of use does not give you the measure of the deduction of club dues. You must also show how much of the use of the club was for entertainment directly related to the active conduct of your business. This percentage of directly related entertainment fixes the amount of your club dues deduction. This means that goodwill entertainment may be counted in determining if you may deduct any club dues at all. But the actual amount of dues to be deducted is based on entertainment directly related to your business and does not include goodwill entertainment.

In making this allocation, you include the cost of your own meals as part of the cost of directly related entertainment.

EXAMPLE
Your dues at a club cost $1,000 a year, and you use the club 75% of the time for the furtherance of your business: 35% of the time for goodwill entertainment and 40% for entertainment directly related to your business. Since more than 50% of the use of the club was for business entertainment, you may deduct club dues. Thus, 40% of your club dues or $400, the part related to direct business entertainment, is deductible. However, this amount is subject to the following reductions. The 80% cost limitation rule reduces the deduction to $320, which, when added to your other miscellaneous expenses, is subject to the 2% adjusted gross income floor.

In reviewing your deduction of club dues, an IRS agent will usually consider the nature of each use, the frequency and duration of your business use as compared with your personal use, and the amount of costs incurred for business use as compared with the amount of personal costs. If your membership entitles your family to use a club, their use will also be considered in determining whether business use exceeds personal use.

> The key to deducting club dues is having records of your use of the club (see below). Even with records, you may find you are entitled to a small deduction of club fees or to none at all. But remember: Whether or not you can take a deduction for club dues, the actual cost of bona fide business entertainment at the club is deductible subject to the 80% limit of ¶19.47. That is, actual entertainment costs, for example, food and beverages, will be deductible under the rules applied to entertainment expenses without regard to the tax treatment of club dues.

RECORD KEEPING FOR CLUB USE

¶ 19.45 To prove you have used a club to further your business, under the more than 50% test, you must have records of (1) when and how the club is used, (2) the cost of the club, and (3) the number of persons entertained. If you do not have these records, the IRS will presume that the club was used for personal purposes. A club is considered to be used primarily for business during a day on which a substantial and bona fide business discussion took place even if it was used for personal or family use during the same day. Days when the club is not used are not counted. For example, if, during the year you used a country club for only 60 days, the 50% test is met if you used the club for business purposes 31 days.

EXCEPTIONS TO THE RESTRICTIVE TESTS

¶ 19.46 The restrictive tests of ¶19.37 do not apply to the following items. Their deductibility is determined under the "ordinary and necessary business expense" rule.
1. Reimbursement of employees' expenses treated as pay and from which income tax is withheld.
2. Expenses paid or incurred by you for your employer or a client where you are reimbursed by the employer or client. To come within this exception, a non-employee such as an attorney or similar independent contractor, must fully account to his client for entertainment expenses incurred on his behalf. In such an accounting, you must keep records in a diary and receipts as required in ¶19.50. You also must report the client's reimbursements as income. After accounting to your client for entertainment expenses, make sure you retain records of these expenses to substantiate your deduction.

Note: The client does not have to obtain records from you to substantiate his reimbursements for travel and gift expenses unless you have accounted to him for the expenses.

EIGHTY PERCENT COST LIMITATION ON MEAL, TICKET, AND OTHER ENTERTAINMENT EXPENSES

¶ 19.47 You may not deduct the full amount of your deductible expenses for business meals and entertainment expenses, such as country club dues and tickets. Only 80% of the otherwise allowable amount for food, beverages, and entertainment is deductible. If your employer reimburses your expenses, the 80% limit applies to him.

EXAMPLES
1. In 1987, you pay meal and entertainment costs of $5,000. Only $4,000 ($5,000 × 80%) is considered deductible.
2. Same facts as above, but your employer reimburses your costs. His deduction is limited to $4,000. You have no deduction.

The deductible amount for a ticket treated as an entertainment expense is restricted to face value of the ticket. Amounts in excess of face value paid to ticket agencies or scalpers are not deductible. The deductible cost of tickets is also subject to the 80% limitation.

EXAMPLE
You buy from a ticket broker five tickets to entertain clients. The face value of the tickets are $250. You paid $300 for them. The deductible amount is $200 (80% × $250).

Exceptions to 80% cost limitation. The 80% limitation does not apply in the following cases:
1. In 1987 and 1988, the 80% cost limitation does not apply to meal costs (if not separately stated) that are provided as an intergral part of a meeting at a convention, seminar, annual meeting, or business meeting (including meetings held at an employee training facility), if (1) the program includes the meal; (2) more than 50% of the participants are away from home; (3) there are at least 40 attendees; and (4) a speaker is present.
2. The costs of meals and entertainment are treated by the employer as taxable compensation to the employee and as wages for purposes of withholding of income tax.
3. Reimbursed expenses of an independent contractor who accounts for expenses in connection with the performance of services for another person. For example, if a law firm separately accounts for meal and entertainment expenses and is reimbursed by a client, the law firm is *not* subject to the 80% limitation on these expenses. The client is subject to the 80% limitation. However, a law firm that pays the expenses for a client but does not separately account for and seek reimbursement is subject to the 80% limitation on such expenses.
4. Expenses for recreational, social or similar activities (including facilities) incurred primarily for the benefit of employees, other than certain highly compensated employees. For example, the expenses of food, beverages, and entertainment for a company-wide summer party are not subject to 80% liability.

5. Expenses for meals and entertainment, including the use of facilities, made available to the general public, such as a free concert.

6. Tax-free *de minimis* fringe benefits. For example, an employer that operates an employee cafeteria for all its employees on its premises and charges amounts for its meals sufficient to cover the direct operating costs of the facility is not subject to the 80% limitation on its cafeteria expenses.

7. The price of tickets to charitable sports events (including amounts in excess of face value) provided the ticket package includes admission to the event. To qualify, a charitable sports event must: (1) be organized for the primary purpose of benefiting a tax-exempt organization; (2) contribute 100% of its net proceeds to such organization; and (3) use volunteers for substantially all work performed in carrying out the event. For example, a golf tournament that donates all its proceeds to charity is eligible to qualify under this exception, even if it offers prize money to the golfers who participate or uses paid concessionaires or security personnel. However, tickets to college or high school football or similar scholastic events generally do not qualify because they do not satisfy the requirement that substantially all work be performed by volunteers.

The cost of a charitable sports ticket may include seating, parking and refreshments.

Allocating payment covering lodging and meals. A hotel may include meals in a room charge or a company may provide employees with one per diem amount to cover both lodging and meal expenses. In such cases, the room charge or per diem rate must be allocated between the meals, and entertainment and lodging. The amount allocated to meals and entertainment is subject to the 80% cost limitation.

Skybox rental costs. A skybox is a facility at a sports arena that is separated from other seating and is available at a higher price than the price applicable to other seating. Skybox seats are generally rented for the season or for a series of games such as the World Series. In 1987, 1988, and 1989, deductions for the extra cost of skybox rentals will be phased out. Starting in 1989, deductions for rentals at more than one event may not exceed the sum of the face values of non-luxury box seat tickets for the number of seats in the box. The allowable amount is also subject to the 80% cost limitation. In 1987 and 1988, there is a partial loss of deductions. In 1987, only one-third of the otherwise disallowed amount is disallowed; in 1988, two-thirds is disallowed. Separately stated charges for food or beverage charges at the box are deductible as entertainment expenses and are subject to the 80% cost rule.

EXAMPLE
To see two events in 1987, Jones paid $1,480 for a skybox containing 10 seats; $740 per event. The cost of 10 non-luxury box seat tickets for each event was $200 or $400 total. Thus, the two-event difference in cost was $1,080, one-third of which is not deductible in 1987. Jones may deduct $896 for the two events: 80% of $400 non-luxury face value plus 80% of 2/3 of $1,080. If he had rented the skybox for one event, he would deduct $592 (80% of $740) for that skybox because the special limitations apply only where the rental is for more than one event.

BUSINESS GIFT DEDUCTIONS ARE LIMITED

¶ **19.48** Deductions for gifts to business customers and clients are restricted. Your deduction for business gifts is limited to $25 a person. You and your spouse are treated as one person in figuring this limitation even if you do not file a joint return and even if you have separate business connections with the recipient. The $25 limitation also applies to partnerships; thus a gift by the partnership to one person may not exceed $25, regardless of the number of partners.

In figuring the $25 limitation to each business associate, do not include the following items:

1. A gift of a specialty advertising item which costs $4 or less on which your name is clearly and permanently imprinted. This exception saves you the trouble of having to keep records of such items as pens, desk sets, plastic bags and cases on which you have your name imprinted for business promotion.

2. Signs, displays, racks, or other promotional material which is used on business premises by the person to whom you gave the material.

3. Incidental costs of wrapping, insuring, mailing or delivering the gift. However, the cost of an ornamental basket or container must be included if it has a substantial value in relation to the goods it contains.

If you made a gift to the spouse of a business associate, the gift is considered as made to the associate. If the spouse has an independent bona fide business connection with you the gift is not considered as made to the associate unless it is intended for the associate's eventual use.

If you made a gift to a corporation or other business group intended for the personal use of an employee, stockholder, or other owner of the corporation, the gift generally is considered as made to that individual.

Theater or sporting event tickets given to business associates are entertainment, not gift, expenses if you accompanied them. If you do not accompany them, you may elect to treat the tickets either as gifts, which are subject to the $25 limitation, or as entertainment expenses subject to the entertainment expense rules such as the requirement to show a business conference before or after the entertainment and the 80% cost limitations. You may change your election at any time within the period allowed for tax assessment (*see* ¶ 38.03).

Packaged food or drink given to a business associate is a gift, if it is to be consumed at a later time.

Gifts not coming within the $25 limit are: (1) scholarships that are tax free under the rules of ¶ 12.7; (2) prizes and awards that are tax free under the rule of ¶ 12.4; (3) gifts to employees, discussed below; (4) death benefit payments coming within the $5,000 exclusion of ¶ 2.7. If a death benefit exceeds $5,000 and is treated as a tax-free gift, the deduction for the excess over $5,000 is limited to $25.

> Employee bonuses should not be labeled as gifts. An IRS agent examining your records may, with this description, limit the deduction to $25 unless you can prove the excess over $25 was pay. By describing the payment as a gift, you are inviting an IRS disallowance of the excess over $25. This was the experience of an attorney who gave his secretary $200 at Christmas. The IRS disallowed $175 of his deduction. The Tax Court refused to reverse the IRS. The attorney could not prove that the payment was for services.

Awards to employees. There is an exception to the $25 gift deduction limitation for achievement awards of tangible personal property given to your employees in recognition of length of service or safety achievement. Special deduction limits apply to such achievement awards provided they are given as part of a presentation under circumstances indicating that they are not a form of disguised compensation. For example, awards will not qualify if given at the time of annual salary adjustments, or as a substitute for a prior program of cash bonuses, or if awards discriminate on behalf of highly compensated employees.

The amount of your deduction depends on whether the achievement award is considered a qualified plan award. You may deduct up to $1,600 for all qualified plan awards (safety and length of service) given to the same employee during the taxable year. If the award is not a qualified plan award, the annual deduction ceiling is $400. The $1,600 limit applies if the same employee receives some qualified plan awards and some non-qualified awards in the same year.

To be a qualified plan award, the award for length of service or safety achievement must be given under an established written plan or program that does not discriminate in favor of highly compensated employees. The average cost of *all* awards under the plan for the year (to all employees) must not exceed $400. In determining this $400 average cost, awards of nominal value are not to be taken into account. In case of a partnership, the deduction limitation applies to the partnership as well as to each member.

Safety and length of service. A length of service award is not subject to the above rules if it is given during the employee's first five years. Further, only one length of service award every five years is considered an employee achievement award.

Safety awards granted to managers, administrators, clerical employees, or professional employees are not considered employee achievement awards. Further, if during the year more than 10% of other employees (not counting managers, administrators, clerical or professional employees) previously received safety awards, none of the later awards are subject to the employee achievement award rules.

Employee's tax. The employer's deductible amount for an employee achievement award is tax free to the employee. *See* ¶ 2.3.

EXAMPLE

You give a qualified plan award costing $1,800 to an employee. You may deduct only $1,600. The employee is not taxed on the award up to $1,600; the balance of $200 is taxable.

TRAVEL AND ENTERTAINMENT RECORDS

¶ 19.49 Your testimony—even if accepted by an IRS agent or a judge as truthful—is not sufficient to support a deduction of travel and entertainment expenses. By law, your personal claim must be supported by other evidence, such as records or witnesses. The most direct and acceptable way is to have records that meet IRS rules discussed in the following pages. Failure to have adequate records will generally result, on an examination of your return, in a disallowance of your travel and entertainment expense deductions. Only in unusual circumstances will evidence other than records provide all of the required details of proof.

> The recordkeeping rules are directed to one event, the possibility that an IRS agent may examine your return and question your travel and entertainment expenses. Your expense account arrangement with your company will determine the type of evidence the agent will ask for.

1. *Are your travel and entertainment expenses fully reimbursed by your company?* The agent will then inquire whether you have submitted expense account statements to your employer. If you answer yes, he will not ask to see your expense account records. *See* ¶ 19.51. Nor will he dispute your travel and entertainment expense arrangement. But note this important point: He or another agent may then review your company's records to determine if you have adequately substantiated your expenses to it by means of a diary and other records. The chances of a current examination of your company's practices are increased if you are an employee of a closely held corporation. In addition, even though you have a reimbursement arrangement, you may have to present your records if you are a stockholder-employee who owns more than 10% of the company stock.

2. *Have you claimed a deduction for travel and entertainment expenses on your return?* That is, your expenses are not reimbursed by your company, or its reimbursements did not cover all of your expenses—or you are self-employed. The agent will then ask for your diary or other account book which lists the amount of these expenses, the time they were incurred, the place they were incurred, and their business purpose. In addition, if the amount of a particular expense is over $25, he will ask to see a receipted bill for the expense. If you do not have the receipts, *your deduction will be disallowed* even though the item is recorded in the diary.

To sum up: Whether or not you have a reimbursement arrangement, you must have records, a diary, or other type of account book, and generally retain receipted bills for costs over $25. But if you have a reimbursement arrangement, your records are primarily for your company which then has the responsibility of seeing that your records are adequate and of paying you for only bona fide business expenses. If this has been done and your return is examined, you generally do not have to show your records to the agent.

The requirement for a business mileage record is discussed at ¶ 19.67.

YOU NEED A DIARY AND, GENERALLY, RECEIPTS

¶ 19.50 Treasury regulations require two types of records to satisfy the IRS requirements, and to substantiate your claims in the event of an audit:

1. A diary, account book, or similar record to list the background and details of your travel and entertainment expenses.
2. Receipts, itemized paid bills, or similar statements for lodging regardless of amount and for other expenses when they exceed $25.

But note these exceptions:

A receipt for travel expenses exceeding $25 is required only when it is readily obtainable, for example, for air travel where receipts are usually provided.

A canceled check by itself is not an acceptable voucher. If you cannot produce a bill or voucher, you may have to present other evidence such as a statement in writing from witnesses.

Recordkeeping rules for attorneys and other independent contractors are discussed separately (*see* ¶ 19.46).

A receipted bill or voucher must show (1) the amount of the expense, (2) the date the expense was incurred, (3) where the expense was incurred, and (4) the nature of the expense.

A hotel bill must show the name, location, date and separate amounts for charges such as lodgings, meals and telephone calls. A receipt for lodging is not needed if its cost is covered by a per diem allowance (*see* ¶ 19.54)

A restaurant bill must show the name and location of the restaurant, the date and amount of the expense, and whether a charge is made for items other than meals or beverages, a description of the charge.

> Your diary does not have to duplicate data recorded on a receipt, provided that a notation in the diary is connected to the receipt. You are also not required to record amounts your company pays directly for any ticket or fare. Credit card charges should be recorded.

Your records must also show: (1) the names of those you entertained, (2) the business purpose served by the entertainment, (3) the business relationship between you and your guests, and (4) the place of entertainment. Inattention to these details of substantiation can cost you the deduction. For example, an executive's company treasurer verified that the executive was required to incur entertainment expenses beyond reimbursed amounts. He also kept a cash diary in which he made contemporaneous notes of the amounts he spent. But he failed to note place, purpose, and business relationship. Consequently, there was no record that tied the expenses to his employment and the deduction was disallowed.

You should keep your diary and supporting records for at least three years after the due date for the return which the records support. However, you may not have to keep these records if the information from them is submitted to your company under the rules applied to reimbursed expenses and allowances described below.

Excuses for inadequate records

Substantial compliance: If you have made a "good faith" effort to comply with the Treasury regulations, you will not be penalized if your records do not satisfy every requirement. For example, you would not automatically be denied a deduction merely because you did not keep a receipt.

> **Accidental destruction:** If receipts or records are lost through circumstances beyond your control, you may substantiate deductions by reasonable reconstruction of your expenditures.

EXAMPLES

1. Bryan's 1966 records were lost by a moving company. He claimed a T&E deduction of $15,301.87. The IRS estimated his T&E and other

business expenses as $8,669 on the basis of his 1971 expense records. The Tax Court affirmed the IRS's approach. True, Bryan's loss of records made his burden of proof difficult, but he had to provide a reasonable reconstruction of his records to support his claimed deduction. His testimony of what he incurred in 1966 was not sufficient. A more accurate method was the IRS's use of his 1971 records and receipts.

2. Jackson claimed the IRS lost his records. He left his records with the IRS when he was audited, and the records were never returned. The Tax Court held that was a good excuse for not producing his records and allowed a deduction on the basis of reconstructed records. Evidence that the IRS lost his records: It turned up Jackson's worksheet a year after the initial audit interview.

3. Murray claimed he lost his records when he was evicted from his apartment for failure to pay rent for a month. The Tax Court accepted his excuse on proof that he had kept records before they were lost. The eviction was beyond his control. However, if the records had been lost during a voluntary move, the loss would not have been excused, as in example (1) above.

4. Canfield testified that his estranged wife destroyed his records. The Court considers the loss beyond his control. Canfield did not move out of his home voluntarily and leave his records; he was under a court order not to enter his former home. His wife either burned or destroyed his records during the time he had no access to his home under the court order.

Exceptional circumstances: If, by reason of the "inherent nature of the situation," you are unable to keep adequate records, you may substantially comply by presenting the next best evidence. A supporting memorandum from your files and a statement from the persons entertained may be an adequate substitute. Treasury regulations do not explain the meaning of "inherent nature of the situation."

HOW TO TREAT REIMBURSED EXPENSES AND ALLOWANCES

¶ **19.51** If the reimbursement or allowance equals your deductible expenses and you adequately account to your employer:

1. You do not report on your tax return the reimbursement or allowance and the expense payment.
2. You do not have to keep your records for a possible IRS audit. That is, you do not have to substantiate your expense account arrangement for the agent. You have already done so with your employer. To deduct his payment to you, your employer must retain the records and receipts submitted by you.

What is an adequate accounting to your employer? You are required to keep for your employer a diary together with supporting paid vouchers and bills according to the recordkeeping requirements explained on the previous pages. These records provide a basis for submitting account statements to your employer. In addition, your company must provide internal control over your account statements. A responsible company employee other than yourself must verify and approve your expense account. If your company does not provide such a check, you will have to keep your records for a possible IRS audit.

If your employer's reimbursements exceed your expenses, you report the excess as additional compensation income and file Form 2106 listing the expenses and reimbursement. You must hold on to your records for a possible audit if your expenses exceed your employer's reimbursements and you deduct the excess amount.

> If you want to avoid detailing your expenses and reimbursements, and retaining your records, do not deduct the excess expenses. Treat your reimbursements as if they equaled your expenses.

EXAMPLE

You charge your business expenses, such as transportation fares, hotel lodgings, meals, and entertainment, through credit accounts paid by your company. At regular intervals, you submit expense account statements to your company explaining the business nature and amounts of these expenses. None of the expenses covered personal

items. You do not have to report the reimbursement and expenses on your return.

Also *see* ¶ 19.55 for the treatment of partially reimbursed expenses.

Are you reimbursed for incidental expenses— such as for running local errands? You do not have to report these or make a statement about them on your return.

CREDIT CARDS

¶ **19.52** Credit card charge statements for traveling and entertainment expenses may meet the IRS tests provided the business purpose of the expense is also shown. Credit card statements provide space for inserting the names of people entertained, their business relationship, the business purpose of the expense, the portion of the expense to be allocated to business and personal purposes. These statements generally meet the IRS requirements of accounting, provided a responsible company official reviews them.

EMPLOYEE-STOCKHOLDERS

¶ **19.53** The IRS's promise that its agent will not ask you to substantiate your expenses if you account to your company does not apply if you are an employee-stockholder who owns more than 10% of the company's stock. You will have to hold on to your records for a possible IRS audit. Further, you may not take advantage of the per diem allowance discussed in ¶ 19.54. The same rule applies if you work for a brother, sister, spouse, parent, or child. However, regardless of this rule, you may take advantage of the 21¢ mileage allowance test below as a means of substantiating your travel expenses.

FIXED REIMBURSEMENT ALLOWANCES

¶ **19.54** The requirements for an adequate *accounting to your employer* are eased if your allowance meets the following limits:

For a fixed mileage allowance for transportation costs away from home: Where your company pays you a fixed mileage allowance of not over 21¢ a mile and you substantiate to your company the time, place and business purpose of the travel, you are considered to have substantiated the amount of the travel costs.

Your employer may give an additional allowance for parking fees and tolls. There is no dollar limit on this additional allowance.

For travel expenses away from home (exclusive of transportation costs): If your company reimburses you for such travel expenses in an amount not exceeding $44 per day, or provides you with a per diem allowance of not over $44, you are considered to have substantiated your expenses if also:

1. Your company reasonably limits the allowance or reimbursement to travel costs which are considered ordinary and necessary in its business. In deciding if your company has set reasonable limits, an IRS agent will check if your expense account is verified and approved by a responsible company employee other than yourself.
2. Where you are paid a per diem allowance, an agent will review company records to determine whether the allowance is based on a reasonably accurate estimate of travel costs.

Rates exceeding $44 per day. More than $44 per day may be paid for travel in areas in which U.S. Government employees are paid allowances exceeding $44 per day. A rate exceeding $44 per day may not generally exceed the Government rate paid in the area.

These travel costs are included in the per diem allowance: lodging, meals, incidental transportation, and all other travel expenses. It does not cover entertainment and general transportation expenses. Car rental costs for a traveling salesman going from town to town would not be included in the per diem limit. Nor would airplane or train fares or the taxi fare from the airport or railroad station. But taxi fares within the city must be included in the $44 limit.

Do not confuse the above allowance rules with the flat mileage allowance for auto costs (*see* ¶ 19.58).

IMPORTANT: Check the Supplement to see if the above rates have been revised since the publication of this book.

HOW TO TREAT PARTIALLY REIMBURSED JOB EXPENSES

¶ **19.55** As a salaried employee (not an outside salesman), you must distinguish between job expenses deductible as itemized deductions and job expenses deductible from gross income even if itemized deductions are not claimed.

You may deduct from gross income *reimbursed* travel expenses away from home, transportation expenses, and entertainment expenses. You file Form 2106 showing the expenses and any reimbursement whether or not included in your pay. You deduct from gross income reimbursed expenses to the extent the reimbursement was included as pay on your Form W-2. Unreimbursed expenses may be deducted only if you itemize deductions. The unreimbursed expenses are also subject to the 2% AGI floor.

EXAMPLE

You receive a company expense allowance of $1,000 for travel. Your employer requires you to give him a statement showing the business nature and amount of expenses paid with this allowance. As you accounted for your expenses, the company does not report the reimbursement on your Form W-2. During the year, the allowance was inadequate and you incurred authorized out-of-pocket traveling expenses of $500. You file Form 2106 on which you report the travel expenses. As the reimbursement was not treated as taxable pay on Form W-2, you also enter the amount of the reimbursement on Form 2106 as a reduction of the travel expenses. To deduct the unreimbursed travel expenses of $500, you must itemize deductions on Schedule A. Further, the $500 is subject to the 2% floor, *see* ¶ 19.1.

Importance of reimbursement arrangements. If your job requires you to incur deductible travel and entertainment expenses, sound tax planning requires that you and your company fix a definite policy of how the expenses will be borne. The best arrangement is for your company to give you an allowance or to reimburse you for the expenses. Try to avoid an understanding that your salary has been set to cover your payment of expenses. If you make an adequate accounting to your employer for reimbursed expenses (¶ 19.51), your employer does not report the reimbursement on your W-2 and you do not have to report the reimbursement of the expenses on your return. Even if you do not make an accounting and the reimbursement is included in your pay, the following example illustrates the advantage of having a reimbursement arrangement which allows you to deduct from gross income those expenses usually treated as itemized deductions.

EXAMPLE

It is understood between you and your company that your job requires paying entertainment expenses of $2,000 annually and that your net salary should be $38,000. If you are paid a straight salary of $40,000, which has to cover your payment of entertainment costs, you report $40,000 as salary income and you may deduct the $2,000 only if you itemize deductions. Further, your deduction is subject to a 2% AGI floor. If 2% of your adjusted gross income exceeds your unreimbursed entertainment expense plus other miscellaneous expenses, your payout is not deductible. Here, assuming $40,000 is also the amount of your adjusted gross income, $800 of your unreimbursed expense is not deductible if it is your only miscellaneous expense. But if your salary is set at $38,000 and your company also pays you for the entertainment costs and includes it in your Form W-2, you report a salary of $38,000 plus $2,000 for the reimbursement and you then deduct from gross income the $2,000 of reimbursed entertainment costs. Your adjusted gross income without the reimbursement arrangement is $40,000; with the reimbursement arrangement, it is $38,000.

If you are entitled to reimbursement from your employer, make sure you receive it. Failure to be reimbursed may prevent you from deducting your out-of-pocket expense. A supervisor whose responsibility was to maintain good relations with his district, and store managers entertained them and their families and also distributed gifts among them. His cost was $2,500 for which he could have been reimbursed by his company, but he made no claim. Consequently, the court disallowed it as a deduction on his return. The expense was the company's; any goodwill he created benefited it. But because he failed to seek reimbursement, he was not allowed to convert company expenses into his own.

DOES AN EMPLOYER HAVE TO REPORT YOUR REIMBURSEMENTS?

¶ **19.56** An employer does not have to file an information return (Forms 1096 and 1099) reporting reimbursements or advances to employees if they submit expense account statements. However, an employer lists on its tax return its top-paid employees, their salaries, and the expenses paid on their behalf. In addition, it also states if it has taken expense deductions in connection with (1) an entertainment facility; (2) living accommodations; (3) employees' families at conventions or meetings; or (4) employee or family vacations. When examining an executive's return, the IRS may confront him with this company information. If he cannot prove the expenses were bona fide business costs, he will be charged with additional compensation.

DEDUCTING AUTOMOBILE EXPENSES

¶ 19.57 Costs of driving on business trips are deductible under rules hedged with restrictions. The new law has added to the restrictions. Under the new law, the recovery system for assets placed in service after 1986 is called MACRS (modified ACRS) instead of ACRS. Under MACRS, there is a lower ceiling on the top annual depreciation deduction. In 1987, the maximum MACRS depreciation deduction for a car purchased in 1987 may not exceed $2,560, even if the car is used only for business travel.

Other restrictions—

Allow MACRS or ACRS depreciation only for autos used for business driving exceeding 50%. Where business driving is less, straight line depreciation must be used.

Recapture ACRS depreciation deductions and the investment credit claimed in prior years if business use declines below certain levels.

Give you an election to avoid accounting for actual auto expenses and depreciation by claiming an IRS mileage allowance. Whatever choice you make, keep a record of mileage of business trips.

Tax the value of personal driving with a company car.

Where to claim auto expense deductions.

Employees. You claim actual auto expenses or the IRS allowance on Form 2106. Form 2106 requires you to list mileage for business, commuting, and other personal trips. If you claim actual costs you may include on Form 2106 interest paid on a car purchase allocated to business use. The balance of the interest may be claimed as itemized deductions on Schedule A. Sales tax allocated to business use is added to the cost basis. The sales tax allocated to personal use is not deductible. If your auto costs are not reimbursed by your employer, you must deduct them as miscellaneous deductions subject to the 2% AGI floor.

Self-employed. You deduct business auto costs on Schedule C; depreciation details are shown on Form 4562.

Buyer of diesel vehicle must offset basis by one-time credit for increased diesel fuel tax. A tax credit is allowed in the year a diesel-powered car or truck weighing 10,000 pounds or less is purchased for a use other than resale. You must be the original purchaser. For a car purchased in 1987, the credit is $102; $198 for a truck or van. The credit is claimed on Form 4136, which is attached to Form 1040. For depreciation purposes, basis must be reduced by the credit. Thus, if you buy a $16,000 diesel car in 1987, basis is reduced by the $102 credit to $15,898. *See also* ¶24.4.

CLAIMING IRS AUTOMOBILE ALLOWANCE

IRS AUTOMOBILE ALLOWANCE

¶ 19.58 You have a choice of either deducting the actual operating costs of your car during business trips or deducting a flat IRS allowance based on the business mileage traveled during the year. The flat mileage allowance takes the place of fixed operating costs such as: gasoline (including state and local taxes), oil, repairs, license tags, insurance, and depreciation. You may not take the allowance and deduct your actual outlays for these expenses. Parking fees and tolls during business trips are allowed in addition to the mileage allowance. You may deduct the business portion of interest on car loans and state and local personal property taxes paid with the purchase of the auto and still use the IRS auto allowance.

The mileage rate may apply also to business trips in pickup or panel trucks.

The rate may not be used to deduct the costs of an automobile used for nonbusiness income-producing activities such as looking after investment property.

Use the IRS allowance in the year you place the car in service if it gives you a larger deduction than the total of the actual operating costs of the car plus depreciation or the MACRS deduction. Deductions based on actual outlays for gas, oil, repairs, and insurance plus the deduction for depreciation or MACRS may exceed the IRS allowance.

Your election also affects later tax years. If in the first year you elect to deduct actual costs and MACRS or elect straight-line recovery under ¶19.65, you may not use the IRS auto allowance for *that car* in a later year. Similarly, claiming the IRS allowance in the first year you put a car in service forfeits your privilege to use MACRS. Therefore before claiming the IRS allowance or actual costs plus MACRS, project your auto deductions over the years you expect to use the car. Compare the total allowable under the IRS allowance for the period and your estimate of costs plus MACRS. Choose the option giving the overall larger deductions for the period.

You may decide to use the allowance if you do not keep accurate records of operating costs. However, you must keep a record of your business trips, dates, customers or clients visited, business purpose of the trips, your total mileage during the year and the number of miles traveled on business. An IRS agent may attempt to verify mileage by asking for repair bills near the beginning and end of the year if the bills note mileage readings.

The IRS will not disallow a deduction based on the allowance even though it exceeds your actual car costs.

You may not claim the allowance if:
1. You first used your car for business and deducted actual operating

costs in that first year. Similarly, you may not use the allowance if you claimed MACRS or first-year expensing for your car.

2. You have depreciated your car using a depreciation method other than the straight line method.
3. You use in your business two or more cars simultaneously, such as in a fleet operation.
4. You use your car for hire. That is, you use it as a taxicab, in carrying passengers for a fare.
5. You lease the car.

Allowance rate. For 1987, the IRS allowance is 22.5¢ per mile for the first 15,000 miles of business travel and 11¢ per mile for business travel over 15,000 miles.

EXAMPLE
You drive your car on business trips. You keep a record of your business mileage. You traveled 20,000 miles on business. You may deduct $3,925 (15,000 × $.225 = $3,375 plus 5,000 × $.11 = $550).

If you have fully depreciated your car, you may not use the top IRS rate; you are limited to the rate applied to travel of over 15,000 miles (*see* ¶ 19.60 and ¶ 19.61 for depreciation rules).

If you use more than one automobile in your business travel and elect the allowance, total the business mileage traveled in both cars.

EXAMPLE
You use one car primarily for business and occasionally your spouse's car for business trips. During the taxable year, on business trips, you drove your car 10,000 miles, your spouse's car, 2,000 miles. Total business mileage is 12,000 miles.

If you replace your car during the year and both cars qualify for the allowance, you total the business mileage of both cars for the year. If you did not use the allowance rate for one of the cars, the following examples illustrate how to total the mileage:

EXAMPLE
1. *Old car does not qualify for allowance; new car does.* During the taxable year, you drove a total of 21,000 business miles, 4,000 miles in a car owned from January until May and 17,000 miles in a new car bought in May. You did not use the allowance for the old car because it was depreciated on the declining balance method. You elect to use the allowance for the new car. Although the allowance does not apply to the old car, you consider the 4,000 miles the old car was driven. As a result you may apply the allowance rate fixed for the first 15,000 miles to only 11,000 business miles. That rate applies to the *first* 15,000 business miles, including the 4,000 miles driven in the old car. You may deduct the actual expenses of operating the old car.
2. *Old car qualifies; new car does not.* Same figures as in example (1), except the old car qualified for the allowance, but you depreciate the new car using MACRS so that you may not use the allowance for the new car. You apply the first 15,000 mile rate to the 4,000 miles driven in the old car and deduct the actual operating costs of the new car.

Where a husband and wife own separate businesses, but use a jointly owned car for individual business trips, business mileages are combined whether they file jointly or separately. The first 15,000 mile rate is applied to the first 15,000 miles of their combined business mileage. Each spouse may not treat his or her travel separately so as to apply the rate to the first 15,000 miles of their individual trips. However, if you and your spouse have separate businesses and you each drive separately owned cars, you do not have to combine mileages; you may compute separate allowances based on your individual travel.

IRS allowance includes depreciation. When you use the IRS allowance, you may not claim a separate depreciation deduction. The IRS mileage allowance includes an estimate for depreciation. After your car reaches the end of its useful life (*see* below), your car is considered fully depreciated and you may no longer use the maximum mileage allowance set for the first 15,000 miles.

If your employer reimburses your auto costs at a rate lower than the IRS allowance, you may use the IRS rate to deduct the excess over your employer's reimbursement. For example, the IRS allowance provides a deduction of $3,000. If your employer reimbursed $1,000 of your auto expenses, you may deduct $2,000 under the IRS allowance. To deduct the excess, the IRS sets these conditions: (1) The amount of your employer's reimbursement must be reported on Form 2106 attached to your return. (2) You must list all the expenses reimbursed by your employer. (3) You must meet the expense-keeping rules of accounting to your employer at ¶19.51. The unreimbursed excess is reported as a miscellaneous deduction subject to the 2% AGI floor.

Assumed depreciation based on mileage. If you have always used the IRS mileage allowance for a car bought after 1979, the IRS measures the useful life of the car by mileage. The car is considered fully depreciated after 60,000 business miles, but for this purpose, only the first 15,000 miles of annual mileage is counted.

EXAMPLE
In 1983, 1984, 1985, and 1986, you drove 20,000 miles a year for business. At the end of 1986, your car is considered fully depreciated (60,000 assumed mileage); in 1987, if you use the same car, you may not use the top rate set for the first 15,000 miles. You must use the lower rate set for mileage over 15,000 miles. If in 1987 you switch to the actual cost deduction method, you may not deduct depreciation.

Switching to allowance. If before 1987 you used a rapid method of depreciation or an ACRS deduction you may not switch to the IRS mileage allowance in 1987. If before 1981 you deducted actual operating costs, including straight line depreciation, and in 1987, you want to use the IRS allowance, your car is considered fully depreciated at the end of the useful life used to figure the straight line depreciation. Thus, unless you figured straight-line recovery using a useful life greater than seven years, you may only use the lower allowance rate for mileage over 15,000 miles in 1987.

Basis adjustment. Where you use the IRS mileage allowance, you reduce the basis of the car for depreciation estimated in the allowance. Basis is reduced by—
7¢ per mile in 1980 and 1981;
7.5¢ per mile in 1982;
8¢ per mile in 1983, 1984 and 1985;
9¢ per mile in 1986, and
10¢ per mile in 1987.
For this purpose, only the first 15,000 miles of business travel each year is taken into account. Depending on the cost of your car, these basis reductions may not in your case reduce the cost basis of your auto to zero, although after 60,000 miles of business travel (at the maximum mileage rate), your car is considered fully depreciated under the IRS rules. Further, after 60,000 business miles, you may not depreciate the remaining basis by electing to deduct your actual auto costs.

DEDUCTING DEPRECIATION AND ACTUAL COSTS

AUTO EXPENSE ALLOCATION RULES

¶ 19.59 If you do not claim the IRS mileage allowance, you may deduct car expenses on business trips such as the cost of gas and oil (including state and local taxes), repairs, parking, tolls, and garage.

If you use your car exclusively for business, all of your operating expenses are deductible. However, if you are an employee, the deduction is limited by the 2% AGI floor. See ¶19.1.

Apportioning car expense between business and personal use. For a car used for business and personal purposes, deduct only the depreciation and expenses allocated to your business use of the car. Depreciation is discussed at ¶19.60 and ¶19.61.

If you claim itemized deductions, you may deduct only that part of the interest and taxes (other than state and local gasoline taxes) not claimed as business expenses. You may not deduct as itemized deductions the non-business part of depreciation, operator's permit and license fees (no part of which is considered as a personal property tax) and state and local gasoline taxes.

The business portion of car expenses is determined by the percentage of mileage driven on business trips during the year.

EXAMPLE

An outside salesman drove his car 15,000 miles during 1987. Of this, 12,000 miles was on business trips. The percentage of business use is 80%:

$$\frac{\text{Business mileage}}{\text{Total mileage}} = \frac{12,000}{15,000} = 80\%$$

His car expenses (gas, oil, repairs, etc.) for the year were $1,000 of which $800 ($1,000 × 80%) is deductible as a miscellaneous itemized deduction subject to the 2% AGI floor.

If you lease a car for business use, you deduct the rental fee plus other costs of operating the car. If the car is also used for personal driving, the rental fee must be allocated between business and personal mileage. See also ¶19.68.

DEPRECIATING A BUSINESS AUTO

¶ 19.60 If you do not elect the IRS allowance, you claim actual operating costs and depreciation. For a car placed in service during 1987, depreciation is figured under the new MACRS (Modified ACRS) rules discussed at ¶19.62. For a car placed in service before 1987, ACRS rates are in the rate table at ¶19.61.

Congress has not only reduced the tax benefits of depreciating business autos but has also set in place complicated rules for figuring depreciation.

If you placed a business auto in service in 1987, here are the tests that you must meet:

Business Auto Depreciation Tests

1. Employer convenience test. If you are an employee and use your own car for work, you must be ready to prove that you use a car for the convenience of your employer who requires you to use it in your job. If you do not meet this employer-convenience test, you may not claim depreciation or first-year expensing. A letter from your employer stating you need the car for business will not meet this test.

The facts and circumstances of your use of the car may show that it is a condition of employment. For example, an inspector for a construction company uses his automobile to visit construction sites over a scattered area. The company reimburses him for his expenses. According to the IRS, the inspector's use of the car is for the convenience of the company and is a condition of the job. However, if a company car were available to the inspector, the use of his own car would not meet the condition of employment and convenience of the employer tests.

2. More than 50% business use test for claiming MACRS depreciation. Whether you are an employee or are self-employed, you may claim

MACRS for a car placed in service during 1987 only if you use it in 1987 more than 50% of the time for business. MACRS depreciation may allow you to deduct larger amounts in the first three years of owning the auto. MACRS rates are discussed at ¶19.61 and ¶19.62.

If business use is 50% or less in the year the auto is placed in service, MACRS is barred; the auto is depreciable over a six-year period under the straight line method. Technically, the recovery period is five years but the period is extended to six years because in the first year, a convention rule limits the deductible percentage. See the rate tables at ¶19.63. The straight line method must be used in future years, even though business use later exceeds 50%.

If a car is used for both business and investment purposes, only business use is considered under the more than 50% business use test to determine the right to claim ACRS. However, in allocating depreciation deductions, investment use is added to business use.

EXAMPLE

Brown buys an automobile for $30,000 and placed it in service in 1987. He uses it 40% for business and 20% for investment activity. Because he does not use his car more than 50% in his business, he may not claim MACRS. He figures depreciation using the straight-line method. The business use allocation rate for depreciation is 60% (40% for business use plus 20% investment use).

Recapture of ACRS deductions if business use fails. If you meet the more than 50% test in the year the car is placed in service but business use falls to 50% or less in a later year, the recapture rules discussed at ¶19.65 apply.

3. Annual deduction ceilings. For a car placed in service during 1987, these so-called luxury car "ceilings" apply both to employees and self-employed persons:

Year	Your depreciation deduction including first-year expensing may not exceed—
1	$2,560
2	4,100
3	2,450
4	1,475
5	1,475
6	1,475

Personal use. Where a deduction is limited by the $2,560 ceiling and the car is also used for personal driving, the business use percentage is applied to the ceiling. For example, in 1987 you buy a car costing $40,000. MACRS is limited by the $2,560 ceiling. You use the car 80% for business travel. The MACRS deduction is limited to $2,048 ($2,560 × 80%).

The more than 50% test and the ceilings do not apply to taxicabs and other vehicles used substantially all of the time to transport persons or property for hire.

First-year expensing. The $2,560 limit applies also to the first-year expensing deduction. Thus, the first-year expensing deduction in 1987 may not exceed $2,560. If your expensing deduction is up to $2,560, no MACRS deduction may be claimed in 1987. First-year expensing is discussed at ¶5.34.

Employee use of company car. In certain cases, an employer who provides a company car to employees as part of their compensation may be unable to count the employee's use as qualified business use, thereby preventing the employer from meeting the more than 50% business test for claiming ACRS and the investment credit. An employer is allowed to treat the employee's use as qualified business use only if: (1) the employee is not a relative and does not own more than 5% of the business, and (2) the employer treats the fair market value of the employee's personal use of the car as wage income and withholds tax on that amount. If such income is reported, all of the employee's use, including personal use may be counted by an employer as qualified business use.

If an employee owning more than a 5% interest is allowed use of a company car as part of his compensation, the employer may not count that use as qualified business use, even if the personal use is reported as income. The same strict rule applies if the car is provided to a person who is related to the employer.

Restrictions on vehicles other than cars. The annual depreciation ceilings discussed above apply only to "passenger automobiles." For this purpose, a passenger automobile is considered to be any four-wheeled vehicle that is manufactured primarily for use on public streets, roads, and highways and that is rated at 6,000 pounds unloaded gross vehicle weight or less. A light truck or van with a gross vehicle weight of 6,000 pounds or less is treated as a passenger automobile. It does not include: (1) an ambulance, hearse, or combination ambulance-hearse used directly in a

business, or (2) a vehicle such as a taxicab used directly in the business of transporting persons or property for compensation or hire.

The more than 50% business use test applies generally to vehicles other than automobiles, such as trucks, vans, boats, motorcycles, airplanes, and buses. However, buses and other vehicles that are exempt from recordkeeping requirements under ¶19.67, such as a school bus, a dump truck, specialty business truck, or farm tractors, are not subject to the more than 50% test or recapture rule. A vehicle not listed at ¶19.67 is subject to the more than 50% test for claiming MACRS depreciation or first-year expensing. If you do not satisfy the more than 50% test, you must apply the straight line recovery rates shown at ¶19.63.

GUIDE TO ACRS AND MACRS DEPRECIATION RATES

¶ 19.61 The following table summarizes both ACRS (Accelerated Cost Recovery System) depreciation and MACRS (Modified ACRS) recently introduced by Tax Reform 1986 for cars placed in service starting in 1987. MACRS further lowers the ceiling on the annual depreciation deduction.

Car placed in service—	Depreciation rate information—
Before 1985	If you used the car 100% for business and placed it in service before June 18, 1984, you have fully depreciated the auto. If you used the car less than 100% for business, you may continue to take ACRS deductions if the percentage of business use (and investment use) exceeds the average business (and investment) use in the first three years. If you show such an increase, the car is treated as placed in service at the start of the taxable year in which the increased use occurs. The first-year ACRS rate is applied, but the deduction is limited by the percentage of increased business use. Basis for this new period is the lower of fair market value at the beginning of the new recovery period or the unadjusted cost basis of the car.

EXAMPLE

In January, 1984, you bought a car for $10,000. During 1984-1986, you claimed ACRS deductions based on 60% business use. Depreciation for the three years was $6,000. In 1987, after the end of the regular three-year ACRS period, business use increased to 70%. In 1987, you may claim an additional ACRS deduction because 70% business use exceeds the 60% average for the first three years. Assuming that fair market value at the beginning of 1987 was $7,500, basis for depreciation purposes is $7,500, the lower of fair market value or $10,000 unadjusted basis. Your 1987 deduction is $187.50; $7,500 basis × .25 (applicable first-year ACRS

Car placed in service—	Depreciation rate information—
	percentage to car placed in service before 1987) × .10 (increase in 1987 business use, or 70%, over 60% average business use during 1984-1986).
	If your car was placed in service after June 18, 1984, and if in the first three years business use was 100%, any remaining basis that could not be deducted because of the annual ceilings of $4,000 (first year) and $6,000 (later years) may be depreciated at a rate of up to $6,000 a year until basis is written off. No ACRS deduction is allowed if you disposed of the car in 1987.
In 1985 but before April 3, 1985	The ACRS rate in 1987 is 37% basis, but the top deduction may not exceed $6,200 in 1987. No ACRS deduction is allowed if you disposed of the car in 1987.
In 1985, but after April 2, 1985	The ACRS rate in 1987 is 37%, but the top deduction may not exceed $4,800. No deduction is allowed if you disposed of the car in 1987.
In 1986	The ACRS rate in 1987 is 38% of cost basis, but the maximum deduction may not exceed $4,800. (In 1988, the ACRS rate will be 37% with a deduction limit of $4,800). No ACRS deduction is allowed if you disposed of the car in 1987.
In 1987	The MACRS rate depends on the convention applied to the car, see ¶19.62. The top 1987 deduction may not exceed $2,560.

Capital improvements. A capital improvement to a business auto is depreciable under MACRS in the year the improvement is made. The MACRS deductions for the improvement and auto are considered as a unit for applying the limits on the annual MACRS deduction.

Converting a pleasure car to business use. The basis for depreciation is the lower of the market value of the car at the time of conversion or its original cost. In most cases, the value of the car will be lower than cost and thus value will be your depreciable basis. For a car converted to business use in 1987, the MACRS rate (¶19.62) is applied to basis allocated to business travel.

MACRS DEPRECIATION OF A BUSINESS AUTO PLACED IN SERVICE IN 1987 AND LATER YEARS

¶ 19.62 Business autos placed in service in 1987 and later years are technically in a five-year MACRS class but because of the half-year or mid-quarter convention (*see* below) and the luxury car limits (¶19.60) the minimum depreciation period is six years.

MACRS rate. To use MACRS, you must meet the more-than-50%

business use test. If you do, the MACRS rate is based on the 200% declining balance method with a switch-over to straight-line. The declining balance rate for a car which is five-year property is 40%. However, the full amount of the deduction is not allowed, because of the convention rules and the annual luxury car limits of ¶19.60. As explained in ¶5.24, each year, the declining balance rate of 40% is applied against the declining balance of the basis of property. As a shortcut, you may apply the following rates against original basis, assuming the half-year convention applies. The dollar limitations reflect the luxury car limits.

Year	Lower of—
1	20% or $2,560
2	32% or $4,100
3	19.20% or $2,450
4	11.52% or $1,475
5	11.52% or $1,475
6	5.76% or $1,475

EXAMPLES

1. In 1987, you place in service a car used 100% in business. The

car cost $20,000. Here is the depreciation schedule assuming the car is kept for the period shown below:

1987	$2,560
1988	4,100
1989	2,450
1990	1,475
1991	1,475
1992	1,152
1993	1,475
1994	1,475
1995	1,475
1996	1,475
1997	888

2. Assume you use the car only 60% for business. You deduct $1,536 in 1987 which is 60% of the annual limit of $2,560. Your deduction may not be based on 60% of depreciable basis; this would give a larger deduction of $2,400 ($20,000 × 60% × 20%) without considering the first-year luxury car limit.

Half-year or mid-quarter convention. Regardless of the time of year you bought the car in 1987, your deduction is limited by a convention rule. If the only business equipment bought in 1987 was the car, then the half-year convention applies, unless you bought the car in the last quarter of 1987 (October, November, or December). Under the half-year convention, the car is treated as if it were placed in service in the middle of the year and the 40% declining balance rate is reduced to 20%. If you bought the car in the last quarter, then the mid-quarter convention applies. Here are the annual MACRS deduction rates applied to original basis under the mid-quarter convention for a car placed in service in the last quarter.

Year	Lower of—
1	5% or $2,560
2	38% or $4,100
3	22.8% or $2,450
4	13.68% or $1,475
5	10.94% or $1,475
6	9.58% or $1,475

If you bought other business equipment in addition to the car, you must consider the total cost bases of property placed in service during the last quarter of 1987. If the total bases of such acquisitions (other than realty) exceed 40% of the total bases of all property placed in service during the year, then a mid-quarter rate applies to all property (other than realty). The mid-quarter rate for each asset then depends on the quarter the asset was placed in service. *See* ¶ 5.26 for further details on mid-quarter conventions. If the 40% test is not met, then the half-year convention applies to all of the property acquisitions.

Straight line election for car if business use exceeds 50%. If business use of your car exceeds 50%, you may elect to write off your cost under the straight line method instead of using MACRS, subject to the annual ceilings discussed at ¶ 19.60. By electing straight line depreciation, you avoid the recapture of excess MACRS deductions if business use drops to 50% or less in a later year. *See* ¶ 19.65.

STRAIGHT LINE RATE REQUIRED FOR BUSINESS USE OF 50% OR LESS

¶ **19.63** You may not use MACRS if your business use of your car is 50% or less. The following chart lists mandatory straight line recovery rates for business use of 50% or less if the half-year or mid-quarter applies. Because of the half-year convention, the straight-line recovery period is extended from five to six years. The depreciation ceilings of ¶ 19.62 apply.

Straight-Line Half-Year Convention

Year	Rate
1	10%
2	20
3	20
4	20
5	20
6	10

In 1987, you place in service an automobile which cost $15,000. You use it 40% for business. The depreciable basis is $6,000 (40% of $15,000). The depreciation deduction in 1987 is $600 (10% of $6,000) if the half-year convention applies. If the mid-quarter convention applies, the write off depends on the quarter the car was placed in service.

Quarter	Deduction
1	$1,050
2	750
3	450
4	150

TRADE-IN OF BUSINESS AUTO

¶ **19.64** If in 1987, you trade in an auto for another auto, no depreciation may be claimed for the old auto. You claim depreciation on the new auto in the year it is placed in service. No gain or loss is recognized on a trade-in of a business auto. Generally, the basis of the new auto is the adjusted basis of the old auto plus any additional payment. However, if you trade in an auto acquired after June 18, 1984, basis for figuring ACRS or MACRS for the new auto is subject to a reduction if it was not used solely for business. To find the basis of the new car, you start with the basis of the car that was traded in, add any cash paid on the trade-in and reduce the total by the excess, if any, of (1) the total depreciation that would have been allowable if the old auto had been used solely for business or investment over (2) the total of the depreciation actually allowed. The same reduction rule applies to involuntary conversion of an auto.

RECAPTURE OF ACRS DEDUCTIONS ON BUSINESS AUTO

¶ **19.65** If you use your car more than 50% for business in the year you place it in service, you may use ACRS or MACRS. If business use drops to 50% or less in the second, third, fourth, fifth or sixth year, earlier ACRS deductions must be recaptured and reported as ordinary income. In the year in which business use drops to 50% or less, you must recapture excess depreciation for all prior years. Excess depreciation is the difference between (1) the amount of ACRS deductions allowed in previous years, including the first-year expensing deduction, if any, and (2) the amount of depreciation that would have been allowed if you claimed straight line depreciation based on a six-year recovery period. *See* ¶ 19.63 for straight line rates.

1. During July 1984, you buy for $18,000 a van weighing 8,000 pounds for business use. The van is subject to the more than 50% test, but because it weighs over 6,000 pounds, the $4,000/$6,000 depreciation limits (¶ 19.61) do not apply. Under ACRS, you completely write off its cost over its three-year recovery period (1984, 1985, 1986). During 1987, you use the van 50% for business and 50% for personal purposes. In 1987, you must recapture excess depreciation for 1984–1986 as follows:

Total ACRS depreciation claimed in prior years		$18,000
Allowable straight line rate over 5-year period (*see* ¶ 19.63)		
1984—10% of $18,000	$1,800	
1985—20% of $18,000	3,600	
1986—20% of $18,000	3,600	9,000
Excess recaptured (ACRS less straight line)		$9,000

In 1987, $9,000 is reported as income and the unrecovered basis of the van treated as $9,000. In 1987, straight line depreciation is $1,800 (original unadjusted basis of $18,000 × 20% fourth-year straight line percent × 50% business use in 1987).

2. Same facts as in example (1) except that in 1988 and 1989, the truck is used exclusively in business. The 1988 depreciation deduction is $3,600 (20% fifth-year straight line rate × $18,000). In 1989, depreciation is $1,800 (10% sixth-year percentage × $18,000).

Recapture is computed on Form 4797 which must be attached to Form 1040. The 50% business use test and recapture rule applies only to cars, trucks, and airplanes placed in service after June 18, 1984. There is an exception for trucks and other specialty vehicles listed at ¶19.67. If you did not use ACRS but instead elected straight line recovery over three, five, or 12 years, the recapture rules do not apply.

Recapture applies where business use is 50% or less in any of the first six years. This means that even if the entire cost of your vehicle has been written off under ACRS within three years, recapture may occur (*see* example below).

Any recaptured amount increases the basis of the property. To compute depreciation for the year in which business use drops to 50% or less, and for later years within the six-year straight line recovery period, you apply the straight line rates shown at ¶19.63.

RECAPTURE OF INVESTMENT CREDIT ON BUSINESS AUTOMOBILES

¶ 19.66 Recapture is triggered if during the recovery period: (1) the percentage of business-investment use drops below the percentage used for the year in which the car was placed in service; or (2) you dispose of the car before the end of the recovery period. A gift, exchange, trade-in, theft or destruction of a car is treated as a disposition. Further, for a car placed in service after June 18, 1984, a drop in business-investment use to 50% or less is treated as a complete disposition of the car as of January 1 of that year.

There are different recapture periods and percentages: (1) for cars on which ACRS was claimed and (2) for cars on which the mileage allowance was originally claimed. The recapture period for ACRS cars is three years starting from the first day of the month the car was placed in service. For IRS mileage allowance cars, it is the useful life elected for the car. The recapture percentage for a complete disposition is based on the number of *full years* that have passed between the first day of the month you placed the car in service and the date of disposition. For a drop in business-investment use, the recapture percentage is based on the number of *full years* between the first day of the month the car was placed in service and January 1 of the year the drop in business-investment use occurs.

Recapture percentage—ACRS cars*

If number of full years is	Recapture percentage is:
0	100 %
1	66
2	33
3 or more	0

*Where IRS mileage allowance is claimed, see Form 4255 for recapture percentage.

EXAMPLE

In July 1985, you bought a car for $20,000. You used the car 70% for business and 10% for investment purposes in 1985. You claimed ACRS and an investment credit of $540 ($675 × 80%). In October 1987, you sell the car. On your 1987 return, $178 of the credit is recaptured and reported as income. The recapture percentage is 33%. Thus, $540 × 33% is $178.

Drop in business use. A decline in business-investment use may require a full or partial recapture of the investment credit.
1. Find the percentage of the decline of business-investment use.

EXAMPLE

You claim an investment credit of $540 in 1985 when initial business use was 80% ($675 × 80%). Business use declines to 60% in 1987. The percentage decline is 25% (20/80).

2. Apply the percentage decline to the credit claimed. The resulting figure is subject to recapture.

EXAMPLE

Same facts as above. Thus, $135 (540 × 25%) is subject to recapture.

3. Apply the regular recapture percentage to the amount in step 2. Assume the recapture percentage is 33% from the above table. The recaptured amount is $33 (100 × 33%).

EXAMPLES

1. On July 2, 1985, you bought a car for $20,000 and used it 80% for business. In 1985, you claim ACRS depreciation and an investment credit of $540 ($675 × 80%). In 1986, you used the car 60% for business. There was a 25% decline in business use (20/80); 25% of the credit or $135 is subject to recapture ($540 × 25%). The recapture percentage from the table is 100%, because less than one full year passed between July 2, 1985, and January 1, 1986. Thus, on your 1986 return, you reported the $135 as income for 1986. You increased the unadjusted basis of the car by $68 (50% of the recaptured $135) before figuring your 1986 depreciation deduction.

2. Same facts as in example (1) except that business use drops from 60% in 1986 to 40% in 1987. Because business use fell to 50% or less, you figure recapture for 1987 as if the car were sold on January 1, 1987. The recapture percentage is 66%; you held the car more than one full year but less than two. Thus in 1987 you recapture $267, 66% of the unrecaptured credit of $405 ($540 credit–$135 recaptured in 1986). Increase basis of the car by $133.50 (50% of the recaptured $267) before figuring your 1987 depreciation deduction.

KEEPING RECORDS OF BUSINESS USE

¶ 19.67 Keep a log or diary or similar record of the business use of a car. Record the purpose of the business trips and mileage covered for business travel. In the record book, also note the odometer reading for the beginning and end of the taxable year. You need this data to prove business use.

The 1984 Tax Act had required the keeping of "contemporaneous" records. Although this requirement has been repealed, it is advisable to keep accurate records. If you do not have a written record of business mileage and your return is examined, you will have to convince an IRS agent of your business mileage through oral testimony. Without written evidence, you may be unable to convince an IRS agent that you use the car for business travel or that you meet the business use tests for claiming ACRS or MACRS. You may also be subject to general negligence penalties for claiming deductions that you cannot prove you incurred.

Mileage records are not required for vehicles that are unlikely to be used for personal purposes, such as, delivery trucks with seating only for the driver or with a folding jump seat, flat bed trucks, dump trucks, garbage trucks, passenger buses (capacity of at least 20), school buses, ambulances or hearses, tractors and other specialized farm vehicles, combines, marked police or fire vehicles, unmarked law enforcement vehicles that are officially authorized for use, and moving vans if personal use is limited by the employer to travel from an employee's home to a move site.

Further, unless the IRS provides otherwise in regulations, mileage records are not required for taxicabs or other vehicles that are used substantially all of the time for transporting persons or property for hire.

Employees using company cars are not required to keep mileage records if (1) a written company policy allows them to use the car for commuting and no other personal driving other than personal errands while commuting home or (2) a written company policy bars all personal driving except for minor stops for lunch between business travel.

LEASED BUSINESS AUTOS: DEDUCTIONS AND INCOME

¶ 19.68 If you lease rather than purchase a car for business use, you may deduct the lease charges as a business expense deduction if you use the car exclusively for business. If you use the car also for personal driving, you may deduct only the lease payments allocated to business travel. You should also keep a record of business use, *see* ¶19.67.

Added income. If you leased the car after June 18, 1984, for at least 30 days, you also have to report an amount as income. Income is imposed to limit your deduction of lease payments to the approximate depreciation ceiling levels placed on deductions for purchased autos. The added income should not exceed your lease deductions. If you do not use the car exclusively for business, reportable income is allocated for business use. Further, if business use is 50% or less a second additional income amount is imposed. *See* IRS Publication 917 for how to make the computation of added income.

20

INVESTMENT AND OTHER NONBUSINESS EXPENSES

	See ¶		See ¶
New tax law pointers	20.1	Deducting legal costs	20.4
Checklist of deductible investment expenses	20.2	Qualified group legal services plans	20.5
Costs of tax returns preparation, tax refunds, and tax audits	20.3		

¶ **20.1** Under the new law, the 2% AGI floor limits the deductible expenses discussed in this chapter, such as investment expenses and other expenses of producing and collecting income; expenses of maintaining income-producing property; expenses of tax return preparation, refunds, and audits; and legal expenses.

EXAMPLE
In 1987, you pay deductible investment management fees of $1,500; a tax preparation fee of $500; and a safe deposit box fee of $40. Your other miscellaneous expense deductions subject to the 2% floor are $500. Your adjusted gross income is $80,000. Your deduction after applying the 2% AGI floor is $940.

Investment management fees	$1,500
Tax preparation fee	500
Safe deposit box fee	40
Other miscellaneous expenses	500
	$2,540
Less 2% of $80,000	1,600
Total deductible	$ 940

Expenses of earning royalty or rental income may be deducted directly from royalty or rental income, rather than as itemized deductions deductible from adjusted gross income (see ¶9.1 and ¶13.8).

CHECKLIST OF DEDUCTIBLE INVESTMENT EXPENSES

¶ **20.2** The following are investment expenses that are deductible as miscellaneous expenses.

Accounting fees for keeping record of investment income.

Fees for collecting interest and dividends. Also deductible are fees paid to a bank that acts as dividend agent in an automatic dividend reinvestment plan of a publicly-owned corporation. Costs of collecting tax-exempt interest are not deductible; expenses deducted on an estate tax return are also not deductible. Fees paid to a broker to acquire securities are not deductible but are added to the cost of the securities. Commissions and fees paid by an investor on the sale of securities reduces the selling price; a dealer, however, may deduct selling commissions as business expenses.

Fees to set up or administer an IRA. The fees must be billed and paid separately from the regular IRA contribution.

Guardian fees or fees of committee for a ward or minor incurred in producing or collecting income belonging to the ward or minor or in managing income-producing property of the ward or minor.

Investment management or counsel fees. But fees allocated to advice dealing with tax-exempt obligations are not deductible.

Legal costs, see ¶20.3.

Mutual fund custodian fees paid for services in collecting and reinvesting dividends, keeping records, and holding the shares. However, fees paid to the sponsor of the plan when entering the fund are *not* deductible, but are capital costs added to the cost of the shares.

Premiums and expenses on indemnity bonds for the replacement of missing securities. If part of the expenses are refunded in the year the expenses are paid, only the excess expense is deductible. A refund in a later year is taxable income to the extent the expenses were deducted and reduced your tax. See ¶12.14.

Proxy fight expenses where the dispute involves legitimate corporate policy issues, not a frivolous desire to gain membership on the board.

Safe deposit box rental fee or home safe to hold your securities, but not if it is used to hold personal effects or tax-exempt securities.

Salary of a secretary, bookkeeper, or other employee hired to keep track of your investment income.

Subscriptions to investment services.

Travel costs of trip away from home to look after investments, confer with your attorney, accountant, trustee, or investment counsel about the production of income.

Expenses incurred in managing property held for income are deductible, even if the property does not currently produce income. Similarly, expenses incurred to avoid further losses or to reduce anticipated losses on such property are deductible.

Nondeductible travel costs. Investors may not deduct the cost of trips to investigate prospective rental property. Further, the IRS does not generally allow deductions for the cost of travel to stockholder meetings. However, in a private letter ruling, one stockholder was allowed a deduction. He owned substantial stockholdings which had lost value because his corporation had been issuing stock to the public at prices below book value. He went to the annual shareholders' meeting to present a resolution requesting management to stop the practice; the resolution passed. Under such circumstances, the IRS held that the trip was directly related to his stockholdings and allowed him the deduction. The IRS distinguished his case from a ruling which bars most stockholders from deducting the cost of travel to an annual meeting. Here the stockholder's purpose in getting the resolution passed was more closely related to his investment activities than if he had attended the meeting, as most stockholders do, to pick up data for future investment moves.

Investors may not deduct travel costs of attending a convention, seminar, or similar meeting that deals with investments, financial planning, or the production or collection of income. Convention costs are deductible only in the case of a business activity. See ¶19.33.

Home office of an investor. An investor may not deduct the costs of an office at home unless investing constitutes a business. For example, you get no deduction for use of a home office in your residence where you read financial periodicals and reports and clip bond coupons. These activities are not considered a business.

229

EXAMPLE

In his home office, Moller spent 40 hours a week managing four stock portfolios worth over $13 million. However, an appeals court held he could not deduct home office expenses despite the time spent there managing his investment. To deduct home office expenses, Moller had to show he was a trader. A trader is in a business; an investor is not. A trader buys and sells frequently to catch daily market swings. An investor buys securities for capital appreciation and income without regard to daily market developments. Here, Moller was an investor. He was primarily interested in the long-term growth potential of stock. He did not earn his income from the short-term turnovers of stocks. He had no significant trading profits.

Hobby expenses. For the limitations on deducting hobby expenses, *see* ¶5.9.

COSTS OF TAX RETURN PREPARATION, TAX REFUNDS, AND TAX AUDITS

¶ **20.3** Subject to the 2% AGI floor, you may deduct your payment of fees charged for:

The preparation of your tax return or refund claim involving any tax, and

Representing you before any examination, trial, or other type of hearing involving any tax.

The term "any tax" covers not only income taxes but also gift, property, estate, or any other tax, whether the taxing authority be federal, state, or municipal.

Deductible fees for services of tax practitioners are claimed as itemized deductions. The deduction is claimed on the tax return for the year in which the fee was paid. For example, if in March 1987, you pay an accountant to prepare your 1986 return, the fee is deductible on your 1987 return. If the tax was directly imposed on your business income, the fee is deductible as a business expense. One exception to this rule is applied to the fees involving federal or state income taxes on self-employed business or professional income. The IRS insists that the expense is a nonbusiness itemized deduction. *See* ¶5.5.

> There have been disputes over the deductibility of fees charged for general tax advice unconnected to the preparation of a return or a tax controversy. A deduction for fees charged for general tax advice not within these areas may be disallowed, unless the fee can be related to the production of business or investment income or the management of income-producing property. The following case distinguished between advice covering tax liabilities and advice concerning the tax consequences of a possible future transaction. According to the court, no deduction was allowed for that part of the fee covering the future transaction.

EXAMPLE

Stockholders of a closely held corporation negotiated with a publicly held company for a tax free exchange of their stock. An accounting firm asked the IRS for a ruling to determine whether the exchange would be taxable or tax free. The accounting fee was $8,602. Of this, $7,602 was for the ruling and $1,000 was for fixing the basis of the new stock. The stockholders deducted the full fee, which the IRS disallowed because the fee was not charged for the preparation of a tax return or representation at a contest of a tax liability.

The Tax Court disagreed in part. The fee paid for the ruling is deductible; it was connected with determining the extent of the stockholders' liability, if any, in the proposed exchange. But a deduction cannot be allowed for the $1,000 charged to determine the basis of the new stock. This was computed for the stockholders' information, not for determining tax liability. The disallowed fee could be added to the cost basis of the stock.

An accountant's fee for arranging the purchase of real estate was deductible where the purchase was part of a plan to minimize taxes.

EXAMPLE

Collins paid an accountant $4,511 for tax advice to reduce his tax on a sweepstake winning. He was advised to buy an apartment house

under a contract obligation to make a large prepayment of interest (which was deductible under prior law). The accountant helped prepare contracts, escrow agreements, and other documents to implement the plan. Collins' deduction of his accountant's fee as a business expense was disallowed. The IRS held that the fee was a capital expense in acquiring the property. The Tax Court disagreed. The accountant was hired to minimize Collins' income tax through the purchase of the building and the terms of the purchase. Therefore, his fee was deductible.

> The purchase of *Your Income Tax* in 1987 is deductible as an itemized deduction in 1987. The cost, when included with other miscellaneous deductions, is subject to the 2% AGI floor.

Personal checking account fees. These are nondeductible, even though the checks are used for tax records. Similarly, the per check fee on an interest-bearing NOW account is nondeductible. However, fees charged on a bank money market account may be deductible if check writing is severely limited and writing excess checks forfeits the status of the account as a money market account.

Appraisal fees. Fees to establish the amount of such tax deductions as a casualty loss or a charitable deduction are claimed as miscellaneous deductions. Appraisal fees in connection with the purchase of your principal residence are not deductible but are added to the basis of your house.

For deductibility of legal costs, *see* ¶20.4.

DEDUCTING LEGAL COSTS

¶ **20.4** A legal expense is generally deductible if the dispute or issue arose in the course of your business or employment or involves income-producing property. Legal expenses for personal matters are generally not deductible. If you are self-employed, your deduction for legal fees arising from a business-related dispute is claimed on Schedule C. Legal expenses related to your job as an employee or to investment activities are claimed as miscellaneous itemized deductions subject to the 2% AGI floor. The IRS may disallow the deduction on the grounds that the legal dispute does not directly arise from the business or income activity. Thus, for example, the cost of contesting suspension of a driver's license for drunken driving is not deductible despite a business need for the license; the suspension arose out of a personal rather than a business-related activity. A deduction may also be disallowed where the dispute involves title to property. Further, the deductibility of a legal expense may depend on whether the damages received are taxable.

For the deductibility of legal fees in organizing a new business, *see* ¶5.10.

Employment suits. The following cases illustrate when legal costs for employment-related matters may be deductible.

EXAMPLES

1. Waldheim, a corporate officer, director, and stockholder, incurred legal fees in a suit to prevent his discharge. His legal costs were deductible.

2. An Army officer was allowed to deduct the cost of successfully contesting a court martial based on charges of misrepresentations in official statements and reports. He would have lost his position had he been convicted.

3. Tellier, a securities dealer, was convicted of mail fraud and securities fraud. He was allowed to deduct legal fees as business expenses related to his securities business. That he was found guilty of the criminal charge does not affect the deductibility of the expense. The deduction of legal expenses is not disallowed on public policy grounds since a defendant has a constitutional right to an attorney.

4. In an alimony action, Gilmore was successful in preventing his wife from securing stock and taking control of corporations from which he earned practically all his income. He was not allowed to deduct his legal costs; the dispute did not arise from an income-producing activity; the fact that an adverse determination of the dispute might affect his income did not make the legal expenses deductible.

5. A doctor who attempted to bribe a judge to suspend his sentence for tax evasion was convicted of the bribe attempt and lost his license to practice medicine. He could not deduct his defense costs. His prac-

tice of medicine did not give rise to his need for an attorney. The fact that the conviction affected his ability to earn income was merely a consequence of personal litigation.

6. Siket, a police officer, was not allowed to deduct expenses of successfully defending a criminal charge of assault while off duty. The origin of the claim was personal, even though a conviction might have been detrimental to his position as a police officer. The arrest did not occur within the performance of his duties; he was off duty and in a different municipality at the time of the arrest.

7. The president of Weight Watchers International, Inc., Jean Nidetch, had a dispute with her fellow directors regarding management of the company. Fearing that her position as president was in jeopardy, she planned a proxy fight, and to solidify her position replaced trustees of a family trust who sided with the other directors. Later, the dispute was settled and the proxy fight never took place. The deduction for $102,500 in legal fees incurred in replacing the trustees was disallowed by the IRS. The Tax Court allowed the deduction. Although a proxy fight never actually took place, the legal expenses of the trustee substitution were a crucial first step in an anticipated proxy contest. To deny deductibility of those expenses while allowing a deduction for actual proxy fight costs would penalize those who are able to amicably settle their disputes.

The legal costs of defending against disbarment are deductible.

> *Legal fees for tax advice and tax return preparation.* You may deduct legal fees paid in 1987 for preparing your tax return or refund claim, or for representing you in a trial, examination, or hearing involving any tax. *See* ¶ 20.3. Legal fees incurred in defending against a tax imposed by a foreign country are also deductible. However, legal fees incurred in reducing an assessment on property to pay for local benefits are not deductible; the fees are capital expenses which are added to basis.

A deductible legal fee, when included with other miscellaneous deductions, is subject to the 2% AGI floor.

Libel suits. The IRS holds that compensatory damages received for injury to personal reputation are tax free; damages received for injury to business reputation are taxable (*see* ¶ 12.16). Thus, legal expenses allocable to an award or settlement for injury to personal reputation are not deductible. If the libel action is for damage to business reputation, legal expenses are deductible as business expenses.

The Tax Court and an appeals court hold that if the libel is considered a "personal" injury under state law, damages allocable to the libel claim are tax free, even if the libel results in lost business income. Thus, under this approach, legal fees related to the libel award would not be deductible.

Will contests and wrongful death actions. Legal costs of a will contest are generally not deductible because an inheritance is not taxable income. Similarly, legal fees incurred to collect a wrongful death award (which is tax free income) are not deductible.

EXAMPLE
Parker, an heir who was left out of his grandmother's estate, sued to recover his inheritance. In a settlement, he received his share of his grandmother's property plus income earned on that property. The allocable portion of legal fees attributed to the income, which was taxable, was deductible; the balance of the fees was not deductible.

Title issues or disputes. Legal costs related to the acquisition of property or to the determination of title to property, whether such property is business or personal, are nondeductible capital expenditures. They are added to the basis of the property. For example, litigation costs to fix the value of shares of dissident shareholders is not deductible because it is related to the purchase of the stock and are part of the cost of acquisition.

Legal fees incurred to quiet title to stock were also held to be nondeductible.

Where a dispute over property does not involve title, such as in a recovery of income-producing securities loaned as collateral, the Tax Court holds that legal fees are deductible.

Personal injury or marital actions. Where you recover taxable damages, you may deduct the legal fees; if the damages are not taxable, legal fees are not deductible (*see* ¶ 12.16). For legal expenses incurred in marital actions, *see* ¶ 1.36.

Estate tax planning fee. Not all of an attorney's fee for estate tax planning services may be deductible in 1987. Estate tax planning usually involves tax and nontax matters. To the extent that the services do not cover tax advice or income-producing property, the fee is not deductible. A bill allocating a fee between deductible and nondeductible services may help support a deduction claimed for the deductible portion of the fee.

EXAMPLE
Estate planning for a doctor involved the drawing of wills, trusts, property transfers, and gift tax returns. The doctor deducted the lawyer's fee of $2,000 in full. The IRS disallowed the deduction because the fee was not allocated between tax and nontax matters. The Tax Court viewed the IRS's position as a concession that fees are deductible to the extent allocable to tax advice in estate planning. All the doctor failed to do was to show how much of the fee was for tax advice. This the majority of the Tax Court did for him. It figured from the evidence that 20% of the attorney's time was spent on tax matters and so allowed a deduction of 20% of the bill.

> Your lawyer should bill you separately or itemize fees for services connected with deductible items (collection of taxable alimony or separate maintenance payments; preparation of tax returns, tax audits, and tax litigation) and nondeductible capital items (expenses incurred in purchase of property or dispute over title).

Recovery of attorney's fees from government. See ¶ 38.10.

QUALIFIED GROUP LEGAL SERVICES PLANS

¶ 20.5 As a tax free fringe benefit, a company may provide employees and their dependents legal services through a qualified group legal service plan.

A qualified legal service plan must be a separate written plan established for the exclusive benefit of the employees and their spouses and dependents; it must not discriminate in favor of officers, shareholders, or highly compensated employees. The plan may be funded by insurance or a special trust, or the company through the plan may pay the attorney providing legal services. The IRS must have notice of the plan within certain time limits.

If you are not required to include the value of legal services in your gross income, you may not claim a deduction for legal services even though you would have been entitled to one under ¶ 20.4 had you paid for the legal services directly.

At the time this book went to press, the exclusion for qualified group legal services was scheduled to expire at the end of 1987. *See* the Supplement for late developments.

21

DEDUCTIBLE EDUCATION COSTS

Under the new law, deductible educational costs, when added to other miscellaneous expense deductions, are subject to the 2% AGI floor. See ¶19.3. Further, costs of travel as a form of education are no longer deductible. See ¶21.9.

GENERAL RULES FOR DEDUCTING EDUCATION COSTS

¶ 21.1 To deduct education costs, you must show that the following conditions are met:
1. You are employed or self-employed;
2. You meet the minimum requirements of your job, business, or profession; and
3. The course maintains or improves your job skills, or you are required by your employer or by law to take the course to keep your present salary or position.

The details of these requirements are explained at ¶21.2.

The cost of courses preparing you for a new profession or for meeting the minimum requirements for your job are not deductible, even if you take them to improve your skills or to meet your employer's requirements. This rule prevents the deduction of law school costs, *see* ¶21.3.

That courses lead to a degree will not bar a deduction provided the above three tests are met. If the courses lead to a change of position or promotion within the same occupation, the deduction for their costs will not be disallowed if your new duties involve the same general type of work.

> Courses qualifying for the deduction may range from refresher courses to advanced academic courses. They may be correspondence school or vocational courses and even private tutoring.

DEDUCTION TESTS FOR EDUCATION COSTS

¶ 21.2 Employment test. Educational costs are not deductible if you are unemployed or inactive in a business or profession. The cost of "brushup" courses taken in anticipation of resuming work are also not deductible. However, in one case, a court allowed an unemployed teacher to deduct the cost of tuition, fees, and books where the IRS conceded that the teacher, although unemployed, remained in the teaching profession while attending college classes.

You are not considered unemployed when you take courses during a vacation or temporary leave of absence. See ¶21.7.

EXAMPLE
A substitute teacher left his job to go to Norway for doctoral studies in linguistics and anthropology. The IRS disallowed his deduction for the cost of travel, room, board, and books, claiming that he abandoned teaching before he went abroad. Also, the studies abroad fitted him for a new career. The Tax Court disagreed. He did not abandon his teaching profession as evidenced by these facts: He applied for work at an American school in Oslo and was available for substitute teaching,

although he only taught one day. He also made arrangements to teach on his return. Furthermore, his studies were appropriate and helpful to his career as a teacher of language and social studies.

If you are practicing your profession, the cost of courses leading to a specialty within that profession are deductible.

EXAMPLE
A practicing dentist returned to school full time to study orthodontics while continuing his practice on a part-time basis. When he finished his training, he limited his work to orthodontics. The IRS ruled he may deduct the cost of his studies. His post-graduate schooling improved his professional skills as a dentist. It did not qualify him for a new profession.

Minimum standards. You may not deduct the cost of courses taken to meet the minimum requirements of your job. The minimum requirements of a position are based on a review of your employer's standards, the laws and regulations of the state you live in, and the standards of your profession or business. That you are presently employed does not in itself prove that you have met the minimum standards for your job.

> *Maintaining or improving skills.* That you are established in your position and that persons in similar positions usually take such education indicates that the courses are taken to maintain and improve job skills. However, the IRS may not allow a deduction for a general education course that is a prerequisite for a job-related course. If, as a consequence of taking a job-related course, you receive a substantial advancement and the IRS questions the deduction of the course costs, be prepared to prove that you took the course primarily to maintain or improve job skills.

If minimum standards change after you enter a job or profession, you are required to meet only the standards that existed when you entered. The minimum standards for teachers are discussed at ¶21.5.

Employer's requirement. If, to retain your present job or rate of pay, your employer requires you to obtain further education, you may deduct the cost of the courses. The fact that you also qualified for a raise in pay or a substantial advancement in your position after completing the courses should not bar the deduction.

The employer's requirement must be for a bona fide business reason, not merely to benefit you. Only the minimum courses necessary for the retention of your job or rate of pay is considered by the IRS as taken to meet your employer's requirement. You must show any courses beyond your employer's minimum requirements were taken to maintain or improve your job skills.

College tuition. You may not deduct tuition costs of undergraduate courses in preparation for a career or employment.

LAW SCHOOL COSTS

¶ 21.3 The IRS does not allow deductions for law school courses because they qualify a person for a new profession. Courts generally support the IRS position.

Bar review courses. The costs of bar review courses and taking the bar exam are not deductible, even where you are seeking admission to the bar of a second state.

An attorney who practices law in one state may not deduct the later costs of getting a degree necessary to the practice of law in another state.

Additional legal education. A lawyer must practice his profession before the expenses of further legal education are deductible. Compare these cases:

EXAMPLES

1. A young lawyer, newly admitted to the Illinois bar, could not deduct the cost of courses for a masters degree in tax law, which he started the fall after he graduated from law school. According to the Tax Court, he never stopped being a full-time student. He earned income to help defray his educational expenses; he did not incur the educational expense to improve his skills as a tax return preparer.

2. The Tax Court allowed a lawyer to deduct educational expenses to obtain an LL.M. degree where he worked for a law firm as a beginning lawyer during the summer between graduating from law school and starting work on the LL.M. degree. He was admitted to the state bar before he graduated from law school, and the work he did during the summer was normally assigned to beginning lawyers rather than to law students.

COURSES TAKEN BY DOCTORS AND NURSES

¶ 21.4 The IRS allows general practitioners to deduct the cost of short refresher courses, even though the courses relate to specialized fields. These courses maintain or improve skills and do not qualify the doctor for a new profession.

A practicing psychiatrist may deduct the cost of attending an accredited psychoanalytic institute to qualify to practice psychoanalysis. A social worker has also been allowed a deduction for the cost of psychoanalysis. In one case, a psychiatrist was allowed by the Tax Court to deduct the cost of personal therapy sessions conducted through telephone conversations and tape cassettes. The court was convinced that the therapy improved his job skills by eliminating psychological blind spots that prevented him from understanding his patient's problems.

> A doctor was allowed by a court to deduct the cost of law school courses. He was a forensic pathologist, and he needed the law background to help in his investigation of sudden, violent, and suspicious deaths for possible criminal prosecution.

A licensed practical nurse may not deduct the costs of a college program which qualifies her as a "physician's assistant," which is a new job. Physician's assistants and practical nurses are subject to different registration and certification requirements under state law, and, more important, the physician's assistant may perform duties, such as physical examinations and minor surgery, which go beyond practical nursing duties.

COURSES TAKEN BY TEACHERS

¶ 21.5 You must meet the minimum level of education for your present position as set down by law or regulations before you may deduct the cost of courses. The educational requirements are those that existed when you were hired. If your employer set no tests fixing a minimum educational level, you meet the minimum requirements when you become a member of the faculty. Whether you are a faculty member depends on the custom of your employer. You are ordinarily considered

a faculty member if (1) you have tenure, or your service is counted toward tenure, (2) the institution is contributing toward a retirement plan based on your employment (other than Social Security or similar program), or (3) you have a vote in faculty affairs.

EXAMPLES

1. A state requires a bachelor's degree for beginning high school teachers, including 30 credit hours of education courses. To retain the position, a teacher must complete a fifth year of preparation within 10 years after beginning employment. If enough teachers with these minimum requirements cannot be found, individuals may be hired if they have completed a minimum of 90 semester hours of college work. However, to remain as a teacher, such an individual must get a bachelor's degree and complete the required education courses within three years. Under these facts, a bachelor's degree is considered to be the minimum educational requirement for qualification as a high school teacher in the state. The IRS says that an individual with a bachelor's degree has met the minimum educational requirements even without completion of 30 credit hours of education courses. Costs of taking education courses are deductible.

2. Because of a shortage of applicants meeting the requirements stated above, Smith is employed as a high school teacher although he has only 90 semester hours of college work toward his bachelor's degree. After his employment, he takes courses leading to a bachelor's degree. These courses (including any courses in professional education) constitute education required to meet the minimum educational requirements. The costs for such education are not deductible.

3. Same facts as above but, after Smith is employed and gets his B.A. degree, the state changes its minimum requirements for beginning teachers to five years of college preparation. As the requirements were changed after he began employment, they do not affect Smith, and he may deduct the cost of his fifth year's courses.

Employed teacher taking courses for teaching certificate. That you are already employed as a teacher, with all the responsibilities of a teacher, may not establish that you have met the minimum educational requirements. A school system which requires a bachelor's degree before granting a permanent teaching certificate may grant temporary or provisional certificates after a person has completed a number of college credits. Renewal of the provisional certificate may be conditioned on the teacher's continuing education for a bachelor's degree. In this case, the IRS will disallow a deduction for the educational costs. The minimum requirements are not met until the teacher has the degree. Current Tax Court decisions follow the IRS position, although in the past the court took a contrary view.

The IRS has allowed a teacher with a provisional certificate to deduct educational costs under these circumstances: She was a fully qualified teacher with a permanent certificate. She moved to another state where the educational requirements for a permanent certificate were greater. The IRS said she was merely fulfilling her new employer's requirements.

> Elementary and secondary school teachers may deduct the cost of courses taken to make any of the following job changes: (1) elementary to secondary school classroom teacher; (2) classroom teacher in one subject (such as mathematics) to classroom teacher in another subject (such as art); (3) classroom teacher to guidance counselor; (4) classroom teacher to principal.
>
> The IRS held that a "discussion leader" in a college adult education program could not deduct the costs of a master's degree program that led to certification as a high school guidance counselor because this was a new business. The Tax Court disagreed, holding that the responsibilities of discussion leader are similar to the responsibilities of a school counselor. The court distinguished an earlier decision in which a classroom paraprofessional assistant was not allowed to deduct education costs that qualified her as a classroom teacher. The court considered this as a change in professions. A paraprofessional does not have the same control and responsibilities for classroom work as a classroom teacher.

PROFESSOR'S RESEARCH EXPENSES

¶ 21.6 Research costs incurred by a college professor are deductible under this condition: He or she is appointed to lecture and teach with the understanding that research in the field will be carried on with the goal of incorporating the findings in teaching and writing. If this test is met, the IRS is satisfied that the research is an express requirement of the teaching position and that research expenses are deductible job expenses.

Deductible research costs include traveling expenses and stenographic and other costs of preparing a manuscript. If income is later realized from the research in the form of lecture or royalty fees, the previously deducted research costs may not again be deducted in determining the income realized from the research.

Expenses of a research project undertaken for a scholarly publication are not deductible if the research is not linked to an income-producing activity or job requirement.

Research expenses incurred in writing a textbook for profit are not deductible but are added to the cost of writing the book.

LEAVE OF ABSENCE TO TAKE COURSES

¶ 21.7 The IRS will allow a deduction for full-time graduate courses taken by a teacher during a leave of absence if these conditions are met: (1) the absence must not be for more than one year; and (2) upon completion of the education courses, the same type of employment must be resumed, although you may take a job with a new employer. You may also have to show that you had more than a vague intention to go back to your employment, for example, that you were actually negotiating for a new teaching position and that, in fact, you did obtain a position soon after finishing the graduate courses.

The IRS has also applied the one-year test to those who leave jobs to pursue MBA degrees.

> The Tax Court considered the IRS "one year" absence rule too narrow and inflexible and allowed a school principal who resigned his position to deduct the cost of full-time courses taken over a three-year period. Similarly, a manager who quit his job to pursue a two-year MBA course was allowed to deduct the cost of his courses. In one case, the IRS did not object to a teacher's two-year absence from the job.

HOW TO DEDUCT EDUCATION COSTS

¶ 21.8 If your courses meet the requirements explained in ¶21.2, you may deduct the following education costs:
1. Tuition, textbooks, fees, equipment, and other aids required by the courses.
2. Certain transportation costs described below.
3. Travel to and from a school away from home.
4. Living expenses (food and lodging) while at the school away from home. The IRS will not disallow traveling expenses to attend a school away from home or in a foreign country merely because you could have taken the course in a local school. But it may disallow your board and lodging expenses at the school if your stay lasts longer than a year.

Transportation expenses. On days you work and attend courses which qualify for an education expense deduction, if your place of employment and school are located within the same general area, you may deduct the cost of travel between your office and school. If you stop off at home on your way to school, you may deduct the cost of travel from your home to the school to the extent it does not exceed the cost you would have incurred in going directly from work to school. If your school is located beyond the general area of your principal place of business, you may deduct your round-trip transportation expenses. The cost of traveling between your home and school on a nonworking day is not deductible.

EXAMPLES

1. After work, you attend classes in the same city in which your office is located. You deduct the costs of going from your office to school, provided you go directly to school.
2. You work in Newark, New Jersey, and attend night classes in New York City. You may deduct your round-trip transportation expenses.

Transportation expenses include tolls and parking fees.

Travel and living expenses away from home. "Away from home" as explained at ¶19.25 has a special tax meaning. You are not away from home unless you are away overnight.

Expenses of sightseeing, social visiting, and entertaining while taking the courses are not deductible. If your main purpose in going to the vicinity of the school is to take a vacation or for other personal reasons, you may deduct only the cost of the courses and your living expenses while attending school. You may not deduct any part of your travel costs.

To determine the purpose of your trip, an IRS agent will pay close attention to the amount of time devoted to personal activities relative to the time devoted to the courses.

The way you deduct educational expenses depends on your occupational status. If you are:

An employee—If your educational expenses are reimbursed by your employer and the reimbursement was included as pay on your Form W-2, you may claim an offsetting deduction from gross income. Reimbursements that are not reported on Form W-2 do not have to be reported as income if the expenses equal or exceed the reimbursement and you do not deduct the expenses. If your employer pays the tuition directly to the institution, you are not required to report the payment in any way on your return.

Unreimbursed costs, such as travel costs, tuition, books, fees, and equipment are deductible only if you claim itemized deductions. They are claimed as miscellaneous itemized deductions and are subject to the 2% AGI floor when included with other miscellaneous deductions.

Payments for substitute teachers. Where a school system has a policy of paying teachers full salary during sabbatical leaves, a teacher on sabbatical may be required to pay a fixed percentage of salary into a fund to pay substitute teachers. A teacher reports the full amount of the salary paid during the sabbatical but may claim payments to the fund as miscellaneous itemized deductions subject to the 2% AGI floor.

An outside salesperson—You deduct all of your unreimbursed education costs as miscellaneous itemized deductions subject to the 2% AGI floor. If you have reimbursed expenses, the rules above for employees apply.

A self-employed business owner or professional—You deduct all of your education costs on Schedule C. You also attach a statement to your return explaining your deduction and the relationship of the education to your position.

A veteran receiving educational benefits from the V.A.—According to the IRS, educational expenses reimbursed by the V.A. are not deductible. This does not apply to a living stipend paid without regard to amounts spent for education.

TRIP TAKEN FOR EDUCATIONAL PURPOSES

¶ 21.9 Under a new law, no deduction is allowed for costs of travel claimed as a form of education. For example, no deduction will be allowed to a French teacher traveling to France to maintain general familiarity with the French language and culture, or to a social studies teacher traveling to learn about or photograph people and customs.

A deduction may still be allowed for travel that qualifies as a business expense. For example, if a teacher must travel abroad to do research that cannot be done elsewhere, the travel costs are deductible because the nontravel research or course costs are deductible business expenses. Such unreimbursed travel costs away from home are deductible only as an itemized deduction subject to the 2% AGI floor. Meal expenses are subject to the 80% cost limitation of ¶19.24.

22

FIGURING YOUR TAX LIABILITY

¶ 22.1 There are two ways to figure your 1987 tax liability: By using the tax tables beginning on page 237 or by using the tax schedules below. You will not have to compute your tax mathematically if you use the tax tables. You use the tables if your taxable income is less than $50,000.

To use the tables, you first figure your taxable income. Then turn to your income bracket and look for the tax liability listed in the column for your filing status. Filing status (single, married filing jointly, head of household, married filing separately) is discussed in chapter 1.

You may *not* use the tax tables and must use the schedules if you claim the foreign income exclusion (*see* ¶36.2) or file for a short period due to a change of accounting period.

Estates and trusts may not use the tax tables.

The amount of your tax liability may be reduced by credits; for details, *see* chapter 24.

Figuring taxable income. By following the line-by-line steps of your tax return, you reach taxable income. If you do not claim itemized deductions, taxable income is adjusted gross income reduced by the standard deduction and exemptions.

If you do claim itemized deductions, taxable income is adjusted gross income reduced by itemized deductions and exemptions.

EXAMPLES

1. You are single and have an adjusted gross income of $15,000. You claim one personal exemption and the standard deduction.

Adjusted gross income		$15,000
Less: Standard deduction	$2,540	
Exemption	1,900	4,440
Taxable income		$10,560

2. You are married and have adjusted gross income of $25,000; itemized deductions of $7,000; and three exemptions.

Adjusted gross income		$25,000
Less: Itemized deductions	$7,000	
Exemptions (3)	5,700	12,700
Taxable income		$12,300

USING THE TAX RATE SCHEDULES AND TAX TABLES

¶ 22.2 You compute your 1987 tax using the tax rate schedules below if you fit into any one of these cases:

Your taxable income is $50,000 or more.

You claim the foreign income exclusion (*see* chapter 36).

Or you file for a short period due to a change of accounting period.

EXAMPLE

A head of household has taxable income of $50,000. Schedule Z

shows that the taxpayer's taxable income falls between $38,000 and $80,000.

Tax on first $38,000	$7,550
Tax on excess $12,000 at	
35%	4,200
Tax	$11,750

The 1988 tax rates. The 1988 Tax Rate Schedules may be found in the Supplement to this book.

Schedule X—Single Taxpayers

Use this schedule if you checked **Filing Status Box 1** on Form 1040—

If the amount on Form 1040, line 36 is:		Enter on Form 1040, line 37	of the amount over—
Over—	But not over—		
$0	$1,800	.......11%	$0
1,800	16,800	$198 + 15%	1,800
16,800	27,000	2,448 + 28%	16,800
27,000	54,000	5,304 + 35%	27,000
54,000	....	14,754 + 38.5%	54,000

Schedule Z—Heads of Household

Use this schedule if you checked **Filing Status Box 4** on Form 1040—

If the amount on Form 1040, line 36 is:		Enter on Form 1040, line 37	of the amount over—
Over—	But not over—		
$0	$2,500	.......11%	$0
2,500	23,000	$275 + 15%	2,500
23,000	38,000	3,350 + 28%	23,000
38,000	80,000	7,550 + 35%	38,000
80,000	....	22,250 + 38.5%	80,000

Schedule Y—Married Taxpayers and Qualifying Widows and Widowers

Married Filing Joint Returns and Qualifying Widows and Widowers

Use this schedule if you checked **Filing Status Box 2 or 5** on Form 1040—

If the amount on Form 1040, line 36 is: Over—	But not over—	Enter on Form 1040, line 38	of the amount over—
$0	$3,000	........11%	$0
3,000	28,000	$330 + 15%	3,000
28,000	45,000	4,080 + 28%	28,000
45,000	90,000	8,840 + 35%	45,000
90,000	....	24,590 + 38.5%	90,000

Married Filing Separate Returns

Use this schedule if you checked **Filing Status Box 3** on Form 1040—

If the amount on Form 1040, line 36 is: Over—	But not over—	Enter on Form 1040, line 37	of the amount over—
$0	$1,500	........11%	$0
1,500	14,000	$165 + 15%	1,500
14,000	22,500	2,040 + 28%	14,000
22,500	45,000	4,420 + 35%	22,500
45,000	....	12,295 + 38.5%	45,000

1987 Tax Table

Based on Taxable Income

For persons with taxable incomes of less than $50,000.

Example: Mr. and Mrs. Brown are filing a joint return. Their taxable income on line 36 of Form 1040 is $25,325. First, they find the $25,300-25,350 income line. Next, they find the column for married filing jointly and read down the column. The amount shown where the income line and filing status column meet is $3,679.

At least	But less than	Single	Married filing jointly *	Married filing separately	Head of a household
			Your tax is—		
25,200	25,250	4,807	3,664	5,374	3,973
25,250	25,300	4,821	3,671	5,391	3,987
25,300	25,350	4,835	(3,679)	5,409	4,001
25,350	25,400	4,849	3,686	5,426	4,015

If taxable income is—

At least	But less than	Single	Married filing jointly *	Married filing separately	Head of a household
			Your tax is—		
0	5	0	0	0	0
5	15	1	1	1	1
15	25	2	2	2	2
25	50	4	4	4	4
50	75	7	7	7	7
75	100	10	10	10	10
100	125	12	12	12	12
125	150	15	15	15	15
150	175	18	18	18	18
175	200	21	21	21	21
200	225	23	23	23	23
225	250	26	26	26	26
250	275	29	29	29	29
275	300	32	32	32	32
300	325	34	34	34	34
325	350	37	37	37	37
350	375	40	40	40	40
375	400	43	43	43	43
400	425	45	45	45	45
425	450	48	48	48	48
450	475	51	51	51	51
475	500	54	54	54	54
500	525	56	56	56	56
525	550	59	59	59	59
550	575	62	62	62	62
575	600	65	65	65	65
600	625	67	67	67	67
625	650	70	70	70	70
650	675	73	73	73	73
675	700	76	76	76	76
700	725	78	78	78	78
725	750	81	81	81	81
750	775	84	84	84	84
775	800	87	87	87	87
800	825	89	89	89	89
825	850	92	92	92	92
850	875	95	95	95	95
875	900	98	98	98	98
900	925	100	100	100	100
925	950	103	103	103	103
950	975	106	106	106	106
975	1,000	109	109	109	109

1,000

At least	But less than	Single	Married filing jointly *	Married filing separately	Head of a household
1,000	1,025	111	111	111	111
1,025	1,050	114	114	114	114
1,050	1,075	117	117	117	117
1,075	1,100	120	120	120	120
1,100	1,125	122	122	122	122
1,125	1,150	125	125	125	125
1,150	1,175	128	128	128	128
1,175	1,200	131	131	131	131
1,200	1,225	133	133	133	133
1,225	1,250	136	136	136	136
1,250	1,275	139	139	139	139
1,275	1,300	142	142	142	142
1,300	1,325	144	144	144	144
1,325	1,350	147	147	147	147
1,350	1,375	150	150	150	150
1,375	1,400	153	153	153	153

At least	But less than	Single	Married filing jointly *	Married filing separately	Head of a household
1,400	1,425	155	155	155	155
1,425	1,450	158	158	158	158
1,450	1,475	161	161	161	161
1,475	1,500	164	164	164	164
1,500	1,525	166	166	167	166
1,525	1,550	169	169	171	169
1,550	1,575	172	172	174	172
1,575	1,600	175	175	178	175
1,600	1,625	177	177	182	177
1,625	1,650	180	180	186	180
1,650	1,675	183	183	189	183
1,675	1,700	186	186	193	186
1,700	1,725	188	188	197	188
1,725	1,750	191	191	201	191
1,750	1,775	194	194	204	194
1,775	1,800	197	197	208	197
1,800	1,825	200	199	212	199
1,825	1,850	204	202	216	202
1,850	1,875	207	205	219	205
1,875	1,900	211	208	223	208
1,900	1,925	215	210	227	210
1,925	1,950	219	213	231	213
1,950	1,975	222	216	234	216
1,975	2,000	226	219	238	219

2,000

At least	But less than	Single	Married filing jointly *	Married filing separately	Head of a household
2,000	2,025	230	221	242	221
2,025	2,050	234	224	246	224
2,050	2,075	237	227	249	227
2,075	2,100	241	230	253	230
2,100	2,125	245	232	257	232
2,125	2,150	249	235	261	235
2,150	2,175	252	238	264	238
2,175	2,200	256	241	268	241
2,200	2,225	260	243	272	243
2,225	2,250	264	246	276	246
2,250	2,275	267	249	279	249
2,275	2,300	271	252	283	252
2,300	2,325	275	254	287	254
2,325	2,350	279	257	291	257
2,350	2,375	282	260	294	260
2,375	2,400	286	263	298	263
2,400	2,425	290	265	302	265
2,425	2,450	294	268	306	268
2,450	2,475	297	271	309	271
2,475	2,500	301	274	313	274
2,500	2,525	305	276	317	277
2,525	2,550	309	279	321	281
2,550	2,575	312	282	324	284
2,575	2,600	316	285	328	288
2,600	2,625	320	287	332	292
2,625	2,650	324	290	336	296
2,650	2,675	327	293	339	299
2,675	2,700	331	296	343	303

At least	But less than	Single	Married filing jointly *	Married filing separately	Head of a household
2,700	2,725	335	298	347	307
2,725	2,750	339	301	351	311
2,750	2,775	342	304	354	314
2,775	2,800	346	307	358	318
2,800	2,825	350	309	362	322
2,825	2,850	354	312	366	326
2,850	2,875	357	315	369	329
2,875	2,900	361	318	373	333
2,900	2,925	365	320	377	337
2,925	2,950	369	323	381	341
2,950	2,975	372	326	384	344
2,975	3,000	376	329	388	348

3,000

At least	But less than	Single	Married filing jointly *	Married filing separately	Head of a household
3,000	3,050	382	334	394	354
3,050	3,100	389	341	401	361
3,100	3,150	397	349	409	369
3,150	3,200	404	356	416	376
3,200	3,250	412	364	424	384
3,250	3,300	419	371	431	391
3,300	3,350	427	379	439	399
3,350	3,400	434	386	446	406
3,400	3,450	442	394	454	414
3,450	3,500	449	401	461	421
3,500	3,550	457	409	469	429
3,550	3,600	464	416	476	436
3,600	3,650	472	424	484	444
3,650	3,700	479	431	491	451
3,700	3,750	487	439	499	459
3,750	3,800	494	446	506	466
3,800	3,850	502	454	514	474
3,850	3,900	509	461	521	481
3,900	3,950	517	469	529	489
3,950	4,000	524	476	536	496

4,000

At least	But less than	Single	Married filing jointly *	Married filing separately	Head of a household
4,000	4,050	532	484	544	504
4,050	4,100	539	491	551	511
4,100	4,150	547	499	559	519
4,150	4,200	554	506	566	526
4,200	4,250	562	514	574	534
4,250	4,300	569	521	581	541
4,300	4,350	577	529	589	549
4,350	4,400	584	536	596	556
4,400	4,450	592	544	604	564
4,450	4,500	599	551	611	571
4,500	4,550	607	559	619	579
4,550	4,600	614	566	626	586
4,600	4,650	622	574	634	594
4,650	4,700	629	581	641	601
4,700	4,750	637	589	649	609
4,750	4,800	644	596	656	616
4,800	4,850	652	604	664	624
4,850	4,900	659	611	671	631
4,900	4,950	667	619	679	639
4,950	5,000	674	626	686	646

* This column must also be used by a qualifying widow(er).

Continued on next page

1987 Tax Table—Continued

If taxable income is—		And you are—				If taxable income is—		And you are—				If taxable income is—		And you are—			
At least	But less than	Single	Married filing jointly *	Married filing separately	Head of a household	At least	But less than	Single	Married filing jointly *	Married filing separately	Head of a household	At least	But less than	Single	Married filing jointly *	Married filing separately	Head of a household
		Your tax is—						Your tax is—						Your tax is—			

5,000 / 8,000 / 11,000

At least	But less than	Single	MFJ*	MFS	HoH	At least	But less than	Single	MFJ*	MFS	HoH	At least	But less than	Single	MFJ*	MFS	HoH
5,000	5,050	682	634	694	654	8,000	8,050	1,132	1,084	1,144	1,104	11,000	11,050	1,582	1,534	1,594	1,554
5,050	5,100	689	641	701	661	8,050	8,100	1,139	1,091	1,151	1,111	11,050	11,100	1,589	1,541	1,601	1,561
5,100	5,150	697	649	709	669	8,100	8,150	1,147	1,099	1,159	1,119	11,100	11,150	1,597	1,549	1,609	1,569
5,150	5,200	704	656	716	676	8,150	8,200	1,154	1,106	1,166	1,126	11,150	11,200	1,604	1,556	1,616	1,576
5,200	5,250	712	664	724	684	8,200	8,250	1,162	1,114	1,174	1,134	11,200	11,250	1,612	1,564	1,624	1,584
5,250	5,300	719	671	731	691	8,250	8,300	1,169	1,121	1,181	1,141	11,250	11,300	1,619	1,571	1,631	1,591
5,300	5,350	727	679	739	699	8,300	8,350	1,177	1,129	1,189	1,149	11,300	11,350	1,627	1,579	1,639	1,599
5,350	5,400	734	686	746	706	8,350	8,400	1,184	1,136	1,196	1,156	11,350	11,400	1,634	1,586	1,646	1,606
5,400	5,450	742	694	754	714	8,400	8,450	1,192	1,144	1,204	1,164	11,400	11,450	1,642	1,594	1,654	1,614
5,450	5,500	749	701	761	721	8,450	8,500	1,199	1,151	1,211	1,171	11,450	11,500	1,649	1,601	1,661	1,621
5,500	5,550	757	709	769	729	8,500	8,550	1,207	1,159	1,219	1,179	11,500	11,550	1,657	1,609	1,669	1,629
5,550	5,600	764	716	776	736	8,550	8,600	1,214	1,166	1,226	1,186	11,550	11,600	1,664	1,616	1,676	1,636
5,600	5,650	772	724	784	744	8,600	8,650	1,222	1,174	1,234	1,194	11,600	11,650	1,672	1,624	1,684	1,644
5,650	5,700	779	731	791	751	8,650	8,700	1,229	1,181	1,241	1,201	11,650	11,700	1,679	1,631	1,691	1,651
5,700	5,750	787	739	799	759	8,700	8,750	1,237	1,189	1,249	1,209	11,700	11,750	1,687	1,639	1,699	1,659
5,750	5,800	794	746	806	766	8,750	8,800	1,244	1,196	1,256	1,216	11,750	11,800	1,694	1,646	1,706	1,666
5,800	5,850	802	754	814	774	8,800	8,850	1,252	1,204	1,264	1,224	11,800	11,850	1,702	1,654	1,714	1,674
5,850	5,900	809	761	821	781	8,850	8,900	1,259	1,211	1,271	1,231	11,850	11,900	1,709	1,661	1,721	1,681
5,900	5,950	817	769	829	789	8,900	8,950	1,267	1,219	1,279	1,239	11,900	11,950	1,717	1,669	1,729	1,689
5,950	6,000	824	776	836	796	8,950	9,000	1,274	1,226	1,286	1,246	11,950	12,000	1,724	1,676	1,736	1,696

6,000 / 9,000 / 12,000

At least	But less than	Single	MFJ*	MFS	HoH	At least	But less than	Single	MFJ*	MFS	HoH	At least	But less than	Single	MFJ*	MFS	HoH
6,000	6,050	832	784	844	804	9,000	9,050	1,282	1,234	1,294	1,254	12,000	12,050	1,732	1,684	1,744	1,704
6,050	6,100	839	791	851	811	9,050	9,100	1,289	1,241	1,301	1,261	12,050	12,100	1,739	1,691	1,751	1,711
6,100	6,150	847	799	859	819	9,100	9,150	1,297	1,249	1,309	1,269	12,100	12,150	1,747	1,699	1,759	1,719
6,150	6,200	854	806	866	826	9,150	9,200	1,304	1,256	1,316	1,276	12,150	12,200	1,754	1,706	1,766	1,726
6,200	6,250	862	814	874	834	9,200	9,250	1,312	1,264	1,324	1,284	12,200	12,250	1,762	1,714	1,774	1,734
6,250	6,300	869	821	881	841	9,250	9,300	1,319	1,271	1,331	1,291	12,250	12,300	1,769	1,721	1,781	1,741
6,300	6,350	877	829	889	849	9,300	9,350	1,327	1,279	1,339	1,299	12,300	12,350	1,777	1,729	1,789	1,749
6,350	6,400	884	836	896	856	9,350	9,400	1,334	1,286	1,346	1,306	12,350	12,400	1,784	1,736	1,796	1,756
6,400	6,450	892	844	904	864	9,400	9,450	1,342	1,294	1,354	1,314	12,400	12,450	1,792	1,744	1,804	1,764
6,450	6,500	899	851	911	871	9,450	9,500	1,349	1,301	1,361	1,321	12,450	12,500	1,799	1,751	1,811	1,771
6,500	6,550	907	859	919	879	9,500	9,550	1,357	1,309	1,369	1,329	12,500	12,550	1,807	1,759	1,819	1,779
6,550	6,600	914	866	926	886	9,550	9,600	1,364	1,316	1,376	1,336	12,550	12,600	1,814	1,766	1,826	1,786
6,600	6,650	922	874	934	894	9,600	9,650	1,372	1,324	1,384	1,344	12,600	12,650	1,822	1,774	1,834	1,794
6,650	6,700	929	881	941	901	9,650	9,700	1,379	1,331	1,391	1,351	12,650	12,700	1,829	1,781	1,841	1,801
6,700	6,750	937	889	949	909	9,700	9,750	1,387	1,339	1,399	1,359	12,700	12,750	1,837	1,789	1,849	1,809
6,750	6,800	944	896	956	916	9,750	9,800	1,394	1,346	1,406	1,366	12,750	12,800	1,844	1,796	1,856	1,816
6,800	6,850	952	904	964	924	9,800	9,850	1,402	1,354	1,414	1,374	12,800	12,850	1,852	1,804	1,864	1,824
6,850	6,900	959	911	971	931	9,850	9,900	1,409	1,361	1,421	1,381	12,850	12,900	1,859	1,811	1,871	1,831
6,900	6,950	967	919	979	939	9,900	9,950	1,417	1,369	1,429	1,389	12,900	12,950	1,867	1,819	1,879	1,839
6,950	7,000	974	926	986	946	9,950	10,000	1,424	1,376	1,436	1,396	12,950	13,000	1,874	1,826	1,886	1,846

7,000 / 10,000 / 13,000

At least	But less than	Single	MFJ*	MFS	HoH	At least	But less than	Single	MFJ*	MFS	HoH	At least	But less than	Single	MFJ*	MFS	HoH
7,000	7,050	982	934	994	954	10,000	10,050	1,432	1,384	1,444	1,404	13,000	13,050	1,882	1,834	1,894	1,854
7,050	7,100	989	941	1,001	961	10,050	10,100	1,439	1,391	1,451	1,411	13,050	13,100	1,889	1,841	1,901	1,861
7,100	7,150	997	949	1,009	969	10,100	10,150	1,447	1,399	1,459	1,419	13,100	13,150	1,897	1,849	1,909	1,869
7,150	7,200	1,004	956	1,016	976	10,150	10,200	1,454	1,406	1,466	1,426	13,150	13,200	1,904	1,856	1,916	1,876
7,200	7,250	1,012	964	1,024	984	10,200	10,250	1,462	1,414	1,474	1,434	13,200	13,250	1,912	1,864	1,924	1,884
7,250	7,300	1,019	971	1,031	991	10,250	10,300	1,469	1,421	1,481	1,441	13,250	13,300	1,919	1,871	1,931	1,891
7,300	7,350	1,027	979	1,039	999	10,300	10,350	1,477	1,429	1,489	1,449	13,300	13,350	1,927	1,879	1,939	1,899
7,350	7,400	1,034	986	1,046	1,006	10,350	10,400	1,484	1,436	1,496	1,456	13,350	13,400	1,934	1,886	1,946	1,906
7,400	7,450	1,042	994	1,054	1,014	10,400	10,450	1,492	1,444	1,504	1,464	13,400	13,450	1,942	1,894	1,954	1,914
7,450	7,500	1,049	1,001	1,061	1,021	10,450	10,500	1,499	1,451	1,511	1,471	13,450	13,500	1,949	1,901	1,961	1,921
7,500	7,550	1,057	1,009	1,069	1,029	10,500	10,550	1,507	1,459	1,519	1,479	13,500	13,550	1,957	1,909	1,969	1,929
7,550	7,600	1,064	1,016	1,076	1,036	10,550	10,600	1,514	1,466	1,526	1,486	13,550	13,600	1,964	1,916	1,976	1,936
7,600	7,650	1,072	1,024	1,084	1,044	10,600	10,650	1,522	1,474	1,534	1,494	13,600	13,650	1,972	1,924	1,984	1,944
7,650	7,700	1,079	1,031	1,091	1,051	10,650	10,700	1,529	1,481	1,541	1,501	13,650	13,700	1,979	1,931	1,991	1,951
7,700	7,750	1,087	1,039	1,099	1,059	10,700	10,750	1,537	1,489	1,549	1,509	13,700	13,750	1,987	1,939	1,999	1,959
7,750	7,800	1,094	1,046	1,106	1,066	10,750	10,800	1,544	1,496	1,556	1,516	13,750	13,800	1,994	1,946	2,006	1,966
7,800	7,850	1,102	1,054	1,114	1,074	10,800	10,850	1,552	1,504	1,564	1,524	13,800	13,850	2,002	1,954	2,014	1,974
7,850	7,900	1,109	1,061	1,121	1,081	10,850	10,900	1,559	1,511	1,571	1,531	13,850	13,900	2,009	1,961	2,021	1,981
7,900	7,950	1,117	1,069	1,129	1,089	10,900	10,950	1,567	1,519	1,579	1,539	13,900	13,950	2,017	1,969	2,029	1,989
7,950	8,000	1,124	1,076	1,136	1,096	10,950	11,000	1,574	1,526	1,586	1,546	13,950	14,000	2,024	1,976	2,036	1,996

* This column must also be used by a qualifying widow(er).

Continued on next page

If taxable income is— At least	But less than	Single	Married filing jointly *	Married filing separately	Head of a household
14,000					
14,000	14,050	2,032	1,984	2,047	2,004
14,050	14,100	2,039	1,991	2,061	2,011
14,100	14,150	2,047	1,999	2,075	2,019
14,150	14,200	2,054	2,006	2,089	2,026
14,200	14,250	2,062	2,014	2,103	2,034
14,250	14,300	2,069	2,021	2,117	2,041
14,300	14,350	2,077	2,029	2,131	2,049
14,350	14,400	2,084	2,036	2,145	2,056
14,400	14,450	2,092	2,044	2,159	2,064
14,450	14,500	2,099	2,051	2,173	2,071
14,500	14,550	2,107	2,059	2,187	2,079
14,550	14,600	2,114	2,066	2,201	2,086
14,600	14,650	2,122	2,074	2,215	2,094
14,650	14,700	2,129	2,081	2,229	2,101
14,700	14,750	2,137	2,089	2,243	2,109
14,750	14,800	2,144	2,096	2,257	2,116
14,800	14,850	2,152	2,104	2,271	2,124
14,850	14,900	2,159	2,111	2,285	2,131
14,900	14,950	2,167	2,119	2,299	2,139
14,950	15,000	2,174	2,126	2,313	2,146
15,000					
15,000	15,050	2,182	2,134	2,327	2,154
15,050	15,100	2,189	2,141	2,341	2,161
15,100	15,150	2,197	2,149	2,355	2,169
15,150	15,200	2,204	2,156	2,369	2,176
15,200	15,250	2,212	2,164	2,383	2,184
15,250	15,300	2,219	2,171	2,397	2,191
15,300	15,350	2,227	2,179	2,411	2,199
15,350	15,400	2,234	2,186	2,425	2,206
15,400	15,450	2,242	2,194	2,439	2,214
15,450	15,500	2,249	2,201	2,453	2,221
15,500	15,550	2,257	2,209	2,467	2,229
15,550	15,600	2,264	2,216	2,481	2,236
15,600	15,650	2,272	2,224	2,495	2,244
15,650	15,700	2,279	2,231	2,509	2,251
15,700	15,750	2,287	2,239	2,523	2,259
15,750	15,800	2,294	2,246	2,537	2,266
15,800	15,850	2,302	2,254	2,551	2,274
15,850	15,900	2,309	2,261	2,565	2,281
15,900	15,950	2,317	2,269	2,579	2,289
15,950	16,000	2,324	2,276	2,593	2,296
16,000					
16,000	16,050	2,332	2,284	2,607	2,304
16,050	16,100	2,339	2,291	2,621	2,311
16,100	16,150	2,347	2,299	2,635	2,319
16,150	16,200	2,354	2,306	2,649	2,326
16,200	16,250	2,362	2,314	2,663	2,334
16,250	16,300	2,369	2,321	2,677	2,341
16,300	16,350	2,377	2,329	2,691	2,349
16,350	16,400	2,384	2,336	2,705	2,356
16,400	16,450	2,392	2,344	2,719	2,364
16,450	16,500	2,399	2,351	2,733	2,371
16,500	16,550	2,407	2,359	2,747	2,379
16,550	16,600	2,414	2,366	2,761	2,386
16,600	16,650	2,422	2,374	2,775	2,394
16,650	16,700	2,429	2,381	2,789	2,401
16,700	16,750	2,437	2,389	2,803	2,409
16,750	16,800	2,444	2,396	2,817	2,416
16,800	16,850	2,455	2,404	2,831	2,424
16,850	16,900	2,469	2,411	2,845	2,431
16,900	16,950	2,483	2,419	2,859	2,439
16,950	17,000	2,497	2,426	2,873	2,446

If taxable income is— At least	But less than	Single	Married filing jointly *	Married filing separately	Head of a household
17,000					
17,000	17,050	2,511	2,434	2,887	2,454
17,050	17,100	2,525	2,441	2,901	2,461
17,100	17,150	2,539	2,449	2,915	2,469
17,150	17,200	2,553	2,456	2,929	2,476
17,200	17,250	2,567	2,464	2,943	2,484
17,250	17,300	2,581	2,471	2,957	2,491
17,300	17,350	2,595	2,479	2,971	2,499
17,350	17,400	2,609	2,486	2,985	2,506
17,400	17,450	2,623	2,494	2,999	2,514
17,450	17,500	2,637	2,501	3,013	2,521
17,500	17,550	2,651	2,509	3,027	2,529
17,550	17,600	2,665	2,516	3,041	2,536
17,600	17,650	2,679	2,524	3,055	2,544
17,650	17,700	2,693	2,531	3,069	2,551
17,700	17,750	2,707	2,539	3,083	2,559
17,750	17,800	2,721	2,546	3,097	2,566
17,800	17,850	2,735	2,554	3,111	2,574
17,850	17,900	2,749	2,561	3,125	2,581
17,900	17,950	2,763	2,569	3,139	2,589
17,950	18,000	2,777	2,576	3,153	2,596
18,000					
18,000	18,050	2,791	2,584	3,167	2,604
18,050	18,100	2,805	2,591	3,181	2,611
18,100	18,150	2,819	2,599	3,195	2,619
18,150	18,200	2,833	2,606	3,209	2,626
18,200	18,250	2,847	2,614	3,223	2,634
18,250	18,300	2,861	2,621	3,237	2,641
18,300	18,350	2,875	2,629	3,251	2,649
18,350	18,400	2,889	2,636	3,265	2,656
18,400	18,450	2,903	2,644	3,279	2,664
18,450	18,500	2,917	2,651	3,293	2,671
18,500	18,550	2,931	2,659	3,307	2,679
18,550	18,600	2,945	2,666	3,321	2,686
18,600	18,650	2,959	2,674	3,335	2,694
18,650	18,700	2,973	2,681	3,349	2,701
18,700	18,750	2,987	2,689	3,363	2,709
18,750	18,800	3,001	2,696	3,377	2,716
18,800	18,850	3,015	2,704	3,391	2,724
18,850	18,900	3,029	2,711	3,405	2,731
18,900	18,950	3,043	2,719	3,419	2,739
18,950	19,000	3,057	2,726	3,433	2,746
19,000					
19,000	19,050	3,071	2,734	3,447	2,754
19,050	19,100	3,085	2,741	3,461	2,761
19,100	19,150	3,099	2,749	3,475	2,769
19,150	19,200	3,113	2,756	3,489	2,776
19,200	19,250	3,127	2,764	3,503	2,784
19,250	19,300	3,141	2,771	3,517	2,791
19,300	19,350	3,155	2,779	3,531	2,799
19,350	19,400	3,169	2,786	3,545	2,806
19,400	19,450	3,183	2,794	3,559	2,814
19,450	19,500	3,197	2,801	3,573	2,821
19,500	19,550	3,211	2,809	3,587	2,829
19,550	19,600	3,225	2,816	3,601	2,836
19,600	19,650	3,239	2,824	3,615	2,844
19,650	19,700	3,253	2,831	3,629	2,851
19,700	19,750	3,267	2,839	3,643	2,859
19,750	19,800	3,281	2,846	3,657	2,866
19,800	19,850	3,295	2,854	3,671	2,874
19,850	19,900	3,309	2,861	3,685	2,881
19,900	19,950	3,323	2,869	3,699	2,889
19,950	20,000	3,337	2,876	3,713	2,896

If taxable income is— At least	But less than	Single	Married filing jointly *	Married filing separately	Head of a household
20,000					
20,000	20,050	3,351	2,884	3,727	2,904
20,050	20,100	3,365	2,891	3,741	2,911
20,100	20,150	3,379	2,899	3,755	2,919
20,150	20,200	3,393	2,906	3,769	2,926
20,200	20,250	3,407	2,914	3,783	2,934
20,250	20,300	3,421	2,921	3,797	2,941
20,300	20,350	3,435	2,929	3,811	2,949
20,350	20,400	3,449	2,936	3,825	2,956
20,400	20,450	3,463	2,944	3,839	2,964
20,450	20,500	3,477	2,951	3,853	2,971
20,500	20,550	3,491	2,959	3,867	2,979
20,550	20,600	3,505	2,966	3,881	2,986
20,600	20,650	3,519	2,974	3,895	2,994
20,650	20,700	3,533	2,981	3,909	3,001
20,700	20,750	3,547	2,989	3,923	3,009
20,750	20,800	3,561	2,996	3,937	3,016
20,800	20,850	3,575	3,004	3,951	3,024
20,850	20,900	3,589	3,011	3,965	3,031
20,900	20,950	3,603	3,019	3,979	3,039
20,950	21,000	3,617	3,026	3,993	3,046
21,000					
21,000	21,050	3,631	3,034	4,007	3,054
21,050	21,100	3,645	3,041	4,021	3,061
21,100	21,150	3,659	3,049	4,035	3,069
21,150	21,200	3,673	3,056	4,049	3,076
21,200	21,250	3,687	3,064	4,063	3,084
21,250	21,300	3,701	3,071	4,077	3,091
21,300	21,350	3,715	3,079	4,091	3,099
21,350	21,400	3,729	3,086	4,105	3,106
21,400	21,450	3,743	3,094	4,119	3,114
21,450	21,500	3,757	3,101	4,133	3,121
21,500	21,550	3,771	3,109	4,147	3,129
21,550	21,600	3,785	3,116	4,161	3,136
21,600	21,650	3,799	3,124	4,175	3,144
21,650	21,700	3,813	3,131	4,189	3,151
21,700	21,750	3,827	3,139	4,203	3,159
21,750	21,800	3,841	3,146	4,217	3,166
21,800	21,850	3,855	3,154	4,231	3,174
21,850	21,900	3,869	3,161	4,245	3,181
21,900	21,950	3,883	3,169	4,259	3,189
21,950	22,000	3,897	3,176	4,273	3,196
22,000					
22,000	22,050	3,911	3,184	4,287	3,204
22,050	22,100	3,925	3,191	4,301	3,211
22,100	22,150	3,939	3,199	4,315	3,219
22,150	22,200	3,953	3,206	4,329	3,226
22,200	22,250	3,967	3,214	4,343	3,234
22,250	22,300	3,981	3,221	4,357	3,241
22,300	22,350	3,995	3,229	4,371	3,249
22,350	22,400	4,009	3,236	4,385	3,256
22,400	22,450	4,023	3,244	4,399	3,264
22,450	22,500	4,037	3,251	4,413	3,271
22,500	22,550	4,051	3,259	4,429	3,279
22,550	22,600	4,065	3,266	4,446	3,286
22,600	22,650	4,079	3,274	4,464	3,294
22,650	22,700	4,093	3,281	4,481	3,301
22,700	22,750	4,107	3,289	4,499	3,309
22,750	22,800	4,121	3,296	4,516	3,316
22,800	22,850	4,135	3,304	4,534	3,324
22,850	22,900	4,149	3,311	4,551	3,331
22,900	22,950	4,163	3,319	4,569	3,339
22,950	23,000	4,177	3,326	4,586	3,346

* This column must also be used by a qualifying widow(er).

Continued on next page

23,000 / 24,000 / 25,000

If taxable income is— At least	But less than	Single	Married filing jointly *	Married filing separately	Head of a household
23,000					
23,000	23,050	4,191	3,334	4,604	3,357
23,050	23,100	4,205	3,341	4,621	3,371
23,100	23,150	4,219	3,349	4,639	3,385
23,150	23,200	4,233	3,356	4,656	3,399
23,200	23,250	4,247	3,364	4,674	3,413
23,250	23,300	4,261	3,371	4,691	3,427
23,300	23,350	4,275	3,379	4,709	3,441
23,350	23,400	4,289	3,386	4,726	3,455
23,400	23,450	4,303	3,394	4,744	3,469
23,450	23,500	4,317	3,401	4,761	3,483
23,500	23,550	4,331	3,409	4,779	3,497
23,550	23,600	4,345	3,416	4,796	3,511
23,600	23,650	4,359	3,424	4,814	3,525
23,650	23,700	4,373	3,431	4,831	3,539
23,700	23,750	4,387	3,439	4,849	3,553
23,750	23,800	4,401	3,446	4,866	3,567
23,800	23,850	4,415	3,454	4,884	3,581
23,850	23,900	4,429	3,461	4,901	3,595
23,900	23,950	4,443	3,469	4,919	3,609
23,950	24,000	4,457	3,476	4,936	3,623
24,000					
24,000	24,050	4,471	3,484	4,954	3,637
24,050	24,100	4,485	3,491	4,971	3,651
24,100	24,150	4,499	3,499	4,989	3,665
24,150	24,200	4,513	3,506	5,006	3,679
24,200	24,250	4,527	3,514	5,024	3,693
24,250	24,300	4,541	3,521	5,041	3,707
24,300	24,350	4,555	3,529	5,059	3,721
24,350	24,400	4,569	3,536	5,076	3,735
24,400	24,450	4,583	3,544	5,094	3,749
24,450	24,500	4,597	3,551	5,111	3,763
24,500	24,550	4,611	3,559	5,129	3,777
24,550	24,600	4,625	3,566	5,146	3,791
24,600	24,650	4,639	3,574	5,164	3,805
24,650	24,700	4,653	3,581	5,181	3,819
24,700	24,750	4,667	3,589	5,199	3,833
24,750	24,800	4,681	3,596	5,216	3,847
24,800	24,850	4,695	3,604	5,234	3,861
24,850	24,900	4,709	3,611	5,251	3,875
24,900	24,950	4,723	3,619	5,269	3,889
24,950	25,000	4,737	3,626	5,286	3,903
25,000					
25,000	25,050	4,751	3,634	5,304	3,917
25,050	25,100	4,765	3,641	5,321	3,931
25,100	25,150	4,779	3,649	5,339	3,945
25,150	25,200	4,793	3,656	5,356	3,959
25,200	25,250	4,807	3,664	5,374	3,973
25,250	25,300	4,821	3,671	5,391	3,987
25,300	25,350	4,835	3,679	5,409	4,001
25,350	25,400	4,849	3,686	5,426	4,015
25,400	25,450	4,863	3,694	5,444	4,029
25,450	25,500	4,877	3,701	5,461	4,043
25,500	25,550	4,891	3,709	5,479	4,057
25,550	25,600	4,905	3,716	5,496	4,071
25,600	25,650	4,919	3,724	5,514	4,085
25,650	25,700	4,933	3,731	5,531	4,099
25,700	25,750	4,947	3,739	5,549	4,113
25,750	25,800	4,961	3,746	5,566	4,127
25,800	25,850	4,975	3,754	5,584	4,141
25,850	25,900	4,989	3,761	5,601	4,155
25,900	25,950	5,003	3,769	5,619	4,169
25,950	26,000	5,017	3,776	5,636	4,183

26,000 / 27,000 / 28,000

If taxable income is— At least	But less than	Single	Married filing jointly *	Married filing separately	Head of a household
26,000					
26,000	26,050	5,031	3,784	5,654	4,197
26,050	26,100	5,045	3,791	5,671	4,211
26,100	26,150	5,059	3,799	5,689	4,225
26,150	26,200	5,073	3,806	5,706	4,239
26,200	26,250	5,087	3,814	5,724	4,253
26,250	26,300	5,101	3,821	5,741	4,267
26,300	26,350	5,115	3,829	5,759	4,281
26,350	26,400	5,129	3,836	5,776	4,295
26,400	26,450	5,143	3,844	5,794	4,309
26,450	26,500	5,157	3,851	5,811	4,323
26,500	26,550	5,171	3,859	5,829	4,337
26,550	26,600	5,185	3,866	5,846	4,351
26,600	26,650	5,199	3,874	5,864	4,365
26,650	26,700	5,213	3,881	5,881	4,379
26,700	26,750	5,227	3,889	5,899	4,393
26,750	26,800	5,241	3,896	5,916	4,407
26,800	26,850	5,255	3,904	5,934	4,421
26,850	26,900	5,269	3,911	5,951	4,435
26,900	26,950	5,283	3,919	5,969	4,449
26,950	27,000	5,297	3,926	5,986	4,463
27,000					
27,000	27,050	5,313	3,934	6,004	4,477
27,050	27,100	5,330	3,941	6,021	4,491
27,100	27,150	5,348	3,949	6,039	4,505
27,150	27,200	5,365	3,956	6,056	4,519
27,200	27,250	5,383	3,964	6,074	4,533
27,250	27,300	5,400	3,971	6,091	4,547
27,300	27,350	5,418	3,979	6,109	4,561
27,350	27,400	5,435	3,986	6,126	4,575
27,400	27,450	5,453	3,994	6,144	4,589
27,450	27,500	5,470	4,001	6,161	4,603
27,500	27,550	5,488	4,009	6,179	4,617
27,550	27,600	5,505	4,016	6,196	4,631
27,600	27,650	5,523	4,024	6,214	4,645
27,650	27,700	5,540	4,031	6,231	4,659
27,700	27,750	5,558	4,039	6,249	4,673
27,750	27,800	5,575	4,046	6,266	4,687
27,800	27,850	5,593	4,054	6,284	4,701
27,850	27,900	5,610	4,061	6,301	4,715
27,900	27,950	5,628	4,069	6,319	4,729
27,950	28,000	5,645	4,076	6,336	4,743
28,000					
28,000	28,050	5,663	4,087	6,354	4,757
28,050	28,100	5,680	4,101	6,371	4,771
28,100	28,150	5,698	4,115	6,389	4,785
28,150	28,200	5,715	4,129	6,406	4,799
28,200	28,250	5,733	4,143	6,424	4,813
28,250	28,300	5,750	4,157	6,441	4,827
28,300	28,350	5,768	4,171	6,459	4,841
28,350	28,400	5,785	4,185	6,476	4,855
28,400	28,450	5,803	4,199	6,494	4,869
28,450	28,500	5,820	4,213	6,511	4,883
28,500	28,550	5,838	4,227	6,529	4,897
28,550	28,600	5,855	4,241	6,546	4,911
28,600	28,650	5,873	4,255	6,564	4,925
28,650	28,700	5,890	4,269	6,581	4,939
28,700	28,750	5,908	4,283	6,599	4,953
28,750	28,800	5,925	4,297	6,616	4,967
28,800	28,850	5,943	4,311	6,634	4,981
28,850	28,900	5,960	4,325	6,651	4,995
28,900	28,950	5,978	4,339	6,669	5,009
28,950	29,000	5,995	4,353	6,686	5,023

29,000 / 30,000 / 31,000

If taxable income is— At least	But less than	Single	Married filing jointly *	Married filing separately	Head of a household
29,000					
29,000	29,050	6,013	4,367	6,704	5,037
29,050	29,100	6,030	4,381	6,721	5,051
29,100	29,150	6,048	4,395	6,739	5,065
29,150	29,200	6,065	4,409	6,756	5,079
29,200	29,250	6,083	4,423	6,774	5,093
29,250	29,300	6,100	4,437	6,791	5,107
29,300	29,350	6,118	4,451	6,809	5,121
29,350	29,400	6,135	4,465	6,826	5,135
29,400	29,450	6,153	4,479	6,844	5,149
29,450	29,500	6,170	4,493	6,861	5,163
29,500	29,550	6,188	4,507	6,879	5,177
29,550	29,600	6,205	4,521	6,896	5,191
29,600	29,650	6,223	4,535	6,914	5,205
29,650	29,700	6,240	4,549	6,931	5,219
29,700	29,750	6,258	4,563	6,949	5,233
29,750	29,800	6,275	4,577	6,966	5,247
29,800	29,850	6,293	4,591	6,984	5,261
29,850	29,900	6,310	4,605	7,001	5,275
29,900	29,950	6,328	4,619	7,019	5,289
29,950	30,000	6,345	4,633	7,036	5,303
30,000					
30,000	30,050	6,363	4,647	7,054	5,317
30,050	30,100	6,380	4,661	7,071	5,331
30,100	30,150	6,398	4,675	7,089	5,345
30,150	30,200	6,415	4,689	7,106	5,359
30,200	30,250	6,433	4,703	7,124	5,373
30,250	30,300	6,450	4,717	7,141	5,387
30,300	30,350	6,468	4,731	7,159	5,401
30,350	30,400	6,485	4,745	7,176	5,415
30,400	30,450	6,503	4,759	7,194	5,429
30,450	30,500	6,520	4,773	7,211	5,443
30,500	30,550	6,538	4,787	7,229	5,457
30,550	30,600	6,555	4,801	7,246	5,471
30,600	30,650	6,573	4,815	7,264	5,485
30,650	30,700	6,590	4,829	7,281	5,499
30,700	30,750	6,608	4,843	7,299	5,513
30,750	30,800	6,625	4,857	7,316	5,527
30,800	30,850	6,643	4,871	7,334	5,541
30,850	30,900	6,660	4,885	7,351	5,555
30,900	30,950	6,678	4,899	7,369	5,569
30,950	31,000	6,695	4,913	7,386	5,583
31,000					
31,000	31,050	6,713	4,927	7,404	5,597
31,050	31,100	6,730	4,941	7,421	5,611
31,100	31,150	6,748	4,955	7,439	5,625
31,150	31,200	6,765	4,969	7,456	5,639
31,200	31,250	6,783	4,983	7,474	5,653
31,250	31,300	6,800	4,997	7,491	5,667
31,300	31,350	6,818	5,011	7,509	5,681
31,350	31,400	6,835	5,025	7,526	5,695
31,400	31,450	6,853	5,039	7,544	5,709
31,450	31,500	6,870	5,053	7,561	5,723
31,500	31,550	6,888	5,067	7,579	5,737
31,550	31,600	6,905	5,081	7,596	5,751
31,600	31,650	6,923	5,095	7,614	5,765
31,650	31,700	6,940	5,109	7,631	5,779
31,700	31,750	6,958	5,123	7,649	5,793
31,750	31,800	6,975	5,137	7,666	5,807
31,800	31,850	6,993	5,151	7,684	5,821
31,850	31,900	7,010	5,165	7,701	5,835
31,900	31,950	7,028	5,179	7,719	5,849
31,950	32,000	7,045	5,193	7,736	5,863

* This column must also be used by a qualifying widow(er).

Continued on next page

If taxable income is— / And you are—

Columns: At least | But less than | Single | Married filing jointly* | Married filing separately | Head of a household — **Your tax is—**

32,000

At least	But less than	Single	Married filing jointly*	Married filing separately	Head of a household
32,000	32,050	7,063	5,207	7,754	5,877
32,050	32,100	7,080	5,221	7,771	5,891
32,100	32,150	7,098	5,235	7,789	5,905
32,150	32,200	7,115	5,249	7,806	5,919
32,200	32,250	7,133	5,263	7,824	5,933
32,250	32,300	7,150	5,277	7,841	5,947
32,300	32,350	7,168	5,291	7,859	5,961
32,350	32,400	7,185	5,305	7,876	5,975
32,400	32,450	7,203	5,319	7,894	5,989
32,450	32,500	7,220	5,333	7,911	6,003
32,500	32,550	7,238	5,347	7,929	6,017
32,550	32,600	7,255	5,361	7,946	6,031
32,600	32,650	7,273	5,375	7,964	6,045
32,650	32,700	7,290	5,389	7,981	6,059
32,700	32,750	7,308	5,403	7,999	6,073
32,750	32,800	7,325	5,417	8,016	6,087
32,800	32,850	7,343	5,431	8,034	6,101
32,850	32,900	7,360	5,445	8,051	6,115
32,900	32,950	7,378	5,459	8,069	6,129
32,950	33,000	7,395	5,473	8,086	6,143

33,000

At least	But less than	Single	Married filing jointly*	Married filing separately	Head of a household
33,000	33,050	7,413	5,487	8,104	6,157
33,050	33,100	7,430	5,501	8,121	6,171
33,100	33,150	7,448	5,515	8,139	6,185
33,150	33,200	7,465	5,529	8,156	6,199
33,200	33,250	7,483	5,543	8,174	6,213
33,250	33,300	7,500	5,557	8,191	6,227
33,300	33,350	7,518	5,571	8,209	6,241
33,350	33,400	7,535	5,585	8,226	6,255
33,400	33,450	7,553	5,599	8,244	6,269
33,450	33,500	7,570	5,613	8,261	6,283
33,500	33,550	7,588	5,627	8,279	6,297
33,550	33,600	7,605	5,641	8,296	6,311
33,600	33,650	7,623	5,655	8,314	6,325
33,650	33,700	7,640	5,669	8,331	6,339
33,700	33,750	7,658	5,683	8,349	6,353
33,750	33,800	7,675	5,697	8,366	6,367
33,800	33,850	7,693	5,711	8,384	6,381
33,850	33,900	7,710	5,725	8,401	6,395
33,900	33,950	7,728	5,739	8,419	6,409
33,950	34,000	7,745	5,753	8,436	6,423

34,000

At least	But less than	Single	Married filing jointly*	Married filing separately	Head of a household
34,000	34,050	7,763	5,767	8,454	6,437
34,050	34,100	7,780	5,781	8,471	6,451
34,100	34,150	7,798	5,795	8,489	6,465
34,150	34,200	7,815	5,809	8,506	6,479
34,200	34,250	7,833	5,823	8,524	6,493
34,250	34,300	7,850	5,837	8,541	6,507
34,300	34,350	7,868	5,851	8,559	6,521
34,350	34,400	7,885	5,865	8,576	6,535
34,400	34,450	7,903	5,879	8,594	6,549
34,450	34,500	7,920	5,893	8,611	6,563
34,500	34,550	7,938	5,907	8,629	6,577
34,550	34,600	7,955	5,921	8,646	6,591
34,600	34,650	7,973	5,935	8,664	6,605
34,650	34,700	7,990	5,949	8,681	6,619
34,700	34,750	8,008	5,963	8,699	6,633
34,750	34,800	8,025	5,977	8,716	6,647
34,800	34,850	8,043	5,991	8,734	6,661
34,850	34,900	8,060	6,005	8,751	6,675
34,900	34,950	8,078	6,019	8,769	6,689
34,950	35,000	8,095	6,033	8,786	6,703

35,000

At least	But less than	Single	Married filing jointly*	Married filing separately	Head of a household
35,000	35,050	8,113	6,047	8,804	6,717
35,050	35,100	8,130	6,061	8,821	6,731
35,100	35,150	8,148	6,075	8,839	6,745
35,150	35,200	8,165	6,089	8,856	6,759
35,200	35,250	8,183	6,103	8,874	6,773
35,250	35,300	8,200	6,117	8,891	6,787
35,300	35,350	8,218	6,131	8,909	6,801
35,350	35,400	8,235	6,145	8,926	6,815
35,400	35,450	8,253	6,159	8,944	6,829
35,450	35,500	8,270	6,173	8,961	6,843
35,500	35,550	8,288	6,187	8,979	6,857
35,550	35,600	8,305	6,201	8,996	6,871
35,600	35,650	8,323	6,215	9,014	6,885
35,650	35,700	8,340	6,229	9,031	6,899
35,700	35,750	8,358	6,243	9,049	6,913
35,750	35,800	8,375	6,257	9,066	6,927
35,800	35,850	8,393	6,271	9,084	6,941
35,850	35,900	8,410	6,285	9,101	6,955
35,900	35,950	8,428	6,299	9,119	6,969
35,950	36,000	8,445	6,313	9,136	6,983

36,000

At least	But less than	Single	Married filing jointly*	Married filing separately	Head of a household
36,000	36,050	8,463	6,327	9,154	6,997
36,050	36,100	8,480	6,341	9,171	7,011
36,100	36,150	8,498	6,355	9,189	7,025
36,150	36,200	8,515	6,369	9,206	7,039
36,200	36,250	8,533	6,383	9,224	7,053
36,250	36,300	8,550	6,397	9,241	7,067
36,300	36,350	8,568	6,411	9,259	7,081
36,350	36,400	8,585	6,425	9,276	7,095
36,400	36,450	8,603	6,439	9,294	7,109
36,450	36,500	8,620	6,453	9,311	7,123
36,500	36,550	8,638	6,467	9,329	7,137
36,550	36,600	8,655	6,481	9,346	7,151
36,600	36,650	8,673	6,495	9,364	7,165
36,650	36,700	8,690	6,509	9,381	7,179
36,700	36,750	8,708	6,523	9,399	7,193
36,750	36,800	8,725	6,537	9,416	7,207
36,800	36,850	8,743	6,551	9,434	7,221
36,850	36,900	8,760	6,565	9,451	7,235
36,900	36,950	8,778	6,579	9,469	7,249
36,950	37,000	8,795	6,593	9,486	7,263

37,000

At least	But less than	Single	Married filing jointly*	Married filing separately	Head of a household
37,000	37,050	8,813	6,607	9,504	7,277
37,050	37,100	8,830	6,621	9,521	7,291
37,100	37,150	8,848	6,635	9,539	7,305
37,150	37,200	8,865	6,649	9,556	7,319
37,200	37,250	8,883	6,663	9,574	7,333
37,250	37,300	8,900	6,677	9,591	7,347
37,300	37,350	8,918	6,691	9,609	7,361
37,350	37,400	8,935	6,705	9,626	7,375
37,400	37,450	8,953	6,719	9,644	7,389
37,450	37,500	8,970	6,733	9,661	7,403
37,500	37,550	8,988	6,747	9,679	7,417
37,550	37,600	9,005	6,761	9,696	7,431
37,600	37,650	9,023	6,775	9,714	7,445
37,650	37,700	9,040	6,789	9,731	7,459
37,700	37,750	9,058	6,803	9,749	7,473
37,750	37,800	9,075	6,817	9,766	7,487
37,800	37,850	9,093	6,831	9,784	7,501
37,850	37,900	9,110	6,845	9,801	7,515
37,900	37,950	9,128	6,859	9,819	7,529
37,950	38,000	9,145	6,873	9,836	7,543

38,000

At least	But less than	Single	Married filing jointly*	Married filing separately	Head of a household
38,000	38,050	9,163	6,887	9,854	7,559
38,050	38,100	9,180	6,901	9,871	7,576
38,100	38,150	9,198	6,915	9,889	7,594
38,150	38,200	9,215	6,929	9,906	7,611
38,200	38,250	9,233	6,943	9,924	7,629
38,250	38,300	9,250	6,957	9,941	7,646
38,300	38,350	9,268	6,971	9,959	7,664
38,350	38,400	9,285	6,985	9,976	7,681
38,400	38,450	9,303	6,999	9,994	7,699
38,450	38,500	9,320	7,013	10,011	7,716
38,500	38,550	9,338	7,027	10,029	7,734
38,550	38,600	9,355	7,041	10,046	7,751
38,600	38,650	9,373	7,055	10,064	7,769
38,650	38,700	9,390	7,069	10,081	7,786
38,700	38,750	9,408	7,083	10,099	7,804
38,750	38,800	9,425	7,097	10,116	7,821
38,800	38,850	9,443	7,111	10,134	7,839
38,850	38,900	9,460	7,125	10,151	7,856
38,900	38,950	9,478	7,139	10,169	7,874
38,950	39,000	9,495	7,153	10,186	7,891

39,000

At least	But less than	Single	Married filing jointly*	Married filing separately	Head of a household
39,000	39,050	9,513	7,167	10,204	7,909
39,050	39,100	9,530	7,181	10,221	7,926
39,100	39,150	9,548	7,195	10,239	7,944
39,150	39,200	9,565	7,209	10,256	7,961
39,200	39,250	9,583	7,223	10,274	7,979
39,250	39,300	9,600	7,237	10,291	7,996
39,300	39,350	9,618	7,251	10,309	8,014
39,350	39,400	9,635	7,265	10,326	8,031
39,400	39,450	9,653	7,279	10,344	8,049
39,450	39,500	9,670	7,293	10,361	8,066
39,500	39,550	9,688	7,307	10,379	8,084
39,550	39,600	9,705	7,321	10,396	8,101
39,600	39,650	9,723	7,335	10,414	8,119
39,650	39,700	9,740	7,349	10,431	8,136
39,700	39,750	9,758	7,363	10,449	8,154
39,750	39,800	9,775	7,377	10,466	8,171
39,800	39,850	9,793	7,391	10,484	8,189
39,850	39,900	9,810	7,405	10,501	8,206
39,900	39,950	9,828	7,419	10,519	8,224
39,950	40,000	9,845	7,433	10,536	8,241

40,000

At least	But less than	Single	Married filing jointly*	Married filing separately	Head of a household
40,000	40,050	9,863	7,447	10,554	8,259
40,050	40,100	9,880	7,461	10,571	8,276
40,100	40,150	9,898	7,475	10,589	8,294
40,150	40,200	9,915	7,489	10,606	8,311
40,200	40,250	9,933	7,503	10,624	8,329
40,250	40,300	9,950	7,517	10,641	8,346
40,300	40,350	9,968	7,531	10,659	8,364
40,350	40,400	9,985	7,545	10,676	8,381
40,400	40,450	10,003	7,559	10,694	8,399
40,450	40,500	10,020	7,573	10,711	8,416
40,500	40,550	10,038	7,587	10,729	8,434
40,550	40,600	10,055	7,601	10,746	8,451
40,600	40,650	10,073	7,615	10,764	8,469
40,650	40,700	10,090	7,629	10,781	8,486
40,700	40,750	10,108	7,643	10,799	8,504
40,750	40,800	10,125	7,657	10,816	8,521
40,800	40,850	10,143	7,671	10,834	8,539
40,850	40,900	10,160	7,685	10,851	8,556
40,900	40,950	10,178	7,699	10,869	8,574
40,950	41,000	10,195	7,713	10,886	8,591

* This column must also be used by a qualifying widow(er).

Continued on next page

1987 Tax Table—Continued

41,000 / 42,000 / 43,000

At least	But less than	Single	Married filing jointly *	Married filing separately	Head of a household
41,000					
41,000	41,050	10,213	7,727	10,904	8,609
41,050	41,100	10,230	7,741	10,921	8,626
41,100	41,150	10,248	7,755	10,939	8,644
41,150	41,200	10,265	7,769	10,956	8,661
41,200	41,250	10,283	7,783	10,974	8,679
41,250	41,300	10,300	7,797	10,991	8,696
41,300	41,350	10,318	7,811	11,009	8,714
41,350	41,400	10,335	7,825	11,026	8,731
41,400	41,450	10,353	7,839	11,044	8,749
41,450	41,500	10,370	7,853	11,061	8,766
41,500	41,550	10,388	7,867	11,079	8,784
41,550	41,600	10,405	7,881	11,096	8,801
41,600	41,650	10,423	7,895	11,114	8,819
41,650	41,700	10,440	7,909	11,131	8,836
41,700	41,750	10,458	7,923	11,149	8,854
41,750	41,800	10,475	7,937	11,166	8,871
41,800	41,850	10,493	7,951	11,184	8,889
41,850	41,900	10,510	7,965	11,201	8,906
41,900	41,950	10,528	7,979	11,219	8,924
41,950	42,000	10,545	7,993	11,236	8,941
42,000					
42,000	42,050	10,563	8,007	11,254	8,959
42,050	42,100	10,580	8,021	11,271	8,976
42,100	42,150	10,598	8,035	11,289	8,994
42,150	42,200	10,615	8,049	11,306	9,011
42,200	42,250	10,633	8,063	11,324	9,029
42,250	42,300	10,650	8,077	11,341	9,046
42,300	42,350	10,668	8,091	11,359	9,064
42,350	42,400	10,685	8,105	11,376	9,081
42,400	42,450	10,703	8,119	11,394	9,099
42,450	42,500	10,720	8,133	11,411	9,116
42,500	42,550	10,738	8,147	11,429	9,134
42,550	42,600	10,755	8,161	11,446	9,151
42,600	42,650	10,773	8,175	11,464	9,169
42,650	42,700	10,790	8,189	11,481	9,186
42,700	42,750	10,808	8,203	11,499	9,204
42,750	42,800	10,825	8,217	11,516	9,221
42,800	42,850	10,843	8,231	11,534	9,239
42,850	42,900	10,860	8,245	11,551	9,256
42,900	42,950	10,878	8,259	11,569	9,274
42,950	43,000	10,895	8,273	11,586	9,291
43,000					
43,000	43,050	10,913	8,287	11,604	9,309
43,050	43,100	10,930	8,301	11,621	9,326
43,100	43,150	10,948	8,315	11,639	9,344
43,150	43,200	10,965	8,329	11,656	9,361
43,200	43,250	10,983	8,343	11,674	9,379
43,250	43,300	11,000	8,357	11,691	9,396
43,300	43,350	11,018	8,371	11,709	9,414
43,350	43,400	11,035	8,385	11,726	9,431
43,400	43,450	11,053	8,399	11,744	9,449
43,450	43,500	11,070	8,413	11,761	9,466
43,500	43,550	11,088	8,427	11,779	9,484
43,550	43,600	11,105	8,441	11,796	9,501
43,600	43,650	11,123	8,455	11,814	9,519
43,650	43,700	11,140	8,469	11,831	9,536
43,700	43,750	11,158	8,483	11,849	9,554
43,750	43,800	11,175	8,497	11,866	9,571
43,800	43,850	11,193	8,511	11,884	9,589
43,850	43,900	11,210	8,525	11,901	9,606
43,900	43,950	11,228	8,539	11,919	9,624
43,950	44,000	11,245	8,553	11,936	9,641

44,000 / 45,000 / 46,000

At least	But less than	Single	Married filing jointly *	Married filing separately	Head of a household
44,000					
44,000	44,050	11,263	8,567	11,954	9,659
44,050	44,100	11,280	8,581	11,971	9,676
44,100	44,150	11,298	8,595	11,989	9,694
44,150	44,200	11,315	8,609	12,006	9,711
44,200	44,250	11,333	8,623	12,024	9,729
44,250	44,300	11,350	8,637	12,041	9,746
44,300	44,350	11,368	8,651	12,059	9,764
44,350	44,400	11,385	8,665	12,076	9,781
44,400	44,450	11,403	8,679	12,094	9,799
44,450	44,500	11,420	8,693	12,111	9,816
44,500	44,550	11,438	8,707	12,129	9,834
44,550	44,600	11,455	8,721	12,146	9,851
44,600	44,650	11,473	8,735	12,164	9,869
44,650	44,700	11,490	8,749	12,181	9,886
44,700	44,750	11,508	8,763	12,199	9,904
44,750	44,800	11,525	8,777	12,216	9,921
44,800	44,850	11,543	8,791	12,234	9,939
44,850	44,900	11,560	8,805	12,251	9,956
44,900	44,950	11,578	8,819	12,269	9,974
44,950	45,000	11,595	8,833	12,286	9,991
45,000					
45,000	45,050	11,613	8,849	12,305	10,009
45,050	45,100	11,630	8,866	12,324	10,026
45,100	45,150	11,648	8,884	12,343	10,044
45,150	45,200	11,665	8,901	12,362	10,061
45,200	45,250	11,683	8,919	12,382	10,079
45,250	45,300	11,700	8,936	12,401	10,096
45,300	45,350	11,718	8,954	12,420	10,114
45,350	45,400	11,735	8,971	12,439	10,131
45,400	45,450	11,753	8,989	12,459	10,149
45,450	45,500	11,770	9,006	12,478	10,166
45,500	45,550	11,788	9,024	12,497	10,184
45,550	45,600	11,805	9,041	12,516	10,201
45,600	45,650	11,823	9,059	12,536	10,219
45,650	45,700	11,840	9,076	12,555	10,236
45,700	45,750	11,858	9,094	12,574	10,254
45,750	45,800	11,875	9,111	12,593	10,271
45,800	45,850	11,893	9,129	12,613	10,289
45,850	45,900	11,910	9,146	12,632	10,306
45,900	45,950	11,928	9,164	12,651	10,324
45,950	46,000	11,945	9,181	12,670	10,341
46,000					
46,000	46,050	11,963	9,199	12,690	10,359
46,050	46,100	11,980	9,216	12,709	10,376
46,100	46,150	11,998	9,234	12,728	10,394
46,150	46,200	12,015	9,251	12,747	10,411
46,200	46,250	12,033	9,269	12,767	10,429
46,250	46,300	12,050	9,286	12,786	10,446
46,300	46,350	12,068	9,304	12,805	10,464
46,350	46,400	12,085	9,321	12,824	10,481
46,400	46,450	12,103	9,339	12,844	10,499
46,450	46,500	12,120	9,356	12,863	10,516
46,500	46,550	12,138	9,374	12,882	10,534
46,550	46,600	12,155	9,391	12,901	10,551
46,600	46,650	12,173	9,409	12,921	10,569
46,650	46,700	12,190	9,426	12,940	10,586
46,700	46,750	12,208	9,444	12,959	10,604
46,750	46,800	12,225	9,461	12,978	10,621
46,800	46,850	12,243	9,479	12,998	10,639
46,850	46,900	12,260	9,496	13,017	10,656
46,900	46,950	12,278	9,514	13,036	10,674
46,950	47,000	12,295	9,531	13,055	10,691

47,000 / 48,000 / 49,000

At least	But less than	Single	Married filing jointly *	Married filing separately	Head of a household
47,000					
47,000	47,050	12,313	9,549	13,075	10,709
47,050	47,100	12,330	9,566	13,094	10,726
47,100	47,150	12,348	9,584	13,113	10,744
47,150	47,200	12,365	9,601	13,132	10,761
47,200	47,250	12,383	9,619	13,152	10,779
47,250	47,300	12,400	9,636	13,171	10,796
47,300	47,350	12,418	9,654	13,190	10,814
47,350	47,400	12,435	9,671	13,209	10,831
47,400	47,450	12,453	9,689	13,229	10,849
47,450	47,500	12,470	9,706	13,248	10,866
47,500	47,550	12,488	9,724	13,267	10,884
47,550	47,600	12,505	9,741	13,286	10,901
47,600	47,650	12,523	9,759	13,306	10,919
47,650	47,700	12,540	9,776	13,325	10,936
47,700	47,750	12,558	9,794	13,344	10,954
47,750	47,800	12,575	9,811	13,363	10,971
47,800	47,850	12,593	9,829	13,383	10,989
47,850	47,900	12,610	9,846	13,402	11,006
47,900	47,950	12,628	9,864	13,421	11,024
47,950	48,000	12,645	9,881	13,440	11,041
48,000					
48,000	48,050	12,663	9,899	13,460	11,059
48,050	48,100	12,680	9,916	13,479	11,076
48,100	48,150	12,698	9,934	13,498	11,094
48,150	48,200	12,715	9,951	13,517	11,111
48,200	48,250	12,733	9,969	13,537	11,129
48,250	48,300	12,750	9,986	13,556	11,146
48,300	48,350	12,768	10,004	13,575	11,164
48,350	48,400	12,785	10,021	13,594	11,181
48,400	48,450	12,803	10,039	13,614	11,199
48,450	48,500	12,820	10,056	13,633	11,216
48,500	48,550	12,838	10,074	13,652	11,234
48,550	48,600	12,855	10,091	13,671	11,251
48,600	48,650	12,873	10,109	13,691	11,269
48,650	48,700	12,890	10,126	13,710	11,286
48,700	48,750	12,908	10,144	13,729	11,304
48,750	48,800	12,925	10,161	13,748	11,321
48,800	48,850	12,943	10,179	13,768	11,339
48,850	48,900	12,960	10,196	13,787	11,356
48,900	48,950	12,978	10,214	13,806	11,374
48,950	49,000	12,995	10,231	13,825	11,391
49,000					
49,000	49,050	13,013	10,249	13,845	11,409
49,050	49,100	13,030	10,266	13,864	11,426
49,100	49,150	13,048	10,284	13,883	11,444
49,150	49,200	13,065	10,301	13,902	11,461
49,200	49,250	13,083	10,319	13,922	11,479
49,250	49,300	13,100	10,336	13,941	11,496
49,300	49,350	13,118	10,354	13,960	11,514
49,350	49,400	13,135	10,371	13,979	11,531
49,400	49,450	13,153	10,389	13,999	11,549
49,450	49,500	13,170	10,406	14,018	11,566
49,500	49,550	13,188	10,424	14,037	11,584
49,550	49,600	13,205	10,441	14,056	11,601
49,600	49,650	13,223	10,459	14,076	11,619
49,650	49,700	13,240	10,476	14,095	11,636
49,700	49,750	13,258	10,494	14,114	11,654
49,750	49,800	13,275	10,511	14,133	11,671
49,800	49,850	13,293	10,529	14,153	11,689
49,850	49,900	13,310	10,546	14,172	11,706
49,900	49,950	13,328	10,564	14,191	11,724
49,950	50,000	13,345	10,581	14,210	11,741

* This column must also be used by a qualifying widow(er).

50,000 or over—use tax rate schedules

HOW CHILDREN ARE TAXED

¶ 22.3 To discourage income splitting of investment income between parents and minor children, the tax law has complicated income reporting for parents and children by—

1. Taxing a child's investment income over $1,000 at the parent's top bracket if the child is under 14 years of age at the end of the taxable year.
2. Barring a dependent child from claiming a personal exemption on his or her own tax return.
3. Limiting the standard deduction to $500 for a dependent child who has only investment income.

Filing tests for dependent child. A 1987 return must be filed by a dependent child with gross income of more than $500, but there is this exception: If a dependent child has salary or other earned income

but no investment income, a return does not have to be filed unless such earned income exceeds $2,540 in 1987. In 1988, a dependent child with only earned income will not have to file unless the earned income exceeds $3,000.

A dependent child whose gross income (earned and unearned) is $500 or less is not subject to tax. Although a dependent child may not claim a personal exemption on his or her tax return, the child is allowed to claim a $500 standard deduction.

Where a child under 14 has investment income exceeding $1,000, Form 8615 must be filed to compute the tax based on a parent's tax bracket. On Form 8615, the parent must provide his tax identification number and taxable income. Form 8615 is attached to the child's return.

CHILDREN WHO ARE NOT SUBJECT TO THE SPECIAL TAX COMPUTATION

¶ 22.4 The special tax computation based on a parent's top tax rate applies only to children under 14 with investment income exceeding $1,000. The computation does *not* apply to—

A dependent child who is 14 years old or over at the end of the taxable year.

A child who has no investment income or whose gross investment income is $1,000 or less. The special computation applies only to investment income exceeding $1,000. Further, children who itemize deductions may in some cases exempt more than $1,000 from the computation; see ¶22.5.

A child under age 14 if neither parent is alive at the end of the taxable year.

EXAMPLES

1. At the end of 1987, a child is age 14. He has interest income of $1,200 and salary income of $750 from his part-time job. His standard deduction is $750, the greater of earned income or $500. No personal exemption may be claimed. Assuming the child has no itemized deductions, taxable income is $1,200 ($1,950 gross income–$750 standard deduction) which will be subject to the 11% tax bracket in 1987. The special tax computation based on a parent's top rate does not apply because the child is at least age 14 at the end of the year.

2. In 1987, a dependent child age five has interest income of $800. Taxable income of $300 is subject to tax at the child's own tax rate. The child uses the tax tables at ¶22.2.

Interest income	$800
Less standard deduction	500
Taxable income	$300

The special tax computation does not apply because investment income does not exceed $1,000.

CHILDREN UNDER 14 SUBJECT TO SPECIAL TAX COMPUTATION

¶ 22.5 The special tax computation based on a parent's top tax rate applies to a child who —

Is under 14 at the end of the taxable year, and

Has either parent alive at the end of the taxable year, and

Has net investment income after reducing gross investment income by $1,000 or other adjustments explained below.

The special tax computation is made on Form 8615 which must be attached to the child's return. A sample Form 8615 is on page 245.

Income subject to the special computation is any income that is *not* compensation for personal services. Therefore investment income—such as interest, dividends, royalties, rents, and profits on the sale of property—is subject to the special tax computation. Income from wages or self-employment is not subject to the special tax computations.

Only net investment income is subject to tax at the parent's top rate. For purposes of this rule, net investment income equals gross investment income minus $1,000 if the child does not itemize deductions on Schedule A. If the child does itemize deductions, net investment income equals gross investment income reduced by the larger of (1) $1,000 or (2) $500 plus itemized deductions that are directly connected with the production of the investment income. Thus, for a child who does not itemize, the first $1,000 of investment income is exempt from the special computation; investment income exceeding $1,000 is considered net investment income subject to the special computation. If a child has itemized deductions of more than $500 that are directly related to the production of investment income, the $1,000 floor is increased, as in example (6) below.

The following examples illustrate whether the special computation applies to a child's investment income. Rules for making the actual computation are at ¶22.6.

EXAMPLES (In all the following examples, assume a child under age 14 as of December 31, 1987)

1. Child has interest income of $480 and no other income. The child has no income tax liability and does not have to file a return.

Interest income	$480
Less standard deduction	480
	–0–

2. Child has interest and dividend income of $900 and no other income. A standard deduction of $500 may be claimed. The balance of $400 is taxed at the child's regular tax bracket. Form 8615 does not have to be filed and the special computation does not apply since investment income does not exceed $1,000.

3. Child has dividend income of $1,300. The child has taxable income of $800 of which $300 is subject to the special computation based on the parent's rate bracket on Form 8615.

Figuring taxable income:
Dividend income	$1,300
Less standard deduction	500
	$ 800

Income subject to tax at parent's rate:
Investment income	$1,300
Less $1,000	1,000
	$ 300

4. Child has wages of $700 and $300 of interest income.

Figuring taxable income:
Total income	$1,000
Less standard deduction (up to wages)	700
Taxable income	$ 300

The parent's tax bracket does not apply because interest income does not exceed the $1,000 floor. Taxable income is taxed at the child's rate.

5. Child has $300 salary and $1,200 dividends and interest income. On Schedule A, the child claims itemized deductions of $400 related to investment income after the 2% AGI floor. The child also has $400 of other itemized deductions. Itemized deductions of $800 are claimed; they exceed the $500 standard deduction.

Figuring taxable income:
Total income	$1,500
Less itemized deductions	800
Taxable income	$700

Income subject to tax at parent's rate:
Investment income	$1,200
Less greater of (1) $1,000 or (2) $500 plus directly related expenses of $400	1,000
Net investment income subject to tax at parent's rate on Form 8615	$ 200

6. Child has $700 of salary income; $3,000 of investment income; and itemized deductions of $800 (net of the 2% AGI floor) directly related to the investment income. The child also has $200 of other itemized deductions.

Figuring taxable income:
Total income	$3,700
Less itemized deductions	1,000
Taxable income	$2,700

Income subject to tax at parent's rate:
Investment income	$3,000
Less greater of (1) $1,000 or (2) $500 plus $800 of deductions related to investment income	1,300
Net investment income subject to tax at parent's rate on Form 8615	$1,700

COMPUTING TAX AT PARENT'S TAX BRACKET

¶ 22.6 Children subject to the special tax computation cannot file their return until their parents have computed their taxable income. If parents file a joint return, net investment income of all of their children under 14 is added on Form 8615 to their joint taxable income. If the parents elect to file separate returns, the net investment income of the children is added on Form 8615 to the income of the parent who has the larger amount of taxable income. If the child's parents are not married, or are divorced or legally separated or living apart, the net investment income is added to the taxable income of the custodial parent. In the case of a foster child, the taxable income of the foster parents is taken into account.

In 1987, the addition of the child's net investment income is merely a tax computation step affecting the child and does not affect the tax liability of the parents or how they compute any limitation on deductions or credits. For example, the addition of the child's net investment income to the parent's taxable income on Form 8615 does *not* affect the adjusted gross income floors for purposes of figuring the parent's deduction for IRA contributions, medical expenses, and miscellaneous expenses.

EXAMPLE

Brown has three dependent children—Ann, Bill, and Betty. At the end of 1987, Ann is 15, Bill is 13, and Betty is 10. Since Ann is at least age 14, she is not subject to the special tax computation. She computes her 1987 tax under regular rules.

For 1987, Bill and Betty each file Form 1040A. Bill has dividend income of $1,800; Betty $1,200. Bill's taxable income after deducting a standard deduction is $1,300. Betty's is $700.

Bill and Betty must each attach Form 8615 to their Form 1040A and make the special computation because they are under 14 and have more than $1,000 of investment income.

To make the special computation on Form 8615, Brown must first determine his own taxable income. Brown and his spouse file a 1987 joint return, reporting taxable income of $52,000. They use the tax rate schedule at the beginning of this chapter: The tax on $52,000 is $11,290. The special computation on Form 8615 does not increase the Browns' joint return tax; it determines only the amount of Bill's and Betty's tax.

As shown on the following sample Forms 8615, Bill's 1987 tax from the tax tables is $336 and Betty's 1987 tax is $126. If the special computation did not apply, Bill's 1987 tax would be $144 and Betty's tax would be $78. Thus, as a result of the special computation, the total tax bill for the children is increased by $240 ($462–$222).

Form 8615 (1987)

Form 8615 — Computation of Tax for Children Under Age 14 Who Have Investment Income of More Than $1,000

Department of the Treasury
Internal Revenue Service

▶ See Instructions below.
▶ Attach to the Child's Form 1040, Form 1040A, or Form 1040NR.

OMB No. 1545-xxxx
1987
Attachment Sequence No. 33

General Instructions

Purpose of Form.—Before 1987, the tax law allowed income-producing property to be given to children so that the investment income from the property could be taxed at the children's lower tax rate. The law was changed for 1987 and later years so that, for children under age 14, investment income (such as interest and dividends) over $1,000 will be taxed at the parent's rate if higher than the child's rate.

Do not use this form if the child's investment income is $1,000 or less. Instead, figure the tax in the normal manner on the child's income tax return. For example, if the child had $900 of interest income and $200 of income from wages, Form 8615 is not required to be completed and the child's tax should be figured on Form 1040A using the Tax Table.

If the child's investment income is more than $1,000, use this form to see if any of the child's net investment income is taxed at the parent's rate and, if so, to figure the child's tax. For example, if the child had $1,100 of interest income and $200 of income from wages, Form 8615 should be completed and attached to the child's Form 1040A.

Investment income.— As referred to in this form, the term investment income includes all taxable income other than earned income as defined on page 2. It includes income such as interest, dividends, capital gains, rents, royalties, etc. It also includes pension and annuity income and income received as the beneficiary of a trust.

Who Must File.—Generally, **Form 8615** must be filed for any child who was under age 14 on December 31, 1987, and who had more than $1,000 of investment income. However, if neither parent was alive on December 31, do not use Form 8615. Instead, figure the child's tax based on his or her own rate.

Additional Information.—For more information about the tax on investment income of children, please get **Publication 922** Tax Rules for Children and Dependents (Rev. Nov. 1987).

Sample 1 (Betty)

Child's name as shown on return: **Betty**
Child's social security number: **X10:00:1111**

Parent's name (first, initial, and last). (Caution: See Instructions before completing.): **Andrew Brown**
Parent's filing status: **Joint Return**
Parent's social security number: **XXX:11:1X11**

Step 1 — Figure child's net investment income

1	Enter the child's investment income, such as interest and dividend income (see Instructions). (If this amount is $1,000 or less, stop here; do not file this form.)	$1,200
2	If the child DID NOT itemize deductions on Schedule A (Form 1040 or Form 1040NR), enter $1,000. If the child ITEMIZED deductions, see the Instructions.	1,000
3	Subtract the amount on line 2 from the amount on line 1. Enter the result. (If zero or less, stop here; do not complete the rest of this form but ATTACH it to the child's return.)	200
4	Enter the child's taxable income (from Form 1040, line 36; Form 1040A, line 17; or Form 1040NR, line 35)	700
5	Compare the amounts on lines 3 and 4 and enter the **smaller** of the two amounts	$200

Step 2 — Figure tentative tax based on the parent's tax rate

Line		Amount
6	Enter the parent's taxable income (from Form 1040, line 36; Form 1040A, line 17; Form 1040EZ, line 7; or Form 1040NR, line 35)	52,000
7	Enter the total, if any, of the net investment income from Forms 8615, line 5, of ALL OTHER children of the parent listed above	800
8	Add the amounts on lines 5, 6, and 7. Enter the total	53,000
9	Tax on the amount on line 8 based on the **parent's** filing status (see Instructions). Check if from ☑Tax Table, ☐Tax Rate Schedule X, Y, or Z, or ☐Schedule D	11,640
10	Enter the parent's tax (from Form 1040, line 37; Form 1040A, line 18; Form 1040EZ, line 9; or Form 1040NR, line 36).	11,290
11	Subtract the amount on line 10 from the amount on line 9. Enter the result. (If no amount is entered on line 7, enter the amount from line 11 on line 13)	350
12a	Add the amounts on lines 5 and 7. Enter the total	1,000
12b	Divide the amount on line 5 by the amount on line 12a. Enter the percentage	x 20
13	Multiply the amount on line 11 by the percentage on line 12b. Enter the result	$70

Step 3 — Figure child's tax

Line		Amount
14	Subtract the amount on line 5 from the amount on line 4. Enter the result.	500
15	Tax on the amount on line 14 based on the **child's** filing status (see Instructions). Check if from ☑Tax Table, ☐Tax Rate Schedule X, or ☐Schedule D	56
16	Add the amounts on lines 13 and 15. Enter the total.	126
17	Tax on the amount on line 4 based on the **child's** filing status. Check if from ☑Tax Table, ☐Tax Rate Schedule X, or ☐Schedule D	78
18	Compare the amounts on lines 16 and 17. Enter the **larger** of the two amounts here and on Form 1040, line 37; Form 1040A, line 18; or Form 1040NR, line 36. Be sure to check the box for "Form 8615".	126

Form **8615** (1987)

Sample 2 (Bill)

Child's name as shown on return: **Bill**
Child's social security number: **0IX:XI:11--**

Parent's name (first, initial, and last). (Caution: See Instructions before completing.): **Andrew Brown**
Parent's filing status: **Joint Return**
Parent's social security number: **XXX:11:1X11**

Step 1 — Figure child's net investment income

Line		Amount
1	Enter the child's investment income, such as interest and dividend income (see Instructions). (If this amount is $1,000 or less, stop here; do not file this form.)	$1,800
2	If the child DID NOT itemize deductions on Schedule A (Form 1040 or Form 1040NR), enter $1,000. If the child ITEMIZED deductions, see the Instructions.	1,000
3	Subtract the amount on line 2 from the amount on line 1. Enter the result. (If zero or less, stop here; do not complete the rest of this form but ATTACH it to the child's return.)	800
4	Enter the child's taxable income (from Form 1040, line 36; Form 1040A, line 17; or Form 1040NR, line 35)	1,300
5	Compare the amounts on lines 3 and 4 and enter the **smaller** of the two amounts	$800

Step 2 — Figure tentative tax based on the parent's tax rate

Line		Amount
6	Enter the parent's taxable income (from Form 1040, line 36; Form 1040A, line 17; Form 1040EZ, line 7; or Form 1040NR, line 35)	52,000
7	Enter the total, if any, of the net investment income from Forms 8615, line 5, of ALL OTHER children of the parent listed above	200
8	Add the amounts on lines 5, 6, and 7. Enter the total	53,000
9	Tax on the amount on line 8 based on the **parent's** filing status (see Instructions). Check if from ☑Tax Table, ☐Tax Rate Schedule X, Y, or Z, or ☐Schedule D	11,640
10	Enter the parent's tax (from Form 1040, line 37; Form 1040A, line 18; Form 1040EZ, line 9; or Form 1040NR, line 36).	11,290
11	Subtract the amount on line 10 from the amount on line 9. Enter the result. (If no amount is entered on line 7, enter the amount from line 11 on line 13)	350
12a	Add the amounts on lines 5 and 7. Enter the total	1,000
12b	Divide the amount on line 5 by the amount on line 12a. Enter the percentage	x 80
13	Multiply the amount on line 11 by the percentage on line 12b. Enter the result	280

Step 3 — Figure child's tax

Line		Amount
14	Subtract the amount on line 5 from the amount on line 4. Enter the result.	500
15	Tax on the amount on line 14 based on the **child's** filing status (see Instructions). Check if from ☑Tax Table, ☐Tax Rate Schedule X, or ☐Schedule D	56
16	Add the amounts on lines 13 and 15. Enter the total.	336
17	Tax on the amount on line 4 based on the **child's** filing status. Check if from ☑Tax Table, ☐Tax Rate Schedule X, or ☐Schedule D	144
18	Compare the amounts on lines 16 and 17. Enter the **larger** of the two amounts here and on Form 1040, line 37; Form 1040A, line 18; or Form 1040NR, line 36. Be sure to check the box for "Form 8615".	336

Form **8615** (1987)

---

*Important: These samples of Form 8615 are based on IRS proof sheet dated June 24, 1987. See the Supplement and your tax form instructions for any changes to the form.

23

ALTERNATIVE MINIMUM TAX

¶ 23.1 The new law changes affect the alternative minimum tax (AMT) as follows:

Starting in 1987, the AMT rate is 21%, up 1% from the prior rate of 20%.

The AMT exemption based on filing status is reduced by 25¢ for each $1 that alternative minimum taxable income exceeds $150,000 for joint filers or a qualifying surviving spouse; $112,500 for single persons; and $75,000 for a married person filing separately. The effect of the exemption phase-out results in a 26% tax for those with income in the phase-out range. The AMT exemption before the phase-out is $40,000 for a joint return or qualifying surviving spouse, $30,000 for a single person, $20,000 for a married person's separate return. The exemption is completely phased out at $310,000 on a joint return, $232,500 on single return, $155,000 on a married separate return.

Passive activity losses and tax shelter farming losses do not reduce AMT taxable income. The full passive loss is denied for AMT purposes although for purposes of the regular income tax, the limits on passive losses will be phased in over five years.

The untaxed appreciation on charitable contributions of property and interest paid on tax-exempt bonds for non-essential private functions issued after August 7, 1986, are AMT preference items.

The computation steps are revised. Under prior law, tax benefits were added back to adjusted gross income for AMT purposes and were described as tax preferences. Under the new law, the starting point for AMT purposes is taxable income. Further, prior law tax preferences and new items are either defined as adjustments or tax preferences. Adjustments generally involve a recalculation of deductions resulting in an increase in AMT income; in some cases, an adjustment may result in a lower AMT taxable income than regular taxable income; a tax preference item always results in the increase of AMT taxable income.

65% rather than 100% of net oil and gas income is used to offset intangible drilling costs for purposes of computing the tax preference for intangible drilling costs.

Net operating losses may not offset more than 90% of remaining tax liability as determined without regard to foreign tax credits and net operating losses.

A new credit based on AMT taxes incurred after 1986 may be deducted from regular tax starting in 1988.

Installment sales of dealer property and rental property with a price of over $150,000 are not recognized for AMT purposes.

The alternative minimum tax (AMT) is designed to recoup tax benefits that reduce or eliminate your regular income tax. AMT is imposed if it exceeds your regular income tax or you have no tax liability after claiming certain tax deductions or credits. You may incur an AMT if you have deductions for accelerated depreciation, percentage depletion, tax shelter losses and intangible drilling and development costs. Even when you do not have the above preference items, you may incur AMT if you have substantial itemized deductions that are not deductible for AMT purposes. For AMT purposes, miscellaneous deductions and state and local income taxes are not deductible, and there is a limited interest deduction.

The following example illustrates how AMT is incurred when substantial itemized deductions are not allowed for AMT purposes.

EXAMPLE

Jones is single. Her taxable income is $27,000 after claiming itemized deductions of $40,000, such as a deduction of state and local taxes, which are not deductible for AMT purposes.

	Regular Tax	AMT
Taxable income	$27,000	$27,000
Adjustment		40,000
		67,000
Less: Exemption		30,000
AMT taxable income		$37,000
Tax	$ 5,304	$ 7,770

The tax benefit realized from the itemized deductions has been offset by the AMT tax of $7,770.

PATTERN OF AMT TAXATION ON FORM 6251

¶ 23.2 For the AMT calculation on Form 6251, taxable income is generally increased by adjustments and tax preferences (*see* below) and decreased by the AMT exemption if not within the phase-out. Taxable income for AMT purposes does not include any refunds of state and local taxes. The result of the above calculations is AMT taxable income. The 21% rate is applied to this amount. The AMT amount may be reduced only by foreign tax credit, *see* ¶23.5. From this amount, you subtract your regular tax. The difference is your alternative minimum tax.

AMT calculation on Form 6251

1. Taxable income (from Form 1040).
2. Add adjustments for:
   Itemized deductions
   Accelerated depreciation on property acquired after 1986

   Mining exploration and development costs
   Long-term contracts
   Net operating losses
   Pollution control facilities
   Certain installment sales of rental property and by dealers
   Circulation and research expenses
   Passive activity and certain farm shelter losses

3. Add tax preference items:
   Accelerated depreciation on property acquired before 1987
   Depletion
   Intangible drilling costs
   Incentive stock options
   Certain tax-exempt interest
   Charitable donations of appreciated capital gain property

4. Less exemption of:
   $40,000 for joint return filer or qualifying surviving spouse
   $30,000 for single taxpayer
   $20,000 for married person filing separate return

   (Exemption phase-out for joint return is between $150,000 and $310,000; $112,500 and $232,500 for single taxpayer; $75,000 and $155,000 for married filing separate return.)

Adjustments are discussed at ¶23.3; tax preferences at ¶23.4.

EXAMPLE

You are married filing jointly. Your taxable income is $45,000 and your regular tax is $8,840. AMT adjustments for unallowed itemized deductions are $40,000; a tax preference item for an incentive stock option exercise is $10,000.

Taxable income		$45,000
Add		
Adjustments	$40,000	
Tax preference	10,000	50,000
		95,000
Less: Exemption		40,000
AMT taxable income		55,000
AMT rate of 21%		11,550
Less regular tax		8,840
Additional tax or AMT		$ 2,710

For AMT purposes, the regular income tax does not include the averaging tax on lump-sum distributions and investment credit recapture.

Make sure that any projected AMT liability is considered in estimating tax payments, *see* chapter 26.

If you do not owe AMT tax and your tax credits are not limited because of the AMT tax (*see* ¶23.5) you are not required to file Form 6251.

ADJUSTMENTS FOR AMT

¶ 23.3 The amount of your regular taxable income will generally be increased by the following adjustments.

Itemized deductions. If you have claimed itemized deductions for state and local taxes, miscellaneous deductions subject to 2% AGI floor, interest, and medical expenses, you will have to add back all or part of such deductions to taxable income. Taxes directly deductible from gross income for business or rental purposes remain deductible for AMT purposes. For AMT purposes only the following itemized deductions are allowed:

  Charitable contributions
  Medical expenses exceeding 10% of adjusted gross income. Do not confuse this limit with the 7.5% limit for regular tax purposes
  Casualty and theft losses exceeding 10% of adjusted gross income
  Unreimbursed moving expenses to a new job location
  Wagering losses
  Claim of right deduction (¶2.11)
  Estate tax deductions for income in respect of a decedent
  Impairment-related work expenses
  Home mortgage interest
  Investment interest to the extent of net investment income

Home mortgage interest is interest paid on a debt incurred to buy, construct, or substantially rehabilitate your principal residence or qualifying second residence. The residence may be a house, apartment, condominium, or mobile home not used on a transient basis. In the case of a refinanced mortgage, less interest may be deductible for AMT purposes than for regular tax purposes. Interest on a refinanced mortgage is deductible for AMT purposes only to the extent the new debt does not exceed the amount of the old debt immediately before the refinancing. Interest on the excess is not deductible for AMT purposes. Interest on a mortgage debt incurred before July 1, 1982, for any purpose qualifies as an AMT deduction if the mortgage is secured by your principal residence or other dwelling in which you or your family reside.

If you did not claim itemized deductions on Form 1040, you may not claim the standard deduction as an AMT deduction.

Exemptions for yourself and your dependents are not allowed for AMT purposes.

MACRS depreciation. Less depreciation is allowed for AMT than for regular tax purposes. For property other than real property acquired after 1986 and depreciable under MACRS, the AMT depreciation rate is the 150% declining balance method, switching to the straight line method when a larger depreciation allowance results. Real property acquired after 1986 is depreciated for AMT over a 40-year period using the straight line method.

When post-1986 depreciation assets are sold, gain for AMT purposes is figured on the basis of property adjusted by depreciation claimed for AMT purposes. (This new AMT basis rule does *not* apply to property placed in service before 1987 except for transitional property within the post-1986 rules.)

The adjustment for MACRS may result in providing more depreciation for AMT purposes where the AMT depreciation computation towards the latter part of the useful life of MACRS property provides larger deductions than the regular MACRS deduction.

Property placed in service before 1987, unless it qualifies under MACRS transitional rules, is subject to prior law tax preference rules. Prior law creates tax preference items when the ACRS deduction exceeds regular straight line, *see* ¶23.4. A tax preference item always increases AMT taxable income.

EXAMPLE

In one taxable year when AMT applies, Jones has two pieces of property acquired after 1986. The regular MACRS depreciation for asset A is $500 and for asset B $400. When applying the AMT rules, the depreciation for asset A is $400 and for asset B $450. AMT taxable income is increased by $50. The adjustment accounts for all post-1987 MACRS property held in the year.

Asset A		
Regular depreciation	$500	
AMT depreciation	400	$100
Asset B		
Regular depreciation	$400	
AMT depreciation	450	(50)
Net adjustment to AMT taxable income		$ 50

Net operating loss deduction. A net operating loss claimed for regular tax purposes must be recomputed for AMT. A net operating loss deductible for AMT purposes is generally the amount of the regular net operating loss with these exceptions: (1) The loss must be reduced by adjustments and tax preference items other than charitable contributions for appreciated property; (2) in figuring the nonbusiness income adjustment, only AMT itemized deductions may be taken. Under the rules of ¶5.18, the nonbusiness income adjustment is reduced by itemized deductions, but for AMT purposes, state and local taxes and certain interest may not reduce nonbusiness income before it is applied to the net operating loss.

In some cases, a net operating loss will eliminate your regular tax liability but not the AMT because the loss for AMT purposes is reduced by tax preference items and the amount of the net operating loss deduction that may be deducted from AMT taxable income may not exceed 90% of AMT taxable income before the deduction. According to Committee reports, net operating losses that are disallowed because of the 90% AMT limit may be carried over to other years under regular tax rules. Carryovers from years beginning after 1982 and before 1987 are figured under prior law rules, subject to the 90% AMT limit.

Mining exploration and development costs. The deduction allowed for regular tax purposes for mining exploration and development costs is amortized ratably over a 10-year period for AMT purposes.

If a mine is abandoned as worthless, all mining exploration and development costs that have not been written off are deductible in the year of abandonment.

Long-term contracts. In the case of a long-term contract entered into after February 28, 1986, the use of the completed contract method of accounting or certain other methods of accounting for long-term contracts is not allowable. For AMT, the percentage of completion method must be used.

Amortization of certified pollution control facilities. For purposes of the alternative minimum tax, the amortization deduction for a certified pollution control facility placed in service after 1986 is determined under alternative MACRS.

Installment sales of certain property. Installment sales of inventory property are not recognized for AMT purposes. For AMT purposes, all gain is treated as realized on the disposition in the year of sale. The same treatment applies to installment sales of dealer property and rental property with a sales price of over $150,000 which are subject to the allocable installment indebtedness rules of ¶6.43. Such installment sales are ignored for AMT purposes. Gain on the sale is recognized in the year of sale.

Research and experimental expenditures. Research and experimental expenditures must be amortized over 10 years beginning with the tax year in which the expenditures were made.

Farm and passive activity losses. No loss from a tax shelter farm activity is allowed in figuring AMT income. Generally, a tax shelter farm activity is any farming syndicate or any other passive farming activity. The loss from a tax shelter farm activity is allowed in figuring alternative minimum taxable income for later years as a deduction against income from the activity or for the year you dispose of your entire interest in the activity.

Passive activity losses are generally not allowed in figuring AMT taxable income. For AMT purposes, there is no phase-in of the passive activity loss disallowance.

A disallowed loss may be reduced if you are insolvent as of the end of the tax year. You are insolvent to the extent that your liabilities exceed the fair market value of your assets.

TAX PREFERENCE ITEMS

¶ **23.4** The following are tax preference items that increase the amount of AMT taxable income.

Incentive stock options. Exercise of an incentive stock option produces a preference item. The amount is the excess of the fair market value of a share at the time of exercise over the option price. No preference is created if there is an early disposition of stock acquired through the exercise of the option which results in immediate income tax; however, this rule may be eliminated by proposed tax legislation.

The basis of stock acquired through the exercise of stock option after 1986 equals the fair market value of the stock for future AMT purposes. For example, in 1987, you pay an exercise price of $10 to buy stock with a fair market value of $15. The preference item is $5. If in a later year you sell the stock, for regular tax purposes, the basis is $10, for AMT purposes $15.

Accelerated depreciation of property acquired before 1987. For property placed in service before 1981, the difference between the depreciation that would have been allowable if the straight line method had been used and accelerated depreciation claimed on real property during the taxable year is a tax preference item. The excess is computed for each asset depreciated through an accelerated method. This rule also applies to accelerated depreciation, including additional depreciation from the use of ADR system, taken on personal property subject to a lease. Five-year amortization of certified pollution control facilities and child care facilities is a preference item to the extent that the claimed deduction exceeds *allowable* depreciation. In the year a building is sold, you do not treat accelerated depreciation as a preference item to the extent that depreciation is recaptured as ordinary income.

The basis of an asset is *not* adjusted for the depreciation element taxed as a preference item.

For property placed in service after 1980, these rules apply. For ACRS recovery property, a tax preference item is the difference between ACRS depreciation and depreciation that would have been allowable if the straight line method (without regard to salvage value) had been used. The excess is computed for each recovery property. In the case of personal property subject to a lease for which an ACRS deduction was claimed, the difference between depreciation that would have been allowable using the straight line method and the following recovery periods (with a half-year convention, but without regard to salvage value) and accelerated cost recovery claimed for the property is an item of tax preference. For three-

year property, the recovery period is five years; for five-year property, the period is eight years, and for 10-year property, 15 years.

Note: In the case of pre-1987 assets, a tax preference is computed for each asset. Excess depreciation, the difference between ACRS and straight line depreciation, is a tax preference. As explained in ¶23.3, the depreciation adjustment for post-1986 assets does not follow this approach and the calculation compares the total AMT depreciation with regular MACRS depreciation, and if MACRS depreciation is greater, any excess is treated as an adjustment to AMT income.

Depletion. The difference between claimed percentage depletion and the adjusted basis of the property at the end of the year (without regard to current depletion) is a preference item. You figure the amount separately for each property for which you claim a depletion allowance. No tax preference occurs until the total depletion claimed over a period of years exceeds the cost basis of the property.

Intangible drilling costs. The preference item is the excess of intangible drilling costs over 65% of net income from oil and gas properties for the taxable year. Excess intangible drilling costs are those expenses in excess of the amount which could have been deducted had the expenses been capitalized and either deducted ratably over ten years or deducted over the life of the well as cost depletion. Net income from oil and gas properties is gross income (excluding rent or royalties paid to another for use of the property) reduced by deductions other than excess intangible drilling costs. Deductions attributable to properties with no gross income are not to be taken into account. Costs incurred in drilling a nonproductive well are not counted as a tax preference.

The preference rule does not apply if you elected to capitalize intangible drilling costs. It does not apply to nonproductive wells. A nonproductive well is one which is plugged and abandoned without having produced oil and gas in commercial quantities for any substantial period of time. According to committee reports, a well which has been plugged and abandoned may have produced some relatively small amount of oil and still be considered a nonproductive well, depending on the amount of oil produced in relation to the costs of drilling. In some cases, it may not be possible to determine whether a well is in fact nonproductive until after the close of the taxable year. In these cases, no preference is included in the minimum tax base to any wells which are later determined to be nonproductive. If a well is proved to be nonproductive after the end of the taxable year but before the tax return for the year in question is filed, that well can be treated as nonproductive on that return. If a well is not determined to be nonproductive by the time the return for the year in question is filed, the intangible expenses related to that well are subject to the minimum tax. However, you may file an amended return and claim a credit or refund for the amount of any minimum tax paid on expenses related to that well if the well later proves to be nonproductive.

Tax benefit rule. You may not have realized a tax benefit from an item subject to an adjustment or treatment as a tax preference. This may happen when non-AMT items would have resulted in a loss without consideration of AMT preference or adjustment items. In such a case, you may not be liable for AMT. The application of this rule is not clear. The Treasury has not released regulations on the subject.

Tax-exempt interest on nonessential private activity bonds. For AMT purposes, you must include the tax-exempt interest on private activity bonds issued after August 7, 1986, except for qualified 501(c)(3) bonds used to benefit tax-exempt groups. Generally, private activity bonds issued after August 7, 1986, are subject to AMT but for certain bonds meeting specific tests, the AMT rule applies to bonds issued on or after September 1, 1986. Interest paid on buying or carrying such bonds is deductible for AMT purposes.

Charitable contributions of appreciated property. If you claimed a charitable contribution of appreciated capital gain property, the appreciation is a tax preference item.

AMT FOREIGN TAX CREDIT AND OTHER TAX CREDITS

¶ **23.5** A foreign tax credit may be deducted from AMT tax liability. It is figured in the same way as the regular foreign tax credits (see ¶36.16) after substituting AMT taxable income for regular taxable income.

The AMT foreign tax credit may not offset more than 90% of AMT tax determined without regard to the foreign tax credit and net operating loss deduction. Any foreign tax credit not allowed by the limit may be carried back and forward; see ¶36.17 and Treasury regulations for further details.

Other credits. Follow the instructions and lines of Form 6251 for the treatment of other tax credits.

The interplay of technical rules and definitions may reduce nonrefundable credits, such as the dependent care credit and the elderly and disabled credit, even when the regular tax applies. The amount of such credits is limited to the regular tax liability less the AMT tax liability.

EXAMPLE
You have regular tax liability of $2,000 and a dependent care credit of $500. The tentative AMT tax is $1,800. The credit may not reduce your regular tax to $1,500. The credit is limited to $200 ($2,000–1,800). It is applied against your regular tax, reducing it to $1,800.

AMT TAX CREDIT FROM REGULAR TAX

¶ **23.6** You may reduce your regular tax by a tax credit based on a prior AMT tax incurred after 1986. Therefore, if you incur AMT in 1987 and a regular tax in 1988, you may be able to deduct your 1987 AMT tax from your 1988 regular tax.

EXAMPLE
In 1987, your AMT tax is $6,000 and your regular tax was $5,000. Your carryforward credit is $1,000 ($6,000–5,000). In 1988, your regular tax is $10,000 and your AMT tax liability is $5,000. You may apply the $1,000 credit against your regular tax.

The credit carryforward period is indefinite. The credit is deductible whenever you have a regular tax liability. However, the credit may not reduce your tax below the AMT tax for that year. To qualify for the credit, your AMT liability must have been triggered by preference and adjustments involving deferred tax benefits. No credit is allowed to the extent the AMT tax was based on disallowed itemized deductions, percentage depletion, charitable donations of appreciated property, and tax-exempt interest.

The credit attempts to even out the differences in AMT and regular tax reporting which over a period of time results in distorted income reporting. Without the credit, the distortion would favor the Government. However, if you are always subject to AMT, you will not be able to take a credit for past AMT taxes.

ELECTION FOR 10-YEAR WRITE OFF OF PREFERENCES

¶ **23.7** You may avoid AMT on certain expenditures by electing to deduct them ratably over a 10-year period beginning with the year in which the expenditure was made. Expenditures qualifying for this election are intangible drilling costs, mining and development costs and research and experimental expenditures. A three-year write off election is allowed for circulation expenses.

Revocation of the election is allowed only with IRS consent. Partners may make separate elections.

AVOIDING AMT TAX

¶ **23.8** If you are close to or within the range of the AMT tax, the following steps can avoid or soften the impact of the tax:

Defer deductible expense items to a later year in which your income will be subject to tax rates exceeding 21%. Consider deferring payment of charitable donations, home mortgage interest, and medical expenses. You will get a larger tax benefit from the deductions in the later year. In the case of certain realty or equipment purchases, consider an election to capitalize taxes and carry charges. Also, do not elect first-year expensing of business equipment.

Defer if possible the exercise of an incentive stock option to a later year. The bargain element of incentive stock option is a preference item subject to AMT. This is the difference between the option price and the fair market price of the stock on the date of exercise. If you exercise the option and it is subject to AMT along with other tax shelter preferences, you may find yourself with an unexpected liability and short of liquid funds to meet your tax liability.

Defer transacting an installment sale that will not be recognized for AMT purposes or elect to report the entire proceeds of such a sale to incur regular tax liability if you have regular tax deductions that will reduce the gain for regular tax purposes but not for AMT purposes.

Accelerating income. If you find that you will be subject to AMT in a current year, you may want to subject additional income in that year to the AMT tax rate. In such a case, consider accelerating the receipt of income to that year. If you are in business, you might ask for earlier payments from customers or clients. If you control a small corporation, you might prepay salary or pay larger bonuses. But here be careful not to run afoul of reasonable compensation rules.

You might also consider paying dividends. If you hold savings certificates with a six-month maturity in a later year, you might consider an early redemption to the current year. But here weigh the penalty cost of an early forfeiture. Similarly you might make an early sale of U.S. Treasury Bills to the current year.

If you are certain that you will be subject to AMT you may consider switching some tax free investments into taxable investments which will give a higher after-tax return after the 21% AMT tax.

24

TAX CREDITS

¶ **24.1** *A credit reduces your tax liability dollar-for-dollar. The following chart lists credits that reduce income tax liability.*

Credit for	For	Rate
Business energy property (¶24.2)	Installation of certain energy saving devices	Biomass and geothermal, 10%, solar, 12%, ocean thermal, 15%
Dependent care (¶1.29)	Care of child under the age of 15 or disabled dependent to enable you to work	20% to 30% (depending on income) of expenses up to $2,400 for one dependent or $4,800 for two or more dependents. Top credit for those with adjusted gross income over $28,000 is $480 for one dependent; $960 for two or more dependents
Diesel vehicles (¶24.4)	To account for increased fuel tax	$102 per car, $198 for van or light truck
Earned income (¶24.10)	Certain low-income wage earners	Top credit $851 subject to reductions for income over $6,920.
Elderly or disabled (¶34.2)	Persons 65 or older or under age 65 who are permanently and totally disabled and receive disability income	Top credit $1,125; limits may reduce or eliminate credit
Federal gasoline and fuels tax (¶24.3)	Gasoline and fuels used for other than highway or aviation vehicles, such as tractors, for a qualified business use	9.1¢ per gallon of gas
Foreign taxes (¶36.15)	Income taxes paid to a foreign country or U.S. possession	Amount of foreign tax not to exceed U.S. tax multiplied by the ratio of foreign taxable income over total taxable income (less zero bracket amount)
Interest on qualified home mortgage certificates (¶24.6)	Interest on home mortgages authorized by special state and local programs	Depends on interest paid and credit rate under certificate
Low-income housing credit (¶24.2)	Constructing or rehabilitating low-income housing units	9% or 4% depending on type of building
Rehabilitation property (¶24.2)	Rehabilitating pre-1936 nonresidential buildings or certified historic structures	20% for historic structures; 10% for pre-1936 buildings
Research credit (¶24.2)	Increasing research costs for developing or improving products, formulas or similar business items	20% of qualifying expenses in excess of three-year average
Targeted jobs (¶24.2)	Employment of disadvantaged persons	40% of first $6,000 of first-year wages
Tax paid by mutual fund on undistributed gains (¶24.5)	Tax paid by mutual fund on capital gains earned by fund and retained	Amount of tax paid by fund on retained capital gains which are reported in your income

BUSINESS CREDITS

GENERAL BUSINESS CREDITS

¶ **24.2** Business credits include the targeted jobs credit, alcohol fuels credit, research credit, low-income housing credit, the rehabilitation property investment credit and business energy investment credit. An investment credit for other property is barred unless you qualify under transition rules (*see* next page).

You compute each credit separately. If you claim only one credit, that credit is considered your *general business credit* for 1987. The credit is subject to a limitation based on tax liability which is figured on the form used to compute that particular credit. You then enter the allowable credit as your general business credit on Form 1040.

If you claim more than one credit, the credits are combined into one general business credit on Form 3800. Each credit is first computed separately and then listed on Form 3800. The combined credit is subject to a limitation based on tax liability. Follow the line-by-line steps of Form 3800 to figure the limitation. You must attach to your return Form 3800 and also the separate forms for each credit you claim.

Carryback and carryforward of unused credits. If your full 1987 general business credit may not be claimed because of the $25,000/75% tax liability limitation, you may carry back the excess three years, starting with the earliest year. After the carryback, any remaining credit may be carried forward 15 years until used up. The carrybacks and carryforwards are listed on Form 3800.

If you have carryforwards from more than one type of unused credit, you report the total carryforward on Form 3800. You do not have to file Form 3800 if you only have one type of carryforward and in 1987 you claim only one type of credit. In that case, you file only the form used to compute the particular credit.

Targeted jobs credit. This credit is designed to encourage business employment of the hard-to-hire. The credit, computed on Form 5884, is based on a percentage of wages. An eligible employee is one who is a member of one of the following targeted groups: A vocational rehabilitation referral, an economically disadvantaged youth (age 18 through 24), an economically disadvantaged Vietnam-era veteran, an SSI recipient, a general assistance recipient, a youth (age 16 through 19) participating in a cooperative education program, or an economically disadvantaged ex-convict. Special rules apply to summer employment of certain disadvantaged youths. Wages paid to related employees do not qualify. Further, an employee must be certified by a designated local agency as qualifying as a member of a targeted group.

The credit is generally 40% of the first $6,000 of first-year wages of an eligible employee. See Form 5884 for details.

Work incentive expense (WIN) credit. This credit may not be claimed for wages paid or incurred in taxable years after December 31, 1981. However, on Form 3800, unused credits may still be used up through carrybacks and carryovers under the general business credit and the credit carryback and carryover provisions.

Alcohol fuels credit. On Form 6478, you compute the credit for sale or use of alcohol fuels and certain alcohol mixture. Different credits apply depending on the type of fuel.

Business energy credits. The following business credits are allowed:

For	Percentage	Property placed in service
Solar energy	12%	1987
	10	1988
Geothermal	10	1987–1988
Ocean thermal	15	1987–1988
Biomass	10	1987

Residential energy credits are no longer allowed.

The business energy credit is treated as an investment credit and is computed on Form 3468.

Investment credit for transition property. Under transition rules, equipment with a class life of at least five years qualifies for the regular investment credit, if you had a binding written contract for its acquisition or construction as of December 31, 1985. Property may also qualify if substantial construction costs were incurred before 1986. For tax years beginning after June 30, 1987, the credit for transition property must be reduced by 35%, except for certain timber property. For taxable years that begin before and end after July 1, 1987, the reduction equals 35% multiplied by this fraction: number of months after June 30, 1987, divided by 12 (number of months in your tax year). If a credit is allowed under transition rules, you must reduce the basis of the property for depreciation purposes by the full credit. See the instructions to Form 3468 for further transition property rules.

Rehabilitation property credit. On Form 3468, you compute the 10% investment credit for rehabilitating pre-1936 nonresidential buildings and the 20% credit for rehabilitating certified historic structures used for either residential or nonresidential purposes.

Low-income housing credit. On Form 8586, you compute the credit which may not exceed the credit allocation given to you on Form 8609 from an authorized low-income housing credit agency. Generally, the credit in 1987 is 9% for new buildings that are not federally subsidized and 4% for new federally subsidized buildings and for existing buildings. The credit is claimed over a 10-year period. For the first year, you must certify on Form 8609 certain information concerning the building and your eligibility for the credit. You must attach both Form 8609 and Form 8586 to your tax return.

Research credit. The research credit may be available if you increase the amount you spend on business research costs. In general, a 20% credit is allowed for qualifying research expenses in excess of average research expenses during the prior three-year period. The credit is computed on Form 6765. See the instructions to Form 6765 and IRS Publication 906 for computation details.

FEDERAL GASOLINE AND FUEL TAX CREDIT

¶ **24.3** For a qualified business use, a refundable credit of 9.1¢ per gallon of gasoline or special motor fuel may be claimed for fuel used in nonhighway vehicles (other than motorboats); 15.1¢ per gallon for diesel fuel. The 9.1¢ and 15.1¢ credits also apply for a qualified farm use. Examples of nonhighway vehicles include generators, compressors, forklift trucks, and bulldozers. A credit may also be claimed for aviation fuel used for farming or commercial aviation.

You must claim the credit on a timely filed income tax return, including extensions. You compute the credit on Form 4136, which you attach to Form 1040. If you do not claim the credit on your tax return, you may do so on a timely filed refund claim or amended return for that year. If the credit exceeds $1,000 during any of the first three quarters of the taxable year, you may file a refund claim on a quarterly basis. A quarterly refund claim must be filed on Form 843 on or before the last day of the quarter following the quarter for which the refund is claimed.

For further explanation, see Publication 378; farmers see Publication 225.

If the cost of the gasoline and special fuel is deducted as a business expense, the credit claimed on these items is reported as income. If you use the cash basis method of reporting, you report the credit as income in the year in which you file a tax return on which the credit is claimed. If you are on the accrual basis, you report the credit in the year the fuel is used.

CREDIT FOR DIESEL VEHICLE FUEL

¶ **24.4** If in 1987, you bought a diesel-powered car or truck weighing 10,000 pounds or less, you may claim a one-time credit for the diesel fuel tax. You must be the original purchaser, that is, the first purchaser for use other than resale. The credit for an auto is $102; for a truck or van, $198. The credit is claimed on Form 4136.

The credit is scheduled to expire after 1987.

For depreciation and investment credit purposes, basis is reduced by the credit. Thus, if a new diesel-powered car is purchased for $16,000, basis is reduced by the $102 credit to $15,898.

CREDIT FOR TAX PAID BY MUTUAL FUND ON UNDISTRIBUTED GAINS

¶ **24.5** A mutual fund that does not distribute all of its capital gains earned during the year pays a tax on the undistributed gain. The law treats this tax payment as made on your behalf. The company will notify you of the amount of tax paid which is the amount of your credit.

To claim a tax credit, you do the following:
1. Report on Schedule D as 1987 long-term capital gain your share of the undistributed capital gain. Your company sends you Form 2439 which lists your share of the undistributed gain and the amount of tax paid on it.
2. You enter your share of the tax the company paid on this gain on Form 1040 on the line reading "Credit from a Regulated Investment Company (attach Form 2439)." Attach Copy B of Form 2439 to your return to support your tax credit.

3. Increase the basis of your stock by the difference between the undistributed capital gain and the amount of tax paid by the mutual fund, as reported on Form 2439.

INTEREST ON QUALIFIED HOME MORTGAGE CERTIFICATES

¶ **24.6** Homebuyers who qualify under special state and local programs may obtain "mortgage credit certificates" to finance the purchase of a principal residence or to borrow funds for certain home improvements. Under the program, a tax credit for interest paid on the mortgage may be claimed. The tax credit equals the interest paid multiplied by the certificate rate set by the governmental authority. The credit rate must be at least 10%, and if it exceeds 20%, the maximum annual credit is $2,000. Interest not qualifying for the credit may be deducted as an itemized deduction.

The credit is computed on Form 8396, which must be attached to Form 1040.

EXAMPLE
You pay $5,000 interest on a mortgage issued under a qualifying mortgage credit certificate. Under its terms, you are allowed a tax credit of $750. You may claim the balance of interest or $4,250 ($5,000–$750) as an itemized deduction.

If the allowable credit exceeds tax liability, a three-year carryover is allowed.

Generally, a qualifying principal residence may not cost more than 110% of the average area purchase price; 120% in certain targeted areas.

CARRYOVERS OF INVESTMENT CREDIT AND HOME ENERGY CREDIT

¶ **24.7** *Investment credit carryovers.* Although the regular investment credit is no longer allowed (except for transition property), you may have a credit carryover from a pre-1987 year. Under the law, the investment credit may be carried back three years and forward 15 years. Credits carried over from earlier years are deducted following a first-in-first-out order.

The 1986 Tax Act substantially reduced the amount of carryover benefits. A carryover to be applied in taxable years beginning after June 30, 1987, must be reduced by 35%. For tax years that straddle July 1, 1987, the 35% reduction is allocated for the months in the taxable year after June 30, 1987. Therefore, for a calendar year 1987 taxpayer, the reduction for 1987 is 17½%. The amount of the reduction may be carried forward to 1988. No carryback of a reduction is allowed. *See* Form 3468 for further details.

Energy credit carryovers. The tax credit for home insulation and other energy-saving expenses is no longer available. However, if you have an unused credit of at least $10 from 1986, you may claim a credit carryforward on your 1987 return. Figure the carryforward credit on Form 5695. Note that 1987 is the last year to take advantage of the energy credit carryover.

INVESTMENT CREDIT RECAPTURE

¶ **24.8** The regular investment credit is no longer allowed except for certain transition property (¶24.2). However, you must report income from credit recapture if in 1987 you dispose of property for which you claimed an investment credit in a prior year and which you held for less than the holding period required for the credit. You figure the recapture on Form 4255 and add the recaptured amount to your regular tax.

Recapture generally occurs when you sell the asset or stop using it for business purposes. Recapture also applies if the percentage of business use drops below the business-use percentage in the year you placed the asset in service.

There is no credit recapture on three-year recovery property if it is held at least three years. There is no recapture on 5-, 10-, or 15-year recovery property held at least five years. If property is disposed of before three or five years, part or all of the credit is recaptured. The credit is deemed to be 2% a year, so that if three-year property, on which a 6%

credit was taken, is sold after two years, 4% of the credit is considered to be earned and 2% is recaptured.

Property disposed within—	Recapture percentage for—	
	3-year property	All other property
First year	100%	100%
Second year	66	80
Third year	33	60
Fourth year	—	40
Fifth year	—	20
Sixth year or later	—	—

To the extent the investment credit did not reduce tax liability in the year claimed, but resulted in a credit carryback or carryover, any recaptured amount will not increase tax liability in the year of recapture but will be used to adjust the credit carrybacks and carryovers.

Special recapture rules not discussed in this book apply to energy property.

Property is considered disposed of whenever it is sold, exchanged, transferred, distributed, involuntarily converted, or given away. A disposal occurs when property is contributed to a partnership or a corporation, but not where the contribution of property is a mere change in the form of operating the business and the owner retains a substantial ownership interest.

If your business use of the property falls below the business use percentage in the year you placed the property in service, you are treated as having disposed of part of the property and part of the credit is subject to recapture. *See* the instructions to Form 4255. If business use of an automobile or computer placed in service after June 18, 1984, falls to 50% or less, follow the recapture rules at ¶19.66.

An election of S corporation status is considered a mere change in form.

If recapture is due on used property, you may avoid recapture if the credit originally was limited by the $125,000 used property limit. You may be able to substitute other used property in order to prevent recapture. Generally, a lease of property is not considered to be a disposition. However, if you lease out property which you would ordinarily dispose of by sale or exchange and it appears that a purpose of the lease is to avoid the recapture of the credit, the lease may be considered a disposition.

A disposal also occurs when property is no longer subject to depreciation because, for example, it is shifted from a business to a personal use. Under Treasury regulations, a reduction in the business use of property is considered a partial disposition triggering recapture.

Recapture does not apply where title to property is transferred as a security interest, for example, where property is mortgaged. The recapture rule also does not apply where property is transferred by reason of the owner's death, or where a successor corporation "stands in the shoes" of the predecessor corporation. Recapture does not result under the Bankruptcy Tax Act when the basis of the property is reduced. This rule reverses a long standing rule that the transfer of property to a trustee in bankruptcy is a disposition.

Involuntary conversions. If property on which an investment credit has been taken is involuntarily converted before the end of the recovery period used in figuring the credit, the recapture rules apply. *See* Treasury regulations for further details.

Basis adjustment. If before 1987 you elected to reduce the basis of property that is subject to recapture in 1987, you may add back to basis 50% of the recaptured amount.

Tax payment credit for farmers who have investment credit carryovers. A qualified farmer may elect to treat as a tax payment credit for 1987 the smallest of the following amounts: $750, one-half of the existing carryovers, or a net tax liability determined for a carryback period. The credit is applied against 1987 tax.

A qualified farmer is one who during a three-year taxable period immediately before the year of election (1987 for calendar year farmers) derived 50% or more of his gross income from farming. The credit carryover must have been based on property used for farming.

EARNED INCOME CREDIT FOR LOW INCOME HOUSEHOLDERS

¶ **24.9** A special tax credit for low income workers with families may provide a refund or subsidy of up to $851 in 1987. An "earned income credit" is available only to low income workers who have dependent children and maintain a household.

> The credit is designed to encourage low income wage earners to file income tax returns. The credit is a form of negative income tax. Even if no tax withholding has been taken from your wages and you do not have to file a return because you do not meet the gross income filing requirements, you may receive a payment from the federal government. If you have a tax liability, the credit will be first applied against your tax liability. Any excess credit is refunded to you. Alternatively, you may elect to have your credit figured into your withholding to receive advanced payment of the credit throughout the year.

The credit is based only on "earned income," wages, salaries and other employee compensation, plus earnings from self-employment. For 1987, the maximum credit is $851.20 or 14% of your first $6,080 of earned income. If you have adjusted gross income over $6,920, the credit is phased out by being reduced by 10% of the excess over $6,920. Thus, the credit is eliminated when your income reaches $15,432. You do not figure the credit; you find your credit in special tables included in the Government's instructions to the 1987 tax forms.

The credit will affect benefits under federal assistance programs.

ARE YOU ELIGIBLE FOR THE CREDIT?

¶ **24.10** You are eligible for the earned income credit for low income householders if you are:
1. Married and entitled to a dependency exemption for a child;
2. A surviving spouse; or
3. Head of household (an unmarried child in your household need not be your dependent, but a married child must be your dependent).

A special rule applies if you are divorced or legally separated, separated under a written agreement, or you live apart from your spouse for the last six months of 1987 and you have custody of your child during a greater portion of the year than does the other parent. You may claim the credit even though you waive the dependency exemption for the child or you may not claim the exemption under a pre-1986 divorce or separation agreement. For this rule to apply, the child must be in your custody, or the custody of you and the other parent for more than half of 1987.

You are not eligible if you are entitled to exclude tax free income from sources outside the United States or within the possessions of the United States (see chapter 36).

Under the household test, you must provide over half of the cost of maintaining a household that is your principal place of abode in the United States. You may qualify whether you are married or single. A single person is considered to be maintaining a household if he provides over half of the cost of maintaining the household. A married person is considered to be maintaining a household if both spouses together furnish over one-half of the cost of maintaining the household. The cost of maintaining a household includes such costs as property taxes, mortgage interest, rent, utility charges, upkeep and repairs, property insurance, and food.

Household costs do not include costs of clothing, education, medical treatment, vacations, life insurance, mortgage principal, and permanent improvements to the premises.

Welfare payments under a state Aid to Families with Dependent Children (AFDC) program for which the recipient is accountable to the state for spending payments for the well-being of the children are treated as not furnished by the recipient. To the extent that AFDC payments are used for household costs, they are counted in the total cost of maintaining the household.

If you maintain a household for a foster child, the child must reside with you for the entire year. In the case of an adopted child or stepchild, your home must be the child's principal place of abode only during the portion of the year the child became your child.

A married person must file a joint return to claim the credit. However, a married individual who is treated as not married may claim the credit as a single person who maintains a household and claims a child as a dependent.

WHAT IS EARNED INCOME?

¶ **24.11** Earned income includes all wages, salaries, tips, and other compensation, plus net earnings from self-employment and pro rata share of partnership income. Net self-employment income of less than $400 qualifies as earned income even though not subject to the self-employment tax. Losses from self-employment reduce earned income. Where there is a net loss from self-employment but you elect to have $1,600 deemed as net earnings from self-employment on Schedule SE, the $1,600 is treated as earned income.

Disability payments, a parsonage allowance, and the value of meals and lodging excluded from gross income qualify as earned income. The IRS has ruled that strike benefits paid by a union to members who may or may not perform strike-related duties is treated as earned income.

Earned income is computed without regard to community property laws. Therefore, you may claim a credit based on the full amount of your own earnings, even though, under community property laws, half of the earnings is treated as gross income of your spouse.

What is not earned income. Pensions and annuity payments are not earned income for purposes of this credit. Income received by nonresident aliens not connected with a U.S. trade or business is not earned income. Interest, dividends, income from an estate or trust, and capital gains are not earned income. Rents will generally not qualify as earned income, except where you render services to tenants or materially help in the production of farm crops grown on rented land. Unemployment benefits and Workmen's Compensation are not earned income.

HOW TO FIGURE THE CREDIT

¶ **24.12** The earned income tax credit for 1987 is 14% of the first $6,080 of earned income. Thus, the maximum credit is $851.20.

EXAMPLE
You earned $3,000. Your earned income tax credit is $420 ($3,000 × 14%).

If your adjusted gross income exceeds $6,920, the maximum credit is reduced under a phase-out formula; see ¶24.9.

You do not have to figure the reduction or the allowable credit yourself. Your allowable credit is taken from a special table included in the Government's instructions to the 1987 tax forms.

ADVANCE PAYMENT OF THE CREDIT

¶ **24.13** If you believe you are entitled to an earned income credit, you may file a certificate, Form W-5, with your employer to have a portion of the credit added to your paycheck throughout the year.

If you receive any advance payments, you must file an income tax return, even though you owe no tax. If you receive payments in excess of the amount you are entitled to, as figured at the end of the year, you are liable for the excess. But if you receive less than the amount you are entitled to, you claim the balance on the tax return.

25

TAX WITHHOLDINGS

¶ **25.1** Taxes are withheld from payments made to you for services that you perform as an employee. The form of payment does not matter. Cash or property payments are subject to withholding tax. There are exceptions and these are listed in ¶25.2.

In fixing the rate of withholding on your pay, pay attention to the new 90% test for determining whether sufficient taxes have been withheld from your pay. A penalty will apply if your wage withholdings plus estimated tax payments do not equal the lesser of 90% of your current tax liability or 100% of the prior year's tax, *see* chapter 26.

By filing Form W-4, you claim exemptions for yourself, spouse, and dependents. The number of exemptions claimed will either lower or increase the amount of withholding. You may also claim withholding allowances for tax reduction items, such as itemized deductions.

A newer simplified withholding form, Form W-4A, may be used instead of the more complicated Form W-4. However, in choosing the W-4A over the W-4, simplicity is obtained at the price of accuracy. The W-4 matches withholdings more closely to tax liability. According to the IRS, filing Form W-4 is advisable if you have a large amount of non-wage income, such as interest or dividends. Further, if you qualify for tax credits other than the child and dependent care credit, you must file Form W-4 to take such credits into account.

WHEN INCOME TAXES ARE WITHHELD ON WAGES

¶ **25.2** The amount of income tax withheld for your wage bracket depends on your marital status and the number of exemptions you claim. Exemptions for withholding correspond with the exemptions allowed on your tax return (*see* ¶1.50). You file a withholding certificate, Form W-4 or W-4A, with your employer, indicating your status and exemptions. Without the certificate, your employer must withhold tax as if you are a single person with no exemptions.

If you failed to file a revised W-4 or W-4A by October 1, 1987, your employer was required to withhold taxes from your pay on the basis of one exemption, or two exemptions if you are married. If you are entitled to more, make sure to file a new W-4 or W-4A.

If you do not expect withholdings to meet your final tax liability, ask your employer to withhold a greater amount of tax (*see* ¶25.3). On the other hand, if the withholding rate applied to your wages results in over-withholding, you may claim extra withholding allowances to reduce withholding during the year (*see* ¶25.5 and ¶25.6).

Cash payments or the cash value of benefits paid to an employee by an employer are subject to withholding unless the payments are specifically excluded.

INCOME TAXES ARE WITHHELD ON:

Payments to employees as salaries, wages, fees, bonuses, commissions, pensions, retirement pay, vacation allowances, dismissal pay, etc. (whether paid in cash or goods). *See* ¶25.11 for withholding on pensions and annuities.

Pay to members of the U.S. Armed Forces.

Prize awarded to a salesman in a contest run by his employer.

Retroactive pay and overtime under Fair Labor Standards Act.

Taxable supplemental unemployment compensation benefits.

Back pay under National Labor Relations Board order and settlements under the Civil Rights Act of 1964 for job applicants refused employment on discriminatory grounds.

Payments to Canadians and Mexicans who cross borders frequently and who are not working in transportation service.

INCOME TAXES ARE NOT WITHHELD ON:

Payments to domestic servants, agricultural workers, college domestics, ministers of the gospel (except chaplains in the Armed Forces), casual workers, nonresident aliens, public officials who receive fees directly from the public—notaries public, jurors, witnesses, precinct workers, etc. (but see voluntary withholding agreements, ¶25.3).

Pay for newspaper home delivery by children under age 18.

Advances for traveling expenses if kept separate from wages. Value of tax free board and lodging furnished by an employer.

Fringe benefits not subject to tax.

Reimbursements for deductible moving expenses or medical care benefits under a self-insured medical reimbursement plan.

Tuition, fees, and supplies paid by an employer under certain educational nondiscriminating assistance plans. (Such plans are scheduled to end after 1987.)

Death benefit payments to beneficiary of employee; wages due but unpaid at employee's death and paid to estate or beneficiary.

Pay for U.S. citizen working abroad or in U.S. possessions to the extent that the pay is tax free (*see* chapter 36 for rules).

Lump-sum settlement of employment contract.

Employer contributions to SEPs (*see* ¶8.12).

Withholding does not apply to earnings of self-employed persons. They pay their income taxes currently through estimated tax.

Taxable group insurance coverage for amount over $50,000.

Form W-2. By the end of January, your employer must give you duplicate copies of Form W-2, which is a record of your pay and the withheld income and Social Security taxes. If you leave your job during the year, you may ask your employer for a W-2 by making a written request within 30 days of leaving the job.

If you have worked for more than one employer during the year, attach all Copies B of Form W-2 to your return. Check to see that a total of no more than $3,131.70 of Social Security (FICA) taxes was withheld. If too much was withheld, claim the excess as a credit on the line on your 1987 return "Excess F.I.C.A. tax withheld."

Employees covered by the Railroad Retirement Tax Act receive Form

W-2 (RR) which lists total wages paid and withholdings of income and Railroad Retirement taxes.

If your employer makes a withholding error, you do not have to wait until filing your return to get a refund; request the refund directly from your employer.

INCREASING WITHHOLDING ON YOUR PAY

¶ **25.3** For withholding tax purposes, you do not have to claim all your exemptions. This will increase the amount withheld and help reduce the final tax payment on filing your tax return. It may also relieve you of making quarterly estimated tax payments, provided the withholdings are sufficient to meet your estimated tax liability. A waiver of exemptions for withholding taxes does not prevent you from claiming the "waived" exemptions on your final tax return. The waiver is merely a bookkeeping aid to your company's payroll department. If you find that even a waiver of exemptions does not cover all of the tax you want withheld you may ask your employer to withhold additional amounts. See the instructions to Form W-4 and W-4A for details.

A domestic or farm worker whose pay is not generally subject to withholding may make a withholding agreement. You may ask your employer to withhold taxes on pay not ordinarily subject to withholding. Your written request should include your name, address, and Social Security number and your employer's name and address. You also give your employer a Form W-4 or W-4A. The employer must agree to this arrangement. Either of you may end the agreement by written notice.

AVOIDING WITHHOLDING ON YOUR PAY

¶ **25.4** If you had no income tax liability in 1987 and expect none for 1988, you may be exempt from income tax withholdings on your 1988 wages. However, if you can be claimed as a dependent on another person's tax return, and you have any investment income, you may claim this special exemption only if you expect total income (wages plus investments) to be $500 or less. If eligible, students working for the summer, retired persons, and other part-time workers do not have to wait for a refund of withheld taxes they do not owe.

To claim exemption, you file a withholding exemption certificate, Form W-4 or W-4A, with your employer. The form may be obtained from an IRS district office or from your employer. If you will file a joint return for 1988, do not file an exemption on Form W-4 or W-4A if the joint return will show a tax.

Social Security taxes are withheld, even though you are exempt from income tax withholding.

WITHHOLDING ALLOWANCES FOR TAX REDUCTION ITEMS

¶ **25.5** Too much may be withheld from your pay if you have tax reduction items. The overpayment will be refunded when you file your return, but you lose the use of your money during the year. By filing Form W-4 or W-4A with your employer, you may avoid this and reduce withholding taxes by claiming additional withholding allowances based on: (1) estimated itemized deductions, (2) IRA contribution deductions, (3) moving expense deduction, (4) alimony deduction, and (5) tax credits. On Form W-4A, the only tax credit that may be claimed is the credit for child or dependent care expenses.

If you are age 65 or older, or blind, you may claim an additional withholding allowance.

Working couples filing jointly figure withholding allowances on combined wage income and may allocate them between employers. On separate returns, the allowances must be figured separately.

If you work for two or more employers at the same time, you may claim withholding allowances from only one employer.

File a new Form W-4 or W-4A each year for withholding allowances based on itemized deductions and credits. Further, you may have to file a new form if your spouse starts work during the year and you have been claiming additional withholding allowances.

A civil penalty of $500 may be imposed if, for purposes of claiming tax withholding allowances, you overstate your itemized deductions and credits or understate your wages without a reasonable basis. There is also a criminal penalty of up to $1,000 plus a jail sentence for willfully supplying false information.

SPECIAL WITHHOLDING ALLOWANCE

¶ **25.6** A special withholding allowance designed to eliminate overwithholding may be claimed on Form W-4 or W-4A by certain employees. The withholding allowance, like an exemption, frees wage income from withholding. An unmarried person may claim this special withholding allowance, provided he is not working for more than one employer. A married person may claim the allowance, provided he also works for only one employer and his spouse does not work, or wages from a second job or your spouse's job are $2,500 or less. This special allowance is only for withholding purposes. You may not claim it on your tax return.

WHEN TO FILE NEW WITHHOLDING EXEMPTION CERTIFICATE, FORM W-4 OR W-4A

¶ **25.7** You may file a new certificate any time the number of your exemptions or withholding allowances increases. For example: A child is born or adopted; you marry; you or your spouse will be 65 during the year.

Your employer may make the new certificate effective with the next payment of wages. However, he may by law postpone the new withholding rate until the payment of wages on or after a date called the first status determination date. This may be January 1, May 1, July 1, or October 1, as the case may be, provided there is at least a 30-day interval between the date of the new certificate and the determination date.

> You do not have to wait until your 65th birthday to file a new withholding certificate to reduce withholding because of your age. If you will be 65 by the end of the year, you are allowed to reduce your withholdings for that entire year.

You must file a new certificate within 10 days if the number of allowances previously claimed by you decreases because: You divorce or legally separate; you stop supporting a dependent; a dependent for whom you claimed an exemption will receive $1,900 ($1,950 in 1988) or more income (except your child who is a student or under 19 years of age).

The death of a spouse or a dependent in a current year does not affect your withholding until the next year, but requires the filing of a new certificate, if possible, by December 1. However, a widow or widower entitled to joint return rates as a surviving spouse need not file a new withholding certificate.

When you file on or before December 1, your employer must reduce your withholding as of January 1 of the next year.

WHEN AND HOW TIPS ARE SUBJECT TO INCOME TAX AND FICA WITHHOLDINGS

¶ **25.8** Tips are subject to income tax and FICA (Social Security) withholding. If you receive cash tips amounting to $20 or more in a month, you must report the total amount of tips received during the month to your employer on Form 4070 (or a similar written report). You make the report on or before the 10th day after the end of the month in which the tips are received. (If the 10th day is a Saturday, Sunday, or legal holiday, you report by the next day that is not a Saturday, Sunday, or legal holiday.) For example, tips amounting to $20 or more and received during January are reported by February 10. Your employer may require more frequent reporting.

You include cash tips paid to you on your own behalf. If you "split" or share tips with others, you include in your report only your share. You do not include tips received in the form of merchandise or your share of service charges turned over to you by your employer.

Your employer withholds the Social Security and income tax due on the tips from your wages or from funds you give him for withholding purposes. If he cannot collect the taxes due on the tips, either from your wages or from voluntary contributions, by the 10th day after the end of the month in which tips are reported, you have to pay the tax when you file your income tax return.

Your employer is required to pay Social Security taxes on the wages he pays you, but not on the tips.

Where wages are insufficient to meet all of the withholding liability, the wages are applied first to Social Security tax.

If your employer is unable to collect enough money from your wages during the year to cover the Social Security tax on the tips reported to him, the uncollected amount is shown on your W-2 Form as "Uncollected Employee Tax on Tips." You compute your Social Security tax on unreported tips on Form 4137. You must file Form 1040 and include the amount of unreported tips from Form 4137 as wage income on Form 1040 and enter any uncollected employee Social Security tax on tips as shown on your W-2. Attach Form 4137 to your Form 1040.

Failure to report tip income of $20 or more received during the month to your employer may subject you to a penalty of 50% of the tax due on the unreported tips, unless your failure was due to reasonable cause rather than to willful neglect.

Tips of less than $20 per month are taxable, but are not subject to withholding.

You are considered to have income from tips when you make your report to your employer. However, if you do not report your tips to your employer, you are considered to have tip income when you receive the tips. For example, if you received tips of $75 during December 1987 and reported the tips to your employer on January 6, 1988; the tips are considered paid to you in January 1988 and the $75 is included in your 1988 income tax return. On the other hand, if your tips during December 1987 totaled only $18, you are not required to report the amount to your employer. The tips are considered paid to you in 1987 and must be included in your 1987 income tax return.

Tip allocation reporting. To help the IRS audit the reporting of tip income, restaurants employing at least 10 people must make a special report of income and allocate tips based on gross receipts. For purposes of the allocation, the law assumes tip income of at least 8%. If you voluntarily report tips equal to your allocable share of 8% of the restaurant's gross receipts, no allocation will be made to you. However, if the total tips reported by all employees is less than 8% of gross receipts and you do not report your share of the 8%, your employer must make an allocation based on the difference between the amount you reported and your share of the 8% amount. The allocated amount is shown on W-2. However, taxes are not withheld on the allocated amount. Taxes are withheld only on amounts actually reported by employees. An employer or majority of employees may ask the IRS to apply a tip percentage of less than 8%, but no lower than 2%.

WITHHOLDING ON GAMBLING WINNINGS

¶ **25.9** Your winnings from gambling may be subject to withholding at the rate of 20%. Winnings subject to withholding include wagering proceeds exceeding:
1. $5,000 from a state-conducted lottery;
2. $1,000 from sweepstakes and wagering pools (whether or not state-conducted) and other lotteries. Wagering pools include all parimutuel betting pools and on- and off-track racing pools;
3. $1,000 from other wagering transactions, if the proceeds are at least 300 times as large as the amount wagered; and
4. gambling proceeds of $1,000 or more from a parimutuel pool on horse races, dog races, or jai alai, if the proceeds are at least 300 times as large as the amount wagered.

Treasury regulations require you to tell the payers of gambling winnings if you are also receiving winnings from identical wagers; winnings from identical wagers must be added together to determine if withholding is required.

Winnings from bingo, keno, and slot machines, however, are not subject to withholding.

Wagering proceeds means winnings less than the amount of the wager.

If tax is withheld from your winnings, you should receive Form W-2G which shows the total winnings and amount withheld.

FICA WITHHOLDINGS

¶ **25.10** FICA (Federal Insurance Contributions Act) withholdings are employee contributions for Social Security coverage. Your employer is liable for the tax if he fails to make proper withholdings. The amount withheld is figured on your wages and is not affected by your marital status or number of exemptions. As long as you have wages, you pay FICA, even though you may be over 65 and are collecting Social Security.

For 1987, the FICA withholding rate was 7.15% on wages up to $43,800. The maximum employee contribution was $3,131.70. If more than this amount was withheld from your wages, see ¶ 25.2. For the 1988 rate and base, see the Supplement.

Subject to FICA tax are your regular salary, bonuses, commissions, vacation pay, Christmas bonuses, lump-sum settlements of wage disputes, and contributions to cash or deferred pay plans or salary-reduction contributions to a simplified employee pension (SEP) or tax-sheltered annuity. Not subject to tax are the value of tax free meals and lodgings under ¶ 2.2 and reimbursements for travel or entertainment expenses or for moving expenses. The first six months of sick pay are subject to FICA withholding; thereafter, sick pay is generally not subject to FICA tax. See Treasury regulations for further details on FICA tax on sick pay.

WITHHOLDING ON PENSIONS AND ANNUITIES

¶ **25.11** Generally, withholding on pensions, IRA distributions, and annuity payments is automatic unless an election to avoid withholding is made either on Form W-4P, W-4AP, or a substitute form furnished by the payer.

No withholding is required if a distribution consists solely of your company's securities and cash of $200 or less in lieu of fractional shares.

Unless you tell the payer otherwise, withholdings on periodic payments are figured according to wage withholding tables as if you were married and claiming three withholding exemptions.

Withholding allowances may be claimed for estimated itemized deductions, alimony payments, and deductible IRA contributions.

You may also request the payor to withhold additional amounts of tax.

Nonperiodic payments are subject to withholding at a flat 10% rate unless the payment is considered a total distribution or you elect to avoid withholding on Form W-4P (or substitute form). IRA distributions that are payable upon demand are considered nonperiodic and thus subject to the 10% withholding rule.

The flat 10% rate does not apply to lump-sum distributions from a qualified pension or profit-sharing plan, stock bonus, or annuity plan. The rate on such distributions approximates the tax that would be due under the averaging method, whether or not you are eligible to elect averaging.

BACKUP WITHHOLDING

¶ **25.12** Backup withholding is designed primarily to pressure taxpayers to report interest and dividend income. You may be subject to backup withholding if you do not give your taxpayer identification number to parties paying you interest or dividend income or if you give an incorrect number. The backup withholding rate is 20%. Each failure to give your number to a payer may also be subject to a $50 penalty. Failure to report interest and dividends is also subject to a 5% penalty based on the deficiency attributed to the failure to report such income.

26

ESTIMATED TAX PAYMENTS

¶ **26.1** Income taxes are collected on a pay-as-you-go basis through withholding on wages and pensions as well as estimated tax payments on other income. Where all or most of your income is from wages, pensions, and annuities, you will generally not have to pay estimated tax, because your estimated tax liability has been satisfied by withholding. But do not assume you are not required to pay simply because taxes have been withheld from your wages. Always check your estimated tax liability. Withholding may not cover your tax; the withholding tax rate may be below your actual tax rate when considering other income such as interest, dividends, business income, and capital gains.

If you are self-employed, include the self-employment tax. Alternative minimum tax liability is also subject to the estimated tax rules.

Failure to pay estimated tax may be subject to a penalty, *see* ¶26.3. Make your estimated tax payment accompanied by the appropriate 1040ES voucher.

You do not have to make estimated tax payments if your estimated tax is less than $500.

Farmers file only one declaration by January 15 of the following year. For example, the 1987 declaration must be filed by January 15, 1988. Or farmers may file a final return by March 1, 1988, instead of making a declaration. To qualify under these rules, a farmer must have two-thirds of his gross income from farming.

Fishermen who expect to receive at least two-thirds of their gross income from fishing pay estimated taxes as farmers do.

Nonresident aliens do not pay estimated tax unless they are residents of Mexico or Canada who enter the United States frequently, but not as employees of a transportation company, *or* they are residents of Puerto Rico during the entire taxable year.

The four installment dates for 1988 estimated tax are:

April 15, 1988
June 15, 1988
September 15, 1988
January 17, 1989.

WHO MUST PAY ESTIMATED TAX?

¶ **26.2** Estimate your income (including wage and salary income subject to withholding), deductions, and exemptions for 1988 and compute the tax using 1988 tax rates. Include in your estimate self-employment tax and alternative minimum tax, if any. If you receive Social Security benefits that may be taxable under the rules of ¶34.9, estimate the taxable portion as part of your projected income. Reduce the estimated tax by tax credits and withholdings from wages, pensions, and annuities.

If your estimated tax liability is $500 or more, you must pay the balance in installments unless withholdings from income will cover at least 90% of your estimated 1988 liability or 100% of your 1987 liability. *See* ¶26.4.

If your estimate changes during the year, you may revise it, *see* ¶26.7.

You may use the worksheet included in Form 1040ES to figure your estimated tax liability.

If you are due a refund when you file your 1987 return, you may credit the refund to your 1988 estimated tax by making an election on your 1987 return. The IRS will credit the refund to the April installment of 1988 estimated tax unless you attach a statement to your return instructing the IRS to apply the refund to later installments.

Members of a partnership declare their estimated taxes in their individual capacities. Each partner's estimate must include his share of the partnership income, whether actually paid to him or not.

The estimated tax may be paid in full with your estimated tax voucher or in four equal installments. This estimate, at your election, may be revised up or down with corresponding changes in your income and exemptions during the year.

EXAMPLE

You estimate a tax of $6,000 on April 15, 1988, for the year 1988. An installment of $1,500 is paid at that time. On June 15, 1988, you amend your estimate showing a tax of $3,000 instead of $6,000. Your next three installments will each be $500.

PENALTY FOR UNDERESTIMATES

¶ **26.3** You are not subject to a penalty if your estimated tax payments for 1987, including withholdings, equal at least 90% of the tax shown on your final return (66⅔% if you are a farmer). Alternatively, if your estimated payments, including withholdings, equal at least 100% of the 1986 final tax, no penalty is imposed even though this is less than 90% of the 1987 liability. The 100% exception applies only if you filed a return for 1986 covering a full 12 months. These are the two basic exceptions to the penalty for underestimating. If your income fluctuates throughout the year, you may be able to avoid a penalty based on an annualized income exception. See ¶26.4 for details.

A penalty is charged if you underpay any installment of estimated tax. In 1987, the penalty rate was 9% for the first three quarters of the year. The rate for the last quarter of 1987 is listed in the Supplement to this book.

Withholding payments are treated as if they were payments of estimated tax. They reduce the amount of your underestimate. In applying them, the total withholdings of the year are divided equally to each quarterly installment date unless you want to show the actual payment dates. Then they are applied in the quarter they are actually withheld.

The penalty is figured separately for each installment date. This means that if after taking into account withholdings, you underpay an early installment, you may owe a penalty for that period even though you overpay later installments to make up the difference. The penalty for each period runs until the amount is paid or until the filing date for the final tax return, whichever is earlier.

Figuring the penalty. Form 2210 is used to determine any 1987 penalty. On Form 2210, the penalty is based on the *lower* of 90% of the 1987 tax or 100% of the 1986 tax (if your return covered 12 months). One fourth of the lower amount is the payment required for each installment period. That is, the penalty for *each* 1987 installment quarter is applied to the difference between your payments for the quarter, if any, and the *lower* of (1) 22.5% of the 1987 tax, or (2) 25% of the 1986 tax (if your return covered 12 months). A special computation applies if you qualify for the annualized income exception.

Withholdings are considered paid in four equal installments unless you elect otherwise.

If you underpaid for any quarter, the amount of the underpayment reduces the payment made in the following quarter. That is, an underpayment of one quarter is carried over to succeeding quarters. If you overpaid in any quarter, the excess carries over to the next quarter. The excess cannot be used to make up an underpayment of the prior quarter. These rules do not apply to withholdings that are allocated equally over the year.

Form 2210. The five penalty exceptions listed at ¶26.4 for 1988 also apply for 1987. File Form 2210 with your 1987 tax return to show that your underestimate of tax liability is within one of the first three exceptions. You do not have to file Form 2210 if you qualify under Exception 4 or 5. If your underestimate is not within one of the exceptions and is subject to a penalty, you may use Form 2210 to figure the penalty. If you owe a penalty and attach Form 2210 to your return, the penalty decreases any refund due or increases any tax balance due. No penalty attaches for failure to file Form 2210.

Waiver of penalty for hardship, retirement, or disability. The IRS may waive the penalty if you can show you failed to pay the estimated tax because of casualty, disaster, or other unusual circumstances. The IRS may also waive a penalty for a 1987 underpayment if in 1987 or 1986 you retired after reaching age 62 or became disabled and you failed to make a payment due to reasonable cause and not due to willful neglect. This rule would apply to a 1988 underpayment if you became disabled or retired (after age 62) in 1987 or 1988. To apply for the waiver, attach an explanation on Form 2210.

AVOIDING THE PENALTY FOR 1988

¶ **26.4** The following are five penalty exceptions for underestimated taxes in 1988.

Exception 1. You avoid any penalty for 1988 if your estimated payments, including withholdings, equal at least 90% of the tax shown on your 1988 return and at least 22.5% of your 1988 tax (25% × 90%) is paid by each installment date.

> *Exception 2.* You avoid the penalty and guesswork by figuring and paying as your 1988 estimated tax an amount that equals or exceeds the tax shown on your 1987 tax return. Pay 25% of your 1987 tax for each installment period. Include 1987 self-employment tax if you are self-employed. To come within this exception, you must have filed a 1987 return covering a period of 12 months.

Exception 3. You may avoid the penalty on an estimated tax installment based on income which was earned in the months ending before the due date of the installment and which was annualized for purposes of computing the estimated tax. This exception may apply if you do not earn income evenly throughout the year, such as where you operate a seasonal business. Form 2210 includes a worksheet for figuring the annualized income exception.

Exception 4. No penalty will be imposed for 1988 if you did not have a 1987 liability, your 1987 taxable year included 12 months, and you were a citizen or resident of the United States throughout 1987.

Exception 5. No penalty is imposed if your estimated tax liability, after taking into account withholdings, is less than $500.

> *Withholdings from pay.* Tax withheld from your pay may help you avoid the penalty for underpayment of estimated tax. You have a choice in allocating your withholdings over the year: (1) You may treat your entire year's withholdings as having been withheld in equal amounts for each quarter; or (2) you may allocate to each quarter the actual withholdings that were taken out of your pay for that quarter. If, toward the end of the year, you find that you have underestimated for an earlier quarter, ask your employer to withhold an extra amount which may be allocated equally over the four quarters. This way you may eliminate the underestimate for the earlier quarters.

FINAL PAYMENT

¶ **26.5** That you paid an estimated tax for 1987 does not excuse you from filing a tax return on or before April 15, 1988. You must file a final return and pay the difference between the total of your withholding plus your estimated tax payments and your final tax. If the tax is less than your withholdings and payments, you get a refund or credit on the 1988 estimated tax. You may also split up the amount due you. You may take part of the overpayment as a refund. The other part may be credited to your next year's estimate. You may get interest only on the part refunded.

Check your mathematics before you apply an overpayment as a credit on your next year's estimate. If you apply too much—even through an unintentional mathematical error—you must pay interest if there is a tax deficiency for that year.

IF YOU USE A FISCAL YEAR

¶ **26.6** A fiscal year is any year other than the calendar year. If you file using a fiscal year, your first estimate installment is due on or before the 15th day of the fourth month of your fiscal year. Amendments may be made on the 15th day of the sixth and ninth months of your year with the final amendment on the 15th day of the first month of your next fiscal year. Your installments are also due then.

AMENDING YOUR ESTIMATE

¶ **26.7** During the year, income, expense, or exemption changes may require you to amend your estimated tax.

If you amend, you merely refigure your estimated tax. You enter the new estimated tax on the currently due voucher and sign the amended voucher. You adjust your payment schedule as explained in ¶26.2.

You do not have to file the January voucher providing you file your final return and pay in full the balance of tax due on or before January 31. For 1987, you do not have to file the January 15, 1988 voucher if you file a final return and pay the balance of tax by February 1, 1988.

If taxes paid in the previous installments total more than your revised estimate, you cannot obtain a refund at that time. You must wait until you file your final return showing that a refund is due.

WHEN TO AMEND 1988 ESTIMATES

If you want to make a change	You amend on
After April 1 and before June 2.	Voucher 2 by June 15, 1988
After June 1 and before September 2.	Voucher 3 by September 15, 1988
After September 1 and before January 1.	Voucher 4 by January 17, 1989

TAX ESTIMATES BY HUSBAND AND WIFE

¶ **26.8** A married couple may pay joint or separate estimated taxes. The nature of the estimated tax does not control the kind of final return you file.

Where a joint estimated tax is paid but the final tax is reported on separate returns, the estimated tax may be treated as the estimate of either the husband or the wife, or divided between them in any proportion. If the couple does not agree, the estimated tax payments are apportioned on the basis of each spouse's tax liability as compared with their total liability.

If separate taxes are paid, overpayment by one spouse is not applied against an underpayment by the other when separate final returns are filed.

A joint estimated tax may be made by husband and wife only if they are both citizens or residents of the United States. Both must have the same taxable year. A joint estimate may not be made by a couple that is divorced or legally separated under a decree.

Responsibility for paying estimated tax rests upon each spouse individually. Each must pay if individually required by the rules.

If a joint estimated tax is made and one spouse dies, the estate does not continue to make installment payments. The surviving spouse is required to pay the remaining installments unless he or she amends. *See* ¶1.14. Amounts paid on the joint estimate may be divided as agreed upon by the spouse and the estate of the deceased. If they do not agree, an apportionment is based on the amount of each spouse's tax liability compared with the total liability.

27

FILING REFUND CLAIMS, AMENDED RETURNS, AND EXTENSIONS

FILING FOR A REFUND ON FORM 1040X

¶ **27.1** File a refund claim on Form 1040X if you have overpaid your tax because you failed to take allowable deductions or credits, overstated income, or want to take advantage of a retroactive change in the law. *See* sample form 1040X at ¶27.9 on the following pages.

File in time. The time limits discussed at ¶27.2 must be strictly observed; otherwise, a valid refund claim will be denied because of late filing.

If you file your 1987 return early and discover an error before April 15, 1988, you may file a corrected return before that date; a corrected return filed before its due date is treated as a regular return, not as an amended return. A corrected return filed after the due date of the return is treated as an amended return and acts as a refund claim.

> Before filing a refund claim for a prior year, carefully review the return of that year for accuracy. A refund claim may subject the return to an examination in which the IRS may find errors that reduce or completely eliminate the refund claim, or may even lead to the assessment of a deficiency.

Income tax overwithholding. You do not have to file a refund claim if you have overpaid your tax due to excessive withholding of taxes on your wages or salary, or if you have overestimated your estimated tax. You get a refund on these overpayments by filing your tax return requesting a refund for these amounts. You may not recover an overpayment of estimated tax until you file your final return.

If you are entitled to a refund due to the earned income credit for certain low income wage earners (¶24.10) you must file your tax return to get your refund, even though your income and filing status would not otherwise require that a return be filed.

Married persons. If a joint return was filed for a year in which a refund is due, both spouses are entitled to recover jointly and both must file a joint refund claim. Where separate returns were filed, each spouse is a separate taxpayer and may not file a claim to recover a refund based on the other spouse's return, except if that spouse becomes fiduciary when one spouse becomes incompetent or dies. If you are divorced and incur a net operating loss or credit that may be carried back to a year in which you were married, you may file a refund claim with your signature alone and the refund check will be made out only to you.

WHEN TO FILE A REFUND CLAIM

¶ **27.2** You may file a claim for refund within three years from the time your return was filed, or within two years from the time you paid your tax, whichever is later. A return filed before its due date is treated as having been filed on the due date.

Failure to file a timely refund claim is fatal, regardless of its merits. Even if you expect that your claim will have to be pursued in court, you must still file a timely refund claim.

The time for filing refund claims based on carrybacks of net operating losses or credits is figured with reference to the return (including extensions) for the year the loss or credit arose.

If you filed an agreement giving the IRS an extended period of time in which to assess a tax against you, you are allowed an additional period in which to file a claim for refund. The claim, up to certain amounts, may be filed through the extension period and for six months afterwards.

If you have failed to take a bad debt deduction or take a loss for worthless securities, you have seven years (instead of three years) in which to file a claim. Refunds based on items from federally registered partnerships may be filed within four years.

> *What a refund claim must contain.* The most important part of a refund claim is a statement of the "reasons" for the refund. A general claim simply noting an overpayment, without supporting facts and grounds, is not sufficient. If a claim is denied by the IRS, it may become the basis of a court suit. If you have not stated all the grounds, you may not be allowed to argue them in court. The courts have limited taxpayers to the exact claim shown on the form. You must make a full claim showing all the:
>   Facts that support the claim. If you need more space than is on the form, the statement and supporting exhibits must be on letter-sized sheets (8½ × 11).
>   Grounds for the claim. If you are uncertain about the exact grounds, alternate and even inconsistent grounds may be given. For example: "The loss was incurred from an embezzlement; if not, from a bad debt."
> To protect against your understating the amount of your claim, you might preface the claim with this phrase: "The following or such greater amounts, as may be legally refunded."

Armed Forces servicemen and veterans. In determining the time limits within which a refund claim may be filed, you disregard intervening periods of service in a combat zone, plus periods of continuous hospitalization outside the United States as a result of combat zone injury, and the next 180 days thereafter. You may also disregard a postponement period if you were missing in action (*see* chapter 35). Servicemen and civilian government employees who were taxed on pay while in "missing" status also have additional time to file refund claims.

HOW TO FILE FOR A REFUND

¶ **27.3** File your claim with the Internal Revenue Service center for the district or region where you filed your return in which the overpayment was made. It should be made on an amended return, Form 1040X, unless you are entitled to file a quick refund on Form 1045. If you made an overpayment of Social Security taxes and you are not required to file a return (see ¶1.1). vou file vour refund claim on Form 843.

QUICK REFUND CLAIMS

¶ **27.4** Form 1045 may be used for filing refunds due to carrybacks from net operating losses, and WIN credit. This form must be filed within 12 months after the loss year. The IRS must act on the claim within 90 days. Payment of quick refund claims is not a final settlement of your return; the IRS may still audit and then disallow the refund claim. This refund process may also be used for certain claim of right adjustments not discussed here. Note that the filing of a quick refund, if rejected, may not be the basis of a suit for refund; a regular refund claim must be filed.

File a separate claim for each year you claim a refund.

The IRS may withhold payment of a quick refund claim if it determines that you have invested in a tax shelter that has misrepresented tax benefits.

INTEREST PAID ON REFUND CLAIMS

¶ **27.5** Interest is not paid on refunds made within 45 days of the day the tax was due (without regard to extensions of time). For example, you file your return on April 1, claiming an overpayment due to overwithholding on your wages. Interest does not begin to run until May 30, which is 45 days after April 15, the day the tax was due. If the overpayment is not refunded within 45 days, interest is paid from the date the tax was overpaid to a date 30 days or less preceding the date of the refund check.

The IRS does not have to pay interest on overpayments resulting from net operating loss carrybacks, net capital loss carrybacks, or carrybacks of investment credit or WIN credit if a refund is paid within 45 days of the filing of the refund claim.

If a refund claim based on a loss or credit carryback is filed and subsequently a quick refund claim is filed on Form 1045 for the same refund, the 45-day period starts to run on the date Form 1045 is filed.

Overpayments resulting in retroactive law changes are generally not entitled to interest as Congress usually puts such stipulation in the retroactive law change.

Interest rates applied to amounts outstanding as follows:

Amounts outstanding between—	Rate—
2/1/78–1/31/80	6%
2/1/80–1/31/82	12
2/1/82–12/31/82	20
1/1/83–6/30/83	16
7/1/83–12/31/84	11
1/1/85–6/30/85	13
7/1/85–12/31/85	11
1/1/86–6/30/86	10
7/1/86–12/31/86	9
1/1/87–3/31/87	8
4/1/87–6/30/87	8
7/1/87–9/30/87	8
10/1/87–12/31/87	See Supplement

TAX SHELTER REFUNDS WITHHELD BY IRS

¶ **27.6** The IRS may withhold refunds based on questionable tax shelter claims. In each IRS service center, returns of tax shelter investors are screened to determine if the tax shelter has fraudulently misrepresented tax benefits or grossly overvalued assets or services. If the tax shelter is considered to be abusive and if claimed deductions or tax credits are not allowable, refunds attributable to the tax shelter items will not be paid. The balance of your refund claim will be paid.

A refund will also be frozen under the above rules if you file your return after receiving a pre-filing notification letter from the IRS warning you not to claim certain tax shelter writeoffs.

The above rules apply to original tax returns showing a refund due as well as to refund claims. Further, if you file a quick refund claim on Form 1045 (¶27.4), and the IRS determines it is likely that excessive tax shelter

benefits have been claimed, the IRS will offset the quick refund claim by a deficiency attributable to the tax shelter items. You will receive the balance and receive a notice of the tax shelter deficiency.

Tax shelter partnerships. The IRS will freeze refunds of investors in tax shelter partnerships if it determines that it is highly likely that the partnership has fraudulently misrepresented tax benefits or grossly overvalued property or services, leading to excessive tax writeoffs by the partners. The refund freeze will continue until completion of the partnership level audit. See ¶10.5 for partnership audits.

APPLY FOR EXTENSION IF YOU CANNOT FILE ON TIME

¶ **27.7** If you cannot file your return on time, apply before the due date to the Internal Revenue Service office with which you file your return for an extension of time to file.

Automatic extension. You may get an extension without waiting for the IRS to act on your request. You receive an automatic four-month extension if you file Form 4868 by April 15 and pay the full amount of tax you estimate that you owe. If you were abroad on April 15 so that your return is not due until June 15, you may receive an additional two-month extension if you file Form 4868 and pay the taxes due by June 15.

Form 4868 must be filed by the date on which the return would otherwise be due. This extension of time on filing does not extend the time for payment of tax. If, on filing Form 4868, you pay less than the final tax you owe, you will be charged interest on the unpaid amount. If the tax paid is less than 90% of the amount due, you may also be subject to a late-payment penalty.

When you file your return within the extension period, you attach a duplicate of Form 4868 and include the balance of the unpaid tax, if any.

While the extension is automatically obtained by a proper filing on Form 4868 (including payment of tax), the IRS may terminate the extension on ten days notice to you.

A general extension of time to file outside of the automatic extension rules above may be granted. You must make a request on Form 2688. An extension of up to six months may be granted if a full explanation showing reasonable cause is shown. The IRS has warned that if the explanation is found to be false or misleading, it will void the extension and apply late filing penalties.

GETTING AN EXTENSION OF TIME TO PAY TAX

¶ **27.8** Do not allow your inability to pay the tax stop you from filing a return. Inability to pay the tax is not a reason for receiving an extension to file. If you cannot pay your tax, file your return and apply for an extension of time to pay your tax. You request an extension on Form 1127.

With Form 1127, you must show that you do not have cash above necessary working capital, liquid assets, or the financial ability to get a loan to meet the tax liability. If you have other assets, such as a house, you must also show that a sale of the asset would be at a sacrifice price and cause you undue financial hardship. You attach to Form 1127 a list of receipts and disbursements for the three months before the due date and also a statement of assets and liabilities as of the end of the month preceding your application.

If the extension is allowed, you are usually given six months from the date the tax was due. An additional six months may be allowed if you are abroad. You may also be required to put up property you own as collateral. Collateral is not required if you do not own property.

Receiving an extension does not stop the running of interest on the tax.

AMENDED RETURNS (FORM 1040X)

¶ **27.9** If, after filing your return, you find that an error has been made, you should file an amended return. Form 1040X may be used to correct a return for 1987 or a return from a prior year. You may also file an amended return on Form 1040. According to the IRS, Form 1040X is processed more rapidly than amended Form 1040. File Form 1040X with the Service Center serving the region or district in which the tax was paid. See also ¶27.1.

Form 1040X (Rev. October 1985)

Department of the Treasury—Internal Revenue Service

Amended U.S. Individual Income Tax Return

OMB No. 1545-0091
Expires 4-30-88

This return is for calendar year ▶ 19 85 , OR fiscal year ended ▶ , 19

Your first name and initial (if joint return, also give spouse's name and initial)	Last name
Daniel & Sarah	Frame

Your social security number: 1X0 :XX :X1X1
Spouse's social security number: X01 :XX :1XX1

Present home address (number and street, including apartment number, or rural route)
16 Emory Avenue

City, town or post office, state, and ZIP code
City, State xxxxx

Telephone number (optional) ( )

Enter below name and address as shown on original return (if same as above, write "Same"). If changing from separate to joint return, enter names and addresses used on original return. (Note: You cannot change from joint to separate returns after the due date has passed.)

"Same"

a Service center where original return was filed

b Has original return for the year being changed been audited? ☐ Yes ☒ No
If "No," have you been notified that it will be? ☐ Yes ☒ No
If "Yes," identify IRS office

c Are you amending your return to include any item (loss, credit, deduction, other tax benefit, or income) relating to a tax shelter required to be registered? ☐ Yes ☒ No
If "Yes," you MUST attach Form 8271, Investor Reporting of Tax Shelter Registration Number.

d Filing status claimed. (Note: You cannot change from joint to separate returns after the due date has passed.)
On original return ▶ ☐ Single ☒ Married filing joint return ☐ Married filing separate return ☐ Head of household ☐ Qualifying widow(er)
On this return ▶ ☐ Single ☒ Married filing joint return ☐ Married filing separate return ☐ Head of household ☐ Qualifying widow(er)

Income and Deductions

		A. As originally reported or as adjusted (see instructions)	B. Net change—Increase or (Decrease)—explain on page 2	C. Correct amount
1	Total income (see instructions)	39,400		39,400
2	Adjustments to income (see instructions)	4,500		4,500
3	Adjusted gross income (subtract line 2 from line 1)	34,900		34,900
4	Deductions (see instructions)	1,225	1,050	2,275
5	Subtract line 4 from line 3	33,675		32,625
6	Exemptions (see instructions)	2,080		2,080
7	Taxable income (subtract line 6 from line 5)	31,595		30,545

Tax Liability

8	Tax (see instructions). (Method used in col. C Tax Tables ..)	5,113	(276)	4,837
9	Credits (see instructions)			
10	Subtract line 9 from line 8. Enter the result, but not less than zero	5,113	(276)	4,837
11	Other taxes (such as self-employment tax, alternative minimum tax)			
12	Total tax liability (add line 10 and line 11)	5,113	(276)	4,837

Payments

13	Federal income tax withheld and excess FICA and RRTA tax withheld	5,400		5,400
14	Estimated tax payments			
15	Earned income credit			
16	Credits for Federal tax on gasoline and special fuels, regulated investment company, etc.			

Refund or Amount You Owe

17	Amount paid with Form 4868, Form 2688, or Form 2350 (application for extension of time to file)	17	
18	Amount paid with original return, plus additional tax paid after it was filed	18	
19	Total of lines 13 through 18, column C	19	5,400
20	Overpayment, if any, as shown on original return (or as previously adjusted by IRS)	20	287
21	Subtract line 20 from line 19 (see instructions)	21	5,113
22	AMOUNT YOU OWE. If line 12, col. C, is more than line 21, enter difference. Please pay in full with this return	22	
23	REFUND to be received. If line 12, column C, is less than line 21, enter the difference.	23	276

Under penalties of perjury, I declare that I have filed an original return and that I have examined this amended return, including accompanying schedules and statements, and to the best of my knowledge and belief this amended return is true, correct, and complete. Declaration of preparer (other than taxpayer) is based on all information of which the preparer has any knowledge.

Please Sign Here

Your signature ▶ Daniel Frame   Date June 10, 1987
Spouse's signature (if filing jointly, BOTH must sign) ▶ Sarah Frame

Paid Preparer's Use Only
Preparer's signature
Date
Check if self-employed ☐
Preparer's social security no.
Firm's name (or yours, if self-employed) and address
E.I. No.
ZIP code

BE SURE TO COMPLETE PAGE 2

For Paperwork Reduction Act Notice, see page 1 of separate instructions.

Form 1040X (Rev. 10-85) Page 2

Part I Exemptions (see Form 1040 or Form 1040A instructions)

If claiming more exemptions, complete lines 1—9.
If claiming fewer exemptions, complete lines 1—6.

		A. Number originally reported	B. Net change	C. Correct number
1	Exemptions—yourself and spouse, 65 or over, blind	2		2
2	Your dependent children who lived with you			
3	If amending your 1985 return, your dependent children who did not live with you			
4	Other dependents			
5	Total exemptions (add lines 1 through 4)	2		2
6	Multiply $1,040 ($1,000, for tax years beginning before 1985) by the total number of exemptions claimed on line 5. Enter this amount here and on page 1, line 6	2,080		2,080

7 First names of your dependent children who lived with you and were not claimed on original return.   Enter number ▶

8 If amending your 1985 return, first names of your dependent children who did not live with you and were not claimed on original return (see instructions). (If pre-1985 agreement, check here ▶ ☐.)   Enter number ▶

9 Other dependents not claimed on original return:

(a) Name	(b) Relationship	(c) Number of months lived in your home	(d) Did dependent have income of $1,040 ($1,000 for tax years beginning before 1985) or more?	(e) Did you provide more than one-half of dependent's support?

Enter number ▶

Part II Explanation of Changes to Income, Deductions, and Credits

Enter the line number from page 1 for each item you are changing and give the reason for each change. Attach all supporting forms and schedules for items changed. Be sure to include your name and social security no. on any attachments.

If the change pertains to a net operating loss carryback, a general business credit carryback, or a research credit carryback, attach the schedule or form that shows the year in which the loss or credit occurred. See the instructions. Also, check here ▶ ☐

Line 4: On original 1985 return, we failed to add to the sales tax allowed by the IRS table sales tax of $1,050 paid on the purchase of a personal automobile on June 20, 1985 from Acme Auto Center, City, State, xxxxx,

Part III Presidential Election Campaign Fund

Checking below will not increase your tax or reduce your refund.

If you did not previously want to have $1 go to the fund, but now want to   Check here ▶ ☐
If joint return and if spouse did not previously want to have $1 go to the fund, but now wants to   Check here ▶ ☐

OFFICES OF DISTRICT DIRECTORS

¶ **27.10** The following is a list of the addresses of the offices of IRS District Directors for filing amended returns. This list gives the location of the main office of each district. There are additional branch offices in principal cities. You can get the address of the nearest branch office by consulting your local post office.

ALABAMA—Birmingham, 35203.
ALASKA—Anchorage, 99501.
ARIZONA—Phoenix, 85025.
ARKANSAS—Little Rock, 72203.
CALIFORNIA—Los Angeles, 90012; San Francisco, 94102.
COLORADO—Denver, 80202.
CONNECTICUT—Hartford, 06103.
DELAWARE—Wilmington, 19801.
DISTRICT Of COLUMBIA—Baltimore, 21202.
FLORIDA—Jacksonville, 32202.
GEORGIA—Atlanta, 30303.
HAWAII—Honolulu, 96813.
IDAHO—Boise, 83707.
ILLINOIS—Chicago, 60602; Springfield, 62704.
INDIANA—Indianapolis, 46204.
IOWA—Des Moines, 50309.
KANSAS—Wichita, 67202.
KENTUCKY—Louisville, 40202.
LOUISIANA—New Orleans, 70130.
MAINE—Augusta, 04330.
MARYLAND—Baltimore, 21201.
MASSACHUSETTS—Boston, 02203.
MICHIGAN—Detroit, 48226.
MINNESOTA—St. Paul, 55101.
MISSISSIPPI—Jackson, 39202.
MISSOURI—St. Louis, 63101.

MONTANA—Helena, 59601.
NEBRASKA—Omaha, 68102.
NEVADA—Reno, 89502.
NEW HAMPSHIRE—Portsmouth, 03810.
NEW JERSEY—Newark, 07102.
NEW MEXICO—Albuquerque, 87101.
NEW YORK—Brooklyn, 11201; 120 Church Street, New York, 10007; Albany, 12210; Buffalo, 14202.
NORTH CAROLINA—Greensboro, 27401.
NORTH DAKOTA—Fargo, 58102.
OHIO—Cincinnati, 45202; Cleveland, 44199.
OKLAHOMA—Oklahoma City, 73102.
OREGON—Portland, 97204.
PENNSYLVANIA—Philadelphia, 19106; Pittsburgh, 15222.
RHODE ISLAND—Providence, 02903.
SOUTH CAROLINA—Columbia, 29201.
SOUTH DAKOTA—Aberdeen, 57401.
TENNESSEE—Nashville, 37203.
TEXAS—Austin, 78701; Dallas, 75201.
UTAH—Salt Lake City, 84110.
VERMONT—Burlington, 05401.
VIRGINIA—Richmond, 23240.
WASHINGTON—Seattle, 98121.
WEST VIRGINIA—Parkersburg, 26101.
WISCONSIN—Milwaukee, 53202.
WYOMING—Cheyenne, 82001.

WHERE TO SEND YOUR RETURN—IRS SERVICE CENTERS

¶ **27.11** Address the envelope containing your return to the Internal Revenue Service Center for the area where you live. No street address is needed. Write -2222 after the five digit ZIP Code listed below for your state, for example, Ogden, UT 84201–2222.

ALABAMA—Atlanta, GA 31101
ALASKA—Ogden, UT 84201
ARIZONA—Ogden, UT 84201
ARKANSAS—Austin, TX 73301
CALIFORNIA—File with the IRS Service Center at Ogden, UT 84201, if you live in the counties of Alpine, Amador, Butte, Calaveras, Colusa, Contra Costa, Del Norte, El Dorado, Glenn, Humboldt, Lake, Lassen, Marin, Mendocino, Modoc, Napa, Nevada, Placer, Plumas, Sacramento, San Joaquin, Shasta, Sierra, Siskiyou, Solano, Sonoma, Sutter, Tehama, Trinity, Yolo, and Yuba. [uls]All other California residents file at Fresco, CA 93888.
COLORADO—Ogden, UT 84201
CONNECTICUT—Andover, MA 05501
DELAWARE—Philadelphia, PA 19255
DISTRICT OF COLUMBIA—Philadelphia, PA 19255
FLORIDA—Atlanta, GA 31101
GEORGIA—Atlanta, GA 31101
HAWAII—Fresno, CA 93888
IDAHO—Ogden, UT 84201
ILLINOIS—Kansas City, MO 64999
INDIANA—Memphis, TN 37501
IOWA—Kansas City, MO 64999
KANSAS—Austin, TX 73301
KENTUCKY—Cincinnati, OH 45999
LOUISIANA—Austin, TX 73301
MAINE—Andover, MA 05501
MARYLAND—Philadelphia, PA 19255
MASSACHUSETTS—Andover, MA 05501
MICHIGAN—Cincinnati, OH 45999

MINNESOTA—Andover, MA 05501
MISSISSIPPI—Atlanta, GA 31101
MISSOURI—Kansas City, MO 64999
MONTANA—Ogden, UT 84201
NEBRASKA—Ogden, UT 84201
NEVADA—Ogden, UT 84201
NEW HAMPSHIRE—Andover, MA 05501
NEW JERSEY—Holtsville, NY 00501
NEW MEXICO—Austin, TX 73301
NEW YORK—*New York City and counties of Nassau, Rockland, Suffolk and Westchester*—Holtsville, NY 00501.
   All Other Counties—Andover, MA 05501
NORTH CAROLINA—Memphis, TN 37501
NORTH DAKOTA—Ogden, UT 84201
OHIO—Cincinnati, OH 45999
OKLAHOMA—Austin, TX 73301
OREGON—Ogden, UT 84201
PENNSYLVANIA—Philadelphia, PA 19255
RHODE ISLAND—Andover, MA 05501
SOUTH CAROLINA—Atlanta, GA 31101
SOUTH DAKOTA—Ogden, UT 84201
TENNESSEE—Memphis, TN 37501
TEXAS—Austin, TX 73301
UTAH—Ogden, UT 84201
VERMONT—Andover, MA 05501
VIRGINIA—Memphis, TN 37501
WASHINGTON—Ogden, UT 84201
WEST VIRGINIA—Cincinnati, OH 45999
WISCONSIN—Kansas City, MO 64999

WYOMING—Ogden, UT 84201
AMERICAN SAMOA—Philadelphia, PA 19255
GUAM—Commissioner of Revenue and Taxation, Agana, GU 96910
PUERTO RICO *(or if excluding foreign income under section 933)*—Philadelphia, PA 19255
VIRGIN ISLANDS: NONPERMANENT RESIDENTS—Philadelphia, PA 19255
VIRGIN ISLANDS: PERMANENT—Bureau of Internal Revenue,

P.O. Box 3186, St. Thomas, VI 00801
FOREIGN COUNTRY: *U.S. citizens and those filing Form 1555 or Form 4563, even if you have an A.P.O. or F.P.O. address*—Philadelphia, PA 19255
A.P.O. or F.P.O. address of: Miami—Atlanta, GA 31101
   New York—Holtsville, NY 00501
   San Francisco—Fresno, CA 93888
   Seattle—Ogden, UT 84201

LIST OF SUPPLEMENTAL FORMS

¶ 27.12 In addition to Form 1040 and its accompanying schedules, the IRS provides other forms for claiming tax credits, for supporting deductions and exemptions, for requests for extensions of time, etc.

These forms, as well as others not listed below, may be obtained from any Internal Revenue Service office. The use of many of these forms is optional; a statement may suffice. Supplemental forms include the following:

Form 1040X—Amended U.S. Individual Income Tax Return
Form 1045—Quick Refund for Carryback Adjustments (*see* ¶27.4)
Form 1116—Foreign Tax Credit (*see* ¶36.15)
Form 1127—Application for Extension of Time for Payment of Tax
Form 1128—Application for Change in Accounting Period
Form 1310—Statement of Claimant to Refund Due Deceased Taxpayer (*see* ¶1.12)
Form 2106—Statement of Employee Business Expenses (*see* ¶19.3)
Form 2119—Statement Concerning Sale or Exchange of Personal Residence (*see* ¶29.2)
Form 2120—Multiple Support Declaration (*see* ¶1.22)
Form 2210—Statement Relating to Underpayment of Estimated Tax (*see* chapter 26). Form 2210F (for farmers and fishermen)
Form 2350—Application for Extension of Time for Filing Tax Return (for U.S. citizens abroad who expect to receive exempt earned income) (*see* ¶36.8)
Form 2439—Notice to Shareholder of Undistributed Long-Term Capital Gains (*see* ¶24.5)
Form 2441—Credit for Dependent Care Expenses (*see* ¶1.29)
Form 2553—Election by Corporation as to Taxable Status Under Subchapter S
Form 2555—Exclusion for Income Earned Abroad (for U.S. citizens abroad; file with Form 1040) (*see* chapter 36)
Form 2688—Application for Extension of Time to File Tax Return (*see also,* Form 4868 below)
Form 2848—Power of Attorney
Form 3115—Application for Change in Accounting Method
Form 3468—Computation of Investment Credit
Form 3621—Net Operating Loss Computation
Form 3621-A—Computation of Net Operating Loss Deduction
Form 3903—Moving Expense Adjustment (*see* ¶19.3)
Form 4070—Employee Tip Income Reported
Form 4070A—Daily Record of Tips
Form 4136—Computation of Credit for Federal Tax on Gasoline and Lubricating Oil (for claiming credit for diesel vehicles, *see* ¶24.3)
Form 4137—Computation of Social Security Tax on Unreported Tip Income
Form 4255—Tax From Recomputing a Prior Year Investment Credit (*see* ¶24.8)
Form 4469—Computation of Excess Hospital Insurance Benefits Tax

Form 4506—Request for Copy of Tax Return
Form 4562—Depreciation (*see* ¶5.22)
Form 4563—Exclusion of Income from Sources in U.S. Possession
Form 4684—Casualties and Thefts (*see* ¶18.)
Form 4782—Employee Moving Expense Information (*see* ¶19.13)
Form 4797—Supplementary Schedule of Gains and Losses (*see* ¶5.44)
Form 4798—Capital Loss Carryover (*see* ¶6.4)
Form 4835—Farm Rental Income and Expenses
Form 4868—Application for Automatic Extension of Time to File Return (*see* ¶27.8)
Form 4952—Investment Interest Deduction (*see* ¶15.11)
Form 4972—Averaging Method for Lump-Sum Distributions (*see* ¶7.4)
Form 5213—Election to Postpone Determination on Presumption That an Activity Is Engaged in for Profit (*see* ¶5.9)
Form 5329—Return for Individual Retirement Savings (*see* ¶8.1)
Form 5500—Annual Return/Report of Employee Benefit Plan (100 or more participants)
Form 5500–C—Annual Return/Report of Employee Benefit Plan (less than 100 participants; filed once every three years)
Form 5500–R—Report of Employee Benefit Plan (to be filed in years Form 5500–C is not filed)
Form 6251—Alternative Minimum Tax (*see* ¶23.2)
Form 6252—Computation of Installment Sale Income (*see* ¶6.33)
Form 6781—Regulated Futures Contracts and Straddles (*see* ¶6.16)
Form 8271—Investor Reporting of Tax Shelter Registration Number
Form 8283—Noncash Charitable Contributions (¶14.12).
Form 8300—Report of Cash Payments Over $10,000 Received in a Trade or Business (¶5.4)
Form 8332—Release of Claim to Exemption for Child of Divorced or Separated Parents (¶1.23)
Form 8396—Mortgage Interest Credit (¶24.6)
Form 8582—Passive Activity Loss Limitations (Chapter 11)
Form 8598—Computation of Deductible Home Mortgage Interest (¶15.11)
Form 8606—Nondeductible IRA Contributions, IRA Basis, and Nontaxable IRA Distributions (Chapter 8)
Form 8615—Reporting Investment Income Exceeding $1,000 of Children Under 14 (¶22.3)

TAX SAVINGS PLANS

It is too late to reduce taxes when it is time to prepare and file your tax return. Make it a practice to plan your tax moves throughout the year. Help yourself by reading this part. Here, you will find chapters that tell you how the new tax law affects tax planning strategies and year-round tax savings plans for homeowners, securities investors, real estate investors, retirees, executives, and family heads.

28

TAX-SAVING IDEAS AND PLANNING

HOW THE 1986 TAX ACT HAS CHANGED TAX PLANNING

¶ **28.1** The 1986 Tax Act has swept away or neutralized these basic tax-saving strategies:

1. **Tax shelter plans that offered up-front deductions for write-offs from salary, interest, and dividend income.** The passive activity rules discourage you from entering into tax shelter plans that offer deduction offsets from other income. The rules do not allow you to deduct tax shelter losses from income such as salary, interest, and dividends. The losses are deductible only from other passive income, such as rents. In striking at tax shelters, Congress also struck at other activities as well. If you do *not* take an active part in a business, your income and loss is treated as passive activity income and loss. The passive activity rules which are discussed in chapter 11 have the opposite effect of tax shelter planning. They defer the deduction of losses until passive income is produced or the business interest is disposed of.

2. **Planning for capital gain income.** Repeal of the capital gains deduction ended the substantial tax benefits afforded long-term capital gains, which in 1986 were subject to rates as low as 4.4% to a high of only 20%. Capital gains are now subject to ordinary income rates. But as the rate differential between ordinary income and capital gains will no longer exist under the projected tax rate schedules, investment objectives have changed. You will generally no longer be concerned to plan strategies for long-term capital gain. The loss of capital gains benefits will also affect your business planning. If you do business in a corporation, in the past you avoided dividend distributions expecting to withdraw accumulated earnings as long-term capital gain on a liquidation or redemption or sale of the stock. With the top personal tax rate now below the top corporate rate, you may prefer to receive current dividend income, especially if you can reinvest the dividends—the income earned on the investment, and they will be taxed at lower rates than income earned on funds held by the corporation.

3. **Family income shifting.** Shifting income to children under 14 will no longer accomplish substantial income tax savings. Starting in 1987, investment income of children under age 14 in excess of $1,000 is taxed to the child at the parent's top marginal rate; *see* chapter 22. Children who have reached age 14 by the close of a taxable year are not subject to this rule. With the reduction of tax rates, the spread between the high and low tax rates is narrowed. As a result, the overall tax saving of income splitting

is reduced. In the 28% bracket, $1,000 after taxes leaves $720; in the 15% bracket, $850. Under prior law where the top tax bracket may have been as high as 50%, the overall saving was substantially greater.

   Tax savings for 10-year and spousal remainder trusts also curtailed. The 10-year (Clifford) trusts were widely used to shift income to relatives in lower tax brackets. Where a trust met the 10-year exception, trust income was taxed to the beneficiary, usually a minor child. Another type of trust used for income splitting was the spousal remainder trust set up for less than 10 years. It allowed income shifting to a child beneficiary when the trust property went to the grantor's spouse after the trust period ended. Under the new law, both types of trust may no longer be used to shift income to the income beneficiary.

4. **Buying equipment to take advantage of tax-incentive benefits.** The tax law no longer allows an investment credit and has severely cut back depreciation deductions for automobiles. It has also taken away accelerated tax advantages for real estate and reduced deductions for many leasehold improvements.

5. **Installment sale deferrals for dealers and for sales of rental property in excess of $150,000.** To the extent that sellers have outstanding debt, the tax deferrals are lost under AII reporting rules. *See* ¶6.43.

6. **Incurring debt providing interest deductions.** Only certain classes of interest are fully deductible. Deductions for consumer interest have been substantially cut back and will end in 1990. *See* chapter 15.

Despite these developments, there still remain opportunities to reduce your taxes as discussed in the following chapters and sections.

WHEN TO DEFER INCOME AND ACCELERATE DEDUCTIONS

¶ **28.2** When you expect to pay less tax in a future year than in a current year, consider deferring income and accelerating deductions. There are two strategies: (1) postpone receipt of income to a year of lower tax rates, and/or (2) claim deductions for losses and expenses in the year you are subject to the higher tax rates. In planning to defer income and accelerate deductions, however, watch these tax rule limitations.

Postponing income. You may not defer salary income by not cashing a paycheck or not taking salary that you have earned and that you can

receive without restrictions. Under certain conditions, you may contract with your employer to defer the taxable receipt of current compensation to future years. To defer pay to a future period, you must take some risk. You cannot have any control over your deferred pay account. If you are not confident of your employer's ability to pay in the future, you should not defer pay.

If you are self-employed and are on the cash basis, you can defer income by delaying your billing at the end of the year or extending the time of collection. If you own a closely held corporation, you can time the payment of dividends and bonuses.

Accelerating deductions. In accelerating deductions, there are these limitations. You may not deduct prepaid interest and rent. Prepaid interest must be deducted over the period of the loan. Rentals must also be deducted over the rental period. However, you can generally deduct prepayments of state income tax and accelerate your payments of charitable contributions. Annual subscriptions to professional journals and business magazines can be renewed before the end of the year. If the subscription is for more than a year, you may deduct only the first-year prepayment. The cost of the later subscription must be deducted in the later year. Contributions, purchases, and expenses charged to credit card accounts are deductible in the year of charge, even though you do not pay your charge account bill until the next year. You can also realize losses by selling property which has lost value in the year you want to incur the loss.

Making an extra donation at the end of the year may also provide an added deduction which may lower your tax. You may deduct a gift made by check on the last day of the year even if the check is not cashed until the new year begins. Charitable donations may be timed to give you the largest possible tax savings. If, toward the end of the year, you find that you need an extra deduction, you may make a deductible donation in late December. Doing so would be especially beneficial if you know that your tax bracket will be lower the following year; *see* ¶ chapter 14 for further planning details.

Deferring interest income to next year. Buying six-month certificates after June 30 can defer interest reporting to the next year. As a general rule, you have to report interest credited to your savings account for 1987,

even though you do not present your passbook to have the amount entered. Similarly, interest coupons due and payable in 1987 are taxable on your 1987 return regardless of when they were presented for collection. For example, a coupon due in December, 1987, but presented for payment in 1988 is taxable in 1987. However, there are opportunities to defer interest in the following ways:

1. Buy a six-month certificate after June 30. Interest is taxable in the next year when the certificate matures, unless you receive interest during the year. Your bank may offer you the choice of when to receive the interest.
2. Buy Treasury bills which come due next year. Six-month bills bought after June 30 will mature in the next year. You can make these purchases through your bank or broker.
3. Buy Series EE bonds. These bonds may be cashed for their purchase price, plus an increase in their value over stated periods of time. The increase in redemption value is taxed as interest. You may defer the interest income until the year you cash the bond or the year the bond finally matures, whichever is earlier.

Timing sales of property. A sale is generally taxable in the year title to the property passes to the buyer. Since you can control the year title passes, you can usually defer income realized on the sale to the year in which you will pay less tax.

Also *see* chapter 13 for claiming standard deduction and itemized deductions in alternate years.

29

TAX SAVINGS FOR HOMEOWNERS

¶ **29.1** The 1986 Tax Act left intact the tax-deferment benefits for personal residence sales and the $125,000 exclusion for homeowners age 55 or over. However, taxable sales of personal residences will be subject to higher tax because of the repeal of the capital gains deduction. Long-term capital gain realized in 1987 on the sale of a personal residence is taxable at rates of up to 28%. *See* chapter 6. Finally, interest paid on home mortgages is fully deductible provided the rules of ¶ 15.11 are met.

TAX CONSEQUENCES OF SELLING YOUR HOME

¶ **29.2** Tax on all or a part of a profit from the sale of your home may be avoided or deferred depending on your age.

If you are 55 or over, you may elect to avoid tax on gain of up to $125,000. *See* ¶29.12.

If you are under 55 or are 55 or over and do not want to elect to avoid tax, you may defer tax by buying or building another residence within the rules of ¶29.3. Tax deferment is not elective but mandatory if the tests are met. If you do not meet the deferment tests, your profit is taxed. In 1987, if you held the house long-term, the profit is taxable as long-term capital gain. Installment sale reporting may be used to defer tax as explained below.

If you sold at a loss, you may not deduct the loss. Losses on the sale of property devoted to personal use are nondeductible (*see* ¶6.8). However, *see* ¶29.11 which explains under what conditions you may claim a loss deduction for a residence which you rent out or inherit.

Reporting a sale. Report the details of a 1987 sale on Form 2119, which must be attached to Form 1040. On Form 2119, you compute gain on the sale and the basis of a new residence and may make the election to exclude gain if over age 55. If you do not qualify for tax deferral or the exclusion, taxable gain from Form 2119 is entered on Schedule D.

The IRS may tax you on the unreported gain from the sale of your residence during a three-year period that starts when you notify the IRS of the cost of your new residence or your intention not to buy one, or your failure to acquire one before the required time limit. In the absence of notice, the IRS may assess the tax on unreported taxable gain at any time.

Installment sale reporting. Where some or all of the sales proceeds will be received after the year of sale and you do not qualify for deferral or elect the exclusion, your gain must be reported on the installment basis, unless you elect to report the entire gain in the year of sale. Sales of residential property on the installment basis are not subject to restrictive rules applied to sales of rental property of more than $150,000, *see* ¶6.43.

DEFERRING TAX ON THE SALE OF A RESIDENCE

¶ **29.3** You defer tax on the gain realized on the sale of your house if you meet the following three tests—

Principal residence test —requires that you have used your old house as your principal residence and now use or intend to use your new house as a principal residence.

Time test —requires you to buy or build your new house and use it within two years before or after you sell your old house.

Investment test —requires you to buy or build a house at a cost at least equal to the amount you received from the sale of the old house. If the replacement property costs less, part or all of the gain is taxed.

If you come within the above three tests, tax deferment is mandatory.

Exchanging houses. When you exchange residences, the trade is considered to be a sale of your old house and a purchase of a new house. If you make an even exchange or pay additional cash, there is no tax on the exchange. If you receive cash in addition to the new house, you generally realize taxable gain.

EXAMPLES

1. Your old house cost $58,000. You exchange it for a new house worth $61,000. You also receive $1,000 in cash. Your gain is $4,000 ($62,000 less your $58,000 cost). As you reinvested $61,000 in the new house, taxable gain is $1,000. Cost basis of the new house is $58,000 ($61,000 purchase price less the $3,000 nontaxed gain).

2. Your old house cost $58,000. You exchanged it for a new house worth $60,000, and pay an additional $2,000. You have no taxed gain. The cost of your new house is $60,000 (the cost of your old house, $58,000, plus the $2,000 cash).

Condemnations. When a residence is condemned by a government authority, a homeowner may elect to treat the condemnation as a sale rather than as an involuntary conversion. Under current law, there is no advantage in making this election, although the involuntary conversion rules (*see* ¶18.21) allow more time to replace the residence than the rules for deferral.

How to claim deferral. You must report a 1987 sale on Form 2119. If by the time you file your return you have already purchased a new home, details of the purchase are shown on Form 2119. You qualify for deferral if the cost of the new home equals or exceeds the adjusted sale price of the old home. If you plan to buy a new home within the two-year replacement period but have not yet done so when you file your 1987 return, you indicate your intention on Form 2119; you do not have to report the gain from the sale on your 1987 return. If you later make a timely replacement that qualifies for full deferral (purchase price exceeds adjusted sales price of old home), you should notify the IRS and attach a new Form 2119 for 1987. If the purchase price of a replacement home does not at least equal the adjusted sales price of the old home, or if you do not make a timely replacement, you must file an amended return on Form 1040X to report taxable gain for 1987 and attach a new Form 2119 and Schedule D; you will also owe interest on the tax due. You may also file an amended return to claim a refund if you paid tax on a 1987 gain and later buy a new home within the two-year replacement period.

PRINCIPAL RESIDENCE TEST

¶ **29.4** You may have only one principal residence for the purpose of deferring tax. You may not defer tax on the profitable sale of a second house, such as a summer cottage. Nor may you defer tax on the sale of a principal residence by buying a summer home.

If you own two houses, only one is considered a principal residence at one time. Assume you sell the unit which you consider your principal residence and decide to use the second house as a principal residence. The cost basis of the second house is not considered in figuring tax deferral unless it was bought during the replacement time period.

EXAMPLE

The Shaws sold their house and immediately moved into a house bought 10 years earlier. They did not report gain from the sale, claiming that the cost basis of the new residence exceeded the sales price of the old house. They treated as cost the market value of the house as of the date they began using it as a principal residence. They argued that, although they owned it for 10 years, they did not acquire it for purposes of tax deferral until they began using it as a principal residence. The IRS and Tax Court held that only reconstruction expenses paid within the replacement period could be considered costs of purchasing a new residence.

Tax deferment is not restricted to one-family houses. You may defer tax on the sale and purchase of a mobile home, trailer, houseboat, cooperative apartment (tied to stock ownership) and condominium apartment, which you use as a principal residence. For example, in a private letter ruling, the IRS allowed deferral of gain recognized on the conversion of a co-op apartment to a condominium. An investment in a retirement home project does not qualify if you do not receive equity in the property.

Tax deferment applies also to your sale of a multifamily building in which you have an apartment. You may defer tax on gain allocated to your apartment (*see* ¶29.10). Similarly, where you actively use part of your house for business purposes, such as in operating a farm or a store while living in an apartment in the same building, an allocation is required. If part of your home was used as an office for which no deduction was allowed, no allocation is required.

If you sell your old house to one buyer and adjacent land to another buyer, the land sale may be treated as part of the sale of your principal residence, and tax on gain is deferred if the other tests are met. However, if the tract of land is substantial, the IRS may attempt to treat the sales as separate transactions. To avoid this possibility where you want to avoid or defer tax on the sale, try to arrange for the sale of the entire property to one buyer who, in turn, may sell the part he does not want to the other buyer.

If you sell only part of a lot on which your residence stands, the gain on the sale may not be postponed by reinvesting in a similar lot or by purchasing a residence. Similarly, if you sell the lot and move your house to a new lot, you may not defer gain on the sale of the old lot. The sale is not of the personal residence.

The location of the principal residences is not relevant. Tax deferment may apply to residences in a foreign country.

Title to both the old and new home must be in your name. If you place title to the new home in someone else's name, the new home does not qualify you for deferral. An exception exists for a married couple who files a consent form. *See* ¶ 29.8.

Delay in sale of old residence after you move. When you cannot find a buyer and must move, you may face a problem in deferring tax on a later sale of the house. If you have bought a new house, there is the possibility that the sale of the old house may not occur within the time limits. If you delay the purchase of a new house until the sale of the old one, you may face this problem: The IRS may charge that, at the time of the sale, you no longer considered the house as your principal residence.

> *Temporary rentals.* You may defer tax if you move into a new home and temporarily rent out your old home while trying to sell it. *See* ¶ 29.17.
>
> You may also defer tax in this case: You buy a new house and rent it before selling your old house in which you continue to live. You later sell your old house and move into the new house.

EXAMPLE

An executive left his residence in suburban New York to live in a New York City apartment near his office; he made no efforts to sell his old home for two years, until just before he purchased a new home in Virginia. The Tax Court held that he had abandoned the old home as a principal residence. He timed the sale merely to take advantage of the tax deferral. In another case, a serviceman rented his residence over a six-year period until he could sell at a profit. He had refused earlier offers which would have given him a loss. The Tax Court held that he had abandoned his home as a residence.

In later decisions, the Tax Court commented that these two cases should not be interpreted as laying down a rule of law that an intention not to return to a home is, by itself, an abandonment of the home as a principal residence. Whether a homeowner has abandoned his residence is a question of fact. The absence of an intention to return is only one fact to be considered.

Separated couples. If you and your spouse agree to live apart, sell your jointly owned home and buy and live in separate new homes, you may each be able to defer tax. You each report the sale on Form 2119 as if two separate homes were sold. For example, assume that under state law, each of you is entitled to half the proceeds. On Form 2119, you each report half of the sales price. If the cost of your new home exceeds your respective half of the old home's adjusted sales price, you defer tax on your half of the gain. The same deferral test applies to your spouse.

TIME TEST

¶ **29.5** If you buy or build a new home, you must do so and begin to use it within two years before or after you sell your old one. The time test is strictly applied; failure to comply will not be excused for any reason.

A contract to purchase a new home is not sufficient to satisfy the time test. A sale is considered to occur at the earlier of the passage of title or the assumption of the benefits and burdens of ownership.

When you build, you must complete and occupy the house within the two-year period.

EXAMPLES

1. Bayley sold his house at a profit, started construction on a new house and elected to defer tax. The new house was not completed before the end of the required time period. A day before the end of the period, Bayley moved some of his furniture into the house but could not live there. The house had no water or sewage connections. He finally moved in two months later. The IRS taxed the gain because the house had not been timely occupied. The Tax Court agreed. Bayley had made the necessary investment but failed to meet the requirement of occupying the house.

2. The Lokans bought land to farm and build a new residence. Several months later, they sold their old house at a profit. During construction, they set up a trailer on the property. When one bedroom and a bath in the new house was completed, three children slept in the house; they and one other child slept in the trailer. The house was not fully completed until three years after the sale. The IRS and the Tax Court held that the Lokans did not reside in the new house; the trailer was their principal residence.

> *Deferment for workers abroad.* If your tax home (¶ 19.26) is outside the United States, the replacement period is suspended while you are abroad. The suspension applies only if your stay abroad began before the end of the replacement period and lasts until you return from abroad or until four years after the sale, whichever occurs first. Your spouse is also protected by the suspension provided that you both used the old home and new home as your principal residence.

Deferment on entering the Armed Forces. If you go on active duty for more than 90 days, the two year replacement period is suspended while you are in the Service. The suspension applies only if your service began before the end of the two-year replacement period. The suspension generally lasts until your discharge, when the two-year replacement period starts to run again, but regardless of the length of service, the replacement period ends four years after the date of sale. Thus, even if you remain in the Service, you must buy and live in a replacement no more than four years after you sell your home. For a sale after July 18, 1984, if you are stationed outside of the U.S. on extended duty or have to live in government quarters at a remote site after returning from a tour of duty outside the U.S., the replacement period may extend beyond the four-year period. The replacement period is suspended while you are at the foreign or remote site plus one year after the last day you were so stationed. However, the replacement period may not exceed eight years after the sale. If your spouse is in the armed forces and you are not, you are also protected by the suspension if you owned the old home and both you and your spouse used the old home and new home as principal residences. If you divorce or separate during the suspension period, your replacement period starts to run again the day after the divorce or separation.

INVESTMENT TEST

¶ **29.6** To defer tax on the full amount of gain, you must buy another principal residence, and your investment must generally equal or exceed the selling price of your old home.

To arrive at your actual gain on the sale and the gain that is not taxed, you have to figure the *amount realized* on the sale, the *adjusted sales price,* and the cost of the new residence. If the cost of the new residence equals or exceeds the adjusted sales price of the old residence, no part of the actual gain is taxed in the year of sale.

If you reinvest proceeds in two homes, one for summer and one for winter, you may not figure the investment in both houses. You consider the investment in the house used as your principal residence.

Amount realized. This is the selling price of your old house less selling expenses for commissions, advertising, preparing the deed, and other legal and title services. "Points" paid by you as the seller also reduce the selling price.

The selling price includes the amount of the mortgages on the old house, whether the buyer has assumed or bought the property subject to them. If immediately after the sale, you discount notes received on a deferred payment contract, include the discounted value of the notes, not the face amounts.

Do not include amounts received for furnishings, such as rugs and furniture, sold with the house. Sale of furnishings is reported separately if sold at a gain. Sales at a loss are not deductible.

Your actual gain is the difference between the amount realized and the cost of the old house. The cost basis of the old house is explained at ¶6.32.

Adjusted sales price. This is the amount realized less fix-up costs spent to make your old house salable, like papering, painting, and other similar repairs. Include costs for work done only within the 90-day period ending on the day on which the contract to sell is entered into and paid for within 30 days after the sale.

If you do not buy or build a house within the rules explained in this section, you may not deduct fix-up costs from the amount realized. Nor may you deduct them separately on your tax return. Furthermore, fix-up costs do not include costs of permanent improvements spent to clinch a sale, for example, installing a new roof or furnace. They are capital expenditures added to the cost basis of the old house.

Cost of the new house. You are not required to reinvest the cash proceeds of the sale of your old house. You may buy the new house with a small cash payment plus a large mortgage loan. The cost of the new house includes not only cash payments but also any mortgages you assume or take subject to. You also include broker's commissions and lawyer's fees. The treatment of "points" is explained at ¶15.13.

The present value of future land lease payments may not be added to the cost of your new house.

> When you build a house, include all costs paid in the construction of the house during the two years prior to the sale and two years after the sale. Costs paid after the two-year period are not included even if you have incurred liability for them before the end of the two-year period. However, these costs do become a part of the cost of the new house to figure gain or loss if you later sell it. Gifts and inheritances of all or part of a new home do not count as part of your purchase price in figuring whether you have reinvested your gain on the sale of your old residence. However, you may include costs of reconstructing an inherited house to make it habitable.

Compare the *adjusted sales price* with the *cost of the new house*. If the cost of the new house is the same or greater than the adjusted sales price of the old house, then none of the actual gain is taxed. But if the cost of the new house is less than the adjusted sales price, you are taxed on the difference—but not on more than your actual gain. Basis of the new home is reduced by nontaxed gain.

Cost basis of a cooperative apartment. Include the price for the stock in the cooperative and part of the mortgage to which the cooperative is subject, if these three tests are met:

1. The mortgage is properly allocated to your apartment. (The IRS will accept a mortgage allocation based on the same ratio as your stock interest bears to the total value of all the stock in the corporation.)
2. The corporation retains your stock as a pledge for payment of your annual charges, such as interest and principal payments on the mortgage.
3. Your share of corporate assets will be reduced by the unpaid balance of your proportionate share of the mortgage if the corporation is liquidated.

EXAMPLES

1. You are under 55. You plan to sell your house, which has a basis of $30,000. To make it more attractive to buyers, you paint the outside at a cost of $300 in April 1987. You pay for the painting when the work is finished. In May 1987 you sell the house for $71,000. Broker's commissions and other selling expenses are $2,000. In October 1987 you buy a new house for $68,000. This is how you compute the amount realized, the adjusted sales price, gain taxable on your 1987 return, and your basis in the replacement property:

Selling price	$71,000
Less: Selling expenses	2,000
Amount realized	69,000
Less: Basis of old house	30,000
Actual gain	$39,000
Amount realized	$69,000
Less: Fix-up costs	300
Adjusted sales price	68,700
Less: Cost of new house	68,000
Taxable gain	$ 700

Of the $39,000 gain $700 is taxable in 1987, the balance, $38,300 is not taxable. The cost basis of the new house is $29,700 ($68,000–$38,300).

2. Same facts as in (1) above except that in 1988 you sell the new house for $68,000 and move to an apartment. Taxed gain is $38,300:

Selling price	$68,000
Less: Cost basis	29,700
Taxed gain	$38,300

The exact amount of additional gain would have been taxed on the sale of your old house if you had not bought the second house. In other words, you merely deferred tax on the sale of your first house until you sold the new house without a further replacement.

Remodeling a vacation home as a permanent residence. A couple, planning to sell their principal home and remodel their vacation home into a permanent residence, asked the IRS if the remodeling costs could be considered as a purchase of a new residence. They planned to add 35% more living space by converting storage space to living areas, put in a new roof, heating and air conditioning systems and expand the basement. The IRS answered that the remodeling qualified because of the substantial structural alterations. Further, the remodeling costs were to be paid within the qualifying replacement period discussed in ¶29.5.

The IRS warned that merely adding a tennis court, pool, or new roof would not have qualified for tax deferral. However, once the major alterations are made, all improvements, such as the construction of a pool, could be considered part of the total cost of the renovation.

REVIEWING PURCHASE AND SALES RECORDS FOR TAX REPORTING

¶ **29.7** Arrange your records into three groups: (1) records of the purchase of the old house and improvements; (2) records of the sale of your old house; (3) records of the new purchase.

Energy conserving capital improvements do not increase your basis to the extent of an energy credit claimed. The basis of your old house is the total costs shown by these records. If you deduct a casualty loss for damage incurred to your house, the basis of the house should be reduced by the amount deducted.

Sale of old house. Here you should have: (1) the sales contract showing the sales price of the old house; (2) a statement showing settlement costs at the closing and allocating taxes and fire insurance; (3) the bill and record of payment of legal fees; (4) record of payment of broker's fees, if any; (5) a closing statement from the bank holding the mortgage on your old house showing final interest charges up to the date of transfer of title and prepayment penalties, if any; (6) if you incurred fix-up costs, records of when the work was done and when payment was made; (7) a record of payments for advertising the sale of the house, if any.

You reduce the selling price of the house by payments for broker's commissions, legal fees, and advertising expenses. The allocated property taxes are deducted according to the rules at ¶16.6. Mortgage interest and the prepayment penalty are deductible as interest if you itemize deductions. You may not deduct fire insurance premium payments. The treatment of fix-up costs is explained at ¶29.6 above. The paying off of the principal balance of the mortgage to the bank does not enter into the tax computation.

Purchase of and improvements to the old house. Your records here should show the purchase price of the old house plus title insurance fees, recording fees, transfer taxes, and attorney's fees. Also, bills or other records detailing capital improvements made to the house for additional rooms, equipment, landscaping and similar capital items (*see* ¶ 9.4). In one case, an accountant forgot to keep adequate records. He bought his house for $5,000 and later sold it for $11,000. In figuring his taxable gain, he claimed he had spent $5,000 for improvements; the IRS allowed him only $2,750. A court permitted him to increase his cost by $4,000. While his proof was not adequate, he was able to show that the house was in dilapidated condition when he bought it. The court estimated that he spent at least $4,000 to make the house habitable.

Purchase of the new residence. Here you should have: (1) your contract showing the cost of the new house plus any additional improvements; (2) the closing statement showing title insurance fees, adjustment of taxes, mortgage fees, and recording fees.

The cost basis of your new house includes the purchase price (even though all or part is covered by a mortgage), attorney's fees, mortgage fees, title insurance fees, and recording fees less the gain not taxed on the sale of your old home. You deduct taxes according to the allocation rules at ¶ 16.6. The payment of fire insurance premiums on the house is not deductible. The treatment of "points" is discussed at ¶ 15.13.

A MARRIED COUPLE MAY HAVE TO AGREE TO TAX DEFERMENT

¶ **29.8** When title to your new house differs from title to your old house, you and your spouse must file consent statements to defer tax. This happens when you or your spouse held title to the old house and now you both hold title jointly to the new house, or title to the old house was in your joint names and now only one of you holds title to the new house. Form 2119 may be used for consent.

EXAMPLES

1. Smith holds title to a condominium which he sells for $40,000. Its cost basis was $30,000, and he realizes a $10,000 gain. However, within the year, he and his wife contribute $20,000 each to buy a new house for $40,000 in their joint names. Smith pays no tax on the gain if he and his wife file consent statements in which they agree to allocate the basis of the new house between them. They file the consent on Form 2119 or on an attached statement in the year gain on the sale is realized. The basis of the new house is $15,000 to Smith and $15,000 to his wife.

2. Same facts as in the above example except the condominium was owned jointly by Smith and his wife, and the new house is bought by Mrs. Smith and placed in her name. Tax on the gain is deferred if both file consent statements. The basis of the new house to Mrs. Smith is $30,000.

Consents are ineffective to defer tax unless the old and new houses were principal residences of the couple.

If a husband and wife separate and sell their common home and each receives one-half the sales proceeds, each may defer tax on the gain by reinvesting his or her share in a new home.

Where a husband and wife each sell separate homes owned before marriage, tax on the gain is postponed if the total proceeds of the two sales is reinvested in a new home within the time limit and each contributes one-half the purchase price and takes joint title to the new home. No consent statement is required.

SALE OF MORE THAN ONE RESIDENCE WITHIN TWO YEARS

¶ **29.9** Tax may not be deferred if, within two years before the sale, you deferred tax on a profitable sale of another principal residence. However, this rule does not apply if you moved to a new job location and your moving expenses qualify under the rules of ¶ 19.13.

EXAMPLES

1. In August 1986, you sell your house at a profit and buy a new principal residence with the sale proceeds in the same month. In July 1987, you sell the new residence at a profit and buy another principal residence in September 1987. You may not defer tax on the July 1987 sale because it was within two years of the August 1986 sale. The house purchased in September 1987 is treated as a new principal residence for purposes of postponing tax on the gain on the August 1986 sale.

2. Same facts as in (1) above, but you had to sell your house in July 1987 because of a job relocation to a new city 500 miles away from your prior area of work and residence. Your moving expenses also meet the other tests of ¶ 19.13. You may defer tax on the sale made in August 1986 and the sale made in July 1987. For deferring tax on the August 1986 sale, you compare the cost of the residence bought in August 1986 with the adjusted sales price of the residence sold in August 1986. For deferring tax on the July 1987 sale, you compare the cost of the new residence bought in September 1987, with the adjusted sales price of the house sold in July 1987.

When you buy a new residence before the sale of the old house and then sell the new house, you may not defer tax on a subsequent sale of the original house, even if all sales and purchases fall within two years. To defer tax on the sale of the original house, you must own the new house at the time of the sale of the old house.

EXAMPLE

You own a house which cost $20,000. In January, you buy another house for $30,000. In July, you sell the house you bought in January for $32,000. In October, you sell your original house for $40,000. You have a $20,000 taxed gain on the October sale. Even though you bought another residence within two years before the October sale, you sold that new residence before you sold the original residence. So you may not avoid tax. You also have a $2,000 gain on the July sale.

SALE OF HOUSE USED PARTLY FOR BUSINESS

¶ **29.10** When you use part of your residence for business or rental to tenants, you treat the sale as if you sold two separate pieces of property. You apportion the sales price and basis of the house between the rented portion and the residential portion. You deduct depreciation from only the rented part.

You do not pay tax on gain allocated to your personal use of the house if your reinvestment in a new residence is at least equal to the selling price of the portion of the old house allocated to your personal use. Similarly, if only part of the new property is used as your personal residence, only the cost allocated to that use is considered as reinvested for purposes of deferring tax on gain.

EXAMPLES

1. You sell for $97,000 a three-family house that cost you $33,000. Selling expenses (commissions and legal fees) were $7,000. You lived in one of the apartments. You rented the other two. On the rental part, you took $4,400 of straight line depreciation. You compute your gain by allocating ⅔ of the selling price and basis to the rental part and ⅓ to the personal part:

		Rental	Personal
Net sales price ($97,000–$7,000)		$60,000	$30,000
Cost ($33,000)	$22,000		
Less: Depreciation	4,400	17,600	11,000
Net gain		$42,400	$19,000

You pay tax on the gain of $42,400. You defer tax on the gain of $19,000, if you invest at least $30,000 in a new residence under the rules at ¶ 29.3. You also defer tax if you buy a new multifamily house and the cost allocated to your apartment in the house is at least $30,000. If you are 55 or over, you can make an election under the rules of ¶ 29.12 and avoid tax on the personal profit even though you do not make a reinvestment.

2. Same facts as in (1) above except the net selling price is only $30,000. Here you have a gain of $2,400 ($20,000 – $17,600) on the rental part, and a loss of $1,000 on the residential part ($10,000–$11,000). You may not offset the $1,000 loss against the gain. Each is

treated as a separate transaction. The loss is not deductible because it is a personal loss.

CLAIMING A LOSS ON SALE OF PERSONAL RESIDENCE

¶ **29.11** Loss on the sale of a personal residence is not deductible. However, a loss may be claimed in these instances: (1) You convert the house from personal use to some profit-making purpose before the sale. (2) You sell a house acquired by gift or inheritance which you did not personally use but rather offered for rental or sale shortly after acquisition. (3) You sell stock in your cooperative apartment in which there were nonstockholder tenants when you acquired your stock.

Profit-making purposes. Renting a residence is a changeover from personal to profit-making purposes. Merely putting the house up for rent or an isolated rental of several months may not be recognized by the IRS as a conversion to rental property.

The Tax Court has approved a loss deduction where a house was rented on a 90-day lease with an option to buy. The court set down two tests for determining when a house is converted to rental property: (1) The rental charge returns a profit. (2) The lease prevents you from using or reoccupying the house during the lease period. Under the Tax Court approach, you have a conversion if you have a lease that gives possession of the house to the tenant during the lease period, and the rent, after deducting taxes, interest, insurance, repairs, depreciation and other charges, returns you a profit.

> You may deduct a loss if you rented part and occupied part for your own purposes. A loss on a sale is allowable on the rented portion.
>
> A loss deduction is also allowed where you acquired the house as an investment with the intention of selling it at a profit even though you occupied it incidentally as a residence prior to sale.
>
> **EXAMPLES**
> 1. An owner bought a house with the intention of selling it. He lived in it for six years, but during that period it was for sale. He was allowed to deduct the loss on its sale by proving he lived in it to protect it from vandalism and to keep it in good condition so it would be attractive to possible buyers.
> 2. An architect and builder built a house and offered it for sale through an agent and advertisements. He had a home and no intention to occupy the new house. On a realtor's advice, he moved into the house to make it more saleable. Ten months later, he sold the house at a loss of $4,065 and promptly moved out. The loss was allowed on proof that his main purpose in building and occupying the house was to realize a profit by a sale; the residential use was incidental.

Rental loss may be barred for temporary rental preceding sale. The IRS and Tax Court disallowed a loss deduction for rental expenses under the "profit motive rules" (¶5.9) where a residence was rented for 10 months until it could be sold. According to the Tax Court, the temporary rental did not convert the residence to rental property. Since the sales effort was primary, there was no profit motive for the rental. Thus, no loss could be claimed; rental expenses were deductible only to the extent of rental income. *See* ¶5.9. The favorable side of the Tax Court position: Since the residence was not converted to rental property, the owners could defer tax on the gain from the sale under the rules of ¶29.3 by buying a new home. An appeals court reversed the Tax Court and allowed both tax deferral and a loss deduction. The rental loss was allowed since the old home was actually rented for a fair rental price. Further, the owners had moved and could not return to the old home, which was rented almost continuously until sold.

Residence acquired by gift or inheritance. You may deduct a loss on the sale of a house which was received as an inheritance or gift if you personally did not use it and you offered it for sale or rental immediately or within a few weeks after acquisition.

If you inherit a residence in which you do not intend to live, it may be advisable to put it up for rent or sale, not for sale alone. If you merely

try to sell, and you finally do so at a loss, you are limited to a capital loss. If you first try to rent but cannot, you will probably get an ordinary loss when you finally sell.

The Tax Court held that a surviving spouse realized a deductible loss on the sale of a house previously held jointly with a deceased spouse.

EXAMPLE

A couple owned a winter vacation home in Florida. When the husband died, his wife immediately put the house up for sale and never lived in it. It was sold at a loss. The IRS disallowed the capital loss deduction, claiming it was personal and nondeductible. The wife argued that her case was no different from the case of an heir inheriting and selling a home, since at the death of her husband her interest in the property was increased. The court agreed with her reasoning and allowed the deduction.

Stock in cooperative apartment. Normally, you get no deduction for a loss on the sale of your stock in a cooperative housing corporation. It makes no difference that you occasionally sublet your apartment. It is still not considered property used in a business. But you may get a loss deduction when there were nonstockholder tenants in the cooperative housing corporation when you bought your stock. Then, you get a partial capital loss deduction if you sell your stock or if it becomes worthless. To figure your capital loss—

First find the difference between your cost and your selling price. This would ordinarily be your capital loss. Then find the percentage of nonstockholding tenants (based on rental values) in the housing corporation when you bought your stock.

Apply this percentage to the loss you figured above. This is the capital loss you are allowed.

See ¶5.16 for when depreciation may be taken on the basis of the cooperative stock ownership.

TAX FREE RESIDENCE SALE BY HOMEOWNERS AGE 55 OR OVER

¶ **29.12** If you are 55 years of age or older and sell or exchange your home at a profit, you may avoid tax on profits up to $125,000. To claim this exclusion, you must: (1) elect to avoid tax; (2) be 55 or over before the date of sale; and (3) have owned and occupied the house as your principal residence for at least three of the five years preceding the day of sale.

The election applies to cooperative apartment ownership tied to stock ownership and to condominiums. It applies also to gain realized from an involuntary conversion of your home through fire, storm or other casualty, or condemnation. Although you avoid tax on gain, you consider the gain as gross income in determining whether you are required to file a return (*see* ¶1.1).

The election to exclude gain does not apply where only a partial interest in the home is sold. In a private letter ruling, the IRS refused to permit an exclusion to a homeowner who sold the remainder interest in her home while retaining the right to live in it for life. However, the exclusion is allowed if a homeowner gives away a remainder interest in the house and then sells the retained life interest. The exclusion may be claimed because the life interest is the owner's entire interest in the residence.

Age test. You must be 55 or over before the date of sale. It is not sufficient that you will be 55 sometime during the year in which the sale occurs. According to the IRS, you reach 55 the day before your birthday. Thus, a sale on the date of your 55th birthday qualifies.

If you receive an offer that you want to accept before your 55th birthday, contract to sell but do not give title or possession until you are 55 if you want to make the election. A sale may be considered to have occurred for tax purposes when you give the buyer possession of the house, although you have not formally passed title.

The use and ownership test. You must have owned and occupied your home as your principal residence for three out of the five years preceding the date of sale. Ownership and use for 36 full months or for 1,095 days (365×3) qualifies. The three years need not be consecutive. Short temporary absences for vacations, although accompanied with rental of the residence, are counted as periods of use.

EXAMPLES

1. You are over 55. You started to use a house as your principal residence in 1950. On January 1, 1986, you move to another state and rent the house. On July 1, 1987, you sell it. You may elect tax free gain. You owned and used the house as your principal residence for three out of the five years preceding the sale.

2. You live with your son and daughter-in-law in a house owned by your son from 1973 through 1984. On January 1, 1985, you buy the house from your son. You sell it on March 31, 1987. You may not make the election in 1987. Although you used the property as your principal residence for more than three years, you did not own it for three of the five years preceding the date of the sale.

3. On January 1, 1984, a teacher, age 55, bought and moved into a house which he used as his principal residence. On February 1, 1985, he went abroad on a one-year sabbatical and, during part of the year, leased the house. On March 1, 1986, one month after his return, he sold the house. He may not make the election. He did not use the residence for the required three years. Under Treasury regulations, his one-year leave is not considered a temporary absence that may be counted as part of the three-year occupancy period.

> **Making the election.** The tax free election is available to you only once in your lifetime. If, at the time you sell your home, you plan to invest the money in another home of sufficient cost to completely defer tax but later change your plans, you can make the election at any time before the end of the period for making a refund claim for the year in which the sale occurred. This is generally within three years from the due date of the return filed for the year of the sale. Similarly, if you make the election and then decide to revoke it, you may do so within the same three-year period.

You make the election on Form 2119 or in a signed statement which you attach to your income tax return for the year of sale. In the statement, you write that you elect to exclude from income the gain realized on the sale. In addition, you give the following data: (1) your name, age, Social Security number, and marital status as of the date of sale; (2) the dates you bought and sold your residence; (3) the adjusted sale price and the adjusted basis of the property on the date of sale; and (4) the length of any absences during the five years preceding the sale.

If you are married at the time of the sale, your spouse must agree to the election. In revoking the election, you must also have your spouse's consent. If you are divorced after the election but then want to revoke, you must get your former spouse's consent to the revocation. If your spouse dies after the sale but before you could make an election, your deceased spouse's personal representative (administrator or executor) must join with you in making an election. Similarly, the personal representative must join in a revocation of any election previously made by you and your deceased spouse. Joint elections and revocations are required, even though the residence was separately owned, separate tax returns are filed, or the nonowning spouse does not meet the three-year residence requirement. Also *see* ¶ 29.14.

In one case, the IRS permitted an election by an executor where a sale was completed after the death of the owner under an executory contract made by the owner prior to his death.

A revocation is made in a signed statement showing: (1) your name and Social Security number; (2) the year in which the election was made and filed; and (3) the Internal Revenue office where you filed the election.

When you might not want to elect the exclusion. If you sell your principal residence at a gain which is substantially less than the exclusion, and you plan to reinvest at least all of the net proceeds from the sale in a new home, consider deferring tax under the rules at ¶ 29.3 rather than electing to exclude gain. You are permitted only one lifetime exclusion. For example, if you have a gain of $10,000 and elect to exclude it, you have used up your once-in-a-lifetime election; a later home sale will not be entitled to a $115,000 exclusion. If you buy a new house at a cost at least equal to the adjusted sales price of the old home (¶ 29.3), the entire gain from the sale of your old home is deferred. If and when you sell the new house without a further home purchase, the election to exclude gain may then be made.

Property used in part as principal residence. An election may be made for that part of the gain attributed to personal use. For example, you use a part of your home as an office for more than two years out of the last five years before the sale. The election does not apply to the gain allocable to the office.

> Rental of the house for periods during the five-year period preceding the date of sale will not disqualify the election. Where you do rent your house and you want to avail yourself of the tax free election, make sure that a rental during the five-year period does not exceed two years. If it does, the three-year residence test will not be met.

Sale by marital trust. Property may be left to marital trust for the benefit of a surviving spouse if there is concern that the survivor may be unable to manage the property. A personal residence may be put into the trust. If the surviving spouse is entitled to all the trust income and has an unlimited power to receive trust corpus upon request or appoint the property to any other person, the surviving spouse is considered the owner of the trust for tax purposes. Thus, if the trust sells the personal residence, the surviving spouse can elect to claim the $125,000 home sale exclusion provided he or she is over age 55 on the date of sale and has (1) owned (through the trust) and used the residence as a principal residence for three of the last five years preceding the date of sale, and (2) the $125,000 exclusion was not previously elected by the surviving spouse or the deceased spouse with respect to a prior sale.

COMBINING THE EXCLUSION WITH TAX DEFERRAL

¶ 29.13 If you sell your principal residence at a gain of over $125,000 and plan to purchase a new home, you may take advantage of the exclusion as well as the tax free deferral rules of ¶ 29.3. Where you qualify for the exclusion, your gain up to the exclusion is tax free. You may then defer all or part of the remaining gain, depending on the amount of your investment in the new home. You may defer all of the remaining gain by making an investment at least equal to the adjusted sales price of the old house (sales price less selling expenses and fix-up costs—*see* ¶ 29.6) less the tax free gain. If you invest less than this amount, the difference between (1) adjusted sales price of the old house less the tax free gain, and (2) the new investment, is taxed, but not exceeding the remaining gain.

In determining whether you have to file a return, the tax free gain realized from the sale of your house is counted as gross income, although not taxed.

EXAMPLE

You sell your home for $180,000. You incurred fix-up costs of $2,000. Basis of the house is $40,000. You make a profit of $140,000. You elect to exclude $125,000 of the profit from tax. You may still defer all or part of the remaining profit of $15,000 of gain by investing in a new home which costs at least $53,000.

Sales price	$180,000
Less: Fix-up costs	2,000
Adjusted sales price	$178,000
Less: Excluded gain	125,000
	$ 53,000

If you buy a new residence for $50,000, $3,000 of the gain is taxable ($53,000–$50,000).

Selling on the installment method. Where you sell your home and take back a purchase money mortgage that will be paid off after the year of sale, you have made an installment sale. Only a portion of each payment is taxable.

EXAMPLE

Smith sold his home which cost him $140,000 for $300,000 and elects the exclusion. The buyer is unable to get outside financing so Smith agrees to take back a purchase money mortgage of $150,000, payable over 15 years. Of the $160,000 profit ($300,000–$140,000), only

$35,000 is taxable; $125,000 is tax free. The $35,000 gain is reported over the 15 years in which payment on the mortgage loan is received. To determine the amount of each payment taxable as income, the gross profit ratio is applied to each payment actually received. The gross profit ratio is figured by dividing the taxable gain by the total contract price (*see* ¶ 6.34). Here, this is $35,000 divided by $300,000, which gives a profit ratio of 11.66%. Thus, in the year of sale, $17,490 (11.66% of the $150,000 down payment) is taxable. Of each annual $10,000 installment payment received over the 15 years, $1,166 is taxable ($10,000 × 11.66%).

THE EXCLUSION AND JOINTLY OWNED RESIDENCES

¶ **29.14** Where you own the house jointly with your spouse and file a joint return in the year the residence is sold, only one of you need meet the age requirement of 55 or over and the residence and ownership requirement of three out of the last five years. Marital status is determined as of the date of the sale.

Where a spouse who has died held and used the house as a personal residence for three out of the last five years and had not previously claimed a tax free exemption election the surviving spouse who is 55 or over and not remarried at the time of the sale may make an election.

EXAMPLE

In 1987, a woman, 56 years old, plans to marry later in the year. She also plans to sell her home at a substantial profit. Her fiance sold his home at a profit of $100,000 in August 1986 and elected on his 1986 return to avoid tax. If she sells the house before the marriage, she may claim the exclusion on her 1987 return. True, only one lifetime election of the exclusion is allowed to a married couple, but for purposes of this test, marital status is determined at the time of sale. Thus, if she sells before she marries, her right to claim the election is not affected by her spouse's prior election. However, if she sells after the marriage, she may not claim the $125,000 exclusion because of her spouse's 1986 election. Once married, the right to claim the election on a sale of her home is forfeited because of a spouse's prior election, even though the spouse's home sale may have taken place prior to her marriage.

Only one lifetime election is allowed to a married couple; you and your spouse do not each have a separate election to claim the exclusion. If either you or your spouse has previously elected the exclusion, neither of you may make another election. If spouses make an election during marriage and later divorce, no further elections are available to either of them or to either of their new spouses should they remarry. If both you and your spouse before your marriage owned and used separate residences and each elected the exclusion, there is no recapture of taxes attributable to the gain excluded on the sale of one of the residences.

What if before your marriage you and your spouse each owned and used a separate residence, and after your marriage both residences are sold? May two elections be made? No. An election may be made for a sale of either residence (but not for both residences) provided the age, ownership, and use requirements are met. To take advantage of two exclusions, the sales should take place before marriage.

A husband and wife selling a jointly owned residence are considered as one taxpayer for purposes of the exclusion limitation. But if joint owners are not married, each owner who meets the tests for age (55), use (principal residence), and holding period (three of five years), may exclude gain up to $125,000 on his or her interest in the residence. That one owner meets the requirements does not qualify the other for the exclusion.

A married person who files a separate return may exclude only up to $62,500 of profit.

Joint ownership with someone other than spouse. If you own the home jointly with someone other than your spouse, each owner who meets the age 55 test and the three out of five year ownership and use test may exclude their share of the gain.

RENTING PERSONAL AND VACATION RESIDENCES

DEDUCTING EXPENSES OF RENTING OUT PART OF YOUR HOME

¶ **29.15** You report rent receipts and deduct expenses allocated to the rented part of the property on Schedule E (*see* Supplement to *Your Income Tax*). Expenses allocated to rental are deductible, whether or not you itemize deductions. You deduct interest and taxes on your personal share of the property as itemized deductions, if you itemize deductions.

EXAMPLE

You bought a three-family house in 1970. You occupy one apartment as a personal residence. The house cost you $30,000 ($27,000 for the building, $3,000 for the land). It has a useful life of 30 years. This is how you deduct expenses:

Depreciation ⅔ of building Cost—$27,000	Cost basis $18,000	Useful life 30 years	Depreciation $600	
	Total	Deduct itemized deductions	Deduct in rent schedule	Not deductible
Taxes	$ 600	$200	$ 400	
Interest	390	130	260	
Repairs	300		200	$100
Depreciation	600		600	
	$1,890	$330	$1,460	$100

The expenses allocated to personal use are deductible provided you do not claim the standard deduction. Repairs allocated to your apartment are nondeductible personal expenses.

If expenses exceed rental income, your loss deduction is subject to the passive activity rules of ¶ 11. The loss, if it comes within the $25,000 allowance, may be deducted from any type of income. If not, the loss may be deducted only from passive activity income. Phase-in exceptions may also allow a partial deduction from income other than passive activity income.

If you or certain close relatives personally use the rented portion during the year and expenses exceed income, the loss deduction may be subject to the rules of ¶ 29.17.

TAKING DEPRECIATION WHEN YOU RENT YOUR RESIDENCE

¶ **29.16** When you convert your residence to rental property, you can begin to take depreciation on the building. You figure depreciation on the *lower* of the building's:

Fair market value at the time you convert it to rental property, or

Adjusted basis (original cost plus or minus capital additions or reductions until time of conversion).

In 1987, you may claim MACRS depreciation; *see* ¶ 5.31. The MACRS straightline rate is 27½ years. A mid-month convention rule applies to the month the house was converted to rental property. The house is treated as placed in service during the middle of the month. This means that one-half of a full month's depreciation is allowed for that month.

273

EXAMPLE

In 1982, you bought a house for $125,000, of which $100,000 is allocated to the house. In June 1987 you move out of the house and rent it. At that time, the fair market value of the house exclusive of land is $150,000. The depreciable basis of the house is the lower adjusted basis of $100,000. Under MACRS, residential property has a 27½ year life or annual rate of 3.64%. In 1987, you may claim depreciation of $1,970 according to the table at ¶5.31 for placing the house in service in June ($100,000 × 1.9697).

Basis to use when you sell a rented residence. If you realize a gain, you use adjusted basis at the time of the conversion, less depreciation. If you realize a loss, you use the *lower* of adjusted basis or fair market value at the time of the conversion, less depreciation. *See* the table below.

Have an appraiser estimate the fair market value of the house when it is rented. The appraisal will help support your basis for depreciation or a loss deduction on a sale if your return is examined.

Depreciation on a vacant residence. If you move from your house before it is sold, you may generally not deduct depreciation on the vacant residence while it is held for sale. The IRS will not allow the deduction, and according to a Tax Court case, a deduction is possible only if you can show that you held the house, expecting to make a profit on an increase in value over and above the value of the house when you moved from it. That is, you held the house for sale on the expectation of profiting on a future increase in value after abandoning the house as a residence.

EXAMPLE

In 1967, Lowry put his summer home up for sale. At the time, it was worth $50,000. However, he decided he would not sell the house for less than $150,000. He expected the value of his land to appreciate greatly during the next few years. He did not rent the house because he felt it would be easier to sell an empty house, and the amount of rental income would not justify the expense of equipping the house for rental. He deducted the maintenance expenses, claiming he held the property as an investment. The IRS disallowed the deduction, claiming that since he did not try to rent it, he held it for personal use.

A federal district court allowed the deduction. Lowry had sound business reasons for not renting. He intended to benefit from post-abandonment appreciation in land values. When he put the house on the market, it was worth $50,000. Six years later, he finally got his asking price of $150,000. That he immediately listed the house for sale did not negate his intention to hold the house for future appreciation.

An investor may claim depreciation on a vacant building held for resale. However, the IRS may dispute the deduction as it has withdrawn a prior acceptance of a court decision which allowed the deduction to an investor.

Loss deductions related to rental operations are limited by the passive activity rules of chapter 11.

RESTRICTIONS ON DEDUCTING RENTAL EXPENSES OF VACATION HOMES AND PERSONAL RESIDENCES

¶ **29.17** Two types of restrictions apply to deducting losses of renting a vacation home or personal residence:

1. Determining whether you are allowed to deduct expenses in excess of income, and
2. If you may deduct the loss, determining whether the losses are deductible from income such as salary and portfolio investment income.

The rules for determining whether you are entitled to the deduction are discussed below. The passive activity rules of chapter 11 determine the type of income from which you may claim the loss deduction. All or part of the deduction may be allowed from all types of income if you qualify for the $25,000 rental allowance or come within the phase-out tests; *see* chapter 11.

The law prevents most homeowners from deducting losses (expenses in excess of income) on renting a personal vacation home or personal residence if the owner or close relatives personally use the premises during the year. Tests based on days of personal and rental use determine whether you may deduct losses. The following tests are designed to disallow losses.

1. *If you rent the home for less than 15 days,* you may not deduct any

expenses attributed to the rental (except for interest, real estate taxes, and casualty losses, if any). If you realize a profit on the rental, you are not taxable on the profit.

2. *If the rental of the home is for 15 days or more,* you then determine if your personal use of the home exceeds a 14-day or 10% time test. If it does, you are considered to have used the unit as a residence during the year and rental expenses are deductible only to the extent of gross rental income. This limitation on loss deductions applies if the number of days you personally *use* the home during your taxable year exceeds the greater of 14 days or 10% of the number of days the home is rented at a fair rental. (The use of rental pool arrangements is discussed below.) If rental income exceeds expenses, your operating gain is fully taxable.

3. *You rent the home for 15 days or more, but the days of your personal use are less than the days fixed by the 14-day/10% test.* You are not considered to have made any personal use of the residence during the year. Therefore, expenses in excess of rental income may be deductible. However, the IRS may disallow the loss deduction if you cannot prove that you rent the residence to make a profit under the "profit motive" tests of ¶5.9.

The Tax Court has allowed loss deductions where the owner made little personal use of the home and proved he bought the house to make a profitable resale.

EXAMPLES

1. *(Loss allowed.)* In 1973, Clancy purchased a house and land in a coastal resort area of California. Prior to the purchase, Clancy was told by a renting agent that he could expect reasonable income and considerable appreciation from the property. Previously, he had sold similar property in the same development at a profit. After the purchase, Clancy spent $5,000 to prepare the house for rental, and gave a rental agency the exclusive right to offer the property for rent. The house was available for rent 95% of the time in 1973, and 100% of the time in 1974. However, rentals proved disappointing, totaling only $280 in 1973 and $1,244 in 1974, despite the active efforts of the agency to rent the property. However, the house did appreciate in value and was eventually sold at a profit of $14,000. In 1973 and 1974, Clancy deducted rental expenses of approximately $21,000 which the IRS disallowed. The IRS claimed that the house was not rental property used in a business. Further, as Clancy knew that he could not make a profit from the rentals, he could not be considered to hold the property for the production of income.

The Tax Court agrees that the expenses are not deductible business expenses. But this does not mean that they are not deductible as expenses of income production. Although the rental income from the property was minimal, Clancy acquired and held the property expecting to make a profit on a sale. He had previously sold similar property at a profit and was told to expect considerable rental income as well as appreciation from the new house. Where an owner holds property, as Clancy did here, because he believes that it may appreciate in value, such property is held for the production of income. Further evidence that Clancy held the property to make a profit: He rarely used it for personal purposes and an agent actively sought to rent it.

2. *(Loss allowed.)* Allen, a banking executive, built a ski lodge near a popular resort at Bromley Mountain in Vermont. The lodge was rented out as a summer or fall vacation home as well as during the ski season. He used the lodge overnight only when preparing it for a tenant. Allen claimed unfavorable weather, gasoline shortages, and a glut of competitors contributed to poor rentals. Deductions of $3,271 in 1971 and $6,500 in 1972 were disallowed by the IRS on the grounds that Allen did not intend to make a profit from the lodge.

The Tax Court disagreed. True, it might be argued that Allen had no profit motive as he had independent income sources. However, he operated the lodge in a businesslike manner, experimenting with different types of rental arrangements in an attempt to turn a profit. The substantial and repeated losses were caused by forces beyond his control: by unfavorable weather and gasoline shortages. Further, he suffered actual economic losses. Finally, he never used the lodge for his own personal enjoyment; he stayed overnight only to get the lodge in rental shape.

3. *(Loss allowed.)* Nelson bought a condominium, hired a rental agent, and even advertised the unit in the Wall Street Journal and Indianapolis Star. He also listed the unit for sale. During 1974, he was unable

to rent the apartment but deducted expenses and depreciation of over $6,100 which the IRS disallowed. The IRS argued he did not buy the unit to make a profit but to tax shelter substantial income. The Tax Court disagreed. Although his efforts to rent were not successful in 1974, he was successful in later years in renting the unit. He rarely visited the apartment other than to initially furnish it. When he went on vacation, he went abroad or to other vacation spots.

4. *(Loss disallowed.)* The Lindows purchased a condominium which they rented out during the prime winter rental season. However, over an eight-year period their expenses consistently exceeded rental income. The Tax Court agreed with the IRS that expenses in excess of rental income were not deductible. Substantial, repeated losses, even after the initial years of operation, indicate that the operation was not primarily profit oriented. The rental return during the prime rental season could not return a profit. Even if the condominium was fully rented for the entire prime rental season, annual claimed expenses would exceed rent income. The couple also used the unit for several months and intended to live there on retirement. They did not consider putting the unit up for sale with an agent. Finally, that they had detailed records of income and expenses did not prove a business venture. Records, regardless of how detailed, are insufficient to permit the deduction of what are essentially personal expenses.

5. *(Loss disallowed.)* A married couple rented their Florida condominium to the husband's parents at less than fair market value. Although the couple might have hoped to realize a profit on resale of the condominium, their failure to profit by renting at the highest possible price indicated that their primary motive for holding the property was personal, rather than to make a profit.

> The loss restrictions apply to any "dwelling unit" you rent out which is also used as a residence during the year by yourself or family members. A "dwelling unit" may be a house, apartment, condominium, house trailer, mini motor home, boat, or similar property, including any environs and outbuildings such as a garage. The term does not include that portion of a dwelling unit that is used exclusively as a hotel, motel, inn, or similar establishment.

The loss limitation rules apply not only to individuals but also to trusts, estates, partnerships, and S corporations owning vacation residences.

Figuring "personal" use time for the 14-day/10% test. A vacation home is considered to have been personally used if for any part of the day the home is used by: (1) you or any other person who owns an interest in the home unless you and the co-owner have a shared equity financing agreement (*see* below); (2) your relatives or the relatives of a co-owner, such as brothers and sisters, spouse, parents, grandparents, children, or spouses of your children. However, if a relative pays a fair rental to use the home as his principal residence, this use is *not* considered personal use; (3) any person who uses the home under a reciprocal arrangement under which you use some other dwelling (whether or not a fair rental is charged); or (4) any other person who uses the vacation home during a day unless for that day the home is rented for a fair rental.

Use by a co-owner is not considered personal use if these tests are satisfied: (1) you have a shared equity financing agreement under which the co-owner pays you a fair rent for using the home as his principal residence; (2) you and your co-owner each have undivided interests for more than 50 years in the entire home and in any appurtenant land acquired with the residence.

Any use by a co-owner which does not meet the above tests is considered personal use by you if, for any part of the day, the home is used by a co-owner or a holder of any interest in the home (other than a security interest or an interest under a lease for fair rental) for personal purposes. For this purpose, any other ownership interest existing at the time you have an interest in the vacation home is counted, even if there are no immediate rights to possession and enjoyment of the vacation home under such other interest. For example, you have a life estate in the home and your friend owns the remainder interest. Use by either of you is personal use.

An owner is not considered to have personally used a vacation home

used by his employee if the value of such use is not taxable under the rules of ¶2.2.

For a home owned by a partnership, trust, estate, or S corporation, the number of days of personal use is the total number of days of use by the owners or beneficiaries. Under proposed regulations, this rule would not apply to a partnership rental of a unit to a partner as his principal residence if there are no special allocations of deductions. If two or more owners or beneficiaries use a home during the same day, that day would constitute only one day of personal use.

Rental of principal residence. You are not considered to have made any personal use of a principal residence which you rent or try to rent at a fair rental for a consecutive period of 12 months or more or for a period of less than 12 months that ends with the sale or exchange of the residence. This means that deductions are not limited by the personal use tests of this section, ¶29.17. However, where the rental precedes a sale, deductions for the period have been limited under the "profit motive rules" of ¶5.9.

EXAMPLE

In July 1977, Bolaris moved into a new home after failing to find a buyer for his old home. He rented the old house for 10 months before its sale in 1978. In 1977, he reported a rental loss of $1,638 and in 1978, $4,727, which the IRS disallowed. The items making up the loss were depreciation, insurance premiums and repair expenses. The IRS did not think the residence could be considered a residence for tax deferral purposes and rental property at the same time. The Tax Court sided with the IRS. An appeals court reversed, allowing the deductions. Bolaris was also allowed to defer tax on the sale of the residence. The IRS did not question his right to do so.

Allocation of expenses to rental activity. When you personally use a home on any day during the taxable year, expenses must be allocated between personal and rental use. By law, deductible expenses of renting, except for interest and taxes, are limited by this fraction:

$$\frac{\text{Days of fair rental}}{\text{Total days of rental and personal use}}$$

Days a vacation home is held out for rent but not actually rented are not counted as rental days.

The IRS has also used the above fraction for allocating interest and taxes to rental use, but the Tax Court and an appeals court disagree, as explained below.

If expenses allocated to rental exceed rental income and your personal use exceeds the 14-day/10% test, allocated expenses are deducted in a specific order. First, gross rental income is reduced by expenses to obtain tenants, such as realtor's fees and advertising expenses. From this balance of rental income, deduct interest and taxes allocated to the rental activity. Next operating expenses (other than depreciation) are deducted to the extent of remaining rental income. Finally, if there is any rental income remaining, depreciation may be deducted up to the balance of income.

EXAMPLE

You rent out your vacation home receiving a rental of $2,000. Assume that, because of your personal use, you may deduct expenses only up to the amount of this income. Assume further that you may deduct two-thirds of the following expenses: Mortgage interest of $1,200; real estate taxes of $600, maintenance and utility costs of $900, and depreciation (if the house had been used only for rental purposes) of $1,200. The allocated expenses are deducted in this order:

Rent income		$2,000
Less: Interest	$800	
Taxes	400	1,200
		800
Less: Maintenance		600
		200
Less: Depreciation		200

The balance of the depreciation is not deductible.

The balance of interest and taxes is deductible as itemized deductions provided you claim itemized deductions. Interest, taxes and casualty losses are deductible, regardless of whether the activity is personal or income producing.

The Tax Court disagrees with the IRS formula for allocating interest and taxes. According to the Tax Court, interest and taxes are allocated on a daily basis. Thus, if the house is rented for 61 days in the year, ⅙ of interest and taxes (61/365) is deducted first from rental income. This rule allows a larger amount of other expenses to be deducted from rental income.

EXAMPLE

The Boltons paid interest and property taxes totaling $3,475 on their vacation home. Maintenance expenses (not including depreciation) totaled $2,693. The Boltons stayed at the home 30 days and rented it for 91 days, receiving rents of $2,700. Because of the personal use for 30 days, the Boltons could deduct rental expenses only up to the gross rental income of $2,700 reduced by interest and taxes allocable to rental. In figuring the amount of interest and taxes deductible from rents, they divided the number of rental days, or 91, by 365, the number of days in the year. This gave them an allocation of 25%. After subtracting $868 for interest and taxes (25% of $3,475) from rental income, they deducted $1,832 of maintenance expenses from rental income.

The IRS argued that 75% of the Boltons' interest and tax payments had to be allocated to the rental income. The IRS used an allocation base of 121 days of personal and rental use. Thus, the IRS allocated 75% (91/121) of the interest and taxes, or $2,606, to gross rental income of $2,700. This allocation allowed only $94 maintenance expenses to be deducted ($2,700– $2,606).

The Tax Court sided with the Boltons and an appeals court agrees. The IRS method of allocating interest and taxes to rental use is bizarre. Interest and taxes are expenses that accrue ratably over the year and are deductible even if a vacation home is not rented for a single day. Thus, the allocation to rental use should be based on a ratable portion of the annual expense by dividing the number of rental days by the number of days in a year.

Interest expenses. Interest paid on a mortgage of a vacation home which qualifies as a second residence (¶15.11) is *not* considered passive activity interest.

Rental pool arrangements. Such arrangements have been devised to avoid the loss restriction by attempting to increase the days the home is held for a fair rental value. They have not been successful.

EXAMPLES

1. Fine, a Florida resort condominium owner, used his home 20 days and rented it for 149 days during the year under a rental pool arrangement that made his home available for rental for 333 days. He received a small fee for the days the home was not rented; a larger sum for the days of actual rental. Under the 14-day/10% test, he could not deduct losses if he counted only the 149 days of actual rental; his 20 days of personal use exceeded 10% of the 149 rental days. However, Fine argued that the home was rented for 333 days under the pool arrangement and, therefore, personal use was less than 10% of 333 days.

The IRS argued that the management company was not a lessee, but merely Fine's agent in arranging rentals; thus, only the 149 days of actual rental could be considered. Further, even if the arrangement is considered a lease, Fine is still considered to have received a fair rental for only the 149 days; the lower pool fee received was not a fair rental value. A federal appeals court agreed that the pool fee was not a fair rental because it did not allow for a profit. Since Fine's personal use of the home for 20 days exceeded 10% of the 149 days for which the home was actually rented at a fair rental value, he may deduct only expenses up to his rental income.

2. Byers bought two condominium units in a Sarasota, Florida resort. Under an agreement, he could use his unit for up to 30 days; during the rest of the year, it was in a rental pool. He deducted losses of $27,000 which the IRS disallowed, claiming that he did not prove how many days his units were actually rented. He could not base the loss deduction on the number of days all of the units were rented from the rental pool. Although the Tax Court agreed with the IRS claims, it allowed part of Byers' deduction. It estimated actual rentals on rental pool records of average pool rentals because there was no record of rentals of individual units. The court accepted the testimony of resort officials that Byers' units were in a popular location and were rented most of the time they were available.

In proposed regulations, the IRS also holds that a rental pool is not a basis for counting fair rental days. However, the proposed regulations permit rental pool participants to elect to average the rental use of their units. The number of rental days for a unit is determined by multiplying the aggregate number of days that all units in the rental pool were rented at fair rental during the pool season by a fraction. The numerator of the fraction is the number of participation days of a particular unit; the denominator is the aggregate number of participation days of all units.

REPORTING GAIN OR LOSS ON SALE OF RENTAL PROPERTY IN 1987

¶ **29.18** Depreciable property held in the business of rental is Section 1231 property. This means that profit may be subject to capital gain treatment; loss may be deductible as an ordinary loss depending on the net result of all Section 1231 transactions occurring during the taxable years. *See* ¶5.44.

Recapture of depreciation. If you rented part of the house or used a part in your business and claimed accelerated depreciation, gain allocated to the rental or business portion may be subject to the recapture rules of ¶5.35. If, before the sale, you used the residence solely for residential purposes, there is no recapture even though it was previously used for rental or business. However, if you buy another principal residence within the rules of ¶29.3, the depreciation recapture element is carried over to the basis of the new residence.

If you are age 55 or over at the time of sale and have used the property solely as your principal residence for the past three out of five years, there is no recapture, even if all or part of the property was previously used for business or rental. This rule applies even if you do not or may not elect to avoid tax on the sale. *See* ¶29.12. On the other hand, if part or all of your home was rented or used in your business for more than two years of the five-year period, there will be recapture under ¶5.35.

30

TAX SAVINGS FOR INVESTORS IN SECURITIES

¶ **30.1** With the repeal of the capital gain deduction, the substantial tax benefits of realizing long-term capital gain are no longer available. Long-term capital gains are subject to ordinary income tax rates. In 1987, there is, however, a 28% tax ceiling placed on the tax on long-term capital gains. The computation of the alternative tax is explained at chapter 6. In 1988, the distinction between short-term capital and long-term capital gain remains effective, although the scheduled ordinary tax rates for 1988 apply equally to both types of gains. Although capital gains will be fully subject to ordinary income tax rates without the application of the 28% alternative tax, the $3,000 limitation on deducting capital losses from other types of income remains as a substantial limitation on capital losses. If you have sub-stantial capital losses limited by the $3,000 rule, it will remain advisable to realize income from capital asset transactions.

As long-term capital gains, interest and dividends become taxable at the same tax rate, your investment strategies will change. In holding securities, you will generally not pay attention to holding periods. Your test for judging the investment return will be the same for both gains and interest and dividend income, which is the net after-tax return over a given period. If the projected after-tax return on a stock held for investment will give only 5% over a two-year period, an investment which will return interest net after tax of 7% during the same period will be the preferred investment.

YEAR-END SALES IN 1987

¶ **30.2** In planning year-end sales, if you want to realize gains in 1987, watch the deadline for recording sales. In the case of a regular sale of publicly-held stock, give your broker instructions no later than December 23, 1987; this assumes a five-day delivery period so that the settlement date should fall before the end of 1987. If you miss this date, you may still be able to get within the deadline if you order a spot cash sale on or before December 31, 1987.

If you are selling at a loss, you can do so until the last business day of the year, regardless of the settlement dates. If you are on the accrual basis, you have until the last business day of the year to realize both gains and losses.

Realizing losses may pose a problem if you believe the security is due to increase in value sometime in the near future. Although the wash sale rule (*see* ¶6.53) prevents you from taking the loss if you buy 30 days before or after the sale, these possibilities are open to you—

If you believe the security will go up, but not immediately, you can sell now, realize your loss, wait 31 days, then recover your position by repurchasing before the expected rise.

You can hedge by repurchasing similar securities immediately after the sale provided they are not identical. They can be in the same industry, of the same quality, without being considered substantially identical. Check with your broker to see if you can use a loss and still maintain your position. Some brokerage firms maintain recommended "switch" lists and suggest a practice of "doubling up," that is, buying the stock of the same company and then 31 days later selling the original shares. Doubling up has disadvantages: It requires additional funds for the purchase of the second lot, exposes you to additional risks should the stock price fall, and the new shares take a new holding period.

> **EXAMPLE**
> You own 100 shares of Steel stock which cost you $10,000. In November, 1987 the stock is selling at $6,000 ($60 a share × 100 shares). You would like to realize the $4,000 loss but at the same time, you want to hold on to the investment. You buy 100 shares at market price of $60 a share (total investment $6,000) and 31 days later, sell your original 100 shares, realizing the loss of $4,000. You retain your investment in the new lot. In 1987, November 30 is the last day to buy new shares to allow a loss sale on December 31.

Postponing taxable gain to 1988. If you do not want to realize taxable gains on a security sale in 1987, but you think that the price of your stock may decline by the time you sell in 1988, you can freeze your profit by ordering a short sale of the stock in 1987. You transact a short sale by selling shares borrowed from your broker. In January 1988, you deliver your shares to the broker as a replacement of the borrowed shares you sold in 1987. By delivering the stock in 1988, the gain on the short sale is fixed in 1988. For tax purposes, a short sale is not completed until the covering stock is delivered.

KEEP RECORDS OF YOUR STOCK PURCHASES

¶ **30.3** Keep a record of all your stock transactions, especially when you buy the stock of one company at varying prices. By keeping a record of each stock lot, you may control the amount of gain or loss on a sale of a part of your holdings.

> **EXAMPLE**
> Over a three-year period, you bought the following shares of Acme Steel stock: In 1970, 100 shares at $77 per share; in 1971, 200 shares at

$84 per share; in 1972, 100 shares at $105 per share. When the stock is selling at $90, you plan to sell 100 shares. You may use the cost of your 1972 lot and get a $1,500 loss if, for example, you want to offset some gains or other income you have already earned this year. Or you may get capital gains of varying amounts by either selling the 1970 lot or part of the 1971 lot. You must clearly identify the lot you want to sell. Say you want a loss and sell the 1972 lot. Unless you identify it as the lot sold, the IRS will hold that you sold the 1970 lot under the "first-in, first-out" rule. This rule assumes that, when you have a number of identical items that you bought at different times, your sale of any of them is automatically the sale of the first you bought. So the cost of your first purchase is what you match against your selling price to find your gain or loss. Here is what to do to counteract the first-in, first-out rule: If the stock certificates are registered in your name, show that you delivered the 1972 stock certificates.

See ¶30.5 for averaging cost on the sale of mutual fund shares.

If your stock is held by your broker, the IRS considers that an adequate identification is made if you grant your broker the power to buy and sell in your name at will. He is to notify you at the time of sale, requesting instructions on which shares he should sell. Before the settlement date (usually four business days from the time of sale), you instruct him by letter which shares to deliver. He, in turn, signs and dates his confirmation, which is printed at the bottom of your letter of instruction, and returns the letter to you. In addition, he submits to you monthly statements of the transactions and your cash position and stock on hand.

PUTS AND CALLS AND INDEX OPTIONS

¶ 30.4 You may buy options to buy and sell stock. On the stock exchange, these options are named calls and puts. A call gives you the right to require the seller of the option to sell you stock at a fixed price during the option period. A put gives you the right to require the seller of the option to buy stock you own at a fixed price during the option period.

Puts and calls allow you to speculate at the expense of a small investment—a call, for expected price rises; a put, for expected price declines. They may also be used to protect paper profits or fix the amount of your losses on securities you own.

You do not have to exercise a put or call to realize your profit. You may sell the option to realize your profit. If you exercise a call, the cost of the call is added to the cost of the stock purchased. If you exercise a put, you reduce the selling price of stock sold by the cost of the put. If you do not exercise a call or put, you realize a capital loss.

The option price depends on the value of the stock, the length of the option period, the volatility of the stock, and the demand and supply for options for the particular stock.

Puts may be treated as short sales. Be careful in using puts when you own stock covered by the put. If you have held the stock short-term, the purchase of the put is a short sale. The exercise or expiration of the put will then be treated as the closing of the short sale. Short sale rules, however, do not apply (1) when you hold stock long-term, and (2) when you buy a put and the related stock on the same day and identify the stock with the put (*see* ¶6.52).

Using a call as leverage. You expect a stock to appreciate in value but you do not have sufficient capital for a further investment. Instead of investing your limited amount of capital in an outright purchase, you might buy a call covering such stock. With a call, the same amount of capital allows you to speculate in many more shares than you could if you purchased stock outright. If the stock rises in value, your call also increases in value.

Exchange option trading. Option market exchanges provide market conditions for trading in puts and call options. The overwhelming number of options transacted are calls. Financial sections of the daily newspapers provide data on the market prices and volume of the options.

HOW TO IDENTIFY SECURITIES WHEN YOU ARE SELLING

If your securities are	Identify them by
Registered in your own name	The number, your name, and any other identification which they bear.
In a margin account registered in a "street" name	A specified block or security bought on a designated day at a particular price. A mere intention to sell a particular share without informing the broker is without significance.
New certificates received for old in a recapitalization	Record the new certificate with the lowest number as being in exchange for the old certificate with the lowest number. Do this until all the new certificates are matched with all the old.
Shares exchanged for shares in a reorganization	Allocate each of the new certificates to each of the old in your records. Where the exchange involves several blocks of stock and there is no specific identification, the IRS says you must average your costs.
Shares received in a split-up	Match the new certificates with the old ones surrendered. Identification of your selling securities as the "highest cost" or "lowest cost" stock is insufficient. You have to match at the time of the split-up.
Stock dividends	The lot of stock on which you received the dividend. The new stock is part of the old lot. But, if you receive one certificate for more than one lot, you may have to apply the rule of first-in first-out to the new stock sold.
Acquired by exercise of nontaxed stock rights	The number, or other identification of the lot you receive by exercising the rights. Each lot you so acquire is considered a separate lot received on the date of subscription.

Option markets are the CBOE, Amex, the Philadelphia Stock Exchange, the Midwest Exchange, and the Pacific Stock Exchange.

Trading in options is highly speculative, attracting those who hope to make profits on minimum investments. At the same time, the market has provided investors and institutions holding large portfolios with an opportunity to earn income through the sale of options based on their holdings. Thus, it takes two to play the option game: (1) the owner of shares who sells an option on his stock, and (2) the option buyer who generally speculates that, by buying an option for a smaller price than he would have to pay for the stock, he will be able to make a profit if the price of the stock goes up. The odds generally favor the option seller.

The income tax consequences of option trading are discussed at ¶6.15.

If you are inexperienced in the use of options, read several technical explanations of the use of options before investing. Master the technical use of options such as straddles and hedges used by professional traders, as the outright purchase of straight calls is generally too speculative. Finally, do not overlook commission costs which can cut into your profits or increase your losses.

Stock index options. Index options give you a chance to speculate on the general movement of stock. The success of the index option has tended to reduce interest in regular stock options given on individual stocks. On the other hand, index options are pegged to the price movement of the stocks that comprise the index option. Thus, with index options, you do not have to be concerned about the market fate of a particular stock. The stock group of the index option follows the general stock market movement. For example, assume that 100 stocks make up the index. The option contract represents an index multiplier of $100 times the index value of the group or basket of 100 stocks. Therefore, when a newspaper reports an index value of 170, which is also called the *strike price*, the contract is worth $17,000. However, as the option is only a right to buy or sell this particular contract, you pay an option price that is only a percentage of the contract value. The particular option price is set by the market in an open auction.

Your role is to weigh how the market will fare within the option period. Should you anticipate lower interest rates within the option period, which can be from approximately a week up to three months, you might buy an index option, betting that the stock market will advance. For example, when the index is at 165, you buy for $1,200 an option with a strike price of 170. If the stock market advances during the option period, pushing the strike price to 177, you have won your bet. At 177, you might sell your option for $7,000, thereby making a $5,800 profit.

Do not let this example encourage you to enter the index option market precipitously. If you guess wrong, you have lost your money. In the example just cited, had the index not moved above 170, you would have lost $1,200.

The S&P 100 index option is offered by the Chicago Board Options Exchange. It is based on Standard & Poor's 100 list of stocks, and it also offers an index option of 500 shares. The Philadelphia Stock Exchange trades the Value Line index option that has an index basket of more than 1,600 stocks traded on several exchanges. The New York Stock Exchange and the American Stock Exchange also offer index options.

If you are interested in playing the index option market, track the market for several months until you get used to the movement of the option. Plot hypothetical purchases and see how you would have fared. You might make a bundle—but, as at roulette, you might lose your shirt in a very short time.

INVESTING IN MUTUAL FUNDS

¶ **30.5** You may buy a tax liability if you invest in a mutual fund which has already realized significant capital gains during the year. Your investment is on the basis of the current value of its portfolio. At the end of the year, the gains realized by the fund before your investment is distributed to you as a capital gain distribution. Then you have to pay tax on the return of your own money. However, an experienced fund adviser can tell you when to make your investment. Or, you can postpone investing until the stock goes ex-dividend. By that time, your buying price is based on an asset value which is reduced by capital gain distribution.

Averaging cost for sale of mutual fund shares. A Treasury regulation sets rules for averaging the cost of purchases made at different times if only part of your holdings are sold. The election applies to open-end mutual fund shares held by an agent, usually a bank, in an account kept for the periodic acquisition or redemption of shares in the fund. Averaging avoids the difficult task of identifying the exact shares being sold where shares were bought at different prices and dates. There are two averaging methods: Single-category method and double-category method.

Single-category method. Under the single-category method, all shares in an account are totaled. The basis of each share is the total basis of all shares in the account at the time of a sale or transfer, divided by the number of shares in the account. For purposes of determining holding period, the shares sold or transferred are considered to be those shares acquired first.

Double-category method. At the time of each sale, you divide all shares in an account into two classes: Shares held long-term and shares held short-term. Shares are deemed transferred from each class without regard to stock certificates. You may tell the agent from which class you are selling. If you do not so specify, the long-term shares are deemed to have been sold first. If the number of shares sold exceeds the number in the long-term class, the excess shares are charged to the short-term class.

Details of these methods are provided in IRS Publication 564.

You make the election to average on your tax return for the first taxable year you want the election to apply. Note on your return which method you have chosen. Keep records to support the average basis used on your return. The election applies to all shares of the particular mutual fund in which the election is initially made.

You may not average shares of a mutual fund acquired by gift, if the adjusted basis of such shares in the hands of the donor was greater than their fair market value at the time of the gift.

REDUCING THE TAX ON DIVIDEND INCOME

¶ **30.6** The tax on dividend income may be reduced by the following types of investments:

Selling stock on which a dividend has been declared but not yet paid. During the period a dividend is declared but not paid, the price of the stock includes the value of the dividend. If you plan to sell stock in this position and figure that the tax on the dividend reflected in the selling price will be less than the tax on the dividend received, transact the sale before the stock goes ex-dividend (*see* ¶3.9).

Investing in companies paying tax free dividends. Some companies pay tax free dividends. A list of companies that do may be provided by your broker. When you receive a tax free dividend, you do not report the dividend as income as long as the dividend does not exceed your stock basis. A tax free dividend reduces the tax cost of your stock; dividends in excess of basis produce capital gain (*see* ¶3.11).

Investing in companies paying stock dividends. On receipt of a stock dividend, you do not generally have taxable income.

INVESTING IN SHORT-TERM PAPER, TREASURY BILLS, CDs, TAX-EXEMPT NOTES, AND OTHER SHORT-TERM OBLIGATIONS

¶ **30.7** Short-term paper (maturity of one year or less) provides an opportunity for earning income on funds during periods of uncertainty in the stock and other investment markets. Funds which you do not wish to tie up long-term and do not want to remain unproductive may be invested in Treasury bills or notes or certificates of deposit. These investments offer safety and negotiability, earning current interest rates from the day of purchase to the day of redemption, either on maturity or sale.

Treasury bills. These are direct obligations of the U.S. Treasury issued to finance budgetary needs. Bills are offered for 3-month, 6-month, and 12-month maturities in minimum amounts of $10,000 and multiples of $5,000 above the minimum. Bills are sold at a discount at Treasury auctions held at the Federal Reserve Banks which serve as agents for the Treasury. They are redeemed at face value. Your return on a Treasury bill is the difference between the discount price you pay for the bill and its face value, if you hold it to maturity, or the amount you receive for it on a sale before maturity. The selling price of a Treasury bill before maturity will vary with changes of current interest rates.

You may buy Treasury bills directly without charge from any Federal Reserve Bank, which gives you a receipt indicating that a book entry has been recorded of your purchase. You may also buy or sell Treasury bills through your bank or your stockbroker who will charge you for handling the transaction.

Most investors submit noncompetitive tenders (bids) for the Treasury bills they wish to buy. To submit a *competitive* tender, you must specify the price you are willing to pay for your bill, and you run the risk of bidding too low and not getting the bills you want. Noncompetitive tenders do not have to specify a price. They are filled at a price which is the average of the accepted competitive tenders for that specific auction. Check the Federal Reserve Bank or branch in your area for auction dates on Treasury bills.

Figuring the yield on your Treasury bill. On the day of the auction, the Treasury will figure the average price bid by those who submitted acceptable competitive tenders. The difference between this average price and the full value of the Treasury bill is the *discount* at which the bill is sold. All noncompetitive tenders are filled at this price. A check for the difference between the purchase price and the face value is mailed to you by first class mail on the issue date of the bills.

EXAMPLE

Assume the accepted average bid on three-month bills is $9,700. You gave the government $10,000. To reflect the actual purchase price of $9,700, a "discount" check of $300 is mailed to you.

The equivalent annual yield on your Treasury bill is figured this way:

1. Find the yield on your investment by dividing discount by purchase price.
2. Convert this yield to the annual rate by dividing the yield by .2500 if the bill is a three-month one; .5000 if a six-month.

On a three-month bill your discount is $150 (cost $9,850); the equivalent annual yield is .0608:

$$\frac{\$150}{\$9,850} = .0152 \qquad \frac{.0152}{.2500} = .0608 \text{ or } 6.08\% \text{ per year}$$

Financial pages of the newspapers report the previous day's auction, including the discount rate and what this amounts to as an annual percentage yield.

Cashing bills before maturity. If you decide you need funds before the maturity date of your bill, you can sell it through a commercial bank or a securities broker. The Federal Reserve Bank and the Treasury do not handle bills which have not matured.

For bills sold before maturity, current interest rates will determine the amount you receive. The market value of Treasury bills is listed daily in the financial section of newspapers and financial periodicals.

At maturity. Redemption is automatic at maturity, unless you notify the Federal Reserve Bank that you wish to roll over matured bills into new bills. The Treasury will mail you a check for the amount of your bill. If you bought your bill through a bank, the bank will credit your account on the date the bill matures. To roll over your maturing bill, you follow the same procedures as in buying a new bill and use your matured bill as payment. A discount check for the difference between the price of the new bills and the face value of your matured bills will be mailed to you on the issue date of the new bills.

Certificates of deposit. Negotiable certificates of deposit, (CDs), are another form of short-term investment which offers a high return with safety and negotiability.

Certificates of deposit represent money lent by investors to a bank for a specified short period of time, generally 30, 60, or 90 days, although in some cases certificates of deposit for six months and a year are available.

The rate of interest banks will pay for these funds is set in advance and depends on supply and demand in the money market. The interest rate may vary with the size of your investment. For deposits of $100,000 or more, you may be able to get a "heavy duty" CD at a higher rate than offered on smaller deposits.

Purchasing CDs. Certificates of deposit are generally purchased through your bank which will have available a list of those banks interested in obtaining funds through such deposits. Banks are careful about their dealings in these instruments and will handle such orders only for known clients. In most cases, your bank will charge a small fee to arrange the transfer of your funds for the certificate of deposit of another bank. Before investing, check with the bank for minimum investment requirements. Also check the status of the broker, insurance, and charges.

Liquidity. CDs may be sold before their maturity date through commercial banks or stockbrokers. However, they are not quite as readily sold as are Treasury bills. As is the case with Treasury bills, you may receive either more or less than you paid for them upon a resale before maturity, depending on the rise or fall of interest rates during the time you hold the certificates of deposit.

CDs may be registered in the name of the purchaser. As a rule, when the intermediary transactions are between two banks, the certificates are made out to bearer to be delivered against payment at the bank where you have deposited your money. That bank will then register the certificate in your name.

Repurchase agreements (repos). This investment offered by banks and thrifts allows you to earn high interest rates by sharing in a portion of the bank's portfolio of government securities. The bank is required to repurchase your investment from you at your request. The minimum investment is $1,000; maturities vary, on average, three months. Repos are not FDIC or FSLIC insured, and there is no interest penalty for early repurchase, as long as you hold them for a minimum of a week or more. There may be a small service charge for early repurchase.

Variable rates. With a variable rate CD the yield fluctuates according to market rates. The rate is guaranteed not to fall below the starting level. When you buy a rising rate certificate, you initially get a return slightly above the current rate for six-month deposits and it matures generally in three years. The rate rises every six months by up to ¼ point. You have the option of cashing in the CD without penalty every time it rises. These certificates are not meant to be long-term investments.

Commercial paper. Many corporations requiring large sums of money periodically during the year to finance short-term customer receivables offer short-term promissory notes at high rates of interest. These notes are generally referred to as commercial paper. Although much of this paper is sold in units of $100,000 or more, commercial paper in denominations of $25,000 and even less is sometimes available.

Finance companies, automobile manufacturers, and large retail stores are types of businesses which typically issue commercial paper for periods ranging from one week to 270 days.

Although companies like General Motors Acceptance Company (GMAC), one of the largest issuers of commercial paper, will sell direct to a buyer, most sales of these notes are made through commercial banks or brokerage houses that can give you information about the paper available, terms and denominations offered, and can complete the sale for you.

Investments in commercial paper may not be as liquid as other short-term paper and are subject to greater risks.

Tax-exempt notes are discussed at ¶30.12.

INVESTING IN MONEY MARKET MUTUAL FUNDS

¶ **30.8** The investor who does not have the capital needed to invest in specific money market obligations may consider a money market mutual fund. A fund portfolio will generally include U.S. government obligations, CDs of major commercial banks, bankers acceptances, and commercial paper of prime-rated firms. Most funds have a minimum investment requirement, varying from $500 to $10,000. Money market funds charge an annual management fee, generally about ½% annually of the fund's average total assets. Investors should check each fund's charges because they differ.

Yields, which change daily, are not guaranteed. Investments are not federally insured. Some state-chartered banks, however, offer money market funds insured by a state insurance fund.

Gains and losses are generally not realized in money market funds; shares are redeemed for exactly what you paid (usually $1 per share) plus accrued interest. Withdrawals may be requested by mail, wire, or telephone. Some funds offer limited checking privileges.

The names of funds which charge commissions may be available through your securities broker. A free list of funds which have no sales charge may be obtained from the No-Load Mutual Fund Association, Valley Forge, Pa. 19481.

Tax free money funds. These funds invest in short-term notes of state and local governments issued in anticipation of tax receipts, bond sales, and other revenues, and in "project notes" issued by local entities and backed by the federal government. The interest paid by these funds is tax exempt. The yields are lower than those of taxable funds, and are attractive only if they provide greater after-tax returns than similar taxable funds. Minimum investments range from $1,000 to $50,000. These funds may offer check writing privileges.

A tax free interest return may also be available through unit-investment trusts holding tax-exempt state and municipal bonds. Offered by certain brokerage houses and other companies, these trusts mature in a specified number of years or as called.

INVESTING IN SAVINGS INSTITUTIONS

¶ **30.9** Banks and savings and loan associations (S&Ls) aggressively compete for funds that would have normally entered the money market. The banking industry, favored by deregulation, offers money market funds and certificates of deposit (CDs) with different maturities and terms.

Bank money market funds are competitive with money market mutual funds. The bank money market funds guarantee for one-week or one-month periods interest rates tied to the Treasury bill rate or the average money market rate. Bank funds also offer this added attraction: They are federally insured. Bank money market accounts require certain average monthly balances which the government is planning to phase out; if the account falls below the minimum, interest is reduced.

Investments in money market funds allow you to take advantage of volatile interest rates which are rising. Investments in CDs allow you to lock into the highest available interest rate for a fixed period of time if you are concerned with a decline of rates during that period.

Current banking regulations allow banks and savings institutions to pay what they please on certificates of deposit and do not require minimum balances on CDs with terms over 31 days.

Withdrawals within certain limits may be made from money market funds without penalty. Premature withdrawals from CDs are penalized.

CD investments in savings institutions allow you to lock into high interest rates only for the short-term, generally up to five years. If you are concerned that rates will substantially decline in the future, you may want to invest in a currently available investment that fixes a high rate over longer periods, such as bonds with long-term maturities. Bond investments are discussed in ¶30.10.

Savings certificates versus Treasury bills. Certificates keyed to the Treasury bill rate may be purchased in fractions once you make a minimum bill rate investment. Treasury bills are only in fixed units. *See* ¶30.7. There is no fee charged for the purchase of certificates, while a fee may be charged to purchase Treasury bills unless purchased directly from the Treasury or a Federal Reserve Bank. Where you do not have the minimum to invest, some institutions may lend the difference at a lower interest rate, typically 1% to 2% over the rate earned on the certificate. Treasury bills have a tax advantage over the certificates. Interest on Treasury bills is exempt from state and local taxes; interest on saving certificates is not. Further, there are penalties for redeeming certificates before maturity. *See* ¶4.1 for taxation of interest and for forfeiture of interest on premature withdrawals.

Investment options vary from bank to bank. Not all banks offer the maximum rates or compound interest in the same manner. Whether interest is compounded daily or annually will affect your rate of return. Each bank also has its own policy on procedures concerning maturity of certificates. Some banks automatically renew the CD for another term at the current rate unless notified to the contrary; some banks will not renew a matured CD without express authority from you. If you fail to act, you may find your funds switched to a day-of-deposit account on maturity. Banking institutions can also change their rules after you have opened an account.

Deferring interest income. You may defer interest income by buying a six-month certificate after June 30. Interest is taxable in the next year when the certificate matures unless you receive interest during the current year. Your bank may offer you the choice of when to receive the interest. You may also defer interest by buying Treasury bills which come due next year.

INVESTING IN CORPORATE BONDS

¶ **30.10** When you buy a corporate bond, you are lending money to the issuer of the bonds. You become a creditor of the issuing company. The corporation pledges to pay you interest on specified dates, generally twice a year, and to repay the principal on the date of maturity stated on the bond.

For investment purposes, a bond may be described according to the length of the period of maturity. Short-term bonds usually mature within one to five years; medium-term bonds in five to 20 years; long-term bonds in 20 or more years.

Where the interest is paid out on a regular schedule, the bond is called a "current income" bond. An accrual or discount bond is a bond on which interest is accumulated and paid as part of the specified maturity value (the bond having been issued at a price lower than the specified maturity value).

Figuring the yield of a bond. The investment value of bonds is generally expressed in rates of yield. There are four types of yield: The nominal or coupon yield; the actual yield; the current market yield; and the net yield to maturity.

The nominal or coupon yield is the fixed or contractual rate of interest stated on the bond. A bond paying 7% has a nominal yield of 7%.

The actual yield is the rate of return based on the price at which the bond was purchased. If bought below par, the actual yield will exceed the nominal or coupon yield. If bought at a premium (above par), the actual

yield will be less than the coupon or nominal yield. For example, if you paid $850 for a $1,000 bond paying 6% interest, the actual yield is 7.06% ($60 divided by $850).

The current market yield is the rate of return on the bond if bought at the prevailing market price. It is figured in the same manner as actual yield. For example, if the 6% bond was quoted at $750, its current yield would be 8%.

Net yield to maturity represents the rate of return on the bond if it is held to maturity, plus appreciation allocated to a discount purchase or less reductions for any premium paid on a bond selling above par. If you buy a bond below par at a market discount, your annual return is proportionately increased by a part of the discount allocated to the number of years before maturity. If the discount was $50 on a bond with a five-year maturity, then your annual income return on the bond is increased by $10 ($50 divided by 5). On the other hand, if you bought at a premium, the extra cost is a reduction against your income because you paid more than can be recovered at maturity. This cost is allocated over the remaining life of the bond. Thus, if you bought a five-year bond at $50 over par, your average annual return is reduced by $10 ($50 divided by 5).

Call privileges may reduce the investment value of the bond. A call privilege gives the issuer a chance to redeem the obligation before maturity if interest rates have declined below the rate fixed by the obligation. The existence of a call is a disadvantage to an investor; it may deprive him of a favorable investment at a time he may not be able to replace it with another. To take some of the "sting" out of a call provision, the issuer may provide for the payment of a "premium" on the exercise of the call and a minimum period during which the bonds will not be called. The call premium is usually expressed as a percentage of the maturity value, for example, 105%. The amount of the premium varies with the length of the period in which the bond may be called. As the maturity date approaches, the call premium will decrease. Some bonds now carry a guarantee that they will not be called for a specified number of years, such as five or ten years.

A call privilege will generally not be exercised if the going interest rate remains about the same as, or is higher than, the interest rate of the bond. If interest rates decline below the interest rate of the bond, the bond will probably be called because the issuer can obtain the borrowed money at lower cost elsewhere.

Interest on bearer bonds issued with coupons attached is paid when a bondholder clips the coupon and deposits it for payment. A registered bond carries the name of the owner who receives his interest by mail from the issuing corporation.

Whether a bond is registered or in bearer form has no effect on its investment quality or yield. A coupon-type or bearer bond may be preferred by institutional investors because it can be transferred by hand without registration. However, this advantage must be weighed against the risks of loss through fire, theft, or casualty.

Issuing and trading bonds. New bond issues are generally placed through investment bankers who usually assist in the preparation of the issue. Often an issue may be sold directly by the issuing organization to an institutional investor. Many newly issued bonds are purchased directly from issuers or from their investment bankers by institutional investors before the bonds are offered to individual investors. Issuers prefer this type of placement as it involves less expense than a public offering. Normally, only the new issues (or part of new issues) which cannot be marketed this way are offered to private investors.

Bonds are also traded on the open market where individuals, as well as institutional buyers, may buy or sell them at competitive, market determined prices, through dealers or brokers.

Investment return on a bond is generally limited to the stated interest. You cannot expect any appreciation of principal as you can in a stock investment, unless you have bought bonds selling at a discount.

Bond sales and prices on the major exchanges are listed in the major financial dailies. Bond prices fluctuate in response to changes in interest rates and business conditions. In setting the daily price of a bond, the market weighs the current status, performance, and future prospects of the issuing corporation, as well as the interest rate and maturity period of the bond.

Quotations are based on 100 as equal to par, even though the basic unit for an actual bond may be in denominations of $1,000. A quote of 90½ simply means a bond with a face value of $1,000 will cost $905 at market.

Calls under sinking fund redemption. A bond may be called in at par under the terms of a sinking fund arrangement. Not all bonds are called and those that are selected are picked by lot. Redemptions for sinking fund purposes account for only a small percentage of a single bond issue. But some issues may retain the right to use a blanket sinking fund under which they may redeem bonds paying interest at their highest rate.

Put privileges. A put privilege is the flip side of a call privilege. It permits the buyer to sell the bonds at par to the issuer after a stated number of years. This feature is valuable to investors for long-term bonds. If interest rates rise, investors are not locked into low yields.

Current interest rates affect the selling price of bonds:

1. *If current interest rates increase over the interest rate of your bond, the market value of your bond will decline.* The decline in value has nothing to do with the credit rating of the issue. It simply means that other investors will buy only at terms that will give them the current higher return. If you bought a bond paying a rate of 8% at par, $1,000, and a few months later, interest rates go to 11%, another investor will not pay $1,000 for the bond for an 8% return. To match the 11% return on a dollar, the market value of the bond will drop to a level which will return 11% on the money invested, based on its actual 8% return and the period remaining before maturity. Thus, during periods of rising interest, the price of bonds issued at lower rates in prior years declines. This occurs to even top quality bonds; the highest credit rating will not protect the market value of a low-interest paying bond. When this happens there may be bond bargains available, as prices on outstanding bonds decrease.

2. *If interest rates decline below the interest rate of your bond, the value of your bond will increase;* but at the same time, the company, if it has an exercisable call option, may redeem the bond to rid itself of the high interest cost and attempt to raise funds at current lower rates. Thus, an early redemption of the bond could upset your long-range investment plans in that particular issue.

With these points in mind, you can understand why in recent years investors have shied away from long-term bonds when volatile interest rates ran into double digits. Investors preferred the high short-term rates. The effect of the investor flight from long-term issues hurt the ability of lenders to raise funds and forced them to devise new types of issues, such as zero coupon bonds and floating rate bonds.

Corporate zero coupon bond. A zero coupon bond is a deep discount obligation issued by companies that have found it difficult to market traditional long-term bonds. The zero coupon bond allows them to compete during periods of high interest rates. The bonds are issued at considerably less than face value and redeemed at face at a set date. No annual interest is paid. A zero coupon bond allows an investor to lock in a return. He knows how much he will receive at maturity and so avoids the problem of turning over his investments at fluctuating short-term rates. Brokers have lists of zero coupon bonds; the prices vary with the credit rating of the companies, current market rates, and maturity dates.

Zero coupon bond discount is reported annually as interest over the life of the bond, even though interest is not received. This tax cost tends to make zero coupon bonds unattractive to investors, unless the bonds can be bought for IRA and other retirement plans which defer tax on income until distributions are made.

Zero coupon bonds may also be a means of financing a child's education. A parent buys the bond for the child. The child must report the income, and if the income is not subject to the parent's marginal tax bracket (*see* chapter 22), the income subject to tax may be minimal.

The value of zero coupon bonds fluctuates sharply with interest rate changes. Consider this fact before investing in long-term zero coupon bonds. If you sell before the maturity term, at a time when interest rates rise, you may lose part of your investment.

Floating rate or variable interest bonds. For investors unwilling to gamble on the future of interest rates, some bonds have been offered with floating interest rates. The rate is updated periodically, but there may be a floor and ceiling limiting the changes. The market price of the bond should remain near par since its interest rate moves with the market. Although this feature is a form of insurance for the investor, it may not be worth its added cost.

INVESTING IN TREASURY BONDS AND NOTES AND OTHER U.S. AGENCY OBLIGATIONS

¶ **30.11** The federal government offers the following obligations for investment opportunities. They are guaranteed by the federal government and are exempt from state and local taxes.

Treasury bonds have maturity dates in excess of 10 years. The minimum denomination is $1,000. Interest is paid semiannually at a rate which varies with each issue. These bonds may be purchased through a commercial bank or directly from the Federal Reserve Bank.

Zero coupon Treasury bonds. Certain major brokerage houses have created zero coupon Treasury bonds by stripping the coupons from Treasury bonds and selling the bonds at deep discounts. They have been promoted under such names as TIGRS, LIONS, COUGARS, and CATS as investments suitable for IRAs, retirement plan trusts, and custodian accounts for minors. The U.S. Treasury itself now offers its own version of the zero coupon bond under the name STRIPS. The government does offer STRIPS directly to individual investors, but sells them to banks and brokers who then sell them to the public. Because STRIPS have the direct backing of the U.S. government, they are considered to be the safest zeros and generally yield up to one tenth of one percent less than TIGRS, CATS or similar brokerage firm or bank created zeros. With all zero coupon Treasury obligations, an investor can select a particular maturity date suited to his or her needs, such as the year the investor will start taking IRA distributions or the year a child will start college. For tax reporting rules, *see* ¶30.10 on corporate zero coupon bonds.

Treasury notes are similar to Treasury bonds but have shorter maturity dates from two to ten years. Minimum investments range from $1,000 to $5,000, depending on the issue. Interest is paid semiannually and interest varies with each issue. Notes are purchased from commercial banks or directly from the Federal Reserve Bank.

Other U.S. obligations, such as savings bonds, are discussed at ¶30.14 and Treasury bills at ¶30.7.

Certain federal agencies, like the Tennessee Valley Authority, offer their own securities. The types of securities offered vary. Such securities must be purchased through brokers or commercial banks.

Federally chartered companies, such as Government National Mortgage Association ("Ginnie Maes") and Federal National Mortgage Association ("Fannie Maes"), authorize certain firms and institutions to issue securities based on insured mortgages. While interest on these securities is generally not exempt from state and local taxes, they offer the investor a higher yield than Treasury securities. Some of these obligations carry a U.S. government full faith and credit guarantee; some have only an implied guarantee; and some no backing from the federal government, but risk is generally considered to be negligible.

Ginnie Maes are offered in minimum denominations of $25,000. Monthly payments to security holders include not only interest, but also a return of principal. Rather than buying Ginnie Maes in the open market, you may consider investing in a fund or trust which has a portfolio of such securities. Minimum investment units typically begin at $1,000.

INVESTING IN TAX EXEMPTS

¶ **30.12** Interest on state and local obligations is not subject to federal income tax. It is also exempt from the tax of the state in which the obligations are issued. In comparing the interest return of a tax exempt with that of a taxable bond, you figure the taxable return that is equivalent to the tax free yield of the tax exempt. This amount depends on your tax bracket. For example, a municipal bond of $5,000 yielding 8% is the equivalent of a taxable yield of 11.1% subject to the tax rate of 28%.

You can compare the value of tax-exempt interest to taxable interest for your tax bracket by using this formula:

Tax-exempt interest return = E
Taxable interest (to be found) = T
Your tax bracket = B

$$T = \frac{E}{1-B}$$

EXAMPLE
You are deciding between a tax-exempt bond and a taxable bond. You want to find which will give you more income after taxes. You have a choice between a tax-exempt bond paying 6% and a taxable bond paying 8%. Your tax bracket is 28%.

Using the above formula, you find that the tax exempt is a better buy in your tax bracket as it is the equivalent of a taxable bond paying 8.3%.

$$T = \frac{.06}{1-.28}$$

$$T = .083\% \text{ or } 8.3\%$$

The following table shows the amount a taxable bond would have to earn to equal the tax-exempt bond, according to the investor's income tax bracket.

If top income tax rate is	*A tax-exempt yield of—					
	6%	7%	8%	9%	10%	11%
	is the equivalent of these taxable yields:					
28%	8.3	9.7	11.1	12.5	13.9	15.3
35%	9.2	10.8	12.3	13.8	15.4	16.9
38.5%	9.7	11.4	13.0	14.6	16.3	17.9

*Exemption from the tax of the state issuing the bond will increase the yield.

To lock in high rates, you may have to invest in a long-term bond. However, consider these drawbacks: You may not want to tie up your capital long-term. There is the possibility that a future increase in interest rates may reduce the value of your investment if you should need the principal before maturity.

Ratings of tax-exempt bonds. As in the case of commercial bonds, tax-exempt issues are rated by services such as Standard & Poor's and Moody's. In rating a bond, the services will consider the size of the issuer, the amount of its outstanding debt, its past record in paying off prior debts, whether it has competent officials and a balanced budget, its tax assessment and collection record, and whether the community is dominated by a single industry which might be subject to economic change. Generally, an issuer with a good credit rating will offer lower interest rates than one plagued with revenue deficits or similar problems. A basic test is the sufficiency of tax yields or revenues even in times of economic stress.

General obligation bonds will normally be rated higher than revenue bonds because they have the support of the taxing power of the community. Revenue bonds (backed by the revenue of the issuer) may receive high ratings once a capacity to produce earnings is shown.

Purchase and trading of tax exempts. Tax-exempt municipals are traded over-the-counter and are generally handled through a firm specializing in this field or having a department for municipals. Prices quoted represent a percentage of par. For example, a par value $5,000 bond quoted at 90 is selling for $4,500 (90% of $5,000); a par value $1,000 bond quoted at 90 is selling for $900 (90% of $1,000). It may not pay to buy tax exempts unless you intend to hold them to maturity because the additional cost of selling a small order might be as much as a year's interest.

The bid and asked prices of tax-exempt bonds are generally not quoted in the daily newspapers, although some brokerage houses which specialize in them do print such prices. As in the general bond market, an offer of unusually high interest compared with the average bond rates may be an indication that the bonds are riskier than others.

The market for tax exempts is not as large as the market for stock. This poses a risk if you ever need ready cash and are forced to sell a tax-exempt bond at a discount. If you are concerned with liquidity, restrict your investments to major general obligation bonds of state governments and revenue bonds of major authorities.

Instead of purchasing the exempts directly, you may consider investing in municipal bond funds. The funds invest in various municipal bonds and thus offer the safety of diversity. Also, an investment in the fund may be as small as $1,000 compared with the typical $5,000 municipal bond. Check on fees and other restrictions in municipal bond funds.

Tax-exempt notes. Although generally bought by banks and large corporations, short-term tax-exempt notes may sometimes be available to individuals. The majority of the notes are offered in face amounts of $25,000 and up, but sometimes in denominations of $5,000 and $10,000. They are issued by states and municipalities to tide them over until expected revenues are received or until longer-term money can be raised through an issue of long-term bonds. Where rising interest rates have made the cost of long-term issues high, a government authority may postpone a long-term offering and try to fill the gap with short-term notes. The interest rates on tax-exempt notes may be higher than on tax-exempt bonds if the authority is willing to pay the extra interest for the short-term in the expectation that a future long-term offering may be placed at lower rates.

Interest on these short-term notes is exempt from federal tax. Many of the notes are from housing authorities and issued to pay construction costs on projects for which bonds will eventually be issued. Housing notes are guaranteed by the FHA and, because of their safety, yields are lower than more speculative paper.

Tax law restrictions. Most municipal bonds issued before July 1, 1983, except for housing issues, are in the form of bearer bonds; the owners are not identified, and interest coupons are cashed as they come due. However, state and municipal bonds issued after June 30, 1983, with a maturity of more than one year, as well as obligations of the federal government and its agencies, are in registered form. Principal and interest are transferable only through an entry on the books of the issuer. The Treasury plans a system for registering obligations now held in street name.

In buying state or local bonds, check the prospectus for the issue date and tax status of the bond. The 1986 Tax Act provided different tax treatment for certain bonds issued after August 7, 1986. Under the 1986 Tax Act, bonds fall within these classes:
1. "Public-purpose" bonds. These include bonds issued directly by state or local governments or their agencies to meet essential government functions, such as highway construction and school financing. These bonds are generally tax-exempt.
2. "Qualified private activity" bonds. These include bonds issued to finance housing and student loans. There are limits on the amount of qualifying private activity bonds an authority may issue. Interest on qualifying bonds issued after August 7, 1986, (or after August 31, 1986, for certain bonds) is tax free for regular income tax purposes, but is a preference item to be added to taxable income if you are subject to alternative minimum tax. Because of the AMT, a nongovernment purpose bond may pay slightly more interest than public-purpose bonds. These may be a good investment if you are not subject to AMT tax or if your AMT liability is not substantial.
3. "Taxable" municipals. These are bonds issued for nonqualifying private purposes, such as building a sports stadium. They are subject to federal income tax, but may be exempt from state and local taxes in the states in which they are issued. Generally, bonds issued after August 15, 1986, are subject to this rule.

INVESTING IN UNIT INVESTMENT TRUSTS

¶ **30.13** A unit investment trust is a closed-end unmanaged portfolio of bonds marketed by investment houses. Yield is fixed for the life of the trust with interest payable semiannually or more frequently. As bonds in the portfolio mature, a unit holder receives a repayment of principal. Unit trusts provide investors with the possibility of locking into high yields for the long-term. However, a trust has this disadvantage: If principal is needed before the end of the trust term, an investor may sacrifice substantial amounts of principal if interest rates rise or if the general investment market is shying away from long-term investments; even where the trust may offer a current return equal to market value, its price may be depressed because there may be few investors willing to take the risk of tying up their funds in long-term investments. Despite these drawbacks, the performance of unit trusts has been rated higher than that of similar mutual funds.

Unit trusts hold varying types of debt instruments. Tax-exempt municipal bond trusts, made up of tax-exempt obligations, are generally favored by investors in the top tax brackets. Taxable unit trusts hold investments such as corporate bonds, bank certificates of deposit, and Treasury obligations. Usually, units are offered in denominations of $1,000. An investor pays a front-end sales charge, but no management fee as there is no need for management once a unit trust is closed.

Maturities of the various trusts range as follows: The short-term, tax-exempt average is three years; intermediate, six to 12 years; and long-term, 18 to 30 years. An average for corporate intermediate is six years; 25 years for long-term.

SAVINGS BOND PLANS

¶ **30.14** Savings bonds purchases give you an opportunity to defer tax (see ¶4.15). Series EE bonds, issued since November 1982, have maturity periods of 10 years. If held at least five years, EE bonds earn interest at a variable market rate tied to five-year Treasury securities, with a guaranteed minimum rate, currently 6%. Bonds held less than five years earn interest on a fixed graduated scale.

Savings bonds can be used to build up values during a lifetime without paying taxes. Heirs may continue to defer tax on the interest. When the bonds are finally cashed, the person cashing them and reporting the income gets a deduction for the estate tax paid (if any) on the income (see ¶4.15).

> Savings bonds can be used in a savings program for a child's college education. Bonds can be bought in a child's name. Tax on interest may be deferred or reported annually. Choose the method that you project gives a greater after-tax return over the period. In making the election, consider the effect of the rules of ¶22.3 on income earned by a minor.

E bonds issued between May 1941 and April 1952 have a 40-year term, after which no interest will accrue. Series H bonds issued between June 1952 and January 1957 have a term of 29 years, eight months and H bonds issued between February 1957 and May 1959 have a 30-year term, after which no interest will accrue. For maturity dates of other E bonds, EE bonds, and H bonds, you may obtain a schedule from the Treasury Department which also shows the interest rate on the bonds.

REPORTING INCOME FROM INVESTMENT CLUBS

¶ **30.15** Investment clubs are a method of pooling funds for stock market investments. The club may be formed by any number of persons who may manage the investments of the club under an informal or a formal agreement or charter. A majority of clubs currently operating are, for tax purposes, partnerships. Some, however, are taxable as corporations or trusts. Corporate or trust status is usually evidenced by formal incorporation or the creation of a trust. However, a group may be taxed as a corporation even though it has not formally incorporated if its manner of operation gives it the characteristics of a corporation. Treasury regulations provide tests for determining when a group is a corporation. If the club is considered a corporation, it reports and pays a tax on the club's earnings. You report dividend distributions made by the club to you. The overall cost of corporate tax reporting is generally more than the tax cost of partnership reporting.

If the club is a partnership, the club files a partnership return on which it reports the tax consequences of its transactions and the shares of each member. The club does not pay a tax. You and the other members pay tax on your shares of dividends, interest, capital gain, and other income earned by the club. You report your share as if you earned the income personally. For example, you report your share of the club's capital gains and losses on your Schedule D on the line provided for partnership gains and losses; you report your share of dividends and interest in the respective dividend and interest schedules of your personal tax return. You may also deduct as itemized deductions your share of the club's investment expenses.

The following is an example of a club treated as a partnership under Treasury regulations:

EXAMPLE

Twenty-five persons each contribute $10 a month for the purpose of jointly investing in securities. They share investment income equally. Under the agreement, the club will operate until terminated by a three-quarter vote of the total membership and will not end upon the withdrawal or death of any member. However, under local law, each member has the power to dissolve the club at any time. Members meet monthly; buy or sell decisions must be voted on by a majority of the organization's membership present. Elected officers perform only ministerial functions, such as presiding at meetings and carrying out the directions of the members. Members of the club are personally liable for all debts of, or claims against, the club. No member can transfer his membership. The club does not have the corporate characteristics of limited liability, free transferability of interests, continuity of life, and centralized management. Therefore, it is treated as a partnership. See chapter 10.

31

TAX SAVINGS FOR INVESTORS IN REAL ESTATE

INVESTMENTS IN REAL ESTATE VENTURES

¶ **31.2** The ideal real estate investment should provide a current income return and an appreciation in the value of the original investment. As an additional incentive, a real estate investment may in the early years of the investment return income subject to little or no tax. That may happen when depreciation and other expense deductions reduce taxable income without reducing the amount of cash available for distribution. This tax savings is temporary and limited by the terms and the amount of the mortgage debt on the property. Mortgage amortization payments reduce the amount of cash available to investors without an offsetting tax deduction. Thus, the amount of tax free return depends on the extent to which depreciation deductions exceed the amortization payments.

To provide a higher return of tax free income, at least during the early years of its operations, a venture must obtain a constant payment mortgage that provides for the payment of fixed annual amounts which are allocated to continually decreasing amounts of interest and increasing amounts of amortization payments. Consequently, in the early years, a tax free return of income is high while the amortization payments are low, but as the amortization payments increase, nontaxable income decreases. When this tax free return has been substantially reduced, a partnership must refinance the mortgage to reduce the amortization payments and once again increase the tax free return.

EXAMPLES

1. A limited partnership of 100 investors owns a building that returns an annual income of $100,000 after deduction of operating expenses, but before a depreciation deduction of $80,000. Thus, taxable income is $20,000 ($100,000 − $80,000). Assuming that there is no mortgage on the building, all of the $100,000 is available for distribution. (Since the depreciation requires no cash outlay, it does not reduce the cash available for distribution.) Each investor receives $1,000. Taxable income being $20,000, only 20% ($20,000 ÷ $100,000) of the distribution is taxable. Thus, each investor reports as income only $200 of his $1,000 distribution; $800 is tax free.

2. Same facts as in (1) above, except that the building is mortgaged, and an annual amortization payment of $40,000 is being made. Consequently, only $60,000 is available for distribution, of which $20,000 is taxable. Each investor receives $600, of which ⅓ ($20,000 ÷ $60,000) or $200 is taxed, and $400 is tax free. In other words, the $60,000 distribution is tax free to the extent that the depreciation deduction of $80,000 exceeds the amortization of $40,000—namely $40,000. If the amortization payment was increased to $50,000, only $30,000 of the distribution would be tax free ($80,000−$50,000).

The tax free return is based on the assumption that the building does not actually depreciate at as fast a rate as the tax depreciation rate. If the building is depreciating physically at a faster rate, the so called tax free return on investment does not exist. Distributions to investors (over and above current income return) that are labeled tax free distributions are in fact, a return of the investor's own capital.

The above advantages are available for investments made by you individually or in partnership with other associates. They are also available to investors in limited partnerships. However, before investing in a limited partnership, consider these disadvantages of limited partnerships.

1. Investors in limited partnerships are by law generally treated as receiving passive activity income or loss. Further, as a limited partner, you may not take advantage of the $25,000 rental loss allowance, as you are not considered an "active participant"; *see* ¶11.4. In view of the passive activity rules, if you and others join together to buy rental property, you should not organize as a limited partnership if any losses are anticipated. Limited partnerships are advisable only if income is expected or where two or more investment activities will produce income and loss, which will offset each other.

2. Although limited partnerships are organized to prevent double taxation, which occurs in doing business as a corporation, there is a danger that the partnership may be taxed as a corporation if its operations resemble those of a corporation.

3. Partnership operations do not provide for the diversification of

investments or for the free transfer of individual interests. Investors may find it difficult to sell their interests because of transferability restrictions and a lack of an open market for the sale of their interests. This liquidity problem may be overcome by buying interests sold through public exchanges. Interests in master limited partnerships (MLP) are offered on the public exchanges. The organization of MLPs has been sparked by the passive activity loss restrictions. MLPs are designed to provide passive income to investors who have passive activity losses which will offset the income. However, MLPs are controversial; the Treasury Department has urged Congress to pass legislation that would tax MLPs as corporations.

Reviewing an investment offer. Consider the following pointers in reviewing an offering.

1. If the venture is constructing a development, discount projected income which may be eroded by increasing construction costs caused by inflation, material shortages, and labor disputes. Escalating costs not accounted for in long-term construction can jeopardize the project or income prospects. Adequate cash reserves should be available for emergencies.
2. Check the market conditions. Has there been overconstruction in the area? Is the area changing socially and economically?
3. Check the fees of managers. See that they are reasonable for your area. A promoter may conceal the amount of money he is drawing from the project. He may be taking a real estate commission by having a commission paid to a company which he controls. A reliable promoter should disclose this fact and be willing to collect the commission only after the investors have recovered their capital. Also check the reasonableness of prepaid management fees and loan fees and whether or not the sale of property to the syndicate is from a corporation in which the syndicator has an interest. If there is such a sale, check its terms, price, interest rates, and whether there is any prepaid interest which may conceal a cash profit payout to the syndicator.
4. Check the experience and reliability of the manager.

Real estate investment trusts (REITS). The tax treatment of real estate investment trusts resembles that of open-end mutual funds. Distributions are taxed to the investors in the trust as ordinary income, but no dividend exclusion is allowed on such distributions. Distributed long-term capital gains are reported by the investors as long-term gains. If the trust operates at a loss, the loss may not be passed on to the investors.

A REIT may not necessarily invest in equities. It may operate for interest return by providing loans. Before investing, check the scope of the REIT's operations and current market conditions and projections.

REMICs. The 1986 Tax Act encourages the creation of real estate mortgage investment companies (REMIC). A REMIC is formed to hold a fixed pool of mortgages. Investors are treated as holding a regular or residual interest.

A corporation, partnership, or trust that meets statutory tests is allowed to be treated as a REMIC. In addition, a segregated pool of assets also may qualify as a REMIC as if it were an entity meeting the requirements.

A REMIC is not a taxable entity for federal income tax purposes. The income from the REMIC generally is reported by holders of regular and residual interests. However, a REMIC may be subject to tax on prohibited transactions and may be required to withhold on amounts paid to foreign holders of regular or residual interests.

The pass-through status of the REMIC applies regardless of whether the REMIC was formed as a corporation, partnership, or trust. For example, where a REMIC is organized as a partnership, the partnership provisions do not apply to any transactions involving the REMIC or any of the holders of regular or residual interest. At the time this book went to press, the Treasury had not released regulations governing REMICs. Income from a REMIC is reported on Schedule E.

Low-income housing. The major tax benefit of investing in low-income housing is a tax credit. Developers of low-income housing projects may claim over a ten-year period an annual tax credit of 9% of the cost of construction or rehabilitation of a building rented to low-income residents; for the purchase of an existing building rented to low-income residents the annual credit is 4%. Over the ten-year period, the credits will equal a present value of 70% of the basis of a new building which is not federally subsidized and of 30% of the basis of an existing building.

The credit is computed on Form 8586. The credit is based on a credit allocation determined by an authorized housing credit agency; the allocation is provided to investors on Form 8609.

Partnerships developing low-income buildings pass through tax credits to limited partners, who may deduct them on their personal tax returns. However, there are these restrictions. The investment must be held for 15 years to qualify for the tax credit claimed during the first 10 years. If not, the credit is subject to recapture. Recapture may also occur if the project fails to comply with legal tests before the end of the 15 years. The amount of the credit is also subject to the general business credit limitations discussed in ¶24. 2. The credit may not exceed the first $25,000 of tax liability plus 75% of tax over $25,000. It is also subject to passive activity rules. The credit is treated as arising from an active rental and may be used to offset tax on up to $25,000 of passive income. However, this tax benefit is subject to a phase-out where adjusted gross income exceeds $200,000, *see* chapter 11.

DETERMINING WHETHER A TENANCY IN COMMON IS A PARTNERSHIP

¶ **31.3** In a tenancy in common, each tenant owns an undivided share in the property. Upon the death of a co-tenant, his interest passes to his heirs, not to the other tenants as in a joint tenancy. Tenants in common may or may not be considered as holding the property in a partnership. The determination of whether they are partners affects whether a partnership return must be filed, whether the involuntary conversion election (¶18.21) and first-year expensing (¶5.34) must be made by the partnership or the co-tenants, and the deductibility of property taxes beyond a co-tenant's percentage of ownership (¶16.9).

Treasury regulations defining partnerships note that the co-ownership of property which is merely maintained, kept in repair, and rented or leased is not a partnership. If you wish to operate the property as a partnership, you may do so by forming a partnership. Even if you do not formally set up a partnership, the IRS may treat your co-ownership as a partnership if the services or other activity in holding the property is considered a business. Collecting rents or hiring agents to collect rents is not considered a business activity. In one case, tenants were held to be partners where the property had been previously owned by a corporation in which they were stockholders. On liquidation, they received interests in the property equal to their former stock interests. As they continued the business of the corporation using the same assets and the same methods of operation they were treated as in business as a partnership.

SALES OF SUBDIVIDED LAND— DEALER OR INVESTOR STATUS?

¶ **31.4** Investors in tracts which they later subdivided aim for capital gain treatment on the sale of the lots. The IRS generally tries to defeat capital gain treatment by arguing that the subdividing and selling made them dealers. Thus, the sales are taxable at ordinary income rates.

For capital gain, the investor generally has to show that his activities did not make him a dealer but were steps in a liquidation of the investment. To convince an IRS agent or a court of investment activity, this type of evidence may present a favorable argument for capital gain treatment:

The property was bought as an investment, or to build a residence, or received as a gift, or by inheritance.
No substantial improvements were added to the tract.
The property was subdivided to liquidate the investment.
Sales came through unsolicited offers. There was no advertising or agents.
Sales were infrequent.
There were no previous activities as a real estate dealer.
The seller was in a business unrelated to real estate.
The property was held for a long period of time.
The sales proceeds were invested in other investment property.

Limited capital gain opportunity is also possible through Section 1237 that applies arbitrary holding period rules and contains restrictions against substantial improvements. Few investors have attempted to meet the terms of this limited tax provision.

After 1987, the distinction between capital gains and ordinary income is retained by the law, but if the scheduled 1988 rates are not increased, the distinction will not affect the tax on capital gains income. Capital gains will be taxed at the same rate as ordinary income. However, capital loss deductions from ordinary income will continue to be limited to $3,000.

Installment sales. The distinction between an investor and dealer will be significant if land is sold on the installment basis. Investor status is preferable if you want to elect the installment basis here. Sales of dealer property are subject to the AII restrictions of ¶6.43. Thus, if you were held to be an investor, you could sell land on the installment basis without running afoul of the AII restrictions. If you were considered a dealer, tax deferment would not be allowed to the extent you held outstanding debt.

Interest expense deductions. The distinction between an investor in land and dealer is also important in the case of interest expenses. Dealer status is preferable here. Interest expenses incurred by an investor are subject to investment interest deduction limitations and phase-ins; *see* chapter 15. On the other hand, interest expenses of a dealer in the course of his business activities are fully deductible.

EXAMPLE
Morley was interested in buying farm acreage to resell at a profit. Two and a half million dollars was set as the purchase price. To swing the deal, Morley borrowed $600,000. A short time later, his attempts to resell the property failed, and he allowed the property to be foreclosed. While he held the property he incurred interest costs of over $400,000, which he deducted. The IRS held the interest was not fully deductible. It claimed the interest was investment interest subject to investment interest restrictions. That is, the debt was incurred to purchase and carry investment property. The IRS position was based on the so-called "one-bite" rule, which holds that a taxpayer who engages in only one venture may not under any circumstances be held to be in a business as to that venture. Morley argued that he bought the property not as an investment property but as business property for immediate resale. The IRS then countered that negotiations for resale were not sufficient to support an ordinary asset classification for the property. He needed a prior binding commitment from the prospective buyer at the time he bought the property.

The Tax Court sides with Morley, holding that he held the acreage as ordinary business property. The court rejects the "one-bite" rule. The fact that he had not previously sold business property does not mean that he cannot prove that he held acreage for resale. Here, he intended promptly to resell it, and the facts support his intention. Further, there was no need to show prior binding commitment for resale as claimed by the IRS.

Passive activity. Income from sales of lots is not considered passive activity income. If you hold rental property and also sell land, make sure that your accounts distinguish between and separate each type of income. This way income and losses from land sales will not be commingled with rent income and subject to the passive activity restrictions of chapter 11. Thus losses from sales of land may offset salary and other investment income.

EXCHANGING REAL ESTATE WITHOUT TAX

¶ **31.5** You may trade real estate held for investment for other investment real estate and incur no tax. The potential tax on the gain is postponed to the time you sell the exchanged property at a price exceeding the tax basis of the property. A tax free exchange may also defer a potential tax due on gain from depreciation recapture and might be considered where the depreciable basis of a building has been substantially written off. Here the building may be exchanged for other property which will give off larger tax deductions.

The postponement of tax is equivalent to receiving an interest free government loan in the amount you would have owed in taxes had you sold the property. With no part of your capital depleted by tax, you can reinvest the full value of your old property.

Although the tax free exchange has this major tax attraction, there are limitations to its use. The primary problem is bringing together suitable

exchange properties and investors interested in trading. This difficulty may sometimes be overcome by brokers specializing in real estate exchanges. Another serious limitation attaches to exchanges dealing with depreciable property. It is posed by the tax rule that requires you to carry over the basis of the old property to the new property.

> To transact a fully tax free exchange, you must satisfy these conditions:
>
> 1. The property traded must be solely for property of a like kind. The words "like kind" are liberally interpreted. They refer to the nature or character of the property, not its grade, quality or use. Some examples of "like kind" exchanges are: Farm or ranch for city property; unimproved land for improved real estate; rental house for a store building; fee in business property for 30-year or more leasehold in the same type of property.
>
> 2. The property exchanged must have been held for productive use in your business or for investment and traded for property to be held for productive use in business or investment. Therefore, trades of property used, or to be used, for personal purposes, such as exchanging a residence for rental property, cannot receive tax free treatment. Special rules, however, apply when you trade your residence for another home; *see* ¶29.3.
>
> 3. The trade must generally occur within a 180-day period and property identification must occur within 45 days of the first transfer; *see* ¶5.49 for further details of this test.
>
> A real estate dealer cannot transact a tax free exchange of property he holds for sale to customers. Furthermore, an exchange is not tax free if the property received is held for immediate resale.

EXAMPLE
You have property with a basis of $25,000, now valued at $50,000, that you exchanged for another property worth $50,000. Your basis for depreciation for the new property is $25,000.

You sell the old property and use the proceeds to buy new property—the tax basis for depreciation is $50,000, giving you larger deductions than you are getting in the exchange transaction. If increased depreciation deductions are desirable, then it may pay to sell the property and purchase new property. Tax on the sale is generally subject to capital gain treatment. Further, tax may be spread by transacting an installment sale. Project the tax consequences of both types of transactions and choose the one giving the greater overall tax benefits. You may find it preferable to sell the property and purchase new property on which MACRS may be claimed.

A tax free exchange may be advantageous in the case of land which is not depreciable. It may be exchanged for a depreciable rental building. The exchange is tax free and depreciation may be claimed on the building.

A tax free exchange is not desirable if the transaction will result in a loss, since you may not deduct a loss in a tax free exchange. To ensure the loss deduction, first sell the property, then buy new property with the proceeds.

A nonresident alien may not defer tax on an exchange of U.S. realty unless he receives realty which, if sold, is subject to U.S. tax.

Partially tax free exchanges. Not all property exchanges are without tax. To be completely tax free, the exchange must be a property-for-property exchange. If the trade includes boot, such as cash or other property, gain is taxed up to the amount of the boot. If property is depreciated under a rapid depreciation method, boot may be subject to ordinary income tax under the rules of ¶5.35.

If you trade mortgaged property, the mortgage released is treated as boot. This holds true whether or not the other party assumes, or takes subject to, the mortgage. Therefore, if you exchange your property worth $50,000 on which there is a $10,000 mortgage, for unmortgaged land worth $45,000, a $2,000 automobile, and $3,000 cash, you would be receiving $15,000 in boot: the release of the $10,000 mortgage, plus $5,000 representing the value of the cash and the car. Whether part or all of the boot is taxed depends on whether you realize gain on the exchange. When you give boot such as cash, other property, or assume or take subject to an existing mortgage, you get no loss deduction. It is simply added to your investment, thereby increasing your basis in the new property.

When there are mortgages on both properties, the mortgages are netted. The party giving up the larger mortgage and getting the smaller mortgage treats the excess as boot.

EXAMPLE

You own a small office building with an adjusted basis of $50,000 on which there is a $30,000 mortgage. You exchange it for Low's building valued at $55,000, having a $20,000 mortgage, and for $5,000 in cash. You compute your gain in this way:

What you received

Present value of Low's property		$55,000
Cash		5,000
Mortgage on building traded		30,000
Total received		$90,000
Less:		
Adjusted basis of building traded	$50,000	
Mortgage assumed by you	20,000	70,000
Actual gain on the exchange		$20,000

However, the actual gain of $20,000 is taxed only up to the amount of boot, $15,000.

Figuring boot

Cash		$ 5,000
Mortgage on building traded	$30,000	
Less: Mortgage assumed on Low's property	20,000	10,000
Total gain taxed to you		$15,000

If the amount of boot exceeds your actual gain, your tax is limited to the amount of your gain.

Cash received as boot may not be netted against a mortgage, except in limited circumstances.

EXAMPLE

Jones exchanges property worth $55,000 (but subject to a $20,000 mortgage) for Smith's property worth $65,000 (but subject to a $30,000 mortgage). Jones did not receive taxable boot because he took subject to a $30,000 mortgage while being relieved of a $20,000 mortgage. But now assume because of certain contract conditions, Smith does not want to assume the $20,000 mortgage; instead he gives $20,000 in cash to Jones to pay off the $20,000 mortgage. The IRS would argue that Jones has received taxable boot in the form of cash; he may not net the cash against the $30,000 mortgage which he assumed. The Tax Court would disagree. It would allow Jones to net the cash against the mortgage because the contract specifically requires him to apply the cash to the mortgage. Here, the court would not treat the cash as ordinary boot because he does not have free use of it.

TIMING YOUR REAL PROPERTY SALES

¶ 31.6 Generally, a taxable transaction occurs in the year in which title or possession to property passes to the buyer. By controlling the year title and possession passes, you may select the year in which to report profit or loss. For example, you intend to sell property this year, but you estimate that reporting the sale next year will incur less in taxes. You can postpone the transfer of title and possession to next year. Alternatively, you can transact an installment sale, giving title and possession this year but delaying the receipt of all or most of the sale proceeds until next year. *See* ¶6.33.

SELLER'S REPOSSESSION OF REALTY AFTER BUYER'S DEFAULT ON PURCHASE MONEY MORTGAGE DEBT

¶ 31.7 When you, as a seller, repossess realty on the buyer's default of a debt which the realty secures, you may realize gain or loss. (If the realty was a personal residence, the loss is not deductible.) A debt is secured by real property whenever you have the right to take title or possession or both in the event the buyer defaults on his obligation under the contract.

Figuring gain on the repossession. Gain on the repossession is the excess of:

1. Payments received on the original sales contract prior to and on the repossession, including payments made by the buyer for your benefit to another party; *over*
2. The amount of taxable gain previously reported prior to the repossession.

Gain computed under these two steps may not be fully taxable. Taxable gain is limited to the amount of original profit less gain on the sale already reported as income for periods prior to the repossession and less your repossession costs.

The limitation on gain does not apply if the selling price cannot be computed at the time of sale as, for example, where the selling price is stated as a percentage of the profits to be realized from the development of the property sold.

EXAMPLE

Assume you sell a house for $25,000. You take a $5,000 down payment plus a $20,000 mortgage, secured by the property, from the buyer, with principal payable at the rate of $4,000 annually. The adjusted basis of the house was $20,000 and you elected to report the transaction on the installment basis. Your gross profit percentage is 20% ($5,000 profit over $25,000 selling price). In the year of sale, you include $1,000 in your income on the installment basis (20% of $5,000 down payment). The next year you reported profit of $800 (20% of $4,000 annual installment). In the third year, the buyer defaults on his payments, and you repossess the property. The amount of gain on repossession is computed as follows:

1. Compute gain.		
Amount of money received ($5,000 plus $4,000)		$9,000
Less: Amount of gain taxed in prior years ($1,000 plus $800)		1,800
Gain		$7,200
2. Compute limited gain, assuming cost of repossession is $500.		
Original profit		$5,000
Reduced by:		
Gain reported as income	$1,800	
Cost of repossession	500	2,300
Taxable gain on repossession		$2,700

The above rules do not affect the character of the gain. Thus, if you repossess property as a dealer, the gain is subject to ordinary income rates. For example, if you, as an investor, repossess in 1987 a tract originally held long-term whose gain was reported on the installment method, the gain is capital gain. According to Treasury regulations, if the sale was originally reported as a deferred payment sale and title was transferred to the buyer who voluntarily reconveyed it, gain on a 1987 repossession is ordinary income. However, if the buyer's obligations are those of a corporation or governmental agency, capital gain treatment may apply.

The basis of repossessed property. It is the adjusted basis of the debt (face value of the debt less the unreported profits) secured by the property, figured as of the date of repossession, increased by (1) the taxable gain, and (2) the amount of money, costs, or other consideration paid by you on the repossession.

EXAMPLE

Same facts as in the example above. The basis of the repossessed property is computed as follows:

1. Face value of debt		$16,000
2. Less: Unreported profit (20% of above)		3,200
3. Adjusted basis at date of repossession		$12,800
4. Plus: Gain on repossession	$2,700	
Cost of repossession	500	3,200
5. Basis of repossessed property		$16,000

If you treated the debt as having become worthless or partially worthless before repossession, you are considered to receive, upon the repossession of the property securing the debt, an amount equal to the amount of the debt treated as worthless; you increase the basis of the debt by an amount equal to the amount previously treated as worthless.

If your debt is not fully discharged as a result of the repossession, the basis of the undischarged debt is zero. No loss may be claimed if the obligations subsequently become worthless. This rule applies to undischarged debts on the original obligation of the purchaser, a substituted obligation of the purchaser, a deficiency judgment entered in a court of law into which the purchaser's obligation was merged, and any other obligations arising from the transaction.

The above repossession rules do not apply if you repurchase the property by paying the buyer a sum in addition to the discharge of his debt, unless the repurchase and payment was provided for in the original sale contract, or the buyer has defaulted on his obligation, or his default is imminent.

Personal residence. The above rules do not apply to repossessions of a personal residence if (1) gain on the original sale was not taxed because you made an election to avoid tax (¶29.12) or to defer gain on the purchase of a new residence (¶29.3), and (2) within a year after the repossession you resell the property. The resale is treated as a part of the transaction comprising the original sale.

FORECLOSURE BIDS BY MORTGAGEES ON MORTGAGES OTHER THAN PURCHASE MONEY MORTGAGES

¶ 31.8 If you, as a mortgagee, bid in on a foreclosure sale to pay off a mortgage that is *not a purchase money mortgage*. your actual financial loss is the difference between the unpaid mortgage debt and the value of the property. For tax purposes, however, you may realize a capital gain or loss and a bad debt loss which are reportable *in the year of the foreclosure sale.*

Your bid is treated as consisting of two distinct transactions:
1. The repayment of your loan. To determine whether this results in a bad debt, the bid price is matched against the face amount of the mortgage.
2. A taxable exchange of your mortgage note for the foreclosed property, which may result in a capital gain or loss. This is determined by matching the bid price against the fair market value of the property.

EXAMPLES

1. *Mortgagee's bid less than market value.* You hold a $40,000 mortgage on property having a fair market value of $30,000. You bid on the property at the foreclosure sale at $28,000. The expenses of the sale are $2,000, reducing the bid price to $26,000. The mortgagor is insolvent, so you have a bad debt loss of $14,000 ($40,000–$26,000). You also have a $4,000 capital gain (the fair market value of the property of $30,000–$26,000).

2. *Mortgagee's bid equal to market value.* Suppose your bid was $32,000, and the expenses $2,000. The difference between the net bid price of $30,000 and the mortgage of $40,000 is $10,000. As the mortgagor is insolvent, there is a bad debt loss of $10,000. Since the net bid price equals the fair market value, there is neither capital gain nor loss.

3. *Mortgagee's bid greater than market value.* Suppose you had bid $36,000 and had $2,000 in expenses. Your bad debt deduction is $6,000—the difference between the mortgage debt of $40,000 and the net bid price of $34,000. You also had a capital loss of $4,000 (difference between the net bid price of $34,000 and the fair market value of $30,000).

Where the bid price equals the mortgage debt plus unreported but accrued interest, you report the interest as income. But where the accrued interest has been reported, the unpaid amount is added to the collection expenses.

Preserve evidence of the property's fair market value. At a later date, the IRS may claim that the property was worth more than your bid and may tax you for the difference. Furthermore, be prepared to prove the worthlessness of the debt to support the bad debt deduction.

Voluntary conveyance. Instead of forcing you to foreclose, the mortgagor may voluntarily convey the property to you in consideration for your canceling the mortgage debt. Your loss is the amount by which the mortgage debt plus accrued interest exceeds the fair market value of the property. If, however, the fair market value exceeds the mortgage debt plus

accrued interest, the difference is taxable gain. The gain or loss is reportable in the year you receive the property. Your basis in the property is its fair market value when you receive it.

HOW MORTGAGEES TREAT PROCEEDS RECEIVED FROM FORECLOSURE SALE TO THIRD PARTY

¶ 31.9 When a third party buys the property in a foreclosure, the mortgagee receives the purchase price to apply against the mortgage debt. If it is less than the debt, the mortgagee may proceed against the mortgagor for the difference. Foreclosure expenses are treated as offsets against the foreclosure proceeds and increase the bad debt loss.

You deduct your loss as a bad debt. The law distinguishes between two types of bad debt deductions, business bad debts and nonbusiness bad debts. A business bad debt is fully deductible. A nonbusiness bad debt is a short-term capital loss that can be offset only against capital gains, plus a limited amount of ordinary income (*see* ¶6.55). In addition, you may deduct a partially worthless business bad debt, but you may not deduct a partially worthless nonbusiness bad debt. Remember this distinction if you are thinking of forgiving part of the mortgage debt as a settlement. If the debt is a nonbusiness bad debt, you will not be able to take a deduction until the entire debt proves to be worthless. But whether you are deducting a business or a nonbusiness bad debt, your deduction will be allowed only if you show the debt to be uncollectible—for example, because a deficiency judgment is worthless, or because the mortgagor is bankrupt or has disappeared.

EXAMPLE

You hold a $30,000 note and mortgage which are in default. You foreclose, and a third party buys the property for $20,000. Foreclosure expenses amount to $2,000. The deficiency is uncollectible. Your loss of $12,000 is figured as follows:

Unpaid mortgage debt		$30,000
Foreclosure proceeds	$20,000	
Less: Expenses	2,000	
Net proceeds		18,000
Bad debt loss		$12,000

TREATMENT OF DISCOUNT ON PURCHASED MORTGAGE

¶ 31.10 According to the IRS, when you buy a mortgage note at a discount, you report each payment as a partial return of principal and discount income. For example, you buy for $10,000 a second mortgage note, the face amount of which is $15,000. If you receive a payment of $1,200, $800 (⅔ of $1,200) is a return of capital; $400 (⅓ of $1,200) is ordinary income. However, taxpayers have disputed the IRS rule which requires a current reporting of discount income and have been allowed to treat all payments as a return of cost (until their investment is fully recovered) when they have been able to convince a court that the mortgage was of a highly speculative nature.

If you decide to defer the reporting of discount income until you recover your cost, anticipate a dispute with the IRS. To support your case, you have to prove that your investment was "speculative." The Tax Court set down these tests for determining whether an obligation is speculative:
1. Is the debtor personally liable? Is there a guarantor? If a party is personally liable, what are his credit standing and resources?
2. The marketability of the note. Is it negotiable?
3. At the time the note is bought, is the debtor in substantial default on payments due?
4. What are the terms of payment? Is the debt a first, second, or other lien?
5. What is the market value of the underlying property?

Even assuming that you can prove that there is a speculative element to the obligation, the next step of proof presents difficulties because the courts are not in agreement on just what part of the note must be proved speculative. In one court, an investment is speculative if you are uncertain that the entire obligation will be paid. This is the most liberal approach. In another court, the test is whether you can expect to recover at least your cost. If you can, then you must currently report part of the discount as income. The Tax Court set down a test that straddles these two tests. The note is speculative if you are uncertain that you will recover your cost and a major portion of the discount. Furthermore, speculativeness of an obligation is to be measured by the facts known at the time of the purchase of the obligation. That the debtor is later able to meet his obligation does not negate the speculative nature of the obligation at the time of its purchase.

TRANSFERRING MORTGAGED REALTY

¶ 31.11 Mortgaging realty that has appreciated in value is one way of realizing cash on the appreciation without current tax consequences. The receipt of cash by mortgaging the property is not taxed; tax will generally be imposed only when the property is sold. However, there is a possible tax where the mortgage exceeds the adjusted basis of the property and the property is given away or transferred to a controlled corporation (ownership of at least 80%).

Where the property is transferred to a controlled corporation, the excess is taxable gain. Further, if the IRS successfully charges that the transfer is part of a tax avoidance scheme, the taxable gain may be as high as the amount of the mortgage liability.

Gifts. The IRS holds that a gift of mortgaged property results in taxable income to the donor to the extent that the mortgage liability exceeds the donor's basis. The IRS position has been supported by the Tax Court and an appeals court.

EXAMPLE

Levine had owned a building for 19 years before transferring it to a trust for his grandchildren. During that period, he obtained nonrecourse loans of $672,000 of which $127,000 was repaid, $334,000 was invested in building improvements and the balance was apparently retained for personal purposes. Upon the transfer, the trust assumed nonrecourse mortgages (with accrued interest) on the building of $785,908, as well as $124,574 in building-related expenses for which Levine was personally liable. The total liabilities taken on by the trust exceeded Levine's adjusted basis by $425,000; the IRS charged that this excess was taxable gain to Levine. The Tax Court agreed and an appeals court affirmed.

Levine had argued that no gain is recognized on the making of a gift; any potential gain is preserved in the donee's basis and will eventually be taxed when the donee sells the property. The appeals court sidestepped this basis argument by noting that no Code provision specifically exempts from taxation gain on a gift of mortgaged property.

32

TAX SAVINGS FOR EXECUTIVES

¶ **32.1** The 1986 Tax Act left intact the basic tax-saving features of employee pay plans but reduced the scale and extent of the tax savings in the following ways:

Reduces the amount of salary income that you may defer in 401(k) plans and imposes stricter nondiscrimination rules. *See* ¶ 32.4.

Restricts averaging opportunities. Special averaging for lump-sum distributions is unavailable to persons under the age of 59½ who were not age 50 as of January 1, 1986. *See* chapter 7 for full details.

Imposes penalties on withdrawals from retirement plans before age 59½ unless because of death or disability, or unless other exceptions listed at ¶7.13 apply.

Eliminates long-term capital gain benefits and so reduces the tax-saving potential of incentive stock options (ISO). *See* ¶32.7.

Imposes 15% penalty on excess retirement distribution, *see* ¶7.14.

Despite these developments, pay plans provide one of the few opportunities of deferring or sheltering income.

GENERAL PRINCIPLES

¶ **32.2** Executive pay plans have one objective—to reduce or eliminate the tax cost of earning salary income. There are pay benefits that are not taxable, such as certain fringe benefits, disability pensions, health and accident and death benefits, and certain housing costs while working abroad. Other tax saving benefits may be developed through pension and profit-sharing plans, stock options, and deferred pay plans. The objective of deferring pay is to postpone the receipt of salary income to a time when you expect to be in a lower tax bracket. However, a deferred pay plan is generally not advisable where a projection of future income shows that there probably will be no substantial income decline, and/or the tax bracket differentials will not be wide. An after-tax dollar in hand for current use is preferable to an expectation of a tax saving that may not materialize.

Fringe benefits. Fringe benefits provided executives by employers increase after-tax income by being either tax exempt or subject to special tax treatment. The tax consequences of fringe benefits and other pay benefits are discussed in the following sections:

PENSION AND PROFIT-SHARING PLANS

¶ **32.3** A company qualified pension or profit-sharing plan offers these benefits: (1) You do not realize current income on your employer's contributions to the plan on your behalf. (2) Funds contributed by both your employer and you compound tax free within the plan. (3) If you receive a lump sum, tax on employer contributions may be reduced by a special averaging rule. (4) If you receive a lump-sum distribution in company securities, unrealized appreciation on those securities is not taxed until you finally sell the stock.

Where you are allowed to choose the type of payout from a qualified plan, make sure that you compare the tax on receiving a lump-sum distribution with the projected tax cost of deferring payments over a period of years or rolling over the distribution to an IRA account. *See* ¶7.3 and ¶7.8.

CASH OR DEFERRED PAY ARRANGEMENTS: 401(k) PLANS

¶ **32.4** If your company has a profit-sharing or stock bonus plan, it has the opportunity of giving you additional tax sheltered pay. The tax law allows the company to add a cash or deferred pay plan, called a 401(k) plan, which can operate in one of two ways:

1. Your employer contributes an amount for your benefit to a trust account. You are not taxed on your employer's contribution. Although there is no income tax, the contribution is subject to Social Security tax.

2. You agree to take a salary reduction or to forgo a salary increase. The reduction is placed in a trust account for your benefit. The reduction is treated as your employer's contribution. In addition, your company may match part of your contribution. The new law limits salary reduction deferrals to $7,000 (*see* below). Taking a pay reduction may be an ideal way to defer income and benefit from a tax free buildup of income.

Income earned on the trust account accumulates tax free until it is withdrawn. By law, you may not withdraw funds attributable to elective salary reduction contributions until you reach age 59½, are separated from service, become disabled, or show financial hardship. Withdrawals are also allowed if the plan terminates, or the corporation sells its assets or its interest in a subsidiary and you continue to work for the buyer or the subsidiary. However, the hardship provision and age 59½ allowance does not apply to certain "pre-ERISA" money purchase pension plans (in existence June 27, 1974). Further, after 1988, hardship withdrawals may include only an employee's elective deferrals; the hardship withdrawal may not include employer contributions or income earned on the employee's elective deferrals.

If withdrawals are allowed before age 59½, such as for hardship you are subject to the 10% penalty for premature withdrawals unless you meet one of the exceptions listed at ¶7.13.

A lump-sum distribution may be eligible for special averaging under the rules of ¶7.2. Lump-sum distributions exceeding $750,000 may be subject to the excess distribution penalty; *see* ¶7.14.

If the plan allows you to borrow from the plan, the loan restrictions at ¶7.15 apply.

$7,000 limit on salary reduction deferrals. Under the new law, the maximum tax free salary reduction contribution you can make is $7,000, although this limit may be increased starting in 1988 by an inflation factor. Deferrals from your pay exceeding $7,000 are taxable in the year of the deferral. Further, if the excess contribution (plus income earned on such excess) is not distributed to you by the first April 15 following the year of the excess deferral, it is taxed again when distributed from the plan.

The $7,000 limit applies to total salary reduction deferrals made to 401(k) plans as well as to simplified employee pension plans (SEPs). If you participate in more than one such plan, the $7,000 limit applies to the total salary reductions for all the plans. According to Congressional Committee reports, if you also contribute to a tax-sheltered annuity (¶7.30), the $7,000 cap is reduced by the amount of salary-reduction contributions made to the tax-sheltered annuity. If salary reductions are made only to the tax-sheltered annuity, a $9,500 limit generally applies (*see* ¶7.30).

The $7,000 tax free limit applies only to an employee's elective deferrals from pay. An employer may make matching or other additional contributions, provided the total does not exceed the lesser of 25% of compensation or $30,000.

Nondiscrimination rules. The law imposes strict contribution percentage tests to prevent discrimination in favor of highly compensated employees. If these tests are violated, the employer is subject to penalties and the plan could be disqualified unless the excess contributions (plus allocable income) are distributed back to the highly compensated employees within specified time limits.

INSURANCE PLANS MAY BE TAX FREE

¶ 32.5 Company-financed insurance for employees is a common method of giving additional benefits at low or no tax cost.

Group life insurance. Group insurance plans may furnish not only life insurance protection but also accident and health benefits. Premium costs are low and tax deductible to the company while tax free to you unless you have nonforfeitable rights to permanent life insurance, or, in the case of group-term life insurance, your coverage exceeds $50,000 (*see* ¶2.4). Even where your coverage exceeds $50,000, the tax incurred on your employer's premium payment is generally less than what you would pay privately for similar insurance.

It may be possible to avoid estate tax on the group policy proceeds if you assign all of your ownership rights in the policy, including the right to convert the policy, and the beneficiary is other than your estate. Where the policy allows assignment of the conversion right, in addition to all other rights, and state law does not bar the assignment, you are considered to have made a complete assignment of the group insurance for estate tax purposes.

The IRS has ruled that where an employee assigns a group life policy and the value of the employee's interest in the policy cannot be ascertained, there is no taxable gift. This is so where the employer could simply have stopped making payments. However, there is a gift by the employee to the assignor to the extent of premiums paid by the employer. That gift is a present interest qualifying for the $10,000 annual exclusion.

Split-dollar insurance. Where you want more insurance than is provided by a group plan, your company may be able to help you get additional protection through a split-dollar insurance plan. Under this type of plan, your employer purchases permanent life insurance on your life. He pays the annual premium to the extent of the yearly increases in the cash surrender value of the policy, and you pay only the balance of the premium. At your death, your employer is entitled to part of the proceeds equal to the cash surrender value or any lesser amount equaling the total premiums he paid. You have the right to name a beneficiary to receive the remaining proceeds which, under most policies, is substantial compared with the employer's share.

You annually report as taxable income an amount equal to the one-year term cost of the declining life insurance protection to which you are entitled, less any portion of the premium provided by you. Simplified somewhat, here is how the tax would be figured in one year. Assume the share of the proceeds payable to your beneficiary (face value less cash surrender value) from a $100,000 policy is $77,535. If the term cost of $77,535 insurance provided by the employer is $567, you pay a tax on $567, less your payment of premium. So, if you paid a premium of $209, you pay tax on $358. Assume in the fourth year, you pay no premium and the amount payable to your family is $69,625. (Under the split-dollar plan, the benefits payable to your beneficiary continuously decline; the employer's share increases annually because of the continued payment of premiums and the increase in the cash surrender value.) The term cost provided by your employer toward $69,625 is $549; you pay tax on the full $549.

Despite the tax cost, you may find the arrangement an inexpensive method of obtaining additional insurance coverage with your employer's help. For example, taking the taxable premium benefit of $549 from the above example, if you are in the 28% bracket, the cost of almost $70,000 insurance protection in that year is $153.72 ($549 × 28%).

Split-dollar insurance policies entered into before November 14, 1964, are not subject to the above tax on the employer's payment of premiums.

STOCK APPRECIATION RIGHTS (SARs)

¶ 32.6 SARs are a form of cash bonus tied to an increase in the price of employer stock. Each SAR entitles an employee to cash equal to the excess of the fair market value of one share on the date of exercise over the value on the date of the grant of the SAR.

EXAMPLE
When a stock is worth $30 a share, you get 100 SARs exercisable within five years. Two years later when the stock price increases to $50 a share, you exercise the SAR and receive $2,000. You are taxed when you receive the cash.

> If the rights increase in value, keep a close watch on the expiration date. Do not let them expire before exercise. If you do, not only will you lose income but you will be taxed on income you never received. According to the IRS, an employee who does not exercise the SARs is taxed as if they had been exercised immediately before they expire. The IRS claims that an employee has constructive receipt of income immediately before they expire. At that time, the amount of gain realized from the SAR is fixed because the employee can no longer benefit from future appreciation in value.

An executive may realize taxable income when he becomes entitled to the maximum SAR benefit allowed by the company plan. For example, in 1984, when company stock is worth $30, an executive is granted 100 SARs exercisable within five years. By exercising the SARs, he may receive cash equal to the appreciation up to $20 per share. If the stock appreciates to $50 per share in 1987, the executive realizes taxable income of $2,000 ($20 per share × 100) in 1986, even if he does not exercise the SARs. The reason: Once the stock value appreciated to $50, the maximum SAR benefit of $20 was realized.

Performance shares. The company promises to make an award of stock in the future, at no cost to you, if the company's earnings reach a set level. You are taxed on the receipt of stock (unless the stock is restricted, as discussed in ¶32.7).

STOCK OPTIONS AND RESTRICTED STOCK

¶ **32.7** *Incentive stock options (ISOs).* A corporation may provide its executives with incentive stock options to acquire its stock (or the stock of its parent or subsidiaries). ISOs are not taxed when granted or exercised. The option spread is generally taxable as capital gain in 1987 if the stock acquired by the exercise of the option was sold in 1987 and was held for two years after the option was granted and for one year after the exercise of the option.

In 1988, if the scheduled tax rate reduction goes into effect, the capital gain feature of ISOs will have no tax significance unless you have capital losses that can offset the capital gains. In 1988, under the scheduled tax rates, there will be no rate distinction between capital gains and ordinary income. Although the loss of capital gain potential reduces the overall tax savings of ISOs, ISOs remain a favorable compensation benefit for executives.

For other restrictions on ISOs, see the terms of your company plan.

Income realized on ISOs sale may be subject to AMT tax, *see* chapter 23.

Nonqualified stock options. If a nonqualified stock option has an ascertainable fair market value, the value of the option is taxable as ordinary income at the time of transfer. On the exercise of the option, no taxable gain is realized; gain or loss is realized on the later sale of the stock. Where the option has no ascertainable fair market value, no income is realized on the receipt of the option. Income is realized when the value of the option is ascertainable. This may occur when the option is exercised. For other details and requirements, *see* Treasury regulations.

Nonqualified stock options may be granted in addition to or in place of incentive stock options. There are no restrictions on the amount of nonqualified stock options that may be granted.

When sale of stock is treated as grant of option. If company stock is purchased on the basis of the executive's promissory note and he is not personally liable, the company can recover only its stock in the event of default on the note. In terms of risk, the executive has given nothing and is somewhat in the same position as the optionee. If the stock value drops, he may walk away from the deal with no personal risk. According to Treasury regulations, the deal may be viewed as an option arrangement. Application of the Treasury regulation would give the executive ordinary taxable income when he pays for the stock if the value of the stock at the time of purchase exceeds the purchase price. For example, on July 1, 1982, a corporation sells 100 shares of its stock to an executive. The stock has a fair market value on that date of $25,000 and the executive executes a nonrecourse note secured by the stock in that amount, plus 8% annual interest. He is required by the note to make annual payment of $5,000 of principal, plus interest, beginning the following year. In 1986, he pays the interest on the note but no principal. He also collects dividends and votes the stock. In 1987, when the stock has appreciated in value to $30,000, he pays off the note. Under the Treasury regulation, the executive would realize ordinary income upon payment of the nonrecourse note to the extent of the difference between the amount paid ($25,000 in 1987) and the value of the stock ($30,000).

> You may elect to be taxed on the unrestricted (market) value of the stock at the time you receive it and to be treated as an investor. If you do, later appreciation in value is not taxed as pay. However, you may not claim a loss deduction if you later forfeit the stock. The election must generally be made not later than 30 days after the date of the transfer of the stock.
>
> The restricted stock rule is not restricted to compensation of employees; it may apply to any type of fee arrangement for services.

Restricted stock. Stock subject to restrictions is taxed as pay in the first year in which it is either transferable or not subject to a substantial risk of forfeiture. A risk of forfeiture exists where your rights are conditioned upon the future performance of substantial services. Generally, taxable income is the difference between the amount, if any, that you pay for the stock and its value at the time the risk of forfeiture is removed. The valuation at the time the forfeiture restrictions lapse is not reduced because of restrictions imposed on the right to sell the property. However, restrictions which will never lapse do affect valuation.

SEC restriction on insider trading is considered a substantial risk of forfeiture, so that receipt of stock subject to such restriction is a nontaxable event. Similarly, if the stock is subject to a restriction on transfer to comply with SEC pooling-of-interests accounting rules the stock is considered to be subject to a substantial restriction.

EDUCATIONAL BENEFITS FOR EMPLOYEES' CHILDREN

¶ **32.8** *Private foundations.* The IRS has published guidelines under which a private foundation established by an employer may make tax free grants to children of employees. If the guidelines are satisfied, employees are not taxable on the benefits provided their children. Advance approval of the grant program must be obtained from the IRS.

IRS guidelines require:

Grant recipients must be selected by a scholarship committee which is independent of the employer and the foundation. Former employees of the employer or the foundation are not considered independent.

Eligibility for the grants may be restricted to children of employees who have been employed for a minimum of up to three years, but eligibility may not be related to the employee's position, services, or duties.

Once awarded, a grant may not be terminated if the parent leaves his job with the employer, regardless of the reason for the termination of employment. If a one-year grant is awarded or a multiyear grant is awarded subject to renewal, a child who reapplies for a later grant may not be considered ineligible because his parent no longer works for the employer.

Grant recipients must be based solely upon objective standards unrelated to the employer's business and the parent's employment, such as prior academic performance, aptitude tests, recommendations from instructors, financial needs, and conclusions drawn from personal interviews.

Recipients must be free to use the grants for courses which are not of particular benefit to the employer or the foundation.

The grant program must not be used by the foundation or employer to recruit employees or induce employees to continue employment.

There must be no requirement or suggestion that the child or parent is expected to render future employment services.

The grant program must also meet a percentage test: The number of grants awarded in a given year to children of employees must not exceed (1) 25% of the number of employees' children who were eligible, applied for the grants, and were considered by the selection committee in that year, or (2) 10% of the number of employees' children who were eligible during that year, whether or not they applied. Renewals of grants are not considered in determining the number of grants awarded.

If all guidelines other than the percentage test are satisfied, the IRS will determine whether the primary purpose of the program is to educate the children, in which case the grants will be considered tax free scholarships or fellowships, or whether the grants are to be taxed to the parent-employee as extra compensation.

Educational benefit trusts and other plans. A medical professional corporation set up an educational benefit plan to provide the payment of college costs to the children of "key" employees. The plan defined a key employee as an employee who was salaried at over $15,000. To receive benefits, the child must have been a candidate for a degree within two years after graduating from high school. If an eligible employee quit for reasons other than death or permanent disability, his children could no longer receive benefits except for expenses actually incurred before termination. The company made annual contributions to the trust for which a bank was trustee. According to the IRS, amounts contributed to the trust are a form of pay to qualified employees, as they are contributed on the basis of employment and earnings record, rather than on the basis of competitive standards, such as need, merit or motivation. However, employees are not currently taxable. The right to have their children receive benefits is conditioned upon each employee's future performance of services. Further, there is a substantial risk of forfeiture. Tax is not incurred until a child has a vested right to receive benefits; here, vesting does not occur until a child becomes a candidate for a degree at an educational institution, has actually incurred educational expenses, and his parent is employed by the company. Once the right to receive a distribution from the plan becomes vested, the parent of the child who has incurred the expenses is taxable on the amount of the distribution. The company may then claim a deduction for the amount reported as income by the employee. The Tax Court and appeals court have upheld the IRS position in similar plans.

PENALTY TAX ON EXCESS GOLDEN PARACHUTE PAYMENTS

¶ **32.9** Executives who receive substantial "golden parachute" payments as compensation following a corporate takeover may be subject to a 20% penalty tax. If the payment exceeds three times the average compensation for the preceding five years, the 20% penalty applies to payments in excess of the five-year compensation average.

The law presumes that excess parachute payments are not reasonable compensation but if it can be shown by clear evidence that the payment represented reasonable compensation, that amount reduces the excess payment subject to penalty. Reasonable compensation for services to be rendered after change of control are not treated as parachute payments. Payments from qualified retirement plans are not treated as golden parachute payments.

Golden parachute payments are subject to income tax withholding as if they were wages; employers must also withhold the 20% penalty tax if applicable. The corporation may not deduct the penalized payment.

Any penalty is reported separately on Form W-2 and must be reported on the executive's tax return.

The above tax does not apply to executives of a small business corporation (a corporation that may qualify to make an S corporation election, see ¶ 10.6). It also does not apply if the stock of the corporation is not readily tradeable and if certain stockholder approval steps are taken.

33

TAX SAVINGS IN FAMILY INCOME PLANNING

¶ **33.1** The new tax law attempts to discourage the income splitting among family members by:

Reducing the difference between the lowest and highest tax brackets. When the range between the tax brackets was between 11% and 50% (and at times as high as 70%), there was an obvious reason for diverting income from such high brackets to the lower brackets of dependents. If the projected two-rate structure is adhered to by Congress, the 13% spread between the 15% and 28% tax brackets may not offer the same motivation for income splitting transfers as in the past.

Taxing investment income exceeding $1,000 of minor children under the age of 14 at the top tax bracket of parents. See ¶ 22.3.

Repealing the income-shifting feature of short-term (ten-year) trusts.

Although the tax-saving advantages of family income splitting have been tarnished by these developments, tax savings are available as discussed in this chapter.

GIFT TAX BASICS

¶ **33.2** As family income planning generally requires the transfer of property, you must consider possible gift tax liability. The gift tax rates and credit are the same as those of the estate tax listed in ¶ 38.12. However, gift tax liability may be avoided by making gifts within the annual exclusion of $10,000 (or $20,000 for joint gifts). To each donee, you may give annually up to $10,000 tax free; further, if your spouse joins in the gift, you may give annually tax free to each donee up to $20,000. Thus, if you (with your spouse's consent) make annual gifts to four persons, you could give away without gift tax up to $80,000 (4 × $20,000

exclusion). Gifts over this exclusion may also avoid tax after applying the unified gift and estate tax credit listed in ¶ 38.12.

If you make an interest-free or low-interest loan to a family member, you may be subject to income tax as well as gift tax, see ¶ 4.17.

HOW INCOME SPLITTING SAVES TAXES

¶ **33.3** Each additional dollar of ordinary income you receive, such as interest, dividends, and rent, is taxed in your highest bracket. If you can deflect income to a lower tax bracket of a child or other dependent relative, he or she will pay a smaller tax on the income than you would pay. This tax-saving technique known as income splitting allows more after-tax income to remain within the family.

To split income, you must do more than make gifts of income. You must transfer the actual property from which the income is produced. For example, you do not avoid tax on interest by instructing your savings bank to credit interest to your children's account. Unless you actually transfer the complete ownership of the account to your children, the interest income is earned on money owned by you and must be reported by you. The same holds true with dividends, rents, and other forms of income. Unless you transfer the property providing the income, the income will be taxed to you.

You may not split earned income; income resulting from your services is taxed to you. You may not avoid this result by setting up trusts to receive your earned income.

CUSTODIAN ACCOUNTS FOR CHILDREN

¶ **33.4** Custodian accounts set up in a bank, mutual fund, or brokerage firm can achieve income splitting; the tax consequences discussed below generally apply to such accounts. Trust accounts which are considered revocable under state law are ineffective in splitting interest income.

> Purchase of securities through custodian accounts provides a practical method for making a gift of securities to a minor child, eliminating the need for a trust. The mechanics of opening a custodian account are simple. An adult opens a stock account for a minor child at a broker's office. He registers the securities in the name of a custodian for the benefit of the child. The custodian may be a parent, a child's guardian, grandparent, brother, sister, uncle or aunt. In some states, the custodian may be any adult or a bank or trust company. The custodian has the right to sell securities in the account, collect sales proceeds and investment income, and use them for the child's benefit or reinvestment.

There are limitations placed on the custodian. He may not take proceeds from the sale of an investment or income from an investment to buy additional securities on margin. While he should prudently seek reasonable income and capital preservation, he generally is not liable for losses unless they result from bad faith, intentional wrongdoing, or gross negligence.

When the minor reaches majority (depending on state law), property in the custodian account is turned over to him. No formal accounting is required. The child, now an adult, may sign a simple release freeing the custodian from any liability. But on reaching majority, the child may require a formal accounting if he has any doubts as to the propriety of the custodian's actions while acting as custodian. For this reason and also for tax record-keeping purposes, a separate bank account should be opened in which proceeds from sales of investments and investment income are deposited pending reinvestment on behalf of the child. Such an account will furnish a convenient record of sales proceeds, investment income, and reinvestment of the same.

Although custodian accounts may be opened anywhere in the United States, the rules governing the account may vary from state to state. The differences between the laws of the states generally do not affect federal tax consequences.

Income tax treatment. Income from a custodian account is taxable to the child as long as it is not used by the parent who set up the account to pay for the child's support. Tax-exempt income from a custodian account is not taxable to the parent even when used for child support. Income from a custodian account in excess of $1,000 is taxed at the parent's tax rate if the child is under 14. Computation of the tax is discussed at ¶ 22.3.

Gift tax treatment. When setting up a custodian account, you may have to pay a gift tax. A transfer of cash or securities to a custodian account is a gift. But you are not subject to a gift tax if you properly plan the cash contributions or purchase of securities for your children's accounts. You may make gifts up to $10,000 to one person, which is shielded from gift tax

by the annual exclusion. The exclusion applies each year to each person to whom you make a gift. If your spouse consents to join with you in the gift, you may give annually tax free up to $20,000 to each person.

If the custodian account is set up at the end of December, another tax free transfer of $20,000 may be made in the first days of January of the following year. In this way, a total of $40,000 is shifted within the two-month period.

Estate tax treatment. The value of a custodian account will be taxed in your estate if you die while acting as custodian of an account before your child reaches his majority. However, you may avoid the problem by naming someone other than yourself as custodian. If you should decide to act as custodian, taking the risk that the account will be taxed in your estate, remember no estate tax is incurred if the tax on your estate is offset by the estate tax credit (*see* ¶ 38.12).

If you act as custodian and decide to terminate the custodianship, care should be taken to formally close the account. Otherwise, if you die while retaining power over the account, the IRS may try to tax the account in your estate.

OTHER TYPES OF INVESTMENTS FOR CHILDREN

¶ **33.5** A minor generally lacks the ability to manage property. Yet, if you exercise control over the property you give to him, the gift may not be recognized for purposes of shifting income. You might appoint a fiduciary for the child, but this step may be costly. Alternatively you might select property which does not require management and which can be transferred by a minor. For example—

1. Bonds may be purchased and registered in a minor's name and coupons or the proceeds on sale or maturity of bonds may be cashed or deposited in a minor's name.
2. Insurance companies will write policies on the lives of minors and recognize their ownership of policies covering the lives of others. Depending on the age of the minor, state law, and company practice, it may be necessary to appoint a guardian for the purpose of cashing in or borrowing on insurance policies given to a minor. A gift of a life insurance policy or an annuity will usually qualify as a gift of a present interest in property for the annual gift tax exclusion.
3. Mutual fund shares, such as money market funds, may be purchased and registered in the name of a minor. The problem of management and sale for reinvestment is minimized because the investment trust itself provides continuous supervision. Changes in the underlying investments of the fund are made without reference to the minor. Most funds provide for automatic reinvestment of dividends in additional shares.

HOLDING PROPERTY AS JOINT TENANTS

¶ **33.6** Owning property jointly with one's spouse seems a reasonable solution to a family estate problem. It is easy to arrange: have both names listed as owners. On the death of one, the surviving spouse becomes sole owner of the property. The property does not pass through the estate incurring probate and other costs. Further, there is no estate tax on the property. One-half the property is included in the deceased spouse's estate, but it is not taxed because of the marital deduction.

> The principal objection to joint ownership is that it deprives each owner of the ability to direct the transfer of ownership of his interest. He cannot specify who is ultimately to inherit it and the time and method of inheritance. The best way to control an estate is through a program of estate planning. While joint ownership offers what seems an easy solution, it involves a fixed disposition of property. Through estate planning it is possible to provide alternatives to meet unexpected events at the lowest possible tax cost.

Jointly owned property may pass to people whom the couple would not have named as heirs. Assume a married man with no children puts nearly all of his property in his and his wife's joint names and then the couple is in an automobile accident that is fatal to the husband. His wife survives for a few weeks. Upon her death, under local law, all the property goes to her brothers and sisters. Both the husband and wife might have wanted to assure his parents of support for their lives. Perhaps the couple might have chosen to distribute the property between both families. The survivorship feature of joint ownership is rigid and cannot be changed once one or both of the joint owners die.

Joint brokerage account in a street name. Setting up a joint brokerage account in a street name is not an effective transfer for gift tax purposes. Securities are held in a "street" name—that is, the name of the broker—when you have a margin account. Even when you have a cash account, securities may be held in a street name to facilitate trading. The IRS has ruled that where you, with your separate funds, have set up a joint brokerage account for yourself and another person, and the securities are registered in the name of a broker, you have not made a gift for gift tax purposes. The gift is completed only when the other party draws on the account without any obligation to account to you. The value of the gift would be the amount of money or property withdrawn. The IRS contends in a ruling that an account in a street name is like a joint bank account set up by one person. He has not given up any control over the funds in either type of account. Income tax consequences were not covered by the ruling. However, a strong inference from the ruling is that the dividends and sales and exchanges are taxable to the party who contributed the funds to the account.

TRUSTS IN FAMILY PLANNING

¶ **33.7** You establish a trust by transferring legal title to property to a trustee who manages the property for one or more beneficiaries. As the one who set up the trust, you are called the grantor or settlor of the trust. The trustee may be one or more individuals or an institution such as a bank or a trust company.

You can create a trust during your lifetime or by your will. A trust created during your lifetime is called an inter vivos trust; one established in your will is a testamentary trust. An inter vivos trust can be revocable or irrevocable. An irrevocable trust does not allow for changes of heart; it requires a complete surrender of property. By conveying property irrevocably to a trust, you may relieve yourself of tax on the income from the trust principal. Further, the property in trust usually is not subject to estate tax, although it may be subject to gift tax. A trust should be made irrevocable only if you are certain you will not need the trust property in a financial emergency.

In a revocable trust, you retain control over the property by reserving the right to revoke the trust. As such, it is considered an incomplete gift and offers no present income tax savings. Further, the trust property will be included as part of your estate. But a revocable trust minimizes delay in passing property to beneficiaries if you die while the trust is in force. When you transfer property to a trust, the property is generally not subject to probate, administration expenses, delays attendant on distributions of estates, or claims of creditors. The interests of trust beneficiaries are generally more secure than those of heirs under a will because a will may be denied probate if found invalid.

Short-term trusts. Ten-year (Clifford) trusts were widely used to shift income to relatives in lower tax brackets. Where a trust met the ten-year exception, trust income was taxed to the beneficiary, usually a minor child. Another type of trust used for income splitting was the spousal remainder trust set up for less than ten years. It allowed income shifting to a child beneficiary when the trust property went to the grantor's spouse after the trust period ends.

Under the new law, both types of trust may no longer be used to shift income to the income beneficiary. The ten-year exemption for grantor trusts is repealed. The grantor of a grantor trust is taxed on the income of the trust. A trust is treated as a grantor trust where the grantor has a reversionary interest (at the time of the transfer) of more than 5% of the

value of the property transferred to the trust. Under an exception, a grantor is not treated as having a reversionary interest if that interest can take effect only upon the death before age 21 of a beneficiary who is a lineal descendent of the grantor. The beneficiary must have the entire present interest in the trust or trust portion for this exception to apply.

Spousal remainder trusts are neutralized as tax-saving techniques by a new law treating the grantor as holding a reversionary interest held by his spouse if the spouse is living with the grantor at the time of the trust transfer. According to Committee reports, a spouse is treated as living with the grantor if they are eligible to file a joint return covering the period in which the trust transfer is made.

The new rules apply to trust transfers made after March 1, 1986. An exception applies to a ten-year trust created pursuant to a binding property settlement entered into before March 2, 1986, which required the taxpayer to establish a grantor trust.

Status of prior ten-year trusts. Trusts created before the effective date continue to shift income to the income beneficiary. However, tax savings are nullified for trust beneficiaries under the age of 14. Unearned income over $1,000 of a child under 14 is taxed to the child at the top marginal rate of the parents. *See* ¶22.3.

Pre-March 2, 1986, ten-year trusts will continue to shift income and provide tax savings to trust beneficiaries 14 or over.

Tax rates for trusts and estates. For taxable years beginning in 1987, a five-tier rate schedule applies with rates of 11%, 15%, 28%, 35%, or 38.5%. The top rate of 38.5% applies to taxable income over $15,150. For taxable years beginning after December 31, 1987, the first $5,000 of taxable income of a trust or estate will be taxed at a 15% rate, with excess income taxed at 28%. The benefit of the 15% bracket will be phased out between $13,000 and $26,000 of taxable income.

OTHER TRANSFERS THAT MAY SAVE TAXES

¶ **33.8** Making a gift of appreciated property that will eventually be sold may reduce income tax. To shift the profit and the tax, the gift must be completed before the sale or before the donor has made a binding commitment to sell. By making a gift of interests in the property to several family members, it is possible to spread the tax among a number of taxpayers in the lowest tax bracket. Note: the IRS may claim that the gift was never completed, if after sale the donor controls the sales proceeds or has the use of them.

Do not make a gift of property which has decreased in value if you want a deduction for the loss. Once you give the property away, the loss deduction is gone forever. Neither you nor your donee can ever take advantage of it. The better way is to first sell the property, get a loss deduction, and then make a gift of the proceeds.

Before transferring appreciated property, consider the fact that the appreciation on property passed by inheritance will escape income tax; the heir takes a basis equal to estate tax value, usually fair market value at the date of death. Further, appreciated property encumbered by mortgage may result in income tax to the donor when a gift of the property is made.

Interest-free loans. The tax law discourages income splitting through interest-free loans by imposing gift and income tax on loans coming within the rules of ¶4.17.

SPLITTING BUSINESS INCOME WITH YOUR FAMILY

¶ **33.9** Tax on your business income may be reduced if you can shift it to members of your family. You may also avoid estate tax on the value of the capital interests transferred to children. If you keep within the annual gift tax exclusion for each donee (on gifts made by husband and wife), there will be no gift tax consequences.

Business income may be shifted by forming a family partnership or by making your family stockholders in a corporation. Generally speaking, an S corporation in which stockholders elect to report income may be used more freely than a partnership to split income.

A minor child will not be recognized as a partner unless he is competent to manage his own property, or control of the property is exercised by another person as fiduciary for his sole benefit. Here, a trust may be set up to hold the partnership interest. The IRS may review not only the terms of the trust and the partnership agreement but also actual operation of the trust to make certain the grantor-partner has not retained any ownership rights over the interest he transferred.

Transfers of stock to a trust for a minor terminate an S election, unless the trust is a qualified trust. For this purpose, a "Subchapter S trust" may be used. Alternatively, stock may be transferred for the minor's benefit to a custodian account in which the parent may act as custodian. Most states allow such transfers.

In order to get the income-shifting benefits from setting up a stock custodian account, there must be a bona fide transfer of stock entailing a complete surrender by you of any control over the transferred stock.

EXAMPLE

Two owners of a beer distributorship operating as an S corporation sold all of their stock to their children. They had two objectives: (1) To shift income to the children, and (2) to avoid the limitations on pension plan contributions applied to shareholder-employees of S corporations. As stockholder-employees, they could contribute only a maximum of $2,500 to the company's pension plan; as non-shareholders, up to $5,700.

The plan failed because the fathers continued to run the corporation as if the stock transfers had not been made. As key employees and directors of the corporation, they retained complete control over the business. The children exercised no voice in corporate affairs. No custodian or guardian was appointed to represent the interests as stockholders of two of the children who were minors. Further, despite substantial company profits, the children received only a small amount as dividends, generally enough only to offset the inclusion of corporate income on their returns. On the other hand, the fathers continued to take sizable unsecured interest-free loans from the corporation as they had before the stock transfer.

With a partnership, shifting income may be more difficult, depending on whether capital is a material income producing factor in the business. If it is, a gift or sale of a partnership interest to a family member is effective. But in a service partnership—real estate or insurance brokers, for example—a mere gift of a partnership interest to a family member will not shift partnership income unless the person actually performs services for the partnership. In one case, the Tax Court held that where substantially all of a family partnership's capital consists of borrowed funds guaranteed by family members, the family partnership interests may be disregarded on the grounds that the borrowed funds are not a material income-producing factor in the business.

In an S corporation, pass-through items must reflect the value of services rendered or capital contributed by family members of the shareholders. If a relative of an S corporation shareholder performs services for the corporation or loans money to the corporation without receiving reasonable pay or interest, the IRS may allocate income to reflect the value of the services or capital provided. The term "family" of an individual includes only spouse, ancestors, lineal descendants, and any trusts for the primary benefit of such persons.

LIFE INSURANCE OFFERS TAX ADVANTAGES

¶ **33.10** Insurance may provide a tax free accumulation of cash. During the time you pay premiums, the value of your contract increases at compound interest rates. The increase is not subject to income tax. In addition, when your policy is paid at death, the proceeds are not subject to income tax.

Estate tax planning. To shelter life insurance proceeds from estate tax, you must not have ownership rights. If you have an existing policy, you must assign your ownership rights, such as the right to change beneficiaries, the right to surrender or cancel the policy, the right to assign it, and the right to borrow against it. An assignment must occur more than three years before death to exclude the proceeds from your estate.

If you are buying a new policy, you must buy the policy in another's name, such as in your spouse's name, or have your spouse buy the policy. For example, a wife bought a policy on her husband's life. She paid the

premiums from household funds. Although he provided household funds, she controlled their use, so there was no indirect premium payment by the husband. Proceeds of the policy were free of estate tax.

> Group insurance provided by an employer may be assigned. The IRS has agreed to follow a court decision holding that the power to convert a group policy into an individual policy when you leave the company will not subject the group-term insurance proceeds to estate tax. Since the conversion privilege is exercisable only by taking an economically disadvantageous step of quitting, this right is too remote to be considered a retained ownership right in the policy. If other incidents of ownership are transferred, such as the power to name beneficiaries and fix the type of benefit payable, the transfer will remove the policy from your estate.

The substitution of a new group carrier does not jeopardize assignments under a prior carrier.

When you plan to assign a policy, review your gift tax liability on such a transfer. In the case of an assignment of a group policy, the cost of the policy is determined by actuarially apportioning the employer's total premium payment among the covered employees. This is difficult for an individual employee to do, particularly where there are many employees, so the IRS generally allows employees to value the assigned policy using the same tax tables used to determine the amount of the employee's compensation where group coverage exceeds $50,000. *See* the tables at ¶2.5. Key employees may not use the table to determine gift tax liability.

EXAMPLE

An employee assigns his $80,000 group-term policy to a family trust. Several months later, when he is age 54, the employer pays the annual premium on the group policy. The value of the gift equals the annual cost of the $80,000 coverage as determined under the table at ¶2.5. Under the table, the value of the gift is $460.80. Gift tax may be avoided under the annual $10,000 gift tax exclusion.

You may want to readjust your coverage to meet new family conditions. You can exchange your policies without tax (*see* ¶12.20).

Using a trust to purchase insurance. If you create a trust to carry a policy on your life by transferring income-producing property the income of which is used to pay the premiums, you are taxable on the trust income. Similarly, if your spouse creates the trust to carry the policy on your life, he or she is taxable on the trust income. This tax rule does not apply to the trust funding of life insurance covering the life of a third party other than your spouse. For example, a grandparent transfers income-producing property to a trust to pay the premiums on a policy on the life of his son. His grandchildren are named trust beneficiaries. The grandparent is not taxed on the income earned by the trust on the transferred property because the trust purchased insurance on his son's life, not his own.

Insurance trust to receive proceeds. A trust may be used to receive insurance proceeds where there is concern that the beneficiary may be unable to manage a large insurance settlement. The trustee may be a bank or a person directed to invest the proceeds and pay income to beneficiaries according to standards provided in the trust. The trustee may be given the discretion to pay out more or less as circumstances warrant. He may be directed to terminate the trust when the beneficiaries reach a certain age, or when they demonstrate their ability to manage money. There may also be investment advantages in a trust. The trust investments may yield a higher rate of return than that of an insurance company under a settlement option.

Insurance proceeds are not subject to income tax whether paid directly to named beneficiaries or to a trust.

Single premium policies. Under current law, single premium policies can give you tax shelter opportunities. Companies offer competitive current return and tax free appreciation on your investment fund. The name of the policy is descriptive: You make a single premium payment—$5,000, $10,000, or $50,000 or more. Part of the premium goes for life insurance coverage and part towards an investment fund.

Two types of contracts are available:

Single-premium whole-life policy, under which the insurance company guarantees the principal. The initial return currently ranges from 7% to 8½% for one to three years. After the initial period, the return fluctuates.

Single-premium variable policy allows you to select an investment fund. Your principal is subject to market risks: If the investment fund makes money, the value of your fund appreciates; if not, the principal loses value.

You can also often borrow up to 90% of the cash value of the policy. You do not have to pay back the loan. At your death, the loan is deducted from the insurance proceeds payable to your beneficiaries.

If you are interested in a single premium policy, shop around. The terms and returns of each company differ.

Universal life insurance plans. Universal life insurance offers tax free buildup of interest income at current high market rates and on death, tax free receipt of insurance proceeds. A universal life insurance policy is made up of (1) life insurance protection and (2) a cash reserve on which interest income accumulates without tax.

Universal life insurance differs from regular whole life in that the interest rate of universal life is pegged to current bond market rates; whole life rates are low, currently about 5%. Further, a universal life policy lets you withdraw the cash reserve if you want to invest it elsewhere and to allocate how much of your premium payment is to cover insurance protection and how much is to go into the cash reserve.

The tax law sets limits to the amount of premiums that may be earmarked for the cash reserve. If these limits are violated, tax free treatment for the proceeds may be lost. For these limits, check with the company issuing the policy.

> *Disadvantage of universal life.* You must incur an up-front commission payment which may be 50% or more of the first premium. There may also be a fee for withdrawing the cash reserve. Therefore, before considering a universal plan, determine the possibility that the purchase of term insurance and an investment in money market funds or long-term bonds may be a better alternative to a universal life plan.

LOSSES MAY BE DISALLOWED ON SALES TO RELATED PERSONS

¶ 33.11 A loss on a sale to certain related taxpayers may not be deductible, even though you make the sale in good faith, the sale is involuntary (for example, a member of your family forecloses a mortgage on your property), or you sell through a public stock exchange and one of the related persons buys the equivalent property.

EXAMPLES

1. You sell 100 shares of A Co. stock to your brother for $1,000. They cost you $5,000. You may not deduct your $4,000 loss even though the sale was made in good faith.

2. The stock investments of a mother and son were managed by the same investment counselor. But neither the son nor mother had any right or control over each other's securities. The counselor followed separate and independent policies for each. Without the son's or his mother's prior approval, the counselor carried out the following trans-

actions: (1) On the same day he sold at a loss the son's stock in four companies and bought the same stock for the mother's account. (2) He sold at a loss the son's stock in a copper company, and 28 days later bought the same stock for his mother. The losses of the first sale were disallowed, but not the losses of the copper stock sale because of the time break of 28 days. However, the court did not say how much of a minimum time break is needed to remove a sale-purchase transaction from the rule disallowing losses between related parties.

Losses are not allowed on sales between the following members of a family: Brothers or sisters (whether by the whole or half blood), ancestors and lineal descendants are the only ones included. Loss is disallowed where the sale is made to your sister-in-law, as nominee of your brother. This sale is deemed to be between you and your brother. But you may deduct the loss on sales to your spouse's relative (for example, your brother-in-law or spouse's stepparent) even if you and your spouse file a joint return. One case allowed the loss on a direct sale to a son-in-law. Other cases disallowed losses upon withdrawal from a joint venture and from a partnership conducted by members of a family. Family members have argued that losses should be allowed because the sales were motivated by family hostility. The Tax Court ruled that family hostility may not be considered; losses between proscribed family members are disallowed in all cases.

Losses are not allowed on sales between an individual or partnership and a controlled corporation (where that individual or partnership owns more than 50% in value of the outstanding capital stock).

EXAMPLES

1. In calculating the stock owned, not only must the stock held in your own name be taken into account, but also that owned by your family. You also add (a) the proportionate share of any stock held by a corporation, estate, trust or partnership in which you are interested as a shareholder, beneficiary, or partner; and (b) the stock owned individually by your partner.

2. You may own 30% of the stock of a company. A trust in which you have a one-half beneficial interest owns 30%. Your partner owns 10% of the stock of the same company. You are deemed the owner of 55% of the stock of that company (30%, plus one-half of 30%, plus 10%).

3. If a father and four sons each owns 20% of the stock of a company *each* member is also deemed to own the stocks of all the others. A family includes brothers, sisters, spouses, ancestors, and lineal descendants.

Losses may also be disallowed in sales between controlled companies, a trust and its creator, a trust and a beneficiary, a partnership and a controlling person, or a tax-exempt organization and its founder. Check with your tax counselor whenever you plan to sell property at a loss to a buyer who may fit one of these descriptions.

Sometimes, the disallowed loss may be saved. Your purchaser gets the benefit of your disallowed loss if he sells at a gain. His gain up to the amount of your disallowed loss is not taxed.

EXAMPLE

Smith bought securities in 1960 which cost $10,000. In 1963, he sold them to his spouse for $8,000. The $2,000 loss is not deductible by Smith. His spouse's basis for the securities is $8,000. In 1984, she sells them for $9,000. The $1,000 gain is not taxed because it is washed out by part of the disallowed loss. If she sold securities for $11,000, then only $1,000 of the $3,000 gain would be taxed.

Sales between spouses are discussed at ¶6.49.

34

TAX POINTERS FOR SENIOR CITIZENS

¶ **34.1** *Increased standard deduction.* When you are 65 or older, you receive an increased standard deduction allowance, if you do not itemize deductions; *see* ¶13.4.

If you or your spouse's 65th birthday is on January 1, 1988, you claim the extra standard deduction amounts on your 1987 tax return. You are considered to be 65 on December 31, 1987.

Tax credit for the elderly. If you are age 65 or over, you may be entitled to a credit. *See* ¶34.2.

Tax free sale of your principal residence. If you are 55 or over and sold your principal residence at a gain, you may elect to avoid tax on up to $125,000 of profit, provided you meet certain tests and file an election. *See* ¶29.12 for details.

TAX CREDIT FOR THE ELDERLY AND DISABLED

¶ **34.2** In 1987, the credit for the elderly is available mainly to those persons 65 or over who do not receive Social Security or Railroad Retirement benefits or persons under 65 who are permanently and totally disabled and receive disability income. For example, if you are single or married but only you are eligible, are over 65 and receive more than $417 each month from Social Security, you may not claim the credit. If you are married and both you and your spouse are over 65 and file a joint return, you may not claim the credit if you receive more than $625 each month from Social Security. The amount of the credit is 15% times the "base amount" after reductions. For a single person, the tax credit for the elderly may be as high as $750; for a married couple, $1,125.

A married couple may claim the credit only if they file a joint return. However, if a husband and wife live apart at all times during the taxable year and file separately, the credit may be claimed on a separate return.

The credit for the elderly and disabled is combined with the credits for dependent care and mortgage credit certificates. The total credits may not exceed regular tax liability without the alternative minimum tax and self-employment tax and penalty taxes for premature retirement distributions. If you also claim a foreign tax credit, the credit for the elderly is deducted first from tax liability before computing the limitation on the foreign tax credit.

The credit is claimed on Schedule R.

WHO QUALIFIES FOR THE CREDIT?

¶ **34.3** You may qualify for the tax credit for the elderly if you meet one of the following conditions:

You are 65 or over before the close of 1987; or
under 65 and permanently and totally disabled and receiving disability income, *see* ¶34.5.

Nonresident aliens. You may not claim the credit if you are a nonresident alien at any time during 1987, unless you are married to a citizen or resident and you have elected to be treated as a resident (*see* ¶1.8).

Prior law allowed retirees from a public retirement system to claim the credit when they were under 65. This provision no longer applies to taxable years after 1983.

INITIAL BASE FOR THE CREDIT

¶ **34.4** The law fixes an initial base amount for figuring the credit. This base amount is reduced by certain tax free benefits and excess adjusted gross income (*see* ¶34.6). The credit is 15% of the base amount after reductions. You do not have to have retirement income to claim the credit.

The base amount is:
$5,000, if you are single.
$5,000, if you file a joint return and only one spouse is eligible for the credit.
$7,500, if you file a joint return and both spouses are eligible for the credit. The credit is figured solely on this base; no separate computation is made for each spouse.
$3,750, if you are married and file a separate return. The credit may be claimed on a separate return only if you and your spouse have lived apart at all times during the year.

INITIAL BASE FOR DISABLED PERSONS

¶ **34.5** If you are under 65 and disabled, the base for figuring the credit is the lower of your 1987 disability income or the initial base amount for your filing status in ¶34.4.

299

EXAMPLES

1. You are single, under 65, and permanently and totally disabled. You received disability income of $4,800. You figure the credit on $4,800, which is less than the base of $5,000 for single persons.

2. Same facts as in (1) above except your disability income is $7,000. You figure the credit on the initial base of $5,000 for singles.

Joint return and both spouses qualify for the credit. If one spouse is 65 or over and one spouse under 65 and receives disability income, the initial base amount is $5,000 plus the disability income of the spouse under 65 but not to exceed $7,500. If both spouses are under 65 and disabled, the initial base amount is the total of their disability income, but not to exceed $7,500.

Disability income is taxable wages or payments in lieu of wages paid while absent from work because of permanent and total disability.

You are considered permanently and totally disabled if you are unable to engage in any substantial gainful activity by reason of any medically determinable physical or mental impairment which can be expected to result in death or which has lasted or can be expected to last for a continuous period of not less than 12 months.

REDUCTION OF BASE AMOUNT

¶ 34.6 The base amount is reduced by the following items:

Social Security and Railroad Retirement benefits which are not taxable under rules of ¶34.8.

Tax free pension, annuity, or disability income paid under a law administered by Veterans' Administration.

Certain tax free pension or annuity income, and

One-half of adjusted gross income exceeding $7,500, if you are single; $10,000 if you are married filing a joint return; $5,000, if you are married and file a separate return. Applying these income floors, the credit is no longer available to a single person when his adjusted gross income reaches $17,500, $20,000 on a joint return where one spouse is age 65 or over, and $25,000, where both spouses are 65 or over.

EXAMPLE

You receive Social Security benefits of $6,000. If under the rules of ¶34.8, $1,500 of the benefits are taxable, only $4,500 of the benefits reduce the base amount.

You do not reduce the base amount for: military disability pensions received for active service in the Armed Forces or in the Coast and Geodetic Survey or Public Health Service; certain disability annuities paid under the Foreign Service Act of 1980; and worker's compensation benefits. However, if Social Security benefits are reduced by worker's compensation benefits, the amount of worker's compensation benefits is treated as Social Security benefits that reduce the base.

EXAMPLES

1. A single person over 65 has adjusted gross income (AGI) of $9,000 and receives Social Security benefits of $4,200 which are not taxable under ¶34.8. His credit is $7.50.

Initial base amount	$5,000
Less: Social Security	4,200
	800
Less 50% of AGI over $7,500	750
Credit base	$ 50
Credit (15%)	$ 7.50

2. A married couple over 65 files a joint return showing adjusted gross income of $12,000. They received tax free Social Security benefits of $5,000.

Initial base amount	$7,500
Less: Social Security	5,000
	2,500
Less: 50% of AGI over $10,000	1,000
Credit base	$1,500
Credit (15%)	$ 225

RETIRING ON SOCIAL SECURITY BENEFITS

¶ 34.7 Benefits are not paid automatically. You must register at the local Social Security office three months before your 65th birthday to allow time for your application to be processed and to locate all necessary information. Even if you do not plan to retire at age 65, you must register to insure your Medicare coverage.

If you retire before age 65, you may elect reduced Social Security benefits. The reduction formula is based on the number of months before age 65. If you retire at the earliest age, 62, the reduction is about 20%. By electing benefits at age 62, a person receives a larger total amount of benefits than the total payable from age 65 provided he or she does not live beyond the age of 77. After age 77, the total benefits paid to those retiring at age 65 is greater than the amount paid to those retiring at age 62.

If you do not retire at age 65, your potential Social Security benefit increases for each year you delay retirement. For those born in 1916 or earlier, the increase is 1% per year for each year of delayed retirement; for those born in 1917 through 1924, the increase is 3% per year. Larger credits for delayed retirement will be available for those born after 1924.

If you are under 70, Social Security benefits are reduced by earned income (wages and self-employment income). If you were 65 or older but under 70 in 1987, you could earn $8,160 without losing benefits. If you were under 65 for the whole year, you could earn $6,000 without losing benefits. These ceilings are subject to inflation adjustments. Once you earn more than these ceilings, benefits are reduced. For each $2 you earn, you lose $1 in benefits. A special monthly rule applies in the year you reach retirement age. After 1989, you will lose $1 in benefits for each $3 you earn above the earnings ceiling.

For those age 70 or over, benefits are not reduced by earnings. You can work, earn any amount, and receive full Social Security benefits.

So long as you continue to work, you pay Social Security taxes on your earnings, regardless of your age.

Regardless of your age, you may receive any amount of income from sources other than work, for example, private pensions or investments, without affecting the amount of Social Security retirement benefits. However, benefits may be taxable if your income exceeds the limits discussed in ¶34.8.

Keep a record of credits. The Social Security Administration has been criticized for not keeping up with workers' earnings records. Do not risk a problem by ignoring your record. At least once every three years, you should mail Form SSA-7004, Request for Statement of Earnings, to the Social Security Administration, Wilkes-Barre Data Operations Center, P.O. Box 20, Wilkes Barre, PA 18703. This form is available at your local Social Security office and the headquarters in Baltimore. You will receive a response in about six weeks.

Social Security forms state that if you wait more than three years, three months and 15 days after an error is discovered to request a correction, a change may not be possible. The agency waived the deadline in 1981 since it had fallen behind in its record keeping, but you should still try to correct any errors immediately.

If you are age 55 or older, your local Social Security office can give you an estimate of your retirement benefits.

HOW SOCIAL SECURITY BENEFITS ARE TAXED

¶ 34.8 If you received or repaid Social Security benefits in 1987, you should receive Form SSA-1099 by February 1, 1988. The form will show the total of paid or repaid benefits. Amounts withheld for Medicare premiums, worker's compensation offset, or attorney's fees are itemized and included in the total benefits you received. Keep Form SSA-1099 for your records; do not attach it to your return.

The *net benefit* shown on Form SSA-1099 (benefits paid less benefits repaid) is the benefit amount used in the following computations to determine taxable benefits.

Part of your net Social Security benefits may be subject to tax if your income exceeds a base amount. The maximum taxable amount is 50% of benefits.

There are two steps in figuring the taxation of Social Security benefits: (1) Figuring whether your income exceeds a base amount for your filing status. (2) Figuring the amount of benefits subject to tax.

Step 1. Start with adjusted gross income (*see* ¶13.8). Add to it 50% of your net Social Security benefits (amount received less amount repaid, if any), tax free interest income, excluded foreign earned income (¶36.3), excluded income from U.S. possessions (¶36.10) and Puerto Rico (¶36.11).

Part of your Social Security benefits are taxable if the total of adjusted gross income plus the other items in step (1) exceed $25,000 and you are single, or $32,000 and you are married filing jointly.

EXAMPLES

1. You are married and have dividend and interest income of $28,000 and tax-exempt interest of $2,000. Your net Social Security benefits are $4,000 and you file a joint return.

Adjusted gross income		$28,000
Plus: Tax-exempt interest	$2,000	
50% of benefits	2,000	4,000
		$32,000
Less: Base amount		32,000
		0

Your benefits are not taxable.

2. Same as in (1) above except your Social Security benefits are $8,000.

Adjusted gross income		$28,000
Plus: Tax-exempt interest	$2,000	
50% of benefits	4,000	6,000
		$34,000
Less: Base amount		32,000
Excess		$ 2,000

Part of your benefits are subject to tax under the rules of Step 2.

Step 2. The amount of benefits subject to tax is 50% of the excess over the base amount or 50% of benefits, whichever is less.

EXAMPLE

In example (2) above, $1,000 of benefits are subject to tax because 50% of the excess over the base amount (50% of $2,000) is less than 50% of benefits (50% of $8,000).

Married filing separately. If you are married and file a separate return, the base amount is zero so that one half of your benefits is subject to tax regardless of their amount or the amount of your other income. However, if you live apart from your spouse at all times during the year and file separately, the $25,000 base applies.

SOCIAL SECURITY BENEFITS SUBJECT TO TAX

¶ 34.9 Social Security benefits subject to tax include your monthly retirement, survivor, or disability benefits. Monthly Tier 1 Railroad Retirement benefits are divided into two parts: One part may be treated as Social Security benefits and is identified on Form RRB-1099 as the Social Security equivalent portion of the Tier 1 benefit; the other part is treated as pension income and like Tier 2 Railroad Retirement benefits is not treated as Social Security benefits subject to tax. If any part of your 1987 Tier 1 benefits is equivalent to Social Security benefits, you should receive Form RRB-1099 from the government by February 1, 1988. Otherwise, you should receive Form RRB-W-2P.

Social Security benefits are not reduced by withholdings for supplementary medical insurance. Your Form SSA-1099 includes the withholdings in total benefits.

Benefits paid on behalf of child or incompetent. If a child is entitled to Social Security benefits, such as after the death of a parent, the benefit is considered to be the child's regardless of who actually receives the payment. Whether the child's benefit is subject to tax will depend on the amount of the child's income.

Workmen's compensation. If you are receiving Social Security disability payments and Workmen's Compensation for the same disability, your Social Security benefits may be reduced by the workmen's compensation. For example, you are entitled to Social Security disability benefits of $5,000 a year. After receiving a $1,000 workmen's compensation award, your disability benefits are reduced to $4,000. For purposes of the 50% of benefits rule, you treat the full $5,000 as Social Security benefits.

Repayment of benefits. If you forfeit part of your Social Security benefits because of excessive outside income, the forfeited amount reduces your benefits for purposes of the 50% inclusion rule. You make the reduction even if the forfeit relates to benefits received in a prior year. For example, your regular 1987 benefit of $5,000 is reduced by $1,000 because of earnings of the prior year. For tax purposes, your 1987 benefits are considered $4,000.

If in 1987, Social Security benefits were subject to tax and in 1988 you must repay 1987 benefits that were taxed, you first reduce 1988 benefits by the amount of repayment. If the repayment exceeds 1988 benefits, you may claim the excess as an itemized deduction. If the repayment exceeds $3,000, you may follow the rules of ¶2.15.

Taxable Social Security benefits may not be the basis of an IRA contribution (¶8.2), earned income credit (¶24.10), or foreign earned income exclusion (¶36.3).

You will receive an information return reporting the amount of benefits received during the year.

In the following chart, the second column lists how much income (*including tax-exempt interest*) you may receive before benefits become taxable. The last column lists the levels at which 50% of benefits become taxable.

Single

Monthly Social Security benefits	No benefits taxed unless other income exceeds—	50% of benefits taxed if other income is at least—
$ 300	$23,200	$26,800
350	22,900	27,100
400	22,600	27,400
450	22,300	27,700
500	22,000	28,000
550	21,700	28,300
600	21,400	28,600
650	21,100	28,900
700	20,800	29,200
750	20,500	29,500
800	20,200	29,800
850	19,900	30,100
900	19,600	30,400
950	19,300	30,700
1,000	19,000	31,000

Married filing jointly

Monthly Social Security benefits	No benefits taxed unless other income exceeds—	50% of benefits taxed if other income is at least—
$ 700	$27,800	$36,200
750	27,500	36,500
800	27,200	36,800
850	26,900	37,100
900	26,600	37,400
950	26,300	37,700
1,000	26,000	38,000
1,050	25,700	38,300
1,100	25,400	38,600
1,150	25,100	38,900
1,200	24,800	39,200
1,250	24,500	39,500
1,300	24,200	39,800
1,350	23,900	40,100
1,400	23,600	40,400

Nonresident aliens. A special rule applies to Social Security and Tier 1 Railroad Retirement benefits received by nonresident aliens. Unless provided otherwise by tax treaty, one half of a nonresident alien's Social

Security benefits will be subject to the 30% withholding tax imposed on U.S. source income that is not connected with a U.S. trade or business (¶37.4).

ELECTION FOR LUMP-SUM BENEFIT PAYMENT COVERING PRIOR YEARS

¶ **34.10** If in 1987 you receive a lump-sum payment of benefits covering prior years, you have a choice: (1) you may treat the entire payment as taxable under the rules of ¶34.8 in 1987 or (2) you may allocate the benefits over the taxable years in which they were payable. The payer will notify you of the years covered by the payments.

When you elect to allocate benefits to a prior year, you do not amend the return for that year. You compute the increase in income (if any) that would have resulted if the Social Security benefits had been received in that year. You then add that amount to the income of the current year.

EXAMPLE

In 1986, you apply for Social Security disability benefits but the Social Security office rules you are ineligible. You appeal and are awarded benefits. In 1987, you receive a lump-sum payment of $8,000 ($3,000 for 1986 and $5,000 for 1987). You may include the $8,000 benefit in 1987 to figure if Social Security benefits are taxable, or you may elect to treat $3,000 of benefits as received in 1986 and $5,000 in 1987. You make the election and figure that in 1986 the inclusion of the award would have resulted in an increase of income of $1,000. You add the $1,000 plus taxable 1987 benefits to your 1987 income. You may not revoke the election unless the IRS consents.

HOW TAX ON SOCIAL SECURITY REDUCES YOUR EXTRA EARNINGS

¶ **34.11** There is an added tax cost of earning income if the earnings will subject your Social Security benefits to tax. Therefore, if your benefits are not currently exposed to tax, you have to figure *not only* the tax on the extra income *but also* the amount of Social Security benefits subjected to tax by those earnings. You should be concerned with the tax cost of extra earnings when your other income is no more than the base amount applied to your status ($25,000 or $32,000) less 50% of your Social Security benefits. If your income is equal to the base amount plus 50% of your Social Security benefits, earning extra pay will not affect the tax on the benefits as the benefits are already subject to tax, even if you do not earn the extra amount.

EXAMPLES

1. You are over 70 and planning to work part-time. You and your spouse receive Social Security benefits of $8,000. Your adjusted gross income before adding 50% of Social Security benefits is $28,000. At this point, no part of your Social Security benefits are taxable.

Adjusted gross income	$28,000
Plus: 50% of benefits	4,000
	32,000
Less: Base	32,000
No excess	–0–

2. Same as in (1) above except that you plan to earn up to $8,000 from a part-time job. The $8,000 will subject $4,000 of Social Security benefits to tax.

Other income	$28,000
Part-time earnings	8,000
	$36,000
50% of benefits	4,000
	$40,000
Less: Base	32,000
Excess	$ 8,000
50% of excess taxable	$ 4,000

Thus, for every dollar of extra earnings above the $32,000 or $25,000 base, 50¢ of your Social Security benefits are taxable. Here, earnings of $8,000 subject $4,000 of Social Security benefits to tax.

If you are under 70, you must also consider that Social Security benefits may be reduced by earnings from a job or self-employment; see ¶34.7.

If you earn extra pay, making a deductible IRA contribution can reduce your income to avoid or reduce a tax on your Social Security benefits.

EXAMPLE

Your other income is $26,000 and your Social Security benefits are $8,000. You have part-time earnings of $4,000. If you make a deductible $2,000 IRA contribution, you will avoid tax on Social Security benefits.

Other Income	$26,000
Earnings	4,000
	$30,000
Less IRA	2,000
	$28,000
Plus 50% of benefit	4,000
Less base	32,000
No excess	–0–

For when you can make deductible IRA contributions, *see* ¶8.

35

TAX SAVINGS FOR VETERANS AND MEMBERS OF THE ARMED FORCES

¶ **35.1** New Law Pointers.

1. *Time period for residence replacements.* If you are a member of the Armed Forces stationed outside the United States or required to reside in quarters on base following your return from a tour of duty outside the United States, the time allowed to defer tax on the sale of your old home has been extended. You now have until one year after the last day you are stationed outside the U.S. or required to reside in quarters on base to buy a new home and defer the tax on the gain from the sale of the old home. The replacement period, plus the period of suspension, is limited to eight years from date of the sale of your old home. The new rule applies to deferment of gain on the sale of an old residence after July 18, 1984; *see* chapter 29.

2. *Relief provisions for those missing in action (MIAs) in the Vietnam conflict have been retroactively reinstated and made permanent for tax years beginning after 1982.* Under these retroactive provisions the following rules apply:

—For purposes of determining whether a widow (or widower) with a dependent child may apply joint return rates, the date of death of a Vietnam MIA is the date determined by the Armed Forces. Joint return rates may be used if a spouse died in either of the two previous years; *see* ¶35.8.

—The income of a Vietnam MIA is exempt from tax for the year in which the determination of death was made and for any prior year that ends on or after the first day that the individual served in a combat zone, *see* ¶35.8.

—A spouse may elect to file a joint return for any taxable year their spouse is in Vietnam MIA status.

—The spouse of a Vietnam MIA may postpone filing a return and paying taxes because of the MIA's combat zone service.

If application of these rules entitles you to a refund, file Form 1040X; *see* chapter 27.

EXTENSION TO PAY YOUR TAX WHEN ENTERING THE SERVICE

¶ **35.2** If you are unable to pay your tax when you enter the Armed Forces, you may get an extension until six months after your initial period of service ends. File your return by April 15, 1988, and get a form at the office of your District Director of Internal Revenue, or write a letter to the District Director (your spouse or parent may do it for you). An extension may be given if payment involves hardship, *and* you actually apply for it.

The extension does not cover your spouse who must file a separate return and pay the tax due. But you and your spouse may file a joint return before the postponement period expires even though your spouse filed a separate return for that particular year. No interest is charged on this postponement of your tax.

Automatic extension of time to file your return. If you are on duty outside the U.S. or Puerto Rico on April 15, 1988, you get an automatic two-month extension to file your return. See ¶27.7.

DISABILITY RETIREMENT PAY

¶ **35.3** Your disability retirement pay may be tax free if you are a former member of the Armed Forces of any country, the Coast Guard, National Oceanic and Atmospheric Administration, or the Public Health Service. For details, *see* ¶2.20.

Tax free treatment of disability retirement pay is retroactive to the date of the application for the benefits.

Readjustment payments to reservists are discussed at ¶35.6.

YOU DO NOT REPORT THIS INCOME

¶ **35.4** The following items need not be reported as income by veterans or members of the Armed Forces:

Adjustments in pay to compensate for losses resulting from inflated foreign currency.

Allotments for dependents. Neither the serviceman nor his dependents are taxed on the government's contribution. But the serviceman may not deduct his contribution from his gross income.

Allowance to an officer for unusual expenses incurred for food and lodgings pending assignment at an overseas station.

Amounts received by former prisoners of war from the U.S. Government in compensation for inhumane treatment suffered at the hands of an enemy government.

Benefits under Servicemen's Group Life Insurance.

Bonuses paid by any state or political subdivision for military service.

Combat pay; *see* ¶35.7.

Death gratuity payments (six months' pay to beneficiaries of servicemen who died in active service).

Dividends on G.I. insurance are not taxed. Many veterans and members of the Armed Forces receive dividend checks on their National Life Insurance. This is merely a return of premiums paid. Nor are the dividends from the U.S. Government Life Insurance (World War I insurance) taxed. Interest on dividends left on deposit is taxed.

Education, training, or subsistence allowances paid under any law administered by the Veterans' Administration. However, deductible education costs must be reduced by the VA allowance.

Family separation allowance received because of overseas assignments.

Grants for homes designed for wheelchair living.

Grants for motor vehicles for veterans who lost their sight or the use of their limbs.

Government endowment policy proceeds paid before the death of the veteran.

Housing and cost-of-living allowances to cover excess cost of quarters and subsistence while on permanent duty outside U.S., whether paid by U.S. government or by government of country in which stationed.

Medical or hospital treatment provided by the United States in government hospitals.

Moving and storage expenses furnished in kind (or reimbursement or allowance for such expenses) to a member on active duty where the move is pursuant to a military order and incident to a permanent change of station.

Mustering-out pay.

Naval attaché's expense money, if used solely in connection with official duties.

Pay forfeited on order of a court martial.

Reduction in retirement benefits to provide survivor annuities. Rental allowance where quarters are not furnished in kind.

Subsistence allowance where subsistence is not furnished in kind and per diem allowance in lieu of subsistence. (However, you are taxed on mileage and per diem subsistence allowance while in travel status or on temporary duty.)

Uniform allowances of officers.

Uniforms furnished.

Veterans' Administration death benefits to families of deceased veterans.

See also the checklist beginning at chapter 40.

YOU MAY DEDUCT

¶ **35.5** Members of the Armed Services may deduct the following items on their returns:

Board and lodging costs over those paid you by the government while on temporary duty away from your home base.

Costs of rank insignia, collar devices, gold braid, etc. The cost of altering rank insignia when promoted or demoted is also deductible.

Cleaning costs of fatigues are deductible if: (1) The fatigues are required to be worn on duty; (2) they cannot under military regulations be worn off duty; (3) the cost and maintenance of the fatigues exceed any tax free clothing allowance received by you.

Contributions to "Company" fund made according to Service regulations. But personal contributions made to stimulate interest and morale in a unit are not deductible.

Court martial legal expenses in successfully defending against the charge of conduct unbecoming an officer and a gentleman.

Dues to professional societies. But you cannot deduct dues for officers' and noncommissioned officers' clubs.

Expense of obtaining increased retirement pay.

Out-of-pocket moving expenses for service connected moves (without meeting either the 35-mile test or the 39-week test).

Subscriptions to professional journals.

Transportation, food and lodging expenses while in official travel status. But you are taxed on mileage and per diem subsistence allowance.

Travel expenses while ship or squadron is away from home post or base. However, a serviceman is not considered "away from home" if he is at his *permanent* duty station or is a naval officer assigned to *permanent* duty aboard a ship. *See also* ¶ 19.26.

Travel expense of reserve personnel where required to be away from home overnight for authorized drill for which they are paid.

In addition, you may deduct all the expenses and losses permitted other persons. (*See* the checklist beginning at chapter 41.)

TAX INFORMATION FOR RESERVISTS

¶ **35.6** **Transportation costs.** If you attend prescribed drills under competent orders, you may deduct the round-trip transportation

costs if the drills are held outside your city or general area in which you work.

If the drills are held within your city or in the general area in which you work on a day you work, you deduct only the one-way cost of traveling between the location of your regular job and the location of the drill even if you first go home for dinner. Do not deduct the cost of the return trip home or the cost of traveling to drill on a day you are not working.

The transportation costs are deductible as miscellaneous deductions and are subject to the 2% adjusted gross income floor.

Readjustment payments. Amounts received by reservists involuntarily released from active duty as readjustment payments are taxed income. If the reservist becomes entitled to retirement pay, he is taxed on only the remainder of the retirement pay after its required reduction by an amount equal to 75% of any readjustment payment previously received.

> **Uniform costs.** You deduct the cost and maintenance of uniforms that you wear at drills or on temporary duty. If you received a tax free uniform allowance, reduce the deduction by the amount of the allowance. Servicemen on full-time duty may not deduct their uniform costs.

TAX FREE COMBAT PAY

¶ **35.7** The combat pay exclusion applies to income earned by a serviceman in a combat zone. Military personnel below the rank of commissioned officer serving in a combat zone are not taxed on any part of their active duty pay, or on pay received while hospitalized as a result of a combat zone wound, disease, or injury. The tax free exclusion for commissioned officers' pay is limited to $500 a month.

The exclusion for a hospitalized serviceman may generally apply during a two-year period after the end of combat.

TAX ABATEMENT FOR MILITARY PERSONNEL KILLED IN ACTION

¶ **35.8** If a member of the Armed Forces is killed in a combat zone or dies from wounds or disease incurred while in a combat zone, any income tax liability for the year of death is waived. In addition, his estate is entitled to a refund for income tax paid by him after he began serving in a combat zone.

If a member of the Armed Forces was a resident of a community property state and his wife reported half of his military pay on a separate return, she may get a refund of taxes paid on her share of his pay for the years he served in a combat zone.

Determination of death for Vietnam MIAs. Under the 1986 Tax Act, the date of death of servicemen missing in action in Vietnam is the date determined by the Armed Forces. Under prior law, MIAs were generally presumed dead as of December 31, 1982. Thus, under the new law, tax abatement may be available for years after 1982. Further, the date of death, as determined by the Armed Forces, also applies for such rules as whether to file as a surviving spouse, and for postponing the due date for filing returns and paying taxes.

Tax abatement for civilian or military personnel killed in terroristic or military action. Tax liability is waived for civilian or military personnel killed in terroristic or military actions outside the U.S. even if the President has not designated the area a combat zone. Tax liability is waived for the period beginning with the last taxable year before the year in which the injuries were incurred and ending with the year of death. The individual must also be a U.S. employee both on the date of injury and date of death.

EXAMPLE
On August 11, 1987, a soldier is killed in a terroristic attack over-

seas; tax liability on the soldier's income is waived for both 1986 and 1987.

Tax abatement does not apply to a U.S. civilian or military employee who dies as a result of an accident or a training exercise. Abatement also does not apply to terroristic action within the United States. However, abatement does apply if the individual dies in the U.S. from a wound or injury incurred in a terroristic or military action outside the United States.

STATE INCOME TAX WITHHOLDING

¶ 35.9 A state that makes a withholding agreement with the Secretary of the Treasury may subject members of the Armed Forces regularly stationed within that state to its payroll withholding provisions. National guardsmen and reservists are not considered to be members of the Armed Forces for purposes of this section.

36

HOW TO TREAT FOREIGN INCOME

¶ 36.1 New Tax Law Pointers:

1. The foreign earned income exclusion is reduced from $80,000 to $70,000.
2. You may not claim the exclusion if you work in areas subject to U.S. government travel restrictions, such as Libya, Cuba, Vietnam, Cambodia, and North Korea.
3. The exclusion for possession income has been revised and the application of new rules may depend on agreements made between foreign tax jurisdictions and the Treasury.

4. U.S. employees of the Panama Canal Commission are not exempt from U.S. taxes. Prior to the new law, courts had split over whether employees of the Panama Canal Commission could avoid U.S. taxes on their wages. The new law provides that the wages are taxable, even for years before the effective date of the new law. However, starting in 1987, U.S. employees of the Panama Canal Commission and civilian employees of the Defense Department in Panama may exclude from income allowances which are comparable to the tax free allowances received by State Department employees stationed in Panama.

RULES FOR REPORTING FOREIGN INCOME

¶ 36.2 In 1987, up to $70,000 of your foreign earned income may be tax free, if you satisfy a foreign residence or physical presence test. In addition, if you are an employee, you may claim an exclusion for housing expenses; if you are self-employed, you may deduct certain housing costs (see ¶ 36.4).

You must file a U.S. return if your gross income meets the filing limits for your personal status, even though all or part of your foreign earned income may be tax free. You claim the foreign earned income exclusion on Form 2555, which you attach to Form 1040.

A separate exclusion is allowed for the value of meals and lodging received by employees living in qualified camps (¶ 36.9).

If you claim the foreign earned income exclusion of $70,000, you may not:

Claim foreign taxes paid on the excluded income as a credit or deduction;
Claim business deductions allocable to the excluded income; or

Make a deductible IRA contribution based on the excluded income.

In deciding whether to claim the exclusion, compare the overall tax (1) with the exclusion and (2) without the exclusion but with the full foreign tax credit and allocable deductions. Choose whichever gives you the lower tax.

See ¶ 36.3 and ¶ 36.7.

CLAIMING THE FOREIGN EARNED INCOME EXCLUSION

¶ 36.3 You may elect the exclusion for foreign earned income only if your tax home is in a foreign country *and* you meet (1) the foreign residence test or (2) the foreign physical presence test of 330 days discussed at ¶ 36.6. Tax home is discussed at ¶ 19.26. If your tax home is in the U.S., you may not claim the exclusion but may claim the foreign tax credit and your living expenses while away from home if you meet the rules at ¶ 19.29.

If you are married and you and your spouse each have foreign earned income and meet the foreign residence or physical presence test, you may each claim a separate exclusion. If your permanent home is in a community property state, your earned income is not considered community property for purposes of the exclusion.

If you qualify under the foreign residence or physical presence test for only part of 1987, the exclusion is reduced on a daily basis.

EXAMPLES

1. You were a resident of France from February 20, 1985, until June 30, 1987, when you returned to the U.S. Since your period of foreign residency included all of 1986, thereby satisfying the foreign residence test, you may claim a prorated exclusion for 1987. As you were abroad for 182 of the 365 days in 1987, you exclude earnings up to 182/365 of the maximum exclusion. If you earned $60,000 from January through June 1987, you would exclude $34,904 ($70,000 × 182/365).

2. You worked in France from June 1, 1986, through September 30, 1987. Your only days outside of France were a 15-day vacation to the U.S. in December 1986. You do not qualify for an exclusion under the foreign residence test because you were not abroad for a full taxable year; you were not abroad for either the full year of 1986 or 1987. You *do* qualify under the physical presence test; you were physically present abroad for at least 330 full days during a 12-month period. The 12-month period giving you the largest 1987 exclusion is the 12-month period starting October 21, 1986, and ending October 20, 1987. *See* ¶36.6 for figuring the 12-month period. Since you were abroad for at least 330 full days during that 12-month period, you may claim an exclusion. In 1987, you were abroad for 293 days within the 12-month period (January 1 to October 20, 1987, is 293 days). Thus, you exclude earnings up to 293/365 of the maximum exclusion. If your earnings in France for 1987 were $70,000, your exclusion is limited to $56,192 ($70,000 × 293/365).

> The exclusion of foreign earned income is not automatic. You elect the exclusion on Form 2555. An election made for a prior year automatically applies in 1987 and future years unless you revoke it. IRS permission is not required for a revocation, but if you do revoke without IRS consent, you may not make another election for five years unless the IRS consents to it.

Foreign earnings from a prior year. Foreign income earned in a prior year but paid in 1987 does not qualify for the 1987 exclusion. However, if the income was attributable to foreign services performed in 1986, the pay is tax free provided you did not use the full 1986 exclusion of $80,000 in 1986. If the services were performed before 1986, no exclusion is available to shelter the pay.

Income for services performed in the U.S. does not qualify for the exclusion, even though it is paid to you while you are abroad.

Foreign tax credit. Foreign taxes paid on tax free foreign earned income do not qualify for a credit or deduction. But if your foreign pay exceeds $70,000, you may claim a foreign tax credit or deduction for the foreign taxes allocated to taxable income. The instructions to Forms 2555 and 1116 and IRS Publication 514 provide details for making the computation.

Countries subject to travel restrictions. You may not claim the exclusion if you work in a country subject to U.S. government travel restrictions. You are not treated as a bona fide resident of, or as present in, a country subject to the travel ban.

HOW TO TREAT HOUSING COSTS

¶ 36.4 The housing costs of employees and self-employed persons are treated differently by the tax law. Employees get a housing exclusion; self-employed persons a deduction from *taxable* foreign earned income. If you live in a special camp provided by your employer, all housing costs are excluded; see ¶36.9.

Exclusion for employer-financed housing costs. If the total of your foreign wage or salary income plus the value of employer-financed housing costs in 1987 does not exceed $70,000, both parts of your pay package are tax free. Your housing costs are considered to be employer-financed as long as they are covered by salary, employer-reimbursements, a housing allowance, or if they are paid directly by your employer. If the total exceeds $70,000, a special housing exclusion will shelter part of your housing costs from tax. The housing exclusion is the difference between the employer's payment of reasonable housing expenses and a "base housing amount." The base housing amount is 16% of the salary for a U.S. government employee at the GS-14, Step 1 level as of the beginning of the year (the 1987 base amount may be found in Form 2555). If you qualify under the foreign residence or physical presence test for only part of 1987, the base housing amount is reduced on a daily basis. Follow instructions to Form 2555. The housing cost exclusion is elected on Form 2555. Employer housing payments exceeding this housing cost exclusion may also escape tax if your foreign salary is below the maximum foreign earned income exclusion; *see* example (1) below. That part of the foreign earned income exclusion not applied to your salary may be applied to housing costs.

On Form 2555, you figure the housing exclusion before the foreign earned income exclusion. The earned income exclusion is limited to the excess of foreign earned income over the housing exclusion.

EXAMPLES

1. In 1987 your salary for work abroad is $59,759 and your employer pays $10,759 for your housing. The total amount of salary and housing costs is tax free. On Form 2555, you list $70,518 (salary plus housing) as your foreign earned income. Assume that the housing cost exclusion is $3,650 (housing costs of $10,759 exceeding a base housing amount of $7,109). Your earned income exclusion is $66,868: $70,518 earned income–$3,650 housing exclusion.

2. In 1987 you earn $62,000 abroad and your employer pays $10,759 for your housing. Assume the housing cost exclusion is $3,650 (housing costs of $10,759 exceeding a base housing amount of $7,109). All of your salary plus the full amount of the housing costs avoids tax: the housing cost exclusion of $3,650 and an earned income exclusion of $69,109 ($72,759 foreign earned income less $3,650 housing exclusion).

3. Same as example (2) above except that you earn $65,000. Foreign earned income is $75,759 ($65,000 plus $10,759), but the total amount of income not subject to tax is $73,650. The total tax free amount is made up of the housing cost exclusion of $3,650 and the maximum foreign earned income exclusion of $70,000.

Reasonable housing expenses of your spouse and dependents living with you include rent, utilities, insurance, parking, furniture rentals, and repairs. The following expenses do not qualify: cost of purchasing a home, furniture, or accessories, home improvements, payments of mortgage principal, domestic labor, and depreciation on a home or on improvements to leased housing. Further, interest and taxes which are otherwise deductible do not qualify for the exclusion.

You may include the costs of a separate household that you maintain outside the U.S. for your spouse and dependents because living conditions at your foreign home are adverse.

Self-employed persons. Self-employed individuals may claim a limited deduction for housing costs exceeding the base housing amount. You may claim this deduction only to the extent it offsets taxable foreign earned income.

EXAMPLES

1. In 1987, you are self-employed and have foreign earnings of $100,000 and qualifying housing expenses of $20,000 in excess of the base amount. You may deduct the expenses of $20,000 from $30,000 of taxable foreign earned income ($100,000 less $70,000 exclusion).

2. Same as in (1) above except that your earnings are $70,000. You may not deduct any housing costs. You have no taxable foreign earned income as your earnings are fully excluded.

Where you may not deduct expenses because you do not have taxable foreign earned income, expenses may be carried forward one year and deducted in the next year to the extent of taxable foreign earned income. The deduction may be claimed whether or not you itemize deductions.

If you are employed and self-employed during the same year. Housing expenses above the base amount are partly excludable and partly deductible. For example, if half of your foreign earned income is from services as an employee, half of the excess housing expenses are excludable. The remaining excess housing costs are deductible to the extent of taxable foreign earned income. Follow the instructions to Form 2555.

Countries ineligible for tax benefits. Housing expenses incurred in a country subject to a U.S. government travel restriction are not eligible for the tax benefits explained above.

WHAT IS FOREIGN EARNED INCOME?

¶ **36.5** Earned income includes salaries, wages, commissions, professional fees, and bonuses. Earned income also includes allowances from your employer for housing or other expenses, as well as the value of housing or a car provided by the employer. It may also include business profits, royalties, and rents, provided this income is tied to the performance of services. Earned income does not include pension or annuity income, payments for nonqualified employee trusts or nonqualified annuities, dividends, interest, capital gains, gambling winnings, alimony, or the value of tax free meals or lodging under the rules at ¶2.2. Foreign earned income does not include amounts earned in countries subject to U.S. government travel restrictions.

If you are an employee of the U.S. government or its agencies, you may not exclude any part of your pay from your government employer. If you are not an employee of the U.S. government or any of its agencies, your pay is excludable even if paid by a government source. You are not an employee of the U.S. if you work under a contract made between your employer and the government.

Under a special law, tax liability is waived for a civilian or military employee of the U.S. government killed in a military action overseas; *see* ¶35.8.

Foreign earned income eligible for the exclusion must be received no later than the taxable year after the year in which you perform the services. Pay is excludable in the year of receipt if you did not use the full exclusion in the year of the services.

Profits from sole proprietorship or partnership. If your business consists solely of services (no capital investment), 100% of net profits is considered earned income. If services and capital are both income-producing factors, no more than 30% of your net profit may be considered earned income.

If you do not contribute any services to a business (for example, you are a "silent partner"), your share of the net profits is *not* earned income.

EXAMPLES
1. A U.S. citizen resides in England. He invests in an English partnership that sells manufactured goods outside the U.S. He performs no services for the business. His share of net profits does not qualify as earned income.
2. Same facts as (1) above, except he devotes his full time to the partnership business. Then 30% of his share of the net profits qualifies as earned income. Thus, if his share of profits is $50,000, earned income is $15,000 (30% of $50,000).
3. You and another person are consultants, operating as a partnership in Europe. Since capital is not an income-producing element, the entire net profits of the business are earned income.

The partnership agreement generally determines the tax status of partnership income in a U.S. partnership with a foreign branch. Thus, if the partnership agreement allocates foreign earnings to partners abroad, the allocation will be recognized unless it lacks substantial economic effect.

Fringe benefits. The value of fringe benefits, such as the right to use company property and facilities, is added to your compensation when figuring the amount of your earned income.

Royalties. Royalties from articles or books may be earned income depending on your royalty agreement. If you write a book and sell the manuscript or "lease" your rights to the book, the royalties are not earned income. However, if you contract to write a book for an amount in cash plus a commission on any sales, your receipts under the contract are earned income.

Royalties from the leasing of oil and mineral lands and from patents are not earned income.

Rental income. Rental income is generally not earned income. However, if you perform personal services, such as an owner-manager of a hotel or rooming house in a foreign country, then up to 30% of your net rents may be earned income.

Reimbursement of employee expenses. Do not include reimbursement of expenses in earned income to the extent they equal expenses which you adequately accounted for to your employer; *see* ¶19.51. If your expenses exceed reimbursements, the excess is allocated according to the rules in ¶36.7. If reimbursements exceed expenses, the excess is treated as earned income.

Straight commission salespersons or other employees who arrange with their employers, for withholding purposes, to consider a percentage of their commissions as attributable to their expenses, treat such amounts as earned income.

Reimbursed moving expenses. Employer reimbursement of moving expenses must be reported on your return in the year of receipt. However, for purposes of claiming the earned income exclusion, the reimbursement may be considered to have been earned in a different year. This is important because an exclusion is allowed only for the year income is earned. If the move is from the U.S. to a foreign country, the reimbursement is considered foreign earned income in the year of the move, if you qualify under the foreign residence or physical presence test for at least 120 days during that tax year. Reimbursement of moving expenses from one foreign country to another is considered foreign earned income in the year of the move, if you qualify under the residency or physical presence test at the new location for at least 120 days during the tax year. If you do not meet one of these tests in the year of the move, the reimbursements are earned income which must be allocated between the year of the move and the following tax year.

Employer reimbursements for moves back to the U.S. are considered income from U.S. sources if you continue to work for the same employer. If you move back to the U.S. and take a job with a new employer, or if you retire and move back to the U.S. and your old employer reimburses your moving expenses under a prior written agreement or company policy, the reimbursement is considered to be for past services in the foreign country and qualifies as foreign earned income eligible for the exclusion. The reimbursement is considered earned in the year of the move if you qualified under the residency or physical presence test for at least 120 days during the tax year. Otherwise, the reimbursement is allocated between the year of the move and the year preceding the move. *See* IRS Publication 54 for details.

MEETING THE FOREIGN RESIDENCE OR PHYSICAL PRESENCE TEST

¶ **36.6** To qualify for the foreign earned income exclusion, you must be either a U.S. citizen meeting the foreign residence test or a U.S. citizen or resident meeting the physical presence test in a foreign country. The following areas are not considered foreign countries: Puerto Rico, U.S. Virgin Islands, Guam, Northern Mariana Islands, any possession of the United States, or the Antarctic region.

If war or civil unrest prevented you from meeting the foreign residence or physical presence test, you may claim the exclusion for the period you actually were a resident or physically present abroad. Foreign locations and the time periods which qualify for the waiver of the residency and physical presence tests are listed in the instructions to Form 2555.

If, by the due date of your 1987 return, you have not yet satisfied the foreign residence or physical presence test, but you expect to meet either test after the filing date, you may either file on the due date and report your earnings or ask for a filing extension under the rules at ¶36.8.

Foreign residence test. You must be a bona fide resident of a foreign country for an uninterrupted period that includes one full tax year. Business or vacation trips to the U.S. or another country will not disqualify you from satisfying the foreign residence test. If you are abroad more than one year but less than two, the entire period qualifies if it includes one full tax year.

EXAMPLE
You are a bona fide foreign resident from September 30, 1986, to March 25, 1988. The period includes your entire tax year 1987. Therefore, up to $70,000 of your 1987 earnings are excludable. Your overseas earnings in 1988 will qualify for a proportionate part of the exclusion which will be available in 1988.

To prove you are a foreign resident, you must show your intention to be a resident of the foreign country. Evidence tending to confirm your intention to stay in a foreign country is: Your family accompanies you; you buy a house or rent an apartment rather than a hotel room; you participate in the foreign community activities; you can speak the foreign language; you have a permanent foreign address; you join clubs there, or you open charge accounts in stores in the foreign country.

Residence does not have the same meaning as *domicile*. Your domicile is a permanent place of abode; it is the place to which you eventually plan to return wherever you go. You may have a residence in a place other than your domicile. Thus, you may go, say, to Amsterdam, and take up residence there and still intend to return to your domicile in the U.S. But your leaving your domicile does not, by itself, establish a bona fide residence in a new place. You must intend to make a new place your residence. For example, you may go to Amsterdam on a short business trip or a short holiday. In neither case have you established a residence. You are a mere transient.

You will not qualify if you take inconsistent positions toward your foreign residency. That is, you will *not* be treated as a bona fide resident of a foreign country if you have earned income from sources within that country, filed a statement with the authorities of that country that you are not a resident there, and have been held not subject to the income tax of that country. However, this rule does not prevent you from qualifying under the physical presence test.

If you cannot prove that you are a resident, check to determine if your stay qualifies under the physical presence test.

Physical presence test. To qualify under this test, you must show you were on foreign soil 330 days (about 11 months) during a 12-month period. Whether you were a resident or a transient is of no importance. You have to show you were physically present in a foreign country or countries for 330 full days during any 12-consecutive-month period. The 12-month period may begin with any day. There is no requirement that it begin with your first full day abroad. It may begin before or after arrival in a foreign country and may end before or after departure from a foreign country. A *full* day is from midnight to midnight (24 consecutive hours). You must spend each of the 330 days on foreign soil. In departing from U.S. soil to go directly to the foreign country, or in returning directly to the U.S. from a foreign country, the time you spend on or over international waters does not count toward the 330-day total.

EXAMPLES
1. On August 9 you fly from New York City to Paris. You arrive there at 10 A.M. of August 10. Your first qualifying day toward the 330-day period is August 11.
   You may count in your 330-day period:
   Time spent traveling between foreign countries.
   Time spent on a vacation in foreign countries. There is no requirement that the 330 days must be spent on a job.
   Time spent in a foreign country while employed by the U.S. government counts towards the 330-day test even though pay from the government does not qualify for the earned income exclusion.
   Time in foreign countries, territorial waters, or travel in the air over a foreign country. However, you will lose qualifying days if any part of such travel is on or over international waters and takes 24 hours or more, or any part of such travel is within the U.S. or its possessions.
2. You depart from Naples, Italy, by ship on June 10 at 6:00 P.M. and arrive at Haifa, Israel, at 7:00 A.M. on June 14. The trip exceeded 24 hours and passed through international waters. Therefore, you lose as qualifying days June 10, 11, 12, 13, and 14. Assuming you remain in Haifa, Israel, the next qualifying day is June 15.

Choosing the 12-month period. You qualify under the physical presence test if you were on foreign soil 330 days during any period of 12 consecutive months. Since there may be several 12-month periods during which you meet the 330 day test, you should choose the 12-month period allowing you the largest possible exclusion if you qualify under the physical presence test for only part of 1987.

EXAMPLE
You worked in France from June 1, 1986, through September 30, 1987, when you left the country. During this period, you left France

only for a 15 day vacation to the U.S. during December 1986. You earned $70,000 for your work in France during 1987. Your maximum 1987 exclusion is $56,192, figured as follows:
1. Start with your last full day, September 30, 1987, and count back 330 full days during which you were abroad. Not counting the vacation days, the 330th day is October 21, 1986. This is the first day of your 12-month period.
2. From October 21, 1986, count forward 12 months, to October 20, 1987, which is the last day of your 12-month period.
3. Count the number of days in 1987 which fall within the 12-month period ending October 20, 1987. Here, the number of qualifying days is 293, from January 1 through October 20, 1987.
4. The maximum 1987 exclusion is $70,000 × 293/365 or $56,192. You may exclude $56,192, the lesser of the maximum exclusion or your actual earnings of $70,000.

CLAIMING DEDUCTIONS IF YOU ELECT THE EARNED INCOME EXCLUSION

¶ **36.7** If you elect the earned income exclusion, you deduct expenses as follows:
Personal or nonbusiness deductions, such as medical expenses, mortgage interest, and real estate taxes paid on a personal residence, are deductible if you itemize deductions. Business expenses attributable to earning excludable income are not deductible. Dependency exemptions are fully deductible.

EXAMPLE
You were a resident of Denmark and elect to exclude your wages of $70,000 from income. You also incurred unreimbursed travel expenses of $2,000. You may not deduct the travel expenses, since the amount is attributable to the earning of tax free income.

If your foreign earnings exceed the exclusion ceiling, you allocate expenses between taxable and tax-exempt income and deduct the amount allocated to taxable earned income.

EXAMPLE
In 1987, you earn $100,000 and satisfy the physical presence test. Your unreimbursed travel expenses are $5,000. If you elect the $70,000 exclusion, you may deduct 30% of the travel expenses, or $1,500 since 30% of your earnings or $30,000 are taxed. The expenses are deductible as a miscellaneous itemized deduction subject to the 2% floor; *see* ¶ 19.1.

If your job expenses are reimbursed and the rules of reporting are met (*see* ¶ 19.51), the reimbursements are not reported to the extent of the expenses incurred. If the reimbursement is less than expenses, the excess expenses are allocated as in the example above.

You may have to allocate state income taxes paid on your income.

If either you or your spouse elect the earned income or housing exclusion, you may not claim an IRA deduction based on excluded income.

Overseas moving expenses. These expenses are generally treated as related to your foreign earnings. Thus, if you move to a foreign country and exclude your income you may not deduct your moving expenses. If your earned income exceeds the exclusion limit, you allocate moving expenses between your tax-exempt and taxable earned income. Employer reimbursement is considered earned income in the year of receipt and is added to other earned income before taking the exclusion and making the allocation. See ¶ 36.5 for allocating reimbursements between the year of the move and the following year for purposes of claiming the exclusion. In allocating moving expenses to taxable earned income, apply the following rules for computing the moving expense deduction: (1) A deduction of up to $6,000 is allowed for the cost of temporary living arrangements at the foreign location, house hunting costs, and expenses incident to the sale of your old home and purchase of a new one at the foreign location; of this amount, up to $4,500 may be claimed for temporary living arrangements and house hunting costs. (2) You may deduct expenses for temporary living arrangements incurred within any 90 consecutive days after obtaining work abroad. (3) You may deduct in full as directly related moving expenses the cost of moving household goods and personal effects to and from storage and the cost of storing the goods or effects while your new foreign work site is your principal place of work.

If, after working in a foreign country, your employer transfers you back to the U.S. or you move back to the U.S. to take a different job, your moving expenses are deductible under the general rules at ¶19.13. If your residence and principal place of work was outside the U.S. and you retire and move back to the U.S., your moving expenses are also deductible under ¶19.13, except you do not have to meet the 39-week test for employees or the 78-week test for the self-employed and partners.

Survivors of workers abroad returning to U.S. If you are the spouse or dependent of a worker who died while his principal place of work was outside the U.S., you may deduct your moving expenses back to the U.S. For the costs to be deductible, the move must begin within six months of the worker's death. The requirements for deducting moving expenses (¶19.13) apply, except for the 39-week test for employees or the 78-week test for the self-employed and partners.

Compulsory home leave. Foreign service officers stationed abroad must periodically return to the U.S. to reorient themselves to American ways of life. Because the home leave is compulsory, foreign service officers may deduct their travel expenses; travel expenses of the officer's family are not deductible.

WHAT TO DO IF YOUR RIGHT TO AN EXCLUSION IS NOT ESTABLISHED WHEN YOUR RETURN IS DUE

¶ **36.8** When your 1987 return is due, you may not have been abroad long enough to qualify for the exclusion. If you expect to qualify under either the residence or physical presence test after the due date for your 1987 return, you may either: (1) Ask for an extension of time for filing your return until after you qualify under either rule, or (2) file your return on the due date, reporting the foreign income in the return, pay the full tax, and then file for a refund when you qualify.

Extension of time to file. If you are abroad on April 15, 1988, you have an automatic extension to June 15, 1988. For an additional two months, file Form 4868 by June 15, 1988, and pay an estimated tax. For a longer extension, in anticipation of owing no tax on your foreign income, you may file Form 2350 either with the Internal Revenue Service, Philadelphia, Pennsylvania 19255, or with a local IRS representative. File Form 2350 before the due date for filing your 1987 return, which is June 15, 1988 if you are abroad and are on a calendar year. If you cannot get Form 2350, apply for the extension on your own stationery. State the facts you rely on to justify the extension and the earliest date you expect to be in a position to determine under which rule you will qualify. You will receive an official letter and copy granting the extension. Generally, you will be granted an extension of time for a period ending 30 days after the date you expect to qualify for the foreign earned income exclusion.

If you will have tax to pay even after qualifying—for example, your earned income exceeds the exclusion—you may file for an extension to file but you will owe interest on the tax due. To avoid interest charges on the tax, you may take one of the following steps:

1. File your return on time and pay the total tax due without the application of the exclusion. When you do qualify, make sure you file a refund claim within the time limits discussed at chapter 27; or
2. Pay estimated tax for the amount of tax you expect to owe and later ask for an extension to file. When you file your return, you apply the estimated tax against the tax due. An estimated tax for 1987 must be made by January 15, 1988, and an extension to file a final return must be made by June 15, 1988. If you fail to make a timely estimate, you cannot use this option.
3. Pay the estimated tax liability when you apply for the extension to file on Form 2350. If the extension is granted, the paid amount is applied to the tax shown on your return when you file.

TAX FREE MEALS AND LODGING FOR WORKERS IN CAMPS

¶ **36.9** If you must live in a camp provided by your employer, you may exclude from income the value of the lodging and meals furnished, if the camp is (1) provided because you work in a remote area where satisfactory housing is not available; (2) located as near as practicable to the worksite; and (3) a common area (enclave) not open to the public normally accommodating at least 10 employees.

You may also qualify for the earned income exclusion under the general rules at ¶36.2.

EARNINGS IN VIRGIN ISLANDS, GUAM, NORTHERN MARIANA ISLANDS, AND U.S. POSSESSIONS

¶ **36.10** The 1986 Tax Act substantially revised prior tax law provisions governing how U.S. citizens working in U.S. possessions, the Virgin Islands, Guam, and Northern Mariana Islands report and file income tax returns. Under prior law, U.S. citizens working in U.S. possessions could exclude from U.S. tax earnings attributed to work in the possessions. Under the new law, for tax years beginning after 1986, a new possession exclusion will apply only for bona fide residents of Guam, American Samoa, or the Northern Mariana Islands.

The application of the new possession exclusion rules may depend on implementing agreements between the jurisdiction and the Treasury. At the time of publication of this book, these agreements had not been reported. Therefore, contact the particular tax authority for the proper treatment of your income and ask the IRS for the 1987 edition of Publication 570, Tax Guide for U.S. Citizens Employed in U.S. Possessions. If you have a mailing address overseas write to Forms Distribution Center, P.O. Box 25866, Richmond, VA 23260, for Publication 570.

For tax information from Guam, write to Commissioner of Revenue and Taxation, Government of Guam, Agana, Guam 96910. For information from the Northern Mariana Islands, write to the Director of Revenues, Saipan, Mariana Islands 96950. For information from American Samoa, write to the Tax Manager, Government of American Samoa, Pago Pago, American Samoa 96799.

New filing rules apply starting in 1987 if you have income derived from the Virgin Islands. For information about tax liability in the Virgin Islands, write to Virgin Islands, Bureau of Internal Revenue, P.O. Box 3186, St. Thomas, Virgin Islands 00801. Also *see* IRS Publication 570.

EARNINGS IN PUERTO RICO

¶ **36.11**

Puerto Rican tax returns. If you are a U.S. citizen who is also a resident of Puerto Rico, you generally report all of your income on your Puerto Rican tax return. Where you report income from U.S. sources on the Puerto Rican tax return, a credit against the Puerto Rican tax may be claimed for income taxes paid to the U.S.

If you are not a resident of Puerto Rico, you report on a Puerto Rican return only income from Puerto Rican sources. Wages earned for services performed in Puerto Rico for the U.S. government or for private employers is treated as income from Puerto Rican sources.

U.S. tax return. As a U.S. citizen, you must file a U.S. tax return reporting income from all sources. But, if you are a bona fide resident of Puerto Rico for an entire tax year, you do not report on a U.S. tax return any income from Puerto Rican sources, except amounts received for services performed in Puerto Rico as an employee of the U.S. government. On a U.S. tax return, you may not deduct expenses or claim tax credits applicable to the excludable income. Personal exemptions are fully deductible.

If you are not a bona fide resident of Puerto Rico for the entire tax year, you report on your U.S. tax return all of your Puerto Rican income as well as all income from other sources. If you are required to report Puerto Rican income on your U.S. tax return, you may claim a credit for income tax paid to Puerto Rico. You figure the credit on Form 1116.

EXAMPLE

You and your spouse are bona fide residents of Puerto Rico during the entire year of 1987. You receive $15,000 in wages as an employee of the U.S. government working in Puerto Rico, a $100 dividend from a Puerto Rican corporation that does business in Puerto Rico, and a $500 dividend from a U.S. corporation that does business in the U.S. Your spouse earned $8,000 in wages from a Puerto Rican corporation for services performed in Puerto Rico. Your exempt and taxable income for U.S. federal tax purposes:

	Taxable	Exempt
Your wages	$15,000	
Your spouse's wages		$8,000
Puerto Rican corporation dividend		100
U.S. corporation dividend	500	
Totals	$15,500	$8,100

You file tax returns with both Puerto Rico and the United States. You have gross income of $15,500 for U.S. tax purposes and $23,600 for Puerto Rican tax purposes. A tax credit may be claimed on the U.S. tax return for income taxes paid to Puerto Rico and on your Puerto Rican return for income taxes paid to the United States.

Information on Puerto Rican tax returns may be requested from Oficina de Apelaciones Administrativas, Consultas y Legislación, Negociado de Contribución sobre Ingresos, Apartado S 2501, San Juan, Puerto Rico 00903.

TAX TREATIES WITH FOREIGN COUNTRIES

¶ **36.12** Tax treaties between the United States and foreign countries modify some of the rules discussed above. The purpose of the treaties is to avoid double taxation. Consult your tax advisor about the effect of these treaties on your income. IRS Publication 54 contains a list of tax treaties between the U.S. and foreign countries.

EXCHANGE RATES AND BLOCKED CURRENCY

¶ **36.13** Income reported on your federal income tax return must be stated in U.S. dollars. Where you are paid in foreign currency, you report your pay in U.S. dollars on the basis of the exchange rates prevailing at the time the income is actually or constructively received. You use the rate that most closely reflects the value of the foreign currency—the official rate, the open market rate or any other relevant rate. You may even be required to use the black market rate if that is the most accurate measure of the actual purchasing power of U.S. dollars in the foreign country. Be prepared to justify the rate you use.

Currency gains and losses. A special statute, Section 988, governs the treatment of gain or loss on currency transactions. In the case of individuals, Section 988 applies if expenses attributable to the transaction would be deductible as business expenses or expenses for the production of income.

Fulbright grants. If 70% of a Fulbright grant is paid in nonconvertible foreign currency, U.S. tax may be paid in the foreign currency. *See* IRS Publication 520 for details.

A citizen or resident alien may be paid in a foreign currency that cannot be converted into American dollars and removed from the foreign country. If your income is in blocked currency, you may elect to defer the reporting of that income until: (1) The currency becomes convertible into dollars. (2) You actually convert it into dollars. (3) You use it for personal expenses (for example, in the foreign country when you go there). Purchase of a business or investment in the foreign country is not the kind of use that is treated as a conversion. (4) You make a gift of it or leave it in your will. (5) You are a resident alien and you give up your U.S. residence.

If you use this method to defer the income, you may not deduct the expenses of earning it until you report it. You must continue to use this method after you choose it. You may only change with permission of the IRS.

You do not defer the reporting of capital losses incurred in a country having a blocked currency.

There may be some disadvantages in making the choice to defer the income—
1. Many years' income may accumulate and all be taxed in one year.
2. You have no control over the year in which the blocked income

becomes taxable. You usually cannot control the events that cause the income to become unblocked.

You choose to defer income in blocked currency by filing a tentative tax return reporting your blocked taxable income and explain that you are deferring the payment of income tax because your income is not in dollars or in property or currency which is readily convertible into dollars. You must attach to your tentative return a regular return, reporting any unblocked taxable income received during the year or taxable income which became unblocked during the year. When the currency finally becomes unblocked or convertible into a currency or property convertible to dollars, you pay tax on the earnings at the rate prevailing in the year the currency became unblocked or convertible. On the tentative return, note at the top: "Report of Deferrable Foreign Income." File separate returns for each country from which blocked currency is received. The election must be made by the due date for filing a return for the year in which an election is sought.

INFORMATION RETURNS ON FOREIGN CURRENCY

¶ **36.14** If you have a financial interest in, or signature or other authority over a foreign bank account, a foreign securities account, or any other foreign financial account, you must report this fact on Form 90-22.1, Report of Foreign Bank and Financial Accounts. The form does not have to be filed if the aggregate value of the accounts at any time during the year does not exceed $10,000, or if the accounts were with a U.S. military banking facility operated by a U.S. financial institution. Taxpayers filing Form 1040 must also indicate on Schedule B whether they had an interest in a foreign account during the year. Form 90-22.1 is not filed with your income tax return. The form must be filed by June 30 of the year following the year in which you had this financial interest. Foreign accounts for 1987 must be reported by June 30, 1988, to the Department of the Treasury, Post Office Box 32621, Detroit, MI 48232.

Treasury regulations impose reporting and record keeping requirements for currency transactions outside the United States. Generally, transactions involving a physical transfer of funds or monetary instruments into or outside the U.S. must be reported if the amount involved exceeds $5,000 on any one occasion.

Financial institutions are also subject to record keeping requirements covering advice, requests or instructions for transfers outside the country of over $10,000 in cash, instruments, securities, or credit (*see* Treasury regulations and Form 4789 for details). *See* Form 4790.

FOREIGN TAX CREDIT

¶ **36.15** You must file Form 1116 to compute your credit. You may not claim a foreign tax credit or deduction for taxes paid on income not subject to U.S. tax. If all of your foreign earned income is excluded, none of the foreign taxes paid on such income may be taken as a credit or deduction on your U.S. return. If you exclude only part of your foreign pay, you determine which foreign taxes are attributable to excluded income and thus disallowed as foreign tax credits by applying the fractional computation provided in the instructions to Form 1116 and IRS Publication 514.

> If you qualify for a credit or deduction, you will generally receive a larger tax reduction by claiming a tax credit rather than a deduction. A deduction is only a partial offset against your tax, whereas a credit is deducted in full from your tax. Also, taking a deduction may bar you from carrying back an excess credit from a later year. However, a deduction may give you a larger tax saving if the foreign tax is levied at a high rate and the proportion of foreign income to U.S. income is small. Compute your tax under both methods and choose the one providing the larger tax reduction.

In one tax year, you may not elect to deduct some foreign taxes and claim others as a credit. One method must be applied to all taxes paid or accrued during the tax year. If you are a cash basis taxpayer, you may claim a credit for accrued foreign taxes, but you must consistently follow this method once elected.

The credit is the amount of foreign taxes paid or accrued, not to exceed the effective U.S. tax on foreign income multiplied by a ratio of foreign taxable income over total taxable income.

The credit may not be claimed if:

You are a nonresident alien. However, under certain circumstances, an alien who is a bona fide resident for an entire taxable year in Puerto Rico may claim the credit. Also a nonresident alien engaged in a U.S. trade or business may claim a credit if he receives income *effectively connected* to that business.

You receive tax-exempt income from a U.S. possession.

Taxes qualifying for the credit. The credit is allowed only for foreign income, excess profits taxes, and similar taxes in the nature of an income tax. It is not allowed for any taxes paid to foreign countries on sales, gross receipts, production, the privilege to do business, personal property, or export of capital. But it may apply to a—

Tax similar to a U.S. tax on income.

Tax paid by a domestic taxpayer in lieu of the tax upon income, which would otherwise be imposed by any foreign country or by any U.S. possession.

Tax of a foreign country imposing income tax, where for reasons growing out of the administrative difficulties of determining net income or basis within that country, the tax is measured by gross income, sales, and number of units produced.

Pension, unemployment, or disability funds of a foreign country; certain foreign social security taxes do not qualify.

Reporting foreign income on your return. You report the gross amount of your foreign income in terms of United States currency. You also attach a schedule showing how you figured the foreign income in United States currency.

EXAMPLE

You earn Canadian dividends of $100 (Canadian dollars), from which $15 of Canadian taxes were withheld. When the dividends were declared, a Canadian dollar could be exchanged for $.82 of United States currency. Therefore, the dividend of $100 (in Canadian dollars) is reported on your return as $82 ($100 × .82). The tax withheld which may be taken as a credit is $12.30 ($15 × .82).

COMPUTING THE FOREIGN TAX CREDIT

¶ **36.16** The foreign tax credit is based on the amount of foreign taxes you paid or accrued. However, the amount of foreign taxes taken into account is limited where the foreign taxes exceed the effective U.S. tax rate on the foreign income. You compute the limitation on Form 1116. You must use the *overall* method of limitation.

The overall limitation is computed according to this formula:

$$\text{U.S. tax} \times \frac{\text{Taxable income from all foreign countries}}{\text{Taxable income from all sources}}$$

Income which is tax free under the foreign earned income exclusion is not taken into account when figuring taxable income. Foreign taxable income, for purposes of computing the ratio, is reduced by all expenses directly related to earning the income. Itemized deductions, such as medical expenses, that are not directly related to foreign sources are allocated to foreign income according to relative gross incomes from foreign and U.S. sources. You do not consider personal exemptions when figuring foreign or total taxable income.

EXAMPLE

Jones, a single individual, receives taxable income from three countries as follows:

	Taxable income	Income taxes paid
Country A	$ 2,000	$ 100
Country B	$ 4,000	$1,200
United States	$ 4,000	
Total taxable income	$10,000	

Assume that the U.S. tax is $2,000.

Tax Credit on Overall Basis

$$\frac{\text{Taxable income from all foreign countries}}{\text{Total taxable income}} \times \text{U.S. tax}$$

	Maximum foreign tax	Actual foreign tax	Foreign tax credit allowable
Countries A and B: $\frac{\$\,6,000}{\$10,000} \times \$2,000 =$	$1,200	$1,300	$1,200

Capital gains. In figuring the overall limitation, taxable income from foreign countries (the numerator) includes gain from the sale of capital assets only to the extent of foreign source capital gain net income, which is the lower of net capital gain from foreign sources or net capital gain from all sources. Gain on the sale of personal property sold outside of the country of your residence may be treated as gain from U.S. sources, unless the gain is subject to a foreign income tax at a rate of 10% or more of the gain. *See* instructions to Form 1116. The same rule applies to personal property (other than corporate stock) sold other than in a country in which such property is used in business or in which you derived more than 50% of your gross income for the three-year period ending with the close of the taxable year preceding the year during which the sale or exchange occurred.

The foreign tax credit allowable may not exceed foreign taxes actually paid or accrued. Where a joint return is filed, the limitation is applied to the aggregate taxable income of both spouses.

A limited foreign tax credit may be applied against the alternative minimum tax; see ¶ 23.5.

Recapture of foreign losses. If you sustain an "overall foreign loss" for any taxable year, a recapture provision treats part of foreign income realized in a later year as income from U.S. sources. By treating part of the later year's foreign income as U.S. income, the numerator of the fraction used to compute the overall limitation (*see* above) is reduced and this in turn reduces the maximum foreign tax credit that may be claimed in the later year. More specifically, the portion of foreign income in succeeding years which is treated as U.S. income equals the lower of (a) the amount of the loss or (b) 50% (or a larger percentage, as you may choose) of taxable income from foreign sources. An "overall foreign loss" means the amount by which the gross income for the taxable year from foreign sources for that year is exceeded by the sum of allocated deductions. For this purpose, the following deductions are not considered and so are not subject to recapture: operating loss deductions, any uncompensated foreign expropriation or casualty loss. Special rules apply to dispositions of property if used predominantly outside the United States in a trade or business.

New law limitations. For tax years beginning after 1986, there is a separate credit limitation for passive income such as dividends, interest, annuities, rents, royalties and gains on certain foreign currency and commodity transactions. Separate limitations also apply to foreign interest income subject to withholding at more than a 5% rate, certain income from banking or similar financed businesses, and certain shipping income.

For further details, *see* IRS Publication 514 and Form 1116.

CARRYBACK AND CARRYOVER OF EXCESS FOREIGN TAX CREDIT

¶ **36.17** Where the amount allowable as a credit under either the per-country (prior law) or overall basis is restricted, the excess may be carried back to the two preceding years and then carried forward to the five succeeding taxable years. Generally, there can be no carryover from a per-country year to an overall basis year, or vice versa. However, exceptions to this rule (not discussed in this book) may be allowed during a transitional period. The carryback or carryover will not be allowed in a year you have no income from foreign sources or the credit limitation already applies to taxes of that year.

For further details, *see* IRS Publication 514.

37

HOW ALIENS ARE TAXED IN THE UNITED STATES

Tax treatment depends on: (1) Whether the alien is a resident or nonresident; (2) if a nonresident, whether he is engaged in a U.S. business; and (3) tax treaties. A treaty prevails over a less favorable tax law.

RESIDENT OR NONRESIDENT?

¶ **37.1** A resident alien, like a U.S. citizen, is taxed on income from all sources.

A nonresident alien is generally taxed only on income from U.S. sources at special rates. However, capital gains from the sale of U.S. real estate are subject to tax at regular U.S. rates. Other capital gains are not taxed unless a nonresident alien has a U.S. business, or is in the U.S. for 183 days during the year. If he is doing business here, business income is taxed differently from investment income.

An alien's mere presence in the U.S. does not make him a "resident."

An alien is generally treated as a "resident" only if he is a lawful permanent resident who has a green card or meets a substantial presence test; see ¶ 37.3.

Dual status. An alien may be both a resident and nonresident in the same year.

EXAMPLE

On June 1, 1987, you arrive on a nonimmigrant visa and are present in the U.S. for the rest of the year. From January 1 to May 31, 1987, you are a nonresident; from June 1 to the end of the year, you are a resident. Despite "dual status," you do not file two returns. You file one return, reporting income on the basis of your status for each part of the year.

Certain restrictions apply to dual status taxpayers. For example, a joint return may not be filed, unless you and your spouse agree to be taxed as U.S. residents for the entire year.

For details on filing a return for a dual status year, *see* IRS Publication 519 and the instructions to Form 1040NR.

HOW A RESIDENT ALIEN IS TAXED

¶ **37.2** A resident alien is taxed like a U.S. citizen. Income earned abroad may be excluded if the foreign physical presence test is satisfied (*see* ¶ 36.6). A resident alien may generally claim a foreign tax credit (*see* ¶ 36.14). He is taxed on a pension from a foreign government. An alien working in the United States for a foreign government is not taxed on his pay if the foreign government allows a similar exemption to American citizens.

WHO IS A RESIDENT ALIEN?

¶ **37.3** The following tests determine whether an alien is taxed as a U.S. resident. Intent to remain in the U.S. is not considered.

You are treated as a resident alien and taxed as a U.S. resident if you meet either of the following tests for 1987:

1. You are a lawful permanent resident of the U.S. *at any time* during the calendar year. If you hold a green card, you meet this test and

are considered a U.S. resident. If you were outside of the U.S. for part of 1987 and then become a lawful permanent resident, *see* the rules below for first year of residency.

2. You meet a substantial presence test. Under this test, you are treated as a U.S. resident if you were in the U.S. for at least 31 days during the calendar year and have been in the U.S. within the last three years for 183 days (the current year and the two preceding calendar years). The 183 day test is complicated and there are several exceptions.

To determine if you meet the 183 day test, the following cumulative times are totaled. Each day in the U.S. during 1987 is counted as a full day. Each day in 1986 counts as ⅓ of a day; each day in 1985 counts as ⅙ of a day.

Note that you must be physically present in the U.S. for at least 31 days in the current year. If you are not, the 183 day test does not apply.

Other exceptions to the substantial presence test are: commuting from Canada or Mexico; keeping a tax home and close contacts or connections in a foreign country; having a diplomatic, teacher, trainee or student status; a professional athlete temporarily in the U.S. after October 22, 1986, to compete in a charitable sports event; or being confined in the U.S. for certain medical reasons. These are explained in the following paragraphs.

Commute from Mexico or Canada. If you regularly commute to work in the U.S. from Mexico or Canada, commuting days do not count as days of physical presence for the 183 day test.

Tax home/closer connection exception. If you are in the United States for less than 183 days during 1987 and show that you had a closer connection with a foreign country than with the U.S. and a tax home there for the year, you will generally not be subject to tax as a resident under the substantial presence test. Under this exception, it is possible to have a U.S. abode and a tax home in a foreign country. A tax home is usually where a person has his principal place of business; if he has no principal place of business, it is the place of his regular abode. Proving a tax home alone is not sufficient; the closer connection relationship must also be shown.

The tax home/closer connection test does not apply to an alien who is present for 183 days or more during a year or who has applied for a green card. A relative's application is not considered as the alien's application.

Exempt-person exception. Days of presence in the U.S. are not counted if you are considered an exempt person, such as a teacher, trainee, student, a foreign government-related person or a professional athlete temporarily in the U.S. (after October 22, 1986) to compete in a charitable sports event.

A foreign government-related person is any individual temporarily present in the U.S. who has (1) diplomatic status, or a visa which the Secretary of the Treasury (after consultation with the Secretary of State) determined represents full-time diplomatic or consular status; (2) is a full-time employee of an intentional organization; or (3) is a member of the immediate family of a diplomat or international organization employee.

A teacher or trainee is any individual other than a student who is temporarily present in the U.S. under a "J" visa—subparagraph (J) of section 101(15) of the Immigration and Nationality Act—and who substantially complies with the requirements for being so present.

A student is any individual who is temporarily present in the U.S. under either an "F" or "J" visa—subparagraph (F) of section 101(15) of the Immigration and Nationality Act or subparagraph (J) of such section 101(15)—and who substantially complies with the requirements for being so present.

The exception generally does not apply to teacher or trainee who has been exempt as a teacher, trainee, or student for any part of two of the six preceding calendar years. However, if during the period you are temporarily present in the U.S. under an "F" or "J" visa, all of your compensation is received from outside the U.S., you may qualify for the exception if you were exempt as a teacher, trainee or student for less than four years in the six preceding calendar years. The exception also does not apply to a student if he has been exempt as a teacher, trainee, or student for more than five calendar years, unless he shows that he does not intend to reside permanently in the U.S. and that he or she has substantially complied with the requirements of the student visa providing for temporary presence in the U.S.

Medical exception. An alien who cannot physically leave the U.S. because of a medical condition that arose in the U.S. may be treated as a nonresident even if present here for more than 183 days during the year.

> *Tax treaty exception.* The lawful permanent residence test and the substantial physical presence test do not override tax treaty definitions of residence. Thus, you may be protected by a tax treaty from being treated as a U.S. resident even if you would be treated as a resident under either test.

First year of residency. If you first became a lawful permanent resident of the U.S. (have green card) during 1987 and were not a U.S. resident during 1986, your period of U.S. residency begins with the first day in 1987 you are present in the U.S. with the status of lawful permanent resident. Before that date, you are a nonresident alien. This means that if you become a lawful permanent resident after January 1, 1987, you have a dual status tax year. On Form 1040, you attach a separate schedule showing the income for the part of the year you are a nonresident.

To figure tax for a dual status year, *see* IRS Publication 519 and the instructions to Form 1040NR.

You may also have a dual status year if you were not a U.S. resident in 1986 and in 1987, you are a U.S. resident under the 183 day presence test. Your period of U.S. residency starts on the first day in 1987 for which you were physically present. However, if you meet the 183 day presence test (but not the green card test) and also spent 10 days or less in the U.S. during a period in which you had a closer connection to a foreign country than to the U.S., you may disregard the 10-day period. The purpose of this exception is to allow a brief presence in the U.S. for business trips or house-hunting before the U.S. residency period starts.

EXAMPLES

1. An alien who has never before been a U.S. resident lives in Spain until May 15, 1987. He moves to the U.S. and remains in the U.S. through the end of the year, thereby satisfying the physical presence test. On May 15, he is a U.S. resident. For the period before May 15, he is taxed as a nonresident.

2. Same facts as in (1) above, but he attends a meeting in the U.S. on February 2 through 8. On May 15, he moves to the U.S. May 15, not February 2, is the starting date of the residency. During February, he had closer connection to Spain than to the U.S. Thus, his short stay in February is an exempt period.

If you were not a resident during 1986 but in 1987 you satisfy both the lawful resident (green card) test and the 183 day presence test, your residence begins on the earlier of the first day you are present in the U.S.

while a lawful permanent resident of the U.S. or the first day of physical presence.

Last year of residence. An alien who does not hold a green card is not treated as a resident after the last day he was present in the U.S. provided (1) he is not treated as a resident during the next calendar year and (2) after leaving the U.S., he had a closer connection to a foreign country than to the U.S. Presence of up to 10 days in the U.S. may be disregarded if during that period you had a closer connection to a foreign country than to the U.S. If an alien who holds a green card gives up his permanent resident status in the current year and meets rules (1) and (2) above, his residency status ends after the day he was no longer a permanent resident.

In the last year of residence, the rules for dual status taxpayers apply. *See* ¶ 37.1.

Interrupted period of residence. If you qualified as a U.S. resident during at least three consecutive calendar years after 1984, and cease to be a U.S. resident, and later return to become a U.S. resident within three calendar years after the end of the initial residency period, you are taxable during the intervening period of nonresidence in the same way as a former U.S. citizen who became expatriated to avoid tax. This treatment applies only if the amount of tax under this rule exceeds the tax that would otherwise apply to you as a nonresident alien. The tax under this special rule is the regular graduated income tax, alternative minimum tax, and tax on lump-sum distributions from an employees' trust, applied only to your gross income effectively connected with a U.S. trade or business and your U.S. source effectively connected gross income. For this purpose, U.S. source gross income includes gains from the sale or exchange of (1) property (other than stock or debt obligations) located in the United States, and (2) stock issued by a U.S. domestic corporation or debt obligations of U.S. persons or of the United States, a state or political subdivision thereof, or the District of Columbia.

This rule is designed to prevent a long-time U.S. resident from disposing of assets free of U.S. tax by leaving the United States for a short period and then resuming U.S. residence. The rule applies regardless of a resident's intention to avoid tax.

First-year choice. If you *do not* meet either the green card test or the substantial presence test for the year of your arrival in the United States or for the immediately preceding year, but you do meet the substantial presence test for the year immediately following the year of your arrival, you may elect to be treated as a U.S. resident for part of the year of your arrival. To do this, you must: (1) be present in the United States for at least 31 consecutive days in the year of your arrival, and (2) be present in the United States for at least 75% of the number of days beginning with the first day of the 31-consecutive-day period and ending with the last day of the year of arrival. For purposes of this 75% requirement, you may treat up to 5 days of absence from the United States as days of presence within the United States.

Do not count as days of presence in the United States days for which you are an *exempt individual* as discussed earlier.

You make the first-year election to be treated as a U.S. resident by attaching a statement to your tax return for the year of your arrival. A first-year election, once made, may not be revoked without the consent of the Internal Revenue Service.

If you make the election, your residence starting date for the year of your arrival is the first day of the earliest 31-consecutive-day period of presence that you use to qualify for the choice. You are treated as a U.S. resident for the remainder of the year.

If you are a nonresident alien, get a copy of IRS Publication 519, U.S. Tax Guide for Aliens. It explains the way aliens pay tax, if any, to the U.S.

WHEN AN ALIEN LEAVES THE UNITED STATES

¶ **37.4** You must obtain a "sailing permit," technically known as a "certificate of compliance," which states that you have fulfilled your income tax obligations to the U.S. Without it, unless you are excused from obtaining one, you will be required at your point of departure to file a tax return and pay any tax due.

The sailing permit is obtained from your local District Director of Internal Revenue about two weeks, but no earlier than 30 days, before your departure. You submit all information pertaining to your income and stay in the U.S., such as passport and alien registration form, copies of U.S. tax returns for the past two years, bank records, and any profit and loss statements. You also file a Form 1040C or Form 2063.

You may avoid paying tax if you satisfactorily convince the District Director that you are returning to the United States. In other cases, you may avoid paying tax on the current year (or previous year if the filing date has not yet passed) by posting a bond for the amount of tax due.

These aliens are not required to obtain a sailing permit: Those traveling under a diplomatic passport, members of their households, and servants accompanying them; employees of foreign governments and international organizations and members of their households whose official compensation is tax exempt and who receive no other income subject to U.S. tax; certain students admitted solely on an F visa; certain industrial trainees admitted solely on an H-3 visa; certain aliens temporarily in the U.S. who have received no U.S. taxable income, such as visitors on a B-2 visa, a C-1 visa, or similar arrangement; aliens admitted to the United States on a border-crossing identification card or for whom passports, visas, and border-crossing identification cards are not required; certain alien military trainees; and an alien resident of Canada or Mexico who frequently commutes between his country and the United States for employment purposes and whose wages are subject to withholding tax.

See IRS Publication 519 for further details.

38

WHAT HAPPENS AFTER YOU FILE YOUR RETURN

HOW THE IRS EXAMINES YOUR RETURN

¶ 38.1 Your return is first checked for arithmetic accuracy. If a mistake is found, you receive either a refund or a bill for additional tax. Special IRS screening also spots the following errors:

1. Income on Form W-2 or Form 1099 incorrectly reported on tax return.
2. Medical expenses without the adjusted gross income limitation.
3. Casualty and theft losses without the adjusted gross income limitation.
4. The use of auto mileage rate for business travel exceeding the allowed IRS rate.
5. Claim for household care expenses of children or disabled dependents claimed by a married person filing a separate return.
6. Use of head of household rates to figure your tax without noting the name of the qualifying dependent.

If you make errors of this type, you will probably be advised by mail of the corrections and of additional tax due, or you may be asked to provide additional information to substantiate tax deductions or credits. If you disagree with an IRS assessment of additional tax, you may request an interview or submit additional information. If you file early and the correction is made before April 15, 1988, interest is not charged.

The IRS also screens returns claiming refunds from tax shelters.

If your return is selected for a more thorough review, you are notified by letter. This may not happen for a year or two.

Your return may command special IRS scrutiny because of your profession, type of transactions reported, or deductions claimed. The chances of being audited are greater under the following circumstances:

You claim tax shelter losses.

You report complex investment or business-transactions without clear explanations.

You receive cash payments in your work that the IRS thinks are easy to conceal, such as cash fees received by doctors or tips received by cab drivers and waiters.

Business expenses are large in relation to income.

Cash contributions to charity are large in relation to income.

You are a shareholder of a close corporation whose return has been examined.

A prior audit resulted in a tax deficiency.

An informer gives the IRS grounds to believe that you are omitting income from your return.

An examination may be held at a local IRS office or at your place of business or home if your return is complex or based on many outside records. If the matter can be settled through correspondence, you may not be asked to appear in person.

You may handle the examination yourself if the issues are simple. If your return is complicated or a large amount of tax is involved, it is advisable to have an experienced tax practitioner represent you.

After the examination, the Revenue Agent may accept your return as filed. If he recommends changes that result in additional taxes and you agree, you sign Form 870. If you disagree, and the examination takes place in an IRS office, you may ask for an immediate meeting with a supervisor to argue your side of the dispute. If an agreement is not reached at this meeting or the audit is at your office or home, the agent prepares a report of his proposed adjustments. You are given the opportunity to request a conference. You may decide not to ask for a conference and await a formal notice of deficiency.

If your case began as an office audit, you do not have to prepare a written protest for a conference. If your case began as a field audit, you must file a written protest if the disputed amount exceeds $2,500. In the protest, you present your reason for disagreeing with the agent's report. At the conference, you may appear for yourself or be represented by an attorney or other agent, and you may bring witnesses.

If you cannot reach a settlement, you will receive a Notice of Deficiency, commonly called a 90-day letter. In it, you are notified that at the end of 90 days from the date it was mailed, the government will assess the additional tax.

When you receive a 90-day letter, if you are still convinced that your position is correct, you may take your case to one of three courts: You may within 90 days file a petition with the Tax Court; or you may pay the additional tax, file a refund claim for it, and after the refund claim is denied, sue for a refund in a federal district court or the U.S. Claims Court.

Generally, the decision to litigate should be considered by an experienced tax practitioner.

The Tax Court has a small tax case procedure for deficiencies of $10,000 or less. Such cases are handled expeditiously and informally. Cases may be heard by commissioners, rather than judges. A small claim case may be discontinued at any time before a decision, but the decision, when made, is final. No appeal may be taken.

TCMP audit. Your return may be selected at random for a special type of audit, a TCMP (Taxpayer Compliance Measurement Program) audit. The TCMP audit is more comprehensive than an ordinary tax examination because the IRS seeks data for setting audit guidelines for others in your tax and economic position. The IRS is protected from having to disclose the standards used in TCMP audits.

AUTOMATIC DATA PROCESSING (ADP)

¶ **38.2** Computers process tax returns. They do not examine returns but facilitate examination by pinpointing returns to be examined and items to be questioned. The IRS uses an automatic formula system to select returns that indicate the "greatest audit potential." The criteria used in the automatic formula system are not made public by the IRS. However, under the Freedom of Information law, the IRS may be forced to make public the standards governing internal procedures except where the IRS determines that such disclosure would seriously impair the assessment, collection, or enforcement of the tax laws.

At regional IRS centers, data is recorded from tax returns and other documents into computers which transfer the data onto magnetic tape. The tape is sent to the National Computer Center in Martinsburg, West Virginia, for posting to the master list of taxpayers arranged by account number. Information from individual tax returns is processed. Failures to file returns, duplicate or multiple filings, and other discrepancies can be detected. Data on information returns can be matched with that reported on individual returns.

To implement ADP, you are required to put your Social Security number on your tax return (*see* ¶38.3). Your number also appears on information returns sent to the IRS reporting the wages, interest, dividends, royalties, etc., paid to you. Your number serves as a basis for posting and cross-referencing data to your account in the master file.

SOCIAL SECURITY NUMBERS FOR TAX RETURNS

¶ **38.3** Your Social Security number must be on your tax return. It must be used on any return, statement or other document filed with the IRS, and should be noted on any check or other remittance sent to the IRS. It must also be furnished to payers of interest or dividends to avoid backup withholding. *See* ¶25.12.

Husband and wife. Your spouse needs a number if she receives dividends or interest in her own name (as distinguished from accounts in your joint names). Both your number and your spouse's number should appear on your return, whether a joint or separate return is filed.

Your minor children need Social Security numbers if they are five or older and you claim dependency exemptions for them. A child of any age who has income also needs a number. You report the number of dependent children age 5 or over on your tax return.

United States citizens outside the United States also need numbers.

Applying for a number. If you do not have a Social Security number, apply for one on Form SS-5 (application for Social Security number). Applications may be obtained at Social Security offices, IRS offices, and most post offices. If you lost your card and do not know your number, the Social Security Administration will send it on request.

You are also required to furnish your number to any payer who in turn must report to the government the dividends, interest or other payments made to you. The number must be given even when a tax return may not be required.

Whose Social Security number should be furnished? When a bank account is owned by two or more individuals, only one Social Security number need be furnished. As between husband and wife, give the husband's number. As between adult and minor, give the adult's number.

If the account reads "John Jones, Custodian, (Guardian or Committee) for Robert Smith, Ward (Minor or Incompetent)," give the number of the ward, minor, or incompetent.

If you are a custodian of stock for your child, give the child's number.

If the account is a valid trust, entitled "John Jones, Trustee under Trust for Robert Smith," give the trust's number.

If the account is entitled "John Jones, Trustee," without disclosing the name of the trust, give the trustee's number.

If John Jones owns stock but arranges with his broker to pay the dividends to Sarah Jones, his mother, give the number of John Jones, who is the registered owner of the stock.

If Alice Jones, a widow, and Thomas Jones, a minor, receive income from the estate of John Jones, give the numbers of both the widow and minor to the executor or administrator of the estate.

If John Jones, Howard Jones and Frank Jones support Sarah Jones, their mother, none contributing more than 50% of the support, but she is claimed by John Jones as a dependent, give the numbers of John, Howard and Frank Jones on the written declaration (Form 2120, Multiple Support Declaration) required to be filed with John Jones's tax return.

If a final income tax return is filed for a decedent, give the decedent's number. If he had no number, his representative should apply for one. In addition, an identification number must also be obtained for his estate for returns it files.

Those who do not need individual numbers are:

1. A widow drawing Social Security benefits who has no number of her own. She may use her deceased husband's number provided she was 62 or over as of January 1, 1963.
2. A nonresident alien who is not engaged in trade or business in the United States.

Penalty. You run the risk of a penalty if you fail to show your Social Security number on your return or if you do not furnish it to a payer.

WHEN THE IRS CAN ASSESS ADDITIONAL TAXES

¶ **38.4** *Three-year statute.* The IRS has three years after the date on which your return is filed to assess additional taxes. When you file a return before the due date, however, the three-year period starts from the due date, generally April 15.

Where the due date of a return falls on a Saturday, Sunday, or legal holiday, the due date is postponed to the next business day.

EXAMPLES

1. You file your 1984 return on February 4, 1985. The last day on which the IRS can make an assessment on your 1984 return is April 15, 1988.

2. You file your 1987 return on May 25, 1988. The IRS has until May 27, 1991, to assess a deficiency (May 25, 1991 is a Saturday).

If the IRS cannot complete an audit within three years, it may request a signed agreement to an extension of time. However, where an individual was "scared" into signing such an agreement, it was held invalid.

EXAMPLE
Robertson, a plumber, won $30,000 in a sweepstakes. An IRS agent asked him to sign an extension agreement. Robertson never had any prior dealings with the IRS, did not know his return was under examination and was not in touch with the lawyer who prepared the return on which his sweepstakes winnings were averaged. Robertson wanted to see his lawyer before signing Form 872, but the agent pressed hard for the signature, phoning him and his wife at home and at work twenty times in a week. The agent did not tell him the amount of additional tax that might be involved, or explain that if he refused to sign he would have an opportunity before the IRS and the courts to contest any additional tax. Instead, the agent's comments gave him the impression that his home could be confiscated if he refused to sign. Robertson signed and the IRS later increased his tax.

Robertson argued that the agreement was not valid. He signed under duress. The Tax Court agreed. He convinced the court that he really believed he could lose his house and property if he did not comply. No adequate explanation of the real consequences of refusal to sign was made, although Robertson asked. Since he signed Form 872 under duress, the IRS could not increase his tax after the three-year period.

Amended returns. If you file an amended return shortly before the three-year limitations period is about to expire and the return shows that you owe additional tax, the IRS has 60 days from the date it receives the return to assess the additional tax, even though the regular limitations period would expire before the 60-day period. This rule applies to amended returns received by the IRS after July 18, 1984.

Six-year statute. When you fail to report an item of gross income which is more than 25% of the gross income reported on your return, the IRS has six years after the return is filed to assess additional taxes.

Where a false or fraudulent return is filed with intent to evade the tax, or where no return is filed, there is no limitation on when the tax may be assessed.

INTEREST ON DEFICIENCIES

¶ **38.5** Interest is charged on a deficiency at rates listed below. For periods after 1986, the rate changes quarterly. Interest begins to accrue from the due date of the return. As of January 1, 1983, interest is compounded daily except for estimated tax penalties. IRS tables on compound interest may be found in Treasury regulations. Where a taxpayer has relied on IRS assistance in preparing a return, and taxes are owed because of a mathematical or clerical error, interest does not begin to accrue until 30 days from a formal demand by the IRS for the payment of additional taxes.

Rates on amounts outstanding are as follows:

From	To	Rate
10/1/87	12/31/87	10%
7/1/87	9/30/87	9
4/1/87	6/30/87	9
1/1/87	3/31/87	9
7/1/86	12/31/86	9
1/1/86	6/30/86	10
7/1/85	12/31/85	11
1/1/85	6/30/85	13
7/1/83	12/31/84	11
1/1/83	6/30/83	16
2/1/82	12/31/82	20
2/1/80	1/31/82	12
2/1/78	1/31/80	6
2/1/76	1/31/78	7
7/1/75	1/31/76	9

*See Supplement for rates.

Higher rate on tax shelter deficiencies. If for any taxable year there is a deficiency of more than $1,000 attributable to a tax shelter transaction, the IRS may charge interest on that deficiency at a rate equal to 120% of the regular rate. The higher rate applies to deficiencies of more than $1,000 due to: (1) disallowed losses or investment credit under the at risk rules; (2) deductions based on overvaluations of property by 150% or more; (3) tax straddles; sham or fraudulent transactions. The IRS may add other items to this list.

Refunds. A lower rate is paid on refunds. For periods after 1986, the interest rate you receive on refunds is 1% less than the rate you must pay on deficiencies. Generally, no interest is paid on a refund made within 45 days of the due date of the return (including extensions). If you file after the due date, no interest is paid on a refund made within 45 days of the actual filing date.

INFORMATION RETURNS ARE IMPORTANT IRS CHECKS

¶ **38.6** The IRS matches tax returns with information returns from employers, payers of interest and dividends, brokers and others to check if income has been omitted from an individual's tax return. In one year, the IRS questioned approximately 8 million taxpayers after finding discrepancies between their tax returns and the income reported on information returns. Here is a checklist of the information returns sent to the IRS by payers:

Employers report wage income to the IRS on Form W-2.

Dividend and interest payments of $10 or more during the calendar year are reported to the IRS on Form 1099. Each payer must furnish you by January 31, 1988, a statement showing the dividend and interest payments made in 1987.

Corporations, banks and other payers, as well as persons or firms who receive such payments for you as nominee, report annually the dividend and interest payments totaling $10 or more per person.

Dividends, for reporting purposes, include dividends paid by corporations, and "dividend equivalents" paid to you while your stock is on loan for a short sale.

Interest, for reporting purposes, includes interest on registered corporate bonds, debentures, notes and certificates; also interest on deposits with savings banks, savings and loan associations, stockbrokers and insurance companies. No returns are required for tax free interest.

Royalty payments of $10 or more are reported on intangible property such as copyrights and interests in oil, gas and other natural resources.

States are required to report income tax refunds of $10 or more.

Similarly, unemployment payments of $10 or more during the year are reported to the IRS on information returns, a copy of which will be furnished to unemployment benefits recipients.

Brokers are required to report to the IRS gross proceeds from sales of stocks, bonds, commodities, and regulated-futures and forward contracts. Commodity options are not covered by this reporting rule.

Information returns are required of persons who in the course of business make payments totaling $600 or more in the calendar year to persons (or partnerships) in the form of:

Compensation for personal services (including salaries, wages, commissions, professional fees) from which no tax is withheld. However, no information return is required for payments to a domestic or other household employee;

Rents (collected by real estate agent on behalf of property owner);

Pensions, annuities, and other gains and profits;

Life insurance, endowment or annuity contracts (unless payment was made by reason of insured's death or surrender or lapse of policy).

Real estate sales are reported to the IRS by the attorney or other party who is responsible for closing the transaction. *See* Form 1099-B.

Distributions from employees' pension or annuity plan—if the total distributions plus the employee's wages equal $600 or more.

Travel or other expense allowances of employee who does not have to account to employer—if the allowance added to the employee's wages totals $600 or more.

Foreign interest or dividends collected for citizen or resident.

Payments of fees to physicians by insurance companies such as Blue

Cross or by a government agency under Medicare or Medicaid. Cooperatives must file annual information returns for patronage dividends to patrons totaling $10 or more during the calendar year. A statement showing the amount reported must be furnished to the patron by the end of January of the following year.

Partnerships. A partnership does not pay income taxes, but must file an annual information return (Form 1065), stating all items of income and deductions. Also included in the return are the names and addresses of all partners, and the amount of each partner's distributive share. The return is filed at the close of the partnership's tax year, whether or not it coincides with that of its partners. Failure to file the return will result in a penalty assessable against the partnership. If a partner sells or exchanges a partnership interest and payment is partly attributable to the partner's share of unrealized receivables or substantially appreciated inventory, the partnership must be notified of the transaction and the partnership must then file an information return with the IRS. The purpose of the reporting requirement is to enable the IRS to verify the income attributable to the receivables and inventory, which is taxable as ordinary income. Statements to the transferor and transferee of the partnership interest must also be provided.

Interest and dividend income information disclosed to Social Security and other agencies. To verify your eligibility for certain government benefits, agencies such as the Social Security Administration, state unemployment compensation agencies and state welfare agencies may obtain from the IRS information on the interest and dividend income shown on your tax return.

REPORTING MORTGAGE INTEREST AND PROPERTY FORECLOSURES AND ABANDONMENTS

¶ **38.7** **Mortgage interest.** Banks, government agencies and businesses receiving mortgage interest of $600 or more for any calendar year report the interest to the IRS on Form 1098. The reporting requirement applies to interest on all obligations secured by real property. If you pay interest on more than one mortgage secured by the same property, the $600 floor applies separately to each obligation. Thus, interest will not be reported if the interest paid on a particular obligation is less than $600.

The lender must provide you a statement of the interest reported to the IRS for 1987 by January 31, 1988.

Cooperative housing corporations also report each tenant-stockholder's share of mortgage interest payments of the co-op.

Foreclosures and abandonments of property. If a business or government agency lends you money and later forecloses on your property or knows that you have abandoned property secured by the loan, the lender must file a report with the IRS on Form 1099-A. A purchase of the property by a party other than the lender at a foreclosure sale is treated also as an abandonment which the lender must report to the IRS.

The reporting rule does not apply to consumer loans for personal property such as an automobile, computer or boat. However, if the lender knows that such property will be used in your business, a foreclosure or abandonment is subject to the reporting requirement.

The purpose of the reporting requirement is to help the IRS check whether you have realized income from discharge or indebtedness or gain on foreclosure, or whether you must recapture a previously claimed investment credit.

If a report to the IRS has been made, you will be sent a statement by the lender by January 31 following the year of the foreclosure or abandonment.

TAX SHELTER REGISTRATION NUMBERS

¶ **38.8** A new tax shelter offering may be required to register with the IRS. If registration is required, the IRS assigns the tax shelter an identification number that must be furnished to investors. As an investor, you must report the registration number on Form 8271. Form 8271 must be attached to your tax return if you report any income or claim any deductions or credits from the shelter.

On Form 8271, the tax shelter must be identified, and you must list from the shelter the gross income, deductions, credits and gains and losses reported on your return; you must identify the forms or schedules on which the income or deductions are reported, such as Schedule D or Schedule E.

A penalty may be imposed if you fail to include the tax shelter registration number on your return.

Promoters of registered tax shelters and any other tax shelter arrangements which the IRS considers as potentially abusive must also keep a list of investors for seven years and provide the list to the IRS upon request. Further, an investor who sells his interest in such a tax shelter to another investor must keep records identifying the buyer.

WHAT ARE THE PENALTIES IN THE LAW?

¶ **38.9** If you are late in paying your taxes, a nondeductible monthly penalty of 0.5% (½ of 1%) is imposed on the net amount of tax due and not paid by the due date. The maximum penalty is 25% of the tax due. The penalty is in addition to the regular interest charge. A similar penalty applies for failure to pay a tax deficiency within 10 days of the date of notice and demand for payment. The penalty does not apply if you can show that the failure to pay is due to reasonable cause and not to willful neglect. The penalty does not apply to the estimated tax. The monthly penalty may be doubled to 1% if after repeated requests to pay and a notice of levy, you do not pay. The increased penalty applies starting in the month after the earlier of these IRS notices: (1) A notice that the IRS will levy upon your assets within 10 days unless payment is made or (2) a notice demanding immediate payment where the IRS believes collection of the tax is in jeopardy. If the tax is not paid after such a demand for immediate payment, the IRS may levy upon your assets without waiting 10 days.

If your return is filed late without reasonable cause, the IRS may impose a penalty of 5% of the net tax due for each month the return is late, with a maximum penalty of 25%. If the return is more than 60 days late, the penalty will not be less than the smaller of $100 or 100% of the tax due.

If you fail to report income shown on any information return, such as interest income or proceeds from a stock sale, the IRS may automatically impose a negligence penalty which you may avoid only by proving you had reasonable cause for omitting the item. This rule applies to returns due (without extensions) after 1986; for returns due before 1987, this rule applied only to interest and dividends.

There are, in addition, penalties for willful evasion of taxes, filing false, fraudulent, or frivolous returns, willful failure to pay taxes or file the proper returns disclosing all the required information, or for willful failure to keep adequate records, file information returns or supply other data required by the IRS.

A "willful failure" generally assumes an act done without a good excuse. There must be an intent to avoid the obligation of the law. If you take an unreasonable position, or make no effort to fairly approximate your deductions, that might also be termed willful failure to observe the law. You *might* avoid penalties if you can prove that you followed the advice of reputable counsel, or you misinterpreted the law; or without request or demand, you later filed the return or you assumed your agent or employee had filed the return or paid the tax.

Overvaluation of property. If you overvalue property, such as by claiming an inflated deduction for a donation of appreciated property to charity, you may be subject to a penalty. The penalty applies if the overvaluation is 150% or more and results in an underpayment of tax of at least $1,000. It does not matter how long the property was held. For returns filed before 1985, the penalty applied only if the property was acquired within five years of the end of the year for which the overvaluation was made.

The amount of the penalty depends upon the extent of overvaluation. If the claimed overvaluation is at least 150% but not more than 200%, the penalty equals 10% of the resulting underpayment of tax. If the overvaluation is over 200% but not over 250%, the penalty is 20% of the resulting underpayment. The maximum penalty is 30% of the underpayment for overvaluations of over 250%. However, if charitable contribution property is overvalued by 150% or more on a return filed after 1984, the penalty is a flat 30% of the tax underpayment due to the overvaluation.

The IRS may generally waive the penalty upon a showing that the overvaluation was made in good faith and had a reasonable basis. However, for overvaluations of charitable contribution property on returns filed after 1984, the penalty will not be waived unless the claimed value was based on an appraisal by a qualified appraiser and, in addition, you show that you made a good faith investigation of the value.

Penalty for substantial underpayment of tax. If you understate tax liability on a return by the greater of $5,000 or 10% of the proper tax, you may be subject to a penalty equal to 25% of the underpayment attributable to the understatement. The 25% penalty applies to penalties assessed after October 21, 1986. Under prior law, the penalty was 10%.

The penalty may be avoided if on your return you provided the IRS with a statement of facts relating to your position, or if you can show that your position was substantially supported by statute, regulations, court decisions, or revenue rulings and procedures. However, if the understatement of tax is due to tax shelter items, you may avoid the penalty only if there is substantial authority for your position and you reasonably believed that your position was "more likely than not" correct.

This penalty does not apply to the extent that a penalty has been imposed for understating tax due to an overvaluation of property (*see* above).

Interest on certain penalties. A higher interest cost is imposed on individuals subject to the following penalties: failure to file a timely return, overvaluation of property, or substantial understatement of tax liability. Generally, for penalties imposed after July 18, 1984, interest will start to run from the due date of the return (including extensions) until the date the penalty is paid. Under prior law, interest on the penalty did not start to run until the IRS imposed the penalty.

RECOVERING ATTORNEYS' FEES FROM THE GOVERNMENT

¶ **38.10** In a tax dispute, you may feel that the IRS has taken an unreasonable position that forced you to incur legal fees and other expenses to win your point. You may be able to recover all or part of your costs under the following rules in a civil tax case.

To win an award, the law requires that you "substantially prevail" in any federal court, including the Tax Court and Claims Court, prove that the IRS was unreasonable, and show that you exhausted all administrative remedies. According to proposed rules, to exhaust administrative remedies, you must ask for an Appeals Office conference before filing a refund action in court or a Tax Court petition. If the Appeals Office asks you to sign Form 872 to extend the time for assessing tax, your administrative remedies will be considered exhausted if you consent to the extension. If the IRS refuses your request for a conference, or if you file a refund claim which the IRS does not act on within six months, you are considered to have exhausted your administrative remedies. You must request an Appeals conference even though there is an IRS ruling contrary to your position and you believe a conference would be unproductive. In actions involving summonses, levies, and liens, administrative remedies will be considered exhausted if a written refund claim is filed with the District Director and it is denied or no action is taken within a reasonable period.

For cases begun after 1985. Generally, prevailing taxpayers who have exhausted all administrative remedies within the IRS may recover up to $75 an hour for attorneys' fees and related litigation expenses by proving that the IRS position was not substantially justified. An award may be based on unjustified conduct by the IRS District Council during pre-trial administrative proceedings as well as on IRS conduct after litigation begins.

PENALTIES FOR TAX LAW VIOLATIONS

Violation	Penalty
Unpaid tax or deficiency.	Generally, 0.5% per month penalty (maximum 25%) and interest from the due date of tax or deficiency (see above).
Negligence (without intent to defraud).	5% of the entire underpayment (including part not due to negligence) plus 50% of the interest due on the portion of the underpayment attributable to negligence.
Attempt to depart from U.S. or conceal property.	25% of tax or deficiency plus interest.
Failure to file return within 60 days of due date plus extensions.	Minimum penalty is lesser of $100 or the taxes due (see above).
Bad check used to pay tax.	1% of amount of check, or, if check is under $500, the penalty is $5, or the amount of the check, whichever is less.
Fraud with intent to evade tax.	50% of the underpayment plus 50% of the interest due on the underpayment attributed to fraud for returns due before 1987. For returns due after 1986, the penalty is 75% of the underpayment attributable to the fraud plus 50% of the interest due on that portion of the underpayment.
Willful failure to pay tax or file return	Misdemeanor—up to $25,000 fine or one year in prison, or both.
Willful making and subscribing to false return.	Felony—up to $100,000 fine or three years in prison, or both.
Willful attempt in any manner to evade or defeat tax.	Felony—up to $100,000 fine or five years in prison, or both.
Failure to file certain information returns.	$50 for each such failure, not to exceed a total of $100,000. Higher penalty and no limit if failures are intentional.
Failure to provide correct information on information return.	$5 for each failure not to exceed $20,000 per calendar year; higher penalty and no maximum limit for intentional failures.
Failure to file partnership return.	$50 times the number of partners for each month (or fraction of a month) not to exceed five months.
Overvaluation of property.	10% to 30% of the resulting underpayment of tax due to the overvaluation of property (see above).
False withholding information.	Civil penalty up to $500; criminal penalty of up to $10,000 plus up to but not more than one year in prison.
Frivolous or incomplete return.	$500, regardless of actual tax liability.
Frivolous Tax Court actions.	Up to $5,000 if taxpayer position is groundless or unreasonably failed to pursue administrative remedies.

Individuals cannot recover legal fees if their net worth exceeds $2 million. No recovery is allowed to sole proprietors, partnerships and corporations if net worth exceeds $7 million or they have more than 500 employees.

The $75 per hour recovery for attorneys' fees replaces the $25,000 limit under prior law. The $75 rate may be increased if the court determines that a higher rate is justified.

You may also recover other reasonable fees, based on prevailing market rates for expert witnesses and special reports, such as an engineer's report necessary to the preparation of your case. However, the recovery for expert witnesses may not exceed the amount paid by the Government to its own expert witnesses.

For cases begun on or after March 1, 1983, and before 1986, you may recover litigation expenses, including attorneys' fees, of up to $25,000 from the government. The $25,000 limit applies to attorneys' fees, fees of expert witnesses, cost of reports or studies necessary for your case, and court costs.

Whether the IRS has acted unreasonably during litigation is a factual issue which courts decide on a case by case basis. Court decisions have split on the issue of whether attorneys' fees may be awarded if the IRS concedes before trial. Some federal courts have allowed awards if the IRS conduct before trial was unreasonable. Other federal courts have held that if the IRS concedes before trial, no award is allowed even if the IRS acted unreasonably before trial.

The Tax Court has held that unreasonable IRS conduct during its administrative proceedings is not a basis for claiming a legal fee award. Only if the IRS acts unreasonably after a Tax Court petition is filed may an award be made. If the IRS concedes the case after a Tax Court petition is filed, the costs of preparing and filing the petition and later legal expenses are recoverable only if the IRS litigating position was unreasonable. The IRS position may be reasonable even though it eventually concedes the case. Expenses paid or incurred during pretrial administrative proceedings may not be recovered. A federal appeals court disagreed with the Tax Court holding and held that unreasonable IRS conduct before litigation may support an award.

INCOME TAX RETURN PREPARERS

¶ **38.11** *Who are preparers?* Anyone who prepares a return or refund claim for a fee.

Where more than one person works on the return or claim, each schedule or entry is reviewed separately to determine the preparer of that schedule or item. A practitioner who gives advice directly relevant to a determination of the existence, characterization, or amount of an entry on a return is considered the preparer of that item. Regulations provide tests for determining whether a part of a return is considered substantial.

A practitioner who prepares entries on a return that affect entries on the return of another taxpayer may be considered the preparer of the other return if the entries are directly reflected on the other return and constitute a substantial portion of that return. For example, a practitioner preparing a partnership return may be considered the preparer of a partner's return if the entries picked up from the partnership return constitute a substantial portion of the partner's individual tax return.

You are not a preparer if you merely type or reproduce a return or claim or prepare a return for your employer or an officer of your employer or fellow employee.

Penalties. Preparers who understate the tax on a taxpayer's return or refund claim are subject to a $100 penalty if the understatement is due to negligence; $500 if willful. A preparer is not subject to penalty for failure to report additions to tax for an underpayment of estimated tax.

A self-employed return preparer and any person who employs people who prepare returns for others must retain a record of the name, Social Security number, and place of work of each employed preparer. The records must be kept for a three-year period following the close of the return period and the records must be made available for inspection upon request of the district director. There is a $100 penalty for each failure to keep and make available a proper record and a $5 penalty for each required item that is missing from the record. The maximum penalty for any return period is $20,000.

In lieu of the $100 or $500 per return penalty, the IRS may impose a $1,000 civil penalty for knowingly understating tax on an individual return ($10,000 on a corporate return). Only one $1,000/$10,000 civil penalty may be imposed on a preparer with respect to the same taxpayer for any taxable year, regardless of the number of returns filed on that taxpayer's behalf.

The IRS has applied the $100 negligence penalty to a preparer's failure to list interest shown on a taxpayer's 1099s which resulted in a substantial underpayment of tax. A mathematical error made in totaling interest statements was not penalized, but a penalty was applied to a preparer who incorrectly totaled the amount of itemized deductions and used the wrong tax table. Although the total understatement of tax was not substantial, the errors, taken as a whole, were considered negligence. Failure to ask a taxpayer whether he had records to support a claimed entertainment expense was penalized, but not where the preparer asked for records which the taxpayer lied that he had.

Tax preparers are subject to a $500 penalty if they endorse or negotiate a refund check issued to a taxpayer whose return they have prepared. Business managers for athletes, actors, or other professionals who prepare their clients' tax returns and handle their tax refunds may also be subject to the penalty. To avoid the penalty, the manager must act only as an agent in depositing the client's refund check.

A preparer must also meet the following requirements:
1. Furnish a completed copy of the return or claim for refund to the taxpayer not later than when it is presented for the taxpayer's signature; a $25 penalty is imposed for each failure.
2. Keep for three years and have available for inspection by the IRS a completed copy of each return or claim prepared, or a list of the names and identification numbers of taxpayers for whom returns or claims were prepared: a $50 penalty is imposed for each failure. A preparer who sells his business is not relieved of the requirement of retaining those records.
3. Sign the return and include his or her identifying number or the identifying number of his or her employer; a $25 penalty is imposed for each failure. Regulations provide that preparers must physically sign the return or refund claim; they may not use a stamped signature or signature label. However, the manual signature requirement may be satisfied by a photocopy of a manually signed copy of a return or refund claim, provided that, before it is photocopied, no one but the preparer has altered entries on the manually signed copy, except to correct arithmetical errors. The individual preparer or the employer-preparer must retain the manually signed copy, as well as a record of any corrected arithmetical errors. If unable to manually sign the return because of a temporary or permanent disability, the words "unable to sign" must be printed, typed, or stamped on the preparer's signature line, together with his name.

In addition to the penalties imposed, the IRS may also seek to enjoin fraudulent or deceptive practice or to enjoin a person from acting as an income tax return preparer. The IRS may seek an injunction against a preparer for "aiding and abetting" a taxpayer to underpay tax. The IRS publishes a list of enjoined preparers in its weekly Internal Revenue Bulletin.

For additional details regarding income tax return preparers, *see* the Professional Edition of Your Income Tax.

A GUIDE TO ESTATE TAXES AND PLANNING

¶ 38.12 The estate you built up may not be entirely yours to give away. The federal government and in all probability at least one state government stand ready to claim their shares.

Do you know what will remain for your family, your favorite philanthropies, your other beneficiaries? If you do not, you cannot intelligently estimate what you can give to each. To help you make such an estimate, we offer this general guide to federal estate taxation. It will alert you to the extent of estate tax costs, and if you find that you have an estate subject to tax, to plan for estate tax savings that you may discuss with your attorney.

WHAT IS THE ESTATE TAX?
The federal estate tax is a tax on the act of transferring property at death. It is not a tax on the right of the beneficiary to receive the property; the estate and the estate alone pays the tax.

Understand what the word *estate* means in estate tax law so that you do not underestimate the value of your taxable estate. The estate includes not only your real estate (foreign and domestic), bank deposits, securities, personal property and other more obvious signs of wealth, but can also include insurance, your interest in trusts and jointly-held property, and certain interests you have in other estates.

TAKE INVENTORY
The first step in estate planning follows a simple business practice of taking inventory of everything you own.

Listing one's belongings takes thought, time, and a surprising amount of work with lists, records of purchases, fire and theft insurance inventories, bank books, brokers' statements, etc. You need to include your cash, real estate (here and abroad), securities, mortgages, rights in property, trust accounts, life insurance payable to your estate or payable to others if you have kept a certain measure of ownership, personal effects, collections and art works.

If you own property jointly with your spouse, include only one-half the value of the property.

If you have had appraisals made of unusual or specially treasured items or collections, or property of substantial value, file such appraisals with your estate papers and enter the value on your inventory.

There are some assets that you might not ordinarily consider as part of your estate. Nevertheless, include in your inventory any trust arrangements created by you in which you have (1) a life estate (the income or other use of property for life); (2) income that is to be used to pay your legal obligations (support of a child, for example); (3) the right to change the beneficiary or his interest (a power of appointment); (4) the right to revoke a trust transfer or gift; (5) a reversionary interest (possibility that the property can come back to you). Also include benefits from any of the following retirement plans: Pension plan, profit sharing plan, Keogh plan, individual retirement account, annuity, or bonds. However, the first $100,000 of benefits payable to a beneficiary other than your estate and not payable in a lump sum *are* excluded from your estate if you were an active participant of a plan as of December 31, 1984, in pay status and before July 18, 1984, you irrevocably elected the form of your beneficiary's benefits. The exclusion does not apply to the extent of your own nondeductible contributions to the plan.

FINDING THE VALUE OF YOUR ESTATE
When you have completed your inventory, assign to each asset what you consider to be its fair market value. This may be difficult to do for some assets. Resist the tendency to overvalue articles which arouse feelings of pride or sentiment and undervalue some articles of great intrinsic worth. For purposes of your initial estimate, it is better to err on the side of overvaluation.

If you have a family business, your idea of its value and that of the IRS may vary greatly. Estate plans have been upset by the higher value placed on such a business by the IRS. You can protect your estate by anticipating and solving this problem with your business associates, accountant and legal counsel.

If your business is owned by a closely held corporation, and there is no ready or open market in which the stock can be valued, get some factual basis for a figure that will be reported on the estate tax return. One of the ways to do this is by arranging a buy-sell agreement with a potential purchaser. This agreement must fix the value of the stock. Generally, an agreement that binds both the estate and the purchaser and restricts lifetime sales of the stock will effectively fix the value of the stock for estate tax purposes. Another way would be to make a gift of some shares to a family member and have value established in gift tax proceedings. Unless there is a drastic change, the valuation thus established will have considerable weight in later estate tax proceedings.

If a substantial part of your estate is real estate used in farming or a closely held business, your executor may be able to elect, with the consent of heirs having an interest in the property, to value the property on the basis of its farming or business use, rather than its highest and best use. The special use valuation, however, may not reduce the gross estate by more than $750,000. But this may mean substantial tax savings. This savings may be recaptured from your heir if he or she stops using the property in farming or business within 10 years of your death.

You can list ordinary personal effects at nominal value.

HOW THE ESTATE TAX IS APPLIED
A single unified rate schedule applies to a decedent's estate and all his post-1976 lifetime gifts over the annual gift tax exclusion. Under the unified gift and estate tax rate, the overall tax on your property holdings is theoretically the same whether or not you make lifetime gifts. In actual cases, however, lifetime gifts may reduce the potential overall tax because of the annual gift tax exclusion.

If you make no taxable gifts during your life, calculating your estate is fairly easy. You start with the total market value of the property in the estate. This is called the gross estate. From the gross estate you subtract certain deductions. The remaining amount is your taxable estate. The unified credit is subtracted from the tax calculated on the taxable estate. Other credits, including the state death tax credit, further reduce the tax on your estate.

If you make gifts after 1976, calculating your estate tax is more complicated. The estate tax is cumulative. That is, the unified tax rate is applied to the sum of: (1) Your taxable estate at death and (2) taxable lifetime gifts made after 1976 (other than gifts included in your estate). The tax you figure on (1) and (2) is reduced by gift taxes payable on gifts made after 1976. The unified credit and other credits are then subtracted from the remaining amount.

UNIFIED TAX CREDIT

The unified tax credit is $192,800 for decedents dying in 1987 and later years. The amount of the credit is the same for gift tax and estate tax purposes. Applying it to the taxable estate, no tax applies to estates under $600,000.

These exempt amounts assume that you did not make any taxable gifts and that the taxable estate is your gross estate less allowable deductions.

The unified tax credit replaces the $60,000 estate tax exemption and $30,000 lifetime gift tax exemption allowed prior to 1977. Where part or all of the $30,000 lifetime gift tax exemption was used after September 8, 1976, and before January 1, 1977, the unified credit is reduced by 20% of the amount allowed as an exemption on those gifts. Thus, if you used the entire $30,000 exemption on a gift made after September 8, 1976, your unified credit is permanently reduced by $6,000 (20% of $30,000).

YOU ARE NOW READY TO ESTIMATE THE FEDERAL ESTATE TAX

Gross estate (your estimated inventory)	$____
Less:	
1. Administration expenses (executor's commissions, attorney's fees, etc.; estimate about 5% to 10% of your estate)	$____
2. Debts, mortgages, liens	____
3. Funeral expenses	____
4. Marital deduction	____
5. Charitable deduction	____
Total of (1), (2), (3), (4) and (5)	$____
Your taxable estate	$____
Plus: Post-1976 taxable gifts (over the annual exclusion)	$____
Total taxable amount	$____
Tentative tax on total	____
Less: Gift tax payable on post-1976 gifts	$____
Unified credit	$____ ____
Estate tax due	$____

EXAMPLE

Assume an unmarried person, who made no taxable gifts after 1976, dies in 1987, leaving a gross estate of $600,000. Debts, administration and funeral expenses total $60,000. The decedent bequeaths $60,000 to charity.

Gross estate		$600,000
Less:		
Debts, administration and funeral expenses		60,000
		$540,000
Less:		
Charitable deduction		60,000
Taxable estate		$480,000
Tentative tax	$149,000	
Less: Unified credit	192,800	
Estate tax due		None

Tax may be less if state tax credit not shown here is claimed.

REDUCING OR ELIMINATING A POTENTIAL ESTATE TAX

Here are general approaches to eliminating or reducing a potential estate tax: You can make direct lifetime gifts. Any appreciation on the property transferred will be removed from your estate. Furthermore, each gift, to the extent of the annual exclusion, reduces your gross estate (see ¶ 33.4). Life insurance can be assigned to avoid estate tax (see ¶ 33.10). You can provide in your will for bequests that will qualify for the marital and charitable deductions.

THE MARITAL DEDUCTION

A married person may greatly reduce or eliminate estate tax by using the marital deduction. Property passing to a spouse is generally free from estate or gift tax because of an unlimited marital deduction.

Weigh carefully the tax consequences of leaving your spouse all of your property. For maximum tax savings, you may want to reduce your taxable estate to the exemption floor (with marital deduction property). The unified credit will then eliminate tax on that amount at the time of your death. By leaving your spouse less than the maximum deductible amount, you may also reduce the tax at the time of his or her death.

To qualify for the marital deduction, the property must generally be given to the spouse outright or by other legal arrangements that are equivalent to outright ownership in law. There is an exception in the case of income interests in charitable remainder annuity or unitrusts and certain other terminable interests (QTIPs) for which the executor makes an election.

Life insurance proceeds may qualify as marital deduction property. Name your spouse unconditional beneficiary of the proceeds with unrestricted control over any unpaid proceeds. If your spouse is not given this control or general power of appointment, then proceeds remaining on your spouse's death must be payable to his or her estate. Otherwise, the insurance proceeds will not qualify for the marital deduction.

What should be done if you believe your spouse cannot manage property? You will not want to give complete and personal control. The law permits you to put the property in certain trust arrangements that are considered equivalent to complete ownership. Your attorney can explain how you can protect your spouse's interest and qualify the trust property for the marital deduction.

A FINAL WORD

You are now aware of the costs of transferring an estate and of the amount of tax that may be levied. But no estate plan is ever really final. Economic conditions and inflation constantly change values. For this reason, your plan must be reviewed periodically as changes occur in your family and business; when a birth or death occurs; when you receive a substantial increase or decrease in income; when you enter a new business venture or resign from an old one; when you sell, retire, bring new persons into business. A member of your family may no longer need any part of your estate, while others may need more. Estate or gift tax laws may be revised, or material changes may occur in the health or life expectancy of one of your beneficiaries.

A final word of caution: Estate tax planning is not a do-it-yourself activity. We suggest that you contact experienced counsel to help you.

UNIFIED GIFT AND ESTATE TAX RATES

If taxable amount is—		The tax is—			
Over	But not over	This—	Plus %	Over	
$ 0	$ 0	$ 0	18	$ 0	
10,000	20,000	1,800	20	10,000	
20,000	40,000	3,800	22	20,000	
40,000	60,000	8,200	24	40,000	
60,000	80,000	13,000	26	60,000	
80,000	100,000	18,200	28	80,000	
100,000	150,000	23,800	30	100,000	
150,000	250,000	38,800	32	150,000	
250,000	500,000	70,800	34	250,000	
500,000	750,000	155,800	37	500,000	
750,000	1,000,000	248,300	39	750,000	
1,000,000	1,250,000	345,800	41	1,000,000	
1,250,000	1,500,000	448,300	43	1,250,000	
1,500,000	2,000,000	555,800	45	1,500,000	
2,000,000	2,500,000	780,800	49	2,000,000	
2,500,000	3,000,000	1,025.800	53	2,500,000	
3,000,000		1,290,800	55	3,000,000	

Beginning in 1988 and thereafter, the top rate will drop to 50% for taxable estates over $2.5 million.

39 WHAT TO INCLUDE IN GROSS INCOME

A

Administrators' and executors' fees; ¶2.16, 12.2
Advance payments of income of which you have unrestricted use, such as rent and commissions; ¶2.10, 2.12, 9.2
Agents—include only your income, not that of your principal
Agreement not to compete, payments from
Aliens; chap. 37
Alimony; *see* ¶1.35 for when taxable
Annuities, in part; ¶7.17, 7.24
Annuity purchased by your employer; ¶7.24
Army or Navy pay; *see* Military and naval personnel
Awards; chap. 2; ¶12.4, 12.8, 12.12, 12.13
Awards to employees under Title VII of the Civil Rights Act of 1964

B

Back pay
Bad debts recovered, if previously deducted; ¶12.14
Bank interest; chap. 4
Bargain purchases under the rules of ¶2.11, 12.3
Beneficiary, distributions of income to you by trusts or estates; ¶10.16
Beneficiary of deceased employee, payment to from deceased's employer in excess of $5,000; ¶2.7
Benefits from your union while on strike; ¶2.14
Board and lodging, not furnished for your employer's convenience; ¶2.2
Bonds, income on retirement or sale of
Bonds, tax-exempt, income from sale of
Bonuses
Breeding fees
Building and Loan Association, dividends and interest received from; ¶4.1
Business overhead insurance proceeds to cover overhead costs while you are unable to work in your business due to illness or injury
Business profits; ¶5.1

C

Cancellation of a lease, receipt for; ¶9.5
Canceled debts owed by you; ¶12.15
Capital gains; ¶6.1
Capital gain dividends; ¶3.3
Christmas bonus
Civil Service retirement payments; ¶7.27
Commissions; ¶2.12
Commodity Credit Corporation loan to farmers
Community income
Compensation; *also see* ¶2.1
    Cancellation of an indebtedness by an employer in payment for services
    Compensation even when deemed "unreasonable" and disallowed by the IRS as a deduction to the employer. If you repay the disallowed portion; ¶2.15
    Compensation received near end of year, though deposited following year
    Compensation set apart or credited to your account on company books, which you have not received but could have withdrawn during the year; ¶2.10
Cost of living allowances to federal employees (except those civilian officers or employees stationed in Alaska, Hawaii, or elsewhere outside continental U.S.)
Cost of living allowances to Red Cross members outside continental U.S.
Dismissal pay
Earned abroad, above exclusion; ¶36.3
Excess drawings (on a salesman's account) which are forgiven by an employer; ¶2.12
Executors' fees; ¶2.16, 12.2
Income taxes paid for you by your employer
Offerings, fees and other contributions received by a clergyman, evangelist or religious worker for funerals, marriages, baptisms, Masses, or other services rendered

Payments received for an agreement not to compete; ¶5.46
Pensions; ¶7.1
Personal expenses paid for you by your company
Prizes and awards; ¶12.4
Retroactive wage adjustments (for example, in settlement of labor disputes) are compensation when received
Severance pay based on the value of employee's services, responsibility, attitude, and general contribution to the company
Sick leave and disability benefits paid; ¶2.17
Stipends paid to student nurses
Tips, prizes, and awards
Withholdings; ¶2.10, 25.3
Condemnation award to the extent of your gain—unless you reinvest in similar property; ¶18.21
Condemnation award for use of your property for a limited time. This is treated as rent income
Conservation payments by Dept. of Agriculture
Contest winnings; ¶12.4
Cost of living allowances; *see* Compensation
County fair prizes; ¶12.4
Crop damage payments
Crop sales
Crop share rentals

D

Damages received in litigation; ¶12.16
Debts, canceled; ¶12.15
Deferred payment sales; ¶6.33
Deposits received as security from your tenant; ¶9.2
Director's fees
Disability, salary payments during; ¶2.17
Discount on advance payment of insurance or annuity premium
Discounts or interest received; ¶4.1
Dividends; ¶3.1
Dividends from mutual funds; ¶3.3
Drawings; ¶2.12

E

E and EE bond interest; ¶4.15
Economic Opportunity Act pay to work-training enrollees
Embezzlement proceeds, in the year of embezzlement
Employees, annuities (in part); ¶7.24
Employees, benefits; ¶2.2, 2.3
Employer's stock; ¶32.7
Employment discrimination, pay for, under Title VII of the Civil Rights Act of 1964
Endowment policy; ¶7.22
Estates and trusts; chap. 11
Excess drawings, forgiven by employer
Exchanges of property; ¶6.44
Executors' fees
Expense allowances; ¶19.36

F

Facilities and privileges received from your employer in certain cases; ¶2.3
Family income; chap. 33
Family, profit on sales between members of; ¶33.11
Federal savings and loan interest; chap. 4
Fellowship awards if they do not meet rules of ¶12.8 and 12.9
Fiduciaries, income from; chap. 11
Foreign government, income from
Foreign income—*but see* chap. 36
Forfeited deposit on agreement to buy real estate; ¶6.20
Forgiven debts, in many cases; ¶12.15
Fringe benefits; ¶2.3

G

Gambling gains; ¶12.6
Golden parachute payments; ¶32.9
Group-term life insurance over $50,000—premiums paid by employer; ¶2.4

H

H and HH bond interest; ¶4.15
Hedging gains; ¶6.6

I

Illegal business or transactions, profits of
Income tax paid for another:
    Employer for employee
    Trustee for beneficiary
Independent contractor's income
Installment obligations, sale of; ¶6.40
Installment sales, profits realized; ¶6.34
Insurance premiums paid for you by your employer on non-group policies, *but see* exception for group-term life; ¶2.3
Insurance proceeds for loss of rent income because of fire; ¶9.2
Insurance proceeds—in some cases; ¶12.17
Insurance, surrender value in excess of cost; ¶12.19
Interest; chap. 4
Interest forgone on loan from employer; ¶4.10
Interest on deferred payment contracts; ¶6.39
Interest reduction payments under National Housing Act; ¶15.12
Involuntary conversion gain, when you do not replace the property; ¶18.20
IRA distributions; ¶8.9

J

Joint tenant—your share of income
Joint venture income; chap. 10
Jury fees

K

Keogh plan distributions; ¶7.3

L

Life insurance; ¶12.17
Life insurance premiums; ¶2.5
Liquidation of a corporation; ¶6.13
Literary work, income from
Living allowance paid civilian employee of Army
Living quarters and meals, etc., furnished by your employer in some cases; ¶2.2
Lottery or raffle winnings; ¶12.4
Lump-sum distributions from pension and profit-sharing plans; ¶7.3

M

Merchant Marine members, pay of
Military and naval personnel; chap. 35
    Allotments to dependents deducted from your pay (portion chargeable against your pay)
    Base pay
    Compensation received from the federal government for services rendered within or without the U.S.
    Drill pay
    Extra pay to work in officers' club
    Foreign duty pay (increase of base pay)
    Lump-sum payments for accrued leave
    Mileage allowance paid in cash for travel under competent orders without troops (your actual expenses may be deducted)
    National Guard pay
    Per diem allowance in lieu of subsistence paid on travel or temporary duty (your actual expenses are deductible)
    Reenlistment bonus
    Salaries received from former employers during military service
    Voluntary allotments
Mortgage liability paid by client in lieu of fee
Moving expense reimbursements; ¶19.13
Mutual funds dividends. Part may be capital gain and part tax free; ¶4.53

N

National Guard pay
NLRB award to employee for illegal discharge
National Teaching fellowships
Notary public fees

O

Option other than I.S.O. to buy employer stock; ¶32.7

Options—sums received by you when option to another is not exercised; ¶6.14
Options—sums received by you not to exercise an option you hold
Overtime pay (but not supper money)

P

Partnership, pool or syndicate income; chap. 10
Patent, royalties, license receipts and any infringement compensation; ¶6.17
Patronage dividends
Pay even if not received in cash
Pension and profit-sharing plan income; ¶7.3, 7.25
Pensions paid by an employer or the U.S.
Performance shares; ¶32.6
Premiums paid by employer on group-term life insurance policies over $50,000; ¶2.5
Prizes; ¶12.4
Proceeds on sale of life insurance policy over premiums paid; ¶7.22
Professional services, fees received for; chap. 5
Profit-sharing income, from:
    All profit-seeking transactions; chap. 5 and chap. 6
    Business operations, joint ventures, pools, syndicates, or partnerships
Profit-sharing plan income; chap. 7
Promissory notes received from your employer, in some cases; ¶2.11
Punitive damages; ¶12.16

R

Radio or TV contest prizes; ¶12.4
Raffle winnings; ¶12.4
Railroad Retirement Tier 1 benefits, if income limits exceeded; ¶34.9
Receivers' compensation
Recovery of bad debts previously charged off; ¶12.14
Recovery of certain medical costs; ¶17.5
Redemption of obligations; ¶12.15
Redemption value of U.S. Savings Bonds, at your election; ¶4.15
Refund of taxes previously deducted; ¶12.14
Regulated investment company dividends; *see* Mutual funds
Reimbursement by employer in excess of actual business expenses; ¶19.54
Reimbursement for medical expenses or casualty loss deducted in earlier year; ¶17.5, 18.11
Reimbursement of personal expense
Rents; chap. 9
Residence sales, profit upon, if you do not buy another residence under rules of ¶29.3 or if you are not 55 or over; ¶29.12
Resident alien—same income that must be reported by a citizen; ¶37.1, 37.2
Restaurant employees' meals—*see* ¶2.2 when tax free
Retirement pay from Armed Forces not for service-connected injury or sickness
Retirement pay when the payments are compensation for past services
Retirement pay to U.S. Public Health Service employee
Retroactive wage payments; *but see* ¶2.10
Rewards; ¶12.4
Rights
    Payment in form of rights which are really compensation. Stock right dividends are usually tax free; ¶3.08
    Sale of; ¶6.51
Royalties received by authors, musicians, inventors, lessors of property
Rural mail carriers' mileage allowance

S

Salaries; *see* Compensation
Sale of property; chap. 6
Salesperson, commissions; ¶2.12
Savings bank deposit, interest on; chap. 4
Securities, sales of; chap. 6
Separation allowances; ¶1.35
Severance pay
Social Security benefits, if income limits exceeded; ¶34.8

State and federal employees' compensation
State tax refunds if prior deduction produced tax benefit; ¶12.14
Stock appreciation rights (SARs), when exercised; ¶32.6
Stock options, nonqualified, even if given for a proprietary interest; ¶32.7
Stock, payment in form of stock which is really compensation
Strike benefits; ¶2.14
Suggestion awards; ¶12.4
Survivor annuity receipts; ¶7.28
Sweepstakes, winnings; ¶12.4
Swindling proceeds
Syndicate, income from; chap. 10

T

Tax refund of tax previously deducted; ¶12.14
Taxes, for which you are liable, paid by another unless the payment is a gift

Income tax of employee paid by employer
Tenant, joint or by the entirety—include income allocated in accordance with the rules in your state
Tips
Traveling expense allowances to the extent not used for travel expenses; see ¶19.36 for further details
Treasure you find
Treble damages in antitrust actions
Trustees fees; ¶2.16
Trust income; ¶10.16

U

Unemployment benefits
Union award for service
University Year for Action program stipend
U.S. Savings Bond interest; ¶4.15
U.S. Savings Bonds, deductions from salary to purchase

Use and occupancy insurance proceeds where reimbursement is for profits lost. Proceeds are taxed as ordinary income
Usurious interest

V

Vacation pay
Value of any property received as compensation
Veterans—
Damages for loss of wages paid by your employer because of failure to give you your former position
Damages for discharge paid by an employer within one year of restoration of your position
National Guard pay
Retirement pay; ¶35.3
Terminal leave pay for service

Wages received for on-the-job training as apprentices
Violation of civil rights, payments for, under Title VII of the Civil Rights Act of 1964 for employment discrimination
VISTA volunteer living expense allowance; ¶2.2

W

Wages
Winnings at exhibitions, fairs, in newspaper or magazine contests, sweepstakes, raffles or TV or radio shows (both money and property); ¶12.4
Withholding from salary, for U.S. Savings Bond purchases, income tax, Social Security tax
Work training program payments under Economic Opportunity Act of 1964

40 WHAT YOU MAY EXCLUDE FROM GROSS INCOME

A

Accident insurance compensation; ¶12.16
Accrued interest included in purchase price of bond or note and later collected; ¶4.4
Adoptive parents' payments received from state agency
Advances drawn from your employer which are repayable (taxable to you if debt is canceled by your employer); ¶2.12
Agent—the income of your principal (taxed to principal)
Alien working for a foreign government here
Alimony, which does not meet rules of ¶1.35
Allotment paid to serviceman's dependent
Allowances
Cost-of-living to civilian officers and employees of U.S. stationed outside U.S.
To widow under applicable state law if required to be paid out of estate principal
Ambassadors or consular officers of foreign governments, compensation to
Annuities; ¶7.17, 7.24
Portion of your annuity payment that is a repayment of your cost
Railroad Retirement Act
Social Security retirement payments
Appreciation in property not yet realized by either sale or exchange
Armed Forces Health Professions Scholarships; ¶12.12
Assigned income received if source is not assigned to you
Award, if turned over to certain philanthropies; see ¶12.4

B

Bad debts, recovery of, where previous deduction did not offset income; ¶12.14
Beneficiary of deceased employee—payments up to $5,000, from deceased's employer; ¶2.7
Benefit payments to veterans—see Veterans
Bequests and devises; ¶12.2
"Black Lung" benefits
Blocked currency income; ¶36.13
Board and lodging furnished by an employer if for convenience of employer; ¶2.2
Bond interest when received on certain obligations of the state or local governments; ¶4.11
Borrowed money returned to you
Breach of promise to marry—see Damages
Building superintendent—value of apartment furnished you for employer's convenience

C

Canceled debts, if forgiveness is gratuitous; ¶12.15
Capital gains of trust required to be added to trust principal are taxed to trust, not to you

Capital return to you
Car pool receipts
Cash rebates on purchase of new car or other items
Casualty insurance proceeds
Check you are holding because payer will not have funds to meet it until a later date
Check you refuse to cash because you claim a larger amount than the payor is then willing to deliver
Child care provided by employer under nondiscriminating plan
Child support payments; ¶1.44
Children's income is not income to parents
Clergymen, rental value of parsonage; ¶2.8
Clergymen, retired—payments by congregation, in addition to pension, motivated by congregation's love and affection
Combat pay up to certain limits; ¶35.7
Compensation—
Compensation depending on happening of certain future events
Compensation if neither computed nor made available to you
Compensation (up to certain limits) earned in a foreign country; ¶36.3
Cost-of-living allowances paid to federal employees stationed outside the U.S.

D

Damages resulting from suit for following (see ¶12.16):
Breach of promise to marry
Injury to goodwill or loss of capital. Recovery for loss of profits or loss of profits and capital combined—without segregating the amounts—is fully taxed.
Libel
Loss of life
Personal injuries
Property settlements; ¶1.70, 6.48
Slander
Support money for minor children
Death benefits of $50,000 payable from Law Enforcement Assistance Administration to surviving dependents of public safety officers killed in the line of duty
Debts collected which, if previously deducted, had not given you a tax benefit; ¶12.14
Devises and bequests; ¶12.2
Diplomatic and consular officers (of foreign governments), compensation of
Disaster Relief Act of 1974 grants to victims of natural disasters
Discount on tax-exempt bonds
Dividends; chap. 3
Distribution from a corporation with no current or accumulated earnings; distribution reduces the cost basis of your stock. Distributions exceeding the cost of your stock give you capital gain
Insurance dividends from mutual insurance companies. These are merely an

adjustment of the premiums paid. However, when amounts received exceed the aggregate premiums or other consideration paid for a policy, then they are taxed. Same rule applies to dividends on paid-up policies whether dividends received or left with company. But interest on such dividends is taxed.
Stock dividend or stock rights under rules of; ¶3.6
VA insurance dividends; ¶3.11
Dwelling furnished a clergyman—or rental allowance paid in lieu of furnishing a residence; ¶2.8

E

Educational assistance allowance paid by Veteran's Administration; ¶12.12
Educational benefits received under War Orphans' Educational Assistance Act of 1956; ¶12.12
Employee death benefits; ¶2.7
Endowment policies proceeds—the part covering your cost. If paid in installments follow annuity rules at ¶7.17. If paid in a lump sum, see ¶7.22
Energy assistance payments by state directly or indirectly to qualified persons to reduce the cost of winter energy use
Escrow, payments held in
Estate, beneficiary may not be taxed on income accumulated in estate; ¶10.17
Exchange of property, tax free exchanges; ¶6.44
Executor's fees if waived before performance of duties; see ¶2.16
Executor's fees if the will provides:
The payment is a form of legacy; ¶12.2
You will have to qualify as executor to receive the money
You receive the fees whether or not you act as executor

F

Facilities and privileges supplied by your employer; ¶2.2, 2.3
Farmers' income of the following type:
Gain on sale of farm residence—if you buy a new residence within two years before or after the sale; see rules at ¶29.3
Increase in value of livestock not sold
Patronage rebate from cooperative for purchases made for personal use
Value of farm produce consumed by farmer and his family. (However, the farmer's expenses must be reduced by the estimated cost of raising such produce)
Federal income tax refunds
Fellowships; ¶12.7
Food benefits under the Nutrition Program for the Elderly

Foreign earned income up to $70,000; ¶36.3
Foreign housing costs, employer-financed; ¶36.5
Foreign income in blocked currency; ¶36.13
Foreign income from country having tax treaty with U.S. to avoid double taxation; ¶36.13
Forgiveness of some types of debts; ¶12.15
Foster parent's payments received from a child-placing agency as reimbursement for expenses of taking care of foster children. These payments are not more than the expenses. Neither the payments received nor the expenses need be shown on the foster parents' tax returns.
Fractional stock dividends under rules of ¶3.6

G

Gains not recognized on certain exchanges; ¶6.44, 12.20, 29.3, 31.5
Gifts; ¶12.2
Government endowment insurance dividends
Group-term life insurance premiums for coverage under $50,000 paid by employer; ¶2.5
Guardian not taxed on ward's income

H

Health and welfare payments; ¶2.18-2.21
Health insurance proceeds; ¶12.19
Home energy assistance payments under SSI or AFDC
House, sale of by owner 55 or over, within certain limits; ¶29.12

I

Impounded payments of compensation
Improvement by lessees (not income to landlord)
Income assigned to you, if the property creating the income was not assigned to you
Income exempt under tax treaty; ¶36.12
Income from sources outside the United States—in certain cases; ¶36.3
Income of the following types:
Appreciation of value of property not yet realized by a sale or exchange of the property
Disputed—the dispute must be settled by litigation or otherwise before it is taxed to you
Escrow—income held by agent. It is not included until available to you; but see ¶6.38
Improvements erected by tenant on your land; ¶9.4
Income assigned to you—if the property creating the income was not assigned to you
Income, fair value of which is not "capable of being ascertained with reasonable certainty." Thus there might be no tax where you have entered restrictive

agreements that make sale or negotiation impossible or require deposit of the property with disinterested persons until clearance under the agreement; ¶ 6.38

Income received by you as agent for others, as—

Proceeds of your family's securities that you retained by agreement

Fees you collected as a lawyer (or physician) in behalf of an associate group of lawyers (or physicians)

Income received by you where you act as nominee for another

Gains from stock trading that is for a group of participants or for another

Recovery of a bad debt, taxes, or interest on delinquent taxes which had been deducted in a previous year when they did not reduce your taxes—usually a year in which you had a loss

Reduction of debt due on purchase of property—when it is an adjustment of purchase price

Income tax refunds from federal government

Indian grants paid by U.S. for relocation and vocational training

Inherited land, monies, and other property

Injury to goodwill, payments received for—see Damage

Insurance payment for excess living costs following casualty; ¶ 18.18

Insurance premium on group-term life policies under $50,000 paid by your employer

Insurance proceeds; ¶ 12.17, 12.20

Interest, if it is:

Interest on the tax-exempt securities listed at ¶ 4.11. But if you detach and sell the coupons separately from the bonds, you include the proceeds

Due, but cannot be collected (it is taxed when collected)

Received in worthless bonds or notes

Interest included in the purchase of an obligation (as a bond or note). You must first recover the amount paid for interest. Any amount in excess is taxed

Interest on bonds in default at time of purchase if coupons mature prior to the date of purchase. These are usually purchased "flat" on the open market. Interest received reduces your cost

Interest accumulated on note to date of gift

Received in property which has no fair market value

Received without any legal obligation and proven to be a gift from your creditor

Received by a surviving spouse under a life insurance policy—and payments are made in installments. Excluded interest is limited annually to $1,000; see ¶ 12.17

Wholly or partially exempt, on obligations of state, territory, any political subdivision thereof, or the District of Columbia

L

Legacies received in lieu of executor's commission; ¶ 12.2

Legal fee turned over to legal aid society by lawyer employed by the society

Legal services under qualified group legal services plan; ¶ 20.5

Lessee's improvements; ¶ 9.8

Libel damages; ¶ 12.16

Life insurance premiums paid by your

employer, within certain limits; ¶ 2.3, 2.5, 32.5

Life insurance received because of the death of the insured, generally; ¶ 12.17

Living quarters and subsistence received from your employer for his convenience; ¶ 2.2

Loans

Loss of life, compensation for; ¶ 12.17

Lump-sum benefits received from Social Security Board

M

Mileage allowance paid to parent for taking children to school where there is no school bus service

Military and naval personnel; ¶ 35.1

Minister's dwelling or rental allowance; ¶ 2.8

Mortgage assistance payments under Section 235 of the National Housing Act

Moving expense payments under Uniform Relocation Assistance and Real Property Acquisition Policies Act of 1970 to persons displaced by federal projects.

Municipal bond interest; ¶ 4.11

Mutual funds' dividends that are returns of capital and pass through of tax free interest; ¶ 3.3

Mutual insurance company dividends (but not interest thereon)

N

National Defense Education Act grants under Title IV to graduate students preparing for college teaching careers

Nominee—the income of the person for whom you act is not your income

Notes received from your employer as security for salary he owes you. (The salary has not been paid because the employer does not have the money)

Nutrition Program for the Elderly food benefits

O

Old Age and Survivors Insurance benefits under Social Security Acts, if income limits are not exceeded; ¶ 34.8

Options to purchase employer's stock in certain cases; ¶ 32.7

Option payments to you as seller until option is given up

P

Parsonage allowances; ¶ 2.8

Partial payments received from a debtor in liquidation are not taxable until capital has been recovered

Payments to union's vacation fund under certain conditions

Payments under the state unemployment laws if income below certain limits; ¶ 2.13

Peace Corps allowances for living and travel expenses

Pensions paid by—

Employees' trusts out of payments by employees; ¶ 7.25

Federal government to soldiers' widows

Federal pension acts enacted prior to March 20, 1933, for World War 1 veterans

Pension plan contributions by employer to qualified plan

Personal injuries, amounts received for; ¶ 12.19

Political campaign contributions used in the campaign and not for candidate's personal use

Premiums paid by employers on group-term life insurance policies under $50,000; ¶ 2.5

Prizes; ¶ 12.4

Proceeds of certain life insurance contracts; ¶ 12.17

Profit on sale of house by owner 55 or over, up to certain limits; ¶ 29.12

Promissory notes, renewal

Property appreciation

Property damages—see Damages

Property which you received as an inheritance, gift, bequest, or devise; ¶ 12.3

Public assistance payments from a general welfare fund

R

Railroad Retirement Act Benefits, if income limits are not exceeded; ¶ 34.8

Rebates of cash on purchase of new car or other items

Receipts in court actions, in certain cases; ¶ 12.16

Recoveries of certain deductions in loss years in the operation of a business; ¶ 12.14

Recovery of medical costs, in certain cases; ¶ 17.9

Reduction of debt due on purchase of property—when it is an adjustment of purchase price; ¶ 12.15

Refunds of federal income tax and state tax if deduction did not give you tax benefits; ¶ 12.14

Regulated Investment Companies' dividends; ¶ 24.5

Reimbursements for out-of-pocket expenses in these volunteer programs: Retired Senior Volunteer Program (RSVP), Foster Grandparent Program, Older American Community Service Program, Senior Corps of Retired Executives (SCORE), Active Corps of Executives (ACE)

Rental allowance or value of home given to minister; ¶ 2.8

Rents collected by mortgagee after taking possession after a default. The rents collected are applied against the mortgage debt

Rent security; chap. 9

Reorganization, certain types of property received in a; ¶ 6.44

Residence sales' gains—if you buy, exchange, or build a new residence under the rules of; ¶ 29.3

Residence, sale of, by owner age 55 or over, tax free up to certain limits; ¶ 29.12

Restaurant employees' meals, in some cases; ¶ 2.2

Restricted, indeterminable, unavailable or disputed income. You pay tax when the income, gains or profits are fully available to you

S

Scholarship awards, meeting tests of; ¶ 12.8

Security paid to landlord; chap. 9

Separation allowances, in some cases; ¶ 1.34

Slander compensation—see Damage

Social Security benefits, if income limits are not exceeded; ¶ 34.8

State unemployment (up to certain limits) and disability payments; ¶ 2.13

Stock appreciation rights; ¶ 32.6

Stock dividends; ¶ 3.6

Stock option to buy employer's stock; ¶ 32.7

Stock rights, received; ¶ 3.6

Support payments for children; ¶ 1.70

T

Tax refunds—see Refunds—(but not interest thereon)

Tax free trades of property

Tax-exempt interest—see Interest

Tax paid for bondholder by corporation under tax free covenant clause; chap. 24.

Tools from your employer, needed in your work

Tenant relocation payments by federal government

Treaty exemptions; ¶ 36.12

U

Uniform allowances for Armed Forces personnel

Uniform supplied by your employer; ¶ 2.3

Use and occupancy insurance proceeds paid on a fixed daily allowance; ¶ 18.20

V

Veterans—

Allowances under Public Law 16 for disabled veterans

Automobile or allowance for automobile given to disabled veteran through Administrator of Veteran Affairs

Transportation in kind from your last station to your home

Disability pension; ¶ 2.20

Free hospitalization or outpatient service in veterans' hospitals

Clothing or clothing allowance on separation

Refund of National Service Life Insurance premiums if you were hospitalized more than six months

Federal Readjustment Allowance

Various other state benefits and bonuses

Proceeds from government endowment insurance contracts of World War I

Payments to veterans of World War I under Adjusted Compensation Act, including interest

Benefits under War Risk Insurance Act

Benefits and pensions received under World War Veterans' Acts or war risk insurance acts

Bonuses paid by any state or political subdivision for military service

Gratuitous medical or hospital treatment provided by U.S. government hospitals

Money paid upon discharge to enlisted men, in place of unused clothing allowance to their credit

Mustering out pay

Prisoner of war payments under 1954 War Claims Act

Value of travel furnished in kind to discharged enlisted men

War risk insurance and government endowment policies (dividends and proceeds)

War risk insurance (dividends and proceeds)

Widows' pension paid by U.S. to soldiers' widows

W

War pensions—benefits, mustering out pay paid to veterans or widows under any Act of Congress relating to veterans

Welfare benefits

Widow of deceased employee, payments received from his employer—up to $5,000; ¶ 2.7

Will contest, amount received in settlement of

Winter energy assistance payments

Workmen's Compensation Acts, amount received under; ¶ 2.19

---

41 WHAT YOU MAY DEDUCT

A

Accelerated cost recovery on business equipment; ¶ 5.30

Accident insurance premiums in your business

Accounting and auditing expenses paid for:
Keeping your books and accounts
Preparation of tax returns

Accrued expenses under economic performance test; ¶ 5.2

Advertising expenses for business

Alimony paid under the rules of; ¶ 1.70

Alterations and repairs on business or income-producing property

Amortization of bond premiums; ¶ 4.5

Amortization of construction period interest and taxes; ¶ 16.5

Appraisal costs for tax and business purposes

Army and Navy; ¶ 35.2

Assessments paid to labor unions for "out of

work" benefit payments

Assessments on worthless bank stock

Attending conventions; ¶ 19.34

Attorney fees related to your job or business
Estate planning; ¶ 20.3
Libel suits, business reputation; ¶ 20.3
Obtaining alimony; ¶ 1.36
Tax advice; ¶ 20.3
See also Expenses paid for the production and collection of income

Automobile—damages to; ¶ 18.13

Automobile expenses incurred during business trips (¶ 19.57); job-related moving (¶ 19.18), trips for charitable organizations (¶ 14.4), and trips for medical care (¶ 17.9)

B

Back pay, expenses to collect

Bad debts; ¶ 6.55

Bank deposit loss by failure of bank; ¶4.2, 6.28, 18.17

Bank charges on business or farm accounts

Blizzard losses; ¶18.1

Board and lodging given employees; ¶2.2

Bonding premium (in business)

Bond premium amortization on fully or partly taxed bonds; ¶4.5

Bonds, worthless; ¶6.11

Bonus to employees

Bonus payment to lessee or lessor; ¶9.2

Bookkeeping expenses (business)

Brokerage fee to obtain a mortgage loan if property is used in business. The fee is amortized over the mortgage term. In the year you sell the property and the buyer assumes the mortgage, you may deduct the unrecovered balance.

Burglary losses; ¶18.5

Bus drivers' uniforms; ¶19.6

Business expense and losses; ¶5.5, 5.6, 5.11

Business expenses of employees in excess of amounts received as reimbursements; ¶19.56

Business overhead insurance premiums for insurance that pays your business operating costs if you are out sick or injured

Business start-up costs, amortizable; ¶5.10

C

Cancellation of lease, payment made by tenant for (as a business expense only)

Cancellation of lease, expenses of lessor in connection with, including unamortized balance of expenses paid in negotiating the lease

Capital asset loss; ¶6.2

Capital loss carryover; ¶6.4

Carrying charges, as interest or taxes, *but see* ¶16.4

Carryover and carryback of a net operating loss; ¶5.20

Casualty losses; chap. 18

Chamber of Commerce dues (business)

Charitable contributions paid to religious, charitable, scientific, literary, educational, and other organizations (including family foundations) which operate in the manner prescribed; ¶14.2

Christmas presents and other holiday gifts to employees, customers or prospects up to $25 per person; ¶19.48

Clothing—uniforms, costumes, and working clothes—cost, laundering, and cleaning if required by your job and not adaptable to general wear; ¶19.6

Cleaning charges for windows, carpets, office furniture, equipment, draperies, etc., in your business

Collection of income and business debts, expenses connected with; ¶20.2

Commissions to employees—for example those paid to obtain business

Commissions paid to agents (press agents, literary agents, booking agents, etc.)

Commissions paid in connection with rented property; ¶9.2

Commissions paid to brokers on sale of property is deducted from sales proceeds; ¶6.27

Compensation paid employees and assistants

Compensation which you have to repay to your employer because of overpayments in former years; ¶2.15

Compromises, of business debts or as a result of litigation

Condominium owners' interest and realty taxes

Conductors' uniforms; ¶19.6

Congressman's salary he returns to the government. This is deductible as a charitable contribution. He must include his entire salary in income—he cannot merely report the net amount he keeps

Contributions, *see* Charitable contributions

Contributions to IRAs if within limits; chap. 8

Contributions to simplified employee pension plans; ¶8.12

Contributions to disability insurance funds in certain states; ¶16.3

Convention expenses; ¶19.33

Cooperative apartment and house owners—
Depreciation if used in business or rented to tenant; ¶5.16
Partial capital loss on worthlessness of stock

Proportionate share of real estate taxes and interest; ¶15.10

Cost depletion; ¶9.13

Costumes, wigs, and makeups (actors and entertainers)

Country club expenses; ¶19.44

Court proceedings, cost of (business only), except when guilty of a criminal offense

Covenant not to compete; ¶6.46

Credit bureau reports and service charges

Custodian fees paid to banks or investment counsel, fees incurred in the management of your investments where they produce taxable income

D

Damage to property held for personal use, as a result of a casualty such as a fire, shipwreck, storm; ¶18.1

Damages paid in connection with suits concerning your business

Debts, cancellation of employees'

Debts, uncollectible; ¶6.55

Delivery and freight charges in your business

Depletion of oil and gas wells, other natural deposits, and timber; ¶9.13

Depreciation on business or income-producing property; ¶5.22

Directors' expenses

Disability insurance deductions in certain states; ¶16.3

Disaster losses; ¶18.12

Disbarment proceedings, expenses in successful defense

Discounts allowed customers

Donations to charities; ¶14.2

Drugs and medicines; ¶17.2

Dues to (*see also* ¶19.5)
Clubs and associations, employer requires you to belong to hold your job
Membership in organized labor unions
Professional societies
Trade associations

E

Education—tuition fees, books, traveling expenses, etc.—if required to keep your employment or professional standards; ¶21.1

Carrying charges on installment payments of tuition

Efficiency expert, fees to

Embezzlement losses; ¶18.5

Employees, payments to

Employment agency fees; ¶19.8

Endorser's losses; ¶6.55

Entertainment of customers; ¶19.36

Estate tax paid on income reported by heirs; ¶10.18

Excess foreign housing costs of self-employed or not employer financed; ¶36.4

Expenses paid for the production and collection of income, and expenses to maintain, manage, and conserve property held for investment; ¶20.1

F

Farm expenses, if operated for profits; ¶10.19

Fees paid—
To bank acting as dividend agent in automatic dividend reinvestment plan; ¶20.2
To secure employment under limits of; ¶19.8
To secure admission to organized labor union
For passports on a business trip
To lawyers, accountants, etc. (See "Attorneys' Fees," and "Accounting and Auditing Expenses")

Fidelity bond—if you pay for it

Finance charges; ¶15.7

Fire insurance premiums (on business or income producing property)

Fire losses—*see* Losses

Firemen's uniforms and equipment; ¶19.6

First-year expensing of depreciable property; ¶5.34

Flood losses; ¶18.2

Food and drinks (for business entertainment); ¶19.36

Forced sales, losses

Foreign taxes paid; ¶16.12, 36.15

G

Gambling losses (only to extent of gambling gains); ¶12.6

Gifts for business purposes; ¶19.48 for limitation

Gifts (*see* under Charitable contributions)

Goodwill
Abandonment of
Loss on sale of
Promotion and maintenance of

Government employee's traveling expense which is necessary to do his job

Group life insurance upon employees

Guarantor's losses; ¶6.55

Guaranty against loss on sale of securities paid by securities' salesman to his customer

H

Health expenses—*see* Medical expenses

Heating (*see* under "Office maintenance")

Home office, limitations; ¶5.11, 19.10

Hotel costs when on a business trip; ¶19.25

Household or personal assets stolen or destroyed by fire or other casualty; ¶18.2

Housing costs while working abroad if self-employed or costs not employer-financed; ¶36.4

Hurricane losses; ¶18.12

I

Income tax return, fees for preparing; ¶20.3

Income tax, state or city

Individual retirement account (IRA) contributions, meeting limits; ¶8.1

Information, cost of obtaining, including cost of standard services for business, tax, or investment use

Injury benefits to employees (not compensated by insurance)

Insurance premiums on policies written in connection with your business. Advance premium payments must be allocated; ¶5.5

Interest paid or imputed; ¶15.1, 4.17, 6.39

Interest, prepaid, must be allocated over life of loan; ¶15.4

Interest, although not stated, on tuition installment plans or personal property purchases; ¶15.7

Interest paid in form of dividends from stock pledged for your loan

Investment counsel fees; ¶20.2

Investor's cost in short selling premiums, dividends, etc.

Involuntary conversion, loss; ¶18.1

J

Job expenses; ¶14.20, 19.3

Jockey's uniforms; ¶19.6

Joint venture losses; chap. 10

K

Keogh plan contributions; ¶8.13

L

Labor expenses

Labor union dues; ¶19.5

Lawsuit expenses—*see* Attorneys' fees

Library expenses used only for business or profession; ¶5.6

License and regulatory fees for your business paid annually

Livestock killed by authorities

Loans, uncollectible; ¶6.55

Lodging on trips to obtain medical care; ¶17.9

Losses (except to the extent covered by insurance) arising from:
Abandoned property
Abandonment of worthless business machinery
Bad debts; ¶6.55
Bonds sold or exchanged; ¶6.10
Bonds—worthless; ¶6.11
Business operations; chap. 5
Capital assets, sale of; chap. 6
Casualties such as fire, theft, storm, shipwreck; chap. 18
Deposit to secure business lease, forfeited
Deposits in closed banks; ¶18.19
Endorser or guarantor compelled to pay for principal when transaction was entered into for profit
Forced sales; ¶18.21
Foreclosures
Forfeitures
Futures account closed by broker
Gambling to the extent of gains; ¶12.6
Goodwill—sale or abandonment

Investments—worthless; ¶6.11

Joint ventures, syndicates, pools, etc., participation in; chap 10

Loans not repaid; ¶6.55

Machinery abandoned

Mortgaged property sold (business or investment)

Net operating loss carried over and back; ¶5.17

Obsolescence of business asset

Partnership operations

Profit-seeking transactions; chap 5

Sale of capital assets; chap 6

Sale of inherited residence; ¶29.11

Sales and exchanges of property; chap 6

Securities—sale or exchange; chap 6

Securities—worthless; ¶6.11

Seizures by the government

Short sales; ¶6.52

Stocks—worthless; ¶6.11

Transactions entered into for profit, even though not connected with a business; chap 20

Worthless securities; ¶6.11

M

Magazines, technical or in waiting room of professional

Malpractice, expenses of professional in defense of suit for

Materials and supplies used in your business

Meals and lodging; ¶19.25

Medical expenses; ¶7.5

Membership dues; ¶19.5

Messenger service (for business)

Military personnel; chap 35

Mortgage foreclosure losses; ¶31.7–31.9

Mortgage brokerage fees; *see* Brokerage fees to obtain a mortgage loan

Moving expense of business property

Moving expenses paid by lessor for prospective lessee (spread ratably over term of lease)

Moving expenses of employees; ¶19.13

Musician—cost of sheet music, arranger's fees, depreciation and repairs on instruments

N

National Defense Education Act grants under Title IV to graduate students preparing for college teaching careers; ¶12.12

Net loss in the operation of a business may be carried back and/or forward; ¶5.17

Net loss resulting from a casualty may be carried back and over; ¶18.16

Non-trade and non-business expense. Be sure to read the deductions allowed; *see* chaps 19 and 20

Nurse's expense for medical kit and drugs; ¶19.7

Nurse's uniforms; ¶19.6

O

Obsolescence; ¶5.22

Office maintenance expenses

Office rent you pay

Office stationery and supplies, including: Bills, cards or envelopes, labels and letterheads

Ordinary and necessary business expenses

Overdrawn advances of employee charged off as compensation

P

Painting expense, rental property; ¶9.3

Parking meter deposits (business car or truck)

Partially worthless business bad debts; ¶6.55

Patents; ¶9.15
Cost of improvement by licensee
Depreciation
Infringement litigation settlement payment
Litigation costs

Payments to Workmen's Compensation Funds

Penalty paid for prepaying mortgage payments

Pension plan contributions to simplified employee pension plan; ¶8.12

Percentage depletion; ¶9.13

Periodicals used in your business or profession

Plane fare for business trips

Points paid for loan under certain circumstances; ¶15.13

Police officers' revolvers, cartridges, etc., paid for by them

Postage (in business)

Premiums on business insurance. The IRS has required cash basis taxpayers to prorate the deduction of prepaid insurance premiums over the life of the insurance policy. One court, however, has allowed a full deduction

Preparation of tax returns, cost of

Professional dues (see "Dues")

Professional's expenses, including books and equipment of short life

Property damage; chap. 18

Property taxes; ¶ 16.6

Publicity costs in your business

R

Rebates on sales

Real estate, expenses of rental or investment property; ¶ 9.3

Real estate sales losses; chap. 6

Real estate taxes; ¶ 16.6

Receivers' fees for services rendered in carrying on business of a bankrupt

Refund by you to your employer of overpayment of compensation in a previous year. Note the special rule if the repayment is over $3,000; ¶ 2.15

Religious organizations, contributions to; ¶ 14.2

Rents, including
Payment to cancel a business lease
Payments assumed to secure tenants
Payments for the use of:
Business property
Safe deposit box used for business investment purposes

Repairs of business or income-producing property

Repairs to a residence or property which you rent to others; ¶ 9.3

Replacing business property damaged by negligence, theft, casualties, etc., when the replacement does not prolong the life of the property damaged

Research and development costs in business amortized over 60 months or more

Research expenses required for courses—the cost of which are deductible under rules of; chap. 21

Reservists' travel expenses; ¶ 35.6

Restaurant and night club bills for entertaining customers under rules at; ¶ 19.36

Royalty expenses

S

Safe deposit box cost for records used in your business or for income-producing or investment property; ¶ 20.2

Salaries or other compensation for services paid

Sales expenses
Discounts and rebates
Entertainment of clients and prospects
Promotion expenses
Special commissions and compensation

Salespersons' expenses; ¶ 19.1

Sample rooms, cost of

Savings, investment and protection
Loss if bank fails (only amount not recovered); ¶ 6.55, 18.12
Sales of securities result in a loss or they become worthless; see ¶ 6.55. (Interest on brokerage account is deductible only when paid, not when charged to the account; ¶ 15.2)
Worthless notes and loans to others
Life insurance loan interest deductible when paid in cash or by check; ¶ 15.2
Health and accident insurance premiums are considered medical expenses; ¶ 17.6

Scrapping of business property, losses caused by

Securities as charitable contributions; ¶ 14.6

Security transactions, cost of

Services of assistants

Shipwreck damages; chap 18

Short sales losses; ¶ 6.52

Short selling costs; ¶ 6.52

Simplified employee pension plan contributions; ¶ 8.12

Social Security taxes paid by you as employer

Soil conservation costs may be deducted currently or capitalized. See Farm deductions

Stamp taxes, if in connection with business or production of income

State income and other taxes; ¶ 16.2

State legislators, living costs

Stationery, supplies, and printing used in business and profession

Stock—see Losses

Stock rights, worthless

Storage charges in business

Storm damage; chap. 18

Subscriptions to professional or trade journals

Substitutes paid by you. Payments to a substitute teacher to take your place are deductible

Supplies used in profession or business

Support of a student, unrelated to you, in your home, up to $50 per month; ¶ 14.5

Surgeons' uniforms

Syndicate losses; chap. 10

T

Tax preparation fees; ¶ 20.3

Taxes paid (property, general sales, income); ¶ 16.2

Taxi fare, on business trips; ¶ 19.5

Teachers' expenses of attending summer school; ¶ 21.5

Technical magazines used in your business

Telegrams and telephones for business

Telephone cost, where you have a telephone at home solely to work (you have no regular hours); ¶ 19.11

Tenants—payment of real estate taxes, interest or other items for your landlord (if property is leased for income-producing purposes)

Termination expenses of lessor

Theater tickets, cost (for business); ¶ 19.48

Theft losses; chap. 18

Tips, in connection with deductible travel or entertainment expenses

Tools, tires, and other assets used in your business having a life of less than a year; ¶ 19.7

Trade associations' dues

Transportation costs; ¶ 19.21

Traveling and entertaining expenses; ¶ 19.25, 19.36, 19.3

Traveling between two jobs

Traveling to professional convention, limits; ¶ 19.33, 19.35

Traveling to get medical care; ¶ 17.9

Traveling to look after income producing property; ¶ 20.2

Trustees' expenses, certain commissions

Tuition costs; see ¶ 19.12 for limitations

U

Uncollectible debts; ¶ 6.55

Uniforms, required for your job and not generally adaptable for ordinary wear; ¶ 19.6

Union assessments; ¶ 19.5

Union dues; ¶ 19.5

Unreimbursed volunteer expenses for charity; ¶ 14.4

Unstated interest; ¶ 6.39, 15.2, 15.12

Upkeep, care and maintenance of real estate held for investment or rented to others; ¶ 9.3

W

Water damage to lakefront property, when caused by a storm—not merely action of waves during high water level periods; chap. 18

Windfall profits tax; ¶ 16.2

Worthless bonds or stocks; ¶ 6.11

Y

Your Income Tax; ¶ 20.3

42 YOU MAY NOT DEDUCT THE FOLLOWING

A

Accident, automobile, loss resulting from, caused by willful negligence; ¶ 18.13

Adoption costs

Alcoholic beverage taxes

Alimony payments (lump sum); ¶ 1.39

Alimony payments, if not part of decree or written separation agreement; ¶ 1.37

Assessments: Labor union members' payment for sickness, accident, and death benefits in some cases

Assessments, local, which benefit property; ¶ 16.6

Attorneys' fees
See below. Expenses not concerned with production or collection of income
See also Litigation expenses

Automobile expenses such as
For personal use
Those incurred going to office from home; ¶ 19.22

B

Bad debts which did not become worthless in this year; ¶ 6.55

Bank fees on personal checking account; ¶ 20.3

Bar examination fees; ¶ 21.3

Betting losses which exceed winnings; ¶ 12.6

Blood donations

Bribes

Brokerage fees or commissions; generally added to purchase price or deducted from sales price

Burial costs

C

Campaign expenses by a public officer or union leader

Capital expenditures

Caretaker expenses for unoccupied residence never offered for rent but merely listed for sale with broker

Carfares for traveling to and from work; ¶ 19.22

Casualty losses as listed at; ¶ 18.15

Child support payments; ¶ 1.44

Cigarette taxes; ¶ 16.2

City permit to build a personal residence

Club dues, if membership is for personal convenience and pleasure, even if club is also used for entertaining visitors; ¶ 19.44

Commissions on sales of real estate

Commissions on purchases and sales of stocks and bonds, if investor or trader; ¶ 6.27, 6.32

Commutation fares; ¶ 19.22

Compensation to domestics

Construction costs

Contributions described in ¶ 14.16

Convention expenses on cruiseship; see limits in ¶ 19.35

Corporation's expenses paid by stockholder

Cost of earning exempt income; see Interest

Cost of proceedings to find mental competency

D

Damages resulting from suits for the following—
Alienation of affections
Breach of promise
Negligence in the operation of your car when used for personal use
Slander, libel, other defamation of character

Debts of another, voluntary payment of

Decrease in the value of property because current market values are less than cost. No loss realized until sale, exchange, or determination of worthlessness

Deductions from your salary for withholding tax, Social Security, U.S. savings bonds, etc.; chap. 2

Defamation of character—libel and slander—see Damages

Defending or clearing title to property, cost

Demolition losses; ¶ 9.6

Depreciation on property held for personal use (such as your home or personal auto)

Development costs for farms, orchards, and ranches; see Farm expenditures

Distribution to beneficiaries of a trust or estate taxable to the trust or estate; ¶ 10.17

Divorce, attorneys' fees, other expenses; ¶ 1.36

Dog licenses; ¶ 16.2

Domestics' Social Security tax paid by the employer and the employee

Dues and fees of a personal nature, unconnected with your trade or profession, such as clubs, societies, fraternities; ¶ 19.5

E

Educational expenses for yourself or family, see exceptions; chap. 21

Employees' Social Security contributions; ¶ 2.10

Entertainment, personal

Estate administration expenditures and fees, other than for the production or collection of income, or for the management, conservation, or maintenance of property held to produce income; ¶ 20.2

Excise taxes; ¶ 16.2

Exempt income expenses

Expenditures to obtain publicity and personal popularity not directly connected with business or the production of income; see Personal expenses

Expenses
Attorneys' fees and costs:
To defend, protect, or perfect title to property
To establish your right to hold a public office to which you were elected
To get a court to allow you to reduce the

interest rate you have to pay on borrowed money
See also Litigation expenses

Carrying on transactions which are primarily a sport, hobby, or recreation and are not prompted by the profit motive

Commuting to your office or place of business

Cost of improving personal appearance

Cost of campaigning for public office or union office

Costs in connection with property used as your personal residence. However, if you rent the residence or convert it to income-producing property, then you are entitled to these deductions

Creditor's payments of life insurance premiums on debtor's life

Payment to another stockholder for his proxy to give you sufficient voting power to prevent a proposed merger

Safe deposit box rentals for personal effects

Stockholder's travel expenses for trips on behalf of the corporation

Expenses for which you are entitled to reimbursement from your employer but fail to claim reimbursement

F

Farms conducted for pleasure, expenses of; ¶ 10.19

Federal income, estate, excise, and gift taxes

Fines for violation of law

Fishing license and fees

Food, clothing, and personal entertainment

Foreclosure of mortgage on personal residence, owner's loss on; ¶ 6.8

Foreign taxes for which a tax credit has been taken; ¶ 36.15

Funeral costs

G

Gasoline, taxes on, for personal driving; ¶ 16.2

Gambling losses exceeding winnings; ¶12.6
Gifts
Gifts to customers or their employees—where it is against the law for them to accept gifts
Gift tax

H

Health or athletic club membership to improve or maintain general good health; ¶17.3
Hobby expenses or losses; ¶5.9
Home expenses, such as—
  Allowances to your children
  Clothing for the family
  Domestics; but *see* ¶1.30
  Education of children
  Electric light, heating and cooking fuel, water, ice, food, liquor, flowers, cleaning
  Home office expenses, unless you meet rules at ¶5.11 and 19.10
  Hunting license fees; ¶16.2

I

Improvements to buildings or equipment
Income anticipated but not received
Inheritance taxes; ¶16.2
Insurance premiums which you pay on:
  Any other personal assets
  Building during construction
  Dwelling which you own and live in
  The life of any executive, employee or stockholder from whose loss by death you are protecting yourself
  Your life
Interest not actually paid, i.e., giving a note, increasing principal, reverse annuity mortgage; ¶15.2, 15.12
Interest paid, such as that paid on: ¶15.8
  Another's note
  Mortgages on another's property
  Life insurance loans if interest is added to the loan and not paid in cash
  A note which is a gift. The interest on such a note is also considered a gift
  Debts incurred or continued to purchase or carry obligations, interest from which is wholly exempt from federal income taxes
  Interest paid or incurred to carry accounts or obligations whose interest is excludable
  Interest paid by Civil Service employees when reinstated under the Civil Service Retirement Act, in order to receive retirement benefits
  On an ordinary margin account with your broker if you do not pay it in cash and the broker has not collected dividends, interest, or proceeds from the sale of securities out of which interest due him may be applied
  Interest incurred or continued to purchase or carry single premium life insurance annuity or endowment contracts

Interest incurred or continued to purchase or carry life insurance, annuity, or endowment contracts (other than single premium) purchased after 8/6/63 under systematic plan for borrowing against increasing cash value; *see* chap. 15
Interest payments where there is no real debt
Interest on obligations originally owed by others but subsequently assumed by you for prior interest due. Interest for the period after you assumed the obligation is deductible
Interest voluntarily paid
Tax deficiencies, where compromised lump-sum payment is less than the total deficiency, penalty, and interest claimed, unless a collateral agreement permits collection of the total deficiency

L

Labor costs—your estimate of your own labor's worth
Laundry service, cost of personal
Legal fees; *see* Litigation
Lessee's expenses to make necessary repairs to leased property—where landlord promised to reimburse him but did not
Libel suits; *see* Damages
Life insurance, personal, premiums on
Life insurance premiums on client's life paid by entertainer's agent (the agent being named as beneficiary)
Light, heat, laundry, etc., for home
Litigation or legal expenses for these personal reasons:
  Breach of promise suit
  Contesting a will
  Defamation of character, by libel or slander
  Defending yourself against a criminal suit which is of a personal nature, as opposed to one connected with business
  Divorce or separation, and dower rights, but *see* ¶1.36
Living and family expenses
Living expenses except when traveling on business; ¶19.25
Local assessments benefiting property; ¶16.6
Losses arising from:
  Difference between the rate of exchange on date you made a loan and the date on which it was repaid (for nonbusiness loans)
  Farms operated for recreation with no intention of making profit
  Fictitious sales
  Gambling—even if it is your business, but *see* ¶12.6
  Gradual sinking of land
  Illegal transactions
  Reduction in value
  Sales of personal residence, car, etc.; ¶6.8
  Sale to family; ¶33.11

M

Military personnel—
  Cost of uniforms
  Cleaning, repairing and laundering of uniforms and equipment
  Cost of packing, crating, freight, etc., in changing official station, of personal effects of members of officer's family
  Cost of additional clothing purchased
  Daily transportation cost between home and station
  Damage to household equipment in moving
  Depreciation in value of uniforms
  Dues to officers' clubs
  Deductions for bonds, allotments or allowances, insurance and hospital fund
  Expense of visiting home while on furlough, leave, or liberty
  Fines imposed by court-martial sentence
  Professional textbooks, school equipment, etc., purchased to secure education in military school
  Premiums paid on war risk, converted government or commercial policies, life insurance policies, and premiums paid for increased insurance to cover hazards of aviation duty
Minor's allowances—*see* Allowances
Missing items—where you cannot prove theft

O

Old-age home, payments to, but *see* ¶17.11

P

Partially worthless securities; ¶6.11
Payments of an employee (teacher, civil service) into a retirement or pension fund; chap. 2
Penalties and fines
Penalties assessed by the IRS
Pensions, trust or profit-sharing payments, by employers unless the trust is organized in the manner provided by law
Permanent improvements, amounts paid for same, if the improvement increases the value of the property or estate; ¶6.32
Personal asset, loss on sale; ¶6.8
Personal expenses, *see* Home expenses
Probate expenses
Professions, expenses for admission to; chap. 21
Propaganda contributions; ¶14.16
Pursuing a hobby, cost of; ¶5.9

R

Recreation, expenses in pursuit of
Related taxpayers, losses, between; ¶33.11
Relief fund withholdings from your pay
Rental cost of keeping a safe deposit box for assets which do not produce income
Rent, when it includes payment for option to purchase property
Repairs to personal automobile or residence
Repayment of loans which you made

S

Sales tax
Securing title—a capital expenditure
Selective sales and excise taxes
Self-employed Social Security tax Separation allowances to a spouse in some cases; ¶1.35
Separation suits—*see* Damages
Servants, domestic, wages paid to
Sewer taxes; ¶16.2, 16.6
Shrinkage in value of property not sold, or exchanged (except inventories)
Slander and libel, damages paid for
Social Security taxes—
  Employee's tax withheld by employer
  Employer's share—paid domestics, unless part of medical expense deduction
Self-employment tax
Sports, expenses incurred in pursuit of (unless business expense)
Spouse's deductions if filing separately; ¶1.4
Stamps, except as a business expense
Stock exchange membership cost—a capital expenditure
Stock in cooperative apartment in which you live, loss for worthlessness
Stockholders' contributions to capital
Supper costs when working overtime
Support payments; ¶1.39

T

Tax penalties
Taxes on gasoline used for personal driving; ¶16.2
Termite damages; ¶18.2
Title to property, cost of defending
Trademark, payment for
Traveling
  Between home and place of work; ¶19.23
  By members of your family who accompany you on business trips; ¶19.23
  By student on a summer job away from home
  To explore general investment possibilities in an area—where there is not already an existing income-producing right or interest
  For pleasure; ¶19.20
Truck overweight fines
Tuition costs to get better position; ¶21.2

U

Uniforms, if adaptable to general wear; ¶19.6
Union assessments—see Assessments
Unemployment insurance payments to state, except in some cases; ¶16.3
Uncollectible judgment based on breach of contract to buy a house

V

Voluntary alimony; ¶1.35

W

"Wash sales," losses in; ¶6.53
Water rents for personal residence; ¶16.2
Will contest, litigation and compromise

PART TWO

WHAT MAKES UP THE TAX LAW

What Makes Up the Tax Law

The federal income tax law is based on statutes passed by Congress. The statutes are organized into a Code, which is currently called the Internal Revenue Code of 1986.

Ideally, there should be no need for legal sources other than the Code, and this is true where a statute as passed by Congress is so clear and specific that no one doubts its application. Where the wording of a statute in the Code is general and may be interpreted in several ways, you must seek interpretations which may help you resolve a tax question or support your point of view in a tax dispute. Authoritative interpretations are made by the Treasury and the Internal Revenue Service in regulations and rulings and by federal courts in specific decisions. The relative authoritativeness of these sources is discussed in this chapter.

LEGISLATIVE SOURCES

THE INTERNAL REVENUE CODE

The 1986 Tax Act redesignates the Internal Revenue Code as the Internal Revenue Code of 1986. The prior designation date was 1954.

The title of the Code remains fixed with the date 1986, although sections of the Code are amended every year. Structurally, the Code is divided into:

Subtitles (for example, Subtitle A: Income Taxes; Subtitle B: Estate and Gift Taxes, etc.);

Chapters (for example, Chapter I of Subtitle A: Normal and Surtaxes);

Subchapters (for example, Subchapter A of Chapter I: Determination of Tax Liability);

Parts (for example, Part I of Subchapter A: Tax on Individuals);

Sections (for example, Section 1 of Part I: Tax Imposed).

Sections run consecutively in the Code from Section 1 up to Section 9602. However, in the sequence many numbers are missing to allow for the further expansion. Each section itself is then broken down as follows:

Lettered subsections: (a), (b), (c), etc.
Numbered paragraphs: (1), (2), (3), etc.
Capital lettered subparagraphs: (A), (B), (C), etc.
Roman-numbered sub-subparagraphs: (i), (ii), (iii), etc.

CONGRESSIONAL COMMITTEE REPORTS

The legislative history of a section may be found in the reports of the Congressional committee that wrote the section. Under the Constitution, tax bills originate in the House of Representatives although in practice, the Senate has sometimes considered tax legislation before the House. In the typical case, the Ways and Means Committee of the House of Representatives holds public hearings and then prepares a tax bill accompanied by a written report explaining its provisions. The House then considers the bill and after it passes the bill, sends it to the Senate. At this point, the Senate Finance Committee holds hearings and prepares its version of the bill, which is also accompanied by a report. The Senate version may differ from the House bill. If the Senate passes the bill, the House and Senate Committee will then meet in a Joint Conference to settle differences between the two bills. The committee will also issue a report. The compromised bill then goes back to each House where it is usually accepted and sent to the President for approval. The bill becomes law after the President signs it. Thus, the legislative history of a section can be found in—

1. The Report of the Ways and Means Committee (cited as H. R. Rep.)
2. The Report of the Senate Finance Committee (cited as S. Rep.)
3. The Conference Report of the Joint Conference Committee (cited as Conf. Rep.)

These reports are published by the Government Printing Office and in recent years have been included in the Cumulative Bulletin (see page 331). Committee reports are helpful authority if Treasury regulations (see below) have not been issued covering the section.

Further, the Joint Committee on Taxation may prepare a general explanation of the law commonly called the "Blue Book," which is also considered part of the legislative history.

ADMINISTRATIVE SOURCES

TREASURY REGULATIONS

The regulations have the force and effect of law and may be relied upon as authority. Failure to comply with a regulation can result in a negligence penalty.

The validity of a regulation can be questioned. Courts are not bound by regulations and can overrule them if they are unreasonable and plainly inconsistent with the Code.

Once a regulation has interpreted a Code provision, passage of a similar law with the exact wording is regarded by the courts as evidence that Congress is satisfied with the regulation and thus the regulation will not generally be overruled. If a regulation is disapproved, the IRS can continue to enforce the regulation unless reversal of the regulation is by the Supreme Court (see below).

New regulations are generally first announced as proposed regulations. During a stated time limit, taxpayers are allowed to suggest changes or additions. Often, the IRS will hold special hearings to discuss the proposals, and then after reviewing the suggestions, will issue final regulations as Treasury Decisions (TD) which are first published in the Federal Register. Afterwards the regulations are printed in a separate pamphlet.

Each section of the regulations is preceded by the section,

subsection, or paragraph of the Internal Revenue Code which it interprets. The sections of the regulations are distinguished from sections of the Code by the arabic numeral 1, followed by a decimal point (1.) before the corresponding provision of the Internal Revenue Code. This designation is then followed by a dash (—) and a number further identifying a section of the regulation. With these numbers you can find regulations interpreting a Code provision. Thus, the regulation explaining IRC Section 301 is designated 1.301, and a section of that regulation is identified as 1.301–1.

A partial comparison of the system of numbering the various divisions of the Code of Federal Regulations and the Internal Revenue Code can be found below.

REVENUE RULINGS

Revenue Rulings make up a large body of IRS interpretations of the tax law. They are generally official replies to specific problems raised by taxpayers. They are published to provide precedent in the disposition of cases having similar facts to those presented in the rulings.

Revenue Rulings are published weekly in the Internal Revenue Bulletin. Every half-year, these rulings are republished in a book, called Cumulative Bulletin, which is available to the public at the Government Printing Office.

References to Revenue Rulings appear as follows:

In the Weekly Internal Revenue Bulletin:

Rev. Rul. 71–419, IRB 1971–38, 10—means that the particular ruling in 1971 is numbered as 419, it appears in the 38th weekly bulletin of that year, and in that bulletin, can be found on page 10.

In the Cumulative Bulletin:

Rev. Rul. 71–419, 1971–2 CB 220—which means that the ruling appears in the second semi-annual Cumulative Bulletin for 1971 and in that book can be found on page 220.

OTHER IRS RULINGS AND RELEASES

After the Revenue Rulings, there are several other IRS releases and rulings that are helpful in determining IRS policy.

Revenue Procedures—These describe internal practices and pro-

cedures within the IRS. They are published in the Internal Revenue Bulletin. References to them are prefixed by the abbreviations *Rev. Proc.*

Technical Information Releases and Announcements—These describe current IRS policy toward a specific issue. They are designed primarily for public release. Newspaper reports of IRS policy usually stem from Technical Information Releases. Sometimes a Technical Information Release will be republished as a Revenue Ruling. Reference to a Release is prefixed by the abbreviation T.I.R.; to an Announcement ANN.

Letter Rulings. These include private rulings, determination letters, and technical advice memoranda. Such rulings resemble Revenue Rulings except that they are not officially published and may not be cited as a precedent by any other taxpayer. However, they may be helpful as they reflect the IRS' policy and interpretation of the law. In one case, the Supreme Court noted that private letter rulings are evidence of an IRS position although they have no authoritative force. Virtually all letter rulings are open to public inspection after all information which could identify the taxpayer involved has been deleted. Letter rulings are referred to by a seven number citation, the first two numbers indicating the year, the next two numbers the week of the year the ruling is issued and the last three numbers are the letter ruling numbers in sequence for that week. For example, Letter Ruling 7821098 was issued in the 21st week of 1978. It was the 98th letter ruling of that week.

General Counsel Memoranda, Actions on Decisions, Technical Memoranda. These are internal IRS documents which provide reasons for rulings, regulations, and acquiescences or nonacquiescences to court decisions. In response to a lawsuit, the IRS has agreed to make available to the public all of these documents, including those dating back to July 1967. The documents are released by the IRS after deletions are made to remove identifying information. General Counsel's Memoranda (GCM's) are legal opinions on proposed revenue rulings, private rulings and technical advice memoranda. Actions on Decisions (AOD's) recommend whether or not to appeal adverse court decisions. Technical Memoranda (TM's) indicate the legal and policy basis for proposed Treasury regulations.

COMPARISON OF NUMBERING FOR REGULATIONS AND CODE

Division	Code of Federal Regulations Description of Number	Example	Internal Revenue Code Description of Number	Example
Section	Arabic numeral separated from the part number by a decimal:		Arabic numeral	31
	Section setting forth law	1.31		
	Section setting forth regulations	1.31–1		
Subsection	(None)		Small letter in parentheses	(a)
* Paragraph	Small letter in parentheses	(a)	Arabic numeral in parentheses	(1)
Subparagraph	Arabic numeral in parentheses	(1)	Capital letter in parentheses	(A)
Subdivision	Small Roman numeral in parentheses	(i)	Small Roman numeral in parentheses	(i)
Inferior subdivisions	Small italic letter in parentheses	(a)	Roman numeral in parentheses	(I)

* The first internal division of a regulations section is "paragraph" and the first internal division of a law section is "subsection."

JUDICIAL SOURCES

COURT DECISIONS

The authority of court decisions varies. When using court decisions, keep these points in mind—

The IRS is not bound to follow a court decision in any other case than in a case in which the decision has been handed down. The only exception to this rule is a decision of the Supreme Court.

Courts are not bound to follow the decision of another court. The only exception again is for Supreme Court decisions.

Court decisions are not of equal weight. A decision of the Tax Court has substantially greater significance than a decision rendered by a Federal District court and often by a Federal Court of Appeals, primarily because the Tax Court hears cases all over the nation and will apply its decisions on a nationwide basis.

Federal District courts are local federal courts and a Court of Appeals hears appeals only on a regional basis. So whereas one decision of the Tax Court will be equally applied through the United States, there may be several conflicting interpretations between district courts in various localities and Courts of Appeal in the various geographical regions. For example, a District Court in California is not bound to follow a decision handed down by a District Court in New York. And a Court of Appeals for one region is not bound to follow a decision of a Court of Appeals for another region. However, the precedent of a Tax Court decision rendered in New York will be controlling authority in a Tax Court hearing held anywhere else in the United States.

SUPREME COURT DECISIONS

Supreme Court decisions are the only decisions which the Internal Revenue Service and lower courts are required to follow. They have the same force as the Code and remain in force until Congress specifically changes the Court's interpretation or unless the Supreme Court in a later decision reverses its own position. Tax cases come before the Supreme Court when either a taxpayer or the Government files a petition for a Writ of Certiorari, asking the Court to review the decision of a U.S. Court of Appeals. However, the Supreme Court limits its review of tax disputes generally to cases where there is a conflict of decisions among several U.S. Courts of Appeals on a specific interpretation of a tax law.

Example of a reference to a Supreme Court decision is:
Beulah Crane, 331 U.S. 1 (1947).

Beulah Crane is the name of taxpayer involved in the case; 331 refers to the official volume in which the case can be found; U.S. designates the official Supreme Court volumes; 1 to the page within the volume; 1947 to the year of the decision. The case can also be found in volumes published by private publishers; citations to these volumes can be found in legal research services once the above official citation is known.

COURT OF APPEALS DECISIONS

There are 12 Courts of Appeal that hear appeals taken by either taxpayers or the government from decisions rendered by the Tax Court or Federal District Court. Eleven of these are regional courts that hear cases arising within their region, which is technically called a circuit; the twelfth hears cases arising within the District of Columbia. The circuits and the states within each circuit are listed below.

Appeals of tax refund decisions from the U.S. Claims Court are heard by a separate appeals court, the U.S. Court of Appeals for the Federal Circuit.

Court of Appeals decisions make up an important part of federal tax law. But the effectiveness of a particular decision may vary because of these factors—

The IRS is not bound to follow any precedent set by an appeals court decision. The IRS will sometimes announce its decision to follow or not to follow a court of appeals decision.

The Tax Court does not consider itself bound to follow any precedent set by an appeals court decision. The Tax Court view is that its nationwide jurisdiction cannot be restricted by the rules of the twelve different appeals courts. However, it will generally follow an appeals court decision in the circuit to which the case before it may be appealed.

A Court of Appeals of one region is not bound to follow the precedent of a Court of Appeals in another region. Consequently, a decision of a particular appeals court is far stronger for taxpayers who can bring their appeals before that court than for taxpayers who must appeal to other appeals courts. A court will generally follow its own precedents unless it is overruled or later decides its original position was wrong.

STATES WITHIN COURT OF APPEALS REGIONS

First Circuit
Maine
Massachusetts
New Hampshire
Rhode Island
Puerto Rico

Second Circuit
Connecticut
New York
Vermont

Third Circuit
Delaware
New Jersey
Pennsylvania
Virgin Islands

District of Columbia

Fourth Circuit
Maryland
North Carolina
South Carolina
Virginia
West Virginia

Fifth Circuit
Canal Zone
Louisiana
Mississippi
Texas

Sixth Circuit
Kentucky
Michigan
Ohio
Tennessee

Seventh Circuit
Illinois
Indiana
Wisconsin

Eighth Circuit
Arkansas
Iowa
Minnesota
Missouri
Nebraska
North Dakota
South Dakota

Ninth Circuit
Alaska
Arizona
California
Hawaii
Idaho
Montana
Nevada
Oregon
Washington
Guam

Tenth Circuit
Colorado
Kansas
New Mexico
Oklahoma
Utah
Wyoming

Eleventh Circuit
Alabama
Florida
Georgia

Court of Appeals decisions are referred in this book to their place in the Federal Series reports published by the West Publishing Company. The first series is cited as "F."; the second series as "F.2d" which began in 1924. For example, take the citation Isaiah Megibow, 218 F.2d 687 (3d Cir. 1955). Isaiah Megibow is the name of the taxpayer, 218 refers to the volume of the second series of Federal reports, 687 to the page within that volume. 3d Cir. refers to the circuit appeals court; 1955 is the year of the decision.

In some instances, cases are not reported in the Federal Series. For example, J. Carl Horneff, 69-2 USTC ¶9727 (3d Cir. 1969) may be found in U.S. Tax Court cases published by Commerce Clearing House. These reports contain tax decisions from all levels of federal courts except the Tax Court. Except for years prior to 1934, two volumes appear for each year. 69-2 refers to the second volume of 1969; ¶9727 is the paragraph at which the case is located.

U.S. TAX COURT

The Tax Court is a special court for taxpayers who appeal tax deficiences imposed by the IRS for income, estate or gift taxes. It is independent of the IRS and the Treasury department; its members are judges, and its decisions are subject to the same judicial review as that of any other federal court. They can be appealed to a Court of Appeals and then to the Supreme Court.

The Tax Court has a small tax case procedure for deficiencies of $10,000 or less. Such cases are handled expeditiously and informally. It is available at the option of the taxpayer. Cases may be heard by commissioners, rather than judges. A small claim case can be discontinued at any time before a decision, but the decision, when made, is final. No appeal can be taken. A decision does not have precedential value.

Between the years 1924 and 1942, the court was known as the Board of Tax Appeals. In 1942, it received the present name of Tax Court. Cases decided by the court before 1942 are referred to, for example, as 20 BTA 45; cases afterwards as 30 TC 43. (The first number of the citation designates the volume of the particular series of court decisions; the second number designates the page within the volume in which the case can be found.)

The IRS is not bound by a Tax Court decision except in the particular case in which the decision has been rendered. It can continue to litigate the same issue in other cases before the Tax Court and in other courts. However, in a tax dispute with a taxpayer involving the same issue which the Court decided against the government, the IRS may be more inclined to negotiate a settlement rather than have the taxpayer bring his case before the Tax Court for another unfavorable decision against its position.

There are two types of Tax Court decisions:

Regular decisions—these are officially reported by the Tax Court and can be found in officially bound reports. They are recognized by the abbreviation TC between the number representing the number of the official volume and the page within the volume, followed by the year of the decision.

Memorandum decisions—these are not collected in any official volumes but are released only in mimeographed form, copies of which go to the litigants. Two private tax services print memorandum decisions: Commerce Clearing House and Prentice-Hall. Commerce Clearing House publishes these decisions in volumes called TAX COURT MEMORANDUM DECISIONS, abbreviation TCM, Prentice-Hall as paragraph numbers in volumes called PRENTICE-HALL MEMORANDUM DECISIONS, abbreviation P-H. In this book, memorandum decisions are referred to in their place within the Commerce Clearing House service, unless only the Prentice-Hall service reported the case.

What is the court test for reporting a case as either a regular decision or as a memorandum decision? The Court says a memorandum decision involves no question of law, but merely facts that the Court believes are limited to a number of cases. If a memorandum decision does involve a question of law, the question is usually one which has been decided previously by the Tax Court and followed by the Court of Appeals. However, taxpayers can and do appeal memorandum decisions to the Court of Appeals as they can reported decisions.

How important are memorandum decisions? Although these are considered by the court as minor decisions, they are further examples of Tax Court policy toward a particular tax issue. Furthermore, memorandum decisions are often appealed and the decision of the appeal court in these cases may become important authority.

The IRS follows a policy of announcing its acceptance of or disagreement with a Tax Court holding against a position held by the IRS in an officially reported decision. No policy statements are made for memorandum decisions. These announcements are made in the weekly Internal Revenue Bulletin, as acquiescences or nonacquiescences. The IRS cautions that an acquiescence of a particular decision merely signifies its acceptance of the court's conclusion. It does not necessarily mean that it has accepted or approved of the court's reasons for the conclusion, and it advises its officials to apply the rule of acquiesced cases to only cases that have substantially the same facts and circumstances as the acquiesced case. An acquiescence or nonacquiescence of a reported case can be recognized by the abbreviation (Acq.) or (Nonacq.) at the end of the case citation. However, if you are going to rely on an acquiesced case, try to find the exact terms of the IRS approval from the weekly Internal Revenue Bulletin or Cumulative Bulletin. Sometimes an acquiescence is limited to only one particular issue of a case. Finally, the IRS is free to withdraw an acquiescence or nonacquiescence.

Current Tax Court policy in issues disputed by two or more Courts of Appeal is to follow the opinion of the Court to which the appeal may be taken.

FEDERAL DISTRICT COURT

There is at least one Federal District Court for each state, with the more populous states having two or more district courts. A Federal District Court can hear only tax cases in which a taxpayer sues for a refund after his claim has been denied by the IRS.

Not all District Court decisions are rendered in written form. But where they are in writing, they may be handed down as an Opinion, Findings of Fact and Conclusions of Law, or both. Generally, a District Court opinion is not strong authority, primarily because of the local nature of a District Court. However, a well-reasoned District Court decision may be accepted by other courts and even the IRS, and in absence of any other authority on a particular issue, a decision of a District Court may prove helpful as presenting at least one published view of the problem.

District Court decisions are referred to in this book to their place in the Federal Supplement series published by the West Publishing Company. For example, take the case Michelin Corp., 137 F. Supp. 798 (S.D.N.Y. 1956). Michelin Corporation is the name of the case; 137 refers to the volume of the Federal Supplement series; and 798 to the page within that volume; S.D.N.Y. to the Southern District of New York; and 1956 to the year of decision. District court decisions not reported in the Federal Supplement Series may be reported in U.S. Tax Court Cases published by Commerce Clearing House. These citations are explained in the section on Court of Appeals decisions above.

U.S. CLAIMS COURT

The United States Claims Court was established in 1982 to take over the trial jurisdiction of the U.S. Court of Claims. The only tax cases heard are those involving refunds of taxes. Decisions by the Claims Court on income tax questions have not had an important effect on the development of the income tax law. However, a favorable decision of the Claims Court on a particular issue which you may be disputing with the IRS may encourage you to choose that court to hear your case. And a well-reasoned Claims Court decision may be followed by the other courts. Appeals from Claims Court decisions are heard by the Court of Appeals for the Federal Circuit.

Claims Court decisions are referred to in this book to their place in the Federal Supplement series published by West Publishing Company and are designated by the abbreviation Ct. Cl.

PART THREE

CITATIONS OF AUTHORITY

Part III contains the citations of authority for the text and material in Part I: YOUR INCOME TAX. The numbers are identical in both Parts. You probably will start your research by using the Contents, Checklists or Index of Part I. The ¶ number of your topic directs you to the place in Part I where your topic is discussed. Authority for the discussion can be found by locating the same ¶ number in Part III. However, regardless of where you find the ¶ number of your topic—from the text, the index, the checklists—you will find the citation of authority under that ¶ number in this Part. The information in the text of Part I is identified further by the use of italics under the identical ¶ number in Part III.

The references to law review, tax journal articles, and private letter rulings in this section are not cited as authority for any position taken in YOUR INCOME TAX. They are provided as a reference for your further study of the topics under which they are cited.

Key to Citations

Revenue Rulings, Treasury Decisions, Releases, and Abbreviations

Law Reviews and Periodicals

Articles are cited according to their title, author, and periodical title. The number before the periodical title is the volume number, the number following is the page number, which is followed by the year of publication.

Filing Your Return

WHO MUST FILE

Income limits
IRC § 6012
IRC § 6017 (self-employed)

Joint returns
IRC § 6013
IRC § 1348 (maximum tax)
IRC § 37 (credit for the elderly)
IRC § 43 (earned income credit)
IRC § 44A (dependent care credit)

File jointly even though spouse had no earnings
IRC § 6013(a)
Reg. § 1.6013–1(a)(1)

Each spouse liable for tax
IRC § 6013(d)(3)
Reg. § 1.6013–4(b)
Vaughn C. Payne, 247 F.2d 481 (8th Cir. 1957), cert. denied, 355 U.S. 923
W. L. Kann, 210 F.2d 247 (3d Cir. 1954), cert. denied, 347 U.S. 967
Myrna S. Howell, 175 F.2d 240 (6th Cir. 1949)
Alma Helfrich, 25 TC 404 (1955) (Acq.)
Virginia M. Wilkins, 19 TC 752 (1953)(Acq.)
Eva M. Manton, 11 TC 831 (1948) (Acq.)
William W. Kellett, 5 TC 608 (1945) (Acq.)
Jane R. Ringler Exrs., 15 TCM 396 (1956)
Jake Krantz, 15 TCM 1205 (1956)

Determination of marital status
IRC § 7703

Surviving spouse
IRC § 2(a)
Reg. § 1.2–2

Spouse missing in combat
IRC § 2(a)(3)

Head of household
IRC § 2(b)

Self-employment income
IRC § 6017

Married, living apart
IRC § 2(c)
IRC § 143(b)

Different tax years bar joint return
IRC § 6013(a)(2)
Reg. § 1.6013–1(c)

Different years before marriage
Frank E. Bertucci, 146 F. Supp. 949 (Ct. Cl. 1957)

Dependent with investment income
IRC § 6012(a)(1)(C)(iv)

Nonresident alien
IRC § 6012(a)(2)(C)(i)

U.S. citizen with income from U.S. possession
IRC § 6012(a)(1)(C)(ii)

Tax year of less than 12 months
IRC § 6012(a)(2)(C)(iii)

Gross income
IRC § 61

WHEN TO FILE YOUR RETURN

IRC § 6072
Reg. § 1.6072–1

Postage meter date ignored
Irving Fishman, 51 TC 869 (1969),

aff'd per curiam, 420 F.2d 491 (2d Cir. 1970)

Combat zone
IRC § 112
Executive Order No. 11216, 1965–1 CB 62

Spouse traveling outside U.S.
Rev. Rul. 82–161, 1982–2 CB 379

WHERE TO FILE YOUR RETURN

IRC § 6091
Reg. § 1.6091–2

Armed forces
"Federal Income Tax Information for Armed Forces Personnel"

Timeliness
IRC § 7502
Reg. § 301.7502–1

APPLY FOR EXTENSION OF TIME IF YOU CANNOT FILE ON TIME

How to get an extension of time
Reg. § 1.6081–4
IRC § 6081
Reg. § 1.6081–1
Reg. § 1.6073–4

Extension of time to pay tax
IRC § 6161
Reg. § 1.6161–1
I.R. 1107, 2/16/71

Automatic extension period
Rev. Rul. 83–27, 83–1 CB 337

Still must pay interest
IRC § 6601(c)(1)

AMENDED RETURNS

Filing amended returns
Reg. § 301.6402–3(a)

¶1
How Your Personal and Family Status Affects Your Taxes

¶1.2 • SIGNING THE JOINT RETURN

Spouse relieved of joint return liability
IRC § 6.013(e)
Reg. § 1.6013–5
William M. Hackney, 35 TCM 420 (1976)

Executor disaffirms
IRC § 6013(a)(3)
Reg. § 1.6013–1(d)(5)

Dependent's joint return used as refund claim
Rev. Rul. 54–567, 1954–2 CB 108

Decision disallowed the exemption
Vonnie M. Hicks, 16 TCM 108 (1957)

Sign as spouse's agent
Reg. § 1.6013–1(a)(2)
Reg. § 1.6012–1(a)(5)

Sick spouse
Rev. Rul. 70–216, 1970–1 CB 265

Intended joint return
Walter M. Ferguson Jr., 14 TC 846 (1950)(Acq.)
Alfred E. Whitehouse Est., 14 TCM 501 (1955)
John Young, 11 TCM 239 (1952)
Jeremy H. Peirce, 43 TCM 400 (1982)

Note: Paragraph numbers refer to Part One. Items marked * are research aids, not citations of authority; see "Key to Citations" on page 337.

338

One spouse agreed to have other spouse handle tax matters
Muriel Heim, 251 F.2d 44 (8th Cir. 1958)
Myrna S. Howell, 10 TC 859 (1948), aff'd, 175 F.2d 240 (6th Cir. 1949)

Answers indicate intent
W. L. Kann, 210 F.2d 247 (3d Cir. 1954), cert. denied, 347 U.S. 967

Explain spouse's failure
Joyce P. Lane, 26 TC 405 (1956) (Acq.)

After joint return filed—may not elect separate returns after due date
Reg. § 1.6013–1(a)(1)
Matthew L. Ladden, 38 TC 530 (1962)(Acq.)
Thomas J. Leger, 29 TCM 101 (1970)

¶1.3 • INNOCENT SPOUSE RULES

IRC § 6013(e)

¶1.4 • MARRIED PERSONS MAY CHOOSE TO FILE SEPARATELY

Non-community property states; joint accounts
Rev. Rul. 59–66, 1959–1 CB 60

Three years to elect joint return after separate returns
Reg. § 1.6013–2

¶1.5 • DEATH OF A SPOUSE DURING THE YEAR

Joint return for decedent and survivor
IRC § 6013
Reg. § 1.6013–1(d), –3, –4

Remarriage
Reg. § 1.6013–1(d)(2)

Change in accounting period
IRC § 6013(a)(2)
IRC § 443(a)(1)
Reg. § 1.6013–1(d)(2)

Nonresident alien
IRC § 6013(a)(1) and (g)(4)(B)
Reg. § 1.6013–1(b)

Disaffirmance by executor
Reg. § 1.6013–1(d)(5) and (6)

Co-executrix could not disaffirm
Frank J. Floyd Est., 51–2 USTC ¶9415 (Orphans' Ct., Del. County, Pa. 1951)

Treat as late return
Reg. § 1.6013–1(d)(5) and (6)

Signing
IRC § 6061
Reg. § 1.6061–1
Reg. § 1.6012–2(b)(1)
Reg. § 1.6013–1(a)(2)

Privilege of treating survivor's return as joint return
IRC § 2
Reg. § 1.2–2
Reg. § 1.6013–1(e)

Survivor bound to joint return liability
Maxine Ruzich, 47 TC 380 (1967)

¶1.6 • DEATH OF SPOUSE IN PRIOR TWO YEARS

IRC § 2(a)

¶1.7 • EFFECT OF DIVORCE OR SEPARATION DECREE ON JOINT RETURN

Divorce or legal separation
IRC § 143(a)(2)
IRC § 6013(d)
Reg. § 1.6013–4(a)
Kenneth T. Sullivan, 256 F.2d 664 (4th Cir. 1958), aff'g 29 TC 71 (1957)

No exemption for divorced wife
IRC § 143(a)(2)
IRC § 151(b)
IRC § 152(b)(4)
Marcel Garsaud, 28 TC 1086 (1957)

Alimony deducted by husband
IRC § 215
Reg. § 1.215–1

Income to wife
IRC § 71
Reg. § 1.71–1

IRS will recognize new marriage
Rev. Rul. 53–29, 1953–1 CB 67

Mexican marriage
Albert Gersten, 267 F.2d 195 (9th Cir. 1959), aff'g in part 28 TC 756 (1957)

Interlocutory divorce decree
William F. Holcomb, 237 F.2d 502 (9th Cir. 1956)
J. R. Calhoun, Jr., 27 TC 115 (1956) (Acq.)
Joyce P. Lane, 26 TC 405 (1956) (Acq.)
Fred F. Davis, 15 TCM 1235 (1956)
Rev. Rul. 75–536, 1975–2 CB 462
Rev. Rul. 57–368, 1957–2 CB 896

IRS position
Rev. Rul. 67–442, 1967–2 CB 65

Decree declared invalid by state law
Harold E. Wondsel, 350 F.2d 339 (2d Cir. 1965), cert. denied, 383 U.S. 935
Herman Borax Est., 349 F.2d 666 (2d Cir. 1965), rev'g 40 TC 1001 (1963), cert. denied, 383 U.S. 935

Year-end divorce may not be recognized
H. D. Boyter, 74 TC 989 (1980), remanded, 668 F.2d 1382 (4th Cir. 1982)
Rev. Rul. 76–255, 1976–2 CB 4

¶1.8 • JOINT RETURN IF SPOUSE IS A NONRESIDENT ALIEN

Nonresident alien spouse
IRC § 6013(a)(1)
Reg. § 1.6013–1(b)

Claim nonresident alien spouse as exemption
IRC § 151
Reg. § 1.151–1

Joint return under election
IRC § 6013(g)

Special election where nonresident alien spouse becomes a resident during the year
IRC § 6013(h)

Community property rules do not apply where couple does not elect joint return
IRC § 879

¶1.9 • COMMUNITY PROPERTY RULES

One-half vested interest
Aimee D. Bagur, 66 TC 817 (1976), rem'd, 72–2 USTC ¶9607 (5th Cir. 1979)

Spouse receiving temporary alimony
Charloette J. Kimes, 55 TC 774 (1971)

Intention to move to a community property state
George D. Hampton, Jr., 38 TC 131 (1962)

Separate returns
IRS Publication No. 555

Renunciation of interest
Anne G. Mitchell, 403 U.S. 190 (1971)

Self-employment tax for spouses
Rev. Rul. 82–39, 1982–1 CB 119

Dependency exemption on joint return,
Thomas R. Jones, 38 TCM 599 (1977)

Community rules inapplicable to certain separated couples
IRC § 66(a)

Community property rules disregarded —spouse not notified of income
IRC § 66(b)

Community property rules disregarded —innocent spouse
IRC § 66(c)

¶1.10 • UNMARRIED "HEAD OF HOUSEHOLD"

IRC § 1(b)
IRC § 2(b)
Reg. § 1.2–2(b), (c) and (d)

Separated or divorced under court decree
Alvin J. Linton 30 TCM 88 (1971)

Status denied when children change residence after separation agreement
Fred J. Stanback Jr., 77–1 USTC ¶9181 (D.N.C. 1977)

Note: Paragraph numbers refer to Part One. Items marked * are research aids, not citations of authority; see "Key to Citations" on page 337.

Parent in rest home
Rev. Rul. 70–279, 1970–1 CB 1

Foster child, adopted child
IRC § 2(b)(1)
IRC § 152(b)(2)
Reg. § 1.151–3

Necessity of physical occupancy
John C. Muse, 434 F.2d 349 (4th Cir. 1970)
Levon P. Biolchin, 433 F.2d 301 (7th Cir. 1970)

Divorced husband in separate residence
W. E. Grace, 51 TC 685 (1969), aff'd per curiam, 421 F.2d 165 (5th Cir. 1970)

Separation
Hans O. Wesemann, 35 TC 1164 (1961), aff'd, 298 F.2d 527 (2d Cir. 1962)

Interlocutory decree
Carole F. Brown, 31 TCM 194 (1972)

Support order pendente lite as interlocutory decree
Walter G. Brusey, 41 TCM 1223 (1981)

Relative resides in your household
IRC § 2(b)(1)
Reg. § 1.2–2(b)

Same residence for taxpayer and dependent
Rev. Rul. 72–43, 1972–1 CB 4

Dependent's residence not same as taxpayers'
Clair Smith, 332 F.2d 671 (9th Cir. 1964)

Special rule for parents
IRC § 2(b)(1)
Reg. § 1.2–2(c)(2)

Old age home
Rev. Rul. 57–307, 1957–2 CB 12
John Robinson, 51 TC 520 (1968) (Acq.), vacated and rem'd, 442 F.2d 873 (9th Cir. 1970)

Marital status determined at close of year
Isaac Hilliard, 310 F.2d 631 (6th Cir. 1963)

Nonresident alien not a dependent
Rev. Rul. 55–711, 1955–2 CB 13, amplified by Rev. Rul. 74–370, 1974–2 CB 7

Spouse who keeps separate household
Hans P. Wesemann, 35 TC 1164 (1961), aff'd, 298 F.2d 527 (2d Cir. 1962)

Two-family house
Jean F. Fleming Est., T.C. Memo. 1974–137

Can still get dependency credit
Katherine Atchison, 17 TCM 718 (1958)

Same person can qualify only once
Reg. § 1.2–2(b)(2)

Residence for whole year
IRC § 2(b)
Reg. § 1.2–2(c)

Illegitimate child
Rev. Rul. 54–498, 1954–2 CB 107

Can move household
Reg. § 1.2–2(c)

Dependent confined in hospital
Reg. § 1.2–2(c)
Abbie D. Reardon, 158 F. Supp. 745 (D. S. Dak. 1958)

Father's absence because of marital dispute
Walter Petlow, 34 TCM 51 (1975)

Probably never return
Harold K. Brehmer, 191 F. Supp. 421 (D. Minn. 1961)
Walter J. Hein, 28 TC 826 (1957) (Acq.)
Rev. Rul. 66–28, 1966–1 CB 31

Pay more than one-half
IRC § 2(b)
Reg. §1.2–2(d)

Figuring household costs
Donald G. Teeling, 42 TC 671 (1964)(Acq.)

Need not be head of family
Rev. Rul. 57–415, 1957–2 CB 13

Custody decree has no effect
Allan L. Blair, 63 TC 214 (1974) (Acq.), aff'd, 538 F.2d 155 (7th Cir. 1976)

¶1.11 • TAX RETURNS FOR YOUR CHILDREN

Minor's earnings and deductions
IRC § 73
Reg. § 1.73–1

Minor's return
IRC § 6012(a)(1)(C)
IRC § 141(e)
Reg. § 1.73–1
Reg. § 1.6012–1(a)(4)

Signing return
Rev. Rul. 82–206, 1982–2 CB 356

Exemptions
IRC § 151(e)
Reg. § 1.151–1
Reg. § 1.151–2
Reg. § 1.151–3

Deduction for pay to minor
Zeno J. Pucci, 10 TCM 529 (1951)
Samuel Rottenberg, 20 BTA 589 (Acq.)
Rev. Rul. 73–393, 1973–2 CB 33

Salary to young children
Nathaniel A. Denman, 48 TC 439 (1967)

Filing for Social Security self-employment tax
IRC § 1401
IRC § 1402
IRC § 6017

Parental responsibility
IRC § 6201(c)

Estimated tax
IRC § 6015
Reg. § 1.6015–1(a)(b)

Minors under age 14
IRC § 1(i)

¶1.12 • TAX RETURN FOR A DECEASED PERSON

Responsibility for filing
IRC § 6012(b)
Reg. § 1.6012–3(b)(1)
Reg. § 1.6012–1(a)(2)(ii)

How reported
IRC § 443
Reg. § 1.443–1(a)(2)
IRC § 451(b)

U.S. Savings Bonds—jointly owned
Rev. Rul. 58–435, 1958–2 CB 370, distinguished by Rev. Rul. 68–145, 1968–1 CB 203

Income received after death
IRC § 691
Reg. § 1.691(a)–1

Income accrued
IRC § 451(b)
Reg. § 1.451–1(b)

Returns
IRC § 6012(b)(1) and (4)
Reg. § 1.6012–3

Deduction for estate tax
IRC § 691(b)
Reg. § 1.691(a)–4
Reg. § 1.691(c)–1

Marital status
IRC § 143
Reg. § 1.143–1

Exemptions
IRC § 153
Reg. § 1.153–1

Estimated tax
IRC § 6015(h)
Reg. § 1.6015(b)–1(c)
Reg. § 1.6015(g)–1(a)

Joint estimation
Reg. § 1.6015(b)–1(c)

Due date
IRC § 6072
Reg. § 1.6071–1(b)
Reg. § 1.6072–1(b)

Refund
Reg. § 301.6402–2

Community property
R. D. Merrill, 211 F.2d 297 (9th Cir. 1954)
Hunt Henderson Est., 155 F.2d 310 (5th Cir. 1946)
Stella W. Bishop, 152 F.2d 389 (9th Cir. 1946)
Rev. Rul. 55–726, 1955–2 CB 24

Death before return filed for previous year
Reg. § 1.6013–1(d)(3)

Note: Paragraph numbers refer to Part One. Items marked * are research aids, not citations of authority; see "Key to Citations" on page 337.

340

Request for prompt assessment
  IRC § 6501(d)

¶1.13 • RETURN FOR AN INCOMPE-TENT PERSON

Guardian files
  IRC § 6012(b)(2)

Reg. § 1.6012–3(b)(3)
Rev. Rul. 55–387, 1955–1 CB 131

Incompetency bars joint return
  David Herman, 38 TCM 119, aff'd in unpublished opinion (3d Cir. Dec. 13, 1979)

Spouse may file
  Rev. Rul. 55–387, 1955–1 CB 131 (joint return for missing spouse)
  Rev. Rul. 56–22, 1956–1 CB 558, modified by Rev. Rul. 58–267, 1958–1 CB 327

Claim All Your Exemptions

¶1.14 • CLAIM ALL YOUR EXEMPTIONS

No exemption for dependent on own return
  IRC § 151(d)(2)

Extra exemptions for elderly and blind repealed by 1986 Tax Act Section 103(b)

¶1.15 • CLAIMING YOUR SPOUSE AS AN EXEMPTION

Taxpayer's and spouse's exemption
  IRC § 151(b)
  Reg. § 1.151–1(b)

Determination of marital status
  IRC § 7703

Spouse not dependent
  IRC § 152(a)(9)
  Reg. § 1.151–1(b)
  Joel Dewsbury, 146 F. Supp. 467 (Ct. Cl. 1954)
  Charles W. Jamieson, 23 TCM 2091 (1964), aff'd 353 F.2d 1 (7th Cir. 1965)

Filing separate return
  IRC § 151 (c)
  Reg. § 1.151–1(b)

Spouse died during year
  IRC § 153(1)
  Reg. § 1.153–1
  Asa C. Epps, 26 TC 843 (1956)
  Rev. Rul. 71–158, 1971–1 CB 50

Remarried before end of year
  Rev. Rul. 71–158, 1971–1 CB 50

Widow remarrying can be exemption
  Rev. Rul. 71–159, 1971–1 CB 50

Divorce or separation
  IRC § 143(a)

Interlocutory decree
  Reg. § 1.6013–4(a)
  William G. Ostler, 237 F.2d 501 (9th Cir. 1956)
  Alice H. Evans, 19 TC 1102 (1953) (Acq.), aff'd, 211 F.2d 378 (10th Cir. 1954)

Rev. Rul. 75–536, 1975–2 CB 462
Rev. Rul. 57–368, 1957–2 CB 896, revoking I.T. 3942, 1949–1 CB 69

¶1.17 • TEST 1. DEPENDENT'S RELATIONSHIP

*"*Who Is a Dependent? Whose Dependent? What is Support?*" George Krawchick, 29 NYU Inst. 1343 (1971)

*"*Who Is a Dependent and How to Support Him Taxwise,*" C. L. Glassberg, 26 NYU Inst. 1 (1968)
*IRS Publication 501

Infants
  Reg. § 1.152–1(b)

Adopted or placed for adoption
  IRC § 152(b)(2)
  Rev. Rul. 54–70, 1954–1 CB 69

Foster child
  IRC § 152(b)(2)

Nephew, niece, uncle, aunt
  IRC § 152(a)(7) and (10)
  Reg. § 1.152–1(a)(1)
  Reg. § 1.152–2(d)

Contributions to a relative
  Lena Hahn, 22 TC 212 (1954)

In-laws
  IRC § 152(a)(8)
  Reg. § 1.152–1(a)(1)

Cannot claim spouse's brother's wife
  Rev. Rul. 1971–72, 1971–1 CB 49

Continue support after divorce of spouse
  Steele v. Suwalski, 75 F.2d 885 (7th Cir.)

Stepchild's husband, wife, child
  IRC § 152
  Reg. § 1.152–1(a)(1)

Close relationship not necessary on joint return
  Reg. § 1.152–2(d)

Close relative not living with you
  IRC § 152(a)(9)

Reg. § 1.151–2(a)
Reg. § 1.152–1(a)(1)

Cousin not allowed
  Rebecca Pettigrew, 24 TCM 745 (1965)

¶1.18 • UNRELATED OR DISTANTLY RELATED DEPENDENT MEMBERS OF YOUR HOUSE-HOLD

Friends
  IRC § 152(a)(9)
  Reg. § 1.152–1(b)
  Robert W. Trowbridge, 30 TC 879 (1958), aff'd per curiam, 268 F.2d 208 (9th Cir. 1959)

Foster children
  IRC § 152(b)

Living in another's house
  Zelta Bombarger, 31 TC 473 (1958)

Friend renders services
  William Thomas Hamilton, 34 TC 927 (1960)

Spouse not dependent
  IRC § 152(a)(9)
  Reg. § 1.152–1(b)
  Joe A. Dewsbury, 146 F. Supp. 467 (Ct. Cl. 1957)
  Rev. Rul. 55–325, 1955–1 CB 18

Divorce void
  Daniel Buckley Est., 37 TC 664 (1962)(Acq.)

Illegal relationship
  IRC § 152(b)(5)
  Leon Turnipseed, 27 TC 758 (1957)
  Leonard J. Eichbauer, 30 TCM 581 (1970)

Unmarried couple: state law controls
  Nevett F. Ensminger, 610 F.2d 189 (4th Cir. 1979) (violates N.C. law)
  L. J. Eichbauer, 30 TCM 581 (1970) (violates Washington law)
  S. J. Martin, 32 TCM 656 (1972) (violates Alabama law)
  In re Mary M. Shackelford, 80–1 USTC ¶9276 (Bankruptcy Ct. 1980) (does not violate Missouri law)

Note: Paragraph numbers refer to Part One. Items marked * are research aids, not citations of authority; see "Key to Citations" on page 337.

¶1.19 • TEST 2. SUPPORT PROVIDED THE DEPENDENT

Dollar amount
 IRC § 152(a)
 Reg. § 1.152–3

Promise to pay is not sufficient
 Rev. Rul. 67–61, 1967–1 CB 27

Obligation to pay in later year
 Rose D. Seraydar, 50 TC 756 (1968)
 (Acq.)

 Rev. Rul. 58–404, 1958–2 CB 56,
 clarified by Rev. Rul. 67–61,
 1967–1 CB 27

Support includes board, lodging, etc.
 Reg. § 1.152–1(a)(2)(i)

Educational expenses
 Ernest W. Herne, 52 TC 572 (1969)

Payment by insurance company
 Rev. Rul. 64–223, 1964–2 CB 50

Parent uses Social Security benefits
 Reg. § 1.152–1(a)(2)(ii)

Social Security to children
 Rev. Rul. 74–543, 1974–2 CB 39
 Ann. 74–115, 1974–52, IRB 29
 Rev. Rul. 57–344, 1957–2 CB 112

Medical care premiums
 Rev. Rul. 64–223, 1964–2 CB 50

Medicare benefits not counted as support
 Alfred H. Turecamo, 64 TC 720
 (1975), aff'd, 554 F.2d 564 (2d
 Cir. 1977) (Acq.)
 Rev. Rul. 79–173, 1979–1 CB 86

Medicaid benefits not counted as support
 Mary Archer, 73 TC 963 (1980)

Use of welfare payments
 Rev. Rul. 71–468, 1971–2 CB 115
 Eddie Carter, 55 TC 109 (1970)
 (Acq.)

Foster care payments
 Rev. Rul. 77–280, 1977–2 CB 14

State payments for adopted child's care
 Rev. Rul. 74–153, 1974–1 CB 20

Summer camp
 Betty A. Shapiro, 54 TC 347 (1970)
 (Acq.)

Singing and drama lessons
 Raymond McKay, 34 TC 1080
 (1960)

Child-care payments
 Paul Lustig, 30 TC 926 (1958)
 (Acq.), aff'd, 274 F.2d 448 (9th
 Cir. 1960), cert. denied, 364 U.S.
 840
 Dorothy H. Limpert, 37 TC 447
 (1961) (Acq.)

Confinement in public hospital
 Hazel Newman, 28 TC 550 (1957)

Veteran's tuition, subsistence allowances
 Reg. § 1.152–1(c)
 Florence L. Long, 30 TCM 588
 (1971)

War orphans payments
 Mary Keegstra, 48 TC 897 (1967)
 (Acq.)
 Rev. Rul. 68–415, 1968–2 CB 65

West Point
 Rev. Rul. 55–347, 1955–1 CB 21

Navy scholarship
 Rev. Rul. 58–403, 1958–2 CB 49

Naval ROTC
 Charles P. Ide, 40 TC 72 (1963),
 aff'd, 335 F.2d 852 (3d Cir. 1964)

Father in religious home
 Rev. Rul. 58–303, 1958–1 CB 61

Dependent inducted into armed forces
 Helena Thompson, 12 TCM 348
 (1953)
 Louis Lindauer, 15 TCM 896 (1956)
 Bennett H. Darmer, 20 TC 822
 (1953)
 Ralph A. Romine, 25 TC 859 (1956)
 (Acq.)

Allotment for member of armed services
 Rev. Rul. 70–87, 1970–1 CB 29

Cost of car and T.V. may be support items
 Rev. Rul. 77–282, 1977–2 CB 52

Surviving spouse receives life insurance
 Rev. Rul. 58–419, 1958–2 CB 57,
 modified by Rev. Rul. 64–222,
 1964–2 CB 47

Does not include life insurance premiums
 Miriam G. Sauer, 12 TCM 1377
 (1953)
 John C. Robertshaw, 38 TCM 935
 (1979)

Not funeral expenses
 Special Ruling, September 17, 1959

Student loan
 John L. Ketterl, 29 TCM 1694
 (1970)
 Philip J. McCauley, 56 TC 48
 (1971)

Value of personal care
 Mildred Bartsch, 41 TC 883 (1964)
 Frank Markarian, 352 F.2d 870 (7th
 Cir. 1965), aff'g 42 TC 640
 (1964), cert. denied, 384 U.S. 988
 Lolita M. Mosher, 29 TCM 251
 (1970)

Child attends school on scholarship
 IRC § 152(d)
 Reg. § 1.152–1(c)
 Charles P. Ide, 335 F.2d 852 (3d
 Cir. 1964), aff'g 40 TC 72 (1963),
 cert. denied, 384 U.S. 988
 Norman Manning, 29 TCM 1707
 (1970)

Student nurse's board and lodging
 Rev. Rul. 58–338, 1958–2 CB 54

State aid to handicapped
 Rev. Rul. 59–379, 1959–2 CB 51,
 clarified by Rev. Rul. 60–190,
 1960–1 CB 51

State aid to educate retarded child is a scholarship
 Rev. Rul. 71–347, 1971–2 CB 114

Musical instrument
 Virginia M. Cramer, 55 TC 1125
 (1955) (Acq.)

¶1.20 • HOW TO VALUE LODGING AND ALLOCATE FOOD COSTS AND SOCIAL SECURITY BENEFITS

Rules for figuring lodgings cost
 Reg. § 1.152–1(a)(2)
 Emil Blarek, 23 TC 1037 (1955)
 (Acq.)
 William C. Haynes, 23 TC 1046
 (1955) (Acq.)
 Norman Reiss, 37 TCM 299 (1978)
 Roy B. Abbott, 13 TCM 113 (1954)
 Rev. Rul. 53–235, 1953–2 CB 23 as
 modified by Rev. Rul. 58–302,
 1958–1 CB 62, distinguished by
 Rev. Rul. 64–222, 1964–2 CB 47,
 and clarified by Rev. Rul. 72–591,
 1972–2 CB 84

Cost of other support expenses
 Rev. Rul. 53–235, 1953–2 CB 23,
 modified by Rev. Rul. 58–302,
 1958–1 CB 62, distinguished by
 Rev. Rul. 64–222, 1964–2 CB 47,
 and clarified by Rev. Rul. 72–591,
 1972–2 CB 84

Allocating Social Security benefits
 Wilfred Abel, 21 TCM 1044 (1962)

¶1.21 • EXAMPLES OF HOW SUPPORT IS ALLOCATED

 Reg. Sec. 1.152–1
 Rev. Rul. 64–222, 1964–2 CB 47,
 clarified by Rev. Rul. 72–591,
 1972–2 CB 84

¶1.22 • MULTIPLE SUPPORT AGREEMENTS

 IRC § 152(c)
 Reg. § 1.152–3

Must actually furnish support
 John L. Donner, 25 TC 1043 (1956)

¶1.23 • DIVORCED OR SEPARATED PARENTS FOLLOW SPECIAL RULES FOR FIGURING SUPPORT OF CHILDREN

 IRC § 152(e)
 Reg. § 1.152–4

Custodial parent denied exemption despite providing more support

Note: Paragraph numbers refer to Part One. Items marked * are research aids, not citations of authority; see "Key to Citations" on page 337.

342

Nicki A. McClendon, 74 TC 1 (1980)

$1,200 support rule requirement for each child
IRC § 152(e)(2)(B)(i)

Noncustodial parent's contribution determinative, not separation agreement
*Letter Ruling 7821098

Arrearages not counted as support
Reg. § 1.152–1(a)(2)(iii)(a)
Frank Bower, 33 TCM 875 (1974)

Retroactive agreement giving exemption to noncustodial parent
Rev. Rul. 70–73, 1970–1 CB 29

Contribution by stepparent deemed made by spouse
Rev. Rul. 78–91, 1978–1 CB 36, clarifying Rev. Rul. 73–175, 1973–1 CB 58

Tests not mandatory
David A. Prophit, 470 F.2d 1370 (5th Cir. 1973), aff'g per curiam 57 TC 507 (1972)

Allocating housing costs
John D. M. Cameron, 33 TCM 725 (1974)

Alimony not fixed for support is not father's contribution
Lory Buccola, 54 TC 1599 (1970)

Standard of proof in courts
Allen F. Labay, 450 F.2d 280 (5th Cir. 1971)

Community property income
Martin Colton, 56 TC 471 (1971)

¶1.24 • TEST 3. GROSS INCOME EARNED BY YOUR DEPENDENT

Gross income test
IRC § 151(c)
Reg. § 1.151–2(a)

Gross receipts from business
Rayburn E. Hahn, 271 F.2d 739 (5th Cir. 1959), aff'g 30 TC 195 (1958)

Gifts not gross income
IRC § 102
Reg. § 1.102–1(a)

Social Security not gross income
Rev. Rul. 70–217, 1970–1 CB 12

Share of partnership gross income
Doris V. Clark, 29 TC 196 (1957) (Acq.)

Dividends excluded by dividend exclusion not gross income
IRC § 116
Reg. § 1.116–1

Capital gains deduction part of gross income
Reg. § 1.1202–1

Certain military pay
IRC § 112
IRC § 113
Reg. § 1.112–1
Reg. § 1.113–1

Insurance proceeds not gross income
IRC § 101
Reg. § 1.101–1

Disability benefit
Reg. § 1.152–1(a)(2)(ii)

¶1.25 • CHILDREN WHO ARE UNDER 19 OR FULL-TIME STUDENTS

No gross income test
IRC § 151(c)(1)(B)
Reg. § 1.151–2

Rule applies to child, stepchild
IRC § 151(c)(3)
Reg. § 1.151–3(a)

Adopted child
IRC § 152(b)(2)

Foster child
IRC § 152(b)(2)

Brother does not meet rule
John E. Young, 19 TCM 1519 (1960)

Full-time course
Reg. § 1.151–3(b)
Rev. Rul. 72–449, 1972–2 CB 83

"Co-op" job
IRC § 151(c)(4)
Reg. § 1.151–3(c)
Rev. Rul. 57–561, 1957–2 CB 114

Education institution
Reg. § 1.151–3(c)

Intern not a student
John F. Bayley, 35 TC 288 (1960) (Acq.)

Child files own tax return
IRC § 6012(a)(1)
Reg. § 1.6012–1(a)(4)

Filing test for dependents
IRC § 6012(a)(1)(C)

¶1.26 • TEST 4. THE DEPENDENT IS A CITIZEN OR RESIDENT

Dependent must be U.S. citizen
IRC § 152(b)(3)
Reg. § 1.152–2(a)
Rev. Rul. 55–413, 1955–1 CB 323

Definition of resident in areas contiguous to U.S.
IRC § 152(b)(3)

Dual citizenship of dependent no bar
Rev. Rul. 71–44, 1971–1 CB 49

Foreign students
Rev. Rul. 54–87, 1954–1 CB 155, amplified by Rev. Rul. 67–159, 1967–1 CB 280
Rev. Rul. 54–485, 1954–2 CB 244

Puerto Ricans as U.S. citizens
U.S. Code Title 8, § 1402

Treating income from U.S. possession as tax free
IRC § 931

¶1.27 • TEST 5. THE DEPENDENT DOES NOT FILE A JOINT RETURN

No exemption for dependent filing joint return
IRC § 151(c)(2)
Reg. § 1.151–2(a)
Benjamin F. Scott, 35 TCM 1563 (1976)
Kotee T. Eason, 26 TCM 240 (1967)
Stephan A. Etersque, 21 TCM 1411 (1962)
Clair F. Martig, 20 TCM 1704 (1961)

Joint return for refund purposes not a tax return
William J. Martino, 71 TC 456 (1978) (Acq.)
Rev. Rul. 65–34, 1965–1 CB 86
Rev. Rul. 54–567, 1954–2 CB 108

¶1.28 • REPORTING SOCIAL SECURITY NUMBER OF DEPENDENTS

IRC § 6109(e)

TAX CREDIT FOR DEPENDENT CARE EXPENSES

IRC § 21

Joint returns
IRC § 21(f)(2)

*IRS Publication 503

¶1.30 • OVERALL VIEW OF THE CARE CREDIT

Amount of the credit
IRC § 21(a)

Dollar limit on expenses
IRC § 21(d) and (e)

Credit limit to tax
IRC § 26

¶1.31 • EARNED INCOME TEST
IRC § 44A(e)

Spouse is student
IRC § 21(d)(2)

Spouse is incapacitated
IRC § 21(d)(2)

¶1.32 • HOUSEHOLD AND DEPENDENT TESTS

Qualifying dependents
IRC § 21(b)
Reg. § 1.44A–1(b)

Maintaining a household
IRC § 21(e)(1)

Note: Paragraph numbers refer to Part One. Items marked * are research aids, not citations of authority; see "Key to Citations" on page 337.

Two or more families
Reg. § 1.44A–1(d)(2)

Monthly proration of household costs
Reg. § 1.44A–1(d)(4)

¶1.33 • EXPENSES QUALIFYING FOR THE CREDIT

IRC § 21(b)(2)

FICA tax
Rev. Rul. 74–176, 1974–1 CB 68

Outside the home care
IRC § 21(b)(2)(B)

Summer camp
Edith W. Zoltan, 79 TC 490 (1982)

Payments to relatives
IRC § 21(e)(6)

Medical expense
Reg. § 1.44A–4(b)

No deduction for travel to day care center
Dorothy E. Warner, 69 TC 995 (1978)

Least expensive alternative not required
Reg. § 1.44A–1(c)(3)(ii)

Allocation between qualifying/nonqualifying service
Reg. § 1.44A–1(c)(6)

Allocation of expenses on daily basis
Reg. § 1.44A–1(c)(1)(ii)

¶1.34 • RULES FOR SEPARATED COUPLES

Marital status
IRC § 21(e)(3)

Spouse is not member of your household
IRC § 21(e)(4)

Special rule if you are divorced or separated
IRC § 21(e)(5)
Reg. § 1.44A–1(b)(2)

Note: Statutory references are to Code Section 21. Regulations are cited under prior law Section 44A.

Alimony

"Alimony and Marital Property Divisions Under the 1986 Act," Michael Asimow, 65 Taxes 352 (June 1987)

¶1.35 • DUAL TAX CONSEQUENCES OF ALIMONY PAYMENTS

Alimony deductible from gross income
IRC § 62(a)(10)
IRC § 215
IRC § 71
Reg. § 1.215–1
Reg. § 1.71

Deductible in year paid
Reg. § 1.71–2
Lily R. Reighley, 17 TC 344 (1951)

No deduction if paid by another
Reg. § 1.215–1(b)

Alimony trusts
IRC § 682

Husband not taxed on payments from transferred property
IRC § 71(d)

Tax-exempt interest from trust
Mary C. Ellis, 288 F. Supp. 168 (W.D. Tenn. 1968), aff'd, 69–2 USTC ¶9665 (6th Cir. 1969)

Deduction for estate
Homer Laughlin Est., 167 F.2d 828 (9th Cir. 1948)
Daniel G. Reid Est., 15 TC 573 (1950), aff'd, 193 F.2d 625 (2d Cir. 1952)

Alimony payments to nonresident alien
IRS Publication 504 ('82 ed.) p. 11

Refund of offsets
Reg. § 304.6402–1

Prior notice to offset
Elinor Nelson, 83–1 USTC ¶9249 560 F. Supp. 1101 (D. Conn. 1983)

¶1.36 • DEDUCTING LEGAL FEES IN MARITAL ACTIONS

Deduction allowed for arranging details of alimony
Reg. § 1.262–1(6)(7)
Barbara B. LeMond, 13 TC 670 (1949)(Acq.)
Harriet C. Flowers, 57–1 USTC ¶9655 (W.D. Pa. 1957)
Ruth K. Wild, 42 TC 706 (1964) (Acq.)
Jimmie T. Jernigen, 34 TCM 615 (1975)

No deduction for wife—property rights in issue
Georgia Leary Neill, 42 TC 793 (1964)

Fee added to basis of property
Shirley H. W. George, 434 F.2d 1336 (Ct. Cl. 1971)

Wife's action to increase alimony
Elsie B. Gale, 13 TC 661 (1949) (Acq.)

Husband's legal expenses
Don Gilmore, 372 U.S. 39 (1963)
Talbot Patrick, 372 U.S. 53 (1963)

Fee allocated to tax advice
Rev. Rul. 72–545, 1972–2 CB 179
Gurnee Munn Jr., 455 F.2d 1028 (Ct. Cl. 1972)

Husband may not deduct wife's legal fees
R. William Johnson, 30 TCM 580 (1971)

Jack Rose, 30 TCM 634 (1971), aff'd, 459 F.2d 28 (6th Cir. 1972), cert. denied, 409 U.S. 879

¶1.37 • DECREE OR AGREEMENT REQUIRED

"Invalid Divorce Decrees," S. Spolter, 24 Tax L. Rev. 163 (1969)

"Tax Consequences of Annulment," J. Tilt and M. Spencer, 61 Taxes 65 (1983)

Decree required—Pre-1985 law
IRC § 71(a)(1)
Reg. § 1.71–1(b)(1)

Decree or separation agreement required—Post 1984 law
IRC § 71(b)(1)(A)
IRC § 71(b)(2)

State decree declared invalid by another state: IRS view
Rev. Rul. 67–442, 1967–2 CB 65
Harold K. Lee, 550 F.2d 1201 (9th Cir. 1977)

State decree declared invalid by another state: other view
Harold E. Wondsel, 350 F.2d 339 (2d Cir. 1965), cert. denied, 383 U.S. 935
Est. of Herman Borax, 349 F.2d 666 (2d Cir. 1965)
George J. Feinberg, 198 F.2d 260 (3d Cir. 1952)

Local support order after out of state divorce
Rev. Rul. 70–61, 1970–1 CB 18

Local support order before Mexican decree
Rev. Rul. 71–390, 1971–2 CB 82

Note: Paragraph numbers refer to Part One. Items marked * are research aids, not citations of authority; see "Key to Citations" on page 337.

344

Roman Catholic ecclesiastical board
Harold L. Clark, 40 TC 57 (1965)

Sample clauses for alimony agreements
Rev. Proc. 82–53, 1982–2 CB 842

Amendment of written agreement after divorce or legal separation
Rev. Rul. 60–140, 1960–1 CB 31
Rev. Rul. 60–141, 1960–1 CB 33
Rev. Rul. 58–152, 1958–1 CB 32

Agreement not incident
Rev. Rul. 60–142, 1960–1 CB 34

Annulment
Andrew M. Newburger, 61 TC 457 (1974) (Acq.)
George F. Reisman, 49 TC 570 (1968) (Acq.)
Anne S. Laster, 48 TC 178 (1967) (Acq.)

Written separation agreement
Howard Bogard, 59 TC 97 (1972) (Acq.)

Oral modification not valid
Eugene H. Bishop, T.C. Memo. 1983–240

Reference to agreement not sufficient
Welford E. Garner Jr., 32 TCM 353 (1973)

Support decree
Rev. Rul. 59–248, 1959–2 CB 31

Support decree valid after divorce
Jeanne S. Knobler, 59 TC 261 (1972)

Support decree not valid after divorce
Benjamin Wolman, 64 TC 883 (1975)

¶1.39 • SUPPORT OBLIGATION— PRE-1985

Must be obligation to support
IRC § 71(a)
Reg. § 1.71–1(b)(4)

Loan repayment
Reg. § 1.71–1(b)(4)

Community property
P. G. Lake, 220 F.2d 341 (5th Cir. 1955)
John S. Thompson, 22 TC 275 (1954) (Acq.)

Two kinds of payments
James M. Fidler, 231 F.2d 138 (9th Cir. 1956)

Edward Bartsch, 203 F.2d 715 (2d Cir. 1953)
Frank C. Smith Est., 208 F.2d 349 (3d Cir. 1953)
Marguerite D. Haldeman Est., 15 TCM 900 (1956)

Assignment of rights to payments
Marjorie J. Campbell, 25 TCM 1355 (1966)

Court increases alimony amount taxable
Elsie B. Gale, 13 TC 661 (1949), aff'd, 191 F.2d 79 (2d Cir. 1951)

Voluntary payment
Natalia D. Murray, 174 F.2d 816 (2d Cir. 1949)
Benjamin B. Cox, 176 F.2d 226 (3d Cir. 1949), aff'g 10 TC 955 (1948)

Permanent alimony after remarriage
Allen Hoffman, 54 TC 1607 (1971), aff'd, 455 F.2d 161 (7th Cir. 1972)
Alfredo Mass, 81 TC 112 (1983)

Voluntary payments after court order denies temporary alimony
Sylvia E. Taylor, 55 TC 1134 (1971)

Payments recommended by state domestic relations master are not deductible
Eugene E. Deyette, 36 TCM 1343 (1977)

Wife taxable on voluntary alimony
Rev. Rul. 81–8, 1981–1 CB 42

Excess payments are voluntary
George H. Moore, 449 F. Supp. 163 (N.D. Tex. 1978)

Gift tax on voluntary payments
Rev. Rul. 79–118, 1979–1 CB 315

Post remarriage payments not alimony
Martha K. Brown, 50 TC 865 (1968) (Acq.), aff'd per curiam, 69–2 USTC ¶9617 (4th Cir. 1969)
Allen Hoffman, 54 TC 1607 (1970) (Acq.), aff'd per curiam, 455 F.2d 161 (7th Cir. 1972)

Husband remains at home
Marion S. DelVecchio, 32 TCM 1153 (1973)

Couple living in same home
Richard J. Sydnes, 577 F.2d 60 (8th Cir. 1978), rev'g 68 TC 170 (1976) (considered separated)
Alexander Washington, 77 TC 601 (1981) (not separated)
William C. Lyddan, 721 F.2d 875 (2d Cir. 1983)

¶1.40 • PERIODIC PAYMENTS— PRE-1985

Must be periodic—Pre-1985
IRC § 71
Reg. § 1.71–1(d)

Installments over 10 years—Pre-1985
IRC § 71(c)
Reg. § 1.71–1(d)

Installments less than 10 years—no fixed total
Reg. § 1.71–1(d)(3)(i)

Supplementary agreement
Randal W. Clark, Jr., 58 TC 519 (1972)

10% limitation not applied to arrears
Antoinette L. Holmhan, 21 TC 451 (1954), aff'd, 222 F.2d 82 (2d Cir. 1955)

10-year rule
Harold J. Lehman, 239 F.2d 139 (7th Cir. 1957)
Marie M. Newman, 248 F.2d 473 (8th Cir. 1957)
A. F. Reis, 214 F.2d 328 (10th Cir. 1954)
Tillie Blum, 187 F.2d 177 (7th Cir. 1951), cert. denied, 342 U.S. 819
Harry Blum, 177 F.2d 670 (7th Cir. 1949)
Rev. Rul. 59–190. 1959–1 CB 23

Measured from agreement
Gordon L. Munderloh, 48 TC 452 (1967) (Acq.)

Measure from date of decree
William M. Joslin Sr., 424 F.2d 1223 (7th Cir. 1970)

Must actually make payments over 10-year period
Harold J. Lehman, 239 F.2d 139 (7th Cir. 1957)

Monthly might mean any time during month
A. F. Reis, 214 F.2d 327 (10th Cir. 1954)

Lump-sum settlement of periodic payments
Alan E. Ashcraft Jr., 28 TC 356 (1957), aff'd, 252 F.2d 200 (7th Cir. 1958)

Payment to wife on remarriage
W. M. Hardy, 59 TC 587 (1973)
Jean Cattier, 17 TC 1461 (1952)

Lump-sum settlement of arrears
Harold C. Holloway, 428 F.2d 140 (9th Cir. 1970)
Jane C. Grant, 18 TC 1013 (1952), aff'd, 209 F.2d 430 (2d Cir. 1954)
Virginia B. A. Davis, 41 TC 815 (1964)
Margaret O. White, 24 TC 452 (1955)

Lump-sum payment less than aggregate due wife
Rev. Rul. 67–11, 1967–1 CB 15

Combine two arrangements
Reg. § 1.71–1(d)(5) (Example 4)

No deduction for payment for remarriage
Jean Cattier, 17 TC 1461 (1952)

No deduction for settlement
Alan E. Ashcraft Jr., 28 TC 356 (1957), aff'd, 252 F.2d 200 (7th Cir. 1958)

Alimony in arrears paid in lump sum
Dorothy Olster, 79 TC 456 (1982)

Settlement partly for unpaid periodic payments
Rev. Rul. 55–457, 1955–2 CB 527

Note: Paragraph numbers refer to Part One. Items marked * are research aids, not citations of authority; see "Key to Citations" on page 337.

345

¶1.41 • RENT-FREE HOME AS ALIMONY—PRE-1985

"When Housing Costs Incurred for an Ex-Spouse Will Qualify for Alimony Treatment," by Albert Feuer, 57 J. Taxation 42 (1982)

Free use of home
Jack Pappenheimer, 164 F.2d 428 (5th Cir. 1947)
James P. Bradley, 30 TC 701 (1958)

Residence owned jointly or in common
Rev. Rul. 62–39, 1962–1 CB 17

Mortgage payments on jointly-held home
Neely B. Taylor, Jr., 45 TC 120 (1965) (Acq. in result only)

Wife personally liable on mortgage
Rev. Rul. 67–420, 1967–2, CB 63, modifying Rev. Rul. 58–52, 1958–1 CB 29 and Rev. Rul. 62–38, 1962–1 CB 15

Rent-free use of co-op apartment is alimony
Jane N. Rothchild, 78 TC 149 (1982)
Dorian K. Grutman, 80 TC 464 (1983)

Utility charges
Rev. Rul. 62–39, 1962–1 CB 17

Rent paid to controlled corporation
Doris B. Marinello, 54 TC 577 (1970)

¶1.42 • PAYMENT OF SPOUSES' MEDICAL OR OTHER EXPENSES—PRE-1985

Payment of wife's medical expenses
Rev. Rul. 62–106, 1962–2 CB 21

Payments to wife's creditor
Robert Lehman, 17 TC 652 (1951) (Acq. in part, nonacq. in part)
Ruth Lehman, 234 F.2d 958 (2d Cir. 1956), aff'g per curiam 14 TCM 928 (1955), cert. denied, 352 U.S. 926

Tuition of relatives
Melvin A. Christianson, 60 TC 456 (1973) (Acq.)

¶1.43 • INSURANCE PREMIUMS AS ALIMONY—PRE-1985

Life insurance premiums
Rev. Rul. 70–218, 1970–1 CB 19

Full amount of premium income to wife
Katherine T. Hyde, 301 F.2d 279 (2d Cir. 1962), aff'g 36 TC 507 (1961)

Policy comes back to husband if wife dies
Frank C. Smith Est., 208 F.2d 349 (3d Cir. 1953), rev'g in part 11 TCM 1167 (1952)
Florence H. Griffith, 35 TC 882 (1961)

James P. Bradley, 30 TC 701 (1958)
Raoul Walsh, 21 TC 1063 (1954) (Acq.)
Aline S. Fisher Exrx., 15 TCM 507 (1956)
Robert L. Montgomery Jr., 13 TCM 578 (1954)

Husband's rights to surrender policy
Lawler B. Reeves, 21 TCM 379 (1962)

Wife may not remarry
Gerard Piel, 22 TCM 1818 (1963), aff'd, 340 F.2d 887 (2d Cir. 1965)
Raoul Walsh, 21 TC 1063 (1954) (Acq.)
Lilian B. Smith, 21 TC 353 (1953) (Acq.)
Aline S. Fisher Exrx., 15 TCM 507 (1956)

Wife is not only life beneficiary
Boies C. Hart Est., 11 TC 16 (1948)

Deduction for premiums to wife, if unmarried
Leon Mandel, 8 TCM 445 (1949), aff'd, 185 F.2d 50 (7th Cir. 1950)

Income to wife
Edna H. Seligman, 207 F.2d 489 (7th Cir. 1953), rev'g 11 TCM 1170 (1952)

Contingency did not bar deduction for premium
Richard E. Stevens, 439 F.2d 69 (2d Cir. 1971)

Absolute assignment where decree intended limited transfer
Austin Cole, 138 F. Supp. 186 (E.D. Ill. 1956)

Term policy
William H. Brodersen Jr., 57 TC 412 (1971)

Purchased policy
Samuel Morrison, 15 TCM 740 (1956)

Later assignment
Huston E. Turpin, 240 F. Supp. 171 (W.D. Mo. 1965)

Cash surrender value
Alan E. Ashcraft, Jr., 28 TC 356 (1957), aff'd, 252 F.2d 200 (7th Cir. 1958)

¶1.44 • CHILD SUPPORT PAYMENTS—PRE-1985

Child support not deductible
IRC § 71(b)
Reg. § 1.71–1(e)

No allocation—deduct entire amount
Reg. § 1.71–1(e)

Agreement must specifically fix amount
Jerry Lester, 366 U.S. 299 (1961), aff'g 279 F.2d 354 (2d Cir. 1960)
Saralee Lust, 30 TCM 281 (1971), aff'd per curiam, 73–2 USTC ¶9627 (9th Cir. 1973)
Rev. Rul. 62–53, 1962–1 CB 41

Arnold A. Abramo, 78 TC 154 (1982)

Tax Court ignores "alimony" label
Grady W. Henry, 76 TC 455 (1981)

New decree changing terms retroactively allowed
Gloria P. Johnson, 45 TC 530 (1965) (Acq.)
Velma B. Vargason, 22 TC 100 (1954) (Nonacq.)
Margaret R. Sklar, 21 TC 349 (1953) (Acq.)

New decree changing terms retroactively not allowed because no original mistake
Josephine D. Cothran, 57 TC 296 (1971)
Michel M. Segal, 36 TC 148 (1961)
Dorothy Turkoglu, 36 TC 552 (1961)
Frances Hummel, 28 TC 1131 (1957)

Decree effective when entered
Grace L. Hunt, 29 TCM 543 (1970)

Apply first to child support obligation
Martha J. Blyth, 21 TC 275 (1953) (Acq.)

Remarriage of wife—payments continued
Arnold B. Glenn, 29 TCM 1640 (1970)

New decree can make all deductible
George R. Joslyn, 230 F.2d 871 (7th Cir. 1956)

Dependent's support contribution
Lory Buccola, 54 TC 1599 (1970)

Paid vacation expenses
Illene Isaacson, 58 TC 659 (1972) (Acq.)

Minor is under age 21
William E. Borbonus, 42 TC 983 (1964) (Acq.)

¶1.45 • PLANNING POST-1984 ALIMONY AGREEMENTS

IRC § 71

Household rule
IRC § 71(b)(c)
Temp. Reg. § 71–1T (Q–9)

Designate nonqualifying payments
IRC § 71(b)(1)B
Temp. Reg. § 1.71–1T (Q–8)

¶1.46 • CASH PAYMENTS REQUIRED—POST-1984

IRC § 71(b)(1)

Payments to third party
Temp. Reg. § 1.71–1T (Q–6)

¶1.47 • MINIMUM PAYMENT PERIOD FOR ALIMONY—POST-1984

IRC § 71(f)(1)
Notice 87–9, IRB 1987–3, 12

Note: Paragraph numbers refer to Part One. Items marked * are research aids, not citations of authority; see "Key to Citations" on page 337.

¶1.48 • RECAPTURE RULES FOR DECLINE OF PAYMENTS—POST-1984

IRC § 71(f)(2)
Notice 87–9, IRB 1987–3, 12

Exceptions
IRC § 71(f)(5)

¶1.49 • PAYMENTS MUST STOP AT DEATH—POST-1984

IRC § 71(b)(1)(D)

¶1.50 • CHILD SUPPORT PAYMENTS ARE ALIMONY—POST-1984

IRC § 71(c)
Temp. Reg. § 1.71–1T (Q–15, 16, 17, 18)

¶2

Taxable Pay and Tax-Free Pay Benefits

TAX-FREE PAY BENEFITS

¶2.1

"Compensation and Fringe Benefits, Current Developments in Compensation Tax Planning," Marcus D. Graycle, 10 Journal of Corporate Taxation, 363 (1984)

¶2.2 • EMPLOYER-FURNISHED MEALS OR LODGING

"Exclusion of Meals and Lodging Under Section 119," D. Braveman, 25 Tax Lawyer 551 (Spring 1972)

Meals and lodging
Pub. L. No. 95–427, § 4
IRC § 119
Reg. § 1.119–1

Utilities
Charles R. Considine, 68 TC 52 (1977)
Rev. Rul. 68–579, 1968–2 CB 61

Lodging off premises
Charles Anderson, 371 F.2d 59 (6th Cir. 1967), rev'g 42 TC 410 (1964), cert. denied, 387 U.S. 906
Gordon S. Dole, 351 F.2d 308 (1st Cir. 1965), aff'g per curiam 43 TC 697 (1964)(Acq.)
Harold T. Giesinger, 66 TC 6 (1976) (Acq.)
Jack B. Lindeman, 60 TC 609 (1973) (Acq.)

Executive luncheon
Carlton R. Mabley 24 TCM 1794 (1965)

Restaurant employees
Reg. § 1.119–1(d)

Waitress's day off
Reg. § 1.119–1(d)

Company cafeteria
Reg. § 1.119–1(d)

Short meal period
Reg. § 1.119–1(a)(2)(ii)(A) and (d)

Emergency
Reg. § 1.119–1(a)(2)(ii)(a)
Reg. § 1.119–1(d)

Living quarters on employer's business premises
IRS Publication No. 17

Employer deducts fixed amount from pay
IRC § 119(b)
Melvin J. Boykin, 260 F.2d 249 (8th Cir. 1958)
Rev. Rul. 59–307, 1959–2 CB 48

Unprepared food
Walter Jacob, 493 F.2d 1294 (3d Cir. 1974)
Michael A. Tougher, Jr., 441 F.2d 1148 (9th Cir. 1971), cert. denied, 404 U.S. 856

Employer gives cash allowance
Reg. § 1.119–1

Hotel manager
Charles N. Anderson, 371 F.2d 59 (6th Cir. 1967), cert. denied, 387 U.S. 906
Jack B. Lindeman, 60 TC 609 (1973) (Acq.)

State civil service employee
Reg. § 1.119–1(d)

No exclusion for purchases at commissary
Michael A. Tougher, Jr., 51 TC 737 (1969), aff'd per curiam, 441 F.2d 1148 (9th Cir. 1971), cert. denied, 404 U.S. 856

Hotel and motel executives, managers
Atlanta Biltmore Hotel Corp., 22 TCM 1266 (1963), mod'd and aff'd, 349 F.2d 677 (5th Cir. 1965)
Adolph Coors Co., 27 TCM 1351 (1968)

Bruce E. Anderson, 1 TCM 227 (1942)
Special Ruling, November 3, 1950

Farm supervision
M. Caratan, 442 F.2d 606 (9th Cir. 1971)

Other employees
Lloyd N. Farnham, 6 TCM 1049 (1947)
Special Ruling, December 3, 1950

Workers in remote area
Reg. § 1.119–1(d)
William L. Olkjer, 32 TC 464 (1959) (Acq.)

Park employee
Robert L. Coyner, 344 F.2d 736 (3d Cir. 1965)

Insufficient eating facilities
Reg. § 1.119–1(a)(2)(ii)(c)

VISTA Volunteer
Carol Goldstein, 73 TC 164 (1979)

Peace Corps volunteer
IRC § 912

¶2.3 • TAX-FREE FRINGE BENEFITS

"Certainty Provided As to the Treatment of Most Fringe Benefits by Deficit Reduction Act," James E. McKinney, 61 Journal of Taxation 134 (Sept. 1984)

Furnishing meals at employer's cost
IRC § 119
Reg. § 1.119–1

Child care services
IRC § 129

Education assistance
IRC § 127

Tuition reductions
IRC § 117(d)

Note: Paragraph numbers refer to Part One. Items marked * are research aids, not citations of authority; see "Key to Citations" on page 337.

Interest-free loans to employees
IRC § 7872

No additional cost service, employee discounts, working condition and de minimus fringes
IRC § 132
Temp. Reg. § 1.132–IT through 1.132–8T

¶2.4 • COMPANY CARS AS FRINGE BENEFITS

"Valuation of Personal Use of Company Car Under Standard Mileage Allowance Rules," Robert M. Brown and David G. Smith, 64 Journal of Taxation 348 (June 1986).
IRS § 132(a)(3)
Temp. Reg. § 1.132–5T

Valuation of benefits
Temp. Reg. § 1.61–2T

¶2.5 • GROUP-TERM LIFE INSURANCE PREMIUMS

"Group Life Insurance," P. H. Walker, 23 NYU Inst. 153 (1965)
IRC § 79
Reg. § 1.79–0 through 3
Reg. § 1.79–3(d)(2)

Assignment of policy
Rev. Rul. 73–174, 1973–1 CB 43

Combination policies
Reg. § 1.79–1(b)

Former employees
IRC § 79(e)

Rates
Reg. § 1.79–3(d)(2)

¶2.6 • GIFTS FROM EMPLOYERS

Mose Duberstein, 363 U.S. 278 (1960)
Lloyd M. Joshel, 296 F.2d 645 (10th Cir. 1962), aff'g 19 TCM 1349 (1960)
Thomas L. Johnson, 48 TC 636 (1967)(Acq.)
Hugh A. Brimm, 27 TCM 1148 (1968)
Abe A. Danish, 19 TCM 1349 (1960)

City's moral obligation to disabled employee
Rev. Rul. 73–346, 1973–2 CB 24

Gift of stock
Rev. Rul. 69–140, 1969–1 CB 46

Employee gifts and awards
IRC § 274(b)
Ann. 82–7, IRB 1982–3, 48

NASA employee taxed
Robert Jones, 79 TC 1008 (1982)

¶2.7 • EMPLOYEES' DEATH BENEFITS MAY BE TAX FREE UP TO $5,000

"Employee Death Benefits," L. A. Rodgers, Jr., 26 Tax L. Rev. 329 (Jan. 1971)

"Employee Death Benefit Plans—A Reappraisal," S. M. Lewis, 50 Taxes 580 (Oct. 1972)

"Corporate Payments to Widows: What Genre Under the Internal Revenue Code?" L. B. Burke, 34 Pittsburgh L. Rev. 91 (1972)

"Estate and Income Tax Aspects of Employee Death Benefits," A. J. McDowell, 25 NYU Inst. 985 (1967)

"How a Corporation Can Protect a Widow's Payment from Taxation," J. A. Thomas, 1 Taxation for Lawyers 222 (1973)

Payments from deceased's employer
IRC § 101(b)
Reg. § 1.101–2(a)

Right to income before death
IRC § 101(b)(2)(B)
Reg. § 1.101–2(a)(2) and (d)

Total death benefit exclusion
Reg. § 1.101–2(a)(3)

More than one beneficiary
Reg. § 1.101–2(c)(1)

Unqualified plan payments
Reg. § 1.101–2(c)(2)

Tax-free death benefit payments
IRC § 101(c)
Reg. § 1.101–3(a)

Benefit exclusion taken in first year of payment
Nordt Co., Inc., 46 TC 431 (1966) (Acq.)

Unless paid from qualified pension plan
IRC § 101(b)(2)(B)
Reg. § 1.101–2(a)(2)
Reg. § 1.101–2(d)(1)

Bonus subject to forfeiture
Rev. Rul. 68–124, 1968–1 CB 44

Nonresident's widow
Rev. Rul. 56–524, 1956–2 CB 504

Voluntary payments of over $5,000
W. R. Olsen Est., 302 F.2d 671 (8th Cir. 1962), cert. denied, 371 U.S. 903
Roy I. Martin, 36 TC 556 (1961), aff'd, 305 F.2d 290 (3d Cir. 1962), cert. denied, 371 U.S. 904
Rev. Rul. 62–102, 1962–2 CB 37
Margaret H. D. Penick, 37 TC 999 (1962)
Jane M. Fanning, 357 F.2d 37 (2d Cir. 1966)
Genevieve E. Frankel, 302 F.2d 666 (8th Cir. 1962), cert. denied, 371 U.S. 903
Mary Fischer, 20 TCM 318 (1961)
Martin Kuntz Est., 300 F.2d 849 (6th Cir. 1962), cert. denied, 371 U.S. 903
Ernest L. Poyner, 301 F.2d 287 (4th Cir. 1962)
Grace P. Reed, 277 F.2d 456 (6th Cir. 1960)

Betty Rodner, 149 F. Supp. 233 (S.D.N.Y. 1957)
Mildred W. Smith, 305 F.2d 778 (3d Cir. 1962), cert. denied, 371 U.S. 904
Eva L. Gaugler, 312 F.2d 681 (2d Cir. 1963)
William Enyart Est., 24 TCM 1447 (1965)

¶2.8 • RENTAL VALUE OF A PARSONAGE IS NOT INCOME

"Who Is a 'Minister of the Gospel' for Purposes of the Parsonage Exclusion?" J. Block, 51 Taxes 47 (1973)

Tax free
IRC § 107
Reg. § 1.107–1

Services performed by minister
Reg. § 1.1402(c)–5

Exclusion limited to amount spent
Fred B. Marine, 47 TC 609 (1967)

Minister's professional expenses not deductible to extent of tax-free income
David E. Deason, 41 TC 465 (1964) (Acq.)

Exclusion allowed for ordained executive directors of parochial schools
Rev. Rul. 62–171, 1962–2 CB 39

No deduction for ordained minister working for a non-religious organization
Rev. Rul. 68–68, 1968–1 CB 51

Not allowed for unordained ministers
Rev. Rul. 59–270, 1959–2 CB 44

Unordained educational director
Robert D. Lawrence, 50 TC 494 (1968)

Cantors
Abraham A. Salkov, 46 TC 190 (1966) (Nonacq.)
Max Silverman, 253 F.2d 849 (8th Cir. 1958)
Rev. Rul. 78–301, 1978–2 CB 103

Traveling evangelist
Rev. Rul. 64–326, 1964–2 CB 37

Retired minister
Rev. Rul. 63–156, 1963–2 CB 79

Widow not entitled to exclusion
Rev. Rul. 72–249, 1972–1 CB 36

Anti-Communist crusade
James D. Colbert, 61 TC 449 (1974)

Priest living as layman
Francis E. Kelley, 62 TC 131 (1974)

Not allowed for unordained executive of tax-exempt nonreligious organization
W. Astor Kirk, 425 F.2d 492 (D.C. Cir. 1970), cert. denied, 400 U.S. 853

Civilian chaplain at VA hospital
Rev. Rul. 72–462, 1972–2 CB 76

Note: Paragraph numbers refer to Part One. Items marked * are research aids, not citations of authority; see "Key to Citations" on page 337.

Administrator of nonreligious old age home
Jesse A. Toavs, 67 TC 897 (1977)
Rev. Rul. 72–606, 1972–2 CB 78

No exclusion for rabbi as director of interreligious affairs
Marc H. Tanenbaum, 58 TC 1 (1972)

Exclusion for rabbi as UJA director
Melvin Libman, 44 TCM 371 (1982)

Allocation for expenses related to tax-free allowance not required through 1986
Rev. Rul. 83–3, 1983–1 CB 72, as modified by Section 1052 of the Tax Reform Act of 1984 and Rev. Rul. 85–96, 1985–2 CB 87

¶2.9 • CAFETERIA PAY PLANS

"Cafeteria Plans: New Law Removes Proposed IRS Restrictions and Adds Certain Operations," Peter L. Knox, 33 Taxation for Accountants 168 (Sept. 1984) and 13 Taxation for Lawyers 102 (Sept. 10 Ct. 1984)

Transition rules for plans falling under proposed Treasury regulations
Sections 531(b)(5) and (6) of the Tax Reform Act of 1984
IRC § 125

WHEN IS YOUR PAY TAXED?

¶2.10 • REPORTING WAGES

"Choosing the Best Annual Accounting Period for Deferral and Other Advantages," Peter L. Knox, 33 Taxation for Accountants 168 (Sept. 1984) and 13 Taxation for Lawyers 102 (Sept. 1984)

Constructive receipt rule
Reg. § 1.451–2

Methods of reporting income
IRC § 446
Reg. § 1.446–1
IRC § 451
Reg. § 1.451–1

Employer payments of FICA and FUTA
IRC § 3121(a)(6)
IRC § 3306(b)(6)

Withholdings for compulsory forfeitable contributions to nonqualified pension plan
Rev. Rul. 72–94, 1972–1 CB 23

Withholdings for U.S. Civil Service retirement funds taxable
George J. Hogan, 347 F. Supp. 1022 (D. Mich. 1974), aff'd, 513 F.2d 170 (6th Cir. 1975), cert. denied, 423 U.S. 836
Laurence J. Cohen, 63 TC 527 (1974), aff'd (2d Cir.) (unpublished opinion)
Eugene G. Feistman, 63 TC 129 (1974)
Rev. Rul. 72–250, 1972–1 CB 22

Wages received by your agent
Richard Pfister, 205 F.2d 538 (8th Cir. 1953)
Samuel E. Diescher, 36 BTA 732 (Acq. and nonacq.), aff'd, 110 F.2d 90 (3d Cir. 1940), cert. denied, 310 U.S. 650
S. W. Forrester, 23 BTA 942 (Acq.)
F. H. Wilson, 12 BTA 403 (Acq.)
Julia A. Strauss, 2 BTA 598
Thomas Watson, 2 TCM 863 (1943)

Check received but not cashed
Hooker Electrochemical Co., 8 TC 1120 (1947)(Acq.)

Employer has no funds in bank
George W. Johnson, 25 TC 499 (1955)(Acq.)

Employee not home to receive check
Beatrice Davis, 37 TCM 42 (1978)

Employer owes you salary
Bourd, 18 BTA 650 (Acq.)

Earnings donated to charity
Rev. Rul. 58–495, 1958–2 CB 27

Fees assigned by doctors to clinic
Rev. Rul. 76–479, 1976–2 CB 20

Deferring tax on pay
Rev. Rul. 71–419, 1971–2 CB 220
Rev. Rul. 69–649, 1969–2 CB 106
Rev. Rul. 69–650, 1969–2 CB 106

Treasury barred from issuing regulations
Sec. 132 of the Revenue Act of 1978

Salary advances
Anson Beaver, 55 TC 85 (1970)

Deferred pay in trust fixed
Candido Jacuzzi, 61 TC 262 (1973)

State or local government deferred pay plan
IRC § 457

Barter transactions
Rev. Rul. 79–24, 1979–1 CB 60

Barter club "credit units" taxable
Rev. Rul. 80–52, 1980–1 CB 100

Barter club must reveal members
In re Columbus Trade Exchange, F.2d (6th Cir. 1982)

Services of child
IRC § 73

Parent taxed on income from children's piecework
Robert Fritschle, 79 TC 152 (1982)

¶2.11 • PAY RECEIVED IN PROPERTY IS TAXED

Reg. § 1.61–1(a)
Reg. § 1.61–2(d)(2)

Employer's note
Reg. § 1.61–2(d)(4)
Samuel Segel, 24 TCM 1131 (1965)
Paul M. Potter, 5 TCM 116 (1946)

Frank B. Essex, 21 BTA 270 (Acq.)
Pratt Est., 7 BTA 621

Debt cancelled by employer
Fred E. Werner, 21 TCM 1435 (1962)

Prize points
Rev. Rul. 70–331, 1970–1 CB 14

¶2.12 • WHEN COMMISSIONS ARE TAXED

Mary Rosenberg, 295 F. Supp. 820 (E.D. Mo. 1969), aff'd per curiam, 422 F.2d 341 (8th Cir. 1970)

Unearned commissions taxable when credited to account
Ada E. Sivley, 75 F.2d 916 (9th Cir. 1935)
C. E. Shockley, 6 TCM 1092 (1947)

Unearned commissions—income in year of advance despite repayment obligation
Rev. Rul. 79–311, 1979–2 CB 25
Rev. Proc. 83–4, 1983–1 CB 577
George Blood Enterprises, Inc., 35 TCM 436 (1976)

Unearned commissions—no repayment required
Kenneth Drummond, 43 BTA 529
James v. United States, 366 US 213 (1961)

Write-off of advances
Rev. Rul. 69–465, 1969–2 CB 27

Repayment of commission when customer defaults
Rev. Rul. 72–78, 1972–1 CB 45

Commission on own purchase taxable
Kenneth W. Daehler, 281 F.2d 823 (5th Cir. 1960), rev'g 31 TC 722 (1959)(Nonacq.)
Sol Minzer, 279 F.2d 338 (5th Cir. 1960), rev'g 31 TC 1130 (1959) (Nonacq.)
J. E. Ostheimer, 264 F.2d 789 (3d Cir. 1959), cert. denied, 361 U.S. 818
Jack Williams, 64 TC 1085 (1975)

Note: Paragraph numbers refer to Part One. Items marked * are research aids, not citations of authority; see "Key to Citations" on page 337.

Commissions waived on policies sold to friends still taxed
Charles O. Mensik, 37 TC 703 (1962), aff'd, 328 F.2d 147 (7th Cir. 1964), cert. denied, 379 U.S. 827

Agent taxed on illegal rebate of commission
James Alex, 70 TC 322 (1978)

¶2.13 • UNEMPLOYMENT BENEFITS ARE TAXABLE

IRC § 85

¶2.14 • STRIKE PAY BENEFITS AND PENALTIES

*Strike Benefits as Income," T. E. Capps, 44 N. Car. L. Rev. 502 (1966)

Emergency benefits funded by federal government
Rev. Rul. 73–154, 1973–1 CB 40

Supplemental payments
IR–156, May 29, 1956

Unemployment benefits from union fund
Halsey L. Williams, 37 TC 1099 (1962)(Acq.)

Strike benefits
Allen Kaiser, 363 U.S. 299 (1960), aff'g 262 F.2d 367 (7th Cir. 1959)
James W. Godwin, 65–1 USTC ¶9121 (D. Tenn. 1965)
William A. Brown, 47 TC 399 (1967) (Acq.), aff'd per curiam, 398 F.2d 832 (6th Cir. 1968), cert. denied, 393 U.S. 1065
John N. Hagar, 43 TC 468 (1965)
Rev. Rul. 58–139, 1958–1 CB 14, mod'd by Rev. Rul. 61–136, 1961–2 CB 20
Rev. Rul. 57–1, 1957–1 CB 15

Pay penalty
Rev. Rul. 76–130, 1976–1 CB 16

¶2.15 • DID YOU HAVE TO RETURN INCOME RECEIVED IN AN EARLIER YEAR?

*"The Claim of Right Doctrine and Section 1341," Robert R. Wootton, 34 Tax Lawyer 297 (1981)
IRC § 1341
Reg. § 1.1341–1

Return of embezzled funds—no claim of right computation

Rev. Rul. 65–254, 1965–2 CB 50

Return of unreasonable salary under agreement business expense deduction
Rev. Rul. 69–115, 1969–1 CB 50
Stewart H. Holbrook, 144 F. Supp. 252 (D. Ore. 1961)
John G. Pahl, 67 TC 286 (1976)

Repayment of supplemental unemployment benefits
IRC § 62(a)(12)

Hedge agreement allows Section 1231 recalculation
Eugene Van Cleave, 718 F.2d 193 (6th Cir. 1983)

¶2.16 • WAIVER OF EXECUTOR'S AND TRUSTEE'S COMMISSIONS

*"Tax Consequences Resulting From the Waiver of Executors' Commissions," E. Everett, E. Chester, M. Loening, 24 NYU Inst. 295 (1966)
George M. Breidert, 50 TC 844 (1968)(Acq.)
Rev. Rul. 66–167, 1966–1 CB 20
Rev. Rul. 64–225, 1964–2 CB 15
Rev. Rul. 56–472, 1956–2 CB 21

¶2.17 • DISABILITY PENSION EXCLUSION REPEALED

IRC § 105(d), repealed by P.L. 98–21 for tax years starting after 1983

¶2.18 • HEALTH AND ACCIDENT INSURANCE BENEFITS

IRC § 104(a)(3)
Reg. § 1.104–1(d)

¶2.19 • WORKER'S COMPENSATION PAYMENTS ARE TAX FREE

Worker's compensation
IRC § 104(a)(1)
Reg. § 1.104–1(b)

Given to employer
Rev. Rul. 56–83, 1956–1 CB 79

In the nature of Worker's Compensation
Madeline G. Dyer, 71 TC 560 (1979) (Acq. in result only)
Rev. Rul. 83–91, 1983–1 CB 38

Civil Service Retirement Act payments not Worker's Compensation
Daniel S. Haar, 78 TC 864 (1982) aff'd per curiam, 709 F.2d 1207 (8th Cir. 1983)

Policeman's sick leave under labor contract not worker's compensation
William Rutter, 48 TCM 1269 (1984), aff'd per curiam, 760 F.2d 466 (2d Cir. 1985)

¶2.20 • DISABILITY PENSION RULES FOR MEMBERS OF THE MILITARY, PUBLIC HEALTH SERVICE AND FOREIGN SERVICE

IRC § 104(a)(4)
IRC § 104(b)

Injuries from terrorist attacks
IRC § 104(a)(5)

¶2.21 • TAX-FREE BENEFITS FROM ACCIDENT AND HEALTH PLANS FINANCED BY EMPLOYER

Employer-paid premiums
IRC § 106(a)

Highly compensated employees subject to tax
IRC § 106(b)

Continuing coverage required
IRC § 162(k)

Specific reimbursements of medical expenses
IRC § 105(b)
Reg. § 1.105–2
Rev. Rul. 63–181, 1963–2 CB 74

Permanent loss of use of part of body
IRC § 105(c)
Reg. § 1.105–3

Hypertension not loss of bodily function
Frank S. Watts, 82–USTC ¶9226 (D. Cal. 1982), aff'd, 83–1 USTC ¶9286 (9th Cir. 1983)

Failing to qualify in any of above two groups
IRC § 105(a)
Reg. § 1.105–1

Close corporations
Alan B. Larkin, 48 TC 629 (1967), aff'd, 394 F.2d 494 (1st Cir. 1968)
Arthur R. Seidel, 30 TCM 1021 (1971)
Sanders & Sons, Inc., 26 TCM 671 (1967)

Medical reimbursement plans
IRC § 105(h)
Reg. § 1.105–11

Note: Paragraph numbers refer to Part One. Items marked * are research aids, not citations of authority; see "Key to Citations" on page 337.

350

¶3

Dividend Income

Note: Paragraph numbers refer to Part One. Items marked * are research aids, not citations of authority; see "Key to Citations" on page 337.

¶4

Interest Income

IRC § 61(4)
Reg. § 1.61-7(a)

Year received
Reg. § 1.446-1(c)(1)(i)

U.S. obligations
IRC § 103

Interest available
Reg. § 1.451-2

"Dividends" on paid-up life insurance
Reg. § 1.72-11(b)

Tax sale certificates
Charles H. Wiltsie, 3 F. Supp. 743
(Ct. Cl. 1933), cert. denied, 291
U.S. 664

Open accounts without specific agreement
Kurtz Bros., 42 BTA 561

Usurious interest
Reg. § 1.61-7(a)

Discount on notes
Reg. § 1.61-7(a)
Reg. § 1.61-7(c)

Interest received in form of property
Reg. § 1.61-1

Autos, boats received for long-term deposits
I.R. 1032, 4/14/70

Coupons from tax-exempt bonds
H. Gates Lloyd, 154 F.2d 643 (3d
Cir. 1946), cert. denied, 329 U.S.
717
Rev. Rul. 55-73, 1955-1 CB 236

Note with accrued interest
Missouri State Life Insurance Co., 78
F.2d 778 (8th Cir. 1935)
Pontiac Commercial and Savings
Bank, 41 F.2d 602 (6th Cir. 1930)
Luther A. Hart, 20 F. Supp. 27,
(E.D. Pa. 1937), aff'd, 99 F.2d 638
(3d Cir. 1938)

G.I. life insurance
Rev. Rul. 57-441, 1957-2 CB 45

Wrap-around annuities
Rev. Rul. 80-274, 1980-2 CB 27

Saving certificates, deferred interest plans
Reg. § 1.1232
Rev. Rul. 73-220, 1973-1 CB 297

Deferred interest as original issue discount
IR-1215, March 13, 1972

Six-month certificates
Prop. Reg. § 1.451-2(a)(2)

Prop. Reg. § 1.1232-3(b)
Rev. Rul. 80-157, 1980-1 CB 186

Interest penalty bars no constructive receipt on C.D. of one-year or less
Reg. Sec. § 1.451-2

Serviceman's interest
Rev. Rul. 67-450, 1967-2 CB 174

Interest on loan arrangement
Rev. Rul. 81-148, 1981-1 CB 207

¶4.1 • FORFEITURE OF INTEREST ON PREMATURE WITHDRAWAL OF TIME SAVINGS ACCOUNT

IRC § 62(2)
Rev. Rul. 75-20, 1975-1 CB 29
Rev. Rul. 73-511, 1973-2 CB 402,
clarified by Rev. Rul. 75-21,
1975-1 CB 367

¶4.2 • INTEREST ON FROZEN ACCOUNTS NOT TAXED

IRC § 451(g)
IRC § 165(1)

¶4.3 • INTEREST INCOME ON DEBTS OWED YOU

Interest uncollectible
Corn Exchange Bank, 37 F.2d 34
(2d Cir. 1930)
Atlantic Coast Line RR Co., 31 BTA
730 (Acq.), aff'd, 81 F.2d 309 (4th
Cir. 1936), cert. denied, 298 U.S.
656

Four restrictions on withdrawal of interest not considered substantial; bonus interest; closing agreements
Reg. § 1.451-2(a)
Rev. Proc. 64-24, 1964-1 CB 693

Agreement with debtor
Annie B. Smith, 12 TCM 131 (1953)
W. H. Hughes, 11 TCM 797 (1952)
Rev. Rul. 63-57, 1963-1 CB 103

Debtor gives new note
George J. Mellinger, 21 F. Supp.
964 (Ct. Cl. 1938)

Interest in advance
Reg. § 1.61-7(a)

Obligations given away
Ida S. Austin, 161 F.2d 666 (6th
Cir. 1947), cert. denied, 332 U.S.
767

¶4.4 • REPORTING INTEREST ON BONDS BOUGHT OR SOLD DURING THE YEAR

Redemption
Special Ruling, February 7, 1949

Included in sales price
Reg. § 1.61-7(d)

Included in purchase price
Reg. § 1.61-7(c)

Tax-free covenant bond
IRC § 32(2)

Guarantor pays interest
Rev. Rul. 54-563, 1954-2 CB 50

Flat price
Reg. § 1.61-7(c)

Payment of contingent rule—flat rule applied
William Sailer, 224 F.2d 641 (5th
Cir. 1955)

¶4.5 • AMORTIZATION OF BOND PREMIUM

Election
IRC § 171
Reg. § 1.171-1
Reg. § 1.171-3

Computing amortization
IRC § 71(b)(3)

Elect on return
IRC § 171(c)(2)
Reg. § 1.171-3(a)

Sale and purchase of similar bonds
Rev. Rul. 55-353, 1955-1 CB 381

Allocate premium for conversions
Reg. § 1.171-2(c)

Premium amortization reduces OID
IRC § 1272(a)(7)

¶4.6 • DISCOUNT ON BONDS AND OTHER OBLIGATIONS

IRC § 1271 (retirement on sale of debt instruments)
IRC § 1272 (current income treatment of OID)
IRC § 1273 (what is OID)
IRC § 1276 (market discount)
IRC § 1281 (short-term debt)

¶4.7 • REPORTING ORIGINAL ISSUE DISCOUNT ON PUBLICLY OFFERED OBLIGATIONS

IRS Publication 1212

¶4.8 • REPORTING INCOME ON MARKET DISCOUNT BONDS

IRC § 1276
IRC § 1278

Note: Paragraph numbers refer to Part One. Items marked * are research aids, not citations of authority; see "Key to Citations" on page 337.

Deferral of interest deduction
IRC § 1277

Election
IRC § 1278(b)

¶4.9 • DISCOUNT ON SHORT-TERM OBLIGATIONS

IRC § 1281
IRC § 1283

Deferred interest deduction
IRC § 1282

¶4.10 • STRIPPED COUPON BONDS

IRC § 1286

¶4.11 • EXEMPT CITY AND STATE INTEREST

State, city obligations
IRC § 103(a)(1)
Reg. § 1.103–1
Rhode Island Hospital Trust Co., 8 BTA 555, vacated and remanded, 29 F.2d 339 (1st Cir. 1929)

Agreement of purchase and sale
Newlin Machinery Corp., 28 TC 837 (1957)(Acq.)

Sale of municipal certificates of indebtedness to municipality
Palm Beach Trust Co., 9 TC 1060 (1947), aff'd per curiam, 174 F.2d 527 (D.C. Cir. 1949), cert denied, 338 U.S. 825

¶4.12 • TAXABLE STATE AND CITY INTEREST

IRC § 103(b)

Qualified private activity bonds not taxed
IRC § 141(d)

Coupons detached from bonds
H. Gates Lloyd, 4 TC 829 (1945), aff'd, 154 F.2d 643 (3d Cir. 1962), cert. denied, 329 U.S. 717

Community open account purchases
Kurtz Bros., 42 BTA 561

Volunteer fire companies
Seagrave Corp., 38 TC 247 (1962)

Tax sale certificates
Charles H. Wiltsie, 3 F. Supp. 743 (Ct. Cl. 1933), cert. denied, 291 U.S. 664

Municipal bond in open market
Rev. Rul. 57–49, 1957–1 CB 62
Rev. Rul. 60–210, 1960–1 CB 38, modified by Rev. Rul. 60–376, 1960–2 CB 38

¶4.13 • TAX-EXEMPT BONDS BOUGHT AT A DISCOUNT

IRC § 1285

Bought bond on original issue
Reg. § 1.103–1

Bond bought at discount
Rev. Rul. 73–112, 1973–1 CB 47
Rev. Rul. 57–49, 1957–1 CB 62
Rev. Rul. 60–210, 1960–1 CB 38

Redeemed old bond at premium
Rev. Rul. 72–587, 1972–2 CB 74
District Bond Co., 1 TC 837 (1943)

Redemption of bonds issued after June 8, 1980
Rev. Rul. 80–143, 1980–1 CB 89, modifying Rev. Rul. 72–587

Market discount rules do not apply to tax exempt bonds
IRC § 1278(a)(1)(B)(ii)

¶4.14 • INTEREST ON U.S. OBLIGATIONS

Taxable interest
Reg. § 1.61–7

Taxed at maturity
IRC § 454(b)

Acquisition discount
IRC § 1281

Interest deductions limitation
IRC § 1282

Gain on sale of short-term obligations
IRC § 1271(a)(3)
Prop. Reg. § 1.1271–3

¶4.15 • HOW U.S. SAVINGS BOND INTEREST IS TAXED

Annual increase
IRC § 454
Reg. § 1.454–1
Rev. Rul. 48–25, 1948–2 CB 12

Election to report interest annually on timely return
Rev. Rul. 55–655, 1955–2 CB 253

Postpone tax during additional 10 years
IRC § 454(c)
Reg. § 1.454–1

Change form of registration of E Bond
Rev. Rul. 55–278, 1955–1 CB 471
Rev. Rul. 54–327, 1954–2 CB 50
IRC § 454(c)
Reg. § 1.454–1

Correction of error in registration
Rev. Rul. 70–428, 1970–2 CB 5

Co-owners
Rev. Rul. 54–143, 1954–1 CB 12
Rev. Rul. 55–278, 1955–1 CB 471
Rev. Rul. 58–435, 1958–2 CB 370, distinguished by Rev. Rul. 68–145, 1968–1 CB 203

Death of owner
Rev. Rul. 64–104, 1964–1 CB 223, distinguished by Rev. Rul. 68–145, 1968–1 CB 203

Transfer to charity
*Letter Ruling 8010082

Bonds transferred by gift without reissue
Edward G. Chandler, 410 U.S. 257 (1973), rev'g 460 F.2d 1281 (9th Cir. 1972)
Mae Elliott Est., 57 TC 152 (1971), aff'd per curiam, 474 F.2d 1008 (5th Cir. 1973)
Lyla C. Curry Est., 409 F.2d 671 (6th Cir. 1969)
Alice H. Silverman, 259 F.2d 731 (3d Cir. 1958)
Helen K. Chambless, 70–1 USTC ¶12,655 (D.S.C. 1970)

Election on decedent's return
Rev. Rul. 68–145, 1968–1 CB 203

H Bond exchange
Announcement, November 19, 1959

¶4.15 (cont.) • TABLE OF REDEMPTION VALUES FOR U.S. SAVINGS BONDS, SERIES E AND EE

Tables of Redemption values for United States Savings Bonds, Series E and EE for all months as of October 1987, Treasury Department, Bureau of Public Debt

¶4.17 • INTEREST-FREE OR BELOW MARKET INTEREST LOANS

*"Interest-Free Loans Can Still Be Used for Tax Planning," David S. Rhine, The Practical Accountant, March 1987
IRC § 7872
Prop. Reg. Secs 1.7872–1 through 1.7872–14

¶4.18 • MINIMUM INTEREST AND REPORTING RULES FOR SELLER FINANCING

*"Planning Real Estate Transactions Under the OID Rules," James W. Banks and Joseph F. Tyrell, The Practical Accountant, March 1987

"Analyzing the far-reaching changes for debt instruments under the new law," John N. Bush, 61 Journal of Taxation 150 (Sept. 1984)

"Debt issued for traded and nontraded property," Jeffrey T. Sheffield, 62 Taxes 12 (1984)
IRC § 1274
IRC § 1275
IRC § 483
Prop. Reg. Secs. 1.1274–1 through 1.1274–7

Minimum interest on sales for $2.8 million or less
Prop. Reg. Sec. 1.1274A–1

Note: Paragraph numbers refer to Part One. Items marked * are research aids, not citations of authority; see "Key to Citations" on page 337.

353

¶5

Income or Loss From Your Business or Profession

¶5.2 • WHAT ACCOUNTING BASIS CAN YOU USE?

*"Some Items Still Deductible Under All-Events Test Despite New Economic Performance Rules," William P. Bowers and Michael K. Stone, 64 Journal of Taxation 354 (June 1986).

*"Advance Payments of Rent for Less than One Year Periods: When Are They Deductible?" R. B. Martin, Jr., 50 J. Taxation 360 (1979)

Permissible methods
IRC § 446(c)
Reg. § 1.446–1

Limits on use of cash method
IRC § 448

Accrual deferral of service income
IRC § 448(d)(5)

Health insurance deduction for self-employed
IRC § 162(m)

More than one business
IRC § 446(d)

Change from cash to accrual method
IRC § 446(e) and (f)
Rev. Proc. 67–10, 1967–1 CB 585, amplified by Rev. Proc. 72–52, 1972–2 CB 833

Constructive receipt
Reg. § 1.451–2

Deductions—generally
IRC § 461
Reg. § 1.461–1(a)

Health insurance deduction for self-employed
IRC § 162(m)

All events test—economic performance test
IRC § 461(h)

Cash basis tax shelters
IRC § 461(i)

Payment through "pay by phone" account
Rev. Rul. 80–335, 1980–2 CB 170

Deferred payments for use of property or services
IRC § 467

Income not deferred by agent
Rev. Rul. 70–294, 1970–1 CB 13

Income deferred on wheat sale
Rev. Rul. 58–162, 1958–1 CB 234, distinguished by Rev. Rul. 70–294, 1970–1 CB 13

Advance payments deductible
R. D. Cravens, 272 F.2d 895 (10th Cir. 1960), rev'g 30 TC 903 (1958)
John Ernst, 32 TC 181 (1959)(Acq.)

Payment to related cash basis taxpayer of salary and interest
IRC § 267(a)(2)

Advance interest payments ("paid or accrued")
IRC § 163

Advance tax payments ("paid or accrued")
IRC § 164

Prepaid insurance—proration
Boylston Market Ass'n, 131 F.2d 966 (1st Cir. 1942)

Prepaid insurance—immediate deduction
Waldheim Realty and Investment, 245 F.2d 823 (8th Cir. 1957)

Accrual—effect of contingency
Safety Car Heating Co., 297 U.S. 88 (1936)
Continental Tie & Lumber Co., 286 U.S. 290 (1932)
American Code Co., 280 U.S. 445 (1930)

Accruals involving related parties
IRC § 267(a)(2)

¶5.3 • TAX REPORTING FOR SELF-EMPLOYED

Taxable year
IRC § 441(b)
Reg. § 1.441–1(b)
*IRS Publication 538

Calendar year
IRC § 441(d)

Fiscal year
IRC § 441(e)

Personal Service Corporation year
IRC § 441(i)

Partnership year
IRC § 706(b)

S Corporation year
IRC § 1378(b)

52–53 weeks
IRC § 441(f)
Reg. § 1.441–2

Period of less than 12 months
IRC § 443
Reg. § 1.443–1

Sole proprietor's tax year
Rev. Rul. 58–389, 1957–2 CB 298,

modified by Rev. Rul. 77–293, 1977–2 CB 91

Change of accounting period
IRC § 442
Reg. § 1.442–1(b)

¶5.4 • REPORTING CASH RECEIPTS

IRC § 6050 I
Temp. Reg. Sec. 1.6050 I–1(T)

Penalty for not providing statement
IRC § 6721 and 6722

¶5.5 • REPORTING INCOME AND EXPENSES ON SCHEDULE C

*IRS Publication 535

Business expenses—adjusted gross income
IRC § 62

Business expenses—in general
IRC § 162
Reg. § 1.162–1

Unreasonable business expense
Palo Alto Town & Country Village, Inc., 32 TCM 1048 (1973), aff'd in part, rev'd in part and rem'd, 565 F.2d 1388 (9th Cir. 1978)

Inventory losses
Reg. § 1.165–7(a)(4)
Reg. § 1.471–2(c)
National Home Products, 71 TC 501 (1979)

Bad debts
IRC § 166

Reserve for bad debts repealed
IRC § 166(c), repealed by 1986 Tax Reform Act Section 805(a)

Insurance premiums
Reg. § 1.162–1

Disability insurance
Marvin J. Blaess, 28 TC 710 (1957)
Rev. Rul. 58–480, 1958–2 CB 62

Prepaid premiums
Waldheim Realty & Investment, 245 F.2d 823 (8th Cir. 1957)
Boylston Market Ass'n., 131 F.2d 966 (1st Cir. 1942)

Premiums for disability insurance
Rev. Rul. 55–331, 1955–1 CB 271, modified by Rev. Rul. 68–212, 1968–1 CB 91

Note: Paragraph numbers refer to Part One. Items marked * are research aids, not citations of authority; see "Key to Citations" on page 337.

Premium for malpractice insurance
Rev. Rul. 60–365, 1960–2 CB 49

Malpractice premiums to physician-owned carrier
Rev. Rul. 80–120, 1980–1 CB 41

Physicians may not deduct cost of setting up insurance carrier
Carl Herman, et al., 84 TC 120

Policies for business overhead expenses
Rev. Rul. 55–264, 1955–1 CB 11

Interest
IRC § 163
Reg. § 1.163–1

Interest deduction limited on employee life insurance
IRC § 264(a)(4)

Interest on funds used in personal affairs
Ebb J. Ford, Jr., 29 TC 499 (1957)

Losses
IRC § 165
Reg. § 1.165–1

Rents
Reg. § 1.162–1
Reg. § 1.162–11
Rev. Rul. 74–209 1974–1 CB 46

Advance rents
Martin J. Zaninovich, 616 F.2d 429 (9th Cir. 1980)

Repairs
Reg. § 1.162–4
Louise Kingsley, 11 BTA 296 (Acq.)

Taxes
IRC § 164
Reg. § 1.164

Salaries and wages
IRC § 162(a)(1)
Reg. § 1.162–7(a)

Legal fees
Rev. Rul. 74–392, 1974–2 CB 10
Rev. Rul. 71–470, 1971–2 CB 12

Deduction for legal fee of unsuccessful defense of criminal charge arising out of business
Walter F. Tellier, 383 U.S. 687 (1966)

Litigation expense of retire officer's rank
Rev. Rul. 72–169, 1972–1 CB 43

Expenses of discontinued business
Rev. Rul. 67–12, 1967–1 CB 29

Wages to your children deductible
Walt E. Eller, 77 TC 934 (1981)
James A. Moriarty, 48 TCM 59; TCM 1984–249

¶5.6 • DEDUCTIONS FOR PRO-FESSIONALS

IRS list of deductible professional expenses
Reg. § 1.162–6

Cost of establishing professional reputation
Miron Kroyt, 20 TCM 1665 (1961)

Amortization of bar admission costs
Joel A. Sharon, 66 TC 515 (1976), aff'd, 591 F.2d 1273 (9th Cir. 1978), cert. denied, *but see contra*, P. L. Johnston, 37 TCM 1112 (1978)

Doctor may amortize patient's records
Los Angeles Central Animal Hospital Inc. 58 TC 269 (Acq.)

Doctor
Richard M. Boe, 35 TC 720 (1961), aff'd, 307 F.2d 339 (9th Cir. 1962)
Chester R. Johnson, Jr., 61–1 USTC ¶9278 (W.D. Tex. 1961)
William Wells-Lee, 360 F.2d 665 (8th Cir. 1966), rev'g and rem'g 23 TCM 1931 (1964)

Payment for hospital rights
S. M. Howard, 39 TC 833 (1963)
E. Vance Walters, 383 F.2d 922 (6th Cir. 1967)

Amortizing cost of right to practice in a hospital
Rev. Rul. 70–171, 1970–1 CB 55

Payment of client's expenses
Reginald G. Hearn, 36 TC 672 (1961), aff'd, 309 F.2d 431 (9th Cir. 1962), cert. denied, 373 U.S. 909
C. Doris Pepper, 36 TC 886 (1961) (Acq.)

Advances to client not deductible
Warren Burnett, 356 F.2d 755 (5th Cir. 1966), cert. denied, 385 U.S. 832

Professionals not in own practice
Wesley J. Rogers, 20 TCM 1515 (1961)

No deduction if failed to make malpractice claim
Rev. Rul. 78–141, 1978–1 CB 380

Extracurricular teaching costs
Samuel F. Patterson, 30 TCM 1003 (1971), on remand from 436 F.2d 359 (9th Cir.), rev'g and rem'g 27 TCM 640 (1968)
Seymour Feinstein, 29 TCM 1338 (1970)
Earl T. Jefferson, 74–1 USTC ¶9205 (N.D. Ga. 1974)

Luncheon discussion
John D. Moss Jr., 758 F.2d 211 (CA–7) S.Ct. cert. denied 106 S.Ct. 382
Richard R. Hankenson, TC Memo. 1984–200

¶5.7 • NONDEDUCTIBLE EXPENSE ITEMS

Capital expenditures
IRC § 263
Reg. § 1.263(a)

Uniform Capitalization rules under 1986 Tax Reform Act
IRC § 263A
Temp. Reg. Sec. 1.263A–1T

New roof on building

George W. Ritter, 163 F.2d 1019 (6th Cir. 1947)
Oberman Mfg., 47 TC 471 (1967) (Acq.)
Thomas J. Locke, 8 BTA 534 (Acq.)
Georgia Car and Locomotive Co., 2 BTA 986 (Nonacq.)

State income taxes not deductible from gross income
Reg. § 1.62–1(d)
Douglas H. Tanner, 45 TC 145 (1965), aff'd per curiam, 363 F.2d 36 (4th Cir. 1966)

State income taxes for net operating loss
Rev. Rul. 70–40, 1970–1 CB 50

Business property tax
E. W. Brown Jr., 439 F.2d 1065 (5th Cir. 1954)

Personal expenses paid with business funds
IRC § 262
Reg. § 1.262–1

Expenses while not in business
Henry G. Owen, 23 TC 377 (1955)

Payment of fines
IRC § 162(f)
Hoover Motor Express Co., Inc., 356 U.S. 38 (1958)
Tank Truck Rentals, Inc., 356 U.S. 30 (1958)
Herbert Davis, 26 TC 49 (1956) (Acq.)
Harry Wiedetz, 2 TC 1262 (1943)

Kickback
IRC § 162(c)
Reg. § 1.162–1(c)

Subcontractor's legal kickback not deductible
Car-Ron Asphalt Paving Co. Inc.; 758 F.2d 132 (6th Cir. 1985), aff'g 46 TCM 1314 (1983).

Contributions to campaigns
IRC § 162(e)

¶5.8 • COSTS OF WRITING A BOOK

IRC § 263A
Prior law IRC § 280 repealed by 1986 Tax Reform Act Section 803 (b)(2)(A)
Arthur T. Hadley, — F.2d — (2d Cir. 1987), reversing 51 TCM 948 (1986)

¶5.9 • DEDUCTING EXPENSES OF A SIDELINE BUSINESS OR HOBBY

*"Hobby Losses," W. M. Horne, Jr., N. W. Goldin, 4 Lasser's Income Tax Techniques, 8A
IRC § 183
IRC § 270
Temp. Reg. § 12.9(b)

Waiver of statute of limitations—items affected
IRC § 183(e)(4)

Determining presumption period
Rev. Rul. 78–22, 1978–1 CB 72

Note: Paragraph numbers refer to Part One. Items marked * are research aids, not citations of authority; see "Key to Citations" on page 337.

Presumption period ends with death
Rev. Rul. 79–204, 1979–2 CB 111

Manner business conducted
Leonard F. Barcus, 32 TCM 660 (1973), aff'd, 492 F.2d 1237 (2d Cir. 1974)
C. West Churchman, 68 TC 696 (1977)

History of income/losses from activity
Warren T. Brown, 280 F. Supp. 854 (D.N. Mex. 1968)
Henry P. White, 23 TC 90 (1954), aff'd per curiam, 227 F.2d 779 (6th Cir. 1956), cert. denied, 351 U.S. 939
Leonard P. Sasso, 20 TCM 1068 (1961)
Charles D. Eggert, 16 TCM 1010 (1957)

Sideline charter boat
John R. Zwicky, 48 TCM 1025 (1984)

Elements of personal pleasure/recreation
Valentine Howell, 41 TC 13 (1963), aff'd per curiam, 332 F.2d 428 (3d Cir. 1964)
Charles H. Carter, 37 TCM 859 (1978)
Peter Hurd, 37 TCM 499 (1978)
Norman D Demler, 25 TCM 620 (1966)

Aspiring authors
Paul Snyder, 674 F.2d 1359 (10th Cir. 1982) (allowed)
Maurice Dreicer, 78 TC 642 (1982) (disallowed), aff'd in unpublished opinion (D.C. Cir. 2/22/83)

Partnerships subject to IRC §183
Rev. Rul. 77–320, 1977–2 CB 78

¶5.10 • DEDUCTING EXPENSES OF LOOKING FOR A NEW BUSINESS

*"Search and Start-Up Expenses for a New Business: When Are They Deductible?": Donald R. Quinn, 17 Practical Accountant 77 (1984)

Amortization of start-up costs
IRC § 195

Expenses of getting a savings and loan charter; loss deduction is allowed

Harris W. Seed, 52 TC 880 (1969) (Acq.)

Funds advanced for mining
Charles T. Parker, 1 TC 709 (1943) (Acq.)

Investigating new business which is not entered into
Frank B. Polachek, 22 TC 858 (1954)
Morton Frank, 20 TC 511 (1953)
Johan Domenie, 34 TCM 469 (1975)
Rev. Rul. 77–254, 1977–2 CB 63

Search for car agency not deductible
William E. Day, 15 TCM 1303 (1956)

¶5.11 • EXCLUSIVE AND REGULAR USE OF HOME OFFICE

*"Tax Ramifications of the Use of a Home," Timothy M. Mulligan, 58 Florida Bar Journal 349 (1984)

*"Does Your Law Office at Home Satisfy the Use Tests Under IRC § 280A," Eugene A. Gargaco Jr., 63 Mich. Bar Journal 570 (July 1984)

*"Home Office Deduction Has Been Narrowed, But Is Still Available After the Tax Reform Act," G. S. Godick and N. B. Godick, Taxation for Accountants, June 1987

*"The Increasing Availability of the Home Office Deduction and the Related Implications of the Tax Reform Act of 1986," John Malloy and Lambert Blank Jr., 65 Taxes 233 (April 1987)

*"An Update on Sec. 280A: Home Office and Vacation Home Deductions," Earl F. Davis & Kenneth H. Heller, 14 Tax Adviser 525–535 (Sept. 1983)
*IRS Publication 587
IRC § 280A
Prop. Reg. § 1.280A–1 through 3

Principal place of business
Rudolph Baie, 74 TC 105 (1980) (roadstand)
Ernest Drucker, 79 TC 605 (1982)

(musician), rev'd 715 F.2d 67 (2d Cir. 1983)
David J. Weissman, 751 F.2d 512 ((CA-2) 1985) (college professor)

Daycare in home
IRC § 280A(c)(4)

Inventory storage
IRC § 280A(c)(2)

Portion of room as office
George H. Weightman, 42 TCM 104 (1981) (allowed); 45 TCM 167 (1982) (disallowed for following year on other grounds).
Sharon L. Gomez. 41 TCM 585 (1980) (failed to prove business use)

Backyard office
Charles A. Scott, 84 TC 683 (1985)

¶5.12 • DEDUCTIBLE EXPENSES OF A HOME AREA USED FOR BUSINESS

Lawn care not deductible
Tom E. Butz, 35 TCM 532 (1976)

¶5.13 • ALLOCATING EXPENSES TO BUSINESS USE

Any reasonable method accepted
Rev. Rul. 62–180, 1962–2 CB 52

¶5.14 • BUSINESS INCOME MAY LIMIT EXPENSE DEDUCTIONS

IRC § 280A(c)(5)
Prop. Reg. § 1.280A-2(i) and 2(iii)
Letter Ruling 8347012

¶5.15 • AN OFFICE IN A HOME FOR SIDELINE BUSINESS

Doctor with rental properties
Edwin R. Curphey, 73 TC 766 (1980)

Investors carrying on business
Joseph Moller, 553 F.2d 1071 (CA–Fed. Cir., 83–2 USTC ¶9698)

¶5.16 • DEPRECIATION ON A CO-OPERATIVE APARTMENT USED AS AN OFFICE

IRC § 216(c)
Reg. § 1.216–2

FIGURING NET OPERATING LOSSES FOR REFUND OF PRIOR TAXES

¶5.17 • NET OPERATING LOSSES FOR REFUND OF PRIOR TAXES

*"What Is a Net Operating Loss?" H. Pomeroy, 14 Western Reserve L. Rev. 233 (1963)

*"Techniques and Computations of the Net Operating Loss," K. B. Sanden, 21 NYU Inst. 1227 (1963)

*"Mechanics of Carrying Losses to

Other Years," 14 Western Reserve L. Rev. 241 (1963)
*IRS Publication 536
IRC § 172
Reg. § 1.172

Accounting change
Rev. Rul. 85–16, 1985–1 CB 180

¶5.18 • YOUR NET OPERATING LOSS

*"Tax Planning for Corporations with

Net Operating Losses," Frederick A. Richman, 32 S. Cal. Tax. Inst. 3–1 (1980)

Product liability
IRC § 172(b)(1)(H) and (i), as added by § 371 of the Revenue Act of 1978

General stock ownership corporations
IRC § 172(b)(1)(H), as added by § 601 of the Revenue Act of 1978

Note: Paragraph numbers refer to Part One. Items marked * are research aids, not citations of authority; see "Key to Citations" on page 337.

Business capital loss
Trammell Crow, 79 TC 541 (1982)

¶5.20 • HOW TO CLAIM NET OPERATING LOSS DEDUCTION

Quick refund

IRC § 6411(a)(1)

Effect of spouse's death on carryback
Rev. Rul. 65–140, 1965–1 CB 127

Widow active in business allowed late husband's carryover
Vivian Rose, 32 TCM 965 (1973)

¶5.21 • ELECTION TO RELINQUISH THE CARRYBACK

IRC § 172(b)(3)(C)

Fifteen-year carryforward
IRC § 172(b)(1)(B)

Election timely-filed return
John H. Young, 83 TC 831 (1984)

CLAIMING DEPRECIATION DEDUCTIONS

*"Election of Post 1986 ACRS Treatment for Pre-ACRS Assets May Be Advantageous," Ken Milani and James L. Wittenbach, 65 Taxes 93 (1987)
*IRS Publication 534
IRC § 168

¶5.22 • WHAT PROPERTY MAY BE DEPRECIATED?

Depreciation not allowed on equipment in suspended medical practice
Rev. Rul. 77–32, 1977–1 CB 38

Depreciation allowed on equipment while owner unemployed
Charles D. Gallagher, 39 TCM 291 (1979)

Ownership interest
Rev. Rul. 78–411, 1978–2 CB 112

Land
Reg. § 1.167(a)–2
Clarence D. Hawkins, 14 TCM 382 (1955), rev'd on another issue, 234 F.2d 359 (6th Cir. 1956)

Cost of education not depreciable
Nathaniel A. Denman, 48 TC 439 (1967)(Acq.)

Good will and customer lists
Reg. § 1.167(a)–3
Haberle Crystal Springs Brewing Co., 280 U.S. 384 (1930)
Frederick C. Renziehausen, 280 U.S. 387 (1930)
Dodge Bros. Inc. 118 F.2d 95 (4th Cir. 1941)
Los Angeles Central Animal Hospital, Inc. 58 TC 269 (1977) (Acq.)

One year or less
W. H. Tompkins Co., 47 BTA 292
International Shoe Co., 38 BTA 81 (Acq.)
Rev. Rul. 59–249, 1959–2 CB 55

Agreement not to compete
Christensen Machine Co., 18 BTA 256
Gazette Telegraph Co., 209 F.2d 926 (10th Cir. 1954)
Frances Silberman, 22 TC 1240 (1954)

Car partly for business
IRC § 280F
J. R. James, 2 BTA 1071 (Acq.)
Kenneth Branchard, 12 TCM 550 (1953)

Paul McWilliams, 9 TCM (1950)
W. H. Wilson, 5 TCM 592 (1946), aff'd, 161 F.2d 556 (4th Cir. 1947), cert. denied, 332 U.S. 769

Offered for sale
Marjorie May, 299 F.2d 725 (4th Cir. 1962)

Depreciation not allowed on idle ranch residence held by business
John T. Steen, 61 TC 298 (1973), aff'd per curiam, 508 F.2d 268 (5th Cir. 1975)

Depreciation on residence put up for sale
Hulet P. Smith, 26 TCM 149 (1967), aff'd per curiam, 397 F.2d 804 (9th Cir. 1968)

Nonproducing property
Reg. § 1.212–1(b)
George W. Mitchell, 47 TC 120 (1966)(Nonacq.)
Maurice H. Connell, 54–1 USTC ¶9119 (S.D. Fla. 1954)
Charles D. Gallagher, 39 TCM 291 (1979)

Work of art not depreciable
Rev. Rul. 68–232, 1968–1 CB 79

Depreciating paintings in office
D. Joseph Judge, 35 TCM 1264 (1976)

Cannot accumulate depreciation
Fort Orange Paper Co., 1 BTA 1230 (Acq.)
First National Bank of Thompson, Iowa, 2 BTA 735
Morris & Bailey Steel Co., 9 BTA 205 (Acq.)

Depreciation on building bought with intention to demolish
Rev. Rul. 67–445, 1967–2 CB 94

Farm property
Reg. § 1–167(a)(6)
When depreciation is claimed
Reg. § 1.167(a)–10

¶5.23 • MACRS CLASS LIVES FOR PROPERTY PLACED IN SERVICE AFTER 1986

IRC § 168(e)

¶5.24 • MACRS BASED ON DECLINING BALANCE METHOD

IRC § 168(b)

¶5.25 • HALF-YEAR CONVENTION FOR MACRS

IRC § 168(d)(1)

¶5.26 • FINAL QUARTER ASSET PLACEMENTS—MID-QUARTER CONVENTION FOR MACRS

IRC § 168(d)(3)

¶5.27 • ALTERNATIVE MACRS DEPRECIATION

IRC § 168(g)

¶5.28 • WRITING OFF THE COST OF A COMPUTER IN 1987

Writing off cost of computer
IRC § 280F

Employee deductions barred
Rev. Rul. 86–129, IRB 1986–45, 4
*Letter Ruling 8710009
*Letter Ruling 8615024
*Letter Ruling 8615071

¶5.29 • ACRS RECOVERY PERIODS FOR BUSINESS ASSETS PLACED IN SERVICE BEFORE 1987

IRC § 168(c) prior to 1986 Tax Act

¶5.30 • FIGURING ACRS ON BUSINESS EQUIPMENT PLACED IN SERVICE BEFORE 1987

IRC § 168(b)(1)(A) prior to 1986 Tax Act

Depreciation of automobiles and home computers
IRC § 280F

¶5.31 • MACRS FOR REAL ESTATE PLACED IN SERVICE AFTER 1986

IRC § 168(e)(2)
IRC § 168(c)
IRC § 167(j)(2)(B)

¶5.32 • DEPRECIATING REAL ESTATE PLACED IN SERVICE BEFORE 1987

The Following Citations Are to Code Sections Before 1986 Tax Act

Recovery period
IRC § 168(c)(2)(D)

Note: Paragraph numbers refer to Part One. Items marked * are research aids, not citations of authority; see "Key to Citations" on page 337.

Low income housing
IRC § 168(b)(4)
IRC § 168(c)(2)(F)

Rate of recovery
IRC § 168(b)(2)

Treasury tables
Notice 81–16, 1981–2 CB 545

Election to use straight line depreciation
IRC § 168(b)(3)

Separate depreciation for components not allowed
IRC § 168(f)(1)

Components added after March 15, 1984
IRC § 168(f)(1)(B)
IRC § 168(g)(4)

¶5.33 • WHEN MACRS IS NOT ALLOWED
IRC § 168(f)

¶5.34 • FIRST-YEAR EXPENSING
IRC § 179

50% business use test for automobiles and computers
IRC § 280F(b)
IRC § 280F(d)

SALES OF BUSINESS ASSETS AND PROPERTY

¶5.35 • PROFITABLE SALES OF DE-PRECIABLE PROPERTY PLACED IN SERVICE BEFORE 1981
IRC § 1245
IRC § 1250
Reg. § 1.1245–1 through 6
Prop. Reg. § 1.1250–1 through 5

¶5.36 • RECAPTURE ON BUSINESS EQUIPMENT PLACED IN SERVICE BEFORE 1981
IRC § 1245
Reg. § 1.1245–1 through 6

¶5.37 • RECAPTURE ON DEPRECIABLE REALTY PLACED IN SERVICE BEFORE 1981
IRC § 1250

Computing excess over straight line
Reg. § 1.1250(b)(1)

Holding period where property is foreclosed
IRC § 1250(d)(10)
Reg. § 1.1250–1 through 5

¶5.38 • RECAPTURE OF ACRS AND MACRS DEDUCTIONS
IRC § 1245(a), as amended by §§ 201(b), 202(b), 204(a)–(d), and 212(d)(2)(F) of the Economic Recovery Tax Act of 1981

¶5.39 • RECAPTURE OF FIRST-YEAR EXPENSING
IRC § 179(d)(10)

¶5.40 • ADDITIONAL AMORTIZATION REALIZED ON LEASEHOLD IMPROVEMENTS
IRC § 1250(f)

¶5.41 • GIFTS AND INHERITANCES OF DEPRECIABLE PROPERTY
IRC § 1245(a)

Tax not imposed at time of gift or inheritance
IRC § 1245(b)(1), (2), and (3)
Reg. § 1.1245–4

¶5.42 • INVOLUNTARY CONVERSIONS AND TAX-FREE EXCHANGES OF DEPRECIABLE PROPERTY
IRC § 1245(b)(4)
IRC § 1250(d)(4)

¶5.43 • INSTALLMENT SALE OF DE-PRECIABLE PROPERTY
Reg. § 1.1245–6(d)

Sales after June 6, 1984
IRC § 453(i)

¶5.44 • PROPERTY USED IN A BUSINESS (SECTION 1231 ASSETS)
*"Capital and Section 1231 Asset Transactions, Status and Planning Opportunities Under the New Law," Philip J. Harmelink and Phyllis V. Copeland, 65 Taxes 176 (March 1987)
IRC § 1231
Reg. § 1.1231–1 and 2

Recapture of ordinary loss
IRC § 1231(c)

¶5.45 • SALE OF A BUSINESS
*"Allocation of Lump-Sum Purchase Price Upon the Transfer of Business Assets After Tax Reform," Rolf Auster, 65 Taxes 545 (August 1987).

*"Deferral of Tax on a Taxable Sale of a Business," J. D. McGaffey, 25 Tax Lawyer 343 (1972)

*"Sale or Exchange of a Partnership Interest: What Constitutes a Sale or Exchange; Treatment of Unrealized Receivables and Inventory Items; Like-kind Exchange," J. S. Brown, 31 NYU Inst. 133 (1973)

*"Steps to Take to Minimize Ordinary Income on the Sale of a Partnership Interest," C. K. Moore, Jr. and H. G. Nagel, 32 Taxation for Accountants, 36 (Jan. 1984) and 12 Taxation for Lawyers 304 (Mar./Apr. 1984)

Allocation of Sales Price to Business Assets—1986 Tax Act
IRC § 1060
Temp. Reg. 1.338(b)–2T

Individual proprietorship
IRC § 1231
Reg. § 1.1231–1
Aaron F. Williams, 152 F.2d 570 (2d Cir. 1946)
Rev. Rul. 55–79, 1955–1 CB 370

Accountant realizes capital gain
Paul J. Kelly, 29 TCM 1090 (1970)

Partnership, joint venture sale
IRC § 741
IRC § 751
Reg. § 1.741–1
Reg. § 1.751–1

Partnership tax year closes for selling partner
IRC § 706(c)(2)
Reg. § 1.706–1(c)(2)

Retirement of partner
IRC § 706(c)(2)
IRC § 736
Reg. § 1.736–1(a)

¶5.46 • CONVENANTS NOT TO COMPETE AND SALE OF GOOD WILL
*"Allocation of Lump-Sum Purchase Price Upon the Transfer of Business Assets After Tax Reform," Rolf Auster, 65 Taxes 545 (August 1987)

*"Handling Covenant Not to Compete Negotiations to Assure Tax Benefits and Preclude Challenges," Bruce A. Rich, 9 Tax for Law 118 (1980)

Allocating sale proceeds to Goodwill—1986 Tax Act
IRC § 1060

Covenant given full effect in absence of fraud, etc.
Carl L. Danielson, 378 F.2d 771 (3d Cir. 1967), cert. denied, 389 U.S. 858
A. A. Proulx, 77–2 USTC ¶9758 (Ct. Cl. 1977)

Covenant may be questioned
J. Leonard Schmitz, 51 TC 306 (1968), aff'd, 457 F.2d 1022 (9th Cir. 1972)

Covenant not to compete—assuring good will
Carl L. Danielson, 44 TC 549 (1965), vacated and rem'd, 378 F. 2d 771 (3d Cir. 1967), cert. denied, 389 U.S. 858

Covenant allowed despite contract's failure to allocate
Peterson Machine Tool Inc., 79 TC 72 (1982)

Corporate good will by stockholder
David H. Ullman, 29 TC 129 (1957), aff'd, 264 F.2d 305 (2d Cir. 1959)

Note: Paragraph numbers refer to Part One. Items marked * are research aids, not citations of authority; see "Key to Citations" on page 337.

358

Professional good will
F. G. Masquelette Est., 239 F.2d 322 (5th Cir. 1957)
Hoyt Butler, 46 TC 280 (1966)
Merle P. Brooks, 36 TC 1128 (1961) (Acq.)
Richard S. Wyler, 14 TC 1251 (1950)(Acq.)
Rodney B. Horton, 13 TC 143 (1949)(Acq.)
Rev. Rul. 64–235, 1964–2 CB 18, modified by Rev. Rul. 70–45, 1970–1 CB 17

¶5.47 • SALE OF SECURITIES PUR-CHASED TO PROTECT BUSINESS INTERESTS

Sales at loss
Charles W. Steadman, 424 F.2d 1 (6th Cir. 1970), cert. denied, 400 U.S. 869

Ordinary loss on sale to protect good-will
Campbell Taggart Inc., 744 F.2d 442 (CA-5, 1985)

Capital loss if investment motive mixed with business motive
W. W. Windle Co., 65 TC 694 (1976), appeal dismissed, 550 F.2d 43 (1st Cir. 1977), cert. denied, 431 U.S. 966

Pressured executive denied ordinary loss
Larrimore Wright, 756 F.2d 1039 (4th Cir. 1985)

Sale at gain
Bell Fibre Products Corp., 36 TCM 182 (1977)

IRS position
Rev. Rul. 78–94, 1978–1 CB 58

Sale of partnership interest
H. Clinton Pollack, 69 TC 11 (1971)

¶5.48 • SALE OF PROPERTY USED FOR BUSINESS AND PERSONAL PURPOSES

Sale of airplane
Hugh Sharp Jr., 199 F. Supp. 743 (D. Del. 1961), aff'd, 303 F.2d 783 (3d Cir. 1962)

¶5.49 • TAX-FREE TRADES OF IN-VESTMENT OR BUSINESS PROPERTY

Exchange solely for like-kind property
IRC § 1031(a)
Reg. § 1.1031(a)–1

Farms exchanged
Rev. Rul. 59–229, 1959–2 CB 180

Farm for city property
L. M. Dyke, BTA Memo. August 12, 1932
E. R. Braley, 14 BTA 1153 (Acq.)

Land for water rights
Rev. Rul. 55–749, 1955–2 CB 295, distinguished by Rev. Rul. 67–255, 1967–2 CB 270

Exchange of partnership interests
Rollin E. Meyers Sr. Est., 503 F.2d

556 (9th Cir. 1974), aff'g per curiam 58 TC 311 (1972)(Non-acq.)
IRC § 1031(a)

Tax-free oil lease for ranch
Rev. Rul. 68–331, 1968–1 CB 352

Exchange of ownership interest in realty for 30 year leasehold
Reg. § 1.1031(a)–1(c)
Rev. Rul. 78–72, 1978–1 CB 258

Taxable oil lease for ranch
William Fleming, 356 U.S. 260 (1958), rev'g 241 F.2d 78 (5th Cir. 1957)

Timber rights
Oregon Lumber Co., 20 TC 192 (1953)(Acq.)

Exchange of cattle of different sexes
IRC § 1031(e)

Must be used in trade or business or for investment
IRC § 1031(a)
Reg. § 1.1031(a)–1

Depreciable equipment on which there is potential gain
IRC § 1245(b)(3)

Exception—residence for other residence
IRC § 1034
Reg. § 1.1034–1
Ethel Black, 35 TC 90 (1960)

Boot is taxed
IRC § 1031(b)
Reg. § 1.1031(b)–1

No loss recognized if boot given
IRC § 1031(c) and (d)
Reg. § 1.1031(c)–1 and (d)–1

Deferred exchanges—time limit
IRC § 1031(a)(3)

Joint tenancy and tenancy in common
Rev. Rul. 56–437, 1956–2 CB 507

Mortgage release is boot
Reg. § 1.1031(d)–2
Beulah B. Crane, 331 U.S. 1 (1947)

Other exchanges
IRC § 1002
Reg. § 1.1002–1

¶5.50 • SHOULD YOU TRADE IN BUSINESS EQUIPMENT?

Loss on trade-in
National Outdoor Advertising Bureau, Inc., 89 F.2d 878 (2d Cir. 1937), on remand, BTA Dec 10,072–C, 6/24/38

Sale to dealer
Rev. Rul. 61–119, 1961–1 CB 395

Trade-ins of personal property
IRC § 1031(d)
Reg. § 1.1031(d)–1
Rev. Rul. 72–111, 1972–1 CB 56

¶5.51 • SELF-EMPLOYMENT TAX RULES

IRC § 6015(c)(2)

Reg. § 1.6015(b)
*IRS Publication 533

Self-employed businessman or professional
IRC § 1401
IRC § 1402
IRC § 1403
Reg. § 1.1401–1
Reg. § 1.1402(a)–1
Reg. § 1.1402(b)–1
Reg. § 1.1402(c)–1

Clergy
IRC § 1402(e)
Temp. Reg. § 1.1402(e)–5T

Consulting
Rev. Rul. 68–595, 1968–2 CB 378
Grosswald v. Schweicker, 653 F.2d 58 (2d Cir. 1981)
Steffens v. United States, 707 F.2d 478 (11th Cir. 1983)
James M. Hornaday, 81 TC 830 (1983)

Director's fees
Rev. Rul. 68–595, 1968–2 CB 378

Employees of foreign government or international organization
Reg. § 1.1402(c)–3(d)
Jessica M. Smart, 63–2 USTC ¶9744 (S.D.N.Y. 1963)

Technical specialists
Section 1706 of 1986 Tax Reform Act
Rev. Rul. 87–41, IRB 1987–23, 7

Fees as executor
Cresence E. Clarke, 27 TC 861 (1957)
Rev. Rul. 58–5, 1958–1 CB 322, distinguished by Rev. Rul. 72–86, 1972–1 CB 273

Nonprofessional executor or administrator
Rev. Rul. 58–5, 1958–1 CB 322, distinguished by Rev. Rul. 72–86, 1972–1 CB 273
Special Ruling, August 19, 1952
Special Ruling, March 5, 1952
Special Ruling, January 10, 1952
Special Ruling, March 20, 1957

Trust beneficiaries not self-employed
Reg. § 1.1402(a)–2(b)

Fee for occasional speech
Rev. Rul. 55–431, 1955–2 CB 312

PIK payments to farmers
Pub. L. No. 98–4
Ann. 83–43, IRB 1983–10, 29

Babysitter
Rev. Rul. 77–279, 1977–2 CB 12

Licensed and practical nurses
Rev. Rul. 75–101, 1975–1 CB 318
Rev. Rul. 61–96, 1961–2 CB 155

Gambling income not subject to self-employment tax
Alfred A. Gentile, 6 TC 1 (1946)

Nonresident alien
IRC § 1402(b)

Public official
IRC § 1402(c)

Note: Paragraph numbers refer to Part One. Items marked * are research aids, not citations of authority; see "Key to Citations" on page 337.

Reg. § 1.402(c)–2

Writer
Rev. Rul. 68–498, 1968–2 CB 377
Rev. Rul. 79–390, 1972–2 CB 308
Rev. Rul. 55–385, 1955–1 CB 100
(professor's writing as self-employment income)

Dealers in commodities and options
IRC § 1402(i)

Real estate salesman and door-to-door salesman
IRC § 3508(a)
Rev. Rul. 85–63, 1985–1 CB 292

¶5.52 • PARTNERS PAY SELF-EMPLOYMENT TAX

IRC § 701
Reg. § 1.701–1

Reg. § 1.702–1
Partner dying during taxable year
Reg. § 1.1402(f)–1

Retirement payments from partnerships
IRC § 1402(a)(10)
Rev. Rul. 79–34, 1979–1 CB 285

Limited partner not subject to self-employment tax
IRC § 1402(a)(12)

¶5.53 • WHAT IS SELF-EMPLOYMENT INCOME?

IRC § 1402
IRC § 6017
Reg. § 1.6017–1(b)
Reg. § 1.1402(a)–1
Reg. § 1.1402(b)–1

Business interruption insurance proceeds not self-employment income
Max G. Newberry, 76 TC 441 (1981)

Rents
Reg. § 1.1402(a)–4

Dividends and interest
Reg. § 1.1402(a)–5

Capital gains and losses
Reg. § 1.1402(a)–6

Net operating loss carryover
IRC § 1402(a)(4) and (5)

Husband and wife
IRC § 6017
Rev. Rul. 82–39, 1982–1 CB 119

Illegal employment
Rev. Rul. 60–77, 1960–1 CB 386

¶6

Capital Gains and Losses on Sales of Property

"Capital Gains and Losses After the Tax Reform Act of 1986," Robert L. Gardner and Dave N. Stewart, 5 Taxes 125 (February 1987)

"Capital and Section 1231 Asset Transactions: Status and Planning Opportunities Under the New Law," Philip J. Harmelink and Phyllis V. Copeland, 65 Taxes 176 (March 1987)

¶6.1 • LONG-TERM CAPITAL GAINS

Maximum 28% capital gains rate after 1986
IRC § 1(j)

60% capital gain deduction repealed
IRC § 1202, repealed by 1986 Tax Reform Act Section 301(a)

¶6.2 • HOW YOUR CAPITAL GAINS ARE REPORTED

IRC § 1(j)
IRC § 1222
*IRS Publication 544

¶6.3 • FIGURING CAPITAL GAINS AND LOSSES

Short-term and long-term transactions
IRC § 1222

Capital losses
IRC § 1211 and 1212
IRC § 62(a)(3)

¶6.4 • CAPITAL LOSS CARRYOVERS

IRC § 1211
IRC § 1212
IRC § 1222(10)
Reg. § 1.1222–1

Loss must be considered even if no tax benefit is realized
Rev. Rul. 76–177, 1976–1 CB 224

Rules for pre-1970 losses repealed for years after 1986
IRC § 1211(b)
IRC § 1212(b)(3)
Reg. § 1.1211–1(b)(3)
Reg. § 1.1212–1(b)(4)

¶6.5 • CAPITAL LOSSES OF MARRIED COUPLES

One capital loss deduction on joint return
John E. Ross, 37 TC 445 (1961)
Reg. § 1.1211–1(d)
Reg. § 1.1212–1(c)

¶6.6 • WHAT ARE CAPITAL ASSETS?

IRC § 1221
Reg. § 1.1221–1

¶6.6(1) • EXAMPLES OF CAPITAL ASSETS

Stock
IRC § 1221
Abraham L. Berman, 14 TCM 406 (1955)
Rev. Rul. 56–153, 1956–1 CB 166

Land not in business
Richard E. Beck, 179 F.2d 688 (7th Cir. 1950)
J. T. G. Crawford, 161 F.2d 315 (5th Cir. 1947)

Goodwill
Ellen J. Franklin, 6 TCM 1099 (1947)
Aaron Michaels, 12 TC 17 (1949) (Acq.)

Rodney B. Horton, 13 TC 143 (1949) (Acq. in result only)

Warehouse receipts
Thomas E. Wood, 16 TC 213 (1951) (Acq.)

Notes
Lehr Est., 18 TC 373 (1952)

Silver futures contracts
Rev. Rul. 77–185, 1977–1 CB 48

Insurance expiration rights
Rev. Rul. 65–180, 1965–2 CB 279, modified by Rev. Rul. 74–456, 1974–2 CB 65

Patents
IRC § 1235

Literary properties for investment
James M. Fidler, 231 F.2d 138 (9th Cir. 1956)
Fred MacMurray, 21 TC 15 (1953) (Nonacq.)
Anatole Litvak, 23 TC 441 (1955) (Nonacq.)

Trademark
Rainier Brewing Co., 7 TC 162 (1946) (Acq. & nonacq.), aff'd, 165 F.2d 217 (9th Cir. 1948)

Dealer's investments
IRC § 1236
C. R. Bondurant, 245 F.2d 265 (6th Cir. 1957)

Tenure of professor
Merrill J. Foote, 81 TC 930 (1983)

¶6.7 • PROPERTY USED FOR PERSONAL PURPOSES

Losses nondeductible
IRC § 165(c)

Note: Paragraph numbers refer to Part One. Items marked * are research aids, not citations of authority; see "Key to Citations" on page 337.

¶6.8 • CAN YOU DEDUCT LOSSES ON SALE OF THESE PERSONAL ASSETS?

Disallowance of loss—general rule
IRC § 165

Pleasure craft—allowed loss
David A. Bellamore, 3 BTA 1133 (Acq.)
Estelle G. Marx, 5 TC 173 (1945) (Acq.)
J. A. Talbot, 23 BTA 792 (Acq.)

Pleasure craft—disallowed loss
C. Bai Lihme, 18 F. Supp. 566 (S.D.N.Y. 1936)

Automobile—loss allowed
Earl King, 9 BTA 502 (Acq.)

Art objects
Juliet P. Hamilton, 25 BTA 1317
Henry B. Twombly, 154 F.2d 293 (3d Cir. 1946)

Sublet
Rev. Rul. 74–28, 1974–1 CB 67

¶6.9 • SALE OR EXCHANGE USUALLY REQUIRED FOR CAPITAL ASSET TREATMENT

Sale or exchange requirement
IRC § 1222

Capital asset treatment for lapse, cancellation, abandonment, etc. of commodity options
IRC § 1234A

Property pledged as collateral
Morgan W. Jopling, 46 BTA 262

Voluntary conveyance of mortgaged property
Rev. Rul. 78–164, 1978–1 CB 264
Eugene L. Freeland, 74 TC 970 (1980)

Gift of depreciable mortgaged property
Aaron Levine Est., 634 F.2d 12 (2d Cir. 1980)
Teofilo Evangelista, 629 F.2d 1218 (7th Cir. 1980)

*"Voluntary Conveyance Sales or Exchanges?" M. M. Caplin, 57 Taxes 287 (1979)

*"The Voluntary Transfer of Real Estate to Creditors: Is It Treated Like 'Abandonment' or Foreclosure?" J. W. Pratt and N. Oestreich, 57 Taxes 293 (1979)

Abandonment treated as sale
Milledge L. Middleton, 77 TC 310 (1981), aff'd, — F.2d — (CA-11, 1982)
James W. Yarbro, 45 TCM 170 (1982) aff'd — F.2d — (5th Cir. 1984)

Executor's transfer
William R. Kenan, 114 F.2d 217 (2d Cir. 1940)
John H. Brinckerhoff, 8 TC 1045 (1947) (Acq.), aff'd, 168 F.2d 436 (2d Cir. 1948)

Marital property settlement
IRC § 1041

Thomas Crawley Davis, 370 U.S. 65 (1962) pre-codification rule

Cancellation of lease
IRC § 1241
Reg. § 1.1241–1

Business lease as § 1231 asset
Rev. Rul. 72–85, 1972–1 CB 234

Distributor's agreement
IRC § 1241
Reg. sec. 1.1241–1

Timber standing or cut
IRC § 631
Reg. § 1.631–1 and 2

¶6.10 • SALE OR RETIREMENT OF BONDS AND NOTES

IRC § 1271
IRC § 1272
*IRS Publication 550

Registered form
IRC § 1287

Retirement defined
Donald S. McClain, 311 U.S. 527 (1941)

Unearned original issue discount is capital gain
Ted Bolnick, 44 TC 245 (1965) (Acq.)

¶6.11 • WORTHLESS SECURITIES

*"Stock Losses Establishing Worthlessness," K. M. Worthy, 22 NYU Inst. 289 (1964)

*"Worthlessness, Debt-Equity and Related Problems," William Natbony, 32 Hastings L.J. 1407 (1981)
IRC § 165(a)
IRC § 165(g)
Reg. § 1.165–5

Partial worthlessness not allowed
Edwin Leo Coyle, 142 F.2d 580 (7th Cir. 1944)
Harry C. Howard, 20 BTA 207, aff'd, 56 F.2d 781 (6th Cir. 1932), cert. denied, 287 U.S. 619

Statute of limitation
IRC § 6511(d)

Sale for nominal amount after worthlessness
J. Graham Brown, 94 F.2d 101 (6th Cir. 1938)
Frank C. Rand, 116 F.2d 929 (8th Cir. 1941), cert. denied, 313 U.S. 594

Insolvency
Alice G. K. Kleburg, 2 TC 1024 (1943)
Arthur C. Ansley, 217 F.2d 252 (3d Cir. 1954)

Potential value in stock despite insolvency
Norman Nelson, 131 F.2d 301 (8th Cir. 1942)

Business continued
Lola G. Bullard, 146 F.2d 386 (2d Cir. 1945)

George P. Snow, 90 F. Supp. 37 (E.D.N.Y. 1950)

Bankruptcy
Joseph A. Jeffrey, 62 F.2d 661 (6th Cir. 1933)
Dennis H. Long, 145 F.2d 234 (6th Cir. 1944)
In re Harrington, 1 F.2d 749 (D.C. Cir. 1924)

Court advice on claiming bad debt deduction
Minnie K. Young, 123 F.2d 597 (2d Cir. 1941)

Payments on note issued for stock
W. P. Tams, Jr., 33 F. Supp. 764 (D.W. Va. 1940)

Small business investment company
IRC § 1242

Loss on short sale of SBIC stock
Rev. Rul. 63–65, 1963–1 CB 142

Political parties
IRC § 271

¶6.12 • SECTION 1244 STOCK (SMALL BUSINESS STOCK)

IRC § 1244
Reg. § 1.1244

¶6.13 • CORPORATE LIQUIDATION

*"General Utilities Repeal: A Transactional Analysis" George Brodie Jr., 66 Journal of Taxation 322 (June 1987)

*"How Liquidations and S Elections May Avoid the Impact of TRA '86," John W. Schmehl, 67 Journal of Taxation 30 (July 1987)

*"Spin-offs, Split-offs and Split-ups Remain Tax Favored Despite the Tax Reform Act of 1986," Ross S. Friedman, Taxation for Accountants, March 1987
IRC § 331
Louis Greenspon, 229 F.2d 947 (8th Cir. 1956)
Susan J. Carter, 170 F.2d 911 (2d Cir. 1948)
L. M. Graves, 11 TCM 467 (1952)
Rev. Rul. 59–228, 1959–2 CB 59

Legal expenses of collecting claim
Otto C. Doering, Jr., 335 F.2d 738 (2d Cir. 1964)

¶6.14 • SALE OF AN OPTION

IRC § 1234
Reg. §1.1234–1

¶6.15 • CALLS OR OPTIONS TRANSACTIONS ON OPTION EXCHANGES

"Selecting the Off-Beat Investments, Puts, Calls, Straddles, Warrants, Commodity Futures and Other Exotica," J. F. Kennedy, 32 NYU Inst. 1093 (1974)

IRC § 1234(b)

Note: Paragraph numbers refer to Part One. Items marked * are research aids, not citations of authority; see "Key to Citations" on page 337.

Index Options
IRC § 1256

¶6.16 • STRADDLE LOSSES AND DEDUCTION RESTRICTIONS

*"An Analysis of the Tax Straddle Provisions of the Economic Recovery Tax Act of 1981," Stuart Strauss, 60 Taxes 163 (1982)

*"Straddle Rules Do Not Apply to Hedging Transactions But Bar Other Tax-Saving Methods," William P. Bowers, 56 J. Taxation 24 (1982) and 55 J. Taxation 338 (1981)

*"An Examination of the Effect of Recent Legislation on Commodity Tax Straddles," Samuel C. Thompson, Jr., 2 Va. Tax Rev. 165 (Winter 1983)
IRC § 1092
IRC § 1256
IRC § 263(g)

Mixed straddles
Temp. Reg. § 1.1092(b)–3T and 4T

¶6.17 • SALES OF PATENTS AND COPYRIGHTS

*"An Interpretation of Section 1235 (a): Obtaining Stock Ownership in a Patent Transfer While Receiving Capital Gains Treatment," S. J. Toll, 28 Tax Lawyer 399 (1975)

*"Capital Gains Treatment for Patents: An Underutilized Fringe Benefit," by Richard B. Byars, 5 Rev. Tax. Individuals 338 (1981) (Review of Taxation of Individuals)

Patents, royalty agreements, etc.
IRC § 1235
Reg. § 1.1235–1 and 2

Royalty payments
IRC § 1235
Reg. 1.1235–1
Halsey W. Taylor, 16 TC 376 (1951) (Nonacq.)

Agreement signed before patent issued
IRC § 1235
Reg. § 1.1235–1

Payments on fixed percent of sales price
Bessie B. Hopkinson, 126 F.2d 406 (2d Cir. 1942)
Franklin S. Speicher, 28 TC 938 (1957) (Acq.)

Professional inventor
IRC § 1235
Reg. § 1.1235–1

Inventor retains legal title
Reg. § 1.1235–2(b)(2)(ii)

Transfer by gift, inheritance, etc.
IRC § 1235
Reg. § 1.1235–1

Nonresident alien transferor
Reg. § 1.871–7(b)(5)(viii)

Employee-inventor allowed capital gain on royalties
Thomas N. Melin, 478 F.2d 1210 (Ct. Cl. 1973)
Thomas H. McClain, 40 TC 841 (1963) (Acq.)

Must meet statutory tests
Myron C. Poole, 46 TC 392 (1966) (Acq.)

Geographic limit
Edwin M. Klein, 84 F.2d 310 (7th Cir. 1936)
Don Kueneman, 68 TC 609 (1977)

Industrial restriction
Thomas L. Fawick, 436 F.2d 655 (6th Cir. 1965)

¶6.18 • GRANTING OF AN EASEMENT

David Fasten, 71 TC 650 (1979) (Acq.)
Inaja Land Co. Ltd., 9 TC 727 (1947) (Acq.)
Rev. Rul. 59–121, 1959–1 CB 212, clarified by Rev. Rul. 68–291, 1968–1 CB 351
Rev. Rul. 72–433, 1972–2 CB 470
Rev. Rul. 73–161, 1973–1 CB 366
Rev. Rul. 72–255, 1972–1 CB 221

¶6.19 • RELEASE OF RESTRICTIVE COVENANT

Rev. Rul. 70–203, 1970–1 CB 171

¶6.20 • TRANSACTIONS NOT SUBJECT TO CAPITAL GAIN OR LOSS

Accounts or notes receivable
IRC § 1221(4)
Laurence Sovic, 92 F. Supp. 202 (N.D.N.Y. 1950), aff'd per curiam, 191 F.2d 895 (2d Cir. 1951)
Dewitt M. Sherwood, 20 TC 733 (1953)

Abandonment of property is sale
James W. Yarbro, 45 TCM 170 (1982) aff'd — F.2d — (5th Cir. 1984)
Milledge L. Middleton, 77 TC 310 (1981) aff'd, — F.2d — (CA–11, 1982)

Abandonment of property not sale
Thomas Stokes, 124 F.2d 335 (3d Cir. 1941)
R. R. Adamson, 107 F.2d 1022 (9th Cir. 1940)
Industrial Cotton Mills, 43 BTA 107 (Acq.)
Robert A. Daily, 81 TC 161 (1983)

Gratuitous voluntary reconveyance of property subject to nonrecourse loan treated as foreclosure sale
Eugene L. Freeland, 74 TC 970 (1980)

Annuity contract surrendered
George M. Cohan, 11 BTA 743, aff'd in part on other issues, 39 F.2d 540 (2d Cir. 1930)

Damages for breach of contract
A. M. Johnson, 32 BTA 156, (Nonacq.), rem'd on compromise, (7th Cir. July 23, 1937)
Aaron E. Greenleaf, 9 TCM 1024 (1950)

Damages for securities fraud
Rev. Rul. 79–279, 1979–2 CB 316

Employment contract canceled
Rev. Rul. 58–301, 1958–1 CB 23, distinguished by Rev. Rul. 74–252, 1974–1 CB 287 and Rev. Rul. 75–33, 1975–1, CB 15

Endowment policy paid on maturity
M. N. Avery, 111 F.2d 19 (9th Cir. 1940)

Estate's collection on claim
Rev. Rul. 55–463, 1955–2 CB 277

F.H.A. loan windfall profits
IRC § 312(j)
Reg. § 1.312–12

Forfeited deposit
George O. Baird, 65 F.2d 911, (5th Cir. 1933), cert. denied, 290 U.S. 690
Samuel Hellerman, 14 TC 738 (1950)
Dexter Sulphite Pulp & Paper Co., 23 BTA 227 (Acq. & nonacq.)
Walter B. Krych, 20 TCM 44 (1961) (nondeductible because for personal purposes)

Franchises
IRC § 1253

Insurance policy sold to third party
Gertrude H. Crocker Est., 37 TC 605 (1962)

Insurance renewal commissions
Floyd L. Turner, 38 TC 304 (1962)
Olmsted Inc., 35 TC 429 (1960) (Nonacq.), aff'd, 304 F.2d 16 (8th Cir. 1962)
Floyd L. Turner, 38 TC 304 (1962)

Notes written off as worthless
Merchants Nat'l Bank of Mobile, 199 F.2d 657 (5th Cir. 1952)

Liquidated damages
Josephine R. Binns, 385 F.2d 159 (6th Cir. 1967)
Ralph A. Boatman, 32 TC 1182 (1959)
Paul F. Myers, 18 TCM 1116 (1959), aff'd, 287 F.2d 400 (6th Cir. 1961) cert. denied, 368 U.S. 828
Alvin B. Lowe, 44 TC 363 (1965) (Acq.) (capital gain allowed on finding of a closed sale)
Phillip Handelman, 32 TCM 249 (1973), rev'd and rem'd, 509 F.2d 1067 (2d Cir. 1975) (closed sale)

Mortgaging property
Woodsam Associates, Inc., 16 TC 649 (1951), aff'd, 198 F.2d 357 (2d Cir. 1952)

Note payment received after judgment
Matilda S. Puelicher, 6 TC 300 (1946)

Note: Paragraph numbers refer to Part One. Items marked * are research aids, not citations of authority; see "Key to Citations" on page 337.

Property received in settlement
Albert C. Becken Jr., 5 TC 498 (1945) (Acq.)
Margery K. Megargel, 3 TC 238 (1944) (Acq.)

Contract right to share profits
Pat O'Brien, 25 TC 376 (1955) (Acq. in part, nonacq. in part)

Land contracts purchased at discount
Arthur E. Wood, 25 TC 468 (1955)

Release of debt
Harry Escher, 78 F.2d 815 (3d Cir. 1935)

Payment for terminating contract
Appalachian Electric Power Co., 158 F.Supp. 138 (Ct. Cl. 1958)
Charles E. McCartney, 12 TC 320 (1949)
William G. H. Finch, 1 TCM 191 (1942)
Marc D. Leh, 27 TC 892 (1957), aff'd, 260 F.2d 489 (9th Cir. 1958)
Salem D. Caplan, 16 TCM 273 (1957)

Release of seniority rights
Rev. Rul. 75–44, 1975–1 CB 15

Release of right to percentage of profits
J. J. Perkins, 301 U.S. 655 (1937)
John D. Hawn, 231 F.2d 340 (5th Cir. 1956)
A. J. Slagter Jr., 238 F.2d 901 (7th Cir. 1956)
W. W. Sutton, 95 F.2d 845 (10th Cir. 1938)
J. Llewellyn, BTA Memo. P-H 42,460

Property returned by borrower
Reg. § 1.61–12

Sale of right to income
Herman W. Rhodes' Estate, 131 F.2d 50 (6th Cir. 1942)

Satisfaction of judgment
Peggy H. Ogilvie, 216 F.2d 748 (6th Cir. 1954)

Termination of insurance agency contract
C. Rogler Elliott, 431 F.2d 1149 (10th Cir. 1970)

Topsoil
Rev. Rul. 78, 1953–1 CB 18

¶6.21 • COUNTING THE HOLDING PERIOD

Long and short term capital gain or loss
IRC § 1222
IRC § 1201
IRC § 1223
Reg. § 1.1222–1
Reg. § 1.1201–1
Reg. § 1.1223–1(a)

Exclude day asset acquired
Harriet M. Hooper, 26 BTA 758

Holding period rules
IRC § 1222

Futures transactions
IRC § 1222

IR 1787, 3/30/77

¶6.22 • SECURITIES TRANSACTIONS

Stock exchange transactions
Rev. Rul. 72–381, 1972–2 CB 233
Rev. Rul. 70–598, 1970–2 CB 168

Year end sales
Rev. Rul. 78–270, 1978–2 CB 215

Stock subscriptions
Mayme C. Sommers, Admtrx., 63 F.2d 551 (10th Cir. 1933)
William J. Wineberg, 20 TCM 1715 (1961), aff'd, 326 F.2d 157 (9th Cir. 1964)

Stock dividends, exercise of rights
IRC § 1223(5)(6)
Reg. § 1.1223–1(f)
Rev. Rul. 56–572, 1956–2, CB 182

"Wash sales"
IRC § 1223(4)
Reg. § 1.1223–1(d)

Commodity satisfaction of futures contract
IRC § 1223(8)
Reg. § 1.1223–1(h)

Different lots
Reg. § 1.1223–1(i)

"When issued" transactions
I.T. 3721, 1945 CB 164, as modified by Rev. Rul. 57–29, 1957–1 CB 519

Employee option stock
John H. Rolfe, 58 TC 361 (1972), aff'd per curiam, 488 F.2d 1092 (9th Cir. 1974)

¶6.23 • REAL ESTATE TRANSACTIONS
Rev. Rul. 54–607, 1954–2 CB 177

New construction
M. A. Paul, 206 F.2d 763 (3d Cir. 1953)
Fred Draper, 32 TC 545 (1959) (Acq.)

¶6.24 • GIFT, INHERITED, OR PARTNERSHIP PROPERTY OR INVOLUNTARY CONVERSIONS

Gift after 1920
IRC § 1223(2)
Reg. § 1.1223–1(b)

Property of decedent sold within one year
IRC § 1223(11)

Inheritance
Nancy K. McFeely, 296 U.S. 102 (1936)
Harry E. R. Hall Est., 38 BTA 1145

Bequest created by will
E. Franklin Brewster, 280 U.S. 327 (1930)

Property purchased by executors
Marjorie K. Campbell, 313 U.S. 15 (1941)
Richard Van Nest Gambrill, 313 U.S. 11 (1941)

Contribution to partnership
Gordon S. Hogg, 214 F.2d 640 (5th Cir. 1954)
Rev. Rul. 55–39, 1955–1 CB 403

Distribution in kind from partnership
IRC § 735(b)
Reg. § 1.735–1

Involuntary conversion
IRC § 1223(1)(A)
Reg. § 1.1223–1(a)

¶6.25 • COMPUTING FRACTIONS OF MONTHS

Rules to compute holding period
Rev. Rul. 66–7, 1966–1 CB 188

¶6.26 • FIGURING YOUR PROFIT OR LOSS

Gain or loss
IRC § 1001
Reg. § 1.1001

¶6.27 • SELLING PRICE AND AMOUNT REALIZED

Selling price
IRC § 1001
Reg. § 1.1001

Mortgage included in price
Beulah B. Crane, 331 U.S. 1 (1947)
Consolidated Coke Co., 70 F.2d 446 (3d Cir.)
Fulton Gold Corp., 31 BTA 519
John F. Tufts, 456 U.S. 960 (1983)

Reduce price by expenses
Seleths O. Thompson, 9 BTA 1342 (Acq.)
Samuel C. Chapin, 12 TC 235 (1949), aff'd, 180 F.2d 140 (8th Cir. 1950)

Legal fee-cost of sale
Fred W. Gunn, 49 TC 38 (1967)

¶6.28 • FINDING YOUR COST

Unadjusted basis
IRC § 1012
Reg. § 1.1012–1

Improvements
IRC § 1016
Reg. § 1.016–2

Adjusted basis
IRC § 1011
Reg. § 1.1011–1

¶6.29 • UNADJUSTED BASIS OF YOUR PROPERTY
*IRS Publication 551

Basis is cash cost
IRC § 1012
Reg. § 1.1012–1

Adjusted cost after depreciation allowed
IRC § 1016
Reg. § 1.1016–3

Rendering services
Reg. § 1.61–2
W. H. Weaver, 25 TC 1067 (1956)
Lawrence S. Vadner, 14 TCM 866 (1955)

Note: Paragraph numbers refer to Part One. Items marked * are research aids, not citations of authority; see "Key to Citations" on page 337.

Taxable exchange of property
Philadelphia Park Amusement Co.,
126 F. Supp. 184 (Ct. Cl. 1954)
Rev. Rul. 56–100, 1956–1 CB 624

Tax-free exchange of property
IRC § 1031
Reg. § 1.1031(d)–1

Gift after December 31, 1920
IRC § 1015
Reg. § 1.1015–1

Gift tax paid increases basis
IRC § 1015(d)(6)

New residence wtihin eighteen months
IRC § 1034(e)
Reg. § 1.1034–1

Gift in trust before January 1, 1921
IRC § 1015(c)
Reg. Sec. 1.1015–3

Distribution from trust before June 2, 1984
Reg. § 1.661(a)–2(f)

Distribution from trust after June 1, 1984
IRC § 643(d)

Life estate or remainder interest
Reg. § 1.1014–5

Sale of life estate—zero basis
IRC § 1001(e)

Inheritance from decedents
IRC § 1014
Reg. § 1.1014–1
Reg. § 1.1014–2

Inheritance of property transferred to decedent within one year of death
IRC § 1014(e)

Estate tax value questioned
Sam F. McIntosh, 26 TCM 1164
(1967)

Property subject to lease
Harriet M. Bryant Trust, 11 TC 374
(1948)(Acq.)

Property subject to mortgage
Beulah B. Crane, 331 U.S. 1 (1947)

Right to buy deceased's property
J. Gordon Mack, 3 TC 390 (1944),
aff'd 148 F.2d 62, (3d Cir. 1945),
cert. denied, 326 U.S. 719

Distribution from trust
IRC § 1015
Reg. § 1.1015–2
IRC § 643

Distribution to settle claim
Rev. Rul. 55–117, 1955–1 CB 233

General power of appointment
IRC § 1015

At age 21
Sherman Ewing, 40 BTA 912 (Acq.)
Lindsay C. Howard, 23 TC 962
(1955)(Acq.)

Compulsory or involuntary conversion
IRC § 1033(c)

Prenuptial agreement
Doris Farid-es-Sultaneh, 160 F.2d

812 (2d Cir. 1947), rev'g 6 TC 652
(1946)

Property purchased prior to March 1, 1913
IRC § 1053
Reg. § 1.1053–1

Distribution on orders of SEC
IRC § 1081
Reg. § 1.1081

Dividends in property
IRC § 301
Reg. § 1.301–1

Bonus on stock owned
Mead Coal Co., 28 BTA 599 (Acq.),
aff'd in part, rev'd in part and
rem'd, 72 F.2d 22 (4th Cir. 1939)
John L. Kirkland, 57 F.2d 608 (D.C.
Cir. 1932)

Variable annuities inherited
Rev. Rul. 79–335. 1979–2 CB 282

Complete liquidation of corporation
IRC § 334
Reg. § 1.334–1

Settlement of debt
Haden Co., 165 F.2d 588 (5th Cir.
1948)
Earl M. Britt, 43 BTA 254 (Acq.)

Contract to buy securities
Rev. Rul. 57–29, 1957–1 CB 519

¶6.30 • JOINT TENANCY BASIS RULES FOR SURVIVING TENANTS

*"Allocating Basis for Jointly-Owned
Property Still Presents Unresolved
Questions," P. Harris 58 J. Taxa-
tion 234 (1983)
IRC § 1014
Reg. § 1.1014–2

¶6.31 • WHEN TO ALLOCATE COST

Apportionment of cost
Frederick Leake, 140 F.2d 451 (6th
Cir. 1944), cert. denied, 323 U.S.
722
Nathan Blum, 5 TC 702 (1945)
Johnson Lumber Corp., 12 TC 348
(1949)(Acq.)
Fairfield Plaza, Inc., 39 TC 706
(1963)(Acq.)

Apportion land
McDonald, BTA Memo. P–H 41,409
Harlan E. McGregor, 14 TCM 897
(1955)

Sale of stock first bought
Reg. § 1.1012–1(c)
A. F. Mack, 31 BTA 1149

¶6.32 • HOW TO FIND ADJUSTED BASIS

*Improvements and betterments to prop-
erty*
IRC § 1016
Reg. § 1.1016–2
B. R. McGrath, 6 BTA 1089 (Acq.)
Edgar S. Appleby Est., 123 F.2d 700
(2d Cir. 1941)

Commissions on security sales
Adolph B. Spreckles, 315 U.S. 626
(1942)

Carrying charges
IRC § 1016
Reg. § 1.1016–2

Interest equalization tax
IRC § 263(d)

Personal residence
Isaiah Megibow, 218 F.2d 687 (3d
Cir. 1955)

Purchaser's share of real estate tax
IRC § 164(d)
Reg. § 1.164–6

Unharvested crops
IRC § 1016(a)(11)
Reg. § 1.1016–5(g)

Demolition cost
Reg. § 1.165–3
Edgar S. Appleby Est., 123 F.2d
700 (2d Cir. 1941)

Deduction from basis
IRC § 1016
Reg. § 1.1016–1 through 8

Return of capital
IRC § 1010(a)(4)
Reg. § 1.1016–5(a)(1–2)

Casualty loss
IRC § 1016(a)(1)
Pasquale Colabella, 17 TCM 704
(1958)

Depletion allowances
IRC § 1016(a)(2)
Reg. § 1.1016–3 and 4

*Depreciation, amortization, obsoles-
cence*
IRC § 1016(a)(2)
Reg. § 1.1016–3 and 4

¶6.33 • REPORTING AN INSTALL-MENT SALE

*"Installment Reporting After the Tax
Reform Act of 1986," Edward
Roche Jr., 66 Journal of Taxation
80 (February 1987)

*"An Analysis of the Changes Made
by the Installment Sales Revision
Act of 1980," Meade Emory and
Roland L. Hjorth, 54 J. Taxation
61 and 130 (1981)

*"Sales of Property Outside Section
453," Dennis S. Karjala, 64 Taxes:
The Tax Magazine 153 (March
1986).

*"Structuring Installment Sales With
Recapture," John O. Everett, 65
Journal of Taxation 66 (August
1986).

*IRS Publication 537
IRC § 453

*Not applicable to year-end sale of se-
curities*
IRC § 453(j)

Not applicable to sale of inventory
Andrew A. Monaghan, 40 TC 680
(1963)(Acq.)
IRC § 453(6)(2)(B)

Note: Paragraph numbers refer to Part One. Items marked * are research aids, not citations of authority; see "Key to Citations" on page 337.

Not applicable to building contractor
Rev. Rul. 73–438, 1973–2 CB 156

Farmer who does not inventory
Temp. Reg. § 15A.453–1(b)(4)

Depreciation recapture
IRC § 453(i)

¶6.34 • FIGURING THE TAXABLE PART OF INSTALLMENT PAYMENTS

*Wraparound Mortgages Considered in the Context of the Commission's Temporary Installment Sales Regulations," Richard W. Kennedy, 65 Taxes 530 (August 1987)

*"Tax Treatment of Wrap-Around Debt Received in Installment Sales Under Temporary Installment Sales Regulations," Gary E. Friedman, 60 Taxes 439 (1982)

Selling price
Temp. Reg. § 15A.453–1(b)(2)(ii)

Contract price
Temp. Reg. § 15A.453–1(b)(2)(iii)

Payments received
Temp. Reg. § 15A.453–1(b)(3)

Gross profit
Temp. Reg. § 15A.453–1(b)(2)(v)

Wrap-around mortgages
Temp. Reg. § 15A.453(b)(3)(ii)

Professional Equities Inc.
89 TC No. 15 (1987)

¶6.35 • ELECTING NOT TO REPORT ON THE INSTALLMENT METHOD

IRC § 453(d)
Temp. Reg. § 15A.453–1(d)

Losses disallowed election denied
Letter Ruling 8338004

Inadvertent election out not revocable
Letter Ruling 8501014

¶6.36 • INSTALLMENT SALES TO RELATIVES AND OTHER RELATED PARTIES RESTRICTED

IRC § 453(e) and (g)

Marketable securities
IRC § 453(f)(2)

Related party
IRC § 453(f)(1)

Controlled entity
IRC § 453(g)

¶6.37 • CONTINGENT PAYMENT SALES

Temp. Reg. § 15A.453–1(c)

¶6.38 • USING ESCROW AND OTHER SECURITY ARRANGEMENTS

Edward Grannemann, 87–1 USTC (E.D. Mo. 1987)
William O. Anderson, 20 TCM 697 (1961)

Big Lake Oil Co., 95 F.2d 573 (3d Cir. 1938), cert. denied, 307 U.S. 638
Marion H. McArdle, 11 TC 961 (1948)(Acq.)
Rev. Rul. 73–451, 1973–2 CB 158

Escrow lacks binding condition
J. Robert Rhodes, 243 F. Supp. 894 (D. S.C. 1965)
Everett Pozzi, 49 TC 119 (1968)
J. Earl Oden, 56 TC 569 (1971)

Escrow under court order
Nannie C. Harris, 477 F.2d 812 (4th Cir. 1973), rev'g 56 TC 1165 (1971)(Nonacq.)

Substitution of escrow for unpaid notes or deed of trust
Rev. Rul. 77–294, 1977–2 CB 173, revoking Rev. Rul. 68–246, 1968–1 CB 198

Certificate of deposit as security
Ulysses G. Trivett Jr., 36 TCM 675 (1977) (disqualified installment sale allowed)
C. J. Porterfield, 73 TC 91 (1979) (installment sale allowed)

¶6.39 • MINIMUM INTEREST REQUIRED ON DEFERRED SALES

IRC § 483
Reg. § 1.483

Patents
IRC § 483(f)(4)

¶6.40 • SALE OR OTHER TRANSFER OR CANCELLATION OF INSTALLMENT NOTES

IRC § 453B

Transfer at death
IRC § 453B(c)
IRC § 691(a)(4)
Reg. § 1.691(a)–5

Receipt of notes in Section 331 corporate liquidation
IRC § 453(h)

¶6.41 • REPOSSESSION OF PERSONAL PROPERTY SOLD ON INSTALLMENT

IRC § 453

¶6.42 • BOOT RECEIVED IN A LIKE-KIND EXCHANGE

IRC § 453(f)(6)

¶6.43 • INCOME ACCELERATION ON CERTAIN INSTALLMENT SALES

IRC § 453C

*"Installment Sales and the New Proportionate Disallowance Rule Under the Tax Reform Act of 1986," James A. Fellows, 64 Taxes 718 (1986)

¶6.44 • TAX-FREE EXCHANGES

IRC §§ 1031–1040

¶6.45 • TAX-FREE EXCHANGES OF STOCK

IRC § 1036
Reg. § 1.1036–1
IRC § 368(a)(1)(E)
Reg. § 1.368–2
IRC § 305(a)

¶6.46 • EXCHANGES OF JOINT OWNERSHIP INTERESTS

Exchange of tenants in common
Rev. Rul. 73–476, 1973–2 CB 300

Joint tenancy and tenancy in common
Rev. Rul. 56–437, 1956–2 CB 507

Boot not offset by assumption of liability
Rev. Rul. 79–44, 1979–1 CB 265

¶6.47 • TAX-FREE TRANSFERS ALLOWED IN SETTING UP A CLOSELY-HELD CORPORATION

IRC § 351

¶6.48 • EXCHANGES OF COINS AND BULLION

IRC § 1031

Mexican pesos for Austrian coronas
Rev. Rul. 76–214, 1976–1 CB 218

Silver bullion for gold bullion
Rev. Rul. 82–166, 1982–2 CB 190

U.S. gold coins for S. African Krugerands
Rev. Rul. 79–413, 1979–2 CB 309

Swiss francs for U.S. double eagle coins
California Fed. Life Ins. Co., 76 TC 107 (1981), aff'd, 680 F.2d 85 (9th Cir. 1982)

¶6.49 • PROPERTY TRANSFERS BETWEEN SPOUSES

IRC § 1041

Gain realized on transfer in trust
IRC § 1041(e)
Temp. Reg. § 1.1041–1T

¶6.50 • SALE OF STOCK RECEIVED AS DIVIDENDS AND IN A STOCK SPLIT

IRC § 1223
Reg. § 1.1223–1

Public utility stock dividend
IRC § 305(e)

¶6.51 • SALE, EXERCISE, OR EXPIRATION OF STOCK RIGHTS

Stockholder rights expire
IRC § 1223
IRC § 307
Reg. § 1.1223–1(e)
Reg. § 1.307–1 and 2
Sidney Z. Mitchell, 18 BTA 994, aff'd, 48 F.2d 697 (2d Cir. 1931), cert. denied, 284 U.S. 646

Stock rights sold
IRC § 1223(5)
Reg. § 1.1223–1(e)

Note: Paragraph numbers refer to Part One. Items marked * are research aids, not citations of authority; see "Key to Citations" on page 337.

Stock rights exercised
IRC § 1223(6)
Reg. § 1.1223–1(f)

Rights purchased
IRC § 1223
Reg. § 1.1223–1

Figuring basis of stock rights
IRC § 307
IRC § 307(b)(1)(B) ("less than 15%" exception)
Reg. § 1.307–1

Election
Reg. § 1.307–2

¶6.52 • HOW TO TREAT SHORT SALES

Special short-sale rules
IRC § 1233(b)
Reg. § 1.1233–1(c)(2)

*"The Application of the Short Sale Rules to Security Investors," J. S. Ehrenkranz, 43 Taxes 85 (1965)

Special rule on short-sale losses
IRC § 1233(d)
Reg. § 1.1233–1(c)(4)

Husband and wife
Reg. § 1.1233–1(d)(3)

Short sale closing
H. S. Richardson, 121 F.2d 1 (2d Cir. 1941), cert. denied, 314 U.S. 684
William P. Doyle, 286 F.2d 654 (7th Cir. 1961), rev'g 19 TCM 677 (1960)

Puts (options to sell)
IRC § 1233(c)
Reg. § 1.1233–1(c)(3)

Expenses of short sales; stock dividends
Rev. Rul. 72–521, 1972–2 CB 178

Cash dividends paid on stock sold short
IRC § 263(h)
1955 Production Exposition Inc., 41 TC 85 (1963)
Main Line Distributors, Inc., 37 TC 1090 (1962), aff'd, 321 F.2d 562 (6th Cir. 1963)

Compensation for use of collateral
IRC § 263(h)(5)

Time of loss
Walter Hendricks, 29 TCM 36 (1970), aff'd, 423 F.2d 485 (4th Cir. 1970)

Arbitrage transactions
IRC § 1233(f)
Reg. § 1.1233–1(f)

Death before sale is closed
Rev. Rul. 73–524, 1973–2 CB 307

Wash sales
IRC § 1091(e)

¶6.53 • SECURITY LOSSES FROM WASH SALES

Wash sales
IRC § 1091

Reg. § 1.1091–1 and 2
Rev. Rul. 74–218, 1974–1 CB 202

Trader
Sol H. Morris, 38 BTA 265 (Acq.)
Richard S. Coulter, 32 BTA 617
IRC § 1236
Reg. § 1.471–5
Wilson, 76 F.2d 476 (10th Cir. 1935)
Walter Hirshon, 116 F. Supp. 135 (Ct. Cl. 1953)
L. B. Maytag, 32 TC 270 (1959)

Dealer
IRC § 1091(a)
Donander Co., 29 BTA 312

Substantially identical securities
Corn Products Refining Co., 215 F.2d 524 (2d Cir. 1954), aff'd, 350 U.S. 46 (1955)
Trenton Cotton Oil Co., 147 F.2d 33 (6th Cir. 1945) rehearing denied, 148 F.2d 208 (6th Cir. 1945)
Marie Hanlin, 197 F.2d 429 (3d Cir. 1939)
Sicanoff Vegetable Oil Co., 27 TC 1056 (1957)
Rev. Rul. 76–346, 1976–1 CB 247
Rev. Rul. 58–210, 1958–1 CB 523
Rev. Rul. 58–211, 1958–1 CB 529

Warrants
Rev. Rul. 56–406, 1956–2 CB 523

Short sales
Reg. § 1.1091–1(g)
William P. Doyle, 286 F.2d 654 (7th Cir. 1961), rev'g 19 TCM 677 (1960)

Contract to sell stock
Rev. Rul. 59–418, 1959–2 CB 184

Foreign currencies are not "securities"
Rev. Rul. 74–218, 1974–1 CB 202

Issue date and interest payments of bonds not material
Marjorie K. Campbell, 39 BTA 916 (Acq.), aff'd, 112 F.2d 530 (2d Cir. 1940), rev'd, 313 U.S. 15 (1941)

Oral agreement
Estate of Maxwell J. Estroff, 47 TCM 234 (1983)

Maturity dates
Marie Hanlin et al., 108 F.2d 429 (3d Cir. 1939)
Rev. Rul. 76–346, 1976–1 CB 247
Rev. Rul. 58–211, 1958–1 CB 259

Interest rates differed
Rev. Rul. 76–346, 1976–1 CB 247
Rev. Rul. 60–195, 1960–1 CB 300

Commodity futures
IRC § 1092(b)
*Letter Ruling 8241006

¶6.54 • CONVERTIBLE STOCKS AND BONDS

No gain or loss
Rev. Rul. 72–265, 1972–1 CB 222

Basis
IRC § 358

Holding period
IRC § 1223(1)

Split holding period
Rev. Rul. 62–140, 1962–2 CB 181

¶6.55 • BAD DEBT DEDUCTIONS

Business bad debt
IRC § 166
Reg. § 1.166–1

*IRS Publication 548

Reserve method repealed
IRC § 166(c) repealed by Section 805(a) of 1986 Tax Reform Act

Debt worthless after termination of business
IRC § 166(d)(2)(A)
Reg. § 1.166–5

Sell merchandise on credit
Reg. § 1.166–6

Business of investing or making loans
Allerton Cushman, 148 F. Supp. 880 (D. Ariz. 1956)
L. Washburn, 51 F.2d 949 (8th Cir. 1931)
Hyman R. Minkoff, 15 TCM 1404 (1956)
Morris H. Cone Estate, 13 TCM 512 (1954)

Sell your business
Reg. § 1.166–5(d)(1)

Liquidate your business
Reg. § 1.166–5(d)(6)

Promoter
Vincent C. Campbell, 11 TC 510 (1948)(Acq.)

Loan to maintain business reputation
Wilfred J. Funk, 35 TC 42 (1960) (Acq.)
Stuart Bart, 21 TC 880 (1954) (Acq.)

Loan to insure merchandise delivery
Robert Haverty Est., 12 TCM 1295 (1953)
J. T. Dorminey, 26 TC 940 (1956) (Acq.)

Loan to controlled corporation to further business
Lawrence M. Weil Est., 29 TC 366 (1957)(Acq.)

Loan to employer
John M. Trent, 291 F.2d 669 (2d Cir. 1961)
Philip W. Fitzpatrick, 26 TCM 1 (1967)

Nonbusiness debt
IRC § 166(d)
IRC § 1211
Reg. § 1.166–5
Reg. § 1.1211–1

Personal advances
Gifford A. Cochran, 14 TCM 206 (1955)

Attorney's loan to client
Robert H. McNeil, 251 F.2d 863 (4th Cir. 1958)

Note: Paragraph numbers refer to Part One. Items marked * are research aids, not citations of authority; see "Key to Citations" on page 337.

366

Payment of another's taxes
Albert Gersten, 28 TC 756 (1957) (Acq.), aff'd in part, rev'd in part on other issues, 267 F.2d 195 (9th Cir. 1959)

Payment of joint tax by spouse
Frank R. Haynes, 27 TCM 1531 (1968)

Loss of deposit
Rev. Rul. 69–457, 1969–2 CB 32

¶6.56 • PROVING A BAD DEBT DEDUCTION

Debtor's refusal to pay
Philip C. Hughes, 10 TCM 204 (1951)

¶6.57 • FOUR RULES FOR BAD DEBT DEDUCTIONS

Advances to insolvent corporation
W. F. Young Inc., 120 F.2d 159 (1st Cir. 1941)

Advances repaid only if profit is shown
Lucia C. Ewing, 20 TC 216 (1953), aff'd, 213 F.2d 438 (2d Cir. 1954)

Usurious loan
William K. Harriman, 26 TCM 941 (1967)

Usurious loan as a business loss
Herbert E. Tharp, 31 TCM 22 (1972)

Debtor-creditor relationship
Kentucky Rock Asphalt Co., 108 F.2d 779 (6th Cir. 1940)
W. M. Robertson, 7 TCM 62 (1948)
Simon Benson, 9 BTA 279

Loan included in income
IRC § 166
Reg. § 1.166–1

Consulting engineer
Jack Shapiro, 20 TCM 579 (1961)

Worthless during year
IRC § 166
Reg. § 1.166–1

Bankruptcy by court order
Reg. § 1.166–2(c)

Final liquidation dividend
Leedom & Worrall Co., 10 BTA 825
First National Bank of Los Angeles, 6 BTA 850 (Acq.)

Corporate liquidation resolution
Pantex Oil Corp., 8 TCM 1079 (1949)

Disappearance of debtor
Fridolin Pabst, 36 F.2d 614 (D.C. Cir. 1930)
John Anthony Barry, 2 BTA 1095 (Acq.)

Revocation of corporate charter
Leila S. Kirby, 35 BTA 578 (Acq. and nonacq.), aff'd in part, rev'd in part, 102 F.2d 115 (5th Cir. 1939)

Canceled debt
Nathan Fink, 29 TC 1119 (1958) (Acq.)

No hope of later value
American Trust Co., 31 F.2d 47 (9th Cir. 1939), aff'g 10 BTA 490
Seldon v. Heiner, 12 F.2d 474 (D. Pa. 1926)
Alemite Die Casting & Manufacturing Co., 1 BTA 548

Worthless before debt due
Clarence Bonynge, 117 F.2d 157 (2d Cir. 1941)

Statute of limitations has run
Ralph H. Cross, 54 F.2d 781 (9th Cir. 1932)
Leo Stein, 4 BTA 1016

Statute ran before death
Clara Burdette, 69 F.2d 410 (9th Cir. 1934)

Debt guaranteed by collateral
Ardis & Co., 12 BTA 679 (Acq.)
Lamb Lumber & Implement Co., 6 BTA 429 (Acq.)
George Leavenworth, 1 BTA 754

Release an endorser
Reg. § 1.166–8
Eleanor A. Bradford, 22 TC 1057 (1954), rev'd, 233 F.2d 935 (6th Cir. 1956)

Breach of contract
Zelma T. Kyle, 242 F.2d 825 (2d Cir. 1957)

Less than full payment
Alexander Co. Nat'l Bank, 12 BTA 1238 (Acq.)
First Nat'l Bank of Durant, Oklahoma, 6 BTA 545 (Acq.)

Embezzled funds
Reg. § 1.165–8

Loan by shareholder-employees to protect job
Edna Generes, 405 U.S. 93 (1972), rev'g 427 F.2d 279 (5th Cir. 1970)
Donald C. Niblock Jr., 417 F.2d 1185 (7th Cir. 1969)
James O. Gould, 64 TC 132 (1975)
Odee Smith, 55 TC 260 (1970), vacated and rem'd per curiam, 457 F.2d 797 (5th Cir. 1972), on rem'd 60 TC 316 (1973) (Acq.)
Lawrence J. Doerfler, 36 TCM 789 (1977)

William G. Young, 33 TCM 397 (1974)

Loans to corporations
Donald C. Van Pelt, 191 F.2d 861 (6th Cir. 1951)
Omaha Nat'l Bank, 183 F.2d 899 (8th Cir. 1950)
Grace N. Spencer, 172 F.2d 638 (9th Cir. 1949)
J. L. Washburn, 51 F.2d 949 (8th Cir. 1931)
Janet McBride, 23 TC 926 (1955) (Acq.)
Weldon D. Smith, 17 TC 135 (1951), rev'd, 203 F.2d 310 (2d Cir. 1953), cert. denied, 346 U.S. 816
Sam Schnitzer, 13 TC 43 (1949) (Acq.), aff'd per curiam, 183 F.2d 70 (9th Cir. 1950), cert. denied, 340 U.S. 911
Hyman R. Minkoff, 15 TCM 1404 (1956)
Alma Spreckels, 8 TCM 1113 (1949)
Rev. Rul. 60–48, 1960–1 CB 112

¶6.58 • LOANS BY STOCKHOLDERS

Unpaid stockholder loans to corporation
A. J. Whipple, 373 U.S. 193 (1963)

Stockholder loan to key employee deductible
Charles W. Carter, 39 TCM 456 (1979)

¶6.59 • FAMILY BAD DEBTS

Reg. § 1.166–1
Ben Perlmutter, 373 F.2d 45 (10th Cir. 1967)
Robert H. Montgomery, 23 F. Supp. 130 (Ct. Cl. 1938), cert. denied, 307 U.S. 632
Robert Redfield, 53 F.2d 293 (D. Conn. 1931)
Griffin Andrew, 54 TC 239 (1970) (Acq.)
E. J. Ellisberg, 9 TC 463 (1947)
Joe E Mellen, 27 TCM 443 (1968)
Robert R Tanner, 21 TCM 645 (1959)
Matthew Edwards Sr, 18 TCM 645 (1959)
Louis Rothbard, 16 TCM 636 (1957)

Debt due from friend
Robert H. Montgomery, 23 F. Supp. 130 (Ct. Cl. 1938), cert. denied, 307 U.S. 632
Charles J Matthews, 8 TC 1313 (1947)

Defaulted support payment
Shirley S. Imeson, 487 F.2d 319 (9th Cir 1973), aff'g per curiam 28 TCM 899 (1969), cert. denied, 418 U.S. 917
M. J. Williford, 34 TCM 354 (1975)

Note: Paragraph numbers refer to Part One. Items marked * are research aids, not citations of authority; see "Key to Citations" on page 337.

367

¶7

Retirement and Annuity Income

¶7.2 • ROUNDUP OF TAX-FAVORED RETIREMENT PLANS

*"How the New Law Affects Saving For Retirement," William W. Chip, 66 Journal of Taxation 30 (1987)

*"Tax Treatment of Plan Distributions After TRA 1986," Dianne Bennett, 66 Journal of Taxation 336 (1987)

*"Retirement Plans: Congress Rewrites the Tax Code," Labh S. Hira, 65 Taxes 99 (1987)

*"Is Your Retirement Plan Alive and Well After the Tax Reform Act of 1986," Paul H. Waldman, The Practical Lawyer, January 1987

¶7.3 • LUMP-SUM DISTRIBUTIONS

*IRS Publication 575

Qualified plans
IRC § 401

Definition of lump sum
IRC § 402(e)(4)(A)
Prop. Reg. § 1.402(e)–2(d)

One-time election for lump-sum treatment
Prop. Reg. § 1.402(e)(4)(B)

IRS lump-sum restriction for pension plans
T.I.R. 1403, Question M–15, 9/17/75

Lump-sum treatment at normal retirement age
Special Ruling, 10/29/76
Letter Ruling 7748053

Five-year participation test for ten-year averaging
IRC § 402(e)(4)(H)
Prop. Reg. § 1.402(e)–2(e)(3)

Irrevocability of rollover election
Temp. Reg. § 1.402(a)(5)–IT

Retroactive revocation of plan qualification
Curtis B. Woodson, 73 TC 779 (1980), rev'd, 651 F.2d 1094 (5th Cir. 1981)
Harold D. Greenwald, 366 F.2d 538 (2d Cir. 1982)
Theodore L. Baetens, 82 TC 152 (1984), rev'd, 85–2 USTC ¶9847
Donald L. Benbow, 82 TC 941 (1984), rev'd, 774 F.2d 740 (7th Cir. 1985)

¶7.4 • TEN-YEAR OR FIVE-YEAR AVERAGING ON FORM 4972

Five-year averaging after age 59½ for those under age 50 at end of 1985
IRC § 402(e)

Ten-year or five-year averaging if age 50 or over before 1986
P.L. 99–514 (1986 Tax Reform Act), Act Section 1122(h)(3) and (h)(5)

1986 averaging for pre-March 16, 1987 distributions
P.L. 99–514 (1986 Tax Reform Act), Act Section 1124

One lifetime election for averaging
IRC § 402(e)(4)(B)

Election to forego capital gain
IRC § 402(e)(4)(L)

Taxable portion; exclusions
IRC § 402(a)(1)
Prop. Reg. § 1.402(a)–1(a)(9)(b)
IRC § 402(e)(4)(D)
Prop. Reg. § 1.402(e)–2(d)(2)

Community property
Prop. Reg. § 1.402(e)–2(e)(2)

"Look-back" rule
IRC § 402(e)(2)
Reg. § 1.402(e)–2(c)(2)

Tax on distribution including annuity contract
Reg. § 1.402(e)–2(c)(1)

¶7.5 • CAPITAL GAIN TREATMENT FOR PRE-1974 PARTICIPATION

Electing 20% capital gain treatment if age 50 before 1986
P.L. 99–415 (1986 Tax Reform Act), Act Section 1122(h)(3)(B)

Election of five-year phaseout of capital gain
P.L. 99–514 (1986 Tax Reform Act), Act Section 1122(h)(4)

¶7.6 • SEPARATION FROM SERVICE TEST FOR EMPLOYEES UNDER 59½

IRC § 402(e)(4)(A)
Reg. § 1.402(e)–2(d)
William L. Haggart, 410 F.2d 449 (8th Cir. 1969), rev'g 274 F. Supp. 817 (D.N. Dak. 1967)
Jack E. Schlegel, 46 TC 706 (1966)
Joseph J. Enright, Jr., 35 TCM 1770 (1976)
Steven Gegax, 73 TC 329 (1979)

Plan termination
Patty Smith, 460 F.2d 1005 (6th Cir. 1972)
Clifford L. Johnson, 331 F.2d 943 (5th Cir. 1964)
Robert A. Stefanowski Est., 63 TC 386 (1974)
Rev. Rul. 72–440, 1972–2 CB 225
Rev. Rul. 79–336, 1979–2 CB 87
Letter Ruling 8327033

Civil Service retirement system with trust fund
Rev. Rul. 70–150, 1970–2 CB 106

Employee who became partner
Rev. Rul. 73–414, 1973–2 CB 144
Rev. Rul. 81–26, 1981–1 CB 200
Harry P. Ridenour, Jr., 83–2 USTC ¶9491 (Cl. Ct. 1983)

Work after retirement
William S. Bolden, 39 TC 829 (1963)

Must be retired
Edward I. Rieben Est., 32 TC 1205 (1959)

¶7.7 • LUMP-SUM PAYMENTS RECEIVED BY DECEASED EMPLOYEE'S BENEFICIARY

IRC § 402(e)(4)(A)(ii)
Richard Gunnison, 461 F.2d 496 (7th Cir. 1972), aff'g 54 TC 1766 (1970)
Robert A. Stefanowski Est., 63 TC 386 (1974)

Five-year participation of employee not required
Prop. Reg. § 1.402(e)–2(e)(3)

Capital gain treatment
Prop. Reg. § 1.403(a)–2(b)
Prop. Reg. § 1.402(e)–2(d)

Lump-sum distribution to more than one beneficiary
T.I.R. 1426, 12/15/75

Distribution to trust or estate
Reg. § 1.402(e)–3
Reg. § 1.402(e)–2(e)(6)

Lump sum of deceased self-employed persons
IRC § 101(b)(3)

¶7.8 • TAX-FREE ROLLOVER OF LUMP SUM

60-day period for multiple distributions
*Letter Ruling 8143057

Extension of 60-day period for frozen assets
IRC § 402(a)(6)(H)

Rollover treatment disallowed for minimum required distributions
IRC § 402(a)(5)(G)
IRC § 408(d)(3)(E)

Rollover of partial distributions
IRC § 402(a)(5)(D) and (E)
IRC § 403(a)(4)
IRC § 408(d)(3)
Reg. § 1.408–4(b)

Rollover by surviving spouse
IRC § 402(a)(7)
IRC § 408(d)(3)

Note: Paragraph numbers refer to Part One. Items marked * are research aids, not citations of authority; see "Key to Citations" on page 337.

Rollover when plan terminates
IRC § 402(a)(5)(A)(i)
IRC § 402(a)(6)

Distribution of life insurance
Rev. Rul. 81–275, 1981–2 CB 75

Tax sheltered annuity rollover
IRC § 403(b)(8)
IRC § 408(d)(3)(A)(iii)

Diversification of rollover permitted
Rev. Rul. 79–265, 1979–2 CB 186

Rollover election after March 20, 1986 irrevocable
Temp. Reg. § 1.402(a)(5)–1T

Changing a rollover election pre-March 20, 1986 distributions
*Letter Ruling 7902022
*Letter Ruling 7945030

¶7.9 • ROLLOVER OF PROCEEDS FROM SALE OF PROPERTY RECEIVED IN LUMP-SUM DISTRIBUTION

Rollover of sales proceeds
IRC § 402(a)(6)(D)

Designation of cash
IRC § 402(a)(6)(D)(iii)(II)

Designation of employee contributions
IRC § 402(a)(6)(D)(iii)(I)

Allocation methods
IR-2083, 2/6/79

¶7.10 • SECURITIES OF EMPLOYER COMPANY RECEIVED AS PART OF A DISTRIBUTION

Unrealized appreciation due to employee's contributions
IRC § 402(a)(1)
Reg. § 1.402(a)–1(b)
Reg. § 1.402(a)–1(a)(9)(B)

Unrealized appreciation due to employer's contributions
IRC § 402(e)(4)(D) and (J)
Reg. § 1.402(a)–1(b)
Reg. § 1.402(a)–1(a)(9)(B)
Reg. § 1.401(e)–2(d)(2)

Shares valued below your cost
Rev. Rul. 71–251, 1971–1 CB 129, amplified by Rev. Rul. 72–15, 1972–1 CB 114

Worthless shares
Rev. Rul. 72–328, 1972–8 CB 224

Holding period
Reg. § 1.402(a)–1(b)

Holding period for post-distribution appreciation
Rev. Rul. 81–122, 1981–1 CB 202

Distribution other than lump-sum
Reg. § 1.402(a)–1(b)(3)
Reg. § 1.402(a)–1(a)(9)(b)

¶7.11 • SURVIVOR ANNUITY BENEFITS GENERALLY REQUIRED FOR SURVIVING SPOUSE

IRC § 401(a)(11)

Survivor annuity requirements
IRC § 417
Temp. Reg. Sec. 1.417(e)-IT

Involuntary cash outs
IRC § 417(e)

¶7.12 • WHEN RETIREMENT BENEFITS MUST BEGIN

Premature distributions
IRC § 72(t)

Age 70½ requirement
IRC § 401(a)(9)(C)

Distribution methods
IRC § 401(a)(9)(A) and (B)
Prop. Reg. § 1.401(a)(9)–1

Penalty for not receiving minimum distributions
IRC § 4974(a)

¶7.13 • PENALTY FOR PREMATURE DISTRIBUTIONS

IRC § 72(t)

¶7.14 • PENALTY FOR EXCESS DISTRIBUTIONS

*"New Tax on Excess Distributions from Retirement Plans Requires Revised Planning," W. Widmann and T. Manning Jr., Taxation for Accountants, June 1987

"Tax Treatment of Plan Distributions After TRA 1986," Dianne Bennett, 66 Journal of Taxation 336 (1987)
IRC § 4981A

¶7.15 • RESTRICTIONS ON LOANS FROM COMPANY PLANS

IRC § 72(p)

Spousal consent
IRC § 417(a)(4)

¶7.16 • COMMERCIAL ANNUITIES

New Unisex actuarial tables
Reg. § 1.72–9

Pre-July 1986 investment and post-June 1986 investment
Reg. § 1.72–6(d)(8)

Annuity exclusion limited to investment
IRC § 72(b)(2)

Premature withdrawals from deferred annuity
IRC § 72(q)

¶7.17 • REPORTING COMMERCIAL ANNUITIES

IRS Publication 575

What is an annuity?
IRC § 72

Investment
IRC § 72(c)(1)
Reg. § 1.72–6

Expected return
IRC § 72(c)(3)
Reg. § 1.72–5

Exclusion limited to investment
IRC § 72(b)(2)

Deduction on final return for unrecovered investment
IRC § 72(b)(3) and (4)

Refund feature
IRC § 72(c)(2)
Reg. § 1.72–7

Exclusion ratio
IRC § 72(b)
Reg. § 1.72–4

Total receipts for year
Reg. § 1.72–4

One annuitant annuity
Reg. § 1.72–5(a)
Reg. § 1.72–9, Table I or Table V

Temporary annuity
Reg. § 1.72–9, Table IV or Table VIII
Reg. § 1.72–5(a)(3)

One annuitant stepped-down annuity
Reg. § 1.72–9, Tables I and IV, or Tables V and VIII
Reg. § 1.72–5(a)(4)

One annuitant stepped-up annuity
Reg. § 1.72–9, Tables I and IV, or Tables V and VIII
Reg. § 1.72–5(a)(5)

Uniform joint and survivor annuities
Reg. § 1.72–5(b)
Reg. § 1.72–9, Tables II or VI

Variable joint and survivor annuities
Reg. §1.72–9, Tables I, II, and IIA, or Tables V, VI, and VIA

Premature withdrawals
IRC § 72(q)

¶7.18 • COST OF ANNUITY WITH A REFUND FEATURE

Reg. § 1.72–7

¶7.19 • FINDING YOUR EXPECTED RETURN

Reg. § 1.72–5

¶7.20 • COMPUTING THE EXPECTED RETURN OF A ONE-ANNUITANT ANNUITY

Reg. § 1.72–5(a)
Reg. § 1.72–9, Table I or Table V

¶7.21 • VARIABLE ANNUITIES

Reg. § 1.72–2(b)(3)
Reg. § 1.72–4(d)(3)
Reg. § 1.72–5(f) and 7(d)

Recompute exclusion
Reg. § 1.72–4(d)(3)

¶7.22 • WHEN YOU CONVERT YOUR MATURED ENDOWMENT POLICY

IRC § 72(e) and (h)

Interest option
Henry L. Blum, 150 F.2d 471 (2d Cir. 1945)
Constance C. Frackelton, 46 BTA 883 (Acq.)

Note: Paragraph numbers refer to Part One. Items marked * are research aids, not citations of authority; see "Key to Citations" on page 337.

Sale of endowment contract
  Percy W. Phillips, 30 TC 866 (1958)
    (Nonacq.), rev'd, 275 F.2d 33 (4th
    Cir. 1960)
  Bolling Jones, 39 TC 404 (1962)

Sale of an annuity contract
  Andrew Wineman Est., 163 F. Supp.
    865 (Ct. Cl. 1958), cert. denied,
    359 U.S. 943
  First Nat'l Bank of Kansas City, 20
    TCM 1411 (1961), aff'd, 309 F.2d
    587 (8th Cir. 1962)
  Harry Roff, 36 TC 818 (1961), aff'd,
    304 F.2d 450 (3d Cir. 1962)

Sale of insurance policies
  Gertrude H. Crocker Est., 37 TC
    605 (1962)

¶7.23 • EMPLOYEE ANNUITIES

Three-year recovery rule repealed
  IRC § 72(d), repealed by 1986 Tax
    Reform Act Section 1122(h)(2)
    (A)

Unisex actuarial tables
  Reg. § 1.72–9, Tables V, VI, VIA,
    VII, and VIII

*Withdrawals before annuity starting
  date*
  IRC § 72(e)(8)

**¶7.24 • REPORTING EMPLOYEE
  ANNUITIES**

  *IRS Publication 575
  IRC § 72
  IRC § 403

**¶7.25 • COST OF EMPLOYEE
  ANNUITY**

Amounts paid
  IRC § 72(b) and (e)

IRC § 403
Reg. § 1.403(a)
Reg. § 1.72–8

Employer's payments
  Reg. § 1.72–8

**¶7.26 • THREE-YEAR RECOVERY
  OF COST**

*Three-year rule allowed only if annuity
  starting date is before July 2, 1986*
  IRC § 72(d), repealed by 1986 Tax
    Reform Act Section 1222(h)(2)

Civil service pension
  Rev. Rul. 71–435, 1971–1 CB 84
  Rev. Rul. 71–18, 1971–1 CB 33
  IRS Pub. No. 568

*Employee taxed on full value of non-
  forfeitable annuity*
  Charles Wilson, 39 TC 362 (1962)

¶7.27 • CIVIL SERVICE RETIREMENT

  *IRS Pub. No. 721

Survivor's civil service annuity
  Rev. Rul. 71–18, 1971–1 CB 33

**¶7.28 • $5,000 DEATH BENEFIT EX-
  CLUSION ADDED TO THE
  COST OF AN ANNUITY**

  IRC § 101(b)
  Reg. § 1.101–2

Allocating the exclusion
  Rev. Rul. 72–555, 1972–2 CB 44

**¶7.29 • WITHDRAWAL FROM EM-
  PLOYEE PLAN BEFORE AN-
  NUITY STARTING DATE**

  *"Planning for Nonannuity Distribu-
    tions from Contribution Plans,"
    Labh S. Hira, 65 Taxes 514 (1987)
  IRC § 72(e)(8)

Notice 87–13, IRB 1987–4, 14

**¶7.30 • ANNUITIES FOR EMPLOYEES
  OF TAX-EXEMPT GROUPS
  AND SCHOOLS**

  *IRS Publication 571
  IRC § 403(b)
  IRC § 415(c)(4)
  Reg. § 1.403(b)–1
  Reg. § 1.403(d)–1
  Temp. Reg. § 11.415(c)–(4)(1)

$9,500 salary reduction limit
  IRC § 402(g)(4)

*$12,500 salary reduction limit for 15-
  year employees*
  IRC § 402(g)(8)

Figuring teacher's exclusion
  Rev. Rul. 84-149, 1984-2 CB 97

Doctor-employee
  Vincent M. Ravel, 26 TCM 885
    (1967)
  Rev. Rul. 68–294, 1968–1 CB 46

Rollovers
  IRC § 403(b)

**¶7.31 • RETIRED MILITARY PER-
  SONNEL ALLOWED TAX
  EXCLUSION ON ANNUITY
  ELECTION**

  IRC § 122
  Reg. § 1.122–1

Reductions previously taxed
  IRC § 122(b)

Cost of contract to survivor
  IRC § 72(n)

Death benefit exclusion
  IRC § 101(b)(2)(D)

¶8

IRAs and Keoghs

**¶8.1 • RETIREMENT SAVINGS
  THROUGH IRAs**

  *"Many Deductible IRAs Repealed;
    Elective SEPS Allowed," Leon E.
    Irish, 66 Journal of Taxation 266
    (1987)
  *IRS Publication 590

**¶8.2 • CONTRIBUTIONS MUST BE
  BASED ON EARNINGS**

  IRC § 219(b)

Time for making contribution
  IRC § 219(f)(3)

Compensation defined
  Reg. § 1.219–1(c)(1)

Earned income
  IRC § 219
  IRC § 401(c)(2)

IRC § 1402(a)

*Self-employment losses do not offset
  ruling*
  Rev. Rul. 79–286, 1979–2 CB 121

Aggregating businesses
  IRC § 1402(a)
  Reg. § 1.1402(a)–2(c)

Trader activities not earned income
  Robert Miller, 77 TC 97 (1981)

Endowment contract
  IRC § 219(d)(3)
  Reg. § 1.408–3(e)

Payment of fees
  Rev. Rul. 84–146, 1984–2 CB 61

*Working for spouse without receiving
  payment of wages*
  *Letter Ruling 8707004

**¶8.3 • FIGURING YOUR IRA CON-
  TRIBUTION AND DEDUCTION**

  *"Deductibility of IRA Contributions
    Under the Tax Reform Act of
    1986," Richard S. Andrews, 65
    Taxes 246 (1987)
  *IRS Publication 590

Deduction limitations after 1986
  IRC § 219(g)
  Notice 87–16, IRB 1987–5, 40

**¶8.4 • ACTIVE PARTICIPATION
  TESTS**

  IRC § 219(g)(5)
  Notice 87–16, IRB 1987–5, 40

**¶8.5 • NONDEDUCTIBLE IRA CON-
  TRIBUTIONS**

  IRC § 408(o)

Note: Paragraph numbers refer to Part One. Items marked * are research aids, not citations of authority; see "Key to Citations" on page 337.

¶8.6 • SETTING UP AN IRA

Individual retirement account
IRC § 408(a)
Reg. § 1.408–2
Rev. Proc. 75–6, 1975–1 CB 646, modified by Rev. Proc. 76–32, 1976–2 CB 654 and Rev. Proc. 77–24, 1977–2 CB 532

Individual retirement annuity
IRC § 408(b)
Reg. § 1.408–3

Loss on surrender of IRA annuity nondeductible
Rev Rul. 80–268, 1980–2 CB 141

Flexible premiums
IRC § 408(b)(2)

Endowment contract
Reg. § 1.408–3(e)

Broker restrictions
Special Ruling, August 24, 1983

Retirement bonds
IRC § 409
Reg. § 1.409–1

Retirement bonds not issued after April 30, 1982
TD News Release April 27, 1982

Time for making contributions
IRC § 219(f)(3)

Tax treatment of distribution
IRC § 408(d)
Reg. § 1.408–4

Diversification of investment permitted
Rev. Rul. 79–265, 1979–2 CB 186

¶8.7 • IRAs FOR MARRIED COUPLES

Deduction limitations for married couples filing jointly
IRC § 219(g)

Married couples filing separately
IRC § 219(g)(4)

Deductions for nonworking spouse
IRC § 219(c)

¶8.8 • IRAs FOR DIVORCEES

IRC § 219(f)(1)

¶8.9 • IRA DISTRIBUTIONS

IRC § 408

Figuring tax if nondeductible contributions have been made
IRC § 408(d)(2)
Notice 87–16, IRB 1987–5, 40

Retirement bonds
IRC § 409

Distribution period
IRC § 408(a)(6)

¶8.10 • PENALTIES FOR PREMATURE DISTRIBUTIONS, EXCESS CONTRIBUTIONS, INSUFFICIENT WITHDRAWALS

*IRS Publication 590

Premature distribution
IRC § 72(t)

Insufficient distribution
IRC § 4974

IRS rules for figuring minimum required distribution
Prop. Reg. § 1.408–8

Reasons for insufficiency
IR–2086, 2/6/79

Life expectancy refigured annually
IRC § 408(a)(6) and 401(a)(9)(D)

Excess contributions
IRC § 4973
Prop. Reg. § 54.4973–1
IRC § 408(d)(4)
Reg. § 1.408–1(c)(1)
IR–2086, 2/6/79

Excess contributions treated as made in subsequent years
IRC § 219(f)(6)

¶8.11 • ROLLOVERS OF IRAs; TRANSFERS INCIDENT TO DIVORCE

IRC § 408(d)(3)
IRC § 409(b)
Reg. § 1.409–1(c)

Rollover treatment disallowed for minimum required distribution
IRC § 408(d)(3)(E)

60-day period extended for frozen deposits
IRC § 408(d)(3)(F)

Transfer because of divorce
IRC 408(d)(5)

Rollover after age 70½
Rev. Rul. 82–153, 1982–2 CB 56

Transfer of account not rollover
Rev. Rul. 78–406, 1978–2 CB 157

Beneficiary can authorize trustee-to-trustee transfer
*Letter Ruling 8716058

¶8.12 • SIMPLIFIED EMPLOYEE PENSION PLANS

IRC § 219(b)(2)
IRC § 404(h)
IRC § 408(j), (k), and (1)
Reg. § 1.219–1(d)(4) and –3
Reg. § 1.404(h)–1
Reg. § 1.408–7 through 9

Overall tax-free SEP contribution limit after 1986
IRC § 402(h)

Salary-reduction SEP
IRC § 408(k)(6)

$7,000 elective salary reduction limit
IRC § 402(g)(1)

Tax Retirement Plans for Self-Employed

¶8.13 • TAX BENEFITS OF KEOGH PLANS

*IRS Publication 560
IRC § 401(a)(7)(8) and (c)
Reg. § 1.401–10–13
Reg. § 1.401(e)

¶8.14 • WHO MAY SET UP A KEOGH PLAN

IRC § 401(c)
Reg. § 1.401–11

More than one trade or business
IRC § 401(d)(10)
Reg. § 1.401–10(b)(2)
Reg. § 1.401–10(c)(4)(ii)
Reg. § 1.401–12(1)(1) and (2)

¶8.15 • CHOOSING A KEOGH PLAN

IRC § 401
Reg. § 401(e)

¶8.16 • TOP HEAVY PLAN RESTRICTIONS

IRC § 416

Prior law premature distribution penalty
IRC § 72(m)(5)

Rollover of retirement bonds
IRC § 402(e)(5)

Key employees
IRC § 416

¶8.17 • HOW MUCH YOU MAY CONTRIBUTE AND DEDUCT

*IRS Publication 560

Contribution limits
IRC § 415(b) and (c)

Penalty for nondeductible contributions
IRC § 4972

Earned income reduced by deductible contributions
IRC § 401(c)(2)(A)(v)
IRC § 404(a)(8)(D)

Deductions
IRC § 404
Reg. § 1.404(e)–1

Deductible contributions up to due date of return
IRC § 404(a)(6)

Deduction limit for profit-sharing plans
IRC § 404(a)(3)

Contributions after age 70½
Reg. § 1.401–11(e)(7)

¶8.18 • HOW TO CLAIM THE DEDUCTION

IRC § 404
Reg. § 1.404(a)–1
TIR 1211, 11/20/72

Note: Paragraph numbers refer to Part One. Items marked * are research aids, not citations of authority; see "Key to Citations" on page 337.

Time for making contributions
  Temp. Reg. § 11.404(a)(6)–1

¶8.19 • HOW TO QUALIFY A PLAN

  IRC § 401
  IRC § 404
  IRC § 405

Failure to set up written plan
  Nelson H. Jones, 51 TC 651 (1969)

¶8.20 • ANNUAL INFORMATION RETURNS

Short form 5500EZ
  Announcement 86–125, IRB 1986–50, 15

¶8.21 • RESTRICTIONS ON LOANS

Prohibited transaction penalties
  IRC § 4975(c) and (d)
  IRC § 4962

Labor Department Exemption
  1986 Tax Reform Act Section 1898(i)

¶ 9

Income from Rents and Royalties

  IRC § 61(a)(5) and (6)
  IRC § 469
  Reg. § 1.61–8
  *IRS Publications 527 and 925

¶9.2 • REPORTING RENT INCOME

Rents received
  Reg. § 1.61–8

Cash basis
  Morris-Poston Coal Co., 42 F.2d 620 (6th Cir. 1930)
  Andrew J. Pembroke, 23 BTA 1176, aff'd 70 F.2d 850 (D.C. Cir. 1935)
  Jas. M. Butler, 18 BTA 718 (Acq.)

Actual basis
  Suffolk & Berks, 40 BTA 1121 (Acq.)
  American Fork & Hoe Co., 33 BTA 1139
  Oregon Terminals Co., 29 BTA 1332 (Nonacq.)

Advance rentals or bonuses
  Reg. § 1.61–8(b)
  Hyde Park Realty, Inc., 211 F.2d 462 (2d Cir. 1954), aff'g 20 TC 43 (1953)
  Chateau Frontenac, 147 F.2d 856 (6th Cir. 1945)
  Clinton Hotel Realty Corp., 128 F.2d 968 (5th Cir. 1945)
  Beach D. Lyon, 97 F.2d 70 (9th Cir. 1938)
  Edward A. Renwick, 87 F.2d 123 (7th Cir. 1937)
  R. L. Harcum, 164 F. Supp. 650 (E.D. Vir. 1958)
  John Mantell, 17 TC 1143 (1952) (Acq.)

Advances transferred to new landlord
  Hyde Park Realty, Inc., 211 F.2d 462 (2d Cir. 1954), aff'g 20 TC 43 (1953)

Security for performance
  Astor Holding Co., 135 F.2d 47 (5th Cir. 1943)
  Clinton Hotel Realty Corp., 128 F.2d 968 (5th Cir. 1942)
  R. L. Harcum, 164 F. Supp. 650 (E.D. Vir. 1958)

Andrew J. Pembroke, 70 F.2d 850 (D.C. Cir. 1935)
John Mantell, 17 TC 1143 (1952) (Acq.)

Taxes, interest, etc. as rent
  Reg. § 1.61–8(c)

Insurance proceeds
  John S. Mellinger, 228 F.2d 688 (5th Cir. 1956)
  Oppenheim's Inc., 90 F. Supp. 107 (D. Mich. 1950)

Canceled lease
  Reg. § 1.61–8(b)
  Walter M. Hort, 313 U.S. 28 (1941)

Amortizing lease cancellation cost over term of old lease
  Handlery Hotels, Inc., 663 F.2d 892 (9th Cir. 1981)

Expenses deductible
  E. M. Godson, 5 TCM 648 (1946)
  Nicollet Associates, Inc., 37 BTA 350
  Louis F. Tucker Sr., 9 TCM 956 (1950)

Improvement by tenant
  IRC § 109
  Reg. § 1.109–1

¶9.3 • CHECKLIST OF DEDUCTIONS FROM RENT INCOME

Management expenses
  IRC § 212
  Reg. § 1.212–1

Maintenance expenses
  IRC § 212
  Reg. § 1.212–1

Salaries and wages
  IRC § 212
  Reg. § 1.212–1

Travel expenses
  E. M. Godson, 5 TCM 648 (1946)

Legal expenses
  Arthur T. Galt, 19 TC 892 (1953), aff'd in part, rev'd in part, 216 F.2d 41 (7th Cir. 1954), cert.

denied, 348 U.S. 951
Louis F. Tucker, Sr., 9 TCM 956 (1950)
E. M. Godson, 5 TCM 648 (1946)

Interest on mortgages
  IRC §163(c)
  Reg. § 1.163–1

Commissions to secure rental
  Mary C. Young, 59 F.2d 691 (9th Cir. 1953), cert. denied, 287 U.S. 652, on remand, 14 TCM 869 (1955)
  John Griffiths, 70 F.2d 946 (8th Cir. 1934)
  Louis A. Meyran, 63 F.2d 986 (3d Cir. 1933)
  Central Bank Block Assn., 57 F.2d 5 (5th Cir. 1932)

Commissions to acquire property
  IRC § 263
  Reg. § 1.263(a)–1 and 2

Abandonment loss
  Reg. § 1.167(a)–8
  Belridge Oil Co., 11 BTA 127
  I. G. Zumwalt, 25 BTA 566
  Rev. Rul. 54–581, 1954–2 CB 112

Insurance premiums
  Reg. § 1.162–1

Year deductible
  Reg. § 1.461–1(a)(1)
  Rev. Rul. 70–413, 1970–2 CB 103

Inherited lease
  Mary Y. Moore, 207 F.2d 265 (9th Cir. 1953), cert. denied, 347 U.S. 942, on remand, 14 TCM 869 (1955)

Release from mortgage
  Rev. Rul. 57–198, 1957–1 CB 94

Tenant in common
  Elmer B. Boyd Est., 28 TC 564 (1957)

Payment of tax by co-tenant
  Lulu Lung Powell, 26 TCM 161 (1967)

Rent for less than fair value
  Nicath Realty (Hummel), 25 TCM 1260 (1966)

Note: Paragraph numbers refer to Part One. Items marked * are research aids, not citations of authority; see "Key to Citations" on page 337.

372

Cost of canceling a lease
Handlery Hotels, Inc., 663 F.2d 892 (9th Cir. 1981)

¶9.4 • DISTINGUISH BETWEEN A REPAIR AND AN IMPROVEMENT

Capital improvements
IRC §263
Reg. § 1.263(a)–1 and –2

Painting
Michael Markovits, 11 TCM 823 (1952)
Charles H. Cohen, 7 TCM 681 (1948)
Jones Hollow Ware Co., 12 BTA 48 (Acq.)
Leedom & Worrall Co., 10 BTA 825
Max Kurtz, 8 BTA 679 (Acq.)

Replacement of roof
George W. Ritter, 163 F.2d 1019 (6th Cir. 1947)
Thomas J. Locke, 8 BTA 534 (Acq.)
Georgia Car & Locomotive Co., 2 BTA 986 (Nonacq.)

Heating system
Republican Co., BTA Memo. (Feb. 20, 1934)

General improvement program
Home News Publishing Co., 18 BTA 1008
Cowell, 18 BTA 997

Repairs and improvements unconnected
W. A. Stoeltzing, 266 F.2d 374 (3d Cir. 1959), aff'g 17 TCM 567 (1958)

¶9.5 • SALE OF A LEASE

Leasehold is capital asset under Section 1231
H. G. Kingsbury, 56 TC 1068 (1971) (Acq.)
S. D. Miller, 48 TC 649 (1967) (Acq.)

Leasehold of land used in business is Section 1231 property
Rev. Rul. 72–85, 1972–1 CB 234

Cancellation of lease
IRC § 1241
Reg. § 1.1241–1

¶9.6 • DEDUCTING COST OF DEMOLISHING A BUILDING

Capitalization required
IRC § 280B

Pre-1984 decisions
Donald S. Levinson, 59 TC 676 (1973)
John A. Lemos, 32 TCM 515 (1973)
J. Alfred Rider, 30 TCM 188 (1971)
Yates Motor Co., 561 F.2d 15 (6th Cir. 1977), rev'g 34 TCM 1235 (1975)
Rossel M. Hightower, 463 F.2d 182 (5th Cir. 1972)
Mayer Feldman, 335 F.2d 264 (9th Cir. 1964)
Herman Landerman, 454 F.2d 338

(7th Cir. 1972), cert. denied, 406 U.S. 967
Thomas P. Foltz, 458 F.2d 600 (8th Cir. 1972)
Ivan Grossman, 74 TC 1147 (1980) (Nonacq.)

¶9.7 • DEDUCTING THE COST OF A BUSINESS LEASE

IRC § 178

Related landlord
G. W. Van Keppel, Inc., 295 F.2d 767 (8th Cir. 1961)

¶9.8 • HOW LESSEES DEDUCT FOR LEASEHOLD IMPROVEMENTS

IRC § 168(i)(8)

Depreciation and amortization
Reg. § 1.167(a)–4

Option to renew
IRC § 178(a)

Unrecovered costs
Alexander J. Cassatt, 137 F.2d 745 (3d Cir. 1943)

¶9.9 • SPECIAL TAX CREDITS FOR CERTAIN REAL ESTATE INVESTMENTS

*"New Tax Credit for Low-Income Housing Provides Incentive," J. William Callison, 66 Journal of Taxation 103 (February 1987)

Rehabilitating old and historic buildings
IRC § 46(b)(4)
IRC § 48(g)

Low-income housing credit
IRC § 42

¶9.10 • DEFERRED OR STEPPED-UP RENTAL AGREEMENTS

IRC § 467

¶9.11 • REPORTING ROYALTY INCOME

License fees for use of patented article
Reg. § 1.61–8(a)

Renting fees
Reg. § 1.61–8(a)

Author's royalties
Reg. § 1.61–8(a)
W. M. Scott, 27 BTA 951
Leon Levy, 2 BTA 1069
Rev. Rul. 60–31, 1960–1 CB 174, modified by Rev. Rul. 64–279, 1964–2 CB 121 and Rev. Rul. 70–435, 1970–2 CB 100

Works of art, etc.
Reg. § 1.61–8(a)

Partial sale of rights
Reg. § 1.61–8(a)

Lessee's payment of taxes
Wallin Coal Corp., 71 F.2d 521 (4th Cir. 1934)
Rev. Rul. 64–91, 1964–1 CB (Part 1) 219

Amortization of production costs of motion pictures, etc.
IRC §280

Royalty taxed as ordinary income
IRC § 61(a)(6)
Reg. § 1.61–8(a)

Depletion allowed
IRC § 611
Reg. § 1.611

Bonus payment
Reg. § 1.612–3(a)(3)
Reg. § 1.613–2(c)(5)
H. H. Weinert Est. 294 F.2d 740 (5th Cir. 1961)
Wesley G. Rogers, 25 BTA 492
Ann. 76–34, IRB 1976–12, 28
Rev. Rul. 73–537, 1973–2 CB 197

Percentage depletion allowed on advanced royalty
Fred Engle, 84–1 USTC ¶9134 (S. Ct. 1984)
Ann. 84–59 IRB 1984–23

Local law
Henry Harmel, 287 U.S. 103 (1932)

Delay rental
Reg. § 1.612–3(c)

Overriding royalty
Reg. § 1.613–2 and 3(b)
E. G. Palmer v. Bender, 287 U.S. 551 (1933)
West Prod. Co., 121 F.2d 9 (5th Cir. 1941), cert. denied, 314 U.S. 682
H. R. Cullen, 118 F.2d 651 (5th Cir. 1941)

Production payments treated as loans
IRC § 636

Oil payments
J. Steve Anderson, 310 U.S. 404 (1940)
Caldwell Oil Corp., 141 F.2d 559 (5th Cir. 1944)
Mamie S. Hammonds, 106 F.2d 420 (10th Cir. 1939)
Roy H. Laird, 97 F.2d 730 (5th Cir. 1938)
William Fleming, 82 F.2d 328 (5th Cir. 1936)
Chester Addison Jones, 82 F.2d 329 (5th Cir. 1936)
Elliott Petroleum Corp., 82 F.2d 193 (9th Cir. 1936)
R. R. Ratliff, 36 BTA 762

Proof of oil payment
J. A. Morgan, 321 F.2d 781 (5th Cir. 1963), on remand, 245 F. Supp. 388 (D. Miss. 1965)

Both oil payment and overriding royalty
J. Steve Anderson, 310 U.S. 404 (1940)
E. G. Palmer v. Bender, 287 U.S. 551 (1933)
H. R. Cullen, 118 F.2d 651 (5th Cir. 1941), rev'g 41 BTA 1042
Marrs McLean, 120 F.2d 942 (5th Cir. 1941), cert. denied, 314 U.S. 670

Note: Paragraph numbers refer to Part One. Items marked * are research aids, not citations of authority; see "Key to Citations" on page 337.

Fred T. Hogan, 1 TCM 208 (1942), aff'd, 141 F.2d 92 (5th Cir. 1944), cert. denied, 323 U.S. 710

Net profits
Kirby Petroleum Co., 326 U.S. 599 (1946)
Thomas A. O'Donnell, 303 U.S. 370 (1938)

Carried interest
Abercrombie Co., 162 F.2d 338 (5th Cir. 1947), aff'g 7 TC 120 (1946) (Nonacq.)
Donald McMurray, 60 F.2d 843 (10th Cir. 1935), cert. denied, 287 U.S. 664

Carved-out oil payments
P. G. Lake, Inc. 356 U.S. 260 (1958)
Murphy J. Foster, 324 F.2d 702 (5th Cir. 1963)

¶9.12 • INTANGIBLE DRILLING COSTS
IRC § 263(c)

Recapture of intangible drilling costs
IRC § 1254
Prop. Reg. § 1.1254

Prepaid expenses—Pre-March 31, 1984
Stephen A. Keller, 725 F.2d 1173 (8th Cir. 1984)

Tax shelter prepayments after March 31, 1984
IRC § 461(i)(2)(D)

¶9.13 • DEPLETION DEDUCTION
IRC § 611
Reg. § 1.611–1
IRC § 612
Reg. § 1.612–1
IRC § 613
Reg. § 1.613–1 and 2

Percentage depletion for gas and oil wells
IRC § 613A

Sales less than $5 million
IRC § 613A(d)(2)

Exceptions to transfer rule
IRC § 613A(c)(9)(iii)

Distributions to trust beneficiaries
IRC § 613A(d)(1)(D)

Windfall profit tax exemption
IRC § 4994(f)(2)

Repeal of production distinctions
IRC § 613(A)(c)

No depletion for lease bonuses
IRC § 613A(d)(5)

¶9.14 • COAL AND TIMBER ROYALTIES
*"Timber and Cattle," by W. E. Murray, 22 NYU Inst. 185 (1964)
*"Federal Income Taxation Relating to Timber," by W. R. Gibson, The Practical Lawyer, Apr. '62

*"An Analysis of the Tax Planning Opportunities Unique to the Mining of Coal," Harry P. Henshaw III, 53 J. Taxation 357 (1980)

Coal royalties
IRC § 631(c)
Reg. § 1.631–3

Timber royalties
IRC § 631(a) and (b)
Reg. § 1.631–1 and 2

¶9.15 • DEDUCTING THE COST OF PATENTS OR COPYRIGHTS
Patent and copyright
Reg. § 1.167(a)–6(a)

Inherited
IRC § 1014
John L. Whitehurst, 12 BTA 1416 (Nonacq.)

Worthless interest
Robert S. Davis, 241 F.2d 701 (7th Cir. 1958)
James Petroleum Corp., 238 F.2d 678 (2d Cir. 1956), cert. denied, 353 U.S. 910
Arthur Finston, 15 TCM 1048 (1956)
Richard B. Lack, 15 TCM 1169 (1956)

¶9.16 • AMORTIZATION OF PRODUCTION COSTS
IRC § 263A

¶ 10

Reporting Income from Partnerships, S Corporations, Trusts, Estates and Farming

¶10.2 • HOW PARTNERS REPORT PARTNERSHIP PROFIT AND LOSS

*"How to Make Sure That Payments to Partners Qualify for Treatment as Guaranteed Payments," Rudolph Ramelli, Taxation for Accountants, June 1987

*"Computation of Partnership and Partner's Income," C. M. Howe, 28 NYU Inst. 521 (1970)

*"Partnerships, What They Are: Definitional Problems," A. S. Rosenberg, 31 NYU Inst. 89 (1973)

*"Many Partnership Planning Opportunities Restricted by Deficit Re-

duction Act of 1984," Timothy M. Larason and Thomas J. Morgan, 33 Taxation for Accountants 140 (Sept. 1984) and 13 Taxation for Lawyers 74 (Sept./Oct. 1984)

*IRS Publication 541

Passive loss limitations
IRC § 469

Failure to file information return
IRC § 6698

Partnership not taxed
IRC § 701
Reg. §1.701–1

What is partnership?
IRC § 761
Reg. § 1.761–1

Organization and syndication fees
IRC § 709
Reg. § 1.709–1

Deduction barred for syndication fees
Rev. Rul. 85-32, 1985–1 CB 186

Special allocations
IRC § 704(b)

Sales to controlled partnership
IRC § 1239(b) and (c)

Substantial economic effect
Reg. § 1.704–1(b)(2)
Mary Ogden, CA–5, 4/25/86, affg. per curiam 84 TC 871 (1985)

Retroactive allocations
IRC § 706(c)(2)(B)

Note: Paragraph numbers refer to Part One. Items marked * are research aids, not citations of authority; see "Key to Citations" on page 337.

374

Partner reports
IRC § 702
Reg. § 1.702–1

Net operating loss
Reg. § 1.702–2

Salary from partnership guaranteed
IRC § 707(c)
Reg. § 1.707–1(c)

Credits deductible
IRC § 702(b)
Reg. § 1.702–2

No advance ruling of partnership pro-
visions re: substantial economic
effect
Rev. Proc. 79–14, 1979–1 CB 496

¶10.3 • WHEN A PARTNER REPORTS INCOME OR LOSS

IRC § 706
Reg. § 1.706–1
Harry W. Lehman, 19 TC 659
(1953)

Fiscal year limitations
IRC § 706(b)(1)

¶10.4 • PARTNERSHIP LOSS LIMITATIONS

IRC § 704
Reg. § 1.704–1
F. A. Falconer, 40 TC 1011 (1963)
(Acq.)

Limitation on losses
IRC § 704(d)
IRC § 465

¶10.5 • UNIFIED TAX AUDITS OF PARTNERSHIPS WITH MORE THAN TEN PARTNERS

IRC §§ 6221 through 6231

"How the TEFRA Partnership Proce-
dures Affect Partners' Adjustments
and Limitations," J. Palmer III,
58 Journal of Taxation 54 (1983)

"Partnership Tax Audits and Litiga-

tion After TEFRA," M. Caplin
and S. Brown, 61 Taxes 75 (1983)

¶10.6 • S CORPORATION ELECTION

"Tax Planning Opportunities Using S
Corporations Under the Tax Re-
form Act of 1986," Jeffrey M.
Gonyo, 65 Taxes 552 (August
1987)

"Electing Subchapter S Via Transi-
tional Rule Can Provide Significant
Tax Advantages," Kenneth S. Apfel
and Andrew T. Wolfe, 67 Journal
of Taxation 66 (August 1987)

"Should a Small Business Make the S
Election After the Tax Reform Act
of 1986," Gary A. Zwick, Taxation
for Accountants, June 1987

¶10.7 • STOCKHOLDER REPORTING OF S CORPORATION INCOME AND LOSS

"An Analysis of the Subchapter S
Revision Act," R. Shaw and J. August, 58 J. Taxation 1, 84 and 300
(1983)
IRC §§ 1361 through 1379

Passthrough of income and losses
IRC § 1366

Distributions
IRC § 1368

Investment income election
Act § 721 of 1984 Tax Reform Act

Income must be included in return
IRC § 1367(b)

Allocation for new and old shareholder
IRC § 1377(a)

Family allocation
IRC § 1366(e)

Expenses of shareholder
IRC § 267(f)

Appreciated property distribution
IRC § 1363(d)

¶10.8 • QUALIFYING TESTS FOR AN S ELECTION

IRC § 1361

¶10.9 • FILING AN S ELECTION

IRS § 1362(a)
IRC § 1362(b)

Effect of election on corporation
IRC § 1363(e)

Built-in gains tax
IRC § 1374
Rev. Rul. 86–141, IRB 1986, 49, 6

¶10.10 • REVOCATION OR TERMINATION OF AN S ELECTION

IRC § 1362(d)

Treatment of termination year
IRC § 1362(e)

¶10.11 • TAX ON FRINGE BENEFITS RECEIVED BY STOCKHOLDERS

IRC § 1372

¶10.12 • PASSIVE INVESTMENT INCOME

IRC § 1362(d)(3)
IRC § 1366(f)(3)
IRC § 1375

Waiver of tax
IRC § 1375(d)

¶10.13 • CORPORATE FISCAL YEAR RESTRICTIONS

IRC § 1378

¶10.14 • TAX ON "ONE-SHOT" CAPITAL GAINS

IRC § 1374

¶10.15 • AUDITS OF S CORPORATIONS AND SHAREHOLDERS

IRC § 6241–6245
Temp. Reg. Secs. 301.6241–1T and
301.6245–1T

INCOME FROM A TRUST OR ESTATE

"Income Taxation of Trusts and Es-
tates Under TRA '86," p. 38, Lisa
Brown Petkun and Deborah Lerner
38 Journal of Taxation, 66 (1987)

"Tax Aspects of Various Types of
Property as Trust Corpus,"
R. M. Orin, 28 NYU Inst. 883
(1970)

"Income and Deductions in Respect of
Decedents and Related Problems,"
M. C. Ferguson, 25 Tax L. Rev. 5
(1969)

"Timing and Effect of Distributions by
Executors and Trustees: Alloca-
tions among Beneficiaries," H. E.
Levine, 27 NYU Inst. 287 (1969)

"Techniques for Controlling Income

Tax Consequences of Trusts and
Estates and Their Beneficiaries,"
M. R. Fremont-Smith, 25 NYU
Inst. 1019 (1967)

"Taxation of Trust Income," J. F.
Gelband, 24 NYU Inst. 233 (1966)
Who files
Reg. § 1.641(b)–2

When beneficiary is taxed
IRC § 652

When grantor is taxed
IRC § 671

¶10.16 • HOW BENEFICIARIES REPORT ESTATE OR TRUST INCOME

IRC § 652
Reg. § 1.652(a) and (b)

Foreign trusts
Sections 1013 and 1014 of the 1976
Tax Reform Act

Depreciation and depletion
IRC § 167(g)
IRC § 611(b)(3)

Losses
IRC § 642(d)
Reg. § 1.642(h)–1
George W. Balkwill, 25 BTA 1147,
aff'd, 77 F.2d 569 (6th Cir. 1935)
cert. denied 296 U.S. 609
George C. Reeves, 15 TCM 394
(1956)

When to report
IRC § 652
Reg. § 1.652(a)–1

Note: Paragraph numbers refer to Part One. Items marked * are research aids, not citations of authority; see "Key to Citations" on page 337.

Multiple trusts
IRC § 643(e)

Distributions of appreciated property
IRC § 643(d)

**¶10.17 • DISTRIBUTIONS OF ACCU-
MULATED TRUST INCOME**

Accumulations
IRC § 662
IRC § 663
IRC § 665
IRC § 666

Trust for spouse
IRC § 677

Method of calculating tax
IRC § 667

*No throwback for years before bene-
ficiary attains age 21*
IRC § 665(b)

Denial of refund
IRC § 666(e)

*Special rule for exchanges within two
years of transfer*
IRC § 644

Foreign trust accumulations
IRC § 667(d)

**¶10.18 • DEDUCTIONS FOR INCOME
SUBJECTED TO ESTATE TAX**

*"Planning for Income in Respect of a
Decedent Can Minimize Effects of
Double Taxation,"* Michael Mulli-
gan, 57 Journal of Taxation 106
(Aug. 1982)

*"How to Compute an Estate's or
Trust's Taxable and Distributable
Net Income for Beneficiaries,"* Wil-
liam A. Raabe, 31 Taxation for
Accountants 46 (July 1983)

*"Tax Aspects of Estate and Trust Dis-
tributions,"* 38 NYU Inst. of Fed
Tax—38–1 (1980)

Deduction for estate tax paid
IRC § 691(c)
Reg. § 1.691(c)–1

No double deduction
IRC § 2053
IRC § 2054

Attorney's fees
IRC § 2053(a)
Reg. § 20.2053–3(c)

Administration expenses
IRC § 2053(b)
Reg. § 20.2053–3(a)

Capital gain reduction
IRC § 691(c)(4)

Lump-sum distributions
IRC § 691(c)

FARM INCOME OR LOSS

¶10.19 • WHO IS A FARMER?

*"Farm and Hobby Losses After Tax
Reform,"* Marvin H. Lewis, 1971
So. Calif. Tax Inst. 627

Who is a farmer?
Reg. § 1.61–4(d)
Reg. § 1.175–3
Reg. § 1.6073–1(b)(2)

Investor as farmer
Perry N. Duggar, 71 TC 147 (1978)
(Acq.)

Hobby losses
IRC § 183

Substantial receipts
Richard T. Wilson, 282 F.2d 38 (2d
Cir.)
Morton F. Plant, 280 F. Supp. 722
(Conn. 1922)

Farm employees
Oscar F. Holcombe, 50–1 USTC
¶9200 (W.D. Tex. 1950)

Not solely for vacations
Reg. § 1.162–12

Follow business principles
Charles B. Irwin, BTA Memo.
(October 28, 1940)

George W. Cutting, 6 TCM 1326
(1947)

Losses are decreasing
Hedi Katz, 13 TCM 188 (1954)

Paying market prices
Richard T. Wilson, 282 F.2d 38 (2d
Cir.)
Oscar F. Holcombe, 50–1 USTC
¶9200 (W.D. Tex. 1950)

Improvements
George R. Heath, BTA Memo.
(March 4, 1936)

Bookkeeping system
George W. Cutting, 6 TCM 1326
(1947)

Farm superintendent
Charles B. Irwin, BTA Memo. (October 28, 1940)
George W. Cutting, 6 TCM 1326
(1947)

Experts consulted
Thomas Watson, 2 TCM 863 (1943)

Tried to cut losses
Dan R. Hanna Jr., 10 TCM 566
(1951)

Personal attention
Iri R Cope, 12 TCM 1258 (1953)

Farm laborers not domestics
Oscar F. Holcombe, 50–1 USTC
¶9200 (W.D. Tex. 1950)

Farm not sideline
Iri R. Cope, 12 TCM 1259 (1953)

Previous farms
David McMorran, BTA Memo.
(March 20, 1939)

Your expressed intention
Norton L. Smith, 9 TC 1150 (1947)
(Acq.)

"At risk" loss limitation
IRC § 465

¶10.20 • FORMS FARMERS FILE

IRC § 6073(b)
Reg. § 1.6073–1(b)
IRC § 6015(f)
Reg. § 1.6015(f)–1

¶10.21 • FARMERS' SOCIAL SECURITY

Self-employment tax
IRC § 1402
Reg. § 1.1402(a)–1

Share farmers
Rev. Rul. 57–58, 1957–1 CB 270
Rev. Rul. 55–538, 1955–2 CB 313

More than one business
Reg. § 1.1402(a)–1

Note: Paragraph numbers refer to Part One. Items marked * are research aids, not citations of authority; see "Key to Citations" on page 337.

¶11
Loss Restrictions: Passive Activities and At Risk Limits

Note: Paragraph numbers refer to Part One. Items marked * are research aids, not citations of authority; see "Key to Citations" on page 337.

¶12
Prizes, Scholarships, Damages, Life Insurance and Other Income

¶12.2 • GIFTS AND INHERITANCES

Gifts and inheritances exempt
IRC § 102
Reg. § 1.102–1

Incompetent's gift taxable
Carl Elmer Henry Bader, 23 TC 813 (1973)

No fixed rule to determine taxability of gifts
Mose Duberstein, 363 U.S. 278 (1960)

Will compromise
Munro L. Lyeth v Hoey, 305 U.S. 188 (1938)

Sale of expected inheritance
Rev. Rul. 70–60, 1970–1 CB 11

Bequest to executor
Frederick L. Merriam, 263 U.S. 179

Bequest to attorney
Lee S. Jones, 23 TCM 235 (1964)
Victor R. Wolder, 493 F.2d 608 (2d Cir. 1974), aff'g 58 TC 974 (1972) (Nonacq.), cert. denied, 419 U.S. 828

Campaign contributions—when taxable
Rev. Rul. 68–19, 1968–1 CB 42

¶12.3 • BARGAIN PURCHASES

Buying at bargain price
Manomet Cranberry Co., 1 BTA 706 (Acq.)

Close relative—gift
Henry F. Robertson, 5 BTA 748 (Acq.)

Your employer—additional compensation
Reg. § 1.61–2

Your corporation—dividend
Reg. § 1.301–1(j)
J. E. Timberlake, 132 F.2d 259 (4th Cir. 1942)
Frank E. Taplin, 41 F.2d 454 (6th Cir. 1930)

Insurance bought from company
Rev. Rul. 59–195, 1959–1 CB 18

¶12.4 • PRIZES AND AWARDS

IRC § 74(a)

Transfer to charity

IRC § 74(b)

Employee achievement
IRC § 74(c)

¶12.5 • SWEEPSTAKES AND LOTTERY WINNINGS

Raffle winnings
Diane M. Solomon, 25 TC 936 (1956)
H. Collings Downes, 30 TC 396 (1958)

Sweepstake winnings divided among family members
Henry Braunstein, 21 TCM 1132 (1962)

Ticket bought for foreign uncle
Alfonso Diaz, 58 TC 560 (1972) (Acq.)

Sweepstake winnings held by court
Rev. Rul. 67–203, 1967–1 CB 105

Lottery prize held by parents as custodians
Joseph Anastasio, 67 TC 814 (1977)

Agreement to share winnings
Samuel L. Huntington, 35 BTA 835 (Acq.)

Agreement to pool winnings
Christian H. Droge, 35 BTA 829 (Acq.)

¶12.6 • GAMBLING WINNINGS AND LOSSES

IRC § 165(d)
Reg. § 1.165–10

Diary supported loss deduction
Leon Faulkner, 40 TCM 1 (1980)

Tickets with sequential numbers supported loss deduction
Theodore L. Wolkomir, 40 TCM 1078 (1980)

Professional gambler may deduct loss as business expense
Anthony J. Ditunno, 80 TC 362 (1983)

Full time gambler is in business
Robert P. Groetzinger, — U.S. — (1987)

¶12.7 • SCHOLARSHIPS, FELLOWSHIPS, AND GRANTS

IRC § 117

¶12.8 • AWARDS TO DEGREE CANDIDATES BEFORE AUGUST 17, 1986

*IRS Publication 520

Determining amount of award
Notice 87–31, IRB 1987–17

Scholarship or fellowship
IRC § 117 pre-1986 Tax Act
Reg. § 1.117–1

Educational institutions
IRC § 151(e)(4)
Reg. § 1.151–3(c)

Amounts to cover expenses—pre-1986 Tax Act
IRC § 117
Reg. § 1.117–1(b)

Teaching or research services—pre-1986 Tax Act
IRC § 117(b)
Reg. § 1.117–2

Primary purpose test
Richard E. Johnson, 394 U.S. 741 (1969)
Reg. § 1.117–4(c)
Elmer L. Reese Jr., 373 F.2d 742 (4th Cir. 1967), aff'g per curiam 45 TC 407 (1966)

Research required for all students—grants tax free
Rev. Rul. 75–280, 1975–2 CB 47

Hospital work required for technology student
Rev. Rul. 73–89, 1973–1 CB 52

Internship teaching in municipal school —grants taxed
Elmer L. Reese Jr., 373 F.2d 742 (4th Cir. 1967), aff'g per curiam 45 TC 407 (1966)
Rev. Rul. 67–443, 1967–2 CB 75

Travel grant
Rev. Rul. 74–86, 1974–1 CB 36

Financial aid to graduate teaching assistant not taxed.
Robert H. Steiman, 56 TC 1350 (1971)(Acq.)

No authority to increase maximum
Rev. Rul. 55–554, 1955–2 CB 36

¶12.9 • AWARDS TO NONDEGREE CANDIDATES BEFORE AUGUST 17, 1986

Not working for degree
IRC § 117(b)(2) pre-1986 Tax Act
Reg. § 1.117–2(b)

Note: Paragraph numbers refer to Part One. Items marked * are research aids, not citations of authority; see "Key to Citations" on page 337.

¶12.10 • FELLOWSHIPS FOR IN-TERNS AND RESIDENT PHYSICIANS PRE-AUGUST 17, 1986

Interns taxed
Rev. Rul. 57–386, 1957–2 CB 107
John E. Adams, 71 TC 477 (1978)

Resident doctors taxed
Joseph D. Woddail, 321 F.2d 721 (10th Cir. 1963), aff'g 21 TCM 1248 (1962)
Frederick Fisher, 56 TC 1201 (1971)
Michael D. Birnbaum, 30 TCM 989 (1971), aff'd, 73–1 USTC ¶9378 3d Cir. 1973)
Aloysius J. Proskey, 51 TC 918 (1969)
Rev. Rul. 65–117, 1965–1 CB 67
Richard F. Bergeron, 31 TCM 1226 (1972)
Leonard T. Fielding, 57 TC 761 (1972)
Eugene T. Hembree Jr., 464 F.2d 1262 (4th Cir. 1972)
Jacob T. Moll, 57 TC 579 (1972)
Walter L. Peterson, 33 TCM 1367 (1974)
Sheldon A. E. Rosenthal, 63 TC 454 (1975)
John E. Adams, 71 TC 477 (1978)

Residents not taxed
Dr. Hollis K. Leathers, 471 F.2d 856 (8th Cir. 1973), cert. denied, 412 U.S. 932 (orthopedics) (pathology)
Jerome Burstein, 79–1 USTC ¶9354 (Ct. Cl. 1979) (radiology) (pediatrics)
Myron W. Mizell *et al*, 663 F.2d 772 (8th Cir. 1981) (university hospital residents)

Public Health official in research program
Frederick A. Bieberdorf, 60 TC 114 (1973)(Acq.)

Training grant at hospital for biochemist not taxed
Gerald F. Falcona, 34 TCM 265 (1975)

Nurses training as specialists
Not taxed: Rev. Rul. 72–568, 1972–2 CB 80
Taxed: Rev. Rul. 71–106, 1971–1 CB 35

VA grants
William Wells, 40 TC 40 (1963)
Richard A. Anderson, 61–1 USTC ¶9162 (D. Minn. 1961)
Paul H. Chesmore, 33 TCM 1226 (1974)
Rev. Rul. 82–57, 1982–1 CB 24

Cardio-renal training program
George L. Bailey, 60 TC 447 (1973) (Acq.)

¶12.11 • TUITION PLANS FOR FAMILIES OF FACULTY MEMBERS

IRC § 117(d)

¶12.12 • CHECKLIST OF NONTAX-ABLE GRANTS MADE BE-FORE AUGUST 17, 1986

Post-doctoral research not taxed
Louis C. Vaccaro, 58 TC 721 (1972)

National Research Service Awards
IRC § 117(c)

National Institute of Health
Rev. Rul. 58–179, 1958–1 CB 57
Theodore Krupin, 439 F. Supp. 440 (D. Mo. 1977)
Frederick A. Bieberdorf, 60 TC 114 (1973)(Acq.)
Peter C. Chen, 39 TCM 273 (1979)

National Science Foundation
Rev. Rul. 58–498, 1958–2 CB 47

National Institute of Public Affairs
Rev. Rul. 64–71, 1964–1 CB 82

American Heart Association
Rev. Rul. 58–76, 1958–1 CB 56

Free tuition to child—Pre 7-1-85
Reg. § 1.117–3(a)

Post June 30, 1985 tuition reduction
IRC § 117(d)

Grants by private person
Rev. Rul. 61–66, 1961–1 CB 19

Armed Forces Health Professions Scholarship Program
Pub. L. Nos. 95–600 and 96–167, amending Pub. L. No. 93–483, 88 Stat. 1457

Interest on student loans paid by HEW
Rev. Rul. 75–537, 1975–2 CB 32

Tax-free benefits for graduate work in 1984 and 1985
IRC § 127(c)(8)

¶12.13 • FULBRIGHT AWARDS

Rev. Rul. 61–65, 1961–1 CB 17

Award paid by U.S. agency
Laurence P. Dowd, 37 TC 399 (1961)(Nonacq.)

Professor on sabbatical leave
Rev. Rul. 62–2, 1962–1 CB 9

¶12.14 • TAX REFUNDS AND OTHER RECOVERIES OF PREVI-OUSLY DEDUCTED ITEMS

IRC § 111
Reg. § 1.111–1

Refund of state income taxes
Rev. Rul. 79–15, 1979–1 CB 80

Overpayment credited against state tax liability
Ralph H. Schultz, 79–1 USTC ¶9199 (D. Wisc. 1979)

Donated property returned
Sidney W. Rosen, 71 TC 226 (1979), aff'd, 80–1 USTC ¶ 9138 (1st Cir. 1980)

Reimbursement of loss absorbed by $100 floor not taxable
Rev. Rul. 80–65, 1980–1 CB 183

Debt forgiveness of accrual basis debtor with carryover
IRC § 111(d), as added by § 2(c) of Pub. L. No. 96–589

¶12.15 • CANCELLATION OF DEBTS YOU OWE

*"How to Handle the Tax Aspects of Bankruptcy for Individuals," Grant W. Newton, The Practical Accountant June 1987

Exclusion for certain discharged debt
IRC § 108

Farm indebtedness
IRC § 108(g)

Election to reduce basis
Bankruptcy Tax Act, Temp. Reg. § 7a.1.

Canceled debts
Reg. § 1.61–12
IRC § 1017
Reg. § 1.1017–1 and 2
IRC § 108
Reg. § 1.108(a)–1 and 2

Prepayment of mortgage at discount
Rev. Rul. 82–202, 1982–2 CB 35

Insolvency of debtor
Rev. Rul. 58–600, 1958–2 CB 29
B. M. Marcus Est., 34 TCM 38 (1975)

Proceedings under Bankruptcy Act
Reg. § 1.61–12
Reg. § 1.1016–7

Property used in trade or business
IRC § 108
Reg. § 1.108(a)–1

Voluntary forgiveness by creditor
American Dental Co., 318 U.S. 322 (1943)

Creditor intended a gift
New York Creditmen's Adjustment Bureau, Inc., 110 F. Supp. 214 (S.D.N.Y. 1953)

Identify debt cancelled
Lewis F. Jacobson, 336 U.S. 28 (1949)

Adjust purchase price
Des Moines Improvement Co., 7 BTA 279 (Nonacq.)
Sobel, Inc., 40 BTA 1263 (Nonacq.)

Decline in value of property
Kalman Hirsch, 115 F.2d 656 (7th Cir. 1940)

Borrow money
Manuel A. Frank, 44 F. Supp. 729 (D. Pa. 1942), aff'd, 131 F.2d 864 (3d Cir.)

No legal obligation
Kern Co., 1 TC 249 (1942)(Acq.)
Hotel Astoria, Inc., 42 BTA 759 (Acq.)
Fulton Gold Corp., 31 BTA 519

Partial cancellation of indebtedness
Gehring Publishing Co., Inc., 1 TC 345 (1942)(Acq.)

Note: Paragraph numbers refer to Part One. Items marked * are research aids, not citations of authority; see "Key to Citations" on page 337.

Unauthorized sale of pledged stock is discharge of indebtedness
Regina A. Poczatek, 71 TC 371 (1978)

Inventory
Rev. Rul. 76–86, 1976–1 CB 37

Contribution to capital
Oregon-Washington R.R. & Nav. Co., 251 F.2d 211 (2d Cir.)
Lawrence, 13 BTA 463

Student loan cancelled
IRC § 108(f)

¶12.16 • RECEIPTS IN COURT ACTIONS FOR DAMAGES

IRC § 104(a)(2)
Reg. § 1.104–1(c)

*"Payments Received in Settlement of Litigation and Claims," J. P. Fouts, 25 NYU Inst. 555 (1967)

*"Payments for Invasion of Privacy," D. H. Gordon, 23 J. Taxation 108 (1965)

*"An Analysis of the Tax Treatment of Post-Termination Personal Injury Settlements," R. I. Barkan, 41 Journal of Taxation 306 (1974)

*"Taxability of Damage Awards," Craig T. Smith, 40 Journal of the Missouri Bar 219 (1984)

*"Tax Consequences of Recoveries for Personal Injuries," Jack B. Middleton and William V. A. Zorn, 25 N. Hampshire Bar Journal 137 (1984)

Personal injuries
IRC § 104(a)(2)
Rev. Rul. 74–77, 1974–1 CB 33

Slander or libel—state law governs
James E. Threlkeld, 87 TC No. 76 (1986)
Paul F. Roemer Jr. 79 TC 398 (1982), rev'd, 716 F.2d 693 (9th Cir. 1983) Nonacq. Rev. Rul. 85–143, 1985–2 CB 55

Defamation legal costs nondeductible to extent of tax-free damages
Wade E. Church, 80 TC 1104 (1983)

Breach of promise to marry
Lyde McDonald, 9 BTA 1340 (Acq.)

Alienation of affection
C. A. Hawkins, 6 BTA 1023 (Acq.)
Rev. Rul. 74–77, 1974–1 CB 33

Support of children
IRC § 71(b)
Reg. § 1.71–1

Loss of profit
Phoenix Coal Co., 231 F.2d 420 (2d Cir. 1956)
D. T. Longino Est., 32 TC 904 (1959)

Business reputation
Mason Knuckles, 23 TCM 182, (1964), aff'd 349 F.2d 610 (10th Cir. 1965)

Paul Draper, 26 TC 201 (1956) (Acq.)

Goodwill
Farmers and Merchants Bank of Catlettsburg, Kentucky, 59 F.2d 912 (6th Cir. 1932)
William Basle, 16 TCM 745 (1957), aff'd per curiam, 256 F.2d 381 (3d Cir. 1958)

Embezzlement forgiven
Rev. Rul. 61–185, 1961–2 CB 9

Extortion
James Rutkin, 343 U.S. 130 (1952), aff'g 189 F.2d 431 (3d Cir. 1951)
James J. Moran, 236 F.2d 361 (2d Cir. 1956), cert. denied, 352 U.S. 909

Swindlers
James A. Akers, 167 F.2d 718 (5th Cir. 1948), cert. denied, 335 U.S. 823

Deducting litigation costs
Rev. Rul. 58–418, 1958–2 CB 18, distinguished by Rev. Rul. 75–230, 1975–1 CB 93
Charles E. Parker, 573 F.2d 42 (Ct. Cl. 1978)
Joseph D. Murphy, 48 TC 569 (1967)

Attorney receives payment
Thomas H. Hannaford, 19 TCM 409 (1960)

Punitive damages in antitrust case taxed
Glenshaw Glass Co. 348 U.S. 426 (1955)

Punitive damages for personal injuries taxed
Maurie Starrels, 304 F.2d 574 (9th Cir. 1962)
Rev. Rul. 84–108, 1984–2 CB 32, revoking Rev. Rul. 75–45, 1975–1 CB 47

Allocating libel suit damages between taxable and nontaxable
Rev. Rul. 85–98, 1985–2 CB 51

Anti-trust
Ralph Freeman, 33 TC 323 (1959)

NLRB award
Hector F. Manseau, 52 F. Supp. 395 (D. Mich. 1943)

Arbitration award
Anna Levens, 10 TCM 1083 (1951)

Settlement of dispute
Dudley G. Seay, 58 TC 32 (1972) (Acq.)
C. H. Hawkins, 6 BTA 1023 (Acq.)

¶12.17 • HOW LIFE INSURANCE PROCEEDS ARE TAXED TO BENEFICIARY

*"Ownership and Transfer of Life Insurance," H. Yohlin, 28 NYU Inst. 765 (1970)
IRC § 101
Reg. § 1.101–1 to 1.101–4

Spouse's exclusion for interest repealed
IRC § 101(d)(1), as amended by Section 1001(a) of 1986 Tax Reform Act

No exclusion for combined insurance-annuity pre-1986 Tax Act
Rev. Rul. 65–57, 1965–1 CB 56

Remarriage does not affect interest exclusion pre-1986 Tax Act
Rev. Rul. 72–164, 1972–1 CB 28

Universal life policy
IRC § 101(f)

¶12.18 • A POLICY WITH A FAMILY INCOME RIDER

Reg. § 1.101–4(h)

¶12.19 • HOW OTHER INSURANCE PROCEEDS ARE TAXED

Dividends as reduction of premium
Special Ruling, December 13, 1940
Special Ruling, September 22, 1941
Veterans Administration Release, February 14, 1957

Endowment policies paid because of death
Reg. § 1.101–1(a)

Gain on surrender of policy
Reg. § 1.72–11(d)
William W. Bodine, 103 F.2d 982, (3d Cir. 1939), cert. denied, 308 U.S. 576
Frank J. Cobbs, 39 BTA 642
Frank Hawkins, 3 TCM 1135 (1944), rev'd on other issue, 152 F.2d 221 (5th Cir. 1946)

Surrender of policy for cash—loss
Standard Brewing Co., 6 BTA 980
London Shoe Co., Inc., 80 F.2d 230 (2d Cir. 1935), cert. denied, 298 U.S. 663
Moses Cohen, 44 BTA 709 (Acq.)

Policy transferred for valuable consideration
IRC § 101(b)
Reg. § 1.101–1(b)

¶12.20 • TAX-FREE EXCHANGES OF INSURANCE POLICIES

*"Income Tax Aspects of Transfers of Life Insurance Policies," R. J. Lawthers, 22 NYU Inst. 1299 (1964)

*"Un-Needed Endowment, Annuity, or Life Insurance Policies, May Be Exchanged Tax Free," Paul J. Streer, 8 Taxation for Lawyers 222 (1980)

Tax free
IRC § 1035
Reg. § 1.1035–1

Not tax free
Reg. § 1.1035–1

Note: Paragraph numbers refer to Part One. Items marked * are research aids, not citations of authority; see "Key to Citations" on page 337.

¶ 13

Claiming the Standard Deduction
or Itemized Deductions

IRC § 63(b)
IRC § 63(c)

Non resident alien
IRC § 63(c)(6)(A)

Estate or trust
IRC § 63(c)(6)(D)

Short tax year
IRC § 63(c)(6)(C)

¶13.2 • ELECT TO ITEMIZE OR TAKE THE STANDARD DEDUCTION

IRC § 63(e)

Changing an election
IRC § 63(e)(3)

¶13.3 • HUSBANDS AND WIVES FILING SEPARATE RETURNS

IRC § 63(c)(b)(A)

Claiming itemized deductions when you are living apart from your spouse
IRC § 63(g)
IRC § 7703

¶13.4 • INCREASED STANDARD DEDUCTION FOR ELDERLY AND BLIND

IRC § 63(b)(3)

Age
IRC § 63(f)(1)

Blindness
IRC § 63(f)(2)
IRC § 63(f)(4)

¶13.5 • STANDARD DEDUCTION FOR DEPENDENTS

IRC § 63(c)(5)

¶13.8 • ADJUSTED GROSS INCOME

Deductions from adjusted gross income
IRC § 62
Reg. § 1.62–1

Interest on rental property
Isaac R. Wharton, 207 F.2d 526 (5th Cir. 1953)

¶ 14

Charitable Contribution Deduction

¶14.2 • DEDUCTIBLE CONTRIBUTIONS

IRC § 170
IRC § 501
IRC § 508

"The Charitable Deduction," J. Y. Taggart, 26 Tax L. Rev. 63 (1970)

"Finalized Regulations Show that Philanthropy Can Still Be Rewarding," D. L. Crumbley, 51 Taxes 227 (1973)

"Charitable Giving and Estate Planning," H. G. Burke, 28 Tax Lawyer 289 (1975)
*IRS Publication. 526

"Charitable Transfers and Estate Planning," Ronald Scott Mangum, 38 NYU Inst. 40-a (1980)

"Outright Charitable Giving: Sophisticated Use of Old Techniques and Development of New Techniques," Malcolm A. Moore, 42 NYU Inst. on Fed. Tax 27 (1984)

"New Substantiation Rules for Chari-

table Contributions," 11 Est. Plan 142 (May 1984)

Legal fees to preserve donation
Anne Archbold, 444 F.2d 1120 (Ct. Cl. 1971)

Records required
Kenneth Lingenfelder, 38 TC 44 (1962)

Contribution by check
Reg. § 1.170A–1(b)
Elie B. Witt Est., 160 F. Supp. 521 (D. Fla. 1956)
Estelle Broussard, 16 TC 23 (1951)
Modie J. Spiegel Est., 12 TC 524 (1949)(Acq.)
Rev. Rul. 54–465, 1954–2 CB 93

Year-end mailing
Stanley G. Reedy, 42 TCM 1401 (1981)

Contribution of note
Sheldon B. Guren, 66 TC 118 (1976)
Norman Petty, 40 TC 521 (1963)

Credit cards
Rev. Rul. 78–38, 1978–1 CB 67

Voluntary payroll deduction
Rev. Rul. 54–549, 1954–2 CB 94

Fund-raising agency
Rev. Rul. 55–192, 1955–1 CB 294

Dues
Eunice A. Horne, 16 TCM 953 (1957)
Rev. Rul. 54–565, 1954–2 CB 95, modified by Rev. Rul. 68–432, 1968–2 CB 104
Rev. Rul. 55–192, 1955–1 CB 294

Treasury guidelines for cash donations
Public Information Fact Sheet, May 14, 1965
Cornelius A. Donelan, 30 TCM 278 (1971)
Dominick Calderazzo, 26 TCM 140 (1967)

¶14.3 • BENEFIT TICKETS, BAZAARS, AND BINGO

Treasury guidelines for deduction
Rev. Rul. 67–246, 1967–2 CB 104, distinguished by Rev. Rul. 74–348, 1974–2 CB 80

Note: Paragraph numbers refer to Part One. Items marked * are research aids, not citations of authority; see "Key to Citations" on page 337.

Dues may be allocable
Rev. Rul. 68–432, 1968–2 CB 104

Benefit tickets
Rev. Rul. 74–348, 1974–2 CB 80

Season ticket
Rev. Rul. 86–63, 1986–1 CB 88

¶14.4 • UNREIMBURSED EXPENSES OF VOLUNTEER WORKERS

No deduction for travel unless elements of personal pleasure absent
IRC § 170(k)
IRS Notice 87–23, IRB 1987–9

Travel expenses
Francois Louis, 25 TCM 1047 (1966)
Rev. Rul. 59–160, 1959–1 CB 59
Rev. Rul. 58–279, 1958–1 CB 145
Rev. Rul. 58–240, 1958–1 CB 141, clarified by Rev. Rul. 71–135, 1971–1 CB 94
Rev. Rul. 57–327, 1957–2 CB 155
Rev. Rul. 55–4, 1955–1 CB 291

No deduction for value of donated services
Reg. Sec. 1.170A–1(g)
William W. Grant, 84 TC 809. (1985)

Per diem allowances
Rev. Rul. 74–433, 1974–2 CB 92
Rev. Rul. 67–30, 1967–1 CB 9

Uniform costs
Rev. Rul. 56–508, 1956–2 CB 126

Delegate
Harris W. Seed, 57 TC 265 (1971)
John R. Wood, 57 TC 220 (1971), aff'd per curiam, 462 F.2d 691 (5th Cir. 1972)
Rev. Rul. 58–240, 1958–1 CB 141, clarified by Rev. Rul. 71–135, 1971–1 CB 94
*Letter Ruling 8242042

Services authorized
Russell Doty, Jr., 62 TC 587 (1974)
Travis Smith, 60 TC 988 (1973) (Acq.)

Replacing engine while doing volunteer work
Rev. Rul. 59–239, 1959–2 CB 100

Nine-cent rate before 1985
Rev. Proc. 80–32, 1980–2 CB 767

Twelve-cent rate after 1984
IRC § 170(j)

Noncompensated minister deducts car expenses
Rev. Rul. 69–645, 1969–2 CB 37

CAP volunteer
Larry A. Miller, 34 TCM 1207 (1975)

Repairs attributable to charitable services deductible
John Orr, 343 F.2d 553 (5th Cir. 1965)
Rev. Rul. 58–279, 1958–1 CB 145

Babysitting costs
Rev. Rul. 73–597, 1973–2 CB 69

¶14.5 • SUPPORT OF A STUDENT IN YOUR HOME

IRC § 170(g)
Reg. § 1.170A–2

¶14.6 • APPRECIATED PROPERTY DONATIONS

"Traps for the Unwary Concerning Gifts of Appreciated Property to Charity," M. I. Sanders, 1972 So. Calif. Tax Inst. 719

"Appreciated Property: Contributions Can Yield Greater Savings Than Cash Despite Restrictions," Philip P. Storrer and Jeffrey P. Shaw, 27 Taxation for Accountants 34 (1981) and 10 Taxation for Lawyers 98 (1981)

Gift of property
IRC § 170
Rev. Rul. 55–410, 1955–1 CB 297
Magnolia Development Corp., 19 TCM 934 (1960)

Gift of mortgaged property
Rev. Rul. 81–163, 1981–1 CB 433
Winston Guest, 77 TC 9 (1981) (Acq.)
Leo Ebben et al; CA–9, 2/25/86, affg. 45 TCM 1283 (1983)

Delivery of stock gift
Jack W. Londen, 45 TC 106 (1965)

No deduction if voting rights retained
Rev. Rul. 81–282, 1981–2 CB 78

Fair market value of property
Philip Kaplan, 43 TC 663 (1965) (Acq.)
Daniel S. McGuire, 44 TC 801 (1965) (Acq.)
Morris Schapiro, 27 TCM 205 (1968)
Alexia DuPont O. De Bie Est., 56 TC 876 (1971) (Acq.)

Deduction limits for tangible personal property
IRC § 170(e)(1)(B)

Bargain sale
IRC § 170(e)(2)
IRC § 1011(b)
Reg. § 1.170A–4(c)(2)

Donated property sold by charity
Stuart A. Rogers, 38 TC 785 (1962) (Nonacq.)

Guidelines for valuations
Rev. Rul. 66–49, 1966–1 CB 36, amplified by Rev. Rul. 72–366, 1972–2 CB 91

Partial interests
IRC § 170(f)(3)(A) and (B)
Reg. § 1.170A–7(d)

Future interests
IRC § 170(a)(3)

Election to reduce appreciation
IRC § 170(b)(1)(C)(iii)
Reg. § 1.170A–8(d)(2)
Rev. Rul. 74–53, 1974–1 CB 60

Ordinary income property
IRC § 170(e)

Reg. § 1.170A–4(b)(1)

Congressman's papers
James H. Morrison, 71 TC 683 (1979), aff'd per curiam, 611 F.2d 98 (5th Cir. 1980)

Capital gain property
IRC § 170(b)(1)(D)
IRC § 170(e)

Special rule for gift of stock to private foundation
IRC § 170(e)(5)

Trust interests
IRC § 170(f)

Prepaid interest
IRC § 170(f)(2)
Reg. § 1.170A–3

Valuation of remainder interests
IRC § 664
Reg. § 1.664–4

Appraisals required after 1984
Tax Reform Act of 1984, Act Section 155

¶14.7 • PROPERTY THAT HAS DECLINED BELOW COST

Deduction limited to cost
LaVar Withers, 69 TC 900 (1978)

¶14.8 • BARGAIN SALES OF APPRECIATED PROPERTY

IRC § 170(e)(2)
IRC § 1011(b)
Reg. § 1.170A–4(2)
Reg. § 1.1011–2

¶14.9 • ART OBJECTS

IRC § 170(b)(1)(B)

Appraising contributions of art works
Adolph Posner, 35 TCM 943 (1976)
Edwin F. Gordon, 35 TCM 1227 (1976)

Appraisal fee an itemized expense
Rev. Rul. 67–461, 1967–1 CB 125

¶14.10 • INTERESTS IN REAL ESTATE

Fractional transfers
IRC § 170(f)(3)(B)(ii)
Rev. Rul. 58–261, 1958–1 CB 143

Remainder interests
IRC § 170(f)(4)
Prop. Reg. § 1.170A–12

Option on realty
Rev. Rul. 82–197, 1982–2 CB 72

Farms or residences
IRC § 170(f)(3)(B)(i)
Rev. Rul. 76–357, 1976–2 CB 285

Vacation use retained
Rev. Rul. 75–420, 1975–2 CB 78

Right to use of property
IRC § 170(f)(3)(A)
Reg. § 1.170A–7(d)
Charles M. Peters, 35 TCM 770 (1976)

Certain partial interests donated for conservation purposes
IRC § 170(f)(3)(B)(iii)

Note: Paragraph numbers refer to Part One. Items marked * are research aids, not citations of authority; see "Key to Citations" on page 337.

382

¶14.11 • LIFE INSURANCE

Deductible if irrevocably assigned
Eppa Hunton, IV, 1 TC 821 (1943) (Acq.)
Ernst R. Behrend, 23 BTA 1037 (Acq.)

Premiums deductible if beneficiary a charity
Mortimer C. Adler, 5 BTA 1063
Rev. Rul. 58–372, 1958–2 CB 99

Contribution of cash surrender value not deductible
Rev. Rul. 76–143, 1976–1 CB 63
Rev. Rul. 76–1, 1976–1 CB 57

¶14.12 • APPRAISALS NEEDED FOR PROPERTY DONATIONS

1984 Tax Act (P.L. 98–369) Section 155
Temp. Reg. Sec. 1.170A–13T

¶14.13 • BUSINESS AND FARM INVENTORY

Corporate inventory
Reg. § 1.170A–4(e)

Gifts at fair market value
IRC § 170(e)
Charles N. Prothro, 209 F.2d 331 (5th Cir. 1954)
David C. White, 104 F. Supp. 213 (D. Kan. 1952)
Rev. Rul. 55–138, 1955–1 CB 223

Crops
Clyde G. Tatum, 46 TC 736 (1966), aff'd, 400 F.2d 242 (5th Cir. 1968)

Certain corporate contributions for care of ill, needy or infants
IRC § 170(e)(3)

¶14.14 • DONATING INCOME AND REMAINDER INTERESTS THROUGH TRUSTS

Income interests
IRC § 170(f)(2)(B)
IRC § 671

Charitable remainder trusts
IRC § 170(f)(2)(A)
IRC § 170(f)(3)(B)
IRC § 170(f)(4)
IRC § 170(f)(7)
IRC § 664

Life income plans
IRC § 170(f)(2)(A)
IRC § 642(c)(5)
IRC § 664
IRS Publication 723(B)

¶14.15 • ORGANIZATIONS QUALIFIED TO RECEIVE DEDUCTIBLE CONTRIBUTIONS

To which organizations
IRC § 170(c)
Rev. Rul. 54–243, 1954–1 CB 92
IRS Publication No. 78 Cumulative List, (supplements published bi-monthly)

United States, state, city, etc.
IRC § 170(b)(1)(a)

IRC § 170(c)(1)
Rev. Rul. 56–126, 1956–1 CB 56

Social Security system
Rev. Rul. 82–169, 1982–2 CB 72

Indian tribes
Rev. Rul. 74–179, 1974–1 CB 279

Land donated to municipality
Mary W. Toole, 63–1 USTC ¶9267 (D. Fla. 1963)
Citizens and Southern Nat'l Bank of S.C., 243 F. Supp. 900 (D.S. Car. 1965)

Religious
IRC § 170(c)(2)(B)
IRC § 501(c)(3)
Clarence Morey, 205 F. Supp. 918 (S.D. Cal. 1962)
Saint Germain Foundation, 26 TC 648 (1956)(Acq.)

Charitable
IRC § 170(c)(2)(B)
IRC § 501(c)(3)
IRC § 509(a)
T. J. Moss Tie Co., 18 TC 188 (1952)(Nonacq.)
Isabel Peters, 21 TC 55 (1953) (Acq.)
William Waller, 39 TC 665 (1963) (Acq.)
Lorain Avenue Clinic, 31 TC 141 (1958)

Scientific, literary and educational
IRC § 170(c)(2)(B)
IRC § 501(c)(3)
IRC § 509(a)
Science and Research Foundation, Inc., 181 F. Supp. 526 (S.D. Ill. 1960)
Rev. Rul. 67–291, 1967–2 CB 184
Rev. Rul. 67–292, 1967–2 CB 184

Prevention of cruelty to children or animals
IRC § 170(c)(2)(B)
IRC § 501(c)(3)
John A. Mustard, Exr., 155 F. Supp. 325 (Ct. Cl. 1957)

Amateur athletic associations
IRC § 170(c)(2)(B)
IRC § 501(c)(3)

Domestic nonprofit war veteran organizations
IRC § 170(c)(3)
Rev. Rul. 57–327, 1957–2 CB 155
Rev. Rul. 59–151, 1959–1 CB 53

Domestic fraternal group
IRC § 170(c)(4)
IRC § 501(c)(8)

Nonprofit cemetery and burial companies
IRC § 170(c)(5)
IRC § 501(c)(13)
Rev. Rul. 58–190, 1958–1 CB 15

Foreign charities
IRC § 170(c)(2)(A)
Reg. § 1.170–2(a)(1)
Dora A. Welti, 1 TC 905 (1943)
Louise K. Herter, 20 TCM 78 (1953)

Rev. Rul. 63–252, 1963–2 CB 101, amplified by Rev. Rul. 66–79, 1966–1 CB 48
Rev. Rul. 69–80, 1969–1 CB 65

¶14.16 • NONDEDUCTIBLE CONTRIBUTIONS

Lobbying
IRC § 170(c)
IRC § 501(c)(3)
IRC § 501(h)
Alan B. Kuper, 332 F.2d 562 (3d Cir. 1964), aff'g 22 TCM 1208 (1963), cert. denied, 379 U.S. 920
Murray Seasongood, 227 F.2d 907 (6th Cir. 1956)
McClintock-Trunkey Co., 19 TC 297 (1952), rev'd on another issue, 217 F.2d 329 (9th Cir. 1955)
Mosby Hotel Co., 13 TCM 996 (1954)
Rev. Rul. 62–71, 1962–1 CB 85

Organization benefiting restricted groups
IRC § 170
Boston Safe Deposit & Trust Co., 30 BTA 679
Colonial Trust Co., Exr., 19 BTA 174 (Acq.)
Montgomery, 63 Ct. Cls. 588

Bar Association donations
Rev. Rul. 77–232, 1977–2 CB 71, clarified by Rev. Rul. 78–129, 1978–1 CB 67

Communist organizations
IRC § 170
Sec. 11(a), Internal Security Act of 1950 (64 Stat. 996; 50 U.S.C. 790)
Reg. § 1.501(e)–1

Foreign governments
R. Hess, 30 TCM 1043 (1971) (State of Israel)

Benefit private individual
IRC § 170(c)
IRC § 501(c)(3)
Dohrman, 18 BTA 66
Emanuel Kolkey, 27 TC 37 (1956) (Acq.), aff'd, 254 F.2d 51 (7th Cir. 1958)
Saint Germain Foundation, 26 TC 648 (1956)(Acq.)
Mark B. Lloyd, 29 TCM 453 (1970)

Purchase of church building bond
Rev. Rul. 75–112, 1975–1 CB 274
Rev. Rul. 58–262, 1958–1 CB 143

Value in return for contribution
Katherine Channing, 67 F.2d 986 (1st Cir.), cert. denied, 291 U.S. 686
Morris N. Scharf, 32 TCM 1247 (1973)
Albin J. Strandquist, 29 TCM 387 (1970)
Rev. Rul. 67–246, 1967–2 CB 104, distinguished by Rev. Rul. 74–348, 1974–2 CB 80
Rev. Rul. 58–303, 1958–1 CB 61

Tuition
Harold De Jong, 309 F.2d 373 (9th

Note: Paragraph numbers refer to Part One. Items marked * are research aids, not citations of authority; see "Key to Citations" on page 337.

383

Cir. 1962), aff'g 36 TC 896 (1961)
Rev. Rul. 71–112, 1971–1 CB 93
Jacob Oppewal, 30 TCM 1177
(1971), aff'd, 468 F.2d 1000 (1st
Cir. 1972)

Rest home
O. J. Wardwell Est., 35 TC 443
(1960), rev'd, 301 F.2d 632 (8th
Cir. 1962)

Donations of services
Reg. Sec. 1.170A–1(g)
Rev. Rul. 67–236, 1967–2 CB 103
Rev. Rul. 57–462, 1957–2 CB 157
William W. Grant, 84 TC 809
(1985)

Blood donations
Rev. Rul. 162, 1953–2 CB 127

Directory of churches
Rev. Rul. 57–525, 1957–2 CB 159

Value of use of property
IRC § 170(f)(3)(A)
Reg. § 1.170A–7(d)

**¶14.17 • CEILING ON CHARITABLE
DEDUCTIONS**

Donations by individuals
IRC § 170(b)(1)(A),(B),(C) and
(D)
Reg. § 1.170A–8(f)

Donations by corporations
IRC § 170(b)(2)

Donations to foundations
IRC § 170(b)(1)(B) and (D)
IRC § 170(c)(2)
IRC § 170(b)(1)(E)

Order of taking deductions
IRC § 170(b)(1)(C) and (D)

**¶14.18 • FIVE-YEAR CARRYOVER
FOR EXCESS DONATIONS
EXCEEDING STATUTORY
CEILING**

Individuals
IRC § 170(d)(1)

Corporations
IRC § 170(d)(2)

Donations to foundations
IRC § 170(b)(1)(B) and (d)

**¶14.19 • ELECTION TO REDUCE
APPRECIATION OF CERTAIN
PROPERTY GIFTS**

Reduction for appreciation
IRC § 170(e)(1)
Electing 50% ceiling
IRC § 170(b)(1)(c)(iii)
Reg. § 1.170A–8(d)(2)

¶15

Deductions for Interest You Pay

¶15.1

*IRS Publication 545
IRC § 163

"The Interest Deduction for Individuals After Tax Reform," Rolf Auster, The Practical Accountant, June 1987

**¶15.2 • SEGREGATE YOUR INTEREST
PAYMENTS**

Personal interest
IRC § 163(h)
IRC § 163(h)(6)

Residential mortgage interest
IRC § 163(h)(2)(D)
IRC § 163(h)(3)

Investment interest
IRC § 163(d)
IRC § 163(h)(2)(B)

Business interest
IRC § 163(h)(2)(A)

Utility's late-payment charge
Rev. Rul. 74–187, 1974–1 CB 48

Loan fees
Robert E. Stewart, 41 TCM 318
(1980)

Dummy corporation loan
Bollinger Jr, — F.2d — (6th Cir.
1986)
Bruce L. Schlosberg, 81–1 USTC
9272 (D. Va. 1981)
Joseph A. Roccaforte Jr., 77 TC 263
(1981), rev'd, 708 F. 2d 986 (5th
Cir. 1983)

*Loans to buy market discount bonds
and T bills*

IRC § 1277
IRC § 1282

Securities held as collateral
I.T. 1666, II–1 CB 64

Usurious interest
Arthur R. Jones Syndicate, 23 F.2d
833 (7th Cir. 1927)

**¶15.3 • YEAR TO CLAIM AN
INTEREST DEDUCTION**

Promissory note is not payment of interest
Francis R. Hart, 54 F.2d 848 (1st
Cir. 1932)

Increasing of loan
Julius I. Peyser, 1 TCM 807 (1943)
Fred W. Leadbetter, 39 BTA 629
(Nonacq.)
S. E. Thomason, 33 BTA 576

Borrow to pay interest
Newton A. Burgess, 8 TC 47 (1949)

Life insurance loan
Nina C. Prime Est., 39 BTA 487
Albert J. Alsberg, 42 BTA 61
L. B. Hirsch, 42 BTA 566 (Acq.),
aff'd, 124 F.2d 24 (9th Cir. 1941)
Arthur A. Beaudry, 1 TCM 838
(1943), modified and rem'd, 150
F.2d 20 (2d Cir. 1945), on remand, 5 TCM 61 (1946)
J. Simpson Dean, 35 TC 1083 (1961)
(Nonacq.)

Margin account with broker
Rev. Rul. 70–221, 1970–1 CB 33

Contested note or obligation
Allegheny Steel Co., 18 F. Supp. 398
(Ct. Cl. 1937)

Shellabarger Grain Products Co., 2
TC 75 (1943)(Acq.), aff'd in
part, rev'd in part, 146 F.2d 177
(7th Cir. 1944)

Partial payment of loan
McConway & Torley Corp., 2 TC 593
(1943)
Theodore R. Plunkett, 41 BTA 700
(Acq.), aff'd on other grounds,
118 F.2d 644 (1st Cir. 1941)
Paul N. Bowen Est., 2 TC 783
(1973)
George R. Newhouse, 59 TC 783
(1973)
John B. Ferenc, 33 TCM 136 (1974)

Full settlement of debt
William J. Petit, 8 TC 228 (1947)
(Acq.)
Warner Co., 11 TC 419 (1948),
aff'd per curiam, 181 F.2d 599 (3d
Cir. 1950)

Using borrowed funds to pay interest
IR–83–93, 7/6/83
Barry L. Battelstein, 631 F.2d 1182
(5th Cir. 1980), cert. denied.
Donald L. Wilkerson, 655 F.2d 980
(9th Cir. 1981)

**¶15.4 • PREPAID INTEREST ALLOCATED OVER TERM OF
LOAN**

IRC § 461(g)

Distortion of income test
Andrew A. Sandor, 536 F.2d 874
(9th Cir. 1976), aff'g per curiam
62 TC 469 (1974)

Nonrefundability clause
Joseph Zidanic, 79 TC 651 (1983)

Note: Paragraph numbers refer to Part One. Items marked * are research aids, not citations of authority; see "Key to Citations" on page 337.

¶15.5 • INTEREST ON DISCOUNT LOANS

Discounted note
Burton Foster, 32 TCM 243 (1973)
Rev. Rul. 75–12, 1975–1 CB 62

Note that is renewed
S. E. Thomason, 33 BTA 576

¶15.6 • RULE OF 78'S

Rev. Proc. 84–27, 1984–1 CB 469
Rev. Proc. 84–28, 1984–1 CB 475
Rev. Proc. 84–29. 1984–1 CB 480

¶15.7 • FINANCE CHARGES

IRC § 163(h)(1)
IRC § 163(h)(6)
IRC § 163(d)(6)(B)
Louise Ross, 23 TCM 2061 (1964)
Rev. Rul. 72–2 1972–1 CB 19
Rev. Rul. 73–137, 1973–1 CB 68

Bank credit card
Rev. Rul. 71–98, 1971–1 CB 57, modified by Rev. Rul. 72–315, 1972–1 CB 49

Revolving charge account
Rev. Rul. 72–315, 1972–1 CB 49

Oil company credit card
Rev. Rul. 73–136, 1973–1 CB 68

¶15.8 • NONDEDUCTIBLE INTEREST

IRC § 163(h)(1)

"Non-deductible Interest," S. Goldstein, 35 N.Y. C.P.A. 21 (1965)

Retirement plan loans
IRC § 72(p)(3)

Interest on another's debts
William A. Colston, 21 BTA 396 aff'd, 59 F.2d 867 (D.C. Cir. 1932), cert. denied 387 U.S. 640
Martin T. O'Brien, 47 BTA 561 (Acq.)
Farmers and Traders Bank, 4 BTA 753
David J. Secunda, 36 TCM 763 (1977)

Parent liable under state law
Joseph E. Walther, 316 F.2d 708 (7th Cir. 1963)

Interest on borrowings to carry tax-exempt obligations
IRC § 265
Reg. § 1.265–2
Constance M. Bishop, 41 TC 154 (1963), aff'd 342 F.2d 757 (6th Cir. 1965)
Rev. Proc. 72–18 1972–1 CB 335, clarified by Rev. Proc. 74–8, 1974–1 CB 419

Interest on minimum deposit life insurance plans
IRC § 264(a)(3) and (c)
Reg. § 1.264–4

Single premium life insurance contract
IRC § 264(a)(2)
Reg. § 1.264–2 and 3

Mutual fund-life insurance plan
Rev. Rul. 74–500, 1974–2 CB 91

Parent made gift to children
William H. Brown, 241 F.2d 827 (8th Cir. 1957)
James Crosby, 36 TCM 1401 (1977)

Parent/child college loan scheme
Rev. Rul. 82–94, 1982–1 CB 31

Private annuities
Rebecca Bell, 76 TC 232 (1981), aff'd, 668 F.2d 448 (8th Cir. 1982)

Loans in tax avoidance schemes
L. Lee Stanton, 34 TC 1 (1960)
George G. Lynch, 273 F.2d 867 (2d Cir. 1960)

GI insurance
George T. Williams, 47 TC 689 (1967), aff'd, 69–1 USTC ¶9115 (6th Cir. 1969), cert. denied, 394 U.S. 997

Charges added to cost of asset
IRC § 266
Reg. § 1.266–1

Loan commitment fee
Rev. Rul. 75–172, 1975–1 CB 145

Bank service charges on checking account
Virginia G. Edgar, 34 TCM 816 (1979)

Consumer loans require allocation
Rev. Rul. 69–189, 1969–1 CB 55

Charges for premium payment schedule
Rev. Rul. 79–187, 1979–1 CB 95

Interest paid voluntarily
Hypotheek Land Co., 200 F.2d 390 (9th Cir. 1953)
D. Loveman & Son Export Corp., 34 TC 776 (1960)(Acq.), aff'd 296 F.2d 732 (6th Cir. 1962), cert. denied, 369 U.S. 860

¶15.9 • INTEREST ON DEBTS TO CARRY TAX-EXEMPT OBLIGATIONS AND SHORT SALES

Frank Batten, 322 F. Supp. 629 (E.D. Vir. 1971)
Amedeo Louis Marionenzi, 32 TCM 681 (1973), aff'd per curiam, 490 F.2d 92 (1st Cir. 1974)

Interest on borrowings to carry tax-exempt obligations
IRC § 265
Reg. § 1.265–2
Constance M. Bishop, 41 TC 154 (1963), aff'd, 342 F.2d 757 (6th Cir. 1965)
Rev. Proc. 72–18, 1972–1 CB 740, clarified by Rev. Proc. 74–8, 1974–1 CB 419

Interest on joint venture mortgage
Max R. Israelson, 367 F. Supp. 1104 (D. Md. 1974), aff'd per curiam, 75–1 USTC ¶9131 (4th Cir. 1975)

Interest on loan to carry mutual fund shares paying exempt-interest dividends
IRC § 265(4)

Short sales
IRC § 265(5)

¶15.10 • DEDUCTIONS FOR OWNERS OF COOPERATIVE AND CONDOMINIUM APARTMENTS

"Tax Aspects of Cooperative and Condominium Housing," P. E. Anderson, 25 NYU Inst. 79 (1967)

"The Cooperative Apartment," M. R. Whitebrook, 9 Practical Lawyer, 25 (1963)

"Calculating Allowable Depreciation for Tenant-Stockholders of Cooperatives," Albert Feuer, 60 Journal of Taxation 268 (1984)

"How to Insure Maximum Benefits for Co-Ops and Condominiums As Well As Their Owners," Douglas R. Holm, 10 Taxation for Lawyers, 158 and 27 Taxation for Accountants 252 (1981)

"Depreciating the Cooperative Apartment," Joel E. Miller, 11 J. Real Estate Tax 307 (Summer 1984)

"Condominium—The Magic in a Word," A. O. Armstrong, Jr. and C. R. Collins, 1964 So. Calif. Tax Inst. 667

"Commercial Condominiums: Tax Considerations for Unit Purchasers and the Association," D. S. Shapiro, 41 Journal of Taxation 204 (1974)

Cooperative apartments
IRC § 216
Reg. § 1.216–1(c) and (d)
Rev. Rul. 59–257, 1959–2 CB 101
Rev. Rul. 53–120, 1953–2 CB 130
Rev. Rul. 73–15, 1973–1 CB 141

Holdover tenants do not jeopardize deductions to coop owners
Rev. Rul. 80–299, 1980–2 CB 82

Condominiums
Rev. Rul. 64–31, 1964–1 (Pt. 1) CB 300
Raymond J. Wachter, 75–1 USTC ¶9172 (D. Wash. 1975)

¶15.11 • TWO RESIDENCE RULE FOR HOME MORTGAGE INTEREST

IRC § 163(h)(3)

Two residence test
IRC § 163(h)(5)(A)

Deductible interest limits
IRC § 163(h)(3)(B)

Married-separate returns
IRC § 163(h)(5)(A)(ii)

Medical expenses
IRC § 163(h)(4)(B)

Educational costs
IRC § 163(h)(4)(C)

Cooperative
IRC § 163(h)(5)(B)

Note: Paragraph numbers refer to Part One. Items marked * are research aids, not citations of authority; see "Key to Citations" on page 337.

¶15.12 • MORTGAGE PAYMENT RULES

Penalty for prepaying mortgage
Rev. Rul. 57–198, 1957–1 CB 94

Joint owners
Barbara S. Finney, 35 TCM 1504 (1976)

Graduated payment mortgages
*Letter Ruling 8031087

Reverse annuity loan
Rev. Rul. 80–248, 1980–2 CB 164

Zero interest mortgages
Rev. Rul. 82–124, 1982–1 CB 89

Shared appreciation mortgage
Rev. Rul. 83–51, 1983–1 CB 48

Mortgage assistance payments under

Sec. 235 of the National Housing Act not deductible
Reg. § 1.163–1(d)
Rev. Rul. 75–271, 1975–2 CB 23

H.U.D. interest reduction payments
Rev. Rul. 76–75, 1976–1 CB 14
Alvin V. Graff, 74 TC 743 (1980)

¶15.13 • "POINTS"
Rev. Rul. 67–297, 1967–2 CB 87
Rev. Rul. 68–650, 1968–2 CB 78
Rev. Rul. 69–188, 1969–1 CB 54, amplified by Rev. Rul. 69–582, 1969–2 CB 29

Refinancing
Rev. Rul. 87–22, IRB 1987–14, 41
Rev. Proc. 87–15, IRB 1987–14, 47

Points withheld from principal not deductible

Roger A. Schubel, 77 TC 701 (1981)

"Points" treated as prepaid interest
IRC § 461(g)

¶15.14 • INVESTMENT INTEREST LIMITATIONS

IRC § 163(d)

Investment interest
IRC § 163(d)(3)

Carryforward
IRC § 163(d)(2)

Phase-in
IRC § 163(d)(6)

¶15.15 • EARMARKING USE OF LOAN PROCEEDS FOR INTEREST DEDUCTIONS

Temp. Reg. Sec. 1.163–8T

¶16

Deductions for Taxes

¶16.2 • GENERAL RULES FOR DEDUCTING TAXES

IRC § 164
Reg. § 1.164–1

Sales tax deduction repealed
1986 Tax Act Section 134(a)(1), repealing prior law Code Sections 164(a)(4), 164(b)(2) and (5).

Sales tax added to basis of business or investment property—post 1986
IRC § 164(a)

Nondeductible taxes
IRC § 275

Federal minimum tax not deductible
Rev. Rul. 77–396, 1977–2 CB 86

Cash basis
IRC § 461
Reg. § 1.461–1(a)(1)
George C. Beidleman, 7 BTA 899
Benjamin I. Powell, 26 BTA 509 (Acq.)
Joseph Shalleck, 1 TCM 292 (1942)

Borrowed funds
In re Barry L. Battelstein, 77–2 USTC ¶9516 (S.D. Tex. 1977)

Payment by bank
Frank J. Hradesky, 65 TC 87 (1975), aff'd per curiam, 540 F.2d 821 (5th Cir. 1976)
Rev. Rul. 78–103, 1978–1 CB 58

Water bills
Benjamin Mahler, 119 F.2d 869 (2d Cir. 1941), aff'g on this point BTA Memo., P-H 39,468, cert. denied, 314 U.S. 660

Rufus K. Steel, 7 TCM 558 (1948)

Assessments not deductible as taxes
Rev. Rul. 77–29, 1977–2 CB 538
Rev. Rul. 76–495, 1976–2 CB 43

Parking meter charges
Rev. Rul. 73–91, 1973–1 CB 71

Sewer fees
Louis M. Roth, 17 TC 1450 (1952) (Acq.)

Postage
Reg. § 1.164–2

Transfer taxes
Rev. Rul. 65–313, 1965–2 CB 47

Turnpike or thruway tolls
Donald L. Cox, 41 TC 161 (1963)

Windfall profit tax
IRC § 164(a)(5)
Rev. Rul. 81–99, 1981–1 CB 312

¶16.3 • DEDUCTING STATE INCOME TAXES

Taxes withheld from pay
Special Ruling, October 15, 1959

State tax paid before end of year
Lillian B. Glassell, 12 TC 232 (1949)
Aaron Lowenstein Est., 12 TC 694 (1949)(Acq.), aff'd on other grounds, 183 F.2d 172 (5th Cir. 1950), cert. denied, 340 U.S. 911
Special Ruling, February 13, 1946
Rev. Rul. 74–140, 1974–1 CB 50
Rev. Rul. 82–208, 1982–2 CB 58

Alabama unemployment tax deductible
Rev. Rul. 75–156, 1975–1 CB 66

Rhode Island disability deductible
James R. McGowan, 67 TC 599 (1976)
IR-1742, January 28, 1977

California disability deductible
Anthony Trujillo, 68 TC 56 (1977)
IR-1967, March 10, 1978

New Jersey disability deductible
IR-1967, March 10, 1978

New York disability deductible
IR-1967, March 10, 1978

¶16.4 • TAXES AND OTHER CARRYING CHARGES YOU CAPITALIZE OR DEDUCT

IRC § 266
Reg. § 1.266–1

Election irrevocable
George Stamos Est., 55 TC 468 (1970)

Prior deduction
Rev. Rul. 72–594 1972–2 CB 199

¶16.5 • AMORTIZATION OF CONSTRUCTION PERIOD INTEREST AND TAXES

IRC § 263A

¶16.6 • DEDUCTING REAL ESTATE TAXES

Payments to bank escrow account deductible when disbursed to tax authorities
Rev. Rul. 78–103, 1978–1 CB 58

Home owner's association fees not deductible
Rev. Rul. 76–495, 1976–2 CB 43

Note: Paragraph numbers refer to Part One. Items marked * are research aids, not citations of authority; see "Key to Citations" on page 337.

Nondeductible governmental charges
IRC § 164(c)(1)

Buyer of foreclosed property
*Letter Ruling 8207030

¶16.7 • TENANTS' PAYMENT OF TAXES GENERALLY NON-DEDUCTIBLE

Deductible
Hawaii real property tax law: Rev. Rul. 64–327, 1964–2 CB 56
California real property tax law: Rev. Rul. 68–84, 1968–1 CB 71

Not deductible
Tax surcharge: Rev. Rul. 75–301, 1975–2 CB 66
U.K. rates tax: Maynard Waxenberg, 62 TC 594 (1974); Rev. Rul. 73–600, 1973–2 CB 47
Maryland-Prince George County renters: Rev. Rul. 75–558, 1975–2 CB 67
New York: Rev. Rul. 79–180, 1979–1 CB 95

¶16.8 • ALLOCATING TAXES WHEN YOU SELL OR BUY REALTY

IRC § 164(d)
Reg. § 1.164–6

Accrual basis
IRC § 461
Reg. § 1.461–1(a)(2) and (4)(C)

Buyer's payment of seller's back taxes capitalized
Al S. Reinhardt, 75 TC 47 (1980)

¶16.9 • WHO MAY DEDUCT REAL PROPERTY TAXES

Husband for his wife
William A. Colston, 59 F.2d 867 (D.C. Cir. 1932), aff'g 21 BTA 396, cert. denied, 287 U.S. 640
Charles F. Dean Est., 1 BTA 27

Mortgage required husband to pay
Eugene W. Small, 27 BTA 1219

Condominium apartment owner
Rev. Rul. 64–31, 1964–1 (Pt. 1) CB 300

Life tenant
Cornelia C. F. Horsford, 2 TC 826 (1943)(Acq.)

Tenant
Reg. § 1.162–11
Denholm & McKay Co., 39 BTA 767
Caroline T. Kissel, 15 BTA 1270 (Acq. and Nonacq.)

Foreclosed for failure to pay taxes
Charles H. McGlue, 54 BTA 761 (Acq.)

Cooperative apartment owner
IRC § 216

Jointly and severally liable for tax
Rev. Rul. 72–79, 1972–1 CB 51

Tenancy by the entirety
Thomas D. Conroy, 17 TCM 21 (1958)
F. C. Nicodemus Jr., 26 BTA 125 (Acq.)
Rev. Rul. 71–268, 1971–1 CB 58

Tenant in common
Lulu Lung Powell, 26 TCM 161 (1967)

Mortgagee
John Hancock Mutual Life Ins. Co., 10 BTA 736 (Acq.)
Lucy S. Schiffelin Est., 44 BTA 137 (Acq.)

Tax on others' property
Albion D. T. Libby, 133 F.2d 203 (3d Cir. 1943), aff'g BTA Memo. P-H 42,252
J. Raymond Batcheller, 5 TCM 746 (1946)
Solomon N. Seale, 9 TCM 48 (1950)
Gordon W. Bonnette Est., 9 TCM 158 (1950)

Eugene W. Small, 27 BTA 1219 (1971)
Virginia N. Cramer, 55 TC 1125 (1971)(Acq.)
Gregory E. Macdonald, 35 TCM 346 (1976)

Have interest in property
Alfred J. Grosso, BTA Memo. P-H 41,581
A. J. Gilbert, 11 TCM 457 (1952)
Archibald R. Watson, 42 BTA 52, aff'd, 124 F.2d 437 (2d Cir. 1942)

Protection of beneficial interest
Rev. Rul. 67–21, 1967–1 CB 45

Trust for life of another
Herman A. Harper, 4 TCM 1097 (1945)
Robert C. Ligget, 4 TCM 598 (1945)
John H. Hord, 95 F.2d 179 (6th Cir. 1944), rev'g 33 BTA 342

Realty owned by parent
J. Raymond Batcheller, 5 TCM 746 (1946)

Stockholder property interest
Fred N. Acker, 258 F.2d 568 (6th Cir. 1958), aff'd, 361 U.S. 87 (1959)
Bula E. Croker, 27 BTA 588
Gustav W. Lembeck, 16 BTA 250 (Acq.)
Samuel Riker Jr., 15 BTA 1160

¶16.10 • AUTOMOBILE LICENSE FEES

Reg. § 1.164–3(c)
Rev. Rul. 74–454, 1974–2 CB 57

¶16.11 • TAXES DEDUCTIBLE AS BUSINESS OR INCOME PRODUCING EXPENSES

IRC § 162
IRC § 212

¶16.12 • FOREIGN TAXES

IRC § 164(a)(3)

¶17
Medical and Dental Expense Deductions

*"Recent Actions Define What Is a Deductible Medical Expense," 11 Est. Plan 167 (May 1984)

¶17.2 • ALLOWABLE MEDICAL CARE COSTS

*IRS Publication 502
IRC § 213
Reg. § 1.213–1

Chiropractor (lic.)
Rev. Rul. 55–261, 1955–1 CB 307

Christian Science practitioners
Rev. Rul. 55–261, 1955–1 CB 307

Dermatologist
Rev. Rul. 55–261, 1955–1 CB 307

Obstetrical services
Reg. § 1.213–1(e)(1)(ii)

Osteopath (lic.)
Rev. Rul. 55–261, 1955–1 CB 307

Nurses
Reg. § 1.213–1(e)(1)(ii)
Jacob Hentz Jr. Est., 12 TCM 368 (1953)
George B. Wendell, 12 TC 161 (1949)
Rev. Rul. 58–339, 1958–2 CB 106
Rev. Rul. 55–261, 1955–1 CB 307

Psychiatrists
Rev. Rul. 53–143, 1953–2 CB 129, modified by Rev. Rul. 63–91, 1963–1 CB 54
Rev. Rul. 55–261, 1955–1 CB 307
Rev. Rul. 56–263, 1956–1 CB 135

Payments to unlicensed practitioners
Rev. Rul. 63–91, 1963–1 CB 54

Dental services
Reg. § 1.213–1(e)(1)(ii)

Equipment and supplies
Reg. § 1.213–1(e)(1)(ii)
Rev. Rul. 55–261, 1955–1 CB 307

Note: Paragraph numbers refer to Part One. Items marked * are research aids, not citations of authority; see "Key to Citations" on page 337.

Auto devices for handicapped
Rev. Rul. 66–80, 1966–1 CB 57

Elevator
Edna G. Hollander, 219 F.2d 934 (3d Cir. 1955), rev'g 22 TC 646 (1954)
James E. Berry, 174 F. Supp. 748 (D. Okla. 1958)
Vance J. Alexander, 57–1 USTC ¶9335 (D. Tenn. 1957)
W. A. Post, 150 F. Supp. 299 (D. Ala. 1956)
W. E. Snellings, 149 F. Supp. 825 (E.D. Vir. 1956)
Rev. Rul. 59–411, 1959–2 CB 100

Elastic hosiery
Bessie Cohen, 10 TCM 29 (1951)

Fluoridation unit
Rev. Rul. 64–267, 1964–2 CB 69

Invalid chair
Rev. Rul. 58–155, 1958–1 CB 156
Rev. Rul. 66–80, 1966–1 CB 57
Rev. Rul. 67–76, 1967–1 CB 70

Wig
Rev. Rul. 62–189, 1962–2 CB 88

Medical treatments
Reg. § 1.213–1(e)(1)(ii)
Rev. Rul. 55–261, 1955–1 CB 307

Laboratory services and X-rays
Reg. § 1.213–1(e)(1)(ii)
Rev. Rul. 55–261, 1955–1 CB 307

Hospital services
Reg. § 1.213–1(e)(1)(ii)
Rev. Rul. 55–261, 1955–1 CB 307

Premiums
Reg. § 1.213–1(e)(1)(i)

Premiums allocable to lost wages, loss of life or limbs
Reg. Sec. 1.213–1(e)(4)

Alcoholic's inpatient care
Rev. Rul. 72–325, 1973–1 CB 75

Birth control pills
Rev. Rul. 73–200, 1973–1 CB 140

Clarinet lessons
Rev. Rul. 62–210, 1962–2 CB 89

Navajo sings
Raymond H. Tso, 40 TCM 1277 (1980)

Health institute
Rev. Rul. 55–261, 1955–1 CB 307

Drug center costs
Rev. Rul. 72–226, 1972–1 CB 96

Face lifting operation
Rev. Rul. 76–332, 1976–2 CB 81

Hair transplant operation
William W. Mattes, 77 TC (1981) (Acq.)

Electrolysis
Rev. Rul. 82–111, 1982–1 CB 48

Legal fees
Carl A. Gerstacker, 414 F.2d 448 (6th Cir. 1969)
Rev. Rul. 71–28, 1971–1 CB 121

Nurses' board and wages
Reg. § 1.213–1(e)(1)(ii)

Federal Insurance Contributions Act
Rev. Rul. 57–489, 1957–2 CB 207

Remedial reading
Rev. Rul. 69–607, 1969–2 CB 40

Seeing-eye dog
Rev. Rul. 55–261, 1955–1 CB 307

Sterilization
Rev. Rul. 73–603, 1973–2 CB 76

Tuition fee
Rev. Rul. 54–457, 1954–2 CB 100

Wages of guide
Rev. Rul. 64–173, 1964–1 (Pt. 1) CB 121

Organ transplant costs
Rev. Rul. 68–452, 1968–2 CB 111

Telephone-teletype
Rev. Rul. 71–48, 1971–1 CB 99, amplified by Rev. Rul. 73–53, 1973–1 CB 139

Television adapter for closed caption service
Rev. Rul. 80–340, 1980–2 CB 81

Braille books
Rev. Rul. 75–318, 1975–2 CB 88

Laetrile
Rev. Rul. 78–325, 1978–2 CB 124

Prescribed drugs
IRC § 213(d)(2)

Extra cost of health food
Theron G. Randolph, 67 TC 481 (1976)
Leona vonKalb, 37 TCM 1511 (1978)

Contact lens replacement insurance protection
Rev. Rul. 74–429, 1974–2 CB 83

Medicare A by persons not automatically covered
Rev. Rul. 79–175, 1979–1 CB 117

Payroll withholding to cover Medicare A not deductible
Rev. Rul. 66–216, 1966–2 CB 100

Car insurance premiums not deductible
Rev. Rul. 73–483, 1973–2 CB 75

¶17.3 • NONDEDUCTIBLE EXPENSES

Toothpaste
Reg. § 1.213–1(e)(2)

Antiseptic diaper service and maternity clothes
Rev. Rul. 55–261, 1955–1 CB 307

Monument
Carolyn W. Libby Est., 14 TCM 699 (1955)

Illegal operations, etc.
Reg. § 1.213–1(e)(1)(ii)

Divorced wife
IRC § 213(a)

Cost of oil furnace
Reg. § 1.213–1(e)(1)(ii)

Special hospital room
Reg. § 1.213–1(e)(i)(iv)

Specially designed car
Rev. Rul. 55–261, 1955–1 CB 307
Rev. Rul. 58–8, 1958–1 CB 154, amplified by Rev. Rul. 67–76, 1967–1 CB 70

Special food or beverages
Rev. Rul. 55–261, 1955–1 CB 307
Leo R. Cohn, 38 TC 387 (1962) (Nonacq.)
John R. Newman, 68–1 USTC ¶9411 (D. Ark. 1968)
T. G. Randolph, 67 TC 481 (1976)

Organically grown food
Becker, — TCM — (1987)

Bottled water
Rev. Rul. 56–19, 1956–1 CB 135

Health programs
Rev. Rul. 57–130, 1957–1 CB 108

Domestic help
Rev. Rul. 58–339, 1958–2 CB 106

Athletic club
Rev. Rul. 55–261, 1955–1 CB 307

Health spa
Jill Ford Murray, 43 TCM 1377 (1982)

Weight loss program for specific ailment deductible
Rev. Rul. 79–151, 1979–1 CB 116
*Letter Ruling 8004111

Healthy child to boarding school
Samuel Ochs, 17 TC 130 (1951), aff'd, 195 F.2d 692 (2d Cir. 1952), cert. denied, 344 U.S. 827

Tuition for problem child
Gordon Pascal, 15 TCM 434 (1956)

Transportation costs
James Donnelly, 28 TC 1278 (1957), aff'd, 262 F.2d 411 (2d Cir. 1959)
Rev. Rul. 55–261, 1955–1 CB 307

Toiletries and sundries
Reg. § 1.213–1(e)(2)
O. G. Russell, 12 TCM 1276 (1953)

Hotel costs
Reg. § 1.213–1(e)(1)(iv)
Loren Wilks, 27 TCM 1086 (1968)

Living costs of outpatient
Harlin H. Lucas, 25 TCM 1312 (1966)

Look for new place to live
Gunnar E. Erickson, 13 TCM 1045 (1954)

Change of environment trip
Rev. Rul. 56–474, 1956–2 CB 157

Dance lessons
John J. Thoene, 33 TC 62 (1959)
Irving A. Adler, 22 TCM 965 (1963), aff'd, 330 F.2d 91 (9th Cir. 1964)
Rose France, 49 TCM 508 (1980), aff'd, 82–1 USTC ¶9225 (6th Cir. 1982)

Fallout shelter
Fred H. Daniels, 41 TC 324 (1963)

Note: Paragraph numbers refer to Part One. Items marked * are research aids, not citations of authority; see "Key to Citations" on page 337.

Travel to golf course
Leon S. Altman, 53 TC 487 (1969)

Scientology fees
Donald H. Brown, 62 TC 551 (1974), aff'd per curiam, 523 F.2d 365 (8th Cir. 1975)
Rev. Rul. 78–190, 1978–1 CB 74

Divorce costs
Joel H. Jacobs, 62 TC 813 (1974)

Marriage counseling fee
Rev. Rul. 75–319, 1975–2 CB 88

Hotel room for sex therapy
Rev. Rul. 75–187, 1975–1 CB 92

Veterinary fees
L. J. Schoen, 34 TCM 736 (1975)

Babysitter expenses
Rev. Rul. 78–266, 1978–2 CB 123

Tattooing and ear piercing
Rev. Rul. 82–111, 1982–1 CB 48

Moving from airport noise
Luke W. Findlay, Jr., 44 TCM 123 (1982)

¶17.4 • INCOME FLOOR APPLIED TO MEDICAL EXPENSE DEDUCTION

7.5% rule
IRC § 213(a)
Reg. § 1.213–1(a)(2)

Loan as payment
William J. Granan, 55 TC 753 (1971)
Rev. Rul. 78–173, 1978–1 CB 73

Credit card charge
Rev. Rul. 78–39, 1978–1 CB 73

¶17.5 • REIMBURSEMENTS OF MEDICAL COSTS

*"*Limitations to the Medical Deduction; Problems on Reimbursement*," J. M. Skilling, Jr., 29 NYU Inst. 1359 (1971)

Reimbursements reduce deduction
IRC § 213(a)
Reg. § 1.213–1(g)

Failure to make claim
*LR 8102010

Excess reimbursements
Rev. Rul. 69–154, 1969–1 CB 46

Loss of earnings, etc.
Reg. § 1.213–1(e)(1)(i)

Injury awards treated as medical cost reimbursements
Benjamin D. Morgan, 55 TC 376 (1970)
Daniel T. Cooney, 30 TCM 845 (1971)

¶17.6 • PREMIUMS OF MEDICAL CARE POLICIES

IRC § 213(a)(2), repealed by § 202 (a) of Pub. L. No. 97–248

¶17.7 • DEPENDENTS' MEDICAL EXPENSES

Deduction allowed
IRC § 213(a)

Reg. § 1.213–1(a)(3)

Dependents
William A. Jewell, 69 TC 791 (1978) (Acq.)

Must contribute half of support
IRC § 152
Reg. § 1.152–1 and 2

Deduction allowed for nondependent children starting in 1985
IRC § 213(d)(5)

Multiple support
IRC § 152(c)
Reg. § 1.152–3
Loring P. Litchfield, 330 F.2d 509 (1st Cir. 1964)

Not related at time of bill
Rev. Rul. 57–310, 1957–2 CB 206

Parent's welfare payments used to pay medical bills
Robert W. Hodge, 44 TC 186 (1965)

Adopted children
Benny L. Kilpatrick, 68 TC 469 (1977)
Rev. Rul. 60–255, 1960–2 CB 105

¶17.8 • DECEDENT'S MEDICAL EXPENSES

IRC § 213(d)
Reg. § 1.213–1(d)
Rev. Rul. 77–357, 1977–2 CB 328

¶17.9 • TRAVEL COSTS MAY BE MEDICAL DEDUCTIONS

Medical deduction for traveling expenses
IRC § 213(e)(1)(B)
Reg. § 1.213–1(e)(1)(iv)

Relieve specific chronic ailments
Rev. Rul. 58–110, 1958–1 CB 155
Rev. Rul. 55–261, 1955–1 CB 307
Sally L. Bilder, 369 U.S. 499 (1963), rev'g 289 F.2d 291 (3d Cir. 1961)

Taxi fare
Rev. Rul. 55–261, 1955–1 CB 307

Nine-cent rate
Rev. Proc. 80–32, 1980–2 CB 767

Out-of-pocket auto expenses
Maurice S. Gordon, 37 TC 986 (1962)

Lodging $50 daily allowance
IRC § 213(d)(2)
Letter Ruling 8576025

Extra cost of salt-free food
Leo Cohn, 38 TC 387 (1962) (Non-acq.)
Leo Cohn, 240 F. Supp. 786 (D. Ind. 1965)

Hotel costs for convalescent
Daniel S. W. Kelly, 440 F.2d 307 (7th Cir. 1971), rev'g 28 TCM 1208 (1969)

Nurses fare
Rev. Rul. 58–110, 1958–1 CB 155

Parent's trip prescribed
Martin J. Lichterman, 37 TC 586

(1961) (Acq.) (to take child to school deductible)
Rev. Rul. 58–533, 1958–2 CB 108 (to visit child deductible)
Robert Rose, 52 TC 21 (1969) (taking child on trip for health reasons—deductible)
*Letter Ruling 7813004 (picking up mentally disturbed son—transportation plus overnight food and lodging deductible)

Visit specialist
Bertha M. Rodgers, 25 TC 254 (1955)(Acq.), aff'd, 241 F.2d 552 (8th Cir. 1957)

Escape bad climate
Reg. § 1.213–1(e)(1)(iv)
L. Keever Stringham, 12 TC 580 (1949)(Acq.), aff'd, 183 F.2d 579 (6th Cir. 1950)
Rev. Rul. 55–261, 1955–1 CB 307

Alcoholics Anonymous
Rev. Rul. 63–273, 1963–2 CB 112

Disabled veterans' commuting
Sanford H. Weinzimer, 17 TCM 712 (1958)

Wife's trip to provide nursing care deductible
Daniel S. W. Kelly, 28 TCM 1208 (1969), rev'd on other grounds, 440 F.2d 307 (7th Cir. 1971)

Travel costs of kidney transplant donor or prospective donor
Rev. Rul. 73–189, 1973–1 CB 139

General improvement
Reg. § 1.213–1(e)(1)(iv)
Margherita Diamond Est., 22 TCM 1073 (1963)

Driving as therapy
Michael R. Bordas, 29 TCM 458 (1970)

Annual trips south are personal expenses
Bertha M. Rodgers, 241 F.2d 552 (8th Cir. 1957), aff'g 25 TC 254 (1955)(Acq.)

Meals en route
Morris C. Montgomery, 428 F.2d 243 (6th Cir. 1970), aff'g 51 TC 410 (1968)

Treatment in distant city
Reg. § 1.213–1(e)(1)(iv), contra:
Stanley D. Winderman, 32 TC 1197 (1959) (Acq.)

Meals and lodging (pre-1984 decisions)
Reg. § 1.213–1(e)(1)(iv)
Max Carasso, 34 TC 1139 (1960), aff'd, 292 F.2d 367 (2d Cir. 1961), cert. denied, 369 U.S. 874
Sally L. Bilder, 369 U.S. 499 (1963), rev'g 289 F.2d 291 (3d Cir. 1961)

Meals and lodging in transit deductible
Morris C. Montgomery, 428 F.2d 243 (6th Cir. 1970), aff'g 51 TC 410 (1968)

Spiritual aid
Vincent P. Ring, 23 TC 950 (1955)

Note: Paragraph numbers refer to Part One. Items marked * are research aids, not citations of authority; see "Key to Citations" on page 337.

Climate more suitable to ill wife's condition
Lawrence Prem, 21 TCM 873 (1962)

Moving household furnishings
C. Earle Phares, 21 TCM 1446 (1962)

Auto for leg condition
Benjamin Ginsberg, 237 F. Supp. 968 (S.D.N.Y. 1965)

Special vehicle
Rev. Rul. 55–261, 1955–1 CB 307
Rev. Rul. 66–80, 1966–1 CB 57
Rev. Rul. 70–606, 1970–2 CB 66

Convalescence cruise
Margherita Diamond Est., 22 TCM 1073 (1963)

Transporting invalid child to public school
Rev. Rul. 65–255, 1965–2 CB 76

Loss on sale of car
Robert K. Weary, 510 F.2d 435 (10th Cir. 1975), cert. denied, 423 U.S. 838

Patient on medical seminar cruise
Rev. Rul. 76–79, 1976–1 CB 70

¶17.10 • SCHOOLING COSTS FOR THE HANDICAPPED

"Private Schooling for Emotionally Disturbed Children: Is It a Medical Expense?" A. B. Muchin, 44 Taxes 699 (1966)

Reg. § 1.213–1(e)
Rev. Rul. 55–261, 1955–1 CB 307
IRS Publication No. 17

Private school with psychologists
C. Fink Fischer, 50 TC 164 (1968) (Acq.)
Hobart J. Hendrick, 35 TC 1223 (1960) (Acq.)

Boarding school recommended by therapist
John A. Dreifus, 36 TCM 368 (1977)

Hyperactive child in regular boarding school
Ernest M. Newkirk, 77–1 USTC ¶9452 (D. Ohio 1977)

Private military academy
H. Grant Atkinson Jr., 44 TC 39 (1965) (Acq.)
Edward S. Enck, 26 TCM 314 (1967)
Rolland T. Olson, 23 TCM 2008 (1964)
Everett F. Glaze, 20 TCM 1276 (1961)

School in Arizona
Martin J. Lichterman, 37 TC 586 (1961) (Acq.)

Cost of college for deaf child (deductible)
Reuben A. Baer Est., 26 TCM 170 (1967)

Blind student at regular school
Arnold P. Grunwald, 51 TC 108 (1968)

Halfway house
*Letter Ruling 7714016

Special public school class for retarded: cost of tuition and travel
Rev. Rul. 70–285, 1970–1 CB 52

Cost of remedial reading school
Paul H. Ripple, 54 TC 1442 (1970)

Cost of private school for epileptic
DeVora R. Shidler, 30 TCM 529 (1971)

¶17.11 • CONVALESCENT HOME COSTS

Reg. § 1.213–1(e)(1)(v)
James J. Matles, 23 TCM 1489 (1964)
W. B. Counts, 42 TC 755 (1964) (Acq.)
Rev. Rul. 67–185, 1967–1 CB 70

Apartment rent
Sidney J. Ungar, 22 TCM 766 (1963)

Lump-sum payment to retirement home
Rev. Rul. 76–481, 1976–2 CB 82
Rev. Rul. 68–525, 1968–2 CB 112

Payment for future lifetime care
Rev. Rul. 75–302, 1975–2 CB 86
Rev. Rul. 75–303, 1975–2 CB 87

Entrance fee to retirement community
Helen Smith Est., 79 TC 313 (1982)

¶17.12 • NURSES' WAGES

Daughter acting as nurse
Myrtle P. Dodge Est., 20 TCM 811 (1961)

Working parents
Maurice Levy Jr., 20 TCM 1534 (1961)

Domestic
John Frier, 30 TCM 345 (1971)
Rev. Rul. 58–339, 1958–2 CB 106

Allocation of medical and household services
Rev. Rul. 76–106, 1976–1 CB 31

Clerk's salary
Sidney J. Ungar, 22 TCM 766 (1963)

Non-professional therapy
Rev. Rul. 70–170, 1970–1 CB 51

Relative providing care
Walter D. Bye, 31 TCM 238 (1972)

¶17.13 • HOME IMPROVEMENTS AS MEDICAL EXPENSES

"Deductibility of Capital Expenditures as Medical Expenses," G. Greer, 36 U. of Colorado L. Rev. 365 (1964)

Reg. § 1.213–1(e)(iii)
John Riach, 302 F.2d 374 (9th Cir. 1962)
Raymon Gerard, 37 TC 826 (1962) (Acq.)
Karlis A. Pols, 24 TCM 1140 (1965)

Air conditioning device
Rev. Rul. 55–261, 1955 CB 307

Removal of lead-based paint
Rev. Rul. 79–66, 1979–1 CB 114

Special bathroom in rented house
Rev. Rul. 70–395, 1970–2 CB 65

Operating costs
Reg. § 1.213(e)(iii)

Swimming pool
Rev. Rul. 83–33 1983–1 CB 70
Collins H. Ferris, 36 TCM 765 (1977), rev'd, 582 F.2d 1112 (7th Cir. 1978)

Buying house with pool
Paul A. Lerew, 44 TCM 918 (1982)

Pool as personal convenience
C. W. Haines, 71 TC 257 (1979)

Handicap exception for ramps, etc.
Conference Committee Report to P.L. 99–514, Act Sec. 133

¶17.14 • COSTS DEDUCTIBLE AS BUSINESS EXPENSES

Medical checkup for job
Rev. Rul. 58–382, 1958–2 CB 59

Throat specialist fee
Rev. Rul. 71–45, 1971–1 CB 51

Services for physically handicapped
Rev. Rul. 75–317, 1975–2 CB 57

Psychoanalysis for social worker
Harry H. Voigt, 74 TC 82 (1980) (Nonacq.)

Spouse accompanying diabetic on business trips
Robert L. Quinn, 77–1 USTC ¶9369 (D. Md. 1977)

Therapy for psychiatrist
Kenneth Porter, TC Memo 1986–70

Note: Paragraph numbers refer to Part One. Items marked * are research aids, not citations of authority; see "Key to Citations" on page 337.

¶ 18

Casualty and Theft Losses and Involuntary Conversion Gains

¶18.2 • DEDUCTIBLE PERSONAL CASUALTY AND THEFT LOSSES

*"The Casualty Loss Deduction," C. C. Pinkerton, 2 Taxation for Accountants 205 (1967)

*"Tax Aspects of Insurance Recoveries for Casualty Losses," W. F. Gleason, Jr., 24 NYU Inst. 489 (1966)

*"How to Prove Casualty Loss Deductions in the Face of Tough Service Attitude," S. Braverman, 22 Journal of Taxation 235 (1965)

*"Casualty Losses," S. A. Champagne, 13 Tulane Tax Inst. 445 (1964)

*"Casualties and Disaster Losses are Deductible: The Do's and Don'ts," J. Rabin, 1964 So. Calif. Tax Inst. 463

*"Nonbusiness Casualty Losses," John N. Kamp, 15 Tax Adviser 289 (May 1984)
*IRS Publication 547

Casualty losses
IRC § 165(c)(3)
Reg. § 1.165–7
Hugh M. Matheson Exr., 54 F.2d 537 (2d Cir. 1931)

10% adjusted gross income floor
IRC § 165(h), as added by § 203(a) of Pub. L. No. 97–248

Great Lakes high water level
Rev. Rul. 76–134, 1976–1 CB 54

Water damage to wall paper
Rupert Stuart, 20 TCM 938 (1961)

Termites
E. G. Kilroe, 32 TC 1304 (1959) (Nonacq.)
Alan M. Winsor, 18 TCM 383 (1959), aff'd, 278 F.2d 634 (1st Cir. 1960)
Rev. Rul. 63–232, 1963–2 CB 97

Southern pine beetle
Paul W. Black, 36 TCM 1347 (1977)
Herbert Nelson, 27 TCM 158 (1968)
Rev. Rul. 79–174, 1979–1 CB 99

Foreseeable damage
Jack R. Farber, 57 TC 714 (1972) (Acq.)
Harry Heyn, 46 TC 714 (1966) (Acq.)

Ring destroyed by disposal unit
William H. Carpenter, 25 TCM 965 (1966)

Ring destroyed by closing of door
John P. White, 48 TC 430 (1967) (Acq.)

Diamond unexplainedly lost
Theodore R. Kielts, 42 TCM 238 (1981)

Fire loss, damage, destruction
IRC § 165
Reg. § 1.165–7

Judgment paid by tenant
Rev. Rul. 73–41, 1973–1 CB 74

Automobile
Tracy V. Buckwalter, 20 BTA 1005, aff'd, 61 F.2d 571 (6th Cir. 1932)

Furniture and home
E. C. O'Rear, 80 F.2d 473 (6th Cir. 1935)
W. B. Brooks, 12 BTA 31, aff'd, 35 F.2d 178 (4th Cir. 1929)

Hurricane
Alfred M. Hickman, 207 F.2d 460 (4th Cir. 1953)
Willard T. Burkett, 10 TCM 948 (1951)

Tornado
Richard E. Stein, 14 TCM 191 (1955)

Heavy rains
Clarence E. Stewart, 12 TCM 921 (1953)

Lightning
S. F. Horn, 18 TCM 177 (1959)

Floods
W. M. Ferguson, 59 F.2d 893 (10th Cir. 1933)
E. T. Hutchings, 41–2 USTC ¶9673 (D. Ky. 1941)

Storms
Webb, 1 BTA 759
Robert B. Honeyman Jr., BTA Memo. P-H 39,021

Landslides
W. K. Stowers, 169 F. Supp. 246 (D. Miss. 1959)

Smog
Rev. Rul. 71–560, 1971–2 CB 126

Drought
Frank Buttram, 87 F. Supp. 322 (D. Okl. 1943)
Rev. Rul. 66–303, 1966–2 CB 55
Rev. Rul. 54–85, 1954–1 CB 58
Norman H. Ruecker, 41 TCM 1587 (1981)

Dust storms
R. F. Barry, 175 F. Supp. 308 (D. Okl. 1959)

Poor construction
Irving J. Hayutin, 31 TCM 509 (1972), aff'd, 508 F.2d 462 (10th Cir. 1975)

Shipwreck
IRC § 165(c)(3)
Edward H. R. Green, 19 BTA 904

Sinking of land
Harry Johnston Grant, 30 BTA 1028 (Acq.)

Tidal wave
M. A. Ferst, 129 F. Supp. 606 (D. Ga. 1955)
Rev. Rul. 76–134, 1976–1 CB 54

Disturbances below earth's surface
Harry Johnston Grant, 30 BTA 1028 (Acq.)

Ice pressure
Paul E. Jackson, 13 TCM 1175 (1954)
Seward City Mills, 44 BTA 173

Underground water
Delbert P. Hesler, 13 TCM 972 (1954)

Car falling through ice
Rev. Rul. 69–88, 1969–1 CB 58

Ice damage
Sherman L. Whipple, 25 F.2d 520 (D. Mass. 1928)
Richard R. Hollington, 15 TCM 668 (1956)
Frederick H. Nash, 22 BTA 482 (Acq.)

Cave-ins
W. K. Stowers, 169 F. Supp. 246 (D. Miss. 1959)
Harry Johnston Grant, 30 BTA 1028 (Acq.)

Quarry blast
Ray Durden, 3 TC 1 (1944)(Acq.)

Severe winter blizzard
Emory M. Nourse, 73 F. Supp. 70 (D. Iowa 1947)

Vandals
Burrell E. Davis, 34 TC 586 (1960) (Acq.)

Rentals for temporary living quarters
Rev. Rul. 59–398, 1959–2 CB 76

Do not have to repair
IRS Publication No. 155

Note: Paragraph numbers refer to Part One. Items marked * are research aids, not citations of authority; see "Key to Citations" on page 337.

Potential buyer's resistance
Harvey Pulvers, 48 TC 245 (1967), aff'd per curiam, 407 F.2d 838 (9th Cir. 1969)
Lewis F. Ford, 33 TCM 496 (1974)
Charles W. P. Kamanski, 29 TCM 1702 (1970), aff'd, 477 F.2d 452 (9th Cir. 1973)

Insurance proceeds
IRC § 165
Reg. § 1.165–1(c)(4)

Adjuster's fee
Ben R. Stein, 31 TCM 663 (1971), aff'd and remanded in unpublished opinion (7th Cir. March 4, 1974)

Voluntary payments from employer
Rev. Rul. 53–131, 1953–2 CB 112, ·distinguished by Rev. Rul. 57–1, 1957–1 CB 15 and Rev. Rul. 64–329, 1964–2 CB 463

Gifts from friends
Rev. Rul. 64–329, 1964–2 CB 58

Jointly owned property
J. H. Anderson, 7 TCM 811 (1948)

Legal life estate
Katherine Bliss, 27 TC 770 (1957) (Acq.), rev'd, 256 F.2d 533 (2d Cir. 1958)

Latent effects not considered
Leonard J. Jenard, 20 TCM 346 (1961)

Decrease in value of land
Bessie Knapp, 23 TC 716 (1955) (Acq.)

Cost less depreciation
Edmund W. Cornelius, 56 TC 976 (1971)(Acq.)
Myron E. Cherry, 26 TCM 556 (1967)

Market value based on inventory
Loy L. Stone, 31 TCM 1042 (1972)

Damage to trees, shrubs, etc.
John M. Winters Jr., 58–1 USTC ¶9205 (D. Okl. 1958), rev'd on other grounds, 261 F.2d 675 (10th Cir. 1959), cert. denied, 359 U.S. 943
Bessie Knapp, 23 TC 716 (1955) (Acq.)

Subsoil shrinkage during drought
Rev. Rul. 54–85, 1954–1 CB 58

Wreck caused by icy road
George L. Shearer, 16 F.2d 995 (2d Cir. 1927)

Collision caused by faulty driving
Reg. § 1.165–7(a)(3)
Elwood J. Clark, 5 TCM 236 (1946), aff'd, 158 F.2d 851 (6th Cir. 1947)

Lawn damage caused by careless use of weed killer
Jack R. Farber, 57 TC 714 (1972) (Acq.)

Defending suit for damages
L. Oransky, 1 BTA 1239

Sonic boom
Rev. Rul. 60–329, 1960–2 CB 67

Property used by dependent
Thomas J. Draper, 15 TC 135 (1950)
Howard Scharf, 32 TCM 1281 (1973), rem'd per curiam, 76–1 USTC ¶9330 (4th Cir. 1976)

Highwater levels
Rev. Rul. 75–134, 1975–1 CB 33

Preventative measures nondeductible
Cade L. Austin, 74 TC 1334 (1980)

Buyer resistance
George W. Finkbohner, Jr., CA–11, 5/6/86.

¶18.3 • WHO MAY CLAIM THE LOSS DEDUCTION

Separate return
Robert M. Loewenstein, 27 TCM 1112 (1968)
Rev. Rul. 75–347, 1975–2 CB 70

Lessee
IRS Publication 17, 1980 ed.

No deduction for cost of repairing rented car
J. Gill, 34 TCM 10 (1975)

Corporate shareholder
Drew Jensen, 39 TCM 163 (1979)

¶18.4 • PROVING A CASUALTY LOSS
IRS Publication No. 155

Appraisal upheld
Doyle E. Collup, 21 TCM 128 (1962)

Auto bluebook
Gus S. Caras, 23 TCM 1103 (1964)

Clean-up expenses
Ralph Walton, 20 TCM 653 (1961)

Dealer's estimate of trade-in not evidence
Gus S. Caras, 23 TCM 1103 (1964)

Fire damage
John Pfalzgraf, 67 TC 784 (1977) (Acq.)

Inventories of property destroyed by fire sustained loss
Loy L. Stone, 31 TCM 1042 (1972)

¶18.5 • THEFT LOSSES
Reg. § 1.165–8

Necessity of proving cost
Jane V. Elliott, 40 TC 304 (1963) (Acq.)
Stanley J. Prescott, 28 TCM 435 (1969)

Must prove property was stolen
Paul Bakewell Jr., 23 TC 803 (1955)
Mary F. Allen, 16 TC 163 (1951)
John L. Seymour, 14 TC 1111 (1950)
Edna M. Oatis, 6 TCM 569 (1947)

State law determines if theft committed
Arthur C. Bromberg, Exr., 232 F.2d 107 (5th Cir. 1956)

Locked valuable pin in compartment
Warner L. Jones, 24 TC 525 (1955) (Acq.)

Report to police
James W. Thomas, 12 TCM 41 (1953)
Henrietta Sava-Goiu, 9 TCM 128 (1950)

Allowed even though not reported
Robert W. Jorg, 52 TC 288 (1969) (Acq.)
Frederick C. Moser, 18 TCM 116 (1959)

Year reported
Reg. § 1.165–1(d)(3)
Reg. § 1.165–8
Virginia M. Cramer, 55 TC 1125 (1971) (Acq.)

Cannot recover property
Henry Kraft Mercantile Co., 14 TCM 833 (1955)

Legal fee
Katherine Ander, 47 TC 592 (1967)

Appraisal value on stamp collection
Max P. Engel, 31 TCM 1223 (1972)

Building contractor absconded
Thomas Miller, 19 TC 1046 (1953) (Acq.)
Allen Hartley, 26 TCM 1281 (1977)

Contractor runs out of money
Otis B. Kent, 12 TCM 1491 (1953)

Additional money to correct defects
IRC § 1016(a)(1)
Reg. § 1.1016–2

Payments to subcontractor
Evelyn Nell Norton, 40 TC 500 (1963)(Acq.), aff'd, 333 F.2d 1005 (9th Cir. 1964)

Theft of trees
Ella Gene Raberge, 20 TCM 1490 (1961)

Embezzlement losses
Mary O. Alsop, 34 TC 606 (1960), aff'd, 290 F.2d 726 (2d Cir. 1961)

Embezzlement not cause of bank depositor's loss
Rev. Rul. 77–383, 1977–2 CB 66

Worthless stock
Paul C. Vietzke, 37 TC 504 (1961) (Acq.)

Illegal sale of unregistered stock not a theft loss
Carroll J. Bellis, 61 TC 453 (1973), aff'd, 540 F.2d 448 (9th Cir. 1976)

Confiscated personal property
William J. Powers, 36 TC 1191 (1961)

Loss from tax avoidance scheme based on fraudulent statements of advisor
Perry A. Nichols et al., 43 TC 842 (1965)(Nonacq.)

Ransom payment
Rev. Rul. 72–113, 1972–1 CB 99

Note: Paragraph numbers refer to Part One. Items marked * are research aids, not citations of authority; see "Key to Citations" on page 337.

Expenses of recovering abducted child nondeductible
Ebrahim Otmishi, 41 TCM 237 (1980)

Seizure of car by creditors
Robert V. Rafter, 489 F.2d 752 (2d Cir. 1974), cert. denied, 419 U.S. 826

Payment for forged divorce decree deductible
*Letter Ruling 8146030

¶18.6 • RIOT LOSSES ARE DEDUCTIBLE

Vandalism
Ann E. Lattimore, 63–1 USTC ¶9485 (N.D. Cal. 1963), rev'd, 353 F.2d 379 (9th Cir. 1966)
Charles Gutwirth, 40 TC 666 (1963) (Acq.)
Burrell E. Davis, 34 TC 586 (1960) (Acq.)

Riot damage
IRC § 165(c)(3) and (e)

Perishable food discarded
Rev. Rul. 69–354, 1969–1 CB 58

¶18.7 • FIGURING YOUR LOSS

IRC § 165
Reg. § 1.165–7

10% adjusted gross income limit
IRC § 165(h)

$100 floor
Reg. § 1.165–7(b)(4)

Proof of cost
Donald Owens, 305 U.S. 468
Hal Millsap Jr., 46 TC 751 (1966) (Acq.), aff'd 387 F.2d 420 (8th Cir. 1968)

Separate computation for each item
Rev. Rul. 66–50, 1966–1 CB 40

Effect of divorce on community property
Armore L. Kamins, 54 TC 977 (1970)

Loss of records in fire no bar
John Pfalzgraf, Jr., 67 TC 784 (1977)(Acq.)

¶18.8 • REPAIRS MAY BE "MEASURE OF LOSS"

Cost of repairs
Reg. § 1.165–7(a)(2)(ii)
S. P. Keith, Jr., 52 TC 41 (1969) (Acq.)

Estimated repairs not measure of loss
Claire E. Lamphere, 70 TC 391 (1978)(Acq.)
Venancio A. Bagnol, 37 TCM 1038 (1978)

Repairs, though not made, may affect post-casualty value
Paul Abrams, 41 TCM 1459 (1981)

Loss of value exceeds repair costs
George E. Conner, 439 F.2d 974 (5th Cir. 1971)

Anne Marie Hagerty, 34 TCM 356 (1975)

¶18.9 • INSURANCE REIMBURSEMENTS

Reimbursements reduce loss
IRC § 165(a)

Disaster relief
Rev. Rul. 76–144, 1976–1 CB 17

Relocation Act payments
Paul J. Smith, 76 TC 459 (1981) (Acq.)

Insurance claim must be filed: 1986 Tax Act
IRC § 165(h)(4)(E)

Failure to make insurance claim pre-1986 Tax Act
David Axelrod, 56 TC 248 (1971)
F. T. Morgan, 37 TCM 524 (1978)
IRS Publication No. 17, 1980 ed.

Deduction allowed despite failure to make claim
Henry L. Hill, 76 TC 484 (1981), aff'd 691 F.2d 997 (1st Cir. 1982)

¶18.10 • HOW THE $100 FLOOR IS APPLIED

Reg. § 1.165–7(b)(4)

¶18.11 • WHEN TO DEDUCT YOUR CASUALTY LOSS

Reimbursement expected
Reg. § 1.165–1(d)
Arthur T. Davidson, 34 TCM 1010 (1975)

Year in which insurance company denies liability is not controlling
Louis Gale, 41 TC 269 (1963)

Flood loss deducted year claim settled
Earl Callan, 235 F.2d 190 (9th Cir. 1956)

Unseasonable blizzard
Emory M. Nourse, 73 F. Supp. 70 (D. Iowa 1947)

Hurricane damage
Willard T. Burkett, 10 TCM 948 (1951)

Loss allowed in year of drought not later year of discovery
Alfred M. Cox, 24 TCM 23 (1965), aff'd per curiam, 354 F.2d 659 (3d Cir. 1966)

Swimming pool
Donald H. Kunsman, 49 TC 62 (1967)

Tax benefit rule
John E. Montgomery, 65 TC 511 (1975)

¶18.12 • DISASTER LOSSES

IRC § 165(h)
Reg. § 1.165–11
Chester Matheson, 74 TC 834 (1980)(Acq. in results only)

Relocation or demolition of house
IRC § 165(k)

¶18.13 • DEDUCTING DAMAGE TO YOUR CAR

Damage to car deductible
Reg. § 1.165–7(a)(3)

No deduction for litigation and settlement expenses
Alexandre R. Tarsey, 56 TC 44 (1971)

Using car on business
Forest Anderson, 81 F.2d 457 (10th Cir. 1936), rev'g 30 BTA 597

Accident between two locations of same business deductible as business expense
Harold Dancer, 73 TC 1103 (1980)

Accident occurring during trip between different jobs nondeductible as business expense
Julian D. Freedman, 35 TC 1179 (1961), aff'd, 301 F.2d 359 (5th Cir. 1962)

Accident costs while commuting nondeductible business expense
Eldon Hall, 41 TCM 282 (1981), aff'd in unpublished opinion (1st Cir. 1981)

Race car
*Letter Ruling 8227010

Deduction allowed only for uninsured losses
Emanuel Hollman, 38 TC 251 (1962)

Damage to engine—not deductible
Emil Wold, 22 TCM 732 (1963)
Lyle W. Mader, 25 TCM 917 (1966)

Towing costs are not deductible
Virginia M. Cramer, 55 TC 1125 (1971)(Acq.)

Car in child's name
Frank W. Oman, 30 TCM 767 (1971)

Damage to rented car
Robert M. Miller, 34 TCM 528 (1975)

¶18.14 • DAMAGE TO TREES AND SHRUBS

Shrubbery
Reg. § 1.165–7(b)(2)

Tree loss
David W. Murray Jr., 20 TCM 7 (1962)

Casualty losses for property
Reg. § 1.165–7
IRS Publication No. 155

Cost of replacing trees
Rev. Rul. 68–29, 1968–1 CB 74

Cost of removing infested trees
Anthony B. Cristo, 44 TCM 1057 (1982)

Winter freeze in Florida
Ben R. Thebaut Jr., 47 TCM 401 (1983)

¶18.15 • NONDEDUCTIBLE LOSSES

Termite damage
Umit Sahkul, 29 TCM 260 (1970)
Rev. Rul. 63–232, 1963–2 CB 97

Note: Paragraph numbers refer to Part One. Items marked * are research aids, not citations of authority; see "Key to Citations" on page 337.

Carpet beetles
J. Peter Meersman, 370 F.2d 109 (6th Cir. 1967)

Dry rot
Rudolph Lewis Hoppe, 42 TC 820 (1964), aff'd, 354 F.2d 988 (9th Cir. 1966)
Worth Rowley, 38 TCM 1297 (1979), aff'd in unpublished opinion (D.C. Cir. 1981)

Personal injuries
Karl Stern, 199 F. Supp. 488 (D. Ohio 1954)
Samuel E. Mulholland, 16 BTA 1331
B. M. Peyton, 10 BTA 1129

Legal expenses in defending suit
L. Oransky, 1 BTA 1239

Personal property wrongfully seized
Fred J. Hughes, 1 BTA 944

Temporary quarters
Rev. Rul. 59–398, 1959–2 CB 76

Personal property lost in storage or transit
Guy I. Rowe, 3 BTA 1228
W. W. Bercaw, 6 TCM 27 (1947), aff'd, 165 F.2d 521 (4th Cir. 1948)

Passenger's luggage lost
Mildred Bauman, 10 TCM 31 (1951)

Accidental loss of ring
Edgar F. Stevens, 6 TCM 805 (1947)

Joint property taken by wife
Grover Tyler, 13 TC 186 (1949) (Acq.)

Loss of dog
Waddell F. Smith, 10 TC 701 (1948)

Damage to crop by insects
Rev. Rul. 57–599, 1957–2 CB 142

Excavation on adjoining property
Daniel F. Ebbert, 9 BTA 1402

Rust of understructure of house
Hugh M. Matheson Exr., 54 F.2d 537 (2d Cir. 1931), aff'g 18 BTA 674

Moth damage
Rev. Rul. 55–327, 1955–1 CB 25

Dry well
James I. Goski, 24 TCM 828 (1965)
Charles E. Springer, 16 TCM 1075 (1957)

Natural phenomena
Texas & Pacific Railway Co., 1 TCM 863 (1943)

Damage to library book
Luther Ely Smith, 3 TC (1944) (Acq. in part, nonacq. in part)

Death of saddle horse
David McMorran, BTA Memo. P–H 39,117

Damage to watch
Williard Thompson, 15 TC 609 (1950), rev'd and rem'd on other grounds, 193 F.2d 586 (10th Cir. 1952)

Jack Ward, 11 TCM 340 (1952)

Drop in securities
Reg. § 1.165–1(d)
Adams, 1 BTA 985
Chicago Railway Equipment Co., 4 BTA 452 (Acq.), aff'd and rev'd in part, 39 F.2d 378 (7th Cir. 1930), rev'd, 282 U.S. 295 (1931)
E. O. Walgren, 4 BTA 1066
W. P. Davis, 6 BTA 1267

Loss due to illness
Jones, BTA Memo. P–H 42,324

Loss of contingent interest
Lillian S. Procter, 19 TC 387 (1952)

Improper police seizure
Fred J. Hughes, 1 BTA 944

Chinaware upset by pet
Robert M. Diggs, 18 TCM 443 (1959), aff'd, 281 F.2d 326 (2d Cir. 1960), cert. denied, 364 U.S. 908
J. Raymond Dyer, 36 TCM 456 (1961) (Acq.)

Temporary fluctuation
Clarence A. Peterson, 30 TC 660 (1958)

Dutch elm disease
Howard F. Burns, 284 F.2d 436 (6th Cir. 1961)
John Alan Appleman, 338 F.2d 729 (7th Cir. 1964), cert. denied, 380 U.S. 956
Arthur Coleman, 76 TC 580 (1981)

Lethal yellowing disease
John A. Maher, 76 TC 593 (1981), aff'd, 680 F.2d 91 (11th Cir. 1982)

Horse eats tree bark
Rev. Rul. 73–123, 1973–1 CB 76

¶18.16 • DO YOUR CASUALTY LOSSES EXCEED YOUR INCOME?

Carryback of losses
IRC § 172
Reg. § 1.172–1
Reg. § 1.172–3(b)

¶18.17 • HOW TO DEDUCT YOUR CASUALTY AND THEFT LOSSES

IRC § 1231
Reg. § 1.1231–1

Appraisal fees
IRS Publication 17, 1980 ed.

¶18.18 • EXCESS LIVING COSTS PAID BY INSURANCE ARE NOT TAXABLE

IRC § 123
Reg. § 1.123–1

¶18.19 • BANK DEPOSIT LOSSES

IRC § 165(l)

¶18.20 • GAINS FROM INVOLUNTARY CONVERSIONS

"A Review of the Tax Aspects of Property Condemnations," C. En-

gler, 36 New York Certified Public Accountant 593 (1966)

"The Tax Factor in Insurance. Recovery," B. M. Ablon, 5 Oklahoma CPA 27 (1966)

"How to Treat Involuntary Conversions," B. Greisman, Lasser's Income Tax Techniques, Chap. 39

"Recognizing Gain from an Involuntary Conversion May Result in Greater Tax Benefits Than Deferred," Barbara T. Olson, 28 Taxation for Accountants 88 (Feb. 1982)

"Planning for Real Estate Condemnation Awards in Light of Recent Favorable Rulings," Charles E. Falbe and William E. Singer, 59 J. Taxation 400 (December 1983)

¶18.21 • INVOLUNTARY CONVERSIONS QUALIFYING FOR TAX DEFERRAL ELECTION

What is an involuntary conversion?
IRC § 1033
Reg. § 1.1033(a)–1

Threat of condemnation by government employee
Frank O. Maixner, 33 TC 191 (1959) (Acq.)
Carson Estate Co., 22 TCM 425 (1963)

Voluntary sale
Harry G. Masser, 30 TC 741 (1958) (Acq.)
Rev. Rul. 59–361, 1959–2 CB 183
Rev. Rul. 63–221, 1963–2 CB 332

Condemnation as unfit for habitation
Rev. Rul. 57–314, 1957–2 CB 523

Threat of building code violation not sufficient
Thorpe Glass Mfg. Corp., 51 TC 300 (1968)

Farmers—irrigation project
Reg. § 1.1033(d)–1

Sale to private party after governmental threat of conversion
Creative Solutions, Inc., 320 F.2d 809 (5th Cir. 1963)

Identity of threatening authority not disclosed
Rev. Rul. 74–8, 1974–2 CB 200

Tax sale
Rev. Rul. 77–370, 1977–2 CB 306

Cattle diseased
Reg. § 1.1033(e)–1

Livestock sales due to drought
IRC § 1033(e)
Reg. § 1.1033(f)–1

Gain on involuntary conversion
IRC § 1033
Reg. § 1.1033(a)–1 and 2
Russel C. Smith, 59 TC 107 (1972)

Advance payment of award
Stewart & Co., 57 TC 122 (1971)

Note: Paragraph numbers refer to Part One. Items marked * are research aids, not citations of authority; see "Key to Citations" on page 337.

Contested award
Conlorez Corp., 51 TC 467 (1968) (Acq.)
Harry D. Aldridge, 51 TC 475 (1968)
Casalina Co., 60 TC 694 (1973) (Acq.), aff'd per curiam, 511 F.2d 1162 (4th Cir. 1975)

¶18.22 • HOW TO ELECT TO DEFER TAX

Election irrevocable
John McShain, 65 TC 686 (1976)

Dissolution of partnership not termination
Morton Fuchs, 80 TC 506 (1983)

¶18.23 • TIME PERIOD FOR BUYING REPLACEMENT PROPERTY

Three-year replacement for condemned realty
IRC § 1033(g)(4)

Estate makes replacement
John E. Morris Est. 55 TC 636 (1971), aff'd per curiam, 454 F.2d 208 (4th Cir. 1972)
Isaac Goodman Est., 199 F.2d 895 (3d Cir. 1952)
Rev. Rul. 64–161, 1964–1 (Pt. 1) CB 298

Investment by widow
George W. Jayne Est., 61 TC 744 (1974)

Must report details of replacement
Reg. § 1.1033(a)–2(c)(2)

File for refund
Reg. § 1.1033(a)–2(c)(2)

¶18.24 • CHARACTER OF REPLACEMENT PROPERTY

Like-kind test
IRC § 1033(g)
Reg. § 1.1031(a)–1(b)

Related use—court rule
Liant Record Inc., 303 F.2d 326

(2d Cir. 1963), on rem'd, 22 TCM 203 (1963)
Clifton Investment Co., 312 F.2d 719 (6th Cir. 1963), cert. denied, 373 U.S. 921
Loco Realty Co., 306 F.2d 207 (8th Cir. 1962)
Thomas McCaffrey Jr., 275 F.2d 27 (2d Cir. 1960), cert. denied, 6/20/60
Steuart Bros., Inc., 261 F.2d 580 (4th Cir. 1959)
Arnold L. Santucci, 32 TCM 840 (1973)
Rev. Rul. 64–237, 1964–2 CB 319

Replacement of rental house by residence does not qualify
Rev. Rul. 76–84, 1976–1 CB 219

Contract to buy does not qualify
Herrick L. Johnston Est., 51 TC 290 (1968), aff'd, 430 F.2d 1019 (6th Cir. 1970)

Purchase of leasehold of at least 30 years
Rev. Rul. 68–392, 1968–2 CB 338

¶18.25 • INVESTMENT IN REPLACEMENT PROPERTY

Replacement
IRC § 1033(a)(3)(B)(i)
Reg. § 1.1033(a)–2(b) and (c)
Rev. Rul. 70–466, 1970–2 CB 165, amplified by Rev. Rul. 76–84, 1976–1 CB 219
John E. Morris Est., 55 TC 636 (1971), aff'd per curiam, 454 F.2d 208 (4th Cir. 1972)

Replacement of livestock—environmental contamination
IRC § 1033(f)

Payments to mortgagee
Reg. § 1.1033(a)–2(c)(1)
Frank W. Babcock, 28 TC 781 (1957)(Nonacq.), aff'd, 259 F.2d 689 (9th Cir. 1958)

Fortee Properties, Inc., 211 F.2d 915 (2d Cir. 1954), cert. denied, 348 U.S. 826

Real property
IRC § 1033(g)

Greater replacement cost
Reg. § 1.1033(c)–2(c)

Insurance proceeds allocated
Rev. Rul. 70–501, 1970–2 CB 163

¶18.26 • HOW TO TREAT SPECIAL ASSESSMENTS AND SEVERANCE DAMAGES

Must allocate or entire award is payment for condemnation
Seaside Improvement Co., 105 F.2d 990 (2d Cir. 1938), cert. denied, 308 U.S. 618
Marshall C. Allaben, 35 BTA 327

Allocation allowed although not fixed in award
L. A. Beeghly, 36 TC 111 (1961) (Acq. in result only)
Rev. Rul. 64–183, 1964–1 (Pt. 1) CB 297

Special assessment
Rev. Rul. 68–37, 1967–1 CB 359

Allocation to purchase of nonadjacent property
Rev. Rul. 72–433, 1972–2 CB 470
John L. McKitrick, 373 F. Supp. 471 (D. Ohio 1974)

IRS computation method
IRS Publication No. 549

Severance damage gain deferred by like kind investment
Rev. Rul. 83–49 1983–1 CB 191

¶18.27 • IF YOU HAVE GAINS AND LOSSES FROM CASUALTIES AND THEFTS

IRC § 165(h)(2)(B)

¶19
Deducting Miscellaneous Expenses

¶19.1 • NEW TWO PERCENT FLOOR

IRC § 67(a)

¶19.3 • DEDUCTING JOB EXPENSES NOT SUBJECT TO FLOOR

IRC § 162(a)
IRC § 212
IRC § 62
IRC § 67(b)

Performing artists
IRC § 62(a)(2)(B)
IRC § 62(b)

¶19.5 • BUSINESS ASSOCIATION AND UNION DUES

Professional society
Henry P. Keith, 1 TCM 184 (1942), aff'd, 139 F.2d 596 (2d Cir. 1944)
Kenneth Blanchard, 12 TCM 550 (1953)

Trade association
Robert S. LeSage, 6 TCM 1263 (1947), aff'd in part and rev'd in part on other issues, 173 F.2d 826 (5th Cir. 1949)

Stock exchange
Charles E. Robertson, 1 BTA 501 (Acq.)

Community "booster" club
Security-First National Bank of Los Angeles, BTA Memo., February 27, 1934

Chamber of Commerce
Smith-Bridgman & Co., 16 TC 287 (1951)(Acq.)
Jeff Rubin, 13 TCM 1094 (1954)

Note: Paragraph numbers refer to Part One. Items marked * are research aids, not citations of authority; see "Key to Citations" on page 337.

Union membership
George A. Tatum Jr., 10 TCM 602 (1951)
Rev. Rul. 54–190, 1954–1 CB 46

Union building fund nondeductible
Carl Briggs, 75 TC 465 (1980), aff'd, 694 F.2d 614 (9th Cir. 1983)
Kenneth M. Ridder, 76 TC 867 (1981)

Union election costs
James P. Carey, 56 TC 477 (1971) (Acq.), aff'd per curiam, 460 F.2d 1259 (4th Cir. 1972), cert. denied, 409 U.S. 990

Union assessments for old age fund
Rev. Rul. 54–190, 1954–1 CB 46

Service charge to nonunion members
Rev. Rul. 68–82, 1968–1 CB 68

Union dues
Rev. Rul. 72–463, 1972–2 CB 93

¶19.6 • EXPENSES FOR UNIFORMS AND WORK CLOTHES

Protective clothing
Oron R. Morgan, 80 F. Supp. 537 (D. Tex. 1948)
Louis M. Roth, 17 TC 1450 (1952) (Acq.)
Lewis F. Cooper, 12 TCM 471 (1953)
T. G. Frazier, Jr., 12 TCM 1129 (1953)

Overalls
Louis M. Roth, 17 TC 1450 (1952) (Acq.)
O. G. Russell, 12 TCM 1276 (1953)

Harder use than customary garments
Louis Drill, 8 TC 902 (1947)

Soiled after day's work
Louis M. Roth, 17 TC 1450 (1952) (Acq.)

Plumber
Vern W. Pratt, 11 TCM 335 (1952)

Sanitation inspector
C. W. Strickler, 11 TCM 252 (1952)

Machinist's helper
Carl E. Noe, 11 TCM 431 (1952)

Carpenter
E. M. Taylor, 11 TCM 651 (1952)
Roy J. Coffman, 16 TCM 353 (1957)

Telephone repairman
John Young, 11 TCM 239 (1952)

Painter
Rev. Rul. 57–143, 1957–1 CB 89

Airline pilots' uniforms
Dean L. Phillips, 9 TCM 501 (1950)

Nurse
Helen K. Harsaghy, 2 TC 484 (1943) (Acq.)
Floyd Gilbert Bickel, II, 25 TCM 1037 (1966)

State highway patrol officer
Marcus O. Benson, 146 F.2d 191 (9th Cir. 1945)

Bakery salesman
Bennie Blatt, 6 TCM 94 (1947)
Marshall J. Hammons, 12 TCM 1318 (1953)

Cement finisher
Williard Thompson, 15 TC 609 (1950) (Acq. in part, nonacq. in part), rev'd and rem'd on other grounds, 193 F.2d 586 (10th Cir. 1952)

Commercial fisherman
Rev. Rul. 55–235, 1955–1 CB 274

Dairy worker
Ben A. Puente, 10 TCM 735 (1951), aff'd without discussion, 199 F.2d 940 (9th Cir. 1952)

Factory foreman's white coat and safety shoes
Oron R. Morgan, 80 F. Supp. 537 (D. Tex. 1948)

Hospital attendant
Oliver W. Bryant, 11 TCM 430 (1952)

Musician's formal wear
Wilson J. Fisher, 23 TC 218 (1954) (Acq. in part), aff'd on other issue, 230 F.2d 79 (7th Cir. 1956)

Paint machine operator
T. G. Frazier, Jr., 12 TCM 1129 (1953)

Plumber's special shoes and gloves
Lewis F. Cooper, 12 TCM 471 (1953)

Railroad fireman
O. G. Russell, 11 TCM 334 (1952)
O. G. Russell, 12 TCM 1276 (1953)

Fashion expert's clothing deductible
Betsy L. Yeomans, 30 TC 757 (1958) (Acq.)

Boutique manager's clothes nondeductible
Barry Pevsner, 38 TCM 1210 (1979), rev'd, 628 F.2d 467 (5th Cir. 1980)

Women's slacks
Oron R. Morgan, 80 F. Supp. 537 (D. Tex. 1948)

Dirty clothes a hazard
Elwood J. Clark, 158 F.2d 851 (6th Cir. 1947), aff'g per curiam 5 TCM 236 (1946)

Clothes worn at work only
Oliver W. Bryant, 11 TCM 430 (1952)

Allowance is taxable
Rev. Rul. 72–110, 1972–1 CB 24

¶19.7 • SMALL TOOLS

Substantiation of tool costs
Donald F. McGraw, 35 TCM 1016 (1976)
Ion Z. Josan, 33 TCM 645 (1974)
Harlan White, 33 TCM 652 (1974)

Hand held calculator deductible
Robert G. Galazin, 38 TCM 851 (1979)

Reimbursements
Rev. Rul. 75–497, 1975–2 CB 29

¶19.8 • EXPENSES OF LOOKING FOR A JOB

Rev. Rul. 75–120, 1975–1 CB 55, clarified by Rev. Rul. 77–16, 1977–1 CB 37

CPA forms partnership
Howard L. Cormutt, 45 TCM 515 (1983)

Tax Court decisions
David J. Primuth, 54 TC 374 (1970) (Acq.)
Leonard F. Cremona, 58 TC 219 (1972) (Acq.)

Remained at same position
Kenneth R. Kenfield, 54 TC 1197 (1970)

Reimbursement of fees
Rev. Rul. 66–41, 1966–1 CB 233, distinguished by Rev. Rul. 73–351, 1973–2 CB 323

Payment of fee by employer
Rev. Rul. 73–351, 1973–2 CB 323

Company interested in your services
Rev. Rul. 63–77, 1963–1 CB 177

Former customers entertained
Harold Haft, 40 TC 2 (1963) (Acq.)

¶19.9 • UNUSUAL JOB EXPENSES

Shoe shine costs
Robert C. Fryer, 33 TCM 122 (1974)

Lobbying
James M. Jordan, 60 TC 770 (1973) (Acq.)

Depreciation on furnishings
LeRoy Gillis, 32 TCM 429 (1973)

Cost of meal assessments
Robert E. Cooper, 67 TC 870 (1977) (Nonacq.)

Executive's purchase of blazers
Norman L. Jetty, 44 TCM 373 (1982)

Repayment of lay off benefits
Rev. Rul. 82–178, 1982–2 CB 59

Salesman's private plan
William F. Sherman, Jr. 44 TCM 1324 (1982)

Job dismissal insurance
*Letter Ruling 8321074

Public officials
Rev. Rul. 84–110, 1984–2 CB 35

¶19.10 • HOME OFFICE EXPENSES OF EMPLOYEES

IRC § 280A

Violinist's studio not principal place of business
Ernest Drucker, 715 F.2d (2d Cir. 1983) rev'g 79 TC 605 (1982)

Professor's home office
David J. Weissman, 751 F.2d 512 (CA-2 1985)

Note: Paragraph numbers refer to Part One. Items marked * are research aids, not citations of authority; see "Key to Citations" on page 337.

Anesthetist employed by hospital
Byron K. Anderson, 44 TCM 1305 (1982)

Phone calls as dealing with clients
John W. Green, 78 TC 428 (1982) rev'd, 707 F.2d 404 (9th Cir. 1983)
Max Frankel, 82 TC 318 (1984)

Teachers not allowed to deduct home office costs
*Letter Ruling 7734023

Professors with sideline writing/consulting business not allowed deduction
*Letter Rulings 8030024, 8030025

Separate structure
Ben W. Heineman, 82 TC 538 (1984)
Charles A. Scott, 84 TC 683 (1985)

No deduction for renting space to employer
IRC § 280A(c)(6)

¶19.11 • PHONE AND TELEGRAPH COSTS

Telephone calls and telegrams for business
Reg. § 1.162–6
Leo R. Marshall, 8 TCM 508 (1949)

Installation of home phone for business
Moline Dispatch Publishing Co., 11 BTA 934 (Acq.)
Charles J. Voigt, 8 TCM 662 (1949)
Robert A. Phillips, 8 TCM 587 (1949)
C. W. Strickler, 11 TCM 252 (1952)
O. G. Russell, 11 TCM 334 (1952)
Robert H. Lee, 19 TCM 317 (1960)

Taxpayer deducted all toll charges
Paul E. Jackson, 14 TCM 1175 (1955)

Businessman confined to home
Dan R. Hanna Jr., 10 TCM 566 (1951)

Deduction allowed for telephone but not for home office
Charles E. Shepherd, 35 TCM 219 (1976), aff'd in unpublished opinion (7th Cir. April 22, 1977)

Allocation of business phone
Robert G. Galazin, 38 TCM 851 (1979)

¶19.12 • IMPAIRMENT RELATED WORK EXPENSES

IRC § 67(d)

¶19.13 • DEDUCTING MOVING EXPENSES TO A NEW JOB LOCATION

IRC § 217
Reg. § 1.217–1 and 2
Rev. Rul. 72–195, 1972–1 CB 95
IRC § 67(b)(6)
*IRS Publication 521

¶19.14 • THE 35-MILE DISTANCE TEST

IRC § 217(c)(1)(A)(B)
Reg. § 1.217–2(a)(3) and (c)(2)

Aliens' moving expenses
Rev. Rul. 69–425, 1969–2 CB 16
Rev. Rul. 68–308, 1968–1 CB 336

Moving overseas
Jon F. Hartung, 484 F.2d 953 (9th Cir. 1973), rev'g per curiam 55 TC 1 (1970)
Richard L. Markus, 486 F.2d 1314 (D.C. Cir. 1973), rev'g 30 TCM 1346 (1971)
William Hughes, 65 TC 566 (1975)

Armed Services
Rev. Rul. 76–2, 1976–1 CB 82
Rev. Rul. 70–520, 1970–2 CB 66

¶19.15 • 39-WEEK TEST FOR EMPLOYEES

Reg. § 1.217–2(c)(4)

Seasonal employee
Reg. § 1.217–2(c)(4)(iv)(a)
Rev. Rul. 68–42, 1968–1 CB 94

¶19.16 • 78-WEEK TEST FOR THE SELF-EMPLOYED AND PARTNERS

Reg. § 1.217–2(c)(4) and (f)(1)(2)

¶19.17 • CLAIMING THE DEDUCTION BEFORE SATISFYING THE TIME TEST

Reg. § 1.217–2(d)(2)

¶19.18 • MOVING EXPENSES YOU MAY DEDUCT

Direct expenses
Reg. § 1.217–2(b)(3),(4)

Indirect expenses
Reg. § 1.217–2(b)(5),(6),(7)

Limit on deductions
Reg. § 1.217–2(b)(9)

Separate returns
TIR 1136, Jan. 19, 1972
Reg. § 1.217–2(b)(9)(iv)(v)(vi)

Cost of moving a pet deductible
Rev. Rul. 66–305, 1966–2 CB 102

Cost of moving car deductible
Rev. Rul. 65–309, 1965–2 CB 77

Depreciation not allowed
Rev. Rul. 70–656, 1970–2 CB 67

Nine-cent rate
Rev. Proc. 80–32, 1980–2 CB 767

Cost of moving a boat nondeductible
William E. Aksomitas, 50 TC 679 (1968)

Furniture purchased en route
Rev. Rul. 70–625, 1970–2 CB 67

Delay of family's move due to child's completing education

Rev. Rul. 78–200, 1978–1 CB 77
Reg. § 1.217–2(a)(3)
Letter Ruling 8346039

¶19.19 • YOU MUST REPORT REIMBURSEMENTS

IRC § 82

Reimbursements for expenses
Homer H. Starr, 399 F.2d 675 (10th Cir. 1968), rev'g 46 TC 743 (1966)
Walter H. Mendel, 351 F.2d 580 (4th Cir. 1965)
Kenneth D. England, 345 F.2d 414 (7th Cir. 1965), cert. denied, 382 U.S. 986
Novel J. McLellan, 51 TC 462 (1968)
John E. Cavanagh, 36 TC 300 (1961) (Nonacq.)
Rev. Rul. 65–158, 1965–1 CB 34

Reimbursement on sale of home
Harris W. Bradley, 324 F.2d 610 (4th Cir), aff'g 39 TC 652 (1963)
Seth E. Keener, Jr., 59 TC 302 (1972)
Willis B. Ferebee, 39 TC 801 (1963)
Otto S. Schairer, 9 TC 549 (1947)

Deduct moving expenses in computing net operating loss
Rev. Rul. 72–195, 1971–1 CB 95

Members of the military
IRC § 217(g)

Note: Paragraph numbers refer to Part One. Items marked * are research aids, not citations of authority; see "Key to Citations" on page 337.

397

¶ 19.20 • TRAVEL AND ENTERTAINMENT EXPENSES

**¶19.21 • DEDUCTING TRANSPORTA-
TION EXPENSES**

Reg. § 1.62–1(g) Pre-1986 Tax Act

**¶19.22 • COMMUNITY EXPENSES:
GENERALLY NOT DEDUCTI-
BLE, BUT THERE ARE
EXCEPTIONS**

Commutation not deductible
Reg. § 1.162–2(e)
Reg. § 1.262–1(b)(5)
Oran R. Morgan, 80 F. Supp. 537
(N.D. Tex. 1948)
Leo M. Verner, 39 TC 749 (1963)
(Acq.)
Joseph M. Winn, 32 TC 220 (1959)
Clarence H. O'Donnell, 21 TCM 609
(1962)

Doctor's emergency calls to hospital
Margaret G. Sheldon, 50 TC 24
(1968)

Commuting from hotel
IRS Publication No. 300 (1956)
Rev. Rul. 63–145, 1963–2 CB 86

Carrying tools to work
Rev. Rul. 75–380, 1975–2 CB 59

*Commuting to temporary job—current
IRS policy—in suspension*
Pub. L. No. 95–427, § 2

Home office of sideline job
Julio S. Mazzotta, 57 TC 427 (1971),
aff'd per curiam, 72–2 USTC
¶9709 (2d Cir. 1972)

Office in home
Thomas C. St. John, 29 TCM 1045
(1970)
Joe J. Adams, 43 TCM 1203 (1982)
Thomas L. Wicker, 51 TCM 225
(1986)

Travel from union hall to job
Russell Anderson, 60 TC 834 (1973)

**¶19.23 • OVERNIGHT-SLEEP TEST
LIMITS DEDUCTION OF
MEAL COSTS ON ONE-DAY
BUSINESS TRIPS**

Sleep or rest rule
Homer O. Correll, 389 U.S. 299
(1968), rev'g 369 F.2d 87 (6th Cir.
1966)

Nap in parked car
Frederick J. Barry, 54 TC 1210
(1970), aff'd per curiam, 435 F.2d
1290 (1st Cir. 1971)

Railroad personnel
Rev. Rul. 75–170, 1975–1 CB 60

Truck drivers
Rev. Rul. 75–168, 1975–1 CB 58

*Meal costs during overtime not de-
ductible*

D. S. Courtney, 32 TC 334 (1959)
W. K. Liang, 34 TCM 1298 (1975)

¶19.24 • IRS MEAL ALLOWANCE

Rev. Proc. 83–71, 1983–2 CB 590

**¶19.25 • DEDUCTING TRAVEL EX-
PENSES AWAY FROM HOME**

Reg. § 1.162–2(a)

Laundry, cab fare
Rev. Rul. 63–145, 1963–2 CB 86

Lavish or extravagant
Rev. Rul. 63–144, 1963–2 CB 129

Limit on cruise ship costs
IRC § 274(m)(1)

**¶19.26 • WHEN ARE YOU AWAY
FROM HOME?**

Place of business as tax home
J. N. Flowers, 326 U.S. 465 (1946)
Lee E. Daly, 72 TC 190 (1979),
rev'd, 631 F. 2d 351 (4th Cir.
1980), aff'g Tax Court and rev'g
after rehearing en banc, 81–2
USTC ¶9721 (4th Cir. 1981)

Ethel Merman case
Robert F. Six, 450 F.2d 66 (2d Cir.
1971)
Robert Rosenspan, 438 F.2d 905 (2d
Cir. 1971), cert. denied, 404 U.S.
864

Residence is tax home
Charles W. Rambo, 69 TC 920
(1978)(Acq. in result only)
Edward M. McKarzel, 30 TCM 366
(1971)
Eli F. McGimsey, 30 TCM 521
(1971)
Rev. Rul. 71–247, 1971–1 CB 54

Unmarried person
Robert Rosenspan, 438 F.2d 905 (2d
Cir. 1971), cert. denied, 404 U.S.
864
Irving M. Sapson, 49 TC 636 (1968)
(Acq.)
Max W. Tugel, 20 TCM 693 (1961)
Curtis L. Ralston, 27 TCM 1312
(1968)
Rev. Rul. 73–529, 1973–2 CB 37
Arthur Crossland, 33 TCM 1278
(1974), aff'd, 76–1 USTC ¶9188
(2d Cir. 1976)

**¶19.27 • FIXING TAX HOME IF YOU
WORK IN DIFFERENT
LOCATIONS**

Francis Markey, 491 F.2d 1249 (6th
Cir. 1974), rev'g 31 TCM 766
(1972)
Joseph Sherman, 16 TC 332 (1951)
(Acq.)
S. M. R. O'Hara, 6 TC 841 (1946)

Richard E. Benson, 27 TCM 1555
(1968)
John H. Webster, 9 TCM 550 (1950)
W. Edward Winterhalter, 10 TCM
268 (1951)
Vincent Treanor, 10 TCM 336
(1951)
Rev. Rul. 55–604, 1955–2 CB 49
Rev. Rul. 63–82, 1963–1 CB 33

*Baseball players, coaches, etc. might
have other business*
Rev. Rul. 54–147, 1954–1 CB 51
Special Ruling, December 29, 1953

**¶19.28 • TAX HOME OF MARRIED
COUPLE WORKING IN
DIFFERENT CITIES**

Robert A. Coerver, 297 F.2d 837 (3d
Cir. 1962), aff'g 36 TC 252 (1951)
Arthur B. Hammond, 213 F.2d 43
(5th Cir. 1954)
Virginia Foote, 67 TC 1 (1976)
George P. Leyland, 34 TCM 1502
(1975)
Charles J. Hundt, 20 TCM 369
(1961)

**¶19.29 • DEDUCTING LIVING COSTS
ON TEMPORARY ASSIGN-
MENT AWAY FROM HOME**

*"A House is Not Necessarily a Tax
Home, An Examination of the Deductibility of Away-From-Home
Expenses," Richard Weber and Edmund Outslay, 65 Taxes 275 (May
1987)

IRS "temporary assignment" guidelines
Rev. Rul. 83–82, 1983–1 CB 45

Family at temporary post
Emil J. Michaels, 53 TC 269 (1969)
(Acq.)

Engineer on 20-month job
Philip Rolbin, 29 TCM 848 (1970)

Retired Florida stenographer
Virginia C. Avery, 29 TCM 1187
(1970)

Student's summer job
Saterios Hantzis, 38 TCM 1169
(1979), rev'd, 638 F.2d 248 (1st
Cir. 1981), cert. denied, 101 S. Ct.
3112

Court rejection of one-year test
David L. Cowger, 25 TCM 513
(1966)
Ronald Brown, 30 TCM 41 (1971)
Louis R. Frederick, 457 F. Supp.
1274 (D.N. Dak. 1978), aff'd,
603 F.2d 1292 (8th Cir. 1979)

Recurrent summer job
Franklin C. Dilley, 58 TC 276
(1972)

Note: Paragraph numbers refer to Part One. Items marked * are research aids, not citations of authority; see "Key to Citations" on page 337.

State judge traveling to other circuits
Frank Fisher, 24 TC 269 (1955)
(Acq.)

State judge who must live in district
James A. Emmert, 146 F. Supp. 322
(S.D. Ind. 1955)

Employed for test period
Richard C. Lipps, 21 TCM 358
(1962)
Rev. Rul. 60–314, 1960–2 CB 48

Employment for part of a year
James R. Whitaker, 24 TC 750
(1955)
George R. Lanning, 34 TCM 1366
(1975)
McGinley, 15 TCM 641 (1956)

*Linesman working out of Oakland,
California*
Max W. Tugel, 20 TCM 693 (1961)

Baseball player's expenses
Rev. Rul. 54–147, 1954–1 CB 51

Professional football player
Ronald C. Gardin, 64 TC 1079
(1975)

Permanent duty station of military personnel
Howe A. Stidger, 386 U.S. 287
(1967), rev'g 355 F.2d 294 (9th
Cir. 1966)

**¶19.30 • CONSTRUCTION WORKER
AT DIFFERENT PROJECTS**

IRS "temporary assignment" guidelines
Rev. Rul. 83–82, 1983–1 CB 45

Temporary assignment
James E. Peurifoy, 358 U.S. 59
(1958)
Michael Kuris, 15 TCM 854 (1956)
Robert K. Denning, 14 TCM 838
(1955)
Rev. Rul. 60–189, 1960–1 CB 60

Itinerant worker
George H. James, 308 F.2d 204 (9th
Cir. 1962), aff'g 176 F. Supp. 270
(D. Nev. 1959)

One-year test disregarded
Ronald Brown, 30 TCM 41 (1971)

**¶19.31 • BUSINESS-VACATION TRIPS
WITHIN THE UNITED
STATES**
Reg. § 1.274–4(e)(2)
IRC § 274(c)(3)
IR–1224, June 1, 1972

**¶19.32 • BUSINESS-VACATION TRIPS
OUTSIDE THE U.S.**
IRC § 274(c)

*Control over trip, managing executive,
etc.*
Reg. § 1.274–4(e)(5)

Definitions of weeks, days, etc.
Reg. § 1.274–4(c)

Allocation formula
Reg. § 1.274(e)(1)

**¶19.33 • DEDUCTING EXPENSES OF
CONVENTION AND
SEMINARS**

*"Convention Expenses—When Are
They Deductible?," E. W. Rowland, 3 Practical Accountant 50
(1970)

*"Company Conventions: Business Discussions Do Not Necessarily Avoid
Tax Problems," Malcolm Osborn,
12 Taxation for Lawyers 268 (Mar/
Apr. 1984)

*"Convention Expenses: Establishing
Business Connection is the Key to
the Deduction," W. F. Sheehan, 1
Taxation for Lawyers 186 (1972)

Business or pleasure trip
Reg. § 1.162–2(b)
Convention expenses
Reg. § 1.162–2(d)
Rev. Rul. 63–266, 1963–2 CB 88

Connection with business
Rev. Rul. 59–316, 1959–2 CB 57,
clarified by Rev. Rul. 63–266,
1963–2 CB 88

Doctor's convention expenses
Cecil M. Jack, 13 BTA 726 (Acq.)
J. Bentley Squier, 13 BTA 1223
(Acq.)
Roy Upham, 16 BTA 950 (Nonacq.)
Robert C. Coffey, 21 BTA 1242
(Acq.)

*No deduction for investment seminars
after 1986*
IRC § 274(h), as amended by 1986
Tax Reform Act

Lawyer's convention expenses
Wade H. Ellis, 50 F.2d 343 (D.C.
Cir. 1931)

Legal secretary's convention expenses
Rita M. Callinan, 12 TCM 170
(1953)

Insurance agent
C. J. D. Rudolph, 291 F.2d 841 (5th
Cir. 1961), aff'g 189 F. Supp. 2
(N.D. Tex. 1960), cert. dismissed,
370 U.S. 269 (1962)

Fraternal organizations' conventions
Reg. § 1.162–2(d)

Business convention in coastal resort
Rev. Rul. 56–168, 1956–1 CB 93
Reg. § 1.162–2(b)(1)

Cruises
DeWitt N. Burnham, 17 TCM 240
(1958)
Reuben B. Hoover, 35 TC 566 (1961)
(Acq.)

**¶19.34 • DEDUCTING YOUR SPOUSE'S
TRAVEL EXPENSES ON A
BUSINESS OR CONVENTION
TRIP**

*"A Wife's Tax Value: Tax Aspects of
a Wife's Attending Conventions,
Sales Meetings," D. R. Rich, 22
NYU Inst. 895 (1964)

"How to Establish That the Expenses
of a Spouse on a Business Trip are

*Deductible," Alan Y. C. Yong, 28
Taxation for Accountants 162
(Mar. 1982)

"Planning to Overcome IRS Opposition
to Deductions for Convention Expenses of a Spouse," Malcolm E.
Osborn, 10 Taxation for Lawyers
294 (Mar./Apr. 1982)

IRS policy
Rev. Rul. 63–144, 1963–2 CB 129

*Spouse's expenses on convention or
business trip*
Reg. § 1.162–2(c)
William N. Clement, Sr., 331 F.
Supp. 877 (E.D.N.C. 1971)
Donald W. Scarborough, 30 TCM
613 (1971)

Company convention policy
J. C. Thomas, 289 F.2d 108 (5th
Cir. 1961), cert. denied, 368 U.S.
837

Spouse acting as nurse
Allenberg Cotton Co., 61–1 USTC
¶9131 (W. D. Tenn. 1961)
William E. Reisner, 34 TC 1122
(1960)(Acq.)
Preston R. Rieley, 23 TCM 449
(1964)

Spouse acting as host or hostess
Pierre C. Warwick, 236 F. Supp. 761
(E.D. Va. 1964)
Ron Merritt, 21 TCM 1011 (1962)
Roy O. Disney, 267 F. Supp. 1 (C.D.
Cal. 1967), aff'd, 413 F.2d 783
(9th Cir. 1969)
Bank of Stockton, 36 TCM 114
(1977)

Spouse as employee
Madyo A. Poletti, 330 F.2d 818 (8th
Cir. 1965)

Spouse of controlling stockholder
Bywater Sales and Service Co., 24
TCM 849 (1965)

Spouse of foreign service employee
Fraser Wilkins, 348 F. Supp. 1282
(D. Neb. 1972)

**¶19.35 • RESTRICTIONS ON DE-
DUCTING FOREIGN CON-
VENTION AND CRUISE
EXPENSES**
IRC § 274(h)

Jamaica not foreign
Treaty, 12/16/81

*U.S. Virgin Islands, Samoa, Guam in
North American Area*
Rev. Rul. 82–151, 1982–2 CB 75

Cruise ship rules
IRC § 274(h)(2)

Reporting rule
IRC § 274(h)(5)

¶19.36 • ENTERTAINMENT EXPENSES

*"Meal, Entertainment and Travel Expenses after TRA 1986," David
A. Schenck, 66 Journal of Taxation 240 (1987)

Note: Paragraph numbers refer to Part One. Items marked * are research aids, not citations of authority; see "Key to Citations" on page 337.

399

*"Vulnerability of Entertainment and Meal Deductions Under the Sutter Rule," Timothy J. McNally 62 Taxes 184 (1984)

*"Substantiation Is the Key to Preventing the Disallowance of Business Entertainment Expenses," by Cary R. Miteles, 32 Taxation for Accountants 342 (June 1984)
IRC § 274(a)

¶19.37 • THE RESTRICTIVE TESTS
IRC § 274(a)
Senate Comm. Report on Pub. L. No. 87–834

Lavish and extravagant entertainment
IRC § 274(k)
Reg. § 1.274–1
Rev. Rul. 63–144, 1963–2 CB 129
Donald G. Harper, 23 TCM 461 (1964)

Entertainment defined
Reg. § 1.274–2(b)(1)(ii)

Business associates
Reg. § 1.274–2(b)(2)(iii)

¶19.38 • DIRECTLY-RELATED ENTERTAINMENT
IRC § 274(a)(1)
Reg. § 1.274–2(a)
Reg. § 1.274–2(c)
Rev. Rul. 63–144, 1963–2 CB 129

Doctor's entertainment
Karl Wolf, 64–1 USTC ¶9211 (W.D. Mo. 1964)
Richard A. Sutter, 21 TC 170 (1953)
C. W. Lokey, 16 TCM 18 (1957)
Kenneth Branchard, 12 TCM 550 (1953)

¶19.39 • GOODWILL ENTERTAINMENT
IRC § 274(a)(1)(A)
Reg. § 1.274–2(a)(1)(ii)
Reg. § 1.274–2(d)
Rev. Rul. 63–144, 1963–2 CB 129

¶19.40 • HOME ENTERTAINING
Reg. § 1.274–2(f)(2)(i)(b)
Rev. Rul. 63–144, 1963–2 CB 129

¶19.41 • YOUR PERSONAL SHARE OF ENTERTAINMENT COSTS
Ray A. Smith, 33 TC 1059 (1960)
Richard A. Sutter, 21 TC 170 (1953)
James P. Fenstermaker, 37 TCM 898 (1978)
Rev. Rul. 63–144, 1963–2 CB 129

¶19.42 • DEDUCTING THE ENTERTAINMENT COSTS OF SPOUSES
Directly related test
Reg. § 1.274–2(d)(4)

Goodwill entertainment
Rev. Rul. 63–144, 1963–2 CB 129

Entertainment of out of town customer's spouse
Rev. Rul. 63–144, 1963–2 CB 129

¶19.43 • COSTS OF MAINTAINING AND OPERATING ENTERTAINMENT FACILITIES ARE NOT DEDUCTIBLE
IRC § 274(a)(1)(B) as amended by § 361 of the Revenue Act of 1978

Luncheon club not facility
Reg. § 1.274–2(e)(3)(ii)

¶19.44 • CLUB DUES
IRC § 274(a)
Reg. § 1.274–2(e)
Rev. Rul. 63–144, 1963–2 CB 129
Harry G. LaForge, 53 TC 41 (1969), rem'd 434 F.2d 370 (2d Cir. 1970)

Club entertainment of CPA
George W. Randall, 56 TC 869 (1971)

¶19.45 • RECORD KEEPING FOR CLUB USE
Reg. § 1.274–5(c)(6)(iii)
Rev. Proc. 63–4, 1963–1 CB 474
Rev. Rul. 63–144, 1963–2 CB 129

Business organizations
IRS Publication No. 463

¶19.46 • EXCEPTIONS TO THE RESTRICTIVE TESTS
IRC § 274(e)
Reg. § 1.274–2(f)

¶19.47 • EIGHTY PERCENT COST LIMITATION ON MEAL, TICKET, AND OTHER ENTAINMENT EXPENSES
80% rule
IRC § 274(n)

Limits on ticket costs
IRC § 274(1)

¶19.48 • BUSINESS GIFT DEDUCTIONS ARE LIMITED
IRC § 274(b)
Reg. § 1.274–3
Rev. Rul. 63–144, 1963–2 CB 129

Gift to secretary
Richard Steel, 28 TCM 1301 (1969), aff'd per curiam, 437 F.2d 71 (2d Cir. 1971)

Gifts to employees
IRC § 102(c)

Employee achievement awards
IRC § 274(j)

¶19.49 • TRAVEL AND ENTERTAINMENT RECORDS
IRC § 274(d)
Reg. § 1.274–5(a)
Rev. Proc. 63–4, 1963–1 CB 474

What your records must show
Reg. § 1.274–5(b)
Reg. § 1.274–5(c)

Business purpose
Reg. § 1.274–5(c)(2)(ii)(b)

Need of receipt with diary
William F. Sanford, 50 TC 823 (1968), aff'd per curiam, 412 F.2d 201 (2d Cir. 1969), cert. denied, 396 U.S. 841

Inadequate travel and entertainment records not a basis for negligence penalties
John Robinson, 51 TC 520 (1968) (Acq.), aff'd, 422 F.2d 873 (9th Cir. 1969)

Oral testimony accepted
Harry G. La Forge, 434 F.2d 370 (2d Cir. 1970)

Oral testimony ignored
Arthur Hughes, 451 F.2d 975 (2d Cir. 1972)
Norman E. Kennelly, 56 TC 936 (1971), aff'd, 72–1 USTC ¶9348 (2d Cir. 1972)

Lost records
Raymond W. Jackson, 34 TCM 1315 (1975)
Joe F. Gizzi, 65 TC 342 (1975)

¶19.50 • YOU NEED A DIARY AND, GENERALLY, RECEIPTS
Diary
Reg. § 1.274–5(c)(2)
Joseph L. Weinfeld, 20 TCM 70 (1961)
Warren Cummings, 20 TCM 1699 (1961)

Hotel bill not needed if per diem allowance received
Rev. Proc. 63–4, 1963–1 CB 494 as updated by Rev. Rul. 80–62, 1980–1 CB 63

Receipts
Reg. § 1.274–5(c)(2)(iii)

Noting expense items
Reg. § 1.274–5(c)
Reg. § 1.274–5(c)(6)

Failure to show business purpose
Norman E. Kennelly, 56 TC 936 (1971), aff'd, 72–1 USTC ¶9348 (2d Cir. 1972)

Time limit for keeping records
Reg. § 1.274–5(c)(2)(iv)

Excuses for inadequate records
Reg. § 1.274–5(c)

Attorney required to keep travel and entertainment records
William Andress Jr., 51 TC 863 (1969), aff'd per curiam, 423 F.2d 679 (5th Cir. 1970)

Loss of records
Lewis M. Bryan, 33 TCM 1188 (1974)

Bills but no other proof
Cam F. Dowell, Jr., 522 F.2d 708 (5th Cir. 1975), cert. denied, 26 U.S. 920

Loss due to eviction
Irvin A. Murray, 41 TCM 337 (1980)

Loss due to destruction by estranged wife
Matthew J. Canfield, 41 TCM 461 (1980)

Note: Paragraph numbers refer to Part One. Items marked * are research aids, not citations of authority; see "Key to Citations" on page 337.

400

¶19.51 • HOW TO TREAT REIM-BURSED EXPENSES AND ALLOWANCES

Reg. § 1.274–5(e)
Reg. § 1.274–5(f)
Rev. Proc. 63–4, 1963–1 CB 474

Repayment agreement of T&E expenses
*Letter Rulings 7811004 and 7811005

¶19.52 • CREDIT CARDS

Reg. § 1.274–5(e)(2)
Rev. Rul. 59–410, 1959–2 CB 64

¶19.53 • EMPLOYEE-STOCKHOLDERS

Reg. § 1.274–5(e)(5)(ii)

¶19.54 • FIXED REIMBURSEMENT ALLOWANCES

Reg. § 1.274–5(f)
Rev. Rul. 71–412, 1971–2 CB 170

¶19.55 • HOW TO TREAT PARTIALLY REIMBURSED JOB EXPENSES

Reg. § 1.62(f)

Failure to get reimbursed
Earl M. Coplon, 18 TCM 166 (1959), aff'd, 277 F.2d 534 (6th Cir. 1960)

Marvin A. Heidt, 18 TCM 149 (1959), aff'd, 274 F.2d 25 (7th Cir. 1960)
Eugene J. Rogers, 18 TCM 866 (1959)
Jack C. Morgan, 24 TCM 644 (1965)

¶19.56 • DOES AN EMPLOYER HAVE TO REPORT YOUR REIMBURSEMENTS?

T.I.R. No. 132, February 13, 1959
T.I.R. No. 198, December 29, 1959
Rev. Rul. 134, 1953–2 CB 199
Weinfeld 20 TCM 70 (1961)

Claiming IRS Automobile Allowance

¶19.57 • DEDUCTING AUTOMOBILE EXPENSES

¶19.58 • IRS AUTOMOBILE ALLOW-ANCE

*"Planning Around the TRA '84 De-preciation Limitations," by John Zimmerman, 64 Taxes 67 (February, 1986)

*"New Law Limits Tax Benefits of Automobiles, Computers, and Other Personal Property," Philip J. Wiesner and David G. Smith, 61 Journal of Taxation 216 (Oct. 1984)

Mileage allowance
Rev. Proc. 82–61, 1982–2 CB 849, as modified by Rev. Proc. 87–49, IRB 1987–38

Deduction for IRS rate which exceeds employer's
Rev. Rul. 73–191, 1973–1 CB 151

Diary record of business mileage
John E. Frankel, 27 TCM 817 (1968)

Useful life
Rev. Proc. 75–3, 1975–1 CB 643

60,000 miles as useful life
Rev. Proc. 81–54, 1981–2 CB 649

Two cars used at one time
Carroll H. West, 63 TC 252 (1974)

Investment credit and IRS rate
Rev. Rul. 67–348, 1967–2 CB 7

Married couple's separately owned cars
Letter Ruling 8343005

¶19.59 • AUTO EXPENSE ALLOCA-TION RULES

Allocation based on mileage
Temp. Reg. Sec. 1.280F–6T(e)

Treasury Department Form 2106
Some car expenses capitalized
Doris Jones, 11 TCM 529 (1952)

Apportioning car expense between busi-ness and personal use
Lawrence Au, 40 TC 264 (1963),

aff'd per curiam, 330 F.2d 1008 (9th Cir. 1964), cert. denied, 379 U.S. 960
Clarence J. Sapp, 309 F.2d 143 (5th Cir. 1962), aff'g 36 TC 852 (1961)(Acq.)

¶19.60 • DEPRECIATING A BUSI-NESS AUTO

IRC § 280F

More than 50% business use test
IRC § 280F(b)
Temp. Reg. Sec. 1.280F–6T(d)(4)

Business-investment percentage
Temp. Reg. Sec. 1.280F–6T(d)(3)
Temp. Reg. Sec. 1.280F–2T(i)

Employer convenience test
IRC § 280F(d)(3)

Employee use of company car
IRC § 280F(d)(6)
Temp. Reg. Sec. 1.280F–6T(d)(2)

Vehicles other than cars
IRC § 280F(d)(4)
Temp. Reg. Sec. 1.280F–6T(b)

Vehicles exempted from more than 50% business use
Temp. Reg. Sec. 1.280F–6T(b)
Temp. Reg. Sec. 1.274–5T(k)

Annual limit on ACRS deduction
IRC § 280F(a)(2)

First-year expensing limitation
IRC § 280F(d)(1)

Personal use percentage reduces ceiling
IRC § 280F(a)(3)
Temp. Reg. Sec. 1.280F–2T(i)

Diesel vehicle credit reduces basis
IRC § 6427(g)(7)

¶19.61 • GUIDE TO ACRS AND MACRS DEPRECIATION RATES

Converting a pleasure car to business use
Prop. Reg. Sec. 1.168–2(j)(1)

Increase in business use after recovery period
Prop. Reg. Sec. 1.168–2(j)(2)

¶19.62 • MACRS DEPRECIATION OF A BUSINESS AUTO PLACED IN SERVICE IN 1987 AND LATER YEARS

IRC § 168(e)(3)(B)(i)
IRC § 168(b)
IRC § 168(c)

Annual deduction limits
IRC § 280 F(a)(2)

Conventions
IRC § 168(d)

¶19.63 • STRAIGHT LINE RATE REQUIRED FOR BUSINESS USE OF 50% OR LESS

Mandatory straight-line recovery
IRC § 280F(b)(2) and (b)(4)
Temp. Reg. Sec. 1.280F–3T(c) and (e)

Optional straight line recovery of busi-ness use exceeds 50%
IRC § 168(f)(2)(c)
Prop. Reg. § 1.168–2(c)

¶19.64 • TRADE-IN OF BUSINESS AUTO

IRC § 1.031(d)
Reg. § 1.1031(d)-1
W. Schmidt, 28 TCM 481 (1969)

¶19.65 • RECAPTURE OF ACRS DEDUCTION ON BUSINESS AUTO

Business use drops to 50% or less
IRC § 280F(b)(2)
Temp. Reg. § 1.280F–3T(c)(2)

¶19.66 • RECAPTURE OF INVEST-MENT CREDIT ON BUSI-NESS AUTOMOBILES

IRC § 47(a)(1)
Reg. § 1.47–1

Note: Paragraph numbers refer to Part One. Items marked * are research aids, not citations of authority; see "Key to Citations" on page 337.

Drop in business use to 50% or less
IRC § 280F(b)(1)
Temp. Reg. § 1.280F–3T(b)

¶19.67 • KEEPING RECORDS OF BUSINESS USE

*"*Substantiation of Automobile Business Use Under the New Regulations*," Donna M. Pawlikowski and

Claireen Herting, 64 Taxes: The Tax Magazine 382 (June 1986)

Recordkeeping requirements after 1985
IRC § 274(d)
Temp. Reg. Sec. 1.274–5T

Vehicles exempted from recordkeeping requirements
IRC § 274(d)(4)
Temp. Reg. Sec. 1.274–5T(k)

Written company policy restricting personal use
Temp. Reg. Sec. 1.274–6T

¶19.68 • LEASED BUSINESS AUTOS: DEDUCTIONS AND INCOME

IRC § 280F(c)
Temp. Reg. § 1.280F–5T
Rev. Rul. 86–87, IRB 1986–28, 8

¶20 INVESTMENT AND OTHER NONBUSINESS EXPENSES

IRC § 212
Reg. § 1.212–1

*"*The Scope of Deductions under Section 212*," Michael B. Lang, F. Rev. Tax Individuals 291 (Autumn 1983)

*"*Accounting and Legal Fees Can Be Structured to Increase Portion That Is Deductible*," Thomas H. Gooding, Jr., 12 Tax for Law 218 (Jan./Feb. 1984)

*"*Deductions for Cost of Tax Advice Are Often Subject to IRS Attack*," H. A. Scott, 22 Journal of Taxation 174 (1965)

*"*Limitation on the Deduction of Legal Fees*," T. L. Caps, 1964 So. Calif. Tax Inst. 163

*"*Deductible Expenses: Transactions Entered Into For Profit: Income Producing Property*," W. D. Kilbourn, Jr., 21 NYU Inst. 193 (1963)

*"*Deductibility of Legal Expenses for Federal Income Tax Purposes*," D. B. Grishman, 1974 So. Calif. Tax Inst. 875

¶20.2 • CHECKLIST OF DEDUCTIBLE INVESTMENT EXPENSES

IRC § 212
Reg. § 1.212–1(b)

2% floor
IRC § 67(a)

Fees to bank in dividend reinvestment plan
Rev. Rul. 75–548, 1975–2 CB 331

Expense of tax exempt income
IRC § 265
Reg. § 1.265–1

Office of investor
Joseph J. Imhoff, 29 TCM 966 (1970)

Safe deposit box for securities
Albina E. Bodell, 1 TCM 395 (1943)
W. N. Fry, 5 TC 1058 (1945)
Daniel S. W. Kelly, 23 TC 682 (1955)(Acq.), aff'd on other issue, 228 F.2d 512 (7th Cir. 1956)

Home safe
*Letter Ruling 8218077

Traveling to check investments, etc.
E. M. Godson, 5 TCM 648 (1946)
Louis H. Mayer, 10 TCM 559 (1951)
Martha E. Henderson, 27 TCM 109 (1968)

Travel expenses for investor in publicly traded securities
William R. Kinney, 66 TC 122 (1976)

Proxy fight expenses
R. Walter Graham, 326 F.2d 878 (4th Cir. 1964)
J. Raymond Dyer, 23 TCM 1208 (1964), aff'd, 352 F.2d 948 (8th Cir. 1965)
Rev. Rul. 64–236, 1964–2 CB 64

Trip to broker not deductible
Stanley S. Walters, 28 TCM 22 (1969)

Prospective investments
Doran S. Weinstein, 420 F.2d 700 (Ct. Cl. 1970)

Mutual fund fees
Rev. Rul. 77–10, 1977–1 CB 62
Rev. Rul. 55–23, 1955–1 CB 275

Business advice to produce income
Reg. § 1.212–1(g)
Andrew Jergens, 2 TCM 385 (1943)
Edward E. Bishop, 4 TC 862 (1945) (Acq.)
Amelia E. Collins, 3 TCM 223 (1944)
Elma M. Williams, 3 TC 200 (1944) (Acq.)
Raymond Fitzgerald, 15 TCM 1450 (1956)

Expenses of fiduciary
Reg. § 1.212–1(i)

Incompetency fees
Elsie Weil Est., 13 TCM 653 (1954)

Reduce income-producing ability
Ann F. Day, 57–1 USTC ¶9270 (D. Ariz. 1957)
Gertrude Lytton-Smith, 57–1 USTC ¶9271 (D. Ariz. 1957)
Robert S. Howard, 32 TC 1284 (1959)(Acq.)

Capital expenditures
IRC § 263
Reg. § 1.263(a)–1 and 2
Reg. § 1.212–1(n)

Stockholder's trip for company
J. D. O'Connor, 13 TCM 623 (1959)

Investment club convention
Walter Gustin, 46 TCM 1505 (1983)

Deduction barred for general investment seminar
Letter Ruling 8451027

Trip to investigate rental property
Patrick L. O'Donnell, 62 TC 781 (1974), aff'd in unpublished decision (7th Cir. July 23, 1975)

Travel cost to stockholders meetings nondeductible
Rev. Rul. 56–511, 1956–2 CB 170

Trip to present stockholder resolution deductible
*Letter Ruling 8220084

No deduction for investor's home office expenses
IRC § 280A
Joseph Moller, 721 F.2d 810 (CA-FC 1983)

¶20.3 • COSTS OF TAX RETURN PREPARATION, TAX REFUNDS, AND TAX AUDITS

IRC § 212(3)
Reg. § 1.212–1(1)

2% floor
IRC § 67(a)

Foreign tax
Philip T. Sharples, 533 F.2d 550 (Ct. Cl. 1976)

Legal fees deductible although underlying transaction is capital
Philip T. Sharples, 533 F.2d 550 (Ct. Cl. 1976)

Tax advice on real estate deal
James A. Collins, 54 TC 1656 (1970) (Acq.)

Tax deficiency imposed on business income
Clarence Wood, 37 TC 70 (1961) (Acq.)

Note: Paragraph numbers refer to Part One. Items marked * are research aids, not citations of authority; see "Key to Citations" on page 337.

Clyde E. Thomas Sr., 41 TC 614 (1964)

Criminal tax fraud charge
Michael Shapiro, 278 F.2d 556 (7th Cir. 1960)

Tax advice on future deals
Basil L. Kaufman, 227 F. Supp. 807 (D. Mo. 1964)

Tax books deductible
Donald W. Fausner, 30 TCM 1170 (1971), aff'd on other issue, 413 U.S. 838 (1973)

Personal checking account fees nondeductible
Florence E. Callander, 75 TC 334 (1980)

NOW account fees nondeductible
Rev. Rul. 82–59, 1982–1 CB 47

Money market account fee
*Letter Ruling 8345067

¶20.4 • DEDUCTING LEGAL COSTS

IRC § 162
IRC § 212
Reg. § 1.212–1(1)

Suspension of license arose from personal activity
Kenneth A. Cameron, 79–2 USTC ¶9477 (C.D. Cal. 1979)

Employment related legal costs
Walter F. Tellier, 383 U.S. 687 (1966)
Don Gilmore, 372 U.S. 39 (1963)
Stanley Waldheim, 25 TC 839 (1956) (Acq.), aff'd on other issue, 244 F.2d 1 (7th Cir. 1957)
M. S. Kaufman, 12 TC 1114 (1949) (Acq.)
Jean Nidetch, 37 TCM 1307 (1978)

Steve Sikey, 37 TCM 548 (1978)
Milton Margoles, 27 TCM 319 (1968)
Rev. Rul. 64–277, 1964–2 CB 55

Libel suits
James E. Threlkeld, 87 TC No. 6 (1986)
Paul F. Roemery Jr. 716 F.2d 693 (9th Cir. 1983), rev'g 79 TC 398
J. Raymond Dyer, 36 TC 456 (1961) (Acq.)
Paul Draper, 26 TC 201 (1956) (Acq.)
Rev. Rul. 58–418, 1958–2 CB 18, distinguished by Rev. Rul. 75–230, 1975–1 CB 93

Allocation of fees where compensatory and punitive damages received
Rev. Rul. 85–98, 1985–2 CB 51

Libel suit of public official
*Letter Ruling 8018077

Will contest
Reg. § 1.212–1(k)
Charles E. Parker, 573 F.2d 42 (Ct. Cl. 1978)

Wrongful death actions
Lawrence E. DeWeese, 276 F. Supp. 901 (D. Ore. 1967)

Title issues or disputes
Reg. § 1.212–1(k)
Fred W. Woodward, 397 U.S. 572 (1970)
Hilton Hotels Corp., 397 U.S. 580 (1970)
Walter W. Cruttenden, 70 TC 191 (1978), aff'd, 644 F.2d 1368 (9th Cir. 1981) (deduction allowed)

Allocation of legal fees where dispute involves title and income
Reg. § 1.212–1(k)

Daniel S. W. Kelly, 228 F.2d 512 (7th Cir. 1956), aff'g 23 TC 682 (1955) (Acq.)
Andrew J. Stormfeltz, 142 F.2d 982 (8th Cir. 1944)
Birdie Kimbrell, 80 F. Supp. 695 (D. Ill. 1948)
Joseph P. Morgan Est., 37 TC 31 (1961) (Acq.), aff'd in part, rev'd in part, 332 F.2d 144 (6th Cir. 1964)
E. W. Brown Jr., 19 TC 87 (1952), aff'd in part, rev'd in part and rem'd, 215 F.2d 697 (5th Cir. 1954)
Agnes P. Coke, 17 TC 403 (1951) (Acq.), aff'd per curiam, 201 F.2d 742 (5th Cir. 1953)
William A. Falls, 7 TC 66 (1946) (Acq.)

Legal fees for tax advice and tax return preparation
IRC § 212(3)
Reg. § 1.212–1(1)

Fees of defending criminal tax fraud charge deductible
Michael Shapiro, 278 F.2d 556 (7th Cir. 1960)
Rev. Rul. 68–662, 1968–2 CB 69

Fee to reduce assessment
Rev. Rul. 70–62, 1970–1 CB 30

Estate planning fee
Sidney Merians, 60 TC 187 (1973) (Acq.)

¶20.5 • QUALIFIED GROUP LEGAL SERVICES PLANS

IRC § 120
Prop. Reg. § 1.120–1 and 2
Reg. § 1.120–3

¶21

Deductible Education Costs

¶21.1 • GENERAL RULES FOR DEDUCTING EDUCATION COSTS

Reg. § 1.162–5

2% floor
IRC § 67(a)

*IRS Publication 508

*"Education Can Take Many Forms and Still Be Deductible," 4 Taxation for Accountants 374 (1970)

*"Tax Aspects of Education," F. C. Niswander, 26 NYU Inst. 27 (1968)

*"Current Climate for Deducting Expenses Is Quite Favorable," D.

Samuels, P. Samuels, 11 Taxation for Accountants 226 (1973)

*"Current Standards Being Used to Determine When Education Expenses Are Deductible," Dale K. Nelson, 10 Taxation for Lawyers 372 (May/June 1982) and 28 Taxation for Accountants 248 (Apr. 1982)

¶21.2 • DEDUCTION TESTS FOR EDUCATION COSTS

Maintain or improve skills
Reg. § 1.162–5(c)(1)
Clark S. Marlor, 251 F.2d 615 (2d Cir. 1958)

Minimum job requirements

Eduardo Antuna, 36 TCM 1778 (1977)
David Cooper, 37 TCM 529 (1978)

Undergraduate courses not deductible by office manager
Theresa M. Malek, 50 TCM 792 (1985)

Undergraduate college costs not deductible by policeman
James A. Carroll, 51 TC 213 (1968), aff'd, 418 F.2d 91 (7th Cir. 1969)

Industrial psychologist
Cosimo A. Carlucci, 37 TC 695 (1962) (Acq.)

Engineering aide to maintain skills

Note: Paragraph numbers refer to Part One. Items marked * are research aids, not citations of authority; see "Key to Citations" on page 337.

Ralph A. Fattore, 22 TCM 1093 (1963)

Attorney attending graduate courses
Albert C. Ruehmann, 30 TCM 675 (1971)
Charles B. Johnson, 332 F. Supp. 906 (D. La. 1971)
Larry R. Adamson, 32 TCM 484 (1973)

Unemployed teacher
Edward J. P. Zimmerman, 71 TC 367 (1978), aff'd, 79-2 USTC ¶9617 (2d Cir. 1979)

Teacher did not abandon profession
John C. Ford, 56 TC 1300 (1971), aff'd per curiam, 487 F.2d 1025 (9th Cir. 1973)

Engineer not established in his profession
Barry Reisine, 29 TCM 1429 (1970)
Thomas W. Gallery, 57 TC 257 (1971)

Orthodontic course
Rev. Rul. 74-78, 1974-1 CB 44

CPA review course—no deduction
Rev. Rul. 69-282, 1969-1 CB 55
William D. Glenn, 62 TC 270 (1974)

Private tutoring in management
Walter G. Lage, 52 TC 119 (1969) (Acq.)

Bar admission fee not deductible
Arthur E. Ryman, Jr., 51 TC 799 (1969)
William J. Brennan, 22 TCM 1222 (1963)

Flying lessons of free lance news photographer
Alan Aaronson, 29 TCM 786 (1970)

Prerequisites not deductible
Neal F. Krauss, 39 TCM 725 (1979)

¶21.3 • LAW SCHOOL COSTS

Law school
Reg. § 1.162-5(b)(2) and (3)
Jeffrey S. Augen, 33 TCM 1022 (1974)
Robert J. Connelly, 30 TCM 376 (1971), aff'd, 72-1 USTC ¶9188 (1st Cir. 1972)

Tax law courses taken by lawyer
Joseph T. Booth, III, 35 TC 1144 (1961)

CFA
Patrick L. O'Donnell, 62 TC 781 (1974), aff'd in unpublished decision (7th Cir. July 23, 1975)

Business law teacher
Juanita Ardavany, 38 TCM 569 (1979)

Bar review
Larry R. Adamson, 32 TCM 484 (1973)
Arthur E. Ryman, Jr., 51 TC 799 (1969)

Costs to practice in second state
Joseph J. Vetrick, 37 TCM 392

(1978), aff'd, 628 F.2d 885 (5th Cir. 1980)

Lawyer must practice profession
Albert C. Ruehmann, III, 30 TCM 675 (1971)
Richard M. Randick, 35 TCM 195 (1976)
Paul R. Wassenaar, 72 TC 1195 (1979)

Not qualified to take bar exam
Rev. Rul. 76-62, 1976-1 CB 12, distinguished by Rev. Rul. 76-352, 1976-2 CB 37

Foreign attorney
Yaroslaw Horodysky, 54 TC 490 (1970)

Pre-law courses
Ben H. Kim, 28 TCM 671 (1969)

¶21.4 • COURSES TAKEN BY DOCTORS AND NURSES

Reg. § 1.162-5(b)(3)
Joseph E. Campbell, 250 F. Supp. 941 (D. Pa. 1966)
John S. Watson, 31 TC 1014 (1959) (Nonacq.)
Ramon M. Greenberg, 367 F.2d 663 (1st Cir. 1966)

Cost of physician's assistant course
Matthew J. Reisinger, 71 TC 568 (1979)

¶21.5 • COURSES TAKEN BY TEACHERS

Reg. § 1.162-5(b)(2)
Clark S. Marlor, 251 F.2d 615 (2d Cir. 1958)
Laurie S. Robertson, 37 TC 1153 (1962)(Acq.)
Elmer R. Johnson, 313 F.2d 668 (9th Cir. 1963)

Effect on tenure
Harold H. Davis, 38 TC 175 (1962), rev'd in unpublished opinion (9th Cir. January 30, 1964)
Evelyn Devereaux, 292 F.2d 637 (3d Cir. 1961)

Change from professor to president
Rev. Rul. 68-580, 1968-2 CB 72

Qualifying in second state
Rev. Rul. 71-58, 1971-1 CB 55

Socialworker denied deduction for education necessary for faculty position
Kenneth C. Davis, 65 TC 1014 (1976)

Provisional license
Howard K. Michaelson, 313 F.2d 668 (9th Cir. 1963)
Elmer R. Johnson, 313 F.2d 668 (9th Cir. 1963)
Woodard W. Hartrick, 22 TCM 145 (1963)

Lonnie R. Lenderman, 22 TCM 511 (1963)
Sandra M. Hering, 33 TCM 1329 (1974)

Teaching assistant denied deduction of graduate study costs
Arthur M. Jungreis, 55 TC 581 (1970)

Paraprofessional
Leonarda Diaz, 70 TC 1067 (1978) aff'd 607 F.2d 995 (2d Cir. 1979)

Discussion leader
Gerald Schwerm, T.C. Memo. 1986-16

¶21.6 • PROFESSOR'S RESEARCH EXPENSES

*"Professors' Taxable Income and Deductions," G. Gibbs, 39 Accounting Review 1004 (1964)
Rev. Rul. 63-275, 1963-2 CB 85
Robert E. Drury, 36 TCM 35 (1977)

¶21.7 • LEAVE OF ABSENCE TO TAKE COURSES

IRS one-year test
Rev. Rul. 68-591, 1968-2 CB 73
*Letter Ruling 8538068

High school teacher's graduate course deductible
Mary O. Furner, 47 TC 165 (1966) rev'd, 393 F.2d 292 (7th Cir. 1968)

Unemployed student's college degree not deductible
Don Cornish, 29 TCM 235 (1970)

Resigned principal—3-year course
Robert Picknally, 36 TCM 1292 (1977)

Manager quits for 2-year MBA
Stephen G. Sherman, 36 TCM 1191 (1977)

IRS does not object to teacher's two-year absence
M. V. Damm, 41 TCM 1359 (1981)
Mary O. Furner, 47 TC 165 (1966), rev'd, 393 F.2d 292 (7th Cir. 1968)
Don Cornish, 29 TCM 235 (1970)
Rev. Rul. 68-591, 1968-2 CB 73

¶21.8 • HOW TO DEDUCT EDUCATION COSTS

Reg. § 1.162-5

Costs of typing
Rev. Rul. 67-421, 1967-2 CB 84

Sightseeing
Reg. § 1.162-5(d) and (e)

Payments from VA
Rev. Rul. 83-3 1983-1 CB 72

Trip between work and school
Gerhard F. B. Boerner, 30 TCM 240 (1971)

Note: Paragraph numbers refer to Part One. Items marked * are research aids, not citations of authority; see "Key to Citations" on page 337.

404

Robert J. Burton, 30 TCM 243 (1971)

Employer reimbursement or direct payment of tuition
Rev. Rul. 76–71, 1976–1 CB 308,

distinguished by Rev. Rul. 76–352, 1976–2 CB 37

Stipend paid by employer is taxable
Rev. Rul. 76–65, 1976–1 CB 46, distinguished by Rev. Rul. 76–352, 1976–2 CB 37

Payment for substitute teacher fund
Rev. Rul. 76–286, 1976–2 CB 41

¶21.9 • TRIP TAKEN FOR EDUCATIONAL PURPOSES
IRC § 274(m)(2)

¶22
Figuring Your Tax Liability

¶22.1 • FIGURING TAX LIABILITY
IRC § 1

Figuring taxable income
IRC § 63(a)

Using the tax tables
IRC § 3

¶22.2 • USING THE TAX RATE SCHEDULES
IRC § 1

¶22.3 • HOW CHILDREN ARE TAXED
IRC § 1(i)

¶22.5 • CHILDREN UNDER 14 SUBJECT TO SPECIAL TAX COMPUTATION
IRC § 1(i)(2)

¶22.6 • COMPUTING TAX AT PARENT'S TAX BRACKET
IRC § 1(i)(1)
IRC § 1(i)(3)

Applicable parent
IRC § 1(i)(5)

¶23
Alternative Minimum Tax

"The Alternative Minimum Tax For Individuals Under the Tax Reform Act of 1986," Beth B. Kern, 65 Taxes 307 (May 1987)

"How the TRA of 1986 Alters the Scope of and Planning for the AMT," George L. Middleton Jr. and Barbara a Newcomb, 67 Journal of Taxation 44 (1987)

"New Minimum Tax Credit May Render Prior Planning Techniques Obsolete," J. D. Finley and Preston Hofer, 67 Journal of Taxation 158 (1987)

¶23.2 • PATTERN OF AMT TAXATION ON FORM 6251
IRC § 55

Exemptions
IRC § 55(d)

Estimated tax requirement
IRC § 6654(f)(1)

¶23.3 • ADJUSTMENTS FOR AMT
IRC § 56

Passive losses
IRC § 58(b)

Farm losses
IRC § 58(a)

¶23.4 • TAX PREFERENCE ITEMS SUBJECT TO TAX
IRC § 57

¶23.5 • AMT FOREIGN TAX CREDIT AND OTHER TAX CREDITS
IRC § 59

Limit on nonrefundable credits
IRC § 26(a)

¶23.6 • AMT TAX CREDIT FROM REGULAR TAX
IRC § 53

¶23.7 • ELECTION FOR 10-YEAR WRITE-OFF OF PREFERENCES
IRC § 59(e)

Note: Paragraph numbers refer to Part One. Items marked * are research aids, not citations of authority; see "Key to Citations" on page 337.

¶24

Tax Credits

EARNED INCOME CREDIT
FOR LOW INCOME HOUSEHOLDERS

Note: Paragraph numbers refer to Part One. Items marked * are research aids, not citations of authority; see "Key to Citations" on page 337.

¶ 25

Tax Withholdings

W–2 Form
IRC § 6051

Social Security maximum
IRC § 31(b)(1)
Reg. § 1.31–2

Graduated withholding rates
IRC § 3402

Indicate marital status on exemption certificate
IRC § 3402(f)(1)

Claim exemptions on W–4
Reg. § 31.3401(e)–1
*IRS Publication 505

¶25.2 • WHEN INCOME TAXES ARE WITHHELD ON WAGES

Wages
IRC § 3401(a)
Reg. § 31.3401(a)–1

Payments other than wages (annuities, supplemental unemployment benefits)
IRC § 3402(o)
Reg. § 31.3402(o)–1

Domestics
Reg. § 31.3401(a)(3)–1

Agricultural workers
Reg. § 31.3401(a)(2)–1

Ministers
Reg. § 31.3401(a)(9)–1

Nonresident aliens
Reg. § 31.3401(a)(6)–1

Public officials
Reg. § 31.3401(a)–2(b)

Traveling advances
Reg. § 31.3401(a)–1(b)(2)

Board, lodging, health benefits, etc.
Reg. § 31.3401(a)(11)–1
Reg. § 31.3401(a)–1(d)(9) and (10)

Foreign government pay
Reg. § 31.3401(a)(5)–1

Foreign residents
Reg. § 31.3401(a)(8)(A)–1

U.S. possessions
Reg. § 31.3401(a)(8)(B)–1

Settlement of contract
Rev. Rul. 58–301, 1958–1 CB 23, distinguished by Rev. Rul. 74–252, 1974–1 CB 287 and Rev. Rul. 75–44, 1975–1 CB 15

Terminated employee
IRC § 6051(a)

Refund of employer overwithholding
Rev. Rul. 82–84, 1982–1 CB 208

¶25.3 • INCREASING WITHHOLDING ON YOUR PAY

IRC § 3402(i) and (p)
Temp. Reg. § 32.1(a) to (g)

¶25.4 • AVOIDING WITHHOLDING ON YOUR PAY

IRC § 3402(n)

¶25.5 • WITHHOLDING ALLOWANCES FOR TAX REDUCTION ITEMS

IRC § 3402(m)
Reg. § 31.3402(m)–1

¶25.6 • SPECIAL WITHHOLDING ALLOWANCES

IRC § 3402(f)(1)(G)

¶25.7 • WHEN TO FILE NEW WITHHOLDING EXEMPTION CERTIFICATE, FORM W–4

IRC § 3402(f)

Change in number of exemptions
Reg. § 31.3402(f)(2)–1(b) and (c)

When new withholding exemption takes effect
IRC § 3402(f)(3)
Reg. § 31.3402(f)(3)–1

¶25.8 • WHEN AND HOW TIPS ARE SUBJECT TO INCOME TAX AND FICA WITHHOLDING

Tax withheld on tips
IRC § 3402(k)
Reg. § 31.3402(k)

Written report
IRC § 6053

FICA tax
IRC § 3101
IRC § 3102

Tip allocation rules
IRC § 6053
Temp. Reg. Sec. 31.6053–3T

¶25.9 • WITHHOLDING ON GAMBLING WINNINGS

IRC § 3402(q)

¶25.10 • FICA WITHHOLDING

IRC § 3121

Rate of tax
IRC § 3101 (employee)
IRC § 3111 (employer)

"Wages" same as for income tax
Rowan Companies, Inc., 81–1 USTC ¶9479 (S. Ct. 1981)

Deferred pay plans
Rev. Rul. 78–263, 1978–2 CB 253

Sick pay
IRC § 3121(a)(2)
IRC § 3231(e)

Spouse and children as employees
IRC § 3121(b)(3)(A)

¶25.11 • WITHHOLDINGS ON PENSIONS AND ANNUITIES

IRC § 3405
Temp. Reg. § 35.3405–1

¶25.12 • BACKUP WITHHOLDING

IRC § 3406
Temp. Reg. § 35a.9999–1
Temp. Reg. § 35a.9999–2

¶ 26

Estimated Tax Payments

IRC § 6654
*IRS Publication 505

Farmers and fishermen
IRC § 6654(i)

$500 threshold
IRC § 6654(e)(1)

Note: Paragraph numbers refer to Part One. Items marked * are research aids, not citations of authority; see "Key to Citations" on page 337.

**¶26.2 • WHO MUST PAY ESTI-
MATED TAX?**

Required installments
IRC § 6654(c)

Partners
Reg. § 1.6654–2(d)(2)

**¶26.3 • PENALTY FOR UNDER-
ESTIMATES—TAX YEARS
BEFORE 1987**

Penalty for underpayments
IRC § 6654(a)
Reg. § 1.6654–1

Reasonable cause no bar to penalty
Barney Ruben Est., 33 TC 1071
(1960)

Underpayment
IRC § 6654(b)

Required amounts
IRC § 6654(d)

Withholding
IRC § 6654(g)

**¶26.4 • AVOIDING THE PENALTY
FOR 1988**

IRC § 6654(d)
IRC § 6654(e)(2)
Rev. Rul. 57–185, 1957–1 CB 454
Rev. Rul. 58–369, 1958–2 CB 894
John A. Guglielmetti, 35 TC 668
(1961)(Acq.)

*Waiver for hardship, retirement, or
disability*
IRC § 6654(e)(3)

¶26.5 • FINAL PAYMENT

Must file final return
IRC § 6012
Reg. § 1.6012–1
IRC § 6072(a)
Reg. § 1.6072–1

Get refund or credit
IRC § 6401
IRC § 6402

Reg. § 301.6402(a)–1
Reg. § 301.6402–1
Reg. § 301.6402–2

Interest on overpayment, not credit
IRC § 6611
IRC § 6513(d)
Reg. § 301.6513–1(d)

Interest if mathematics wrong
IRC § 6601
Rev. Rul. 55–448, 1955–2 CB 595

**¶26.6 • IF YOU USE A FISCAL
YEAR**

IRC § 6654(j)

**¶26.7 • AMENDING YOUR
ESTIMATE**

IRC § 6654(c)

January 31
IRC § 6654(h)

¶ 27

Filing a Refund Claim

*"The Imperfect Claim for Refund,"
D. N. Adams, 22 Tax Lawyer 309
(1969)

**¶27.1 • FILING FOR A REFUND
ON FORM 1040X**

IRC § 6401
IRC § 6402
Reg. § 301.6401–1
Reg. § 301.6402–2(c) and –3

**¶27.2 • WHEN TO FILE A REFUND
CLAIM**

Overpayment of estimated tax
Rev. Rul. 54–149, 1954–1 CB 159

*Divorce and net operating loss carry-
back*
Rev. Rul. 75–368, 1975–2 CB 480

*Credit against future estimated tax
liability*
IRC § 6402(b)

**¶27.3 • HOW TO FILE FOR A
REFUND**

¶27.4 • QUICK REFUND CLAIMS

Reg. § 1.6411–1(a)

Tax shelter refunds
Rev. Proc. 84–84, 1984–2 CB 782

**¶27.5 • INTEREST PAID ON REFUND
CLAIMS**

Interest from date of overpayment
Reg. § 301.6611–1(a)

*Interest on net operating loss carry-
back*
IRC § 6611(f)
Reg. § 301.6611–1(e)

**¶27.6 • TAX SHELTER REFUNDS
WITHHELD BY IRS**

Rev. Proc. 84–84, 1984–2 CB 782

**¶27.7 • EXTENSIONS OF TIME TO
FILE**

IRC § 6081
Reg. § 1.6081–4
Reg. § 1.6081–1
Reg. § 1.6073–4
Tax Practitioner Series 68–1, 69–2 N.
Atlantic Region

**¶27.8 • EXTENSIONS OF TIME TO
PAY**

Extension of time to pay tax

IRC § 6161
Reg. §1.6161–1
I.R. 1107, 2/16/71

Automatic extension period
Rev. Rul. 83–27, 83–1 CB 337

Still must pay interest
IRC § 6601(c)(1)

¶27.9 • AMENDED RETURNS

Reg. § 301.6402–3(a)

**¶27.10 • OFFICES OF DISTRICT
DIRECTORS**

IRC § 6091
Reg. § 1.6091–2

Armed forces
"Federal Income Tax Information
for Armed Forces Personnel"

Timeliness
IRC § 7502
Reg. § 301.7502–1

Note: Paragraph numbers refer to Part One. Items marked * are research aids, not citations of authority; see "Key to Citations" on page 337.

Tax-Saving Plans

¶ 28 • TAX SAVING IDEAS AND PLANNING

Tax shelter investments—passive loss limitations
IRC § 469

Children under 14
IRC § 1(i)

Interest deductions
IRC § 163

¶ 29 • TAX SAVINGS FOR HOME OWNERS

¶29.2 • TAX CONSEQUENCES OF SELLING YOUR HOME

*"Tax-Free Sales and Exchanges of Residences," A. L. Margolis, 1965 So. Calif. Tax Inst. 483

*"The Tax Position of the Home-owner," A. Aronsohn, 26 NYU Inst. 287 (1968)

*"How to Obtain the Most Favorable Tax Results When Client Disposes of Real Estate," Lloyd W. Herrold and James L. Mohr, 9 Taxation for Lawyers 140 (1980)

*"Selected Tax Strategies Involving the Principal Residence," Rolf Auster, 64 Taxes: The Tax Magazine 229 (April 1986).
*IRS Publication 523

To avoid tax on gain
IRC § 1034
Reg. § 1.1034–1

Sale by owner 55 and over
IRC § 121

Personal losses
Reg. § 1.262–1(b)(4)

Statute of limitations
IRC § 1034(j)
Reg. § 1.1034–1(i)

Installment sale reporting
Rev. Rul. 53–75, 1953–1 CB 83, amplified by Rev. Rul. 56–396, 1956–2 CB 298, as modified by Rev. Rul. 65–297, 1965–2 CB 152, as amplified by Rev. Rul. 76–44, 1976–1 CB 127
John F. Bayley, 35 TC 288 (1960) (Acq.)

¶29.3 • DEFERRING TAX ON THE SALE OF A RESIDENCE
IRC § 1034

Condemnations
IRC § 1033(a)(3)(B)
IRC § 1034(i)(2)
Reg. § 1.1034–1(h)

¶29.4 • PRINCIPAL RESIDENCE TEST

*"The Sale of a Personal Residence

That Has Been Used for Business," Stevens, J. K. Rice, 89 J. Real Estate Tax 264 (Spring 1983)

Principal residence
IRC § 1034(a)
Reg. § 1.1034–1(c)(3)
William H. Evans, 21 TCM 339 (1962)
Rev. Rul. 76–541, 1976–2 CB 246

Co-op converted to condominium
*Letter Ruling 8210054

Second house used as residence
Charles M. Shaw, 69 TC 1034 (1978)

Separated couple
Rev. Rul. 74–250, 1974–1 CB 202

Condominium apartment
Rev. Rul. 64–31, 1964–1 CB (Part 1) 300

Accommodations in retirement home
Rev. Rul. 60–135, 1960–1 CB 298

Part of house used for business
Charles T. Grace, 20 TCM 1313 (1961); but *see* Letter Ruling 7935003, home office as nonresidential use

No allocation required for nondeductible home office
Rev. Rul. 82–16, 1982–1 CB 461

Rent house and then later sell
IRC § 280A
Robert G. Clapham, 63 TC 505 (1975) (Acq.) (allowed)
Richard T. Houlette, 48 TC 350 (1967) (not allowed deferral)
Ralph L. Trisko, 29 TC 515 (1957) (Acq.) (deferral allowed)
Rev. Rul. 59–72, 1959–1 CB 203
William C. Stolk, 40 TC 345 (1963), aff'd, 326 F.2d 760 (2d Cir. 1964) (not allowed deferral)

Prolonged use of apartment
William C. Stolk, 326 F.2d 760 (2d Cir. 1964), aff'g 40 TC 345 (1964) (Acq.)

New residence in foreign country
Rev. Rul. 54–611, 1954–2 CB 159

Purchase of foreign residence by resident alien
Rev. Rul. 71–495, 1971–2 CB 311

Sale of land; house moved to new lot
Rev. Rul. 83–50, 1983–1 CB 41

Sale of vacant land
Benjamin A. O'Barr, 44 TC 501 (1965)

Separate sale of land and residence
Samuel E. Bogley, 263 F.2d 746 (4th Cir. 1959)
Rev. Rul. 65–541, 1976–2 CB 246

¶29.5 • TIME TEST
IRC § 1034(a) and (c)(5)
Reg. § 1.1034–1(c)
Joseph T. Gelinas, 35 TCM 498 (1976)

Strict application of time test
Andrew J. Marinko, 38 TCM 26 (1979)
James A. Henry, 44 TCM 844 (1982)

Contract to purchase insufficient
F. Occipinti, 28 TCM 968 (1969)

Construction start
Rev. Rul. 68–594, 1968–2 CB 339

Living in house
IRC § 280A
John F. Bayley, 35 TC 288 (1960) (Acq.)
Edwin L. Sheahan, 323 F.2d 383 (5th Cir. 1963)
Paul Bazzell, 26 TCM 981 (1967)
Nelson C. Elam, 477 F.2d 1333 (6th Cir. 1973), aff'g 58 TC 238 (1972)
Harry Lokan, 39 TCM 168 (1979)

Armed Forces
IRC § 1034(h)
Reg. § 1.1034–1(g)
Rev. Rul. 69–343, 1969–1 CB 305

Divorce affects postponed period
Rev. Rul. 78–136, 1978–1 CB 259

Combat zone suspension
Rev. Rul. 69–353, 1969–1 CB 49

¶29.6 • INVESTMENT TEST
IRC § 1034(a)
Richard E. Boesel Jr., 65 TC 378 (1975)

Note: Paragraph numbers refer to Part One. Items marked * are research aids, not citations of authority; see "Key to Citations" on page 337.

Reinvest in two homes
Rev. Rul. 66–114, 1966–1 CB 181

Amount realized
Reg. § 1034–1(b)(4)

Adjusted sales price
IRC § 1034(b)
Reg. § 1.1034–1(b)(3)

Fix-up expenses
IRC § 1034(b)
Reg. § 1.1034–1(b)(6)

Cost of new house
IRC § 1034(c)(2)
Reg. § 1.1034–1(b)(7)
Reg. § 1.1034–1(c)(4)
Grace Kern, 291 F.2d 29 (9th Cir.
1961), aff'g 185 F. Supp. 769 (D.
Ore. 1960)

Basis of new house
IRC § 1034(e)
Reg. § 1.1034–1(e)

Holding period
IRC § 1223(7)

Title in another's name
Rev. Rul. 55–37, 1955–1 CB 347

Moving house to a new lot
Rev. Rul. 54–156, 1954–1 CB 112

Remodeled vacation home
Letter Ruling 854802

**¶29.7 • REVIEWING PURCHASE
AND SALES RECORDS FOR
TAX REPORTING**

Charles O. Gunther Jr., 13 TCM 98
(1954)

**¶29.8 • A MARRIED COUPLE MAY
HAVE TO AGREE TO TAX
DEFERMENT**

IRC § 1034(g)
Reg. § 1.1034–1(f)

Husband and wife buy separate homes
Rev. Rul. 74–250, 1974–1 CB 202

*Husband and wife sell separate homes
and buy jointly*
Rev. Rul. 74–238, 1975–1 CB 257

**¶29.9 • SALE OF MORE THAN ONE
RESIDENCE WITHIN TWO
YEARS**

IRC § 1034(c)(4)
Reg. § 1.1034–1(d)
Robert W. Aagaard, 56 TC 191
(1971)(Acq.)
Richard P. Koehn, 16 TC 1378
(1951)
Theo Gutman Est., 18 TC 112
(1952)(Acq.)

*Sale of new house before sale of old
one*
IRC § 1034(c)(3)
Reg. § 1.1034–1(d)

Employment-related sale
IRC § 1034(d)

**¶29.11 • CLAIMING A LOSS ON
SALE OF PERSONAL
RESIDENCE**

IRC § 165(c)(2)
Reg. § 1.165–1(c)(2)
IRC § 262
Reg. § 1.262–1(b)(4)

Sale of partly rented house
Virginia V. Gary, BTA Memo., P–H
32,174, December 1, 1932 (capital
gain on rental part; nondeductible
loss on personal part)

Short-term lease returning a profit
Paul H. Rechnitzer, 26 TCM 298
(1967)

No loss unless move out
Peter Seletos, 254 F.2d 794 (8th
Cir. 1958)

Annual rent
Austin F. Stillman, 9 TCM 425
(1950)

Conversion to business property
Reg. § 1.165–9(b)

Isolated rental
Charles A. Foehl Jr., 20 TCM 418
(1961)

Intent to sell at profit
Lucille H. Gaunt, 69 F. Supp. 747
(W.D. Ky. 1938)
Sidney W. Sinsheimer, 7 BTA 1099
(Acq.)
John N. Hughes, 8 BTA 206 (Acq.)
Richard Croker Jr., 12 BTA 408
Henry J. Gordon, 12 BTA 1191
(Nonacq.)
Minnie L. Campe, 17 BTA 575 (Non-
acq.)
W. W. Holloway Admr., 19 BTA 378
Marjorie G. Randall, 27 BTA 475
Albert W. Bassett, 35 TCM 40 (1976)
Edward C. Quinn, 65 TC 523 (1975)

Vandalism
Elbert S. Tillotson, 12 TCM 171
(1953)

Architect
Leonard Hyatt, 20 TCM 1635 (1961),
supplemented by 20 TCM 1712
(1961), aff'd, 325 F.2d 715 (5th
Cir. 1964), cert. denied, 379 U.S.
832

Listing for sale or rent
George D. Morgan, 76 F.2d 390 (5th
Cir. 1935), cert. denied, 296 U.S.
601
Walden E. Sweet, 68–2 USTC ¶9656
(N.D. Cal. 1968)
James J. Sherlock, 31 TCM 383
(1972)

Rental to buyer
Henry B. Dawson Jr., 31 TCM 5
(1972)

Expenses of rental attempt
Paul F. Stutz, 24 TCM 888 (1965)

*Deducting expense of vacant building
put up for sale*
George W. Mitchell, 47 TC 120
(1966)(Nonacq.)

*Limit on expense deductions where
house used for personal purposes
during the year*
IRC § 280A

*Residence acquired by gift or inherit-
ance*
IRC § 1231
Robert W. Williams, 1 BTA 1101
(Acq.)
N. Stuart Campbell, 5 TC 272
(1945)(Acq.)
Maria Assmann Est., 16 TC 632
(1951)
Reed A. Watkins 32 TCM 1260
(1973)
George W. Carnrick, 9 TC 756
(1947)(Acq.)
Pauline Miller Est., 26 TCM 229
(1967)

Stock in co-op apartment
Rev. Rul. 60–76, 1960–1 CB 296
Cecil P. Stewart, 5 TCM 229 (1946)
Leon Chooluck, 13 TCM 864 (1954)
William M. Calder, Jr., 16 TC 144
(1951)(Acq.)

**¶29.12 • TAX-FREE RESIDENCE SALE
BY HOMEOWNERS AGE
55 OR OVER**

IRC § 121
Reg. § 1.121–1

Sale on 55th birthday qualifies
Rev. Rul. 77–382, 1977–2 CB 57

*Tax-free gain from sale counts as gross
income*
IRC § 6012(c)

Executor's completion of sale
Rev. Rul. 82–1, 1982–1 CB 366

Allocation for business use
Reg. § 1.121–4(e)

*Ownership and use need not be con-
current*
Rev. Rul. 80–172, 1980–2 CB 56

*Sale of remainder interest does not
qualify*
* Letter Ruling 8029088

Sale by marital trust
Rev. Rul. 85–45, 1985–1 CB 183

**¶29.13 • COMBINING THE EXCLU-
SION WITH TAX DEFERRAL**

Reg. § 1.121–5(g)

**¶29.14 • THE EXCLUSION AND
JOINTLY-OWNED RESI-
DENCES**

**¶29.15 • DEDUCTING EXPENSES OF
RENTING OUT PART OF
YOUR HOME**

Three-way allocation
Rev. Rul. 76–287, 1976–2 CB 80

Note: Paragraph numbers refer to Part One. Items marked * are research aids, not citations of authority; see "Key to Citations" on page 337.

¶29.16 • TAKING DEPRECIATION WHEN YOU RENT YOUR RESIDENCE

"Determining Deductibility of Expenses Related to Residence Rental: A Current Analysis," Richard P. Weber, 60 J. Taxation 158 (Mar. 1984)

"Rental of Principal Residence Before Sale: Retaining 1034 Treatment and Rental Deductions," James E. Maule, 55 J. Taxation 8 (1981)

"Real Property Depreciation and the Homeowner," David G. Harris, 62 Taxes 54 (1984)

Take depreciation
IRC § 167(a)
Reg. § 1.212–1(h)

Cost basis or value
Reg. § 1.167(f)–1
J. Russell Parsons, 227 F.2d 437 (3d Cir. 1956)
Louise Biesek, 22 TCM 464 (1963)

Basis when you sell
Reg. § 1.165–9
Tindle and Union Trust Co., 276 U.S. 582 (1928)
Mary Louise Bok, 46 BTA 678 (Acq.), aff'd, 132 F.2d 365 (3d Cir. 1942)
Bert P. Newron, 11 TC 512 (1948) (Acq.)
Alan H. Colcord, 9 TCM 729 (1950)

Need of appraisal
Sam Perry Robinson, 19 TCM 1374 (1960)

Depreciation on vacant residence
Hulet P. Smith, 26 TCM 149 (1967), aff'd, 397 F.2d 804 (9th Cir. 1968)
George W. Mitchell, 47 TC 120 (1966)(Nonacq.)
Frank A. Newcombe, 54 TC 1298 (1970)
James J. Sherlock, 31 TCM 383 (1972)
Edward G. Lowry Jr., 384 F. Supp. 257 (D. N.H. 1974)

Recapture of depreciation
IRC § 1250(d)(7)
Reg. § 1.1250–3(g)

¶29.17 • RESTRICTIONS ON DEDUCTING RENTAL EXPENSES OF A VACATION HOME AND PERSONAL RESIDENCES
IRC § 280A

"Maximizing After-Tax Return on Vacation Property Requires Special Care," Craig Dalton, Jr. and Richard Bristow, 32 Taxation for Accountants 348 (1984) 12 Taxation for Lawyers 338 (1984)

"An Update on Section 280A: Home Office and Vacation Home Deductions," Earl F. Davis and Kenneth H. Heller, 14 Tax Adviser 525 (Sept. 1983)

"Bolaris Decision Makes Temporary Rentals More Attractive to Homesellers," Karen J. Boucher and William A. Raabe, 65 Taxes 28 (January 1987)

"Tax Planning for Vacation Properties: A Comparison of Three Alternatives," Camille Blommer and William B. Pollard, 64 Taxes: The Tax Magazine 322 (May 1986)

"Tax Implications of the Rental Use of a Vacation Home: IRC, Section 280A," Timothy M. Mulligan, 88 Dickinson Law Review 109 (1983)

Income limitation on deductions
IRC § 280A(c)(5)

"Mini motorhome" as vacation home
Ronald L. Haberkorn, 75 TC 259 (1980)

Length of time vacation home used for personal purposes
IRC § 280A(d)

Rental for less than 15 days
IRC § 280A(g)

Profit motive
IRC § 183
Terence D. Clancy, 37 TCM 400 (1978)
Marvin Eisenstein, 37 TCM 441 (1978)
Truett E. Allen, 72 TC 28 (1979) (Acq.)
Lester W. Lindow, 37 TCM 1257 (1978)
Richard H. Nelson, 37 TCM 1204 (1978)

No deductions for rental of home space to employer
IRC § 280A(c)(6)

Mobile home not rented for profit
James E. Wittstruck, 645 F.2d 618 (8th Cir. 1981), aff'g per curiam 39 TCM 1168 (1980)

Qualified rental period
IRC § 280A(d)(3)

Rental pool arrangements
Prop. Reg. § 1.280A–3(e)
Richard S. Fine, 493 F. Supp. 540 (D. Ill. 1980), aff'd, 647 F.2d 763 (7th Cir. 1981)
Kenneth G. Byers, Jr., 82 TC 919

Allocation method
Dorance D. Bolton, 77 TC 104 (1981), aff'd, 694 F.2d 556 (9th Cir. 1982)
Edith McKinney,__F.2d__(10th Cir. 1983)

Rental of personal residence
IRC § 280A(d)(4)
Stephen Bolaris, 776 F.2d 1428 (9th Cir. 1985), revg. 81 TC 840 (1983)

Interest expense
IRC § 163(h)
IRC § 469(j)(7)

¶29.18 • REPORTING GAIN OR LOSS ON SALE OF RENTAL PROPERTY

"Handling the Treatment of Renting a Former Residence While Awaiting Its Sale," R. Lipton, 58 Journal of Taxation 170 (1983)

IRC § 1231
Leland Hazard, 7 TC 372 (1946) (Acq.)
Irving R. Stratton, 17 TCM 1066 (1958)
Stephen P. Wasnok, 30 TCM 39 (1971)

Courts contra
Isabel H. Grier, 120 F. Supp. 395 (D. Conn. 1954), aff'd per curiam, 218 F.2d 603 (2d Cir. 1955)
Charlotte A. Bauer, 168 F. Supp. 539 (Ct. Cl. 1959)

No recapture for principal residence
IRC § 1250(d)(7)
Reg. § 1.1250–3(g)

¶30 • TAX SAVINGS FOR INVESTORS IN SECURITIES

¶30.1

"Capital Gains and Losses After the Tax Reform Act of 1986," Robert L. Gardner and Dave N. Stewart, 65 Taxes 125 (February 1987)

"Capital and Section 1231 Asset Transactions: Status and Planning Opportunities, Under the New Law," Philip J. Harmelink & Phillis V. Copeland, 65 Taxes 176 (March 1987)

¶30.2 • YEAR-END SALES IN 1987
Capital gain holding period
IRC § 1222

Capital loss deduction against ordinary income
IRC § 1211(b)

Installment treatment barred for year end sale of publicly traded securities—post 1986
IRC 453(j)

Note: Paragraph numbers refer to Part One. Items marked * are research aids, not citations of authority; see "Key to Citations" on page 337.

Installment election for year-end sale
Rev. Rul. 82–227, 1982–2 CB 89

¶30.3 • KEEP RECORDS OF YOUR STOCK PURCHASES

Registered in own name
Reg. § 1.1012–1(c)(5)
James E. Davidson, 305 U.S. 44 (1938)

Margin account registered in "street" name
James L. Rankin, Exr., 295 U.S. 123 (1936)
Laura M. Curtis, 101 F.2d 40 (2d Cir. 1939)
James L. Rankin, Exr., 84 F.2d 551 (3d Cir. 1936)

Recapitalization
Robert E. Ford, 33 BTA 1229 (Acq.)

Reorganization—identified
Amelia D. Bloch, 148 F.2d 452 (9th Cir. 1945)

Failure to show certificate numbers
Kluger Associates, 69 TC 925 (1978), aff'd, 617 F.2d 323 (2d Cir. 1980)

Reorganization—average cost
Christian W. Von Gunten, 76 F.2d 670 (6th Cir. 1935)
Harry M. Runkle, 39 BTA 458
Pio Crespi, 126 F.2d 699 (5th Cir. 1942)
Big Wolf Corp., 2 TC 751 (1943) (Acq.)

Split-up
Robert E. Ford, 33 BTA 1229 (Acq.)
Herbert H. Franklin, 37 BTA 471 (Acq.)
Solomon B. Kraus, 88 F.2d 616 (2d Cir. 1937)

Stock dividends
George Vawter, 83 F.2d 11 (10th Cir. 1936), cert. denied, 299 U.S. 578

Stock rights
Williams R. Perkins, 12 F. Supp. 481 (Ct. Cl. 1935), cert. denied, 297 U.S. 710

¶30.4 • PUTS AND CALLS AND INDEX OPTIONS

Capital gain

IRC § 1234
Reg. § 1.1234–1

"Puts, Calls and Other Options," H. O. Colgan, Jr., 27 NYU Inst. 1157 (1969)

"How to Freeze Stock-Trading Profits; Get Capital Gains, with a Call and Short Sales," A. J. Hoffman, 16 J. Taxation 110 (1962)

Convert to long-term profits
Rev. Rul. 58–384, 1958–2 CB 410

¶30.5 • INVESTING IN MUTUAL FUNDS

Capital gain
IRC § 852(b)(3)
IRC § 854(a)

"Federal Income Tax Aspects of Mutual Funds," H. G. Salamy, 9 Practical Lawyer 33 (1963)

Averaging cost on sale of shares
Reg. § 1.1012–1(e)(i)

Interfund transfers
Rev. Rul. 56–246, 1956–1 CB 316

Dividend relief
IRC § 854(b)

¶30.6 • REDUCING THE TAX ON DIVIDEND INCOME

Sale after declaration of dividend
Reg. § 1.61–9(c)

Accrue from time of dividend default
Reg. § 1.61–7(c)

Stock dividends
IRC § 305
IRC § 307

¶30.7 • INVESTING IN SHORT-TERM PAPER, TREASURY BILLS, CDs, TAX-EXEMPT NOTES, AND OTHER SHORT-TERM OBLIGATIONS

IRC § 103

¶30.12 • INVESTING IN TAX EXEMPTS

IRC § 103

Qualified activity boards
IRC § 141

Tax preference item
IRC § 57(a)(5)

¶30.14 • SAVINGS BOND PLANS

Reporting E and EE Bond interest annually
IRC § 454(c)
Reg. § 1.454–1

Deduction for estate tax
Rev. Rul. 58–435, 1958–2 CB 370, distinguished by Rev. Rul. 68–145 1968–1 CB 203

¶30.15 • REPORTING INCOME FROM INVESTMENT CLUBS

"How to Obtain the Most Favorable Tax Results When Client Disposes of Real Estate," Lloyd W. Herrold and James L. Mohr, 9 Taxation for Lawyers 140 (1980)

"How to Convert an Apartment Complex into Condominium Units at Capital Gain Rates," J. V. Stewart, 8 Taxation for Lawyers 342 (1980)

"Can a Straight Condominum Conversion Produce a Capital Gain? An Analysis," Joel E. Miller, 54 Journal of Taxation 8 (1981)

"Capital Gains in Condominum Conversions? Internal Rev. Code See 1237," Roger Bolling and William Brent Carper, 13 R.E. Law Journal 45 (1984)

"Checklist of Tax Considerations When Real Property Is Acquired As Investment or Business," David F. Smith, 33 Tax for Accounting 104 (Aug. 1984)

"How TEFRA Affects Real Estate Investments: Analyzing Direct and Indirect Consequences," Stefan F. Tucker, 58 Journal of Taxation 66 (Feb. 1983)

"Depreciating Dealer Real Property," William Notbony, 62 Taxes 363 (1984)

"When Capital Gains Can Be Obtained Upon the Sale of Subdivided Real Estate," Tony A. Flesher and William Wallace, 31 Taxation for Accountants 98 (Aug. 1983)
Reg. § 301.7701–2(g), Example 7
Rev. Rul. 75–523, 1975–2 CB 257

¶31 • TAX SAVINGS FOR INVESTORS IN REAL ESTATE

"TRA 1986 Will Have a Pervasive Impact Upon Real Estate Transactions," Stefan Tucker, David Schwinger, 66 Journal of Taxation 130 (March 1987)

"Real Estate Financing Techniques; Equity Aspects of Debt Arrangements," B. Fisher, 60 Taxes 1040 (1982)

¶31.2 • INVESTMENTS IN REAL ESTATE VENTURES

"Real Estate Investment Trusts: Tax Problems of Equity Trusts," M. J. Rabinowitz, 31 NYU Inst. 1773 (1973)

"Tax Problems of Mortgage Real Estate Investment Trusts," C. A. Agger, 31 NYU Inst. 1739 (1973)

"Real Estate Investment Trusts," W. A. Kelley, 32 NYU Inst. 1637 (1974)

Syndicates
Reg. § 301.7701–1

Limited partnership not taxable as corporation
Phillip G. Larson, 66 TC 159 (1976) (Acq.)

Note: Paragraph numbers refer to Part One. Items marked * are research aids, not citations of authority; see "Key to Citations" on page 337.

Rev. Rul. 79–106, 1979–1 CB 448

IRS to study minimum capitalization requirement
Ann. 83–4, IRB 1983–2, 31

Real estate investment trusts
IRC § 856
IRC § 857
IRC § 858
Reg. § 1.856
Reg. § 1.857
Reg. § 1.858

REMICs
IRC § 860A–860G

Low-income housing credit
IRC § 42

¶31.3 • DETERMINING WHETHER A TENANCY IN COMMON IS A PARTNERSHIP

Collecting rents
Reg. § 1.761–1

Partnership return
Est. of R. L. Langer, 16 TC 41 (1951), aff'd per curiam, 194 F.2d 288 (9th Cir. 1952)
Lana Halen, 21 TC 212 (1954)
Louis Greenspan, 229 F.2d 947 (8th Cir. 1956)

Lack of partnership agreement
Craig M. Smith Est., 313 F.2d 724 (8th Cir. 1963)
Ayrton Metal Company, 229 F.2d 741 (2d Cir. 1962)

State law not determinative
Hubert M. Luna, 42 TC 1067 (1964)

Intent
William O. Culbertson, 337 U.S. 733 (1949)

Business activities
Edgar S. Appleby Est., 41 BTA 18 (1940), aff'd, 123 F.2d 700 (2d Cir. 1941)

¶31.4 • SALES OF SUBDIVIDED LAND—DEALER OR INVESTOR STATUS?

IRC § 1237
Reg. § 1.1237–1

All restrictions on dealer and rental real estate
IRC § 453C

Liquidation of business property—no capital gain
John W. Kelley, 18 TCM 329 (1959), aff'd, 281 F.2d 527 (9th Cir. 1959)

No sales effort
Robert E. Austin, 263 F.2d 460 (9th Cir. 1959)
William T. Minor Jr., 18 TCM 14 (1959)
James G. Hoover, 32 TC 618 (1959) (Acq.)
Allen Moore, 30 TC 1306 (1958) (Acq.)
Sam E. Broadhead Est., 32 TCM 1047 (1973)

Robert L. Adams, 60 TC 996 (1973) (Acq.)

Sale to controlled corporation
Ralph E. Gordy, 36 TC 855 (1961) (Acq.)

Real estate dealer
Richard H. Pritchett, 63 TC 149 (1974) (Acq.)

Effect of condemnation
Thomas K. McManus, 65 TC 197 (1975)
Tri S. Corp., 400 F.2d 862 (10th Cir. 1968) (capital gains allowed)
Theodore H. Case, 633 F.2d 1240 (6th Cir. 1980) (capital gains denied)

Developer allowed capital gains on sale to city
Est. of Eileen Knudsen, 40 TCM 510 (1980)

¶31.5 • EXCHANGING REAL ESTATE WITHOUT TAX

**"Tax Treatment of Like-Kind Exchanges of Property Used in a Trade or Business or for Investment,"* Gersham Goldstein and Charles S. Lewis, 5 Rev. Tax Individuals 201 (1981)

**"Section 1031 Like-Kind Property Exchanges: Possibilities and Pitfalls,"* L. A. Huskins, 1978 So. Calif. Tax Inst. 459

Basis
IRC § 1031(d)
Reg. § 1.1031(d)–1 and –2

Boot
Reg. § 1.1031(b)–1

Loss not recognized
IRC § 1031(a)
Reg. § 1.1031(a)–1

"Like kind"
Reg. § 1.1031(a)–1(b) and (c)
Rev. Rul. 59–229, 1959–2 CB 180
E. R. Braley, 14 BTA 1153 (Acq.)
George E. Hamilton, 30 BTA 160
P. G. Lake, Inc., 356 U.S. 260 (1958)

Productive use in trade or business
IRC § 1031
Reg. § 1.1031(a)–(1)(a)

Dealer
IRC § 1031
Luther A. Harr, 15 F. Supp. 1004 (E.D. Pa. 1936)

Resale
Ethel Black, 35 TC 90 (1960)

Exchanges of remainder and life interests
Rev. Rul. 72–601, 1972–2 CB 467

Partially tax-free exchanges
IRC § 1031(b)
Reg. § 1.1031(b)–1

Receipt of cash contractually obligated to be applied against liabilities not boot
Earlene T. Barker, 74 TC 555 (1980)

Planning tax-free exchange
Rev. Rul. 77–297, 1977–2 CB 304

99-year lease for fee hold
Carl E. Koch, 71 TC 54 (1978) (Acq.)

Sale/leaseback
Century Electric, 192 F.2d 155 (8th Cir. 1951), cert. denied, 342 U.S. 954

Time limit
IRC § 1031(a)(3)

Nonresident alien
IRC § 897(l)

¶31.6 • TIMING YOUR REAL PROPERTY SALES

Tax in year of sale
Milton S. Yunker, 26 TC 161 (1956), rev'd on other issue, 256 F.2d 130 (6th Cir. 1958)

Title passes
Alfred M. Bedell, 30 F.2d 622 (2d Cir. 1929)

Completion of terms of contingent sale
E. F. Baertschi, 412 F.2d (6th Cir. 1969), rev'g 49 TC 289 (1967)

Deliver deed and possession
William C. King, 10 BTA 308 (Acq.)
Big Western Oil & Gas Co., 9 BTA 427 (Acq.)

Possession this year, deed next year
J. T. Pittard, 5 BTA 929 (Acq.)
Standard Lumber Co., 28 BTA 352

Buyer in possession
Ted F. Merrill, 40 TC 66 (1963), aff'd per curiam, 366 F.2d 771 (9th Cir. 1964)
Marshall E. Boykin, 344 F.2d 889 (5th Cir. 1965)

Property held in escrow
Arthur Long, 1 BTA 796
Harry C. Moir, 14 BTA 23, (Nonacq.), aff'd, 45 F.2d 356 (7th Cir. 1930)

Deed delivered
William F. Scruggs, 281 F.2d 900 (10th Cir. 1960)

Option to sell exercised next year
Samuel C. Chapin, 180 F.2d 140 (8th Cir. 1950)

Contract to sell
Rev. Rul. 69–93, 1969–1 CB 139

No fair market value
A. M. Nichols, 44 F.2d 157 (3d Cir. 1930)
Nina Ennis, 17 TC 465 (1951)

Purchase price held
George I. Bumbaugh, 10 BTA 672
R. M. Waggoner, 9 BTA 629 (Nonacq.)
Preston R. Bassett, 33 BTA 182, aff'd per curiam, 90 F.2d 1004 (2d Cir. 1950)
K. E. Merren, 18 BTA 156 (Acq.), aff'd, 51 F.2d 44 (5th Cir. 1931)

Note: Paragraph numbers refer to Part One. Items marked * are research aids, not citations of authority; see "Key to Citations" on page 337.

Installment sales
IRC § 453

¶31.7 • SELLER'S REPOSSESSION OF REALTY AFTER BUYER'S DEFAULT ON MORTGAGE DEBT

"Repossession of Real Property," A. B. Willis, 1966 So. Calif. Tax. Inst. 601

"Effect of Repossessions Under Section 1038," C. C. Hauser, 25 NYU Inst. 47 (1967)

"Gain on Repossession Will Depend on Whether Property Was Real or Personal and Its Use," Ollie S. Powers and Caroline D. Strobel, 26 Tax for Accounting 36 (1981)
IRC § 1038
Reg. § 1.1038–1 through 3

End of holding period for depreciation recapture purposes where property foreclosed
IRC § 1250(d)(10)

¶31.8 • FORECLOSURE BIDS BY MORTGAGEES ON MORTGAGES OTHER THAN PURCHASE MONEY MORTGAGES

You bid in property at foreclosure sale
Reg. § 1.166–6(a)(1) and (b)(1)
Hadley Falls Trust Co., 110 F.2d 887 (1st Cir. 1940)

Unreported but accrued interest as income in foreclosure
Midland Mutual Life Ins. Co., 300 U.S. 216 (1937)

Bid price as fair market value
West Production Co., 121 F.2d 9 (5th Cir. 1941), cert. denied, 314 U.S. 682
Harold S. Weil, 111 F. Supp. 390 (D. La. 1953)

Must prove worthlessness of debt
Reg. § 1.166–2

Property voluntarily conveyed in satisfaction of debt
Achilles H. Kohn, 197 F.2d 480 (2d Cir. 1952)

Unreported but accrued interest as income in voluntary conveyance
Reserve Loan Life Ins. Co., 18 BTA 359 (Acq. and nonacq.)
Prudential Ins. Co. of America, 33 BTA 332 (Nonacq.)

Year deductible
Hadley Falls Trust Co., 110 F.2d 887 (1st Cir. 1940)
William C. Heinemann & Co., 40 BTA 1090

¶31.9 • HOW MORTGAGEES TREAT PROCEEDS OF FORECLO- SURE SALE TO THIRD PARTY

Foreclosure expenses
Coeur d'Alene Hotel Inc., BTA Memo., Dec. 12,097–A
Bowles Lunch, Inc., 33 F. Supp. 235 (Ct. Cl. 1940)

Foreclosure sale at less than your mortgage
Reg. § 1.166–6(a)(1)

Business bad debt is fully deductible
IRC § 166(a)

Nonbusiness bad debt is a limited capital loss
IRC § 166(d)

Partially worthless debts
IRC § 166(a)(2) and (d)(1)(A)

Business and nonbusiness bad debt must be uncollectible
IRC § 166(a)(1) and (d)

¶31.10 • TREATMENT OF DISCOUNT ON PURCHASED MORT- GAGE

*IRS Publication 17

Speculative test
Morton Liftin, 317 F.2d 234 (4th Cir. 1963), aff'g 36 TC 909 (1961)
Darby Investment Corp., 315 F.2d 551 (6th Cir. 1963), aff'g 37 TC 839 (1962)
Walter H. Potter, 44 TC 159 (1965)
Mark L. Grinsten, 23 TCM 390 (1964)
Joseph J. Weiss, 24 TCM 79 (1965)
Wingate E. Underhill, 45 TC 489 (1966)

¶31.11 • TRANSFERRING MORT- GAGED REALTY

Corporation
IRC § 351
IRC § 357
F. W. Drybrough, 376 F.2d 350 (6th Cir. 1967)

Gifts
Est. of Aaron Levine, 634 F.2d 12 (2d Cir., 1980)

¶32 • TAX SAVINGS FOR EXECUTIVES

¶32.2 • GENERAL PRINCIPLES

"How the New Tax Law Will Affect Executive Compensation," Robert K. Johnson, 65 Journal of Taxation 318 (November 1986)

¶32.3 • PENSION AND PROFIT- SHARING PLANS

IRC §§ 401 through 403

Restriction on S stockholder-employees
IRC § 1379(b)(1)

¶32.4 • CASH OR DEFERRED PAY ARRANGEMENTS: 401(K) PLANS

"Loss of IRA Deductions Makes 401(k) Plans More Attractive Despite New Limits," Peter L. Knox, Taxation of Accountants, March 1987

Qualified cash or deferred arrangements
IRC § 401(k)
Prop. Reg. § 1.401(k)–1

$7,000 salary reduction limit
IRC § 402(g)

Nondiscrimination rules
IRC § 401(k)(8)

¶32.5 • INSURANCE PLANS MAY BE TAX FREE

"Life Insurance in Executive Benefit Plans," Edward R. Hall and Peter W. Mullina, 1979 S. Cal. Tax Inst. 525

Assignment of group policy
Rev. Rul. 76–490, 1976–2 CB 300
Rev. Rul. 68–334, 1968–1 CB 403

Permanent and paid-up insurance— taxed to employee
Reg. § 1.61–2(d)(2)
Frank D. Yuengling, 69 F.2d 971 (3d Cir. 1934)
W. F. Parker, 38 BTA 989
Rev. Rul. 56–400, 1956–2 CB 116

Split-dollar
"Split Dollar Insurance," J. R. Lyons, 104 Trusts and Estates 15 (1965)

"Split Dollar Insurance: New Developments Suggest Planning Techniques That Save Taxes," Charles

C. Morgan, 58 Taxes 269 (1980)
Rev. Rul. 78–420, 1978–2 CB 67
Rev. Rul. 64–328, 1964–2 CB 11, amplified by Rev. Rul. 66–110, 1966–1 CB 112

Qualified group legal services plan
IRC § 120

¶32.6 • STOCK APPRECIATION RIGHTS

No tax on receipt of SARs
Rev. Rul. 80–300, 1980–2 CB 165

Tax on expiration of SARs
* Letter Ruling 8120103

No constructive receipt on SAR tied to stock option
Rev. Rul. 82–121, 1982–1 CB 79

¶32.7 • STOCK OPTIONS AND RE- STRICTED STOCK

"How the New Tax Law Will Affect Executive Compensation," Robert K. Johnson, 65 Journal of Taxation 318 (November 1986)

*"Planning for the New Incentive Stock

Note: Paragraph numbers refer to Part One. Items marked * are research aids, not citations of authority; see "Key to Citations" on page 337.

Options in Light of the Temporary Regs.," William L. Sollee, 56 Journal of Taxation 194 (1982)

*"Incentive Stock Options: Their Place in History, in Policy, and in Compensation Packages," D. Bennett, 40 NYU Inst. ¶9.00 (ERISA) (1983)

*"Impact of the New Alternative Minimum Tax on Employee Stock Options," C. Hartwell, 61 Taxes 407 (1983)
IRC § 83
Reg. § 1.83–1 through 8
IRC § 421
IRC § 422
IRC § 422A
IRC § 423
IRC § 424

Incentive stock options
IRC § 422A
Temp. Reg. § 14a–422A–1

Restricted stock
IRC § 83(c)

Executive cannot deduct loss on sale of

restricted stock to key employees
Henry C. Tilford, Jr., 75 TC 134 (1980), rev'd, 705 F.2d 828 (6th Cir. 1983)

Nonqualified stock options
IRC § 83(e)(3) and (4)
Reg. § 1.421–6(c)(1)

Electing tax on unrestricted value within 30 days
IRC § 83(b)

Finder's fee
Pasquale N. Cassetta, 39 TCM 188 (1979)

Sale treated as option
Reg. § 1.83–3(a)(2)

Not given in option exercise
John H. Rolfe, 488 F.2d 1092 (9th Cir. 1974), aff'g 58 TC 361 (1972)

Restricted stock options
IRC § 424

Qualified stock options
IRC § 422

Lapsed restrictions disregarded
IRC § 422A(e)(10)

¶32.8 • EDUCATIONAL BENEFITS FOR EMPLOYEES' CHILDREN

Grants by private foundations
Rev. Proc. 76–47, 1976–2 CB 670, amplified by Rev. Proc. 77–32, 1977–2 CB 541

Educational benefits trusts
Rev. Rul. 75–448, 1975–2 CB 55
Richard T. Armantrout, 67 TC 996 (1977), aff'd per curiam, 570 F.2d 210 (7th Cir. 1978)
Grant-Jacoby, Inc., 73 TC 700 (1980)
John C. Saunders,__F.2d__(5th Cir., 1983)

¶32.9 • PENALTY TAX ON EXCESS GOLDEN PARACHUTE PAYMENTS

IRC § 4999

No corporate deduction for excess parachute
IRC § 280G

¶33 • TAX SAVINGS IN FAMILY INCOME PLANNING

¶33.2 • GIFT TAX BASICS

IRC § 2502
IRC § 2503
IRC § 2505
IRC § 2523

Loans to relatives taxable
Esther C. Dickman, 84–1 USTC ¶9240

¶33.3 • HOW INCOME SPLITTING SAVES TAXES

Investment income of children under age 14
IRC § 1(i)

Cannot assign income
Paul R. G. Horst, 311 U.S. 112 (1940)
Guy C. Earl, 281 U.S. 111 (1930)
Edward T. Blair, 300 U.S. 5 (1937)

Excessive wages paid to children not deductible
Anthony R. Furmanski, 33 TCM 225 (1974)

Gift of right to collect rent
Wareham C. Seaman, 14 TCM 1123 (1955)

Family trust for earned income is tax avoidance scheme
Richard L. Wesenberg, 69 TC 1005 (1978) (Nonacq.)

Family trust materials not deductible
Louis P. Contini, 76 TC 447 (1981) (Acq.)
Rev. Rul. 79–324, 1979–2 CB 119

¶33.4 • CUSTODIAN ACCOUNTS FOR CHILDREN

Income taxed to child
Rev. Rul. 55–469, 1955–2 CB 519
Rev. Rul. 56–484, 1956–2 CB 23
Rev. Rul. 59–357, 1959–2 CB 212

Child remains dependent and exemption allowed
IRC § 151(e)
Reg. § 1.151–2

Gift tax
IRC § 2501
IRC § 2503
Reg. § 25.2503–2
Reg. § 25.2503–4
IRC § 2505
IRC § 2513
Rev. Rul. 56–86, 1956–1 CB 449

Estate tax
IRC § 2001
IRC § 2010
Rev. Rul. 57–366, 1957–2 CB 618

No estate tax where securities purchased with jointly owned funds in which deceased custodian had no interest
Estate of Jack F. Chrysler, 361 F.2d 508 (2d Cir. 1966)

No estate tax on estate of deceased spouse who was custodian and agreed to gift splitting
Rev. Rul. 74–556, 1974–2 CB 300

No estate tax where custodian made gift of custodial securities before death

Antonia B. Vogel Est., 36 TCM 875 (1977)

Trust accounts ineffective to split interest income
Roy K. Heintz, 41 TCM 429 (1980)

¶33.5 • OTHER TYPES OF INVESTMENTS FOR CHILDREN

Assignment of licensing agreement by inventor
Lewis R. Heim, 262 F.2d 887 (2d Cir. 1959)

¶33.6 • HOLDING PROPERTY AS JOINT TENANTS

*"Tax, Legal, and Practical Problems Arising from the Way in Which Title to Property Is Held by Husband and Wife," 1966 So. Calif. Tax Inst. 35
IRC § 2040

Street account
Rev. Rul. 69–148, 1969–1 CB 226

¶33.7 • TRUSTS IN FAMILY PLANNING

Repeal of 10-year trust rule
1986 Tax Reform Act Section 1402, amending IRC § 673

5% grantor trust rule
IRC § 673(a)

Minor liberal descendants
IRC § 673(b)

Grantor trusts: spouse living with grantor
IRC § 672

Note: Paragraph numbers refer to Part One. Items marked * are research aids, not citations of authority; see "Key to Citations" on page 337.

Tax rates for trusts and estates
IRC § 1(h)—1987 rates
IRC § 1(e)—1988 rates

Division of income
T. N. Mauritz, 206 F.2d 135 (5th Cir. 1953)
Estelle Morris Trusts, 51 TC 20 (1968), aff'd per curiam, 427 F.2d 1361 (9th Cir. 1970)

Trust for spouse may be taxed to creator
IRC § 677(a)

"Apocalypse" family trust
Rev. Rul. 75–257, 1975–2 CB 251
Rev. Rul. 75–258, 1975–2 CB 503
Rev. Rul. 75–259, 1975–2 CB 361
Rev. Rul. 75–260, 1975–2 CB 376

Trust sale of appreciated property within two years
IRC § 644

Escape estate tax
IRC § 2038

Gift tax
IRC § 2511
Reg. § 1.2511–1

Revocable trust—no tax changes
IRC § 676
IRC § 2038

Short term
IRC § 673
IRC § 2037
IRC § 2511
Reg. § 1.2511–1

Testamentary trust—estate tax
IRC § 2037

Accumulation trust
IRC §§ 665 through 667

Foreign trusts with U.S. beneficiaries
IRC § 643
IRC § 668
IRC § 679

Generation-skipping transfers
IRC §§ 2601 through 2622

¶33.8 • OTHER TRANSFERS THAT MAY SAVE TAXES

Give appreciated property
W. G. Farrier, Est., 15 TC 277 (1950)(Acq.)
Charles N. Prothro, 209 F.2d 331 (5th Cir. 1954)
Elsie Sorelle, 22 TC 459 (1954) (Acq.)
Marvin Berry, 11 TCM 301 (1952)
Emily J. Haley, 381 F. Supp. 431 (M.D. Ga. 1974)
Rev. Rul. 55–531, 1955–2 CB 520, distinguished by Rev. Rul. 63–66, 1963–1 CB 13, as modified by Rev. Rul. 75–11, 1975–1 CB 27

Avoid claim gift not completed
William R. Tracy, 70 F.2d 93 (6th Cir. 1934)
Rev. Rul. 58–337, 1958–2 CB 13
Richard G. Shafto, 246 F.2d 338 (4th Cir. 1957)

Jeannette W. Fitz Gibbon, 19 TC 78 (1952)

Get loss deduction by selling first
Reg. § 1.165–1(b)

Private annuities—gain reported ratably over life expectancy
Rev. Rul. 69–74, 1969–1 CB 43

Gain immediately taxed on secured private annuity
Bell Est., 60 TC 469 (1973)
212 Corp., 70 TC 788 (1978)

Recovery of basis defers gain in private annuity
Esther LaFargue, 689 F.2d 845 (9th Cir. 1982)

No interest deduction for annuity payments
Rebecca Bell, 76 TC 233 (1981), aff'd per curiam, 82–1 USTC ¶9148 (8th Cir. 1982)

¶33.9 • SPLITTING BUSINESS INCOME WITH YOUR FAMILY

Stock transfers to family members
IRC § 1375(c)
Reg. § 1.1375–3
Edwin D. Davis, 64 TC 1034 (1975)

Trust can be partner
Frank Trust, 44 BTA 934

Trust ignored
Max J. Kuney, 448 F.2d 22 (9th Cir. 1971)

S transfer disregarded
Gino A. Speca, 38 TCM 544 (1979), aff'd, 630 F.2d 554 (7th Cir. 1980)

Control kept by parent
Henry D. Duarte, 44 TC 193 (1965)

Transfer to children recognized where mother was active custodian
Donald O. Kirkpatrick, 36 TCM 1122 (1977)

Court reporter still taxed on his corporation's income
Elvin V. Jones, 64 TC 1066 (1975)

Corporation to split commission income
Frederick H. Foglesong, 621 F.2d 865 (7th Cir. 1982), rev'g 35 TCM 1309 (1976)

Family partnership interests disregarded where capital comes from borrowed funds
Carriage Square, Inc., 69 TC 10 (1977)

Family partnership in CPA firm disregarded
Melvin P. Ketter, 70 TC 637 (1978)

S corporation allocation
IRC § 1366(e)

¶33.10 • LIFE INSURANCE OFFERS TAX ADVANTAGES

"Insurance Programs as Non-Taxable Compensation," J. M. Skilling, Jr., 27 NYU Inst. 29 (1970)

"Use of Life Insurance in Estate Planning—Recent Developments," F. S. Berall, 31 NYU Inst. 1053 (1973)

Interest on installment payments
IRC § 101(c)
Reg. § 1.101–3

$1,000 tax free
IRC § 101(d)(1)(B)
Reg. § 1.101–4(a)

Interest deductible
IRC § 163

Estate tax eliminated
IRC § 2042
Reg. § 20.2042–1(c)

Policy transferred within three years of death included in taxable estate
IRC § 2035

Assignment of group-term policy
Rev. Rul. 84–147, 1984–2 CB 201

Substitution of group carrier does not jeopardize prior assignments
Rev. Rul. 80–289, 1980–2 CB 270

Assigned policy used by husband as collateral for loan
Hilton W. Goodwyn Est., 32 TCM 1026 (1973)
Max Krischer Est., 32 TCM 821 (1973)

Son paid premiums
Morris R. Silverman Est., 61 TC 338 (1974)(Acq.), aff'd, 521 F.2d 574 (2d Cir. 1975)

Right to select type of payment defeats assignment
Est. of James H. Lumpkin Jr., 474 F.2d 1092 (5th Cir. 1973)

Assigned flight insurance subject to estate tax
Fay L. Berman Exrx, 487 F.2d 70 (5th Cir. 1973)

Veto power subjects assigned policy to tax
Rev. Rul. 75–70. 1975–1 CB 301

Gift tax
Reg. § 25.2512–6
Reg. § 25.2503–2

Marital deduction
IRC § 2056

Funding buy-and-sell contracts
Rev. Rul. 59–184, 1959–1 CB 65

¶33.11 • LOSSES MAY BE DISALLOWED ON SALES TO RELATIVES

Nondeductible losses
IRC § 267
Reg. § 1.267(a)–1(a)

Bona fide
Reg. § 1.267(a)–1(c)
Nathan Blum, 5 TC 702 (1945)

Stock exchange
John P. McWilliams, 331 U.S. 694 (1947)
John B. Shethar, 28 TC 1222 (1957)

Note: Paragraph numbers refer to Part One. Items marked * are research aids, not citations of authority; see "Key to Citations" on page 337.

Foreclose mortgage
Thomas Zacek, 8 TC 1056 (1947)

Pledgee's sale
Charles E. Cooney, 1 TCM 55 (1942)

Members of family
IRC § 267(b)(1) and (c)(4)
Reg. § 1.267(c)–1(a)(4)

Nominee
Charles J. Stamler, 45 BTA 37
O. Phil Nordling, 166 F.2d 703 (9th Cir. 1948), cert. denied, 337 U.S. 938

Wife's relative
J. Henry DeBoer, 194 F.2d 989 (2d Cir. 1952) (Nonacq.)

Son-in-law
Fervel Topek, 9 TC 763 (1947)

Family hostility may not be considered
David L. Miller, 75 TC 182 (1980)

Withdrawal from joint ventures and partnerships
T. N. Mauritz, 205 F.2d 135 (5th Cir. 1953)
Fritz Busche, 229 F.2d 437 (5th Cir. 1956)

Henry V. B. Smith, 5 TC 323 (1945)

Controlled corporation
IRC § 267
Reg. § 1.267(b)–1
Reg. § 1.267(c)–1

Other losses disallowed
IRC § 267
Reg. § 1.267(b)–1

Partnership and controling persons
IRC § 707(b)(1)(A)

¶34 • TAX SAVINGS FOR SENIOR CITIZENS

¶34.1 • TAX RULES FOR PERSONS 65 OR OVER

*IRS Publication 554

¶34.2 • CREDIT FOR ELDERLY AND DISABLED

IRC § 22
*IRS Publication 524

¶34.3 • WHO QUALIFIES FOR THE CREDIT?

IRC § 22(b)

Nonresident alien ineligible
IRC § 22(f)
*IRS Publication 524

¶34.4 • INITIAL BASE FOR THE CREDIT

IRC § 22(c)(2)

¶34.5 • INITIAL BASE FOR DIS-ABLED PERSONS

IRC § 22(c)(2)(B)

Disability income
IRC § 22(c)(2)(B)(iii)

Disability defined
IRC § 22(e)(3)

¶34.6 • REDUCTION OF BASE AMOUNT

IRC § 22(c)(3)
IRC § 22(d)(3)

¶34.8 • HOW SOCIAL SECURITY BENEFITS ARE TAXED

IRC § 86
*IRS Publication 915

Base
IRC § 86(c)

¶34.9 • SOCIAL SECURITY BENE-FITS SUBJECT TO TAX

IRC § 86(d)

Benefits to child
House and Ways and Means Committee Report to P.L. 98–21

Workmen's Compensation
IRC § 86(d)(3)

Repayments
IRC § 86(d)(2)

Nonresident alien
IRC § 871(a)(3)

¶34.10 • ELECTION FOR LUMP-SUM PAYMENT COVERING PRIOR YEARS

IRC § 86(e)

¶35 • TAX SAVINGS FOR VETERANS AND MEMBERS OF THE ARMED FORCES

¶35.2 • TIME EXTENSION TO PAY YOUR TAX WHEN ENTER-ING SERVICE

Rev. Proc. 57–25, 1957–2 CB 1092
Soldiers' and Sailors' Civil Relief Act of 1940, Sec. 513
T.D. 5279, 1943 CB 952, amended by T.D.'s 5293, 5429, 5444, 5959

Filing extension for spouse of MIA's
IRC § 7508(b)

Joint return election by spouse of MIA
IRC § 6013(f)(1)

¶35.3 • DISABILITY RETIREMENT PAY

IRC § 104
Career Compensation Act of 1949, Sec. 402
Pub. L. No. 78–314
Zebulon L. Strickland, Jr., 540 F.2d 1196 (4th Cir. 1976)
IR 1979, 3/31/78

¶35.4 • YOU DO NOT REPORT THIS INCOME

Exclusion for qualified military benefits
IRC § 134

Adjustments for inflated foreign currency
IT 3725, 1945 CB 60

Allotments for dependents
Special Ruling, Jan. 10, 1946
Rev. Rul. 70–87, 1970–1 CB 29

Former prisoners of war
Rev. Rul. 55–132, 1955–1 CB 213
Rev. Rul. 56–462, 1956–2 CB 20

Bonuses
Rev. Rul. 56–610, 1956–2 CB 25

State bonus
Rev. Rul. 68–158, 1968–1 CB 47

Gratuity
Rev. Rul. 55–330, 1955–1 CB 236

Dividends on GI insurance
Special Ruling, February 3, 1947

Serviceman's Readjustment Act
Veterans Administration Release, February 14, 1957
Ephraim Banks, 17 TC 1386 (1952)

Family separation allowance
Clifford Jones, 60 Ct. Cls. 552
Rev. Rul. 70–281, 1970–1 CB 16

Pay forfeited on court martial order
Armed Forces Fed. Income Tax, '77 ed.

Subsistence allowance
Rev. Rul. 55–572, 1955–2 CB 45, distinguished by Rev. Rul. 63–64, 1963–1 CB 30

Moving and storage
IRC § 217(g)

Mustering out pay
IRC § 113
Reg. § 1.113–1

Note: Paragraph numbers refer to Part One. Items marked * are research aids, not citations of authority; see "Key to Citations" on page 337.

Naval attache expense money
Rev. Rul. 77–351, 1977–2 CB 23

Retirement pay reduction to provide survivor annuity
IRC § 122

Injuries or sickness
Career Compensation Act of 1949, Sec. 402

Return to active duty
Special Ruling, January 24, 1945

Medical and pension benefit from Veteran's Administration
Rev. Rul. 72–605, 1972–2 CB 35

Subsistence payments
Veterans Administration Release, February 14, 1957

Travel expenses—permanent duty station
W. W. Bercaw, 165 F.2d 521 (4th Cir. 1948)
Rev. Rul. 55–571, 1955–2 CB 44

Uniforms; uniform allowances
Reg. § 1.61–2(b)

VA death benefits
Veterans Administration Release, February 14, 1957

¶35.5 • YOU MAY DEDUCT

Board and lodging costs
Rev. Rul. 55–571, 1955–2 CB 44, modified by Rev. Rul. 67–438, 1967–2 CB 82

Cost of insignia
Charles A. Harris, 12 TCM 42 (1953)

Fatigues
Rev. Rul. 67–115, 1967–1 CB 30

Contributions to "Company" fund
Rev. Rul. 73–296, 1973–2 CB 67
Rev. Rul. 55–201, 1955–1 CB 269
B. O. Mahaffey, 1 TC 176 (1942), rev'd, 140 F.2d 879 (8th Cir. 1944)
Morris Investment Corp., 156 F.2d 748 (3d Cir. 1946), cert. denied, 329 U.S. 788
Jacob Kaplan, 21 TC 134 (1953) (Acq.)
William F. Krahl, 9 TC 862 (1947)

Trade in open market
Richard W. Norton Jr., 250 F.2d 902 (5th Cir. 1958)

Sale to family
IRC § 267(b)(1) and (c)(4)
Reg. § 1.267(c)–1(a)(4)

Court martial expenses
Lindsay C. Howard, 202 F.2d 28 (9th Cir. 1953), aff'g 16 TC 157 (1951)(Acq.)

Professional societies
Rev. Rul. 55–250, 1955–1 CB 270

Increased retirement pay
IRC § 212

Professional journals
Charles A. Harris, 12 TCM 42 (1953)

Travel status and duty expenses
Rev. Rul. 67–438, 1967–2 CB, 82, modifying Rev. Rul. 55–571, 1955–2 CB 44
Charles A. Harris, 12 TCM 42 (1953)

Temporary lodging allowance
Rev. Rul. 76–2, 1976–1 CB 82

¶35.6 • TAX INFORMATION FOR RESERVISTS

Transportation
Rev. Rul. 76–453, 1976–2 CB 86, suspended by Pub. L. No. 95–427 until June 1, 1981

Readjustment payments
Rev. Rul. 67–350, 1967–2 CB 58

*"The Armed Forces Reservist and IRC Section 162," J. J. Smith Jr. 47 Taxes 167 (1969)

*"Many Tax Deductions Are Overlooked by Military Reservists," R. A. Behren, 16 Journal of Taxation 232 (1962)

¶35.7 • TAX-FREE COMBAT PAY

IRC § 112
Executive Order No. 11216, 4/26/65
Rev. Rul. 73–187, 1973–1 CB 51
Ben C. Land, 61 TC 675 (1974)

Hospitalized serviceman
IRC § 112(a)(2)

"Missing" status
IRC § 112(d)

Waiver of tax
Rev. Rul. 68–393, 1968–2 CB 292
Rev. Rul. 72–169, 1972–1 CB 43

¶35.8 • ABATEMENT FOR COMBAT DEATHS

IRC § 692

MIAs
IRC § 692(b)

¶36 • HOW TO TREAT FOREIGN INCOME

¶36.2 • RULES FOR REPORTING FOREIGN INCOME

*"Tax Planning for U.S. Executives Moving Abroad," R. Voll, 61 Taxes 342 (1983)

*IRS Publication 54

Foreign earned income exclusion
IRC § 911

$70,000 exclusion after 1986
IRC § 911(b)(2)

Must file return even if exclusion is available
Reg. § 1.911–6
IRC § 6012
Reg. § 1.6012–1(a)(3)

Panama Canal Commission employees
1986 Tax Act Section 1232

¶36.3 • CLAIMING THE FOREIGN EARNED INCOME EXCLUSION

*"Employment Overseas and the Tax Home Issue: Exclusion versus Deduction," L. Stillabower and L. Phillips, 61 Taxes 202 (1983)

Foreign residence and foreign physical presence test
IRC § 911(d)(1)

Foreign tax home
IRC § 911(d)(1); § 911(d)(3)

Exclusion allowed in year services performed
IRC § 911(b)(2)(B)

Pro-rating exclusion on daily basis
IRC § 911(b)(2)

Exclusion must be elected
IRC § 911(a)

No foreign tax credit on excluded income
IRC § 911(d)(6)

No exclusion for countries under U.S. travel ban
IRC § 911(d)(8)
Rev. Rul. 87–35, IRB 1987–18, 4

¶36.4 • HOW TO TREAT HOUSING COSTS

Exclusion for employer-financed housing
IRC § 911(c)

Qualifying housing expense
IRC § 911(c)(2)

Deduction for housing costs not paid for by employer
IRC § 911(c)(3)

Note: Paragraph numbers refer to Part One. Items marked * are research aids, not citations of authority; see "Key to Citations" on page 337.

¶36.5 • WHAT IS FOREIGN EARNED INCOME?

IRC § 911(b)

Reimbursed moving expenses
Rev. Rul. 75–84, 1975–1 CB 236, amplified by Rev. Rul. 76–162, 1976–1 CB 197
Clifford Dammers, 76 TC 835 (1981)

¶36.6 • MEETING THE FOREIGN RESIDENCE OR PHYSICAL PRESENCE TEST

Bona fide residence test
IRC § 911(d)(1)(A)
IRC § 911(d)(5)

Physical presence test—330 day/12 month requirement
IRC § 911(d)(1)(B)

Waiver of time tests due to war or civil unrest
IRC § 911(d)(4)

¶36.7 • CLAIMING DEDUCTIONS IF YOU ELECT THE EARNED INCOME EXCLUSION

No deduction for expenses attributable to excluded income
IRC § 911(d)(6)

Deducting expenses of moving overseas
IRC § 217(h)

Retirees and survivors of workers abroad returning to U.S.
IRC § 217(i)

Deduction for compulsory home leave expenses
Rev. Rul. 82–2, 1982–1 CB 367
Bruce C. Stratton, 448 F.2d 1030 (9th Cir. 1971)

¶36.8 • WHAT TO DO IF YOUR RIGHT TO AN EXCLUSION IS NOT ESTABLISHED WHEN YOUR RETURN IS DUE

IRS Form 2350

¶36.9 • TAX-FREE MEALS AND LODGING FOR WORKERS IN CAMPS

IRS § 119(c)

¶36.10 • EARNINGS IN VIRGIN ISLANDS, GUAM, NORTH-ERN MARIANA ISLANDS, AND U.S. POSSESSIONS

Guam, Samoa, No. Mariana Islands
IRC § 931

Virgin Islands
IRC § 932
IRC § 934

Tax Guide for U.S. Citizens Employed in U.S. Possessions
*IRS Publication No. 570

U.S. or agencies
IRC § 931(d)
Rev. Rul. 54–612, 1954–2 CB 169

¶36.11 • EARNINGS IN PUERTO RICO

IRC § 933
Reg. § 1.933–1
Rev. Rul. 56–585, 1956–2 CB 166

Moving expenses allocable to tax-exempt income from Puerto Rico not deductible
Alberto Roque, 65 TC 920 (1976)

¶36.12 • TAX TREATIES WITH FOR-EIGN COUNTRIES

IRC § 894
Reg. § 1.894–1
IRC § 7852(d)

¶36.13 • EXCHANGE RATES AND BLOCKED CURRENCY

*IRS Publication 54

Foreign currency gains and losses
IRC § 988

¶36.14 • INFORMATION RETURNS ON FOREIGN CURRENCY

IRS Forms 4789 and 4790

¶36.15 • FOREIGN TAX CREDIT

*IRS Publication 514

Foreign tax credit or deduction
IRC § 33
IRC § 901
Reg. § 1.901–1 and 2

Foreign tax defined
Temp. Reg. § 4.901–2

¶36.16 • COMPUTING THE FOREIGN TAX CREDIT

*"New Tax Law Makes Major Changes to the Foreign Tax Credit Limita-tion," Gerald T. Ball, Donald Car-ter and Tom B. Wight, 66 Journal of Taxation 140 (March 1987)

Overall limitation
IRC § 904

Capital gains
IRC § 904(b)(2)

Recapture of overall foreign loss
IRC § 904(f)

Credit limitation for passive income and other items
IRC § 904(d)

¶36.17 • CARRYBACK AND CARRY-OVER OF EXCESS FOREIGN TAX CREDIT

IRC § 904(c)

¶37 • HOW ALIENS ARE TAXED IN THE UNITED STATES

IRC § 871
*IRS Publication 519

*"The 'Trade or Business' of Foreign Taxpayers in the United States," Joseph Isenbergh, 61 Taxes 972 (1983)

*"The Scope of the Withholding Tax on Payments to Aliens: A Survey," Max Holmes, 22 Columbia Jour-nal of Transnational Law 359 (1984)

¶37.1 • RESIDENT OR NON-RESIDENT?

*"Defining Resident Alien Status for Income Tax Purposes," James D. Herbert, 24 Virginia Journal of In-ternational Law 667 (1984)

Resident taxed as U.S. citizen
Reg. § 1.871–1
Prop. Reg. § 1.871–1(a)

Nonresident
IRC § 871
Prop. Reg. § 1.871–1(b)

Capital gains
IRC § 871(a)(2)

Doing business
IRC § 871(b)

Who is a resident—Pre-1985
Reg. § 1.871–2
David O. Tilburn, 14 TCM 950 (1955)
Rudolf Jellinek, 36 TC 826 (1961) (Acq.)
Dorothy C. Ingram, 47 F.2d 925 (S.D.N.Y. 1931), aff'd, 57 F.2d 65 (2d Cir. 1932)
Federico Stallforth, 77 F.2d 548 (D.C. Cir. 1935), cert. denied, 296 U.S. 606
Orlando Hechavarria, 374 F. Supp. 128 (S.D. Ga. 1974)

Indefinite stay—Pre-1985
Zareh Nubar, 185 F.2d 584 (4th Cir. 1951), cert. denied, 341 U.S. 925

Foreign students
U.S. Treasury Doc. No. 5588
Rev. Rul. 54–87, 1954–1 CB 155, amplified by Rev. Rul. 67–159, 1967–1 CB 280

¶37.2 • HOW A RESIDENT ALIEN 18 TAXED

Same as U.S. citizen
Reg. § 1.871–1
Prop. Reg. § 1.871–1(a)

Work for foreign government
IRC § 893
Reg. § 1.893–1

Joint return
IRC § 6013(a)(1)
IRC § 6013(g) and (h)

Note: Paragraph numbers refer to Part One. Items marked * are research aids, not citations of authority; see "Key to Citations" on page 337.

Unused zero bracket amount
IRC § 63(e)

Dual status-zero bracket amount
Rev. Rul. 83–90 1983–1 CB 15
(No zero bracket amount)
Nino, 565 F.2d 1234 (2d Cir. 1977)
(full standard deduction allowed)

Split year
Georges Simenon, 44 TC 820 (1965)

Mary A. Marsman, 205 F.2d 335
(4th Cir. 1953) cert. denied, 348
U.S. 943

¶37.3 • WHO IS A RESIDENT ALIEN?
IRC § 7701(b)

First-year election to be treated as resident
IRC § 7701(b)(4)

*IRS Publication 519

¶37.4 • WHEN AN ALIEN LEAVES THE U.S.
IRS Doc. No. 5589, "U.S. Tax Guide for Aliens"
Nino Sanzogno, 60 TC 947 (1973)
(Acq.)

¶ 38 • WHAT HAPPENS AFTER YOU FILE YOUR RETURN

¶38.1 • HOW THE IRS EXAMINES YOUR RETURN
Reg. § 301.6103(a)
Reg. § 301.6213–1

Penalty for frivolous Tax Court suit
Roger D. Wilkinson, 71 TC 633 (1979)

¶38.2 • AUTOMATIC DATA PROCESSING (ADP)
TCMP audits: IRS summons upheld
George Flagg, 634 F.2d 1087 (8th Cir. 1980), cert. denied, 101 S. Ct. 1977 (1981)

¶38.3 • SOCIAL SECURITY NUMBERS FOR TAX RETURNS
IRC § 6109
Reg. § 1.6109–1
Rev. Rul. 64–122, 1964–1 CB 484
Rev. Rul. 64–151, 1964–1 CB 484

¶38.4 • WHEN THE IRS CAN ASSESS ADDITIONAL TAXES
IRC § 6501(a) through (e)
Reg. § 301.6501(a)–1 through (h)–1
Leslie Robertson, 32 TCM 955 (1973)

Mathematical or clerical error
IRC § 6213(b)(1) and (2) and (f)

Amended return following fraudulent return does not start limitations period
Ernest Bodaracco,__U.S.__(1984)

IRS has 60 days to assess tax on amended return
IRC § 6501(c)(7)

¶38.5 • INTEREST ON DEFICIENCIES
IRC § 6621

Higher rate for deficiencies than refunds after 1986
IRC § 6621(a)

Quarterly rates after 1986
IRC § 6621(b)

Deposit stops interest accrual
Rev. Proc. 82–51, 1982–2 CB 841

Interest and dividend information disclosed to government agencies
IRC § 6103(l)(7)

¶38.6 • INFORMATION RETURNS ARE IMPORTANT IRS CHECKS
IRC § 6041
Reg. § 1.6041–1 through 6

Tax-exempt interest must be reported on return
IRC § 6012(d)

¶38.7 • REPORTING MORTGAGE INTEREST AND PROPERTY FORECLOSURES AND ABANDONMENTS
Mortgage interest
IRC § 6050H

Real estate sales closing after 1986
IRC § 6045(e)
Announcement 87–39, IRB 1987–18, 49

Abandonment and foreclosures
IRC § 6050J
Temp. Reg. Sec. 1.6050J–IT

¶38.8 • TAX SHELTER REGISTRATION NUMBER
IRC § 6111

List of investors
IRC § 6112

¶38.9 • WHAT ARE THE PENALTIES IN THE LAW?
*"Compliance, Administration Provisions Greatly Changed by TRA '86," Stephen C. Struntz, 67 Journal of Taxation 2 (1987)

Monthly penalty for late filing
IRC § 6651(a)

Monthly penalty for late payment
IRC § 6651(a)(2)

Penalties generally
IRC §§ 7201–7207, as amended by §§ 327 and 329 of the 1982 Tax Equity and Fiscal Responsibility Tax Act

Negligence penalty for grossly overstating charitable contribution
Jack R. Olken, 41 TCM 1255 (1981)

No fraud penalty for overstating charitable contribution
Russell R. Owens, Jr., 41 TCM 1312 (1981)

Willful failure
Harry Murdock, 290 U.S. 389 (1933)
Thomas W. Banks, 223 F.2d 884 (8th Cir. 1955), cert. denied, 350 U.S. 986
Sam M. Hargrove, 67 F.2d 820 (5th Cir. 1933)
Murray R. Spies, 317 U.S. 492 (1943)
Clarence A. Zacher, 227 F.2d 219 (8th Cir. 1955), cert. denied, 350 U.S. 993
John J. Gannon, 244 F.2d 541 (2d Cir. 1957)

Might avoid penalties
Joseph C. Lurding, 179 F.2d 419 (6th Cir. 1950), aff'g unreported opinion, on remand 191 F.2d 921 (6th Cir. 1951)
George Phillips, 217 F.2d 435 (7th Cir. 1954)

Unpaid tax or deficiency
IRC § 6601
Reg. § 301.6601–1

Negligence
IRC § 6653(a)
Reg. § 301.6653–1(a)

Negligence penalty applies to entire underpayment
Asphalt Products Co. Inc., — U.S. — (June 1, 1987)

File on time
IRC § 6652
Reg. § 301.6652–1
Corwin L. Hulbert, 32 TCM 1024 (1973)

Bad check
IRC § 6657
Reg. § 301.6657–1

Fraud with intent to evade
IRC § 6653(b)
Reg. § 301.6653–1(b)

Attempt to depart or to conceal property
IRC § 6658
Reg. § 301.6658–1
IRC § 6851

Willful failure to pay or file
IRC § 7203

Willful false return
IRC § 7206

Note: Paragraph numbers refer to Part One. Items marked * are research aids, not citations of authority; see "Key to Citations" on page 337.

Willful evasion
IRC § 7201

Information returns
IRC § 6721 and 6722

Failure to file correct information returns
IRC § 6723

Failure to report Social Security number of dependents
IRC § 6676(e)

Failure to file partnership return
IRC § 6698

Allocating interest on underpayments and overpayments
TIR 1345, February 2, 1975

Overvaluation of property
IRC § 6659

Substantial underpayment of tax
Act Section 8002 of the Omnibus Budget Reconciliation Act of 1986 (P.L. 99–509)
IRC § 6661
Reg. Sec. 1.6661–1 through 1.6661–6

Interest on penalties
IRC § 6601

Failure to keep log of business travel expenses
IRC § 274(d)

Interest on certain penalties
IRC § 6601(e)(2)(B)

Frivolous returns penalty
IRC § 6702
Martin Bradley, — F.2d — (9th Cir. 1987)

¶38.10 • RECOVERING ATTORNEYS' FEES FROM THE GOVERNMENT

Pre-March 1, 1983 cases
Pub. L. No. 96–481

Cases begun after March 1, 1983 and before 1986
IRC § 7430, before amendment by 1986 Tax Reform Act
Reg. Sec. 301–7430–1

Cases begun after 1985
IRC § 7430, as amended by Section 1551(a) of the 1986 Tax Reform Act

IRS settles before litigation: pre-1986 cases
David Kaufman, Dist. Ct.; Me.; 84–1 USTC ¶9500
Philip Hallam, Jr.; Dist. Ct., Ga.; 84–1 USTC ¶9230
William Eidson, Dist. Ct., Ala.; 84–1 USTC ¶9182
Robert Baker, 83 TC 822 (1984)

¶38.11 • INCOME TAX RETURN PREPARERS

"The Responsibilities of Tax Professionals in Preparing Returns and Rendering Tax Advice Under the Tax Return Preparer Rules," Ira H. Shapiro, 38 NYU Inst. ¶17.00 (1980)

* *"Under New Rules, Preparers Penalties May Be Restricted to More Flagrant Violators,"* John Brockhouse, 54 J. Taxation 2 (1981)

"Avoiding Civil Liability in Tax Practice," Frank E. Puryear, Jr., 14 Tax Adviser 668 (Nov. 1983)

Penalties
IRC § 6694
IRC § 6695

Penalty for knowingly aiding in understatement of tax
IRC § 6701

No penalty for failure to report estimated tax additions
T.D. 7572, 11/15/78

Unable to sign
Rev. Proc. 79–7, 1979–2 CB 403

Failure to keep copy of return or list
IRC § 6107(b)
IRC § 6695(d)

Keep record of taxpayers filed with IRS
IRC § 6060
IRC § 6695(e)

Negotiating client's refund check
IRC § 6695(f)
*Letter Ruling 8720021

Sale of business; retention of records required
Rev. Rul. 79–400, 1979–2 CB 403

Penalty for failure to list interest from Form 1099
Rev. Rul. 80–262, 1980–2 CB 375

Penalty for using wrong table
Rev. Rul. 80–263, 1980–2 CB 376

Penalty for not asking about entertainment records
Rev. Rul. 80–266, 1980–2 CB 378

Penalty for depositing refund checks
Rev. Rul. 80–35, 1980–2 CB 305

Software seller treated as preparer
Rev. Rul. 85–189, 1985–2 CB 341
IR–86–62 (5–5–86)

Computerized tax preparer service
Rev. Rul. 85–187, 1985–2 CB 338

¶38.12 • A GUIDE TO ESTATE TAXES AND PLANNING

"Estate Planning Strategies after 1986," Rolf Auster, 65 Taxes 116 (February 1987)

Tax rates
IRC § 2001

Unified credit
IRC § 2010

Marital deduction
IRC § 2056

Note: Paragraph numbers refer to Part One. Items marked * are research aids, not citations of authority; see "Key to Citations" on page 337.

PART FOUR

PRACTICE BEFORE THE IRS

Practice Before the IRS

HOW RETURNS ARE EXAMINED

WHEN WILL A RETURN BE EXAMINED?

Because the IRS is unable to examine every return it follows a policy of examining returns which, upon preliminary inspection, indicate the largest possible source of potential tax deficiency. In the past, about 2% of all individual income tax returns have been examined.

Returns are rated for audit according to a mathematical formula called the discriminant function system (DIF). Various weights are assigned to separate items on each tax return, thus permitting the ranking of returns for the greatest potential error. The method is based on data the IRS compiled from extensive audits of taxpayers under the Taxpayer Compliance Measurement Program (TCMP).

The factors entering into the DIF formula are not disclosed by the IRS. However, its general procedure for selecting returns for audit may be found in IRS Handbook, IRM (41(12)0), which is substantially reproduced at the end of this chapter.

THE TYPE OF EXAMINATION

An examination may be held by correspondence, at a local IRS office or at the taxpayer's place of business, office or home. An examination at an IRS office or by correspondence is called a desk or office examination; an examination at a place of business or home is called a field examination. The complexity of the transactions reported on a return generally determines whether a return will be reviewed at an office or field examination.

An office examination is initiated by a letter of notification listing the items to be examined. The Agent will ordinarily not go beyond these items. However, the Agent may, in his judgment, extend the examination to other items. When a low-income return is examined, an office examination is generally made to substantiate deductions. On the other hand, a field examination may involve a review of the entire return.

A correspondence examination may be used to question simple individual returns; it is a type of office examination handled entirely through correspondence. The taxpayer is asked to explain a particular item or to send supporting evidence. A correspondence examination may end up as an interview type of office examination or a field examination. Whether it does or not will depend on how satisfactory the answers to correspondence are and also whether or not the answers indicate problems not appearing on the face of the return. If you feel that it is impractical to handle the examination through correspondence or that it places you at a disadvantage, request an office examination conference. Practitioners generally feel that the absence of personal contact and discussion is a disadvantage. The use of this type of examination is decreasing since the IRS has found that many taxpayers, especially those who do not use professional advisors, have been unable to adequately handle the questionnaires.

You may request a transfer of a case from an office examination to a field examination. Requests for transfers have been granted because of voluminous records or physical incapacity. A request will be denied if it is clear that you have no legitimate reason for the transfer.

A field examination may be shifted to the office of the taxpayer's representative if he has the client's records and it is more convenient to hold the examination there.

An individual taxpayer may appear at an examination in his own behalf, and a corporation may be represented by an officer. The preparer of a tax return may, if authorized, represent his client before an Agent in connection with the return although he is not enrolled to practice before the IRS. An attorney or CPA may also represent a taxpayer before IRS.

If you represent a taxpayer, file a power of attorney, and ask the IRS to send you all correspondence involving the examination. In your correspondence with the IRS, always use the IRS code symbols found on the IRS's letter to you.

Before the examination, review not only the return in question but also the records of prior examinations of the client's return. The Agent, in preparing his examinations, has reviewed these records and will use them as a starting point for the present examination.

Correspondence notices are used to correct the following types of obvious errors spotted at IRS service centers: Medical expenses without the adjusted gross income limitation; personal casualty and theft losses without the 10% adjusted gross income limitation; auto mileage rates for business transportation in excess of 22.5¢ per mile for the first 15,000 miles or 11¢ per mile over 15,000 miles; income on Form W-2 or 1099 incorrectly reported on tax return; fractional exemptions. Taxpayers are advised by mail of the corrections and of additional tax due. The taxpayer may request an interview or submit additional information if he disagrees. Where the correction is made and additional tax paid before the due date for filing the return, the taxpayer may avoid interest charges.

Where an underpayment of tax results from a mathematical or clerical error, the taxpayer does not have a right to appeal to the Tax Court, as provided in other cases. In the past, the IRS allowed taxpayers time to explain and substantiate claims that there was no error made. The IRS must give the taxpayer an explanation of the error, and 60 days within which to file a request for the abatement of the assessment. The IRS must honor that request. It must then follow the normal deficiency procedures described in this chapter. This procedure is followed for the following types of mathematical and clerical errors: (1) arithmetic errors (addition, subtraction, multiplication, or division), (2) errors in transferring amounts on the tax forms; (3) missing schedules or forms; (4) incorrect use of any Treasury table; and (5) entries that exceed statutory limitations.

Where an arithmetic error is made by an IRS taxpayer service representative, the IRS may abate any interest due on the underpayment of tax for any period ending on or before the 30th day following the date of notice and demand for payment of the deficiency.

Further, under the 1986 Tax Act, the IRS has discretion to abate interest attributable to procedural or mechanical errors by IRS officials that delay processing of a deficiency. Only delays caused by an IRS failure to perform a "ministerial" act are subject to the abatement rule; interest is not eligible for abatement if delay is due to IRS work priorities, discretionary judgments, or decisions concerning the application of tax laws. Requests for abatement are made on Form 843.

RESTRICTIONS ON IRS EXAMINATIONS OF BOOKS

The IRS may not make more than one examination of a taxpayer's books of accounts for any taxable period unless the taxpayer requests otherwise, or the IRS, after investigation, notifies the taxpayer in writing that an additional inspection is necessary. However, this restriction does not bar the IRS from examining public records or bank accounts. Nor does it bar examination of the books of a third party, such as the taxpayer's corporation, unless the identities of the taxpayer and his corporation are so inextricable that the examination of the books of one constitute an examination of the books of the other.

A taxpayer may protest a second examination by refusing to give the Agent access to his books. The IRS may then issue a summons. If the taxpayer still refuses access, the IRS may seek enforcement of the summons in district court. The taxpayer then has the opportunity at a hearing in the district court to show that a second examination is unnecessary.

The IRS tries to avoid examining the same items appearing on a taxpayer's returns for more than one year, such as the treatment of installment sale payments. Thus, where the taxpayer's return was examined in either of the two years prior to the current examination for the same items, and that examination resulted in no change in tax liability, the IRS will suspend the current examination, upon the taxpayer's notifying the appointment clerk or the examiner, pending a review of its files to determine whether the examination should proceed. If the IRS decides to proceed with examination the taxpayer has no recourse.

Handwriting samples. The Supreme Court has ruled that the IRS can compel a taxpayer to furnish handwriting samples in the same manner as it can demand other physical evidence. (Eugene F. Euge, 100 S. Ct. 874 (1980)).

DISCLOSURE OF IRS POLICY

Court decisions interpreting the Freedom of Information Act have led to release of manuals and other data explaining the internal operations of the IRS. It may be possible to obtain private letter rulings and a list of prime issues the IRS will not compromise.

Knowledge of operating procedures and positions may provide you with a perspective on the overall techniques and strategies suggested to agents in dealing with taxpayers. One such training manual discussing investigations of possible tax fraud is reproduced at the end of this chapter.

Some taxpayers have tried to force the IRS to disclose the statistical data obtained from its Taxpayer Compliance Measurement Program (TCMP), which is used to establish audit criteria. After federal courts ordered the IRS to disclose this data, Congress passed a law allowing the IRS to refuse disclosure of the standards used to select returns for audit or the data used for determining such standards.

HOW TO HANDLE THE EXAMINATION

Common sense rules of courtesy should be your guide in your contacts with the Agent. Avoid personality clashes; they can only interfere with a speedy and fair resolution of the examination. However, be firm in your approach and, if the Agent appears to be unreasonable in his approach, make it clear that, if necessary, you will go all the way to court to win your point. A vacillating approach may weaken your position in reaching settlement.

Where a practitioner is handling the audit, the taxpayer should not be present during discussions with the Agent. He can add nothing to the discussion that the practitioner does not already know after becoming thoroughly acquainted with the return. The taxpayer's presence may damage his case if he volunteers information harmful to his position.

In a field audit, the Agent will want to review the original books and records. If he also wants supporting secondary records, ask him to give you a list of his needs, which you can then present as a unit.

The Agent should not be allowed to take original records out of your office or the client's office. Give him copies of relevant records. Do not volunteer data. He will make his needs known. Also, try to provide him with an adequate area in which to work.

After his review and before he prepares his report, the Agent will discuss his findings and recommendations. At this stage, disputes generally involve questions of fact. The Agent will readily use his discretion in compromising issues of fact where, for example, there are inadequate primary records but other evidence convinces him that the taxpayer has made a valid claim. As for conflicting interpretations of law, the Agent will abide by well-defined IRS policy. He will not lean to an interpretation conflicting with or not covered by IRS policy. Compromises involving open issues or conflicts between IRS and court positions are possible at a higher level conference in the Appeals office. Occasionally, a disputed point in an examination may be resolved by asking the IRS for technical advice (*see* the chapter on rulings).

In some instances, you may be asked by the Agent to submit a legal memorandum. This may be a signal that the Agent is not sure of the legal issues involved in your case and wants your help. You are not required to do this and you may refuse where the memo might reveal more of your case than you would care to divulge at this level. However, where the facts are not in dispute and you feel a clarification of the law might expedite the case, a memo may be advisable. Keep in mind that anything submitted to the Agent becomes part of the record that is passed through the levels of IRS review.

Your readiness to compromise will depend on the extent of the Agent's examination and the amount of the proposed deficiency or refund. Sometimes an Agent will pick up one point but fail to develop another issue that could lead to a substantial deficiency. Here, it may be tactically advisable to accept his proposal, although you might successfully resist it in a later conference. Carrying the case beyond the Agent might lead to an opening of other items on the return.

IF YOU AGREE WITH THE EXAMINER

When you agree to the Agent's proposed changes, he will ask your client to sign a Form 870 or other appropriate agreement form. When signed, it permits an immediate assessment of a deficiency. Its full title is "Waiver of Restrictions on Assessment and Collection of Deficiency in Tax and Acceptance of Overassessment." It is used in the District Director's office at any stage when an agreement is reached.

The only advantage in signing is to stop the running of interest on the tax deficiency within 30 days after the date the waiver is filed. In an overassessment, that is, where a refund is due, a signed waiver is merely an acknowledgment of the overassessment.

A signed Form 870 does not prevent the IRS from reopening the case to assess an additional deficiency. If on review the deficiency is increased, you will receive a revised Form 870. Your client can refuse to sign the form. The signed first form has the effect of stopping the interest on the original deficiency. As a matter of practice, however, waivers or acceptances ordinarily result in a closing of the case.

If your client signs a Form 870 after a formal deficiency notice (90-day letter) has been mailed, he still retains his right to appeal to the Tax Court. But if he signs the Form 870 before a deficiency notice has been mailed, he loses his right to appeal to the Tax Court. Unless your client agrees in the Form 870 not to seek a refund later, he may still file suit for a refund even though he cannot appeal to the Tax Court.

The payment of a tax before the deficiency notice is mailed is, in effect, a waiver of the restrictions on assessment and collection. If the payment satisfies your client's entire tax liability for that year, he cannot appeal to the Tax Court. He must sue for a refund in either the District Court or Court of Claims.

If a refund is due and a Form 870 is signed, you may file a protective refund claim. Generally, the Agent will process the refund, but if he fails to do so or the review staff puts it aside for some reason and the limitations period expires, the refund will be lost. The refund claim will protect your client from such a mishap.

AN AGREED CASE IS ALWAYS REVIEWED

Once a Form 870 is signed, the Agent prepares his report, which is sent to a review group in the Examination Division of the District Director's office. While the Agent's report is approved in most cases, do not assume that this review is a mere formality. Agreed cases receive closer review than unagreed cases. Once approved, an agreed case has, except for isolated cases, "reached the end of the line." A reviewer thus realizes that he has a greater responsibility in checking the agreed case than in an unagreed case where he knows that the facts and law may be reviewed several times as the case proceeds through administrative channels. The reviewer will check the following points:

Facts appearing in the Agent's report and in the return filed by the taxpayer. During his review, he may find facts that the Agent overlooked or emphasize facts that did not appear important to the Agent.

Agent's interpretation of the Code and the manner in which he applies its provisions to the facts in the case.

Agent's judgment. The taxpayer might not have substantiated all of his claimed deductions by primary evidence. But the Agent allowed a portion of the deduction on the basis of secondary evidence. The reviewer may question the judgment of the Agent. He may believe that the Agent was too lenient. The Agent may try to justify his position. If the reviewer and Agent cannot agree, the chief reviewer will resolve the problem.

Other tax returns. Where an individual's return shows income from an estate, trust, or partnership, the reviewer will usually ask the Agent to check the estate, trust, or partnership return, or to transfer the case to an Agent who may be examining one of these returns.

Tax returns of prior tax years. The Agent may be required to examine the facts on the prior returns. The inquiry may result in the development of new facts which may widen the scope of the audit. The number of ways in which a reviewer may develop new facts depends only on his ingenuity, experience, and zeal. Therefore, remember that even after an agreement is signed (Form 870), the Agent may ask for additional facts, and confront you with new interpretations.

You will not be allowed to argue your case directly with the reviewer. But you may be sure that the Agent will present your case in the best light, if for no other reason than to justify his own judgment.

WHAT TO DO IF YOU DISAGREE WITH THE AGENT

If you disagree with the Agent at an *office* examination, the Agent explains the adjustments and available appeal procedure. If you desire an immediate conference with his supervisor, it will be granted if practicable. Otherwise, you will receive a report of the examination from the District Director and a 30-day letter providing the following alternatives: (1) You can agree to the proposed adjustments and sign an enclosed Form 870; (2) you can request an Appeals office conference by written protest; or (3) you may ignore the letter in which case you will eventually receive a statutory notice of deficiency (90-day letter).

If you disagree with the Agent at the *field* examination, he will prepare a complete examination report fully explaining his proposed adjustments. He will then send it to the district examination review staff for a technical and procedural review. After the review, you will receive a 30-day letter as in the case of the office examination. The 30-day letter is accompanied by a copy of the examination report and a detailed explanation of the available appeal procedures, with a request that you inform the District Director of your choice of action. You have the following alternatives:

1. Sign a Form 870 (which precludes appeal to the Tax Court);
2. Request an Appeals office conference by written protest;
3. Ignore the 30-day letter and wait for the statutory notice of deficiency (90-day letter);
4. Pay the tax and file a claim for refund.

A 30-day letter is not required by the Code and, if the IRS wants to, it may dispense with it and send you the 90-day letter. The 30-day letter is merely an additional attempt by the IRS to settle the case without going to trial. If necessary, you may get additional time to file your protest. However, if the limitation period for the assessment of tax is running out on the tax year in question, you will not get a 30-day letter nor an extension unless a waiver is signed extending the limitation period.

SHOULD YOU ASK FOR A CONFERENCE?

The answer lies in the nature of your disagreement with the auditing Agent. You may feel his authority to accept proposals for settlement is too limited. You may believe he has over-emphasized certain facts, disregarded or failed to give proper weight to other facts. Perhaps he has misinterpreted applicable tax law or misapplied it to your case. He may even have ignored law that supports your claim.

The very existence of the conference procedure is in itself a recognition that your objection to the Agent's decision may be right. If the IRS were convinced that the auditing Agent was always correct, there would be no purpose to the conferences.

It is usually advisable to take your case to the Appeals office. The chances of a settlement are favorable. Most cases, about 85%, are settled in conference. But before going ahead, consider these points:

1. When the IRS has an established policy regarding the disputed issue, taking a case further in the IRS usually gains nothing. All IRS personnel are bound by the same rules.
2. Interest continues to run. It does not stop unless you deposit money with the District Director.
3. The IRS will find out your position on all issues. If the case comes to trial, there can be no element of surprise.
4. The IRS can always find additional issues.

HOW TO WRITE YOUR PROTEST

The protest is simply your written explanation of the reasons for your disagreement with the Agent. In it, you give the ap-

HOW YOUR DISAGREED FIELD CASE IS PROCESSED

Step 1	*Step 2*	*Step 3*
AGENT'S EXAMINATION	REVIEW STAFF Examination Division	APPEALS OFFICE CONFERENCE
If you do not agree to his adjustments, he will prepare his report and send it to the District Review Staff.	You receive a 30-day letter from the District Director. You may ask for an Appeals office conference or wait for a 90-day letter.	You appear before an Appeals officer.

Step 4	*Step 5*
REVIEW	IN THE TAX COURT
You receive a 90-day letter from which you move for appeal as outlined in *Step 5*.	Before trial, you may have a chance to settle your case at a hearing with the Appeals office or District Counsel.

peals officer your side of the dispute. A written protest is required for cases going to the Appeals office if the case began as a field examination and the amount in issue exceeds $2,500. If your case began as an office examination, a written protest is not required, but it would be wise to prepare a written protest if your case has difficult questions of law or fact.

There is no special form for the protest. The important thing is to include information and arguments that will present your case in the best light.

Seven specific points must be included in the protest:

1. Taxpayer's name and address.
2. Date and symbols on the 30-day letter.
3. Years covered and the amounts of tax liability in dispute for each year. List here only the amount of the proposed deficiency with which you disagree. This is often less than the entire proposed deficiency.
4. An itemized schedule of the Agent's findings with which you disagree. Make sure you cover every item you contest. Where more than one finding is involved, list each one separately and number it.
5. State the facts supporting your position for each of the items named in (4). Use separate numbered paragraphs for each issue; make sure the number of each paragraph corresponds with the number of the item in (4) which it covers.
6. State the law on which you rely for each of the items listed in (4); use separate paragraphs, numbered to correspond with the items in (4).
7. If you want a hearing with the Appeals office, you must make such request in the protest. Otherwise, you will get no hearing and the case will be decided on the basis of what you submit as your protest.

The most important part of the protest is the presentation of your arguments. These you divide into three parts: (1) Give the arguments in summary form, numbered. (2) A statement of facts covering the disputed items. (3) Develop each argument and support it by citations of authority.

Separate protests do not have to be filed if more than one tax year is involved. All the tax years covered in the 30-day letter may be covered in one protest.

An original and a copy of the protest must be filed.

Stress the equities of your case. A case that shows that a decision against you would be unfair may be stronger than one where you have the technicalities on your side.

Write the facts so that they can be understood. They should be clear and accurate. List them in the order in which they happened.

Do not omit the facts that seem to be against you. When explained, they may not be as detrimental to your case as they first appear.

Substantiate the facts with exhibits, affidavits, or any other proof.

Try to avoid unimportant facts which are not relevant to the issue. Make sure you understand the principles of law affecting any fact you state. Otherwise, the argument you will later make may be weak.

Discuss the issues in the order of their importance. Leave the least important for last. Say what is involved, who is involved.

Write short headings before each issue. But they must accurately state the point you are making. Repeat important facts if they help your argument.

Summarize the point you are making and show how it applies to your case.

Sometimes a short quotation from a leading case is effective if you can relate the case to your facts. But do not give

Be sure that every case you cite stands for what you say it does.

Try to put yourself in the place of the conferee who is going to read the protest. Ask yourself what you would want to know in order to answer the questions, and then try to supply the information.

Take the time to write a well-organized, succinct, and interesting protest.

Consider the appearance of the letter. Give it eye appeal. Use side heads to break up solid pages of type. Sometimes graphs, photographs, charts and other illustrations help make your point in an attractive manner.

How the protest is signed. Your client must certify, under penalty of perjury, that the statements of facts in the protest are true. Add the following signed statement to the protest: "Under penalties of perjury, I declare that I have examined the statement of facts presented in this protest and in any accompanying schedules and, to the best of my knowledge and belief it is true, correct and complete." A taxpayer's representative who submits a protest for the taxpayer may substitute a declaration stating that he prepared the protest and indicating whether he personally knows that the statements of facts are true and correct.

You file the original and one duplicate copy of the protest with the District Director who sends the protest along with your case to the Appeals office. No filing fee is necessary.

District Directors may have screening groups to review protests before they are sent to the Appeals office. If, after reading a protest, a reviewer believes that there is a basis for settlement, he will refer the case back to the Examination Division for settlement. For this reason, make sure that your protest presents your case well so that a reviewer can have a basis for such a decision.

HOW THE APPEALS OFFICE OPERATES

In the Appeals office, your case is assigned to an appeals officer. After he acquaints himself with your case, he sets the time of the conference. If it is inconvenient, you may ask for another date or time. An immediate hearing may be granted if you have some unusual reason for it. The hearing may be held in a Regional Commissioner's office, a District Director's office, a local branch office of the Service, or "on circuit" (appeals officers sometimes travel to outlying districts to save taxpayers the expense and time involved in a trip to a metropolitan area).

The Appeals office is separated functionally from the District Director's office. The major purpose of the separation is to provide an appellate procedure which, organizationally at least, will tend to produce free and unbiased opinions. An officer in the Appeals office is not responsible to the District Director who controls the Revenue Agent and his supervisor. He is thus less likely to be unduly influenced by the conclusions reached in that office and more likely to reach his decisions objectively. The officer does not need, nor does he seek, the approval of the Revenue Agent, Supervisor, or District Director for any decision he may make.

When you protest the conclusions reached in the District Director's office, the entire case file is sent to the Appeals office, and the District Director's control over the case ceases.

In the majority of cases, neither the Agent nor any other representative of the District Director will attend your conference with the appeals officer. If, in a few situations, the Agent does attend a conference, it will be at the invitation of the Appeals office and only for the purpose of establishing the facts. Since you are appealing from the recommendations of the Agent, do not reargue the case with him. Your sole problem will be to convince the appeals officer. In all cases, however, you should remember that the officer has a copy of the Agent's recommendations and his confidential report of the Agent, which you never see.

Cases which reach the Appeals office after the 90-day letter has been issued are known as "90-day cases." Conferences at this stage are not easily granted. You must generally show that you have not had a previous conference for reasons beyond your control, and there is a reasonable expectation that a settlement will be reached.

The settlement authority in the Appeals office is broader than in the Examination Division. The Appeals office may trade or split issues where substantial uncertainties exist either in law or in fact, or in both, as to the correct application of the law. They may also settle issues based on their judgment as to the hazards of litigation. The Agents have no authority to consider litigation hazards. One explanation for the reluctance of district office personnel to close a case is that they realize there is another administrative step following theirs. If they have any doubts about the acceptability of a settlement proposal, they can resolve their doubts by recommending that the case be considered by the Appeals office. The appeals officer thinks in terms of the cost and possible result of extended litigation. Cases are generally settled on the "merit approach." That is, the merits of each issue are considered, regardless of the amount of tax involved. A second, less preferred method of settlement is on the basis of a flat sum or percentage of the dollars involved. This second method is limited in use and may not be used, for example, where an issue will recur in subsequent years or where the issue is present in other similar cases unless they are all to be disposed of together upon the same basis.

Settlement authority of appeals officers may also depend on whether or not the issue is on an IRS appeals coordinated issue list. If the issue is on the list, the officer does not have independent settlement authority; he must submit his proposed settlement to a person within the regional office who is in charge of reviewing issues placed on the coordination list. If this person does not agree to the settlement, the appeals officer may present the dispute to an appeals director in the region for a decision. You will not be given the chance to argue your position at this stage because the appeal coordination list procedure is internal administration measure through which the IRS attempts to provide a consistent national settlement policy on certain issues which involve large numbers of taxpayers who have cases involving the same issue.

HOW TO HANDLE THE CONFERENCE

The conference is held in an informal manner. No stenographic record is made. Testimony is generally not under oath. Your approach to the conference will vary, depending on whether your client wishes to settle, whether the issues in dispute are factual or legal, how strong you feel your case is on a specific issue.

You can assume the conferee:

Has the Agent's recitation of the facts, his opinions, and recommendations—all of which appear in a transmittal memo which you do not receive. He also has a record of the informal conference and copies of reports covering examinations of prior years.

Has read your protest with your version of the facts and your arguments. He will read the cases you cite. When you cite a case, make sure that it is on point. If you cite it for the dicta incorporated in the opinion, indicate that fact. There is nothing more discouraging than wading through a case only to find that it is not on point. The appeals officer may well conclude that you do not understand the issue, that you think he does not or cannot, or that you believe he is careless enough to accept citations without reading the cases. Such conclusions will affect you adversely.

Knows the strengths and weaknesses of your position and what you would settle for. If your case is the type that should be settled, the appeals officer has thought of possible settlements. As a general proposition, an officer would rather settle cases than send them to the Tax Court. But rarely is he more anxious to settle than you are. To you, the problem represents dollars and cents.

You may bring witnesses. However, do not plan on using witnesses unless they are absolutely necessary to prove your case and you are sure they will not testify beyond your objectives. Instead of the personal appearance of witnesses, you may present their statements in affidavit form. Facts brought up for the first time will be referred back to the District Director's office for reconsideration.

Sufficient time is given you to present your side of the case. Additional hearings are granted as needed.

An attorney may become aware that his client has no hope of winning but is stalling the date of actual payment of the deficiency by going through the various appellate procedures.

To support his tactic violates IRS rules of practice and professional canons of ethics.

DOES IT PAY TO SETTLE YOUR TAX DISPUTE WITH THE SERVICE?

Here are some approaches followed by practitioners:

If you want rapid settlement of the dispute and cannot convince the IRS of your position, consider paying the deficiency—then suing for refund in the District Court or Claims Court. But check the docket of the District Court where you will sue first. Some District Courts are as overloaded as the Tax Court.

In a dispute involving a difference of opinion over the facts, accept a fair offer from the IRS. You may not do any better before the Tax Court. Where the IRS refuses to accept any settlement offer, you may take your case to court. You will have to wait for a hearing, but you stand a good chance of getting a better break.

In a complicated case or one involving a difficult point of law, the Tax Court is favored over the District Court. There is less risk of judicial misinterpretation of the tax law since the Tax Court judges are more familiar with the intricacies of the Code.

Where you have a question of fact and your position is appealing to the average person, pay the deficiency and then sue for a refund in the District Court where a jury will determine the facts. In the Tax Court, the facts are determined by judges who may be less sympathetic. You are not entitled to a jury trial in Tax Court. Your case is also decided by a judge if you pay the deficiency and sue for a refund in the Claims Court.

WHAT HAPPENS WHEN YOU PROPOSE A SETTLEMENT

Settlement proposals are generally made orally but more complicated proposals may be in writing. If your proposal is accepted, you are asked to sign either a Form 870 or 870-AD. (Forms 890 and 890-A, respectively, are used in nondocketed estate and gift tax cases.) Form 870 is signed for a settlement based on a complete agreement with the changes originally recommended by the Agent. Where the IRS makes concessions in reaching a settlement in the Appeals office, a conditional consent, Form 870-AD, is signed. Unlike Form 870 which is effective when handed to the Agent, Form 870-AD is not effective until it is signed by the Commissioner of Internal Revenue or his delegate.

Form 870-AD has been called an informal closing agreement. It is an agreement not to file a claim for refund, except for overassessments shown on the agreement form and amounts attributed to a net operating loss carryback deduction. Similarly, the IRS agrees not to assert further deficiencies for the year in question, except where there is fraud, malfeasance, concealment or misrepresentation of a material fact, mathematical error, an excessive tentative allowance of a net operating loss carryback or investment credit carryback, or deficiencies determined at a partnership level audit or S corporation level audit.

ADVANCE CASH DEPOSIT STOPS INTEREST ACCRUAL ON DEFICIENCY WHILE RETAINING APPEAL RIGHTS

An individual who faces a potentially large interest charge on a tax deficiency may cut off the accrual of interest by making an advance deposit against an estimated deficiency. Before a deficiency notice is mailed, this may be done by identifying a payment as a "deposit in the nature of a cash bond." Interest stops running on the deposit as of the date it is received by the IRS. However, interest continues to accrue on accrued interest unless the deposit is large enough to cover the interest. If an agreement is not reached, the IRS will send a deficiency notice which may be appealed to the Tax Court. If you agree to the deficiency, no deficiency notice is mailed as the deposit is applied to the deficiency. You also lose the right to petition the Tax Court.

Details of making a cash bond deposit are in Rev. Proc. 84–58, 1984–2 CB 50.

WHAT TO DO AFTER RECEIVING A 90-DAY LETTER

Before the IRS can assess a deficiency, it must send out by registered or certified mail a statutory notice of deficiency. This notice is called a "90-day letter." It gives your client the chance, within 90 days from the date of its mailing, to file a petition to the Tax Court of the United States. If the notice is mailed to an address outside of the United States, you are allowed 150 days. In the event the 90th or 150th day falls on a Saturday or Sunday, or on a legal holiday in the District of Columbia, you have until the next business day to file a petition with the Tax Court.

Your client receives a 90-day letter at the end of the period allowed in the 30-day letter if he has not signed a Form 870 or filed a formal protest, or after an Appeals Office conference. At the end of the 90 (or 150) days, the deficiency is assessed.

The effect of an 870-AD is one-sided. The taxpayer agrees to an immediate assessment of the deficiency, whereas the IRS does not agree to pay an immediate refund as, for example, the agreement covers two years, and one year involves an over-assessment. It may, therefore, be advisable to file a protective claim for refund at the same time as the Form 870-AD is signed, or at least before the expiration of the refund period for the year in question. The refund claim should be accompanied by a letter explaining that the purpose of the claim is to protect the taxpayer against an unfavorable disposition of the waiver issue, and that the claim will be withdrawn upon the IRS's favorable action on the waiver.

Whether or not Form 870-AD is binding on the IRS and the taxpayer as a closing agreement has been litigated. The decisions present conflicting opinions on the issue.

Filing a Form 870-AD does not automatically stop the running of interest. Interest stops 30 days after the date the IRS accepts the form. In any event, the accumulation of interest can be avoided by prepaying the deficiency.

After Form 870-AD is signed, the appeals officer presents his report to an Appellate Branch official, such as an Associate Chief. If he approves the proposed settlement, he will accept the agreement and the case is then ready for closing.

What if the settlement on review is rejected by the Associate Chief or other official? He will then discuss the case with the appeals officer. If the case remains unapproved, you may ask for a hearing before the reviewer who turned down the settlement.

What if you do not submit a settlement or the appeals officer rejects your proposal? The officer then prepares his report together with a proposed statutory notice of deficiency. This is sent to an Associate Chief or other official for review. If he approves the report, the case is then reviewed by the Chief, Appellate Branch Office. The statutory notice of deficiency is checked by the Regional Counsel. After final approval by both offices, a 90-day letter is then mailed to your client.

On receipt of the 90-day letter, you can do one of the following:

File a petition with the Tax Court. No assessment can be made until its decision (which includes all appeals) becomes final.

Do nothing and wait for the assessment of the deficiency.

Sign the Form 870. This limits the interest on the deficiency. Your client can still take his case to the Tax Court. Or, he can pay the disputed deficiency and file a refund claim. When it is rejected, he can sue in a Federal District Court or the Claims Court.

For a deficiency involving a joint return, the 90-day letter is mailed as a single joint notice. So, where a husband and wife have separated, notify the IRS of their separate addresses to insure receipt of the notice. The IRS will then send a duplicate original of the joint notice to both the husband and wife.

The IRS may issue more than one 90-day letter for the same year before the earliest of the following events: (1) Expiration of the assessment period; (2) execution of a final closing agreement or compromise; or (3) filing of a timely petition to the Tax Court.

WHEN A 90-DAY LETTER IS NOT NECESSARY

The 90-day letter is the only notice of deficiency which the law requires the IRS to send. Without it, you cannot go to the Tax Court to litigate your matter. However, there are situations in which the 90-day letter is not required and you have no recourse to the Tax Court.

(1) A 90-day letter is not sent where a mathematical error has been made in your return. Taking an excessive credit on your tax liability for taxes withheld or for estimated taxes paid is considered a mathematical error.

(2) A voluntary payment "paid as a tax or in respect of a tax" may be assessed without the issuance of a 90-day letter.

(3) An immediate assessment may be made without issuance of a 90-day letter whenever the IRS believes that assessment or collection will be jeopardized by delay. For example, if the IRS finds out that a taxpayer is leaving the country with all his assets before paying his tax liability, it is not necessary to send a 90-day letter first and then wait 90 days before assessment.

(4) In the case of bankruptcy or receivership, an assessment may be made before a 90-day letter is sent.

(5) If you sign a Form 870 before a 90-day letter is sent, you are not thereafter entitled to a 90-day letter.

GETTING A SETTLEMENT AFTER FILING A PETITION WITH THE TAX COURT

You may still be able to get a settlement even after you have filed a petition in the Tax Court. If you have brought your case to the Tax Court without first appealing to the Appeals office for a conference to settle the dispute, you will be asked to discuss a settlement with the Appeals office. The District Counsel's office may refer your case to the Appeals office for settlement for up to six months if the deficiency is $10,000 or less, with a possible extension where a settlement is considered likely.

Even if you have filed a Tax Court petition after an unsuccessful conference in the Appeals office, your case will still be referred back to the Appeals office for settlement unless Counsel determines that there is little likelihood of a settlement. The Appeals office may enter into a binding settlement. If the case is returned to the Counsel's office, it determines whether to settle or proceed to trial.

POST-REVIEW CHECKUP

Each Regional Commissioner is charged with the responsibility of arranging the post-review check for his region. The reviews are general and determine:

Quality and technical accuracy of examinations.

Extent and degree of uniformity in the application of tax law and policy questions.

Categories in which the most frequent procedural and technical errors are made in closed cases. (Closed cases are not reopened unless there is a substantial error or evidence of fraud or collusion.)

After the review, exception and advisory letters are sent to the District Directors' offices advising them of cases that are to be reconsidered and of the types of error that will cause a reopening of cases.

To provide for nationwide uniformity, the National Office at Washington receives reports from each review office on those cases for which advisory and exception letters were issued. From these reports, a study is published and sent to the review offices in each region. In this way, a regional office gets the chance to compare its policies with the policies of other regions. If it finds that its policies differ from those applied throughout the country, it changes them to conform with policies of the other regions.

IRS CLASSIFICATION PROCEDURES FOR
SELECTION OF RETURNS FOR AUDIT

The following chapter presents IRM (41(12)0) edited to highlight the major points of the IRS method for selecting returns for audit.

Due to limited resources, the Service can examine only a small percentage of the returns filed. The classifier's role is to ensure that these resources are used effectively. The classifier must decide which returns are most in need of examination and through examination will promote the highest degree of voluntary compliance. A classifier should be alert to items that would result in potential overassessments as well as items that would result in potential deficiencies.

STANDARDS FOR CLASSIFICATION

Discriminant Function (DIF) returns are selected for screening by computer. Each selected DIF return will be screened by an experienced examiner to eliminate those returns not worthy of examination.

Non-DIF returns are manually classified by experienced examiners to select returns that contain significant issues.

All returns are identified for assignment to a revenue agent, tax auditor, or tax examiner based on the complexity of the issues involved and the degree of accounting and auditing skills required to conduct a quality examination.

During the classification process, the scope of the examination is determined for all tax auditor and tax examiner returns except for pre-contact analysis returns and for designated revenue agent returns.

SORTING OF CLASSIFIED SCREENED RETURNS

During the course of classification, returns should be separated as follows:

Selected returns for office examination—interview and pre-contact analysis.

Selected returns for field examination.

Selected returns for service center correspondence examination (CORR).

Returns that are unusual in nature.

DISCRIMINANT FUNCTION (DIF) SYSTEM

Most returns, both individual and corporate, that are examined each year are DIF returns. For each examination class, different items on the return are scored. The total DIF score for a return is the sum of the scores of the individual items, and the higher the score, the greater the probability of tax change. The DIF score indicates the overall tax change potential of the return as a whole.

SIGNIFICANT ITEMS

There are several factors that must be considered when determining whether an item is significant. These are:

Comparative size of the item. A questionable expense item of $6,000 with total expenses of $30,000 would be significant; however, if total expenses are $300,000, ordinarily the item would not be significant.

Inherent character of the item. Although the amount of an item may be insignificant, the nature of the item may be significant, i.e., airplane expenses claimed on a plumber's schedule C.

Evidence of intent to mislead. This may include missing, misleading, or incomplete schedules, or incorrectly showing an item on the return.

Beneficial effect of the manner in which an item is reported. Expenses claimed on a business schedule rather than claimed as an itemized deduction may be significant.

Relationship to other items on a return. Business expenses without corresponding income. Similarly, the lack of dividends reported when Schedule D shows sales of stocks.

DETERMINATION OF OFFICE/FIELD EXAMINATION

Once you determine that the return will not be accepted as filed, it must be decided if the examination should be conducted by a revenue agent or a tax auditor. In making this determination, you must give consideration to the types of issues identified for field examination:

Issues which require on site inspection of the taxpayer's books, records or assets.

Complex Schedule D transactions.

Returns with unusually complex rental income and expenses.

Tax shelter returns.

Donations of real property which would involve an engineering specialist.

Alimony, if it appears there is a property settlement involving business property (i.e., accounts receivable, inventory.)

CORRESPONDENCE EXAMINATION

Returns selected with the following criteria should be flagged for correspondence within the service center:

All the questioned items are susceptible to direct verification from records that could be easily submitted by mail. You should not exclude substantial items for the checksheet to convert what might be an interview examination to a correspondence examination.

Inspection of the previous or subsequent year return is not necessary.

Some examples of issues which can be verified by correspondence are:

Simple itemized deductions (exclusive of office in the home, and education expense).

Payments to an IRA/Keogh Plan.

Interest penalty on early withdrawal of savings.

Child care credit.

Credit for the elderly.

Residential energy credit.

Self-employment tax.

Single issues should generally not be examined as experience has shown that such examinations frequently result in insignificant or no tax change when other questionable items are not present on the return.

Certain issues do not lend themselves to a correspondence examination, such as—

Exemptions.

Income from tips, pensions and annuities, rents and royalties, and income not subject to tax withholding.

Determination of whether income reported constitutes capital gain or ordinary income.

Deductions for travel and entertainment.

Deductions for bad debts.

Determinations of basis of property.

Complex miscellaneous itemized deductions such as casualty and theft losses where determination of a fair market value is required.

Returns in which the classifier feels an office interview is needed to ensure the taxpayer's rights under the law, or the appearance of the return (writing, grammar, neatness, etc.) indicates that the taxpayer may not be able to communicate effectively in writing.

REGULAR INTERVIEW EXAMINATION

Returns selected for office interview examinations should contain issues which lend themselves to an analytical approach and require individual judgment, in addition to direct verification.

Returns may contain issues which, based on the classifiers'

judgment and experience, require examination planning and analysis by a tax auditor before contacting the taxpayer. Local instructions as provided by the districts will be followed in selecting a return for pre-contact analysis. This type of return must be kept to a minimum to utilize centralized files and scheduling efficiently.

Examples of types of returns which may be subject to pre-contact analysis are:

Returns with complex issues requiring research before contacting the taxpayer for examination.

Returns with income low in relation to the taxpayer's financial responsibilities and the audit technique may involve a net worth statement, gross profit reconstruction, or statement of application of funds (indirect methods).

Returns exhibiting factors which indicate a need for visual inspection of the taxpayer's place of business or residence.

Any return (business or non-business) selected for 13 or more issues.

Any return selected for district or service center examination identified as an employee return.

IDENTIFYING SIGNIFICANT ISSUES

Here are suggested guidelines to assist in the identification of significant issues on individual nonbusiness returns.

Itemized deductions. Look first at overall potential based on the amount of itemized deductions. Verify that itemized deductions are not claimed elsewhere on the return when the standard deduction has been elected (i.e., personal real estate taxes and mortgage interest deducted on rental schedule).

Exemptions. Exemptions claimed by the noncustodial parent have proven to have high potential for adjustment. When married persons file separately, both taxpayers may not have made the same election for standard, or itemized deductions. If dependent children are claimed, the other spouse may also be claiming them.

Medical expenses. High medical expenses for large families, deceased taxpayers, or older taxpayers are usually not productive.

Taxes. Real estate taxes, consider changes in address (i.e., W-2, 1040, 2119). Sales tax, consider significant amounts above table allowance or nonqualifying items.

Interest expense. Interest is generally not productive when questioning all the small items that might be listed, or combined. Productive issues could come from payments to individuals, and closing costs on real estate transactions. Home mortgage interest usually is unproductive.

Contributions. Check to see if contributions exceed 50 percent of adjusted gross income. Check large donations made to questionable miscellaneous charities; check for payments which may represent tuition. Check for large donations of property, other than cash.

Casualty or theft losses. Watch for business assets, valuation methods and limitations.

Miscellaneous deductions. Scrutinize large, unusual, or questionable items.

Capital transactions. Gains on sales of rental and other depreciable property, where the taxpayer has been using an accelerated method of depreciation or ACRS, should be questioned since the taxpayer may have to report ordinary income. Loss on the sale of rental property, recently converted from a personal residence, is usually productive. Current year installment sales and exchanges of property should be carefully scrutinized as taxpayers frequently make errors in computing the recognized gain. Check to see if the gain on a sale is large enough to require the alternative minimum tax computation.

Pension or annuity. Verify if distribution qualifies under the three-year rule. Check whether distribution qualifies as a lump sum distribution.

Rental properties. Consider fair rental value. If the rental property is located at the same address as the taxpayer's residence, consider whether the allocation is proper between the rental portion and the portion used personally by the taxpayer. Repairs may be capital improvements. Consider whether the cost of land is included in the basis. The rental of vacation/resort homes should be scrutinized.

Sales of residence. Check to be sure that the taxpayer purchases a more expensive residence to qualify for deferral of the gain.

Unreported income. Check for the following:

Is the income sufficient to support the exemptions claimed? Installment sale of property but no interest reported.

Does the taxpayer show interest and real estate tax deductions for two residences but no rental income?

If a taxpayer lists his/her occupation as waiter, cab driver, porter, beautician, etc. tip income is a productive issue.

Are there substantial interest expenses with no apparent source of funds to repay the loans?

Does the taxpayer claim business expenses for an activity that shows no income on the return (i.e., beautician supplies, but no Form 1099 or W-2 for that occupation)?

Copy of Schedule K-1. Returns containing office examination type issues will be selected for office examination without regard to distributive type income from Forms 1065, 1120S, and 1041. However, if the Schedule K-1 requires inspection, the entity's name and year of Schedule K-1 should be listed on the classification checksheet.

Items of self-employment income shown on Schedule K-1 should be matched to Schedule SE to ensure that the amounts are properly included in the self-employment tax computation.

Employee business expenses. Amounts should be reasonable when compared to the taxpayer's income level. Avoid auto expenses as an issue where the standard mileage computation is used and the mileage shown does not appear excessive. Transportation expenses for construction workers, carpenters, etc., who appear to have several different employers at different locations, have not proven to be productive. However, be alert for expenses claimed for travel to remote job sites. Expenses for clubs, yachts, airplanes, etc., must meet the facilities requirements of IRC 274 and therefore, are usually productive issues.

Taxpayer's previous/subsequent year return. Determine whether the previous/subsequent year return should be inspected. If so, you must note the checksheet. Situations where inspection may be warranted are:

Probable carryover adjustments (i.e., capital loss carryover, substantial depreciation changes).

Items which, if disallowed in the selected year, may be allowable in the following year.

Business individual returns. Generally, business returns should be selected for Field Examination when the following conditions occur:

Voluminous records.

Complex accounting method.

Extensive timeframe required to complete the examination.

Advisability of on-site inspection of business.

Inventories are substantial and material.

Termination of business before the end of the taxable year.

Unusual issues that appear to be complex and time consuming to develop, such as nontaxable transfers, complex oil or mineral explorations, sale of IRC 1231 assets and unstated interest (IRC 483).

The size of a business is also an indicator of what may be involved when an actual examination is made of the books and records of any particular taxpayer.

Net profit. Is the taxpayer engaged in the type of business or profession normally considered to be more profitable than reflected on the return? Is the zero bracket amount used with high gross income and low net profit shown on the business schedule? Experience has shown that the incidence of fraud is greater on low business returns when the return reflects large receipts ($100,000 or more), a sizable investment, and the standard deduction is used. Does the address, real estate taxes and mortgage interest indicate a higher mode of living than justified by the reported income? Does the return reveal large amounts of interest/dividend income not commensurate with current sources of income?

Cost of goods sold. Check for the possibility of withdrawal of items for personal use. Is the ending inventory inclusive of all costs, direct and indirect?

Bad debt deduction. Is it a cash business? Is the deduction disproportionate for the indicated value of sales?

Depreciation. Does the schedule contain an adequate description of the asset? Are personal assets being depreciated? Consider investment credit aspects and sales of property simultaneously with depreciation issues.

Sale of assets. Is there a sale of business assets during the year without investment credit or depreciation recapture? Is the gain large enough to require the alternative minimum tax computation?

Self-employment tax. All returns should be screened for self-employment tax issues, including returns with Schedule SE attached. Look for income such as director's fees, janitorial services, miscellaneous income, partnership income, etc., which may be subject to self-employment tax. Some items of income earned by independent contractors may be reported as wages or other income. Where the income appears to be personal service income, it must be considered for Social Security tax purposes.

Burned-out tax shelters. Burned-out tax shelters are shelters that have reached the crossover point or have become insolvent. Since there may be deferred tax consequences involved, these shelters are potentially abusive even though large losses are not being claimed.

Some shelters may try to postpone recognizing the deferred gain by filing returns showing zero income and expenses or a nominal loss from accrual of interest on non-recourse notes. You should be alert for instances of burned-out shelters.

Some elements for identifying burned-out shelters are being provided for your consideration. The following listing is not intended to be all inclusive: Negative capital accounts; decrease in assets and/or non-recourse accounts; disposition of shelter property through sales, abandonment or voluntary conveyance or like kind exchanges; incorporation of shelter property; transfer of shelter property due to bankruptcy.

Frequently, when these transactions are present, there is nothing left in the shelter to distribute to investors, but because

non-recourse liabilities are wiped out, the investors may realize gain for income tax purposes. Since no distributions are made, it may appear that no transaction has taken place.

Also, you should be alert for the following situations which may involve burned-out shelters:

Charitable contribution. Some taxpayers attempt to dispose of their interest in a burned-out shelter partnership by donating it to a charitable organization and claiming a contribution deduction.

Ordinary or capital loss. Once the shelter has burned out, taxpayers may claim an ordinary or capital loss for their initial cash investment.

Capital gains. Some taxpayers may recognize the deferred tax consequences and report it as capital gain. In most cases, some of the gain should be reported as ordinary income.

These are only a few situations involving burned-out shelters. This is an abuse area which you should be alert to in the classifying/screening of all individual, partnership, and corporate returns.

Commodity options and commodity futures tax shelters. Tax shelter transactions involving commodity straddles can be found on all types of income tax returns, divided between various returns as partnership and partner returns, or scattered through different parts of the same return. They may involve different investment houses or different commodities.

Classifiers/screeners should be aware that transactions involving commodity shelters may be reflected on a return in several ways. The various ways, with references to Exhibits for examples, are listed below:

Form 6781, Gains and Losses from Regulated Futures Contracts and Straddles, is used to report gains and losses from commodity futures contracts and straddle positions.

"Other income" on Form 1040.

Capital Gains and Losses reported on Schedule D.

On Schedule C, Profit and Loss from Business or Profession.

Additional indicators of possible commodity tax shelter schemes on Schedule D are: Transactions with no description given (particularly short-term gains and losses). Transactions reported with a commodity or option shown as the "kind of property and description." Transactions with an ambiguous description and the date sold is prior to the date acquired. Ordinary losses from options with almost equal capital gains.

All returns identified as commodity tax shelters will have Form 5546, Examination Return Charge-Out stamped "Tax Shelter'" by the classifier/screener.

AUDIT RULES FOR PARTNERSHIPS AND S CORPORATIONS

The IRS determines the tax treatment of partnership items at the partnership level in a unified administrative proceeding rather than in separate proceedings with the individual partners. All partnerships with more than ten partners are subject to the rules; partnerships with ten or fewer partners, all of whom are individuals or an estate, may elect to have the rules apply.

The tax treatment of S corporation items is determined at the corporate level in a manner similar to the rules discussed below for partnerships.

AUDIT PROCEDURES AND JUDICIAL REVIEW

The IRS generally may not audit individual partners but must bring proceedings at the partnership level. The IRS must conduct an administrative proceeding to challenge the partnership's treatment of income, deduction, or credit items (I.R.C. § 6223). The IRS determination is called a final partnership administrative adjustment (FPAA). Partners must report partnership items as they are reported on the partnership return or

identify the inconsistency on their return; otherwise, the IRS may assess a deficiency against the partner without having to conduct the partnership proceeding (I.R.C. § 6222). Notice of the proceeding is first given to a so called "tax matters partner" (TMP). The TMP is a specially designated general partner or in the absence of a designation, the general partner having the largest interest in partnership profits at the end of the taxable year involved (I.R.C. § 6231). Notice of the proceeding is given to the other partners within 60 days after the TMP is notified. All partners are entitled to participate in the partnership proceeding.

If the IRS enters into a settlement with some partners, similar settlement terms must be offered to other partners (I.R.C. § 6224).

Within 90 days of the IRS FPAA determination, the TMP may petition the Tax Court for review; individual partners are given an additional 60 days to file a court petition if the TMP does not do so. An appeal from the FPAA may also be filed in a federal district court or the Claims Court if the petitioning partner first deposits with the IRS an amount equal to the tax that would be owed if the FPAA determination were sustained. A petition filed in the Tax Court takes precedence over petitions filed in other courts. The first Tax Court petition filed is heard; if other partners have also filed petitions, their cases will be dismissed. If no Tax Court petitions are filed, the first petition filed in federal district court or the Claims Court takes precedence. Regardless of which petition takes precedence, all partners who hold an interest during the taxable year involved will be bound by the decision (unless the statute of limitations with respect to that partner has run) (I.R.C. § 6226).

STATUTE OF LIMITATIONS

To assess tax against a partner, the IRS must do so within three years following the later of the actual filing date or the due date for the partnership return. If the IRS and the TMP so agree, the limitations period may be extended for all partners. Extension agreements may also be made with each partner. If the partnership understates gross income by more than 25%, the limitations period increases to six years. If the partnership return is fraudulent, there is an unlimited limitations period for partners participating in the fraud and a six-year period for other partners. If the IRS mails notice of an FPAA to the TMP, the statute of limitations stops running until one year after a final court decision is made, or if the FPAA is not appealed, the limitation period is extended until one year after the period for filing a petition for court review expires. (I.R.C. § 6229).

REFUND REQUESTS BY PARTNERS

Partners must make refund claims by filing a "request for an administrative adjustment," or RAA (I.R.C. § 6227). The RAA request must be filed within three years of the actual filing date of the partnership return or the due date for the return (without extensions), whichever is later. It must also be filed before the IRS has notified the partners that it plans to conduct a partnership proceeding. The IRS may decide to conduct a partnership proceeding in response to the refund request.

If an RAA on behalf of all the partners is filed by the tax matters partner (TMP) and the IRS has not allowed any part of it within six months of filing, the TMP may petition the Tax Court, a federal district court or the Claims Court to uphold the claim. A court petition must be filed between six months and two years after the RAA was filed. If the IRS conducts a partnership proceeding and notice of an FPAA determination is given to the TMP, a subsequent court petition on the RAA is barred; the TMP must seek review of the FPAA. All partners may participate in a court proceeding relating to an RAA.

If an RAA is filed by a partner other than the TMP and the IRS does not allow any part of the request within six months, that partner may sue for a refund in a federal district court or the Claims Court; the suit must generally commence within two years of the filing of the RAA. Once a refund action is filed, the partner will not be bound by a subsequent FPAA or judicial review of an FPAA. If the IRS notifies the partner that the items in question are to be treated as nonpartnership items, the partner may sue for a refund within two years of the IRS notice.

IRS PROCEDURES IN AUDITING SUSPECTED TAX FRAUD

The following is a reproduction of an IRS training manual for agents. It suggests techniques for examining taxpayers suspected of tax fraud. Although most tax audits do not involve fraud or suspicion of fraud, the manual should be of general interest in revealing how thorough an examination can be and the range of methods, both technical and psychological, an agent may employ.

The manual is IRS Training No. 3158–01(5–73) Relating to the Principles of Reconstructing Income By the Indirect Methods.

TABLE OF CONTENTS

1 INTRODUCTION

1.01 Objectives

The objectives of this training are to enable examiners:

(A) To use the principles of reconstructing income by the indirect methods
(B) To efficiently and effectively perform a quality audit
(C) To insure the audit was pursued to the point of making a substantially correct determination of the tax liability.

This course gives examiners tools and techniques to enforce taxpayer compliance by auditing the taxpayer and not just his books and records.

The course follows the normal sequence of an examination showing the basic information necessary to adequately and professionally direct the examination.

The primary emphasis is examination of gross receipts.

Practical problems have been prepared for practice in reconstructing income by four methods: the Cash Transaction Account, Net Worth, Source and Application of Funds, and Bank Deposit Analysis.

Each problem is based on the practical approach that the gross income test involves information from four basic sources.

(A) Tax return
(B) Notes of interview
(C) Analysis of books and records
(D) Analysis of bank accounts

Instructions on what information to obtain and how to secure it is a vital part of this course. The examiner must know what information is needed for a gross income test before starting an examination. He should realize that tax examinations should not be limited to verifying specific deductions even if the books and records balance and agree with the tax return. If the preliminary test shows that the amount of the understatement would not warrant more time, then the understatement should be explained, refined, or adjusted.

Solving simulated problems in this course offers effective guides to methods of determining facts, or recognizing and resolving issues, of placing emphasis where it is proper, and of orienting an examiner to develop factual and technical issues.

Methods presented in this text are not an exact science, nor will they result in an absolutely correct answer. Many variables beyond the control of the taxpayer and the examining officer may require pursuing the audit by other means. Generally, however, the methods presented have proved successful tools in ascertaining the substantially correct tax liability. The methods and techniques presented are guidelines; they do not constitute all the requirements for an audit. Similarly, not all the guidelines and techniques are used in every case. The examining officer must choose those guidelines and techniques which he believes appropriate to the situation, and which follow Service policies and procedures. In other words, the examiner must use his own judgment in determining the scope and depth of an examination.

2 PRE-CONTACT ANALYSIS

2.01 Scrutiny of the Return

The beginning of any examination is pre-contact analysis. Pre-contact analysis is an overview of the return which brings out issues and data needed to plan the examination. The analysis should cover all aspects of the return. Make notes as you analyze the return and use them later to prepare workpapers and outline the initial interview.

2.011 Cost of Living Indicators

Some items on the return which are important in a pre-contact analysis are as follows:

(A) Page One
  (1) Filing status
  (2) Size of family
  (3) Address
  (4) Wage income
  (5) Miscellaneous income
  (6) Age
  (7) Estimated tax, if any
(B) Schedule A
  (1) Itemized deductions
    (a) Sales tax—Any capital items purchased?
    (b) Real estate tax—Compare with taxpayers address. Do the taxes suggest taxpayer owns more property than just a personal residence?
    (c) Interest—Does interest expense indicate loans or property holdings?
    (d) Miscellaneous deductions—Any unusual items?
  (2) Dividends and Interest Income—Interest on contracts implies contract payments were received in addition to interest income. Estimate balances in savings accounts by doubling the interest and adding a digit. For example, if the interest income was $500, the estimated balance would be $10,000 using an interest factor of five percent.
(C) Miscellaneous Income
  (1) Rents
  (2) Distributions from Partnership and Sub-Chapter S Returns
  (3) Pensions and Annuities
(D) Schedule D
  (1) Property sold
  (2) Property purchased
(E) Schedule C or F
  (1) Type of business
  (2) Accounting method
  (3) Gross profit percentage—See Revenue Agent's Handbook, Exhibit 19, M.T. 4231–17.
  (4) Net Income
  (5) Interest expense—Does taxpayer pay cash or finance the purchase of business assets?
  (6) Depreciation Schedule—Determine if taxpayer purchased assets during the year.
  (7) Specific unusual items.

These are just some of the items to keep in mind when first looking at a return. As you gain more experience, this procedure will become automatic.

2.012 Books and Records

Once the analysis has been made, determine the books and records needed to answer your specific questions. These records include, but are not limited to, ledgers, journals, bank statements, cancelled checks, savings passbooks, contracts, vouchers, etc.

2.013 Consideration of General Items

In addition to the specific considerations of the pre-contact analysis already listed, the following general items must be considered during the pre-contact analysis.

(A) Evaluate overall composition of the return. Is the return complete, with all necessary information? Who prepared the return? Is it neat and legible?
(B) Analyze the data in relation to the business or industry of the taxpayer.
(C) Consider the location of the business. This could have a bearing on the volume of business.
(D) Use industry percentages of gross profit and net profit to verify the general accuracy of the income and expenses reported.
(E) Find out whether an earlier audit has been made; if so, review these RAR's. (Revenue Agent's Report)
(F) Begin to consider one of the indirect income ap-

proaches to verify the correctness of gross income. Start listing the information needed to make a gross income test.

2.02 Workpapers

Once the pre-contact analysis is completed, you are ready to prepare the formal workpapers which are a guide during the interview. Each workpaper should have a clear heading, showing the name of the taxpayer, year under examination, date prepared, and name of the examiner. The pages should be numbered.

Form 4318 or 4700 is a cover sheet listing technical issues and summarizing those covered.

Immediately following the cover sheet write out or outline specific questions to be asked during the initial interview. Leave space to record answers obtained during the examination, whether or not the item changed the tax liability. Additional issues or areas covered during the examination should be listed and the answers recorded.

If research is necessary, the workpapers should contain summary notes and citations.

The importance of workpapers, especially in unagreed cases, cannot be stressed too highly, not only for your own use as examiners but also for anyone later reviewing the case.

2.03 Scheduling Appointments

2.031 Planning

Upon completion of the pre-contact analysis and before an examining officer makes an appointment, he must plan and organize what he wants to accomplish in the initial contact. What is the best way to do this? What effect will an appointment date have in keeping up with the rest of his workload? He must ask himself, "What am I going to do? How am I going to do it? And when, where and to what degree will I do it?" The governing factors in his answers are effective use of time and good public relations.

2.032 Books and Records Required

The methods for making an appointment will vary according to your district. Whether you use the telephone or a letter, be specific when requesting information or records, which generally include the following:

(A) All books and records used in preparing the return.
(B) Retained copies of Employment Tax Returns, copies of Excise Tax Return, other related returns.
(C) Retained copies of individual income tax returns, including the year before and the year after.
(D) Retained copies of related partnership returns.
(E) All personal and business bank accounts, savings and checking, cancelled checks, and deposit slips.
(F) Invoices to support purchase of assets.
(G) Legal documents, i.e., contracts, inventory records, or others necessitated by your pre-contact analysis.

2.033 Choosing a Date

In making an appointment, do not insist on a specific date, but try to select a mutually convenient time. To insure keeping appointments, record them in a pocket diary. To best use time, closely schedule appointments far enough in advance to allow intermittent blank dates to be used for report writing, research of law, and follow-up previous examinations.

2.034 Initial Contact

We strongly emphasized making the initial contact with the taxpayer, not with his representative. If your case is a corporation, contact an executive directly connected with preparing the return, such as the treasurer. In partnerships, contact a partner. Often taxpayers will refer you to an attorney or accountant. If the representative has a power of attorney, the request will normally be complied with. However, if the representative engages in dilatory or delaying tactics, bring it to the attention of your immediate supervisor for necessary action.

You must record in the case file sufficient facts to show how the examination was being delayed or hindered.

The question of where the appointment will take place will be answered by taking into consideration the bulk of the taxpayer's records, the location of all records, including underlying supporting data, and the policies of the district on such points.

2.035 Taxpayer Relations

In dealing with taxpayers remember you are not only an officer of the Government but also, in effect, a representative of the taxpayer. An examining officer must insure the tax is neither understated nor overstated. When the examiner puts himself in the taxpayer's place, he may better understand the taxpayer problems and thereby avoid premature recommendation that will later be reversed. The examiner should explain the provisions of the law and give full weight to all evidence and information the taxpayer furnishes.

2.036 Interview Site

Knowing what you want, where you are going to do it, and when you are going to do it is only half the job. Insuring the taxpayer knows and agrees with you is mandatory. Often it will save time if you confirm your appointments with the taxpayer at least a day or so before the appointment date. Don't take for granted you know how to get to the interview. Also check to see if there is a place where you can work without disturbance to either the taxpayer's normal business activity or yours. What facilities are available, rest rooms, eating, electric power, adding machines? If they are not available, what is the next best bet? These are samples of secondary areas of consideration when planning an appointment.

2.037 Delays

Now that you have considered the what, where, when, how and how much, be prepared to cope with undue delays. It may be necessary to invent or use methods to keep taxpayers or their representatives from putting off the interview. When delays are necessary, get a definite commitment from the taxpayer or his representative concerning appointments or when the additional information will be forthcoming. Try to complete a case without unnecessary lapse of time.

3 CASH TRANSACTIONS (T) ACCOUNT

3.01 Introduction

The primary method of testing the income reported is an analysis of cash transactions or T Account.

The theory is to consider all types of income and all types of expenditures as "cash transactions" flowing in and out of the cash account in double entry accounting records. Income items will appear in the "T" account as "debits" (left column) and expenditure items will appear in the "T" account as "credits." (Right column) If the total credits exceed the total debits, the difference represents an understatement of gross receipts.

3.02 Computation

After the pre-contact analysis has been made, prepare a T account and enter the known items from the return. The remainder are added after the interview and after the books and records have been examined. An example follows:

T ACCOUNT

Gross Receipts (Per Return)	Business expenses (less depr.)
Gross Rents	Rental expenses (less depr.)
Miscellaneous Income	Personal living expenses
Interest Income and Dividends	Purchase of assets
Cash on hand	Cash on hand
(at beginning of year)	(at the end of year)
Cash in banks	Cash in banks
(at beginning of year)	(at the end of year)
Loans	Loan payments
Accounts receivable	Accounts receivable
(at beginning of year)	(at the end of year)
Accounts payable	Accounts payable
(at the end of year)	(at beginning of year)
Nontaxable income	
Wages	

Only items representing cash transactions should be entered.

   (A)   Adjustments are needed if the taxpayer is on an accrual basis. Beginning and year-end balances of accounts receivable and accounts payable must be entered. Accounts receivable are the same as cash and are similarly entered, with the beginning balance on the debit side of the T Account. Accounts payable are the reverse. The ending balance is a debit, since it represents expenses deducted but not paid and therefore, does not require cash.

   (B)   Only those dividends representing cash payments should be entered. Neither the exclusion nor dividends reinvested appear.

   (C)   Cash on hand or cash hoard represents the money which the taxpayer has in his pocket or "in the mattress."

   (D)   Cash in banks requires several adjustments, as the bank statements do not reflect checks or deposits which have not cleared the bank at beginning and year end.

   (E)   Business expenses do not include such items as depreciation, bad debts, spoilage, inventory, etc., as they do not represent cash transactions.

   (F)   Loan payment and specific asset purchases should be checked carefully to avoid duplication.

   (G)   Personal withdrawals affect the figure entered for purchases. Enter the net figure in business expenses. Personal withdrawals will be picked up later in the personal living expense figure.

   (H)   Sources of possible nontaxable income might include:
      (1) Income tax refunds
      (2) Loan repayments to taxpayer
      (3) Social Security benefits
      (4) Unemployment
      (5) Gifts and Inheritances
      (6) Sale of Personal Assets
      (7) Insurance Proceeds
      (8) Reimbursements
      (9) Gambling, prizes, etc.
      (10) Other

These examples merely suggest possible items and not a complete list. As an examiner you will have to develop these items during the interview and from the records submitted.

3.03   Technical Adjustment

A problem may develop when you recognize personal expenses claimed as business expenses. Do you adjust these items by reducing business expenses and also eliminating such items from the personal living expense computation, or leave them as business expenses and include them as personal living expenses? If the former computation were chosen specific adjustments would be required after determining the correctness of the gross receipts by the "T" account method.

The preferred computation considers all expenses representing cash expenditure on the Schedule "C" as business expenses and includes in the personal living expenses all the personal living expenses you can identify. Therefore, the only difference in the figure used as Schedule "C" expenses in the "T" account and those reported on the return is noncash expenditures.

Because the gross income test is designed to verify the correctness of gross receipts any understatement calculated will not require any other adjustments to items representing cash expenditures claimed as business expenses.

As an overstatement of expenses creates an understatement, additional adjustments to the business cash expenditure items would duplicate the adjustment considered in the gross receipts.

When the test results in no understatement, indicating the gross receipts are correct as reported, specific adjustments are applicable.

Technical adjustments to depreciation, bad debts, or other items representing noncash expenditures are always applicable.

3.04   Cash On Hand at Beginning of Period

It is important to get complete information about nontaxable income as your efforts may be wasted if the taxpayer provides information regarding a nontaxable source of funds which explains the understatement. This is especially true of cash on hand or cash hoard. This information is a must in every indirect method. The best adjustment for unreported income will be lost if this item is not determined from the beginning. Once the taxpayer is faced with an understatement, he will try to explain it. He cannot use the defense of "cash in the mattress" if he has already furnished the amount.

3.05   Example

The following example illustrates the T Account method.

CASH TRANSACTIONS (T) ACCOUNT

1/1 Cash on hand and in banks (B)	$ 2,000	12/31 Cash on hand and in banks (B)	$ 7,000
Wife's Salary (A)	5,000	Expenses Sch. C (less depr.) (A)	287,000
Gross Receipts (A)	285,000	Personal living expenses (estimated) (C)	14,000
		Assets purchased (B)	2,000
	$292,000		$310,000

   (A)   Amounts taken from the return.
   (B)   Amounts determined from the initial interview and/or the bank statements.
   (C)   Personal living expenses estimated from the initial interview. You may ask the taxpayer for a weekly or monthly estimate which can be later refined if necessary. This subject will be covered later.

This example indicates that income was understated by $18,000 ($310,000 less $292,000).

3.06   Identification of Understatement

This understatement may result from unreported gross receipts, from overstated expenses, from omitted nontaxable income, or from a combination of these items. Enlist the taxpayer's cooperation in explaining the discrepancy. You may use one of the other methods (covered later) to reinforce your position. If the understatement is resolved, make any technical adjustments and close the case.

If the cash transactions method indicates that taxpayer had sufficient money to cover the known expenditures, accept the income reported and no-change the return, if there are no technical adjustments. Do not try to refine figures to the point of perfection. Time is important and should be kept to a minimum if possible. As soon as you have enough information to satisfy yourself that income appears properly reported, conclude the examination.

Should you discover that the "Debit" column is substantially larger than the "Credit" column, you have a different situation that warrants further investigation. More than likely there are investments or other personal expenses of which you are not aware. You might then assume that these investments would create additional income. Because there are no sure answers to any imbalance, be very careful before concluding that an under- or overstatement exists. You will need to be sure of your ground before presenting your findings to the taxpayer. Here experience will help, but until you thoroughly understand the theory, check with your O.J.T. Coach or supervisor before approaching the taxpayer again.

Using the cash transactions, or T account, cannot be stressed too highly. It is a simple method that can accommodate varied situations without becoming over technical. This method can be used in any examination because of the relatively short time it takes to develop the information necessary. Use it for all examinations requiring testing income. The results are accurate and the information easy to obtain.

4 EXAMINATION

4.01 Initial Interview

4.011 Introduction

The initial interview is an auditing technique used in every examination involving one of the indirect methods of determining income. Frequently, the information developed by this method will determine the eventual outcome of the case, although most evidence exists in some tangible form, such as, cancelled checks, invoices, books, records, and other items; much needed information can be obtained only through discussion with the taxpayer. Developing skill in interviewing is a personal matter in which the examiner's personality plays a dominant role. A successful examiner can improve his interviewing technique by concentration, practice, and a knowledge of human nature. Ask yourself! What do I want to know? Why? In all indirect methods of determining income you must know how much money the taxpayer spends and where he spends it. Voice variations and facial expressions may indicate a need for more extensive questioning. Don't just hear the taxpayer's reply, but observe his reaction. It may be more important than the answer.

4.012 Planning the Interview

Careful planning of each interview is necessary; however, an outline is not always required. Often more information can be obtained without direct questioning, while at other times the examiner will want to lead the interview with the specific questioning technique. This technique should be used when the taxpayer wants to "ramble" and avoids giving pertinent information.

4.013 Purpose of Interview

The primary purpose of the interview is to secure, by conversation with the taxpayer, sufficient facts which will present an overall financial picture of the taxpayer. Such a picture will include savings plans, investments, approximate standard of living, inheritances, and other items of income and expense common to the man's status in life. After the interview, the examiner should be in a position to see if the reported taxable income bears the necessary relationship to the taxpayer's financial picture.

There is no substitute for good sound judgment and friendliness in contacting the taxpayer for an interview. The examiner should attempt to establish a rapport with the taxpayer. After identifying himself in a friendly, affable manner, and telling the taxpayer the purpose of his visit, he should conduct himself to establish the confidence of the taxpayer as early in the examination as possible. Begin the discussion by commenting on a topic of apparent interest to the taxpayer. Display pleasant emotional responses and avoid unpleasant expressions. Do not immediately attempt to discuss involved technical matters but keep the conversation informal and easy. Be fair and keep an open mind that is receptive to all information. Attempt to properly evaluate the taxpayer's mental ability.

The interview techniques set forth in this text are not infallible. They are suggested as aids or guides and should be used when apropriate. The most important point to remember about this subject is that a good interview is a basic part of a quality audit.

4.014 Development of Interview

The following list contains some of the items which an examiner should try to develop in making a quality audit.

(A) Information about the taxpayer's family and dependents. The family size, dependents living outside the home, children in college, etc.

(B) Unusual expenditures, extended trips, gambling, acquisition of unusual assets, and the taxpayer's hobbies should be considered. Although such expenditures are personal, they should be considered as a lead into the personal living statement.

(C) Establish annual estimated personal and family living expenses, if feasible. It may be that all living expenses are paid through a personal bank account and the taxpayer makes such a statement. The examiner may utilize that data without acquiring a complete living expense statement. On occasions the examiner may take a living expense statement form and question the taxpayer as to the items listed thereon and write in the estimates.

(D) Data relating to the taxpayer's business history and related businesses. If the taxpayer owns controlling interest in various business or is a partner, this should be developed.

(E) Secure information about accounts receivable, loans receivable, inventories, and a general statement as to how the inventories are valued and method used. Ask that a record of the inventory be made available.

(F) Acquire positive statements about business bank accounts and those personal accounts of the immediate family. Be specific about all open or closed accounts—business, personal, savings, certificate of deposits, and other forms of money deposits. If the taxpayer does not have such records available, request that he obtain them after the interview.

(G) Request information about bank loans, personal loans, accounts payable, and other borrowed funds. It may be more practical to cover loans made outside the business which do not appear in the regular books.

(H) Determine the taxpayer's security holdings in stocks, bonds, mutual funds, etc.

(I) Obtain a listing of the real estate holdings. Be specific about the personal residence and monthly payments. This could be a good indication that the taxpayer is living beyond his reported income. Ask specifically about purchases of real estate because this may disclose use of funds which have not been reported.

(J) Request a record of personal loans made to others—this may be to a member of the family, a friend, or someone else. (NOTE: The material requested on various assets and liabilities may vary if the examiner has considered a gross income test by a specific technique.)

(K) Since many taxpayers will attempt to explain away an understatement by saying that it is from cash hoards, it is imperative that cash on hand be covered during the interview. Also, any increase or decrease in cash on hand is a part of the gross income test.

(L) Ask about cash control and understand the mechanics of how cash is handled in the business and how expenses are paid—if certain expenses are paid in currency, this is a good indication that receipts may not be handled correctly.

(M) Ask about other assets—those that appear on the return and those that do not appear on the return.

(N) In developing the information, if a specific item appearing on the tax return or pre-planning sheet needs some comment, it should be included in the interview.

(O) Find out if financial statements, independent audit reports, applications for loans, workpapers used to prepare the return, and other information may be available. If so, request that it be made available since a verification of the return to records is to follow.

(P) If the taxpayer's prior or subsequent returns have been made available, there may be items appearing thereon that would have a bearing on the current year—if so, this should be covered.

(Q) At the conclusion of the interview, the examiner would have jotted down notes of various records required. If the taxpayer or his employees do not have such records readily available, ask that the taxpayer secure such information—the examiner should not have to go find the data.

(R) Determine whether the taxpayer received any nontaxable income such as gifts, inheritances, proceeds from life insurance, etc.

(S) Be discreet and find out whether or not the taxpayer

received funds or handled funds other than those reported. For example, in certain instances a taxpayer may be trustee for certain funds and such must be known.

The examiner should remember in following through with the interview that he is examining the taxpayer and not just the taxpayer's books and records. The most satisfaction can come by using ingenuity, common sense, and being a little suspicious.

4.015 Personal Living Expenses

The initial interview is the proper time to secure as much data as possible to determine personal living expenses. Personal living expenses are a very important aspect of any of the indirect methods of determining income. In a quick test of gross receipts, a rough estimate of personal living expenses may be sufficient. However, if this quick test shows a possible understatement of gross receipts, these expenses should be as accurate as possible. Many taxpayers, who are skimming off the top, put the diverted funds directly into increasing their personal standard of living. Without a reasonably accurate determination of these expenses the understatement will not be disclosed. Many personal living expenses can be determined directly by analyzing the checking account, while other expenses can be obtained during the initial interview by skillfully asked questions. Hence, these two sources become very important in determining taxpayer's style of living. During the initial interview the taxpayer may answer more honestly, because he does not know why the questions are asked. The Personal Living Expense Form should be completed after analyzing the bank account and the initial interview. Many items can be safely estimated. Only as a last resort should the Form be presented to the taxpayer to complete. This suggestion depends upon the policy of the individual districts.

A sample format for obtaining an estimate of personal living expenses is provided in Exhibit A at the end of this chapter. Recurring items can better be obtained on a weekly or monthly basis and then converted to a yearly basis.

4.02 Evaluation of Documents

4.021 Introduction

Books and records vary depending on the type and volume of business. There are two types of records for each business. The secondary or formal records are the permanent books, worksheets, etc., which list or summarize the information from the primary or informal records.

Usually the secondary records will agree with the return. Scan these records for unusual items, but do not examine them extensively unless a specific issue is part of the formal work plan or classification. The primary records will be of more concern to the examiner. Of major importance are the bank accounts.

4.022 Bank Accounts

Relate the information obtained in the interview to the analysis of all bank and savings accounts. Develop a picture of the total operation of the taxpayer. Determine where the money came from. Scan the duplicate deposit tickets, if available, and investigate substantial or unusual deposits. A large cash deposit made by a taxpayer whose receipts normally consist primarily of checks needs an explanation. Identification of small check deposits by a taxpayer whose receipts normally consist of cash may indicate dividends, interest, or other income. Repeated or semi-annual, monthly, quarterly deposits of the same amount may indicate rental, dividend, interest or other income accruing to the taxpayer. Observe the ratio of cash deposits to checks. Is there a relative absence of cash, or a relative absence of checks that would normally be accumulated in the taxpayer's business? If the taxpayer's normal operations is primarily cash receipts and his deposits are primarily checks, probably he is cashing customer checks, or he may be pocketing the cash and using it for personal expenses. Compare the annual deposits to the sources of gross income reported on the return. Banks frequently show the total deposits at the top of each monthly

statement. Totaling the twelve monthly deposits will thus give the total of annual deposits. Deposits greater than Gross Receipts require an analysis to determine if loans, repayment of loans, or extraneous items are reflected in the deposits. Another point to consider is that the nature of the business or the convenience of the depository may require the taxpayer to follow a pattern in making deposits. Deviation from this pattern should bear questioning.

The examination of deposit slips may indicate checks drawn on out-of-state banks. From the American Banking Association identification number on the deposit slip the name and location of the bank can be readily determined by reference to a banker's guide. In all cases, if the location of the bank on which the check for deposit has been drawn bears little relation to the taxpayer's business locality or sources of income, it may need further investigation.

Find out whether deposits in personal or nonbusiness bank accounts can be accounted for by withdrawals from business or other known sources of funds.

When necessary analyze the cancelled checks and group by categories of personal, business, capital expenditures and loans. If the taxpayer is present, ask him to help identify them. Notations on check stubs and the face of the check may provide leads to various nonbusiness expenditures. Use of adding machine tapes will avoid listing personal checks. Compare the name of the payee with the endorsement. If they do not agree, or if the name of any officer, partner, etc., appears as a secondary endorser, determine why. If the checks are drawn payable to Bearer or Cash, glance at the check book to see if the payee is the same one named on the check itself. Look for unusual amounts and to whom paid and for what reason. Determine whether the check cleared the bank and note it. Often in small operations the owner will issue a check to an employee for payroll and have the employee endorse the check. The employer will then cash the check for the employee and keep the check as a record of payment. Similarly, the employer may write a check to cash, withdraw cash, and not deposit the check. Checks to the taxpayer and members of his family, the bank, and department store may also list account numbers belonging to the taxpayer. This information may disclose hidden bank accounts or unknown expenditures.

The examining officer should glance at the endorsements, the clearing bank, and bank markings when he inspects checks. Third-party checks endorsed by the taxpayer may mean a fictitious deduction or endorsements not by a firm stamp may indicate forgeries by the taxpayer. The location of the clearing bank on checks to cash may indicate a vacation in another city.

Upon a detailed analysis of the checks the amounts and frequency of payments can be observed for personal items such as food, clothing, rent, home mortgage and capital expenditures. If relatively few personal items are being paid by check, the rest of the annual expenses were paid by cash.

In general, if the examining officer were in the taxpayer's shoes and wanted to hide income or claim personal expenses as business expenditures, how would he go about it? Now what is a method to detect this evasion? Original approaches are left to the imagination of the examining officer; however, there is no substitute for prudent judgment in determining the extent to which the bank account analysis should be pursued.

Analyzing the taxpayer's check disbursements is not only a means of verifying expenses and deductions, but also a way of determining how the taxpayer is spending his money. It is not necessarily what the taxpayer says concerning his personal and nondeductible expenses, but what his checks indicate to substantiate his mode of living. In short, the checks may establish that the taxpayer is spending more than his reported income.

4.023 Other Documents

Other important primary documents are sales and purchases invoices. These should be at least spot-checked to make sure that the secondary records contain accurate postings. Since the records vary for each business, it is not practical to explain in detail the extent to examine records. The training you receive on the job will provide the necessary guidelines on a case-by-case basis.

If you have any questions or problems in interpreting the taxpayer's records, always stop what you are doing and ask the taxpayer. What is obvious to him is not always obvious to you. Much time will be wasted if you attempt to solve the problem yourself when a simple question may clear up the confusion. In discussing the records with the taxpayer, it is often advantageous to feign ignorance and let him tell you about his business and records. More information can be obtained from this method than by merely looking at the records and making assumptions.

The prior year return should be looked at for a comparison and any major differences noted and considered. The taxpayer must file related returns, such as payroll, excise, etc. Look at these to see if they were properly filed. Copies of Partnership (Form 1065) or Sub-Chapter S Corporations (Form 1120-S) returns should be glanced over to see if the distribution was correctly shown on Form 1040. Contributions to capital and withdrawals will be items needed for income testing by an indirect method.

As you analyze records, make notes of unusual items to consider along with the interview notes.

4.03 Analysis of Evidence

Once the initial interview has been completed and the records examined, there will be additional facts to consider. The taxpayer may provide further information and various conclusions will be drawn from analysis of the records. These additional facts are then considered with reference to your pre-contact analysis. You are now ready to elaborate on the T account which you began during pre-contact analysis. By entering various items you can determine whether income was understated or overstated. If at this point you feel that further elaboration is necessary, you may test your findings by one of the other methods (net worth, source and application of funds, bank deposit analysis).

4.04 Concluding the Examination

An examiner must use sound judgment in deciding when an examination should be terminated. It is rarely, if ever, necessary to verify every item on the return or to analyze every account on the books. An examiner, however, is expected to extend the audit to cover all unusual and questionable items, including all items noted on his examination planning sheet. Conclude the audit when you have considered all items necessary for substantially proper determination of the tax liability.

If the examination results in an understatement, it is your job to explain the understatement to the taxpayer in terms he understands. If he agrees to your determination, you will not need to refine your computation. If he does not agree, you may need to use another method to reinforce your position.

Previously you have been told that you should examine the taxpayer and not just his books and records. This is true. However, when concluding the examination your arguments should be with the books and records rather than with the taxpayer. In other words, try to avoid a situation where personalities become involved. You will be more successful in concluding examinations.

Closing a case is possibly the most difficult part of an examination. You must be tactful in pointing out errors in the books or records so that you do not criticize the work of the taxpayer's employees or his representatives. You must be patient in explaining the provisions of law, bearing in mind that what is clear to you as an examiner is not so clear to persons in other fields of work. The written explanation of adjustments should be clear to the taxpayer and concise. The schedules should guide the reader to a conclusion which is easily followed and understood. Always keep an open mind and listen to the taxpayer's explanation. The possibility that you may be wrong always exists and you should readily admit any errors. Always remember that your job is to determine the correct tax, regardless of the outcome.

5 NET WORTH

5.01 Introduction

The net worth method is probably the best known of the

IRS's weapons for detecting unreported income. Historically it has been used primarily in fraud cases. Courts have recognized the net worth method probably because it is presented in the familiar balance sheet format readily recognized in the business world. The net worth method is based on a complete financial picture and on the theory that increases or decreases in the taxpayer's net worth during a taxable period, adjusted for nontaxable expenditures and nontaxable income, must result from taxable income.

5.02 Basic Theory of the Net Worth

In this type of examination the taxpayer's net worth, that is, the difference between his assets and his liabilities, must be determined at the beginning and at the end of the taxable year. The difference between these two amounts is the increase or decrease in his net worth. Adjustments are then made for nondeductible and nontaxable items to arrive at taxable income.

The net worth method is an excellent one to use when the accounts on the taxpayer's books appear false, incomplete, or missing. It is also recommended when two or more years are under examination and when the taxpayer has several assets and liabilities which changed during the year.

A net worth statement prepared and submitted by the taxpayer can save much of the examining officer's time. The statement should be checked carefully for inaccuracies and omissions. A net worth statement in the file on the taxpayer would always be available as a starting point for any future income verification.

A study of the taxpayer's insurance coverage can suggest the extent of unreported income. Life insurance and annuities might be a good reflection of the taxpayer's own opinion of his earning power. Insurance on the stock of merchandise might give a clue to the true inventory value. Burglary and theft insurance could disclose the existence and value of furs, jewelry, antiques and rare collections. However, some caution will be necessary before relying on these valuations; taxpayers may have some reasons of their own for over insuring or under insuring their assets.

If the taxpayer is an alien or a naturalized citizen, the Immigration and Naturalization Service may have the taxpayer's sworn statement of the value of property brought into the country. This information may supply an excellent starting point in some cases.

5.03 The Net Worth Computation

The formula for computing income by the net worth method is:

(A) Assets less Liabilities = Net Worth
(B)

Net Worth—End of Year	$ XXX
Less: Net Worth—Beginning of Year	XXX
Increase or Decrease in Net Worth	$ XXX
Add: Nondeductible Expenditures	XXX
Total	$ XXX
Less: Nontaxable Income	XXX
Adjusted gross income (This figure would be net or taxable income in the case of partnerships and corporations.)	$ XXX

(C) To arrive at the correct taxable income, reduce the adjusted gross income figure by allowable itemized deductions (or standard deduction) plus the personal exemptions.

In the net worth method you must use the same accounting method the taxpayer used in his return, unless the examination shows that the accounting method should be changed. If the taxpayer reports on the cash basis, items like business accounts receivables and payables would not be used. However, if the taxpayer is on the accrual method, all accrued business assets and business liabilities would be used. If the taxpayer elects to report on the installment basis, the element of unrealized gross profit should be set up in the liability section of the balance sheet. If returns are filed on a Fiscal year basis, the balance sheet dates should conform to that basis.

The net worth computation consists of preparing balance

sheets for the beginning and end of each year, including reserves for depreciation and amortization computed on the correct basis. Asset values should be listed at cost or taxpayer's basis.

After computing the net worth for each year, determine the increase or decrease in net worth by comparing the net worth at the beginning and end of each year.

5.04 Below-the-Line Adjustments

Next, make adjustments to account for expenditures not included in the assets and liabilities, as well as various nondeductible and nontaxable items. These adjustments are commonly referred to as below-the-line adjustments.

Following are some examples of items which should be added to the increase or decrease in net worth:

(A) Personal living expenses
(B) Income tax payments
(C) Nondeductible portion of capital losses
(D) Losses on sale of personal assets (if included as assets on the balance sheet)
(E) Gifts made

The following items should be subtracted from the increase or decrease in net worth:

(A) Nontaxable portions of capital gains
(B) Tax-exempt interest
(C) Nontaxable pensions
(D) Nontaxable portion of proceeds from life insurance
(E) Gifts received
(F) Inheritances
(G) Veterans benefits
(H) Dividend exclusions
(I) Excludable sick pay

The result of the adjustments to the increase or decrease in net worth is adjusted gross income as corrected.

To arrive at the correct taxable income, reduce the adjusted gross income figure by allowable itemized deductions (or standard deduction) plus the personal exemptions.

It may be difficult or even impossible to accurately determine the exact amount of taxpayer's personal assets at the beginning of the year. This is particularly true for personal furniture, residence, etc. The beginning balances of such items can be estimated. The workpapers should clearly reflect which items are estimates and how the other amounts were determined.

The question may arise why items that do not change should be included in the net worth statement, particularly since they have no bearing on the final result. First, the net worth statement should be as complete as possible so that the taxpayer will have no grounds to successfully contest its credibility because items were omitted. Second, net worth statements are frequently used as a starting point in future examinations of the same taxpayer, and a complete net worth would be valuable to the next examiner.

5.05 Example

For an illustration of the net worth method, see Attachment A at the end of this chapter.

5.06 Cash On Hand at the Beginning of the Period

One of the most important factors in a net worth computation is establishing a correct and "tight" opening net worth statement. This usually involves the sound determination of cash on hand in the opening net worth. Often the taxpayer or his representative will claim sizable cash accumulation at the beginning of the period in an attempt to counteract the increases determined by this method of computation. The examining officer is faced with the difficult problem of verifying the truthfulness of the taxpayer's statement.

5.07 Methods of Verifying Taxpayer's Statement of Cash Accumulation

As mentioned previously, the initial interview with the taxpayer can be, and usually is, the most important phase of an examination. At this time, the taxpayer may give accurate, de-

pendable, and useful information which he may be reluctant or unwilling to give later. If the subject of cash on hand is approached emphasizing the taxpayer's present cash accumulations compared to the past, he may make statements which may solve this problem. If so, be sure to make comprehensive notes in workpapers of the date of the statement and the information given. It even may be advisable at that time to prepare an affidavit to be signed by the taxpayer pertaining to this type of information.

At the initial interview a casual discussion of the taxpayer's financial history may give information which will disclose that the taxpayer had once been in some financial difficulty, perhaps in bankruptcy or subject to a lawsuit, in which his assets and liabilities in the past were determined.

Often the taxpayer may have filed balance sheets with financial or credit organizations. This fact may assist the examiner in determining the opening cash accumulations.

On other occasions loans and chattel mortgages on automobiles, personal furniture and other equipment, especially if at a high interest rate, may be evidence that the taxpayer had no sizable cash accumulations during that period.

Another consideration in determining and allowing cash on hand at the beginning of the period is the taxpayer's filing history. An analysis of the income reported in prior years may indicate that cash accumulations claimed would be impossible when compared to the income previously reported.

NET WORTH COMPUTATION

Assets	12-31-71	12-31-72
Cash in Bank	$ 2,000.00	$ 1,500.00
Accounts Receivable	3,200.00	5,300.00
Equipment	10,000.00	15,000.00
Personal Residence	25,000.00	25,000.00
Personal Furniture	5,000.00	5,000.00
Personal Auto	2,500.00	2,500.00
Total Assets	$47,700.00	$54,300.00
Liabilities		
Accounts Payable	$ 4,700.00	$ 3,700.00
Notes Payable—Equipment	0.00	4,000.00
Accumulated Depreciation	8,000.00	9,000.00
Total Liabilities	$12,700.00	$16,700.00
Net Worth	$35,000.00	$37,600.00
Net Worth at the Beginning of Year		35,000.00
Increase in Net Worth		$ 2,600.00
Add: Personal Living Expenses		9,000.00
		$11,600.00
Less: Sec. 1202 Deduction for Capital Gains		1,200.00
Adjusted Gross Income as Corrected		$10,400.00
Adjusted Gross Income per Return		8,100.00
Understatement of Adjusted Gross Income		$ 2,300.00

6 SOURCE AND APPLICATION OF FUNDS METHOD

6.01 Definition

The Source and Application of Funds Method is a comparison of all known expenditures with all known receipts. When using this method, we determine where the taxpayer's money came from (source) and what the taxpayer did with his income (application). In this method, however, only the increases and decreases in assets and liabilities are considered along with other nondeductible expenses and nontaxable receipts. When the taxpayer has several assets and liabilities that remain unchanged during the year, they are not listed. The Source and Application of Funds Method is often preferred by the examiner because of its simplicity and its ease of explanation to the taxpayer.

6.02 Cash on Hand at the Beginning of the Period

It is imperative that the cash on hand at the beginning of the period is carefully tied down. Otherwise, the taxpayer may contend that cash accumulations at the beginning of the year, were an additional source. During your previous study of the Net Worth Method, you learned the importance of and methods for verifying cash on hand at the beginning of the period.

6.03 Accrual Method Taxpayer

By including the increase or decrease of the accounts receivable account, accounts payable account, and inventory in the computation of the source and application of funds method, no separate adjustments are necessary when the taxpayer uses the accrual method of accounting.

6.04 Computation

In the computation of the source and application of funds method, items to be considered are:

6.041 Application

(A) Increase in Cash on Hand
(B) Increase in Bank Accounts
This includes both checking and saving accounts used for business and nonbusiness purposes.
(C) Increase in Inventory
(D) Increase in Accounts Receivable
(E) Decrease in Accounts Payable
(F) Decrease in Loan Principal
(G) Payments on Business Equipment Purchased
(H) Payments on Real Estate Purchased
(I) Payments on Personal Assets Acquired
(J) Personal Living Expenses

6.042 Source

(A) Business Profit Reported per Return
(B) Depreciation Deduction per Return
(Include separate Rental Schedule Depreciation, if applicable.) Any change in depreciation from the tax return will result in a separate specific adjustment.
(C) Sale of Assets (Gross)
(D) Increase in Loan Principal
(E) Decrease in Cash on Hand
(F) Decrease in Bank Accounts
(G) Salaries (Gross)
(H) Net Rental Profit
(I) Other Income Items Per Return
(Interest, Gross Dividends, Pensions, Annuities, Partnership, and Estate 1120-S Distributions)
(J) Nontaxable Receipts
(Gifts, Inheritances, Social Security, Tax-exempt Interest, etc.)

Any excess of Application of Funds over Source of Funds results in understatement of Taxable Income.

6.05 Example

The following example illustrates the Source and Application of Funds Method.

Application

Merchants National Bank—Increase	$ 108.13
Notes Receivable	2,150.00
Inventory—Increase	576.00
Accounts Receivable—Increase	1,500.00
Payments on Business Equipment Purchased	1,000.00
Payments on Personal Assets Acquired	750.00
Personal Living Expenses	14,175.26
Total Application	$20,259.39

Source

Jot-em-Down Grocery—Net Profit Per Return	$ 3,654.11
Depreciation—Per Return	755.32
Basis of Stock Sold	1,300.00
Notes Payable (Principal)—Increase	2,500.00
Federal Savings and Loan Association—Decrease	1,000.00
Salaries	6,050.00
Total Source	$15,259.43
Understatement	$ 4,999.96

6.06 When to Use

The use of the Source and Application of Funds Method is generally recommended in the following situations:

(A) Only one or two years are under examination.
(B) The taxpayer has several assets and/or liabilities which do not change during the year.
(C) In nonbusiness returns, in which the deductions claimed appear out of proportion to the income reported or there are indications of unreported income.
(D) Comparative balance sheets are available.
(E) There is little or no apparent net worth and most of the expenditure of funds constitutes nondeductible personal living expenses.

7 BANK DEPOSIT

7.01 Introduction

The bank deposits method is simple in theory. It ascertains the taxpayer's total receipts by showing what happened to the money. If you can determine the disposition of the money, it is possible to determine the total amount of the money. This is basically the theory used in any indirect income determination.

The bank deposits method is a cash basis computation. If the taxpayer is using the accrual method, an adjustment must be made for accounts receivable and accounts payable.

For instance, an increase in accounts receivable would be added to "total receipts."

7.02 Basic Formula

The basic formula for the simplified bank deposits method is:

NET DEPOSITS + CASH EXPENDITURES =
TOTAL RECEIPTS

For a better understanding of the formula, assume that a taxpayer receives money. He can put the money in a bank account, spend it for living expenses in cash, purchase assets with cash, pay expenses with cash, or hoard it. He must either *Deposit* the money or handle it in the form of *Cash*. It is apparent that a good interview is required to determine the taxpayer's expenditures, whether by cash or check; to identify all his bank accounts, and to determine all loans and other nontaxable receipts. The following are basic sources of information for the bank deposits computation:

(A) Tax Return
(B) Interview
(C) Analysis of books and records
(D) Analysis of bank accounts

7.03 Comparison of Lengthy vs. Simplified

This Simplified Bank Deposit Method is not the same as the Lengthy Bank Deposit Method in the Revenue Agent's or Tax Auditor's Handbooks. There are two basic differences in these two methods.

(A) In the simplified method bank transfers and redeposits are not eliminated in the computation but are included in net deposits. Therefore deposits are overstated by these amounts. Likewise, included in total checks written are all withdrawals for redeposit or transfer. Hence this overstatement offsets the overstatement in net deposits.
(B) The simplified method includes all outlays paid by either check or cash, while the more lengthy method requires a specific determination of disbursements made by cash and disbursements made by check.

7.04 Computation

7.041 Net Deposits

Net deposits consist of total deposits less non-income receipts. Total deposits includes deposits for all bank accounts, i.e. business, personal, savings, and checking. You need not always reconcile the accounts if the amounts (deposits in transit and checks outstanding) at the end of the year are substantially the same as they were at the beginning of the year. Total non-income receipts consist of only money actually received from such sources as loans, inheritances, pensions, gifts, life insurance proceeds, etc. These items must be deducted regardless of

Form **4822** (Rev. 6-83)	Department of the Treasury - Internal Revenue Service **STATEMENT OF ANNUAL ESTIMATED PERSONAL AND FAMILY EXPENSES**			
TAXPAYER'S NAME AND ADDRESS				TAX YEAR ENDED

	ITEM	BY CASH	BY CHECK	TOTAL	REMARKS
1. PERSONAL EXPENSES	Groceries and outside meals				
	Clothing				
	Laundry and dry cleaning				
	Barber, beauty shop, and cosmetics				
	Education (tuition, room, board, books, etc.)				
	Recreation, entertainment, vacations				
	Dues (clubs, lodge, etc.)				
	Gifts and allowances				
	Life and accident insurance				
	Federal taxes (income, FICA, etc.)				
2. HOUSEHOLD EXPENSES	Rent				
	Mortgage payments (including interest)				
	Utilities (electricity, gas, telephone, water, etc.)				
	Domestic help				
	Home insurance				
	Repairs and improvements				
	Child care				
3. AUTO EXPENSES	Gasoline, oil, grease, wash				
	Tires, batteries, repairs, tags				
	Insurance				
	Auto payments (including interest)				
	Lease of auto				
4. DEDUCTIBLE ITEMS	Contributions				
	Medical Expenses — Insurance				
	Medical Expenses — Drugs				
	Medical Expenses — Doctors, hospitals, etc.				
	Taxes — Real estate (not included in 2. above)				
	Taxes — Personal property				
	Taxes — Income (State and local)				
	Interest (not included in 2. and 3. above)				
	Miscellaneous — Alimony				
	Miscellaneous — Union dues				
5. PERSONAL ASSETS, ETC.	Stocks and bonds				
	Furniture, appliances, jewelry				
	Loans to others				
	Boat				
	TOTALS ▶				

whether they were actually deposited. However, the examiner should have determined the disposition of loans and other non-income items during the interview. He must be reasonably certain that he picks up in Total Outlays (discussion to follow) the costs of assets acquired with non-income receipts. The items under discussion do not include bank transfers and redeposits.

Subtract Total Non-income receipts from Total Deposits. The balance is "Net Deposits," which is the first part of the formula.

7.042 Cash Expenditures

Cash expenditures consist of total outlays less checks written.

Total outlays includes all outlays by either check or cash. There is no need to determine which part was paid by cash and which part was paid by check. Total outlays include, but are not limited to, the following:

(A) Tax Return—Purchases, business expenses (less non-cash items), capital assets, rental expenses, etc.

(B) Loans Repaid—Principal only—Determine from the loan ledger of bank or other creditor.

(C) Investments or capital assets—Total expenditures for such acquisitions during the year. Determine from the invoices or contracts. Includes asset purchased with non-income receipts.

443

(D) Personal expenditures—For the gross income test these may be estimated. However, the taxpayer may furnish these amounts during the interview or analysis of the bank accounts.

Total checks written for all bank accounts are determined by adding the Total Deposits, as determined above, to the beginning bank balances and deducting the ending bank balances. The difference representing "total checks written" represents all withdrawals from the bank accounts including withdrawals from savings accounts.

From the Total Outlays subtract "total checks written." The difference is "cash expenditures" and should be added to "Net Deposits" to arrive at "Total Receipts" on a cash basis.

7.05 Accrual Method Taxpayer

For the taxpayer on the accrual basis, adjustments will be made at this point for receivables and payables.

Total Receipts as corrected should now be compared with the total receipts per return to determine any understatement.

7.06 Example

An example of a simplified Bank Deposits computation follows:

Total Deposits		$90,000.00
Less: Total Non-income Items:		
Loan Proceeds	$ 5,000.00	
Veterans Pension	3,000.00	8,000.00
Net Deposits		$82,000.00
Total Outlays		
Purchases—from Schedule C	$60,000.00	
Business Expenses (less Depreciation)— from Schedule C	5,000.00	
Loans repaid—from ledger sheet	3,000.00	
Equipment purchased—from tax return	7,000.00	
Personal expenses—Interview and cancelled checks	8,000.00	
Total Outlays	$83,000.00	
Less: Total Checks Written	78,000.00	
Cash Expenditures		5,000.00
Total Receipts		$87,000.00
Accrual Adjustments		
Increase in Accounts Receivable		700.00
Total Receipts As Corrected		$87,700.00
Total Receipts Per Return		82,000.00
Understatement		$ 5,700.00

THE TIME LIMITS WITHIN WHICH THE IRS MUST ACT FOR ADDITIONAL TAXES

THE THREE-YEAR RULE

Generally, the IRS has *three* years after the date on which your tax return is filed to proceed against you. However, when you file a return before the due date, the period does not start from the filing date but from the day after the due date. To illustrate, instead of filing your last quarterly estimated tax payment on January 15, you file a *final* return on January 31. The limitation period on the final return begins the day after April 15, the date the final return is due, not on January 31, the date the return is filed.

To start the running of the statute of limitations, the District Director or your regional Service Center must receive your return. In any controversy concerning the statute, you must prove that you filed a return. If you fail to do this, there is no limit on the time during which the government may make an assessment against you. Similarly, filing a return containing insufficient information of your tax liability does not start the running of the statute.

WHAT IS THE STARTING DATE FOR THE LIMITATION PERIOD?

Amended return. The statute starts running when the original return was filed. For amended returns received by the IRS after July 18, 1984, the IRS has 60 days from the date of receipt to assess additional tax, even though the regular limitations period would expire before the end of the 60-day period.

Incorrect return form. The statute starts running when you file (or from the due date), if the return has all of the information on which the correct tax liability can be figured.

Declaration of estimated tax or final return in lieu of amended tax declaration. The statute starts running from due date of final return. Filing before does not start the statute running ahead of time.

Tax information on a form other than a return. The statute starts running when you file the information (or from the due date), if it contains the information on which your tax liability can be figured. If you claim you do not have to pay a tax, notify the IRS of your claim and the basis for it. A tentative return does not start the period running since it does not specifically state the items of gross income and deductions.

Improperly executed return. The statute starts running when the return is properly executed. Example: A corporate return must be signed by one of the corporation's officers. A return signed by an unauthorized person is not good, and the filing of such a return does not start the running of the statute.

Sometimes, a taxpayer or a group of taxpayers may operate as a trust or as a partnership without knowing that the organization under the tax law is really a corporation, and so must file a corporate return rather than a trust or partnership return. Even though a partnership or trust return is filed, this filing can be treated as the filing of a corporate return for purposes of starting the statute. To obtain this result, the taxpayer or taxpayers must prove that the determination of the trust or partnership status was made in good faith.

A similar rule covers a situation where a taxpayer, in good faith, determines that it is an exempt organization. In such cases, the filing of a return for an exempt organization starts the statute—even though it is later held to be a taxable corporation for that tax year.

There are several exceptions to the general rule that the filing of a return starts the running of the statutory period:

Where a false or fraudulent return is filed with intent to evade tax, tax may be assessed at any time. The Supreme Court has held that a later filing of an amended nonfraudulent return does not start the running of the three-year period of limitations.

Where a willful attempt in any manner is made to defeat or evade the tax, tax may be assessed at any time.

Where a return is executed by the IRS, the statute does not run with the making of the return.

Where no return is filed, the tax may be assessed at any time, but the subsequent filing of a nonfraudulent return starts the running of the three-year limitations period.

IF MORE THAN 25% OF GROSS INCOME IS OMITTED

If you omit an amount which is more than 25% of the gross income shown on your return, the IRS may make an assessment within six years after the return is filed rather than three years. For example, in the 1981 return (which was filed on April 15, 1982), gross income of $5,000 is reported. But a $2,000 gain from the sale of a home has been omitted. In this case, the IRS has until April 15, 1988, to assess a deficiency on the 1981 return. The reason: The omitted $2,000 gain is more than 25% of the gross income reported on the return (25% of $5,000 or $1,250). However, if gross income is $10,000, the three-year statute applies rather than the six-year statute because the omission is not more than 25% of the reported gross income (25% of $10,000 or $2,500).

To apply the six-year statute, the IRS has the burden of proving that there is an omission and that it exceeds 25% of the reported gross income. If it fails to sustain its claim, the three-year statute applies. To be successful against such a claim, you must then show that the items were not omitted; for example, that the item was tax free or not taxable in the particular year, or that the IRS's valuation is incorrect. You cannot base your defense on a plea of an honest mistake or the use of an incorrect method of accounting, or that the omission was reduced to less than 25% by an amended return. The statute runs from the filing of the original return. It is not affected by the filing of an amended return.

In figuring gross income, *do not confuse the way income is reported on a tax return with the concept of gross income.* The tax return does not provide for the term gross income. For example, when reporting capital gains and losses, the net gain or loss is reported on a return. But this amount is not gross income. For purposes of computing the gross income omission, gross income would include the capital gains *before* they are reduced by either capital losses or by the capital gain deduction, or by both. Where you are in business, gross income means gross receipts, that is, the total amount received from the sale of goods or services unreduced by the cost of such goods or services. Gross income of a partner's share of partnership income means the partner's share of the partnership gross income, not partnership net income.

If you omit a questionable item from gross income, you may prevent an extension of the statute by adequately disclosing the fact of the omission on the return or in an attached statement. If the disclosure *adequately* tells the IRS of the nature and amount of the item omitted, that item will not be counted in determining whether there has been an omission of more than 25% of gross income.

The following are examples of adequate disclosure: (1) sales receipts were fully stated, but claimed deductions were excessive; (2) opening inventory was overstated, resulting in understated profits; (3) total income was revealed by a schedule attached to the return; and (4) total income was disclosed on the return, but was erroneously claimed as exempt.

There was not an adequate disclosure where the taxpayer liquidated his real estate corporation, attaching a statement of depreciation on the liquidation property, but failed to report gain realized on the liquidation.

WHEN THE LIMITATION PERIOD MAY BE REDUCED

To expedite the closings of income tax cases of estates and of liquidated corporations, the statutory period may be reduced to 18 months. After you have filed a return reporting income received by a decedent in his lifetime, an estate during administration, or a corporation being liquidated, send the Commissioner a letter specifically asking for prompt assessment on the return in the following 18 months. Make this request after the return is filed, or it will not be effective. Send your letter in a separate envelope. Do not mail it with the return.

When the request is made for a corporation, you must notify the Commissioner that liquidation is contemplated within 18 months; begin the liquidation in good faith within that time, and complete the liquidation.

When you request a prompt assessment for an estate, send evidence of your authority to act for the estate along with the application.

The filing of the request for prompt assessment starts the 18-month period. The shortened limitation period will not apply if more than 25% of gross income is omitted from the return or if there is fraud or a willful attempt to evade tax.

LIMITATION RULES FOR CARRYBACK

Net operating loss or capital loss carryback. A deficiency resulting from an erroneous carryback may be assessed within the statutory period of the loss year in which the carry-

back originated. For example, a net operating loss in 1983 carried back to 1980 results in a refund of $5,000; in an audit of the 1983 return, the carryback is reduced and it is determined that the refund should have been $1,000. The IRS has until April 15, 1987 to recover $4,000 of the refund attributed to the carryback to 1980.

Foreign tax credit carryback. A deficiency resulting from an improper carryback of the foreign tax credit may be assessed within one year after the period for assessment for the year producing the excess foreign tax credit.

Investment credit and work incentive credit carryback. A deficiency resulting from an erroneous carryback may be assessed within the statutory period of the year producing the credit.

Where a quick refund was elected, the IRS has an extended time to audit the year to which the carryback was made (except in the case of foreign tax credit). The IRS may assess within the statutory period for the year which produced the carryback a tax deficiency not to exceed the amount of the refund or credit arising from the carryback.

EXAMPLES—
1. For 1980, a calendar year corporation files a quick refund claim claiming an unused investment credit for $50,000 arising in 1983 and receives a refund of $50,000. In 1986, the IRS reduces the unused investment credit for 1983 to $30,000. As the corporation filed its 1983 return on March 15, 1984, the period for assessing the excess $20,000 does not expire until March 15, 1987.
2. Same facts as in example 1 but the IRS also finds that the corporation owes $40,000 of additional tax for 1980 because of its failure to report certain income for that year. The IRS may assess on or before March 15, 1987, a deficiency not in excess of $30,000.

OTHER LIMITATION RULES

Where separate returns were originally filed and later a joint return is filed, the period of limitations must extend to at least one year after the time the joint return was actually filed. The regular limitation periods are figured from the following filing dates, but if those periods would expire before one year after the joint return was filed, then the period is extended until the end of that one year.

Where both spouses previously filed separate returns, the period begins on the last date that either spouse could have filed his separate return.

Where only one spouse filed a return because the other had gross income under the requirement for filing a return, the period begins on the last date the spouse who filed could have filed his return.

Where only one spouse filed a return, even though the other had gross income requiring the filing of a return, the period begins when they file the joint return.

LIMITATION PERIODS WHERE RECOGNITION OF GAIN IS DEFERRED

Where an involuntary conversion has occurred, tax on the gain may be deferred by investing the proceeds in similar property. When tax on gain has been deferred, instead of the regular three-year period from the time a return is filed, the three-year period starts when the District Director is notified that the property has been replaced or no replacement has been made.

If a replacement is made before the beginning of the last year in which any part of the gain is received on the conversion, then the limitation period for any year before that year (during which the election to replace was in effect) ends when the limitation period for the last year ends.

Warning: Failure to notify the District Director prevents the statute from closing.

Where a residence is sold and a new one is bought within two years before or after the sale, part or all of the gain may not be taxed. But the three-year period of limitations on assessments does not begin until the District Director is notified that a new residence is bought, giving its cost, or that no residence has been bought within the time limit.

WAIVING THE LIMITATION PERIOD

If a return is being examined during a time close to the expiration of the statutory period for assessing deficiencies, the IRS may ask for a waiver of the statute of limitations on a Form 872.

SHOULD A WAIVER EXTENDING THE STATUTE BE SIGNED?

A return is subject to a possible deficiency assessment for at least three years. An extension of the statute of limitations may be an advantage because the time to file refund claims is extended by the extension period plus six months. However, taxpayers generally regard an extension as a disadvantage. They assume that the IRS, in making the request, has become suspicious of the return after a preliminary examination and a more thorough examination is likely to lead to a deficiency assessment.

It is advisable to agree to the consent if it is anticipated that disputed items may be amicably compromised.

If consent is refused, the statute of limitations binds both the taxpayer and the Commissioner. Neither is obliged to agree to an extension.

What is the practical result of a refusal to consent? If the refusal comes:

Before the Agent has had an opportunity to make an examination, he can recommend the disallowance of every claimed deduction. A statutory notice of deficiency (90-day letter) can be sent on that basis. Since the refusal to an extension prevented any reasonable determination, he is forced to do this to protect the government's interest. He can, in appropriate cases, also recommend a jeopardy assessment. If a 90-day letter is issued without an audit, the IRS's action may be attacked as arbitrary.

Before the Agent has completed his examination, or before he has time to consider the merits of your position, his recommendations will be based on the assumption that there is no merit to your position.

Before the Group Chief or in the appeals office and before either has an opportunity to consider the merits of your position, the Agent's recommendations might be sustained.

In all of these situations, the case may have to go to court. There will be delay and expense. Give all these facts thought before you object to signing a Form 872.

You may stipulate on the Form 872 how long the statute of limitations is to be extended.

Form 872-A is used to extend the limitation period for cases under Appeals office consideration. It permits flexibility by extending the limitation to a date 90 days after you are notified of a determination or 90 days after you terminate the agreement.

WHEN THE RUNNING OF THE STATUTE IS SUSPENDED

The limitation period is automatically suspended in the following cases:

When a 90-day letter is sent, the period of limitation is automatically suspended for 150 days. (Technically, this includes the 90-day period during which the IRS cannot assess a deficiency, plus an additional 60 days.) However, if the period would have expired during the suspended period, the IRS cannot assess an additional deficiency after that time, though it can still assess the original deficiency. Note: Where a deficiency notice is sent to a corporation, the suspension covers not only the corporation but any other corporation with which it filed a consolidated return for the year covered by the notice.

If you file a timely petition in the Tax Court, the period is extended until the Tax Court decision (including all appeals) becomes final and for 60 days afterwards.

Where there is a bankruptcy or a receivership, the period is suspended for the period beginning with the date of the institution of bankruptcy or receivership proceedings until 30 days after the Commissioner in Washington is notified of the receivership or bankruptcy. But the period cannot be extended for more than two years because of bankruptcy or receivership.

Where assets are in the custody or control of a court, the period of limitation is suspended for the period in which the assets are in the hands of the court and for six months thereafter.

When a taxpayer is out of the country for a continuous period of six months or more, the limitation period is suspended during his absence. The period of limitation does not expire until six months after he or she returns to the United States.

Where property of a third party is wrongfully seized by the government, the limitation period is suspended. The suspension begins when the property is wrongfully seized or received and ends 30 days after the IRS determines the levy was wrongful and returns the property. If the third party goes to court, the suspension ends 30 days after entry of a final judgment that the levy was wrongful.

If the IRS is attempting to obtain records from a third party and a dispute over the records is not solved within six months after the IRS issues an administrative summons, the period is suspended until the issue is resolved. Further, if you intervene in a dispute between the IRS and the third-party recordkeeper, the limitation period is suspended from that date until the entire dispute is resolved.

MITIGATING THE EFFECT OF THE LIMITATION PERIOD TO AVOID DOUBLE TAX

Suppose income which should have been reported in a 1983 return is reported in a 1982 return. In 1987, after the limitation period for filing a refund claim for 1982 has expired, the IRS asserts a deficiency on this item for the year 1983. You take the case to the Tax Court, but it upholds the government's position.

Can you get a refund for the tax paid on this item in 1982 even though the statute has run out on that year?

The answer is yes. In this and in certain other cases, the limitation period is lifted, not only to prevent double taxation of the taxpayer, but also to protect the government in cases where an item of income might otherwise escape taxation.

EXAMPLES—
1. For the year 1982, a trustee, directed to accumulate trust income, made no distribution to the income beneficiary. So, the entire trust income was taxed to the trust; the return was filed in 1983. In 1984, a state court held invalid the trust clause directing the accumulation. The trustee then filed a refund claim for the tax paid in 1983. In 1987, a federal court sustained the claim. Even though the limitation period for assessing a deficiency against the beneficiary for the year 1982 has expired, the government may assess a deficiency against him.

In this example, the limitation period of the beneficiary, not that of the trustee, was lifted. This kind of adjustment is permitted only between the following *"related taxpayers":*

Husband and wife
Grantor and fiduciary
Grantor and beneficiary
Decedent and decedent's estate
Partners
Fiduciary and legatee, heir, or beneficiary
Members of an affiliated group of corporations

2. Jones and his son were partners. Each was entitled to one-half of partnership profits. In his 1982 return, Jones, Sr. included the entire partnership profits. In 1986, he filed a refund claim for that portion of tax he paid on his son's share for the year 1982. In 1987, a federal district court approved the claim. The IRS then could assess a deficiency against the son for that portion of the 1982 profits on which he did not pay tax.

3. Howe assigned his salary in 1982 to his wife. She reported it

in her return for the year. In 1985, the IRS assessed a deficiency against Howe for the omission of the salary in 1982. In 1987, the Tax Court upheld the IRS's position, Mrs. Howe was then entitled to a refund on the tax paid on his salary for 1982, even though the statute had expired for that year.

WHEN A CLOSED YEAR MAY BE REOPENED

Before the limitation period can be lifted, the taxpayer or the IRS must show there has been a *final determination* that requires an adjustment *specifically covered by the relief statute.* A final determination may be a:

Closing agreement—It is considered final when the agreement is approved.

Decision of the Tax Court or other competent court—It is considered final at the end of the time allowed for taking an appeal if no appeal has been taken.

Final disposition of a refund claim—It is considered final as to:
Allowed items either on the date of the allowance of the refund or the credit or on the date of mailing a notice of disallowance. The last situation arises when the allowed items are offset by other items.

Disallowed items when time for filing a refund suit expires (unless a suit is started before that time). This rule covers items disallowed in whole or in part, or items which have reduced a refund.

Informal agreement—signed by the taxpayer and the IRS. (Form 2259)

As pointed out above, a closed year may be reopened for an adjustment only in limited cases. The law allows for a reopening in the following seven situations (an eighth situation involving affiliated companies is not discussed here):
1. The determination includes in gross income an item which was erroneously included in the taxpayer's gross income or in the gross income of a related taxpayer in a tax year now closed.

EXAMPLE—Smith, who keeps his books on the cash basis, included in his 1982 return an item of accrued rent. In 1987, after the limitations period for 1982 has expired, the IRS claims that the rent was received in 1983, and asserts a deficiency. It is upheld by the Tax Court. Smith can get a refund for tax paid on the rent in his 1982 return.

2. The determination allows a deduction or a credit which was erroneously allowed to the taxpayer or to a related taxpayer in a tax year now closed.

EXAMPLE—Green, in his 1982 return claimed and was allowed a deduction for the destruction of his house by a tornado. The tornado actually occurred in 1983. After the end of the period of limitations for the assessment of a deficiency in 1982, Green files a refund claim for 1983 based upon a deduction for the casualty loss in that year. The refund claim is allowed for 1983, and the IRS may make an assessment for the deduction taken in 1982.

3. The determination excludes from gross income an item on which the taxpayer paid a tax or which he included in a filed return (whether or not he paid a tax on it). However, in a closed year, the item was erroneously excluded or omitted from his gross income or from the gross income of a related taxpayer.

EXAMPLE—Brown, in 1983, received under a contract, payments which were included in his 1983 return. Thereafter, he filed a refund claim for 1983, asserting he was on the accrual basis, and since the payments had accrued in 1982, they should have been taxed then. The claim is allowed in 1987. An assessment may be made for 1982 even though the statute has run out on that year.

4. The determination involves the correction of a deduction or income item of an estate, or a trust, or beneficiaries of either. *See* the Regulations of the particular situations which may arise under such a determination.

EXAMPLE—A trustee claimed in a trust's return for 1982 a deduction for income distributed to the beneficiary. The beneficiary was taxed. In 1986, the IRS asserted a deficiency against the trust on the ground that the amount given to the beneficiary was corpus, not income. In 1987, the deficiency is sustained by the Tax Court. Even though the period for filing claims for refund by the beneficiary for 1982 has expired, he may get a refund.

5. The determination fixes the basis of property for any purpose. And the adjustment affects either an error made in the treatment of a transaction on which the basis depends or an error made in treating the transaction as one involving basis in the first place. In applying this rule, the following two tests have to be met:
   a. This error has to be one of the following types: an erroneous—
      Inclusion in or omission from gross income
      Recognition or nonrecognition of gain or loss
      Deduction of an item that should have been charged to a capital account
      Charge to a capital account that should have been deducted from income
   b. Before any one of the above mistakes may be corrected in a closed year, the taxpayer or the IRS must show that a determination was made in:
      The taxpayer's case; or
      A tax case of a party who received property from the taxpayer after he acquired it in a transaction in which he treated improperly the basis of the property; or
      A tax case of a party who received title from the taxpayer by gift after he erroneously treated a transaction which affected the basis of the donated property. Note that the improperly treated transaction does not have to be the one in which the taxpayer acquired the property. Compare this with the above rule in which the transaction is required to be the one in which he acquired title.

EXAMPLE—In 1981, Stone transferred property which had cost him $5,000 to A Co. in exchange for an original issue of stock worth $10,000. In his 1981 return, he treated the exchange as tax free.
   In 1987, A Co. claims that gain should have been recognized and so the property should have a $10,000 basis. If its argument is sustained, there can be no adjustment in the 1981 tax of A Co. There was no erroneous inclusion in or omission from its gross income or an erroneous recognition or nonrecognition of gain or loss. Nor was there an erroneous deduction of an item which should have been charged to a capital account or a charge to a capital account which should have been deducted from income. As for Stone, the determination did not affect his tax. Nor does the determination relate to a transaction in which he acquired the property. It applies to the property A Co. acquired.
   In 1987, Stone sells stock and claims that since gain should have been recognized on the exchange in 1981, the basis for figuring gain or loss should be $10,000. If his claim is allowed, an adjustment will be made to his 1981 tax. The basis for computing gain on the sale depends on the 1981 transactions. Here there was an erroneous nonrecognition of gain to Stone. He was the taxpayer for whom the determination was made.
   Stone does not sell the stock but gives it to his son, who later sells it and claims the $10,000 basis. A closing agreement sustains his claim. Stone's 1981 tax will be adjusted. The basis for computing gain or loss on the sale by his son depends on the 1981 transaction where there was an erroneous nonrecognition of gain. Stone is deemed the person who acquired title to the property in the transaction and from whom his son derived title subsequent to the transaction.

6. The determination disallows a deduction or a credit which should have been allowed, but was not allowed to the taxpayer or to a related taxpayer in a tax year now closed.
   Important: Here, a refund or a credit is allowed only if the deduction was not barred at the time the taxpayer first claimed it in writing. That is, when he files a return, a refund claim, or a petition to the Tax Court.

EXAMPLE—Burns reports on the accrual basis. In 1984, he deducted an expense item which he paid in that year. (At the time he filed his 1984 return, the statute had not expired for 1983.) Later, the IRS claimed that the item should have been accrued in 1983. In 1987, the Tax Court disallows the deduction for 1984. But Burns can get an adjustment for 1983 even though it is now a closed year. The reason: When he took the 1984 deduction, 1983 was still an open year. Note: Suppose the liability should have been accrued in 1977 instead of 1983—Burns could not get an adjustment if a refund or credit for the year 1976 was already barred when he took the deduction by error in 1983.

7. The determination excludes a gross income item which has not been reported or on which a tax has not been paid. However, the income item is includable in the taxpayer's gross income or in the gross income of a related taxpayer in a tax year now closed. *Important:* Here, an adjustment is allowed only if a deficiency assessment was not barred at the time the IRS first claimed, either in a deficiency notice or before the Tax Court, that the item should be reported for the tax year to which the determination relates.

EXAMPLE—Jones reports on the accrual basis. In 1981, he did some work for A Co. He got paid in 1981 and 1982. He did not report the 1982 payment in either year. In 1983, the IRS sent him a deficiency notice for 1981 claiming he should have reported all the payments then. Jones contested the deficiency notice on the basis that in 1981 he had no accruable right to the payments received in 1982. In 1986, the Tax Court agrees with him. But the IRS can assess a deficiency for 1982 even though it is now a closed year. The reason: A deficiency assessment for 1982 was not barred at the time the deficiency notice for 1981 was sent.

In the first five cases, *before the statute can be lifted,* one more requirement must be met. The taxpayer or the IRS must have maintained an *inconsistent position* in the determination. This means that either party would benefit unfairly if the closed year was not reopened for an adjustment (either for a refund or an assessment of a deficiency). Here is how the rule works:

For an additional assessment: The taxpayer—not the IRS—must have maintained an inconsistent position.

EXAMPLE—Adam, in his 1982 return, claimed and was allowed a deduction for a fire loss. In 1987, he filed a refund claim for the year 1983, claiming that the fire loss took place in 1983. The claim finally was allowed. Adam maintained a position inconsistent with the allowance of the deduction for 1982, by filing a refund claim for 1983 based on the same deduction. So, the Commissioner may assert an additional assessment for 1982.

For a refund or credit: The Commissioner—not the taxpayer—must have maintained an inconsistent position.

EXAMPLE—Evans, in his 1980 return, erroneously included an item of income which should have been reported in his 1981 return. After the limitations period for 1980 has expired, the Commissioner asserts a deficiency for the year 1981 on this item. The Tax Court sustains the deficiency. Here, the Commissioner has maintained an inconsistent position. He got his tax for both 1980 and 1981. Evans may get a refund for the year 1980.

Important: A deficiency adjustment may not affect a related taxpayer unless his relationship to the taxpayer was maintained when the inconsistent position was taken in a return, in a refund claim, or in a Tax Court petition. If a taxpayer does not hold an inconsistent position, then the relationship must be fixed at the time of the final determination. These rules do not apply to the situation described in case No. 7 above.

IF THE STATUTE IS LIFTED

If your client receives an additional assessment for any of the adjustments described above, he will receive a statutory notice of deficiency (90-day letter). He can pay the deficiency and sue for a refund, or appeal to the Tax Court. The IRS must send him a deficiency notice within one year from the date of the determination.

If he is entitled to a refund or credit, he must file a refund claim within one year from the date of the determination, unless the IRS makes the refund without a claim. If the claim is turned down, he can sue for a refund.

An informal agreement involving a closed year can be revoked or altered. When this happens, a later readjustment is treated in the same way as the original adjustment was treated.

Where the adjustment results in an additional assessment by the IRS, you will be charged with interest and penalties. Where the adjustment results in a refund to you, the IRS will pay interest. However, the adjustment which is made by lifting the statute of limitations is not affected by any item other than the one that is the subject of the adjustment.

FILING FOR REFUNDS

The technical rules outlined in this chapter should be strictly observed. Often, refunds are denied because of a taxpayer's failure to comply with a technical rule. Moreover, the filing of a refund claim is the first step that must be taken before suing the government. Unless a proper claim has been filed, a suit will be dismissed.

But before you decide to file a refund claim, carefully review the return involved for accuracy. A refund claim opens the return to a thorough investigation in which the IRS may find errors that reduce or completely eliminate the refund claim, and may even lead to the assessment of a deficiency.

Some practitioners wait until the end of the limitations period to file refund claims. If the IRS, after the limitations period, finds a deficiency, it can use the deficiency only to offset the claimed refund.

If, in good faith, you accept an erroneous refund and the IRS later discovers its mistake, repay the refund promptly. Otherwise, you will be liable for interest.

FILE TIMELY REFUND CLAIMS

A refund claim for income taxes must meet a time limitation and a dollar limitation.

Time limitation. The claim must be made within three years from the time the return was filed or two years from the time the tax was paid, whichever period is later. For purposes of determining the three-year period, a return which is filed before the original due date is deemed to have been filed on the due date. For example, a return due on April 15 but filed April 1 is deemed filed on April 15, the due date. However, where an extension for filing is obtained, a return filed before the extended due date is deemed to have been filed on the actual date of filing and not on the extended due date. For example, if your due date for filing is April 15 but you get an extension to August 15 and actually file the return on August 1, your return is deemed to have been filed on August 1.

You may file a protective refund claim when a particular issue is being litigated by other taxpayers and you want to await the outcome. This type of claim is generally accompanied by a cover letter to the IRS explaining its nature. Filing the protective refund claim preserves your right to sue for a refund. A suit must be brought before the expiration of two years from the date of mailing by the District Director of his notice of disallowance of your claim.

With agreement of the IRS, Form 907 may be used to extend the two-year period for filing suit. The two-year period may not be extended once it has run out.

Dollar limitation. The amount of the refund is limited to the amount of tax paid within the three-year period (plus any extension of time for filing) preceding the filing of the claim, or, if the claim is not filed within the three-year period, to the amount of tax paid within the two-year period preceding the filing of the claim.

EXAMPLE—Smith's 1982 return is due on April 15, 1983. He obtains an extension for filing until June 15, 1983. His return is actually filed on June 1, 1983, and he remits a check with his return for a tax liability of $2,000. On May 15, 1986, Smith files a claim for a refund for $1,000 on his 1982 return. The claim is timely filed since he meets the time limitation (within three years of the actual date of filing, June 1, 1983) and the amount limitation (tax paid within three years of filing of the return).

All estimated taxes and taxes withheld by an employer are deemed to have been paid on the original due date of the return. For example, your return was due on April 15, 1983, but because of an extension you filed the return on June 1, 1983. Any estimated tax or withholding tax paid before April 15, 1983 is deemed paid on April 15, not June 1. Now suppose you file a claim for a refund of a portion of the estimated or withholding tax on May 15, 1986. The claim is timely, even though the estimated or withholding tax is deemed paid on April 15, 1983, or more than three years prior to the claim for refund. You meet the time limitation since the claim is filed within three years of the date the return was filed, June 1, 1983. Also the dollar limitation is met since the claim is filed within three years, *plus any extensions of time for filing the return,* of the date of payment of estimated or withholding tax, April 15, 1983.

If no return is filed, the claim must be made within two years from the time the tax was paid, and the amount of refund cannot be more than the tax paid during the two years immediately preceding the filing of the claim.

When you agree with the IRS to extend the time during which it can assess your tax, you may file a refund claim during this extended period plus an additional six months afterwards. A refund made during this time includes the refund you would have received if you had filed a claim at the time the extension was signed, plus the tax paid after the agreement was signed, but before you filed your claim.

EXAMPLE—A 1981 return, filed on April 15, 1982, is under audit. In January 1985, an agreement is made to extend the statutory period of assessment to June 30, 1986. But for this extension, the period during which a refund claim may be filed would have closed on April 15, 1985. With the extension, you now have until January 2, 1987 to file a refund claim on your 1981 return.

Where your claim is filed more than six months after the end of the extended period, the refunded amount cannot be more than the tax paid during the two years before the filing of the claim.

Note: These extension period rules do not apply to refunds of estate taxes.

Other limitation periods for filing a claim for refund are: (1) You have three years from the date of tax payment for claiming a refund of estate and gift taxes; (2) If you file a claim for a failure to take a bad debt deduction or worthless security deduction, you have seven years from the due date of your return. Here, all you get back is the tax related to the bad debt or worthless security deduction; (3) You have four years from the due date of your return to claim a refund resulting from a partnership item in a federally registered partnership.

WHAT REFUND FORM TO USE

Refund claims must be filed on Form 1040X (for an individual who originally filed on Form 1040, 1040A, or 1040EZ) or on 1120X (for a corporation which filed Form 1120). Where a form other than Form 1040, 1040A, 1040EZ or 1120 was filed, a refund claim is made on an amended return. Form 843 may be used for claiming refund for employment taxes or certain other nonincome taxes. A sample copy of Form 1040X may be found in ¶27.00 of Part I.

Overwithheld taxes. You need not file a formal claim for overpayment of personal income tax resulting from excessive withholding of taxes on wages or excessive estimated tax payments. In these two cases, a tax return requesting a refund of the overpayment acts as a claim for refund. But, there is one exception. On the death of an individual who has overpaid his tax, the administrator or executor of his estate files a refund claim on Form 1310.

Generally, refunds for excessive withholding or estimating of tax are made soon after a tax return is filed. However, a return may be subject to a "pre-refund" audit. Especially where the income shown on the return is less than $10,000 or there are large deductions or many exemptions that require substantiation.

Filing an amended return. If you file an amended return as a refund claim, write "amended return" on the top of the return. The data shown on the original return does not have to be repeated on the amended return, except for the amended items. A statement explaining the circumstances and grounds for the refund must accompany the return. The return must be signed. If it is a joint return, both spouses must sign.

To correct an error on a return filed before its due date, you can file a corrected return on or before its due date. This return is not considered an amended return. However, a corrected return filed after the due date is an amended return and acts as a refund claim.

Letters to the IRS are usually held by the courts as not satisfying the requirements for an adequate refund claim.

PREPARING YOUR REFUND CLAIM

The most important part of a refund claim is stating the "reasons" for the refund. A general claim where you just note an overpayment, without supporting facts and grounds, is not sufficient. If a claim is denied by the IRS, it may become the basis of a court suit. If you have not stated all the grounds, you may not be allowed to show them in court. The courts have limited taxpayers to the exact claim shown on the form. Make a full claim and show:

All the facts that support the claim. You may attach to the form as much evidence as is helpful. Be sure your facts are simply and fully stated. If you need more space than is on the form, the statement and supporting exhibits must be on letter-sized sheets (8½ x 11).

All the grounds for the claim. You may hedge if you are uncertain about the exact grounds; alternate and even inconsistent grounds may be given. For example:

The loss was incurred from an embezzlement; if not, from a bad debt.

The gain from the sale is entitled to capital gain treatment as the property sold was a capital asset; if not, it was depreciable property used in business.

The loss was due to a loss on the acquisition of real estate and from a partial bad debt (where the claim arose from the extinguishing of a mortgage by a deed in lieu of a foreclosure).

While it is necessary to be complete and precise in specifying the facts and reasons for your claim, you are not required to present your evidence, but must merely inform the IRS of the basis for your claim.

To protect against your understating the amount of your claim, it may be advisable to preface the claim with this phrase: "The following or such greater amounts as may be legally refunded." However, neither this nor any other "protective clause" will allow you to support your refund claim on grounds other than those mentioned in the original claim or in amendments made before the period of limitations has expired.

A separate claim must be made for each year in which a refund is claimed. It must be made in duplicate and signed under oath by the taxpayer or his duly authorized agent. If an agent signs, he must attach to the claim evidence of his authority. If the claim is based on a joint return, it must be signed by both spouses.

A refund claim filed before there is an overpayment is invalid unless the IRS waives the defect.

When you file a petition to the Tax Court, thus giving that court jurisdiction over your case, you may no longer file a refund claim for any part of the tax for the taxable year in question.

AMENDING THE REFUND CLAIM

You may generally amend your refund claim before the occurrence of either of the following events: (1) Expiration of the period for filing the original claim (generally two years after paying the tax or three years after filing the return, whichever is later), or (2) final action taken by the IRS on the refund claim. After the expiration of the time limitation, you may not raise new issues or grounds in an amended refund claim, even though the original claim was timely.

Regardless of the time limitations above, file your amended claim immediately upon discovering the need for the amendment. Make certain that your amended claim meets all the technical standards discussed in previous paragraphs.

FILING AN INFORMAL CLAIM

There is no advantage in filing an informal claim for refund. An informal claim must meet the same requirements as a formal claim. Although some informal claims have been allowed, many more have been denied and have not been permitted to be the basis of refund suits. For example, you may not base a refund suit on an informal claim that is limited to a:

Letter suggesting a change in tax computation;
Request for a ruling which stated the facts and grounds for a refund; or
Sworn statement which states the facts and grounds for a refund but does not include a demand for one.

Refunds based on informal claims have been allowed where an informal claim was accompanied by a brief that gave the basis of the claim or where, as a result of a conference, letters and memoranda stating the taxpayer's position were filed and a general claim referring to these papers was later filed.

FILING YOUR REFUND CLAIM ON TIME

File your refund claim with the Service Center serving the district in which the tax was paid. When circumstances have forced you to wait until the last minute to file a refund claim, make sure that you meet the filing deadline. This does not mean that the claim must be received on or before the last day of the statutory period. You can make a timely filing if you mail a claim so that the enclosing envelope is postmarked on the last day of the statutory period. Where the claim is sent by registered mail, the registration date takes the place of the postmark date.

To insure a timely mailing, deliver the claim's mailing package at the post office for a postmark cancellation. Also, make certain that it is properly addressed and that the postage is prepaid. Failure to do this will invalidate the timely mailing. Another safe method of getting a timely filing is to deliver the claim at the District Director's office. Here, a receiving clerk will stamp the duplicate copy of the claim with the date of the filing.

Where the last day for filing falls on a Saturday, Sunday, or legal holiday—a timely filing is made if the return is filed or postmarked on the next work day. A legal holiday includes a legal holiday in the District of Columbia as well as a legal holiday in the State in which you have to file the claim.

EXAMPLE—The last day for filing a refund claim falls on a Saturday. You can make a timely filing by delivering the claim at the District Director's office on Monday, or by mailing the claim to the Service Center so that it is postmarked on or before Monday.

You may file a protective claim when the statutory period is about to expire. It may omit facts or grounds, but it must be amended with the complete data and grounds before it is rejected by the IRS.

GETTING A PARTIAL REFUND IN A CONTESTED CASE

The IRS, in three situations, may allow partial refunds in cases where contested issues still remain to be settled.

1. Two or more refund issues where some issues are settled and others are still contested. Here, a refund may be allowed on the settled issues.

EXAMPLE—You file a refund claim based on two issues. The first one, which would result in a $1,000 refund, is settled. The second one, which would result in a $500 refund, is contested. The IRS may give you a partial refund of $1,000.

2. Two or more issues where some issues will result in a refund and the others in a deficiency, but the overall netting results in a refund.

EXAMPLE—A case involves a refund issue which is not contested and a deficiency issue which is contested. The allowance of the refund issue would result in a net overassessment of $5,000 after offsetting the deficiency issue. A $5,000 refund may be allowed even though the contested issue is still pending.

3. Two or more years are under examination. In one year, there is a contested proposed deficiency. In the other year, there is an agreement on an overassessment which is greater than the proposed deficiency.

EXAMPLE—For the year 1985, the IRS proposes a deficiency of $4,000 which you contest. But for the year 1986, the IRS agrees that it owes you a refund of $7,000. A partial refund of not more than $3,000 may be made.

Note: The IRS will not give partial refunds in cases which involve partial refunds of over $100,000, or in cases where there may be an overall deficiency, even though there is no dispute on the tax refunding issue.

If the refund differs from the amount you sought, you usually get a notice of adjustment explaining the difference before receiving the refund. But sometimes the refund is received without prior explanation. In that case the IRS recommends this action: If the refund is smaller than you claimed, cash the check and write to your Service Center asking why the refund was less than the amount claimed. If the refund exceeds your claim, return the check to your Service Center with a request for an explanation.

AFTER A REFUND CLAIM IS FILED

No matter how small a refund claim is, it is thoroughly scrutinized by the Examination Division of the District Director's office.

The examination procedure is like the one used in examining your return. It provides for an agent's examination in a desk examination or in the field, and if the agent disputes your claim you may ask for a conference at a higher level. If you cannot settle your case at a conference, you may sue for a refund in a Federal District Court or in the U.S. Claims Court.

If your claim is finally turned down, you are notified by registered mail. A disallowed claim may not be amended. Sometimes the IRS will reconsider a denied claim. But this reopening cannot extend the time in which you can sue for a refund. Of course, you may file a new claim so long as the limitations period within which a claim may be filed has not expired, but it must be on new grounds.

If a claim is allowed, you receive a Certificate of Overassessment. Check it for accuracy. Interest is calculated from the date of overpayment to a date preceding the date of the check by no more than 30 days.

Before the check is mailed, the District Director's office investigates to see that no taxes are owed by the taxpayer for other years. If his record is clear, the check is mailed. If not, the check is held up until payment of the taxes, or it is credited against the outstanding balance.

SOME REFUNDS ARE CHECKED BY CONGRESS

A tax refund or credit over $200,000 may not be made until 30 days after a report is made to Congress' Joint Committee on Taxation. These cases do not require greater documentation and are not subject to closer examination than regular cases. The right to appeal within the IRS is the same as in other cases. If a protest is not made and no Tax Court petition is filed, the report to the Joint Committee will be prepared by regional specialists in the Examination Division, called Joint Committee Coordinators. If a protest is made, the report is prepared either by an Appeals officer or Counsel attorney.

The report contains:
The name of the person to whom the refund or credit is to be made;
The amount of the refund or credit;
A summary of the facts of the case;
The decision of the Commissioner.
The Joint Committee makes an annual report to Congress of such refunds and credits.

This provision of the law does not apply to refunds or credits resulting from tentative amortization adjustments and tentative carryback adjustments.

QUICK REFUND FOR CARRYBACK OF LOSS OR UNUSED CREDIT

You may file an application for a tentative carryback adjustment of prior years' taxes due to a carryback of net operating loss, unused investment credit, unused work incentive program credit (for wages paid before January 1, 1982), new employee credit (from prior law), unused research credit (for expenses paid or incurred after June 30, 1981), corporate capital loss, or a previously reported income item under claim of right. If accepted, you may receive a quick refund without extensive audit procedures.

The application, on Form 1045 (Form 1139 for corporations), must be filed within twelve months from the end of the taxable year in which the loss or unused credit occurs. The IRS must act on your application within 90 days of filing or 90 days from the last day of the month in which your return is due, whichever is later. In the case of a quick refund based on a claim of right under Section 1341(b)(1), the IRS must act within 90 days from the date on which the application is filed or the date of overpayment (the last day for the payment of tax for the year in which a deduction is allowed for the restoration of income held under a claim of right), whichever is later.

The IRS may refuse your application if there are computational errors or material omissions which cannot be corrected within the 90-day period. Further, quick refund claims attributable to questionable tax shelter losses may be withheld by the IRS. If the IRS determines that a carried back net operating loss is "highly likely" the result of a gross valuation statement or false or fraudulent tax shelter promotion (under Code Section 6700), the IRS may reduce the refund to take into account the improper loss (*see* Rev. Rul. 84–175, 1984–2 CB 296).

The application does not act as a claim for refund. You may file a separate claim for refund before, at the same time, or after you file your application.

Even though the IRS allows the carryback adjustments according to your application and refunds prior taxes to you, it is not barred from later assessing a deficiency. The purpose of the quick refund procedure is to give you cash immediately when you most likely need it.

HOW TO ARRANGE CLOSING AGREEMENTS AND COMPROMISES

A closing agreement may be used to fix the final tax liability of a taxable period or to determine the tax consequences of specific items without settling the final tax liability of that period.

You may want a closing agreement even though no tax is due for the period to which the agreement relates. You may enter into a series of agreements relating to the tax liability of a single period. To cover these and other situations, the IRS provides the following closing agreement forms:
Form 866—which covers liability for any past period.
Form 906—which closes specific items of tax liability for either past, current, or future periods.
A Closing Agreement Handbook, prepared by the IRS for its staff has been released to the public under the Freedom of Information Act. If you can obtain a copy, you may find it useful in preparing your case.

Before entering into a closing agreement, make sure that you understand all of its consequences. After both you and the IRS sign, you cannot change your position. A closing agreement is final on the matter expressly stated in the agreement, unless there is a showing of fraud, or misrepresentation of a material fact. It cannot be modified, set aside, or disregarded in a later suit, action, or proceeding. A closing agreement, however, is subject to any change in or modification of the agreement, with respect to any taxable period ending after the date of the law enacted after the date of the agreement and applicable to such taxable period.

Closing agreements are not widely used for income tax purposes. Instead, IRS policy is almost always obtained through requests for rulings.

WHY USE A CLOSING AGREEMENT?

The main object of a closing agreement is to protect the individual against the reopening of an agreed matter at some later date by the IRS. It also stops an individual from suing or filing other claims for refund. A closing agreement may also be used to fix tax liability for a year barred or arguably barred by the statute of limitations.

You may want a closing agreement for recurring transactions. Cost, fair market value, or adjusted basis as of a given date in the past may be established.

Establishing tax liability may facilitate a transaction such as the sale of stock.

A corporation in the process of liquidation or dissolution may want an agreement to wind up its affairs.

In estate tax proceedings, a closing agreement can assure the fiduciary that the estate is closed for federal tax purposes.

WHEN IS FORM 866 USED?

Form 866, called Agreement as to Final Determination of Tax Liability, is used for tax periods ending before the agreement. It closes the total liability of the individual for those periods. It is used where the tax period for which the agreement is asked has ended, and tax liability for the period has been determined.

The total tax liability determined has to be separated into tax periods and types of taxes. Also, the exact section of the law under which each tax covered was imposed must be noted.

Whenever Form 866 is used, the tax liability stated for each period shown in the agreement has to be the total tax liability determined for each period, without any penalty or interest. But the government may want the closing agreement to include ad valorem penalties which have been incurred. Then the tax and penalty are described in the agreement. Three copies of Form 866 must be completed.

WHEN IS FORM 906 USED?

Closing agreements on specific items are made on Form 906. This is so whether they are related to past, current, or future periods. A closing agreement of a year ending after the agreement is always made on Form 906. It relates only to a specific item or items affecting tax liability. It cannot attempt to conclude total tax liability for any period. Specific items on past periods which it may cover are items like:

Amount of gross income, deductions for losses, depreciation or depletion;
Year for which an item of income is to be included in gross income;
Year for which an item of loss is to be deducted;
Value of property on a specified date.

EXAMPLE—You own 500 shares of stock acquired by gift from someone who purchased them before March 1, 1913, and you plan to sell 200 shares. Either before or after the sale, a closing agreement on Form 906 may be used to fix the basis for the 500 shares.

COMBINED AGREEMENTS

Neither Form 866 nor Form 906 is designed to determine both tax liability and tax consequences of specific items. Instead, a typed combined agreement may be used. The format is shown in the IRS Handbook. The main reason for a combined agreement is that a determination of liability does not fix the amount of income or deductions taken into account in reaching liability. Later, you may be able to prove a net operating loss for the year liability was determined, even though the tax was based on facts showing taxable income. In such a case, while the tax liability has been fixed, the effect of transactions of that year on other years has not. If agreed, the problem may be avoided by a combined agreement determining taxable income for such year and any carryovers from the year.

HOW TO APPLY FOR CLOSING AGREEMENTS

The office to which you apply is determined by whether the agreement relates to a past tax period or a present or future tax period. If a past tax period, send your request to the District Director with audit jurisdiction over the returns, or to the Appeals Office if your request relates to a case pending before it. If a present or future period, send your request to the Commissioner of Internal Revenue, Washington, D.C. 20224.

A request is only an offer. It may be withdrawn any time before it is accepted. The closing agreement may be prepared by the taxpayer or the examining agent, but in most cases collaboration is preferable. The taxpayer executes the agreement first, but may withdraw prior to the signing on behalf of the Commissioner.

If it covers a joint return, both spouses have to sign. When an attorney or agent signs, he has to include papers proving his authority to sign. Specific instructions for the preparation of closing agreements are contained in Revenue Procedure 68–16, 1968–1 CB 770.

When preparing a closing agreement:
Fill in the required number of forms. All copies have to be exactly the same. Avoid erasures or corrections; do *not* switch typewriters.
Include a statement of how you want the liability fixed and your reasons.
Use words describing the kind of tax liability involved, like "Federal income tax."
Mention all statutes, regulations, and decisions supporting your case, and show how they apply to your facts.
Describe the taxes involved.
Include anything else that will help the IRS decide the case.

When a closing agreement is submitted on Form 866 or Form 906, the taxpayer is asked to sign a Form 870. This permits the immediate assessment and collection of the agreed deficiency. But it may be conditioned on the approval of the final closing agreement. The IRS will insert a paragraph stating this.

Under IRS policy, most closing agreements are signed without having to be approved and signed at the National Office.

Commissioner Delegation Order No. 97 (Rev. 23, May 31, 1984) lists the IRS officials authorized to enter into closing agreements.

IRS POLICY ON CLOSING AGREEMENTS

The policy is to enter into a closing agreement in any case in which you can show:
An advantage in having the case permanently closed, as for example, where in the settlement of disputed issues, you and the government have made mutual concessions.
Good and sufficient reasons for desiring a closing agreement, and that the government will suffer no disadvantage if the agreement is entered into.
The purpose is to mitigate the effect of the statute of limitations, or to allow a deficiency dividend.
Properly executed amended returns have been filed, after the expiration of the period in which assessments might have been made, and no fraud was involved.

A request for a closing agreement is reviewed much more closely than a request for a ruling. The very fact that the IRS is being asked to enter into a binding agreement often makes it suspicious of your motives. Because of the involved nature of the procedure connected with a closing agreement, the IRS is not anxious to use this form. It prefers the much simpler rulings procedure.

There is no assurance in the case of a closing agreement that the Commissioner will agree to it. But no application for a closing agreement can or will be rejected solely because it gives no apparent advantage to the IRS.

OFFERS IN COMPROMISE

The IRS may compromise any civil or criminal case. An offer in compromise is a proposal by you, the taxpayer, to pay a sum in full satisfaction of your unpaid tax liability. When an offer has been accepted and you have been notified by letter of the acceptance, the compromise is a legally enforceable contract between the IRS and you. All questions of tax liability for the years in question are conclusively and finally settled. Neither you nor the IRS may reopen the case except for the showing of falsification or concealment or a mutual mistake of a material fact.

The compromise of a tax liability may rest upon one or both of two grounds: (1) Doubtful liability and (2) doubtful collectibility. The IRS does not have authority to compromise a tax liability which is undisputed where there is no doubt of the ability of the IRS to collect.

You file the offer on Form 656 with the District Director's office in which the liability is pending. If the offer is based on doubtful collectibility, the Form 656 is accompanied by Form 433, a statement of your financial condition.

Under the terms of Form 656, you agree that any refunds or overpayments due you will be retained by the IRS, that you waive the statute of limitations applicable to the assessment and collection of the compromised liability, and that, if the offer is accepted, you will not contest the amount of the compromised liability. You also agree that if there is a default in the payment of a deferred payment offer, the IRS may assess and collect the balance without further notice.

District Directors may accept compromise offers involving liability under $100,000 subject to approval by District Counsel, and reject offers regardless of the amount involved. Service Center Directors may accept or reject compromise offers limited to specific penalties, and to certain ad valorem delinquency penalties relating to excise and employment taxes.

Your offer may be withdrawn at any time prior to final acceptance by the IRS. If your offer is rejected, you may submit a written request for a hearing before the Regional Appeals office which may act on compromise offers rejected by a District Director or Service Center. The determination is subject to approval by the Commissioner if the amount involved is over $100,000.

HOW TO GET THE IRS'S OPINION ON A TAX PROBLEM

The IRS provides an invaluable service in giving, through letter rulings and determination letters, opinions on tax questions asked by taxpayers. Any taxpayer may ask for an opinion, and requesting one is often a necessary step in making business decisions. Not every tax problem may be satisfactorily resolved, and where an adverse tax holding might disrupt a planned transaction, requesting an IRS opinion before undertaking the proposed move is advisable.

An IRS opinion may also be requested for a closed transaction to determine how to report it on a tax return.

The IRS's discretion to rule on taxpayers' problems is broad. But as a matter of policy, it does not give opinions in certain areas and also distinguishes between the type of opinions that can be given by IRS personnel. Here, an important distinction is made between letter rulings and determination letters. A *letter ruling* is issued by the National Office in Washington and is in response to questions involving prospective transactions or completed transactions before a return is filed. A *determination letter* is issued by a District Director in response to questions involving completed transactions. As for prospective transactions, determination letters are issued for determining the qualification of proposed pension or profit sharing plans or the exempt status of certain organizations.

Revenue rulings are generally modifications of letter rulings that have been selected because of their importance or interest for publication in the Internal Revenue Bulletin.

Procedures for requesting rulings and determination letters are detailed in Revenue Procedure 87–1, IRB 1987–1, 7.

SHOULD YOU ASK FOR AN IRS RULING?

Before requesting a ruling, it is advisable to carefully research the tax law applying to your problem. If your review shows that IRS policy is against your position, do not ask for a ruling. If you proceed without a ruling, there is always the chance that, if the transaction is examined, a settlement might be reached at that time.

Ask for a ruling if you have a fair chance of receiving a favorable ruling or have an alternative plan if you receive an unfavorable reply. Even if the request is turned down, at least you know that you will encounter possible litigation if you proceed with the transaction. This knowledge may also be important in planning and executing the transaction.

GETTING ADVICE FOR FUTURE TRANSACTIONS

If your question involves a prospective transaction, then only the National Office in Washington has the authority to answer in a letter ruling. Unless the law or regulations specifically provide otherwise, the issuance of an answer is a matter that rests within the discretion of the National Office.

If the question is about the qualification of proposed pension, profit-sharing, or stock bonus plans, then a District Director has the authority to issue a determination letter.

Only certain District Directors are authorized to issue determination letters involving exempt status under IRC Sec. 501. The 10 key districts and the areas covered are listed in Revenue Procedure 85–32, 1985–2 CB 414. Application procedures are detailed in Revenue Procedure 84–46, 1984–1 CB 541.

GETTING ADVICE ON CLOSED TRANSACTIONS

A problem concerning a completed transaction may be answered by the National Office in a ruling if no return has been filed, and the answer requires the establishment of principles and policies in the interpretation of the law.

If the answer to the question requires simply the routine application of established principles and policies, a District Director may answer in a determination letter. For a District Director to answer, the return to be affected must be filed in his district.

In a particular case, it may be difficult to draw the line between a novel or routine problem. If you are not sure of your position, you can send your question to the National Office in Washington. The final decision on whether a question is routine or novel, simple or complex, rests with the IRS. If you send a question to a District Director on the theory that the matter is routine, he may decide that it is novel and refer the question to the National Office. You will be notified of the change.

If the closed transaction has been reported in a filed return but has not been examined as yet, you may let well enough alone and wait out the limitation period. However, if future transactions are affected, you may need a present opinion. If you do decide to ask for an opinion, send your request to the District Director. If he answers before an examination by a Revenue Agent, the response is considered a tentative finding and not a determination letter. If the question is novel or complex, rather than routine and simple, the National Office will take the question and its decision will be forwarded to the District Director. Normally, however, the request results in an examination by a Revenue Agent. The transaction will be considered by him in the usual way.

YOU CANNOT GET A RULING FOR—

Questions of facts involving:
  Market value of property
  Reasonableness of compensation
  Accumulated earnings penalty.
Matters involving a court decision adverse to IRS policy and the IRS has not decided to follow or litigate the issue.
Hypothetical transactions.
An issue that is identical to an issue involved in a return filed by the taxpayer for an earlier year and that issue is under examination or has been examined by a District Director or has been considered by an Appeals office, and the statute of limitations has not yet expired.
Questions involved in pending tax cases—if the government's position would be hurt by giving you a ruling.
Tax avoidance schemes (you must have a legitimate business purpose in carrying out your transaction).
Questions that the IRS thinks it cannot properly settle by rulings.
An issue that is expected to be covered by imminent legislation.
Questions on replacing involuntarily converted property, even though replacement has not been made, if a return has been filed for the year in which the property was converted. The District Director can give a determination letter on this issue.

You cannot, by court action, force the IRS to give you a ruling or to apply a ruling in your favor.

Generally, rulings are not issued to business, trade or industrial associations, or to other similar groups, relating to the application of the tax laws to members of the groups. However, rulings may be issued to such groups or associations relating to their own tax status or liability.

In addition to the above limits, there are other areas in which the IRS will not issue rulings or determination letters. A specific area or list of these areas is published from time to time in the Internal Revenue Bulletin. (*See* Rev. Proc. 87–3, IRB 1987–1, 27). The list is not all-inclusive since the IRS may decline to issue rulings or determination letters on other questions whenever warranted by the facts or circumstances of a particular case. Finally, when there has been new legislation, the IRS hesitates to rule on issues involving Code sections for which regulations have not been made final.

HOW TO REQUEST A RULING

Your request must be in writing. The IRS does not issue rulings or determination letters upon oral requests. IRS employees ordinarily will not discuss a substantive tax issue prior to the receipt of a written request for a ruling. If they do, their oral opinions are not binding upon the IRS. This should not discourage an inquiry on whether the IRS will rule on a particular question or a discussion on the procedure for submitting a request for a ruling.

Conference before making a request. Sometimes, it is advisable to ask for a conference before you make your request for a ruling. There are advantages in a conference before submitting your request. If you are uncertain whether you will get the ruling, the conference allows you to sound out the IRS without exposing the essential facts of the proposed transaction. In making a formal request for a ruling, you are required to supply the National Office with abundant materials and data, such as financial statements, minutes, and balance sheets. These are not returned if the ruling request is denied but are transmitted to the District Director where they become part of your file.

If a conference is held, understand that what is said during the meeting is merely an aid. It does not bind the IRS. Before going to the conference, prepare your case well. Take with you the draft of your request for a ruling and any proposed contracts or other documents.

Making a request. Your request for a determination or ruling will be processed quickly if you follow these rules detailed in Rev. Proc. 87-1, IRB 1987-1, 7.

1. Submit the request in duplicate if:
   More than one issue is presented in the request.
   A closing agreement is requested on the issue presented.

   It is not necessary to present requests in duplicate under other circumstances.

   A declaration under penalties of perjury that the facts presented are true, correct and complete must be signed by the person on whose behalf the request is made.

2. Address:
   Rulings: Internal Revenue Service, Associate Chief Counsel (Technical), Attention CC: IND: D:C, Room 6545, 1111 Constitution Avenue, N.W., Washington, D.C. 20224
   Determination letters: District Director—Office which has or will have audit jurisdiction.

3. Do *not* submit alternative plans in requests for a ruling.

4. Be sure to include:
   Complete facts.
   Names, addresses and taxpayer account numbers of all interested parties.
   The district office which has audit jurisdiction.
   Copies, not originals, of all pertinent documents. The copies should be attested to be the same as the originals. Do not send originals as they become part of the IRS file and are not returned.
   The balance sheet nearest the date of the transaction, if a corporate reorganization, distribution, or similar transaction is involved.
   If documents are submitted, they must be accompanied by an analysis of their relevancy to the issue.

5. Give the business reason for the transaction (favorable rulings often depend upon the existence of a bona fide business reason for the transaction).

6. Give the grounds for your stand and your supporting authority, and specify what ruling or rulings you want. If you want a particular determination, explain the basis for your contentions, together with a statement of relevant authorities. If you do not urge a particular determination, give your view of the tax result, supported by a statement of relevant authorities, such as statutes and regulations.

7. Sign the request. Include your power of attorney and evidence of enrollment with the Treasury Department. The request is signed by the taxpayer or by his authorized representative, who is (1) an attorney, who has filed a written declaration that he is currently qualified as an attorney and he is authorized to represent the taxpayer; (2) a certified public accountant who files with the IRS written declaration that he is currently qualified as a certified public accountant and he is authorized to represent the taxpayer, or (3) a person, other than an attorney or certified public accountant, enrolled to practice before the Service. An unenrolled preparer of a return may not ask for a ruling or a determination letter for a taxpayer.

8. Add the request that, in the event the IRS decides not to grant a favorable ruling, you will be afforded a conference before the issuance of an unfavorable ruling. This request is usually honored.

9. The IRS encourages the disclosure of any legislation, regulations, revenue rulings or revenue procedures contrary to the taxpayer's position, but it is not required. However, the IRS believes that disclosure will lead to more rapid action. (Rev. Proc. 87–1, IRB 1987–1, 7.)

Requests that do not comply with the above requirements will be acknowledged, and the requirements which have not been met will be pointed out. If the missing information is not supplied within 30 days, the request will be followed by a closing letter. If you supply the missing information after the closing letter is mailed, your request will be reopened and treated as a new request as of the date of the receipt of the information.

The IRS has an alternate procedure to expedite the processing of ruling requests. Under the procedure, you may submit, together with the detailed statement of facts, documents, other required information and a summary statement of the controlling facts which support your request. If the National Office finds your summary satisfactory, the ruling will be based on these facts. This procedure has the advantage of eliminating many of the facts which the reviewer must assess. In addition, it removes some of the subjectivity exercised by the reviewer in determining whether the transaction was carried out substantially as proposed and whether minor deviations are material. On the other hand, this procedure poses the problem of what is a sufficient statement of the facts.

Withdrawing your request. You may withdraw your request for a ruling or a determination letter at any time prior to the signing of the letter of reply. However, this may prove futile. The National Office may give its views on your request to the District Director. The information you submitted with your request will be considered by the District Director in a later audit or examination of your return. Even though you withdraw your request, all correspondence and exhibits are retained by the IRS and are not returned to you.

YOUR RULING WILL BE OPEN TO PUBLIC INSPECTION

Code Sec. 6110 requires the IRS to open to public inspection virtually all letter rulings, determination letters, and technical advice memoranda (called "written determinations") and related background files. Before your ruling is made public, it must be "sanitized" by deleting the following information:

1. Identifying details, such as names, addresses, social security numbers, and any other information which would identify any person (other than certain third parties who communicate with the IRS regarding the determination). Identifying details include information that would permit a person in the appropriate community (such as an industry or geographic location) to identify any person.

2. Information specifically authorized to be kept secret in the interest of national defense or foreign policy.

reviews the taxpayer's return and after concluding that no changes are necessary, mails it to the IRS under the taxpayer's instructions. In any of these circumstances, the consultant must sign the return as a preparer or be subject to the $25 penalty for failure to sign, unless there is reasonable cause for not signing.

Sellers of tax software. A company or individual that prepares and sells software programs to customers is considered a "tax preparer" by the IRS because the software program is used to calculate tax return items based on information punched into the computer by the customer.

The software seller is potentially subject to a negligence penalty if the program is incomplete or inadequate and results in an underpayment of tax by the taxpayer using the program. The penalty for willfully attempting to underestimate the liability could also be imposed in extreme cases.

In one case a software company was held to be potentially subject to the $100 negligence penalty, per return, for not updating its program to include a 1983 law change that required a 50% basis reduction if an investment credit was claimed. The IRS picked up the error during an audit of a taxpayer who used the program. However, the IRS did not specifically rule on whether the penalty would be imposed. Before imposing a penalty, the IRS will consider the nature, frequency and materiality of the errors. If the software seller's normal office procedures indicate that a particular error would rarely occur, the IRS may consider this a mitigating factor in deciding whether to apply penalties.

Computerized tax return preparer services. Firms that provide tax practitioners with worksheets and then feed the information from the practitioners into computers to prepare completed tax returns are potentially subject to penalties if the program used contains errors or is incomplete, leading to an understatement of tax liability. Penalties for negligence or willful understatement of tax liability may be imposed after the IRS takes into account the nature, frequency and materiality of the errors, as well as the preparer's normal office practice. The $500 penalty for endorsing or negotiating a client's refund check may also be imposed.

Substantial preparation. Where more than one person worked on the preparation of a return or claim for refund, a determination of who is the "preparer" will be made according to the rules of substantial preparation described below.

Under Treasury regulations, each schedule, entry, or other portion of the return or refund claim is reviewed separately to determine who is the preparer. (Reg. § 301.7701–15 (b)(1)). You are considered the preparer of an entry if you rendered advice that is directly relevant to a determination of the existence, characterization, or amount of an entry or a return or refund claim. Further, regulations provide a mechanical test for determining whether a part of a return or refund claim is considered substantial. An item is *not* considered substantial if it involves an amount which is (1) less than $2,000, or (2) less than $100,000 and less than 20 percent of adjusted gross income. Where more than one schedule, entry, or other portion is involved, the items are aggregated. (Reg. § 301.7701–15(b)(2)).

EXAMPLE—

You prepare a schedule on a taxpayer's return for dividend income which totals $1,500 and also give advice on a schedule of medical expenses which results in a medical expense deduction of $1,500. You are not a preparer of the return if the taxpayer's adjusted gross income on the return exceeds $15,000, as $3,000 is 20% of $15,000.

This mechanical test does not apply to a person who prepares the entire return or claim for refund.

WHAT FORMS ARE "INCOME TAX RETURNS"?

The penalties for income tax return preparers stem from the preparation of only certain forms specified in the regulations. (Reg. § 301.7701–15(c)): These are:

Individual or corporation income tax return

Fiduciary income tax return for trust or estate
Regulated investment company undistributed capital gains tax return
Charitable remainder trust return
Return of a transferor of stock or securities to a foreign corporation, trust, or partnership
Subchapter S corporation return
Partnership's return
Disc return
Small business corporation income tax return
Refund claim for a credit against any income tax
Information return by or on behalf of a person or entity that is not a taxable entity and which reports information which is or may be reported on the return of a taxpayer under the income tax provisions.

Tax returns do *not* include an estate or gift tax return, any other return of excise taxes or income taxes collected at source on wages, an individual or corporate declaration of estimated tax, an application for an extension of time to file an individual or corporation income tax return, or an informational statement on Form 990, any Form 1099, or similar form.

PENALTIES

As a preparer, you are subject to a penalty of $100 if the tax on the return is understated or claim for refund is overstated because of your negligent or intentional disregard of Treasury rules or regulations. (IRC § 6694(a).) If you willfully understated tax liability, the penalty is $500. (I.R.C. § 6694(b).) In lieu of the $100 or $500 per return penalty, the IRS may impose a $1,000 civil penalty on a preparer for assisting in the preparation of a return which he knows understates tax, or for giving advice with respect to the return (I.R.C. § 6701). The penalty is $10,000 for knowingly understating tax on a corporate return. The $1,000/$10,000 penalty also applies to the presentation of a return or other document (such as an affidavit) at an IRS examination if the preparer knows that the document understates tax liability. Only one $1,000/$10,000 civil penalty may be imposed on a preparer with respect to the same taxpayer for any taxable year, regardless of the number of returns filed on that taxpayer's behalf.

Understatement of tax liability refers to the tax on the entire return. Thus, the understatement of a particular item on the return will not trigger the penalty if there is an overstatement of an offsetting item. Except for abatement of penalties, discussed below in *Penalty Assessment Procedures,* understatement of tax liability is made without regard to any administrative or judicial determination involving the client. (IRC § 6694(e)).

The $100 penalty for negligent or intentional disregard of rules does not apply where you dispute the IRS's interpretation of the law in good faith, even if your position is ultimately determined to be incorrect. For example, if you reasonably believe that case law reflects a more accurate interpretation of the Internal Revenue Code than does a Treasury regulation or rule, you may complete a return on the basis of such case law without being subject to the penalty. The case law relied upon does not have to be identified in the return. However, a Committee Report states that some form of disclosure on a return might be necessary to avoid the penalty in some cases. (Conf. Rept. Pub. L. No. 94–455, 94th Cong., 2d Sess. 484 (1976).)

A preparer will not avoid penalties where he has an opinion on a particular issue which is supported by the IRS, but which he disregards in favor of the taxpayer's view (Letter Ruling 7813019) or where, without consulting regulations, omits income items on the basis of the taxpayer's advice (Rev. Rul. 78–344, 1978–2 CB 334). These are not considered to be good faith disputes with the IRS interpretation of the law.

Neither the $100 nor the $500 penalty is imposed on an employer solely because he employs a preparer who becomes subject to penalty. The employer or one of its officers must actually participate in the prohibited conduct before the penalty applies to the employer. (Reg. § 1.6694–1(b)(1).) The $1,000 civil penalty will not apply to an employer unless he knows that the subordinate is understating tax and does not attempt to prevent it. (I.R.C. §§ 6701(c))

Generally, you may rely without verification upon information supplied by a taxpayer. (Reg. § 1.6694–1(b)(2)(ii).) You are not required to ferret out documents or other evidence supporting the taxpayer's information. However, you may not ignore the implications of furnished information. Where the taxpayer's information appears incorrect or incomplete, you must make reasonable inquiries. For example, a penalty was imposed on an attorney who prepared a client's return when he knew that in a prior year deductions claimed on a return prepared by another person had been disallowed. He was on notice that the records were improper. (Letter Ruling 8022027)

EXAMPLE—

A taxpayer tells the preparer that he paid $2,500 in doctor bills when he actually paid a smaller amount. The preparer, having no reason to question the accuracy of the information, uses it as the basis for calculating the medical expense deduction. No penalty will be imposed in this case, even though the preparer did not request bills or other documentation.

The IRS has ruled that a preparer is negligent if he overlooks the minimum tax. The preparer's claim that he did not know about the minimum tax was no defense; the minimum tax is not an unusual item and the tax return itself states that capital gains may be a preference item. (Rev. Rul. 80–28, 1980–1 CB 304)

If you negligently overstate a net operating loss on a return and carryback the loss to prior years on amended returns, you may be subject to a penalty for the current year and also the prior years. Further, if the loss is not exhausted by the carryback and you carry it forward to a subsequent return, you may be penalized for the later year as well. You may be penalized for the subsequent year even where a different preparer prepares the return for such subsequent year. A preparer who carried forward an overstated loss from returns prepared by another preparer was not penalized where he was unaware of the original preparer's overstatement of the loss, and he checked the earlier returns to determine the proper amount to be carried forward to the return for the subsequent year. (Rev. Rul. 81–171, 1981–1 CB 589)

If you knowingly disregard facts supplied by a taxpayer or others in an attempt to reduce the taxpayer's tax liability, the $500 penalty or $1,000 penalty will be imposed. For example, a taxpayer tells you that he has two dependents, but you report six dependents on the return, knowing the statement to be incorrect. A federal district court upheld a $500 penalty for willful understatement of tax on a corporate return where the preparer ignored the bookkeeper's warning that the corporation had paid the personal expenses of the stockholders and their children. (Pickering, 691 F.2d 853 (8th Cir. 1982))

When the law requires specific facts or other circumstances before the deduction may be properly claimed, you must ask for information concerning such facts. For example, where travel and entertainment expenses are claimed, you should ask if the taxpayer has the records required by law to support the deductions.

You could be subject to more than one penalty for the same offense. (I.R.C. § 6694(b).)

EXAMPLE—

A preparer who deducts all of a taxpayer's medical expenses, intentionally disregarding the applicable floors limiting deductibility of such expenses, may have both intentionally disregarded rules and regulations and willfully understated tax liability. However, the total amount collectible through both penalties may not exceed $500 per return. If the $100 penalty for intentional or negligent disregard of rules and regulations is assessed first, and then the penalty for willful understatement is assessed with respect to the same return, the later assessment for willful understatement is limited to $400.

An appeals court agrees that both penalties apply if a preparer intentionally disregards the law or Treasury rules or regulations for the purpose of understating a client's tax liability (Clara Judisch, 755 F. 2d 823 (11th Cir. 1985)).

DISCLOSURE AND RECORD-KEEPING REQUIREMENTS

Apart from the above penalties for understating tax liability, you, as a preparer, must keep records of returns and meet certain notation requirements in preparing returns.

Retention of records on preparers. Self-employed preparers and preparers who employ other preparers must retain a record of the name, social security number, and place of work of each employed preparer. The records must be retained for a three-year period following the close of the return period (defined as a 12-month period beginning on July 1 of each year) and the records must be made available for inspection upon request by the District Director (Reg. § 1.6060–1(a). There is a $100 penalty for each failure to retain and make available a proper record and a $5 penalty for each required item that is missing from the record. The maximum penalty for any return period is $20,000 (I.R.C. § 6695(e)).

Return or refund claim requirements. A preparer has four responsibilities towards each return or refund claim he prepares.

Each return must be signed;

Each return must contain the preparer's identification number;

A copy of the return must be furnished to the client;

A copy of the return must be retained by the preparer or a list containing the names of clients for whom returns were prepared.

Signing. A preparer must sign a return or refund claim in the space provided and include his address and identification number (see below). There is a $25 penalty for each return or refund claim not signed by the preparer. (I.R.C. § 6695(b)) Preparers must physically sign the return or refund claim after it is completed but before it is presented to the client. They may not use a stamped signature or signature label. Initialling a return does not satisfy the signature requirement. If physically unable to manually sign due to a disability, the words "unable to sign" must be printed, typed or stamped on the preparer's signature line, followed by the preparer's name which is printed, typed, or stamped. (Rev. Proc. 79–7, 1979–1 CB 486)

If more than one person worked on the return, the person with the primary responsibility for the return's overall accuracy is considered the preparer who must sign. If the preparer is unavailable to sign the return, another preparer must so advise the client, review the entire preparation of the return or claim, and then sign it.

The manual signature requirement may be satisfied by a photocopy of a manually signed copy of a return or refund claim. (Reg. § 1.6695–1(b)(4)(i)). Before it is photocopied, no one but the preparer may alter entries on the manually signed copy except to correct arithmetical errors. The individual preparer or the employer-preparer must retain the manually signed copy, as well as a record of any corrected arithmetical errors. If the return or refund claim is prepared by a computer not under the individual preparer's control, and no other person has altered the information in the return or refund claim except for corrections of arithmetical errors, the preparer may satisfy the manual signature requirement by attaching a manually signed attestation that the information in the return or refund claim was obtained from the taxpayer and is correct to the best of his or her knowledge. The information submitted to the computer must be retained by the individual preparer or the employer-preparer along with a record of any arithmetical corrections.

In addition to a signature, a return or claim for refund prepared by a preparer must also list the street address, city, state, and postal zip code of the place of business where the return or claim for refund was prepared. If the place of business is not maintained on a year-round basis, the return or claim for refund must bear the street address, city, state, and postal zip code of his or her principal office or business location, or if none, his or her residence. (Reg. § 1.6109–2(b)(1).) Preparers, after written notice to the IRS, may satisfy the address requirement by disclosing only the postal zip code of the applicable place of business. (Reg. § 1.6109–2(b)(2).)

3. Information exempt from disclosure under other laws.

4. Trade secrets and privileged or confidential commercial or financial information.

5. Information the disclosure of which would constitute a clearly unwarranted invasion of personal privacy. This would include, for example, details not yet made public of a pending divorce or of medical treatment.

6. Information concerning agency regulation of financial institutions.

7. Geological and geophysical information and data, including maps, concerning wells.

Requesting deletions before written determination is issued. When you request a determination letter, ruling or technical advice memorandum, you must also submit a separate statement of proposed deletions. Before issuing the determination, the IRS will inform you of the material you had proposed to be deleted which is likely to appear in the final version. Within ten days, you may submit further information and arguments in support of your position. The IRS will attempt to resolve the differences, but will not grant a conference specifically for that purpose. However, you may discuss issues involving deletions at any conference scheduled with respect to the requested determination.

Requesting deletion when the determination is issued. At the same time the determination on your case is issued, you will receive a notice that it will be disclosed to the public. You will also receive a copy of the text the IRS proposes to disclose on which is indicated the material the IRS proposes to delete, any substitutions, and any third-party communications. (In the case of a background file or written determination that is disclosed only on written request for disclosure, the disclosure notice will be mailed to you within a reasonable time after the IRS receives its first request for disclosure.) You then have 20 days after the notice is mailed to submit a written statement identifying those items which you believe should be deleted but were not. You must also submit your version of the determination you believe should be disclosed, and indicate by brackets further deletions. Generally, the IRS will not delete any material which you had not earlier proposed be deleted. The IRS will mail to you its final administrative conclusions regarding deletions within 20 days of receiving your response.

Court remedies when you and the IRS do not agree on deletions. If you are still not satisfied with the deletions proposed by the IRS, you may file a petition in the Tax Court (anonymously, if appropriate) within 60 days after the date on which the IRS mailed the disclosure notice. You must have exhausted your remedies within the IRS prior to petitioning the Tax Court. If you have not received the IRS's final administrative conclusions regarding deletions within 50 days of the mailing of the disclosure notice, you may then file a petition in the Tax Court.

Within 15 days, the IRS will notify by registered or certified mail any other person interested in keeping information confidential that a petition has been filed in the Tax Court. Such person may intervene in the Tax Court action (anonymously, if appropriate).

The Tax Court will make a decision as soon as possible on the extent of deletions and may close its proceedings on the issue to the public.

WHEN WRITTEN DETERMINATIONS ARE OPEN TO PUBLIC INSPECTION

Generally, written determinations and background files will be open to public inspection not less than 75 days and not more than 90 days after the IRS mailed you the disclosure notice. If you sued in the Tax Court regarding deletions, the written determination or background file will be open to the public within 30 days after the court order becomes final, although the court may extend the 30-day period to give the IRS time to comply with its order.

REQUEST FOR DELAY OF DISCLOSURE

Where the transaction which is the subject of the written determination is not complete when the determination is issued, you may request that the IRS postpone disclosure until 15 days after the transaction is completed. However, disclosure generally must occur within 180 days after the IRS mailed you the disclosure notice. If the transaction is still not completed within the 180-day period, and disclosure would interfere with the transaction, you may again request a postponement until 15 days after the transaction. Overall, postponement may not exceed 360 days after the mailing of the disclosure notice.

Your request for postponement must be in writing and state the date on which you expect to complete the transaction. To get the first postponement, send your request so the IRS receives it within 60 days after the disclosure notice. To get the second postponement, send your request so the IRS receives it within 15 days before the date you stated you expected to complete the transaction.

You must notify the IRS when you complete the transaction if that happens earlier than you expected. The written determination will be open to public inspection 30 days after notice of completion or on the date originally scheduled for disclosure, whichever is earlier.

WHAT TO DO WHEN THE IRS FAILS TO MEET THE TIME LIMITATIONS OR FAILS TO MAKE DELETIONS

Where the IRS fails to meet the time limitations, such as disclosing before 75 days after the disclosure notice was mailed to you or failing to postpone disclosure pursuant to your request, you may sue the government in the Claims Court. You or any other person identified in the determination may sue the government in the Claims Court if the IRS fails to make deletions as required by its own agreement or by court order. Where the court determines that any employee of the IRS intentionally or willfully failed to make a deletion or failed to act within the time limits, you may recover your actual damages (but not less than $1,000) plus costs and reasonable attorney's fees for bringing the action.

HOW SOON MAY YOU RECEIVE AN ANSWER?

Rulings and determination letters are issued on a first-come-first-served basis. You may get a preference by showing a clear need for a faster consideration. But the IRS will not assure you that your request will be processed within the time set by you. You cannot avoid this policy by sending a telegram. Also the IRS will not generally answer by telegram.

You may learn the status of an income tax ruling by contacting the Director, Individual Tax Division, Area Code 202, 566-3767 or 566-3788, or the Director, Corporate Tax Division, Area Code 202, 566-4504 or 566-4505.

YOU MAY GET AN INFORMATION LETTER

Even though you request a ruling or a determination letter, you may receive an information letter. This is a statement issued either by the National Office or by a District Director. It does no more than call attention to a well-established interpretation or principle of tax law without applying it to a specific set of facts. You may receive an information letter if your request seeks general information or does not meet all the requirements for a ruling or determination letter.

CAN YOU RELY ON A RULING?

You can usually rely on a ruling sent to you, although the IRS has the power to revoke the ruling retroactively. However, the IRS only under rare circumstances exercises this power. If the ruling is changed or revoked, the effect is almost always prospective. Be sure, in applying a ruling to the actual transaction, that the facts of the transaction are as you had stated them in your request and that the law has not changed in the meantime.

When preparing the return for the year in which the transaction involved takes place, attach a copy of the ruling or letter to the return. IRS personnel compare the facts reported on the return with the representations upon which the ruling was based. They do this to find if there has been a misstatement or omission of a material fact, or if the transaction upon which the ruling was based was actually carried out in a manner materially different from that represented.

When you receive a ruling, the IRS will generally audit the return reporting the transaction that is the subject of the ruling.

You are not justified in relying on a written determination issued to another taxpayer. The law specifically states that written determinations may not be used as precedent by either the IRS or taxpayers. The Supreme Court has stated that although the law bars the use of private rulings as precedents, they are nonetheless "evidence" of IRS views. The IRS may designate in a widely circulated official government publication (such as the Internal Revenue Bulletin) that a determination will be used as precedent.

You may not rely on a Letter Ruling issued to another taxpayer although the ruling may be helpful in discerning the IRS position on a particular issue.

You may rely on Revenue Rulings published in the Internal Revenue Bulletin in determining the rule applicable to your own case if the facts and circumstances of your transaction are substantially the same as in the published ruling.

REVIEW AND REVOCATION OF DETERMINATION LETTERS

Determination letters involving income taxes are not generally reviewed by the National Office, as they merely repeat a position previously established in a regulation, ruling, or court decision published in the Internal Revenue Bulletin. If you believe a determination letter to be in error, you may ask the District Director to reconsider the matter. You may also ask the District Director to request advice from the National Office. At his discretion, he may refuse to request such advice.

A District Director may revoke a determination letter on re-examination of the issue on an audit of the taxpayer's return. The revocation is automatically retroactive because the letter was issued for a completed transaction. Therefore, you did not rely upon the letter when entering into the transaction. The revocation of a determination letter on the status of pension and profit-sharing plans and exempt organizations, however, is generally prospective in effect.

HOW LETTER RULINGS BECOME REVENUE RULINGS

Revenue Rulings are generally revised letter rulings that the IRS believes have value as precedents or guides for taxpayers and IRS personnel.

Although on the same subject matter, a Revenue Ruling differs from a letter ruling. A letter ruling will list in detail the facts followed by a statement of conclusions, but without the statement of general principles or rules. When a letter ruling is edited for publication as a Revenue Ruling, the taxpayers' names and identifying facts are deleted. However, the ruling retains relevant facts with modifications to fit within the IRS's intention to propound a general rule. Finally, Revenue Rulings are subject to higher review, whereas many letter rulings are issued with no review above the branch level.

REQUESTING TECHNICAL ADVICE FROM THE NATIONAL OFFICE

During an audit or conference, you may request that an issue be referred to the National Office for technical advice. You may do this on the grounds that the issue has not been handled by the IRS in a uniform manner, or the issue, because of its complexity or unusualness, warrants consideration by the National Office. Request for technical advice should be made as early as possible. If you wait until the case is in the Appeals office, the request for technical advice may be made before the Appeals office conference.

The IRS official handling your case may agree that technical advice should be given. However, if your statement of facts and points at issue are not wholly acceptable, you will be advised in writing and will have ten days to reply. If agreement cannot be reached, your statements and those of the district official will be forwarded to the National Office. Similarly, if the IRS initiates the request for technical advice, you may challenge its statement of facts and points at issue within ten days after receipt of the proposed questions. Your statement explaining your position on the issues and citing precedents will be forwarded to the National Office with the request for advice.

Whether the request for technical advice is initiated by you or by the IRS, you must also submit, within the ten-day period, a statement of proposed deletions. If the IRS does not receive your statement of proposed deletions within ten days, it may decline to request technical advice.

The list of information that may be deleted and the procedure to follow when you and the IRS do not agree on deletions are outlined above. Technical advice memoranda and related background files are subject to the same rules on disclosure as letter rulings and determination letters.

You will be informed of your right to a conference in the National Office in the event an adverse decision is indicated. If you ask for a conference, it will be arranged by telephone, if possible, and must be held within 21 days after contact has been made. Extensions of time are granted only if justified in writing and approved by the appropriate Technical branch chief. Generally, you are entitled to only one conference, but, under special circumstances, the National Office may invite you back for another conference.

Within 21 days after the conference, you may furnish the National Office with any additional data, lines of reasoning, and precedents, proposed by you and discussed at the conference but not previously or adequately presented in writing. The National Office will forward a copy to the IRS office handling your case. It may verify the additional facts and data presented and comment.

You obtain information as to the status of your case by contacting the Director, Corporate Tax Division, Area Code 202, 566-4504, or 566-4505, or the Director, Individual Tax Division, Area Code 202, 566-3767 or 566-3788.

IRS officials may turn down your request for technical advice. You will be informed and have ten days to appeal to the office handling your case. Your appeal must include a statement of the facts, law and arguments with respect to the issue, and the reason why you believe the matter should be referred to the National Office for advice.

The examining officer or conferee will submit your statement to the chief of the office handling your case. If he determines that technical advice should not be requested, you will be informed in writing of his intention to deny the request, and generally, his reasons for the proposed denial. You then have 10 days to notify the office chief, if you do not agree. The data will be submitted to the National Office, which will, within 30 days, notify the office whether the request is appropriate. The decision is made solely on the basis of the written record, and no conference will be held in the National Office.

The reply by the National Office to the requests for technical advice is called the *Technical Advice Memorandum.* It contains: (1) A recitation of the pertinent facts; (2) a discussion of the facts, precedents and reasoning of the National Office; and (3) the conclusions of the National Office. Accompanying the technical advice memorandum is a notice of intention to disclose the memorandum and a copy of the version proposed to be open to public inspection.

The conclusions of the National Office in the memorandum give direct answers, whenever possible, to the specific questions of the IRS officials handling your case. Generally, the IRS will give you a copy of the technical advice memorandum, including the notice of intention to disclose and the version proposed to be disclosed, after it has been adopted. However, you will not receive a copy where the case involves criminal or civil fraud investigation or jeopardy or termination assessment until all proceedings with respect to the investigation or assessment are completed. The National Office may advise the office handling your case not to give you a copy of the memorandum, and you will be so advised when you request a copy.

You have no right of appeal from an action of the National Office.

Other details on the furnishing of technical advice are in Revenue Procedure 87–2, IRB 1987–1, 19.

Effect of technical advice. A technical advice memorandum represents the IRS's views of the law, applied to the facts of a specific case. Generally, a technical advice memorandum has the same effect as a ruling on a closed and completed transaction. It usually disposes of the matter in which it was requested and usually applies retroactively. But note: (1) Technical advice is not binding in a subsequent year, even though it is not revoked. (2) The IRS office handling your case may raise an issue in any taxable period even though it has received technical advice concerning the same issue in another taxable period.

Technical advice memoranda often form the basis for revenue rulings.

HOW TO GET WRITTEN DETERMINATIONS ISSUED TO OTHER TAXPAYERS

While you may not use letter rulings, determination letters, or technical advice memoranda issued to other taxpayers as precedent, they may be helpful as they reflect IRS policy and interpretation of the law. Written determinations are available in government reading rooms; background files are open to inspection only on written request.

Disclosure is not required of any technical advice memorandum (and its related background file) where the case involves civil fraud or criminal investigation or jeopardy or termination assessment until any action relating to the investigation or assessment is completed. Further, a determination relating to IRS approval of the adoption or change in accounting method or period, qualified retirement plan funding method or plan year, or taxable year of a partner or partnership need not be open to public inspection, although the IRS must honor a written request for inspection.

WHERE YOU MAY INSPECT WRITTEN DETERMINATIONS

Rulings and technical advice memoranda are located in the National Office Reading Room. Determination letters are available in the Reading Room of the Regional Office in which is located the district office that issued the determination letter. Written determinations available only on written request are available only from the National Office Reading Room. Background files must be requested from the reading room where the written determination is located (Reg. § 301.6110–1(c)).

Addresses of the reading rooms:

National Office
Location: 1111 Constitution Avenue, N.W., Washington, D.C. 20224.
Mailing address: Director, Disclosure Operations Division, Internal Revenue Service, P.O. Box 388, Ben Franklin Station, Washington, D.C. 20044.

North-Atlantic Region
Freedom of Information Reading Room, Internal Revenue Service, 120 Church Street, Room 805, New York, New York 10007.

Mid-Atlantic Region
Location: 5th Floor, Federal Office Building, 600 Arch Street, Philadelphia, Pennsylvania 19106
Mailing address: Freedom of Information Reading Room, In-

ternal Revenue Service, Box 12805, Philadelphia, Pennsylvania 19106.

Southeast Region
Location: 275 Peachtree Street, N.E., Atlanta, Georgia.
Mailing address: Freedom of Information Reading Room, Internal Revenue Service, P.O. Box 926, Atlanta, Georgia 30301.

Midwest Region
Freedom of Information Reading Room, Internal Revenue Service, 230 South Dearborn Street, Room 2896, Chicago, Illinois 60604.

Central Region
Location: Federal Office Building, 550 Main Street, Cincinnati, Ohio.
Mailing address: Freedom of Information Reading Room, Internal Revenue Service, P.O. Box 1699, Cincinnati, Ohio 45201.

Southwest Region
Freedom of Information Reading Room, Internal Revenue Service, 1100 Commerce Street, Dallas, Texas 75222.

Western Region
Freedom of Information Reading Room, Internal Revenue Service, 450 Golden Gate Avenue, Box 36040, San Francisco, California 94102

You may request copies of documents and the IRS may assess actual costs for publication and searching. Such costs are generally $5.00 per hour per person involved in searching for documents and 10¢ per page for photocopying.

Some private publishing firms, such as Commerce Clearing House, regularly publish such written determinations.

ACTIONS TO OBTAIN ADDITIONAL DISCLOSURE

You may seek disclosure of additional information on any written determination or background file open to public inspection. You must request the additional disclosure from the Internal Revenue Office which issued the written determination, specifying the deleted information which you believe should be disclosed and why. The IRS says it will not disclose names, addresses or identifying numbers.

The IRS will notify all people identified by name and address in the determination or background file that additional disclosure is sought. If all of them agree to the additional disclosure within 20 days, the determination or background file will be revised to reflect the additional disclosure. If anyone objects to the additional disclosure, the IRS will deny your request.

You may then file a petition in Tax Court or the District Court for the District of Columbia for the additional disclosure. The IRS will notify anyone identified by name and address in the determination or background file of the suit within 15 days by registered or certified mail, and such person may intervene in the suit (anonymously, if appropriate). The court may order disclosure of names and addresses, but generally only if such disclosures would be in the public interest.

INSPECTION OF GENERAL COUNSEL MEMORANDAS, TECHNICAL MEMORANDAS, ACTIONS ON DECISIONS

After identifying details are deleted to protect confidentiality, IRS documents relating to proposed rulings, technical advice memoranda, and pending tax litigation are available for inspection and copying at the IRS National Office Reading Room, 1111 Constitution Ave., N.W., Washington D.C. General Counsel Memoranda (GCMs) are legal opinions that advise the assistant commissioner on proposed revenue rulings, letter rulings and technical advice memoranda. Technical memoranda (TMs) provide the legal and policy basis for proposed Treasury regulations. Actions on decisions (AODs) recommend whether or not the IRS should appeal adverse Tax Court or district court rulings.

GCMs relating to revenue rulings are available for public inspection within ten days of the ruling's publication. GCMs relating to private letter rulings and technical advice memoranda are available for inspection no earlier than 75 days and no later than 90 days after the IRS notifies the taxpayer involved in the ruling that the ruling will be disclosed. If the taxpayer sues to restrain disclosure of the private ruling, the GCM will be available for public inspection within 30 days of the final court decision. TMs are available within ten working days after publication of the regulation to which they relate. AODs are available within ten working days after they are distributed, except that AODs for regular Tax Court decisions are available within ten working days after an acquiescence or nonacquiescence is published in the Internal Revenue Bulletin.

GCM's, TMs and AODs are also available from some private publishing firms, such as Commerce Clearing House and Prentice Hall.

WHO MAY PRACTICE BEFORE THE INTERNAL REVENUE SERVICE

Anybody may fill out a tax return for anyone else. But if the return is questioned, only a qualified practitioner may represent a taxpayer before the IRS.

To represent anyone at conferences above the audit level, you have to meet certain requirements. If you are not an attorney or a certified public accountant, you must, in most cases, be enrolled to practice before the IRS.

The requirements, privileges, and duties of persons qualified to practice before the IRS are described in Circular No. 230, which is available from the Director of Practice, Internal Revenue Building, Washington, D.C. 20009. The following discussion is a summary of Circular No. 230.

ATTORNEYS AND CPAs FILE A DECLARATION

Any attorney or certified public accountant may practice before the IRS by filing a written declaration that he is currently qualified as an attorney or certified public accountant and is authorized to represent the particular party on whose behalf he acts.

What the declaration should contain. If you are an attorney, the declaration should show the State bar of which you are a member, your name, address, and telephone number, and a statement that you are authorized to represent the particular taxpayer, giving the taxpayer's name and address.

If you are a certified public accountant, the declaration should show the State in which you are qualified to practice, your name, address and telephone number, and a statement that you are authorized to represent the particular taxpayer, giving the taxpayer's name and address.

The declaration may be filed with a power of attorney (Form 2848) or Authorization and Declaration (Form 2848-D).

ENROLLMENT REQUIREMENTS FOR PRACTICE BEFORE THE IRS

You must demonstrate technical competence in tax matters by passing a written examination given by the IRS. No particular experience or educational background is required, but the IRS suggests that knowledge of income tax accounting on an intermediate college course level is indicated. Publication 693 provides a sample examination. The test is generally given annually, in September. Applications should be filed on Form 2587 by August 15. There is a fee.

Former IRS employees. You may not be required to take the examination if you were an employee within a period of three years preceding the application, and you show five years of continuous service in the IRS. Within those five years, you must have been engaged in applying and interpreting the provisions of the Internal Revenue Code and regulations. The permission to practice may, at the discretion of the IRS, be limited to certain areas.

Continuing education required to renew enrollment. IRS rules require enrolled agents, other than attorneys and certified public accountants, to renew enrollment status and to complete educational courses as a requirement for renewal. Agents enrolled before 1986 were required to complete 24 hours of tax or tax-related courses such as accounting, financial management or business computer science during 1986 in order to have their enrollments renewed as of April 1, 1987 for a three-year period. Within the three-year period ending April 1, 1990, all enrolled agents generally have to complete 72 hours of qualifying courses, with at least 16 hours per year, to qualify for another renewal. Similar rules apply for each later three-year period. Individuals who receive initial enrollment during a three-year cycle have to complete two hours of courses for each month (or part of month) enrolled during the initial enrollment cycle. Writing articles or teaching courses are given partial credit towards the minimum education requirement.

GOVERNMENT EMPLOYEES

Federal government officers and employees. You may not practice before the IRS except to represent a member of your immediate family, or a person or estate you represent as a fiduciary (guardian, executor, administrator, trustee).

State government officers and employees. If your employment duties deal with taxation and may disclose information applicable to federal taxation, you are not permitted to practice before the IRS.

NO ENROLLMENT REQUIRED IN SPECIAL CASES

No enrollment is required if you represent yourself or a member of your immediate family without compensation. In addition, enrollment is not required in the following cases: (1) You represent your regular full-time employer or a partnership in which you are a partner or full-time employee. (2) You are an officer or regular full-time employee representing a corporation, trust, estate, association or organized group. (3) You are a fiduciary or full-time employee, representing your trust, receivership, guardianship or estate. (4) You are an officer or regular employee in the course of your official business, representing a governmental unit, agency or authority. (5) You are serving as representative outside of the United States before personnel of the IRS. (6) You prepared and signed a tax return for a taxpayer, and you present proper authorization from the taxpayer; representation, here, is limited to appearances before revenue agents and examining officers of the Audit Division in the offices of District Directors, and to questions regarding the tax liability of the year, or period covered by that return. You may not represent the taxpayer at conferences.

The Commissioner may also authorize any person to represent another without enrollment for the purpose of a particular matter.

APPLICATION FOR ENROLLMENT

Individuals who have passed the special enrollment examination and former Internal Revenue Service employees who qualify without examination may apply for enrollment on Form 23.

Mail Form 23, with a check or money order for the fee noted on Form 23 payable to the Internal Revenue Service, to Internal Revenue Service, P.O. Box 85854, Dallas TX 75285. The fee is not refundable if your application is rejected.

Upon receipt of a properly executed application, the Commissioner may grant you temporary recognition to practice pending a determination as to whether permanent enrollment should be granted.

If your application is denied, you will be informed of the reasons for the denial. You may then, within 30 days after receipt of the notice of denial, file a written notice of appeal, together with supporting reasons, to the Director of Practice. If the denial of enrollment is sustained by the Director of Practice, you have 30 days after its receipt to appeal to the Secretary of the Treasury.

Upon enrollment, you will be issued a permanent enrollment card. The card remains valid so long as you remain in good standing.

You should carry your enrollment card whenever you appear before the IRS. Revenue agents generally ask to see it.

WHAT ATTORNEYS, CERTIFIED PUBLIC ACCOUNTANTS, AND ENROLLED AGENTS CAN DO

You may appear for hearings, conferences, and discussions. But in doing so, you also agree to: (1) Advise your client promptly when you know anything indicating that he has not complied with the law, or has made an error in or omission from any return or document; (2) exercise due diligence in preparing, approving and filing returns, documents, affidavits and other papers relating to tax matters, or in any representations you make to your client or to the IRS; (3) produce records or evidence upon proper demand; (4) disclose upon request from the Director of Practice violations of the enrollment regulations unless you believe in good faith that the information is privileged.

ETHICAL CONSIDERATIONS

You are under a duty not to mislead the IRS by your statements or silence; or by permitting your client to mislead. Where your client's case is arguable, you are not required to disclose its weaknesses.

WHAT ATTORNEYS, CERTIFIED PUBLIC ACCOUNTANTS, AND ENROLLED AGENTS MUST NOT DO

You must not unreasonably delay the prompt disposition of any matter before the IRS. Thus, an IRS request for or attempt to obtain records or information should be refused only if you believe in good faith and on reasonable grounds that the information sought is privileged or that the effort to obtain it is of doubtful legality.

You must not, as notary public, with respect to any matter administered by the IRS take acknowledgments, administer oaths, certify papers or perform any official act in connection with matters in which you are employed as counsel, attorney or agent, or in which you are in any way interested before the IRS.

You must not employ or accept assistance from any person who has been suspended or disbarred from practice before the IRS. Nor may you share fees with such a person.

You must not charge an unconscionable fee for representation of a client in any matter before the IRS.

You must not represent conflicting interests in your practice before the IRS except by express consent of all directly interested parties after full disclosure has been made.

Solicitation of employment in matters related to the IRS is prohibited. However, advertising of professional services, including fee information and the statement that you are enrolled to practice before the IRS, is permitted in professional lists, telephone directories, print media, radio and television and certain mailings. Professional ethical standards must be adhered to.

If you are also an income tax return preparer, you may not

endorse or otherwise negotiate any check made to a taxpayer other than yourself.

Any attorney, certified public accountant or enrolled agent may be disbarred or suspended from practice before the IRS if he willfully violates any of the Treasury regulations. Circular 230 makes clear that the penalty of disbarment or suspension from practice is not limited solely to the specifically enumerated forms of disreputable conduct.

Further, a $1,000 penalty ($10,000 with respect to corporate returns) may be imposed on a representative who presents a return or other document (such as an affidavit) at an IRS examination, knowing that it understates tax (I.R.C. 6701).

PRACTICE BY FORMER GOVERNMENT EMPLOYEES

As a former government employee, you may not represent a client in a matter on which you previously worked as a government employee. The matter may have involved a decision, a finding, a letter ruling, technical advice, or approval or disapproval of a contract. You are considered to have participated in a matter if you were substantially involved in making decisions. You are also disqualified if you prepared or reviewed documents (with or without the right to exercise a judgment of approval or disapproval), or participated in conferences or investigations, or gave substantial advice.

You may also be disqualified where you had official responsibilities for a transaction within a period of one year before you left government service. In such a case, you may not represent or assist in that transaction any person who is or was a specific party to that transaction, within one year after your government employment ended. You are considered to have had official responsibility if you had direct administrative or operating authority, whether intermediate or final, exercisable alone or with others, to approve, disapprove, or otherwise direct government action.

Within one year after leaving government service, you may not appear before the IRS in a matter involving the publication, withdrawal, amendment, modification, or interpretation of a rule if you participated in its development or, within a period of one year prior to the termination of your government employment, you had official responsibility for developing the rule. However, you may appear on your own behalf or represent a client in a transaction involving the application or interpretation of the rule provided you do not use or disclose any confidential information you acquired in the development of the rule and do not argue that the rule is invalid or illegal. A rule includes Treasury Regulations, whether issued or under preparation for issuance as Notices of Proposed Rule Making or as Treasury Decisions, and revenue rulings and revenue procedures published in the Internal Revenue Bulletin.

Firm representation. A firm of which you are a member may not represent or knowingly assist a person who was or is a specific party in any transaction in which you participated as a government employee, unless:

(1) No member of the firm who knew of your participation in the transaction initiated discussions with you concerning your becoming a member of the firm until your government employment ended or six months after the termination of your participation in the transaction, whichever is earlier;

(2) You did not initiate any discussions concerning becoming a member of the firm while participating in the transaction or, if such discussions were initiated, they conformed with the requirements of 18 U.S.C. § 208(b); and

(3) The firm isolates you in such a way that you do not assist in the representation.

If you had official responsibility for a transaction, no member of your firm may represent or knowingly assist a person who was or is a specific party in that transaction, unless you are isolated in such a way that you do not assist in the representation. You and another member of your firm must sign a statement under oath that you will be isolated from participating in the transaction, and the statement must be filed with the Director of Practice.

WHEN UNENROLLED TAX RETURN PREPARERS MAY REPRESENT TAXPAYERS AT AUDITS

Any unenrolled person who signs an income tax return as having prepared it may appear as the taxpayer's representative at an audit in the office of a District Director. He may also appear where no space is provided on a return for a preparer's signature or where the regulations do not require his signature. However, the preparer of the return must show he has been authorized by the taxpayer to represent him. He may use Form 2848-D or any other written authorization which the taxpayer signs before a notary public or two disinterested witnesses.

An unenrolled preparer is strictly limited to an audit on the return he has prepared. He cannot represent a taxpayer at conferences after an examination. Where net operating losses are involved, he cannot deal with prior or later returns he has not prepared and signed. He cannot execute claims for refunds, receive checks in payment of any refund, execute waivers, consents or closing agreements, or a "30-day letter." If the taxpayer wants to have an informal conference or file a protest to the regional Appeals Office, he must do it himself or engage an enrolled representative.

WHO MUST FILE A POWER OF ATTORNEY?

You must file a power of attorney to receive a check from the Treasury in payment of a client's refund and to execute a client's Form 870, a waiver of notice of disallowance of a claim for credit or refund, a Form 872, or a closing agreement.

The power must be acknowledged before a notary public or by two disinterested individuals. An attorney or CPA need not have the signature verified, if he has filed a qualifying declaration. He merely certifies that he is qualified.

The power of attorney must be signed according to the following rules:

1. For an individual taxpayer, by the taxpayer.
2. For a joint return, by both spouses unless one spouse has authorized the other in writing to sign for him.
3. For a partnership, by all the partners, or by one in the name of the partnership, if he has been duly authorized to sign.
4. For a corporation or association, by an officer, authorized in writing to bind the corporation or association.
5. For a guardian or other court-appointed fiduciary, by the fiduciary. In addition there must accompany the power of attorney an official court document as proof of the appointment and that the appointment has not terminated.

A power of attorney may be filed on Form 2848 and 2848-D.

WHEN MUST A TAX INFORMATION AUTHORIZATION BE FILED?

If you do not file a power of attorney, you have to file a tax information authorization in order to receive certain confidential tax information of your client, such as his tax return, and to receive certain information, such as the IRS's position towards his liability. A tax information authorization is also needed for conferences dealing with the merits of a request for a ruling or determination letter and the receipt of a deficiency notice, a "30-day letter," and an examining officer's report.

The tax information authorization is signed by the taxpayer and specifies the particular authorization given.

No tax information authorization is required where: (1) A power of attorney has already been filed for the same matter, or (2) the taxpayer himself is present when the information is divulged, such as at a conference, or (3) the receipt of notices and other matters are not of a confidential nature.

INCOME TAX RETURN PREPARERS

Preparers are subject to penalties for negligent or fraudulent preparation of returns and for violation of specific disclosure and record requirements. Thus, the rules discussed in this chapter deserve careful consideration by all tax practitioners.

WHO IS A PREPARER?

Anyone who prepares or employs another to prepare a substantial part of any income tax return or refund claim for compensation is considered an income tax return preparer. (IRC § 7701(a)(36)(A)). You need not physically make the entries on the return to be a preparer. You may be considered a preparer where you:

Provide advice or information that reduces the filling out of the return to a clerical matter; or

Provide advice on matters of tax law or IRS policy concerning a particular deduction or income item. You are considered a preparer in relation to those items if the advice is given in connection with the preparation of a return and is directly related to a specific entry on the return or refund claim. The advice must be for events that have already occurred rather than for the consequences of contemplated actions.

A person may be considered a preparer regardless of educational qualifications or professional status. (Reg. § 301.7701-15(a)(3)) But an IRS employee performing his official duties is not considered an income tax preparer. (Reg. § 301.7701-15(a)(6))

You are *not* a preparer if you perform only the following (Reg. § 301.7701-15(d)):

Merely type or reproduce returns; or

Prepare a return or refund claim for your employer, officer of your employer, or a fellow employee, or for a general partner in a partnership in which you are a general partner or an employee. An employee of a subsidiary corporation is also considered an employee of the parent corporation; or

Prepare a return as fiduciary; or

Prepare a return for a friend, a relative, or neighbor with no implicit or explicit agreement for compensation, even though you receive a gift or return service or favor. (Reg. § 301.7701-15(a)(4))

Prepare a claim for refund in response to a notice of deficiency issued to the taxpayer or a waiver of restriction after initiation of an audit of the taxpayer or another taxpayer of a determination if the audit of that other taxpayer affects the liability of the taxpayer for tax.

Even though entries on a return you prepare affect entries on the return of another taxpayer, you are not the preparer of the other return, unless the entries on the return you prepared are directly reflected on that other return and constitute a substantial portion of that return. For example, if you prepare a partnership return, you are not the preparer of a partner's return unless the entries on the partnership return reportable on the partner's return constitute a substantial portion of his return. (Reg. § 301.7701-15(b)(3))

Consultants. The IRS has listed four situations in which a tax "consultant" is considered to be a "preparer." (1) He fills out a return, (2) he prepares a statement which the taxpayer may mechanically follow to fill out the return, (3) he recommends substantial changes to a taxpayer's draft of a return which the taxpayer follows in completing the return or (4) he

No penalties are imposed for failure to furnish the required address.

Identification number. A $25 penalty is also charged a preparer who does not include an identification number on each return or refund claim. (I.R.C. § 6695(c).) Individual preparers with no employees use their social security numbers as identification numbers. (I.R.C. § 6109(a)(4).) A preparer with one or more employees uses both his employer identification and social security numbers, and an individual employed by another should use the employer identification number of the employer as well as his social security number. (Reg. § 1.6109–2(a).) For this purpose, a partner in a partnership is considered an employee and should use the partnership's identification number in addition to his social security number.

Instructions to Form 1040 require a self-employed preparer to check the box before his or her social security number if self-employed.

The $25 penalty is not imposed on a preparer who is an employee of another preparer of the return or refund claim, nor is it imposed on a partner of a partnership which is also a preparer of the return or refund claim. (Reg. § 1.6695–1 (c)(2).) Neither is the penalty imposed on one who merely gives advice on specific issues of law or who prepares another return which affects amounts reported on the return. (Reg. § 1.6695–1(c)(1).)

Furnishing client with copy of return or refund claim. Before the return or refund claim is presented to the client for signature, a copy of the return or claim must be furnished. (I.R.C. § 6107(a).) Where there is an employment relationship, the employer is responsible for furnishing the copy; where there is a partnership relationship, the partnership must furnish the copy. (Reg. § 1.6107–1(c).) Where two or more persons are considered preparers with respect to the same return, compliance by any preparer will be considered compliance by all. (I.R.C. § 6107(c).)

Failure to furnish a copy results in a penalty of $25 for each failure unless it can be shown that failure was due to reasonable cause and not due to willful neglect. (I.R.C. § 6695(a).)

The preparer may request a receipt as proof of having satisfied this requirement. (Reg. § 1.6107–1(a).)

No penalty will be imposed on a preparer who deletes information from the copy of a client who holds an elected or politically appointed office on the federal, state, or local level and who, in order to faithfully carry out his official duties, has so arranged his affairs that he has less than full knowledge of his property or debts. (Reg. § 1.6695–1(a)(2).)

Records. A preparer must keep for three years copies of all returns and refund claims he or she prepares *or* a list of the taxpayers for whom returns were prepared, including each name, taxpayer identification number, taxable year of the taxpayer for whom the return or refund claim was prepared and the type of return or refund claim prepared. (I.R.C. § 6107(b)) A $50 penalty may be imposed for each failure, with a maximum penalty of $25,000 for each return period. (I.R.C. § 6695(d).)

A tax preparer who sells his business is not relieved of the obligation to keep the returns he prepared. (Rev. Rul. 79–400, 1979–2 CB 403)

If the preparer is a corporation or partnership which goes out of business before the end of the three-year period, the person who is responsible for winding up the affairs of the corporation or partnership under state law must retain the records until the three-year period ends. If state law does not specify who is responsible for winding up, the directors or general partners are subject to the record-retention rules. These individuals will be jointly and severally liable for the $50 penalty for each failure to retain records, up to the maximum penalty of $25,000 per return period (Reg. Sec. 1.6107–1).

Where there is an employment relationship or a partnership relationship, see *Furnishing client with copy of return or refund claim* above.

Negotiation of refund checks prohibited. A preparer is subject to a $500 penalty for each endorsement or negotiation of a refund check resulting from a return which he or she prepared. (I.R.C. § 6695(f).) However, the penalty does not apply to a preparer-bank where the full amount of the refund check is deposited to the taxpayer's account. (IRC § 6695(f).) A preparer who endorses a client's refund check is subject to the penalty even if he has a power of attorney from the client authorizing him to negotiate the refund check (Letter Ruling 872–0021).

A preparer who operates a check-cashing business and who occasionally cashes refund checks of clients is not exempted from the penalty where the client endorses the check prior to negotiation or endorsement by the preparer. (Rev. Rul. 78–220, 1978–1 CB 447, revoking Rev. Rul. 77–184, 1977–1 CB 407.)

A business manager for athletes, actors, or other professionals who prepares his client's tax returns and handles their tax refunds may avoid penalty where he acts only as an agent in depositing a client's refund check. Thus, the manager who receives the refund check pursuant to a power of attorney and deposits the check in a client's checking account is not liable for the penalty since he is not "negotiating" the check, but merely acting in his capacity as agent. (Rev. Rul. 80–35, 1980–1 CB 305)

PENALTY ASSESSMENT PROCEDURES

The penalties must be assessed within three years after a return or refund claim is filed; no court proceeding for collection of the penalty without assessment may be begun after the three-year period. Penalties for willful understatement of tax liability may be assessed (or court proceedings for collection without assessment may begin) at any time. (I.R.C. § 6696 (d)(1).)

The IRS will issue a preparer a 30-day letter notifying a preparer of a proposed penalty and offering an opportunity to pursue administrative remedies prior to assessment of the penalty. The preparer has the burden of proving that he did not intend to intentionally or willfully disregard Treasury rules or regulations. However, the IRS bears the burden of proof on the issue of whether the preparer willfully attempted to understate a taxpayer's tax liability. (I.R.C. § 7427.) If the preparer appeals the determination, the IRS cannot assess the penalties until after a final determination is made. (Reg. § 1.6694–2(a)(1).)

If a penalty for understatement of tax is assessed and the preparer does not pursue an administrative remedy or pursues such a remedy but receives an adverse final administrative determination from the IRS, the preparer has two alternatives:

Pay the entire amount assessed and file a claim for refund of the amount paid not later than three years from the date the penalty is paid, or

Pay 15% of the penalty within 30 days of the IRS's statement of notice and demand for payment and file a claim for refund of the amount paid within the same 30-day period. (I.R.C. § 6694(c).)

If the preparer timely pays 15% of the penalty, the IRS may not seek collection of the remaining 85% while the claim for refund is pending. If the IRS denies a claim for refund of the paid portion of the penalty, the preparer may bring an action for refund in a federal district court within 30 days of the date of denial. The action must be brought within the 30-day period to postpone or avoid collection measures by the IRS as to the remaining 85% of the penalty under the second alternative above. If the IRS does not deny a claim for refund by the end of six months after the claim is made, the preparer may bring an action in federal district court within 30 days after the expiration of the six-month period. If such an action is not brought, the IRS may pursue collection of the remaining 85% of the penalty (second alternative above).

If at any time there is a final determination that there was no understatement of liability in a return or refund claim prepared by the preparer for which a negligence or willful penalty has been assessed, such assessment is abated. (I.R.C. § 6694(d).) If any penalties have been paid, they will be refunded without regard to the statute of limitations.

The above assessment procedures also apply to the $1,000 penalty for knowingly understating tax. (I.R.C. § 6703)

IRS MAY SEEK INJUNCTION AGAINST PREPARER

The IRS may seek an injunction in a federal district court to prohibit improper conduct by an income tax return preparer. (I.R.C. § 7407) An injunction may be sought regardless of whether penalties have been or may be assessed against the preparer. An injunction may be issued where the court finds that the preparer has:

Engaged in conduct subject to the disclosure requirement penalties or the understatement of tax liability penalties;

Engaged in conduct subject to criminal penalties under the Internal Revenue Code;

Misrepresented his or her eligibility to practice before the Treasury or his or her experience or education as a tax return preparer;

Guaranteed payment of any tax refund or the allowance of any tax credit; or

Engaged in other fraudulent or deceptive conduct that interferes with administration of the tax laws.

A court may also enjoin the person from acting as a preparer if it finds that the person has repeatedly engaged in the above practices. (I.R.C. § 7407(b).) A preparer may prevent an injunction action based on the penalties for violating disclosure requirements or understatement of tax liability by filing with the IRS a $50,000 bond as surety for payment of any penalties that might be assessed.

The IRS may also seek a court injunction against a preparer who is subject to the $1,000 penalty for willfully understating tax under I.R.C. § 6701. If an injunction is issued, the preparer will be listed in the Internal Revenue Bulletin for five weeks; a cumulative list of those enjoined during each six month period will be published in the Bulletin at the end of the period and will also appear in the Cumulative Bulletin. The listing will include the name and address of the enjoined preparer, the court that issued that injunction, and if a tax shelter promotion was involved, the name or nature of the shelter.

PART FIVE

PREPARING A FEDERAL ESTATE TAX RETURN

Preparing a Federal Estate Tax Return

THE ESTATE TAX RETURN—GENERAL REQUIREMENTS

The estate tax return, Form 706, is due nine months after death. Form 706 must be filed if the gross estate of a citizen or resident dying in 1987 or a later year exceeds $600,000, valued at the date of death.

The $600,000 filing floor is reduced by post-1976 taxable gifts *not* treated as part of the gross estate. Generally, these are gifts made after December 31, 1976, exceeding the annual gift tax exclusion.

The value of the gross estate on the date of death governs filing the return, even though the executor or administrator elects the alternate valuation date and value at that date is less.

The return must be verified and filed in the district in which the decedent was domiciled at his death. If the return is filed in the wrong district, it generally will be transferred to the proper district. In exceptional cases, the IRS, upon application, may permit the return to be filed in another district.

The executor or administrator is required to file the return. If there is no qualified executor or administrator, the responsibility falls on any person in actual or constructive possession of property belonging to the decedent.

Where there is more than one executor or administrator, the return must be made jointly by all. If the executor is unable to make a return reporting the complete gross estate, he should give all the information he has concerning the property, including a full description and the name of every person holding a legal or beneficial interest in the property. The District Director can require that every such person make a return reporting that part of the gross estate that he holds.

Tax practitioners generally advise delaying the filing of the return until after the alternate valuation date which is six months after date of death. Until this time, it is not possible to determine whether values will be lower at the date of death or the alternate valuation date.

COLLECTING INFORMATION FOR THE RETURN

Immediately after the death of the decedent, the executor or administrator and his attorney should begin to collect information for filing the estate tax return. They should save the stock market pages of the newspaper for the date of death, the alternate valuation date and date on which any security is sold. The decedent's files and records should also be reviewed. Recent income tax returns will provide valuable data. The size and nature of a decedent's income usually indicate the make-up of the estate. Schedules of dividends furnish a list of decedent's stocks. These may also be obtained from his broker's statement of recent sales and purchases. Deductions for real estate taxes and expenses disclose the existence and, frequently, the location of land and buildings. Deductions for interest paid indicate the existence of debts.

If appraisals of estate property are to be submitted with the return, the closer to the date of death they are made, the more accurate and valuable they will be. Select an experienced appraiser soon after decedent's death. An appraisal by an expert is usually desirable to establish the value of both personal and real property. A combination of factors, such as sales of comparable property, rentals, mortgages, and local market conditions, is important in arriving at a conclusion as to the value of the property in question. Assessed valuation usually is not a reliable indication of the fair market value of real estate.

All gift tax returns for gifts made after September 9, 1976, should be collected. Gifts of certain interests, such as life insurance, made within three years of death are included in the gross estate. Further, gift tax paid on gifts made after 1976 and within three years of death is also included in the estate. Gifts not included in the gross estate affect the computation of the estate tax.

CHECKLIST OF PROPERTY SUBJECT TO ESTATE TAX

Although the gross estate includes all property to the extent of decedent's interest at the time of death, this checklist may prevent the omission of includible property:

Real estate wherever located

Stocks

Dividends payable to decedent as stockholder of record on date prior to date of death, even though not paid at date of death

Bonds

Accrued interest to date of death

Mortgages and notes

Joint and survivor annuity

Refund annuity

Insurance proceeds payable to estate or to others where decedent owned the policy

Tax-exempt bonds, even though exempt from income tax

Accrued income to date of death, including salaries, commissions, annuity payments

Value of dower, curtesy or similar interests

Community property to the extent of decedent's interest

Interest in land contracts

Jointly-held property (one-half if co-owner is spouse; otherwise subtract the proportion of other joint tenant's contribution)

Vested remainders

Cash on hand and in bank accounts

Partnership interests

Household and personal belongings such as furniture, jewelry, automobiles, art objects

All taxable gifts (and life insurance, whether or not taxable) made after December 31, 1976, and made within three years of death (including gift tax)

Transfers in which decedent retained some legal or beneficial interest in property

Refund claims

Vested death benefits

General powers of appointment

Patent and copyright rights

Flight insurance

Lump-sum distributions from pension plans, Keogh plans, and IRAs

Annuities from pension plans, Keogh plans, and IRAs are includable in estates of individuals dying before 1985 if payable to the executor, or if payable to another beneficiary, to the extent of value over $100,000. The $100,000 exclusion was generally repealed for estates of individuals dying after 1984. Under an exception, the exclusion is allowed for estates of decedents who were participants in a plan and in pay status as of December 31, 1984, provided that before July 18, 1984 they irrevocably elected the beneficiary and form of benefits.

Also included in the gross estate are the following items:

Tax refund claims. Report the value of decedent's interest in a claim for refund of income taxes, even if it is being contested by the government. If a tax refund is made, report the amount actually received.

Wrongful death claim. The proceeds of a wrongful death action are not generally includible in the decedent's estate. However, where the wrongful death proceeds represent damages to which the decedent became entitled during his lifetime (such as pain and suffering and medical expenses), rather than damages for his premature death, the IRS will include the proceeds in decedent's estate.

Compensation for services. Include compensation and commissions earned by decedent prior to his death to which he had a contractual or other legal claim. This would include severance pay, which his employer agreed to pay in installments to his widow. Do not include a gratuitous payment made by an employer. Contingent fee claims of an attorney-decedent are also includible in his estate.

Contingent claims. Any contingent claim is includible unless defeated by the decedent's death.

PROPERTY NOT SUBJECT TO ESTATE TAX

Federal survivors insurance benefits paid under the Social Security Act to widow(er), children, or parents

Dividends declared but not payable to decedent as stockholder of record at time of his death

Life estate held by decedent created by another

Insurance payable to beneficiaries other than estate where incidents of ownership are not held by decedent

Death benefit payments in which decedent did not hold any vested rights

Contingent remainders defeated by decedent's death

Profits or income earned after decedent's death

Unenforceable claims

Retired U.S. serviceman's survivor annuity

For estates of individuals dying before 1985, annuities from qualified pension plans, Keogh plans, and IRAs are excludable up to $100,000, but only if payable to a beneficiary other than the estate. The exclusion may be allowed for estates of certain individuals dying after 1984. *See* checklist of taxable property.

In addition do not include claims of the decedent which were barred by a statute of limitations at date of decedent's death. The estate has the burden of proving that the claim was barred.

PREPARING FORM 706

A filled-in Form 706 may be found at the end of this chapter. Generally, the instructions accompanying each schedule of the form adequately explain the treatment of common items held by an estate. As a supplement to the instructions, a discussion of selected points is presented in the following pages. A complete discussion of estate tax problems is beyond the scope of this chapter. Where the official instructions and the following material do not cover a particular item, an estate tax service should be consulted. An extensive treatment of estate taxes may be found in J. K. Lasser's ESTATE TAX TECHNIQUES, a three-volume loose-leaf service for professionals in estate and gift tax practice.

ALTERNATE VALUATION DATE

An executor may elect to value assets as of the date of death or six months later. The election may not be made if the value of the gross estate was below the filing threshold on the date of death. An election applies to all the assets of the estate. It may not be made for some assets and not for others.

The principal purpose of the election is to protect the estate from the effects of a falling market. Assets of the estate are generally not distributed until several months after decedent's death. If, in the interim, the assets depreciated substantially and the executors were forced to use the date of death value, there might not be sufficient cash to meet the estate tax liability.

Alternate valuation may be elected for estates of individuals dying after July 18, 1984 only if the election decreases both the value of the gross estate and the estate tax liability. This rule prevents an estate with appreciated assets from electing alternate valuation in order to provide a surviving spouse with a stepped-up basis although the assets are not subject to estate tax because of the unlimited marital deduction.

If the election is made, values are fixed according to these rules: (1) For property distributed, sold, exchanged, or otherwise disposed of within six months after death, the value on the date of distribution, sale, or exchange. (2) If the property is not distributed, sold, or exchanged within six months, the value six months after the date of death. Changes in value due to mere lapse of time are disregarded. Examples of "limited life" property are patents or life estates which steadily decrease in value with the passage of time. However, changes in the value of limited life property attributable to other causes may be reflected in setting estate tax valuation.

When the alternate valuation date is elected and the property is disposed of during the six-month period, the value on the date of disposition fixes the value for estate tax purposes. Later dispositions or sales by transferees of the estate are disregarded. Thus, if four months after the death of a decedent, the executor distributes stock valued at $10,000 to a beneficiary who sells it for $12,000 one month later, $10,000 is the value used on the estate tax return if the executor elects the alternate valuation date.

Filing the election. An alternate valuation election for the estate of a decedent dying after July 18, 1984 must be made on an original estate tax return filed no later than one year after the filing date including extensions. An election is irrevocable once made, even though adjustments on audit might make it disadvantageous. Under a transitional rule, the one-year late-filing rule also applies to an election made on an original estate tax return for a decedent dying before July 18, 1984, provided the election reduces both the value of the gross estate and the tax liability.

EXAMPLE—

Decedent died on February 1, 1987. His estate consisted of the following assets at date-of-death values: 1,000 shares of oil stock, $64,000; cash, $30,000; investment in a joint venture, $100,000; the family home, $425,000, and miscellaneous items such as the family car, painting, jewelry, etc., $20,000.

On June 1, 1987, four months later, the executor distributed to the beneficiaries 500 shares of oil stock when their value was $30,000. Value on August 1, 1987, six months after decedent's death, was $25,000. The remaining 500 shares were distributed October 1, 1987. The joint venture suffered substantial reverses immediately after decedent's death, and the executor, on July 1, 1987, accepted a $50,000 payment for the decedent's interest in the venture. A painting was sold on June 1, 1987, at a loss of $2,000, although by August 1, 1987, the painting (now in the hands of the purchaser) had risen to its former value.

The table below illustrates how each of the items is treated. If the alternate valuation date were elected by the executor, the gross estate would be $278,000; if no election were made, the gross estate would be $339,000.

Asset	Value at Date of Death	Value on Date of Distribution or Sale	Value Six Months After Death	Alternate Valuation
500 shares of oil stock	$ 32,000	$30,000	$25,000	$ 30,000
500 shares of oil stock	32,000	—	25,000	25,000
Cash	30,000	—	—	30,000
Joint venture	100,000	50,000	—	50,000
Family home	425,000	—	425,000	425,000
Miscellaneous including paintings	20,000	18,000	20,000	18,000
Total Value	$639,000	—	—	$578,000

VALUING STOCKS AND BONDS

Publicly-traded stocks. If there were sales on the valuation date, report the mean between the highest and lowest quoted selling price on that date. If there were no sales on the valuation date, the value is the weighted average of the means between the highest and lowest sales on the nearest dates before and after the valuation date. The average, however, must be weighted inversely by the number of trading days between the sales dates and the valuation date.

EXAMPLES—

1. The valuation date is Friday, May 20. The mean sales prices per share on the nearest sales dates were $10 on Wednesday, May 18, two trading days before, and $15 on Wednesday, June 25, three trading days after the valuation date. The value of the stock is fixed at $12 per share arrived at as follows:

$$\frac{(3 \times 10) \text{ plus } (2 \times 15)}{5} = \frac{60}{5} = \$12$$

2. Same facts as (1) except that the mean sale prices per share were $15 on May 18 and $10 on May 25. The value is fixed at $13 per share as follows:

$$\frac{(3 \times 15) \text{ plus } (2 \times 10)}{5} = \frac{65}{5} = \$13$$

3. The decedent died on Sunday. The mean prices per share were $20 on Friday and $23 on Monday. (Saturday and Sunday were not trading days.) Each share of stock is valued at $21.50.

$$\frac{(1 \times 23) \text{ plus } (1 \times 20)}{2} = \frac{43}{2} = \$21.50$$

If there were no actual sales within a reasonable period before and after the valuation date, value is fixed by use of *bona fide* bid and asked prices. Take the mean between the bid and asked prices, if any, on the valuation date, or use the nearest trading dates before and after the valuation date and prorate according to the weighted average method described above.

If actual sales prices or bid and asked prices are not available either before or after the valuation date, then take as the value the mean between the highest and lowest available sales or bid and asked prices.

If a security is listed on more than one exchange, use the records of the exchange where the security is principally dealt in.

If price quotations of unlisted securities are obtained from brokers, attach letters furnishing such quotations to the return. Evidence of the sale of securities obtained from officers of the issuing companies should also be attached.

Blockage. If the quantity of stock to be valued is relatively large, the "blockage" method of valuation may be used. Under the blockage method, value is based on an estimate of the prices at which the quantity could be sold for during a reasonable time.

Valuing unlisted or closely-held stocks. The methods of valuing stocks and bonds described above may not be used if there are no sales or other market activity. This would be the case where a company shares are closely held by one or a relatively limited number of stockholders. In fixing the value of inactive securities, all available financial data and all relevant factors are considered. In valuing stock of closely-held corporations or the stock of corporations where market quotations are either lacking or too scarce to be recognized, the IRS requires that certain factors be given careful analysis. See Revenue Ruling 59–60, 1959–1 CB 237 as modified by Revenue Ruling 65–193, 1965–2 CB 370 and amplified by Revenue Rulings 77–287, 1977–2 CB 319, Revenue Ruling 80–213, 1980–2 CB 101, and Revenue Ruling 83–120, IRB 1983–33, 8. Treasury regulations also include a list of these facts. Buy-sell agreements may serve to fix valuation where decedent is bound during life and his estate is bound after death to sell or offer for sale his share at a fixed or determinable price.

Valuing mutual fund shares (open end). Open end mutual fund shares are valued at redemption (bid) price and not at the higher "asked" price.

REPORTING U.S. SAVINGS BONDS

Include U.S. Savings Bonds owned by decedent at their redemption values. Redemption values for savings bonds are determined as follows: For Series E and EE Bonds, consult the book of redemption values which may be obtained for a small charge from the Superintendent of Documents, Government Printing Office, Washington, D.C. 20402. Specify the date of

decedent's death in your request. For Series H bonds, report par value plus accrued interest to date of death.

If a savings bond is registered in the name of decedent and another as co-owners, it is included in decedent's estate to the extent that he furnished the purchase price.

Most savings bonds records are maintained alphabetically by name and address of the registered owner or first-named co-owner. To obtain savings bond information from the Treasury Department, give the following data:

1. The complete name, including middle name or initial, if any, which appears first on the bonds, together with information as to any other names also appearing on the bonds.

2. All addresses (street and number, city and state) which may be shown in the inscriptions on the bonds.

3. The series and denomination, if known, and the approximate date (month and year) bonds were purchased.

4. A description of all savings bonds held by the legal representative or persons entitled.

5. Date of decedent's death.

6. The names and addresses, if known, of issuing agents of the bonds.

Send the request to the Claims Department, Bureau of Public Debt, P.O. Box 1328, Parkersburg, West Virginia 26106-1328, together with proof of your appointment as legal representative, certified under the court seal.

REPORTING HOUSEHOLD GOODS AND PERSONAL EFFECTS

All household effects owned by a decedent at the time of his death are included in the gross estate, including articles owned by him but used by other members of his family.

The IRS requires an itemized list of all personal and household tangible property, with descriptions and specific valuations. For articles valued in excess of $3,000 (jewelry, furs, paintings, etc.), or a collection of similar articles valued in excess of $10,000, an appraisal should be submitted by an expert under oath, with a statement by the executor describing the expert's qualifications, as required by Treasury regulations.

The closer to the death date the appraisal is made, the more accurate it is, and the more acceptable it will be for estate tax purposes. Where an executor has an appraisal made, he will be able to dispose of decedent's property before filing the return or waiting for an audit.

In the case of an item of property generally obtained by the public in the retail market, its fair market value is the price at which the item or a comparable item would be sold at retail. Thus, the fair market value of an automobile is the price for which an automobile of the same or approximately the same description, make, model, age, condition, could be purchased by a member of the general public, and not the price for which the particular automobile of decedent would be purchased by a dealer in used automobiles.

VALUING FARM AND CLOSELY-HELD BUSINESS REAL PROPERTY

The executor may elect, with the consent of the heirs, to value real property used in farming or a closely-held business on the basis of its farming or business use, rather than its highest and best use. The special valuation, however, may not reduce the gross estate by more than $750,000 and applies only to the extent of the property passing to a qualified heir (explained below). The election must be made on the estate tax return by the due date for filing, plus extensions. The law provides standards for calculating the special use valuation and a method which may be used for valuing farm property.

To qualify for special use valuation: (1) The decedent must have been a citizen or resident of the United States at his death; (2) the value of the farm or closely-held business assets in the decedent's estate, including both real and personal property (but reduced by debts attributable to the real and personal property), must be at least 50 percent of the decedent's gross estate (reduced by debts and expenses) without regard to its special use value; (3) at least 25 percent of the adjusted value of the gross estate without regard to the special use value must be qualified farm or closely-held business real property; (4)

the real property qualifying for special use valuation must pass to a member of the decedent's family (a "qualified heir"); (5) such real property must have been owned by the decedent or a member of his family and used or held for use as a farm or closely-held business for five of the last eight years prior to the decedent's death; and (6) there must have been material participation in the operation of the farm or closely-held business by the decedent or a member of his family in five years out of the eight years immediately preceding the decedent's death.

If, within 10 years after the decedent's death (unless the heir dies sooner), the heir stops using the property as a farm or closely-held business or sells or otherwise disposes of the property to nonfamily members, the tax savings from the special valuation are subject to recapture. The amount potentially subject to recapture is the excess of the estate tax liability which would have been incurred had the special use valuation provision not been utilized over the actual estate tax liability. The qualified heir remains personally liable for additional tax but instead may furnish a bond for the maximum additional tax that could be imposed should recapture result. However, no recapture occurs where involuntary conversion proceeds are invested in similar property.

OTHER VALUATION CONSIDERATIONS

Retention of voting rights to stock in controlled corporation. Where a decedent gives away the stock but retains voting rights, the stock is included in his estate. The corporation is considered to be controlled if at any time after the transfer and within three years of death, the decedent owned (through the attribution rules), or had the right to vote, at least 20 percent of the total combined voting power of all classes of stock. This rule applies for gifts after June 22, 1976.

Tax on gifts within three years of death. Where post-1976 gifts are included in the gross estate, the gift taxes paid on such gifts are also included. However, a surviving spouse's payment of gift tax on a "split gift" is not included in a deceased spouse's estate.

Requiring the IRS to submit its reasons for valuing estate or gift property. An executor or a donor may request in writing a statement from the IRS of its basis for valuing an item of property subject to estate or gift tax. The IRS must supply the information within 45 days of the request or the date it determined the value, whichever is later. The statement must explain the basis on which the value was determined, any computation used in arriving at the value, and a copy of any expert appraisal made by or for the IRS. The IRS, however, is not bound by its determination of value. By obtaining the IRS's statement, the executor or donor may be in a better position to decide whether to accept the IRS valuation or to litigate.

PENALTY FOR UNDERVALUING PROPERTY

A penalty may be imposed on estate tax or gift tax returns filed after 1984 if the value claimed for any property is 66⅔% or less of the correct value. There is no penalty unless the undervaluation results in a tax deficiency of at least $1,000. The IRS has discretion to waive the penalty if the claimed valuation had a reasonable basis and was made in good faith. The amount of the penalty depends on the extent of the undervaluation. The penalty equals 10% of the underpayment if the claimed value is 50% to 66⅔% of the correct value. If the claimed value is 40% to less than 50% of the correct value, the penalty is 20% of the underpayment. The maximum penalty of 30% of the underpayment applies to valuations that are less than 40% of the correct amount.

REPORTING JOINTLY-HELD PROPERTY

Different rules apply to joint tenancies between husbands and wives and between tenants who are not married.

Joint tenant is surviving spouse. One-half the value of jointly-owned property is included in the estate of the first spouse to die, regardless of who paid for the property. This means that jointly-held property will not be taxed in the estate of the first spouse to die; although one-half is included in the estate, it is offset by the marital deduction.

This rule has important income tax consequences to the surviving spouse. The half included in the estate is valued at fair market value used for estate tax purposes.

EXAMPLES—
1. Jones and his wife jointly own a house which cost them $50,000 in 1970. In 1987 Jones dies when the house is worth $200,000. $100,000 is included in his estate. For income tax purposes, Mrs. Jones' basis for the house is $125,000.

Her original basis	$25,000
Basis for inherited portion	100,000
	$125,000

On a sale of the home in 1988 for $200,000, Mrs. Jones would realize a $75,000 long-term capital gain ($200,000—$125,000).

2. If Jones had owned the house in his own name and left it to Mrs. Jones, the house would have been included in his estate at $200,000. However, it would be offset by the marital deduction and Mrs. Jones' income tax basis would be $200,000. Thus, if she sold the house in 1988, there would be no taxable gain.

Some tax authorities suggest that the family home should be owned solely by the spouse who is expected to die first. Upon death, the home would pass tax free to the surviving spouse due to the unlimited marital deduction. Further, the house would get a full stepped-up basis to its estate tax value, a decided advantage if the surviving spouse sells the house. However, such ownership arrangement may not be necessary where the surviving spouse is age 55 or over and would owe no tax on a sale due to the $125,000 home sale exclusion or because the surviving spouse does not anticipate a sale. Tax considerations in arranging ownership of property should be weighed with personal and financial requirements.

Joint tenant is someone other than surviving spouse. The full value of jointly-held property is included in the gross estate. There is an exception if the estate can prove that a part of the property originally belonged to the surviving owner and was never received from the decedent for less than its value, or part of the property was acquired with funds originally belonging to the surviving owner. With the return, an affidavit should be filed setting forth the circumstances.

If the property was acquired by decedent and other joint owners by gift or inheritance, only the decedent's fractional interest is taxed. To figure the value of decedent's interest, divide the full value of the property by the number of joint tenants.

EXAMPLES—
1. Decedent and his brother acquired the property by gift as joint tenants. Include one-half of the value of the property in decedent's gross estate.
2. Decedent and his two surviving brothers acquired property as joint tenants by will. Include one-third of the value of the property in decedent's gross estate.

Where the decedent furnished only part of the consideration, that proportionate part of the entire value is included in his estate.

EXAMPLE—
The fair market value of the jointly held property at the date of decedent's death is $60,000. The property originally cost $30,000, $25,000 of which was paid by the decedent. The amount included in decedent's estate is $50,000; that is, the value of the property at the date of death, $60,000, multiplied by the fraction $\frac{\$25,000}{\$30,000}$.

If the decedent, before acquiring the property, gave the surviving owner money or other property which was later used to help purchase the property, the value of the entire property is included in decedent's estate, even though the property received as a gift may have appreciated in value between the time of the gift and the time of the purchase of the jointly-held property. However, if the decedent made a gift of property during his life and income from that property was used to purchase jointly-held property, the value attributable to that income is not includible.

The estate tax rules applicable to joint tenancies apply as well to funds on deposit in the joint names of decedent and another. In the common forms of joint bank accounts, the survivor is entitled to the entire balance at his co-owner's death. However, not every bank account in the names of two or more persons is a joint tenancy. The owners of the account might be tenants in common. State law should be consulted to determine the property rights created by the language of the account.

If the funds on deposit in a joint account are payable to the surviving owner, they are includible in decedent's estate unless the executor can prove that part of the funds originally belonged to the survivor. Proof of this nature is particularly difficult since it involves proving not only deposits but also withdrawals.

Where the decedent created joint property out of corporate stock, stock dividends issued are included in decedent's gross estate unless the executor can show that the dividends were capitalized out of corporate profits earned after the date of the gift.

Where tenants by the entirety or joint tenants assume a purchase money mortgage on the joint property, each is considered as having made an original contribution of one-half the amount of the mortgage. Thus, where decedent created a tenancy by the entirety out of the family home, having a value of $100,000 and his spouse personally assumed one-half of a $50,000 mortgage on the property, only $75,000 is included in decedent's gross estate.

Where the decedent registered U.S. Savings Bonds in co-ownership form, full redemption value of the bonds is included in decedent's gross estate, even if he tried to give his interest to the other co-owner. He can only make such a gift and so avoid estate tax by having the bonds re-issued in the name of the donee.

ANNUITIES AND LUMP-SUM DISTRIBUTIONS UNDER QUALIFIED PENSION OR PROFIT-SHARING PLANS

Estates of individuals dying before 1985. Up to $100,000 of annuity benefits from IRAs and qualified plans are excludable from the estate. Benefits from a qualified plan are excludable if they do not qualify as a lump-sum distribution and are attributable to the employer's contributions to the plan. The benefits must be payable to someone other than the decedent's estate or his executor. The same rule applies to Keogh plans; benefits attributed to nondeductible contributions are included in the estate. Lump-sum distributions are excluded from the gross estate if the recipient elects not to apply ten-year averaging or capital gains treatment.

The value of an annuity (but not a lump sum) from an IRA receivable by a beneficiary other than the decedent's estate or his executor is excludable, subject to the overall $100,000 limitation. The annuity must be payable in substantially equal periodic amounts over the beneficiary's life or for at least 36 months after the decedent's death. Benefits attributable to nondeductible contributions to the account or plan are included in the estate, unless the nondeductible contributions were returned to the decedent before his death. However, the exclusion covers a "rollover" account from a qualified plan.

Estates of individuals dying after 1984. All benefits are includable in the estate with this exception: The prior law $100,000 exclusion is allowed for estates of decedents who were participants in a plan and in pay status as of December 31, 1984 if before July 18, 1984 an irrevocable election of the form of benefits was made.

DEDUCTIONS FROM THE GROSS ESTATE

Funeral expenses. The reasonable cost of a tombstone, monument, mausoleum, or burial plot, including the cost of future care, is deductible.

Executor's or administrator's commissions. The commissions that have actually been paid or, at the time of filing the estate tax return, may reasonably be expected to be paid are deductible. If the commissions have not been fixed by court decree, the deduction will be allowed when the return is finally audited if the following three conditions are satisfied: (1) The District Director is reasonably satisfied that the commissions claimed will be paid, (2) the amount claimed is within the legally allowable limits of the law of the state in which the estate is being administered, and (3) it is usually accepted practice in the state to allow such an amount in estates of similar size and character. If the fees claimed have not been paid by the time the final audit of the return is made, the executor must submit an affidavit, stating that the amount claimed by him as a deduction has been agreed upon and will be paid.

The executor is under a continuing obligation to inform the District Director of any change in the status of his commissions. Thus, if he waives them after they have been allowed on the final audit, the additional tax must be paid with interest.

A bequest or devise to the executor in lieu of commissions is not deductible. If the decedent fixed in his will the amount of commissions to be paid, this amount is deductible, provided it is not in excess of state law or practice.

Deduction for attorneys' fees. The rules applicable to the deduction of the executor's commissions are equally applicable to the deduction of attorneys' fees. A deduction for attorneys' fees incurred in contesting an asserted deficiency or in prosecuting a claim for refund should be claimed when the deficiency is contested or when the refund claim is prosecuted. The additional fees actually paid in contesting the deficiency or prosecuting the refund claim will be allowed whether or not the fees were claimed as a deduction on the estate tax return or refund claim.

Attorneys' fees incurred by beneficiaries incident to litigation as to their respective interests are not deductions of the estate.

Miscellaneous administration expenses. These include court costs, surrogate's fees, accountants' fees, and appraisers' fees. Expenses necessarily incurred in collecting assets, preserving and distributing the estate, including the cost of storing, insuring, or maintaining property of the estate, are deductible where immediate distribution to the beneficiaries is not feasible.

Expenses of selling property of the estate are deductible if the sale is necessary to pay the decedent's debts, administration expenses or taxes, to preserve the estate, or to effect distribution. These expenses include brokerage fees, auctioneers' fees, etc., if they are reasonably necessary. The IRS disallows expenses incurred in a sale made for the benefit or convenience of heirs. Courts conflict on this issue.

Where an item included in gross estate is disposed of in a *bona fide* sale to a dealer in such items at a price below its fair market value, the expense of selling the item is the lesser of the following amounts: (a) The amount by which the fair market value of the property on the applicable valuation date (date of death or alternate valuation date) exceeds the proceeds of the sale, or (b) the amount by which the fair market value of the property on the date of the sale exceeds the proceeds of the sale.

The handling of the deductions from the gross estate is also affected by the community property laws. The deduction for administrative and funeral expenses depends on whether the expenses are deemed to be an expense of the community estate or of the decedent's separate estate. If it is an expense of the community estate, only one-half the amount expended is deductible. If such expenses are allowable against the separate estate of the decedent, they are deductible to the extent so allowable. Similarly, if losses have been incurred with property which had been held in community, only one-half the loss is deductible. Also, if debts or mortgages are community obligations, only one-half the amounts should be listed as obligations of the estate.

Charitable bequests. A deduction is allowable for bequests to most charitable and nonprofit organizations. Unlike the charitable deduction for income tax purposes, there is no percentage limitation on the amount of the deduction. Further, an outright bequest to a foreign charity is also deductible.

Local law should be consulted in cases where close relatives are disinherited in favor of a charity. Some states may preclude all or a portion of such a bequest.

These considerations should also be noted:

If administration expenses or estate or inheritance taxes are payable out of a charitable bequest, the deduction is limited to the amount the charity actually receives.

Where, as a result of a qualified disclaimer executed by a legatee, a charity receives part of a decedent's estate, a charitable deduction may be allowed. The disclaimer must be irrevocable, timely (see below), voluntary and made without consideration paid to the disclaiming legatee.

Subscriptions or pledges made by a decedent during his life are generally deductible if legally enforceable against his estate.

Where the will creates a trust for both private and charitable purposes, a deduction may be allowable for the charitable interest. The deduction is for the value of the charitable interest at the date of decedent's death, computed actuarially according to Treasury tables. Bequests of both income interests and remainder interests will qualify for the charitable deduction only if the trust is either in an annuity trust or unitrust form. An annuity trust is one which fixes the noncharitable interest as a specific dollar amount payable each year. A unitrust fixes the noncharitable interest at a fixed percentage of the trust assets, as valued annually, and payable each year.

Deductions are allowable for remainder bequests that are not in trust form where the property is a personal residence or a farm.

THE MARITAL DEDUCTION

Almost all property passing to the surviving spouse qualifies for the marital deduction. There are no percentage or dollar limitations. Further, certain terminable income interests may qualify for the marital deduction. The surviving spouse's income interest in a charitable remainder annuity trust or unitrust qualifies for the marital deduction as long as the decedent and spouse are the only noncharitable interests.

The marital deduction may also be claimed for a qualified life income interest (QTIP). For example, a will may leave the surviving spouse income from trust property for life and direct that her son is to receive the property after her death. If the executor makes a special election, the decedent's estate may claim the marital deduction for the value of the entire property, not just for the surviving spouse's life income interest. The election postpones tax until the earlier of two events: A sale or other disposition of the interest by the surviving spouse or the death of the surviving spouse. If the property is held to death, it is included in the surviving spouse's estate. The estate of the spouse is entitled to recover the tax imposed on the life income interest from the person or persons receiving the property unless the surviving spouse's will provides otherwise.

The terminable interest election does not apply to an income interest fixed for a term of years or which ends on the happening of an event, such as remarriage. Further, during the surviving spouse's life, principal may be withdrawn only for the surviving spouse's benefit. The decedent may give the surviving spouse or other person the power to appoint the principal remaining at the surviving spouse's death; this power is exercisable only at or after the surviving spouse's death.

The executor elects to treat a life income interest as a qualified life income interest on the estate tax return. Once elected, it is irrevocable.

The rules for providing a life QTIP interest in trust are similar to the rules applied to power of appointment trusts

under prior law. The basic difference is that a QTIP income interest qualifies for the marital deduction even though the surviving spouse does not have a power of appointment. The power to choose the final beneficiaries remains with the spouse who owns the property. Thus the QTIP rules provide an important planning technique for a spouse who wants to provide for his survivor but at the same time wants to control who is to take the property on the death of the survivor.

Marital deduction planning. The unlimited marital deduction may lure an individual into leaving everything to a spouse in an effort to save taxes. While it is true that this will save taxes for the first estate, such a complete bequest may be unnecessary and unwise. This is because each estate has a credit which protects a sizable portion of it from tax. Moreover, what is saved by the first estate from leaving everything to a spouse may be at the expense of the surviving spouse's estate.

To utilize the marital deduction most effectively, estimate the estate taxes that will be due on both estates under alternative dispositions of property. After deducting the value of marital deduction property passing to the surviving spouse, estimate the tax liability on the estate of the spouse who is assumed, for purposes of the estimate, to be the first to die. Then calculate the potential estate tax liability of the surviving spouse's estate which includes the property inherited from the first estate. Compare the combined tax liability after distributions for the marital deduction with the combined tax liability without these distributions. Vary the amounts qualifying for the deduction and figure the tax costs. By doing this, you can determine how much each estate should hold so that the "combined estate tax" will be in the range that will best achieve tax saving while providing for your surviving spouse. You may find that you can shelter property from tax through the unified credit rather than leave marital deduction property which may be subject to tax in the estate of the surviving spouse. If the estate is not greater than the amount that would be offset by the unified credit, you need not be concerned with the amount of the marital deduction as an estate tax reducing item. The minimum amount to be left the spouse is determined by state law and the maximum amount by personal desires.

For decedents dying in—	An estate can pass tax-free (without marital deduction) up to:
1987 and later years	600,000

Here is a chart listing the minimum amount of marital deduction property that must be left to a spouse to avoid estate tax on the estate of the first spouse to die. For example, in 1987, in an estate of $800,000, leaving a spouse property of at least $200,000 will avoid tax; along with the unified credit equivalent of $600,000. Property which does not qualify for the marital deduction and which is sheltered by the credit equivalent may still benefit a spouse by being placed in a nonmarital deduction or by-pass trust.

Marital deduction property should be at least the following amount to avoid estate tax if your estate is:

In	$600,000	$700,000	$800,000	$900,000	$1,000,000	$1,100,000	$1,200,000
1987 or later	–	100,000	200,000	300,000	400,000	500,000	600,000

You may want to take advantage of the unlimited marital deduction if the major asset of the estate is a business or major income producing asset. The marital deduction permits the asset to pass free of taxes which, if incurred, might have required a sale of the asset. On the other hand, in some situations, it may be advisable to leave only up to 50% of estates to a spouse. If

both estates are subject to tax, they will be subject to lower graduated estate tax rates.

Expenses, debts, and state death taxes may limit the deduction. In planning for the marital deduction, a planner should be aware that even when the unlimited marital deduction is used and all property is left to your spouse, an estate tax may be incurred in these situations: (1) administration expenses of the estate are taken as an income tax deduction, (2) debts against the estate are charged against marital deduction property, and (3) state death taxes are incurred and charged against marital deduction property.

EXAMPLE—

An estate of $1,200,000 is left entirely to a surviving spouse. The estate has administration expenses of $300,000. The marital deduction is $900,000. There is no estate tax if the expenses are claimed as an estate tax deduction. But if the expenses are claimed as an income tax deduction, there may be an estate tax based on a taxable estate of $300,000 unless credits eliminate the tax.

If the couple has a large estate and also lives in a state which has a substantial estate tax, especially one which does not permit an unlimited marital deduction, federal estate tax may be incurred on the first estate. The large state death tax which exceeds the federal credit allowed for state death taxes may reduce the amount of the marital deduction and thus subject the estate to federal estate tax.

Formula clauses. Between the time an estate plan is drawn and the time of death, property values may change, new assets may be acquired, and others disposed of. These changes will affect the amount of the marital deduction. Property going to the spouse may be worth more or less than the amount projected as the deduction. This projected tax saving may be lost. Periodic reviews which may lead to revisions of the will or other property dispositions are the most direct way to meet changes in property holdings. But this is not always practical, and you may prefer to solve the difficulty by using a formula clause. With the increase in the exemption equivalent, a formula clause may be based on an amount directed to an heir other than the spouse or to a nonmarital deduction or by-pass trust with the balance of your estate passing directly to a surviving spouse or to a marital deduction trust.

The composition of the "estate" on which the percentage will be computed should be defined carefully. The clause should select the date on which the property will be valued; whether or not administrative expenses will be deducted before computing the value of the estate; whether or not assets which pass outside of the will will be considered.

Rather than use a formula clause, a couple may rely on the surviving spouse to decide how much of the marital deduction property should be taken through the exercise of a disclaimer.

You may consider combining a disclaimer with an unlimited marital deduction disposition. If there is no need for the unlimited provision, the survivor can disclaim part of the bequest. The disclaimer must be made within nine months after death of the first spouse. A QTIP election may also serve a similar purpose.

Wills in existence prior to September 12, 1981 in which formula clauses were defined in terms of the old marital deduction limitation should be reviewed. Unless the clause is amended, the formula clause in the will may apply to limit property passing to the surviving spouse and will limit the amount of the marital deduction.

A "survivorship presumption" clause. Where a couple dies at the same time and the order of death is unknown, state laws generally presume that the person whose estate is being distributed survived the person who was to inherit from the estate. For example, a married couple perish together in an air accident; the order of their deaths is not known. Under state law, neither would inherit from the other, and no marital deduction could be claimed by the estate of either spouse. To prevent this result, a will may state that the spouse shall be presumed to have survived the testator if the order of their deaths cannot be established. If the couple do, in fact, die simultaneously, two estates will automatically come into being. The estate of the spouse considered first to die may claim the marital deduction. A survivorship-presumption clause will have no effect if the order of death from a common disaster is known, as where, for a time after the accident, one spouse survives.

Bequests to spouse subject to a condition. If the spouse's right to property is subject to a condition, the marital deduction may not be allowed. For example, a spouse is given life income in a trust, remainder to her estate. But the trust is subject to this condition: "If my wife should remarry, then her interest will terminate." No part of the trust qualifies for the marital deduction.

By law, the following condition will not disqualify a bequest from the marital deduction: That a surviving spouse outlive the decedent by at least six months or not die as a result of a common disaster in which the decedent died. A will may combine the six-month condition with the common disaster condition and qualify property for the marital deduction.

Life insurance qualifying for the marital deduction. Insurance proceeds may qualify for the marital deduction if these tests are met: The proceeds are payable to the surviving spouse in a lump sum or in installments. Installments, including interest, are payable annually or more frequently, starting not later than 13 months after the decedent's death. The surviving spouse alone has the power to have the proceeds paid to herself or her estate. This power is usually expressed in terms of a "right of withdrawal" or "right to direct payment." If a policy provides for the proceeds to go to secondary beneficiaries in the event of the spouse's death, the proceeds will not qualify unless there is an overriding provision that, notwithstanding any other provision contained in the policy, the spouse may exercise a power of appointment over all or a specific portion of the proceeds.

Life insurance policies generally allow for an election of a settlement payment plan under which the insured may designate the manner in which the proceeds will be paid out to the beneficiary. These options vary, and it is possible that a particular settlement plan in a policy may fail to meet one or more of the above tests. Following are examples of terms frequently found in settlement payment plans and their estate tax consequences:

(1) The policy provides that the spouse receives the entire interest in the policy and either the installments are to continue for her (his) life, or the installment or interest payments generally extend for a definite time (for example, 10 years in annual payments), with the remainder to her (his) estate. The proceeds qualify for the marital deduction as she (he) is entitled to all of the proceeds.

(2) The policy provides that payments are to be made to the spouse for a guaranteed period. This does not satisfy the requirement that she (he) is to receive all of the proceeds because she (he) is not entitled to the entire proceeds or a specific portion of the proceeds. Therefore, no part of the proceeds qualify for the marital deduction.

(3) The policy provides that a specific portion of the proceeds are earmarked for the spouse, for example, one-half, payable in installments for her (his) life, remainder to her (his) estate. Only one-half the proceeds qualify for the marital deduction.

(4) The policy provides that the spouse is entitled to $2,000 per year, with a power of appointment over the entire proceeds. The present value of her (his) right to $2,000 per year may or may not qualify for the marital deduction. The IRS may contend that the spouse's right to a specific portion must be expressed in terms of a percentage of the entire proceeds. Court authority does not tend to support the IRS position.

The insurance company may require that the right of withdrawal be exercised on a particular form or that it receive reasonable notice. The company's requirement would not disqualify the proceeds for the marital deduction.

Effect of a disclaimer by spouse. A surviving spouse may want to disclaim an interest in property bequeathed to her. She may prefer that the property go directly to her children. When the surviving spouse's present wealth is sufficient to sustain her according to her own desires for the rest of her life, it might be advisable to disclaim property that does not qualify for the marital deduction. A qualified disclaimer may also reduce taxes on her estate and/or avoid a later gift tax if she gives away the property during her life. A disclaimer by a surviving spouse will not be disqualified where the interest disclaimed passes to such a spouse as, for example, where the disclaimed property passes to a trust in which the spouse is income beneficiary.

Where a surviving spouse is entitled to receive a property interest in decedent's estate as a result of a disclaimer made by another person, such interest will be treated as property passing from decedent to the spouse if such person made a qualified disclaimer as explained below.

Valuation of the interest passing to the surviving spouse. It is the value of the property less claims against the property, or claims of the spouse against the decedent which the property was intended to satisfy.

EXAMPLES—

1. Jones devised a residence valued at $125,000 to his wife, with a direction that she pay $5,000 to his sister. For the purpose of the marital deduction, the value of the property interest passing to his wife is $120,000.

2. Smith devised real property to his wife in satisfaction of a debt owing to her. The debt is a deductible claim under Schedule K. If the wife is obligated to relinquish the claim as a condition to acceptance of the devise, the value of the devise is, for the purpose of the marital deduction, reduced by the amount of the claim.

3. Brown bequeathed securities to his wife in lieu of her interest in property held by them as community property under state law. The wife elected to relinquish the community property interest and take the bequest. For the purposes of the marital deduction, the value of the bequest is reduced by the value of the community property interest relinquished by her. If the bequest had been in lieu of the wife's dower interest (or statutory estate created in lieu of dower or courtesy), the value of the bequest is *not* reduced by the value of the dower interest relinquished by her.

If, under the terms of decedent's will or under local law, the executor is required to discharge a mortgage or other encumbrance on property passing from decedent to his spouse out of other assets of the estate or is required to reimburse the spouse for the amount of the mortgage, the payment or reimbursement constitutes an additional interest passing to the surviving spouse.

SHOULD AN EXPENSE BE CLAIMED AS AN ESTATE TAX OR AS AN INCOME TAX DEDUCTION?

Administrative expenses and losses of an estate generally may not be claimed on both the estate tax return and the estate's income tax return. The executor must decide on which return the deduction will provide the larger tax reduction.

To claim the deduction on the income tax return, he must file in duplicate a statement that the item has not already been allowed as a deduction for estate tax purposes, and waive the right to have it allowed.

When the executor claims the deduction on the estate tax return, he may do so without filing a statement and waiver. Thus, if it later develops that the deduction will benefit the estate more by taking it on the income tax return, the executor may do so if: (1) the statute of limitations for the year in which the income tax deduction is sought has not expired, and (2) the estate tax return on which the deduction has already been claimed is not closed.

Where it is not known immediately on which return to claim the deduction, the best procedure is to claim the deduction on the estate tax return and make the election when all the facts necessary for a proper determination become known.

EXAMPLE—

Decedent died January 1, 1987. The executor retains an attorney for the estate whose fee is an allowable deduction from the gross estate and also from the estate's gross income for that year. The estate tax return is filed in September 1987. On it, the attorney's fee is taken as a deduction. The estate's income tax return is filed April 15, 1988, without having claimed the fee as a deduction. The executor has until April 15, 1991 (or earlier, if the estate tax deduction is finally allowed before that date), to make the election on the income tax return.

A deduction for estate tax purposes is finally "allowed" (at which time the election may no longer be made) at the expiration of the statute of limitations for assessment of a deficiency or when the estate has been closed by a closing agreement.

It is not necessary that all of one deductible item be treated the same way. The executor may claim part of the item for income tax purposes by filing the waiver and claim the balance for estate tax purposes.

Certain expenses may be claimed on both returns where the expenses relate to "income in respect of a decedent," such as interest, taxes, and business expenses which accrued at the date of death. These items are deductible, not only as claims against the estate, but also as income tax deductions. For example, real property tax or interest accrued, but unpaid at the time of decedent's death, may be deducted on both returns.

Selling expenses. A double deduction is not allowed for expenses incurred by an estate in selling securities to pay taxes and other expenses. Commissions and other selling expenses are deductible as administration expenses on the decedent's estate tax return or as an offset against the selling price in computing gain on the estate's income tax return. An expense item may not be used to offset the sales price for income tax purposes if the same expense item is deducted for estate tax purposes.

DISCLAIMERS

A qualified disclaimer not to accept property will be recognized for federal tax purposes, even if local law does not technically characterize the refusal as a "disclaimer," or if the person refusing the property was considered to have been the owner of the legal title to the property before disclaiming it.

A "qualified disclaimer" is an irrevocable and unqualified refusal to accept an interest in property that meets four tests: (1) It is in writing. (2) It is received by the transferor of the interest, his legal representative, or the holder of the legal title to the property not later than nine months after the day on which the transfer creating the interest is made. Persons under age 21 have until nine months after their 21st birthday to deliver the disclaimer. (3) The person must not have accepted the interest or any of its benefits before making the disclaimer. (4) The interest must pass to a surviving spouse or a person other than the person making the disclaimer as a result of the disclaimer.

The person making a qualified disclaimer will not be treated as having made a gift to the person to whom the interest passes by reason of the disclaimer.

COMPUTING THE ESTATE TAX

If the decedent did not make taxable gifts, the tax rates are applied to the amount of the taxable estate. The resulting tax is then reduced by the applicable unified credit.

EXAMPLE—

A decedent dying in 1987 leaves a taxable estate of $665,000. He did not make any gifts subject to gift tax.

Taxable estate		$665,000
Tax on $500,000	$155,800	
Tax on excess of $165,000 at 37%	61,050	
Tentative tax		$216,850
Less: Unified credit*		$192,800
Tax		$ 24,050

* The unified credit is explained below.

If the decedent made taxable gifts after 1976, the tax rates are applied to the sum of the: (1) Taxable estate, and (2) adjusted taxable gifts, *less* (3) the amount of gift tax paid on gifts made after 1976. Adjusted taxable gifts are gifts made after 1976 which exceed the $3,000 annual exclusion ($10,000 exclusion after 1981) and which are not included in the taxable estate because of the three-year gift rule or rights retained by the decedent until his death.

Credit for gift taxes paid. The credit for gift taxes paid is abolished for gifts made after 1976. The "credit" for post-1976 gifts is built into the computation under item (3) above. That is, gift tax paid on post-1976 gifts is subtracted from the tentative tax computed on the taxable estate and adjusted taxable gifts.

Credit for gift taxes paid on pre-1977 gifts is still available where such gifts are included in the estate. Pre-1977 gifts may be included because of rights retained by the decedent until his death.

CREDITS

The following credits are deductible from the estate tax if they apply to the estate.

Unified tax credit. The unified tax credit is the same for gift tax and estate tax purposes.

For estate of decedent dying in—	Credit is—
1987 and thereafter	192,800

The unified tax credit replaces the $60,000 estate tax exemption and $30,000 lifetime gift tax exemption allowed prior to 1977. Where part or all of the $30,000 lifetime gift tax exemption was used against gifts made after September 8, 1976, and before January 1, 1977, the unified credit is reduced by 20% of the amount allowed as an exemption on those gifts. Thus, if the entire $30,000 exemption was used on a gift made after September 8, 1976, the unified credit is permanently reduced by $6,000 (20% of $30,000).

State death tax credit. State death taxes are credited against the Federal estate tax. Most states impose death taxes that are at least equal to the maximum credit allowed. The credit is computed on the taxable estate reduced by $60,000. Note that the unified tax credit is deducted from the tentative estate tax before applying the state death tax credit.

Credit for federal estate tax on prior transfers. It sometimes happens that part of the property in an estate was taxed in another estate. Federal estate tax credit is provided to save the second estate from paying full tax again on such property. To get the benefit of this credit, the property must have been included in a taxable estate within ten years before or two years after the death of the person in question. The amount of the credit is in proportion to the time lapse between the date the property was previously taxed and the date of death of the person whose estate is claiming the credit. The credit is computed on Schedule Q of Form 706.

Foreign death credit. Sometimes when a person dies, part of his property is in a foreign country to which death taxes must be paid. The IRS allows a credit to the estate for such taxes. This credit is fixed by law or tax treaty.

EXTENSION OF TIME TO FILE FORM 706

If a reasonably complete return cannot be filed within nine months from the date of death, the District Director, upon a showing of reasonable cause, may extend the time to file up to six months from the due date. The application for an extension, Form 4768, must be made within the nine-month period after death. A full explanation of the cause for delay must be furnished with the application.

An extension of time for filing a return does not postpone the time for payment of the estate tax, or the running of interest, which starts after the due date of the return.

Even where all the data or assets of the estate cannot be determined by the filing date, a return should be filed on time with an attached statement, explaining and specifying which information or assets have not been included and the reasons for their exclusion. When the information is obtained, the District Director should be notified; or, at the time of the examination of the return, the information can be given to the examining officer.

EXTENSIONS OF TIME FOR PAYMENT OF TAX

The IRS has authority to grant extensions for payment of tax of up to ten years for reasonable cause. Under prior law, the standard for obtaining an extension of up to ten years was that timely payment would result in undue hardship to the estate. An extension of up to 12 months could be obtained on the lesser showing of reasonable cause. Under current law, the same reasonable cause test applies to applications for ten-year extensions and 12-month extensions.

The following cases were published in a Congressional report to illustrate undue hardship. These situations would qualify for payment extension under the more liberal reasonable cause test.

1. A closely-held business makes up a significant portion of an estate. It does not meet the percentage requirements for an election to postpone payment without approval of the District Director (see below), but sufficient funds for payment of estate tax are not available. Although the business could be sold to an unrelated person for fair market value, the executor needs time to raise cash from other sources to pay the tax.

2. A gross estate has sufficient liquid assets to pay the tax, but the assets are located in several jurisdictions and not under the executor's immediate control. Although the executor has used due diligence, he cannot readily marshal the liquid assets.

3. A substantial part of the estate consists of payments to be made in the future (royalties and accounts receivable). These assets do not provide present cash for payment of the tax, and the only terms upon which the estate could borrow against such assets would inflict a loss upon the estate.

4. The estate includes a substantial claim which cannot be collected without litigation. The actual size of the taxable estate is unascertainable when the tax is due.

5. The assets of the estate, which must be liquidated to provide cash for the tax, must be sold at a sacrifice price or in a depressed market.

6. Without borrowing at a rate higher than usually available, the estate does not have sufficient funds with which to pay the entire estate tax and, at the same time, satisfy claims due against it and make a reasonable allowance for the widow and children during the administration period.

In the above cases, the amount of the tax subject to the extension would be limited to the amount of cash which the estate cannot raise to pay the tax.

The granting of an extension of time to pay the estate tax does not relieve the executor from the duty of filing the return on or before the date it is due. Nor will an extension operate to prevent the running of interest.

Election if estate has large interest in a closely-held business. In some cases, the executor may elect to extend the payment of the tax attributable to an interest in a closely-held business without permission from the District Director. The first payment may be postponed until the end of the fifth year after the regular due date. Thereafter, the entire tax is due in two or more installments over not more than ten years. Interest on the tax for the five-year deferral period accrues at the rate of four percent on the first $1,000,000 of closely-held business property; that is, 4% interest is charged on the first $345,800 of estate tax due. The regular prevailing interest rate is charged on estate tax exceeding this amount.

To qualify for the 14-year extension, the value of the interest in a closely-held business must exceed 35% of the adjusted gross estate. An interest in a closely-held business is one of the following:

Stock in close corporation. For corporate stock (where there are no more than 15 shareholders), at least 20% in value of the voting stock must be included in decedent's gross estate.

Indirect ownership of a close corporation through a holding company may qualify if certain tests are met.

Partnership. For a partnership interest (where there are 15 or fewer partners), at least 20% of the total capital interest must be included in decedent's gross estate.

Proprietorship. For a proprietorship, there are no percentage limitations.

Stock or partnership interests held by the decedent's family is to be treated as being held by a single stockholder or partner.

When the election is made. The executor may make the election at any time up to the due date of the return. Where an election is made, the executor may elect a special lien provision and be discharged from personal liability for the estate tax.

REDEEMING STOCK TO PAY DEATH TAXES

Generally, the redemption of stock runs the risk of being treated as a dividend and taxed at ordinary income rates. However, where stock is included in an estate, the redemption proceeds may be taxable as capital gain under special rules. Capital gain treatment is allowed where the value of stock of the redeeming corporation included in the estate of a decedent exceeds 35% of the excess of the gross estate over the deductions for expenses, debts, taxes and losses. If the stock is included in the estate, capital gain treatment extends to a redemption from the estate, a beneficiary, or a third party (such as a donee who received it as a gift within three years of decedent's death), but only if the owner's interest is reduced either directly or through a binding obligation to contribute toward the payment of debts, expenses, or taxes.

The redemption generally must be made within four years after the decedent's death. However, where the executor elects to defer payment of estate tax, the redemption may be made up to the due date of the last installment. Capital gain treatment on any redemption made after four years is limited to the lesser of (1) The remaining unpaid taxes and funeral and administration expenses, or (2) The amount of taxes and funeral and administration expenses paid during the one-year period following the redemption.

ESTATE TAX RETURN FOR NONRESIDENT ALIENS

No return is required unless the gross estate subject to U.S. estate tax is greater than $60,000, reduced by taxable gifts after 1976.

Form 706NA for nonresident aliens is filed with the Internal Revenue Service Center, Philadelphia, Pa. 19255.

A unified rate schedule also applies to gifts and estates of nonresident aliens subject to U.S. tax. A unified credit of $3,600 is allowed against the tax.

If the taxable amount is—	Tentative tax is—
Not over $100,000	6%
Over $100,000 but not over $500,000	$6,000, plus 12% of excess over $100,000
Over $500,000 but not over $1,000,000	$54,000, plus 18% of excess over $500,000
Over $1,000,000 but not over $2,000,000	$144,000, plus 24% of excess over $1,000,000
Over $2,000,000	$384,000, plus 30% of excess over $2,000,000

Table A—Unified Rate Schedule

Column A	Column B	Column C	Column D
Taxable amount over	Taxable amount not over	Tax on amount in column A	Rate of tax on excess over amount in column A
			(Percent)
0	$10,000	0	18
$10,000	20,000	$1,800	20
20,000	40,000	3,800	22
40,000	60,000	8,200	24
60,000	80,000	13,000	26
80,000	100,000	18,200	28
100,000	150,000	23,800	30
150,000	250,000	38,800	32
250,000	500,000	70,800	34
500,000	750,000	155,800	37
750,000	1,000,000	248,300	39
1,000,000	1,250,000	345,800	41
1,250,000	1,500,000	448,300	43
1,500,000	2,000,000	555,800	45
2,000,000	2,500,000	780,800	49
2,500,000	See Table A (1) for year of decedent's death.		

Table A(1)—Decedents dying in 1984, 1985, 1986 and 1987

Column A	Column B	Column C	Column D
Taxable amount over	Taxable amount not over	Tax on amount in column A	Rate of tax on excess over amount in column A
			(Percent)
$2,500,000	$3,000,000	$1,025,800	53
3,000,000	--------	1,290,800	55

Table B

Maximum Unified Credit Against Estate Tax	
For decedents dying—	The credit is—
1981 and earlier	Use the November 1981 revision of Form 706
1982	$ 62,800
1983	79,300
1984	96,300
1985	121,800
1986	155,800
1987 and later	192,800

Table C

Computation of Maximum Credit for State Death Taxes							
(Based on Federal adjusted taxable estate which is the Federal taxable estate reduced by $60,000)							
Adjusted taxable estate equal to or more than—	Adjusted taxable estate less than—	Credit on amount in column (1)	Rate of credit on excess over amount in column (1)	Adjusted taxable estate equal to or more than—	Adjusted taxable estate less than—	Credit on amount in column (1)	Rate of credit on excess over amount in column (1)
(1)	(2)	(3)	(4)	(1)	(2)	(3)	(4)
			(Percent)				
0	$40,000	0	None	2,040,000	2,540,000	106,800	8.0
$40,000	90,000	0	0.8	2,540,000	3,040,000	146,800	8.8
90,000	140,000	$400	1.6	3,040,000	3,540,000	190,800	9.6
140,000	240,000	1,200	2.4	3,540,000	4,040,000	238,800	10.4
240,000	440,000	3,600	3.2	4,040,000	5,040,000	290,800	11.2
440,000	640,000	10,000	4.0	5,040,000	6,040,000	402,800	12.0
640,000	840,000	18,000	4.8	6,040,000	7,040,000	522,800	12.8
840,000	1,040,000	27,600	5.6	7,040,000	8,040,000	650,800	13.6
1,040,000	1,540,000	38,800	6.4	8,040,000	9,040,000	786,800	14.4
1,540,000	2,040,000	70,800	7.2	9,040,000	10,040,000	930,800	15.2
				10,040,000	--------	1,082,800	16.0

Form **706** (Rev. March 1985) Department of the Treasury Internal Revenue Service	**United States Estate Tax Return** Estate of a citizen or resident of the United States (see separate instructions) To be filed for decedents dying after December 31, 1981, and before January 1, 1988. Section references are to the Internal Revenue Code.	OMB No. 1545-0015 Expires 12-31-87

Decedent's first name and middle initial (and maiden name, if any)	Decedent's last name	Date of death
William P.	Johnston	February 1, 1987

Domicile at time of death	Year domicile established	Date of birth	Decedent's social security no.
19 Douglas Lane, Yonkers, N.Y.	1952	6/2/13	000 : 00 : 0000

Name of executor (see instructions)	Executor's address (number and street including apartment number or rural route, city, town or post office, state and ZIP code)
Elizabeth Johnston	
Executor's social security number (see instructions)	
xx : xx : xxxx	19 Douglas Lane, Yonkers, N.Y. 10XXX

Name and location of court where will was probated or estate administered	Case number
Surrogate's Court, White Plains, N.Y.	0000-1983

If decedent died testate, check here ▶ ☒ and attach a certified copy of the will. If Form 4768 is attached, check here ▶ ☐

Authorization to receive confidential tax information under regulations section 601.502(c)(3)(ii), to act as the estate's representative before the Internal Revenue Service, and to make written or oral presentations on behalf of the estate if return prepared by an attorney, accountant, or enrolled agent for the executor:

Name of representative (print or type)	State	Address (number and street, city, state and ZIP code)
Louis Weaver	N.Y.	17 Amer Place, White Plains, N.Y. 100XX

I declare that I am the attorney/accountant/enrolled agent (strike out the words that do not apply) for the executor and prepared this return for the executor. I am not under suspension or disbarment from practice before the Internal Revenue Service and am qualified to practice in the State shown above—

Signature *Louis Weaver*	Date October 10, 1987	Telephone number 914-999-9999

Tax Computation

1	Total gross estate (from Recapitulation, page 3, item 10).	1	718,331 57
2	Total allowable deductions (from Recapitulation, page 3, item 20)	2	522,145 53
3	Taxable estate (subtract line 2 from line 1).	3	196,186 04
4	Adjusted taxable gifts (total taxable gifts (within the meaning of section 2503) made by the decedent after December 31, 1976, other than gifts that are includible in decedent's gross estate (section 2001(b))).	4	0
5	Add line 3 and line 4	5	196,186 04
6	Tentative tax on the amount on line 5 from Table A in the instructions	6	53,579 53
7	Total gift taxes payable with respect to gifts made by the decedent after December 31, 1976. Include gift taxes paid by the decedent's spouse for split gifts (section 2513) only if the decedent was the donor of these gifts and they are includible in the decedent's gross estate	7	0
8	Gross estate tax (subtract line 7 from line 6)	8	53,579 53
9	Unified credit against estate tax from Table B in the instructions [9] 192,800		
10	Adjustment to unified credit. See instructions [10] 0		
11	Allowable unified credit (subtract line 10 from line 9).	11	192,800
12	Subtract line 11 from line 8 (but do not enter less than zero).	12	0
13	Credit for State death taxes. Do not enter more than line 12. Compute credit by using amount on line 3 less $60,000. See Table C in the instructions and **attach credit evidence** (see instructions).	13	0
14	Subtract line 13 from line 12.	14	0
15	Credit for Federal gift taxes on pre-1977 gifts (section 2012) (attach computation) [15]		
16	Credit for foreign death taxes (from Schedule(s) P). (Attach Form(s) 706CE) [16]		
17	Credit for tax on prior transfers (from Schedule Q) [17]		
18	Total (add lines 15, 16, and 17).	18	0
19	Net estate tax (subtract line 18 from line 14)	19	0
20	Prior payments. Explain in an attached statement. [20]		
21	United States Treasury bonds redeemed in payment of estate tax [21]		
22	Total (add lines 20 and 21)	22	0
23	Balance due (subtract line 22 from line 19)	23	0

Note: *Please attach the necessary supplemental documents.* **You must attach the Death Certificate.**

Under penalties of perjury, I declare that I have examined this return, including accompanying schedules and statements, and to the best of my knowledge and belief, it is true, correct, and complete. Declaration of preparer other than the executor is based on all information of which preparer has any knowledge.

Elizabeth Johnston	October 10, 1987
Signature(s) of executor(s)	Date

Louis Weaver	17, Amer Place, White Plains, N.Y.	October 10, 1987
Signature of preparer other than executor	Address (and ZIP code)	Date

Estate of: William P. Johnston

Elections by the Executor

Please check the "Yes" or "No" box for each question.	Yes	No
1 Do you elect alternate valuation?		X
2 Do you elect special use valuation?		X
If "Yes," complete and attach Schedule N and the agreements required by the instructions to Schedule N.		
3 Are you excluding from the decedent's gross estate the value of a lump-sum distribution described in section 2039(f)(2)?		X
If "Yes," you must attach the information required by the instructions.		
4 Do you elect to claim a marital deduction for qualified terminable interest property (QTIP) under section 2056(b)(7)?.		X
If "Yes," please attach the additional information required by the instructions.		
5 Do you elect to pay the tax in installments as described in section 6166?		X
If "Yes," you must attach the additional information described in the instructions.		
6 Do you elect to postpone the part of the tax attributable to a reversionary or remainder interest as described in section 6163?		X
7 Do you elect to have part or all of the estate tax liability assumed by an ESOP as described in section 2210?		X
If "Yes," enter the amount of tax assumed by the ESOP here $ - - - - - - - - - - - - - - - - - and attach the supplemental statements described in the instructions.		

General Information

1   Death certificate number and issuing authority (attach a copy of the death certificate to this return).

      #84XXX

2   Decedent's business or occupation. If retired check here ▶ [x] and state decedent's former business or occupation.

      Certified Public Accountant

3   Marital status of the decedent at time of death:

[x] Married

[ ] Widow or widower—Name and date of death of deceased spouse ▶ -

[ ] Single

[ ] Legally separated

[ ] Divorced—Date divorce decree became final

4a Surviving spouse's name	4b Social security number	4c Amount received (see instructions)
Elizabeth	000 : X1 : 001X	411,994.98

5   Individuals (other than the surviving spouse), trusts, or other estates who receive benefits from the estate (do not include charitable beneficiaries shown in Schedule O) (see instructions). For Privacy Act Notice (applicable to individual beneficiaries only), see the Instructions for Form 1040.

Name of individual, trust or estate receiving $5,000 or more	Identifying number	Relationship to decedent	Amount (see instructions)
Edgar Johnston	xxx-xx-xxx1	Son	$100,000
All unascertainable beneficiaries, and those who receive less than $5,000 . . . . ▶			
Total			$100,000

SCHEDULE A—Real Estate

(For jointly owned property that must be disclosed on Schedule E, see the Instructions for Schedule E.)

(Real estate that is part of a sole proprietorship should be shown on Schedule F.)

Item number	Description	Alternate valuation date	Alternate value	Value at date of death
1	House and lot, 19 Douglas Lane, Yonkers, County of Westchester, State of New York (Lot No. 5, Block 1) Value based on attached appraisal of W. Murphy, 33 Moller Street, Yonkers, N.Y.			106,000.00
	Total from continuation schedule(s) (or additional sheet(s)) attached to this schedule			
	TOTAL. (Also enter on the Recapitulation, page 3, at item 1.)			106,000.00

(If more space is needed, attach the continuation schedule from the end of this package or additional sheets of the same size.)

Estate of: William P. Johnston

Please check the "Yes" or "No" box for each question.

		Yes	No
6	Does the gross estate contain any section 2044 property (see instructions)?		X
7a	Have Federal gift tax returns ever been filed?		X
	If "Yes," please attach copies of the returns, if available, and furnish the following information		
7b	Period(s) covered		
7c	Internal Revenue office(s) where filed		

If you answer "Yes" to any of questions 8-16, you must attach additional information as described in the instructions.

		Yes	No
8a	Was there any insurance on the decedent's life that is not included on the return as part of the gross estate?		X
8b	Did the decedent own any insurance on the life of another that is not included in the gross estate?		X
9	Did the decedent at the time of death own any property as a joint tenant with right of survivorship in which (1) one or more of the other joint tenants was someone other than the decedent's spouse and (2) less than the full value of the property is included on the return as part of the gross estate?		X
10	Did the decedent, at the time of death, own any interest in a partnership or unincorporated business or any stock in an inactive or closely held corporation?		X
11	Are any of the contents of any safe deposit box which the decedent either owned or had access to not included on the return as part of the gross estate?		X
12	Did the decedent make any transfer described in section 2035, 2036, 2037 or 2038 (see the instructions for Schedule G)?		X
13	Were there in existence at the time of the decedent's death		
a	Any trusts created by the decedent during his or her lifetime?		X
b	Any trusts not created by the decedent under which the decedent possessed any power, beneficial interest or trusteeship?		X
14	Did the decedent ever possess, exercise or release any general power of appointment?		X
15	Was the marital deduction computed under the transitional rule of Public Law 97-34, section 403(e)(3) (Economic Recovery Tax Act of 1981)?		X
	If "Yes," attach a separate computation of the marital deduction, enter the amount on item 18 of the Recapitulation, and note on item 18 "computation attached."		
16	Was the decedent, immediately before death, receiving an annuity described in the "General" paragraph of the instructions for Schedule I?		

Recapitulation

Item number	Gross estate	Alternate value	Value at date of death
1	Schedule A—Real Estate		106,000 00
2	Schedule B—Stocks and Bonds		395,593 60
3	Schedule C—Mortgages, Notes, and Cash		24,700 89
4	Schedule D—Insurance on the Decedent's Life (attach Form(s) 712)		100,000 00
5	Schedule E—Jointly Owned Property (attach Form(s) 712 for life insurance)		2,501 08
6	Schedule F—Other Miscellaneous Property (attach Form(s) 712 for life insurance)		89,536 00
7	Schedule G—Transfers During Decedent's Life (attach Form(s) 712 for life insurance)		None
8	Schedule H—Powers of Appointment		None
9	Schedule I—Annuities		None
10	Total gross estate (add items 1 through 9) Enter here and on page 1, line 1		718,331 57

Item number	Deductions	Amount
11	Schedule J—Funeral Expenses and Expenses Incurred in Administering Property Subject to Claims	34,374 00
12	Schedule K—Debts of the Decedent	8,064 07
13	Schedule K—Mortgages and Liens	32,712 48
14	Total of items 11 through 13	75,150 55
15	Allowable amount of deductions from item 14 (see the instructions for item 15 of the Recapitulation)	75,150 55
16	Schedule L—Net Losses During Administration	None
17	Schedule L—Expenses Incurred in Administering Property Not Subject to Claims	None
18	Schedule M—Bequests, etc. to Surviving Spouse	411,994 98
19	Schedule O—Charitable, Public, and Similar Gifts and Bequests	35,000 00
20	Total allowable deductions (add items 15 through 19) Enter here and on page 1, line 2	522,145 53

Estate of: William P. Johnston

SCHEDULE C—Mortgages, Notes, and Cash

(For jointly owned property that must be disclosed on Schedule E, see the Instructions for Schedule E.)

Item number	Description	Alternate valuation date	Alternate value	Value at date of death
1	Cash on hand			457.00
2	County Trust Co., checking account			2,500.75
3	County Savings & Loan Co., savings account #8571-256			3,856.85
4	Federal National Bank, savings account #25867			4,808.29
5	$1,000 Promissory note of Jones Corp. dated April 11, 1983 due on demand Interest 10%, payable annually Interest accrued to Feb. 1, 1985			1,000.00 / 10.00
6	12,068 shares Ready Cash Fund			12,068.00

Total from continuation schedule(s) (or additional sheet(s)) attached to this schedule . . . .

TOTAL. (Also enter on the Recapitulation, page 3, at item 3) 24,700.89

(If more space is needed, attach the continuation schedule from the end of this package or additional sheets of the same size)

Estate of: William P. Johnston

SCHEDULE B—Stocks and Bonds

(For jointly owned property that must be disclosed on Schedule E, see the Instructions for Schedule E.)

Item number	Description including face amount of bonds or number of shares and par value where needed for identification. Give CUSIP number if available.	Unit value	Alternate valuation date	Alternate value	Value at date of death
1	680 shares Telephone & Telegraph Co., common (New York Stock Exchange)	61			41,480.00
2	Dividend on Item 1 of $2.35 per share payable on March 1, 1985 to holders of record on January 31, 1985				1,598.00
3	120 shares Tobacco Co., common (New York Stock Exchange)	66			7,920.00
4	300 shares Motor Corp., common (New York Stock Exchange)	51			15,300.00
5	Dividend on Item 4 of $1.00 per share payable on March 1, 1985 to holders of record on January 31, 1985				300.00
6	1,468 shares Business Machines Corp., common (New York Stock Exchange)	78			114,504.00
7	142 shares Textile Co. common (New York Stock Exchange)	47			6,674.00
8	473 shares Steel Sheet & Tube, common (New York Stock Exchange)	42			19,866.00
9	$20,000 State of New York 6% due 12/1/91	96.55			19,310.00
10	Interest payable May 1 and Nov. 1 Accrued interest on Item 9 from Nov. 1, 1984 to Feb. 1, 1985 (Value obtained from Jones Bros. Inc.)				200.00
11	200,000 shares Hartco Inc. (unlisted closed corporation)	.55			110,000.00
12	18,604 shares Uranium Inc., common (over-the-counter)	.40			7,441.60
13	2,400 shares Speculative Stock Fund	16			38,400.00
14	1,800 shares Solid Bond Fund	7			12,600.00

Total from continuation schedule(s) (or additional sheet(s)) attached to this schedule . . . .

TOTAL. (Also enter on the Recapitulation, page 3, at item 2) 395,593.60

(If more space is needed, attach the continuation schedule from the end of this package or additional sheets of the same size)

Estate of: William P. Johnston

SCHEDULE D—Insurance on the Decedent's Life

Item number	Description	Alternate valuation date	Alternate value	Value at date of death
1	$100,000 policy #56925, Mutual Insurance Co. of New York, payable to decedent's estate in one lump sum			100,000
	$25,000 policy #817625, Manhattan Life Insurance Co., payable to decedent's widow, Elizabeth Johnston, who has owned all incidents of ownership and paid the premiums on the policy.			
	See Form 712 attached			
	Total from continuation schedule(s) (or additional sheet(s)) attached to this schedule . .			
	TOTAL. (Also enter on the Recapitulation, page 3, at item 4) . . .			100,000

(If more space is needed, attach the continuation schedule from the end of this package or additional sheets of the same size)

Estate of: William P. Johnston

SCHEDULE E—Jointly Owned Property

Interests Held by the Decedent and His or Her Spouse as the Only Joint Tenants

PART I.— Qualified Joint Interests—Interests Held by the Decedent and His or Her Spouse as the Only Joint Tenants (Section 2040(b)(2))

Item number	Description — For securities, give CUSIP number, if available	Alternate valuation date	Alternate value	Value at date of death
1	Checking account #87-10863, White Plains Commercial Bank			2,751.70
2	Savings Account #85712, Gunty Savings & Loan Company			2,250.45
	Total from continuation schedule(s) (or additional sheet(s)) attached to this schedule. . .			
1(a)	Totals . . .			5,002.15
1(b)	Amounts included in gross estate (½ of line 1(a)) . . .			2,501.08

PART II.— All Other Joint Interests

2(a) State the name and address of each surviving co-tenant. If there are more than 3 surviving co-tenants list the additional co-tenants on an attached sheet.

	Name	Address (Number and street, city, State, and ZIP code)
A.		
B.		
C.		

Item number	Enter letter for co-tenant	Description (including alternate valuation date (if any) For securities, give CUSIP number, if available	Percentage includible	Includible alternate value	Includible value at date of death
		Total from continuation schedule(s) (or additional sheet(s)) attached to this schedule . .			
2(b)		Total other joint interests . . .			

Total includible joint interests (add lines 1(b) and 2(b)). Also enter on the Recapitulation, page 3, at item 5 . | | | | | 2,501.08

(If more space is needed, attach the continuation schedule from the end of this package or additional sheets of the same size.)

Estate of: William P. Johnston

SCHEDULE F—Other Miscellaneous Property Not Reportable Under Any Other Schedule

(For jointly owned property that must be disclosed on Schedule E, see the Instructions for Schedule E.)

		Yes	No
1	Did the decedent, at the time of death, own any articles of artistic or collectible value in excess of $3,000 or any collections whose artistic or collectible value combined at date of death exceeded $10,000?	X	
	If "Yes," full details must be submitted on this schedule.		
2	Has the decedent's estate, spouse, or any other person, received (or will receive) any bonus or award as a result of the decedent's employment or death?		X
	If "Yes," full details must be submitted on this schedule		
3	Did the decedent at the time of death have, or have access to, a safe deposit box?		X
	If "Yes," state location, and if held in joint names of decedent and another, state name and relationship of joint depositor.		

If any of the contents of the safe deposit box are omitted from the schedules in this return, explain fully why omitted

Item number	Description For securities, give CUSIP number, if available	Alternate valuation date	Alternate value	Value at date of death
1	Household possessions located at 19 Douglas Lane, Yonkers, N.Y. Value based on appraisal by Smith Co., 756 County Place, White Plains, N.Y.			13,480.00
2	One 1981 Cadillac Seville			9,000.00
3	One 1974 Saab			1,800.00
4	One U.S. gold coin			256.00
5	One mobile by Alexander Calder Value based on appraisal by Arnold Co., 600 Madison Ave., N.Y., N.Y.			65,000.00

Total from continuation schedule(s) (or additional sheet(s)) attached to this schedule . .	
TOTAL. (Also enter on the Recapitulation, page 3, at item 6.) . . .	89,536.00

(If more space is needed, attach the continuation schedule from the end of this package or additional sheets of the same size.)

Estate of: William P. Johnston

SCHEDULE G—Transfers During Decedent's Life

Item number	Description For securities, give CUSIP number, if available	Alternate valuation date	Alternate value	Value at date of death
	A. Gift tax paid by the decedent or the estate for all gifts made by the decedent or his or her spouse within 3 years before the decedent's death (section 2035(c)) . . .	X X X X		
1	B. Transfers includible under sections 2035(a), 2036, 2037 or 2038			

Total from continuation schedule(s) (or additional sheet(s)) attached to this schedule . .	
TOTAL. (Also enter on the Recapitulation, page 3, at item 7.) . . .	None

SCHEDULE H—Powers of Appointment

Item number	Description	Alternate valuation date	Alternate value	Value at date of death
1				

Total from continuation schedule(s) (or additional sheet(s)) attached to this schedule . .	
TOTAL. (Also enter on the Recapitulation, page 3, at item 8.) . . .	None

(If more space is needed, attach the continuation schedule from the end of this package or additional sheets of the same size.)

Estate of: William P. Johnston

SCHEDULE J—Funeral Expenses and Expenses Incurred in Administering Property Subject to Claims

Note: Do not list on this schedule expenses of administering property not subject to claims. For those expenses, see the Instructions for Schedule L. If executors' commissions, attorney fees, etc. are claimed and allowed as a deduction for estate tax purposes, they are not allowable as a deduction in computing the taxable income of the estate for Federal income tax purposes. They are allowable as an income tax deduction on Form 1041 (see Form 1041 instructions). They are allowable as an income tax deduction on Form 1041 if a waiver is filed to waive the deduction on Form 706 (see Form 1041 instructions).

Item number	Description	Expense amount	Total Amount
1	**A. Funeral expenses:**		
	Edwards Funeral Home, Yonkers, N.Y.	1,500.00	
	Yonkers Florists (funeral flowers)	100.00	
	Kensico Cemetery (for perpetual care)	15,000.00	
	Tombstone	1,000.00	
	Total funeral expenses		17,600.00
	B. Administration expenses:		
1	Executors' commissions—amount estimated/agreed upon/paid. (Strike out the words that do not apply.)		6,650.00
2	Attorney fees—amount estimated/agreed upon/paid. (Strike out the words that do not apply.) . .		8,500.00
3	Accountant fees—amount estimated/agreed upon/paid. (Strike out the words that do not apply.) .		
4	Miscellaneous expenses:	Expense amount	
	W. Murphy, 33 Moller Street, Yonkers, N.Y., appraisals	200.00	
	Smith Co., 756 County Place, White Plains, N.Y., appraisals	250.00	
	Arnold Co., 600 Madison Avenue, N.Y., N.Y. appraisals	325.00	
	J. Cuoller Co., Certified Public Accounts,	375.00	
	Surrogate's Court, White Plains, N.Y., Surrogate's fees	474.00	
	Total miscellaneous expenses from continuation schedule(s) (or additional sheet(s)) attached to this schedule		
	Total miscellaneous expenses		1,624.00

TOTAL. (Also enter on the Recapitulation, page 3, at item 11.) 34,374.00

(If more space is needed, attach the continuation schedule from the end of this package or additional sheets of the same size.) **Schedule J—Page 12**

Estate of: William P. Johnston

SCHEDULE I—Annuities

Note: The total combined exclusion for lump sum distributions and "Annuities Under Approved Plans" is $100,000 for the estates of certain decedents dying after December 31, 1982. No exclusion is generally allowed for the estates of decedents dying after December 31, 1984 (see instructions).

Item number	Description Show the entire value of the annuity before any exclusions.	Alternate valuation date	Includible alternate value	Includible value at date of death
1				

Total from continuation schedule(s) (or additional sheet(s)) attached to this schedule . . .

TOTAL. (Also enter on the Recapitulation, page 3, at item 9.) . . . . None

(If more space is needed, attach the continuation schedule from the end of this package or additional sheets of the same size.)

Estate of: William P. Johnston

SCHEDULE K—Debts of the Decedent, and Mortgages and Liens

Item number	Debts of the Decedent—Creditor and nature of claim, and allowable death taxes	Amount
1	Dr. S. Miller, Medical	400.00
2	White Plains Hospital	300.00
3	District Director of Internal Revenue - 1984 income tax	4,896.85
4	State Tax Commissioner - 1984 State income tax	1,259.79
5	Socony Mobile Oil Company - auto expenses	300.00
6	Zone Pharmacy - drugs	124.35
7	Senate Ambulance and Oxygen Co. - medical	65.00
8	Chemical Bank Master Charge - personal items	718.08

Total from continuation schedule(s) (or additional sheet(s)) attached to this schedule

TOTAL. (Also enter on the Recapitulation, page 3, at item 12.) — 8,064.07

Item number	Mortgages and Liens—Description	Amount
1	Mortgage on decedent's residence, 19 Douglas Lane, Yonkers, N.Y. (Schedule A, item 1). Decedent was personally liable. Mortgagee is County Savings and Loan Co., Yonkers, N.Y. This is a 25-year mortgage dated Feb. 1, 1973. Face amount $45,000. Interest rate of 7% per annum. Unpaid principal to date of death	32,518.05
	Accrued interest to date of death	194.43

Total from continuation schedule(s) (or additional sheet(s)) attached to this schedule

TOTAL. (Also enter on the Recapitulation, page 3, at item 13.) — 32,712.48

SCHEDULE L—Net Losses During Administration and Expenses Incurred in Administering Property Not Subject to Claims

Item number	Net losses during administration	Amount
	(Note: Do not deduct losses claimed on a Federal income tax return.)	
1		

Total from continuation schedule(s) (or additional sheet(s)) attached to this schedule

TOTAL. (Also enter on the Recapitulation, page 3, at item 16.) — None

Item number	Expenses incurred in administering property not subject to claims (Indicate whether estimated, agreed upon, or paid.)	Amount
1		

Total from continuation schedule(s) (or additional sheet(s)) attached to this schedule

TOTAL. (Also enter on the Recapitulation, page 3, at item 17.) — None

Schedules K and L—Page 13

(If more space is needed, attach the continuation schedule from the end of this package or additional sheets of the same size.)

Estate of: William P. Johnston

SCHEDULE M—Bequests, etc., to Surviving Spouse

1 Did any property pass to the surviving spouse as a result of a qualified disclaimer?. **No** (X)
If "Yes," attach a copy of the written disclaimer required by section 2518(b).

Item number	Description of property interests passing to surviving spouse	Value
1	Checking account, White Plains (Commercial Bank, jointly with Elizabeth Johnston (Widow of decedent). (Schedule E, Part item 1)	1,375.85
2	Savings Account # 85712, County Savings and Loan Co., jointly with Elizabeth Johnston (widow of decedent). (Schedule E, Part 1, Item 2)	1,125.23
3	Specific bequests listed in Paragraphs Three and Ten of decedent's will	409,493.90

Total from continuation schedule(s) (or additional sheet(s)) attached to this schedule — 411,994.98

2 Total

3 (a) Federal estate tax payable out of property interests listed above — None
(b) Other death taxes payable out of property interests listed above — None
(c) Add items (a) and (b) — None

4 Net value of property interests listed above (subtract 3(c) from 2). Also enter on the Recapitulation, page 3, at item 18. — 411,994.98

Schedule M—Page 14

(If more space is needed, attach the continuation schedule from the end of this package or additional sheets of the same size.)

Form 706 (Rev. 3-85)

Estate of: William P. Johnston

SCHEDULE P—Credit for Foreign Death Taxes

List all foreign countries to which death taxes have been paid and for which a credit is claimed on this return.

If a credit is claimed for death taxes paid to more than one foreign country, compute the credit for taxes paid to one country on this sheet and attach a separate copy of Schedule P for each of the other countries.

The credit computed on this sheet is for .... **None**
              (Name of death tax or taxes)

Credit is computed under the   imposed in _____
                     (Name of country)

Credit is computed under the _____
              (insert title of treaty or statute)

Citizenship (Nationality) of decedent at time of death

(All amounts and values must be entered in United States money)

1	Total of estate, inheritance, legacy and succession taxes imposed in the country named above attributable to property situated in that country, subjected to these taxes, and included in the gross estate (as defined by statute).	
2	Value of the gross estate (adjusted, if necessary, according to the instructions for item 2)	
3	Value of property situated in that country, subjected to death taxes imposed in that country, and included in the gross estate (adjusted, if necessary, according to the instructions for item 3)	
4	Tax imposed by section 2001 reduced by the total credits claimed under sections 2010, 2011, and 2012 (see instructions)	
5	Amount of Federal estate tax attributable to property specified at item 3 (Divide item 3 by item 2 and multiply the result by item 4)	
6	Credit for death taxes imposed in the country named above (the smaller of item 1 or item 5). Also enter on page 1, line 16	

SCHEDULE Q—Credit for Tax on Prior Transfers

Name of transferor	Social security number	IRS office where estate tax return was filed	Date of death
A			
B			
C			

Check here ▶ ☐ if section 2013(f) (special valuation of farm, etc., real property) adjustments to the computation of the credit were made (see instructions)

Check here ▶ ☐ if section 2013(g) (generation-skipping transfers) adjustments to the computation of the credit were made (see instructions)

	Item	Transferor			Total A B & C
		A	B	C	
1	Transferee's tax as apportioned (from worksheet, (line 7 ÷ line 8) x line 35 for each column)				
2	Transferor's tax (from each column of worksheet, line 20)				
3	Maximum amount before percentage requirement (for each column, enter amount from line 1 or 2, whichever is smaller)				
4	Percentage allowed (each column) (see instructions)	%	%	%	
5	Credit allowable (line 3 x line 4 for each column)				
6	TOTAL credit allowable (add columns A, B and C of line 5). Enter here and on line 17 of the Tax Computation.				**None**

Schedules P and Q—Page 16

Form 706 (Rev. 3-85)

Estate of: William P. Johnston

SCHEDULE N—Section 2032A Valuation

Enter the requested information for each party who received any interest in the specially valued property. **Also complete and attach the required agreements described in the instructions.**

	Name	Address
A		
B		
C		
D		
E		
F		
G		
H		

	Identifying number	Relationship to decedent	Fair market value	Special use value
A				
B				
C				
D				
E				
F				
G				
H				

SCHEDULE O—Charitable, Public, and Similar Gifts and Bequests

		Yes	No
1(a)	If the transfer was made by will, has any action been instituted to have interpreted or to contest the will or any provision thereof affecting the charitable deductions claimed in this schedule?		X
	If "Yes," full details must be submitted with this schedule		
1(b)	According to the information and belief of the person or persons filing the return, is any such action designed or contemplated?		X
	If "Yes," full details must be submitted with this schedule		
2	Did any property pass to charity as the result of a qualified disclaimer?		X
	If "Yes," attach a copy of the written disclaimer required by section 2518(b)		

Item number	Name and address of beneficiary	Character of institution	Amount
1	New York University, N.Y., N.Y. Cash gift under Paragraph Fifteen of decedent's will	Educational Institution	35,000
	Total from continuation schedule(s) (or additional sheet(s)) attached to this schedule		
3	Total		35,000
4 (a)	Federal estate tax payable out of property interests listed above	None	
(b)	Other death taxes payable out of property interests listed above	None	
(c)	Add items (a) and (b)		0
5	Net value of property interests listed above (subtract 4(c) from 3). Also enter on the Recapitulation, page 3, at item 19		35,000

(If more space is needed, attach the continuation schedule from the end of this package or additional sheets of the same size.)

Schedules N and O—Page 15

INDEX TO PARTS ONE AND THREE

488

INDEX TO PART FOUR

INDEX TO PART FIVE

FINANCIAL SECURITY BEGINS WITH GOOD PLANNING... ALL YEAR LONG

To get ahead, you have to plan ahead. Good planning and smart money management are fundamental to establishing the financial base for the kind of life you want.

HOW TO PLAN YOUR FINANCIAL FUTURE

What financial plan is right for you based on both your present income? Your current life situation? Your future needs? Can you afford to be risky or should you invest conservatively?

The new *J.K. Lasser's Personal Financial Planner* will help you answer these questions. The book offers a three-part strategy that will help you determine what your needs are, explain what investment opportunities are available, and show you how to develop a personal plan.

- Part I works on personal profiling. Questions and exercises show you where you fit in today's financial market.

- Part II acts as a database of money-making instruments and opportunities. Includes a glossary, a review of the basics of financial planning, and a guide to approximately 100 investing opportunities.

- Part III deals with the actual creation and execution of your customized financial plan, from initial goal setting to choosing the right financial advisors.

Special design elements facilitate easy use through symbols identifying specific types of investments by their risk, complexity, and potential yield. Hands-on charts, tables, record-keeping forms, and a year-round financial planning calendar help you write your own financial security blueprint.

As the tax tips throughout *J.K. Lasser's Your Income Tax* make clear, there's much more to personal finances that just paying your taxes. Achieve success through smart money management with this new, one-stop financial planner.

WE'VE DISCOUNTED THE PRICE OF SUCCESS

Now it costs less to get ahead. For a limited time only, purchasers of *J.K. Lasser's Your Income Tax 1988* can receive a $2.00 rebate off the price of *J.K. Lasser's Personal Financial Planner 1988*. Just buy a copy of *J.K. Lasser's Personal Financial Planner 1988* (0-13-510504-8, $14.95. Available December 1987) and send the Proof of Purchase found at the back of the book, your cash register receipt, and the completed coupon below to: Personal Financial Planner, J.K. Lasser Rebate Coupon, P.O. Box 9700, Clinton, Iowa 52736.

Special offer expires May 30, 1988. Allow 4-6 weeks of delivery for rebate check.

Special! $2.00 off the purchase price of *J.K. Lasser's Personal Financial Planner 1988*.

Personal Financial Planner
J.K. Lasser
Rebate Coupon
P.O. Box 9700
Clinton, Iowa 52736

Yes, send my $2.00 rebate to the address below. Along with this completed coupon, I am sending the Proof of Purchase found in *J.K. Lasser's Personal Financial Planner 1988* and the cash register receipt.

Name

Address

City   State   Zip

SPECIAL REBATE OFFER EXPIRES 5/30/88. ALLOW 4-6 WEEKS FOR DELIVERY OF REBATE CHECK.

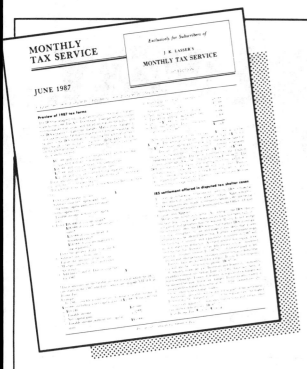

FREE HOME DELIVERY...
ORDER TODAY

- J.K. Lasser publishes an entire library of time- and money-saving tax publications.

- We even bring them to your home postage paid.

- Simply select the titles you want below and mail to:

J.K. Lasser Tax Institute • c/o Simon & Schuster
200 Old Tappan Road • Old Tappan, N.J. 07675
(Payment must be enclosed; or use your credit card).

Enclosed is my check for $ _____	or charge my ☐ MasterCard ☐ VISA
Account # _____	Exp. Date _____
Signature _____	(order invalid without signature)
Name _____	
Address _____	
City _____ State _____	Zip _____

J.K. LASSER'S MONTHLY TAX SERVICE

Keep abreast of tax law changes throughout the year with 12 monthly issues of J.K. Lasser's Monthly Tax Service $24.00 ☐

The J.K. Lasser Library

___ [1] J.K. Lasser's Retirement Plan Handbook 1988	[67-51033]	$ 8.95
___ [2] J.K. Lasser's Personal Financial Planner 1988	[67-51050]	$14.95
___ [3] Lasser Business Tax Deduction Master Guide	[67-51032]	$29.95
___ [4] J.K. Lasser's Small Business Tax Guide	[67-51041]	$29.95
___ [5] 1988 Professional Edition of Your Income Tax	[67-51043]	$19.95

For PC OWNERS
J.K. Lasser's Your Income Tax — Software Version

☐ IBM PC, AT, XT, PS/2, and 100% compatible computers   [40-66004] $69.95
Requires 256K, DOS 2.1 or higher, mono or color monitor

J.K. Lasser's Your Money Manager — Software Version
[All versions require monitor and one disk drive; printer recommended]

☐ Apple II+, IIe, IIc	[40-53208] $89.95	
	Requires 64K	
☐ Apple Macintosh	[40-53209] $99.95	
	Requires 128K	
☐ Commodore 64/128	[40-65749] $39.95	
	Requires 64K	